Writers' & Artists' YEARBOOK 2019

Other Writers & Artists titles include

Writers' & Artists' Companions
Series Editors: Carole Angier and Sally Cline
Each title is full of expert advice and tips from bestselling authors.

Crime and Thriller Writing by Michelle Spring and Laurie R. King
Life Writing by Sally Cline and Carole Angier
Literary Non-fiction by Sally Cline and Midge Gillies
Writing Children's Fiction by Yvonne Coppard and Linda Newbery
Writing Historical Fiction by Celia Brayfield and Duncan Sprott
Writing Short Stories by Courttia Newland and Tania Hershman
Novel Writing by Romesh Gunesekera and A.L. Kennedy
Playwriting by Fraser Grace and Clare Bayley
Writing for TV and Radio by Sue Teddern and Nick Warburton

NEW in July 2018
Children's Writers' & Artists' Yearbook 2019
Take the great advice that's in this Yearbook'
David Almond

'Whenever people ask me about how to get their work for children published . . . the first words to come out of my mouth are always: *Children's Writers' & Artists' Yearbook*'
Michael Rosen

You can buy copies from your local bookseller or online at www.writersandartists.co.uk/shop

Writers' & Artists' YEARBOOK 2019

ONE HUNDRED AND TWELFTH EDITION

THE ESSENTIAL GUIDE TO THE MEDIA AND PUBLISHING INDUSTRIES

The perfect companion for writers of fiction and non-fiction, poets, playwrights, journalists, and commercial artists

B L O O M S B U R Y
LONDON • OXFORD • NEW YORK • NEW DELHI • SYDNEY

BLOOMSBURY YEARBOOKS
Bloomsbury Publishing Plc
50 Bedford Square, London, WC1B 3DP, UK

BLOOMSBURY YEARBOOKS, WRITERS' & ARTISTS' and the Diana logo are trademarks of Bloomsbury Publishing Plc

First published in Great Britain 1906
This edition published 2018

A catalogue record for this book is available from the British Library

ISBN: PB: 978-1-4729-4749-9; eBook: 978-1-4729-4748-2

2 4 6 8 10 9 7 5 3 1

Typeset by DLxml, a division of RefineCatch Limited, Bungay, Suffolk
Printed and bound in Italy by Grafica Veneta S.p.A., Trebaseleghe (PD)

To find out more about our authors and books visit www.bloomsbury.com and sign up for our newsletters.

Writers' & Artists' team
Editor Alysoun Owen
Articles Editor Virginia Klein
Listings Editors Lisa Carden, Rebecca Collins, Lauren Simpson
Editorial assistance Sophia Blackwell (poetry), Eden Phillips Harrington
Production Controller Ben Chisnall

This edition of the *Yearbook* is dedicated to the memory
of bestselling novelist Penny Vincenzi:
'the doyenne of the modern blockbuster' (*Glamour* magazine).

Penny died in February 2018; her article on
Writing bestselling women's fiction starts on page 311.

A note from the Editor

The Editor welcomes readers to this edition of the *Writers' & Artists' Yearbook*

This *Yearbook* is full of advice, practical suggestions and thousands of updated contacts. Think of it as your little black book (or rather as your rather sizeable red reference resource) of all the individuals and organisations across the media that will be useful to you as you write and prepare your work for publication.

New articles this year celebrate the range of non-fiction being published. Frances Jessop suggests what makes for a well-conceived sports book (*Writing sports books*, page 348). Ruby Tandoh provides her recipe for success in *Writing a cookbook* on page 341 and Jane Robinson charts her route to becoming a bestselling writer of social history books (see *Making facts your mission: the pleasure of writing non-fiction*, page 329). The joys of writing fiction are captured in David Lodge's *For the love of language and books* (page 249) and *Writing speculative fiction* by Claire North (page 300). Andrew McMillan shares his advice on *How to become a poet* on page 357 and Helen Chaloner provides details of organisations that support writers in *Developing talent: support and opportunities for writers* (page 515).

For those of you starting out, you might be inspired by Wyl Menmuir's *Debut success with an indie publisher* (page 111) and surprised by how little authors earn when reading *The mathematics of publishing* by Scott Pack (page 149). If you want to know more about the money side of writing, take a look at *Managing a successful writing career* by Tony Bradman on page 254, *Crowdfunding your novel* by Alice Jolly on page 104, and at our annually updated features by Tom Tivnan (*News, views and trends: review of the publishing year*, page 119) and Philip Jones (*Electronic publishing*, page 124).

New, too, is practical advice from agents Andrew Lownie (*How to submit a non-fiction proposal*, page 429) and Hellie Ogden (*Putting together your submission*, page 424), as well as a list of *Software for writers* on page 659. James Peak gives his insider knowledge of a blossoming area of publishing in *Should I make an audiobook?*, page 626. Also aimed at authors considering the indie or self-publishing route is Sheila O'Reilly's *Getting your book stocked in a high-street bookshop* on page 611. If your ambitions lie in the journalistic direction, read Suzanne Elliott's *Writing for online and print*, page 6. Lynette Owen in *UK copyright law and publishing rights* (page 699) distils her professional expertise on the subject for the non-lawyer.

As always, our intention is that you find much here to guide and inspire you in your writing and in your quest for publication. Joanne Harris, in this year's *Foreword* (page xiii), describes how she became a writer (and consulted this tome along the way).

Alysoun Owen

All articles, listings and other material in this *Yearbook* are reviewed and updated every year in consultation with the bodies, organisations, companies and individuals that we select for inclusion. To the best of our knowledge the websites, emails and other contact details are correct at the time of going to press.

More than a book

The Writers & Artists **website** (www.writersandartists.co.uk) provides up-to-the-minute writing advice, blogs, competitions and the chance to share work with other writers. You can sign up to our regular **newsletter**; browse our **Writing Calendar**; and learn about the **editorial services** we offer. We also run **courses, workshops** and other events, including **How to Hook an Agent** lunches and one-day **How to Get Published** conferences around the country.

Our **listings service** can be accessed at www.writersandartists.co.uk/listings. In addition to all the contacts in this edition of the *Yearbook*, subscribers are able to search hundreds of additional organisations and companies.

Whatever your needs, we hope that Writers & Artists resources, whether delivered in print, online or at our events, will provide you with the information, advice and inspiration you are looking for.

Short story competition

The annual *Writers' & Artists' Yearbook* Short Story Competition offers published and aspiring writers the chance to win a place on an Arvon residential writing course (worth £1,000). In addition, the winner's story will be published on the Writers & Artists website.

To enter the competition, submit a short story (for adults) of no more than 2,000 words, on any theme by 13 February 2019 to competition@bloomsbury.com. For full details, terms and conditions, and to find out more about how to submit your entry, visit www.writersandartists.co.uk/competitions.

You might like to read *Writing short stories* on page 267 of this *Yearbook*.

ARVON runs three historic writing houses in the UK, where published writers lead week-long residential courses. Covering a diverse range of genres, from poetry and fiction to screenwriting and comedy, Arvon courses have provided inspiration to thousands of people at all stages of their writing lives. You can find out more and book a course online at www.arvon.org.

Contents

Praise for the *Yearbook*

'... the book which magically contains all other books ... an entrance ticket to the world you long for.'
Fay Weldon

'So much the budding writer needs.'
Martina Cole

'Read this book very carefully. Treasure it.'
Rachel Joyce

'... buy a copy of the current *Writers' & Artists' Yearbook* and get yourself out there.'
Donal Ryan

'Full of useful stuff.'
J.K. Rowling

'Everything you need to know about the business of being a writer.'
Lawrence Norfolk

'When you're looking to get published, it's your Bible.'
The Association of Illustrators

'Every writer can remember her first copy of the *Writers' & Artists' Yearbook*.'
Rose Tremain

'The wealth of information ... is staggering.'
The Times

'I went out and bought myself a copy of the *Writers' & Artists' Yearbook* ... and talked to editors about ideas for stories. Pretty soon I found myself hired to do interviews and articles.'
Neil Gaiman

'The one-and-only, indispensable guide to the world of writing.'
William Boyd

Foreword

Joanne Harris

I wrote my first book when I was nine. It was a 17-page adventure story, handwritten, lavishly illustrated, entitled *Flesh-Eating Warriors of the Forbidden City*. My best friend and I micro-published it by copying it out a dozen times, packaged it with a suitably bloodthirsty cover and blurb and sold it, for sweets, to our schoolfriends. We basked in an abundance of sweets, which we ate without telling our parents, and for a week became the richest and most popular kids in the class. It was the most lucrative book deal I was to have for the next 30 years.

Encouraged by this early success, I announced to my family my plan to become a novelist when I grew up. My mother (a teacher, the child of a teacher, married to a teacher) looked surprised, and not in a good way. She led me to a room in our house that was filled with books, mostly by 19th-century French novelists who had died (as she informed me) penniless, in the gutter, of syphilis, and asked me to reconsider my career choice. To no one's surprise, I grew up to become a teacher, and remained in teaching for 15 years.

That said, I never gave up my passion for writing. I kept it a secret from everyone, writing my stories by hand in a series of notebooks, until my soon-to-be husband bought me my first word processor as a birthday present and, having taught myself to type by transcribing my work-in-progress, I began to experiment with the idea of sending my novel to publishers.

In those pre-internet days, I knew nothing about the process of submission. I had no idea that most publishers did not read unsolicited manuscripts, or that my manuscript should be double-spaced and printed on only one side of the paper. My one rejection letter was devastatingly kind: 'This is quite well written, but far too long and complicated for a children's book. PS: illustrations should be of professional quality.' The rest of the publishers I approached did not reply at all.

I sought help at my local library, where I discovered a copy of the *Writers' & Artists' Yearbook*. From it, I began to learn something about the role of literary agents, as well as some of the things I now think of as blindingly obvious. Realizing that the library's copy was out of date I bought my own, and continued to do so for many years afterwards. Every year there were different features, covering different aspects of the trade. For someone living in Barnsley with no creative writing qualifications, no writer friends and no contact with the publishing world, the book was a lifeline; it gave me the chance to benefit from the experience of people I thought (wrongly, as it happened) I would never meet, and introduced me both to my first agent and to the Society of Authors, an organization that helped me connect with the writing community and which continues to provide me with invaluable help and advice. Though it took me some years, and many more rejections, finally to become an overnight success, what I read in that first (and slightly outdated) copy of *Writers' & Artists' Yearbook* helped me formulate my goals and set my feet on the tortuous path that would eventually lead me to this point in my career – a career I'd once thought impossible.

If you are reading this as a new arrival to the world of publishing, let me pass on a few of the things I wish I'd been told when I was unknown. First, there is no such thing as an 'aspiring' artist or writer. If you write, you're a writer. Welcome to the neighbourhood. We're all of us at different points on the same learning curve, and we all rely on practice, experience and the input of others to help us improve. Second, nothing you create is ever wasted. If your work is rejected at first, you may find that it gains an unexpected lease of life in later years (that too-hard-for-a-children's book with the bad illustrations grew up to become my *Runemarks* series and has been published all over the world). And even if it doesn't, the repeated act of creation itself makes you a better artist.

So go on, stop worrying, make mistakes, collect your rejection letters, dust yourself off and start again – stronger and knowing more. You are in excellent company, and your failures are nothing to be feared; they are simply the milestones on the road to success. Lastly and most importantly, love what you do. Love writing, love making art, and try to make it as good as you can. There are as many different ways of making art as there are people making it, and for as many different reasons. But the love of it brings us together – as readers, as writers, as artists – and when things go wrong and we may be tempted to give everything up, it is the love of this curious thing we do that will keep us going.

Joanne Harris, MBE is the author of 18 novels including *Chocolat* (Doubleday 1999), which was made into an Oscar-nominated film starring Juliette Binoche and Johnny Depp, plus collections of short stories, cookbooks, novellas, game scripts, libretti and screenplays. Her books are now published in over 50 countries and have won a number of British and international awards. She is an honorary Fellow of St Catharine's College, Cambridge, has honorary doctorates in literature from the universities of Sheffield and Huddersfield, and has been a judge for the Whitbread Prize, the Orange Prize, the Desmond Elliott Prize, the Betty Trask Prize and the Royal Society Winton Prize for Science. She is currently an elected member of the Management Committee of the Society of Authors.

Newspapers and magazines

Getting started

Of the titles included in the newspapers and magazines section of this *Yearbook*, almost all offer opportunities to the writer. Many publications do not appear in the lists because the market they offer for the freelance writer is either too small or too specialised, or both. To help writers get started, we offer some guidelines for consideration before submitting material.

Study the market

• The importance of studying the market cannot be overemphasised. It is an editor's job to know what readers want, and to see that they get it. Thus, freelance contributions must be tailored to fit a specific market; subject, theme, treatment, length, etc must meet the editor's requirements. This is discussed further in *Writing features for newspapers and magazines* on page 3.

• Magazine editors complain about the unsuitability of many submissions, so before sending an article or feature, always carefully study the editorial requirements of the magazine – not only for the subjects dealt with but for the approach, treatment, style and length. These comments will be obvious to the practised writer but the beginner can be spared much disappointment by consulting copies of magazines and studying their target market in depth.

• For additional information on markets, see the UK & Ireland volume of *Willings Press Guide*, which is usually available at local reference libraries and also online (www.cision.co.uk/resources/white-papers/willings).

Check with the editor first

• Before submitting material to any newspaper or magazine it is advisable to first contact the relevant editor. The listings beginning on page 15 give the names of editors for each section of the national newspapers. A quick telephone call or email to a magazine will establish the name of the relevant commissioning editor.

• Most newspapers and magazines expect copy to be sent by email.

• It is not advisable to send illustrations 'on spec'; check with the editor first. For a list of publications that accept cartoons see page 766.

Explore the overseas market

• For newspapers and magazines outside the UK, visit www.writersandartists.co.uk/listings. For fuller listings, refer to the *Willings Press Guide* Volume for World News Media.

• Some overseas magazine titles have little space for freelance contributions but many of them will consider outstanding work.

• It is worth considering using an agent to syndicate material written for the overseas market. Most agents operate on an international basis and are more aware of current market requirements. Listings for *Syndicates, news and press agencies* start on page 97.

Understand how newspapers and syndicates work

• The larger newspapers and magazines buy many of their stories, and the smaller papers buy general articles, through well-known syndicates. Another avenue for writers is to send printed copies of their stories published at home to an agent for syndication overseas.

• For the supply of news, most of the larger UK and overseas newspapers depend on their own staff and press agencies. The most important overseas newspapers have permanent representatives in the UK who keep them supplied, not only with news of special interest to the country concerned, but also with regular summaries of British news and with articles on events of particular importance. While many overseas newspapers and magazines have a London office, it is usual for freelance contributions to be submitted to the headquarters' editorial office overseas. Listings of *National newspapers UK and Ireland* start on page 15.

Payment

• The *Yearbook* has always aimed to obtain and publish the rates of payment offered for contributions by newspapers and magazines. Many publications, however, are reluctant to state a standard rate, since the value of a contribution may be dependent not upon length but upon the standing of the writer or the information supplied. Many other periodicals prefer to state 'by negotiation' or 'by arrangement', rather than giving precise payment information.

See also...

- *Writing features for newspapers and magazines,* page 3
- *Life's a pitch: how to get your ideas into print,* page 11
- *Regional newspapers UK and Ireland,* page 23

Writing features for newspapers and magazines

Merope Mills outlines a route to success for prospective feature writers to follow.

Newspapers and magazines are experiencing their most profound change in a century. Every title – be it broadsheet, tabloid or glossy magazine – is finding its way in these increasingly digital times. It's a revolution that is both frightening and exciting in equal measure. ABC figures are largely in decline but online 'unique users' are, mostly, on the up. Feature writers these days can reach enormous audiences from around the world, but finances at many titles have never been tighter. For several years now, budgets have been cut, staff numbers slashed and freelancers' contracts have been terminated. But just when you think it's all doom and gloom for print, there are unexpected success stories – such as the launch of the *Independent's* sister title *i*; the launch of the free magazines *Stylist* and *ShortList*, and the huge popularity of the now free *Evening Standard*.

No one could accurately predict what shape the industry will take a few years from now, but one thing is for sure: every title needs great writers, ideas and well-written content. But be it for the print or online arm of its operation, making the right approach, especially if you are unknown to an editor, is more essential than ever.

Starting out

If you're new to writing, thc best thing you can do is play to your strengths. Do your friends tell you your emails make them fall off their chairs laughing? Then maybe a humorous column beckons. Do you have specialist knowledge? A green-fingered writer might be able to spot a gap in the market in a gardening title, for example. When starting out in journalism, it is often best to stick to factual journalism that you can write about entertainingly. Most comment and analysis columnists these days are personalities who already carry authority – novelists, television celebrities or journalists who have built up a reputation across many years. If you're at the start of your career, your opinion (though extremely valid) will count for very little unless it's backed up by something solid. The majority of newspaper and magazine freelances are feature writers as news reporters tend to be on staff.

The internet

As a freelance writer, the internet is your friend. A newspaper or magazine has a finite number of pages and therefore a limited number of people that can write for it. Its online equivalent, on the other hand, can accommodate many more voices. If you have a niche subject and a valid angle on a story and the newspaper or magazine editor can't accommodate you in print, they may be able to include your piece online.

If you already have your own blog, so much the better. In the newspaper industry, it used to be traditional for writers to work their way up the ladder through local papers. Today, the talent seems increasingly to come from the internet. Its advantages are plain: a writer with a blog has a stash of readily available, easily accessible cuttings that clearly establish their identity. Better still for an editor, if it's a good blog it may even have built up its own raft of followers who would keenly follow the blogger if they were to shift to print.

The rise of Twitter presents endless opportunities for the freelance writer. The trick is learning how to exploit it. The master at this, in my opinion, is the freelance writer Sali Hughes – who appears regularly in womens' magazines such as *Red* and *Grazia*, as well as writing comment pieces for the *Guardian*. When I found her on Twitter she seemed smart and funny, so I became one of her many thousands of followers. Eventually, off the back of that digital relationship, I hired her for the beauty column in *Weekend*. She told me that Twitter is invaluable to her freelance career: one of her editors will see something she's tweeted and then ask her to write a longer feature on the subject. She is also comfortable having conversations with her readers – both on Twitter and 'below the line' (with people who comment on her column). Embracing new technology and fostering a community of fans in this way is a fantastic example of how to make social media work for you.

Ideas

Good ideas are the essence of a good journalist. But you must avoid the obvious. Don't write to a magazine or newspaper editor suggesting an interview with Madonna – it's likely they've already had that idea and probably aren't casting around for writers. If you're just starting out, think laterally. Look in the less obvious sections or supplements for columns that an editor might struggle to fill. In a travel magazine or newspaper travel section, for example, you probably won't be able to bag a 2,000-word commission on a Maldives beach holiday, but there may be a small regular section on B&Bs or budget holidays around the UK that grander, established writers probably won't be pitching for. Don't be shy of writing about yourself and your own experiences. Again, the rise of the internet means that newspapers and magazines increasingly see the value of readers' stories and contributions. Look for those 'first person' slots and think if you've got a good personal story that would suit. From tiny acorns like that, whole careers can grow. Once you've established contact and written something, however small, bigger things may well flourish.

Respond quickly to time-sensitive ideas that are the lifeblood of newspaper features and weekly magazines, and if there is something in the news or something trending on Twitter that you think you can spin a feature out of – act fast. When something is big news or goes viral and you have an idea, get in quick – before someone beats you to it.

Contacting the publication

Whether you are published or unpublished, the most important thing is to write a convincing email or letter. Keep your idea succinct – no more than two paragraphs. (Think of it like the newspaper or magazine's stand first. On publication, they have to sell the idea to the readers in a few brief sentences – so you should be able to do the same.) If you've written before, include a few links to your most relevant work. Lots of people tell me they write for the *Guardian*, but all too often I find myself searching the archive for their byline, never to find it. It's so much easier to point to your work within your pitch.

It sounds obvious, but make sure your idea is right for the publication you're contacting. Don't blanket-email every title you can think of with the same idea, hoping that somewhere it will stick. It's good for an editor to know that you're familiar with their product and that you're suggesting an idea specifically for their section and readership. I get way too many ideas that are a completely wrong fit for the *Guardian*. It's a waste of everybody's time.

Above all, the most important thing you can do is *read* the publication you're pitching to, before getting in contact.

It's a writer's instinct to send things to the editor of the publication, but there's often someone else who will consider your idea quicker and give you an answer. Perhaps it's the deputy editor, the commissioning editor or the features editor. If it's a more specific idea – to do with fashion, health or food, for example – find out who is in charge of that area and contact them. Make a call first to see who the best person to receive your pitch is, if you're not sure. Always address them by name. If you can't be bothered to write a personal email, it doesn't suggest you're likely to be a thorough journalist.

Style

Again, read the publication, and writers you particularly admire. They might be owned by the same company – Murdoch's News International – but there's a world of difference between writing for the *Sun* and *The Times*. They might both deal in celebrity and fashion, but *Grazia* and *Vogue* have completely different styles and sections. You must adapt to the publication, and think about whether the way you've written a piece is suitable.

There is no formula to writing features you can follow for every publication, but it is common to start a piece with some 'colour'. This means beginning a piece by focusing on one anecdote or one particular person's story or quote before broadening it out to explain why their tale matters and what it represents. By the third or fourth paragraph there should really be an explanation of what trend/event/issue your piece is about. The body of any feature should have enough case studies (usually at least three people) to back up the facts and opinions that make the thrust of the piece.

Money

You've had an idea accepted – now what? The first thing to do is agree a fee. Most commonly you will be offered the publication's lineage fee (a standard rate, paid by the word). This can vary widely, so make sure you're happy with this before you start. The National Union of Journalists (www.nuj.org.uk) offers a guide to freelance rates that is worth checking. Also make it clear if you will be submitting expenses receipts and give a rough estimate of what these might be, so your editor can budget for them. Establish who owns copyright beforehand, in case you want to sell second rights to another publication. Having said that, most titles have a syndication service and are more likely to be able to place it elsewhere for you, taking a cut if they do. This is worth investigation.

Deadlines and editing

Don't miss a deadline – even if you are sure that the piece won't be printed imminently. You probably aren't familiar with the title's production schedule and deadlines are usually there for a reason, so don't ignore them. It's also better to be open to your editor's thoughts and rewriting suggestions. Their job is to make the piece better, not worse, so it's in everyone's best interest not to be a prima donna about your copy. If you're not sure of the reason for the changes, just ask.

Breaking into the industry isn't easy, but writing for newspapers and magazines can have many rewards – from meeting interesting people, to seeing your name in print for the first time, to receiving a cheque for your first published piece of work. All you need is a nice style, some good ideas and a little bit of luck!

Merope Mills currently lives in San Francisco and is West Coast Editor of *Guardian US*. She was formerly Editor of the Saturday *Guardian* and the *Guardian*'s *Weekend* magazine in London.

Writing for online and print

Experienced freelance journalist Suzanne Elliott has sound advice on how to work successfully as a writer across different platforms in the age of fake news, social media and new technology.

Not long ago journalists were split into web or print specialists, with a certain snottiness reserved for the online usurpers. But that attitude has changed and writing for online is no longer considered the poor cousin of print journalism. There is now far more of a content and staff crossover. Magazines, in particular, have embraced a more fluid relationship between the two platforms, with many pulling everything under a single 'content' umbrella.

Having worked in print and online, in newsrooms, for fashion magazines, creative agencies and press agencies, I've ridden the wave of a shifting media world over the last 20 years. Having lived through the eye of the storm, it's been fascinating watching the shift, as the internet changed how we consumed news and, as a consequence, how journalists write.

While this changing environment has proven challenging for traditional news outlets, it does provide exciting opportunities for freelancers and I hope these tips I've picked up in my time as a freelance journalist will make it easier for newcomers to exploit.

News writing

Despite the changing landscape, the '*when, where, who, what, why*' formula applies – whether you are writing for online or print, newspaper or magazine.

The inverted triangle method puts the most important detail – the five 'Ws' – in the first one or two sentences. The reader should be able to stop reading at this point and still have grasped the main points of the story. This journalism 101 may have been around since the printing press but, in a world where people consume news at a rapid pace, it has never been more appropriate. For example:

Two people have died after their car was involved in a collision with a lorry on the M25 near Leatherhead.

After this initial scene setting, you move on to the middle section that fleshes out the story, identifying victims, giving their ages, explaining how the accident happened.

The final third will include other relevant background information, quotes and perhaps a reference to a similar story.

Writing for online *v* print

While the foundations of journalism apply across all formats, there are some differences between writing for online and print. Online articles traditionally follow several other formats: news pieces; listicles (also popular in magazines); picture-led galleries (usually reserved for fashion, beauty and celebrity content); and short, blog-like articles.

Until recently, the emphasis had been to keep online articles short and, while that rule still applies to a lot of online content, more traditional long-form pieces of between 1,000 and 20,000 words are gaining popularity with publishers and readers.

Many of the regular, daily-updated and news-focused articles will be written in-house, so you will find that focusing on evergreen articles (content that is always relevant and does not date like news stories) can be a more successful route to catching an editor's eye.

Comment or opinion (op-ed) pieces are common in both print and digital. Timely pieces, these differ from news articles as they enable a writer to express their own, often provocative or controversial, opinion on a topical subject. They are usually personal and conversational and, unlike a news piece, they entertain as well as stimulate conversation.

What is fake news?

An article no longer has to be a comment or opinion piece to merit discussion. The internet enables readers to give immediate feedback on features and news stories, not all of it positive.

Increasingly, the term 'fake news' has become an accusation aimed at journalists by people who don't like what is been reported. It is also an increasing frustration for journalists trying to unearth the truth in a world full of false chatter. Fake news is nothing new, but in a 'post-truth' world, fuelled by social media and with a US president fixated on it, fake news has become a mainstream problem. Its impact on journalism is not to be underestimated. As it gains traction, fake news makes it difficult for journalists to cover high-profile news stories and undermines reports from reputable publications. Put simply, when we're telling the truth the world is not listening. A study by Buzzfeed found the top 20 fake news stories about the 2016 US presidential election received more engagement on Facebook than the top 20 *real* news stories from 19 major media outlets.

Never assume anything that appears on social media – or even other news outlets – is true until you have verified the source yourself. After the Manchester Arena bombing in May 2017, several posts of fake victims went viral within hours of the attack. One of the photos used in a montage was of Jayden Parkinson who was murdered in 2013, while another showed a picture of a young boy who had been used as a model for a fashion line several years before. Following the Grenfell Tower fire, a story of a baby being thrown from a window and caught was published in many newspapers and websites, but a BBC investigation discovered that the incident probably never happened.

Journalists need to play their part in fighting fake news, not fuelling it. Real news will always take a while to filter through, even in a world where everything is so immediate. Taking time to fact-check in the middle of a frantic breaking news story requires confidence and conviction. But it's better to be slow than to be wrong.

Style, accuracy and sources

Every publication has its own house style to ensure stylistic consistency and tone of voice. An editor may give you guidelines in the commission, but the best way to get a clear idea of style is to read the magazine, newspaper or website thoroughly.

Fact-check meticulously and don't be tempted to fudge facts. Choose your words carefully – simply replacing one word for another can alter the meaning of a sentence completely.

Record all interviews and ensure your sources are reliable and trustworthy. Many a journalist has been tripped up by failing to check the credibility of a too-good-to-be-true scoop. In 2004, Piers Morgan was sacked as editor of the *Daily Mirror* after printing fake photos of British soldiers abusing an Iraqi, claiming he had fallen victim to a 'calculated and malicious hoax'.

A working knowledge of **libel laws** is an absolute necessity for any journalist. Writing anything potentially libellous can, at best, end with the publication having to print an apology, and, at worse, land them and you in court.

The Defamation Act was updated in 2013 to include social media. You can defame someone by publishing material:

- in newspapers, magazines and other printed media;
- in radio and TV broadcasts;
- on the internet, including online forums, social media and blogs;
- by email.

Spreading 'false' news, through sloppiness and errors of judgement, is only going to further discredit journalism and fuel accusations of fake news in the mainstream media.

The rise of the internet has given a voice to citizen, or public, journalism. American journalist Courtney Radsch, author of *Cyberactivism and Citizen Journalism in Egypt: Digital Dissidence and Political Change* (Palgrave Macmillan 2016) defines it as an 'activist form of news gathering' that is 'driven by different objectives and ideals and relies on alternative sources of legitimacy than traditional or mainstream journalism.'

Technology, including smart phones and social media, have enabled members of the public to report a breaking news story more quickly than journalists, particularly in countries where foreign media access is limited. Citizen journalism played a key role in the 2010 Arab Spring, the war in Syria – especially during the battle of Aleppo – and in the 2018 economic protests in Iran.

While citizen journalism plays a significant role in unfolding news stories, a degree of caution should be applied to reports from non-professional journalists, as citizen journalism by its very nature is subjective. This doesn't devalue its worth, but its objectives and reference points should always be understood before taking it as verbatim.

Online journalism – the ins and outs

Flexibility and an open mind are important when working as a freelance journalist across different platforms. Working online involves embracing technology and usually means going beyond a traditional journalist's job description. It is common to be asked to picture edit, sub-edit, promote articles on social channels such as Twitter and Facebook and, increasingly, video edit. A grasp of content management systems (CMS) is essential for if you work online. No two systems are the same, but they are increasingly user-friendly.

Online headlines have to work extra hard. They not only have to grab a reader's attention, they must contain the right *keywords* to make it more visible to a search engine. Most search queries are two to four words long and consist of proper names and keywords. Ensuring that your headline and copy are search engine optimisation (SEO)-friendly without compromising the quality of your writing is an important skill for online journalists. The journalistic maxim 'man bites dog' – used to describe how unusual events are more likely to be reported as news – would need to be rewritten for online purposes using keywords and proper names to make it SEO-friendly, for example: '*Hampshire man, 39, bites golden retriever on leg at Centerparcs*'.

How to find a story

- Social media and news wires can be great sources of breaking news and a way of monitoring popular campaigns (e.g. #MeToo or the ice bucket challenge), but you certainly won't have been the only journalist to have spotted a trending topic – so don't rely too heavily on these.
- Social media can be helpful in other ways. Got a story and need case studies? Twitter and Facebook can be excellent ways to find people, under the hashtag #journorequest.

• Online journalist communities also offer excellent resources for freelancers to broaden their network, ask for contacts and stay up-to-date with the latest media news and jobs. Try JournoAnswers (www.facebook.com/groups/JournoAnwers) and Freelance Journalist UK (www.facebook.com/groups/FreelanceJournalistsUK), or the online reporters and editors group on LinkedIn (www.linkedin.com/groups/75711).
• Have something (a pen, a smartphone) to jot down any light-bulb story ideas. A seemingly irrelevant observation or off-hand remark can be the first germ of a far bigger idea.
• Sometimes a more interesting story is hidden *within* the story you are going after, or hidden within a seemingly unexceptionable press release.
• Think locally – read the local papers, talk to local people. Big news stories can be buried in bin collection disputes or fundraising efforts.
• Be curious and ask questions. People love talking about themselves, especially about something they are passionate about.

Pitching

While print and digital formats are more symbiotic that ever, they often still exist and are structured as two separate publications within an organisation. In a row with the *Guardian* in 2017 over commentator Katie Hopkins, *Daily Mail* editor Paul Dacre distanced himself from *MailOnline*, declaring in an editorial that the online version was 'a totally separate entity that has its own publisher, its own readership, different content and a very different world view'. It's therefore important to find out who the editor, or section editor, is within each platform.

Do not approach publications with a one-size-fits-all pitch. Think about how you consume articles online and pitch those ideas accordingly.

The dos and don'ts of pitching

DO include your pitch within an email. No busy editor will want to download and then open a Word document, or equivalent.

DO explain who you are and why the piece you are pitching is relevant to the publication.

DO read the site you are pitching to thoroughly. Don't skim through the home page and assume you've seen everything. How often do they publish? What kind of article formats do they publish (galleries, long-form, etc)? Look at the word count for each one.

DON'T send a pitch email on a Friday afternoon or first thing on a Monday.

DON'T jump on the news bandwagon assuming you're the first person to think of a pitch.

DO flag up time-sensitive features and include a deadline if it is a news–related piece.

DON'T be precious about being edited. Even the most hard-nosed and experienced of journalists can bristle at an edit, but learning not to is an important skill.

DO get the tone of the publication right in the pitch. Pitching to a music website aimed at people in their 20s is different to pitching a long-form piece to a gardening print magazine with readers over 60.

DO keep the pitch short. Avoid going beyond four paragraphs; start with a brief sentence introducing yourself; then a sentence or two on the topic, why you want to write it, who you plan to interview, your suggested word count and any possible leads; finish with why you are the person to write it.

DO follow up the email within a few days if you have not heard back.

Tips for starting out

1. Start a blog

A blog can be an effective way to promote yourself and your writing. It is particularly useful if you're a freelance journalist just starting out, as it allows you to establish yourself as an authority, on a subject and as a writer. A well-managed blog can help create writing opportunities and at the same time demonstrate your initiative and interests. It's a great way to help find your voice as a writer and to sharpen your CMS and SEO skills.

2. Have a social media presence

A Twitter profile will not only give you visibility; used well, it can also give you credibility. Use your full name (not a cheeky nickname from school) for your handle. In your bio, include your email address, your job title, publications you've written for and any speciality areas you work in. Tweet regular, appropriate updates that signpost your interests, and don't be afraid to let your personality come through.

And don't ignore LinkedIn. As well as being an excellent resource for journalists looking for scoops and jobs, by showing an up-to-date CV and a list of your skills and areas of expertise, LinkedIn makes it easier for editors who are looking for freelancers to find you.

3. Explore other writing opportunities

Content marketing, writing for a brand who want to behave like publishers, is a path increasingly open to journalists and writers. While it may not fit with your dreams of being the next Bob Woodward and Carl Bernstein, the essence of good editorial remains the same. Journalists know how to tell a good story; they know how to a hook a reader with quality writing and present clear, compelling content – skills much in demand by brands.

4. Build relationships

One of the best pieces of advice I was given when I went freelance was to 'batter my contacts'. Do not be shy to approach people you have a connection with – whether it's a former colleague, someone you studied with, or an editor you met fleetingly at a party.

Do not assume they remember you, and keep your contact email formal, but people are far more likely to commission you if there is a trusted link there. Remember you are often a solution to someone's fix – you are looking for the work and they need someone to do it.

The essential bookshelf for the budding journalist

As Stephen King says: 'If you don't have time to read, you don't have the time (or the tools) to write.' Reading great journalists and writers can inspire, educate and galvanise.

- *How to write* – George Orwell, in *Politics and the English Language* (Horizon 1946)
  Orwell's advice to 'Never use a long word when a short one will do' rings in my head whenever I write.
- *Bliss to be alive: the collected writings of Gavin Hills* (Penguin 2000)
  Hills was what the *Independent* described as one of the 'serious boys of the Loaded generation'. His hugely engaging and vital pieces covered everything from civil war to football violence.
- *On Writing: a memoir of the craft* – Stephen King (New English Library 2001)
  Read this and you'll never look at an adverb the same way again.
- *Scoop* – Evelyn Waugh (Chapman & Hall 1938)
  While journalism has changed a great deal since William Boot, the *Daily Beast*'s timid nature correspondent, is sent to cover a socialist insurrection in (fictional) Ishmaelia, so much of this biting satire still rings true.
- *The Journalist and the Murderer* – Janet Malcolm (Knopf 1990)
  A fascinating exploration of journalism ethics and the strange relationship between a reporter and their subject – in this case a man accused of murdering his wife and daughters.

Suzanne Elliott is a freelance journalist who has worked for Sky.com, *Vogue*, *Men's Fitness*, *Shortlist*, ITV News, *Huffington Post*, *Glamour*, *Marie Claire*, the *National* and MSN, and written editorial for companies including Global Radio, Shell, EE and Debenhams. For more information see https://suzanneelliott.wordpress.com or https://theviewfromtheuppercircle.com. Follow her on Twitter @CakeSuzette.

Life's a pitch: how to get your ideas into print

Mike Unwin has lots of valuable advice for would-be freelance writers keen to see their work in print, and explains what magazine and newspaper editors are looking for in a pitch.

Dear Editor

I'm desperate to write for you. Please let me. I'm not yet sure what to write – and I hesitate to share my ideas, in case you don't like them. But if you could just explain what you're looking for I'm sure I could do the job. I know you've never heard of me, but I'm a great writer – all my friends say so – and I could certainly match what you usually publish. Other editors haven't yet recognised my talent but you can change all that. Commission me and you won't regret it. What do you say?

Kind regards

A.D. Luded-Freelance

How does an aspiring freelance get into print? The answer, short of blackmail or nepotism, is via the 'pitch'. This is a written proposal to a commissioning editor. Get it right and it can bag you a commission, complete with brief, fee and deadline. Get it wrong, and the first impression you make may well be your last.

Pitching is a notoriously tricky art. With editors' inboxes already groaning, the odds are stacked against freelances, especially first-timers. The example above may be ridiculous but it nonetheless expresses the frustration felt by many freelances. How on earth do you break through?

Every freelance has a subjective take on this dilemma, depending on their field. Mine is travel and wildlife, so my advice is drawn from experience in this particular part of the industry. But the challenges are likely to be pretty similar whatever you write about. If there is a foolproof formula for success, I've yet to find it. What follows reflects 15 years of trial and error.

'Some pitches are good, most are OK, but many are dire,' says freelance commissioning editor Sue Bryant. You may never learn why your pitch succeeds or fails, but you *can* ensure that it always falls into the first of those three categories. The rest may just come down to luck.

Do your homework

First, before you write a word, familiarise yourself with your target publication. Trawl the website – or splash out on a paper copy. Establish how often it comes out: pitching a story about an imminent one-off event to a quarterly whose next edition won't appear for three months is wasting the editor's time. And check that nothing similar has already appeared. 'My bugbear is when people pitch something we've recently covered,' says Andrew Purvis, commissioning editor at *Telegraph Travel.*

Second, consider the readership. 'This is where people most often go wrong,' says Lyn Hughes, publisher of travel magazine *Wanderlust*. 'It's vitally important that you understand who the readers are and what interests them.' You don't need demographics: the ads and letters pages speak volumes. Hughes describes how *Wanderlust* has received pitches for articles on golf – utterly irrelevant to readers interested in adventure travel and the natural world. Ignorance shows. 'You can always tell if they've not thought about the magazine and the target audience,' confirms Laura Griffiths-Jones of *Travel Africa* magazine, who would never entrust a fact-finding commission to a writer who can't even be bothered to research the magazine.

Don't cut corners. An all-purpose pitch to several publications simultaneously may save you time but will seldom get past the editor, who has a nose for the mail shot. Mistakes can be excruciating. 'We see a lot of cut-and-pasting,' says Hughes. 'The giveaway is the different font.'

Finally, address your pitch to the right person. Larger publications may have different commissioning editors for different sections, including their website, and a misdirected pitch may disappear without trace. Heed protocol: copying in the commissioning editors of rival publications in your address line – a common mistake, according to Griffiths-Jones – will *not* endear you to the editor you're addressing. And don't pull rank. 'Never go over the editor's head and talk to the publisher,' warns Bryant. 'That used to make me furious.'

Most commissioning editors would rather not receive a pitch by phone: it can feel confrontational – and they will, in any case, seldom be able to say yes or no without investigating further. Social media is also seen by many as too throw-away for the initial pitch – although, if you establish a relationship, it may become useful further down the line.

Get to the point

Once you've worked out where to direct your pitch, your challenge is to make it stand out from all the others. First comes the subject line, which must convey the gist in as few words as possible. 'You've almost got to put in as much effort on the subject line as in the pitch,' stresses Hughes. Bear in mind that longer lines may half disappear on the screen of a smartphone. Thus 'New snow leopard safari to Ladakh' is more effective than 'Proposal to write a travel feature about visiting the Himalayas in search of snow leopards'.

If the editor takes the bait, the pitch that follows must flesh out that subject line succinctly. 'Ideally one paragraph, explaining what the story is,' recommends Griffiths-Jones. I aim for one paragraph of no more than 100 words, sometimes adding a few brief supplementary details (see example opposite). It can help to think of your pitch as being like a 'standfirst': the introductory paragraph that a magazine often places above an article.

Your 'angle' is critical. In travel journalism this might be a new means of experiencing an old destination or a topical hook, such as a forthcoming movie. In reality, your angle may not be very original – in travel, as elsewhere, subjects are revisited and dusted down on rotation – but your job is to make it sound novel and convince the editor that you are the one to write it. 'If I think: "So what? I could write that from my desk," then it's a non-starter,' warns Bryant.

A scattergun approach suggests lack of focus, so don't cram too many ideas into one story and certainly don't bundle several stories into one pitch. Settling on one idea can be difficult: in travel writing, almost any trip could yield multiple stories and it can feel risky to cram all your eggs into one basket. But editors are commissioning a story, not a destination. If torn, one compromise is to lead with a main angle but allow a little room for manoeuvre by including two or three brief subsidiary points that might suggest other angles should the main idea not appeal. Here's an example:

New snow leopard safari to Ladakh
In January I join a new tour to Ladakh, India, in search of snow leopards. This endangered big cat recently starred on BBC's *Planet Earth* and is one of the world's most sought-after wildlife sightings. Confined to the high Himalayas, it has long been off the tourist agenda. This pioneering venture (www.snowleopardsafaris.com) now offers snow leopard tracking for the first time. Accommodation is in community home-stays, from where expert local trackers guide small groups in to the mountains. Tourism revenue helps fund community-based conservation.
Highlights include:

- Tracking snow leopards
- Wolves, ibex, eagles and other wildlife
- Trekking in the high Himalayas
- The ancient Ladakh capital of Leh (3,500m)
- Buddhist culture: monasteries, festivals, village home-stays
- Snow leopard conservation project

Peak season Jan–April; could file story from end January.

If the editor doesn't know you, some brief credentials might help: a simple sentence at the end explaining who you are, plus a sample or two of your work. Keep any attached files small: the editor won't want PDFs clogging up their inbox. Any weblinks should be to articles relevant to your pitch. 'Don't just say "visit my website",' warns Bryant. 'It sounds really arrogant and I haven't got time.'

Mind your language

Even the most perfectly structured pitch can founder on the detail. Typos happen, but this is one place where they mustn't. Hughes describes how *Wanderlust* regularly receives pitches for stories about 'Equador' and 'Columbia'. Remember, you are trying to persuade an editor to trust your ability with words. What will they think if you stumble at the first hurdle? Editors work to tight budgets and schedules so the last thing they want is more work. 'If it's riddled with errors, and they can't construct a sentence or a paragraph correctly,' asks Purvis, 'why would I waste all that time – and budget – sorting it out?'

So double-check your pitch before sending. If in doubt, print it out: research shows that we all spot errors more easily on the printed page. To guard against embarrassing disasters, never insert the recipient's address in your email until you're ready to press 'Send'.

Style is important too. In general, less is more: the pitch is not a place for purple prose. And try to avoid journalistic faux pas, such as opening with long subordinate clauses or overusing the passive voice. And avoid cluttering your pitch with clichés: 'land of contrasts' and 'best-kept secret' are travel industry horrors that spring to mind. Editors are writers too. It doesn't take much for them to sniff out a weakness.

Me, me, me . . .

Perhaps the worst error in pitching your story is to make yourself its subject. 'Don't make the pitch about you,' insists Bryant, 'unless you're really famous or really funny.' A travel editor is not generally looking for a Bruce Chatwin or Bill Bryson; they have no use for your hilarious anecdotes or journey of discovery. They want your writing to sell an experience that their readers can go out and buy. 'We're not interested in you,' confirms Hughes. 'We're interested in our readers.' That's why any travel article will have at the end a fact box 'call to action', with all the details that the reader will need in order to replicate your experience.

Any hint of neediness is an instant deterrent. Your needs are not important, so don't suggest that by publishing your work the editor will be helping launch your career. A particular bugbear for travel editors is 'blagging': securing a commission in order to get yourself a free trip. 'I was recently offered a place on an Amazon River trip, but couldn't find a sponsor for the flights to Lima,' began one pitch that Bryant instantly rejected. Whilst a commission is a part of the equation that enables freelance travel writers to travel, the publication in question does not generally want to be caught up in the mechanics. You're a freelance; that's *your* lookout.

And beware how you present yourself. Editors talk to one another and reputations are quickly acquired. Social media can be a minefield: Bryant recalls discovering a long rant on Twitter from a writer she was considering commissioning that threatened to have a PR fired because the writer had not received a flight upgrade. 'When you're on the road on a commission,' she stresses, 'you are representing the publication and our advertisers.'

Editor empathies

If in doubt, try placing yourself in the shoes of the commissioning editor. Invariably they will be overburdened, against deadline and quite possibly battling some cost-cutting edict from on high. The last thing they're looking for, usually, is unsolicited pitches from writers that they've never heard of. 'Editors can be lazy,' admits Bryant. 'They don't like surprises.'

What's more, an editor's job is not to showcase your writing but to publish material that trumps the competition. Ultimately all editorial decisions are commercial. 'You're going to be held accountable for spending the money,' points out Purvis. Your job is to make their life easier by offering something that meets their needs.

Remember, too, that it was you who made the approach. An editor is under no obligation to justify their decision. Indeed – common courtesy aside – they are not even obliged to reply. The frustrating reality for freelances is that responses may be very slow and, at times, non-existent. Your pitch may never reach the front of the queue.

If you don't hear back, do send a gentle reminder. I usually leave it a couple of weeks and if I still hear nothing after that, I drop it. But never express your frustration; swallow it and look elsewhere. Who knows? Your name or idea may have struck a chord. The editor may get back to you months later, when you least expect it. It has happened to me. Don't burn your bridges.

And never give up. Somewhere out there is an article with your byline on it.

Mike Unwin is a freelance writer, editor and photographer who specialises in travel and wildlife. He worked for 14 years in book publishing before leaving to pursue a freelance career. Today he writes for a variety of newspapers and magazines, including the *Telegraph*, the *Independent*, *BBC Wildlife*, *Wanderlust*, *National Geographic Traveller* and *Travel Africa*. Among his 30 published books for both adults and children are *The RSPB Guide to Birdwatching* (Bloomsbury 2008), *Swaziland* (Bradt Travel Guides 2012) and *Endangered Species* (Aladdin Books 2000). His awards include BBC Wildlife Nature Travel writer of the year 2000, the British Guild of Travel Writers' UK Travel Writer of the Year 2013 and Cruise Lines International 'Best-off-the beaten-track feature' 2016.

National newspapers UK and Ireland

Daily Express

Northern & Shell Building, 10 Lower Thames Street, London EC3R 6EN
tel 020-8612 7000
email news.desk@express.co.uk
website www.express.co.uk
Facebook www.facebook.com/DailyExpress
Twitter @Daily_Express
Editor Lloyd Embley
Daily Mon–Fri 55p, Sat 80p
Supplements **Daily Express Saturday**

Exclusive news; striking photos. Leader page articles (600 words); facts preferred to opinions. Payment: according to value.

Deputy Editor Michael Booker
Diary Editor Jack Teague
Environment Editor John Ingham
Fashion & Beauty Editor Mernie Gilmore
Features Editor Natasha Weale
News Editor Geoff Maynard
Online Editor Emily Fox
Political Editor Macer Hall
Sports Editor Howard Wheatcroft
Travel Editor Jane Memmler
Women's Editor Mernie Gilmore

Daily Express Saturday Magazine

Editor Graham Bailey
Free with paper

Daily Mail

Northcliffe House, 2 Derry Street, London W8 5TT
tel 020-7938 6000
email news@dailymail.co.uk
website www.dailymail.co.uk
Facebook www.facebook.com/DailyMail
Twitter @MailOnline
Editor Paul Dacre
Daily Mon–Fri 65p, Sat £1
Supplements **Weekend**

Founded 1896.

Senior Deputy Editor Gerard Greaves
Deputy Editor Ted Verity
City Editor Alex Brummer
Diary Editor Sebastian Shakespeare
Education Correspondent Eleanor Harding
Executive Editor of Features Leaf Kalfayan
Good Health Editor Justine Hancock
Literary Editor Sandra Parsons
Moneymail Editor Dan Hyde
Executive News Editor Ben Taylor
Picture Editor Paul Silva
Political Editor Jason Groves
Head of Sport Lee Clayton
Travel Editor Mark Palmer

Daily Mirror

1 Canada Square, Canary Wharf, London E14 5AP
tel 020-7293 3000
email mirrornews@mirror.co.uk
website www.mirror.co.uk
Facebook www.facebook.com/DailyMirror
Twitter @DailyMirror
Editor Alison Phillips
Daily Mon–Fri 75p (England and Wales), 80p (Scotland), Sat £1.20
Supplements **We Love TV**

Top payment for exclusive news and news pictures. Freelance articles used, and ideas bought: send synopsis only. Unusual pictures and those giving a new angle on the news are welcomed; also cartoons. Founded 1903s.

Executive Features Editor Barry Rabbetts
Head of Business Graham Hiscott
Head of News Tom Carlin
Picture Editor Ben Jones
Political Editor Andrew Gregory
Head of Politics Jason Beattie
Head of Sports Dominic Hart

Daily Record

1 Central Quay, Glasgow G3 8DA
tel 0141 309 3000
email reporters@dailyrecord.co.uk
website www.dailyrecord.co.uk
Facebook www.facebook.com/TheScottishDailyRecord
Twitter @Daily_Record
Daily Mon–Fri 65p, Sat 90p
Supplements **Saturday, Seven Days, Living, TV Record, Road Record, Recruitment Record, The Brief**

Topical articles, from 300–700 words; exclusive stories of Scottish interest and exclusive colour photos.

Editor David Dicke
Assistant Editor & Head of News Kevin Mansi
Assistant Editor & Head of Sports Austin Barrett
Health & Education Editor Vivienne Aitken
Online Editor Graeme Thomson
Political Editor David Clegg

Saturday

Free with paper

Lifestyle magazine and entertainment guide. Reviews, travel features, shopping, personalities, colour illustrations. Payment: by arrangement.

Daily Star

Express Newspapers, The Northern & Shell Building, 10 Lower Thames Street, London EC3R 6EN

tel 020-8612 7000
email news@dailystar.co.uk
website www.dailystar.co.uk
Facebook www.facebook.com/thedailystar
Twitter @Daily_Star
Editor Lloyd Embley
Daily Mon–Fri 30p, Sat 50p
Supplements **Hot TV, Seriously Football**

Hard news exclusives, commanding substantial payment. Major interviews with big-star personalities; short features; series based on people rather than things; picture features. Illustrations: line, half-tone. Payment: by negotiation. Founded 1978.

Editor-in-Chief Jon Clark
Digital Showbiz Editor Nadia Mendoza
News Editor John McJannet
Deputy Sports Editor Andy Rose

Daily Star Sunday

Express Newspapers, The Northern & Shell Building, 10 Lower Thames Street, London EC3R 6EN
tel 020-8612 7424
website www.dailystar.co.uk/sunday
Editor Stuart James
Sun 50p
Supplements **OK! Extra**

Opportunities for freelancers.

Daily Telegraph

111 Buckingham Palace Road, London SW1W 0DT
tel 020-7931 2000
email dtnews@telegraph.co.uk
website www.telegraph.co.uk
Facebook www.facebook.com/telegraph.co.uk
Twitter @Telegraph
Editor Chris Evans
Daily Mon–Fri £1.80, Sat £2.20
Supplements **Gardening, Motoring, Property, Review, Sport, Telegraph Magazine, Travel, Weekend, Your Money**

Articles on a wide range of subjects of topical interest considered. Preliminary letter and synopsis required. Length: 700–1,000 words. Payment: by arrangement. Founded 1855.

Executive Editor Ben Clissitt
Defence & Foreign Editor Con Coughlin
Education Editor Camilla Turner
Environment Editor Geoffrey Lean
Fashion Editor Lisa Armstrong
Health Editor Laura Donnelly
Director of Lifestyle & Deputy Editor Jane Bruton
Political Editor Robert Winnett
Weekend Editor Kylie O'Brien

Telegraph Magazine

Free with Sat paper

Short profiles (about 1,600 words); articles of topical interest. Preliminary study of the magazine essential. Illustrations: all types. Payment: by arrangement. Founded 1964.

Telegraph Online

email dtnews@telegraph.co.uk
website www.telegraph.co.uk
Based on the *Daily Telegraph*. Founded 1994.

Financial Times

1 Southwark Bridge, London SE1 9HL
tel 020-7873 3000
email ean@ft.com
website www.ft.com
Facebook www.facebook.com/financialtimes
Twitter @FT
Editor Lionel Barber
Daily Mon–Fri £2.70, Sat £3.90
Supplements **Companies & Markets, FTfm, FT Reports, FT Executive Appointments, FT Weekend Magazine, House and Home, FT Money, How To Spend It, FT Wealth, Life & Arts**

One of the world's leading business news organisations, the FT provides premium and essential news, commentary and analysis. The FT aims to make its authoritative, award-winning and independent journalism available to readers anytime, anywhere and on whichever device they may choose.

Deputy Editor Roula Khalaf
Associate & Managment Editor Andrew Hill
Business Editor Sarah Gordon
Digital Comment Editor Sebastian Payne
House & Home Editor Jane Owen
Markets Editor Michael Mackenzie
Political Editor George Parker
FT Weekend Editor Alec Russell

The Guardian

Kings Place, 90 York Way, London N1 9GU
tel 020-3353 2000
email national@theguardian.com
website www.theguardian.com
Facebook www.facebook.com/theguardian
Twitter @guardian
Editor Katharine Viner
Daily Mon–Fri £2, Sat £2.90
Supplements **Sport, G2, Film & Music, The Guide, Weekend, Review, Money, Work, Travel, Family, Cook**

Few articles are taken from outside contributors except on feature and specialist pages. Illustrations: news and features photos. Payment: apply for rates. See contributors' guide https://www.theguardian.com/info/1999/nov/22/contributors-guide-and-contacts. Founded 1821.

Deputy Editor Paul Johnson
Business Editor Fiona Walsh
Economics Editor Larry Elliott
Education Editor Richard Adams
Fashion Editor Jess Cartner-Morley
Music Editor Tim Jonze
Head of National News Owen Gibson
Deputy Opinion Editors Joseph Hacker
Review Editor Lisa Allardice

Society Editor Alison Benjamin
Head of Travel Andy Pietrasik

theguardian.com/uk
website www.theguardian.com/uk

Weekend
Editor Abigail Radnor
Free with Sat paper

Features on world affairs, major profiles, food and drink, home life, the arts, travel and leisure. Also good reportage on social and political subjects. Illustrations: b&w photos, line drawings and cartoons. Payment: apply for rates.

Herald

Herald & Times Group, 200 Renfield Street, Glasgow G2 3QB
tel 0141 302 7000
email news@theherald.co.uk
English office 58 Church Street, Weybridge, Surrey KT13 8DP
tel (01932) 821212
website www.heraldscotland.com
Editor Graeme Smith
Daily Mon–Fri £1.30, Sat £1.70

Articles up to 1,000 words. Founded 1783.
Arts Editor Keith Bruce
Business Editor Ian McConnell
Foreign Affairs Editor David Pratt
Political Editor Magnus Gardham
Chief Sports Editor Stewart Fisher

Independent

Northcliffe House, 2 Derry Street, London W8 5HF
tel 020-7005 2000
email newseditor@independent.co.uk
website www.independent.co.uk
Facebook www.facebook.com/TheIndependentOnline
Twitter @independent
Editor Christian Broughton

Online only. Occasional freelance contributions; preliminary letter advisable. Payment: by arrangement. Ceased publishing in print May 2016. Founded 1986.
Arts Editor David Lister
City Editor Jim Armitage
Education Editor Richard Garner
Features Editor Rebecca Armstrong
International Editor Chris Stevenson
Literary Editor Arifa Akbar
Political Editor Joe Watts
Sports Editor Simon Rice

Irish Examiner

Linn Dubh, Assumption Road, Blackpool, Cork T23 RCH6, Republic of Ireland
tel +353 (0)21 4272722 (newsroom)
email news@examiner.ie
website www.irishexaminer.com
Acting Editor Allan Prosser
Daily Mon–Fri €2.20, Sat €2.80

Features. Material mostly commissioned. Length: 1,000 words. Payment: by arrangement. Founded 1841.
Executive Editor (news & digital) Dolan O'Hagan
Features Editor Vickie Maye
Picture Editor Jim Coughlan
Sports & Deputy Editor Tony Leen

Irish Independent

27–32 Talbot Street, Dublin D01 X2E1, Republic of Ireland
tel +353 (0)17 055333
email info@independent.ie
website www.independent.ie
Facebook www.facebook.com/independent.ie
Twitter @independent_ie
Editor Fionnan Sheahan
Daily Mon–Fri €2, Sat €2.50

Special articles on topical or general subjects. Length: 700–1,000 words. Payment: editor's estimate of value.
Business Editor Donal O'Donovan
Group Business Editor Dearbhail McDonald
Education Editor Katherine Donnelly
Opinion Editor Frank Coughlan
Group Political Editor Kevin Doyle

The Irish Times

The Irish Times Building, PO Box 74, 24–28 Tara Street, Dublin D02 CX89, Republic of Ireland
tel +353 (0)16 758000
email newsdesk@irishtimes.com
website www.irishtimes.com
Facebook www.facebook.com/irishtimes
Twitter @IrishTimes
Editor Paul O'Neill
Daily Mon–Fri €2, Sat €2.90
Supplements **The Irish Times Magazine, The Ticket (Sat), Health + Family (Tue), Business (Daily), The Ticket (Fri), Sport (Mon, Wed, Sat)**

Mainly staff-written. Specialist contributions (800–2,000 words) by commission on basis of ideas submitted. Illustrations: photos and line drawings. Payment: at editor's valuation.
Arts Editor Hugh Linehan
Business Editor Ciaran Hancock
Digital Editor Paddy Logue
Education Editor Carl O'Brien
Daily Features Editor Roisin Ingle
Deputy Features Editor Róisín Ingle
Features Weekend Review Conor Goodman
Foreign Editor Chris Dooley
Literary Editor Martin Doyle
Magazine Editor Rachel Collins
News Editor Mark Hennessy
Opinion Editor John McManus
Picture Editor Frank Miller/Brendan Fitzsimons

Political Editor Pat Leahy
Social Media Editor David Cochrane
Sports Editor Malachy Logan

Mail on Sunday

Northcliffe House, 2 Derry Street, London W8 5TT
tel 020-7938 6000
email news@mailonsunday.co.uk
website www.mailonsunday.co.uk
Editor Geordie Greig
Sun £1.80
Supplements **You, EVENT**

Articles. Illustrations: line, half-tone; cartoons. Payment: by arrangement. Founded 1982.

Arts Editor Dominic Connolly
City Editor Simon Watkins
Deputy Features Editors Nicholas Pyke, Kate Mansey
Literary Editor Susanna Gross
News Editor David Dillon
Political Editor Jason Groves
Sports Editor Alison Kervin

Financial Mail on Sunday

tel 020-7938 6984
Part of main paper

City, industry, business and personal finance. News stories up to 1,500 words. Full colour illustrations and photography commissioned. Payment: by arrangement.

EVENT

Editor Gordon Thomson
Free with paper

Fresh and exclusive take on celebrity, film, music, TV and radio, books, theatre, comedy, food, technology and cars. Founded 2013.

You

Editor Jo Elvin
Free with paper

Women's interest features. Length: 500–2,500 words. Illustrations: full colour and b&w drawings commissioned; also colour photos. Payment: by arrangement.

Morning Star

People's Press Printing Society Ltd,
William Rust House, 52 Beachy Road,
London E3 2NS
tel 020-8510 0815
email enquiries@peoples-press.com
website www.morningstaronline.co.uk
Editor Ben Chacko
Daily Mon–Fri £1.20

Newspaper for the Labour movement. Articles of general interest. Illustrations: photos, cartoons, drawings. Founded 1930.

Arts & Media Editor Cliff Cocker
Features Editor Ros Sitwell
News Editor Will Stone
Political Editor John Haylett

The National

200 Renfield Street, Glasgow G2 3QB
tel 0141 302 7000
email reporters@thenational.scot
website www.thenational.scot
Facebook www.facebook.com/thenationalnewspaperscotland
Twitter @ScotNational
Editor Callum Baird
Mon–Sat 80p

Scottish daily newspaper owned by Newsquest and the first daily newspaper in Scotland to support Scottish independence. Founded 2014.

The New European

tel (01603) 628311
email theneweuropean@archant.co.uk
website www.theneweuropean.co.uk
Facebook www.facebook.com/theneweuropean
Twitter @TheNewEuropean
Editor Matt Kelly
Weekly Thurs £2.50

A pro-EU weekly newspaper. Writers include Alastair Campbell, Michael White, Bonnie Greer, Hardeep Singh-Kohli, Yasmin Alibhai-Brown and AC Grayling. Founded 2016.

The Observer

Kings Place, 90 York Way, London N1 9GU
tel 020-3353 2000
email observer.news@observer.co.uk
website www.guardian.com/observer
Editor Paul Webster
Sun £3
Supplements **The Observer Magazine, The New Review, Sport, Observer Food Monthly**

Some articles and illustrations commissioned. Payment: by arrangement. Founded 1791.

Associate Editor & Comment Editor Robert Yates
Assistant Editor (national & international news) Julian Coman
Arts Editor Sarah Donaldson
Books Editor Ursula Kenny
Fashion Editor Jo Jones
The New Review Editor Jane Ferguson
Deputy News Editor Lisa Bachelor
Oberver Food Monthly Editor Allan Jenkins
Picture Editor Greg Whitmore
Political Editor Toby Helm
Readers' Editor Paul Chadwick
Sports Editor Matthew Hancock
Design Director Lynsey Irvine

The Observer Magazine

tel 020-3353 2000
email magazine@observer.co.uk
Editor Harriet Green

Free with paper

Commissioned features. Length: 2,000–3,000 words. Illustrations: first-class colour and b&w photos. Payment: NUJ rates; see website for details.

Observer Online
website www.theguardian.com/observer

Scotland on Sunday

Orchard Brae House, 30 Queensferry Road, Edinburgh EH4 2HS
tel 0131 311 7311
email reception@scotsman.com
website www.scotsman.com
Editor Frank O'Donnell
Sun £2

Features on all subjects, not necessarily Scottish. Payment: varies. Founded 1988.
Deputy Editor Euan McGrory
Arts Editor Roger Cox
Sports Editor Graham Bean

Spectrum Magazine
Editor Alison Gray
Free with paper

Scotsman

Orchard Brae House, 30 Queensferry Road, Edinburgh EH4 2HS
tel 0131 311 7311
email reception@scotsman.com
website www.scotsman.com
Facebook www.facebook.com/TheScotsmanNewspaper/
Twitter @TheScotsman
Editor Frank O'Donnell
Daily Mon–Fri £1.50, Sat £1.95
Supplements **Saturday Magazine, Critique, Property, Motoring, Recruitment**

Considers articles on political, economic and general themes which add substantially to current information. Prepared to commission topical and controversial series from proved authorities. Length: 800–1,000 words. Illustrations: outstanding news pictures, cartoons. Payment: by arrangement. Founded 1817.
Deputy Editor Donald Walker
Arts Editor Roger Cox
Head of Content Alan Young
Picture Editor Kayt Turner
Scottish Political Editor Tom Peterkin
Sports Editor Graham Bean

Scottish Sun

News International Newspapers, Scotland, 6th Floor, Guildhall, 57 Queen Street, Glasgow G1 3EN
tel 0141 420 5200
email scottishsundigital@news.co.uk
website www.thescottishsun.co.uk
Facebook www.facebook.com/thescottishsun
Twitter @ScottishSun
Editor Alan Muir
Daily Mon–Fri 50p, Sat 70p, Sun £1
Supplements **Fabulous**

Scottish edition of the *Sun*. Illustrations: transparencies, colour and b&w prints, colour cartoons. Payment: by arrangement. Founded 1985.

Sun

The News Building, 1 London Bridge Street, London SE1 9GF
tel 020-7782 4100
email exclusive@the-sun.co.uk
website www.thesun.co.uk
Facebook www.facebook.com/thesun
Twitter @TheSun
Editor Tony Gallagher
Daily Mon–Fri 50p, Sat 70p
Supplements **Cashflow, TV Magazine**

Takes freelance material, including cartoons. Payment: by negotiation. Founded 1969.
Deputy Editor Simon Cosyns
Business Editor Tracey Boles
Digital Editor Keith Poole
Political Editor Tom Newton Dunn
Sports Editor Jim Munro
Travel Editor Lisa Minot
TV Editor Andy Hall

Sun on Sunday

News International Newspapers Ltd, 1 London Bridge Street, London SE1 9GF
tel 020-7782 4100
email exclusive@the-sun.co.uk
website www.thesun.co.uk
Editor Victoria Newton
Sun £1
Supplements **Fabulous**

Takes freelance material. Founded 2012 replacing the *News of the World*.

Sunday Business Post

Hambleden House, 19/26 Pembroke Street Lower, Dublin D02 WV96, Republic of Ireland
tel +353 (0)16 026000
email editor@sbpost.ie
website www.businesspost.ie
Editor Ian Kehoe
Sun €3.20

Features on financial, economic and political topics; also lifestyle, media and science articles. Illustrations: colour and b&w photos, graphics, cartoons. Payment: by negotiation. Founded 1989.
Managing Editor Gillian Nelis
Deputy Editor Tony Lyons
Books & Arts Editor Nadine O'Regan
Political Editor Michael Brennan

Sunday Express

Northern & Shell Building, 10 Lower Thames Street, London EC4R 6EN
tel 020-8612 7000
email sundaynews@express.co.uk
website www.express.co.uk/news/sunday
Editor Martin Townsend
Sun £1.40
Supplements **'S' Sunday Express, Property, Review, Sport, Travel, Financial**

Exclusive news stories, photos, personality profiles and features of controversial or lively interest. Length: 800–1,000 words. Payment: top rates. Founded 1918.

Arts & Entertainment Editor Clair Woodward
City Editor Geoff Ho
Features Editor Amy Packer
Health Editor Lucy Johnston
Literary Editor Charlotte Heathcote
Political Editor Caroline Wheeler
Sports Editor Scott Wilson
Television Editor David Stephenson

'S' Sunday Express

tel 020-8612 7257
email sundaymag@express.co.uk
Editor Margaret Hussey
Free with paper

Sunday Herald

200 Renfield Street, Glasgow G2 3QB
tel 0141 302 7000
email news@sundayherald.com
website www.heraldscotland.com
Sun £1.80
Supplements **Sport, Sunday Herald Magazine**

News and stories about Scotland, the UK and the world. Opportunities for freelancers with quality contacts. Founded 1999.

Executive Editor Neil Mackay
Features Editor Garry Scott
Foreign Editor David Pratt
Opinion Editor Susan Flockhart

Sunday Independent

27–32 Talbot Street, Dublin D01 X2E1, Republic of Ireland
tel +353 (0)17 055333
email info@independent.ie
website www.independent.ie
Editor Cormac Bourke
Sun €3

Special articles. Length: according to subject. Illustrations: topical or general interest, cartoons. Payment: at editor's valuation.

Business Editor Nick Webb
Deputy Business Editor Fearghal O'Connor
Life Magazine Editor Brendan O'Connor
Sports Editor John Greene

Sunday Mail

1 Central Quay, Glasgow G3 8DA
tel 0141 309 3000
email reporters@sundaymail.co.uk
London office 1 Canada Square, Canary Wharf, London E14 5AP
website www.dailyrecord.co.uk
Editor David Dick
Sun £1.30
Supplements **Entertainment, Fun on Sunday, Jobsplus!, 7-Days, Right at Home**

Exclusive stories and pictures of national and Scottish interest; also cartoons. Payment: above average.

Deputy Editor Russell Findlay
Head of Images Andrew Hosie
Political Editor Mark Aitken
Sports Editor George Cheyne

Sunday Mirror

1 Canada Square, Canary Wharf, London E14 5AP
tel 020-7293 3000
email scoops@sundaymirror.co.uk
website www.mirror.co.uk
Editor Peter Willis
Sun £1.40
Supplements **Notebook, Holidays & Getaways**

Concentrates on human interest news features, social documentaries, dramatic news and feature photos. Ideas, as well as articles, bought. Payment: high, especially for exclusives. Founded 1963.

Deputy Editor Caroline Waterstone
Head of Features Gemma Aldridge
Head of News Nick Owens

Sunday People

1 Canada Square, Canary Wharf, London E14 5AP
tel 020-7293 3842
email feedback@people.co.uk
website https://www.mirror.co.uk/all-about/sunday-people
Editor Peter Willis
Sun £1.50
Supplements **Take it Easy**

Exclusive news and feature stories needed. Investigative and campaigning issues. Features and human interest stories as speciality. Strong sports following. Payment: rates high, even for tips that lead to published news stories.

Executive Editorial Kate Coyne
Political Editor Nigel Nelson

Take it Easy

Editor Samantha Cope
Free with paper

Sunday Post

2 Albert Square, Dundee DD1 1DD
tel (01382) 223131
email mail@sundaypost.com
website https://www.sundaypost.com/

Editor Richard Prest
Sun £1.70
Supplements **Travel & Homes, TV & Entertainment**

Human interest, topical, domestic and humorous articles, and exclusive news. Payment: on acceptance.

in10 magazine
tel (01382) 223131
Head of Content Dawn Donaghey
Monthly Free with paper

General interest articles. Length: 1,000–2,000 words. Illustrations: colour transparencies. Payment: varies. Founded 1988.

Sunday Telegraph

111 Buckingham Palace Road, London SW1W 0DT
tel 020-7931 2000
email stnews@telegraph.co.uk
website www.telegraph.co.uk
Editor Allister Heath
Sun £2
Supplements **Business Reporter, Life, Money, Seven, Sport, Stella, Discover**

Occasional freelance material accepted.
Group Head of Books Gaby Wood
Group Business Editor James Quinn
Group City Diary Editor Anna White
Film Editor Ross Jones
London Editor Andrew Gilligan
Picture Editor Mike Spillard

Stella
tel 020-7931 2000
email stella@telegraph.co.uk
Editor Marianne Jones
Free with paper

All material is commissioned. Founded 1995.

The Sunday Times

The News Building, 1 London Bridge Street, London SE1 9GF
tel 020-7782 5000
email newsdesk@sunday-times.co.uk
website www.thetimes.co.uk
Facebook www.facebook.com/timesandsundaytimes
Twitter @thesundaytimes
Editor Martin Ivens
Sun £2.50
Supplements **Appointments, Business, Culture, Driving, Home, Money, News Review, Sport, Style, The Sunday Times Magazine, Travel**

Special articles by authoritative writers on politics, literature, art, drama, music, finance, science and topical matters. Payment: top rate for exclusive features. Founded 1822.
Deputy Editor Sarah Baxter
Editorial Director Eleanor Mills
Culture Editor Helen Hawkins
Economics Editor David Smith
Literary Editor Andrew Holgate
Political Editor Tim Shipman
Social Affairs Editor Greg Hurst
Sports Editor David Walsh

The Sunday Times Magazine
tel 020-7782 5000
Editor Sarah Baxter
Free with paper

Articles and pictures. Illustrations: colour and b&w photos. Payment: by negotiation.

The Times

The News Building, News UK,
1 London Bridge Street, London SE1 9GF
tel 020-7782 5000
email home.news@thetimes.co.uk
website www.thetimes.co.uk
Facebook www.facebook.com/timesandsundaytimes
Twitter @thetimes
Editor John Witherow
Daily Mon–Fri £1.60, Sat £1.70
Supplements **Books, Bricks & Mortar, Crème, Football Handbook, The Game, The Knowledge, Money, Times 2, Times Law, The Times Magazine, Times Sport, Travel, Arts and Entertainment, Fashion, Saturday Review, Technology Review, Weekend**

Outside contributions considered from experts in subjects of current interest and writers who can make first-hand experience or reflection come readably alive. Phone appropriate section editor. Length: up to 1,200 words. Founded 1785.
Deputy Editor Emma Tucker
Managing Editor Craig Tregurtha
Business Editor Richard Fletcher
Head of Digital at The Times & Sunday Times Alan Hunter
Health Editor Chris Smyth
Foreign Editor Roland Watson
Literary Editor Andrew Holgate
Political Editor Francis Elliott
Head of Sport Tim Hallissey
Travel Editor Jane Knight

The Times Magazine
Editor Louise France
Free with Sat paper

Features. Illustrated.

The Voice

GV Media Group Ltd, Unit 235,
Elephant and Castle Shopping Centre,
London SE1 6TE
tel 020-7510 0340
email newsdesk@gvmedia.co.uk
website www.voice-online.co.uk
Managing Director & Editor George Ruddock
Weekly £1

Weekly newspaper for black Britons. Includes news, features, arts, sport and a comprehensive jobs and business section. Illustrations: colour and b&w photos. Open to ideas for news and features on sports, business, community events and the arts. Founded 1982.

Wales on Sunday

6 Park Street, Cardiff CF10 1XR
tel 029-2024 3604
email newsdesk@walesonline.co.uk
website www.walesonline.co.uk
Editor Alan Edmunds
Sun £1.60
Supplements **Life on Sunday, Sport on Sunday**

National Sunday newspaper of Wales offering comprehensive news, features and entertainment coverage at the weekend, with a particular focus on events in Wales. Accepts general interest articles, preferably with a Welsh connection. Founded 1989.

Political Editor David Williamson
Head of Sport Paul Abbandonato

Regional newspapers UK and Ireland

Regional newspapers are listed in alphabetical order under region. Some will accept and pay for letters to the editor, brief fillers and gossip paragraphs, as well as puzzles and quizzes.

BELFAST

Belfast Telegraph

33 Clarendon Road, Clarendon Dock,
Belfast BT1 3BG
tel 028-9026 4000
email editor@belfasttelegraph.co.uk
email newseditor@belfasttelegraph.co.uk
website www.belfasttelegraph.co.uk
Facebook www.facebook.com/belfasttelegraph
Twitter @beltel
Editor Gail Walker
Group Managing Editor Edward McCann
Daily Mon–Sat £1

An Independent News & Media publication. Any material relating to Northern Ireland. Payment: by negotiation. Founded 1870.

Irish News

115–117 Donegall Street, Belfast BT1 2GE
tel 028-9032 2226
website www.irishnews.com
Facebook www.facebook.com/IrishNewsLtd
Twitter @irish_news
Editor Noel Doran
Daily Mon–Sat £1

Founded 1855.

News Letter

Ground Floor, Metro Building,
6–9 Donegall Square South, Belfast BT1 5JA
tel 028-3839 5577
email newsdesk@newsletter.co.uk
website www.newsletter.co.uk/news
Facebook www.facebook.com/belfastnewsletter
Twitter @News_Letter
Editor Mike Nesbitt
Daily Mon–Sat £1.10

Pro-Union. Founded 1737.

Sunday Life

Belfast Telegraph House, 33 Clarendon Road,
Clarendon Dock, Belfast BT1 3BG
tel 028-9026 4000
email sinews@sundaylife.co.uk
website https://www.belfasttelegraph.co.uk/sunday-life/
Editor Martin Breen
Sun £1.60

Items of interest to Northern Ireland Sunday tabloid readers. Illustrations: colour and b&w pictures and graphics. Payment: by arrangement. Founded 1988.

CHANNEL ISLANDS

Guernsey Press and Star

PO Box 57, Braye Road, Vale, Guernsey GY1 3BW
tel (01481) 240240
website http://guernseypress.com/
Facebook www.facebook.com/GuernseyPress
Twitter @guernseypress
Editor Shaun Green
Daily Mon–Sat 65p

News and feature articles. Length: 500–700 words. Illustrations: colour and b&w photos. Payment: by negotiation. Founded 1897.

Jersey Evening Post

PO Box 582, Five Oaks, St Saviour, Jersey JE4 8XQ
tel (01534) 611611
email news@jerseyeveningpost.com
website https://jerseyeveningpost.com/
Facebook www.facebook.com/jerseyeveningpost
Twitter @jepnews
Editor Andy Sibcy
Daily Mon–Sat 70p

News and features with a Channel Islands angle. Length: 1,000 words (articles/features), 300 words (news). Illustrations: colour and b&w. Payment: £110 per 1,000 words. Founded 1890.

CORK

Evening Echo (Cork)

Linn Dubh, Assumption Road, Blackpool,
Cork T23 RCH6, Republic of Ireland
tel +353 (0)21 4272722
email news@eecho.ie
website www.eveningecho.ie
Facebook www.facebook.com/eveningecho
Twitter @CorkEveningEcho
Editor Maurice Gubbins
Daily Mon–Sat €1.50

Articles, features and news for the area. Illustrations: colour prints.

DUBLIN

Herald

Independent House, 27–32 Talbot Street,
Dublin D01 X2E1, Republic of Ireland
tel +353 (0)17 055722

email hnews@independent.ie
website www.herald.ie
Facebook www.facebook.com/Herald.ie
Twitter @HeraldNewsdesk
Editor Stephen Rae
Daily Mon–Sat €1.20

Articles. Illustrations: line, half-tone, cartoons. Payment: by arrangement.

EAST ANGLIA

Cambridge News

Building 100, Cambridge Research Park, Waterbeach, Cambs. CB25 9PD
tel (01223) 632200
email newsdesk@cambridge-news.co.uk
website www.cambridge-news.co.uk
Facebook www.facebook.com/cambridgenews
Twitter @CambridgeNewsUK
Editor David Bartlett
Daily Mon–Fri 60p, Sat 70p

The voice of the Cambridge region – news, views and sport. Illustrations: colour prints, b&w and colour graphics. Payment: by negotiation. Founded 1888.

East Anglian Daily Times

Portman House, 120 Princes Street, Ipswich IP1 1RS
tel (01473) 230023
email newsroom@archant.co.uk
website www.eadt.co.uk
Facebook www.facebook.com/eadt24
Twitter @eadt24
Editor Brad Jones
Daily Mon–Fri 90p, Sat £1.80

Features of East Anglian interest, preferably with pictures. Length: 500 words. Illustrations: NUJ rates. Payment: negotiable. Founded 1874.

Eastern Daily Press

Prospect House, Rouen Road, Norwich NR1 1RE
tel (01603) 628311
London office House of Commons Press Gallery, House of Commons, London SW1A 0AA
tel 020-7219 3384
website www.edp24.co.uk
Facebook www.facebook.com/edp24/
Twitter @edp24
Editor David Powles
Daily Mon–Fri 95p

Limited market for articles of East Anglian interest not exceeding 900 words. Founded 1870.

Ipswich Star

Portland House, 120 Princes Street, Ipswich, Suffolk IP4 1AN
tel (01473) 230023
website www.ipswichstar.co.uk
Facebook www.facebook.com/ipswichstar24
Twitter @ipswichstar24
Editor Brad Jones
Daily Mon–Fri 80p

Founded 1885.

Norwich Evening News

Prospect House, Rouen Road, Norwich NR1 1RE
tel (01603) 628311
website www.eveningnews24.co.uk
Facebook www.facebook.com/NorwichEveningNews
Twitter @EveningNews
Editor David Powles
Daily Mon–Sat 80p

Interested in local news-based features. Length: up to 500 words. Payment: Agreed rates. Founded 1882.

EAST MIDLANDS

Burton Mail

Burton Daily Milton House, Burton on Trent DE14 1BQ
tel (01283) 245000
email editorial@burtonmail.co.uk
website www.burtonmail.co.uk
Facebook www.facebook.com/BurtonNews
Twitter @BurtonMailNews
Editor Julie Crouch
Daily Mon–Sat 60p

Features, news and articles of interest to Burton and south Derbyshire readers. Length: 400–500 words. Illustrations: colour and b&w. Payment: by negotiation. Founded 1898.

Chronicle & Echo, Northampton

Northamptonshire Newspapers Ltd, Albert House, Victoria Street, Northampton NN1 3NR
tel (01604) 467000
email editor@northantsnews.co.uk
website www.northamptonchron.co.uk
Facebook www.facebook.com/northamptonchron
Twitter @ChronandEcho
Editor David Summers
Weekly Thurs £1.50

Articles, features and news – mostly commissioned – of interest to the Northampton area. Length: varies. Payment: by negotiation. Founded 1931.

Derby Telegraph

2 Siddals Road, Derby DE1 2PB
tel (01332) 411888
website www.derbytelegraph.co.uk
Facebook www.facebook.com/derbytelegraph
Twitter @DerbyTelegraph
Editor Steve Hall
Daily Mon–Sat 60p

Articles and news of local interest. Payment: by negotiation.

Leicester Mercury
16 New Walk, Leicester LE1 6TF
tel 0116 251 2512
website www.leicestermercury.co.uk
Facebook www.facebook.com/leicestermercury
Twitter @Leicester_Merc
Editor George Oliver
Daily Mon–Fri 75p, Sat 85p

Occasional articles, features and news; submit ideas to editor first. Length/payment: by negotiation. Founded 1874.

Nottingham Post
3rd Floor, City Gate, Tollhouse Hill, Nottingham NG1 5FS
tel 0115 948 2000
email newsdesk@nottinghampostgroup.co.uk
website www.nottinghampost.com
Facebook www.facebook.com/TheNottinghamPost
Twitter @Nottingham_Post
Editor Mike Sassi
Daily Mon–Sat 65p

Material on local issues considered. Founded 1878.

Peterborough Telegraph
Unex House, Suite B, Bourges Boulevard, Peterborough PE1 1NG
tel (01733) 555111
email news@peterboroughtoday.co.uk
website www.peterboroughtoday.co.uk
Facebook www.facebook.com/peterboroughtoday
Twitter @peterboroughtel
Editor Mark Edwards
Weekly Thurs £1.40

LONDON

London Evening Standard
Evening Standard Ltd, 2 Derry Street, London W8 5TT
tel 020-3367 7000
email news@standard.co.uk
website https://www.standard.co.uk/
Facebook www.facebook.com/eveningstandard
Twitter @standardnews
Editor George Osborne
Daily Mon–Fri Free

Founded 1827.

ES-Magazine
Editor Laura Weir
Weekly Free with paper on Fri

Feature ideas, exclusively about London. Illustrations: all types. Payment: by negotiation.

Homes & Property
email homesandproperty@standard.co.uk
Editor Janice Morley
Weekly Free with paper on Wed

UK property. Payment: by negotiation.

NORTH EAST

Berwick Advertiser
90 Marygate, Berwick-upon-Tweed, Northumberland TD15 1BW
tel (01289) 334700
email advertisernews@tweeddalepress.co.uk
website www.berwick-advertiser.co.uk
Facebook www.facebook.com/BAdvertiser
Twitter @BAdvertiser
Editor Paul Larkin
Daily Mon–Fri £1.30

Articles, features and news.

The Chronicle
Groat Market, Newcastle upon Tyne NE1 1ED
tel 0191 201 6446
email ec.news@ncjmedia.co.uk
website www.chroniclelive.co.uk
Facebook www.facebook.com/NewcastleChronicle
Twitter @EveningChron
Editor Darren Thwaites
Daily Mon–Sat 65p

News, photos and features covering almost every subject of interest to readers in Tyne & Wear, Northumberland and Durham. Payment: by prior arrangement.

Darlington and Stockton Times
PO Box 14, Priestgate, Darlington DL1 1NF
tel (01325) 381313
email newsdesk@nne.co.uk
website www.darlingtonandstocktontimes.co.uk
Facebook www.facebook.com/darlingtonstocktontimes
Twitter @DAndSTimes
Editor Andy Richardson
Weekly Fri £1

Founded 1847.

Durham Advertiser
Ribble House, Mandale Business Park, Belmont Industrial Estate, Durham DL1 1TH
tel 0191 384 4600
email newsdesk@nne.co.uk
website www.durhamadvertiser.co.uk
Facebook www.facebook.com/durhamadvertiser
Head of Content Nigel Burton
Weekly Fri Free

The Gazette
1st Floor, Hudson Quay, The Halyard, Middlehaven, Middlesbrough TS3 6RT
tel (01642) 234262

email news@gazettemedia.co.uk
website www.gazettelive.co.uk
Facebook www.facebook.com/TeessideGazette
Twitter @EveningGazette
Editor Chris Styles
Daily Mon–Sat 65p

News, topical and lifestyle features. Length: 600–800 words. Illustrations: line, half-tone, colour, graphics, cartoons. Payment: £75 per 1,000 words; scale rate or by agreement for illustrations. Founded 1869.

Hartlepool Mail

Northeast Press Ltd, 9–13 Scarborough Street, Hartlepool TS24 7DA
tel (01429) 235197
email mail.news@northeast-press.co.uk
website www.hartlepoolmail.co.uk
website www.peterleestar.co.uk
Facebook www.facebook.com/hartlepoolmailnews
Twitter @HPoolMail
Editor Joy Yates
Daily Mon–Sat 70p

Features of local interest. Length: 500 words. Illustrations: colour, b&w photos, line. Payment: by negotiation. Founded 1877.

The Journal

Groat Market, Newcastle upon Tyne NE1 1ED
tel 0191 201 6446
email ec.news@ncjmedia.co.uk
website www.chroniclelive.co.uk
Facebook www.facebook.com/newcastlejournal
Twitter @TheJournalNews
Editor Darren Thwaites
Daily Mon–Fri 80p, Sat £1.30

News, sport items and features of topical interest considered. Payment: by arrangement.

The Northern Echo

PO Box 14, Priestgate, Darlington, Co. Durham DL1 1NF
tel (01325) 381313
email newsdesk@nee.co.uk
website www.thenorthernecho.co.uk
Facebook www.facebook.com/thenorthernecho/
Twitter @thenorthernecho
Editor Andy Richardson
Daily Mon–Fri 75p, Sat 95p

Articles of interest to North-East and North Yorkshire; all material commissioned. Preliminary study of newspaper advisable. Length: 800–1,000 words. Illustrations: line, half-tone, colour – mostly commissioned. Payment: by negotiation. Founded 1870.

The Shields Gazette

7 Beach Road, South Shields, Tyne & Wear NE33 2QA
tel 0191 501 7436
website www.shieldsgazette.com
Facebook www.facebook.com/shieldsgazette
Twitter @shieldsgazette
Editor Joy Yates
Daily Mon–Sat 80p

The Sunday Sun

Groat Market, Newcastle upon Tyne NE1 1ED
tel 0191 201 6201
email scoop.sundaysun@ncjmedia.co.uk
website www.chroniclelive.co.uk/all-about/sunday-sun
Editor Matt McKenzie
Weekly Sun £1

Looking for topical and human interest articles on current problems. Particularly welcomed are special features of family appeal and news stories of special interest to the North of England. Length: 200–700 words. Illustrations: photos. Payment: normal lineage rates, or by arrangement. Founded 1919.

Sunderland Echo

2nd Floor, Alexander House, 1 Mandarin Road, Houghton-le-Spring, Sunderland, Tyne & Wear DH4 5RA
tel 0191 501 5800
email echo.news@northeast-press.co.uk
website www.sunderlandecho.com
Facebook www.facebook.com/sunderlandechoonline
Twitter @SunderlandEcho
Editorial Director Joy Yates
Daily Mon–Sat 75p

Local news, features and articles. Length: 500 words. Illustrations: colour and b&w photos, line, cartoons. Payment: by negotiation. Founded 1875.

NORTH WEST

Blackpool Gazette

Blackpool Gazette and Herald Ltd, Avroe House, Avroe Crescent, Blackpool Business Park, Squires Gate, Blackpool FY4 2DP
tel (01253) 400888
email editorial@blackpoolgazette.co.uk
website www.blackpoolgazette.co.uk
Facebook www.facebook.com/blackpoolgazette
Twitter @the_gazette
Editor Chris Dixon
Daily Mon–Sat 70p

Local news and articles of general interest, with photos if appropriate. Length: varies. Payment: on merit. Founded 1929.

Bolton News

The Wellsprings, Civic Centre, Victoria Square, Bolton, Lancs. BL1 1AR
tel (01204) 522345

email newsdesk@nqw.co.uk
website www.theboltonnews.co.uk
Facebook www.facebook.com/theboltonnews
Twitter @TheBoltonNews
Editor-in-Chief Ian Savage
Daily Mon–Sat 65p

Founded 1867.

Carlisle News and Star

CN Group, Newspaper House, Dalston Road, Carlisle CA2 5UA
tel (01228) 612600
website www.newsandstar.co.uk
Facebook www.facebook.com/newsandstar
Twitter @newsandstar
Associate Editor Chris Story
Daily Mon–Sat 65p

The Chester Chronicle

Maple House, Park West, Sealand Road, Chester CH1 4RN
tel (01244) 340151
email newsroom@cheshirenews.co.uk
website www.chesterchronicle.co.uk
Facebook www.facebook.com/chesterchronicle
Twitter @ChesterChron
Editor Michael Green
Weekly Thurs £1.10

Local news and features. Founded 1775.

Lancashire Evening Post

Stuart House, 89 Caxton Road, Fulwood, Preston PR2 9ZB
tel (01772) 254841
email lep.newsdesk@lep.co.uk
website www.lep.co.uk
Facebook www.facebook.com/lancashireeveningpost
Twitter @leponline
Editor Gillian Parkinson
Daily Mon–Sat 70p

Topical articles on all subjects. Area of interest: Wigan to Lake District, Lancs. and coast. Length: 600–900 words. Illustrations: colour and b&w photos, cartoons. Payment: by arrangement.

Lancashire Telegraph

50–54 Church Street, Blackburn, Lancs. BB1 5AL
tel (01254) 678678
email lt_editorial@nqnw.co.uk
website www.lancashiretelegraph.co.uk
Facebook www.facebook.com/lancashiretelegraph
Twitter @lancstelegraph
Editor Steven Thompson
Daily Mon–Sat 65p

Will consider general news items from East Lancashire. Payment: by arrangement. Founded 1886.

Liverpool Echo

PO Box 48, Old Hall Street, Liverpool L69 3EB
tel 0151 227 2000
website www.liverpoolecho.co.uk
Facebook www.facebook.com/theliverpoolecho
Twitter @LivEchonews
Editor Alastair Machray
Daily Mon–Fri 70p, Sat £1, Sun 60p

Articles of up to 600–800 words of local or topical interest; also cartoons. Payment: according to merit; special rates for exceptional material. Connected with, but independent of, the *Liverpool Post*: articles not interchangeable.

The Mail

Newspaper House, Abbey Road, Barrow-in-Furness, Cumbria LA14 5QS
tel (01229) 840100
email news.em@nwemail.co.uk
website www.nwemail.co.uk
Facebook www.facebook.com/northwesteveningmail
Editor James Higgins
Daily Mon–Fri 60p, Sat 70p

Articles, features and news. Length: 500 words. Covering the whole of South Cumbria. Illustrations: colour photos and occasional artwork. Founded 1898.

Manchester Evening News

Mitchell Henry House, Hollinwood Avenue, Chadderton OL9 8EF
tel 0161 832 7200 (editorial)
email newsdesk@men-news.co.uk
website www.manchestereveningnews.co.uk
Facebook www.facebook.com/ManchesterEveningNews
Twitter @MENNewsdesk
Editor Rob Irvine
Daily Mon–Sat 75p

Feature articles of up to 1,000 words, topical or general interest and illustrated where appropriate, should be addressed to the Features Editor. Payment: on acceptance.

SCOTLAND

The Courier

D.C. Thomson & Co. Ltd, 2 Albert Square, Dundee DD1 9QJ
tel (01382) 223131
London office 185 Fleet Street, London EC4A 2HS
tel 020-7400 1030
website www.thecourier.co.uk
Facebook www.facebook.com/thecourieruk
Twitter @thecourieruk
Editor (acting) Catriona MacInnes
Daily Mon–Fri £1, Sat £1.20
Supplements **Motoring, House & Home, What's On, Menu, Weekend, Beautiful Homes, Perfect Weddings, Farming, Business, Sport**

One of Britain's biggest regional morning newspapers and an established title in east central Scotland.

Publishes four daily editions and covers local news for Perthshire, Fife, Angus & The Mearns and Dundee. Founded 1816.

Dundee Evening Telegraph and Post

2 Albert Square, Dundee DD1 1DD
tel (01382) 575888
email newsdesk@eveningtelegraph.co.uk
London office 185 Fleet Street, London EC4A 2HS
tel 020-7400 1030
website www.eveningtelegraph.co.uk
Facebook www.facebook.com/eveningtele
Twitter @Evening_Tele
Editor Andrew Kellock
Daily Mon–Fri 65p

Evening Express (Aberdeen)

Aberdeen Journals Ltd, PO Box 43, Lang Stracht, Mastrick, Aberdeen AB15 6DF
tel (01224) 344150
email ee.news@ajl.co.uk
website www.eveningexpress.co.uk
Facebook www.facebook.com/EveningExpressAberdeen
Twitter @eveningexpress
Editor Alan McCabe
Daily Mon–Sat 55p

Lively evening paper. Illustrations: colour and b&w. Payment: by arrangement.

Evening News (Edinburgh)

Orchard Brae House, 30 Queensferry Road, Edinburgh EH4 2HS
tel 0131 311 7311
email reception@scotsman.com
website www.edinburghnews.scotsman.com
Facebook www.facebook.com/edinburgh.evening.news
Twitter @edinburghpaper
Editorial Director Frank O'Donnell
Daily Mon–Sat 80p

Features on current affairs, preferably in relation to the circulation area. Women's talking points; local historical articles; subjects of general interest; health, beauty and fashion. Founded 1873.

Glasgow Evening Times

200 Renfield Street, Glasgow G2 3QB
tel 0141 302 7000
website www.eveningtimes.co.uk
Facebook www.facebook.com/eveningtimes
Twitter @TheEveningTimes
Editor Donald Martin
Daily Mon–Sat 68p

Founded 1876.

Greenock Telegraph

2 Crawfurd Street, Greenock PA15 1LH
(01475) 726511
email editorial@greenocktelegraph.co.uk
website www.greenocktelegraph.co.uk
Facebook www.facebook.com/greenocktelegraph
Twitter @greenocktele
Editor Brian Hossack
Daily Mon–Fri 48p

News and features from the area in and around Greenock. Founded 1857.

Inverness Courier

New Century House, Stadium Road, Inverness IV1 1FG
tel (01463) 233059
email editorial@inverness-courier.co.uk
website www.inverness-courier.co.uk
Facebook www.facebook.com/invernesscourier/
Twitter @InvCourier
Editor Brian Hossack
Biweekly Tue 85p, Fri £1.15

Articles of Highland interest only. Unsolicited material accepted. Illustrations: colour and b&w photos. Payment: by arrangement. Founded 1817.

Paisley Daily Express

Scottish and Universal Newspapers Ltd, 14 New Street, Paisley, Renfrewshire PA1 1YA
tel 0141 887 7911
website www.dailyrecord.co.uk/all-about/paisley
Facebook www.facebook.com/paisleydailyexpress
Twitter @PDEofficial
Editor Cheryl McEvoy
Daily Mon–Sat 50p

Articles of Paisley interest only. Considers unsolicited material.

Press and Journal

PO Box 43, Lang Stracht, Aberdeen AB15 6DF
tel (01224) 343311
email pj.newsdesk@ajl.co.uk
website https://www.pressandjournal.co.uk/
Facebook www.facebook.com/ThePressandJournal
Twitter @pressjournal
Editor Richard Neville
Daily Mon–Fri £1, Sat £1.20

Contributions of Scottish interest. Illustrations: half-tone. Payment: by arrangement. Founded 1747.

SOUTH EAST

The Argus

Dolphin House, 2–5 Manchester Street, Brighton BN2 1TF
tel (01273) 021400
email editor@theargus.co.uk
website www.theargus.co.uk
Facebook www.facebook.com/brightonargus
Twitter @brightonargus

Editor Aaron Hendy
Daily Mon–Fri 70p, Sat 85p

Established 1880.

Banbury Guardian

The Colin Sanders Business Innovation Centre, Mewburn Road, Banbury OX16 9PA
tel (01295) 227758
email editorial@banburyguardian.co.uk
website www.banburyguardian.co.uk
Facebook www.facebook.com/banburyguardian
Twitter @banburynews
Editor Jason Gibbins
Daily Mon–Sat £1.10

Local news and features. Founded 1838.

Echo

Newspaper House, Chester Hall Lane, Basildon, Essex SS14 3BL
tel (01268) 522792
email echonews@nqe.com
website www.echo-news.co.uk
Facebook www.facebook.com/echo.essex
Twitter @Essex_Echo
Editor Chris Hatton
Daily Mon–Fri 68p

Mostly staff-written. Only interested in local material. Payment: by arrangement. Founded 1969.

Essex Chronicle

Kestrel House, Hedgerows Business Park, Chelmsford Business Park, Chelmsford CM2 5PF
tel (01245) 602700
email newsdesk@essexlive.news
website www.essexlive.news/news
Twitter @totalessex
Editor Paul Dent-Jones
Weekly Thurs 90p

Local news and features for Essex. Founded 1764.

Hampshire Chronicle

5 Upper Brook St, Winchester, Hants SO23 8AL
tel (01962) 861860
email news@hampshirechronicle.co.uk
website www.hampshirechronicle.co.uk
Facebook www.facebook.com/hampshire.chronicle
Twitter @hantschronicle
Editor Gordon Sutter
Weekly Thurs £1.10

Founded 1772.

Isle of Wight County Press

Brannon House, 123 Pyle Street, Newport, Isle of Wight PO30 1ST
tel (01983) 535007
email editor@iwcp.co.uk
website www.iwcp.co.uk
Facebook www.facebook.com/iwcponline
Twitter @iwcponline
Editor Alan Marriott
Weekly Fri 80p

Articles and news of local interest. Founded 1884.

Kent and Sussex Courier

Courier House, 80–84 Calverley Road, Tunbridge Wells, Kent TN1 2UN
tel (01892) 239042
email westkentreporters@kentlive.news
website www.kentlive.news
Facebook www.facebook.com/kentlivenews
Twitter @kentlivenews
Editor Roger Kasper
Weekly Fri £1

Local news, articles and features. Founded 1872.

Medway Messenger

Medway House, Ginsbury Close, Sir Thomas Longley Road, Medway City Estate, Strood, Kent ME2 4DU
tel (01634) 227800
website www.kentonline.co.uk
Facebook www.facebook.com/MedwayMessenger
Twitter @MedwayMessenger
Editor Matt Ramsden
Biweekly Mon 80p, Fri £1.40

Emphasis on news and sport from the Medway Towns. Illustrations: line, half-tone.

The News, Portsmouth

100 Lakeside, North Harbour, Portsmouth PO6 3EN
tel 023-9266 4488
email newsdesk@thenews.co.uk
website www.portsmouth.co.uk
Facebook www.facebook.com/portsmouthnews
Twitter @portsmouthnews
Editor Mark Waldron
Daily Mon–Fri 83p, Sat 90p

Articles of relevance to South-East Hampshire and West Sussex. Payment: by arrangement. Founded 1877.

Oxford Mail

Newspaper House, Osney Mead, Oxford OX2 0EJ
tel (01865) 425262
email newsdesk@nqo.com
website www.oxfordmail.co.uk
Twitter @TheOxfordMail
Editor John Carter (acting)
Daily 70p

The Oxford Times

Newspaper House, Osney Mead, Oxford OX2 0EJ
tel (01865) 425262
email news@nqo.com
website www.oxfordtimes.co.uk
Facebook www.facebook.com/TheOxfordTimes/
Twitter @oxfordtimes

Acting Editor John Carter
Weekly Thurs £1.30
Supplements **Oxford Limited Edition, In Business**

Local weekly newspaper for Oxford. Founded 1862.

Reading Chronicle

2–10 Bridge Street, Reading, Berks. RG1 2LU
tel 0118 955 3333
email news@readingchronicle.co.uk
website www.readingchronicle.co.uk
Facebook www.facebook.com/readingchronicle
Twitter @rdgchronicle
Group Editor Samantha Harman
Weekly Thurs 70p

Southern Daily Echo

Newspaper House, Test Lane, Redbridge, Southampton SO16 9JX
tel 023-8042 4777
email newsdesk@dailyecho.co.uk
website www.dailyecho.co.uk
Facebook www.facebook.com/dailyecho
Twitter @dailyecho
Editor Gordon Sutter
Daily Mon–Sat 68p

News, articles, features, sport. Length: varies. Illustrations: line, half-tone, colour, cartoons. Payment: NUJ rates. Founded 1888.

Swindon Advertiser

100 Victoria Road, Old Town, Swindon SN1 3BE
tel (01793) 528144
email newsdesk@swindonadvertiser.co.uk
website www.swindonadvertiser.co.uk
Facebook www.facebook.com/swindonadvertiser
Twitter @swindonadver
Editor Paul Gavan
Daily Mon–Sat 65p

News and information relating to Swindon and Wiltshire only. Considers unsolicited material. Founded 1854.

SOUTH WEST

Cornish Guardian

High Water House, City Wharf, Malpas Road, Truro TR1 1QH
tel (01872) 271451
email cgedit@c-dm.co.uk
website www.cornishguardian.co.uk
Facebook https://www.facebook.com/cornwallivenews/
Twitter @CornishGuardian
Editor Scott Harrison
Weekly Wed £1.20

Items of interest for Cornwall. Founded 1901.

Cornishman

Harmsworth House, Lemon Quay, Truro TR1 2LP
tel (01872) 271451
email newsdesk@cornishman.co.uk
website www.cornishman.co.uk
Facebook www.facebook.com/cornwalllivenews
Twitter @cornishmanpaper
Editor Jacqui Walls
Weekly Thurs £1.20

Local news and features. Founded 1878.

Daily Echo

Richmond Hill, Bournemouth BH2 6HH
tel (01202) 554601
email newsdesk@bournemouthecho.co.uk
website www.bournemouthecho.co.uk
Facebook www.facebook.com/bournemouthdailyecho
Twitter @bournemouthecho
Editor Andy Martin
Daily Mon–Fri 68p, Sat 85p

Founded 1900.

Dorset Echo

Fleet House, Hampshire Road, Weymouth, Dorset DT4 9XD
tel (01305) 830930
email newsdesk@dorsetecho.co.uk
website www.dorsetecho.co.uk
Facebook www.facebook.com/dorsetecho
Twitter @Doresetecho
Editor Diarmuid MacDonagh
Daily Mon–Fri 65p, Sat 60p

News and occasional features, length: 1,000–2,000 words. Illustrations: b&w photos. Payment: by negotiation. Founded 1921.

Express & Echo

Queens House, Little Queen Street, Exeter EX4 3LJ
tel (01392) 349000
email echonews@expressandecho.co.uk
website www.exeterexpressandecho.co.uk
Facebook www.facebook.com/devonlivenews/
Twitter @devonliveexeter
Editor Patrick Phelvin
Weekly Thurs 50p

Features and news of local interest. Length: 500–800 words (features), up to 400 words (news). Illustrations: colour. Payment: lineage rates; illustrations: by negotiation. Founded 1904.

Gloucester Citizen

6–8 The Oxebode, Gloucester GL1 2RZ
tel (01452) 420621
website www.gloucestershirelive.co.uk
Facebook www.facebook.com/GlosLiveOnline/
Twitter @GlosLiveOnline
Editor Jenny Eastwood
Daily Mon–Fri 75p

Local news and features for Gloucester and its

districts. Length: 1,000 words (articles/features), 300 words (news). Illustrations: colour. Payment: by negotiation.

Gloucestershire Echo

Third Floor, St James's House, St James's Square, Cheltenham, Glos. GL50 3PR
tel (01242) 278000
email echo.news@glosmedia.co.uk
website www.gloucestershirelive.co.uk
Facebook www.facebook.com/GlosLiveOnline/
Twitter @GlosLiveOnline
Editor Matt Holmes
Daily Mon–Fri 70p, Sat 80p

Specialist articles with Gloucestershire connections; no fiction. Founded 1873.

The Herald

The Plymouth Herald, 3rd Floor, Studio 5–11, Millbay Road, Plymouth PL1 3LF
tel (01752) 765500
email news@plymouthherald.co.uk
website www.plymouthherald.co.uk
Facebook www.facebook.com/theplymouthherald
Twitter @heraldnewslive
Editor Paul Burton
Daily Mon–Fri 55p, Sat 60p

Local news, articles and features. Will consider unsolicited material. Welcomes ideas for articles and features. Illustrations: colour and b&w prints.

Herald Express

Harmsworth House, Barton Hill Road, Torquay, Devon TQ2 8JN
tel (01803) 676767
website www.devonlive.com
Editor Jim Parker
Weekly Thurs £1

Hereford Times

Holmer Road, Hereford HR4 9UJ
tel (01432) 845873
email news@herefordtimes.com
website www.herefordtimes.com
Facebook www.facebook.com/herefordtimes
Twitter @HTnewsroom
Editor John Wilson
Weekly Thurs £1.20

Local news, sports and features. Founded 1832.

Post

Temple Way, Bristol BS2 0BU
tel 0117 934 3000
website www.bristolpost.co.uk
Facebook www.facebook.com/bristolpost
Twitter @BristolPost
Editor Mike Norton
Daily Mon–Thurs 60p, Fri 75p

Takes freelance news and articles. Payment: by arrangement. Founded 1932.

Sunday Independent

Oakland Mews, Owen Sivell Close, Liskeard PL14 3UX
tel (01579) 556972
email newsdesk@sundayindependent.co.uk
website www.sundayindependent.co.uk
Twitter @thesundayindy
Editor John Collings
Weekly Sun £1

Sport and news features on West Country topics; features/articles with a nostalgic theme; short, quirky news briefs (must be original). Length: 600 words (features/articles), 300 words (news). Illustrations: colour, b&w. Payment: by arrangement. Founded 1808.

Western Daily Press

Bristol Evening Post and Press Ltd, Temple Way, Bristol BS99 7HD
tel 0117 934 3000
website www.westerndailypress.co.uk
Facebook www.facebook.com/WesternDaily
Twitter @WesternDaily
Editor Gavin Thompson
Daily Mon–Fri 80p, Sat £1.30

National, international or West Country topics for features or news items, from established journalists, with or without illustrations. Payment: by negotiation. Founded 1858.

Western Morning News

Western Morning News, 3rd Floor, Studio 5–11, Plymouth PL1 3LF
tel (01752) 765500
website https://www.devonlive.com/
Facebook www.facebook.com/devonlivenews
Twitter @WMN
Editor Bill Martin
Daily Mon–Fri 70p, Sat 85p

Articles plus illustrations considered on West Country subjects. Founded 1860.

WALES

Cambrian News

7 Science Park, Aberystwyth, Ceredigion SY23 3AH
tel (01970) 615000
email edit@cambrian-news.co.uk
website www.cambrian-news.co.uk
Facebook www.facebook.com/CambrianNews
Twitter @CambrianNews
Editor Beverly Thomas
Weekly Wed 90p for the Aberystwyth, South and Machynlleth & Llanidloes editions; Thurs 80p for the Meirionnydd and Arfon & Dwyfor editions

Wales' biggest-selling weekly newspaper. Payment for freelance articles and pictures by arrangement. Founded 1860.

Daily Post

Bryn Eirias, Colwyn Bay LL29 8BF
(01492) 574452
email welshnews@dailypost.co.uk
website www.dailypost.co.uk
Facebook www.facebook.com/dailypostwales
Twitter @dailypostwales
Editor Andrew Campbell
Daily Mon–Sat 70p

The Leader

NWN Media Ltd, Mold Business Park,
Wrexham Road, Mold, Flintshire CH7 1XY
tel (01352) 707707
website www.leaderlive.co.uk
Facebook www.facebook.com/LeaderLive
Twitter @leaderlive
Editor Susan Perry
Mon–Fri 70p

South Wales Argus

Cardiff Road, Maesglas, Newport, Gwent NP20 3QN
tel (01633) 810000
email newsdesk@gwent-wales.co.uk
website www.southwalesargus.co.uk
Facebook www.facebook.com/southwalesargus/
Twitter @southwalesargus
Editor Nicole Garnon
Daily Mon–Sat 65p

News and features of relevance to Gwent. Length: 500–600 words (features); 350 words (news). Illustrations: colour prints and transparencies. Payment: £30 (features), £20 (news) per item; £20–£25 (photos). Founded 1892.

South Wales Echo

6 Park Street, Cardiff CF10 1XR
tel (02920) 223333
email echo.newsdesk@walesonline.co.uk
website www.walesonline.co.uk
Editor Tryst Williams
Daily Mon–Sat £1

Evening paper: news, sport, features, showbiz, news features, personality interviews. Length: up to 700 words. Illustrations: photos, cartoons. Payment: by negotiation. Founded 1884.

South Wales Evening Post

South Wales Evening Post, Urban Village,
High Street, Swansea SA1 1NW
tel (01792) 510000
email postnews@mediawales.co.uk
website www.southwales-eveningpost.co.uk
Facebook www.facebook.com/SWEveningPost
Twitter @SWEveningPost
Editor Jonathan Roberts
Daily Mon–Sat 50p

Western Mail

6 Park Street, Cardiff CF10 1XR
tel 029-2022 3333
website www.walesonline.co.uk
Editor Alan Edmunds
Daily Mon–Fri 75p, Sat Free

Articles of political, industrial, literary or general and Welsh interest are considered. Illustrations: topical general news and feature pictures, cartoons. Payment: according to value; special fees for exclusive news. Founded 1869.

WEST MIDLANDS

Birmingham Mail

Embassy House, 60 Church Street,
Birmingham B3 2DJ
tel 0121 234 5000
email newsdesk@birminghammail.co.uk
website www.birminghammail.co.uk
Facebook www.facebook.com/birminghammail
Twitter @birminghammail
Editor-in-Chief Marc Reeves
Daily Mon–Sat 65p

Features of topical Midland interest considered. Length: 400–800 words. Payment: by arrangement. Founded 1870.

Birmingham Post

Embassy House, 60 Church Street,
Birmingham B3 2DJ
tel 0121 234 5000
website www.birminghampost.co.uk
Facebook www.facebook.com/birminghampost
Twitter @birminghampost
Editor-in-Chief Marc Reeves
Weekly Thurs £2

Authoritative and well-written articles of industrial, political or general interest are considered, especially if they have relevance to the Midlands. Length: up to 1,000 words. Payment: by arrangement.

Coventry Telegraph

Corporation Street, Coventry CV1 1FP
tel 024-7663 3633
email news@coventrytelegraph.net
website www.coventrytelegraph.net
Facebook www.facebook.com/coventrytelegraph
Twitter @covtelegraph
Editor Keith Perry
Daily Mon–Fri 65p, Sat 75p

Topical, illustrated articles with a Coventry or Warwickshire interest. Length: up to 600 words. Payment: by arrangement.

Express & Star

51–53 Queen Street, Wolverhampton WV1 1ES
tel (01902) 313131
email newsdesk@expressandstar.co.uk
website www.expressandstar.com
Facebook www.facebook.com/expressandstar

Twitter @expressandstar
Editor Keith Harrison
Daily Mon–Sat 65p, Sat 80p

Founded 1874.

Sentinel

Staffordshire Sentinel News & Media Ltd,
Sentinel House, Bethesda Street, Hanley,
Stoke-on-Trent ST1 3GN
tel (01782) 864100
email newsdesk@thesentinel.co.uk
website www.stokesentinel.co.uk
Facebook www.facebook.com/sentinelstaffs
Twitter @SentinelStaffs
Editor Martin Tideswell
Daily Mon–Sat 60p

Articles and features of topical interest to the north Staffordshire and south Cheshire area. Illustrations: colour and b&w. Payment: by arrangement. Founded 1873.

Shropshire Star

Waterloo Road, Ketley, Telford TF1 5HU
tel (01952) 242424
website www.shropshirestar.com
Facebook www.facebook.com/ShropshireStar
Twitter @ShropshireStar
Editor Martin Wright
Daily Mon–Fri 70p, Sat 75p

Daily paper: news and features. No unsolicited material; write to Features Editor with outline of ideas. Payment: by arrangement. Founded 1964.

Sunday Mercury

Embassy House, 60 Church Street,
Birmingham B3 2DJ
tel 0121 234 5000
website www.birminghammail.co.uk/authors/sunday-mercury
Print Editor Paul Cole
Sun £1.40

News specials or features of Midland interest. Illustrations: colour, b&w, cartoons. Payment: special rates for special matter.

Worcester News

Berrows House, Hylton Road, Worcester WR2 5JX
tel (01905) 748200
website www.worcesternews.co.uk
Facebook www.facebook.com/theworcesternews
Twitter @worcesternews
Editor Michael Purton
Daily Mon–Sat 70p

Local and national news, sport and features. Will consider unsolicited material. Welcomes ideas for articles and features. Length: 800 words (features), 300 words (news). Illustrations: colour jpg files. Payment: by negotiation.

YORKSHIRE/HUMBERSIDE

Grimsby Telegraph

First Floor, Heritage House, Fisherman's Wharf,
Grimsby DN31 1SY
tel (01472) 808000
email newsdesk@grimsbytelegraph.co.uk
website www.thisisgrimsby.co.uk
Facebook www.facebook.com/grimsbytel
Twitter @GrimsbyTel
Editor Michelle Lalor
Daily Mon–Sat 55p

Considers general interest articles. Illustrations: line, half-tone, colour, cartoons. Payment: by arrangement. Founded 1897.

Halifax Courier

The Fire Station, Dean Clough Mills,
Halifax HX3 5AX
tel (01422) 260200
email editor@halifaxcourier.co.uk
website www.halifaxcourier.co.uk
Facebook www.facebook.com/HalifaxCourier
Twitter @HXCourier
Editor John Kenealy
Weekly Fri £1.40

Huddersfield Daily Examiner

Pennine Business Park, Longbow Close,
Bradley Road, Huddersfield HD2 1GQ
tel (01484) 430000
email editorial@examiner.co.uk
website www.examiner.co.uk
Facebook www.facebook.com/HuddersfieldExaminer
Editor Wayne Ankers
Daily Examiner 70p, Weekend Examiner 80p

No contributions required at present. Founded 1851.

Hull Daily Mail

Blundell's Corner, Beverley Road, Hull HU3 1XS
tel (01482) 327111
website www.hulldailymail.co.uk
Facebook www.facebook.com/HullDailyMail
Twitter @hulldailymail
Editor Neil Hodgkinson
Daily Mon–Sat 65p

Lincolnshire Echo

Ground Floor, Witham Wharf, Brayford Wharf East,
Lincoln LN5 7HY
tel (01522) 820000
website www.lincolnshirelive.co.uk
Facebook www.facebook.com/LincsLive/
Twitter @LincsLive
Editor Charles Walker
Weekly Thurs £1.10

The Press

Newsquest York, PO Box 29, 76–86 Walmgate,
York YO1 9YN
tel (01904) 567131
email newsdesk@thepress.co.uk

website www.yorkpress.co.uk
Facebook www.facebook.com/thepressyork
Twitter @yorkpress
Editor Joanna Norris
Daily Mon–Sat 60p

Articles of North and East Yorkshire interest. Length: 500–1,000 words. Illustrations: line, half-tone. Payment: by arrangement. Founded 1882.

Scarborough News

Newchase Court, Hopper Hill Road, Scarborough YO11 3YS
tel (01723) 860161
email newsdesk@jpress.co.uk
website www.thescarboroughnews.co.uk
Facebook www.facebook.com/thescarboroughnews
Twitter @thescarboronews
Editor Ed Asquith
Weekly £1.25

Scunthorpe Telegraph

4–5 Park Square, Scunthorpe, North Lincolnshire DN15 6JH
tel (01724) 273273
email newsdesk@scunthorpetelegraph.co.uk
website www.scunthorpetelegraph.co.uk
Facebook www.facebook.com/thisisscunny
Twitter @ScunTelegraph
Editor David Atkin
Weekly Thurs £1.20

Local news and features. Founded 1937.

Sheffield Star

York Street, Sheffield S1 1PU
tel 0114 276 7676
website www.thestar.co.uk
Facebook www.facebook.com/sheffieldstar/
Twitter @sheffieldstar
Editor Nancy Fielder
Daily Mon–Sat 75p

Well-written articles of local character. Length: about 500 words. Illustrations: topical photos, line drawings, graphics, cartoons. Payment: by negotiation. Founded 1887.

Telegraph & Argus

Hall Ings, Bradford BD1 1JR
tel (01274) 729511
email newsdesk@telegraphandargus.co.uk
website www.thetelegraphandargus.co.uk
Facebook www.facebook.com/telegraphandargus
Twitter @Bradford_TandA
Editor Perry Austin-Clarke
Daily Mon–Sat 65p

Daily paper: news, articles and features relevant to or about the people of West Yorkshire. Length: up to 1,000 words. Illustrations: line, half-tone, colour. Payment: features from £15; line from £5, b&w and colour photos by negotiation. Founded 1868.

Yorkshire Evening Post

No 1 Leeds, 26 Whitehall Road, Leeds LS1 1BE
tel 0113 238 8917
website www.yorkshireeveningpost.co.uk
Facebook www.facebook.com/YEP.newspaper
Twitter @LeedsNews
Editor Hannah Thaxter
Daily Mon–Sat 72p

News stories and feature articles. Illustrations: colour and b&w, cartoons. Payment: by negotiation. Founded 1890.

Yorkshire Post

No 1 Leeds, 26 Whitehall Road, Leeds LS1 1BE
tel 0113 243 2701
London office 292 Vauxhall Bridge Road, London SW1V 1AE
tel 020-7963 7646
website www.yorkshirepost.co.uk
Facebook www.facebook.com/yorkshirepost.newspaper
Twitter @yorkshirepost
Editor James Mitchinson
Daily Mon–Fri 90p, Sat £1.70
Supplements **Yorkshire Post Magazine**

Authoritative and well-written articles on topical subjects of general, literary or industrial interests. Founded 1754.

Magazines UK and Ireland

Listings for regional newspapers start on page 23 and listings for national newspapers start on page 15. For quick reference, magazines are listed by subject area starting on page 735.

Accountancy

145 London Road, Kingston-upon-Thames, Surrey KT2 6SR
tel 020-8247 1379
email accountancynews@wolterskluwer.co.uk
website www.cchdaily.co.uk
Editor Sara White
Monthly £95 p.a.

Articles on accounting, taxation, audit, financial, tax law and regulatory compliance targeted at accountants, tax advisers and finance professionals in practice or industry. All feature ideas to be submitted by email in the form of a brief, bullet-pointed synopsis. Founded 1889.

Accountancy Age

Contentive, 1 Hammersmith Broadway, London W6 9DL
tel 020 8000 9513
email emma.smith@contentive.com
website www.accountancyage.com
Twitter @AccountancyAge
Editor Emma Smith
Online

Articles of accounting, financial and business interest. Freelance assignments commissioned. Payment: by arrangement. Founded 1969.

Accounting & Business

Association of Chartered Certified Accountants, The Adelphi, 1–11 John Adam Street, London WC2N 6AU
tel 020-7059 5000
email info@accaglobal.com
website www.accaglobal.com/uk/en/member/ab.html
Editor-in-Chief Jo Malvern
10 p.a. £10, £85 p.a. (non-members)

Journal of the Association of Chartered Certified Accountants. Features accountancy, finance and business topics of relevance to accountants and finance directors. Length: 1,100 words. Illustrated. Founded 1998.

Acumen Literary Journal

6 The Mount, Higher Furzeham, Brixham, South Devon TQ5 8QY
tel (01803) 851098
email patriciaoxley6@gmail.com
website www.acumen-poetry.co.uk
Editor Patricia Oxley
3 p.a. £5.50, £15.50 p.a.

Poetry, literary and critical articles, reviews, literary memoirs, etc. Send sae with submissions; online submissions also accepted (see website for guidelines). Payment: small. Founded 1985.

Aeroplane Monthly

Key Publishing Group, Units 1–4, Gwash Way Industrial Estate, Ryhall Road, Stamford, Lincs. PE9 1XP
email ben.dunnell@keypublishing.com
website www.aeroplanemonthly.com
Editor Ben Dunnell
Monthly £4.50

Articles and photos relating to historical aviation and aircraft preservation. Length: up to 5,000 words. Illustrations: line, colour. Payment: £100 per 1,000 words, payable on publication; photos £25 or more depending on size. Founded 1973.

Aesthetica Magazine

PO Box 371, York YO23 1WL
tel (01904) 629137
email info@aestheticamagazine.com
website www.aestheticamagazine.com
Editor Cherie Federico
Bi-monthly £5.95

Sets out to provide a 'visual bridge' between the latest developments in Visual Arts, Architecture, Fashion and Design by means of the current socio-political climate. Aimed at art and culture lovers across the world, each edition includes coverage of the most important artists at work today, both established and emerging, exhibitions news and photography features. Hosts of the annual Aesthetica Art Prize, Creative Writing Award and Aesthetica Short Film Festival for international practitioners. Founded 2002.

Africa Confidential

37 John's Mews, London WC1N 2NS
email andrew@africa-confidential.com
website www.africa-confidential.com
Editor Patrick Smith, *Deputy Editor* Andrew Weir
Fortnightly £850 p.a. (print), £730 p.a. (online only)

News and analysis of political and economic developments in Africa. Unsolicited contributions welcomed, but must be exclusive and not published elsewhere. Length: 1,200-word features, 500-word pointers. No illustrations. Payment: from £300 per 1,000 words. Founded 1960.

Africa: St Patrick's Missions

St Patrick's Missionary Society, Kiltegan, Co. Wicklow W91 YO22, Republic of Ireland
tel +353 (0)59 6473600
email africa@spms.ie
website www.spms.org
Facebook www.facebook.com/AfricaMagazineKiltegan
Editor Rev. Tim Redmond
9 p.a. €15 p.a.

Articles of missionary and topical religious interest. Length: up to 1,000 words. Illustrations: colour.

African Business

IC Publications Ltd, 7 Coldbath Square, London EC1R 4LQ
tel 020-7841 3210
email editorial@icpublications.com
website www.africanbusinessmagazine.com
Monthly £4 or from £17.99 p.a.

Articles on business, economic and financial topics of interest to businessmen, ministers and officials concerned with African affairs. Length: 1,000–1,400 words; shorter coverage 500 words. Illustrations: line, half-tone, cartoons. Payment: £90–£100 per 1,000 words; £1 per column cm for illustrations. Founded 1978.

Agenda

Harts Cottage, Stonehurst Lane, Five Ashes, Mayfield, East Sussex TN20 6LL
tel (01825) 831994
email editor@agendapoetry.co.uk
website www.agendapoetry.co.uk
Editor Patricia McCarthy
Quarterly £28 p.a. (individuals), £22 p.a. (concessions), £35 p.a. libraries and institutions

Poetry and criticism. Study the journal and visit the website for submission details before submitting via email (submissions@agendapoetry.co.uk). Young poets and artists aged 16–38 years are invited to submit work for the online publication *Broadsheet*. Detailed criticism of poems available to subscribers.

AIR International

Key Publishing Ltd, PO Box 100, Stamford, Lincs. PE9 1XQ
tel (01780) 755131
email airint@keypublishing.com
website www.airinternational.com
Editor Mark Ayton
Monthly £47 p.a.

Technical articles on aircraft; features on topical aviation subjects – civil and military. Length: up to 3,000 words. Illustrations: colour transparencies/prints, b&w prints/line drawings. Payment: £50 per 1,000 words or by negotiation; £20 colour, £10 b&w. Founded 1971.

Amateur Gardening

Time Inc. (UK) Ltd, Pinehurst 2, Pinehurst Road, Farnborough Business Park, Farnborough Hants GU14 7BF
tel (01202) 440840
email amateurgardening@timeinc.com
website www.amateurgardening.com
Group Editor Garry Coward-Williams
Weekly £1.99

No longer accepts any form of unsolicited material. Founded 1884.

Amateur Photographer

(incorporating Photo Technique)
Time Inc. (UK), Pinehurst 2, Pinehurst Road, Farnborough, Hampshire GU14 7BF
email amateurphotographer@timeinc.com
website www.amateurphotographer.co.uk
Facebook www.facebook.com/amateur.photographer.magazine
Twitter @AP_Magazine
Editor Nigel Atherton
Weekly £2.99

Unsolicited editorial submissions are not encouraged. Founded 1884.

Ambit

Staithe House, Main Road, Brancaster Staithe, Norfolk PE31 8BP (correspondence)
tel 07715 233221
email contact@ambitmagazine.co.uk
website www.ambitmagazine.co.uk
Twitter @ambitmagazine
Editor Briony Bax
Quarterly £29.99 p.a. (UK)

Literary magazine. Publishes poetry, fiction, flash fiction and art in a full-colour quarterly magazine. Accepts submissions via online portal (see website for details). Contributors may send up to five poems in one document or a story of up to 5,000 words; flash fiction no more than 1,000 words. Payment: see website. Founded 1959 by Dr Martin Bax.

Angler's Mail

Time Inc. (UK), Pinehurst 2, Pinehurst Road, Farnborough Business Park, Farnborough, Hampshire GU14 7BF
tel (01252) 555213
email anglersmail@timeinc.com
website www.anglersmail.com
Twitter @AnglersMail
Editor Tim Knight
Weekly £1.99

News items about coarse fishing. Payment: by agreement.

Angling Times

Bauer Media Group, Media House, Lynchwood, Peterborough Business Park, Peterborough PE2 6EA

tel (01733) 395097
email steve.fitzpatrick@bauermedia.co.uk
website www.gofishing.co.uk/Angling-Times
Twitter @AnglingTimesEd
Editor Steve Fitzpatrick
Weekly £86 p.a.

Articles, pictures, news stories, on all forms of angling. Illustrations: line, half-tone, colour. Payment: by arrangement. Founded 1953.

Apollo

22 Old Queen Street, London SW1H 9HP
tel 020-7961 0150
email editorial@apollomag.com
website www.apollo-magazine.com
Editor Thomas Marks
Monthly £6.95

Scholarly and topical articles of c. 2,000–3,000 words on art, architecture, ceramics, photography, furniture, armour, glass, sculpture and any subject connected with art and collecting. Interviews with collectors. Exhibition and book reviews, articles on current developments in museums and art galleries, regular columns on the art market and contemporary art. Illustrations: colour. Payment: by arrangement. Founded 1925.

The Architects' Journal

EMAP, Telephone House, 69–77 Paul Street, London EC2A 4NW
tel 020-3033 2741
website www.architectsjournal.co.uk
Twitter @ArchitectsJrnal
Editor-in-Chief Christine Murray, *Acting Editor* Emily Booth
Bimonthly £10

Articles (mainly technical) on architecture, planning and building, accepted only with prior agreement of synopsis. Illustrations: photos and drawings. Payment: by arrangement. Founded 1895.

Architectural Design

John Wiley & Sons, 25 John Street, London WC1N 2BS
tel 020-8326 3800
email architecturaldesign@wiley.com
website www.architectural-design-magazine.com
Editor Helen Castle
6 issues p.a. £136 p.a. (print, individual; other rates available)

International architectural publication comprising an extensively illustrated thematic profile and magazine back section, *AD Plus*. Uncommissioned articles not accepted. Illustrations: drawings and photos, line (colour preferred). Payment: by arrangement. Founded 1930.

The Architectural Review

EMAP, Telephone House, 69–77 Paul Street, London EC2A 4NW
tel 020-3033 2741
email editorial@architectural-review.com
website www.architectural-review.com
Editorial Director Paul Finch
Monthly £15.99

Articles on architecture and the allied arts (urbanism, design, theory, history, technology). Writers must be thoroughly qualified. Length: up to 3,000 words. Illustrations: photos, drawings, etc. Payment: by arrangement. Founded 1896.

Architecture Today

34 Pentonville Road, London N1 9HF
tel 020-7837 0143
email editorial@architecturetoday.co.uk
website www.architecturetoday.co.uk
10 p.a. £50 p.a. Circulated free of charge to architects

Mostly commissioned articles and features on today's European architecture. Length: 200–800 words. Illustrations: colour. Payment: by negotiation. Founded 1989.

Areté

8 New College Lane, Oxford OX1 3BN
tel (01865) 289193
email craigraine@aretemagazine.co.uk
website www.aretemagazine.co.uk
Editor Craig Raine
3 p.a. £27 p.a. (UK)

Literary magazine covering many aspects of contemporary culture, from novels to film, poetry and prose. Contributors include Julian Barnes, Tom Stoppard and Ian McEwan. Submissions should be sent as hard copy to the postal address above; send sae with any unsolicited pieces.

Art + Framing Today

2 Wye House, 6 Enterprise Way, London SW18 1FZ
tel 020-7381 6616
email info@fineart.co.uk
website www.fineart.co.uk/art_and_framing_today.aspx
Managing Editor Lynn Jones, *Publisher* Louise Hay
5 p.a. £33 p.a.

Distributed to the fine art and framing industry. Covers essential information on new products and technology, market trends and business analysis. Length: 800–1,600 words. Illustrations: colour photos, cartoons. Payment: by arrangement. Available on iTunes App store. Founded 1905.

Art Monthly

12 Carlton House Terrace, London SW1Y 5AH
tel 020-7240 0389
email info@artmonthly.co.uk
website www.artmonthly.co.uk
Twitter @ArtMonthly
Editor Patricia Bickers
10 p.a. £49 p.a. (print)

Features on modern and contemporary visual artists and art history, art theory and art-related issues; exhibition and book reviews. All material commissioned. Length: 750–1,500 words. Illustrations: b&w photos. Payment: features £100–£200; none for photos. Founded 1976.

The Art Newspaper

70 South Lambeth Road, London SW8 1RL
tel 020-3416 9000
email londonoffice@theartnewspaper.com
website www.theartnewspaper.com
Acting Editor Julia Michalska
11 p.a. £85 p.a. (print and digital subscription)

International coverage of visual art, news, politics, law, exhibitions with some feature pages. Length: 200–1,000 words. Illustrations: colour and b&w photos. Payment: £350+ per 1,000 words. Founded 1990.

Art Quarterly

The Art Fund, 2 Granary Square, London N1C 4BH
tel 020-7225 4800
email info@artfund.org
website www.artfund.org
Editor Helen Sumpter
Quarterly Free to members

Magazine of the Art Fund. Features on art, exhibition previews and coverage of the Art Fund's campaigns and grant-giving activities.

ArtReview and ArtReview Asia

1 Honduras Street, London EC1Y 0TH
tel 020-7490 8138
email office@artreview.com
website www.artreview.com
Facebook www.facebook.com/ArtReview.Magazine
Twitter @ArtReview_
Editor Mark Rappolt
ArtReview 9 p.a. £39 p.a. (print and online); ArtReviewAsia 4 p.a. £24 p.a. (print and online)

Contemporary art features and reviews. Proposals welcome. Illustrations: colour. Payment: £350 per 1,000 words. Founded 1949.

ARTEMISpoetry

3 Springfield Close, East Preston, West Sussex BN16 2SZ
email editor@poetrypf.co.uk
website www.secondlightlive.co.uk/artemis.shtml
Contact Dilys Wood
2 p.a. £6, £11 p.a. or free to members of Second Light Network

Bi-annual journal of women's poetry and writing about poetry. Published in May and November each year by the Second Light, membership of which is open to female poets over the age of 40 (associate membership if under 40). Submissions should be hitherto unpublished work by women authors. See website for full details and specific information on forthcoming issues.

The Artist

The Artists' Publishing Co. Ltd, Caxton House, 63–65 High Street, Tenterden, Kent TN30 6BD
tel (01580) 763673
email info@tapc.co.uk
website www.painters-online.co.uk
Editor Sally Bulgin
13 p.a. (issues published every four weeks) £4.40

Practical, instructional articles on painting for all amateur and professional artists. Illustrations: line, half-tone, colour. Payment: by arrangement. Founded 1931.

Artists & Illustrators

Jubilee House, 2 Jubilee Place, London SW3 3TQ
tel 020-7349 3700
email info@artistsandillustrators.co.uk
website www.artistsandillustrators.co.uk
Twitter @AandImagazine
Editor Sally Hales
Monthly £4.40

Practical and inspirational articles for amateur and professional artists. Length: 500–1,500 words. Illustrations: hi-res digital images, hand-drawn illustrations. Payment: variable. Founded 1986.

Astronomy Now

Pole Star Publications, PO Box 175, Tonbridge, Kent TN10 4ZY
tel (01732) 446110
email editorial2018@astronomynow.com
website https://astronomynow.com/
Facebook www.facebook.com/astronomynow
Twitter @astronomynow
Editor Keith Cooper
Monthly £5.25

Specialises in translating exciting astronomy research into articles for the lay reader. Also covers amateur astronomy with equipment reviews and observing notes. Please submit article pitches to the editorial email address. Length: 800–2,000 words. Payment: 15p per word; from £10 per photo. Founded 1987.

Athletics Weekly

22 Long Acre, London WC2E 9LY
email jason.henderson@athleticsweekly.com
website www.athleticsweekly.com
Facebook www.facebook.com/athleticsweekly
Twitter @athleticsweekly
Editor Jason Henderson
Weekly £4.95

News and features on track and field athletics, road running, cross country, fell and race walking. Material mostly commissioned. Length: 300–1,500 words. Illustrations: colour and b&w action and head/shoulder photos, line. Payment: varies. Founded 1945.

Attitude

Attitude Media, 33 Peartree Street,
London EC1V 3AG
tel 020-7608 6363
email attitude@attitude.co.uk
website www.attitude.co.uk
Editor-in-Chief Cliff Joannou
13 p.a. £4.95

Men's style magazine aimed primarily, but not exclusively, at gay men. Covers style/fashion, interviews, reviews, celebrities, humour. Illustrations: colour transparencies, b&w prints. Payment: £150 per 1,000 words; £100 per full-page illustration. Founded 1994.

The Author

84 Drayton Gardens, London SW10 9SB
tel 020-7373 6642
email theauthor@societyofauthors.org
website www.societyofauthors.org/author
Editor James McConnachie
Quarterly £14.25 or free to Society members

Organ of the Society of Authors. Commissioned articles from 1,000–2,000 words on any subject connected with the legal, commercial or technical side of authorship. Little scope for the freelance writer: preliminary letter advisable. Illustrations: line, occasional cartoons. Payment: by arrangement. Founded 1890.

Auto Express

Dennis Publishing Ltd, 31–32 Alfred Place,
London WC1E 7DP
tel 020-3890 3890
email editorial@autoexpress.co.uk
website www.autoexpress.co.uk
Editor-in-Chief Steve Fowler
Weekly £3

News stories, and general interest features about drivers as well as cars. Illustrations: colour photos. Payment: features, £350 per 1,000 words; photos, varies. Founded 1988.

Aviation News

Key Publishing Group, Units 1–4,
Gwash Way Industrial Estate, Ryhall Road,
Stamford, Lincs. PE9 1XP
tel (01780) 755131
email dino.carrara@aviation-news.co.uk
website www.aviation-news.co.uk
Editor Dino Carrara
Monthly £4.70

Covers all aspects of aviation. Many articles commissioned. Payment: by arrangement.

BackTrack

Pendragon Publishing, PO Box 3, Easingwold,
York YO61 3YS
tel (01347) 824397
email pendragonpublishing@btinternet.com
website www.pendragonpublishing.co.uk
Editor Michael Blakemore
Monthly £4.75

British railway history from 1820s to 1980s. Welcomes ideas from writers and photographers. Articles must be well researched, authoritative and accompanied by illustrations. Length: 3,000–5,000 words (main features), 500–3,000 words (articles). Illustrations: colour and b&w. Payment: £30 per 1,000 words, £18.50 colour, £10 b&w. Founded 1986.

Banipal

1 Gough Square, London EC4A 3DE
tel 07979 540594
email editor@banipal.co.uk
website www.banipal.co.uk
Editor-in-Chief Samuel Shimon, *Publisher* Margaret Obank
3 p.a. £10 per issue; digital and print subscription options available

Showcases contemporary Arab authors in English translation. Welcomes inquiries from authors and translators; see website for full submission guidelines. Features prose and poetry. Complete archive now available online for digital subcribers.

The Banker

FT Business, 1 Southwark Bridge, London SE1 9HL
tel 020-7873 3000
email brian.caplen@ft.com
website www.thebanker.com
Editor-in-Chief Brian Caplen
Monthly £825 p.a. (print and digital)

Global coverage of retail banking, corporate banking, banking technology, transactions services, investment banking and capital markets, regulation and top 1,000 bank listings.

Baptist Times

129 Broadway, Didcot, Oxon OX11 8RT
tel (01235) 517677
email editor@baptisttimes.co.uk
website www.baptisttimes.co.uk
Twitter @baptisttimes
Editor Paul Hobson
Website only.

Religious or social affairs, news, features and reviews. Founded 1855.

Bare Fiction

177 Copthorne Road, Shrewsbury SY3 8NA
info@barefiction.co.uk
website www.barefictionmagazine.co.uk
Twitter @barefiction
Editor Robert Harper
3 p.a. £20 p.a., including free digital access

New creative writing in poetry, fiction and plays. Also includes articles, reviews and interviews. See website for information on forthcoming submission windows; all material submitted during those times should be original and unpublished. Authors' names should not be included. Unsolicited work is not accepted.

BBC Countryfile Magazine

Immediate Media Co. Ltd, Tower House, Fairfax Street, Bristol BS1 3BN
tel 0117 927 9009
email editor@countryfile.com
website www.countryfile.com
Twitter @BBCCountryfile
Editor Fergus Collins
Monthly £4.50

Articles and features on making the most of the UK's countryside, and the lives of its rural communities.

BBC Focus

Immediate Media Co. Ltd, Tower House, Fairfax Street, Bristol BS1 3BN
tel 0117 314 8779
email daniel.bennett@immediate.co.uk
website www.sciencefocus.com
Editor Daniel Bennett
Monthly £4.99

Science and technology magazine featuring articles from popular scientists and leading academics, as well as news. Submissions accepted for articles only from experienced and previously published science writers: send 2–8pp overview along with feature pitch form provided on the website to jason.goodyer@immediate.co.uk. Photography and illustration submissions also accepted: see website for full specifications.

BBC Gardeners' World Magazine

Immediate Media Co. Ltd, Vineyard House, 44 Brook Green, London W6 7BT
tel 020-7150 5770
email magazine@gardenersworld.com
website www.gardenersworld.com
Twitter @GWmag
Editor Lucy Hall, *Deputy Editor* Kevin Smith, *Features Editor* Catherine Mansley
Monthly £4.50

Advice, support and features for gardeners of all levels of expertise. Fully illustrated.

BBC Good Food

Immediate Media Co. Ltd, Vineyard House, 44 Brook Green, London W6 7BT
email enquiries@bbcgoodfoodmagazine.com
website www.bbcgoodfood.com
Twitter @bbcgoodfood
Editor-in-Chief Christine Hayes
Monthly £4.25

Inspiration for everyday, weekend and seasonal cooking for cooks of all levels. Features recipes from many BBC TV chefs as well as other leading food writers, along with an extensive range of hints, tips and features.

BBC History Magazine

Immediate Media Co. Ltd, Tower House, Fairfax Street, Bristol BS1 3BN
tel 0117 314 7377
email historymagazine@historyextra.com
website www.historyextra.com
Facebook www.facebook.com/historyextra
Twitter @historyextra
Editor Rob Attar
Monthly £4.99

Popular history writing on a wide range of topics, from Ancient Egypt to the Second World War. Contents include feature spreads, book reviews, opinion and news. Contributors include Mary Beard, Tracy Borman, Dan Snow and Michael Wood. Illustrated. Founded 2000.

BBC Music Magazine

Immediate Media Co. Ltd, Tower House, Fairfax Street, Bristol BS1 3BN
email oliver.condy@immediate.co.uk
website www.classical-music.com
Twitter @MusicMagazine
Editor Oliver Condy
Monthly £5.99

Reviews and articles on all aspects of classical music. Also interviews with leading practitioners, information on technical equipment and forthcoming tours. Free CD with every issue.

BBC Sky at Night Magazine

Immediate Media Co. Ltd, Tower House, Fairfax Street, Bristol BS1 3BN
tel 0117 314 8758
email contactus@skyatnightmagazine.com
website www.skyatnightmagazine.com
Twitter @skyatnightmag
Editor Chris Bramley
Monthly £4.99

Offers a mix of practical stargazing tips and information, space science and dark skies travel features, and equipment news to both experienced astronomers and those new to the subject. Founded 2005.

BBC Top Gear

Immediate Media Co. Ltd, Vineyard House, 44 Brook Green, London W6 7BT
tel 020-7150 5559
email charlie.turner@bbctopgearmagazine.co.uk
website www.topgear.com
Twitter @BBC_TopGear
Editor Charlie Turner
13 p.a. £4.50

Articles and photographic features on motoring, lifestyle and cars.

BBC Wildlife Magazine

Immediate Media Co. Ltd, Tower House, Fairfax Street, Bristol BS1 3BN
email wildlifemagazine@immediate.co.uk
website www.discoverwildlife.com
Twitter @WildlifeMag
Editor Sheena Harvey
Monthly £4.25

Natural history magazine. Expert-written articles and features, along with award-winning photography.

Bella

H. Bauer Publishing, Academic House, 24–28 Oval Road, London NW1 7DT
tel 020-7241 8000
website www.bellamagazine.co.uk
Editor Julia Davis
Weekly £1

Women's magazine with celebrity interviews, exclusive photos, real-life stories, high-street fashion, diet advice, health, food and travel. Payment: by arrangement. Founded 1987.

Best

Hearst Magazines UK, 33 Broadwick Street, London W1F 0DQ
tel 020-7339 4500
email siobhan.wykes@hearst.co.uk
Editor Siobhan Wykes
Weekly £1.10

Unsolicited work not accepted, but always willing to look at ideas/outlines. Payment: by agreement. Founded 1987.

The Big Issue

43 Bath Street, Glasgow G2 1HW
tel 0141 352 7260
email editorial@thebigissue.com
website www.bigissue.com
Editor Paul McNamee
Weekly £2.50

Features, current affairs, reviews, interviews – of general interest and on social issues. Length: 1,000 words (features). No short stories or poetry. Illustrations: colour and b&w photos and line. Payment: £160 per 1,000 words. Founded 1991.

Bike

Bauer Media Group, Media House, Lynchwood, Peterborough Business Park, Peterborough PE2 6EA
tel (01733) 468181
email bike@bauermedia.com
website www.bikemagazine.co.uk
Editor Hugo Wilson
Monthly £4.30

Motorcycle magazine. Interested in articles, features, news. Length: articles/features 1,000–3,000 words. Illustrations: colour and b&w photos. Payment: £140 per 1,000 words; photos per size/position. Founded 1971.

Bird Watching

Bauer Media Group, Media House, Lynchwood, Peterborough Business Park, Peterborough PE2 6EA
tel (01733) 468201
email birdwatching@bauermedia.co.uk
website www.birdwatching.co.uk
Editor Matthew Merritt
13 p.a. £4.20

Broad range of bird-related features and photography, particularly looking at bird behaviour, bird news, reviews and UK birdwatching sites. Limited amount of overseas features. Emphasis on providing accurate information in entertaining ways. Send synopsis first. Length: up to 1,200 words. Illustrations: emailed jpgs and photo images on CD, bird identification artwork. Payment: by negotiation. Founded 1986.

Birdwatch

Warners Group Publications, The Chocolate Factory, 5 Clarendon Road, London N22 6XJ
tel 020-8881 0550
website www.birdguides.com
Managing Editor Dominic Mitchell
Monthly £4.20

Topical articles on all aspects of British and Irish birds and birding, including conservation, identification, sites and habitats and equipment, as well as overseas destinations. Length: 700–1,500 words. Illustrations: hi res jpgs (300 dpi at 1,500 pixels min. width) of wild British and European birds considered; submit on CD/DVD or full size via email or file-sharing site. Artwork: by negotiation. Payment: by negotiation. Founded 1991.

Black Beauty & Hair

Hawker Publications, 2nd Floor, Culvert House, Culvert Road, London SW11 5DH
tel 020-7720 2108
email info@blackbeautyandhair.com
website www.blackbeautyandhair.com
Editor Irene Shelley
Bi-monthly £3.50

Beauty and style articles relating specifically to the black woman; celebrity features. True-life stories and salon features. Length: approx. 1,000 words. Illustrations: colour and b&w photos. Payment: £100 per 1,000 words; photos £25–£75. Founded 1982.

Black Static

TTA Press, 5 Martins Lane, Witcham, Ely, Cambs. CB6 2LB
website www.ttapress.com
Twitter @TTApress
Editor Andy Cox
Bi-monthly £5.99

New horror and dark fantasy stories. Also features interviews with, and profiles of, authors and film-makers. Send sae with all submissions. Considers unsolicited material and welcomes ideas for articles and features. Length: 3,000–4,000 words (articles and features), short stories unrestricted. Illustrations: send samples and portfolios. Payment: by arrangement. Founded 1994.

Blithe Spirit

email blithespirit.editor@gmail.com
website www.britishhaikusociety.org.uk
Editor Shrikaanth Krishnamurthy
Quarterly Free to members

80pp journal of the British Haiku Society. Includes original poems, articles, news and letters to the editor from Society members only. Four submission windows (see website for up-to-date details); poems must not have appeared, or be under consideration, elsewhere.

Boat International

41–47 Hartfield Road, London SW19 3RQ
tel 020-8545 9330
email stewart.campbell@boatinternationalmedia.com
website www.boatinternational.com
Twitter @boatint
Editor Stewart Campbell
12 p.a. £7

News and features on superyachts and the lifestyles of those who own them. Also yacht listings in a brokerage section and reviews.

The Book Collector

(incorporating Bibliographical Notes and Queries)
39 Melrose Gardens, London W6 7RN
tel 020-7602 0502
email editor@thebookcollector.co.uk
website www.thebookcollector.co.uk
Editor James Fergusson
Quarterly £60 p.a. (UK), €90 (Europe), US$125 (RoW; airmail)

Articles, biographical and bibliographical, on the collection and study of printed books and MSS. Payment: for reviews only. Founded 1952.

Books Ireland

Unit 9, 78 Furze Road, Dublin 8, Republic of Ireland
tel +353 (0)1 2933568
email una@wordwellbooks.com
email tony@booksirelandmagazine.com
website www.booksirelandmagazine.com
Twitter @booksirelandmag
Editor Tony Canavan
Bi-monthly €5.95, €35 p.a. (€45 p.a. to UK mainland)

Reviews of Irish-interest and Irish-author books, as well as articles of interest to librarians, booksellers and readers. Length: 800–1,400 words. Founded 1976.

The Bookseller

Floor 10, Westminster Tower,
3 Albert Embankment, London SE1 7SP
tel 020-3358 0365
email lisa.campbell@thebookseller.co.uk
website www.thebookseller.com
Twitter @thebookseller
Editor Philip Jones, *Features and Insight Editor* Tom Tivnan
Weekly £4.95

Journal of the UK publishing, bookselling trade and libraries. While outside contributions are welcomed, most of the journal's contents are commissioned. Length: about 1,000–1,500 words. Payment: by arrangement. Founded 1858.

Bowls International

Oyster Media Group Ltd, 71-75 Shelton Street, London WC2H 9JQ
tel 07791 696718
email sian.honnor@keypublishing.com
website www.bowlsinternational.com
Facebook www.facebook.com/BowlsInternational
Twitter @BowlsInt
Editor Sian Honnor
Monthly £4.20

Sport and news items and features; occasional, bowls-oriented short stories. Illustrations: colour transparencies, b&w photos, occasional line, cartoons. Payment: sport/news approx. 25p per line, features approx. £50 per page; colour £25, b&w £10. Founded 1981.

Breathe

GMC Publications Ltd, 86 High Street, Lewes BN7 1XN
tel (01273) 477374
email hello@breathemagazine.com
website www.breathemagazine.com
Publisher Jonathan Grogan
Monthly £5.99

Mindfulness magazine aiming to help readers achieve a healthier life across five key areas: wellbeing, living, creativity, mindfulness and escape. Submissions welcomed from experienced or new writers, and from illustrators. See www.teenbreathe.co.uk/submissions for specific requirements for each type of potential contributor.

British Birds

4 Harlequin Gardens, St Leonards-on-Sea TN37 7PF
tel (01424) 755155
email editor@britishbirds.co.uk
website www.britishbirds.co.uk
Twitter @britishbirds
Editor Dr Roger Riddington
Monthly £60 p.a. (print)

Publishes major papers on identification, behaviour, conservation, distribution, ecology, movements, status and taxonomy with official reports on: rare breeding birds, scarce migrants and rare birds in Britain. Payment: token. Founded 1907.

British Chess Magazine

Albany House, Shute End, Wokingham, Berks. RG40 1BJ
email editor@britishchessmagazine.co.uk
website www.britishchessmagazine.co.uk
Monthly £5.50

Authoritative reports and commentary on the UK and overseas chess world. Payment: by arrangement. Founded 1881.

British Journal of Photography

1854 Media Ltd, Anchorage House, 9th Floor, 2 Clove Street, London E14 2BE
tel 020-7993 2243
email izabela@1854.media
website www.bjp-online.com
Editorial Director Simon Bainbridge, *Assistant Editor* Izabela Radwanska Zhang
Monthly £9.99

Focus on all aspects of contemporary photography: articles on fine art, commercial, fashion, documentary and editorial, alongside trend reports and technical reviews. Founded 1854.

British Journalism Review

SAGE Publications, 1 Oliver's Yard, 55 City Road, London EC1Y 1SP
tel 020-7324 8500
email editor@bjr.org.uk
website www.bjr.org.uk
Editor Kim Fletcher
Quarterly £47 p.a. for individuals (print only; institutional rates also available)

Comment, criticism and review of matters published by, or of interest to, the media. Length: 1,500–3,000 words. Illustrations: b&w photos. Payment: by arrangement. Founded 1989.

British Medical Journal

BMJ Publishing Group, BMA House, Tavistock Square, London WC1H 9JR
tel 020-7387 4410
email fgodlee@bmj.com
website www.bmj.com/thebmj
Editor Dr Fiona Godlee
Weekly Free to members of BMA; for subscription details see website

Medical and related articles. Payment: by arrangement. Founded 1840.

British Philatelic Bulletin

Royal Mail, 185 Farringdon Road, Floor MP-03, London EC1A 1AA
email bulletin.enquiries@royalmail.co.uk
website www.royalmail.com/stamps
Editor Tim Noble
Monthly £1.95

Articles on all aspects of British philately – stamps, postmarks, postal history; also stamp collecting in general. Length: up to 1,500 words (articles); 250 words (news). Illustrations: colour. Payment: £75 per 1,000 words. Founded 1963.

Brittle Star

Diversity House, 72 Nottingham Road, Arnold, Nottingham NG5 6L
email production@brittlestar.org.uk
website www.brittlestar.org.uk
Twitter @brittlestarmag
Editors Jacqueline Gabbitas, Martin Parker
2 p.a. £15 p.a. (UK), £25 p.a. (Rest of World)

Not-for-profit literary magazine run by volunteers. Seeks high-quality contemporary literature for adults, including all forms of poetry as well as literary short fiction. Send submissions by post, having first read a copy of the magazine, along with a covering letter and an sae (see website for further details and up-to-date postal address). Submitted work should not be under consideration elsewhere.

Broadcast

Media Business Insight Ltd, Zetland House, 5–25 Scrutton Street, London EC2A 4HJ
tel 020-8102 0827
email chris.curtis@broadcastnow.co.uk
website www.broadcastnow.co.uk
Editor Chris Curtis
Weekly From £257 p.a.

For people working or interested in the UK and international broadcast industry. News, features, analysis and opinions across a variety of platforms. Covers the latest developments in programming, commissioning, digital, technology and post-production.

Building

UBM EMEA, 240 Blackfriars Road, London SE1 8BF
tel 020-7560 4000
email building@ubm.com
website www.building.co.uk
Editor-in-Chief Tom Broughton
49 p.a. From £110 p.a. (digital only; premium subscriptions, including print, are available)

Covers all aspects of the construction industry and built environment, from architecture to property development. Sectors include housing, commercial property, education and health buildings, and infrastructure. Will consider articles on the built environment in the UK and abroad; including news, comment, analysis and photos. Payment: by arrangement. Founded 1843.

Building Design

UBM EMEA Built Environment, 240 Blackfriars Road, London SE1 8BF

tel 020-7921 5000
email buildingdesign@ubm.com
website www.bdonline.co.uk
Facebook www.facebook.com/BDmagazine
Twitter @BDonline
Editor Thomas Lane
Annual subscriptions from £63.85 p.a.

Daily online newspaper and magazine plus monthly digital edition. News and features on all aspects of architecture and urban design. All material commissioned. Length: up to 1,500 words. Illustrations: colour and b&w photos, line, cartoons. Payment: £150 per 1,000 words; illustrations by negotiation. Founded 1970.

Bunbury Magazine

5 Chester Street, Bury, Lancs. BL9 6EU
tel 07446 025630
email submissions@bunburymagazine.com
website www.bunburymagazine.com
Twitter @BunburyPublish
Directors and Editors Christopher Moriarty, Keri-Ann Moriarty

Online arts and literature magazine committed to providing a platform for both grass-roots and established writers and artists. Submissions welcomed on a variety of subjects, from poetry to artwork, flash fiction to graphic stories, life writing to photography, but see website for full guidelines. Also offers editorial services and a regular writers' group and spoken word events, called Just Write. Founded 2013.

The Burlington Magazine

14–16 Duke's Road, London WC1H 9SZ
tel 020-7388 8157
email editorial@burlington.org.uk
website www.burlington.org.uk
Editor Michael Hall
12 p.a. £25

Deals with the history and criticism of art; book and exhibition reviews; illustrated monthly Calendar section. Potential contributors must have special knowledge of the subjects treated; MSS compiled from works of reference are unacceptable. Length: 500–5,000 words. Illustrations: colour images. Payment: up to £150 (book and exhibition reviews only). Founded 1903.

Buses

Key Publishing Ltd, Foundry Road, Stamford, Lincs. PE9 2PP
tel (01780) 755131
Editor Alan Millar, PO Box 14644, Leven KY9 1WX
tel (01333) 340637
email buseseditor@btconnect.com
website www.busesmag.com
Monthly £4.70

Articles of interest to both road passenger transport operators and bus enthusiasts. Preliminary enquiry essential. Illustrations: digital (first preference), colour transparencies, half-tone, line maps. Payment: on application. Founded 1949.

Business Traveller

41 Maddox Street, London W1S 2PD
tel 020-7821 2700
email enquiries@panaceapublishing.co.uk
website www.businesstraveller.com
Editor-in-Chief Tom Otley
10 p.a. £3.95

Articles, features and news on consumer travel aimed at individual frequent international business travellers. Submit ideas with recent clippings and a CV. Length: varies. Illustrations: colour for destinations features. Payment: on application. Founded 1976.

Campaign

Haymarket Ltd, Bridge House, 69 London Road, Twickenham TW1 3SP
tel 020-8267 8032
email maisie.mccabe@haymarket.com
website www.campaignlive.co.uk
Editor Rachel Barnes
Monthly £46 per quarter

News and articles covering the whole of the mass communications field, particularly advertising in all its forms, marketing and the media. Features should not exceed 2,000 words. News items also welcome. Payment: by arrangement.

Candis

Newhall Publications Ltd, Newhall Lane, Hoylake, Wirral CH47 4BQ
tel 0151 632 3232
email fiction@candis.co.uk
website www.candis.co.uk
Twitter @candismagazine
Editor Debbie Attewell
Monthly Subscription only

Commissions one 2,500-word short story each month by a well-known published author. Unsolicited material is no longer received and will be returned unread. Writers willing to share a personal life story or experience for real lives feature may send a synopsis to editor@candis.co.uk. Also covers health, news, celebrity interviews, family issues, fashion and beauty.

Car

Bauer Media Group, Media House, Lynchwood, Peterborough Business Park, Peterborough PE2 6EA
tel (01733) 468379
email car@bauermedia.co.uk
website www.carmagazine.co.uk
Editor-in-Chief Phil McNamara, *Editor* Ben Miller
Monthly £4.60

Top-grade journalistic features on car driving, car

people and cars. Length: 1,000–2,500 words. Illustrations: b&w and colour photos to professional standards. Payment: minimum £350 per 1,000 words. Founded 1962.

Car Mechanics

Bauer Media Group, Media House, Lynchwood, Peterborough Business Park, Peterborough PE2 6EA
tel (01733) 468000
email carmechanics@bauermedia.co.uk
website www.carmechanicsmag.co.uk
Twitter @CarMechanics
Editor Martyn Knowles
Monthly £4.30

Practical articles on maintaining, repairing and uprating modern cars for DIY plus the motor trade. Always interested in finding new talent for our rather specialised market, but study a recent copy before submitting ideas or features. Email outlining feature recommended. Illustrations: line drawings, colour prints, digital images. Supply package of text and pictures. Payment: by arrangement. Founded 1958.

Caravan Magazine

Warners Group Publications, The Maltings, West Street, Bourne, Lincs. PE10 9PH
tel (01778) 391000
email johns@warnersgroup.co.uk
website www.caravanmagazine.co.uk
Managing Editor John Sootheran
Monthly £4.20

Lively articles based on real experience of touring caravanning, especially if well illustrated by photos provided by the author or from regional Tourist Boards, attractions etc. Payment: by arrangement. Founded 1933.

Cat World

PO Box 2258, Pulborough RH20 9BA
tel (01903) 884988
email support@ashdown.co.uk
website www.catworld.co.uk
Editor Jill Mundy
Monthly £3.25

Bright, lively articles on any aspect of cat ownership. Articles on breeds of cats and veterinary articles by acknowledged experts only. No unsolicited fiction. All submissions by email or on disk. Illustrations: colour prints, tiffs. Payment: by arrangement. Founded 1981.

The Caterer

Jacobs Media Group, 52 Grosvenor Gardens, London, SW1W 0AU
tel 020-7881 4803
email info@caterer.com
website www.thecaterer.com
Editor Chris Gamm, *Associate Editor* Janet Harmer, *Deputy Editor* James Stagg, *News Editor* Emma Lake
Weekly £4

Multimedia brand for the UK hospitality industry. In print and online, offers content, job news and a digital platform for hotel, restaurant, food service, and pub and bar operators across the country. Article length: up to 1,500 words. Illustrations: line, half-tone, colour. Payment: by arrangement. Founded 1878.

The Catholic Herald

Herald House, Lamb's Passage, Bunhill Row, London EC1Y 8TQ
tel 020-77448 3603
email editorial@catholicherald.co.uk
website www.catholicherald.co.uk
Editor Luke Coppen
Weekly £2.50

Independent newspaper covering national and international affairs from a Catholic/Christian viewpoint as well as church news. Length: articles 800–1,200 words. Illustrations: photos of Catholic and Christian interest. Payment: by arrangement.

Catholic Pictorial

36 Henry Street, Liverpool L1 5BS
tel 0151 522 1007
email p.heneghan@rcaol.co.uk
website www.catholicpic.co.uk
Editor Peter Heneghan
Monthly Free

News and photo features (maximum 800 words plus illustration) on Merseyside, regional and national Catholic interest only. Payment: by arrangement. Founded 1961.

Catholic Times

The Universe Media Group Ltd, Guardian Print Centre, Longbridge Road, Trafford Park, Manchester M17 1SN
email kevin.flaherty@thecatholicuniverse.com
website www.thecatholicuniverse.com
Editor Kevin Flaherty
Weekly £1.30

News (400 words) and news features (800 words) of Catholic interest. Illustrations: colour photos. Relaunched 1993.

The Catholic Universe

The Universe Media Group Ltd, Guardian Print Centre, Parkway, Longbridge Road, Trafford Park, Manchester M17 1SN
tel 0161 214 1249
email joseph.kelly@thecatholicuniverse.com
website www.thecatholicuniverse.com
Editor Joe Kelly
Weekly £1.30

Catholic Sunday newspaper. News stories, features and photos on all aspects of Catholic life required;

also cartoons. Send sae with MSS. Payment: by arrangement. Founded 1860.

Central and Eastern European London Review

161 Fordwych Road, London NW2 3NG
tel 07983 918170
email ceel.org@gmail.com
website www.ceel.org.uk
Editor Robin Ashenden

Online magazine. Voluntary contributions sought on any aspect of Central and Eastern European life in the capital. Book/film reviewers especially welcome. Submissions: via email. Founded 2014.

Ceramic Review

63 Great Russell Street, London WC1B 3BF
tel 020-7183 5583
email editorial@ceramicreview.com
website www.ceramicreview.com/
Facebook www.facebook.com/ceramicreview
Twitter @ceramicreview
Editor Karen Bray
6 p.a. £9.90

International magazine containing critical features, reviews and practical information on all forms of ceramics and clay art and craft. Welcomes article proposals – critical, profile, technical, historical or experiential – and also looks at the role of ceramics within contemporary culture. Feature articles run from 800 to 1,400 words and must include large, hi-res images. Payment: offered at current rates on publication.

Chat

Time Inc. (UK), 161 Marsh Wall, London E14 9AP
tel 020-3148 5000
email chat_magazine@timeinc.com
website www.chatmagazine.co.uk
Facebook www.facebook.com/ChatMagazine
Twitter @ChatMagazine
Editor Matthew Davis
Weekly 96p

Tabloid weekly for women. Includes readers' letters, tips and true-life features. Payment: by arrangement. Founded 1985.

Church of England Newspaper

Religious Intelligence Ltd, 14 Great College Street, London SW1P 3RX
tel 020-7878 1001
email cen@churchnewspaper.com
website www.churchnewspaper.com
Twitter @churchnewspaper
Editor Colin Blakely
Weekly £75 p.a. (print and digital)

Anglican news and articles relating the Christian faith to everyday life. Evangelical basis; almost exclusively commissioned articles. Prior study of paper desirable. Length: up to 1,000 words. Illustrations: photos, line drawings, cartoons. Payment: c. £40 per 1,000 words; photos £22, line by arrangement. Founded 1828.

Church Times

108–114 Golden Lane, London EC1Y 0TG
tel 020-7776 1060
email news@churchtimes.co.uk
website www.churchtimes.co.uk
Managing Editor Paul Handley
Weekly £2.20

Articles on religious topics are considered. No verse or fiction. Length: up to 1,000 words. Illustrations: news photos, sent promptly. Payment: £100 per 1,000 words. Negotiated rates for illustrations. Founded 1863.

Classic Boat Magazine

The Chelsea Magazine Co., Jubilee House, 2 Jubilee Place, London SW3 3TQ
tel 020-7349 3755
email rob.peake@classicboat.co.uk
website www.classicboat.co.uk
Editor Rob Peake
Monthly £4.95

Cruising and technical features, restorations, events, new boat reviews, practical, maritime history; news. Study of magazine essential: read three to four back issues and send for contributors' guidelines. Length: 500–2,000 words. Illustrations: colour and b&w photos; line drawings of hulls. Payment: £75–£100 per published page. Founded 1987.

Classic Cars

Bauer Consumer Media, Media House, Lynchwood, Peterborough Business Park, Peterborough PE2 6EA
tel (01733) 468000
email classic.cars@bauermedia.co.uk
website www.classiccarsmagazine.co.uk
Facebook www.facebook.com/classiccarsmagazine
Editor Phil Bell
Monthly £4.60

Specialist articles on older cars and related events. Length: from 150–4,000 words (subject to prior contract). Photography: classic car event photography on spec; feature photography on commission basis. Payment: by negotiation. Founded 1973.

Classical Music

Rhinegold Publishing Ltd, 20 Rugby Street, London WC1N 3QZ
tel 020-7333 1729
email classical.music@rhinegold.co.uk
website www.classicalmusicmagazine.org
Twitter @ClassicalMusic_
Deputy Editor Katy Wright
Monthly From £53.45 p.a.

News, opinion, features on the classical music business. All material commissioned. Illustrations:

colour photos and line; colour covers. Payment: minimum £130 per 1,000 words. Founded 1976.

Climber

email climbereditorial@gmail.com
website www.climber.co.uk
Twitter @climbermagazine
6 p.a. £4.95

Articles on all aspects of rock climbing/ mountaineering in Great Britain and abroad, and on related subjects. Study of magazine essential. Length: 1,500–2,000 words. Illustrations: colour transparencies. Payment: according to merit. Founded 1962.

Closer

Bauer Consumer Media, Endeavour House, 189 Shaftesbury Avenue, London WC2H 8JG
tel 020-7437 9011
email closer@closermag.co.uk
website www.closeronline.co.uk
Editor Lisa Burrow
Weekly £1.80

Women's celebrity weekly magazine with real-life stories, lifestyle, fashion, beauty and TV entertainment and listings sections. Payment by negotiation.

Coin News

Token Publishing Ltd, 40 Southernhay East, Exeter, Devon EX1 1PE
tel (01404) 46972
email info@tokenpublishing.com
website www.tokenpublishing.com
Editor John W. Mussell
Monthly £4

Articles of high standard on coins, tokens, paper money. Send text in digital form. Length: up to 2,000 words. Payment: by arrangement. Founded 1983.

Commercial Motor

6th Floor, Chancery House, St Nicholas Way, Sutton, Surrey SM1 1JB
tel 020-8912 2163
email christopher.walton@roadtransport.com
website www.commercialmotor.com
Group News Editor Christopher Walton
Weekly £3

Technical and road transport articles only. Length: up to 1,500 words. Illustrations: drawings and photos. Payment: varies. Founded 1905.

Community Care

St Jude's Church, Dulwich Road, Herne Hill, London SE24 0PB
tel 020-3915 9444
email communitycare@markallen.com
website www.communitycare.co.uk

Online magazine site with articles, features and news covering the Social Services sector.

Computer Arts

Future Publishing Ltd, Quay House, The Ambury, Bath BA1 1UA
tel (01225) 442244
email hello@computerarts.co.uk
website www.creativebloq.com/computer-arts-magazine
Monthly £6

Magazine for digital artists and designers with in-depth tutorials together with tips for web design, typography, 3D, animation, motion graphics and multimedia. Also reviews the latest hardware and software releases and includes interviews with leading figures in the global design world.

Computer Weekly

25 Christopher Street, London EC2A 2BS
email cw-news@computerweekly.com
website www.computerweekly.com
Facebook www.facebook.com/computerweekly
Twitter @computerweekly
Editor Bryan Glick
Weekly Free to registered subscribers

Feature articles on IT-related topics for business/ industry users. Length: 1,200 words. Illustrations: colour photos. Payment: £250 per 1,000 words. Founded 1966.

Computeractive

Dennis Publishing Ltd, 31–32 Alfred Place, London WC1E 7DP
website http://getcomputeractive.co.uk
Editor Daniel Booth
Fortnightly £1.99

Computing magazine offering plain-English advice for PCs, tablets, phones and the internet, as well as product reviews and technology news.

Condé Nast Traveller

Condé Nast Publications Ltd, Vogue House, Hanover Square, London W1S 1JU
tel 020-7499 9080
email editorcntraveller@condenast.co.uk
website www.cntraveller.com
Editor Melinda Stevens
Monthly £4.30

Lavishly photographed articles on all aspects of travel, featuring exotic destinations and those close to home. Specialist pieces include food and wine, motoring, health, foreign correspondents, travel news, hotels. Illustrations: colour. Payment: by arrangement. Founded 1997.

Cosmopolitan

Hearst Magazines UK, National Magazines House, 72 Broadwick Street, London W1F 9EP
tel 020-7439 5000
website www.cosmopolitan.co.uk
Editor Farrah Storr

Monthly £2

Commissioned material only. Payment: by arrangement. Illustrated. Founded 1972.

Cotswold Life

Cumberland House, Oriel Road, Cheltenham, Glos. GL50 1BB
tel (01242) 216050
email candia.mckormack@archant.co.uk
website www.cotswoldlife.co.uk
Facebook www.facebook.com/cotswoldlife/
Twitter @cotswoldlife
Editor Mike Lowe, *Deputy Editor* Candia McKormack
Monthly £4.50

Articles on the Cotswolds, including places of interest, high-profile personalities, local events, arts, history, interiors, fashion and food. Founded 1967.

Country Homes and Interiors

Time Inc. (UK), 161 Marsh Wall, London E14 9AP
tel 020-3148 5000
email countryhomes@timeinc.com
website www.housetohome.co.uk/countryhomesandinteriors
Facebook www.facebook.com/countryhomesandinteriors
Twitter @countryhomesmag
Editor Rhoda Parry
Monthly £3.99

Articles on country homes and gardens, interiors, food, lifestyle. Payment: from £250 per 1,000 words. Founded 1986.

Country Life

Time Inc. (UK), Pinehurst 2, Pinehurst Road, Farnborough Business Park, Farnborough, Hants GU14 7BF
tel (01252) 555062
website www.countrylife.co.uk
Editor Mark Hedges, *Deputy Editor* Kate Green
Weekly £3.50

Illustrated journal chiefly concerned with British country life, social history, architecture and the fine arts, natural history, agriculture, gardening and sport. Length: about 1,000 or 1,300 words (articles). Illustrations: mainly colour photos. Payment: according to merit. Founded 1897.

Country Living

Hearst Magazines UK, National Magazines House, 72 Broadwick Street, London W1F 9EP
tel 020-7439 5000
email country.living@hearst.co.uk
website www.countryliving.co.uk
Twitter @countrylivinguk
Editor Susy Smith
Monthly £4.30

Up-market home-interest magazine with a country lifestyle theme, covering interiors, gardens, crafts, food, wildlife, rural and green issues. Do not send unsolicited material or valuable transparencies. Illustrations: line, half-tone, colour. Payment: by arrangement. Founded 1985.

Country Smallholding

Archant SW, Unit 3, Old Station Road, Barnstaple EX32 8PB
tel (01271) 341652
email editorial.csh@archant.co.uk
website www.countrysmallholding.com
Editor Simon McEwan
Monthly £3.99

The magazine for smallholders. Practical, how-to articles and seasonal features on organic gardening, small-scale poultry and livestock keeping, country crafts, cookery and general subjects of interest to smallholders and others. Approach the Editor in writing or by phone or email with ideas. Length: up to 1,200 words. Payment: on application. Founded 1975 as *Practical Self-Sufficiency*.

Country Walking

Bauer Consumer Media, Media House, Lynchwood, Peterborough Business Park, Peterborough PE2 6EA
tel (01733) 468205
website www.livefortheoutdoors.com/countrywalking
Editor Guy Procter
13 p.a. £4.50

Features. Length: 1,000 words on average. Illustrations: digital images. Payment: by arrangement. Founded 1987.

The Countryman

Country Publications Ltd, The Water Mill, Broughton Hall, Skipton, North Yorkshire BD23 3AG
tel (01756) 701381
email editorial@thecountryman.co.uk
website www.countrymanmagazine.co.uk
Twitter @Countrymaned
Editor Mark Whitley
Monthly £3.99

Features rural life, wildlife and natural history, country people, traditions, crafts, covering whole of UK. Positive view of countryside and rural issues. Non-political, and no bloodsports. Unusual or quirky topics welcomed. Copy must be well written and accurate, for well-informed readership who are generally 40+ with strong affection for countryside. Articles between 600–1,000 words. Illustrations: good-quality digital images. Study magazine before submitting ideas. Send detailed outline first. Payment: by agreement. Founded 1927.

Crafts Magazine

44A Pentonville Road, London N1 9BY
tel 020-7806 2538
email crafts@craftscouncil.org.uk
website www.craftsmagazine.org.uk

Editor Grant Gibson
Bi-monthly £6.50

Magazine for contemporary craft, published by the Crafts Council. Specialist features, craft news and reviews, archive articles from the magazine's 35-year history and contributors from iconic institutions such as the V&A, Royal College of Art and Central St Martins. Submissions for review should include pictures and applicants should be mindful of the lead times associated with a bi-monthly schedule.

Crannóg

email editor@crannogmagazine.com
website www.crannogmagazine.com
Editors Sandra Bunting, Tony O'Dwyer, Ger Burke, Jarlath Fahy
3 p.a. €7.00

Literary magazine aiming to bring together the best poetry and fiction from Irish and international contributors. Published triannually in February, June and October. Contributor's fee paid: see detailed submissions information online (www.crannogmagazine.com/submissions.htm). Founded 2002.

Criminal Law & Justice Weekly (incorporating Justice of the Peace)

LexisNexis, 30 Farringdon Street, London EC4A 4HH
tel 020-7400 2828
email diana.rose@lexisnexis.co.uk
website www.criminallawandjustice.co.uk
Twitter @crimlawjustice
Editor Diana Rose
Weekly Online subscription £99 p.a.

Delivers information and acts as a resource for the criminal law professional and those working within criminal justice areas. Articles on criminal law and associated subjects including news, local authorities, professional, criminology, coroners, prison, police and probation, international law, news, blogs and reports. Length: 700 words for comment pieces; 1,700 words for features. Founded 1837.

Critical Quarterly

Newbury, Crediton, Devon EX17 5HA
tel (01359) 242375
email cs-journals@wiley.com
website http://onlinelibrary.wiley.com/journal/10.1111/(ISSN)1467-8705
Editor Colin MacCabe
Quarterly £42 p.a. (individual, print and online)

Fiction, poems, literary criticism. Length: 2,000–5,000 words. Study magazine before submitting MSS. Payment: by arrangement. Founded 1959.

Crystal Magazine

3 Bowness Avenue, Prenton, Birkenhead CH43 0SD
tel 0151 608 9736
email christinecrystal@hotmail.com
website www.christinecrystal.blogspot.com
Editor Christine Carr
6 p.a. £18 p.a. (UK), £22 p.a. (overseas)

Poems, stories (true and fiction), articles. Also: Wordsmithing, a humorous and informative look into the world of writers and writing; readers' letters; subscribers' news; and surprise competitions – entry £1, small surprise gifts as prizes. Founded 2001.

Cumbria Magazine

Country Publications Ltd, The Water Mill, Broughton Hall, Skipton, North Yorkshire BD23 3AG
tel (01756) 701381
email johnm@dalesman.co.uk
website www.cumbriamagazine.co.uk
Editor John Manning
Monthly £3.20

Articles of rural interest concerning the people and landscapes of the Lake District and surrounding county of Cumbria. Short length preferred; articles should be of a journalistic nature and no more than 1,200 words. Illustrations: first-class photos, illustrations. Payment: £70 per 1,000 words. Pictures extra. Founded 1947, New Series 1951.

Custom Car

Kelsey Media, Cudham Tithe Barn, Berry's Hill, Cudham, Kent TN16 3AG
tel (01959) 541444
email cc.ed@kelsey.co.uk
website www.customcarmag.co.uk
Editor David Biggadyke
Four-weekly £4.80

Hot rods, customs and drag racing. Length: by arrangement. Payment: by arrangement. Founded 1970.

Custom PC

Dennis Publishing Ltd, 31–32 Alfred Place, London WC1E 7DP
tel 020-8390 3890
website www.custompc.co.uk
Editor Ben Hardwidge
Monthly £5.99

Magazine covering performance PC hardware, technology and games with full-page and DPS single-product reviews, group tests, and practical and technical features.

Cycling Weekly

Time Inc. (UK), Pinehurst 2, Pinehurst Road, Farnborough Business Park, Farnborough, Hants GU14 7BF
tel (01252) 555100
email cycling@timeinc.com
website www.cyclingweekly.com
Facebook www.facebook.com/CyclingWeekly
Twitter @cyclingweekly
Editor Simon Richardson
Weekly £2.99

Racing, fitness, features and technical reviews. Illustrations: topical cycling racing photos considered; cartoons. Length: not exceeding 2,000 words. Payment: by arrangement. Founded 1891.

Cyphers

3 Selskar Terrace, Ranelagh, Dublin D06 DW66, Republic of Ireland
tel +353 (0)1 4978866
website www.cyphers.ie
Editors Eiléan Ní Chuilleanáin, Macdara Woods
3 p.a. €21 p.a.

Poems, fiction, translations. Submissions cannot be returned unless accompanied by postage (Irish stamps or International Reply Coupons.) Payment: €35 to 50 per page. Founded 1975.

Dalesman

Country Publications Limited, The Water Mill, Broughton Hall, Skipton, North Yorkshire BD23 3AG
tel (01756) 693479
email editorial@dalesman.co.uk
website www.dalesman.co.uk
Editor Adrian Braddy
Monthly £3.10

Articles and stories of genuine interest concerning Yorkshire (1,000 to 1,200 words). Payment: £70 per 1,000 words plus extra for useable photos/ illustrations. Founded 1939.

Dancing Times

36 Battersea Square, London SW11 3RA
tel 020-7250 3006
email editorial@dancing-times.co.uk
website www.dancing-times.co.uk
Editor Jonathan Gray
Monthly £3.95

Ballet, ballroom, Latin, contemporary dance and all forms of stage and social dancing from general, historical, critical and technical angles. Well-informed freelance articles used occasionally, but only after preliminary arrangements. Illustrations: occasional line, action photos preferred; colour welcome. Payment: by arrangement. Founded 1910.

Dare

16 Connaught Place, London W2 2ES
tel 020-7420 7000
website www.therivergroup.co.uk
Free

Superdrug magazine. Predominantly features aspirational yet affordable beauty and fashion.

The Dark Horse

3A Blantyre Mill Road, Bothwell, South Lanarkshire G71 8DD
website www.thedarkhorsemagazine.com
Editors Gerry Cambridge, Jennifer Goodrich, Marcia Menter
1 or 2 p.a. £18 for three editions

International literary magazine, focusing on British, Irish and American poetry. Has published work from both new and established poets, including Wendy Cope, Robert Nye and Anne Stevenson. Submissions welcomed by hard copy; allow sixteen weeks for work to be considered, and include return postage or International Reply Coupons if the return of submitted work is required. Founded 1995.

Darts World

11 Octavian Way, Kingsnorth, Ashford, Kent TN23 3RN
tel (01233) 220011
email editor@dartsworld.co.uk
website www.dartsworld.co.uk
Monthly £2.95

Articles and stories with darts theme. Illustrations: half-tone, cartoons. Payment: £40–£50 per 1,000 words; illustrations by arrangement. Founded 1972.

The Dawntreader

24 Forest Houses, Cookworthy Moor, Halwill, Beaworthy, Devon EX21 5UU
email dawnidp@indigodreams.co.uk
website www.indigodreams.co.uk
Facebook www.facebook.com/ indigodreamspublishing
Twitter @IndigoDreamsPub
Editor Dawn Bauling
Quarterly £4.50, £17 p.a.

Poetry, short stories and articles up to 1,000 words encompassing themes of the mystic, myth, legend, landscape, nature and love. New writers welcome. Lively feedback pages. No payment. Sae essential. Founded 2007.

Decanter

Time Inc. (UK), The Blue Fin Building, 110 Southwark Street, London SE1 0SU
tel 020-3148 4488
email editor@decanter.com
website www.decanter.com
General Manager Lindsay Greatbatch
Monthly £4.95

Articles and features on wines, wine travel and food-related topics. Welcomes ideas for articles and features. Length: 1,000–1,800 words. Illustrations: colour. Payment: £275 per 1,000 words. Founded 1975.

delicious.

Axe & Bottle Court, 3rd Floor, 70 Newcomen Street, London SE1 1YT
tel 020-7803 4115
email info@deliciousmagazine.co.uk
website www.deliciousmagazine.co.uk
Editor Karen Barnes
Monthly £4.50

Articles on food, recipes, preparation, trends, chefs, wine and ingredients. Founded 2003.

Derbyshire Life and Countryside

Archant Life, c/o The Barn, Elms Farm, Hobb Lane, Daresbury, Warrington WA4 5LS
tel (01332) 227851
email joy.hales@derbyshirelife.co.uk
website www.derbyshirelife.co.uk
Editor Joy Hales
Monthly £3.99

Articles, preferably illustrated, about Derbyshire life, people, places and history. Length: up to 1,200 words. Some short stories set in Derbyshire accepted; no verse. Illustrations: photos of Derbyshire subjects. Payment: according to nature and quality of contribution. Founded 1931.

Descent

Wild Places Publishing, PO Box 100, Abergavenny NP7 9WY
tel (01873) 737707
email descent@wildplaces.co.uk
website www.wildplaces.co.uk
Editor Chris Howes
Bi-monthly £5.95

Articles, features and news on all aspects of cave and mine sport exploration (coalmines, active mining or showcaves are not included). Submissions must match magazine style. Length: up to 2,000 words (articles/features), up to 1,000 words (news). Illustrations: colour. Payment: on consideration of material based on area filled. Founded 1969.

Devon Life

Archant South West, Newbery House, Fair Oak Close, Exeter Airport Business Park, Clyst Honiton, Exeter, Devon EX5 2UL
tel (01392) 888423
email andy.cooper@archant.co.uk
website www.devonlife.co.uk
Editor Andy Cooper
Monthly £4.20

Articles on all aspects of Devon, including inspiring people, fascinating places, beautiful walks, local events, arts, history and food. Some articles online, plus a lively community of Devon bloggers. Unsolicited ideas welcome: 'ideal' articles comprise a main section of 650–700 words alongside two sections of associated facts/points of interest on the subject material. Founded 1963.

The Dickensian

The Dickens Fellowship, The Charles Dickens Museum, 48 Doughty Street, London WC1N 2LX
email M.Y.Andrews@kent.ac.uk
website www.dickensfellowship.org/dickensian
Editor Prof. Malcolm Andrews, School of English, Rutherford College, University of Kent, Canterbury, Kent CT2 7NX
3 p.a. £19 p.a. (UK individuals), £29 p.a. (UK institutions); £21 p.a. (overseas individuals), £32 (overseas institutions); reduced rate for Dickens Fellowship members

Welcomes articles (max. 5,000 words) on all aspects of Dickens's life, works and character. Send contributions by email attachment to the Editor. See website for house-style conventions and specifications for any photographic material. Payment: none.

Digital Camera

Future Publishing Ltd, Quay House, The Ambury, Bath BA1 1UA
tel (01225) 442244
website www.digitalcameraworld.com
Editor Benedict Brain
Monthly £4.99

Practical guide to creating better photographs. Each issue contains inspirational images, expert techniques and essential tips for capturing great images and on how to perfect them on a computer. Also includes reviews of the latest cameras, accessories and software.

Director

Seven, 3–7 Herbal Hill, London EC1R 5EJ
email directormagazine@seven.co.uk
website www.director.co.uk
6 p.a. Free to Institute of Directors members; £20 p.a. for UK non-members (print)

Authoritative business related articles. Send synopsis of proposed article and examples of printed work. Length: 500–2,000 words. Payment: by arrangement. Illustrations: colour. Founded 1947.

Diva

Twin Media Group, Room 32, Spectrum House, 32–34 Gordon House Road, London NW5 1LP
tel 020-3735 7873
email editorial@divamag.co.uk
website www.divamag.co.uk
Editor Carrie Lyell
Monthly £4.50

Lesbian and bisexual women's lifestyle and culture: articles and features. Length: 200–2,000 words. Illustrations: colour. Payment: £15 per 100 words; variable per photo; variable per illustration. Founded 1994.

Diver

Suite B, 74 Oldfield Road, Hampton, Middlesex TW12 2HR
tel 020-8941 8152
email enquiries@divermag.co.uk
website www.divernet.com
Publisher and Editor-in-Chief Nigel Eaton, *Editor* Steve Weinman

Monthly £4.40

Articles on recreational scuba-diving and related developments. Length: 1,500–2,000 words. Illustrations: colour. Payment: by arrangement. Founded 1963.

DIY Week

15A London Road, Maidstone, Kent ME16 8LY
tel (01622) 687031
email fgarcia@datateam.net
website www.diyweek.net
Twitter @diyweeknews
Editor Fiona Garcia
Fortnightly From £128 p.a.

Product and city news, promotions and special features on recent developments in DIY houseware and garden retailing. Payment: by arrangement. Founded 1874.

Dogs Today

The Old Print House, 62 High Street, Chobham, Surrey GU24 8AA
tel (01276) 858880
email enquiries@dogstodaymagazine.co.uk
website www.dogstodaymagazine.co.uk
Publisher Beverley Cuddy
Monthly £3.99

Study of magazine essential before submitting ideas. Interested in human interest dog stories, celebrity interviews, holiday features and anything unusual – all must be entertaining and informative and accompanied by illustrations. Length: 800–1,200 words. Illustrations: colour, preferably digital. Payment: negotiable. Founded 1990.

The Dolls' House Magazine

Guild of Master Craftsman Publications Ltd, 86 High Street, Lewes, East Sussex BN7 1XN
tel (01273) 488005
website www.craftsinstitute.com
Twitter @DollsHouseMag
Monthly £4.50

Step-by-step projects, news and features.

Dorset Life – The Dorset Magazine

7 The Leanne, Sandford Lane, Wareham, Dorset BH20 4DY
tel (01929) 551264
email editor@dorsetlife.co.uk
website www.dorsetlife.co.uk
Editor Joël Lacey
Monthly £2.90

Articles (c. 1,000 or 1,500 words), photos (colour) with a specifically Dorset theme. Payment: on acceptance: text £100 per 1,000 words; photos dependent on size used. Founded 1968.

Drapers

EMAP, Telephone House, 69–77 Paul Street, London EC2A 4NQ
tel 020-3033 2770
email keely.stocker@emap.com
website www.drapersonline.com
Facebook www.facebook.com/Drapersonline
Twitter @Drapers
Editor Keely Stocker
From £210 p.a. online and print

Online only. Business editorial aimed at fashion retailers, large and small, and all who supply them. Illustrations: colour and b&w photos. Payment: by negotiation. Founded 1887.

Dream Catcher

Stairwell Books, 161 Lowther Street, York YO31 7LZ
tel (01904) 733767
email rose@stairwellbooks.com
website www.dreamcatchermagazine.co.uk
Editor John Gilham
2 p.a. £8

International literary and arts journal. Welcomes poetry, short stories (optimum length of 2,000 words), artwork, interviews and reviews. Each issue features a selected artist whose work is reproduced on the cover and inside. Promotes reading and workshops across the UK. Founded 1996 by Paul Sutherland.

The Dublin Review

PO Box 7948, Dublin 1, Republic of Ireland
tel +353 (0)1 6788627
email enquiry@thedublinreview.com
website www.thedublinreview.com
Editor Brendan Barrington
Quarterly €11.25

Essays, memoir, reportage and fiction for the intelligent general reader. Payment: by arrangement. Founded 2000.

Early Music

c/o Faculty of Music, University of Cambridge, 11 West Road, Cambridge CB3 9DP
email earlymusic@oxfordjournals.org
website http://em.oxfordjournals.org/
Editors Helen Deeming, Alan Howard, Stephen Rose
Quarterly £75 p.a. (individual)

Lively, informative and scholarly articles on aspects of medieval, renaissance, baroque and classical music. Payment: £20 per 1,000 words. Illustrations: line, half-tone, colour. Founded 1973.

East Lothian Life

1 Beveridge Row, Belhaven, Dunbar, East Lothian EH42 1TP
tel (01368) 863593
website www.eastlothianlife.co.uk
Twitter @eastlothianlife
Editor Pauline Jaffray
Quarterly £3

Articles and features with an East Lothian slant.

Length: up to 1,000 words. Illustrations: b&w photos, line. Payment: negotiable. Founded 1989.

Eastern Art Report

EAPGROUP International Media, PO Box 13666, London SW14 8WF
tel 020-8392 1122
email ear@eapgroup.com
website www.easternartreport.net
Twitter @easterneap
Publisher/Editor-in-Chief Sajid Rizvi
Quarterly £14.95

Original, well-researched articles on all aspects of the visual and performing arts, cinema and digital media – Asian and diasporic, Buddhist, Islamic, Judaic, Indian, Chinese and Japanese; reviews. Length of articles: min. 1,500 words. Illustrations: colour or b&w, hi-res digital format. No responsibility accepted for unsolicited material. Payment: by arrangement. Founded 1989.

Economica

STICERD, London School of Economics, Houghton Street, London WC2A 2AE
tel 020-7955 7855
website http://onlinelibrary.wiley.com/journal/10.1111/(ISSN)1468-0335
Editors Nava Ashraf, Oriana Bandiera, Tim Besley, Francesco Caselli, Maitreesh Ghatak, Stephen Machin, Ian Martin,and Gianmarco Ottaviano
Quarterly From £54 p.a. (other subscription rates on application)

Learned journal covering the fields of economics, economic history and statistics. Payment: none. Founded 1921; New series 1934.

The Economist

1–11 John Adam Street, London WC2N 6HT
tel 020-7576 8000
website www.economist.com
Facebook www.facebook.com/TheEconomist
Twitter @TheEconomist
Editor Zanny Minton Beddoes
Weekly £5.99

Articles staff-written. Founded 1843.

Electrical Review

SJP Business Media Ltd, 6 Laurence Pountney Hill, London EC4R 0BL
tel 020-7933 8999
email elinorem@electricalreview.co.uk
website www.electricalreview.co.uk
Editor Elinore Mackay
Monthly Free (restricted qualification; see website for details) or £232 p.a. (print and digital subscription)

Technical and business articles on electrical and control engineering; outside contributions considered. Good quality imagery an advantage. Electrical news welcomed. Payment: according to merit. Founded 1872.

ELLE (UK)

Hearst Magazines UK, National Magazines House, 72 Broadwick Street, London W1F 9EP
tel 020-7150 7000
website www.elleuk.com
Facebook www.facebook.com/Ellemagazine
Twitter @Ellemagazine
Editor-in-Chief Anne-Marie Curtis
Monthly £4.40

Commissioned material only. Illustrations: colour. Payment: by arrangement. Founded 1985.

Embroidery

The Embroiderers' Guild, c/o Bucks County Museum, Church Street, Aylesbury, Bucks. HP20 2QP
mobile 07742 601501
email embroidery@embroiderersguild.com
website www.embroiderersguild.com/embroidery
Twitter @johalleditor
Editor Jo Hall
6 p.a. £4.90

News and illustrated features on all aspects of embroidery in contemporary design, fashion, illustration, interiors, art, general textiles and world embroidery. Features on internationally renowned makers, artists and designers working with textiles, stitch and embroidery. News covering exhibitions, books, interiors and products, plus event listings, book and exhibition reviews and opportunities. Length of articles accepted: exhibition reviews, 500 words; book reviews, 250 words; profile features, 1,000 words. Published every two months from January each year. Founded 1932.

Empire

Endeavour House, 189 Shaftesbury Avenue, London WC2H 8JG
tel 020-7295 6700
website www.empireonline.com
Facebook www.facebook.com/empiremagazine
Twitter @empiremagazine
Editor-in-Chief Terri White
13 p.a. £4.70

Guide to film on all its platforms: articles, features, news. Length: various. Illustrations: colour and b&w photos. Payment: approx. £300 per 1,000 words; varies for illustrations. Founded 1989.

Energy Engineering

Media Culture, Pure Offices, Plato Close, Leamington Spa, Warks. CV34 6WE
tel (01926) 671338
email info@energyengineering.co.uk
website http://energyengineering.co.uk
Managing Editor Steve Welch
6 p.a. £65 p.a.

Features and news for those engaged in technology, manufacturing and management. Contributions considered on all aspects of engineering. Illustrations: colour. Founded 1866.

The Engineer

Centaur Media Plc, 79 Wells Street,
London W1T 3QN
tel 020-7970 4437
email jon.excell@centaurmedia.com
website www.theengineer.co.uk
Twitter @TheEngineerUK
Editor Jon Excell
Monthly £3.70

Features and news on innovation and technology, including profiles, analysis. Length: up to 800 words (news), 1,000 words (features). Illustrations: colour transparencies or prints, artwork, line diagrams, graphs. Payment: by negotiation. Founded 1856.

Engineering in Miniature

Warners Group Publications Plc, The Maltings,
West Street, Bourne, Lincs. PE10 9PH
tel (01778) 391000
website www.worldofrailways.co.uk
Twitter @TEEandEIM
Publisher (Railways) Steve Cole
Monthly £3.75

Articles containing descriptions and information on all aspects of model engineering. Articles welcome but technical articles preferred. Payment dependent on pages published. Founded 1979.

The English Garden

Jubilee House, 2 Jubilee Place, London, SW3 3TQ
tel (020)7 349 3700
email theenglishgarden@chelseamagazines.com
website www.theenglishgarden.co.uk
Facebook www.facebook.com/theenglishgardenmagazine/
Twitter @TEGmagazine
Editor Clare Foggett
13 times p.a. £4.20

Features on gardens in the UK and Ireland, plants, practical gardening advice and garden design. Length: 800–1,200 words. Illustrations: colour photos and botanical artwork. Payment: variable. Founded 1997.

Envoi

Meirion House, Glan yr afon, Tanygrisiau,
Blaenau Ffestiniog, Gwynedd LL41 3SU
tel (01766) 832112
email envoi@cinnamonpress.com
website www.cinnamonpress.com
Editor Jan Fortune
3 p.a. £5.50

New poetry, including sequences, collaborative works and translations; reviews; articles on modern poets and poetic style. Sample copy: £5. Payment: complimentary copy. Founded 1957.

EQY (Equestrian Year)

Fettes Park, 496 Ferry Road, Edinburgh EH5 2DL
tel 0131 551 1000
email rbath@scottishfield.co.uk
website www.eqymagazine.co.uk
Editor Richard Bath
1 p.a., distributed free with *Scottish Field*

Scottish equestrianism, all disciplines. Length of article accepted: 1,200 words. Founded 2015.

Erotic Review

120 New Kings Road, London SW6 4LZ
email editorial@ermagazine.org
website http://eroticreviewmagazine.com/
Editor Jamie Maclean
Online

Online literary eZine with fiction, reviews and sophisticated erotic lifestyle for sensualists, libertarians and libertines. Commissions features (500–2,500 words) and short fiction (1,000–5,000 words). Information on submissions can be found online at http://eroticreviewmagazine.com/contributor-guidelines. Founded 1995.

Esquire

Hearst Magazines UK, National Magazines House,
72 Broadwick Street, London W1F 9EP
tel 020-7439 5601
website www.esquire.co.uk
Editor-in-Chief Alex Bilmes
Monthly £4.35

Quality men's general interest magazine – articles, features. No unsolicited material or short stories. Length: various. Illustrations: colour and b&w photos, line. Payment: by arrangement. Founded 1991.

Essex Life

Portman House, 120 Princes Street, Ipswich IP1 1RS
tel 07834 101686
email julian.read@archant.co.uk
website www.essexlifemag.co.uk
Editor Julian Read
Monthly £4.20

No unsolicited material. Founded 1952.

Evergreen

The Lypiatts, Lansdown Road, Cheltenham,
Glos. GL50 2JA
tel (01242) 225780
email editor@evergreenmagazine.co.uk
website www.evergreenmagazine.co.uk
Editor Angeline Wilcox
Quarterly £17 p.a.

Articles about Great Britain's heritage, culture, countryside, people and places. Length 250–2,000 words. Illustrations: digital only. Payment: £15 per 1,000 words, £4 poems (8–24 lines). Founded 1985.

Families First

(formerly Home & Family)
Mothers' Union, Mary Sumner House, 24 Tufton Street, London SW1P 3RB
tel 020-7222 5533
email familiesfirst@mothersunion.org
website www.mothersunion.org
Editor Tola Fisher
Bi-monthly £2.75

Short articles on Mothers' Union projects, parenting, marriage, family life, Christian faith, reviews, health, fair trade and community life and events. Illustrations: colour photos and occasionally illustrations. Few unsolicited articles are accepted. Enclose sae. Payment: from £80 per 1,000 words. Founded 1954.

Family Law journal

LexisNexis, 30 Farringdon Street, London EC4A 4HH
tel 0330 161 1234
email editor@familylaw.co.uk
website www.familylaw.co.uk
Facebook www.facebook.com/JordansFamilyLaw
Twitter @JPFamilyLaw
Editor Elizabeth Walsh
Monthly £350 p.a.

Practitioner journal, aimed at helping family law professionals keep abreast of latest developments in the field and their impact. Each issue includes news on legislative change, case reports, articles and news items. Length between 2,000 and 3,000 words, no illustrations. Founded 1971.

Family Tree

Warners Group Publications Plc, The Maltings, West Street, Bourne, Lincs. PE10 9PH
tel (01778) 395050
email editorial@family-tree.co.uk
website www.family-tree.co.uk
Facebook www.facebook.com/familytreemaguk
Twitter @familytreemaguk
Editor Helen Tovey
Every 4 weeks £5.25, £48 p.a. Digital issues also available.

Features on family history, genealogy and related topics. Payment: by arrangement. Founded 1984.

Farmers Weekly

Reed Business Information, Quadrant House, The Quadrant, Sutton, Surrey SM2 5AS
tel 020-8652 4911
email farmersweekly@proagrica.com
website www.fwi.co.uk
Editor Karl Schneider
Weekly £3.50

Commissions freelance contributors to write articles; willing to consider pitches. Founded 1934.

Feminist Review

Springer, The Macmillan Building, 4 Crinan Street, London N1 9XW
tel (01256) 329242
website https://link.springer.com/journal/41305
Twitter @FeministReview_
Edited by a Collective
3 p.a. Subscriptions from £42.90 p.a.

Aims to unite research and theory with political practice and contribute to the development of both as well as the exploration and articulation of the socio-economic realities of women's lives. Welcomes contributions from the spectrum of contemporary feminist debate. Empirical work – both qualitative and quantitative – is particularly welcome. In addition, each issue contains some papers which are themed around a specific debate. Founded 1979.

The Fenland Reed

email thefenlandreed@gmail.com
website www.thefenlandreed.co.uk
Editors Mary Livingstone, Jonathan Totman
2 p.a. £5.50 or £10 p.a.

East Anglian literary magazine. Published biannually, with one themed and one non-themed issue each year. Includes poetry and short stories. Founded 2015.

The Field

Time Inc. (UK), Pinehurst 2, Pinehurst Road, Farnborough Business Park, Farnborough, Hants GU14 7BF
tel (01252) 555000
email thefield@timeinc.com
website www.thefield.co.uk
Facebook www.facebook.com/TheFieldMagazine
Twitter @TheFieldmag
Editor Jonathan Young
Monthly £4.90

Specific, topical and informed features on the British countryside and country pursuits, including natural history, field sports, gardening and rural conservation. Overseas subjects considered but opportunities for such articles are limited. No fiction or children's material. Articles of 800–2,000 words by outside contributors considered; also topical 'shorts' of 200–300 words on all countryside matters. Illustrations: colour photos of a high standard. Payment: on merit. Founded 1853.

Financial Adviser

Financial Times Business, 1 Southwark Bridge, London SE1 9HL
tel 020-7775 3000
email emma.hughes@ft.com
website www.ftadviser.com
Editor Emma Ann Hughes
Weekly £118.80 p.a.

Topical personal finance news and features. Length: variable. Payment: by arrangement. Founded 1987.

FIRE

Ground Floor, Rayford House, Hove BN3 5HX
tel (01273) 434943
email andrew.lynch@pavpub.com
website www.fire-magazine.com
Managing Editor Andrew Lynch
Monthly £86.50 p.a.

Articles on firefighting and fire prevention from acknowledged experts only. Length: 1,500 words. No unsolicited contributions. Illustrations: dramatic firefighting or fire brigade rescue colour photos. Payment: by arrangement. Founded 1908.

Fishing News

Kelsey Media, Cudham Tithe Barn, Berry's Lane, Cudham, Kent, TN16 3AG
tel (01434) 607375
email dave@linkie.co.uk
website www.fishingnews.co.uk
Twitter @YourFishingNews
Editor Dave Linkie
Weekly £122 p.a.

News and features on all aspects of the commercial fishing industry. Length: up to 1,000 words (features), up to 500 words (news). Illustrations: colour and b&w photos. Payment: negotiable. Founded 1913.

Flash: The International Short-Short Story Magazine

Department of English, University of Chester, Parkgate Road, Chester CH1 4BJ
tel (01244) 513 152
email flash.magazine@chester.ac.uk
website www.chester.ac.uk/flash.magazine
Editors Dr Peter Blair, Dr Ashley Chantler
Bi-annual £6, £11 p.a. Subscription includes membership of International Flash Fiction Association (IFFA)

Quality stories of up to 360 words (title included); see website for submission guidelines. Suggestions for reviews and articles considered. Payment: complimentary copy. Founded 2008.

Flora International

Wimborne Publishing, 113 Lynwood Drive, Merley, Wimborne, Dorset BH21 1UU
tel (01202) 880299
email enquiries@flora-magazine.co.uk
website www.flora-magazine.co.uk
Editor Nina Tucknott
Bi-monthly £3.70

Magazine for flower arranging and floristry; also features flower-related crafts and flower arrangers' gardens. Unsolicited enquiries and suggestions welcome on any of these subjects. Send brief synopsis together with sample illustrations attached. Illustrations: hi-res files on CD or email. Payment: £60 per 1,000 words, £10–£20 illustrations. Founded 1974.

Fly Fishing & Fly Tying

Rolling River Publications, The Locus Centre, The Square, Aberfeldy, Perthshire PH15 2DD
tel (01887) 829868
email MarkB.ffft@btinternet.com
website www.flyfishing-and-flytying.co.uk
Editor Mark Bowler
12 p.a. £3.75

Fly-fishing and fly-tying articles, fishery features, limited short stories, fishing travel. Length: 800–2,000 words. Illustrations: colour photos. Payment: by arrangement. Founded 1990.

Fortean Times

Dennis Publishing Ltd, 31–32 Alfred Place, London WC1E 7DP
tel 020-3890 3890
email drsutton@forteantimes.com
website www.forteantimes.com
Twitter @forteantimes
Editor David Sutton
13 p.a. £4.25

Journal of strange phenomena, experiences, related subjects and philosophies. Includes articles, features, news, reviews. Length: 500–5,000 words; longer by arrangement. Illustrations: colour photos, line and tone art, cartoons. Payment: by negotiation. Founded 1973.

FourFourTwo

Haymarket Ltd, Bridge House, 69 London Road, Twickenham TW1 3SP
tel 020-8267 5000
email contact@fourfourtwo.com
website www.fourfourtwo.magazine.co.uk
Editor Hitesh Ratna
Monthly £4.99

Football magazine with interviews, in-depth features, issues pieces, odd and witty material. Length: 2,000–3,000 (features), 100–1,500 words (Up Front pieces). Illustrations: colour transparencies and artwork, b&w prints. Payment: £200 per 1,000 words. Founded 1994.

France

Archant House, Oriel Road, Cheltenham, Glos. GL50 1BB
tel (01242) 216050
email editorial@francemag.com
website www.completefrance.com
Editor Lara Dunn
Monthly £3.99

Informed quality features and articles on the real France, ranging from cuisine to culture to holidays exploring hidden France. Length: 800–2,000 words. Payment: £100 per 1,000 words; £50 per page/pro rata for illustrations. Founded 1989.

The Friend

173 Euston Road, London NW1 2BJ
tel 020-7663 1010
email editorial@thefriend.org
website www.thefriend.org
Editor Ian Kirk-Smith
Weekly From £69 p.a. online or £86 p.a. print

Material of interest to Quakers and like-minded people; spiritual, political, social, economic, environmental or cultural, considered from outside contributors. Length: up to 1,200 words. Illustrations: b&w or colour photographs and line drawings by email preferred. Payment: not usually but will negotiate a small fee with professional writers. Founded 1843.

Frieze

1 Montclare Street, London E2 7EU
tel 020-3372 6111
email infolondon@frieze.com
website www.frieze.com
8 p.a. £8.95

Magazine of European contemporary art and culture including essays, reviews, columns and listings. Frieze Art Fair is held every October in Regent's Park, London, featuring over 150 of the most exciting contemporary art galleries in the world. Founded 1991.

The Furrow

St Patrick's College, Maynooth,
Co. Kildare W23 TW77, Republic of Ireland
tel +353 (0)1 7083741
email furrow.office@spcm.ie
website www.thefurrow.ie
Editor Rev. Padraig Corkery
Monthly €3.50

Religious, pastoral, theological and social articles. Length: up to 3,500 words. Articles are available through JSTOR and from the Secretary at *The Furrow* office. Illustrations: line, half-tone. Payment: average €20 per page (450 words). Founded 1950.

Galleries

Barrington Publications, Riverside Studios,
65 Aspenlea Road, London W6 8LH
tel 020-8237 1180
email features@galleries.co.uk
website www.galleries.co.uk
Contact (features) Nicholas Usherwood
Monthly £28 p.a.

Art listings and editorial magazine describing current exhibitions and stock of commercial and public art galleries, galleries for hire and art services.

GamesMaster

Future Publishing Ltd, Quay House, The Ambury,
Bath BA1 1UA
tel (01225) 442244
email gamesmaster@futurenet.co.uk
website www.gamesradar.com/gamesmaster/
Editor Robin Valentine
Every 4 weeks £4.99

The UK's longest running video games magazine, covering the biggest and best games across all formats.

Garden Answers

Bauer Media Group, Media House, Lynchwood,
Peterborough Business Park, Peterborough PE2 6EA
tel (01733) 468000
email gardenanswers@bauermedia.co.uk
website www.gardenanswersmagazine.co.uk
Twitter @GardenAnswers
Editor Liz Potter
Monthly £4.10

Some commissioned features and articles on all aspects of gardening. Reader garden photo and interview packages considered. Study of magazine essential. Approach by email with examples of published work. Length: approx. 750 words. Illustrations: digital images and artwork. Payment: by negotiation. Founded 1982.

Garden News

Bauer Media Group, Media House, Lynchwood,
Peterborough Business Park, Peterborough PE2 6EA
tel (01733) 468000
email gn.letters@bauermedia.co.uk
website www.gardennewsmagazine.co.uk
Facebook www.facebook.com/GardenNewsOfficial
Twitter @GardenNewsMag
Editor Simon Caney
Weekly £1.99

Up-to-date information on everything to do with plants, growing and gardening. Payment: by negotiation. Founded 1958.

Gay Times – GT

Spectrum House, 32–34 Gordon House Road,
London NW5 1LP
tel 020-7424 7400
email edit@gaytimes.co.uk
website www.gaytimes.co.uk
Twitter @gaytimesmag
13 p.a. £3.99

Celebrity, gay lifestyle, health, parenting, music, film, technology, current affairs, opinion, culture, art, style, grooming, features and interviews. Length: up to 2,000 words. Payment: by arrangement. Founded 1984.

Geographical

3.20 QWest, 1100 Great West Road,
London TW8 0GP

tel 020-8332 8434
email magazine@geographical.co.uk
website www.geographical.co.uk
Facebook www.facebook.com/GeographicalMagazine
Twitter @Geographicalmag
Editor Paul Presley
Monthly £4.50

Magazine of the Royal Geographical Society (with the Institute of British Geographers). Covers culture, wildlife, environment, science and travel. Illustrations: top-quality hi-res digital files, vintage material. Payment: by negotiation. Founded 1935.

The Geographical Journal

Royal Geographical Society (with the Institute of British Geographers), 1 Kensington Gore, London SW7 2AR
tel 020-7591 3026
email journals@rgs.org
website www.rgs.org/GJ
Editor Keith Richards
4 p.a. Subscriptions from £264 p.a.

Papers range across the entire subject of geography, with particular reference to public debates, policy-oriented agendas and notions of 'relevance'. Illustrations: photos, maps, diagrams. Founded 1893.

Gibbons Stamp Monthly

Stanley Gibbons Ltd, 7 Parkside, Ringwood, Hants BH24 3SH
tel (01425) 481042
email dshepherd@stanleygibbons.co.uk
website www.stanleygibbons.co.uk
Editor Dean Shepherd
Monthly £4.25

Articles on philatelic topics. Contact the Editor first. Length: 500–2,500 words. Illustrations: photos, line, stamps or covers. Payment: by arrangement, £60 or more per 1,000 words.

Glamour

13 Hanover Square, London W1S 1HN
tel 020-7499 9080
email glamoureditorialmagazine@condenast.co.uk
website www.glamourmagazine.co.uk
Principally online, but two print editions p.a.

Lifestyle magazine containing fashion, beauty, real-life features and celebrity news aimed at women aged 18–34. Feature ideas welcome; approach with brief outline. Length: 500–800 words. Payment: by arrangement. Founded 2001.

Golf Monthly

Time Inc. (UK), Pinehurst 2, Pinehurst Road, Farnborough Business Park, Farnborough, Hants GU14 7BF
tel (01252) 555197
email golfmonthly@timeinc.com
website www.golf-monthly.co.uk
Editor Michael Harris
Monthly £4.30

Original articles on golf considered (not reports), golf clinics, handy hints. Illustrations: half-tone, colour, cartoons. Payment: by arrangement. Founded 1911.

Golf World

Bauer Media Group, Media House, Lynchwood, Peterborough Business Park, Peterborough PE2 6EA
tel (01733) 468000
email nick.jwright@bauermedia.co.uk
Twitter @GolfWorld1
Editor Nick Wright
13 p.a. £4.50

Expert golf instructional articles, 500–3,000 words; general interest articles, personality features 500–3,000 words. No fiction. No unsolicited material. Illustrations: line, half-tone, colour, cartoons. Payment: by negotiation. Founded 1962.

Good Housekeeping

Hearst Magazines UK, National Magazines House, 72 Broadwick Street, London W1F 9EP
tel 020-7439 5590 (editorial enquiries)
email goodh.mail@hearst.co.uk
website www.goodhousekeeping.co.uk
Executive Editor Michelle Hather
Monthly £4.40

Articles on topics of interest to women. No unsolicited features or stories accepted. Homes, fashion, beauty and food covered by staff writers. Illustrations: commissioned. Payment: magazine standards. Founded 1922.

Governance and Compliance

Institute of Chartered Secretaries and Administrators, Saffron House, 6–10 Kirby Street, London EC1N 8TS
tel 020-7580 4741
email hker@icsa.org.uk
website www.govcompmag.com
Editor Henry Ker
Monthly £90 p.a. (free to members)

Published by ICSA: The Governance Institute. Offers news, views and practical advice on the latest developments in governance and compliance.

GQ

Condé Nast Publications, Vogue House, Hanover Square, London W1S 1JU
tel 020-7499 9080
website www.gq-magazine.co.uk
Editor Dylan Jones
Monthly £3.99

Style, fashion and general interest magazine for men. Illustrations: b&w and colour photos, line drawings, cartoons. Payment: by arrangement. Founded 1988.

Granta

12 Addison Avenue, London W11 4QR
tel 020-7605 1360

website www.granta.com
Twitter @GrantaMag
Editor Sigrid Rausing
Quarterly £12.99, £32 p.a.

Original literary fiction, non-fiction, memoir, reportage and photography. Study magazine before submitting work. No academic essays or reviews. Note that submissions are accepted only via online submissions system (https://granta.submittable.com/submit). Length: determined by content. Illustrations: photos and original artwork. Payment: by arrangement. Founded 1889; reconceived 1979.

Grazia

Bauer Consumer Media, Endeavour House, 189 Shaftesbury Avenue, London WC2H 8JG
tel 020-7437 9011
email graziadaily@graziamagazine.co.uk
website https://graziadaily.co.uk/
Weekly £2.20

Women's magazine with the latest trends, gossip, fashion and news in bite-size pieces.

Greetings Today

(formerly Greetings Magazine)
Lema Publishing, 1 Churchgates, The Wilderness, Berkhamsted, Herts. HP4 2AZ
tel (01442) 289930
email tracey@emapublishing.co.uk
website www.greetingstoday.co.uk
Editor Tracey Bearton
Monthly Controlled circulation

Trade magazine with articles, features and news related to the greeting card industry. Mainly written in-house; some material taken from outside. Length: varies. Illustrations: line, colour and b&w photos. Payment: by arrangement.

The Grocer

William Reed Publishing Ltd, Broadfield Park, Crawley, West Sussex RH11 9RT
tel (01293) 613400
website www.thegrocer.co.uk
Facebook www.facebook.com/TheGrocer
Twitter @TheGrocer
Editor Adam Leyland
Weekly £4.20

Trade journal: articles, news or illustrations of general interest to the grocery and provision trades. Payment: by arrangement. Founded 1861.

Grow Your Own

25 Phoenix Court, Hawkins Road, Colchester CO2 8JY
tel (01206) 505979
email laura.hillier@aceville.co.uk
website www.growfruitandveg.co.uk
Editor Laura Hillier
Monthly £5.99

Magazine for kitchen gardeners of all levels of expertise. Will consider unsolicited material. Welcomes ideas for articles and features. Length: 1,000 words (articles), 1,500 words (features) 200 words (news). Illustrations: transparencies, colour prints and digital images. Payment: varies.

guiding Magazine

17–19 Buckingham Palace Road, London SW1W 0PT
tel 020-7834 6242
email newsletters@girlguiding.org.uk
website www.girlguiding.org.uk
3 p.a. Free download

Official magazine of Girlguiding. Articles of interest to women of all ages, with special emphasis on youth work and the guide movement. Illustrations: line, half-tone, colour. Payment: £300 per 1,000 words. Please email with proposal in the first instance.

Guitarist

Future Publishing Ltd, Quay House, The Ambury, Bath BA1 1UA
tel (01225) 442244
website www.musicradar.com/guitarist
Editor Jamie Dickson
13 p.a. £6.25

Aims to improve readers' knowledge of the instrument, help them make the right buying choices and assist them in becoming a better player. Ideas for articles welcome. Founded 1984.

Gutter

49–53 Virginia Street, Glasgow G1 1TS
email contactguttermagazine@gmail.com
website www.guttermag.co.uk
Facebook www.facebook.com/guttermag
Twitter @freightbooks
Editors Colin Begg, Kate MacLeary, Laura Waddell, Robbie Guillory, *Managing Editor* Henry Bell
Bi-annual £14 p.a.

Award-winning print journal for fiction and poetry from writers born or living in Scotland. Invites submissions of up to 3,000 words of fiction or 120 lines of poetry, and seeks provocative work that challenges, reimagines or undermines the individual or collective status quo. See website for more information. Payment: a free two-year subscription to Gutter (worth £22). No longer offering editorial review.

H&E naturist

Hawk Editorial Ltd, PO Box 545, Hull HU9 9JF
tel (01482) 342000
email editor@henaturist.net
website www.henaturist.net
Editor Sam Hawcroft
Monthly £4.20

Articles on naturist travel, clubs, beaches and naturist lifestyle experiences from the UK and beyond.

Length: 800–1,200 words. Illustrations: prints and digital images featuring naturists in natural settings; also cartoons, humorous fillers and features with naturist themes. Payment: by negotiation but guidelines for contributors and basic payment rates available on request.

Harper's Bazaar

Hearst Magazines UK, 72 Broadwick Street, London W1F 9EP
tel 020-7439 5000
website www.harpersbazaar.co.uk
Editor-in-Chief Justine Picardie
Monthly £4.60

Features, fashion, beauty, art, theatre, films, travel, interior decoration – some commissioned. Founded 1867.

Health Club Management

Leisure Media Company Ltd, Portmill House, Portmill Lane, Hitchin, Herts. SG5 1DJ
tel (01462) 431385
email healthclub@leisuremedia.com
website www.healthclubmanagement.co.uk
11 p.a. £55 p.a. (UK)

Europe's leading publication for the health and fitness industry, covering the latest news, interviews, new openings and trends across the public and private health and fitness sectors. Print and digital editions of the magazine are available, as is *Health Club Management Handbook*, an annual reference book for buyers and decision-makers in the health and fitness sector. Founded 1995.

Healthy

The River Group, Garden Floor, 16 Connaught Place, London W2 2ES
tel 020-7420 7000
email healthy@therivergroup.co.uk
website www.healthy-magazine.co.uk
Editorial Director Ellie Hughes
8 p.a. From £15.99 p.a.

Holland & Barrett magazine. Health and nutrition information, features, tips, news and recipes, all from a holistic health angle. Ideas from freelances welcome, with a view to commissioning. It does not do product reviews, will not mention products not available in Holland & Barrett and cannot cite any brand names in the copy. Email ideas in first instance. Payment: by negotiation. Founded 1996.

Heat

Bauer Media, Endeavour House, 189 Shaftesbury Avenue, London WC2H 8JG
tel 020-7437 9011
email heatEd@heatmag.com
website www.heatworld.com
Editor Julia Davis
Weekly £2.09

Features and news on entertainment and popular media. Founded 1999.

Hello!

Wellington House, 69–71 Upper Ground, London SE1 9PQ
tel 020-7667 8700
website www.hellomagazine.com
Editor-in-Chief Rosie Nixon
Weekly £2

News-based features – showbusiness, celebrity, royalty; exclusive interviews. Illustrated. Payment: by arrangement. Founded 1988.

Here Comes Everyone

email Matt@herecomeseveryone.me
website www.herecomeseveryone.me
Facebook HCEmagazine
Twitter @HereComesEvery1
Editors Matthew Barton, Raef Boylan
Quarterly £5

Original prose, poetry, non-fiction and art written to fit a theme. Submissions are accepted via online submissions form found at www.herecomeseveryone.me/submit. Submission guidelines also available on the website, where current and past issues can be previewed and purchased in print and digital forms.

Hi-Fi News

MyTime Media Ltd, Enterprise House, Enterprise Way, Edenbridge, Kent TN8 6HF
tel 0844 8488822
email paul.miller@hifinews.com
website www.hifinews.com
Editor Paul Miller
Monthly £4.99

Articles on all aspects of high-quality sound recording and reproduction; also extensive record review section and supporting musical feature articles. Audio matter is essentially technical, but should be presented in a manner suitable for music lovers interested in the nature of sound. Length: 2,000–3,000 words. Illustrations: line, half-tone. Payment: by arrangement. Founded 1956.

High Life

Cedar Communications Ltd, 85 Strand, London WC2R 0DW
tel 020-7550 8000
email high.life@cedarcom.co.uk
website www.cedarcom.co.uk
Content Director Kerry Smith, *Editor* Andy Morris
Monthly

Inflight consumer magazine for British Airways passengers. Articles on entertainment, travel, fashion, business, sport and lifestyle. Founded 1973.

History Today

2nd Floor, 9 Staple Inn, London WC1V 7QH
tel 020-3219 7810
email admin@historytoday.com
website www.historytoday.com
Editor Paul Lay
Monthly £6.75

History in the widest sense – political, economic, social, biography, relating past to present; world history as well as British. Length: 3,500 words (articles); 600–1,200 words (news/views). Illustrations: prints and original photos. Do not send original material until publication is agreed. Accepts freelance contributions dealing with genuinely new historical and archaeological research. Send sae for return of MS. Payment: by arrangement. Founded 1951.

Homes & Gardens

Time Inc. (UK), 161 Marsh Wall, London E14 9AP
tel 020-3148 5000
email hgcontactus@timeinc.com
website www.housetohome.co.uk/homesandgardens
Twitter @homesandgardens
Editor-in-Chief Deborah Barker
Monthly £3.90

Articles on home interest or design, particularly well-designed British interiors (snapshots should be submitted). Length: 900–1,000 words (articles). Illustrations: all types. Payment: generous, but exceptional work required; varies. Founded 1919.

Horse & Hound

Time Inc. (UK), Pinehurst 2, Pinehurst Road, Farnborough Business Park, Farnborough, Hants GU14 7BF
tel (01252) 555029
email pippa.roome@timeinc.com
website www.horseandhound.co.uk
Content Director Sarah Jenkins, *Magazine Editor* Pippa Roome, *Website Editor* Carol Phillips
Weekly £2.90

News, reports, features and opinion, covering all areas of equestrianism, particularly the Olympic disciplines of eventing, showjumping and dressage, plus showing and hunting. Payment: by negotiation.

Horse & Rider

DJ Murphy Publishers Ltd, Marlborough House, Headley Road, Grayshott, Surrey GU26 6LG
tel (01428) 601020
email editor@djmurphy.co.uk
website www.horseandrideruk.com
Editor Louise Kittle
Monthly £4.20

Covers all forms of equestrian activity at home and abroad. Good writing and technical accuracy essential. Length: 1,500–2,000 words. Illustrations: photos and drawings, the latter usually commissioned. Payment: by arrangement. Founded 1959.

Hortus

Bryan's Ground, Stapleton, Nr Presteigne, Herefordshire LD8 2LP
tel (01544) 260001
email all@hortus.co.uk
website www.hortus.co.uk
Editor David Wheeler
Quarterly £38 plus postage

Articles on decorative horticulture: plants, gardens, history, design, literature, people; book reviews. Length: 1,500–5,000 words, longer by arrangement. Illustrations: line, half-tone and wood-engravings. Payment: by arrangement. Founded 1987.

Hot Press

13 Trinity Street, Dublin D02 W228, Republic of Ireland
tel +353 (0)1 2411500
email info@hotpress.ie
website www.hotpress.com
Twitter @hotpress
Editor Niall Stokes
Fortnightly €69.95 p.a. (Ireland), €79.95 p.a (UK)

High quality, investigative stories, or punchily written offbeat pieces, of interest to 16–39 year-olds, including politics, music, sport, sex, and religion. Length: varies. Illustrations: colour with some b&w. Payment: by negotiation. Founded 1977.

House & Garden

Vogue House, 1 Hanover Square, London W1S 1JU
tel 020-7499 9080
email houseandgarden@condenast.co.uk
website www.houseandgarden.co.uk
Editor Hatta Byng
Monthly £4.20

Articles (always commissioned), on subjects relating to domestic architecture, interior decorating, furnishing, gardens and gardening, exhibitions, travel, food and wine.

House Beautiful

Hearst Magazines UK, National Magazines House, 72 Broadwick Street, London W1F 9EP
tel 020-7439 5000
email house.beautiful@hearst.co.uk
website www.housebeautiful.com
Executive Editor Lizzie Hudson
Monthly £3.90

Specialist features for the homes of today. Unsolicited submissions are not accepted. Illustrated. Founded 1989.

Housebuilder

27 Broadwall, London SE1 9PL
tel 020-7960 1630

email info@house-builder.co.uk
website www.house-builder.co.uk
Twitter @housebuildermag
Publishing Director Ben Roskrow
10 p.a. £93 p.a.

Official Journal of the Home Builders Federation published in association with the National House-Building Council. Technical articles on design, construction and equipment of dwellings, estate planning and development, and technical aspects of house-building, aimed at those engaged in house and flat construction and the development of housing estates. Preliminary letter advisable. Length: articles from 500 words, preferably with illustrations. Illustrations: photos, plans, construction details, cartoons. Payment: by arrangement.

The Huffington Post UK

email HuffPostUK@huffingtonpost.com
website www.huffingtonpost.co.uk
Facebook www.facebook.com/HuffPostUK
Twitter @HuffPostUK
Editor-in-Chief Polly Curtis

Online news and commentary magazine, covering topics such as politics, sport, business, technology and entertainment. To submit an idea for a blog post, email the blog team direct (UKBlogTeam@Huffingtonpost.com).

ICIS Chemical Business

Reed Business Information, Quadrant House, The Quadrant, Sutton, Surrey SM2 5AS
tel 020-8652 3500
email icbeditorial@icis.com
website www.icischemicalbusiness.com
Weekly Subscription optiions available upon enquiry

Articles and features concerning business, markets and investments in the chemical industry. Digital-only format. Length: 1,000–2,000 words; news items up to 400 words. Payment: £150–£200 per 1,000 words.

Icon Magazine

Media 10, Crown House, 151 High Road, Loughton, Essex IG10 4LF
tel 020-3235 5200
email icon@icon-magazine.co.uk
website www.iconeye.com
Editor James McLachlan
Monthly £5

Articles on new buildings, interiors, innovative design and designers. Payment by negotiation. Founded 2003.

Ideal Home

Time Inc. (UK), The Blue Fin Building, 110 Southwark Street, London SE1 0SU
tel 020-3148 5000
email ideal_home@timeinc.com
website www.idealhome.co.uk
Twitter @idealhome
Editor Vanessa Richmond
Monthly £3.99

Lifestyle magazine, articles usually commissioned. Contributors advised to study editorial content before submitting material. Illustrations: usually commissioned. Payment: according to material. Founded 1920.

Improve Your Coarse Fishing

Bauer Media Group, Media House, Lynchwood, Peterborough Business Park, Peterborough PE2 6EA
tel (01733) 395134
email james.furness@bauermedia.co.uk
website www.anglingtimes.co.uk/magazines/improve-your-coarse-fishing/
Editor James Furness
13 p.a. £3.70

Articles on technique and equipment, the best venues, news and features. Ideas welcome by email. Founded 1991.

The Independent Publishing Magazine

website www.theindependentpublishingmagazine.com
Facebook www.facebook.com/TheIndependentPublishingMagazine
Twitter @theindiepubmag
Editor-in-Chief Mick Rooney

Online magazine for writers and publishers with a focus on providing essential information, news, resources, reviews of publishing service providers and an overview of the changing landscape of the publishing industry. Provides a regularly updated publishing service index. Guest posts welcome, but see website for full guidelines. Also offers one-on-one online consultancy services: see website for details. Founded 2007.

Index on Censorship

Vauxhall Bridge Road, London SE1 2TH
tel 020-7260 2660
email info@indexoncensorship.org
website www.indexoncensorship.org
Twitter @Index_Magazine
Editor Rachael Jolley
Quarterly £35 p.a. (print), £18 p.a. (digital)

Articles up to 3,000 words dealing with all aspects of free speech and political censorship. Illustrations: b&w, cartoons. Payment: £200 per 1,000 words. Founded 1972.

Ink Sweat & Tears

website www.inksweatandtears.co.uk
Twitter @InkSweatTears
Editor Helen Ivory, *Publisher and Social Media Officer* Kate Birch
Online

Poetry, short prose, and word and image webzine.

Accepts previously unpublished submissions of up to 750 words. Publishes something new every day. Has a 'Pick of the Month' feature voted for by readers (see website for full information). Publishes both new and more established writers and welcomes submissions of well-written reviews. The IS&T/Café Writers Commission is open every two to three years, to write a pamphlet of poems published by IS&T Press; recent winner Jay Bernard 's 'The Red and Yellow Nothing' was shortlisted for the 2017 Ted Hughes Award, and the 2018 winners of the Commission are Jo Young and Gail McConnell.

Inside Soap

Hearst Magazines UK, 33 Broadwick Street, London W1F 0DQ
tel 020-7339 4588
email editor@insidesoap.co.uk
website www.insidesoap.co.uk
Facebook www.facebook.com/insidesoap
Twitter @InsideSoapMag
Editor Steven Murphy
Weekly £1.85

Gossip and celebrity interviews with soap and popular TV characters on terrestrial and satellite channels. Submit ideas by email in first instance. Payment: by negotiation.

Insurance Age

InfoPro Digital Services, Haymarket House, 28–29 Haymarket, London SW1Y 4RX
tel 020-7316 9653
email emmanuel.kenning@infopro-digital.com
website www.insuranceage.co.uk
Editor Emmanuel Kenning, *Deputy Editor* Siân Barton, *Senior Reporters* Judith Ugwumadu, Ida Axling
10 p.a. £150 p.a. (free to FCA registered brokers)

News and features on general insurance and the broker market, personal, commercial, health and Lloyd's of London. Payment: by negotiation. Founded 1979.

Insurance Post

InfoPro Digital, Haymarket House, 28–29 Haymarket, London SW1Y 4RX
tel 020-7484 9700
email postonline@infropro-digital.com
website www.postonline.co.uk
Editor Stephanie Denton
Weekly From £515 p.a.

Commissioned specialist articles on topics of interest to insurance professionals in the UK, Europe and Asia; news. Illustrations: colour photos and illustrations, colour cartoons and line drawings. Payment: £200–250 per 1,000 words; photos £30–£120, cartoons/line by negotiation. Founded 1840.

InterMedia

International Institute of Communications, Highlands House, 165 Broadway, London SW19 1NE
email jgrimshaw@iicom.org
website www.iicom.org
Editor Mark Beishon

Quarterly Free to IIC members

International journal concerned with policies, events, trends and research in the field of communications, broadcasting, telecommunications and associated issues, particularly cultural and social. Founded 1970.

International Affairs

The Royal Institute of International Affairs, Chatham House, 10 St James's Square, London SW1Y 4LE
tel 020-7957 5728
email adorman@chathamhouse.org
website www.chathamhouse.org/publications/ia
Editor Andrew Dorman
6 issues p.a. From £91 p.a. individuals, £552 p.a. institutions

Peer-reviewed academic articles on international affairs; up to 50 books reviewed in each issue. Unsolicited articles welcome; submissions on ScholarOne: mc.manuscriptcentral.com/inta. Article length: 7,000-10,000 words. Illustrations: none. Payment: by arrangement. Founded 1922.

The Interpreter's House

'Scrimshaw', 63 Strait Path, Seatown, Gardenstown, Bannffshire AB45 3ZQ
tel (01261) 851096
email theinterpretershouse@aol.com
website www.theinterpretershouse.com
Twitter @theinterpreter6
Editor Martin Malone, *Deputy Editor* Charles Lauder Jnr
3 p.a. (February/June/October) £5.00, £15.00 p.a.

Poetry, short stories, flash fiction and reviews. Bi-annual poetry competition. Send sae with submissions; online submissions preferred (see website for guidelines and submission windows). Payment: contributor's copy. Note that from Issue #69 onwards (Autumn 2018), the magazine will have a new editorial team: Georgi Gill (Editor) and Andrew Wells (Deputy Editor). Please consult the website at that time for new address and contacts.

Interzone

TTA Press, 5 Martins Lane, Ely, Cambs. CB6 2LB
website www.ttapress.com
Twitter @TTAPress
Bi-monthly £4.99

Science fiction and fantasy short stories, articles, interviews and reviews. Read magazine before submitting. Length: 2,000–6,000 words. Illustrations: colour. Payment: by arrangement. Founded 1982.

Investors Chronicle

Number One, Southwark Bridge, London SE1 9HL
tel 020-7873 3000
email ic.cs@ft.com
website www.investorschronicle.co.uk
Editor John Hughman
Weekly £4.90

Journal covering investment and personal finance. Occasional outside contributions for features are accepted. Payment: by negotiation.

Ireland's Own

Channing House, Upper Rowe Street,
Wexford Y35 TH2A, Republic of Ireland
tel +353 (0)53 9140140
email info@irelandsown.ie
website www.irelandsown.ie
Editor Seán Nolan, *Assistant Editor* Shea Tomkins
Weekly €1.70

Short stories: non-experimental, traditional with an Irish orientation (1,800–2,000 words); articles of interest to Irish readers at home and abroad (750–900 words); general and literary articles (750–900 words). Monthly special bumper editions, each devoted to a particular seasonal topic. Suggestions for new features considered. Payment: varies according to quality and length. Founded 1902.

Irish Arts Review

15 Harcourt Terrace, Dublin D02 TD65,
Republic of Ireland
tel +353 (0)1 6766711
email editorial@irishartsreview.com
website www.irishartsreview.com
Twitter @IrishArtsReview
Editor John Mulcahy
Quarterly €75 p.a. (UK)

Magazine committed to promoting Irish art and heritage around the world with reviews of Irish painting, design, heritage, sculpture, architecture, photography and decorative arts.

Irish Farmers Journal

Irish Farm Centre, Bluebell, Dublin D12 YXW5,
Republic of Ireland
tel +353 (0)1 4199530
email jmccarthy@farmersjournal.ie
website www.farmersjournal.ie
Editor Justin McCarthy
Weekly From €2.60 per week

Readable, technical articles on any aspect of farming. Length: 700–1,000 words. Payment: £100–£150 per article. Illustrated. Founded 1948.

Irish Journal of Medical Science

Royal Academy of Medicine in Ireland,
Setanta House, 2nd Floor, Setanta Place, Dublin 2,
Republic of Ireland
tel +353 (0)1 6334820
email helenmoore@rcpi.ie
website www.springer.com/medicine/internal/journal/11845
Editor William P. Tormey, *Managing Editor* Helen Moore
Quarterly

Official Organ of the Royal Academy of Medicine in Ireland. Original contributions in medicine, surgery, midwifery, public health, etc; reviews of professional books, reports of medical societies, etc. Illustrations: line, half-tone, colour.

Irish Medical Times

Merchants House, 25 Merchants' Quay,
Dublin D08 NT3K, Republic of Ireland
tel +353 (0)1 8176300
email editor@imt.ie
website www.imt.ie
Editor Lloyd Mudiwa
Weekly €298 p.a. (Ireland), €434 p.a. (UK, Europe and RoW)

Medical articles. Opinion column length: 850–1,000 words.

Irish Pages: A Journal of Contemporary Writing

129 Ormeau Road, Belfast BT7 1SH
tel 028-9043 4800
email editor@irishpages.org
website www.irishpages.org
Twitter @irishpages
Editor Chris Agee
Bi-annual £14/€22

Poetry, short fiction, essays, creative non-fiction, memoir, essay reviews, nature writing, translated work, literary journalism, and other autobiographical, historical and scientific writing of literary distinction. Publishes in equal measure writing from Ireland and abroad. Accepts unsolicited submissions by post only. Payment: pays only for certain commissions and occasional serial rights. Founded 2002.

The Irish Post

88 Fenchurch Street, London EC3M 4BY
tel 020-8900 4137
email editor@irishpost.co.uk
website www.irishpost.co.uk
Twitter @theirishpost
Editor-in-Chief Siobhán Breatnach
Weekly (Wed) £1.30

Coverage of all political, social and sporting events relevant to the Irish community in Britain. Also contains a guide to Irish entertainment in Britain. Annual events include The Irish Post Awards. The Post also has links to some of the biggest Irish festivals and events in Britain, including the Mayor of London St Patrick's Day Festival and the GAA All-Britain Competition. Among The Irish Post's annual magazines are Building Britain, which promotes the

Irish construction industry; Companies100, a guide to the top one hundred Irish companies in Britain; and In Business, an informative list Irish business leaders across Britain. Founded 1970.

Irish Tatler

Harmonia Ltd, Rosemount House, Dundrum Road, Dublin D14 P924, Republic of Ireland
tel +353 (0)1 2405300
email sohalloran@harmonia.ie
website www.irishtatler.com
Twitter @irishtatler
Editor Shauna O'Halloran
Monthly €37.40 p.a. (Ireland)

General interest women's magazine: fashion, beauty, interiors, cookery, current affairs, reportage and celebrity interviews. Length: 2,000–4,000 words. In association with ivenus.com. Payment: by arrangement.

Jane's Defence Weekly

Sentinel House, 163 Brighton Road, Coulsdon, Surrey CR5 2YH
tel 020-3253 2100
website www.janes.com
Editor Peter Felstead
Weekly From £262 p.a.

International defence news; military equipment; budget analysis, industry, military technology, business, political, defence market intelligence. Illustrations: colour. Payment: minimum £200 per 1,000 words used. Founded 1984.

Jewish Chronicle

28 St Albans Lane, London NW11 7QE
tel 020-720 7415 1639
email editorial@thejc.com
website www.thejc.com
Twitter @JewishChron
Editor Stephen Pollard
Weekly £90 p.a. (print and digital)

Authentic and exclusive news stories and articles of Jewish interest from 500–1,500 words are considered. Includes a lively arts and leisure section and regular travel pages. Illustrations: of Jewish interest, either topical or feature. Payment: by arrangement. Founded 1841.

Jewish Telegraph

Telegraph House, 11 Park Hill, Bury Old Road, Prestwich, Manchester M25 0HH
tel 0161 740 9321
email manchester@jewishtelegraph.com
The Galehouse Business Centre, Chapel Allerton, Leeds LS7 4RF
tel 0113 295 6000
email leeds@jewishtelegraph.com
120 Childwall Road, Liverpool L15 6WU
tel 0151 475 6666
email liverpool@jewishtelegraph.com
May Terrace, Giffnock, Glasgow G46 6LD
tel 0141 621 4422
email glasgow@jewishtelegraph.com
website www.jewishtelegraph.com
Facebook www.facebook.com/jewishtelegraph/
Twitter @JewishTelegraph
Editor Paul Harris
Weekly Price varies per location

Non-fiction articles of Jewish interest, especially humour. Exclusive Jewish news stories and pictures, international, national and local. Length: 1,000–1,500 words. Illustrations: line, half-tone, cartoons. Payment: by arrangement. Founded 1950.

Kent Life

Archant Kent, Kent House, 81 Station Road, Ashford, Kent TN23 1PP
tel 07809 551221
email sarah.sturt@kent-life.co.uk
website www.kent-life.co.uk
Facebook www.facebook.com/kentlife
Twitter @kentlife
Editor Sarah Sturt
Monthly £3.45

Local lifestyle magazine, celebrating the best of county life. Features local people, entertainment, Kent towns, walks, history and heritage. Welcomes ideas for articles and features, length: 1,000 words (articles/features). Illustrations: hi-res jpgs. Payment: contact editor. Founded 1962.

Kerrang!

Wasted Talent, 90–92 Pentonville Road, London N1 9HS
website www.kerrang.com
Twitter @KerrangMagazine
Editor Sam Coare
Weekly £3

News, reviews and interviews; music with attitude. All material commissioned. Illustrations: colour. Payment: by arrangement. Founded 1981.

Kitchen Garden

Mortons Media Group Ltd, Media Centre, Morton Way, Horncastle, Lincs. LN9 6JR
tel (01507) 529396
email sott@mortons.co.uk
website www.kitchengarden.co.uk
Editor Steve Ott
Monthly £4.99

Magazine for people with a passion for growing their own vegetables, fruit and herbs. Includes practical tips and inspirational ideas. Specially commissions most material. Welcomes ideas for articles and features. Length: 700–2,000 (articles/features). Illustrations: colour transparencies, jpgs, prints and artwork; all commissioned. Payment: varies. Founded 1997.

The Lady

39–40 Bedford Street, London WC2E 9ER
tel 020-7379 4717
email editors@lady.co.uk
website www.lady.co.uk
Facebook www.facebook.com/TheLadyMagazine
Twitter @TheLadyMagazine
Editor Sam Taylor
Weekly £3.20

Features, interviews, comment, columns, arts and book reviews, fashion, beauty, interiors, cookery, health, travel and pets. Plus classified ads, holiday cottages and pages of puzzles. Brief pitches by email preferably. Founded 1885.

The Lancet

125 London Wall, London EC2Y 5AS
tel 020-7424 4922
email editorial@lancet.com
website www.thelancet.com
Twitter @TheLancet
Editor Dr Richard Horton
Weekly £155 p.a. (digital, UK), £182 p.a. (digital and print, UK)

Research papers, review articles, editorials, correspondence and commentaries on international medicine, medical research and policy. Material may be submitted directly through a dedicated online system. Founded 1823.

The Lawyer

79 Wells Street, London W1T 3QN
tel 020-7970 4000
email editorial@thelawyer.com
website www.thelawyer.com
Editor Catrin Griffiths
Weekly From £440 p.a. (for online premium content access)

News, articles, features and views relevant to the legal profession. Length: 600–900 words. Illustrations: as agreed. Payment: £125–£150 per 1,000 words. Founded 1987.

Legal Week

Cheapside House, 138 Cheapside, London EC2V 6BJ
tel 020-3868 7552
email GStanley@alm.com
website www.legalweek.com
Editor Georgina Stanley
Online From £29 per month

News and features aimed at business lawyers. Length: 750–1,000 words (features), 300 words (news). Payment: £200 upwards (features), £75–£100 (news). Considers unsolicited material and welcomes ideas for articles and features. Founded 1999.

Leisure Painter

Caxton House, 63–65 High Street, Tenterden, Kent TN30 6BD
tel (01580) 763315
email ingrid@tapc.co.uk
website www.painters-online.co.uk
Editor Ingrid Lyon
Every four weeks £4.40

Instructional articles on painting and fine art. Payment: £75 per 1,000 words. Illustrations: line, half-tone, colour, original artwork. Founded 1967.

LGC (Local Government Chronicle)

EMAP, Telephone House, 69–77 Paul Street, London EC2A 4NW
tel 020-3033 2787
email lgcnews@emap.com
website www.lgcplus.com
Editor Nick Golding
Weekly £74.75 quarterly

Aimed at senior managers in local government. Covers politics, management issues, social services, education, regeneration, industrial relations and personnel, plus public sector finance and Scottish and Welsh local government. Length: 1,000 words (features). Illustrations: b&w and colour, cartoons. Payment: by arrangement. Founded 1855.

Life and Work: The Magazine of the Church of Scotland

121 George Street, Edinburgh EH2 4YN
tel 0131 225 5722
email magazine@lifeandwork.org
website www.lifeandwork.org
Editor Lynne McNeil
Monthly £2.50

Articles not exceeding 1,200 words and news; occasional stories and poetry. Study the magazine and contact the Editor first. Illustrations: photos and colour illustrations. Payment: by arrangement.

Lighthouse Literary Journal

32 Grove Walk, Norwich NR1 2QG
email submissions@lighthouse.gatehousepress.com
website www.gatehousepress.com/lighthouse
Poetry Editors Andrew McDonnell, Julia Webb, Meirion Jordan, Jo Surzyn; *Prose Editors* Anna De Vaul, Philip Langeskov, Scott Dahlie
Quarterly £18 p.a. plus postage

Publishes poetry, short fiction and artwork from new writers/artists from within the UK and beyond. Submissions by email only; see website for details. Payment: none at present, but all published receive a free copy of the journal and are able to purchase more at a discounted rate. Founded 2012.

Lincolnshire Life

County House, 9 Checkpoint Court, Sadler Road, Lincoln LN6 3PW
tel (01522) 527127
email editorial@lincolnshirelife.co.uk
website www.lincolnshirelife.co.uk

Monthly £29 p.a.

Articles and news of county interest. Approach in writing. Length: up to 1,500 words. Illustrations: colour photos and line drawings. Payment: varies. Founded 1961.

The Linguist

The Chartered Institute of Linguists,
Dunstan House, 14A St Cross Street,
London EC1N 8XA
tel 020-7940 3100
email linguist.editor@ciol.org.uk
website www.ciol.org.uk
Editor Miranda Moore
Bi-monthly Free online to CIOL members or subscriptions available from £48 p.a.

Articles of interest to professional linguists in translating, interpreting and teaching fields. Most contributors have special knowledge of the subjects with which they deal. Articles usually contributed, but payment by arrangement. Length: 800–2,000 words.

Literary Review

44 Lexington Street, London W1F 0LW
tel 020-7437 9392
email editorial@literaryreview.co.uk
website www.literaryreview.co.uk
Facebook www.facebook.com/LiteraryReviewLondon
Twitter @lit_review
Editor Nancy Sladek
Monthly (double issue December/January) £4

Reviews, articles of cultural interest, interviews and profiles. Material mostly commissioned. Length: articles and reviews 800–1,500 words. Illustrations: line and b&w photos. Payment: by arrangement; none for illustrations. Founded 1979.

Litro

1–5 Cremer Street, Studio 9.1, London E2 8HD
tel 020-3371 9971
email info@litro.co.uk
website www.litro.co.uk
Editor-in-Chief Eric Akoto
Monthly £6

Literary magazine featuring fiction, non-fiction, reviews, articles of cultural interest, interviews, profiles and a monthly short story competition. Length: short stories, 2,500 words; articles and reviews, 800–1,500 words. Illustrations: line and b&w photos. Founded 2006.

Little White Lies

TCOLondon, 71A Leonard Street,
London EC2A 4QS
tel 020-7729 3675
email hello@tcolondon.com
website http://lwlies.com/
Editor David Jenkins
Bi-monthly From £25 p.a.

Independent movie magazine that features cutting-edge writing, illustration and photography to get under the skin of cinema. Also explores the worlds of music, art, politics and pop culture as part of its mission to reshape the debate across the movie landscape. Length: various. Illustrations and photography. Payment: varies for illustration, articles and reviews. Founded 2005.

Living France Magazine

Archant Life, Archant House, Oriel Road,
Cheltenham, Glos. GL50 1BB
tel (01242) 216050
email editorial@livingfrance.com
website www.livingfrance.com
Facebook www.facebook.com/LFmagazine
Twitter @livingfrance
Editor Vicky Leigh
13 p.a. £3.99

Articles on travel, property and aspects of living in France, from having a baby to setting up utilities. Interviews with expats also featured. Founded 1990.

The London Magazine: A Review of Literature and the Arts

Administration 11 Queen's Gate, London SW7 5EL
email info@thelondonmagazine.org
website www.thelondonmagazine.org
Editor Steven O'Brien
Bi-monthly £6.95; subscriptions from £17 p.a.

The UK's oldest literary magazine. Poems, stories (2,000–5,000 words), memoirs, critical articles, features on art, photography, theatre, music, architecture, etc. Submission guidelines available on our website. Founded 1732.

London Review of Books

28 Little Russell Street, London WC1A 2HN
tel 020-7209 1101
email edit@lrb.co.uk
website www.lrb.co.uk
Twitter @LRB
Editor Mary-Kay Wilmers
Fortnightly £3.95

Features, essays, poems. Payment: by arrangement.

Long Poem Magazine

20 Spencer Rise, London NW5 1AP
email mail@longpoemmagazine.org.uk
website www.longpoemmagazine.org.uk
Facebook www.facebook.com/groups/longpoemmagazine
Twitter @LongPoemMag
Co-editors Linda Black, Claire Crowther
Biannual £9.25 (inc. p&p)

Publishes a wide range of poetry, including sequences and translations, plus one essay per issue on an aspect of the long poem. Publishes online reviews. See website for up-to-date details of current submission windows. Send no more than two original, unpublished poems of at least 75 lines by email only inside the dates indicated. Contributors should familiarise themselves with the magazine before sending in material. Editors will read all submissions, but simultaneous submissions will not be accepted. Founded 2008.

Lothian Life

4/8 Downfield Place, Edinburgh EH11 2EW
tel 07905 614402
email office@lothianlife.co.uk
website www.lothianlife.co.uk
Twitter @LothianLife
Editor Anne Hamilton
Online publication only

Articles, profiles, etc with a Lothians angle. Length: 500–2,000 words. Payment terms can be found on the website. Founded 1995.

Magma Poetry

23 Pine Walk, Carshalton SM5 4ES
email info@magmapoetry.com
website www.magmapoetry.com
Twitter @magmapoetry
3 p.a. £8.60 (inc. p&p)

Contemporary poetry and prose magazine, each issue of which has a different editor. Features new and established writers: previous contributors include George Szirtes, Gillian Clarke and Don Paterson. Submissions of previously unpublished poems are welcome via post (from UK writers) or via Submittable (https://magmapoetry.submittable.com/submit), but potential contributors should check the website first for calls for submission and any specific requirements.

Management Today

Bridge House, 69 London Road, Twickenham, TW1 3SP
email adam.gale@haymarket.com
email kate.bassett@haymarket.com
website www.managementtoday.co.uk
Editor Adam Gale, *Head of Content* Kate Bassett
Online only From £67 p.a.

Company profiles and analysis, features up to 3,000 words. Payment: £350 per 1,000 words. Founded 1966.

Marie Claire

Time Inc. (UK), The Blue Fin Building, 110 Southwark Street, London SE1 0SU
tel 020-3148 7513
email marieclaire@timeinc.com
website www.marieclaire.co.uk
Editor-in-Chief Trish Halpin
Monthly £4.20

Feature articles of interest to today's woman; plus fashion, beauty, health, food, drink and travel. Commissioned material only. Illustrated in colour. Payment: by negotiation. Founded 1988.

Maritime Journal

Mercator Media Ltd, Spinnaker House, Waterside Gardens, Fareham, Hants PO16 8SD
tel (01329) 825335
email editor@maritimejournal.com
website www.maritimejournal.com
Editor Jake Frith
Monthly £134.50 p.a.

Industry information and news for the European commercial marine business. Also reviews products and services. Founded 1987.

Market Newsletter

Bureau of Freelance Photographers, Vision House, PO Box 474, Hatfield AL10 1FY
tel (01707) 651450
email mail@thebfp.com
website www.thebfp.com
Monthly Free to members of BFP

Current information on markets and editorial requirements of interest to writers and photographers. Founded 1965.

Marketing Week

Wells Point, 79 Wells Street, London W1T 3QN
tel 020-7970 4000
email mw.editorial@centaur.co.uk
website www.marketingweek.co.uk
Editor Russell Parsons
Weekly £199 p.a.

Aimed at marketing management. Accepts occasional features and analysis, but no bylined pieces. Length: 1,000–2,000 words. Payment: £250 per 1,000 words. Founded 1978.

MBUK (Mountain Biking UK)

Immediate Media Co., Tower House, Fairfax Street, Bristol BS1 3BN
tel 0117 927 9009
email danny.walter@immediate.co.uk
website www.mbuk.com
Editor-in-Chief Danny Walter
Every 4 weeks £5.50

Magazine for mountain bike enthusiasts with features, reviews, news and world and domestic racing coverage.

MCN (Motor Cycle News)

Bauer Media Group, Media House, Lynchwood, Peterborough Business Park, Peterborough PE2 6EA
tel 0845 601 1356
email mcn@motorcyclenews.com
website www.motorcyclenews.com
Editor Andy Calton

Weekly £2.20

Features (up to 1,000 words), photos and news stories of interest to motorcyclists. Founded 1955.

Medal News

Token Publishing Ltd, 40 Southernhay East, Exeter, Devon, EX1 1PE
tel (01404) 46972
email info@tokenpublishing.com
website www.tokenpublishing.com
Editor John Mussell
10 p.a. £4

Well-researched articles on military history with a bias towards medals. Send text in digital form. Length: up to 2,000 words. Illustrations: if possible. Payment: by arrangement; none for illustrations. Founded 1989.

Men's Fitness

Dennis Publishing Ltd, 31–32 Alfred Place, London WC1E 7DP
tel 020-3890 3890
email joe@ilmedia.co.uk
website www.coachmag.co.uk
Twitter @MensFitnessMag
Editor Joe Warner
Monthly £4.20

Magazine for men who want to get more out of their lives, focusing on an upbeat, optimistic, proactive lifestyle. Focuses on both mental and emotional fitness.

Men's Health

Hearst Magazines UK, 33 Broadwick Street, London W1F 0DQ
tel 020-7339 4400
email contact@menshealth.co.uk
website www.menshealth.co.uk
Editor Toby Wiseman
10 p.a. £3.99

Active pursuits, grooming, fitness, fashion, sex, career and general men's interest issues. Length 1,000–4,000 words. Ideas welcome. No unsolicited MSS. Payment: by arrangement. Founded 1994.

Methodist Recorder

3–5 Lambeth Road, London SE1 7DQ
email editorial@methodistrecorder.co.uk
website www.methodistrecorder.co.uk
Twitter @MethRecorder
Weekly £3.10

Methodist newspaper; ecumenically involved. Limited opportunities for freelance contributors. Preliminary contact advised. Founded 1861.

Military Modelling

Enterprise House, Enterprise Way, Edenbridge, Kent TN8 6HF
email contribeditor@militarymodelling.com
Samples to Martyn Chorlton (Military Modelling), 39 Backgate, Cowbit, Spalding, Lincs. PE12 6AP
website www.militarymodelling.com
Editor Martyn Chorlton
Monthly £5.10

Articles on military modelling. Length: up to 2,500 words. Illustrations: line, half-tone, colour. Payment: by arrangement.

Mixmag

Wasted Talent, 90–92 Pentonville Road, London N1 9HS
tel 020-7078 8400
email mixmag@mixmag.net
website www.mixmag.net
Twitter @Mixmag
Global Editorial Director Nick DeCosemo
Monthly £40 p.a.

Dance music and clubbing magazine. No unsolicited material. Illustrations: colour and b&w. Payment: £200 per 1,000 words. Founded 1983.

MMM - the motorhomers' magazine

Warners Group Publications, West Street, Bourne, Lincs. PE10 9PH
tel (01778) 391154
email danielattwood@warnersgroup.co.uk
website www.outandaboutlive.co.uk
Managing Editor Daniel Attwood
Every four weeks £4.20

Articles including motorcaravan travel, owner reports and DIY. Length: up to 2,500 words. Illustrations: line, half-tone, colour prints and transparencies, high-quality digital. Payment: by arrangement. Founded 1966 as *Motor Caravan and Camping*.

Model Boats

MyTime Media Ltd, Suite 25, Enterprise House, Enterprise Way, Edenbridge, Kent TN8 6HF
tel (01689) 869840
email editor@modelboats.co.uk
website www.modelboats.co.uk
Editor Graham Ashby
Monthly £4.95

Founded 1964.

Model Engineer

MyTime Media Ltd, Enterprise House, Enterprise Way, Edenbridge, Kent TN8 6HF
tel (01689) 86984
email diane.carney@mytimemedia.com
website www.model-engineer.co.uk
Editor Diane Carney
Fortnightly £3.40

Detailed description of the construction of engineering models, small workshop equipment, machine tools and small electrical and mechanical devices; articles on small power engineering, mechanics, electricity, workshop methods, clocks and experiments. Relevant event reporting and visits. Illustrations: line, half-tone, colour. Payment: up to £50 per page. Founded 1898.

Modern Language Review

Modern Humanities Research Association, Salisbury House, Station Road, Cambridge CB1 2LA
email mail@mhra.org.uk
website www.mhra.org.uk/journals/MLR
General Editor Derek Connon
Quarterly

Articles and reviews of a scholarly or specialist character on English, Romance, Germanic and Slavonic languages, literatures and cultures. Payment: none, but electronic offprints are given. Founded 1905.

Modern Poetry in Translation

The Queen's College, Oxford OX1 4AW
email editor@mptmagazine.com
website www.mptmagazine.com
Twitter @mptmagazine
Editor Clare Pollard
3 p.a. £23 p.a.

Features the work of established and emerging poets and translators from around the world. Welcomes translated work that has not been previously been published; contemporary pieces preferred. Up to six poems may be submitted (email to submissions@mptmagazine.com or send via the website form), but potential contributors should familiarise themselves with the magazine before sending their work. See website for full guidelines and to keep up to date with open calls.

Mojo

Bauer Media Group, Endeavour House, 189 Shaftesbury Avenue, London WC2H 8JG
tel 020-7208 3443
email mojo@bauermedia.co.uk
website www.mojo4music.com
Editor John Mulvey
Monthly £5.25

Serious rock music magazine: interviews, news and reviews of books, live shows and albums. Length: up to 10,000 words. Illustrations: colour and b&w photos, colour caricatures. Payment: £250 per 1,000 words; £200–£400 illustrations. Founded 1993.

Moneywise

Standon House, 21 Mansell Street, London E1 8AA
tel 020-7680 3600
email editorial@moneywise.co.uk
website www.moneywise.co.uk
Editor Moira O'Neill
Monthly £3.95

Financial and consumer interest features, articles and news stories. No unsolicited MSS. Length: 1,500–2,000 words. Illustrations: willing to see designers, illustrators and photographers for fresh new ideas. Payment: by arrangement. Founded 1990.

The Moth

Ardan Grange, Milltown, Belturbet, Co. Cavan, Republic of Ireland
tel +353 (0)8 72657251
email editor@themothmagazine.com
website www.themothmagazine.com
Facebook www.facebook.com/themothmagazine
Twitter @themothmagazine
Founders Rebecca O'Connor, Will Govan, *Editor* Rebecca O'Connor
Quarterly €7, €28 p.a.

Original poetry, short fiction and interviews alongside full-colour artwork. Submissions welcome, although potential contributors should familiarise themselves with the magazine first. Send no more than six poems and two short stories (max. 2,500 words) by email or post (with sae). Annual Moth Poetry Prize (€10,000 for a single unpublished poem, plus three runner-up prizes of €1,000), *Moth* Short Story Prize (first prize, €3,000; second prize, week-long retreat at Circle of Misse plus €250 stipend; and third prize, €1,000) and *Moth* Art Prize (€1,000 plus a two-week stay at The Moth Retreat). Also runs an artists' and writers' retreat and publishes a junior version, *The Caterpillar*. Founded 2010.

Mother & Baby

Bauer Media Group, Media House, Lynchwood, Peterborough Business Park, Peterborough, PE2 6EA
tel (01733) 468000
website www.motherandbaby.co.uk
Twitter @MotherAndBaby
Editor Emily Bailey
Monthly £3.99

Features and practical information including pregnancy and birth and babycare advice. Expert attribution plus real-life stories. Length: 1,000–1,500 words (commissioned work only). Illustrated. Payment: by negotiation. Founded 1956.

Motor Boat and Yachting

Time Inc. (UK), The Blue Fin Building, 110 Southwark Street, London SE1 0SU
tel 020-3148 4651
email mby@timeinc.com
website www.mby.com
Editor Hugo Andreae
Monthly £43.99 p.a.

General interest as well as specialist motor boating material welcomed. Features up to 2,000 words considered on all sea-going aspects. Payment: varies. Illustrations: hi-res photos. Founded 1904.

The Motorship

Mercator Media Ltd, Spinnaker House, Waterside Gardens, Fareham, Hants PO16 8SD

tel (01329) 825335
email editor@motorship.com
website www.motorship.com
Twitter @Motorship
Editor Gavin Lipsith
11 p.a. £168.50 p.a.

News, information and insight for marine technology professionals.

Moving Worlds

School of English, University of Leeds, Leeds LS2 9JT
email mworlds@leeds.ac.uk
website www.movingworlds.net
General Editors Shirley Chew, Stuart Murray
Biannual From £14 p.a.

International magazine, describing itself as a 'journal of transcultural writings'. Features creative writing, literary criticism, visual texts, and translations into and from English. Submissions should be of previously unpublished work.

Mslexia

PO Box 656, Newcastle upon Tyne NE99 1PZ
tel 0191 204 8860
email postbag@mslexia.co.uk
website www.mslexia.co.uk
Twitter @Mslexia
Editorial Director Debbie Taylor, *Books Editor* Danuta Kean
Quarterly £8.95

Magazine for women writers which combines features and advice about writing with new fiction and poetry by women. Considers unsolicited material within specific submission slots. Length: up to two short stories of no more than 2,200 words, up to four poems of no more than 40 lines each, in any style, or up to two short scripts of no more than 1,000 words, which must relate to current themes (or adhere to poetry or short story competition rules). Also accepts submissions for other areas of the magazine, including Confession, Bedtime stories, Poet Laureate, etc., variously themed and unthemed. Articles/features by negotiation. Illustrations: by commission only; email submissions welcome. Payment: by negotiation. Founded 1998.

Muscle & Fitness

Weider Publishing, 10 Windsor Court, Clarence Drive, Harrogate, North Yorkshire HG1 2PE
tel (01423) 504516
website www.muscleandfitness.com
Facebook www.facebook.com/musclefitnessuk
Twitter @MuscleFitnessUK
Editor John Plummer
Monthly £4.20

A guide to muscle development and general health and fitness. Founded 1988.

Music Teacher

Rhinegold House, 20 Rugby Street, London WC1N 3QZ
tel 07785 613417
email alex.stevens@rhinegold.co.uk
website www.rhinegold.co.uk/rhinegold-publishing/magazines/music-teacher
Twitter @MusicTeacherMag
Editor Alex Stevens
Monthly £45.99 p.a. (print), £17.99 p.a. (digital)

Information and articles for both school and private instrumental teachers, including reviews of books, music, software, CD-Roms and other music-education resources. Articles and illustrations must both have a teaching, as well as a musical, interest. Length: articles 600–1,700 words. Payment: £120 per 1,000 words. Founded 1908.

Music Week

The Emerson Building, 4–8 Emerson Street, London SE1 9DU
tel 020-7226 7246
email msutherland@nbmedia.com
website www.musicweek.com
Editor Mark Sutherland
Weekly £5.50

News and features on all aspects of producing, manufacturing, marketing and retailing music, plus the live music business and all other aspects of the music industry. Payment: by negotiation. Founded 1959.

Musical Opinion

1 Exford Road, London SE12 9HD
tel 020-8857 1582
email musicalopinion@hotmail.co.uk
website www.musicalopinion.com
Editor Robert Matthew-Walker
Bi-monthly £28 p.a.

Suggestions for contributions of musical interest, scholastic, educational, anniversaries and ethnic. DVD, CD, opera, festival, book, music reviews. Illustrations: colour photos. Founded 1877.

Musical Times

7 Brunswick Mews, Hove, East Sussex BN3 1HD
email mted@gotadsl.co.uk
website http://themusicaltimes.blogspot.co.uk
Editor Antony Bye
4 p.a. £43 p.a.

Musical articles, reviews, 500–6,000 words. All material commissioned; no unsolicited material. Illustrations: music. Founded 1844.

My Weekly

D.C. Thomson & Co. Ltd, 80 Kingsway East, Dundee DD4 8SL
tel (01382) 223131

email myweekly@dcthomson.co.uk
website www.myweekly.co.uk
Twitter @My_Weekly
Acting Editor-in-Chief Sally Hampton, *Assistant Editor* Sally Rodger, *Health Editor* Moira Chisholm, *Fiction Editor* Karen Byrom
Weekly £1.20

Modern women's magazine aimed at 50+ age group. No unsolicited MSS considered. Send ideas or pitches to relevant department editor. Illustrations: colour. Payment by negotiation. Founded 1910.

The National Trust Magazine

The National Trust, Heelis, Kemble Drive, Swindon SN2 2NA
tel (01793) 817716
email magazine@nationaltrust.org.uk
website www.nationaltrust.org.uk
Editor Sally Palmer
3 p.a. Free to members or £4.75

Lifestyle title with focus on the National Trust, encompassing interiors, gardens, food, UK travel, wildlife, environment, topical features and celebrity content. No unsolicited articles. Length: 1,000 words (features), 200 words (news). Illustrations: colour transparencies and artwork. Payment: by arrangement; picture library rates. Founded 1932.

Nature

Springer Nature, The Macmillan Building, 4 Crinan Street, London N1 9XW
tel 020-7833 4000
email nature@nature.com
website www.nature.com/nature
Editor Magdalena Skipper
Weekly £135 p.a.

Devoted to scientific matters and to their bearing upon public affairs. All contributors of articles have specialised knowledge of the subjects with which they deal. Illustrations: full colour. Founded 1869.

NB magazine

Studio 20, Glove Factory Studios, Brook Lane, Holt, Wilts. BA14 6RL
tel (01225) 302266
email info@nudge-book.com
website www.nudge-book.com
Managing Director Alistair Giles, *Publishing Liaison Executive* Alice Beazer
4 p.a. £27.60 p.a. (UK, including p&p)

Aimed at book lovers and book clubs. Includes extracts from new books, articles and features about and by authors, focusing on how the book trade works, how books reach publication and then find a readership. A diverse range of genres are covered within the magazine, and readers voices and opinions are represented. Also covers news from the book world, including updates on awards and prizes. A sample magazine is available for £6.90 from the website (strictly UK only). Free copies of featured books in each issue may be claimed as long as post and packing costs are covered.

net

Future Publishing Ltd, Richmond House, 33 Richmond Hill, Bournemouth BH2 6EZ
tel (01225) 442244
website www.creativebloq.com
Twitter @netmag
Editor Philip Morris
Monthly £5.99

Articles, features and tutorials news on web design and development. Length: 1,000–3,000 words. Illustrations: colour. Payment: negotiable. Founded 1994.

New Humanist

The Rationalist Association, Development House, 56–64 Leonard Street, London EC2A 4LT
tel 020-3633 4633
email editor@newhumanist.org.uk
website https://newhumanist.org.uk
Editor Daniel Trilling
Quarterly £27 p.a. (print), £10 p.a. (digital)

Articles on current affairs, philosophy, science, the arts, literature, religion and humanism. Length: 750–4,000 words. Illustrations: colour photos. Payment: nominal. Founded 1885.

New Internationalist

The Old Music Hall, 106–108 Cowley Road, Oxford OX4 1JE
tel (01865) 403345
email ni@newint.org
website http://newint.org
Twitter @newint
Co-editors Vanessa Baird, Chris Brazier, Hazel Healy, Dinyar Godrej, Yohann Koshy
Monthly £4.45

World issues, ranging from food to feminism to peace; one subject examined each month. Length: up to 2,000 words. Illustrations: line, half-tone, colour, cartoons. Payment: £250 per 1,000 words. Founded 1973.

New Law Journal

LexisNexis Butterworths, Lexis House, 30 Farringdon Street, London EC4A 4HH
tel 020-7400 2580
email newlaw.journal@lexisnexis.co.uk
website www.newlawjournal.co.uk
Twitter @newlawjournal
Editor Jan Miller
48 p.a. £8, £389 p.a.

Articles and news on all aspects of civil litigation and dispute resolution. Length: up to 1,900 words. Payment: by arrangement.

New Musical Express (NME)

(incorporating Melody Maker)
Time Inc. (UK), The Blue Fin Building,
110 Southwark Street, London SE1 0SU
tel 020-3148 5000
email karen.walter@timeinc.com
website www.nme.com
Facebook www.facebook.com/nmemagazine
Twitter @nme
Editor-in-Chief Mike Williams
Online only

The latest music news, the best new bands, world exclusive features and new album reviews every week. Length: by arrangement. Preliminary letter or phone call desirable. Illustrations: action photos with strong news angle of recording personalities, cartoons. Payment: by arrangement. Founded 1952.

New Scientist

25 Bedford Street, London WC2 9ES
tel 020-7611 1202
email enquiries@newscientist.com
website www.newscientist.com
Editor Emily Wilson
Weekly £4.50

Authoritative articles of topical importance on all aspects of science and technology. Potential contributors should study recent copies of the magazine and initially send only a 200-word synopsis of their idea. Illustrations: all styles, cartoons; contact art dept.

New Statesman

(formerly New Statesman & Society)
71–73 Carter Lane, London, EC4V 5EQ
tel 020-7936 6400
email editorial@newstatesman.co.uk
website www.newstatesman.co.uk
Editor Jason Cowley
Weekly £4.50

Interested in news, reportage and analysis of current political and social issues at home and overseas, plus book reviews, general articles and coverage of the arts, environment and science seen from the perspective of the British Left but written in a stylish, witty and unpredictable way. Length: strictly according to the value of the piece. Illustrations: commissioned for specific articles, although artists' samples considered for future reference; occasional cartoons. Payment: by agreement. Founded 1913.

New Welsh Reader

(formerly New Welsh Review)
PO Box 170, Aberystwyth, Ceredigion SY23 1WZ
tel (01970) 628410
email submissions@newwelshreview.com
website www.newwelshreview.com
Editor Gwen Davis
3 p.a. From £16.99 p.a.

Literary – critical articles, creative non-fiction, short stories, poems, book reviews and profiles. Especially, but not exclusively, concerned with Welsh writing in English. Length: up to 3,000 words (articles). Send by email or hard copy with a sae for return of material. Decisions within three months of submission. See website for information on New Welsh Writing Awards and *New Welsh Rarebyte* (ePub). Illustrations: colour. Payment: £68 per 1,000 words (articles); £28 per poem, £100 per short story, £47 per review. Founded 1988.

The North

Submissions Department, The Poetry Business,
Campo House, 45 Campo Lane, Sheffield S1 2EG
tel 0114 438 4074
email office@poetrybusiness.co.uk
website www.thepoetrybusiness.co.uk
Twitter @poetrybusiness
Editor Ann Sansom
2 p.a. £10

Contemporary poetry from new and established writers, as well as book reviews, critical articles and a range of features. Up to six poems may be submitted by post only; full information on submission windows given on the website.

Now

Time Inc. (UK), The Blue Fin Building,
110 Southwark Street, London SE1 0SU
tel 020-3148 5000
email nowletters@timeinc.com
website www.nowmagazine.co.uk
Weekly £1.80

Celebrity gossip, news, fashion, beauty and lifestyle features. Most articles are commissioned or are written by in-house writers. Founded 1996.

Nursery World

MA Education, St Jude's Church, Dulwich Road,
London SE24 0PB
tel 020-8501 6693
email liz.roberts@markallengroup.com
website www.nurseryworld.co.uk
Editor Liz Roberts
Weekly £102 p.a. (print and digital)

For all grades of primary school, nursery and childcare staff, nannies, foster parents and all concerned with the care of expectant mothers, babies and young children. Authoritative and informative articles, 800 or 1,300 words, and photos, on all aspects of child welfare and early education, from 0–8 years, in the UK. Practical ideas, policy news and career advice. No short stories. Illustrations: line, half-tone, colour. Payment: by arrangement.

Nursing Times

EMAP, Telephone House, 69–77 Paul Street,
London EC2A 4NQ

tel 020-3953 2707
email jenni.middleton@emap.com
website www.nursingtimes.net
Twitter @nursingtimes
Twitter @nursingtimesed
Editor Jenni Middleton
Monthly £9.50

Articles of clinical interest, nursing education and nursing policy. Illustrated articles not longer than 2,000 words. Press day: first or last Friday of the month. Illustrations: photos, line. Payment: NUJ rates; by arrangement for illustrations. Founded 1905.

OK!

Northern & Shell Building, 10 Lower Thames Street, London EC3R 6EN
tel 0871 434 1010
website www.ok.co.uk/home
Editor Kirsty Tyler
Weekly £2

Exclusive celebrity interviews and photographs. Submit ideas in writing. Length: 1,000 words. Illustrations: colour. Payment: £150–£200 per feature. Founded 1993.

The Oldie

65 Newman Street, London W1T 3EG
tel 020-7436 8801
email editorial@theoldie.co.uk
website www.theoldie.co.uk
Editor Harry Mount
Monthly £4.25

General interest magazine reflecting attitudes of older people but aimed at a wider audience. Features (600–1,000 words) on all subjects, as well as articles for specific sections. Potential contributors should familiarise themselves with the magazine prior to submitting work. See website for further guidelines. Enclose sae for reply/return of MSS. No poetry. Illustrations: welcomes b&w and colour cartoons. Payment: approx. £100–£150 per 1,000 words; £100 for cartoons. Founded 1992.

Olive

Immediate Media Co. Ltd, Vineyard House, 44 Brook Green, London W6 7BT
tel 020-7150 5000
website www.olivemagazine.com
Editor Laura Rowe
Monthly £4.50

Upmarket food magazine which aims to encourage readers to cook, eat and explore. Each edition includes a range of recipes for both everyday and weekend cooking, as well as information on techniques, trends and tips; restaurant recommendations across the UK; and foodie-inspired travel ideas from around the world.

Opera

36 Black Lion Lane, London W6 9BE
tel 020-8563 8893
email editor@opera.co.uk
website www.opera.co.uk
Editor John Allison
13 p.a. £70.50 p.a.

Reviews of opera from the UK and around the world, including profiles of opera's greatest performers and a comprehensive calendar of productions and events. Length: up to 2,000 words. Illustrations: photos. Payment: by arrangement.

Opera Now

Rhinegold House, 20 Rugby Street, London WC1N 3QZ
tel 020-7333 1729
email opera.now@rhinegold.co.uk
website www.rhinegold.co.uk
Editor-in-Chief Ashutosh Khandekar
Monthly £4.95

Articles, news, reviews on opera. All material commissioned only. Length: 150–1,500 words. Illustrations: colour and b&w photos, line, cartoons. Payment: £120 per 1,000 words. Founded 1989.

Orbis International Literary Journal

17 Greenhow Avenue, West Kirby, Wirral CH48 5EL
tel 0151 625 1446
email carolebaldock@hotmail.com
website www.orbisjournal.com
Editor Carole Baldock
Quarterly £5, £18 p.a. (UK)

Literary magazine; provides feedback with proofs. Publishes poetry, fiction (1,000 words maximum), flash fiction, non-fiction, and translations. UK submissions: four poems; please include C5-sized sae. Overseas: two submissions via email. Readers' Award: £50, plus £50, split between four runners-up. Subscribers also receive the Xtra Kudos Newsletter, which typically appears weekly. Two sample issues may be obtained for £7 (inc. p&p) for UK readers, or £16 for those based overseas. Founded 1969.

Our Dogs

Northwood House, Greenwood Business Centre, Regent Road, Salford M5 4QH
tel 0844 504 9001
email editorial@ourdogs.co.uk
website www.ourdogs.co.uk
Twitter @OURDOGSNEWS
Editor Alison Smith
Weekly £4

Articles and news on the breeding and showing of pedigree dogs. Illustrations: b&w photos. Payment: by negotiation; £10 per photo. Founded 1895.

Oxford Poetry

Magdalen College, Oxford OX1 4AU
email editors@oxfordpoetry.co.uk
website www.oxfordpoetry.co.uk

Editors Mary Jean Chan, Theophilus Kwek
2 p.a. £13 p.a. (plus postage)

Previously unpublished poems (in English) and translations, both unsolicited and commissioned; also interviews, articles and reviews. Submissions via email, either as attachments or in the body of a message. Founded 1910; refounded 1983.

PC Pro

Dennis Publishing Ltd, 31–32 Alfred Place, London WC1E 7DP
020-3890 3890
email editor@pcpro.co.uk
website subscribe.pcpro.co.uk
Facebook www.facebook.com/pcpro
Twitter @pcpro
Editor-in-Chief Tim Danton
Monthly £5.99 (DVD edition), £4.99 (CD edition)

Expert advice and insights from IT professionals, plus in-depth reviews and group tests, aimed at IT pros and enthusiasts. Email feature pitches to editor@pcpro.co.uk but only after reading the magazine first. Founded 1994.

Peace News

5 Caledonian Road, London N1 9DY
tel 020-7278 3344
email editorial@peacenews.info
website www.peacenews.info
Editors Milan Rai, Emily Johns
6 p.a. From £10 p.a.

Political articles based on nonviolence in every aspect of human life. Illustrations: line, half-tone. No payment. Founded 1936.

People Management

Haymarket Ltd, Bridge House, 69 London Road, Twickenham, TW1 3SP
tel 020-8267 5013
email PMeditorial@haymarket.co.uk
website www.peoplemanagement.co.uk
Twitter @PeopleMgt
Editor Robert Jeffrey
10 p.a. Free to CIPD members

Magazine of the Chartered Institute of Personnel and Development. News items and feature articles on recruitment and selection, training and development; pay and performance management; industrial psychology; employee relations; employment law; working practices and new practical ideas in personnel management in industry and commerce. Length: up to 2,500 words. Illustrations: contact art editor. Payment: by arrangement.

People's Friend

D.C. Thomson & Co. Ltd, 2 Albert Square, Dundee DD1 1DD
tel (01382) 223131
email peoplesfriend@dcthomson.co.uk
website www.thepeoplesfriend.co.uk
Facebook www.facebook.com/PeoplesFriendMagazine
Twitter @TheFriendMag
Editor Angela Gilchrist
Weekly £1.30

Fiction magazine for women of all ages. Serials (60,000–70,000 words) and complete stories (1,000–4,000 words) of strong romantic and emotional appeal. Includes knitting and cookery. No preliminary letter required; send material for the attention of the Editor. Illustrations: colour. Payment: on acceptance. Founded 1869.

People's Friend Pocket Novel

D.C. Thomson & Co. Ltd, 80 Kingsway East, Dundee DD4 8SL
tel (01382) 223131
email tsteel@dcthomson.co.uk
website www.thepeoplesfriend.co.uk
Editor Tracey Steel
2 per month £3.49

38,000-word family and romantic stories aimed at 30+ age group. No illustrations. Payment: by arrangement.

Period Living

Future Publishing Ltd, 2 Sugar Brook Court, Aston Road, Bromsgrove, Worcs. B60 3EX
email period.living@futurenet.com
website www.realhomes.com/period-living
Twitter @PeriodLivingMag
Editor Melanie Griffiths
Monthly £4.35

Articles and features on decoration, furnishings, renovation of period homes; gardens, crafts, decorating in a period style. Illustrated. Payment: varies, according to work required. Founded 1990.

The Photographer

BIPP, Ardenham Court, Oxford Road, Aylesbury, Bucks HP19 8HT
tel (01296) 642020
email editor@bipp.com
website www.bipp.com
Editor Chris Harper FBIPP
Quarterly £20 p.a. (UK residents), £40 p.a. (EU residents), £50 (Rest of World); free to all members of British Institute of Professional Photography

Journal of the British Institute of Professional Photography. Authoritative reviews, news, views and high-quality photographs.

Picture Postcard Monthly

6 Camarthen Avenue, Portsmouth, PO6 2AQ
tel 023-9242 3527
email info@picturepostcardmagazine.co.uk
website www.picturepostcardmagazine.co.uk
Twitter @Postcard_World

Contact Mark Wingham
Monthly £38 p.a. (UK)

Articles, news and features for collectors of old or modern picture postcards. Length: 500–2,000 words. Illustrations: colour and b&w. Payment: by negotiation prior to articles/images being submitted. Founded 1978.

Planet: The Welsh Internationalist

PO Box 44, Aberystwyth, Ceredigion SY23 3ZZ
tel (01970) 611255
email planet.enquiries@planetmagazine.org.uk
website www.planetmagazine.org.uk
Twitter @Planet_TWI
Editor Emily Trahair
Quarterly £22 p.a. (UK)

Articles on culture, society, Welsh current affairs and international politics, as well as short fiction, poetry, photo essays and review articles. Article length: 1,500–2,500 words. Payment: £45 per 1,000 words, £30 per poem. Submissions by post or email, preferably by email. For articles, email enquiry in first instance. Founded 1970.

PN Review

(formerly Poetry Nation)
Carcanet Press Ltd, 4th Floor, Alliance House, 30 Cross Street, Manchester M2 7AQ
tel 0161 834 8730
email info@carcanet.co.uk
website www.pnreview.co.uk
Editor Michael Schmidt
6 p.a. £39.50 p.a. UK (print and digital; other subscription rates are available)

Poems, essays, reviews, translations. Submissions by post only. Payment: by arrangement. Founded 1973.

Poetry Ireland Review/Iris Éigse Éireann

11 Parnell Square East, Dublin D01 ND60, Republic of Ireland
tel +353 (0)1 6789815
email publications@poetryireland.ie
website www.poetryireland.ie
Editor Eavan Boland, *Irish-language Editor* Caitlín Nic Íomhair
3 p.a. €12, €38 p.a. (Republic of Ireland and Northern Ireland), €43 p.a. (Rest of World)

Poetry. Features and articles by arrangement. Payment: €40 per contribution; €75 reviews. Founded 1981.

Poetry London

The Albany, Douglas Way, London SE8 4AG
tel 020-8691 7260
email admin@poetrylondon.co.uk
website www.poetrylondon.co.uk
Facebook www.facebook.com/poetrylondon
Twitter @Poetry_London
Editors Ahren Warner and Martha Kapos (poetry), Sam Buchan-Watts (reviews)
3 p.a. £25 p.a.

Poems of the highest standard, articles/reviews on any aspect of contemporary poetry. Comprehensive listings of poetry events and resources. Contributors must be knowledgeable about contemporary poetry. Payment: £20 minimum. Founded 1988.

The Poetry Review

The Poetry Society, 22 Betterton Street, London WC2H 9BX
tel 020-7420 9880
email poetryreview@poetrysociety.org.uk
website www.poetrysociety.org.uk
Editor Emily Berry
Quarterly From £37 p.a.

Poems, features and reviews. Send no more than six poems with sae. Preliminary study of magazine essential. Payment: £50+ per poem.

Poetry Wales

57 Nolton Street, Bridgend CF31 3AE
tel (01656) 663018
email info@poetrywales.co.uk
website www.poetrywales.co.uk
Editor Nia Davies
3 p.a. £9.99

Poetry, criticism and commentary from Wales and around the world. Payment: by arrangement. Founded 1965.

The Police Journal: Theory, Practice and Principles

SAGE Publications, 1 Oliver's Yard, 55 City Road, London EC1Y 1SP
tel 020-7324 8500
website https://uk.sagepub.com/en-gb/eur/journal/police-journal
Editors Jason Roach, Michelle Rogerson
Quarterly From £66 p.a. for individual print issues; see website for further details

Articles of technical or professional interest to the Police Service throughout the world. Illustrations: line drawings. Payment: none. Founded 1928.

The Political Quarterly

Wiley-Blackwell, 9600 Garsington Road, Oxford OX4 2DQ
tel (01865) 776868
website www.politicalquarterly.org.uk
Twitter @po_qu
Editors Deborah Mabbett, Ben Jackson
4 p.a. From £11 p.a. for personal online subscription; see website for full list

Topical aspects of national and international politics and public administration; takes a progressive, but not a party, point of view. See website for submissions information. Length: average 5,000 words. Payment: about £125 per article. Founded 1930.

The Pool

email hello@thepoolltd.com
website www.the-pool.com
Twitter @thepoolUK
Co-founders Sam Baker, Lauren Laverne

Online news and comment platform for women, covering a range of issues including arts and culture, work, food, beauty, fashion and health. Pitches welcomed by editorial and art teams, but potential contributors should clearly indicate any time-sensitive ideas and also send examples of previous work.

Popshot Quarterly

Jubilee House, 2 Jubilee Place, London SW3 3TQ
tel 020-7349 3700
email hello@popshotpopshot.com
website www.popshotpopshot.com
Twitter @popshotmag
Editor Laura Silverman
2 p.a. From £20 p.a. for four print editions and digital issue

Original short stories, flash fiction and poetry paired with bespoke illustrations. Study magazine before submitting work. Each issue is themed and submissions should be tailored accordingly – visit www.popshotpopshot.com/submit for latest details. Length: maximum 3,000 words, shorter is preferable. Illustrations: send portfolios to illustration@popshotpopshot.com. Founded 2009.

Poultry World

Reed Business Information, Quadrant House, The Quadrant, Sutton, Surrey SM2 5AS
tel 020-8652 4927
email jake.davies@proagrica.com
website www.poultryworld.net
Editor Jake Davies
Monthly £3.90

Articles on poultry breeding, production, marketing and packaging. News of international poultry interest. Illustrations: photos, line. Payment: by arrangement.

PR Week

Haymarket Ltd, Bridge House, 69 London Road, Twickenham TW1 3SP
tel 020-8267 5000
email john.harrington@haymarket.com
website www.prweek.com
Twitter @prweekuknews
Editor-in-Chief Danny Rogers
Bi-monthly p.a. £6

News and features on public relations. Length: approx. 800–3,000 words. Payment: by arrangement. Founded 1984.

Prac Crit

email editors@praccrit.com
website www.praccrit.com
Twitter @praccrit
Editors Sarah Howe, Dai George, Vidyan Ravinthiran

Online journal of poetry and criticism, published three times a year. Features interviews, essays and the reflections of poets themselves; close analysis of poems a hallmark.

Practical Boat Owner

Pinehurst 2, Pinehurst Road, Farnborough Business Park, Farnborough GU14 7BF
tel (01252) 555000
email pbo@timeinc.com
website www.pbo.co.uk
Facebook www.facebook.com/practicalboatownermag
Twitter @p_b_o
Editor Rob Melotti
Monthly £4.60

Yachting magazine. Hints, tips and practical articles for cruising skippers. Send synopsis first. Illustrations: photos or drawings. Payment: by negotiation. Founded 1967.

Practical Caravan

Haymarket Ltd, Bridge House, 69 London Road, Twickenham TW1 3SP
tel 020-8267 5712
email practical.caravan@haymarket.com
website www.practicalcaravan.com
Group Editor Alastair Clements
Every four weeks £4.20

Caravan-related travelogues, caravan site reviews; travel writing for existing regular series; technical and DIY matters. Illustrations: colour. Payment negotiable. Founded 1967.

Practical Fishkeeping

Bauer Media Group, Media House, Lynchwood, Peterborough Business Park, Peterborough PE2 6EA
tel (01733) 468000
website www.practicalfishkeeping.co.uk
Twitter @PFKmagazine
Editor Karen Youngs
13 p.a. £4.50

Practical fishkeeping in tropical and coldwater aquaria and ponds. Heavy emphasis on inspiration and involvement. Good colour photography always needed, and used. No verse or humour, no personal biographical accounts of fishkeeping unless practical. Payment: by worth. Founded 1966.

Practical Photography

Bauer Media Group, Media House, Lynchwood, Peterborough Business Park, Peterborough PE2 6EA
tel (01733) 468000
website www.practicalphotography.com
Twitter @practphoto
Editor Ben Hawkins
13 issues p.a. £5.49

Aimed at photographic enthusiasts of all levels who want to improve their skills, try new techniques and learn from the experts. Excellent potential for freelance pictures: must be technically and pictorially superior and have some relevance to photographic technique. Ideas for features are welcome but must be considered, original and relevant. Send brief of idea in first instance. Rates are negotiable but are typically £60 per page pro rata for images and £120 per 1,000 words. Founded 1959.

Practical Wireless

Warners Group Publications Ltd, The Maltings, West Street, Bourne, Lincs. PE10 9PH
tel (01778) 391000
email practicalwireless@warnersgroup.co.uk
website www.radioenthusiast.co.uk
Editor Don Field
Monthly £3.99

Articles on the practical and theoretical aspects of amateur radio and communications. Constructional projects. Telephone or email for advice and essential *PW* author's guide. Illustrations: in b&w and colour; photos, line drawings and wash half-tone for offset litho. Payment: by arrangement. Founded 1932.

The Practising Midwife

Saturn House, Mercury Rise, Altham Industrial Park, Altham, Lancs. BB5 5BY
email info@all4maternity.com
website www.all4maternity.com
Twitter @TPM_Journal
Editor Anna Byrom, *Managing Editor* Laura Yeates
Monthly Subscription rates available on application; see website for full list.

Disseminates evidence-based material to a wide professional audience. Research and review papers, viewpoints and news items pertaining to midwifery, maternity care, women's health and neonatal health with both a national and an international perspective. All articles submitted are peer-reviewed anonymously. Length: 1,200–1,750 words (articles) or 2,400 words (research articles). Illustrations: colour transparencies and artwork; hi-res jpgs or pdfs. Payment: by arrangement. Founded 1997.

The Practitioner

Practitioner Medical Publishing Ltd, 10 Fernthorpe Road, London SW16 6DR
tel 020-8677 3508
email editor@thepractitioner.co.uk
website www.thepractitioner.co.uk
Editor Corinne Short
Monthly From £69 p.a.

Clinical journal for GPs. The articles, on advances in evidence-based medicine, are written by hospital consultants who are specialists in their field. The articles are independently commissioned. Unsolicited material, placed copy or suggestions from third parties not accepted. Founded 1868.

Press Gazette

40 Hatton Garden, London EC1N 8EB
tel 020-7936 6433
email pged@pressgazette.co.uk
website www.pressgazette.co.uk
Editor Dominic Ponsford
Weekly Online only

News and features of interest to journalists and others working in the media. Length: 1,200 words (features), 300 words (news). Payment: approx. £230 (features), news stories negotiable. Founded 1965.

Pride

1 Garratt Lane, London SW18 4AQ
tel 020-8714 467
email editor@pridemagazine.com
website www.pridemagazine.com
Publisher C. J. Cushnie
Monthly £30 pa. (UK)

Lifestyle magazine incorporating fashion and beauty, travel, food and entertaining articles for the woman of colour. Length: 1,000–3,000 words. Illustrations: colour photos and drawings. Payment: £100 per 1,000 words. Founded 1991; relaunched 1997.

Prima

Hearst Magazines UK, National Magazines House, 72 Broadwick Street, London W1F 9EP
tel 020-7439 5000
email prima@hearst.co.uk
website www.prima.co.uk
Facebook www.facebook.com/primamagazine
Twitter @primamag
Editor Gaby Huddart
Monthly £3.49

Articles on fashion, home, crafts, health and beauty, cookery; features. Founded 1986.

Private Eye

6 Carlisle Street, London W1D 3BN
tel 020-7437 4017
email strobes@private-eye.co.uk
website www.private-eye.co.uk
Twitter @PrivateEyeNews
Editor Ian Hislop
Fortnightly £2

News and current affairs. Satire. llustrations and cartoons: colour or b&w. Payment: by arrangement. Founded 1961.

Prole

15 Maes-y-Dre, Abergele, Conwy LL22 7HW
email admin@prolebooks.co.uk
website www.prolebooks.co.uk
Twitter @Prolebooks
Editors Brett Evans, Phil Robertson
3 p.a. (April/August/December) £6.70 (UK inc. p&p), £18.60 p.a. (UK inc. p&p)

Submissions of poetry, short fiction and creative non-fiction (7,500 words max) and photographic cover art welcome (see website for submission guidelines). Annual poetry competition. Payment: profit share. Founded: 2010.

Prospect Magazine

5th Floor, 23 Savile Row, London W1S 2ET
tel 020-7255 1281
email editorial@prospect-magazine.co.uk
website www.prospectmagazine.co.uk
Twitter @prospect_uk
Editor Tom Clark
Monthly £5.95

Political and cultural monthly magazine. Essays, features, special reports, reviews, short stories, opinions/analysis. Length: 3,000–6,000 words (essays, special reports, short stories), 1,000 words (opinions). Illustrations: colour and b&w. Payment: by negotiation. Founded 1995.

Psychologies

Kelsey Media, Cudham Tithe Barn, Berry's Hill, Cudham, Kent TN16 3AG
tel (01959) 541444
email editor@psychologies.co.uk
website www.psychologies.co.uk
Editor-in-Chief Suzy Greaves
Monthly £4.20

Women's magazine with a focus on 'what we're like, not just what we look like'; features cover relationships, family and parenting, personality, behaviour, health, wellbeing, beauty, society and social trends, travel, spirituality and sex. Welcomes new ideas by email which fit into one of these areas, and suggestions should offer a combination of psychological insight and practical advice.

Pulse

140 London Wall, London EC2Y 5DN
tel 020-7214 0500
email feedback@pulsetoday.co.uk
website www.pulsetoday.co.uk
Twitter @pulsetoday
Editor Nigel Praities
Weekly Free on request

Articles and photos of direct interest to GPs. Purely clinical material can be accepted only from medically qualified authors. Length: 600–1,200 words. Illustrations: b&w and colour photos. Payment: £150 average. Founded 1959.

Pushing Out the Boat

email info@pushingouttheboat.co.uk
website www.pushingouttheboat.co.uk
Facebook www.facebook.com/pushingouttheboat
Twitter @POTB13
Biennial £7

North-East Scotland's magazine of new writing and visual arts. Features new prose, poetry and art from the area and the wider world, all selected (anonymously) from online submissions. A not-for-profit magazine run as a charity by volunteers, its costs are met by sales revenue, plus events.

Q Magazine

Bauer Media Group, Endeavour House, 189 Shaftesbury Avenue, London WC2H 8JG
tel 020-7437 9011
email qmail@qthemusic.com
website www.q4music.com
Editor Ted Kessler
Monthly £4.50

Glossy music guide. All material commissioned. Length: 1,200–2,500 words. Illustrations: colour and b&w photos. Payment: £350 per 1,000 words; illustrations by arrangement. Founded 1986.

RA Magazine

Royal Academy of Arts, Burlington House, Piccadilly, London W1J 0BD
tel 020-7300 5820
email ramagazine@royalacademy.org.uk
website www.royalacademy.org.uk/ra-magazine
Editor Sam Phillips
Quarterly £5.95 (£24 p.a.)

Visual arts and culture articles relating to the Royal Academy of Arts and the wider British and international arts scene. Length: 150–1,800 words. Illustrations: consult the Editor. Payment: average £250 per 1,000 words; illustrations by negotiation. Founded 1983.

Racing Post

Floor 23, 1 Canada Square, Canary Wharf, London E14 5AP
tel (01635) 246505
email editor@racingpost.co.uk
website www.racingpost.com
Editor Bruce Millington
Mon–Fri £2.90, Weekender edition (Wednesday to Sunday) £3.40

News on horseracing, greyhound racing and sports betting. Founded 1986.

Radio Times

Immediate Media Co. Ltd, Vineyard House, 44 Brook Green, London W6 7BT
tel 020-7150 5429
email feedback@radiotimes.com
website www.radiotimes.com
Editorial Director Mark Frith
Weekly £2.80

Articles and interviews that preview the week's programmes on British TV and radio as well as on-demand programming. All articles are specially commissioned – ideas and synopses are welcomed but not unsolicited MSS. Length: 600–2,500 words.

Illustrations: mostly in colour; photos, graphic designs or drawings. Payment: by arrangement.

RAIL

Bauer Media Group, Media House, Lynchwood, Peterborough Business Park, Peterborough PE2 6EA
tel (01733) 468000
email rail@bauermedia.co.uk
website www.railmagazine.com
Facebook www.facebook.com/Railmagazine
Twitter @RAIL
Managing Editor Nigel Harris
Fortnightly From £79 p.a.

News and in-depth features on current UK railway operations. Length: 1,000–3,000 words (features), 250–400 words (news). Illustrations: colour and b&w photos and artwork. Payment: £75 per 1,000 words; £15–£40 per photo except cover (£100). Founded 1981.

Railway Gazette International

7th Floor, Chancery House, St Nicholas Way, Sutton, Surrey SM1 4JB
tel 020-8652 5200
email editor@railwaygazette.com
website www.railwaygazette.com
Twitter @railwaygazette
Editor Chris Jackson
Monthly £110 p.a.

Deals with management, engineering, operation and finance of railway, metro and light rail transport worldwide. Articles of business interest on these subjects are considered and paid for if accepted. No 'enthusiast'-oriented articles. Phone or email to discuss proposals. Illustrated articles, of 1,000–2,000 words, are preferred.

The Railway Magazine

Media Centre, Morton Way, Horncastle, Lincs. LN9 6JR
tel (01507) 529589
email railway@mortons.co.uk
website www.railwaymagazine.co.uk
Editor Chris Milner
Monthly £4.40

Illustrated magazine dealing with all railway subjects; no fiction or verse. Articles from 1,500–2,000 words accompanied by photos. Preliminary email or letter desirable. Illustrations: digital; black and white and colour transparencies. Payment: by arrangement. Founded 1897.

Reach Poetry

Indigo Dreams Publishing Ltd, 24 Forest Houses, Cookworthy Moor, Halwill, Beaworthy, Devon EX21 5UU
email publishing@indigodreams.co.uk
website www.indigodreams.co.uk
Facebook www.facebook.com/indigodreamspublishing
Twitter @IndigoDreamsPub
Editor Ronnie Goodyer
Monthly £4.50, £51.00 p.a.

Unpublished and original poetry. Submit up to three poems for consideration by post (include sae for reply) or email (preferred). New poets encouraged. Features lively subscribers' letters and votes pages. No payment; £50 prize money each issue. The editors were recipients of the Ted Slade Award for Services to Poetry 2015; Indigo Dreams won the Most Innovative Publisher Award (Saboteur Awards for Literature 2017). Founded 1998.

Reader's Digest

PO Box 7853, Ringwood BH24 9FH
tel 0845 601 2711
email info@readersdigest.co.uk
website www.readersdigest.co.uk
Monthly £3.79

Original anecdotes, short stories, letters to the editor and jokes may be submitted online for consideration. Founded 1922.

Real People

Hearst Magazines UK, National Magazines House, 72 Broadwick Street, London W1F 9EP
tel 020-7339 4570
website www.realpeoplemag.co.uk
Weekly 67p

Magazine for women with real-life tales of ordinary people coping with extraordinary events, plus puzzles section.

Reality

Redemptorist Communications, Unit A6, Santry Business Park, Swords Road, Dublin D09 X651, Republic of Ireland
tel +353 (0)1 4922488
email info@redcoms.org
website www.redcoms.org
Editor Fr. Gerry Moloney CSSR
Monthly €2.50

Illustrated magazine for Christian living. Illustrated articles on all aspects of modern life, including family, youth, religion, leisure. Length: 1,000–1,500 words. Payment: by arrangement; average £50 per 1,000 words. Founded 1936.

Record Collector

7th Floor, Vantage London, Great West Road, London TW8 9AG
email rc.editorial@metropolis.co.uk
website www.recordcollectormag.com
Reviews Editor Jamie Atkins
Monthly £4.90

Covers all areas of music, with the focus on collectable releases and the reissues market. Specially commissions most material but will consider unsolicited material. Welcomes ideas for articles and features. Length: 2,000 words for articles/features; 200 words for news. Illustrations: transparencies, colour and b&w prints, scans of rare records; all commissioned. Payment: negotiable. Founded 1980.

Red

Hearst Magazines UK, National Magazines House, 72 Broadwick Street, London, W1F 9EP
tel 020-7150 7600
email red@redmagazine.co.uk
website www.redonline.co.uk
Twitter @RedMagDaily
Executive Editor Sarah Tomczak
Monthly £4.30

High-quality articles on topics of interest to women aged 25–45: humour, memoirs, interviews and well-researched investigative features. Approach with ideas in writing in first instance. Length: 900 words upwards. Illustrations: transparencies. Payment: NUJ rates minimum. Founded 1998.

Red Pepper

44–48 Shepherdess Walk, London N1 7JP
email submissions@redpepper.org.uk
website www.redpepper.org.uk
Facebook www.facebook.com/redpeppermagazine
Twitter @redpeppermag
Co-editors Hilary Wainwright, Michael Calderbank, Ruth Potts
Bi-monthly From £2 per month

Independent radical magazine: news and features on politics, culture and everyday life of interest to the left and greens. Material mostly commissioned. Length: news/news features 200–800 words, other features 800–2,000 words. Illustrations: photos, graphics. Payment: for investigations, otherwise only exceptionally. Founded 1994.

Reform

(published by United Reformed Church)
86 Tavistock Place, London WC1H 9RT
tel 020-7916 8630
email reform@urc.org.uk
website www.reform-magazine.co.uk
Twitter @Reform_Mag
Editor Stephen Tomkins
10 p.a. £4 (£2.85 for subscribers), £28.50 p.a.

Explores theology, ethics, personal spirituality and Christian perspectives on social and current affairs. Offers articles about Christian ideas from a range of viewpoints, as well as interviews and reviews. Published by the United Reformed Church but has readers from all Christian denominations, as well as readers from other faiths and from no faith tradition. Illustrations: graphic artists/illustrators. Payment: by arrangement. Founded 1972.

Report

ATL, 7 Northumberland Street, London WC2N 5RD
tel 020-7930 6441
email report@atl.org.uk
website www.atl.org.uk/report
Twitter @ATLReport
Editors Alex Tomlin, Charlotte Tamvakis
9 p.a. Free

Magazine from the Association of Teachers and Lecturers (ATL). Features, articles, comment, news about nursery, primary, secondary and further education. Payment: minimum £120 per 1,000 words.

Restaurant Magazine

William Reed Business Media, Broadfield Park, Crawley RH11 9RT
tel (01293) 613400
email joe.lutrario@wrbm.com
website www.bighospitality.co.uk
Twitter @RestaurantMagUK
Editor Stefan Chomka
Monthly £4.99

Articles, features and news on the restaurant trade. Specially commissions most material. Welcomes ideas for articles and features. Illustrations: colour transparencies, prints and artwork. Payment: variable. Founded 2001.

Resurgence & Ecologist

The Resurgence Trust, Fort House, Hartland, Bideford, Devon EX39 6EE
tel (01237) 441293
email greg@resurgence.org
website www.resurgence.org
Editor-in-Chief Greg Neale
6 p.a. £4.95

Interested in environment and social justice investigations and features, green living advice and ideas, grassroots activism projects, artist profiles and reviews. Proposal first in most cases. Payment: various. See website for further guidance.

Retail Week

Ascential Information Services Ltd, 33 Kingsway, London WC2B 6UF
tel 020-3033 4220
email content@retail-week.com
website www.retail-week.com
Twitter @retailweek
Executive Editor George MacDonald
Weekly £7.99

Features and news stories on all aspects of retail management. Length: up to 1,400 words. Illustrations: colour photos. Payment: by arrangement. Founded 1988.

The Rialto

PO Box 309, Aylsham, Norwich NR11 6LN
email info@therialto.co.uk
website www.therialto.co.uk
Editor Michael Mackmin
3 p.a. £8.50 per issue, £24 p.a. for UK subscriptions; for overseas subscriptions, please consult the website

68pp A4 magazine, mainly poetry but with occasional prose pieces. Prose is commissioned, poetry submissions are very welcome: up to six poems may be submitted either by post (sae essential) or online via Submittable. See website for details of submission windows. Payment: by arrangement. Founded 1984.

Royal National Institute of Blind People (RNIB)

105 Judd Street, London WC1H 9NE
tel 0303 123 9999
email helpline@rnib.org.uk
website www.rnib.org.uk
Twitter @RNIB

RNIB publishes a variety of titles in a range of formats (including audio, email, braille and Daisy) for adults and young people who have sight loss.

Rugby World

Time Inc (UK) Ltd, 2nd Floor, Pinehurst 2, Pinehurst Road, Farnborough Business Park, Farnborough, Hants GU14 7BF
tel (01252) 555271
email rugbyworld@timeinc.com
website www.rugbyworld.com
Twitter @Rugbyworldmag
Editor Sarah Mockford
Monthly £4.90

Features and exclusive news stories on rugby. Length: approx. 1,200 words. Illustrations: colour photos, cartoons. Payment: £120. Founded 1960.

Runner's World

Hearst Magazines UK, 33 Broadwick Street, London W1F 0DG
tel 020-7339 4400
website www.runnersworld.co.uk
Facebook www.facebook.com/runnersworlduk
Twitter @runnersworlduk
Editor Andy Dixon
Monthly £4.70

Articles on running, health and fitness, and nutrition. Payment: by arrangement. Founded 1979.

RUSI Journal

Whitehall, London SW1A 2ET
tel 020-7747 2600
email publications@rusi.org
website https://rusi.org/publication/rusi-journal
Editor Emma De Angelis
Bi-monthly; available as part of RUSI membership (see website for full list; concessions available) or a subscription in conjunction with RUSI Whitehall Papers.

Journal of the Royal United Services Institute for Defence and Security Studies. Articles on international security, military science, defence technology and procurement, and military history; also book reviews and correspondence. Length: 3,000–3,500 words. Illustrations: colour photos, maps and diagrams.

Saga Magazine

Saga Publishing Ltd, The Saga Building, Enbrook Park, Sandgate, Folkestone, Kent CT20 3SE
tel (01303) 771523
website www.saga.co.uk/magazine
Monthly From £12 p.a. (special rate; normal rates may be higher)

General interest magazine aimed at the intelligent, literate 50+ reader. Wide range of articles from human interest, real-life stories, intriguing overseas interest (not travel), some natural history, celebrity interviews, photographic book extracts – all subjects are considered in this general interest title. Articles mostly commissioned or written in-house, but genuine exclusives welcome. Illustrations: colour, digital media; mainly commissioned but top-quality photo feature suggestions sometimes accepted. Payment: competitive rate, by negotiation. Founded 1984.

Sainsbury's Magazine

Seven, 3–7 Herbal Hill, London EC1R 5EJ
tel 020-7775 7775
email feedback@sainsburysmagazine.co.uk
website www.sainsburysmagazine.co.uk
Editor-in-Chief Helena Lang
Monthly £2

Features: general, food and drink, health, beauty, homes; all material commissioned. Length: up to 1,500 words. Illustrations: colour and b&w photos and line illustrations. Payment: varies. Founded 1993.

Salomé

email salomeliterature@gmail.com
website www.salomelit.com
Twitter @salome_lit
Founder Jacquelyn Guderley
Quarterly £3.50, £13.50 p.a.

Online literary magazine for emerging female writers of fiction, non-fiction, flash fiction and poetry. Aims to give anyone who identifies as female the platform to get their work published, to support and improve the writing skills of female writers, and to provide high-quality reading material for readers. Submission windows and guidelines are provided online: detailed feedback given to everyone who submits, whether their work is publshed or not. Founded 2017.

Sarasvati

24 Forest Houses, Cookworthy Moor, Halwill, Beaworthy, Devon EX21 5UU
email dawnidp@indigodreams.co.uk
website www.indigodreams.co.uk
Facebook www.facebook.com/indigodreamspublishing
Twitter @IndigoDreamsPub

Editor Dawn Bauling
Quarterly £4.50, £17 for 4 issues

International poetry and short story magazine. New writers/poets encouraged. Lively feedback pages. Several pages given to each subscriber. Prose length: 1,000 words or under. Founded 2008.

The School Librarian

School Library Association, 1 Pine Court, Kembrey Park, Swindon SN2 8AD
tel (01793) 530166
email sleditor@sla.org.uk
website www.sla.org.uk
Features Editor Barbara Band, *Reviews Editor* Joy Court
Quarterly Free to SLA members

Official journal of the School Library Association. Articles on school library management, use and skills, and on authors and illustrators, literacy, publishing. Reviews of books, CD-Roms, websites and other library resources from preschool to adult. Length: 1,800–2,500 words (articles). Payment: by arrangement. Founded 1937.

Scientific Computing World

4 Signet Court, Cambridge CB5 8LA
tel (01223) 275464
email editor.scw@europascience.com
website www.scientific-computing.com
Editor Robert Roe
6 p.a. Free to qualifying subscribers, other subscription rates apply (see website)

Features on hardware and software developments for the scientific community, plus news articles and reviews. Length: 800–2,000 words. Illustrations: colour transparencies, photos, electronic graphics. Payment: by negotiation. Founded 1994.

The Scots Magazine

D.C. Thomson & Co. Ltd, 80 Kingsway East, Dundee DD4 8SL
tel (01382) 223131
email mail@scotsmagazine.com
website www.scotsmagazine.com
Editor Robert Wright
Monthly £3.75

Articles on all subjects of Scottish interest, but authors must also be Scottish. Illustrations: colour and b&w photos. Unsolicited material considered but preliminary enquiries advised. Payment: on acceptance. Founded 1739.

The Scottish Farmer

Newsquest, 200 Renfield Street, Glasgow G2 3QB
tel 0141 302 7732
email ken.fletcher@thescottishfarmer.co.uk
website www.thescottishfarmer.co.uk
Editor Ken Fletcher
Weekly £3.10

Articles on agricultural subjects. Length: 1,000–1,500 words. Illustrations: line, half-tone, colour. Payment: £80 per 1,000 words. Founded 1893.

Scottish Field

Fettes Park, 496 Ferry Road, Edinburgh EH5 2DL
tel 0131 551 1000
email rbath@scottishfield.co.uk
website www.scottishfield.co.uk
Facebook www.facebook.com/scottishfield/
Twitter @scottishfield
Editor Richard Bath
Monthly £4.25

Scottish lifestyle magazine: interiors, food, travel, wildlife, heritage, general lifestyle. Length of article accepted: 1,200 words. Founded 1903.

Screen International

MBI Ltd, Zetland House, 5–25 Scrutton Street, London EC2A 4HJ
tel 020-8102 0900
email matt.mueller@screendaily.com
website www.screendaily.com
Editor Matt Mueller
Monthly From £163 + VAT p.a.

International news and features on the international film business. No unsolicited material. Length: variable. Payment: by arrangement.

Sea Angler

Bauer Media Group, Media House, Lynchwood, Peterborough Business Park, Peterborough PE2 6EA
tel (01733) 395134
website www.seaangler.co.uk
Editor Cliff Brown
Monthly £3.60

Topical articles on all aspects of sea-fishing around the British Isles. Illustrations: colour. Payment: by arrangement. Founded 1972.

Sea Breezes

Media House, Cronkbourne, Tromode, Douglas, Isle of Man IM4 4SB
tel (01624) 696573
website www.seabreezes.co.im
Editor Hamish Ross
Monthly From £49.50 p.a.

Factual articles on ships and the sea past and present, preferably illustrated. Length: up to 4,000 words. Illustrations: line, half-tone, colour. Payment: by arrangement. Founded 1919.

Seen and Heard

Nagalro, PO Box 264, Esher, Surrey KT10 0WA
tel (01372) 818504
email mail@rodneynoon.co.uk
website www.nagalro.com/seen-and-heard-journal/seen-and-heard.aspx
Editor Rodney Noon
Quarterly £35 p.a.

Professional journal of Nagalro, the professional association of children's guardians, family court advisers and independent social workers. Publishes high-quality articles and academic papers on issues relating to, the professional practice of child-protection social workers, child abuse and protection, adoption and the law relating to children. Potential contributors are advised to contact the editor initially with proposals. Payment: on publication, ranging from £50 to £100.

SelfBuild & Design

151 Station Street, Burton on Trent, Staffs. DE14 1BG
tel (01584) 841417
email ross.stokes@sbdonline.co.uk
website www.selfbuildanddesign.com
Editor Ross Stokes
Monthly £4.50

Articles on house construction for individual builders. Welcomes ideas for articles. Illustrations: colour prints, transparencies and digital. Payment: £100–£200 per 1,000 words.

The Sewing Directory

11A Tedders Close, Hemyock, Cullompton, Devon, EX15 3XD
tel (01823) 680588
email julie@thesewingdirectory.net
website www.thesewingdirectory.co.uk
Facebook www.facebook.com/thesewingdirectory
Twitter @sewingdirectory
Content Editor Julie Briggs

Online directory of UK sewing business – sewing courses, fabric shops and sewing groups. Plus free sewing projects and technique guides. Payment: £40 per article/project. Founded 2010.

Sewing World

MyTimeMedia Ltd, Eden House, Enterprise Way, Edenbridge, Kent TN8 6HF
tel (01689) 869840
email sw@mytimemedia.com
website www.sewingworldmagazine.com
Twitter @sewingworldmag
Editor Emma Horrocks
13 p.a. £5.25

Contemporary sewing magazine for sewing machine enthusiasts. Features, in-depth techniques and step-by-step projects including garments, quilts, home accessories, bags, small makes etc. Length: 1,000–1,500 words (articles). Illustrations: hi-res colour. Payment: dependent on complexity of project/article. Founded 1995.

SFX Magazine

Future Publishing Ltd, Quay House, The Ambury, Bath BA1 1UA
tel (01225) 442244
email sfx@futurenet.com
website www.gamesradar.com/sfx
Facebook www.facebook.com/SFXmagazine
Twitter @SFXmagazine
Editor Richard Edwards
Every 4 weeks (13 p.a.) £4.99

Sci-fi and fantasy magazine covering TV, films, DVDs, books, comics, games and collectables. Founded 1995.

Ships Monthly

Kelsey Media, Cudham Tithe Barn, Berry's Hill, Cudham, Kent TN16 3AG
tel (01959) 541444
email ships.monthly@btinternet.com
website www.shipsmonthly.com
Editor Nicholas Leach
Monthly £4.50

Illustrated articles of shipping and maritime interest – both mercantile and naval, preferably of 20th- and 21st-century ships. Well-researched, factual material only. No short stories or poetry. 'Notes for contributors' available. Mainly commissioned material; preliminary letter or email essential. Illustrations: half-tone and line, colour transparencies, prints and digital images via email, DVD or CD. Payment: by arrangement. Founded 1966.

Shooter Literary Magazine

98 Muswell Hill Road, London N10 3JR
email shooterlitmag@gmail.com
website www.shooterlitmag.com
Facebook www.facebook.com/shooterliterarymagazine
Twitter @ShooterLitMag
Editor Melanie White

Submissions of short fiction and non-fiction (2,000–7,500 words) and poetry welcome. Annual story and poetry competitions. Please visit the website for guidelines, current theme and deadline information. Payment: £25 for prose, £5 for poetry, plus complimentary issue. Founded 2015.

Shooting Times and Country Magazine

Time Inc. (UK), Pinehurst 2, Pinehurst Road, Farnborough Business Park, Farnborough, Hants GU14 7BF
tel (01252) 555000
email shootingtimes@timeinc.com
website www.shootingtimes.co.uk
Editor Patrick Galbraith
Weekly £2.40

Articles on fieldsports, especially shooting, and on related natural history and countryside topics. Unsolicited MSS not encouraged. Length: up to 2,000 words. Illustrations: photos, drawings, colour transparencies. Payment: by arrangement. Founded 1882.

The Shropshire Magazine

Shropshire Newspapers, Ketley, Telford TF1 5HU
tel (01952) 241455
website www.shropshiremagazine.com
Editor Neil Thomas
Monthly £3.50

Articles on topics related to Shropshire, including countryside, history, characters, legends, education, food; also home and garden features. Length: up to 1,500 words. Illustrations: colour. Founded 1950.

Sight and Sound

BFI, 21 Stephen Street, London W1T 1LN
tel 020-7255 1444
website www.bfi.org.uk/sightandsound
Twitter @SightSoundmag
Editor Nick James
Monthly From £35 p.a.

Topical and critical articles on world cinema; reviews of every film theatrically released in the UK; book reviews; DVD reviews; festival reports. Length: 1,000–5,000 words. Illustrations: relevant photos, cartoons. Payment: by arrangement. Founded 1932.

Ski+board

(formerly Ski Survey)
The Ski Club of Great Britain, The White House, 57–63 Church Road, London SW19 5SB
tel 020-8410 2000
email ben.clatworthy@skiclub.co.uk
website www.skiclub.co.uk
Editor Colin Nicholson
Monthly in winter (Oct, Nov, Dec/Jan, Feb/Mar, plus April online only)

Online only. Articles, features, news, true-life stories, ski tips, equipment reviews, resort reports – all in connection with skiing and snowboarding. Please pitch during the first two weeks of the month. Payment: £180 per 1,000 words; £20–£150 per photo/illustration. Founded 1972.

The Skier and Snowboarder Magazine

The Lodge, West Heath, Ashgrove Road, Sevenoaks TN13 1ST
tel 07768 670158
email frank.baldwin@skierandsnowboarder.com
website www.skierandsnowboarder.com
Editor Frank Baldwin
5 p.a. Free

Ski features, based around a good story. Length: 800–1,000 words. Illustrations: colour action ski photos. Payment: by negotiation. Founded 1984.

Slightly Foxed

53 Hoxton Square, London N1 6PB
tel 020-7033 0258
email all@foxedquarterly.com
website www.foxedquarterly.com
Facebook www.facebook.com/foxedquarterly
Twitter @foxedquarterly
Publisher/Co-editor Gail Pirkis
Quarterly Single issue £11 (UK and Ireland), £12 (Overseas); annual subscription £40 p.a. (UK and Ireland), £48 (Overseas)

Independent-minded magazine of book reviews. Each issue contains 96pp of recommendations for books of lasting interest, old and new, both fiction and non-fiction – books that have inspired, amused, and sometimes even changed the lives of the people who write about them. Unsolicited submissions are welcome; see website for guidelines.

Slimming World Magazine

Clover Nook Road, Alfreton, Derbyshire DE55 4SW
tel (01773) 546071
email editorial@slimmingworld.com
website www.slimmingworld.com/magazine/latest-issue.aspx
Editor-in-Chief Elise Wells
7 p.a. £2.95 (£1.95 group members)

Magazine about healthy eating, fitness and feeling good with real-life stories of how Slimming World members have changed their lives, as well as recipes and menu plans, health advice, beauty and fitness tips, features, competitions and fashion.

Smallholder

Newquest Media, Falmouth Business Park, Bickland Water Road, Falmouth, Cornwall TR11 4SZ
tel (01326) 213340
email editorial@smallholder.co.uk
website www.smallholder.co.uk
Twitter @smallholdermag
13 p.a. £3.95

Articles of relevance to small farmers and rural dwellers about livestock, poultry, grow your own, allotments, wildlife, conservation, land management, equipment and true-life stories. Items and submissions relating to the countryside considered; please email the Editor. Length: single-page article 500 words; double-page spread 1,000–1,500 words with pictures.

Snooker Scene

Hayley Green Court, 130 Hagley Road, Halesowen, West Midlands B63 1DY
tel 0121 585 9188
email info@snookerscene.com
website www.snookerscene.co.uk
Facebook www.facebook.com/snooker.scene
Twitter @Snookerscene
Editor Clive Everton
Monthly £3.50

News and articles about the snooker and billiards scene for readers with more than a casual interest in the games. Illustrations: photos. Payment: by arrangement. Founded 1971.

The Songwriter

International Songwriters Association, PO Box 46, Limerick City, Republic of Ireland
tel +353 (0)61 228837
email jliddane@songwriter.iol.ie
website www.songwriter.co.uk
Editor James D. Liddane
Quarterly

Articles on songwriting and interviews with songwriters, music publishers and recording company executives. Length: 1,000–10,000 words. Illustrations: photos. Payment: by arrangement. Founded 1967.

Songwriting and Composing

Westland House, 2 Penlee Close, Praa Sands, Penzance, Cornwall TR20 9SR
tel (01207) 500825
email gisc@btconnect.com
website www.songwriters-guild.co.uk
Editor Colin Eade
Quarterly Free to members

Magazine of the Guild of International Songwriters and Composers. Profiles/stories, articles, contacts relating to songwriting, music publishing, recording and the music industry. Illustrations: line, half-tone. Payment: negotiable upon content £25–£60. Founded 1986.

SOUTH

PO Box 4228, Bracknell, Berks. RG42 9PX
email south@southpoetry.org
website www.southpoetry.org
Contacts Anne Peterson, Andrew Curtis, Peter Keeble, Patrick Osada and Chrissie Williams
2 p.a. £7

Poetry magazine featuring previously unpublished poems written in English. Poems featured in the magazine are chosen by a selection panel which changes for every issue. Up to three poems (two copies required) may be submitted for each issue, but see website for full details, including annual deadlines. Potential contributors are advised to study the magazine prior to sending in their work.

Spear's Magazine

John Carpenter House, John Carpenter Street, London EC4Y 0AN
tel 020-7936 6445
email christopher.silvester@spearwms.com
website www.spearsmagazine.com
Twitter @SpearsMagazine
Editor-in-Chief William Cash
Bi-monthly £25 p.a. (print), £22.99 p.a. (print and digital)

Guide to wealth management, business and culture. Topics covered include wealth management, the law, art, philanthropy, luxury, food and wine and global affairs. Readership includes ultra-high-net-worths, private bankers, top lawyers, philanthropists etc. Standard length of articles 850–1,300 words (features). Colour and b&w illustrations. Payment: 40p per word; £150+ for illustrations. Founded 2003.

Speciality Food

Aceville Publications, 21–23 Hawkins Road, Colchester CO2 8JY
email holly.shackleton@aceville.co.uk
website www.specialityfoodmagazine.com
Editor Holly Shackleton
9 p.a. £3.25

Trade magazine for the fine food industry, combining expert insight, product recommendations and independent retail-focused features with the sector's latest news and opinion.

The Spectator

22 Old Queen Street, London SW1H 9HP
tel 020-7961 0200
email editor@spectator.co.uk
website www.spectator.co.uk
Editor Fraser Nelson
Weekly £4.50

Articles on current affairs, politics, the arts; book reviews. Illustrations: colour and b&w, cartoons. Payment: on merit. Founded 1828.

The Stage

Stage House, 47 Bermondsey Street, London SE1 3XT
tel 020-7403 1818
email alistair@thestage.co.uk
website www.thestage.co.uk
Editor Alistair Smith, *Features Editor* Nick Clark, *Reviews Editor* Natasha Tripney, *News Editor* Matthew Hemley
Weekly £2.30

Original and interesting articles on the theatre and performing arts industry may be sent for the Editor's consideration. Features range in length from 800 to 3,000 words. Payment: £100 per 1,000 words. Founded 1880.

Stamp Magazine

MyTime Media Ltd, Enterprise House, Enterprise Way, Edenbridge, Kent TN8 6HF
tel 0844 848 88 22
email Guy.Thomas@mytimemedia.com
website www.stampmagazine.co.uk
Editor Guy Thomas
13 p.a. £42 p.a. (print)

Informative articles and exclusive news items on stamp collecting and postal history. Preliminary letter. Payment: by arrangement. Illustrations: line, half-tone, colour. Founded 1934.

The Strad

Newsquest Specialist Media, 4th Floor, 120 Leman Street, London E1 8EU

tel 020-7618 3095
email thestrad@thestrad.com
website www.thestrad.com
Twitter @TheStradMag
Editor Charlotte Smith
12 p.a. plus occasional supplements. £5.50

Features, news and reviews for stringed instrument players, teachers, makers and enthusiasts – both professional and amateur. Specially commissions most material but will consider unsolicited material. Welcomes ideas for articles and features. Length: 1,000–2,250 (articles/features), 100–150 (news). Illustrations: transparencies, colour and b&w prints and artwork, colour cartoons; some commissioned. Payment: £150–£350 (articles/features), varies for news. Founded 1890.

Structo

email editor@structomagazine.co.uk
website http://structomagazine.co.uk
Facebook www.facebook.com/structomagazine
Twitter @structomagazine
Editor Euan Monaghan
2 p.a. £15 p.a.

Fiction, poetry, author interviews and essays. Nominally based in the UK, but with a worldwide staff, readership and contributor base. Invites submissions of short stories and poetry, both originals and translations into English, specifically: original and previously unpublished fiction of up to 3,000 words; up to three original and previously unpublished poems per issue. Contributors should indicate any translation rights issues in their cover note. Payment: issues, plus any additional copies at cost. Founded 2008.

Stuff

Haymarket Ltd, Bridge House, 69 London Road, Twickenham TW1 3SP
tel 020-8267 5052
email stuff@haymarket.com
website www.stuff-magazine.co.uk
Editor Will Findlater
Monthly £4.99

Articles on technology, games, films, lifestyle, news and reviews. Payment by negotiation. Founded 1999.

Style at Home

Time Inc. (UK), The Blue Fin Building, 110 Southwark Street, London SE1 0SU
email styleathome@timeinc.com
website www.housetohome.co.uk/styleathome
Facebook www.facebook.com/StyleAtHomeMag
Twitter @styleathomemag
Editor Vanessa Richmond
Monthly £1.99

Interiors magazine aimed at woman interested in updating, styling and decorating their home. With an emphasis on achievable, affordable home make-overs, the magazine has regular articles showing transformed rooms as well as step-by-step projects, shopping ideas and a recipe section for keen cooks.

Suffolk Norfolk Life

Today Magazines Ltd, The Publishing House, Station Road, Framlingham, Suffolk IP13 9EE
tel (01728) 622030
email editor@suffolknorfolklife.com
website www.suffolknorfolklife.com
Editor Kevin Davis
Monthly £2.50

Articles relevant to Suffolk and Norfolk – current topics plus historical items, art, leisure, etc. Considers unsolicited material and welcomes ideas for articles and features. Send via email. Length: 900–1,500 words. Illustrations: transparencies, digital colour and b&w prints, b&w artwork and cartoons. Payment: £60–£80 per article. Founded 1989.

Surrey Life

c/o 28 Teville Road, Worthing, West Sussex, BN11 1UG
tel (01903) 703730
email editor@surreylife.co.uk
website www.surreylife.co.uk
Facebook www.facebook.com/SurreyLife
Twitter @SurreyLife
Editor Rebecca Younger
Monthly £3.99

Articles on Surrey, including places of interest, high-profile personalities, local events, arts, history, food, homes, gardens and more. Founded 1970.

Swimming Times Magazine

Swimming Times Ltd, SportPark, Pavilion 3, 3 Oakwood Drive, Loughborough, Leics. LE11 3QF
tel (01509) 640230
email swimmingtimes@swimming.org
website www.swimming.org/swimmingtimes
Monthly £20.30 p.a. (print)

Official journal of the Amateur Swimming Association and the Institute of Swimming. Reports of major events and championships; news and features on all aspects of swimming including synchronised swimming, diving and water polo, etc; accompanying photos where appropriate; short fiction with a swimming theme. Unsolicited material welcome. Length: 800–1,500 words. Payment: by arrangement. Founded 1923.

The Tablet

1 King Street Cloisters, Clifton Walk, London W6 0GY
tel 020-8748 8484
email thetablet@thetablet.co.uk
website www.thetablet.co.uk
Twitter @The_Tablet
Editor Brendan Walsh
Weekly £3.20

Catholic weekly: religion, philosophy, politics, society, books and arts. International coverage. Freelance work commissioned: do not send unsolicited material. Length: various. Illustrations: cartoons and photos. Payment: by arrangement. Founded 1840.

Take a Break

H. Bauer Publishing Ltd, Academic House, 24–28 Oval Road, London NW1 7DT
tel 020-7241 8000
email tab.features@bauer.co.uk
website www.takeabreak.co.uk
Weekly 96p

Lively, illustrated tabloid women's weekly. True-life features, health and beauty, family; lots of puzzles. Payment: by arrangement. Founded 1990.

Take a Break's Take a Puzzle

H. Bauer Publishing, Academic House, 24–28 Oval Road, London NW1 7DT
email take.puzzle@bauer.co.uk
website www.puzzlemagazines.co.uk/takeapuzzle
Editor Babetta Mann
Monthly £2.30

Puzzles. Fresh ideas always welcome. Illustrations: colour transparencies and b&w prints and artwork. Payment: from £25 per puzzle, £30–£90 for picture puzzles and for illustrations not an integral part of a puzzle. Founded 1991.

TATE ETC

Tate, Millbank, London SW1P 4RG
tel 020-7887 8724
email tateetc@tate.org.uk
website www.tate.org.uk/about/business-services/tate-etc-magazine
Twitter @TateEtcMag
Editor Simon Grant
3 p.a. £18 p.a. (UK)

Independent visual arts magazine: features, interviews, previews and opinion pieces. Length: up to 3,000 words but always commissioned. Illustrations: colour and b&w photos. Payment: negotiable.

Tatler

Vogue House, Hanover Square, London W1S 1JU
tel 020-7499 9080
website www.tatler.co.uk
Twitter @TatlerUK
Editor Richard Dennen
Monthly £4.70

Smart society magazine favouring sharp articles, profiles, fashion and the arts. Illustrations: colour, b&w, but all commissioned. Founded 1709.

Taxation

Quadrant House, The Quadrant, Sutton SM2 5AS
tel 020-8212 1949
email taxation@lexisnexis.co.uk
website www.taxation.co.uk
Twitter @Taxation
Editor Richard Curtis
49 issues p.a. £410 p.a.

Updating and advice concerning UK tax law and practice for accountants and tax experts. All articles written by professionals. Length: 2,000 words (articles). Founded 1927.

The Teacher

National Education Union (NUT section), Hamilton House, Mabledon Place, London WC1H 9BD
tel 020-7380 4708
email teacher@neu.org.uk
website www.teachers.org.uk/teacher-online
Editor Helen Watson
6 p.a. Free to NUT members

Articles, features and news of interest to all those involved in the teaching profession. Email outline in the first instance. Length: 500 words (single page), 1,000 (double page). Payment: NUJ rates to NUJ members. Founded 1872.

Tears in the Fence

Portman Lodge, Durweston, Blandford Forum, Dorset DT11 0QA
email tearsinthefence@gmail.com
website https://tearsinthefence.com
Twitter @TearsInTheFence
Editor David Caddy
Monthly £10, or £25 p.a. for three issues

Socially aware literary magazine with an international outlook and author base. Includes regular columnists as well as critical reviews of recent books and essays on English and American poets, flash fiction, translations and interviews. See website for up-to-date information on forthcoming submission windows. Submissions of original, unpublished work should be made by email to the address above in the body of the message and as an attachment.

Television

RTS, Kildare House, 3 Dorset Rise, London EC4Y 8EH
tel 020-7822 2810
email publications@rts.org.uk
website www.rts.org.uk
Editor Steve Clarke
Monthly

Articles on the technical aspects of domestic TV and video equipment, especially servicing, long-distance TV, constructional projects, satellite TV, video recording, teletext and viewdata, test equipment, monitors. Illustrations: by agreement. Payment: by arrangement. Founded 1950.

Tempo

Cambridge University Press,
The Edinburgh Building, Shaftesbury Road,
Cambridge CB2 8RU
email tempoeditor@cambridge.org
website https://www.cambridge.org/core/journals/tempo
Editor Christopher Fox
Quarterly Various subscription rates apply; see website for details

Authoritative articles on contemporary music. Length: 2,000–4,000 words. Illustrations: music type, occasional photographic or musical supplements. Payment: by arrangement.

TES (The Times Educational Supplement)

26 Red Lion Square, London WC1R 4HQ
tel 020-3194 3000
email newsdesk@tes.com
email features@tes.com
website www.tes.com
Twitter @tes
Editor Ann Mroz
Weekly £30 per quarter print and digital; £15 per quarter digital only

Education magazine and website. Articles on education written with special knowledge or experience; news items; features; book reviews. Outlines of feature ideas should be emailed. Illustrations: suitable photos and drawings of educational interest, cartoons. Payment: by arrangement.

TESS (The Times Educational Supplement Scotland)

tel 07825 033445
email scoted@tess.co.uk
website www.tes.com/
Twitter @TESScotland
News Editor Henry Hepburn
Weekly £30 per quarter print and digital

Education newspaper. Articles on education, preferably 800–1,000 words, written with special knowledge or experience. News items about Scottish educational affairs. Illustrations: line, half-tone. Payment: by arrangement. Founded 1965.

TGO (The Great Outdoors) Magazine

Kelsey Media, Cudham Tithe Barn, Berry's Hill,
Cudham, Kent TN16 3AG
tel (01959) 541444
email emily.rodway@tgomagazine.co.uk
website www.tgomagazine.co.uk
Twitter @TGOmagazine
Editor Emily Rodway
13 p.a. £4.50

Articles on walking or lightweight camping in specific areas, mainly in the UK, preferably illustrated with photography. Apply for guidelines. Length: 700–2,000 words. Illustrations: colour. Payment: by arrangement. Founded 1978.

that's life!

H. Bauer Publishing Ltd, Academic House,
24–28 Oval Road, London NW1 7DT
tel 020-7241 8000
email stories@thatslife.co.uk
website www.thatslife.co.uk
Editor-in-Chief Sophie Hearsey
Weekly 76p

Dramatic true-life stories about women. Length: average 1,000 words. Illustrations: colour photos and cartoons. Payment: up to £2,000. Founded 1995.

This England

The Lypiatts, Lansdown Road, Cheltenham,
Glos. GL50 2JA
tel (01242) 225780
email editor@thisengland.co.uk
website www.thisengland.co.uk
Editor Stephen Garnett
Quarterly £5.25

Articles about England's traditions, customs and places of interest. Regular features on towns, villages, the English countryside, notable men and women, and readers' recollections. Length 250–2,000 words. Illustrations: digital; colour transparencies accepted only when accompanying articles. Payment: £25 per 1,000 words, £10 poems (12–24 lines). Founded 1968.

Time Out London

Time Out Group Ltd, 4th Floor,
125 Shaftesbury Avenue, London, WC2H 8AD
tel 020-7813 3000
email hello@timeout.com
website www.timeout.com
Facebook www.facebook.com/TimeOutLondon/
Twitter @timeoutlondon
Editorial Director Caroline McGinn
Weekly Free

Listings magazine for London covering all areas of the arts, plus articles of consumer and news interest. Illustrations: colour and b&w. Payment by negotiation. Founded 1968.

Times Higher Education

26 Red Lion Square, London WC1R 4HQ
tel 020-3194 3000
email john.gill@tesglobal.com
website www.timeshighereducation.co.uk
Facebook www.facebook.com/timeshighereducation
Twitter @timeshighered
Editor John Gill
Weekly £3.80

Articles on higher education written with special knowledge or experience, or articles dealing with academic topics. Also news items. Illustrations: suitable photos and drawings of educational interest. Payment: by arrangement. Founded 1971.

TLS (The Times Literary Supplement)

1 London Bridge Street, London SE1 9GF
tel 020-7782 4985
email queries@the-tls.co.uk
website www.the-tls.co.uk
Editor Stig Abell
Weekly £3.50

Will consider poems for publication, literary discoveries and articles on literary and cultural affairs. Payment: by arrangement.

Today's Golfer

Bauer Media Group, Media House, Lynchwood, Peterborough Business Park, Peterborough PE2 6EA
tel (01733) 468000
email chris.jones@bauermedia.co.uk
website www.todaysgolfer.co.uk
Facebook www.facebook.co.uk/Today'sGolfer
Twitter @TheTodaysGolfer
Editor Chris Jones
Every 4 weeks £4.50

Specialist features and articles on golf instruction, equipment and courses. Founded 1988.

Top Santé Health & Beauty

Kelsey Media, Cudham Tithe Barn, Berry's Hill, Cudham, Kent TN16 3AG
tel (01959) 541444
website www.topsante.co.uk
Twitter @topsanteuk
Editor Katy Louise Sunnassee
Monthly £3.70

Articles, features and news on all aspects of health and beauty. Ideas welcome. No unsolicited features. Payment: illustrations by arrangement. Founded 1993.

Total Film

Future Publishing Ltd, 1–10 Praed Mews, London W2 1QY
tel 020-7042 4831
email jane.crowther@futurenet.com
website www.gamesradar.com/totalfilm
Editor-in-Chief Jane Crowther
Monthly £4.50

Movie magazine covering all aspects of film. Email ideas before submitting material. Length: 400 words (news items); 1,000 words (funny features). Payment: 20p per word. Founded 1996.

Total Off-Road

Repton House G11, Bretby Business Park, Burton on Trent, Staffs. DE15 0YZ
tel (01283) 553243
email alan.kidd@assignment-media.co.uk
website www.toronline.co.uk
Editor Alan Kidd
Monthly £4.50

Features on off-roading: competitions, modified vehicles, overseas events. Length 1,200–3,000 words. Illustrations: colour and b&w prints, transparencies and digital images. keen to hear from photographers attending UK/overseas off-road events. Preliminary email strongly advised. Payment: £100 per 1,000 words.

Total Politics

Dods Group Plc, The Shard, 32 London Bridge Street, London SE1 9SG
email david.singleton@dods.co.uk
website www.totalpolitics.com
Twitter @TotalPolitics
Editor David Singleton
Online only

News site for politicians and people interested in politics. Looking for relevant articles and features. Length: up to 2,200 words. Illustrations: colour and b&w photos and bespoke artwork. Payment: negotiable. Founded 2008.

Trail

Bauer Consumer Media, Media House, Lynchwood, Peterborough Business Park, Peterborough PE2 6RA
tel (01733) 468363
email simon.ingram@lfto.com
website www.livefortheoutdoors.com
Editor Simon Ingram
Monthly £4.60

Outdoor activity magazine focusing mainly on high level walking with some scrambling and climbing. Some opportunities for freelancers. Good ideas welcome.

Trout & Salmon

Bauer Media Group, Media House, Lynchwood, Peterborough Business Park, Peterborough PE2 6EA
tel (01733) 468000
email troutandsalmon@bauermedia.co.uk
website www.troutandsalmon.com
Editor Andrew Flitcroft
13 p.a. £3.70, £37 p.a.

Articles of good quality with strong trout or salmon angling interest. Length: 400–2,000 words, accompanied if possible by good quality colour prints. Illustrations: line, colour transparencies and prints, cartoons. Payment: by arrangement. Founded 1955.

Truck & Driver

DVV, Road Transport Media Ltd, Sixth Floor, Chancery House, St Nicholas Way, Sutton, Surrey SM1 1JB
tel 020-8912 2142
email chris.turner@roadtransport.com
website www.truckanddriver.co.uk
Twitter @TRUCKNDRIVER

Monthly £3.85

News, articles on trucks, personalities and features of interest to truck drivers. Words and picture packages preferred. Preferred feature length: 500-1,500 words. Illustrations: digital; cartoons. Payment: negotiable. Founded 1984.

Trucking

Kelsey Media, Cudham Tithe Barn, Berrys Hill, Cudham, Kent TN16 3AG
tel (01733) 347559
email trucking.ed@kelsey.co.uk
website www.truckingmag.co.uk
Twitter @truckingmag
Editor Andy Stewart
Monthly £4.20

For truck drivers, owner–drivers and operators: news, articles, features and technical advice. Length: 750–2,500 words. Illustrations: mostly 35mm digital. Payment: by negotiation. Founded 1983.

TV Times Magazine

Time Inc. (UK), 161 Marsh Wall, London, E14 9AP
tel 020-3148 5615
email tvtimes@timeinc.com
website www.whatsontv.co.uk
Editor-in-Chief Colin Tough
Weekly £1.80

Features with an affinity to ITV, BBC1, BBC2, Channels 4 and 5, satellite and radio personalities and TV generally. Length: by arrangement. Photographs: commissioned only. Payment: by arrangement.

25 Beautiful Homes

Time Inc. (UK), 161 Marsh Wall, London E14 9AP
email 25beautifulhomes@timeinc.com
website www.idealhome.co.uk/25-beautiful-homes
Twitter @25BHomesMag
Editor-in-Chief Deborah Barker
Monthly £4.30

Interiors magazine aiming to inspire affluent readers in their love for their homes. Each edition shows a selection of properties in the UK and Europe that have been renovated or built to a high standard. The magazine also features a selection of best buys in decorative accessories to help make beautiful homes achievable.

U magazine

Rosemount House, Dundrum Road, Dublin D14 P924, Republic of Ireland
tel +353 (0)1 2405300
email AOToole@harmonia.ie
website http://umagazine.ie
Twitter @U_Magazine
Editor Aisling O'Toole
Fortnightly €25.20 p.a. (Republic of Ireland), €76.20 p.a. (UK)

Fashion and beauty magazine for Irish women aged 18 to 25, with celebrity interviews, talent profiles, real-life stories, sex and relationship features, plus regular pages on the club scene, movies, music and film. Also travel, interiors, health, food, horoscopes. Material mostly commissioned. Payment: varies. Founded 1978.

Under 5

Pre-school Learning Alliance, 50 Featherstone Street, London EC1Y 8RT
tel 020-7697 2504
email editor.u5@pre-school.org.uk
website www.pre-school.org.uk
Twitter @under5mag
Editor Rachel Lawler
10 p.a. Free to members, £28.57 p.a. otherwise

Articles on the role of adults, especially parents/preschool workers, in young children's learning and development, including children from all cultures and those with special needs. Length: 750–1,000 words. Founded 1962.

Vanity Fair

The Condé Nast Publications Ltd, Vogue House, Hanover Square, London W1S 1JU
tel 020-7499 9080
website www.vanityfair.com
Twitter @VanityFair
Editor-in-Chief Radhika Jones
Monthly £4.90

Media, glamour and politics for grown-up readers. No unsolicited material. Payment: by arrangement. Illustrated.

The Vegan

The Vegan Society, Donald Watson House, 21 Hylton Street, Birmingham B18 6HJ
tel 0121 523 1730
email editor@vegansociety.com
website www.vegansociety.com
Editor Elena Orde
Quarterly £3, £12 p.a., free to members

Articles on health, nutrition, cookery, vegan lifestyles, land use, climate change, animal rights. Length: approx. 1,000 words. Illustrations: photos, cartoons, line drawings – foods, animals, livestock systems, crops, people, events; colour for cover. Payment: contributions are voluntary. Founded 1944.

VEGAN Life

Prime Impact, The Old School, Colchester Road, Wakes Colne, Colchester, Essex CO6 2BY
tel (01787) 224040
email olivia@primeimpact.co.uk
website www.veganlifemag.com
Editor Olivia Middlebrook
Monthly £4.99

Lifestyle magazine covering all things vegan. Interested in: vegan news; recipes; food and drink; celebrities, athletes, and artists; compassion pieces and animal rescue stories; restaurant reviews and vegan chefs; travel and leisure; health and nutrition; and in-depth features on the food industry, animal agriculture and exploitation, vegan advocacy etc. Length: generally 1,000–2,000 words, but flexible according to value of the article/feature. Images: writers and contributors should try to source their own large, hi-res images wherever possible. Payment: all contributions are voluntary. Writers credited for the pieces and bylines offered on request.

Vegetarian Living

Select Publisher Services Ltd, PO Box 6337, Bournemouth BH1 9EH
tel (01202) 586848
email lindsey@vegmag.co.uk
website www.vegetarianliving.co.uk
Editor Lindsey Harrad
Monthly £4.95

Aimed anyone interested in vegetarian and vegan cooking. Articles on high-profile chefs, food writers and celebrities; kitchen skills tutorials; healthy living and nutrition; eco/green ideas and community schemes/projects. Welcomes ideas for articles and features.

Veggie

Aceville Publications, 25 Phoenix Court, Hawkins Road, Colchester CO2 8JY
tel (01206) 508627
email holly.treacy@aceville.co.uk
website www.vegetarianrecipesmag.com
Contact Holly Treacy
Monthly £4.99

Aimed at fans of meat-free cookery. Features recipes from a variety of cuisines and for diverse dietary requirements.

Viz

Dennis Publishing Ltd, 31–32 Alfred Place, London WC1E 7DP
tel 020-3890 3890
email viz@viz.co.uk
website www.viz.co.uk
10 p.a. £3.20

Cartoons, spoof tabloid articles, spoof advertisements. Illustrations: half-tone, line, cartoons. Payment: £300 per page (cartoons). Founded 1979.

Vogue

Vogue House, 1 Hanover Square, London W1S 1JU
tel 020-7499 9080
email vogue.com.editor@condenast.co.uk
website www.vogue.co.uk
Editor Edward Enninful
Monthly £3.99

Fashion, beauty, health, decorating, art, theatre, films, literature, music, travel, food and wine. Length: articles from 1,000 words. Illustrated.

Waitrose Food

John Brown Media, 8 Baldwin Street, London EC1V 9NU
tel 020-7565 3000
email waitrosefood@waitrose.co.uk
Editor William Sitwell
Monthly £2 (free to MyWaitrose members)

In-house magazine of the Waitrose Group. Features seasonal recipes, menu ideas and interviews.

walk

The Ramblers, 2nd Floor, Camelford House, 87–90 Albert Embankment, London SE1 7TW
tel 020-7339 8540
email matthew.jones@ramblers.org.uk
website www.walkmag.co.uk
Editor Matthew Jones
Quarterly £3.60 Free to members

Magazine of the Ramblers, Britain's walking charity. Articles on walking, access to countryside and related issues. Material mostly commissioned. Length: up to 1,500 words. Illustrations: colour photos, preferably hi-res, digitally supplied. Payment: by agreement. Founded 1935.

Wallpaper*

Time Inc. (UK), The Blue Fin Building, 110 Southwark Street, London SE1 0SU
email contact@wallpaper.com
website www.wallpaper.com
Twitter @wallpapermag
Editor Sarah Douglas
12 p.a. £8.75

Design, interiors, art, architecture, fashion and travel. For payment information, see: www.magazinesdirect.com/wallpaper. Founded 1996.

Wanderlust

PO Box 1832, Windsor SL4 1YT
tel (01753) 620426
email editorial@wanderlust.co.uk
website www.wanderlust.co.uk
Editor-in-Chief Lyn Smith
8 p.a. £4.50

Features on independent, adventure and special-interest travel. Visit www.wanderlust.co.uk/about for contributor guidelines. Length: up to 2,500 words. Illustrations: hi-res colour slides or digital. Payment: by arrangement. Founded 1993.

The War Cry

The Salvation Army, 101 Newington Causeway, London SE1 6BN
tel 020-7367 4900
email warcry@salvationarmy.org.uk
website salvationarmy.org.uk/warcry
Editor Major Nigel Bovey
Weekly 20p

Voluntary contributions: Human interest stories of personal Christian faith. Founded 1879.

Wasafiri

School of English and Drama,
Queen Mary University of London, Mile End Road,
London E1 4NS
email wasafiri@qmul.ac.uk
website www.wasafiri.org
Editor-in-Chief Susheila Nasta
4 p.a. £51 p.a. (print only), £51 (online only), £61 p.a. (print and online)

International contemporary literature. Accepts submissions for fiction, poetry, articles and interviews; see website for details. Founded 1984.

Waterways World

Waterways World Ltd, 151 Station Street,
Burton-on-Trent DE14 1BG
tel (01283) 742950
email editorial@waterwaysworld.com
website www.waterwaysworld.com
Editor Bobby Cowling
Monthly £4.50

Feature articles on all aspects of inland waterways in Britain and abroad, including historical material; factual and technical articles preferred. No short stories or poetry. See website for notes for potential contributors (under the contact section). Illustrations: digital, colour transparencies or prints, line. Payment: £70 per page (including illustrations). Founded 1972.

The Week

32 Queensway, London W2 3RY
tel 020-3890 3890
email editorialadmin@theweek.co.uk
website www.theweek.co.uk
Editor-in-Chief Jeremy O'Grady
Weekly £3.50

Magazine that distils the best from the British and foreign press into 44pp, including news, art, science, business, property and leisure. Founded 1995.

The Weekly News

D.C. Thomson & Co. Ltd, 2 Albert Square,
Dundee DD1 1DD
tel (01382) 575850
email weeklynews@dctmedia.co.uk
Weekly £1.30

Send fiction submissions to weeklynewsfiction@dctmedia.co.uk.

Weight Watchers Magazine

The River Group, 16 Connaught Place,
London WC2 2ES
tel 020-7420 7000
email wwmagazine@riverltd.co.uk
12 p.a. £2.99, £2 for members

Features: health, beauty, news; food-orientated articles; success stories: weight-loss, motivation, wellbeing. All material commissioned. Length: up to 3pp. Illustrations: colour photos and cartoons. Payment: by arrangement.

What Car?

Haymarket Motoring Magazines Ltd, Bridge House,
69 London Road, Twickenham TW1 3SP
tel 020-8267 5688
email editorial@whatcar.com
website www.whatcar.com
Editorial Director Jim Holder
Monthly £5.99

Road tests, buying guide, consumer stories and used car features. No unsolicited material. Illustrations: colour and b&w photos, line drawings. Payment: by negotiation. Founded 1973.

What's On TV

Time Inc. (UK), 161 Marsh Wall, London E14 9AP
tel 020-3148 5928
email wotv.enquiries@timeinc.com
website www.whatsontv.co.uk
Editor-in-Chief Colin Tough
Weekly 65p

Features on TV programmes and personalities. All material commissioned. Length: up to 250 words. Illustrations: colour and b&w photos. Payment: by agreement. Founded 1991.

The White Review

243 Knightsbridge, London SW7 1DN
email editors@thewhitereview.org
website www.thewhitereview.org
Twitter @TheWhiteReview
Editors Ben Eastham, Jacques Testard
Quarterly £14.99

Contemporary arts and literature journal. Welcomes submissions of fiction, poetry, essays and interviews. See website for full submission details, but briefly: all fiction and non-fiction submissions should be in English, not have been published elsewhere and (poetry excepted) be at least 1,500 words long. Interview pitches also accepted, but see previous editions for style and tone. Email no more than three poems to poetry@thewhitereview.org; all other submissions should be sent to submissions@thewhitereview.org. Founded 2011.

WI Life

(formerly WI Home & Country)
104 New King's Road, London SW6 4LY
tel 020-7731 5777
email wilife@nfwi.org.uk
website www.thewi.org.uk/wie-and-wi-life
Twitter @WILifemagazine
Editor Sarah Drew Jones
8 p.a. as part of the WI subscription

Journal of the National Federation of Women's Institutes for England and Wales. Publishes material related to the Federation's and members' activities with articles of interest to active women engaged in their communities and campaigns, mainly written in-house and by WI members but some freelance opportunities. Illustrations: colour photos and artwork. Payment: by arrangement.

Woman

Time Inc. (UK), 161 Marsh Wall, London E14 9AP
tel 020-3148 5000
email woman@timeinc.com
website www.womanmagazine.co.uk
Editor-in-Chief Catherine Westwood
Weekly £1.15

News, celebrity and real-life features, of no more than 1,000 words. Particular interest in celebrity and diet exclusives. Digital images only. Read magazine prior to submission. Fiction not published. Payment: by negotiation. Founded 1937.

Woman Alive

(formerly Christian Woman)
Christian Publishing and Outreach, Garcia Estate, Canterbury Road, Worthing, West Sussex BN13 1BW
tel (01903) 604352
email womanalive@cpo.org.uk
website www.womanalive.co.uk
Editor Jackie Harris
Monthly £3.95

Aimed at women aged 25 upwards. Celebrity interviews, topical features, Christian issues, profiles of women in interesting occupations, Christian testimonies and real-life stories, fashion, beauty, travel, health, crafts. All feature articles should be illustrated. Length: 700–1,800 words. Payment £55–£160. Founded 1982.

woman&home

Time Inc. (UK), 161 Marsh Wall, London E14 9AP
tel 020-3148 5000
email W&Hmail@timeinc.com
website www.womanandhome.com
Editorial Director Kath Brown
Monthly £4.50

Centres on the personal and home interests of the lively minded mature, modern woman. Articles dealing with fashion, beauty, leisure pursuits, gardening, home style; features on topical issues, people and places. Fiction: complete stories from 3,000–4,500 words in length. Illustrations: commissioned colour photos and sketches. Non-commissioned work is not accepted and cannot be returned. Founded 1926.

Woman's Own

Time Inc. (UK), 161 Marsh Wall, London E14 9AP
tel 020-3148 5000
email womansown@timeinc.com
website www.womansown.co.uk
Editor-in-Chief Catherine Westwood
Weekly £1.15

Modern women's magazine aimed at the 35–50 age group. No unsolicited features. Address work to relevant department editor. Payment: by arrangement.

Woman's Way

Harmonia Ltd, Rosemount House, Dundrum Road, DublinD14 P924, Republic of Ireland
tel +353 (0)1 2405318
email atoner@harmonia.ie
website www.womansway.ie
Editor Áine Toner
Weekly €1.59

Human interest, personality interviews, features on fashion, beauty, celebrities and investigations. Founded 1963.

Woman's Weekly

Time Inc. (UK), 161 Marsh Wall, E14 9AP
tel 020-3148 5000
email womansweeklypostbag@timeinc.com
website www.womansweekly.com
Facebook www.facebook.com/WomansWeekly
Editor Diane Kenwood
Weekly £1.05

Lively, family-interest magazine. Unsolicited short stories currently not accepted. Celebrity and strong human interest features, health, finance and consumer features, plus beauty, diet, travel, homes, craft, knitting, gardening and cookery; also inspirational and entertaining personal stories. Illustrations: full colour fiction illustrations, small sketches and photos. Payment: by arrangement. Founded 1911.

Woman's Weekly Fiction Special

Time Inc. UK, 161 Marsh Wall, E14 9AP
tel 020-3148 5000
email womansweeklypostbag@timeinc.com
Editor Gaynor Davies
12 issues p.a. £1.99

Minimum 20 stories each issue of 1,000–8,000 words of varied emotional interest, including romance, humour and mystery. Payment: by arrangement. Illustrations: full colour. Founded 1998.

Women Together

(formerly Scottish Home and Country)
19 Victoria Street, Aberdeen AB10 1UU
tel (01224) 646491
email magazine@theswi.org.uk
website www.swri.org.uk
Monthly £2

Articles on crafts, cookery, travel, personal experience, rural interest, women's interest, health, books. Length: up to 1,000 words, preferably illustrated. Illustrations: hi-res jpg/tif files, prints, cartoons and drawings. Payment: by arrangement. Founded 1924.

The Woodworker

MyTime Media Ltd, Enterprise House,
Enterprise Way, Edenbridge, Kent TN8 6HF
tel 0844 848 8822
website www.getwoodworking.com
Editor Mark Cass
Monthly £4.75

For the craft and professional woodworker. Practical illustrated articles on cabinet work, carpentry, polishing, wood turning, wood carving, rural crafts, craft history, antique and period furniture; also wooden toys and models, musical instruments; timber procurement, conditioning, seasoning; tools, machinery and equipment reviews. Illustrations: line drawings and digital photos. Payment: by arrangement. Founded 1901.

World Fishing & Aquaculture

Spinnaker House, Waterside Gardens,
Fareham PO16 8SD
tel (01329) 825335
email editor@worldfishing.net
website www.worldfishing.net
Editor Quentin Bates
11 issues p.a. £132 p.a.

International journal of commercial fishing. Technical and management emphasis on catching, processing and marketing of fish and related products; fishery operations and vessels covered worldwide. Length: 500–1,500 words. Illustrations: photos and diagrams for litho reproduction. Payment: by arrangement. Founded 1952.

The World of Interiors

The Condé Nast Publications Ltd, Vogue House,
1 Hanover Square, London W1S 1JU
tel 020-7499 9080
website www.worldofinteriors.co.uk
Editor-in-Chief Rupert Thomas, *Editorial Manager* Augusta Pownall
Monthly £4.99

All material commissioned: send photographs/synopsis for article ideas. Length: 1,000–1,500 words. Illustrations: colour photos. Founded 1981.

World Soccer

Time Inc. (UK), The Blue Fin Building,
110 Southwark Street, London SE1 0SU
tel 020-3148 5000
email worldsoccer@timeinc.com
website www.worldsoccer.com
Editor Gavin Hamilton
Monthly £4.90

Articles, features, news concerning football, its personalities and worldwide development. Length: 600–2,000 words. Payment: by arrangement. Founded 1960.

The World Today

Chatham House, 10 St James's Square,
London SW1Y 4LE
tel 020-7957 5712
email afrimston@chathamhouse.org
website www.chathamhouse.org/publications/twt
Editor Alan Philps, *Deputy Editor* Agnes Frimston
6 p.a. £38 p.a. (£137 p.a. institutions, £30 p.a. students)

Analysis of international issues and current events by journalists, diplomats, politicians and academics. Length: 800–1,500 words. Payment: nominal. Founded 1945.

Writing Magazine

Warners Group Publications, 5th Floor,
31–32 Park Row, Leeds LS1 5JD
tel 0113 200 2929
email jonathant@warnersgroup.co.uk
website www.writers-online.co.uk
Facebook www.facebook.com/writingmagazine
Twitter @writingmagazine
Editor Jonathan Telfer
Monthly £4.10, £39.90 p.a. (by Direct Debit; £45 p.a. otherwise. Includes *Writers' News*.)

Articles on all aspects of writing. Length: 800–2,000 words. Payment: by arrangement. Founded 1992. In addition, *Writers' News* (now part of *Writing Magazine*) features news, competitions and market information. Length: up to 350 words. Payment: by arrangement. Founded 1989.

Yachting Monthly

Time Inc. (UK), Pinehurst 2, Pinehurst Road,
Farnborough Business Park, Farnborough GU14 7BF
tel (01252) 555213
email yachting.monthly@timeinc.com
website www.yachtingmonthly.com
Editor Theo Stocker
Monthly £4.80

Articles on all aspects of seamanship, navigation, the handling of sailing craft, and their design, construction and equipment. Well-written narrative accounts of cruises in yachts. Length: up to 1,500 words. Illustrations: colour transparencies and prints, cartoons. Payment: quoted on acceptance. Founded 1906.

Yachting World

Time Inc. (UK), Pinehurst 2, Pinehurst Road,
Farnborough Business Park, Farnborough GU14 7BF
tel (01252) 555000
email yachting.world@timeinc.com
website www.yachtingworld.com
Editor Elaine Bunting

Monthly From £19.99 p.a. (print)

Practical articles of an original nature, dealing with sailing and boats. Length: 1,500–2,000 words. Illustrations: digital files, drawings, cartoons. Payment: varies. Founded 1894.

Yachts and Yachting

The Chelsea Magazine Company, Jubilee House, 2 Jubilee Place, London SW3 3TQ
email georgie.corlett-pitt@chelseamagazines.com
website www.yachtsandyachting.co.uk
Editor Georgie Corlett-Pitt
Monthly £6

Technical sailing and related lifestyle articles. Illustrations: line, half-tone, colour. Payment: by arrangement. Founded 1947.

Yorkshire Life

PO Box 163, Ripon HG4 9AG
tel (01765) 692586
website www.yorkshirelife.co.uk
Editor Esther Leach
Monthly £3.99

Articles on Yorkshire, including places of interest, high-profile personalities, local events, arts, history and food. Unsolicited ideas welcome. Founded 1946.

You & Your Wedding

Immediate Media Co. Ltd, Vineyard House, 44 Brook Green, London W6 7BT
tel 020-7150 5373
website www.youandyourwedding.co.uk
Facebook www.facebook.com/youyourwedding/
Twitter @YouYourWedding
7 p.a. £5.50

Features, trends and news covering all aspects of planning a wedding. Submit ideas by email. Illustrations: colour. Payment: negotiable.

Your Cat Magazine

BPG Media, 1–6 Buckminster Yard, Buckminster, Grantham, Lincs. NG33 5SB
tel (01476) 859820
email editorial@yourcat.co.uk
website www.yourcat.co.uk
Facebook www.facebook.com/yourcatmagazine
Contact Mel Hudson
Monthly £3.60

Practical advice on the care of cats and kittens, general interest items and news on cats, and true-life tales and fiction (commission only). Length: 800–1,500 words (articles), 200–300 words (news), up to 1,000 words (short stories). Illustrations: hi-res digital, colour transparencies and prints. Founded 1994.

Your Dog Magazine

BPG Media, 1–6 Buckminster Yard, Buckminster, Grantham, Lincs. NG33 5SB
tel (01476) 859830
email editorial@yourdog.co.uk
website www.yourdog.co.uk
Facebook www.facebook.com/yourdogmagazine
Twitter @yourdog
Editor Sarah Wright
Monthly £3.99

Articles and information of interest to dog lovers; features on all aspects of pet dogs. Length: approx. 800–1,500 words. Payment: £140 per 1,000 words. Founded 1994.

Your Horse Magazine

Bauer Media Group, Media House, Lynchwood, Peterborough Business Park, Peterborough PE2 6EA
tel (01733) 395052
email aimi.clark@bauermedia.co.uk
website www.yourhorse.co.uk
Facebook www.facebook.com/YourHorse
Editor Aimi Clark
13 issues p.a. £4.20

Practical horse care, riding advice and inspiration for riders and owners. Send feature ideas with examples of previous published writing. Specially commissions most material. Welcomes ideas for articles and features. Length: 1,500 words. Payment: £140 per 1,000 words. Founded 1983.

Yours

Bauer Consumer Media, Media House, Lynchwood, Peterborough Business Park, Peterborough PE2 6EA
tel (01733) 468000
email yours@bauermedia.co.uk
website www.yours.co.uk
Facebook www.facebook.com/Yoursmagazine
Twitter @yoursmagazine
Editor Sharon Red
Fortnightly £1.55

Features and news about and/or of interest to the over-50s age group, including nostalgia and short stories. Study of magazine essential; approach in writing in the first instance. Length: articles up to 300 words, short stories up to 1,200 words. Payment: at the Editor's discretion or by agreement. Founded 1973.

Syndicates, news and press agencies

Before submitting material, you are strongly advised to make preliminary enquiries and to ascertain terms of work. Strictly speaking, syndication is the selling and reselling of previously published work although some news and press agencies handle original material.

Academic File Information Services

Academic File International Syndication Services, EAPGROUP International Media, PO Box 13666, London SW14 8WF
tel 020-8392 1122
email afis@eapgroup.com
email main@eapgroup.com
website www.eapgroup.com
Twitter @eapgroupnews
Commissioning Editor Sajid Rizvi

Feature and photo syndication with special reference to the developing world diasporic and migrant and and immigrant communities in the West. Founded 1985.

AFP (Agence France-Presse)

Floor 15, 200 Aldersgate, Aldersgate Street, London EC1A 4HD
tel 020-776 2740
email london.economics@afp.com
website www.afp.com

Major news agency with journalists in more than 150 countries across five geographical zones.

Neil Bradley Puzzles

Linden House, 73 Upper Marehay, Ripley, Derbyshire DE5 8JF
tel (01773) 745599
email bradcart@aol.com
Director Neil Bradley

Supplies visual puzzles to national and regional press; emphasis placed on variety and topicality with work based on current media listings. Daily single frame and strip cartoons. Founded 1981.

Brainwarp

23 Chatsworth Avenue, Culcheth, Warrington, Cheshire WA3 4LD
tel (01925) 765878
email sarah@brainwarp.com
website www.brainwarp.com
Contacts Trixie Roberts, Tony Roberts, Sarah Simmons

Writes and supplies original crosswords, brainteasers, wordsearches, quizzes and word games to editors for the printed page. Does not accept work from external sources. Standard fees for syndicated puzzles. Customised work negotiable. Founded 1987.

Bulls Presstjänst AB

Box 1228, 13128 Nacka Strand, Sweden
tel +46 8-55520600
website www.bullspress.com

Market: newspapers, magazines, weeklies and advertising agencies across Northern Europe. Syndicates human-interest picture stories; topical and well-illustrated background articles and series; photographic features dealing with science, people, personalities, glamour; genre pictures for advertising; condensations and serialisations of bestselling fiction and non-fiction; cartoons, comic strips, film and TV rights, merchandising and newspaper graphics online.

Cartoons & Wordgames

341 Stockport Road, Mossley, Ashton-under-Lyne OL5 0RS
tel (01457) 834883
email email@wordgames.co.uk
website www.wordgames.co.uk
Managing Editor Tom Williams

Long-term supplier to *Daily Mail* of crosswords and variety puzzles. Syndicated puzzles, plus gag cartoons, are available for UK and worldwide dailies, weeklies and magazines. Founded 1980.

Europress Features (UK)

18 St Chad's Road, Didsbury, Nr Manchester M20 4WH
tel 0161 445 2945
email europressmedia@yahoo.com

Representation of newspapers and magazines in Europe, Australia, United States. Syndication of top-flight features with exclusive illustrations – human interest stories – showbusiness personalities. 30–35% commission on sales of material successfully accepted; 40% on exclusive illustrations.

FAMOUS*

13 Harwood Road, London SW6 4QP
tel 020- 7485 1005
email pictures@famous.uk.com
website www.famous.uk.com/index.jsp

Celebrity picture and feature agency. Supplies showbiz content to newspapers, magazines, websites, TV stations, mobile phone companies, books and advertisers worldwide. Represents celebrity journalists and photographers from Los Angeles, New York, Europe and Australia, syndicating their copy around the globe. Open to new material. Founded 1990.

Foresight News

Centaur Media Plc, Profile Group, 79 Wells Street, London W1T 3QN
tel 020-7970 4299
email info@foresightnews.co.uk
website www.foresightnews.com
Editor and Associate Publisher Nicole Wilkins

Offers a vast, fully searchable database featuring thousands of forthcoming events and news from across the UK and around the world, spanning a variety of sectors including politics, business, crime and home affairs, health, entertainment and sport.

Guardian Syndication

Kings Place, 90 York Way, London N1 9GU
tel 020-3353 2539
email permissions.syndication@guardian.co.uk
website http://syndication.theguardian.com/
Contact Helen Wilson

International syndication services of news and features from the *Guardian*, the *Observer* and theguardian.com. Unable to syndicate content which has not been published in its own titles. All permission requests to be submitted via online form.

Hayters Teamwork

47 Dean Street, London W1D 5BE
tel 020-7183 6727
email sport@hayters.com
website www.hayters.com
Twitter @HaytersTeamwork

Sports news, features and data supplied to all branches of the media. Commission: negotiable according to merit. Founded 1955.

Headliners

Rich Mix, 35–47 Bethnal Green Road, London E1 6LA
tel 020-7749 9360
email enquiries@headliners.org
website www.headliners.org
Twitter @HeadlinersUK
Director Fiona Wyton

UK-wide news agency. Offers young people aged 8–18 the opportunity to write on issues of importance to them, for newspapers, radio and TV. Founded 1995.

Independent Radio News (IRN)

Academic House, 24–28 Oval Road, London NW1 7DJ
tel 020-3227 4044
email news@irn.co.uk
website www.irn.co.uk
Managing Director Tim Molloy

National and international news.

Knight Features Ltd

Trident Business Centre, 89 Bickersteth Road, London, SW17 9SH
tel 020-3051 5650
email info@knightfeatures.co.uk
website www.knightfeatures.com
Contacts Gaby Martin, Andrew Knight, Sam Ferris

Worldwide selling of puzzles, strip cartoons, crosswords, horoscopes and serialisations for print and digital media. Agent in the UK and Republic of Ireland for Creators Syndicate, Tribune Content Agency. Founded 1985.

London at Large Ltd

Canal Studios, 3–5 Dunston Road, London E8 4EH
tel 020-7275 7667
email laura@londonatlarge.com
website www.londonatlarge.com
Twitter @LdnAtLarge
Editor Chris Parkinson

Forward planner serving the media: lists press contacts for parties, celebrities, launches, premieres, music, film, video and book releases. Founded 1985.

National Association of Press Agencies

c/o Cavendish Press (Manchester) Ltd, 5th Floor, The Landing, BLUE, MediaCityUK, Salford Quays, Manchester M50 2ST
email enquiries@napa.org.uk
website www.napa.org.uk
Membership £250 p.a.

NAPA is network of independent, established and experienced press agencies serving newspapers, magazines, TV and radio networks. Founded 1983.

New Blitz Literary and Editorial TV Agency

Via di Panico 67, 00186 Rome, Italy
postal address CP 30047–00193, Rome 47, Italy
tel +39 06-4883268
email blitzgacs@inwind.it
Manager Giovanni A.S. Congiu

Syndicates worldwide: cartoons, comic strips, humorous books with drawings, feature material, topical. Average rates of commission 60/40%, monthly report of sales, payment 60 days after the date of sale.

PA (The Press Association)

292 Vauxhall Bridge Road, London SW1V 1AE
tel 020-7963 7001
website www.pressassociation.com
Chief Executive Clive Marshall, *Managing Director* Tony Watson

Provider of multimedia content and services, and the national news agency for the UK and Ireland. Customers include major national, regional and international media and digital brands, as well as businesses and public sector organisations. Services include: pictures; video; data APIs; hosted live blogs; graphics; listings pages; social media curation; and page production. Part of the PA Group of specialist media companies. Founded 1868.

The Puzzle House

Ivy Cottage, Battlesea Green, Stradbroke, Suffolk IP21 5NE
tel (01379) 384656
email enquiries@thepuzzlehouse.co.uk
website www.the-puzzle-house.co.uk
Partners Roy Preston & Sue Preston

Supply original crosswords, quizzes and puzzles of all types. Commissions taken on any topic, with all age ranges catered for. Wide selection of puzzles available for one-off usage. Founded 1988.

Rann Media

120 Molesworth Street, North Adelaide, SA 5006 Australia
tel + (61) 418 832 512
website www.rann.com.au
Managing Director Chris Rann

Professional PR, press releases, special newsletters, commercial and political intelligence, media monitoring. Welcomes approaches from organisations requiring PR representation or press release distribution. Founded 1982.

Sirius Media Services Ltd

Suite 3, Stowmarket Business Centre, Stowmarket Business Park, Stowmarket, Suffolk IP14 2AH
tel (01449) 678878
email info@siriusmedia.co.uk
website www.siriusmedia.co.uk

Crosswords, puzzles and quizzes.

Solo Syndication dmg media

Northcliffe House, 2 Derry Street, London W8 5TT
tel 020-7566 0360
website www.solosyndication.co.uk
Managing Director William Gardiner

Worldwide syndication of newspaper features, photos, cartoons, puzzles and strips. Represents the international syndication of Associated Newspapers Ltd (*Daily Mail*, *Mail on Sunday*, *Mail Online*, *Metro*) and Andrews McMeel Syndication (US) and Creators Syndicate (US) in Great Britain and Ireland, Africa and the Middle East.

The Telegraph – Content Licensing & Syndication

Telegraph Media Group, 111 Buckingham Palace Road, London SW1W 0DT
tel 020-7931 1010
email syndication@telegraph.co.uk
website www.telegraph.co.uk/topics/syndication-services/

News, features, photography & graphics, video, worldwide distribution and representation. Content licensing packages available for print or online use.

Visual Humour

5 Greymouth Close, Stockton-on-Tees TS18 5LF
tel (01642) 581847
email peterdodsworth@btclick.com
website www.businesscartoonshop.net
Contact Peter Dodsworth

Daily and weekly humorous cartoon strips; also single panel cartoon features (not gag cartoons) for possible syndication in the UK and abroad. Picture puzzles also considered. Submit photocopy samples only initially, with sae. Founded 1984.

WENN

4A Tileyard Studios, Tileyard Road, London N7 9AH
tel 020-7607 2757
email enquiries@wenn.com
website www.wenn.com

Provides the world's media with up-to-the-minute entertainment news and photos. Offices in Los Angeles, New York and Berlin. (Formerly World Entertainment News Network.)

Wessex News, Features and Photos Agency

Little Mead, Lower Green, Inkpen, Berks. RG17 9DW
tel (01488) 668308
email news@britishnews.co.uk
website www.britishnews.co.uk
Editor Jim Hardy

Freelance press agency with a network of writers and photographers across the UK. Providing real-life new stories and features for the national and international newspapers and magazines. Founded 1981.

Books

How to get published

The combined wisdom of the writers of the articles in this *Yearbook* provide some of the most up-to-date and best practical advice you will need to negotiate your way through the two main routes to publication. Whether you opt for the traditional route via an agent or the self-publishing model, there are key things it would be useful to consider before you begin.

There is increasing competition to get published. Hundreds of manuscripts appear in the inboxes of publishers and literary agents every week. Potential authors have to be really dedicated (and perhaps very lucky) to get their work published. That is one of the reasons so many writers are turning to self-publishing. So how can you give yourself the best chance of success whichever route you take?

1. Know your market

• Be confident that there is a readership for your book. Explore the intended market so you are sure that your publishing idea is both commercially viable and desirable to the reading public, agent or publisher.
• Know your competition and review the latest publishing trends: look in bookshops, at ebook stores, at online book sites, take an interest in publishing stories in the media and, above all, *read*. See *News, views and trends: review of the publishing year* on page 119.

2. Agent, publisher or do-it-yourself?

• First decide if you want to try and get signed by a literary agent and be published by an established publisher. Self-publishing in both print and electronically has never been easier, quicker or cheaper and can be a viable alternative to the traditional approach.
• If you opt for the agent/publisher model, decide whether you prefer to approach an agent or to submit your material direct to a publisher. Many publishers, particularly of fiction, will only consider material submitted through a literary agent. For some of the pros and cons of each approach, see *How literary agencies work* on page 419, *How to get an agent* on page 422, and *Understanding publishing agreements* on page 114. Whether you choose to contact an agent or a publisher, your work will be subjected to rigorous commercial assessment – see *Getting hooked out of the slush pile* on page 433.
• For information about self-publishing, consult *What do self-publishing providers offer?* on page 619, *Self-publishing online: the emerging template for sales success* on page 607 and *The Alliance of Independent Authors* on page 525.

3. Choose the right publisher, agent or self-publishing provider

• Study the entries in this *Yearbook*, examine publishers' lists and their websites, and look in the relevant sections in libraries and bookshops for the names of publishers which might be interested in your material.
• Take a look at the Contents list and the indexes in this *Yearbook* for lists of publishers, agents and other providers across all genres and forms of writing, everything from film scripts, to poetry and biography.

• Consult the *Children's Writers' & Artists' Yearbook 2019* (Bloomsbury 2018) for in-depth coverage of writing and publishing for the children's and young adult markets.
• Authors should not pay publishers for the publication of their work. There are many companies that can help you self-publish your book, for a fee; see *What do self-publishing providers offer?* on page 619. Make sure you know what it is the company will actually do and agree any fees in advance.
• Crowdfunding is becoming a viable option for some (see page 104).

4. Prepare your material well

• Presentation is important. If your material is submitted in the most appropriate electronic format an agent or publisher will be more inclined to give attention to it.
• Numerous manuscripts are rejected because of poor writing style or structure. A critique by an experienced editorial professional can help to iron out these weaknesses.
• It is understandable that writers, in their eagerness to get their work published as soon as possible, will send their manuscript out in a raw state. Do not send your manuscript to a literary agent or publisher and do not self-publish your script until it is *ready* to be seen. Wait until you are confident that your work is as good as it can be. Have as your mantra: edit, review, revise and then edit again. See *Editing your work* on page 661.

5. Approach a publisher or literary agent in the way they prefer

• Submit your work to the right person within the publishing company or literary agency. Look at the listings in this *Yearbook* for more details. Most agents will expect to see a synopsis and up to three sample chapters or the complete manuscript. Most publishers' and literary agents' websites give guidance on how to submit material, and should make clear if they accept unsolicited scripts by email or only by post. Many agents have a 'submissions' email link or button on their site.
• Always keep a backed-up copy of your manuscript. Whilst reasonable care will be taken of material in the possession of a publisher or agent, responsibility cannot be accepted if material is lost or damaged.

6. Write a convincing cover letter or email

• Compose your preliminary letter or email with care. It will be your first contact with an agent or publisher and needs to make them take notice of your book for the right reasons.
• When submitting a manuscript to a publisher, it is a good idea to let them know that you know (and admire!) what they already publish. You can then make your case about where your submission will fit in their list. Show them that you mean business and have researched the marketplace.
• What is the USP (unique selling point) of the material you are submitting? You may have an original authorial 'voice', or you may have come up with an amazingly brilliant idea for a series. If, after checking out the marketplace, you think you have something truly original to offer, then believe in yourself and be convincing when you offer it around.

7. Network

• Writing can be a lonely business – don't work in a vacuum. Talk to others who write in the same genre or share a similar readership. You can meet them at literature festivals, conferences and book or writers' groups. Consider doing a course – see *Writers' retreats and creative writing courses* on page 678.

• Go to a festival and be inspired. There are numerous literature festivals held throughout the year at which authors appear (see *Festivals and conferences for writers, artists and readers* on page 597).

• Join one of the numerous online communities, book review and manuscript share sites; see *Book sites, blogs and podcasts* on page 639.

Publishers' contracts

Following a publishing company's firm interest in a MS, a publisher's contract is drawn up between the author and the publisher (see *Understanding publishing agreements* on page 114). If the author is not entirely happy with the contract presented to them or wishes to take advice, he/she could ask their literary agent, the Society of Authors (see page 519) or the Writers' Guild of Great Britain (see page 522) to check the contract on their behalf – providing the author has an agent and/or is a member of those organisations. Or you can seek advice from a solicitor, but before consulting one, make sure that they are familiar with publishing agreements and can give informed advice. Many local firms have little or no experience of such work and their opinion can often be of limited value meaning that the cost may outweigh any possible benefit they can provide.

8. Don't give up!

• For an agent and publisher, there are many factors that have to be taken into consideration when evaluating the hundreds of submissions they receive each week, the most important of which is: 'Will it sell?'. See *What do publishers do?* on page 107.

• Be prepared to wait for a decision on your work. Editors and agents are very busy people so be patient when waiting for a response. Don't pester them too soon.

• Publishing is big business and it is more competitive than ever. Even after an editor has read your work, there are many other people involved before a manuscript is acquired for publication. People from the sales, marketing, publicity, rights and other departments all have to be convinced that the book is right for their list and will sell.

• The harsh reality of submitting a manuscript to a publisher or literary agent is that you have to be prepared for rejection. But many successful authors have received such rejections at some time so you are in good company.

• For advice from established writers on how they first got into print see the articles under *Writing advice* that start on page 267.

• Have patience and persevere. If the conventional route doesn't produce the results you were hoping for, consider the self-publishing route as a viable alternative.

Good luck!

Crowdfunding your novel

Alice Jolly discusses why she turned to crowdfunding to publish her memoir and subsequent novels, how the system works, its place as an alternative to mainstream and self-publishing, and the pros and cons of this new publication option.

It is April 2014. I am in a bar in Soho, talking to John Mitchinson, one of the founders of the crowdfunding publisher Unbound. He is interested in publishing a memoir I have written called *Dead Babies and Seaside Towns*. Our conversations about the book itself are straightforward but the wider purpose of our meeting is more problematic. He is thinking – *not the ideal person to crowdfund a book*. And I would have to agree with his unspoken assessment.

I'm a country mum, a quiet, academic type, who doesn't attend literary events. I have never used social media. On top of that, mainstream publishers have already told me that, no matter how good my memoir is, there is simply no market for it. Yet, despite these inauspicious omens, John has already decided he wants the book. And I agree to the crowdfunding idea because I am absolutely determined to get my memoir published.

Cut to June 2016 and I'm standing on a platform being awarded the Pen/Ackerley prize for that same memoir. John is in the audience and I catch his eye. Neither of us need to say – *well, that's stuck it to them!* It turns out that my book *did* need to be published ... and that crowdfunding was as good a way to publish it as any other.

On the basis of this experience, you might assume that I am something of an expert on crowdfunded publishing and that I would unreservedly recommend it to other writers. But the reality is more complicated. Although I have subsequently crowdfunded another two books with Unbound (both novels), I only really know about what *I* have done – and not much more; and although crowdfunding has been a good choice for me, that does not mean I would suggest every other writer should go down the same road.

The crowdfunding process

So how does a writer decide if crowdfunding might be a good choice for them? First, let me give a quick summary of how it works. The process starts with the writer submitting his or her idea (or book) to a crowdfunder such as, in my case, Unbound. Unbound are 'curated' crowdfunders and so (like any mainstream gate-keeping publisher) they decide whether or not they want that book. The important difference from a mainstream publishing is, however, that the company is run by three people who are writers themselves. If one of them wants to publish a certain book, then it will happen. This means that you won't be told: '*The editors loved your book but unfortunately the Sales and Marketing team just couldn't....*'

If Unbound agree to work with you, then they help you to put together a page on their website which will include a biography and an extract from your book. A short film will also be made which explains the book. This web page then becomes the tool which you will use to bring in pledges or – to put it more simply – to pre-sell copies of the book. This idea is far from new. It is actually the same as 'publishing by subscription', which was how many books were published in the 19th century.

If you chose Unbound's digital option, then you might need to raise £3,000 or £4,000. If you are going to be producing a hard-copy book, then the cost rises to £10,000 or £12,000, depending on length, illustrations, etc. The budget is something you discuss with Unbound and it can be adjusted. Once all of this has been agreed, then you have to bring in the pledges. Unbound have a well-developed social media presence and a huge mailing list, so that helps spread the word but, fundamentally, it is down to you, as the writer, to raise that money. That process is tough – very tough. You need thick skin, persistence and confidence in what you are doing. You will suffer many dark moments – but you will also regularly be amazed by the random generosity of people you have never even met.

Writers have a hundred different crowdfunding strategies. Some authors are highly professional and imaginative; others, like me, shamble through the whole thing, relying on the support of family and friends, slowly and painfully spreading the word by doing readings, and events and workshops.

Once the money is raised, Unbound operate in just the same way as any other publisher. They do the editing, proofreading, cover design, publicity and distribution. When the book is published, the writer does not get royalties as such but they receive a profit share of 50% (obviously much higher than the usual 10%). Although they are a small publisher, until recently Unbound had a distribution agreement with Penguin Random House and they now have a similar agreement with independent sales force PGUK.

From my own experience with my memoir, I know that Unbound can publicise and distribute a book widely. But, of course, the experience of one writer may be wildly different from that of another. How often have you actually heard a writer say how pleased they were by the publicity for their new book? More or less never, I would bet. As a breed, we tend to be naturally ungrateful and disappointed, even when we don't really have a reason to be so. All the same, we know that it is not the case that big publisher equals big publicity and small publisher equals small publicity. It all depends on the type of book, the timing, the status of the author, the personnel in the publicity department. A junior and inexperienced book publicist in a small publishing house can sometimes achieve great things if they have a passion for a particular title.

Comparisons with self-publishing

Of course, I am regularly asked – why don't you self-publish? I take my hat off to those who have chosen that route. I know that the potential financial gains are much greater. Those who do self-publish also tell me that the Unbound £10,000 budget is too high. But I've looked into it (comparing the cost with quality self-publishing) and I rather doubt that. If you want a beautiful book then the process is long, slow and expensive.

Book production values are a matter of personal choice but, as ever, if you want quality you have to pay for it. Personally I don't necessarily expect my books to sell thousands of copies but I would be desperately disappointed if they looked shoddy. I do not do curly, shiny covers and homespun cover design (daft, I know, but we've all got our petty little prejudices).

Although I know that self-publishing has worked well for some genre writers, there is little evidence that it works for more literary books. There is also the intractable question of time. I don't have IT or marketing skills and I don't particularly want to acquire them. I struggle to find time for my writing – there is no chance that I'd manage to be a publisher as well.

At a more fundamental level, I also want to be part of a collaborative process. Writing is a horribly lonely business. I need some people to celebrate with when it goes well, and to down a consoling glass with when it does not. Mainstream publishers, in general, seem to take a 'divide and rule' attitude to writers (... *For God's sake don't get more than two of them in a room together or they'll whinge incessantly*). Unbound, by contrast, have created an online forum for their authors. And yes, in that forum there are some challenging discussions, but there is also a huge amount of camaraderie, consolation and support, plus many examples of writers clubbing together to promote each other's books and organise readings and events.

A developing role for crowdfunding

I've described my experience with Unbound, but what other crowdfunding options are available? There are many on-line organisations who offer crowdfunding to novelists, although none (as far as I know) are 'curated' crowdfunders. Kickstarter is a platform which anyone can use to raise money, but that still leaves the writer with all the book production work. Might this approach be the worst of both worlds? I'm not qualified to judge. But do remember – publishing is not the same as printing.

So far Unbound have done well – their books have won major prizes, reached the bestseller lists and, perhaps most importantly, fuelled important debate, meaning that there are real benefits to being published by them. But what are the limits of this approach? Well, sadly, I don't think it can do much to improve diversity in publishing. It does return more money to the author than the mainstream model. And that's important given that the median earnings for a professional writers is approximately £11,000 (according to ALCS figures from 2013), far below the £17,900 which the Joseph Rowntree Foundation suggests is needed for a single person to reach the minimum income standard.

In addition, Unbound bravely publish anthologies which look at issues of social justice (notably *The Good Immigrant*, edited by Nikesh Shukla, 2016 and *Trans Britain*, edited by Christine Burns, 2018). However, the crowdfunding model itself will tend to favour those who already have a name, a reputation, a network.

Although a recent Arts Council report (*Literature in the 21st Century: Understanding Models of Support for Literary Fiction*, 2017) suggests that crowdfunding may be able to play a role in addressing the difficulties in publishing literary fiction, as one of the guinea pigs, I remain less than certain at this stage. But the reality is that, if a book is going to be hard to sell, it will usually to be hard to crowdfund as well.

As Unbound are still a new company, they are navigating a route through uncharted waters. Despite these challenges, I remain proud to be published by Unbound. I never really wanted to man the barricades with a bunch of publishing revolutionaries, but I am acutely aware that the range of books published by the mainstream industry has become increasingly narrow and that does need to change.

Unbound have made it possible for some of those challenging, difficult, eccentric books to be published which would otherwise languish in a box under a writer's bed. That matters to me. I passionately believe in a world where all the voices are heard, a world we need now more than ever. I've always preferred the 'out-crowd' to the in-crowd.

Alice Jolly is a novelist and playwright whose memoir *Dead Babies and Seaside Towns* (Unbound Digital 2015) won the 2015 Pen/Ackerley Prize. Her short story *Ray the Rottweiler* won the V.S. Pritchett Memorial Prize in 2014. She has published two novels with Simon and Schuster, *What The Eye Doesn't See* (2002) and *If Only You Knew* (2006), and with Unbound has two further novels: *Mary Ann Sate, Imbecile*, due out in June 2018 and *Between the Regions of Kindness* in 2019. Alice teaches Creative Writing at Oxford University. Her website is http://alicejolly.com/wp. Follow her on Twitter @JollyAlice.

What do publishers do?

Now that authors can successfully publish their own work, why are publishers still needed? Bill Swainson makes clear how vital the editor's experience and expertise – and that of designers, publicists and sales teams – are in bringing a book to market. Publishers manage and pay for all parts of the publishing process, with all departments working together to give your book the greatest chance of success.

In the age of digital publishing, when self-published authors can occasionally achieve spectacular success, you might think that publishers would by now have become extinct. After all, some types of book and book distribution have ceased to exist, so why not the people and companies who make them?

In 1894, when the private lending libraries like WH Smith and Mudie's stopped buying the popular three-decker novel (150,000 words of genteel excitement spun out to three volumes – the nice little earner that had sustained the private libraries and publishers for half a century) it was not so much the public's taste that had changed overnight, but a row over the costs of production and distribution and competing one-volume cheap editions that brought things to a head. Agreement could not be reached, with the result that the triple-decker disappeared almost at once. The publishers adapted, so did the writers and so, even, did the private lending libraries – at least for a while – and into the gap left by the three-decker slipped the slim modern novel by the likes of E.M. Forster, H.G. Wells and Virginia Woolf.

If one of today's commercially more challenging forms is the literary novel, the descendant of Forster et al., could this be the moment when the triple-decker wreaks its revenge? (One thinks, for example, somewhat mischievously of E.L. James' originally self-published *Fifty Shades of Grey*.) Maybe.

One of Britain's most successful writers, Rachel Abbott, has this to say about the realities of DIY publishing: 'The self-publishing model can look attractive because, depending on the price of the book, the author can take up to 70% of the proceeds of each sale – which is a bigger return than they would get through a traditional publisher. But it takes a lot of work to make those sales: when I started to follow my marketing plan for *Only the Innocent*, I was working 14 hours a day, seven days a week. For three months, not a word of a novel was written.' [*Guardian*, 30 March 2016] Rachel Abbott has made a hard-earned fortune with her self-published psychological thrillers and the writer in her has clearly decided to accept the periodic downside of long hours and no writing in exchange for 'the variety and the challenge' each self-publication presents.

And there's the point. It takes 'a lot of work' and, it should be remembered, a fair bit of money to publish a book successfully. While there will always be some energetic self-publishers – craftsmen like William Blake, William Morris and Walt Whitman – there have also been those who believed so strongly in what they had written that they paid for their own work to be published. Jane Austen (*Sense and Sensibility*, 1811), Marcel Proust (*Swann's Way*, 1913) and rather more recently Sergio de la Pava (*A Naked Singularity*, 2008, winner of the 2013 Pulitzer for Debut Fiction once it was commercially published) all took this route. In the end the books and their authors were vindicated and sustained even greater success when an enterprising publisher (John Murray for Jane Austen,

Gallimard for Proust, Chicago University Press for De la Pava) saw the opportunity that self-publishing had revealed and took on writers previously rejected.

Acquiring a book

So what is it that publishers actually do and how do they do it? In brief, they decide to back a writer's work and take on the financial risk involved in exchange for an advance against royalties in anticipation of income from print books, ebooks and rights sales that will exceed the initial outlay and yield a profit.

Every publishing company acquires its books from similar sources: from literary agents, publishers in other countries, direct commissions to authors and, very occasionally, from unsolicited submissions taken from what is unceremoniously dubbed the 'slush pile', although this is becoming very much rarer.

The in-house selection process goes something like this: the commissioning editor finds a book from among his or her regular weekly reading and makes a case for taking it on at an 'acquisitions meeting', which is usually attended by all the other departments directly involved in publishing the book, including editorial, digital, sales, marketing, publicity and rights; lively discussions follow and final decisions are determined by a mixture of commercial good sense (estimated sales figures, likely production costs and the author's track record) on the one hand, and conviction and taste (and remember the tastes of every company and every editor are different) on the other.

Paying for the rights

Traditionally authors earn royalties, a guarantee of which is paid up front in the form of an advance, and once that advance has earned out (i.e. once the royalties earned have matched the advance paid) all future royalties are paid to the author, usually via his or her agent. Often the returns are modest. Below are typical figures for a contemporary novel:

Advance: £10,000	***Earnings***	
	2,500 HBs @ £16.99 x av. 8% royalty =	£3,200
	5,000 PBs @ £8.99 x av. 6% royalty =	£2,697
	Total	**£5,897**

The starting hardback royalty is traditionally 10% of cover price (7.5% for the paperback), but there is usually a reduced royalty (typically four fifths of the agreed rate) on high discount sales which for most hardbacks start at about 50%, hence 8% in the example above. Export sales would be paid at the home royalty but on price received, so 10% of what's left after a, say, 70% discount.

These figures may look modest, and they are, but once a book really takes off they can also be substantial, even though such success is all too rare a phenomenon.

Other costs: design, production, distribution

There are also a whole host of other expenses, namely for: cover and text design; typesetting (styling and formatting of text); print, paper and binding; distribution (shipping the book to the bookseller and dealing with the return of unsold books); and marketing, sales and publicity costs. To these must be added the cost of converting the text to digital format for ebook (although soon this conversion stage and the associated editorial checking costs will be obviated by the preparation of all text in XML format) and the posting of the book with the e-distributor; in the UK, for example, that includes Amazon, iPad, Kobo, Tablet.

And finally there are the overheads: the office space; IT maintenance; photocopiers, etc.; and staffing costs – everyone from the receptionist and post-room staff to the sales team, publicists, marketeers, purchase ledger and royalty accountants, the MD or Ceo, and the person in a publishing house the author will usually have most to do with, the editor.

What do editors do?

Given all these costs, not to mention the booksellers' and e-tailers' costs, why not just self-publish digitally and cut out the middleman? Well, Rachel Abbott provides part of the answer: 'It's a lot of work'. Even when ebooks are successful (at peak moments in a traditionally published book's life digital sales can match or exceed print sales), what they cannot yet do, or rather what publishers have not yet found a way to do with any guarantee of success, is regularly generate the publicity that will attract readers. It doesn't mean it won't happen, but print and broadcast media, for all that they have a strong online presence (you only have to think of the *Guardian*, BBC or the *Daily Mail*'s internet reach), do not yet compete with what's left of traditional media for bringing a book to the public's attention, and ebook sales are still mostly driven by those in the 55–75 age range buying titles, usually for their Kindles and iPads.

However, digital publishing does not suit every kind of book and, while some writers might be confident in their ability to produce a word-perfect text, there are many – whether novelists or historians, scientists or chefs – who value the collaborative process that editing involves. Like translators, who must be the closest readers of all, editors must also stand at a distance and coolly assess the text the writer has slaved over and is now perhaps too close to review clearly. Here is William Plomer of Jonathan Cape writing to Ian Fleming after his first reading of the typescript of *Moonraker*: 'Have just finished and much enjoyed the new book . . . I have been through it with minute care and a pencil & have applied both to your punctuation and spelling. You don't have to accept my corrections but they are reasoned ones.' And here is Ian Fleming responding to Plomer, whom he had come to trust completely, about the latter's notes on *Doctor No*: 'I note the ghastly clichés. How awful it is that so many slip by when one is making little effort to write "well". I will attend to them.' The editorial process almost always improves the quality of a book, focusing on continuity, tone, pacing, argument, plot or characterisation. It is a kind of peer review but, in the editor's case, a peer whose ultimate aim is to help the writer to achieve the best possible expression of his or her narrative or argument. And, while that work could be dispensed with, readers would be the poorer for it.

Sales, rights, marketing and publicity

Getting the text right is one thing, but taking it to market is quite a different matter. Here publishing is at its most collaborative with marketing, sales and publicity working closely together to interest retailers and potential readers. There used to be clearer divisions between these roles, with marketing providing the sales team with the material to get the books into the shops and publicity working with both to get the books out of the shops and into the readers' hands. Today – while publishing is no longer exclusively about physical books, or even ebooks sold through e-tailers, but includes internet subscription models like Drama Online (www.dramaonlinelibrary.com) or Encyclopædia Britannica (www.britannica.com), or online magazines like *Words without Borders* (www.wordswithoutborders.org) and Salon.com, or a mixture, like the enterprising And

Other Stories (www.andotherstories.org) – the aim remains to persuade customers to buy what the publisher is selling. The means at the disposal of marketing, sales and publicity departments, now including Twitter, YouTube, vimeos, specialist blogging and vlogging, etc, may have changed, but publishers still have to get a reader's and, crucially, a purchaser's attention. Generally, this is easier for a professional company to achieve than the individual, however well connected, working alone.

Good luck

How the publisher balances these costs against income in order to create a company that pays its bills and makes the profits that allow reinvestment in new books and production is one of the great conjuring tricks of publishing. Whether you're publishing graphic novels, erotica, fine art, commercial, historical or literary fiction, history, current affairs, natural history or sports, a publisher is involved in curation. His or her reputation is built on the quality of that curation and the effectiveness with which works and authors are championed in the marketplace. In a lively and energetic publisher there will always be a healthy and creative tension between curation and promotion, a sensitivity both to new talent and to new ways of finding readers for your authors. This creative tension between good commercial sense and taste, often driven by conviction and aided by luck, is at the heart of good publishing.

Bill Swainson has worked for small, medium and large publishers since 1976 and was a senior commissioning editor at Bloomsbury Publishing Plc for 15 years, where he edited non-fiction and fiction, including in translation. He is currently a literary consultant and freelance editor, who also publishes a portfolio list under his own name at MacLehose Press, and is editor at large for non-fiction at Oneworld.

See also...

- *Editing your work, page 661*
- *Understanding publishing agreements*, page 114

Debut success with an indie publisher

Wyl Menmuir describes the long, often uncertain and obscure path that led to his debut novel being written, and the encouragement, support and belief of others that helped him reach completion and success.

To say I achieved unexpected success with my debut novel is serious understatement. When I started to write *The Many*, I knew I would finish it and that was all. I would finish it – if only to prove to myself that I could. But a novel that would appear on bookshop shelves? A novel that people might buy? That was still the same vague dream I'd had since I first visited the library as a child.

Depending on which article you read, my first novel took me between two and three years to write. The truth is, I probably started three years earlier than that. I just didn't realise that was what I was doing when I was writing the stack of impenetrable short stories and novel openings on which I cut my fictional teeth (stories, incidentally, that remain locked in a drawer where they belong). It wasn't until something clicked, while I was on an Arvon 'Starting to Write' residential week (see page 678), that I worked out what I should really be working on. One of the tutors, Nikita Lalwani, challenged me to write the story that was at the back of my head, bugging me to be written, the one I thought that I could not write. How she knew it was there still mystifies me but, of the tens of thousands of words I discarded as I wrote the novel, the thousand-word story I wrote that afternoon sits at the heart of *The Many*, pretty much as I wrote it. When I got home though, when the rush of the course dissipated, I realised I had no idea where I was going with it, or how to take those first few words and turn them into the novel I wanted it to be.

There's a vastly overused but useful metaphor which suggests that writing a novel is like going into the woods; it looks like a great idea from a distance, the canopy gleaming in the sunlight. At that point, there seem to be endless possibilities for taking your reader on a journey through those woods and leading them blinking into the sunlight at the other side, bemused and enlightened by the journey they've just taken. As a writer, what actually happens when you get to the edge of these literary woods is that there's no sign of a path at all. Or if there is a path, it's so well-worn – a fictional hollow-way trodden by too many before – that there's no point in following it. You discount the hollow-way but start to worry that you're going to lose your way immediately. Or step on a snake. Or get caught in the brambles. When I started, I had no idea of my destination. I had my thousand words from my week at Arvon but, aside from that, I felt I was picking my way through increasingly dense forest. For me at least, the novel-writing process is one in which I have to feel my way and most days I have no idea what I will write next.

My practice consisted of walking around Cornwall's coast out of season and spending hours in the small fishing villages I used as inspiration for the novel's setting. I skulked around fishing boats, watched the changing sea, took countless photographs and talked to obliging fishermen, and by the time I was back at my desk the next scene was ready to be uncovered. That's the part of the process with which no one can help you. As for everything else, I say take as much help as you can get.

Once I realised I had a novel on my hands, I signed up for an MA in Creative Writing at Manchester Metropolitan University. The course gave me much-needed deadlines and the support of a community of writers, all of whom were finding their way through their own literary woods. I signed up for an early version of the tracking and productivity app, Prolifiko (https://prolifiko.com; some writers might roll their eyes at the idea, but it worked for me, and I'm currently tracking my second novel in the same way). A novel happens in increments, in an incalculable number of changes so small it's often impossible to see the progress. That's where tracking my writing comes in. I have a marvellous capacity for self-deception, but the app made me accountable for getting words on the page. I set myself a modest target – 500 words a day – and over the weeks and months it helped me not only to see the progress I'd made but to keep going, which is invaluable when you're ready to throw the whole thing out of the window (a more common state than many writers would like to admit). As novelist and friend Liz Jenson so eloquently put it to me when I was despairing recently, 'We may lose hope, but we can still keep our appointment with the manuscript.' Anything that helps you to keep your appointment with the manuscript is worth its weight.

By the time you come to rewrites and editing, everything changes. You don't have to know what your novel is when you start, but by the time you're at the end you'd better be unambiguous about it. You have to be able to look back through the woods and see the wrong turns and dead ends as clearly as you do the path you want your reader to follow. After I'd written my first draft, I asked the author Steve Voake for his advice on editing and rewriting and he suggested I should summarise the novel in a single sentence, pin it up, and ask myself continually whether or not each scene moves the reader towards an understanding of this central statement. I was still looking at that note ten or eleven drafts in.

When I was close to finishing, my MA tutor, Nicholas Royle, suggested that Salt Publishing, for whom he is a commissioning editor, would be interested in publishing my novel. Choosing a publisher, like choosing an agent, is a matter of trust. You've spent possibly years crafting your novel, so you have to trust that your editor and publisher will care for it, that they will lift it further and help it to find the readers it deserves. It wasn't a hard choice. I already loved Salt's fiction list, in particular the work of Alice Thompson and Alison Moore. I had worked with Nicholas on the novel already through my MA; he understood the book I wanted to write and I trusted his judgement. Then there was the question about going with a small, independent publisher. At its best, small and independent means nimble and risk-taking. It means committed. Knowing Nicholas and the novels I'd read of theirs, I felt that Salt was all of the above. And whether or not a larger publisher would have put the novel up for the Man Booker Prize over the other titles on their list, I'll never know. What I do know is that Salt did. They believed in my strange, short novel.

The day before the Man Booker longlist came out in 2016, I wrote my predictions in the margin of the *Guardian*. My novel wasn't on the list I wrote, and it didn't even cross my mind that it might be. It seemed too far removed, the domain of Kazuo Ishiguro, Hilary Mantel and Graham Swift, writers who occupied another space entirely. Only then it wasn't. When the longlist was announced, I wasn't even listening out for it. I ignored my phone when it rang. 'You realise this changes everything?' my publisher asked me when I finally answered. I didn't. But it did. It continues to change everything. It has meant a huge boost in confidence, readers in far greater numbers than I could have hoped for, festival appearances, articles and another novel on the way. I wrote the novel I needed to write, the one that was nagging at the back of my head and wouldn't leave me be until it was down on paper, not the one I thought I ought to write. And that (to paraphrase a prince of the woodland metaphor) has made all the difference.

Shortly after I started writing, I stuck a Post-it® above my desk repeating Neil Gaiman's singularly useful piece of advice: 'Finish what you start'. It sounds prosaic, but I need that advice so much that I now have it carved into the surface of my desk as a constant reminder. It took me three, four, or seven years (take your pick), eleven drafts and countless incremental changes to finish *The Many*. And I'd like to pass Gaiman's sage words on to you. However long it takes – however many drafts, wrong turns, dead ends and backtracking it takes to get there – finish what you start. You never know where it might take you.

Wyl Menmuir is author of the novel *The Many* (Salt Publishing 2016), longlisted for the 2016 Man Booker Prize, *Rounds* (Nightjar Press 2016) and *In Dark Places* (National Trust 2017). He is based in Cornwall and is co-creator of the Cornish writing centre, The Writers' Block. Wyl teaches creative writing at Falmouth University and Manchester Metropolitan University and works as a freelance editor and literacy consultant. His website is http://wylmenmuir.co.uk. Follow him on Twitter @Wylmenmuir.

Understanding publishing agreements

Publishers usually require authors or their agents to sign a written legal contract when they decide to publish a book. Gillian Haggart Davies demystifies some of the clauses in such agreements.

Publishing agreements are contracts governed by contract law, the defining feature of which is that it treats parties to the contract as being of equal standing. In other areas the law deems that there is a 'weaker party' who needs to be protected, for example in employment law a person with a disability/physical impairment or a pregnant employee is deemed 'weaker' than the employer organisation. But this is not so with publishing agreements, albeit that we all know the reality of the situation: the author/writer is the one (usually) who wants a publishing deal and the publisher, in certain circumstances, can take it or leave it so can dictate the terms.

If you have a literary agent, she or he should handle all these issues for you; and if you are a member of the Writers' Guild (see page 522), the NUJ (page 538) or the Society of Authors (see page 519), they will help review the details of a contract. The main resource for lawyers in this field is *Clark's Publishing Agreements* (ed. Lynette Owen; Bloomsbury Professional, 9th edn 2013) which sets out standard form contracts for various kinds of publications. The contract for 'General book–author–publisher' has 35 clauses, some of which are 'legal nuts and bolts' and need not concern us too much – they are there to ensure the contract operates properly and can be enforced (e.g. 'Arbitration', 'Interpretation', 'Entire Agreement', '*force majeure*', 'Notices'). According to *Clark's*, 'The contract should empower both author and publisher with the confidence that each party will do its job to mutual advantage', and that a simple structure underlies all publishing contracts:

> 'The author owns the copyright in their work. In return for various payments, he/she licenses to the publisher, primarily exclusively, the right principally as readable text (printed book and ebook) to create multiple copies of that book and the further right to license others to exploit it in both readable text and other forms. The author writes; the publisher invests; from sales of copies of the book that they create together and the licensing of rights in it, the author earns royalties and other earnings, and the publisher makes its profit. It is as simple – and as complicated – as that.'

You may also want to refer to the Publishers Association Code of Practice on Author Contracts (www.publishers.org.uk) to see what the publishing industry suggested standards are and consult *The Media and Business Contracts Handbook* by Deborah Fosbrook and Adrian C. Laing (Bloomsbury Professional, 5th edn 2014).

So, there is a basic structure, and some clauses are 'more fundamental' than others. We do have judicial precedent suggesting that at the very least a publishing contract, to be accepted by the courts as such, must have terms dealing with royalties (or fees), print run and form of publication (e.g. hardback, paperback, digital). It can be a contract with those three things alone, and even if it is an implied or a verbal agreement, and as such can be enforced (in that case successfully by an author against the publisher).

What follows are some of the other more significant clauses which will be key for writers. Whatever kind of contract you see, remember that in principle you can add, delete and amend any of the clauses in it. In practical terms, it will depend on how much clout you or your agent have as to whether your publisher will be happy to negotiate or not, and on the time available.

Rights

Rights are multiple and sub-divisible. You can license them outright or in part (e.g. sound recording not images, script not film, illustrations not text, English translation not other languages), and do so for a set period of time or forever (i.e. the duration of the copyright). You can choose the territory. You can grant exclusive or non-exclusive rights. *Clark's* lists 23 varieties of rights but that is not necessarily exhaustive.

It is key that you license and do not *assign* your rights, as assignation is almost impossible to reverse. If you must assign copyright, note that you would have a small chance of legal protection because the publisher may owe you 'fiduciary duties', i.e. be obliged to look after your best interests; but this would be very difficult and costly to enforce and the best advice would always be to *never* assign rights.

Most publishers will want 'all rights' and 'world rights', but you/your agent may want to negotiate to retain certain rights. Consider whether the publisher would consult you before transferring the rights to a third party: they should. Would the publisher act on your behalf if someone else is in breach of your copyright? Would the publisher protect your work to the best possible extent? For example, if the work is posted online, would it be tagged for permissions information to allow anyone who wants to reuse it to find you or the publisher to ask permission? Subsidiary rights include, for example, anthology rights.

Serial rights are generally offered as 'first' and 'second'. First serial rights are often retained by authors and refer to the right to publish elsewhere (e.g. in a magazine feature in advance of a book's publication). Second serial rights can belong to a different party and are often controlled by the publisher. They concern rights to reprint after publication.

There have been calls for less slicing up of the copyright cake into so many individual rights, with the industry increasingly accepting the need to take a '360-degree' approach to intellectual property. However, this is work in progress.

All of the above relates to the 'economic copyright' rights, but authors have moral rights too; see the PA Code of Practice on Author Contracts and the government's IPO website (www.gov.uk/government/organisations/intellectual-property-office).

Delivery, acceptance and approval

The publisher will want to ensure it is not committing itself to publishing work which is not what it commissioned, or not as expected, and should of course be able to reject or not proceed to publish work which is poor, or which seems factually incorrect or libellous (on which see new developments under Scots law below, referring to 'defamation' rather than libel under Scottish law) , or unlawfully copied from someone else. But what can you do if a publisher wants to reject your work for another reason, perhaps because the market or competition has changed since you were commissioned? The Society of Authors in the past used to advise writers not to sign 'acceptance' clauses for this type of reason, arguing that publishers should fully assess the work by asking for a synopsis and specimen chapters, rather than letting an author complete the work, submit it to them and have it rejected. You may be powerless to remove such a clause, but it is something to be aware of.

The Scottish Law Commission's draft Bill for 2018 includes:
- 'a defence of publication on a matter of public interest;
- a serious harm test, meaning that claimants would be required to prove serious harm before a claim can proceed;
- a single publication rule, so that the time limit for bringing a defamation claim applies from the first publication of a statement and is not reset every time that statement is shared, for example by re-tweeting;
- a reduction of the time limit for bringing a claim from three years to one year.'

Timing of publication may also be important. For example, if you are writing a law book and the publisher fails to send it to press within a reasonable time, the book may be so out of date as to be useless/unlawful, so your reputation would suffer as well as sales. You won't want to revise it without payment of a further fee. Another example may be that the publisher has budgetary reasons for the timing of publication or may want to link, say, a sports book with an event. These types of situations may be covered in a clause about 'Date of publication' or 'Publisher's responsibility to publish'.

Think about the details as well. What are you agreeing to deliver? For example, with some textbooks you may also be agreeing to deliver pictures as well as text, but is it clear who clears copyright permissions for the pictures? And who pays for this? The publisher may give you a budget to do this work or may just expect it to have been done, and if so, and if you have not done it, that could jeopardise the whole enterprise because it can be not only an expensive but potentially very lengthy process.

Some contracts may also require you to be around for editing queries within a certain time-period – failing which the publisher will bring someone else in to edit. Would you be happy with that? Is that a term in the contract? This also touches moral rights. Are you agreeing to future updates of the book within the fee?

Remember to check the termination clause ('break clause') too. No one is thinking about a relationship breaking down when a deal is being signed, but the reality is that things can go wrong and one party may want to get out. Publishing relationships tend to be personal and so in reality, if one party wants to go, the other party would probably be best served simply letting this happen.

If a publisher decides to shelve publication of your book, the publisher might be in breach of contract; but in practice, it would be very difficult for an author in that situation to get an order from the court forcing the publisher to honour the contract and publish – especially if the book hasn't been edited yet. The author would have to claim for damages, and probably for payment of advances as yet unclaimed (subject to the contract terms), and possibly for loss of earnings for future editions if this pivots around cancellation of a first edition. But this is all about power and reputation and the lesser-known/unknown author may struggle to win such a fight or be able to afford to go into battle in the first place. However, there is some hope here if you are looking for it – in *Malcolm* v. *OUP* [1994] EMLR 17 Court of Appeal, around £17,500 was awarded against the publisher in favour of the disappointed author (although the court costs could easily be around the same again for such an author).

Outside the law of contract, any author who considers they have been wrongfully treated may also look to other areas of the law to support their case (for damage to goodwill and reputation under copyright moral rights; defamation; passing off, etc).

Alternatively, a publisher may have to enforce its rights and publish despite an author wishing to back out (say, to go with another publisher). The publisher will be legally entitled to do so depending on what the author signed up to, so be mindful of how long you are agreeing to tie yourself into a deal and how soon you can get out of it, if it is possible to do so. Ultimately, if authors break their side of the deal they will probably have to pay back any advances, and potentially damages too (although the courts do say that the damages sum claimed must be reasonably quantifiable by the party claiming loss: a difficult point to prove if the book wasn't even written, never mind marketed). Again, it is about reputation and clout: see Penguin's legal action in 2012 against Elizabeth Wurtzel for failure to deliver a follow-up to *Prozac Nation* (and for return of a $33,000 advance).

Warranties and indemnities

With warranties and indemnities you 'warrant' to the publisher that you have done certain things like fact-checking, copyright clearance, checking there are no libellous or blasphemous or plagiarised statements and promise to 'indemnify' them against any losses they may suffer as a result of anything like that happening after publication. Indeed, careful publishers may want a lawyer to read your text to check for these things before publication. Is there a clause saying if this happens the publisher will bill you the author for the 'legalling'? I have seen some lawyer–authors strike warranties and indemnities out. In practice, you need to consider whether you would be in a financial position to indemnify a publisher against its loss – most individuals wouldn't be, especially against libel actions. (Remember, you cannot defame the dead but you can defame a business entity, so beware when writing blogs.) However, you may be confident that no issues will arise; or you may be happy that you are 'decree proof' (no point suing you, you have no money); or you may have professional indemnity or other insurance. Insurance is something authors should consider especially if writing on particular subjects (e.g. writing about medical dosages) or are of a certain profile.

Exclusion clauses and limitations of liability

The publisher may wish to exclude liability for certain eventualities. It may wish to exclude liability for any damage the author might suffer to her name because of the publication (loss of reputation), or might suffer 'loss of opportunity' (say if the contract is exclusive to one publisher and prevents it from taking the content off elsewhere). Note, however, that some contractual exclusions of liability – or purported exclusions – may fail (i.e. be legally unenforceable). This may be the case if a publisher tried to prevent an author from including parody or satire in her work, fearing it may cause offence to some other author. Such a clause would technically now be unenforceable (in copyright terms anyway) because parody, pastiche and satire are now 'allowed' as a defence to breach of copyright. That said, in practice, the subject of the parody could have other civil law remedies against the publisher and/or author. The late Ronnie Barker hated Ben Elton's *Not the Nine O'Clock News* pastiche entitled 'The Two Ninnies', but Ronnie Barker would probably never have thought that this was a copyright issue; it was insult and injury to his reputation and goodwill that mattered to him. The separate legal issues of libel and passing-off would arise. A publisher could also seek to avoid liability for those issues by including an exclusion clause in a publishing contract.

Royalty advances and payment

An 'advance' is an advance on royalties which will be earned on book sales. This is different from a flat fee that is paid for a commission. Obviously, royalties are a very good thing if sales are to be significant, but they are perhaps less useful to authors whose markets are small, i.e. academic or specialised areas, like children's book authors who receive lower royalty rates (5% of the book's published price rather than the 10% a writer of fiction for adults might receive), albeit perhaps dealing with larger volumes. Some novelists receive huge advances that are never recouped by the publisher; the writers will receive royalty statements reporting a deficit but most publishers do not expect that deficit to be repaid. Clarifying what would happen about a recouped advance is therefore crucial. (Keep royalty statements for tax reasons: declare royalties as 'income' not 'other expenses'; losses/recouped advances are 'expenses' for income tax.)

If you are to receive royalties only, or an advance on royalties, it is important that someone is actually going to market the book. The clause 'Production and promotion responsibility' refers to this.

If the royalties payable to you are expressed as a percentage of estimated receipts (what the publisher actually earns from the sale of your book) rather than as a percentage of the book's published price, you will want to ask the publisher what it estimates receipts will be. However, the publisher may wish that information to be confidential.

Date of payment

As an author, when do you want to be paid? Probably on receipt by the publisher of your typescript at the latest, if not on commission – depending on the job and your status. You do not want to be paid 'on publication' because for reasons beyond your control the book may never be published, for example due to the publisher going bust.

When does a publisher want to pay? Possibly not on receipt of the typescript because there is still the copy-editing, typesetting and printing to carry out.

Payment in three stages is pretty standard – on signature; on delivery of the typescript; and on the day of first UK publication. Four stages are also possible, the third stage broken down into publication of hardback and of paperback editions.

The contract

It is best to avoid adversity and dispute wherever possible. Bear in mind that most publishers will be using a precedent form, i.e. a pro forma document. This may be historical or inherited from another part of the publishing group or a subsidiary/parent group and edited for your particular publication, so do not be surprised if it needs tweaking or renegotiating on issues important to you. Perhaps try to be firm and understanding. The contract is possibly not the author's preferred focus, but it might also be a chore for the publisher.

Note too that you may have legal rights and remedies from areas of the law which are external to the contract, i.e. some things that are not explicitly written down in a contract may be enforceable by you under equity, breach of confidence, etc. The Contracts (Rights of Third Parties) Act 1999 might be interpreted by lawyers to mean that if an author tells the publisher to 'pay my royalties to my friend', the friend gains the legal right to sue the publisher under the contract if this does not happen.

Publishing agreements are a minefield but if you can think about what is most important for you, your publication and its markets, whilst also being aware of some of the issues noted above, you will at least be off to a good start.

Gillian Haggart Davies MA (Hons), LLB is the author of *Copyright Law for Artists, Designers and Photographers* (A&C Black 2010) and *Copyright Law for Writers, Editors and Publishers* (A&C Black 2011).

News, views and trends: review of the publishing year

Tom Tivnan reflects on a steady if unspectacular year in the book industry, but a third consecutive year of growth, with a rise in sales of middle-range authors and the children's sector, and featuring a marked feminist trend in both non-fiction and fiction and further revival of physical bookshops.

A good word to describe the last year in the books world might be 'meh'. Solid but unspectacular, there were no real blow-the-doors-off hits or breakout trends. Don't just take my word for it, listen to Waterstones' James Daunt. In the run-up to Christmas 2017, the boss of the UK's biggest specialist book chain called the previous 12 months a 'funny old year' and 'fallow' time, with few 'walloping bestsellers coming through'.

Daunt was not wrong, as some of the most anticipated books and authors did not quite perform up to expectations. Dan Brown's latest Robert Langdon thriller *Origin* (Bantam 2017) had £4.4m in hardback sales, but that was 20% down on his previous effort, *Inferno* (Bantam 2013). Paula Hawkins' *Into the Water* (Doubleday 2017) sold a not-too-shabby £1.7m, but that didn't come close to her all-conquering *The Girl on the Train* (Doubleday 2015). Despite two new titles in 2017, fitness and cookery star Joe Wicks' overall sales plummeted 56% compared to his monster 2016 (the poor lamb only sold £6.1m). E.L. James had another go with the money-for-old-rope rewriting of her original *Fifty Shades of Grey* series from the point of view of kinkster billionaire Christian Grey. But James's *Darker* (Arrow), released in November 2017, sold 205,000 copies in its first month on sale; her previous outing, *Grey* (Arrow 2016), shifted 887,000 units in its initial four weeks.

Yet (what do you know?) despite some of those big hitters swinging and missing, the books market still grew, albeit by the barest of margins. Print revenue in the UK through industry sales monitor Nielsen BookScan for the full year 2017 was £1.592bn, a wafer-thin 0.2% up on 2016. A tiny upwards bump, but if we look at this in context we can cheer, as this continues a winning run. In 2014, the books market plummeted to £1.395bn, the lowest point in 12 years, but 2017's slim rise means that booksellers and publishers have enjoyed the third year of growth on the trot.

If there is an emblematic book of the last 12 months, it might be Tim Marshall's *Prisoners of Geography*. Published in 2016 by the well-respected indie Elliott & Thompson, the title was championed by booksellers and a hit in its first year, earning £1.2m. Its 2017 matched 2016, but in – yes – a solid but unspectacular fashion. Marshall's book only hit the weekly top 50 twice during the course of the year, but was always in the top 200, selling between 2,500 to 3,000 copies, week in and week out, and it ended up the 35th bestselling book of the year.

The middle class

Perhaps the most interesting thing of the past year is that the jump in sales was not driven by the big brand authors but by that often much-maligned group, the midlist. There had been a trend over the last decade or so of rich authors getting richer, with the top 50 writers each year earning more and claiming a greater share of the overall market. But that changed in 2017, with the top 50 writers generating a smidgeon under £200m in print sales for the year. That's a decent chunk of change, but 13% down on what the top 50 chalked up in 2016. Conversely, there was growth for the middle range. There were 1,233 authors with sales between £100,000 and £250,000 last year, 128 more than 2016. Collectively, those writers shifted £188.9m, 11% up on 2016's cohort in the same sales range (I should underscore that that those figures are bookshop and online sales, not actual author earnings which are, alas, far lower).

In fact, it is astonishing to see how much of the UK book trade depends on vast swathes of authors who, quite frankly, aren't making all that much money from their blood, sweat and tears. Consider this: 5,093 authors had print sales of more than £10,000 in 2017, the bulk of whom (3,147) were in the £10,000 to £100,000 range. Collectively, those 5,093 authors shifted £893.4m last year, or 56% of the industry's £1.592bn in sales. This means that a massive part of the market – 44%, or £699m – came from authors having sub-five-figure sales through the tills last year. We often speak of the likes of J.K. Rowling, Lee Child, David Walliams and Julia Donaldson who rule the top of the bestseller lists. But they are standing on the shoulders of many authors who unfortunately earn very little.

Belle of the fall

But, of course, there were some authors who enjoyed a fab past 12 months. Walliams (helped by his illustrator Tony Ross) continued a winning run of form. The author's sales rose 20% to £16.5m and had *nine* titles on the 2017 top 50; no one has ever had more than six books chart in a year-end top 50 since accurate records began. He is certainly valuable to his publisher, HarperCollins (HC): he had the three top sellers of the year for the wider HC group, and almost £1 in every £2 spent on a HC Children's Books title in 2017 was on a book authored by Walliams.

It was a year when a lot of the energy was in the children's sector. Rowling (£15.5m) and Donaldson (£14.7m) were the second and third bestselling authors of the year, and the unquestionable publishing event was Philip Pullman's *La Belle Sauvage* (co-published by Penguin and David Fickling Books, DFB). The first in an 'equel' (i.e. 'equal') trilogy to Pullman's much-beloved *His Dark Materials* series, the book launched in October 2017 with high-profile events and midnight bookshop openings, earning Pullman his first-ever UK number one. Ah, but in the book world minor controversies are always ready to rear their heads. Indie booksellers were incensed that Waterstones was given 5,000 copies of an exclusive, signed special edition of the title. Penguin and DFB responded by offering indies Pullman-signed book plates – but that was two weeks after publication, and indies were decidedly unimpressed.

Knock out sales for rebel girls

The past year has not been completely devoid of hot trends, either. One that has spanned both the children's and adult sectors is feminism. Leading this was Elena Favilli and Francesca Cavallo's kids' title *Good Night Stories for Rebel Girls*, an illustrated collection of '100 stories of extraordinary women'. The path to publication was interesting, with the writers first financing the project on Kickstarter in 2016, obliterating the crowdfunding platform's record for a children's book by raising just over $675,000 (it probably helped the cause that the duo are in tech, having co-founded Silicon Valley start-up Timbuktu). The book was then taken up by traditional publishers with rights feverishly snapped up in 30 territories, including Penguin in the UK. *Rebel Girls*' cross-generational appeal has helped it become a sensation in Britain, with £3.1m in sales and counting since its March 2017 release. The public is hungry for more: Cavallo and Favilli are doing a sequel along the same crowdfunded model, and in its first day it became the fastest-funded project in Kickstarter history ($229,000 pledged in 24 hours).

Inevitably when there is a success in books, there is a raft of 'me too' publishing. Enter a typical bookshop in 2018 and you will see the shelves groaning with *Rebel Girls*-esque … um… homages, including Rachel Ignotofsky's *Women in Science: 50 Fearless Pioneers Who Changed the World* (Wren & Rook 2017), Libby Jackson's *A Galaxy of Her Own: Amazing Stories of Women in Space* (Century 2017) and Kate Pankhurst's *Fantastically Great Women Who Changed the World* (Bloomsbury 2016). To be fair to Pankhurst – who is a descendant of the suffragette Emmeline Pankhurst – her book preceded *Rebel Girls*, but only truly hit its stride in sales terms after Favilli and Cavallo's success. Heck, the trend is so hot even the fellas are getting a shot: in April 2018 Quercus released Ben Brooks and Quinton Winters' *Stories for Boys Who Dare to Be Different*, tales for youngsters who 'don't conform to the stereotype of masculinity'. One can easily imagine the wild-eyed staffer bursting into Quercus editorial meeting shouting, 'Boss, I've got it – girls stories ... *but for boys*.'

The power and the furore

It was an excellent year for feminism in adult fiction, too. Naomi Alderman's *The Power* (Viking 2016) – depicting a world in which young women suddenly gain the ability to inflict pain and death on men and its effect on society (spoiler: it doesn't work out well for the patriarchy) – won the Women's Prize for Fiction. Here's what nabbing a major award can do for a writer: since winning the gong, *The Power* has gone on to shift almost 180,000 copies in the UK. Alderman's next bestselling title, *Disobedience* (Penguin), has sold a comparatively modest 19,000 units since its 2007 publication. Margaret Atwood's feminist dystopian classic *The Handmaid's Tale* (McClelland & Stewart 1985) sold over 270,000 copies in 2017, helped by the hugely successful Hulu/Channel 4 TV series starring Elisabeth Moss (you know, Peggy off of *Mad Men*). There is a lesson for writers here. Atwood revealed in early 2018 that she did not make any money off the series itself as she sold the production rights to MGM in 1990 for a movie adaptation, rights the film company retained and was therefore the beneficiary of the hefty profits from Hulu (Atwood still benefited from the massive rise in book sales).

The feminist books surge is partly a response to a wider focus on women's issues in the 100th anniversary celebrations of some women getting the right to vote in the UK, and the larger public conversation on gender pay imbalance and sexual harassment, in the wake of the #metoo and #timesup movements that have mushroomed after Harvey Weinstein's and other Hollywood stars' scandals. Commissioning editors seem keen to snap up stories that, if not overtly 'feminist', at least feature compelling female leads. Historical fiction is a particularly strong area in this respect, with a number of successful debuts in 2017 and 2018 including Beth Underdown's *The Witchfinder's Sister* (Viking 2017), Imogen Hermes Gowar's *The Mermaid and Mrs Hancock* (Harvill Secker 2018) and Anna-Marie Crowhurst's *The Illumination of Ursula Flight* (Allen & Unwin 2018).

While the #metoo campaign has brought out scads of stories from women subjected to sexual harassment in Hollywood, the Houses of Parliament, and seemingly almost every industry on the planet, the UK books sector to date has been scandal-free. Perhaps this is because about 75% of those employed by UK publishers are female. But #metoo has started widespread debates about gender balance in the top jobs and in the boardroom (despite the overwhelming dominance of women in the trade as a whole, only three of the top 20 British publishers are run by women). Publishers are also looking at what and who they publish, spurred on by author Kamila Shamsie's call for 2018 to be a year of publishing only women, to redress gender imbalances in review coverage and the top books prizes. While many were sympathetic to Shamsie, only literary press And Other Stories has committed to the scheme.

Working class heroes

Who and what is published – and who is employed by the industry – is also being increasingly scrutinised in terms of diversity. Book trade bosses have in recent years recognised that their workforce is overwhelming white and middle class (perhaps by simply looking around the table at company meetings) and have consequently implemented a number of programs to aid inclusivity. This ramped up another notch last year, with the likes of the UK's biggest publisher Penguin Random House (PRH) creating an 'inclusion tracker', data that measures the diversity in its staff and the authors it publishes with its goal to 'reflect UK society' by 2025. Little, Brown in 2017 launched an imprint called Dialogue Books, spearheaded by former literary scout Sharmaine Lovegrove, to 'source, nurture and publish writing talent – and reach audiences – from areas currently underrepresented or not covered by the mainstream publishing industry'.

'Underrepresented' is the key word. Finding new communities surely appeals to the well-meaning liberals who make up the bulk of publishing. But there is a hard, commercial case, too: with book sales flattening, the industry needs to reach out to as many potential readers as it can to expand the market. A demographic often neglected by publishers is working class readers. In a November 2017 Radio 4 documentary *Where Are All the Working Class Writers?*, Penguin Random House Ceo Tom Weldon said he was 'sick in my stomach when I realise books and publishing don't reflect the world we live in'. To help widen access to publishing beyond the upper and middle classes, Weldon said PRH had removed the need for university degrees in its recruitment, banned all personal referrals for work experience, and set up an author mentoring program Write Now, which encourages writers from 'communities whose stories aren't often told'.

High times on the high street

For some time, the reviews of the book trade in *Writers' & Artists' Yearbooks* have had one consistent and depressing commonality: the decline of the bricks and mortar bookshop, particularly in the indie sector. But the Booksellers Association (BA) revealed that, in 2017, 39 new independents opened their doors, while 25 closed – the first net gain since the BA began tracking these figures in 1995. Before you begin popping the champagne corks, it should be pointed out that we are a long way from the heyday: there are 881 indie bookshops in the UK and Ireland, just over 1,000 fewer than there were in the mid-1990s. Still, the figures reflect an industry that has weathered the perfect storm in recent years of digitalisation, rising business rates, competition from Amazon and other deep discounters, to name just a few of the challenges.

Daunt's Waterstones is bouncing along. The 275-store chain saw its pre-tax profit rise 80% to £18m (on turnover of £403.8m) in its last set of results, cementing the recovery that began when Russian oligarch Alexander Mamut bought the company in 2011 and installed Daunt at the helm. It continued to expand, with five new sites opened in November and December 2017, and a similar number are expected to launch in 2018. Some openings have been controversial, with the chain accused of 'subterfuge' as several of the shops have been 'unbranded' – usually named after their locations in the style of an indie store with no Waterstones livery (the late 2017 cohort included The Deal Bookshop, The Weybridge Bookshop and The Blackheath Bookshop). That minor kerfuffle aside, the firm faces a new chapter as Mamut put Waterstones up for sale. Though most expect a smooth transition (hedge fund Elliott Advisors became the new owner in April 2018), any disruption of what has been a remarkable return from the brink worries the trade. Daunt has stayed on after the sale – which publishers certainly hoped for – but might an acquisitive hedge fund put its own, rather than the wider book trade's, interests first. Stay tuned.

Tom Tivnan is features and insight editor of the *Bookseller*. Previously Tom was a freelance writer and his work has appeared in the *Glasgow Herald*, the *Independent*, the *Daily Telegraph* and *Harper's Bazaar*. He has also worked as a bookseller for Blackwell's in the UK and Barnes & Noble in the US. He wrote the text for *Tattooed by the Family Business* (Pavilion 2010) and his debut novel is *The Esquimaux* (Silvertail 2017).

See also...

- *Electronic publishing*, page 124
- *The mathematics of publishing*, page 149

Electronic publishing

Ebooks continue to change the face of the publishing industry and possibilities for e-publishing are rapidly developing all the time. With new author-to-reader routes opening up, Philip Jones sets the scene and explains the implications for authors.

Markets, growth and sales

In the UK, the ebook market is a fixed reality, with digital sales for most trade publishers now making up about 30% of their total books revenue – for commercial fiction, the ratio of ebook to print book sales may be more even.

But the market growth that was extreme between 2010 and 2013 has plateaued, and most trade publishers saw their ebook sales numbers slow from 2014 onwards, a consequence of rising prices and tax (VAT is levied on ebooks, but not print books), as well as device fatigue (Waterstones stopped selling Kindles in 2015). Some regard this slowdown as temporary, others suggest it indicates that the book trade's digital transition will be complicated, with smart-speakers as well as mobiles having as much impact on reading as the more humble e-reader.

In 2017 there was better news for the big trade publishers, with the digital market lifting slightly – a result of more experimentation in pricing following their move back to so-called agency ebook deals, whereby they have full control over the price consumers pay for ebooks. Growth has also continued to pick up in the audiobook download sector (driven primarily by the Amazon-owned retailer Audible), with many trade publishers pointing to audio as the fastest growing segment of their digital content business.

Smaller publishers, digital specialists and self-published authors continue to do well, particularly at the very low price points favoured by ebook buyers. Amazon, though, refuses to release sales data about this new market, so no one really knows. What we do know is that print book sales are also growing – first in 2015, a likely consequence of the spectacular growth in sales of colouring books, but again in 2016 and 2017, when most of the major segments, including fiction, grew.

Overall, though, don't be fooled into thinking that digital is losing its edge. The truth about digital publishing is that its significance is, if anything, even more fundamental than first imagined. Even if the pace of ebook growth continues to slow and stabilise – as many predict it will – the wider impact of digital on the book business runs deep and by no means in one direction. The importance now of self-published writers or smaller digital-only publishers, such as Bookouture, Endeavour Media, Canelo and even Amazon Publishing, is not necessarily measured just in market share growth: in offering higher royalty rates and more regular payment terms these alternative routes are creating a different way of doing business today for some authors, and in some cases it is a satisfactory alternative to traditional publishing. It is perhaps for this reason, rather than simply as a boost to its topline, that Hachette bought Bookouture in March 2017.

At the beginning of 2018 the ebook market was dominated – as it has been throughout its creation and growth – by Amazon and its Kindle device. Challengers came – Apple, Google, Nook, Kobo, Blinkboxbooks – but did not make a dent. In the case of some the effort was too much, with Tesco closing its ebook retailer Blinkboxbooks at the beginning of 2015, while Nook fled the UK at the beginning of 2016. Subscription services such as

Oyster, Scribd and Mofibo (among others), who were briefly in vogue having inked deals with many major publishers in an attempt to expand the market beyond those readers already locked into Amazon, have also faded from view. Oyster was swallowed by Google. Mofibo was bought by fellow Scandinavian start-up Storytel that has grown a formidable audiobook download operation out of its Sweden base. Scribd is only just now emerging from a period of readjustment; profitable, the company has recently reintroduced its *all-you-can-eat* model, but says it may cap some users who over-read. Amazon's own Kindle Unlimited subscription model continues to grow too – though it is primarily focused on self-published writers and smaller publishers.

However, where once we expected new retailers to look to the growing ebook market, no new entrants emerged during the past year, and it is highly unlikely this situation will change much until there is a dedicated shift to reading (or listening) on mobile devices or tablets. It reflects a certain torpor around the ebook market, a consequence of a market dominated by one company – Amazon. In 2017 the European Commission concluded its investigation into the Seattle-based giant, contending that it considered Amazon's behaviour (in particular around Most Favoured Nation clauses in its ebook contracts, that meant publishers could not price promote their titles on other retailer websites or sign up to new business models without also offering Amazon the same terms) might violate EU antitrust rules that prohibit abuses of a dominant market position and restrictive business practices. Amazon has offered to remove such clauses for five years, and the impact of this on the overall ebook market will be interesting to follow. It may stimulate competition, despite Amazon's continuing dominance.

In terms of tracking the size of the digital content market in 2017, we are, as before, stymied by the lack of verifiable data from this new marketplace; Amazon does not share its numbers either with its investors, the news media, or third-party data companies such as Nielsen BookScan, which tracks physical book sales. Nevertheless, as in previous years, the *Bookseller* has collated the digital sales numbers from all the major trade publishers, providing a good view of most of the digital market. In early 2018, the *Bookseller* noted that the combined digital volume of the Big Five publishers (Hachette Livre, HarperCollins (HC), Penguin Random House (PRH), Simon & Schuster (S&S) and Pan Macmillan), stood at 46.2 million units in 2017, up 1.2% against 2016. It ended a three-year run of decline for the sector.

The raw numbers reflected how publishers chose to address the market in 2017. Both Hachette and S&S saw double-digit increases, with S&S up 12.2% to 2.7 million (ebooks sold) and Hachette jumping 20.5% to 17 million. Both totals are the best on record, said the *Bookseller*. Hachette's 17 million figure does not include Bookouture's sales, so its growth is reflective of how it has priced more aggressively over the year. It had previously set relatively high ebook prices, but in the past year or so Hachette has experimented with dynamic pricing, particularly with backlist and new writers.

As the *Bookseller* also noted, determining what these numbers mean for the digital market as a whole is, as always, tough. These five publishers contributed 55% of the print market in volume terms in 2017; extrapolating that ratio to digital sales equates to a 'total' volume of around 84 million ebooks sold in 2017. We do not have value figures, but it is unlikely to be up. The great unknowns remain self-publishing authors, and Amazon's own digital publishing business, Amazon Publishing.

How do these numbers chime with those reported elsewhere? A recent consumer survey from Nielsen Book confirmed that purchases of ebooks are in decline, with consumers buying 4% fewer in 2016 – a trend which coincides with a slowing in the growth of device ownership and the increasing of ebook prices. In addition, multi-function devices, such as mobile phones and tablets, overtook dedicated e-reading devices as the most commonly used for e-reading, with a 48%-44% split respectively, according to Nielsen. The latest figures are not yet available, but according to the Publishers Association the invoiced value of consumer ebooks dropped by close to 17% in 2016 to £204m.

The upshot is that even if the big publishers are no longer growing their ebook businesses (significantly), the market itself continues to shift and offer opportunities for smaller players and individual authors, especially those prepared to sell their ebooks at the kind of low prices prevalent on the Kindle. A good example is the ebook specialist Bookouture (now owned by Hachette). Bookouture was founded in 2012 by former Harlequin/Mills & Boon marketing controller Oliver Rhodes, and made its first book signing in November of that year. In 2013 it sold 81,000 ebooks, in 2014 362,000, in 2015 it sold 2.5m ebooks, and in 2016 6m. In short, it could be said that a tiny digital press has outperformed the bigger publishers. The rub: Bookouture prices its bestselling titles extremely aggressively – resulting in a turnover (by value) that is not much bigger than its volume number.

The context is important to understand when trying to figure out the growth rates of a market that is still in its infancy, and prone to tantrums. Four years ago in the *Yearbook* I wrote that – in the UK at least – the rate of growth in the ebook market was exaggerated in 2012 because of the *Fifty Shades* trilogy, which also then further skewed the perceived slowdown in sales growth in 2013; for example in 2012 the companies that would become Penguin Random House reported ebook sales volume growth of 169%, but one year later their ebook sales business fell by 20%. As the ebook market has become part of the overall reading market, its fortunes look to be also partly based on what is selling well elsewhere; in short, the success of print books, from colouring books to the adult Ladybird Christmas books, will also impact what sells in digital formats.

Others have suggested that there is also a visibility issue, with Amazon promoting its own publishing and self-publishing as well as subscription service, Kindle Unlimited, at the expense of traditional bestsellers, putting off discerning readers. As HarperCollins UK chief executive Charlie Redmayne put it to the *Bookseller* recently: 'There has been a lot of focus on the plateauing of ebooks because of price, but it is also about relevance: Amazon is focused on building Kindle Unlimited, its own publishing and self-publishing, and that means that books from the bigger publishing companies tend not to get the same exposure. But it is also ghettoising them, as consumers are not seeing the kinds of books they see and are buying elsewhere.'

That does not mean there are not huge successes to be had in ebook publishing. *The Girl on the Train* (Doubleday 2015) by Paula Hawkins was a runaway success in print during 2015 and 2016, and did as well, if not better, in ebook format. But there was no runaway hit in 2017 (in print or ebook), and that impacts the market.

The biggest question mark, however, remains over how big the market is that we do *not* see, as represented by authors who choose to self-publish, whether that is via Amazon's Kindle Direct Publishing platform, or those rivals offered by Nook (in the USA) and Kobo, or by using one of the print-on-demand players such as Blurb or Ingram. No sales made via these routes are being tracked (or indeed are trackable without the intervention of a third party such as Amazon), and many authors do not use an ISBN, meaning that even the number of titles being published annually is not measured.

Author Earnings, the website established by bestselling ebook writer Hugh Howey and the anonymous Data Guy, which looks at the relative rankings of ebooks in the Amazon Kindle charts, continues to push its view that indie-published (or self-published) ebooks are the dominant movement in the ebook market. As it notes: 'Self-published indie authors are verifiably capturing at least 24%–34% of all ebook sales in each of the five English-language markets; it's not just a US-only phenomenon. When you also include the uncategorized authors, the vast majority of whom are also self-published, the true indie share in each market lies somewhere between 30% and 40%. The Big Five, on the other hand, are letting themselves progressively get squeezed out of nearly every English-language ebook market.'

There is no reason to think this situation has not developed further in 2017 – the ebook market is one dominated by very low-priced commercial fiction, and self-published authors are often most well placed to take advantage. Amazon also has a tendency to showcase these titles, either because they come from an Amazon Publishing imprint, or because they feature in its Kindle Unlimited or Prime Reading programmes. But keep in mind that Author Earnings' figures are an extrapolation, and at best an indication of market change, and its figures for UK publishers (as reported in last year's *Yearbook*) are inaccurate.

Individual writers and smaller publishers can still have huge success in the Kindle store, even while the wider market ebbs and flows. But, as with much about the self-publishing market, anything said as fact should be re-interpreted as supposition.

With due irony, I add that self-publishing is, without doubt, a big part of the digital book business and a growing one, but it is not usurping the role of the traditional publisher. Both now accommodate and feed off each other – and authors transition in both directions.

Publishers' horizons

Two years ago I wrote that, for publishers, a stable market is a good one, and we should begin to see a trickle-down effect in terms of better publishing and greater investment in authors. And I was right. Publishing seems as confident today as I have known it for some time. The high street is in growth again, all of the major booksellers are in profit (or close to it), and some are even opening new stores. Waterstones – purchased by hedge fund Elliott Advisors in April 2018 – is in a particularly good state, after years in the wilderness.

From the perspective of digital, the important thing is not to assume that what may be a short period of print growth leads to a longer period of digital decline. I have noted that some publishers got burnt betting the bank on continued strong ebook growth, but the concern now is that they may get caught out simply by looking the other way. How publishers ready themselves for what happens now that the first wave of digital has come to an end will be key. At Penguin Random House its main focus appears to be on discoverability and marketing to the consumer, not on selling direct. 'We want to connect. We don't need to make the transaction,' said its chief executive Markus Dohle in 2015. In early 2016 it launched its consumer website Penguin.co.uk to do just that, and it has continued to build its consumer networks in 2016. Publishers are thinking hard about three things: how they reach readers; what tools they use to reach readers; and what they should do once they've reached those readers.

But Hachette's acquisition of Bookouture was also important, and evidence that now the wild west days of the ebook market are behind us, publishers may once again begin to think strategically about this sector – great news for authors if true. Bookouture has profited from an ebook market many in the trade misread; while the bigger publishers have focused on ebook sales in relation to print, and priced accordingly (pegging ebook prices to print book costs), digital-only publishers faced no such quandaries and concentrated just on selling ebooks at whatever prices ebooks could be sold at.

Lots of ebooks appear to work better at lower prices, and Bookouture – as with Amazon Publishing, Head of Zeus, Endeavour Press (now Endeavour Media), Canelo, and numerous self-publishing writers – have taken advantage. Hachette, in buying a fast-growing ebook specialist, will be trying to figure out if its traditional print business can accommodate a digital operation without one curbing or cannibalising the other. It is worth remembering that for years publishers were split between hardback houses and paperback imprints. It took decades for these two entities to figure out that they had more in common than just the content they published. Now most publishers publish across all formats simultaneously. Ironically, the ebook bit of their business might benefit from a specialist approach.

Hachette is also one of the few big publishers thinking outside of the ebook. Hachette Group Ceo Arnaud Nourry recently expressed his frustration with the ebook format, calling it a 'stupid product' and forecasting its sales would continue to plateau because of a lack of innovation. Of course publishers are creative and they want to be creative in the digital space, as well as in print, but it is also true that many are concerned that a healthier market for digital content has not yet emerged.

What's in it for writers?

How does this changing market affect writers? When we talk about the fundamental impact digital is having on the book business, nowhere is this more apparent than in the traditional publishing world's relationship with authors.

Authors now have more ways to find readers than ever before, and often without the intervention of an intermediary. Successful self-publishing is now no longer the exception that proves the rule, it is becoming the exception that threatens the rule. Writers such as Hugh Howey, whose fiction title *Wool* was 2012's stand-out self-published hit, are showing not only that they publish successfully, but that they can bring publishers to heel. Simon & Schuster in the USA bought print rights to *Wool*, but the author refused the company digital rights. Other writers following this path include Mark Edwards, Mark Dawson and Rachel Abbott.

Howey's way is not for every writer, but what it shows is that publishers now have to market themselves to each and every writer, not just in competition against other publishers, but in competition to not having a publisher at all. Most publishers have a strong message. The biggest-selling book of many years, *Fifty Shades of Grey*, sold far more copies after it was traditionally published by Random House than it did before this, and ever could have done. Paula Hawkins was a jobbing writer until her agent and her publisher alighted on *The Girl on the Train*. There is an alchemy to the publishing process that remains mysterious, but can still work. Each year the *Bookseller* compiles a list of top 50 bestselling writers, each raking in millions for their publisher and a good proportion of that for themselves. It doesn't stop working because self-publishing also works and, in sheer numbers, traditional publishing still sells far more books across a far wider range of titles and authors. Furthermore, if you are writing a book that is not commercial fiction or a genre title, traditional publishing remains the only viable route to market.

But as in other creative sectors, digital flattens the market, and punches the nose of the corporates. In a world with so many new options open to writers, is big publishing's 'value-add' still significant enough to prevent authors taking what promises to be a more lucrative route sideways? Probably. But it is a question that is not going away.

There remain plenty of questions for authors, and a raft of possible routes to market. Do you wait for a publisher to discover you? Or do you publish direct to a retailer's website? Do you use a third-party aggregator? Or pay for professional help? Should you publish everything you have written?

Whichever approach you take, digital has not changed one thing: authors struggle to make an income from their published writing, with the DIY option suitable for some but not all. A report commissioned by the ALCS (Authors' Licensing and Collecting Society; see page 707) in 2014 noted that the most successful self-publishing ventures had an average rate of return of 154% (and a typical 'median' rate of return of 40%). But it remained a risky option, partly because of the costs associated with self-publishing. The report found that the bottom 20% of self-publishers made losses of £400 or more.

Of course Indie writers make a huge noise about their success, but even self-publishing companies such as Smashwords noted a slowdown in sales growth for this sector, as has Author Earnings, which believes Amazon Publishing is making greater strides than it once was.

There has been a shift too, to suggesting authors should also self-publish in print, with Amazon's paperback programme, making use of its print-on-demand services, and the launch of new indie services. Though a few rare indie hits do break through into print – such as *The Rabbit Who Wants To Fall Asleep* (Ladybird 2015), created by Swedish behavioural psychologist and linguist Carl-Johan Forssén Ehrlin – most do not. Having said that, Amazon's POD imprint CreateSpace always performs well in the *Bookseller*'s end of year round-ups, regularly posting double-digit rises in sales of physical books (possibly through Amazon!).

All that glisters

Amazon's success in digital and its dominance within the self-publishing market is also its biggest problem. The lack of genuine competition, beyond that provided by Nook Press (now US only) and Kobo Writing Life, is also limiting the noise. Sites such as WattPad, where writers promote and improve their work, are increasingly being used by both self-publishers and publishers as ways of meeting and interacting with readers in a more neutral territory. They are also slowly figuring out ways for contributors to make money from their activities, but again this is in its infancy.

That said, should you choose to self-publish, then Amazon's Kindle Direct Publishing platform remains the compelling option. It offers clarity, high rewards, and a route to the largest audience of ebook readers. But it is not a risk-free decision. During 2014 it launched Kindle Unlimited, a subscription offer seemingly hurried out in order to compete with the perceived threat of newer ebook vendors Oyster and Scribd, whose business model was the near mythical 'Spotify for ebooks'. Amazon placed many independently published titles into the service without asking authors to opt-in, and set up a pool of money that they would share based on the number of reads. Many authors quickly opted out as they feared (like traditional publishers) that their sales would be cannibalised. Though the jury is out on this, there was a sense of a bond of trust between platform and author having been stretched – though perhaps not quite to breaking point.

Over the next couple of years Amazon has continued to grow the pot of money made available to writers participating in this scheme (though not with any accounting transparency), but has also had to change how it measures the rates paid to books read after it discovered some authors gaming the system by using shorter novels that triggered full payments after 10% was read; the change meant it would pay based on total pages actually read. It is also worth noting the following clause in the Amazon self-publishing contract – 'The Program will change over time and the terms of this Agreement will need to change over time as well. We reserve the right to change the terms of this Agreement at any time in our sole discretion.' Never forget: Amazon is the *de facto* monopoly in this space and remains in control. A traditional publishing deal, even one from a digital specialist, will offer a broader publishing strategy and a safety net should things go wrong.

The range of services marketed to authors has grown exponentially, with the arrival and growth in importance of the Alliance of Independent Authors (ALLi) helping to add an informed voice within the community. Because – and this is important – as an author you will at some point need to engage an expert. Even successful self-published writers will engage an editor, a cover designer, and perhaps even a 'social media guru'. This market is now well served, and certainly more honourable than it was even a few years ago. But, as ever, be careful what you pay for up front, and make sure you understand what you are getting in return for your money. The rebranding of the self-published into 'indie' writers has not meant an end to the traditional vanity operations; many have simply transformed into online author platforms offering to publish a book and make it available worldwide for a fee. Just as there is much more to publishing than simply printing a book, there is also much more to digital publishing than merely acquiring an ISBN or distribution. As the author Ros Barber wrote in a *Guardian* blog two years ago, 'If you self-publish your book, you are not going to be writing for a living. You are going to be marketing for a living. Self-published authors should expect to spend only 10% of their time writing and 90% of their time marketing.'

It is worth consulting the giant ebook aggregators, such as Ingram (www.ingrambook.com), Lulu (www.lulu.com) and Smashwords (www.smashwords.com); these companies will ensure the ebook basics are covered and that the ebooks are featured on third-party websites at a fraction of the cost of a typical vanity publisher.

First and foremost remember this: the traditional publishing route invests in a writer and their book, with 'risk' part of the publishing deal. Of course authors have invested their time and effort in the writing; but it is the publisher's job to invest in the publishing, production, marketing, PR, copy-editing, cover design, distributions and sales relationships with retailers. Self-publishing works in exactly the opposite way: the author invests in the publication of their work, and as such takes on all of the risk. You will find many websites and author service platforms talking about a revolution, parading their wares as a type of freedom: believe some of that, but not all of it. Any entity taking money for publication from an author upfront is not really invested in making that book a success: it is debatable that they are really a publisher.

But it is true that digital has shaken up the market, with new style publishers such as Unbound or Bookouture demonstrating that authors are no longer tied to the old routes. Digital-only lists such as Little, Brown's Blackfriars, HarperCollins' Impulse, Canelo, Bonnier Zaffre's twenty7, or even Amazon Publishing's growing suite of imprints, have become more sophisticated, having recognised that they too can publish outside of the ebook format. Endeavour Press (now Endeavour Media) is just the latest to launch a printed book imprint. As many have remarked, digital can be used to create a story around a book or author that can then lead to a different type of publishing – usually print publication.

Talent does out, however. Publishers are beginning to look for new talent more aggressively, and they are prepared to look outside the usual routes. Publishers such as HarperCollins' Borough Press and even Random House's Jonathan Cape have been experimenting with a period for 'open submissions', suggesting that even as more gets published, and the routes to readers clear, publishers remain desperate to root out the talent. Perhaps the biggest burden to getting published these days is not that a gatekeeper won't entertain you, but that they are so busy dealing with the rush through the gates!

Listen for the future

For a number of years now, I've written about what might happen as readers transition to using mobile devices rather than dedicated e-reading devices. As the Nielsen data suggested earlier in this piece, there is now good evidence that we are living through this transition, with many pundits anticipating a decline in long form digital reading (simply because it is harder on the eyes). Many also wondered if it would lead to a re-awakening of the enhanced ebook – that heady mix of words, pictures, sound, movies, animation, etc. In 2017 Amazon published Patricia Cornwell's *Ripper: The Secret Life of Walter Sickert* as Kindle in Motion ebook, that featured words and animation for Kindle readers. But the results are mixed, and the enhancements minimal (though not ineffective). Either way, there is little sense that the enhanced ebook has arrived – though some companies, such as Orson & Co and The Pigeonhole, continue to believe there is a market for such mash-ups. Publishers are continuing to show a willingness to try and reinvent the product (of which Orion's Belgravia app is yet another good example). Virtual reality is a coming trend too, with opportunities for writers. In 2016 the literary agent Sarah Such struck what she described as the world's first VR deal for a YA series, the *Fallow Trilogy* written by Amy Lankester-Owen. It remains to be seen if such projects have legs.

By far the biggest impact from the arrival of smartphones has not been on reading, but listening. Every trade publisher speaks now not just of ebooks, but of audiobook downloads, a market driven in the UK, as in the USA, by Amazon subsidiary Audible, whose own sales increased by 54% in 2016, with similar growth expected in 2017. Overall, the audiobook download market is thought to be worth as much as £100m in the UK. In 2015 the *Bookseller* began running a monthly audio download chart in its pages for the first time, and in 2016 relaunched its dedicated audiobook conference. Audible has even put the tools into the hands of authors via its ACX platform (recently launched in the UK), meaning that authors can now create their own audiobook versions. But other players are emerging, and some are significant. BookBeat and Storytel from Sweden, AudioBooks.com, Kobo, Google, with iTunes and Spotify the sleeping giants.

If the UK market follows the USA, then further rises can be predicted: the Audio Publishers' Association in the US estimates that audiobook sales in 2016 totalled more than $2.1bn, up 18.2% on 2015, and with a corresponding 33.9% increase in units. It was the third consecutive year that audio sales grew by nearly 20% in volume.

The bigger publishers, such as HarperCollins and Penguin Random House, are investing heavily in their audio production teams, with many observers expecting this market to develop and grow quickly over the next few years as the availability of listening tools on mobile devices proliferates. There are also numerous third-party producers who may vie for audio rights, such as Naxos or Bolinda, while Audible too has its own production arm. Audio, it seems, is the enhanced ebook already here.

The real push, though, will come as smart-speakers such as Amazon's Echo and Google's Home device infiltrate people's homes, providing ready access to spoken-word content. It is said that in the evening the primary activity for those using smart-speakers is listening to spoken-word content, primarily audiobooks. Of course, some of the predictions about adoption and usage bring back memories of the early days of the iPad, but there is little doubt that we are once again witnessing a major shift in consumer behaviour, pioneered by the big tech giants.

Reading rules

So, having lived through this first wave of digital, what can we say with any kind of certainty about the future? Readers like reading, and many of them like writing too. Despite the great disruptions we've seen, the bits in between the reader and writer remain largely stable and stabilising. The shift in 2017 was, again, not at either pole but in this middle ground; publishers simply got better at getting books from authors to readers – both digitally and in print. But anyone who expected the ebook market to develop as it had done over the previous half-decade was mistaken. The major action was in the print book market, and in audio.

As I said at the beginning of this article, digital is now ever-present in the publishing business. It has changed the market, and will continue to change it, creating opportunities and challenges for publishers and authors alike.

Philip Jones is Editor of the *Bookseller*, and co-founder of the digital blog FutureBook.net.

See also...

- *News, views and trends: review of the publishing year*, page 119
- *Self-publishing online: the emerging template for sales success*, page 607
- *Alliance of Independent Authors*, page 525
- *Notes from a hybrid author*, page 630
- *The dos and don'ts of self-publishing*, page 615

ISBNs: what you need to know

The Nielsen ISBN Agency for UK & Ireland receives a large number of enquiries about the ISBN system. The most frequently asked questions are answered here and for more information visit www.nielsenisbnstore.com.

What is an ISBN?

An ISBN is an International Standard Book Number and is 13 digits long.

What is the purpose of an ISBN?

An ISBN is a product number, used by publishers, booksellers and libraries for ordering, listing and stock control purposes. It enables them to identify a particular publisher and allows the publisher to identify a specific edition of a specific title in a specific format within their output.

Contact details

Nielsen ISBN Agency for UK and Ireland
3rd Floor, Midas House, 62 Goldsworth Road, Woking GU21 6LQ
tel (01483) 712200
email isbn.agency@nielsen.com
website www.nielsenisbnstore.com

What is a publisher?

The publisher is generally the person or organisation taking the financial and other risks in making a product available. For example, if a product goes on sale and sells no copies at all, the publisher loses money. If you get paid anyway, you are likely to be a designer, printer, author or consultant of some kind.

What is the format of an ISBN?

The ISBN is 13 digits long and is divided into five parts, as shown below, separated by spaces or hyphens.

- Prefix element: for the foreseeable future this will be 978 or 979
- Registration group element: identifies a national, geographic, or national grouping. It shows where the publisher is based
- Registrant element: identifies a specific publisher or imprint
- Publication element: identifies a specific edition of a specific title in a specific format
- Check digit: the final digit which mathematically validates the rest of the number

The four parts following the prefix element can be of varying length.

Prior to 1 January 2007 ISBNs were ten-digit numbers; any existing ten-digit ISBNs must be converted by prefixing them with '978' and the check digit must be recalculated using a Modulus 10 system with alternate weights of 1 and 3. The ISBN Agency can help you with this.

Do I *have* to have an ISBN?

There is no legal requirement in the UK and Ireland for an ISBN and it conveys no form of legal or copyright protection. It is simply a product identification number.

Why should I use an ISBN?

If you wish to sell your publication through major bookselling chains, independent bookshops or internet booksellers, they will require you to have an ISBN to assist their internal processing and ordering systems.

The ISBN also provides access to bibliographic databases, such as the Nielsen Book Database, which use ISBNs as references. These databases help booksellers and libraries to provide information for customers. Nielsen Book has a range of information, electronic trading and retail sales monitoring services which use ISBNs and are vital for the dissemination, trading and monitoring of books in the supply chain. The ISBN therefore provides access to additional marketing opportunities which could help sales of your product.

Where can I get an ISBN?

ISBNs are assigned to publishers in the country where the publisher's main office is based. This is irrespective of the language of the publication or the intended market for the book.

The ISBN Agency is the national agency for the UK and Republic of Ireland and British Overseas Territories. A publisher based elsewhere will not be able to get numbers from the UK Agency (even if you are a British Citizen) but can contact the Nielsen ISBN Agency for details of the relevant national Agency.

If you are based in the UK and Ireland you can purchase ISBNs online from the Nielsen ISBN Store: www.nielsenisbnstore.com.

How long does it take to get an ISBN?

If you purchase your ISBNs online from the Nielsen ISBN Store (www.nielsenisbnstore.com) you will receive your ISBN allocation within minutes. If you are purchasing ISBNs direct from the ISBN Agency via an off-line application, it can take up to five days, but there is a Fast-Track service of three working day processing period. The processing period begins when a correctly completed application is received in the ISBN Agency and payment is received.

How much does it cost to get an ISBN?

Please refer to www.nielsenisbnstore.com or email the ISBN Agency: isbn.agency@nielsen.com.

What if I only want one ISBN?

ISBNs can be bought individually or in blocks of ten or more; visit the ISBN Store to find out more: www.nielsenisbnstore.com.

Who is eligible for ISBNs?

Any publisher who is publishing a qualifying product for general sale or distribution to the market. By publishing we mean making a work available to the public.

Which products do NOT qualify for ISBNs?

Any publication that is without a defined end should not be assigned an ISBN. For example, publications that are regularly updated and intended to continue indefinitely (such as journals, serials, magazines, newspapers, updating loose-leafs, updating websites) are ineligible for ISBN.

Some examples of products that do not qualify for ISBN are:

- Journals, periodicals, serials, newspapers in their entirety (single issues or articles, where these are made available separately, may qualify for ISBN);
- Abstract entities such as textual works and other abstract creations of intellectual or artistic content;
- Ephemeral printed materials such as advertising matter and the like;
- Customised print-on-demand publications (Publications that are available only on a limited basis, such as customised print on demand publications with content specifically

tailored to a user's request shall not be assigned an ISBN. If a customised publication is being made available for wider sale, e.g. as a college course pack available through a college book store, then an ISBN may be assigned);

- Printed music;
- Art prints and art folders without title page and text;
- Personal documents (such as a curriculum vitae or personal profile);
- Greetings cards;
- Music sound recordings;
- Software that is intended for any purpose other than educational or instructional;
- Electronic bulletin boards;
- Emails and other digital correspondence;
- Updating websites;
- Games;
- Non text-based publications.

Following a review of the UK market, it is now permissible for ISBNs to be assigned to calendars and diaries, provided that they are not intended for purely time-management purposes and that a substantial proportion of their content is textual or graphic.

What is an ISSN?

An International Standard Serial Number. This is the numbering system for journals, magazines, periodicals, newspapers and newsletters. It is administered by the British Library, *tel* (01937) 546959; *email* issn-uk@bl.uk; *website* www.bl.uk/bibliographic/issn.html

How do I contact the ISBN Agency?

Registration Agencies: ISBN Agency; *tel* (01483) 712215; *fax* (01483) 712214; *email* isbn.agency@nielsen.com.

Who's who in publishing

agent

See **literary agent**.

aggregator

A company or website that gathers together related content from a range of other sources and provides various different services and resources, such as formatting and distribution, to ebook authors.

art editor

A person in charge of the layout and design of a magazine, who commissions the photographs and illustrations and is responsible for its overall appearance and style.

audio editor

A person who edits the raw audio from the recording into the final, retail-ready audiobook.

audio producer

A person who supervises the entire production process of the audiobook.

author

A person who has written a book, article, or other piece of original writing.

book packager

See **packager**.

columnist

A person who regularly writes an article for publication in a newspaper or magazine.

commissioning editor

A person who asks authors to write books for the part of the publisher's list for which he or she is responsible or who takes on an author who approaches them direct or via an agent with a proposal. Also called **acquisitions editor** or **acquiring editor** (more commonly in the US). A person who signs up writers (commissions them to write) an article for a magazine or newspaper. See page 107.

contributor

A person who writes an article that is included in a magazine or paper, or who writes a chapter or section that is included in a book.

copy-editor

A person whose job is to check material ready for printing for accuracy, clarity of message, writing style and consistency of typeface, punctuation and layout. Sometimes called a **desk editor**. See page 661.

distributor

Acts as a link between the publisher and retailer. The distributor can receive orders from retailers, ship books, invoice, collect revenue and deal with returns. Distributors often handle books from several publishers. Digital distributors handle ebook distribution.

editor

A person in charge of publishing a newspaper or magazine who makes the final decisions about the content and format. A person in book publishing who has responsibility for the content of a book and can be variously a senior person (editor-in-chief) or day-to-day contact for authors (copy-editor, development editor, commissioning editor, etc). See page 661.

editorial assistant

A person who assists senior editorial staff at a publishing company, newspaper, or similar business with various administrative duties, as well as editorial tasks in preparing copy for publication.

illustrator

A person who designs and draws a visual rendering of the source material, such as characters or settings, in a 2D media. Using traditional or digital methods, an illustrator creates artwork manually rather than photographically.

journalist

A person who prepares and writes material for a newspaper or magazine, news website, television or radio programme, or any similar medium.

literary agent

Somebody whose job is to negotiate publishing contracts, involving royalties, advances and rights sales on behalf of an author and who earns commission on the proceeds of the sales they negotiate. See page 419; page 422.

literary scout

A person who looks for unpublished manuscripts to recommend to clients for publication as books, or adaptation into film scripts, etc.

marketing department

The department that originates the sales material – catalogues, order forms, blads, samplers, posters, book proofs and advertisements – to promote titles published. See page 107.

narrator

A person who reads a text aloud into a recording device to create an audiobook. This may be the author of the text, or a professional voice artist.

packager

A company that creates a finished book for a publisher. See page 245.

picture researcher

A person who looks for pictures relevant to a particular topic, so that they can be used as illustrations in, for example, a book, newspaper or TV programme.

printer

A person or company whose job is to produce printed books, magazines, newspapers or similar material. The many stages in this process include establishing the product specifications, preparing the pages for print, operating the printing presses, and binding and finishing of the final product.

production controller

A person in the production department of a publishing company who deals with printers and other suppliers. See page 107.

production department

The department responsible for the technical aspects of planning and producing material for publication to a schedule and as specified by the client. Their work involves liaising with editors, designers, typesetters, printers and binders.

proofreader

A person whose job is to proofread texts to check typeset page presentation and text for errors and to mark up corrections. See page 661.

publicity department

The department that works with the author and the media on 'free' publicity – e.g. reviews, features, author interviews, bookshop readings and signings, festival appearances, book tours and radio and TV interviews – when a book is published.

publisher

A person or company that publishes books, magazines and/or newspapers. See page 107.

rights manager

A person who negotiates and coordinates rights sales (e.g. for subsidiary, translation or foreign rights). Often travels to book fairs to negotiate rights sales.

sales department

The department responsible for selling and marketing the publications produced by a publishing company, to bring about maximum sales and profit. Its tasks include identifying physical and digital outlets, ensuring orders and supplies of stock, and organising advertising campaigns and events.

sub-editor

A person who corrects and checks articles in a newspaper before they are printed. See page 0.

translator

A person who translates copy, such as a manuscript, from one language into another. See page

typesetter

A person or company that 'sets' text and prepares the final layout of the page for printing. It can also now involve XML tagging for ebook creation. See page 661.

vanity publisher

A publisher who charges an author a fee in order to publish his or her work for them, and is not responsible for selling the product. See page

web content manager

A person who controls the type and quality of material shown on a website or blog and is responsible for how it is produced, organised, presented and updated.

wholesaler

A person or company that buys large quantities of books, magazines, etc from publishers, transports and stores them, and then sells them in smaller quantities to many different retailers.

Print on demand

David Taylor explains how print on demand is keeping books alive.

What is 'print on demand'?

Ever since mankind first started committing words to a physical form of delivery, whether on wood, stone, papyrus, illuminated text or moveable type, the method of supplying these for sale has largely followed a similar pattern: produce first and then sell. Of course, the risk in this is that the publisher can overproduce or underproduce. Overproduction means that the publisher has cash tied up in books that are waiting to be sold. Underproduction means that the publisher has run out and sales are being missed because the book is not available to buy.

If you walk around any publisher's distribution centre you will see huge quantities of printed books that are awaiting sale, representing large amounts of cash tied up in physical inventory. This is often referred to as 'speculative inventory' because the publisher has printed the books in anticipation of selling them. One of the hardest decisions that a publisher has to make is how many copies of a title to print upon publication; equally hard is how many to reprint if the initial print run is sold. Get these wrong and it can cost the publisher dearly and, in some extreme cases, prove mortal to the business.

For others in the supply chain, this model is also deeply flawed. The author whose title sells well can fall into the limbo of 'out of stock' pending a reprint decision by the publisher. The bookseller, who has orders for a title but cannot supply them, also loses sales and disappoints customers. In some cases, those orders are of the moment and when that moment passes, so does the sale. Last but by no means least, the book buyer is frustrated as they are unable to buy the book that they wish to read.

The supply model is also famously inefficient, characterised as it is by large amounts of speculative stock being printed, transported, stored in warehouses, transported again, returned from the bookseller if it does not sell and, in many cases, being pulped. Not only is this commercially inefficient, it is also environmentally costly, involving large amounts of energy being used to print and transport books that may end their life as landfill.

In the mid-1990s, developments in the then emerging field of digital printing started to hold out the possibility that this traditional 'print first then sell' model might be changed to a more commercially attractive 'sell first and then print' model. Such a supply model was premised upon a number of things coming together.

- First, the technology of digital printing advanced to the stage where simple text-based books could be produced to a standard that was acceptable to publishers in terms of quality.
- Second, the speed of digital presses advanced so that a book could be produced upon the receipt of an order and supplied back to the customer within an acceptable timeframe.
- Third, models started to emerge which married these digital printing capabilities to wholesaling and book distribution networks such that books could be stored digitally, offered for sale to the market with orders being fulfilled on a 'print-on-demand' (POD) basis from a virtual warehouse rather than a physical warehouse full of speculative inventory. This hybrid model requires a highly sophisticated IT infrastructure to allow the swift routing and batching of orders to digital print engines so that genuine single copy orders can be produced 'on demand'.

The first mover in developing this model was the US book wholesaler Ingram Book Group which, in 1997, installed a digital print line in one of their giant book wholesaling warehouses and offered a service to US publishers called Lightning Print. This service presented to publishers the option of allowing Ingram to hold their titles in a digital format, offer them for sale via Ingram's vast network of bookselling customers and print the title when it was ordered. In addition, the publisher could order copies for their own purposes.

Twenty-one years on, Lightning Source, which operates as the POD service for what has now become Ingram Content Group, has operations in the USA, the UK, Australia, a joint venture with Hachette in France, a research and training facility in Germany and agreements with POD vendors in Spain, Russia, Poland, South Korea, China, India, Italy and Germany. Lightning Source prints millions of books from a digital library of 15 million titles from tens of thousands of publishers. The average print run per order is less than two copies.

POD service companies

Digital printing technology has developed at a staggering pace and the quality of digitally printed titles is now almost indistinguishable from titles printed using offset machines. Ink jet digital print engines, now into their second generation, are well established in the market and have taken the quality of digitally printed books to the next level, especially for full-colour titles. Speed of production has also improved at amazing rates. For example, Lightning Source now produces books on demand for Ingram customers within four hours of receiving the order, thereby allowing orders to be shipped within 24 hours to the bookseller. Ingram also recently acquired some robotic technology, taking the POD model to a true status of virtual wholesaler. Ingram's fourth American POD facility opened in California in late 2014 and deploys this next generation of capability.

The number and types of players in the POD market continues to expand. In the UK, Antony Rowe established a POD operation in partnership with the UK's biggest book wholesaler, Gardners, in early 2000. Antony Rowe's POD facility supplies orders on demand for Gardner's bookselling customers using a very similar model to that of Ingram and Lightning Source in the USA. Other UK printers have been scrambling to enter the fast-growing POD space with significant investments being made in digital printing equipment. Rather ironically, the arrival of the ebook is fuelling the growth of POD as publishers move more titles into shorter print runs or opt to operate from a virtual stock position as they attempt to cope with the shift from 'p' to 'e'. The last thing a publisher wants is a warehouse full of titles that are selling faster in an 'e' format. Publishers are increasingly moving to a 'p' and 'e' model of supply and using POD to offer a print alternative as well as an 'e' version.

In Germany, the book wholesaler Libri has a POD operation, Books on Demand, which also offers a self-publishing service to authors. Lightning Source and Antony Rowe deal only with publishers. Books on Demand have recently extended their offer into both France and the Netherlands and have an arrangement with Ingram so that their self-published authors can use the Lightning Source network to get their titles into North America, the UK and Australia. In the French market, the joint venture between Lightning Source and Hachette Livre and the arrival of the genuine single copy POD model has fuelled the growth of French self-publishing businesses which previously lacked this supply model.

In the Australian market, the arrival of Lightning Source in mid-2011 has had a dramatic impact on Australian self-publishing companies. Now that they have a POD model in their market, they are actively growing their title base and are able to offer Australian authors easy access to a global selling network in addition to local services. One of the most significant moves in this area was the purchase in 2005 by Amazon of a small US POD business called Booksurge. Like Libri's Books on Demand model, Amazon also offers a self-publishing service to authors and is actively leveraging its dominance of the internet bookselling market to develop innovative packages for authors via this model and their CreateSpace brand. The consensus within the book trade appears to be that Amazon sees POD as a very important part of the way in which they manage their supply chain and as a key opportunity to improve service levels to their customers. Amazon is now also a publisher in the traditional sense of the word and is using its own POD service to support the availability of many of these titles within their supply chain. In the wider world, traditional publishing and self-publishing did seem to be moving ever closer together as witnessed by the rather surprising purchase in 2012 by Penguin of Author Solutions, which was at the time probably the largest self-publishing company in the market. However, in 2016 Penguin Random House sold Author Solutions to private investors, so perhaps the trend is now moving the other way. Time will tell.

Elsewhere in the world, there are emerging POD supply models in an increasing number of countries including South America, India, China, Japan and Europe. Self-publishing in India is especially vibrant. Ingram is actively building supply partnerships with many of these organisations via its Global Connect programme, thereby offering publishers and authors an increasingly global option to make their books available on demand to their readers.

As digital print technology has improved, many traditional book printers have tried to enter this market and offer POD. However, without significant investment in the IT infrastructure needed to deliver single copy production at scale and speed and without allying that capability to an established book distribution or wholesaling network, many of these offers are effectively ultra short-run printing offers and cannot replicate the genuine POD supply model of a single copy printed when an order is received. Increasingly, as well, that supply model needs to be built on a global scale to offer authors and publishers the maximum exposure for their titles.

What POD means for self-published authors

POD is impacting aspiring and published authors in different ways. The existence of POD has led to a whole set of new publishing models and platforms. Removing the need to carry speculative inventory has reduced the barriers to entry for organisations which want to enter the publishing space. For example, in the US market, Ingram's Lightning Source supply model has enabled a large number of self-publishing companies to flourish and to offer aspiring authors a wide range of services to get their work into print. These companies will typically use a POD service to do the physical printing and distribution of a title, and also use them to list the titles for sale via book wholesalers like Amazon and Gardners, internet booksellers like Amazon, and physical bookshop chains such as Barnes & Noble and Waterstones. Authors may also have the opportunity to order copies of their own titles. They would also offer the aspiring author a set of support services covering editorial, marketing, design, etc. See *Editorial services and self-publishing providers* on page 644. In addition, in 2013, Ingram launched a new platform called IngramSpark, specifically designed to help self-published authors and smaller publishers with POD (via Lightning Source) as well as ebook distribution. IngramSpark makes it easy to upload POD and ebook formats and then make those formats available to Ingram's 39,000 global retail and library partners. Growth has been really quite significant and perhaps one of the trends is that individual authors have become far more adept at managing the whole publishing and distribution process themselves, rather than relying completely upon a self-publishing company. The market would seem to be maturing in that sense.

No longer does an author wanting to self-publish have to commit upfront to buying thousands of copies of his or her title. The previously mentioned self-publishing organisations are large, sophisticated and have many tens of thousands of authors whose books are available for sale in mainstream book reselling outlets. In addition, traditional publishers who have historically been a little snooty about self-published books now view them in a slightly different light, perhaps as a less risky way of testing the market with new authors who are willing to pay for the privilege of being published. They trawl self-published titles for potential: there have been several well-publicised cases of authors who started out by self-publishing before being picked up by one of the established publishing houses (e.g. E.L. James' *Fifty Shades of Grey*).

The published author

The POD picture for the published author is a little more mixed. There is no doubt that traditional publishers are engaging more than ever before with the benefits that POD brings. The ability to reduce speculative inventory or get out of it completely, to ensure that sales are not missed, to reduce the risk of getting a reprint decision wrong, and even to bring titles back to life from the out-of-print graveyard, are all very attractive financial propositions. For the author who has a book already published, POD means sales are not missed and therefore royalties are forthcoming. Many books can languish in 'reprint under consideration' limbo for years: POD removes that category and ensures that books are available for sale. Probably the thorniest issue is around the decision to put a book out of print and here most author contracts have simply not caught up with the new technologies. Some contracts still require that the publisher has to keep physical inventory of a title to show that it is in print, yet many millions of books are in print and there is no physical inventory held anywhere. An author may therefore find their title being put out of print because of such a clause even though the publisher is willing to keep it in print but does not want to keep speculative inventory before an order is received.

The flip side of this, of course, is that a publisher might use POD to retain the rights to the title by printing a small amount of inventory when really the best thing for the author might be to allow the title to go out of print and get the rights back. There have been many cases where rights have reverted to the author who has then either set himself up as an independent publishing company or utilised the services of one of the self-publishing companies mentioned earlier. There have also been examples of literary agents using POD to offer a new publishing service to authors who may have the rights as the title has gone out of print at their original publisher.

In conclusion, the advice for both aspiring authors and published authors is to do your homework. For an aspiring author, look carefully at the various self-publishing organisations out there and do your sums. Are you better off using them or do you want to set up your own publishing company? For published authors, take a long hard look at how your contract defines 'out of print'. The old definition was typically based on 'no physical copies in existence': POD has made that irrelevant and your contract should reflect these new realities if you are to take full advantage of them.

And finally, here is one of the most delicious ironies of this whole model. The death of the physical book has been predicted many times now that we live in a digital age. POD has digital technology at its core and yet it is giving life to one of the oldest products on the planet: the paper book. POD is set to be at the heart of the way in which paper books are published, printed and distributed for many years to come. Without this new model, there would be far fewer books available to buy and read and I, for one, think that the world would be a duller place for that.

David Taylor has worked in the book trade since 1983 and spent most of his time in bookselling. He has worked at Ingram Content Group since 2003 and is currently Senior Vice President, Content Acquisition International, Ingram Content Group and Group Managing Director, Lightning Source UK Ltd. He is also the Director of Lightning Source Australia, President of Lightning Source France and Managing Director of National Book Network International, a UK-based book distributor which was acquired by Ingram in mid 2017.

See also...

- *News, views and trends: review of the publishing year*, page 119
- *Electronic publishing*, page 124

Public Lending Right

Under the PLR system, payment is made from public funds to authors and other contributors (writers, illustrators/photographers, translators, adapters/retellers, ghostwriters, editors/compilers/abridgers/revisers, narrators and producers) whose books (print, audiobook and ebook) are lent from public libraries. Payment is annual; the amount authors receive is proportionate to the number of times that their books were borrowed during the previous year (July to June).

How the system works

From the applications received, the PLR office compiles a database of authors and books (the PLR Register). A representative sample of book issues is recorded, consisting of all loans from selected public libraries. This is then multiplied in proportion to total library lending to produce, for each book, an estimate of its total annual loans throughout the country. The estimated loans are matched against the database of registered authors and titles to discover how many loans are credited to each registered book for the calculation of PLR payments, using the ISBN printed in the book (see below).

Parliament allocates a sum each year (£6.6 million for 2017/18) for PLR. This fund pays the administrative costs of PLR and reimburses local authorities for recording loans in the sample libraries (see below). The remaining money is divided by the total estimated national loan figure for all registered books in order to work out how much can be paid for each estimated loan of every registered ISBN.

Since July 2014 the UK PLR legislation has been extended to include public library loans of audiobooks and ebooks downloaded to library premises for taking away as loans ('on-site' ebook loans). On 27 April 2017 the Digital Economy Bill, which included provision to extend the UK PLR legislation to include remote loans of ebooks from public libraries, received Royal Assent. The new arrangements are expected to take effect officially from 1 July 2018, when remote ebook loans data will start to be collected, and any payments arising from the newly eligible loans will be made in February 2020. The PLR website will keep authors informed of the progress of this legislation.

Further information

Public Lending Right
PLR Office, First Floor, Richard House, Sorbonne Close, Stockton-on-Tees TS17 6DA (until 30 September 2018)
Public Lending Right, British Library, Boston Spa, Wetherby, West Yorkshire (from 1 October 2018)
tel (01642) 604699 (until 30 September 2018)
tel (01937) 546030 (from 1 October 2018)
websites www.bl.uk/plr, www.plrinternational.com
Contact Head of PLR Operations

The UK PLR scheme is administered by the British Library from its offices in Stockton-on-Tees (the 'PLR office'). Please note that the operation will move to Boston Spa in autumn 2018. The UK PLR office also provides registration for the Irish PLR scheme on behalf of the Irish Public Lending Remuneration office.

Application forms, information and publications are all obtainable from the PLR Office. See website for further information on eligibility for PLR, loans statistics and forthcoming developments.

British Library Advisory Committee for Public Lending Right

Advises the British Library Board, the PLR Head of Policy and Engagement and Head of PLR Operations on the operation and future development of the PLR scheme.

Limits on payments

If all the registered interests in an author's books score so few loans that they would earn less than £1 in a year, no payment is due. However, if the books of one registered author score so high that the author's PLR earnings for the year would exceed £6,600, then only £6,600 is paid. (No author can earn more than £6,600 in PLR in any one year.) Money that is not paid out because of these limits belongs to the fund and increases the amounts paid that year to other authors.

The sample

Because it would be expensive and impracticable to attempt to collect loans data from every library authority in the UK, a statistical sampling method is employed instead. The sample represents only public lending libraries – academic, school, private and commercial libraries are not included. Only books which are loaned from public libraries can earn PLR; consultations of books on library premises are excluded.

The sample consists of the entire loans records for a year from libraries in more than 30 public library authorities spread through England, Scotland and Wales, and whole data is collected from Northern Ireland. Sample loans represent around 20% of the national total. All the computerised sampling points in an authority contribute loans data ('multi-site' sampling). The aim is to increase the sample without any significant increase in costs. In order to ensure representative sampling, at least seven libraries are replaced every year and a library cannot stay in the sample for more than four years. Loans are totalled every 12 months for the period 1 July–30 June.

An author's entitlement to PLR depends on the loans accrued by his or her books in the sample. This figure is averaged up to produce first regional and then finally national estimated loans.

ISBNs

The PLR system uses ISBNs (International Standard Book Numbers) to identify books lent and correlate loans with entries on the PLR Register so that payments can be made.

Summary of the 35th year's results

Registration: authors. When registration closed for the 35th year (30 June 2017) there were 61,364 authors and assignees.

Eligible loans. The loans from UK libraries credited to registered books – approximately 42% of all library borrowings – qualify for payment. The remaining loans relate to books that are ineligible for various reasons, to books written by dead or foreign authors, and to books that have simply not been applied for.

Money and payments. PLR's administrative costs are deducted from the fund allocated to the British Library Board annually by Parliament. Total government funding for 2017/18 was £6.6 million. The amount distributed to authors was just over £6 million. The Rate per Loan for 2017/18 was 8.20 pence.

The numbers of authors in various payment categories are as follows:

*294	payments at	£5,000–6,600
382	payments between	£2,500–4,999.99
760	payments between	£1,000–2,499.99
829	payments between	£500–999.99
3,271	payments between	£100–499.99
16,572	payments between	£1–99.99
22,108	TOTAL	

* Includes 195 authors whose book loans reached the maximum threshold

ISBNs are required for all registrations. Different editions (e.g. 1st, 2nd, hardback, paperback, large print) of the same book have different ISBNs. See *ISBNs: what you need to know* on page 133.

Authorship

In the PLR system the author of a printed book or ebook is any contributor such as the writer, illustrator, translator, compiler, editor or reviser. Authors must be named on the book's title page, or be able to prove authorship by some other means (e.g. receipt of royalties). The ownership of copyright has no bearing on PLR eligibility. Narrators, producers and abridgers are also eligible to apply for PLR shares in audiobooks.

Co-authorship/illustrators. In the PLR system the authors of a book are those writers, translators, editors, compilers and illustrators as defined above. Authors must apply for registration before their books can earn PLR and this can be done via the PLR website. There is no restriction on the number of authors who can register shares in any one book as long as they satisfy the eligibility criteria.

Writers and/or illustrators. At least one contributor must be eligible and they must jointly agree what share of PLR each will take based on contribution. This agreement is necessary even if one or two are ineligible or do not wish to register for PLR. The eligible authors will receive the share(s) specified in the application.

Most borrowed authors

Children's authors

1. Julia Donaldson
2. Daisy Meadows
3. Roderick Hunt
4. Francesca Simon
5. Adam Blade
6. Jacqueline Wilson
7. Roald Dahl
8. Fiona Watt
9. Michael Morpurgo
10. Lucy Cousins
11. David Walliams
12. Jeff Kinney
13. Enid Blyton
14. Holly Webb
15. Claire Freedman
16. Jeanne Willis
17. Mick Inkpen
18. Giles Andreae
19. Terry Deary
20. Eric Hill

Authors of adult fiction

1. James Patterson
2. M.C. Beaton
3. Nora Roberts
4. Anna Jacobs
5. Lee Child
6. David Baldacci
7. Danielle Steel
8. Clive Cussler
9. Michael Connolly
10. John Grisham
11. Peter James
12. Harlan Coben
13. Ann Cleeves
14. Alexander McCall Smith
15. Katie Flynn
16. Ian Rankin
17. J. D. Robb
18. Jeffrey Archer
19. Agatha Christie
20. Susan Lewis

These two lists are of the most borrowed authors in UK public libraries. They are based on PLR sample loans in the period July 2015–June 2016 (data for 2016–17 not available before going to press; this will be published on the PLR website in summer 2018). They include all writers, both registered and unregistered, but not illustrators where the book has a separate writer. Writing names are used; pseudonyms have not been combined.

Please note that these top 20 listings are based on the February 2017 UK PLR payment calculations.

Translators. Translators may apply for a 30% fixed share (to be shared equally between joint translators).

Editors and compilers. An editor or compiler may apply to register a 20% share if they have written at least 10% of the book's content or more than ten pages of text in addition to normal editorial work and are named on the title page. Alternatively, editors may register 20% if they have a royalty agreement with the publisher. In the case of joint editors/ compilers, the total editor's share should be divided equally.

Audiobooks. PLR shares in audiobooks are fixed by the UK scheme and may not be varied. *Writers* may register a fixed 60% share in an audiobook, providing that it has not been abridged or translated. In cases where the writer has made an additional contribution (e.g. as narrator), he/she may claim both shares. *Narrators* may register a fixed 20% PLR share in an audiobook. *Producers* may register a fixed 20% share in an audiobook. *Abridgers* (in cases where the writer's original text has been abridged prior to recording as an audiobook) qualify for 12% (20% of the writer's share). *Translators* (in cases where the writer's original text has been translated from another language) qualify for 18% (30% of the writer's share). If there is more than one writer, narrator, etc the appropriate shares should be divided equally. If more than one contribution has been made, e.g. writer and narrator, more than one fixed share may be applied for.

Dead or missing co-authors. Where it is impossible to agree shares with a co-author because that person is dead or untraceable, then the surviving co-author or co-authors may submit an application to register a share which reflects their individual contribuation to the book.

Transferring PLR after death. First applications may not be made by the estate of a deceased author. However, if an author registers during their lifetime the PLR in their books can be transferred to a new owner and continues for up to 70 years after the date of their death. The new owner can apply to register new titles if first published one year before, or up to ten years after, the date of the author's death. New editions of existing registered titles can also be registered posthumously.

Residential qualifications. To register for the UK PLR scheme, at the time of application authors must have their only home or principal home in the UK or in any of the other countries within the European Economic Area (i.e. EC member states plus Iceland, Norway and Liechtenstein).

Eligible books

In the PLR system each edition of a book is registered and treated as a separate book. A book is eligible for PLR registration provided that:

- it has an eligible author (or co-author);
- it is printed and bound (paperbacks counting as bound);
- it has already been published;
- copies of it have been put on sale, i.e. it is not a free handout;
- the authorship is personal, i.e. not a company or association, and the book is not crown copyright;
- it has an ISBN;
- it is not wholly or mainly a musical score;
- it is not a newspaper, magazine, journal or periodical.

Audiobooks. An audiobook is defined as an 'authored text' or 'a work recorded as a sound recording and consisting mainly of spoken words'. Applications can therefore only be accepted to register audiobooks which meet these requirements and are the equivalent of a printed book. Music, dramatisations and live recordings do not qualify for registration. To qualify for UK PLR in an audiobook contributors should be named on the case in which the audiobook is held; OR be able to refer to a contract with the publisher; OR be named within the audiobook recording.

Ebooks. At April 2017 only ebooks downloaded to fixed terminals in library premises and then taken away on loan on portable devices to be read elsewhere qualify for PLR payment. Information provided by libraries suggests that the vast majority of ebook and digital audio lending is carried out 'remotely' to home PCs and mobile devices, which means the loan did not qualify for PLR. That is not to say libraries will not make on-site lending available in the future. There is nothing to stop eligible contributors from registering their ebook and audio download editions for PLR, but it is unlikely at present that loans of this material will generate PLR earnings until remote loans of ebooks qualify under the scheme.

On 27 April 2017 the Digital Economy Bill, which included provision to extend the UK PLR legislation to include remote loans of ebooks from public libraries, received Royal Assent. The new arrangements are expected to take effect officially from 1 July 2018, when remote ebook loans data will start to be collected, and any payments arising from the newly eligible loans will be made in February 2020. The PLR website will keep authors informed of the progress of this legislation.

Statements and payment

Authors with an online account may view their statement online. Registered authors without an online account receive a statement posted to their address if a payment is due.

Sampling arrangements

To help minimise the unfairness that arises inevitably from a sampling system, the scheme specifies the eight regions within which authorities and sampling points have to be designated and includes libraries of varying size. Part of the sample drops out by rotation each year to allow fresh libraries to be included. The following library authorities were designated for the year beginning 1 July 2017 (all are multi-site authorities). This list is based on the nine government regions for England plus Northern Ireland, Scotland and Wales.

- East – Bedfordshire/Bedford, Hertfordshire
- East Midlands – Derbyshire
- London – Lambeth, Luton, Southwark, Triborough Libraries (Hammersmith and Fulham/Kensington and Chelsea/Westminster)
- North East – North Tyneside, Sunderland
- North West & Merseyside – Cheshire East/Cheshire West/Chester, Cumbria, Halton, Stockport, Warrington
- South East – Hampshire, Kent
- South West – Bournemouth, Poole
- West Midlands – Worcestershire
- Yorkshire & The Humber – Barnsley, Wakefield
- Northern Ireland – The Northern Ireland Library Authority
- Scotland – Aberdeenshire, Edinburgh, Falkirk, South Lanarkshire
- Wales – Caerphilly, Conwy, Gwynedd.

Participating local authorities are reimbursed on an actual cost basis for additional expenditure incurred in providing loans data to the PLR Office. The extra PLR work mostly consists of modifications to computer programs to accumulate loans data in the local authority computer and to transmit the data to the PLR Office.

Reciprocal arrangements

Reciprocal PLR arrangements now exist with the German, Dutch, Austrian and other European PLR schemes. Authors can apply for overseas PLR for most of these countries through the ALCS (Authors' Licensing and Collecting Society) (see page 707). The exception to this rule is Ireland. Authors should now register for Irish PLR through the UK PLR Office. Further information on PLR schemes internationally and recent developments within the EC towards wider recognition of PLR is available from the PLR Office or on the international PLR website.

The mathematics of publishing

Scott Pack reveals the numbers underlying the publishing business and spells out the important, surprising and sobering figures – for publisher and author alike – to be considered when publishing a book, even a bestseller.

When you think about the world of writing and publishing you probably picture an industry built upon words. And rightly so. The book world would be nothing without the written word. But numbers play a crucial part too, and some of the numbers that crunch away behind the scenes of publishing may surprise you.

How many copies does a book need to sell to become a bestseller?

100,000? 50,000? 10,000? Each week the *Sunday Times* publishes four separate book charts: top tens in Hardback Fiction, Hardback Non-fiction, Paperback Fiction and Paperback Non-fiction. For a book to be able to feature the three magic words '*Sunday Times* Bestseller' on the cover, it needs to have appeared in one of these charts for at least one week.

To sit at the top of these charts, especially Paperback Fiction, you generally need to sell thousands of copies. But pick a quiet time of year, perhaps February or March, and you could sneak in at number 10 in the Hardback Non-Fiction chart by selling around 500 copies, a somewhat less daunting figure.

Let's put that in perspective. There are close to 5,000 book outlets in the UK. A book could sell one copy in just 10% of these locations in any given week and hit the bestseller chart. 90% of shops wouldn't need to have sold any at all, and you'd still have a bestseller on your hands.

Things are very different at the top of the charts, of course. The bestselling paperback novel in the UK would typically have to sell well into five figures, although that could be anywhere between 10,000 and 90,000 depending on the time of year and what books are out that week.

And things get more interesting when you start to delve into the chart data a bit more. The *Sunday Times* top tens are taken from a much larger sales report generated by Nielsen Bookscan. They create a Top 5,000 chart each week that is distributed widely within the book trade, with retailers and publishers poring over the figures in some detail.

Let's say the bestselling book in the country sold 25,000 copies in a week. That's a lot of books, but not many titles can deliver that level of sales. In the same week it is likely that the tenth bestselling book sold around 7,000 copies – still a lot, but quite a drop-off. The book at number 100 in the charts will have sold 1,500 or so. The book at 500 may actually have sold 500 copies, and you can often get into the bottom regions of the Top 5,000 by selling 50 or so copies in a week.

So how does this pan out across an entire year? In a very good year, the bestselling book in the UK can sell close to a million copies, but it would more often be about half that number. The tenth bestseller may have sold half that again. The book at number 500 might have sold around 50,000, and you could have the 5,000th bestselling book of the year by selling 5,000 copies – or just one copy in every bookshop in the land.

It is important to stress that with the many tens of thousands of books published every year, and the hundreds of thousands already in circulation, the vast majority of books never even get close to the top 5,000 at all.

How much does it cost to publish a book?

These sales figures are all well and good, and may prove fascinating, but you cannot sell a single book until it is printed and distributed to shops, and that can prove to be a costly exercise.

Different types of books have different budgets – a big, illustrated, coffee-table book will usually cost several times more to produce than a fairly straightforward paperback – but for this example we are going to look at the costs for a standard novel with no fancy design elements or illustrations.

To get the manuscript ready for publication, with a developmental edit, copy edit, typesetting and proofread, you are rarely going to have much change from £2,500. A designer will charge around £750 to create a cover. Printing costs vary depending on the size of the print run, but 75p per copy is not untypical. So, to produce and print 3,000 copies of a paperback novel will cost a publisher in the region of £5,500. Of course, the major publishing houses manage a lot of these services in-house, but most medium- and small-sized publishers will be paying freelancers to do much of this work.

And that £5,500 is without spending any money on warehousing, distribution, sales, marketing or publicity, the combined costs of which could easily bring the total outlay to £10,000.

Example P&L

Sales

Book RRP
£7.99

Book sales
3000

Discount
55.00%

NET BOOK SALES £10,787

Production costs

Editorial
£1,750

Typesetting
£750

Cover design
£750

Printing costs

Print costs
£2,700

Sales and marketing costs

Sales and distribution
£2,500

Marketing and publicity
£1,500

TOTAL COSTS £9.950

Other deductions

Returns @ 15%
£1,618

Royalties
£1,798

Total costs + deductions £13,366

TOTAL PROFIT: -£2,579

How much money does a publisher make from a book?

So, a publisher has spent £10,000 to produce, sell, distribute and promote 3,000 copies of a new novel. Let's assume all 3,000 copies sell to bookshops, a rare feat but one that makes our maths a little easier, and that it has an RRP of £7.99.

Book retailers receive discount from publishers which can be anywhere from 30% to 70%, depending on the size of the retailer, how many copies they are ordering and whether or not the book goes into a big promotion – but let's use 55% as an average. That means that for every copy sold to bookshops the publisher receives £3.59. Across 3,000 copies that comes to £10,770 of revenue.

Cast your eye back a few paragraphs and you'll be reminded that it cost around £10,000 to produce these books in the first place, so even by selling the whole of the first print run, the publisher is only just breaking even. But wait! We forgot returns. In the UK, most books are sold to retailers on a sale-or-return basis. This means that shops can return unsold stock and typically 15-20% of all books sold to retailers are sent back. So that £10,770 mentioned above may end up being more like £8,600 once the returns are accounted for.

So how do publishers make any money from their books? Well, the truth is that many do not. They are often reliant on one or two books selling in excess of 10,000 copies, and ideally lots more than that, in order to generate the income needed to fund the other books on the list that sell below 3,000. Over time, they can build up a backlist of older titles that tick over, generating ongoing revenue. And ebooks can help too; they are cheaper to sell, as there are no warehouse costs and no returns, and many a book these days moves into profit on the back of healthy digital sales.

And how much money can an author make?

You probably know the score when it comes to royalties: for every copy of a book that sells, the author receives a percentage of the revenue. There are many variations on the basic deal but, if we continue with our example of a paperback novel, typically an author will receive 7.5% of the RRP for each copy that sells. On our £7.99 paperback that would be just under 60p – but I am feeling generous so will round it up.

Again, sticking with our example, if we sell 3,000 copies then the author will have made £1,800 in royalties. Hardly a life-changing amount, but not to be sniffed at either.

But let's not focus on such tiny numbers. Instead, let's be ambitious and bold and go back the bestsellers that we discussed earlier. Remember that bestselling book that sold 25,000 copies in a week, taking it to the top of the charts? Assuming it was a £7.99 paperback, that book will have earned its author £15,000 in just one week. The book at number 10, selling 7,000, will have generated £4,200. And even the number 500 book will have made £300, which isn't bad for one week's work. Although don't forget that the agent will take 15% of that!

What does this all add up to?

It is important that authors understand the numbers behind the publishing world. If a book becomes a bestseller, then it is possible for both author and publisher to make a lot of money, and even a moderate seller can, over time, generate some decent income. However, the majority of books published will only make a small amount of money for their authors.

For most of us, this is not a get-rich-quick industry. Does that matter? Only you can answer that, but if you have decided to write a book in order to make your fortune, you are probably going to be disappointed. If, however, you are writing a book because you want to share your story, and you value a connection with readers above all else, then great fortune may await – it just may not be a financial one.

Scott Pack is a writer, editor and publisher. He was formerly head of buying for Waterstones and spent many years at HarperCollins. He is now editor-at-large for Eye & Lightning Books and associate editor for Unbound. Scott also works as a freelance editor. For more information see https://reedsy.com/scott-pack.

Book publishers UK and Ireland

There are changes to listings in this section every year – publishers cease to exist, new ones emerge and others merge with each other. We aim to provide a comprehensive list of publishing imprints, the name or brand under which a specific set of titles are sold by a publisher. Any one publisher might have several imprints, for example Bloomsbury publishes cookery books under the Absolute Press imprint and nautical books under Adlard Coles. The imprint usually appears on the spine of a book. Imprints are included either under a Publisher's main entry or in some cases as an entry itself. Information is provided in a way that is of most use to a reader. The subject indexes which start on page 735, list publishers and imprints for different genres and forms of writing. The listings that follow are updated by the Writers' & Artists' editors based on information supplied by those listed.

*Member of the Publishers Association or Publishing Scotland
†Member of the Irish Book Publishers' Association
sae = self-addressed envelope, MS = manuscript (MSS = manuscripts)

AA Publishing

AA Media Ltd, Fanum House, Basing View, Basingstoke, Hants RG21 4EA
tel (01256) 491524
email aapublish@theaa.com
website www.theaa.com

Atlases, maps, leisure interests, travel including City Packs and AA Guides. Founded 1910.

Abacus – see Little, Brown Book Group

Absolute Press – see Bloomsbury Publishing Plc

Academic Press – see Elsevier Ltd

ACC Art Books Ltd

Sandy Lane, Old Martlesham, Woodbridge, Suffolk IP12 4SD
tel (01394) 389950
email uksales@accpublishinggroup.com
website www.accartbooks.com
Facebook www.facebook.com/ACCPublishing
Twitter @ACCPublishing
Publisher James Smith

Publisher and distributor of books on art, photography, decorative arts, fashion, gardening, design and architecture. Founded 1966.

Acorn Editions – see James Clarke & Co. Ltd

Airlife Publishing – see The Crowood Press

Akasha Publishing Ltd

20–22 Wenlock Road, London N1 7GU
tel 07939 927281
email info@akashapublishing.co.uk
Facebook www.facebook.com/akashapublishing
Twitter @Akashic84
Director Segun Magbagbeola

Trade (fiction and non-fiction), African and Caribbean interest, fantasy/sci-fi, spirituality, metaphysical, mind, body & spirit, ancient and classical history, alternative history, mythology, children's, Nuwaubian books, biographies and autobiographies. Currently accepting submissions. Founded 2012.

Ian Allan Publishing Ltd

Heritage House, 52–54 Hamm Moor Lane, Addlestone, Surrey KT15 2SF
tel (01932) 834950
email lewismasonic@gmail.com
website wwww.lewismasonic.co.uk
Managing Director Nick Lerwill, *General Manager* Martin Faulks

Lewis Masonic is the oldest Masonic imprint in the world. The company has been part of Ian Allan Publishing since 1973 and continues to produce Masonic books and rituals as well as the quarterly magazine *The Square*. Founded 1886.

J.A. Allen

The Crowood Press Ltd, The Stable Block, Crowood Lane, Ramsbury, Wilts. SN8 2HR
tel (01672) 520320
email enquiries@crowood.com
website www.crowood.com

Horse care and equestrianism including breeding, racing, polo, jumping, eventing, dressage, management, carriage driving, breeds, horse industry training, veterinary and farriery. Books usually commissioned but willing to consider any serious, specialist MSS on the horse and related subjects. Imprint of The Crowood Press (page 165). Founded 1926.

Allison & Busby Ltd

12 Fitzroy Mews, London W1T 6DW
tel 020-7580 1080

email susie@allisonandbusby.com
website www.allisonandbusby.com
Facebook www.facebook.com/allisonandbusbybooks
Twitter @allisonandbusby
Publishing Director Susie Dunlop, *Publishing Manager* Lesley Crooks, *Head of Sales* Daniel Scott

Fiction, general non-fiction, young adult and preschool. No unsolicited MSS. Founded 1967.

Allyn & Bacon – see Pearson UK

Alma Books

3 Castle Yard, Richmond TW10 6TF
tel 020-8940 6917
website www.almabooks.com, www.almaclassics.com
Directors Alessandro Gallenzi, Elisabetta Minervini

Contemporary literary fiction, non-fiction, European classics, poetry, drama, art, literary, music and social criticism, biography and autobiography, essays, humanities and social sciences. No unsolicited MSS. Inquiry letters must include a sae. Series include: Alma Classics, Overture Opera Guides, Calder Publications. Around 40% English-language originals, 60% translations. Founded 2005.

The Alpha Press – see Sussex Academic Press

Amazon Publishing

1 Principal Place, Worship Street, London EC2A 2FA
tel 0843 504 0495
email amazonpublishing-pr@amazon.com
website www.amazon.com/l/16144524011
EU Publisher Dominic Myers

Amazon Publishing is the full-service publishing arm of Amazon. Imprints: AmazonEncore, AmazonCrossing, Montlake Romance, Thomas & Mercer, 47North, Montlake Romance, Grand Harbor Press, Little A, Jet City Comics, Two Lions, Skyscrape, Lake Union Publishing, StoryFront, Waterfall Press, Kindle Press. Also publishes ebooks via its Kindle Direct publishing platform. Currently not accepting unsolicited MSS. Amazon Media EU Sarl is Amazon Publishing's EU entity. The address is: 31–33 Rives de Clausen, 2165 Luxembourg. Founded 2009.

Amber Books Ltd

United House, North Road, London N7 9DP
tel 020-7520 7600
email enquiries@amberbooks.co.uk
website www.amberbooks.co.uk
Facebook www.facebook.com/amberbooks
Twitter @amberbooks
Managing Director Stasz Gnych, *Rights Director* Sara McKie, *Publishing Manager* Charles Catton, *Head of Production* Peter Thompson, *Design Manager* Mark Batley, *Picture Manager* Terry Forshaw

Illustrated non-fiction publisher for adults and children. Subjects include history, photography, music, gift books, military technology, military history, survival, natural history and family reference. Works include encyclopedias and highly illustrated reference series. Children's titles created under Tiptoe Books imprint. Opportunities for freelancers. Founded 1989.

Amberley Publishing

The Hill, Stroud, Glos. GL5 4EP
tel (01453) 847800
email info@amberley-books.com
website www.amberley-books.com
Facebook www.facebook.com/amberleybooks
Twitter @amberleybooks
Chief Executive Nick Hayward

General history and local interest; specialisations include transport (railways, road transport, canals, maritime), industry, sport, biography and military history. Founded 2008.

Amgueddfa Cymru – National Museum Wales

Cathays Park, Cardiff CF10 3NP
tel 029-2057 3235
email post@museumwales.ac.uk
website www.museumwales.ac.uk
Twitter @AmgueddfaBooks
Head of Publishing Mari Gordon

Books based on the collections and research of Amgueddfa Cymru for adults, schools and children, in both Welsh and English.

And Other Stories

Central Library, Surrey St, Sheffield S1 1XZ
email info@andotherstories.org
website www.andotherstories.org/about/contact-us
Facebook www.facebook.com/AndOtherStoriesBooks
Twitter @andothertweets
Publisher Stefan Tobler

Contemporary literary fiction and non-fiction from around the world. Has an open submissions policy, but has strict submissions guidelines. Please read carefully before submitting: www.andotherstories.org/about/contact-us/. Submissions not complying with these guidelines will be disregarded. Founded 2011.

Andersen Press Ltd*

20 Vauxhall Bridge Road, London SW1V 2SA
tel 020-7840 8703 (editorial), 020-7840 8701 (general)
email anderseneditorial@penguinrandomhouse.co.uk
website www.andersenpress.co.uk
Managing Director Mark Hendle, *Publisher* Klaus Flugge, *Directors* Philip Durrance, Joëlle Flugge, Libby Hamilton (editorial picture books), Charlie Sheppard (editorial fiction), Sarah Pakenham (rights)

Children's books: picture books, fiction for 5–8 and 9–12 years and young adult fiction. Will consider unsolicited MSS. Include sae and allow three months

Books

for response. For novels, send three sample chapters and a synopsis only. No poetry or short stories. Do not send MSS via email. Founded 1976.

The Angels' Share – see Neil Wilson Publishing Ltd

Angry Robot Books

20 Fletcher Gate, Nottingham NG1 2FZ
tel 0115 933 8456
email incoming@angryrobots.com
website https://www.angryrobotbooks.com/
Facebook www.facebook.com/angryrobotbooks
Twitter @angryrobotbooks
Publisher Marc Gascoigne

Publishes modern adult science fiction, fantasy and everything inbetween. Part of Watkins Media (page 214). Founded 2009.

Anness Publishing

Head office 108 Great Russell Street, London WC1B 3NA
email info@anness.com
Distributed by Marton Book Services, 160 Eastern Avenue, Milton Park, Oxford OX14 4SB
website www.annesspublishing.com
Managing Director Paul Anness, *Publisher* Joanna Lorenz

Practical illustrated books on lifestyle, cookery, crafts, reference, gardening, health and children's non-fiction. Imprints include: Lorenz Books, Armadillo, Southwater, Peony Press, Hermes House and Practical Pictures (www.practicalpictures.com). Founded 1988.

Appletree Press Ltd†

164 Malone Road, Belfast BT9 5LL
tel 028-9024 3074
email reception@appletree.ie
website www.appletree.ie
Director John Murphy

Gift books, guidebooks, history, Irish interest, Scottish interest, photography, sport, travel. Founded 1974.

Arc Publications

Nanholme Mill, Shaw Wood Road, Todmorden, Lancs. OL14 6DA
tel (01706) 812338
email arc.publications@btconnect.com
website www.arcpublications.co.uk
Facebook www.facebook.com/arcpublications
Twitter @arc_poetry
Directors Tony Ward (founder & managing editor), Angela Jarman (publisher & editor of Arc Music); *Editors* James Byrne (international), Jean Boase-Beier (translation), John W. Clarke (UK & Ireland), Ben Styles (digital editor)

Specialises in contemporary poetry and neglected work from the past: poetry from the UK and Ireland; world poetry in English; and bilingual translations mainly from the smaller languages (individual poets and anthologies). Imprints: Arc Publications and Arc Music. Refer to website for current publication list/catalogue and submissions policy. Email editors at: editorarcuk@btinternet.com. No unsolicited MSS. Founded 1969.

Architectural Press – see Elsevier Ltd

Arena Publishing

6 Southgate Green, Bury St. Edmunds IP33 2BL
tel (01284) 754123
email arenabooks.bse@gmail.com
website www.arenabooks.co.uk
Director James Farrell

Publishers of quality fiction, travel, history and current affairs, also of specialised social science, politics, philosophy and academic dissertations suitable for transcribing into book format. Special interest in publishing books analysing the debt-fuelled financial crisis from a non-party standpoint. New authors welcome. IPG member.

The Armchair Traveller *at the* bookHaus Ltd

4 Cinnamon Row, Plantation Wharf, London SW11 3TW
tel 020-7838 9055
email info@hauspublishing.com
website www.hauspublishing.com
Publisher Harry Hill

Publishes travel literature, the *Literary Traveller* series and the Armchair Traveller's *Histories* series.

Arrow Books Ltd – see Cornerstone

Ashgate Publishing Ltd – see Taylor & Francis Group

Ashmolean Museum Publications

Beaumont Street, Oxford OX1 2PH
tel (01865) 288070
email dec.mccarthy@ashmus.ox.ac.uk
website www.ashmolean.org
Contact Declan McCarthy

Publisher of exhibition catalogues, fine and applied art of Europe and Asia, archaeology, history, numismatics. Photographic archive and picture library. Museum founded 1683.

Atlantic Books*

Ormond House, 26–27 Boswell Street, London WC1N 3JZ
tel 020-7269 1610
email enquiries@atlantic-books.co.uk
website http://atlantic-books.co.uk/
Ceo & Publisher Will Atkinson

Literary fiction, thrillers, history, current affairs, politics, reference, biography and memoir. Strictly no unsolicited submissions or proposals. In 2009 Atlantic Books entered a partnership with Australian publisher Allen & Unwin. Founded 2000.

Atlantic Europe Publishing Co. Ltd

The Barn, Bottom Farm, Bottom Lane,
Henley-on-Thames, Oxon RG8 0NR
tel (01491) 684028
email info@atlanticeurope.com
website www.atlanticeurope.com, www.curriculumvisions.com
Director Dr B.J. Knapp

Children's primary school class books: science, geography, technology, mathematics, history, religious education. No MSS accepted by post; submit by email only, no attachments. Founded 1990.

Atrium – see Cork University Press

Attic Press – see Cork University Press

Aureus Publishing Ltd

Castle Court, Castle-upon-Alun, St Bride's Major, Vale of Glamorgan CF32 0TN
tel (01656) 880033
email info@aureus.co.uk
website www.aureus.co.uk
Director Meuryn Hughes

Rock and pop, autobiography, biography, sport; also music. Founded 1993.

Aurora Metro

67 Grove Avenue, Twickenham TW1 4HX
tel 020-3261 0000
email info@aurorametro.com
website www.aurorametro.com
Facebook www.facebook.com/AuroraMetroBooks
Twitter @aurorametro
Managing Director Cheryl Robson

Adult fiction, young adult fiction, biography, drama (including plays for young people), non-fiction, theatre, cookery and translation. Submissions: send synopsis and three chapters as hard copy to: Submissions Editor, at address above or via email to submissions@aurorametro.com. Biennial Competition for women novelists (odd years): The Virginia Prize For Fiction. Supernova Books publishes non-fiction titles on the arts, culture and biography.

Authentic Media Ltd

PO Box 6326, Bletchley, Milton Keynes MK1 9GG
tel (01908) 268500
email info@authenticmedia.co.uk
website www.authenticmedia.co.uk
Facebook www.facebook.com/authenticmedia
Twitter @authenticmedia
General Manager Donna Harris

Biblical studies, Christian theology, ethics, history, mission, commentaries. Imprints: Paternoster, Authentic.

The Authority Guides

Unit 3 Spike Island, 133 Cumberland Road,
Bristol BS1 6UX
tel (01789) 761345
email hello@authorityguides.co.uk
website http:authorityguides.co.uk
Facebook www.facebook.com/groups/theauthorityclub/
Twitter @SRA_TAG
Director Sue Richardson

Pocket-sized business books for entrepreneurs and business professionals. Concise and practical, our titles range across business subjects from finance to leadership, sales and marketing to personal development. Submissions welcomed, please email for guidelines.

Avon – see HarperCollins Publishers

Award Publications Ltd

The Old Riding School, The Welbeck Estate,
Worksop, Notts. S80 3LR
tel (01909) 478170
email info@awardpublications.co.uk
Facebook www.facebook.com/awardpublications
Twitter @award_books

Children's books: full-colour picture story books; early learning, information and activity books. No unsolicited material. Founded 1972.

Bernard Babani (publishing) Ltd

The Grampians, Shepherds Bush Road,
London W6 7NF
tel 020-7603 2581/7296
email enquiries@babanibooks.com
website www.babanibooks.com
Director M.H. Babani

Practical handbooks on radio, electronics and computing. Founded 1942.

Bailliere Tindall – see Elsevier Ltd

Bantam Press – see Penguin Random House Children's UK

Barrington Stoke*

18 Walker Street, Edinburgh EH3 7LP
tel 0131 225 4113
email info@barringtonstoke.co.uk
website www.barringtonstoke.co.uk
Chairperson Lucy Juckes

Short fiction for children, specially adapted and presented for reluctant, struggling and dyslexic readers, including picture books up to young adult fiction. No unsolicited submissions. Founded 1998.

Batsford – see Pavilion Books

Bennion Kearny Ltd

6 Woodside, Churnet View Road, Oakamoor, Staffs. ST10 3AE
tel (01538) 703591
email info@BennionKearny.com
website www.BennionKearny.com
Publisher James Lumsden-Cook, *Marketing* Adam Walters

Specialises in non-fiction, with an emphasis on sport, biography, STM, computing and business. Founded 2008.

Berg Publishers – see Bloomsbury Publishing Plc

Berlitz Publishing – see Insight Guides/Berlitz Publishing

BFI Publishing

Palgrave Macmillan, The Macmillan Building, 4 Crinan Street, London N1 9XW
tel 020-7833 4000
email bfipublishing@palgrave.com
website https://www.macmillanihe.com/page/bfi-publishing/
Head of Publishing Jenna Steventon

Film, TV and media studies; general, academic and educational resources on moving image culture. Founded 1982.

Birlinn Ltd

West Newington House, 10 Newington Road, Edinburgh EH9 1QS
tel 0131 668 4371
email info@birlinn.co.uk
website www.birlinn.co.uk
Directors Hugh Andrew, Neville Moir, Jan Rutherford, Andrew Simmons, Laura Poynton, Joanne Macleod

Based in Newington in Edinburgh and run by a small team. Publisher of the reissue of Neil Munro's *Para Handy* which has been in print since 1992. Publishes both in the UK and internationally. Genres include Scottish history, local interest/history, Scottish humour, guides, military, adventure, history, archaeology, sport, general non-fiction. Founded 1992.

Birlinn

Scottish and general UK interest books, biography, history, military history, mapping, cookery and Scottish Gaelic.

BC Books

Children's imprint providing quality illustrated books for young readers. Founded 2015.

Polygon

Imprint of classic and modern literary fiction and poetry. Authors include: Robin Jenkins, George Mackay Brown and Alexander McCall Smith. Publishes music and film titles including Stuart Cosgrove's *Young Soul Rebels.* International authors include Jan-Philipp Sendker.

Arena Sport

Sport imprint. Subjects include football, rugby, golf, running and cycling.

John Donald

Academic books.

A&C Black – see Bloomsbury Publishing Plc

Black Ace Books

PO Box 7547, Perth PH2 1AU
tel (01821) 642822
website www.blackace.co.uk
Publisher Hunter Steele

Fiction, Scottish and general; new editions of outstanding recent fiction. Some biography, history, psychology and philosophy. No submissions without first visiting website for latest list details and requirements. Imprints: Black Ace Books, Black Ace Paperbacks. Founded 1991.

Black & White Publishing Ltd*

Nautical House, 104 Commercial Street, Edinburgh EH6 6NF
tel 0131 625 4500
email mail@blackandwhitepublishing.com
website www.blackandwhitepublishing.com
Directors Campbell Brown (managing), Alison McBride (publishing)

Non-fiction: general, sport, cookery, biography, humour, crime. Fiction: women's fiction, contemporary, historical, psychological thrillers, crime, young adult (Ink Road imprint). Also publisher of *Itchy Coo*, *The Broons* and *Oor Wullie books.* New submissions should be sent via the website: http://blackandwhitepublishing.com/submissions. Founded 1999.

Black Lace – see Virgin Books (in partnership with Virgin Group), page 168

Black Swan – see Transworld Publishers

Blackstaff Press Ltd†

Colourpoint House, Jubilee Business Park, 21 Jubilee Road, Newtownards, Co. Down BT23 4YH
tel 028-9182 6339 (within the UK), 048-9182 6339 (Republic of Ireland)
email info@blackstaffpress.com
website www.blackstaffpress.com
Facebook www.facebook.com/Blackstaffpressni
Twitter @BlackstaffNI

Managing Editor Patsy Horton

Local interest titles, particularly memoir, history and humour. See website for submission guidelines before sending material. Acquired by Colourpoint Creative Ltd in 2017 (page 163) Founded 1971.

John Blake Publishing Ltd

3 Bramber Court, 2 Bramber Road,
London W14 9PB
tel 020-7381 0666
email help@johnblakebooks.com
website www.johnblakebooks.com
Facebook www.facebook.com/johnblakebooks
Twitter @jblakebooks
Publishing Director Kelly Ellis

Incorporating Metro Books, Blake Publishing, Dino Books, Independent Music Press and Max Crime and Smith Gryphon Ltd. Popular non-fiction, including biographies, true crime, food and drink, humour, health and lifestyle. Imprints include Dino Books and Music Press Books. No unsolicited fiction. Acquired by Bonnier Publishing in 2016. Founded 1991.

Blink Publishing

107–109 The Plaza, 535 Kings Road, Chelsea,
London SW10 0SZ
tel 020-3770 8888
email info@blinkpublishing.co.uk,
submissions@blinkpublishing.co.uk
website www.blinkpublishing.co.uk
Publishing Director Matthew Phillips, *Editorial Director* Kelly Ellis, *Editor* Beth Eynon, *Publicity Director* Karen Browning

Blink is an imprint focussed on general non-fiction, popular culture, sport, business, humour, vloggers, true crime, biography and inspirational memoir. Imprint of Kings Road Publishing (page 184), which is part of Bonnier Publishing UK.

Lagom

Acquistions Director & Publisher Natalie Jerome, *Senior Editor* Oliver Holden-Rea

Health and wellbeing, diet and fitness, cookery, lifestyle and memoir.

535

Senior Editor Joel Simons

Narrative non-fiction, popular science, quirky memoir, humour and entertaining reference.

Bloodaxe Books Ltd*

Eastburn, South Park, Hexham,
Northumberland NE46 1BS
tel (01434) 611581
email editor@bloodaxebooks.com
website www.bloodaxebooks.com
Directors Neil Astley, Simon Thirsk

Poetry. Check submissions guide on website and send sample of up to a dozen poems with sae only if the submission fits the publisher's guidelines. No email submissions or correspondence. Founded 1978.

Bloomsbury Publishing Plc*

50 Bedford Square, London WC1B 3DP
tel 020-7631 5600
website www.bloomsbury.com (main),
www.bloomsbury-ir.co.uk (investor relations)
Co-founder & Chief Executive Nigel Newton, *Executive Directors* Jonathan Glasspool, Richard Charkin, *Group Finance Director* Wendy Pallot, *Non-executive Chairman* Sir Richard Lambert, *Independent Non-executive Directors* John Warren, Jill Jones, Steven Hall, *Group Company Secretary* Michael Daykin, *media enquiries: tel* 020-7631 5670, *email* publicity@bloomsbury.com

A medium-sized independent book publishing house and digital content services provider with two worldwide publishing divisions: Consumer and Non-Consumer. It has a global footprint served from offices in the UK, the USA (see page 228), India and Australia (see page 217). Has acquired imprints dating back to 1807. Listed on the London Main Market stock exchange (code: BMY). MSS must normally be channelled through literary agents. Bloomsbury runs training for authors on getting published via *Writers' & Artists'* publications and Bloomsbury Institute events. Founded 1986.

Bloomsbury Consumer Division

Managing Director Emma Hopkin, *Adult Editor-in-Chief* Alexandra Pringle, *Children's Editor-in-Chief* Rebecca McNally

Imprints include: Absolute Press, Bloomsbury Activity Books, Bloomsbury Children's Books, Bloomsbury Circus, Bloomsbury India, Bloomsbury Press, Bloomsbury Publishing, Bloomsbury USA, Bloomsbury USA Children's Books, Raven Books.

Bloomsbury Adult Trade Publishing

Adult Editor-in-Chief Alexandra Pringle, *Publishing Director* Alexis Kirschbaum, *Publishing Director* Michael Fishwick, *Editorial Director Raven Books* Alison Hennessey

Part of **Bloomsbury Consumer Division**, Bloomsbury Adult Trade publishes a wide variety of fiction, non-fiction and cookery titles under the Absolute Press Bloomsbury, Bloomsbury Circus and Raven Books imprints. Known for literary fiction it publishes, amongst others, Neil Gaiman, Elizabeth Gilbert, Khaled Hosseini, Madeleine Miller, Ann Patchett and in 2017 George Saunders won the Man Booker prize with *Lincoln in the Bardo*. The successful non-fiction list features authors such as Reni Eddo-Lodge, Peter Frankopan and Johann Hari. The cookery list features chefs such as Hugh Fernley-Whittingstall, Paul Hollywood and Tom Kerridge.

Bloomsbury Children's Books

Publishing Director & Editor-in-Chief Rebecca McNally, *Publishing Director Non-fiction* Sharon

Hutton, *Publishing Director Illustrated Books* Emma Blackburn, *Editorial Directors* Ellen Holgate (fiction), Saskia Gwinn (non-fiction)

Part of **Bloomsbury Consumer Division**, Bloomsbury Children's Books is a global publisher for children of all ages up to 16 years including titles such as the *Harry Potter* novels by J.K. Rowling, *Holes* by Louis Sachar and *The Graveyard Book* by Neil Gaiman. Recent highlights include the bestselling *Throne of Glass* series by Sarah J. Maas, *One* by Sarah Crossan (winner of the Carnegie Medal), *The Bombs That Brought Us Together* by Brian Conaghan (winner of the Costa Children's Book Award), *You Can't Take an Elephant on the Bus* by Patricia Cleveland-Peck and David Tazzyman and *Harry Potter and the Philosopher's Stone* Illustrated Edition by J.K. Rowling and Jim Kay. Recent non-fiction highlights include *Fantastically Great Women Who Changed the World* by Kate Pankhurst and *My Epic Book of Epicness* by Adam Frost, winner of Blue Peter's Best Book with Facts award 2016. No complete MSS; send a synopsis with three chapters.

Bloomsbury Non-Consumer Division

website www.bloomsburyprofessional.com, www.bloomsburyacademic.com
Managing Director Non-Consumer Division Jonathan Glasspool, *Executive Director (Special Interest)* Richard Charkin

Imprints include: The Adlard Coles; Andrew Brodie; Arden Shakespeare; Bloomsbury Academic, Business, Berg Publishers, Caravel, Continuum, Education, Natural History, Professional, Reader, Shire Publications, Sigma, Sport and Visual Arts; Burns & Oates; Conway; Fairchild Books; Featherstone; Green Tree; Hart Publishing (page 178); Helm; Methuen Drama; Osprey Publishing; Osprey Games; Poyser; Reeds; T&T Clark; Wisden; and Bloomsbury Yearbooks. I.B. Tauris & Co. Ltd (page 209) was acquired in May 2018.

Bloomsbury Education

Head of Education Rachel Lindley, *Editorial Director* Helen Diamond, *Commissioning Editors* Hannah Rolls (fiction & poetry), Hannah Marston (education)

Part of **Bloomsbury Non-Consumer Division**, Bloomsbury publishes 75 titles a year for children, young people and those working with them. Titles for teachers and practitioners cover the areas of early years, primary and secondary education, and include both practical resources and professional development titles. Recent titles include *Mark. Plan. Teach.* by Ross Morrison McGill, *Effective Transition into Year 1* by Alistair Bryce-Clegg and *Will You Be My Friend?* by Molly Potter. Educational fiction and poetry publications include Terry Deary's *Historical Tales*, Joshua Seigal's *I Don't Like Poetry* and *Classic Nursery Rhymes*, with illustrations by Dorothy M. Wheeler. Imprints include Bloomsbury Education, A&C Black, Andrew Brodie, Featherstone Education and Herbert Press.

Digital Resources

Managing Director, Digital Resources Division Kathryn Earle

Digital Resources is part of **Bloomsbury Non-Consumer Division** and is developing new digital content services to expand Bloomsbury's portfolio across the humanities and social sciences. Recent launches include Bloomsbury Design Library, Bloomsbury Food Library, Bloomsbury Cultural History, and the Bloomsbury Encyclopedia of Philosophers.

Blue Guides Ltd

Winchester House, Dean Gate Avenue, Taunton TA1 2UH
tel 020-8144 3509
email editorial@blueguides.com
website www.blueguides.com
Facebook www.facebook.com/blueguides
Twitter @blueguides

Blue Guides and *Blue Guide Travel Companions*. Detailed guide books with a focus on history, art and architecture for the independent traveller.

Bluemoose Books

25 Sackville Street, Hebden Bridge HX7 7DJ
email kevin@bluemoosebooks.com
website www.bluemoosebooks.com
Twitter @ofmooseandmen
Publisher Kevin Duffy

Publisher of literary fiction. No children's, young adult or poetry. Founded 2006.

Bodleian Library Publishing

Bodleian Library, Broad Street, Oxford OX1 3BG
tel (01865) 283850
email publishing@bodleian.ox.ac.uk
website www.bodleianshop.co.uk
Facebook www.facebook.com/bodleianlibraries
Twitter @BodPublishing
Head of Publishing Samuel Fanous

The Bodleian Library is the main library of the University of Oxford. The publishing programme creates gift, trade and scholarly books on a wide range of subjects drawn from or related to the Library's rich collection of rare books, manuscripts, maps, postcards and other ephemera.

The Bodley Head – see Vintage

Bodley Head Children's Books – see Penguin Random House Children's UK

Bonnier Zaffre*

80–81 Wimpole Street, London W1G 9RE
tel 020-7490 3875

email info@bonnierzaffre.co.uk
website www.bonnierzaffre.co.uk
Facebook www.facebook.com/BonnierZaffre
Twitter @BonnierZaffre
Ceo Mark Smith, *Executive Director* Kate Parkin (adult), *Executive Director* Jane Harris (children's), *Executive Director* James Horobin (sales & marketing)

Publishes award-winning fiction for all ages, including crime, thrillers, women's fiction, general fiction, children's fiction and picture books and young adult. Imprints include: Zaffre Publishing, Twenty7 Books, Hot Key Books (page 180), Piccadilly Press (page 198) and Manilla Publishing. A division of Bonnier Publishing. Founded 2015.

The Book Guild Ltd

14 Priory Business Park, Wistow Road, Kibworth, Leics. LE8 0RX
tel 0800 999 2982
email info@bookguild.co.uk
website www.bookguild.co.uk
Facebook www.facebook.com/thebookguild
Twitter @BookGuild
Directors Jeremy Thompson (managing), Jane Rowland (operations)

Offers traditional and partnership publishing arrangements, with all titles published being funded or co-funded by The Book Guild Ltd (does not offer self-publishing). MSS accepted in fiction, children's and non-fiction genres, please see the website for details. The Book Guild is part of parent company Troubador Publishing Ltd (page 212).

Bookouture

Carmelite House, 50 Victoria Embankment, London EC4Y 0DZ
email pitch@bookouture.com
website www.bookouture.com
Facebook www.facebook.com/bookouture
Twitter @bookouture
Managing Director & Publisher Oliver Rhodes, *Publishing Directors* Claire Bord, Jenny Geras, *Associate Publishers* Natasha Harding, Keshini Naidoo, Lydia Vassar-Smith, Kathryn Taussig, Isobel Akenhead, *Commissioning Editors* Abigail Fenton, Jessie Botterill, Helen Jenner, Christina Demosthenous, *Head of Talent* Peta Nightingale

Bookouture is a digital imprint publishing commercial fiction. Welcomes submissions via the website: www.bookouture.com. Part of Hachette UK isince March 2017 (page 176). Founded 2012.

Booth-Clibborn Editions

Studio 83, 235 Earls Court Road, London SW5 9FE
tel 020-7565 0688
email info@booth-clibborn.com
website www.booth-clibborn.com

Illustrated books on art, popular culture, graphic design, photography. Founded 1974.

Bounty – see Octopus Publishing Group

Bowker

ProQuest/Dialog/Bowker, 3 Dorset Rise (5th Floor), London EC4Y 8EN
tel 020-7832 1700
email sales@bowker.co.uk
website www.bowker.com
Managing Director Doug McMillan

Publishes bibliographic information and management solutions designed to help publishers, booksellers and libraries better serve their customers. Creates products and services that make books easier for people to discover, evaluate, order and experience. Also generates research and resources for publishers, helping them understand and meet the interests of readers worldwide. Bowker, an affiliated business of ProQuest and the official ISBN agency for the United States has its headquarters in New Providence, New Jersey, with additional operations in the UK and Australia.

Boxtree – see Pan Macmillan

Marion Boyars Publishers Ltd

26 Parke Road, London SW13 9NG
email catheryn@marionboyars.com
website www.marionboyars.co.uk
Director Catheryn Kilgarriff

Literary fiction, film, cultural studies, jazz, cookery. Not currently accepting submissions. Founded 1975.

Boydell & Brewer Ltd

Bridge Farm Business Park, Top Street, Martlesham IP12 4RB
tel (01394) 610600
email editorial@boydell.co.uk
website www.boydellandbrewer.com

Medieval studies, early modern and modern history, maritime history, literature, archaeology, art history, music, Hispanic studies. No unsolicited MSS. See website for submission guidelines. Founded 1969.

James Currey

website www.jamescurrey.com

Academic studies of Africa and developing economies.

Bradt Travel Guides Ltd

IDC House, The Vale, Chalfont St Peter, Bucks. SL9 9RZ
tel (01753) 893444
email info@bradtguides.com
website www.bradtguides.com
Twitter @BradtGuides
Managing Director Adrian Phillips

Travel and wildlife guides with emphasis on unusual destinations and ethical/positive travel. Founded 1974.

Nicholas Brealey Publishing

Carmelite House, 50 Victoria Embankment, London EC4Y 0DZ
tel 020-3122 6000
email rights@nicholasbrealey.com
website www.nicholasbrealey.com
Directors Nick Davies (managing), Holly Bennion (editorial)

Publishes subjects related to coaching, crossing cultures and the big ideas in business. Also popular psychology, science and philosophy, and includes an expanding travel writing/adventure list. Founded 1992 in London; also has offices in Boston. Part of Hachette UK (page 176).

Brilliant Publications Limited*

Unit 10, Sparrow Hall Farm, Edlesborough, Dunstable LU6 2ES
tel (01525) 222292
email info@brilliantpublications.co.uk
website www.brilliantpublications.co.uk
Facebook www.facebook.com/Brilliant-Publications-340005555138
Twitter @Brilliantpub, @BrillCreative
Managing Director Priscilla Hannaford

Brilliant Publications creates easy-to-use educational resources, featuring engaging approaches to learning, across a wide range of curriculum areas, including English, foreign languages, maths, art and design, thinking skills and PSHE. No children's picture books, non-fiction books or one-off fiction books. See Guidelines for Authors on website before sending proposal. Founded 1993.

Bristol University Press/Policy Press

University of Bristol, 1–9 Old Park Hill, Clifton, Bristol BS2 8BB
tel 0117 954 5940
email pp-info@bristol.ac.uk
website www.policypress.co.uk, www.bristoluniversitypress.co.uk
Facebook www.facebook.com/PolicyPress
Twitter @policypress, @BrisUniPress
Ceo Alison Shaw, *Journals Director* Julia Mortimer, *Sales & Marketing Director* Jo Greig, *Head of Commissioning* Victoria Pittman

Social science. Bristol University Press specialising in politics and international relations, sociology, human geography, business & management, economics and law. Policy Press, specialising in social and public policy, criminology, social work and social welfare. Bristol University Press founded 2016, Policy Press founded 1996.

The British Library (Publications)*

Publishing Office, The British Library, 96 Euston Road, London NW1 2DB
tel 020-7412 7535
email publishing_editorial@bl.uk
website www.bl.uk/aboutus/publishing

Publishes around 40 non-fiction books a year: arts, bibliography, music, maps, oriental, manuscript studies, history, literature, facsimiles, audio and multimedia. Founded 1979.

The British Museum Press

38 Russell Square, London WC1B 3QQ
tel 020-3073 4946
email publicity@britishmuseum.org
website www.britishmuseum.org/about_us/services/the_british_museum_press.aspx
Head of Business Planning Susan Walby

Award-winning illustrated books for general readers, families, academics and students, inspired by the famous collections of the British Museum. Titles range across the fine and decorative arts, history, archaeology and world cultures. Division of The British Museum Company Ltd. Founded 1973.

Andrew Brodie – see Bloomsbury Publishing Plc

Brown, Son & Ferguson Ltd*

Unit 1, 426 Drumoyne Road, Glasgow G51 4DA
tel 0141 883 0141 (24 hours)
email info@skipper.co.uk
website www.skipper.co.uk
Editorial Director Richard B.P. Brown

Nautical books, plays. Founded 1860.

Bryntirion Press

Bryntirion, Bridgend CF31 4DX
tel (01656) 655886
email office@emw.org.uk
website www.emw.org.uk
Publications Officer Shâron Barnes

Formerly Evangelical Press of Wales. Theology and religion (in English and Welsh). Founded 1955.

Buster Books – see Michael O'Mara Books Ltd

Butterworth-Heinemann – see Elsevier Ltd

Butterworths – see LexisNexis

Calisi Press

100 Somerset Road, Folkestone CT19 4NW
tel (01303) 272216
email info@calisipress.com
website www.calisipress.com
Facebook www.facebook.com/CalisiPress
Twitter @CalisiPress
Publisher Franca Simpson

Small independent publishing company specialising in the publication of works by Italian women writers. Founded 2014.

Cambridge University Press*

University Printing House, Shaftesbury Road, Cambridge CB2 8BS

tel (01223) 358331
email information@cambridge.org
website www.cambridge.org
Facebook www.facebook.com/CambridgeUniversityPress
Twitter @CambridgeUP
Chief Executive Peter Phillips; *Managing Directors* Mandy Hill (academic), Michael Peluse (ELT), Rod Smith (Cambridge Education)

Anthropology and archaeology, art history, astronomy, biological sciences, classical studies, computer science, dictionaries, earth sciences, economics, engineering, history, language and literature, law, mathematics, medical sciences, music, philosophy, physical sciences, politics, psychology, reference, technology, social sciences, theology, religion. ELT, educational (primary, secondary, tertiary), e-learning products, journals (humanities, social sciences, science, technical and medical). The Bible and Prayer Book. Founded 1534.

Campbell Books – see Pan Macmillan

Candy Jar Books

Mackintosh House, 136 Newport Road, Cardiff CF24 1DJ
tel 029-2115 7202
email shaun@candyjarbooks.co.uk
website www.candy-jar.co.uk/books
Facebook www.facebook.com/CandyJarLimited
Twitter @Candy_Jar
Head of Publishing Shaun Russell

Publishes science fiction, biography, general non-fiction, children's, military history, fantasy. Publishes about 15 titles per year. Unsolicited material welcome; submissions form on website. No children's picture books. Founded 2010.

Canongate Books Ltd*

14 High Street, Edinburgh EH1 1TE
tel 0131 557 5111
email support@canongate.co.uk
Alternative address Eardley House, 4 Uxbridge Street, London W8 7SY
website www.canongate.co.uk
Ceo Jamie Byng, *Publishing Director* Francis Bickmore, *Rights Director* Andrea Joyce, *Editorial Director* Simon Thorogood, *Senior Commissioning Editor* Hannah Knowles, *Editor* Jo Dingley

Adult general non-fiction and fiction: literary fiction, translated fiction, memoir, politics, popular science, humour, travel, popular culture, history and biography. The independent audio publisher CSA WORD was acquired by Canongate in 2010, with audio now published under the Canongate label. Founded 1973.

Canopus Publishing Ltd

15 Nelson Parade, Bedminster, Bristol BS3 4HY
tel 07970 153217
email robin@canopusbooks.com
website www.canopusbooks.com
Twitter @robin_rees
Directors Robin Rees, Sarah Tremlett

Packager of books on astronomy, aerospace, photography and rock music; publisher for the London Stereoscopic Company and Starmus. Founded 1999.

Canterbury Press – see Hymns Ancient and Modern Ltd

Jonathan Cape – see Vintage

Capuchin Classics – see Stacey Publishing Ltd

Carcanet Press Ltd*

4th Floor, Alliance House, 30 Cross Street, Manchester M2 7AQ
tel 0161 834 8730
email info@carcanet.co.uk
website www.carcanet.co.uk
Managing Director Luke Allan

Poetry, *Fyfield* series, Oxford Poets, translations. Imprints include Anvil Press Poetry, Comma Press, Lintott Press, Northern House, Sheep Meadow Press. Founded 1969.

Carlton Publishing Group

20 Mortimer Street, London W1T 3JW
tel 020-7612 0400
email enquiries@carltonbooks.co.uk
website www.carltonbooks.co.uk
Editorial Director Piers Murray Hill

No unsolicited MSS; synopses and ideas welcome, but no fiction or poetry. Founded 1992.

Carlton Books

Sport, music and film, history, puzzles, lifestyle, fashion, art, photography, popular culture, crime, science.

André Deutsch

Autobiography, biography, military history, history, current affairs.

Goodman

High-end illustrated books on popular culture and the arts.

Prion Books

Humour, nostalgia.

Caterpillar Books – see Little Tiger Group

Catholic Truth Society

42–46 Harleyford Road, London SE11 5AY
tel 020-7640 0042
email il.gregoire@ctsbooks.org
website www.ctsbooks.org, www.onefifties.org

Publisher Fergal Martin, *Managing Editor* Lisa Gregoire

General books of Roman Catholic and Christian interest, liturgical books, missals, bibles, prayer books, children's books and booklets of doctrinal, historical, devotional or social interest. MSS of 11,000–13,600 words with up to six illustrations considered for publication as booklets. Founded 1868.

Cengage Learning*

Cheriton House, Andover SP10 5BE
tel (01264) 332424
email emea.editorial@cengage.com
website www.cengage.co.uk

Actively commissioning texts for further education and higher education courses in the following disciplines: IT, computer science and computer applications; accounting, finance and economics; marketing; international business; human resource management; operations management; strategic management; organisational behaviour; business information systems; quantitative methods; psychology; hairdressing and beauty therapy; childcare; catering and hospitality; motor vehicle maintenance. Submit proposal either by email or by post.

Century – see Cornerstone

Chapman Publishing

4 Broughton Place, Edinburgh EH1 3RX
tel 0131 557 2207
email chapman-pub@blueyonder.co.uk
website www.chapman-pub.co.uk
Editor Joy Hendry

Poetry and drama: *Chapman New Writing Series*. Also the *Chapman Wild Women Series*. Founded 1986.

Chartered Institute of Personnel and Development

CIPD Publishing, 151 The Broadway, London SW19 1JQ
tel 020-8612 6200
email publish@cipd.co.uk
website www.cipd.co.uk/bookstore
Head of Publishing Sinead Costello

People management, training and development.

Chatto & Windus – see Vintage

Chicken House

2 Palmer Street, Frome, Somerset BA11 1DS
tel (01373) 454488
email hello@chickenhousebooks.com
website www.chickenhousebooks.com
Twitter @chickenhsebooks
Managing Director & Publisher Barry Cunningham, *Deputy Managing Director* Rachel Hickman

Fiction for ages 7+ and young adult. No unsolicited MSS. Successes include James Dashner (the *Maze Runner* series), Cornelia Funke (*Inkheart* and the *Dragon Rider* series) and Kiran Millwood Hargrave (*The Girl of Ink & Stars*). See website for details of *Times*/Chicken House Children's Fiction Competition for unpublished writers. Part of Scholastic Ltd (page 205).

Child's Play (International) Ltd

Ashworth Road, Bridgemead, Swindon, Wilts. SN5 7YD
tel (01793) 616286
email office@childs-play.com
website www.childs-play.com
Facebook www.facebook.com/ChildsPlayBooks
Twitter @ChildsPlayBooks
Chairman Adriana Twinn, *Publisher* Neil Burden

Children's educational books: board, picture, activity and play books; fiction and non-fiction. Founded 1972.

Christian Education*

5/6 Imperial Court, 12 Sovereign Road, Birmingham B30 3FH
tel 0121 472 4242
email anstice.hughes@christianeducation.org.uk
website http://shop.christianeducation.org.uk/, www.retoday.org.uk
Facebook www.facebook.com/RETodayServices
Twitter @IBRAbibleread

Incorporating RE Today Services and International Bible Reading Association. Publications and services for teachers and other professionals in religious education including *REtoday* magazine, curriculum booklets and classroom resources. Also publishes bible reading materials.

Churchill Livingstone – see Elsevier Ltd

Churchwarden Publications Ltd

PO Box 420, Warminster, Wilts. BA12 9XB
tel (01985) 840189
email enquiries@churchwardenbooks.co.uk
website www.churchwardenbooks.co.uk
Directors J.N.G. Stidolph, S.A. Stidolph

Publisher of *The Churchwarden's Yearbook*. Care and administration of churches and parishes.

Cicerone Press

Juniper House, Murley Moss Business Village, Oxenholme Road, Kendal, Cumbria LA9 7RL
tel (01539) 562069
email info@cicerone.co.uk
website www.cicerone.co.uk
Managing Director Jonathan Williams

Guidebooks: walking, trekking, mountaineering, climbing, cycling in Britain, Europe and worldwide.

Cico Books – see Ryland Peters & Small

Cisco Press – see Pearson UK

Claret Press

51 Iveley Road, London SW4 0EN
tel 020-722 0436
email contact@claretpress.com
website www.claretpress.com
Facebook www.facebook.com/ClaretPublisher
Twitter @Claret_Press
Founder & Editor-in-Chief Katie Isbester

Claret Press is an indie boutique publishing house which selects on the basis of quality and readability in the belief that those criteria create modern classics. Publishes quirky, tilt to young adult cross-over. Flexible about genre. Founded 2016.

James Clarke & Co. Ltd

PO Box 60, Cambridge CB1 2NT
tel (01223) 350865
email publishing@jamesclarke.co.uk
website www.jamesclarke.co
Facebook www.facebook.com/JamesClarkeandCo
Twitter @JamesClarkeLtd
Managing Director Adrian Brink

The company began by publishing the religious magazine *Christian World*. It now publishes academic, scholarly and reference works. Recent titles include *The Human Icon: A Comparative Study of Hindu and Orthodox Christian Beliefs* by Christine Mangala Frost, *Divine Remaking: St Bonaventure and the Gospel of Luke* by Douglas Dales and *The Books of Homilies: A Critical Edition* by Gerald Bray. Publishes books and ebooks on: theology, philosophy, history and biography, biblical studies and reference books including the *Libraries Directory*. Imprints: The Lutterworth Press, Acorn Editions, Patrick Hardy Books. Founded 1859.

Classical Comics

PO Box 177, Ludlow, Shrops. SY8 9DL
tel 0845 812 3000
email info@classicalcomics.com
website www.classicalcomics.com
Managing Director Gary Bryant

Graphic novel adaptations of classical literature.

Cló Iar-Chonnachta Teo†

Indreabhán, Co. Galway,
H91 CHO1 Republic of Ireland
tel +353 (0)91 593307
email eolas@cic.ie
website http://www.cic.ie/
Director & Chairman Micheál Ó Conghaile, *Director & Secretary* Tadhg Ó Conghaile

Irish-language – novels, short stories, plays, poetry, songs, history; CDs (writers reading from their works in Irish and English). Promotes the translation of contemporary Irish fiction and poetry into other languages. Founded 1985.

Cloud Lodge Books Ltd

Niddry Lodge, 51 Holland Street, London W8 7JB
tel 020-7225 1623
email info@cloudlodgebooks.co.uk
website www.cloudlodgebooks.co.uk
Facebook www.facebook.com/cloudlodgebooks
Twitter @CLBPressUK
Managing Director William Campos, *Fiction Editor* Oliver Walton, *Science Fiction Editor* Alexander Hernandez, *Sales & Marketing* David Wightman

London-based publisher of daring literary fiction, crime fiction and sci fi. Publishes up to four original titles per year, which are made available in print, digital and audio formats. Features writers (and characters) of every race, religion, nationality, gender and sexual orientation. In short, diversity is regarded as vitally important and a hallmark of all imprints. Founded 2016.

Co & Bear Productions

63 Edith Grove, London SW10 0LB
tel 020-7351 5545
email info@cobear.co.uk
website www.scriptumeditions.co.uk
Publisher Beatrice Vincenzini

High-quality illustrated books on lifestyle, photography and art. Imprints: Scriptum Editions, Cartago. Founded 1996.

Collins & Brown – see Pavilion Books

Collins Learning – see HarperCollins Publishers

Colourpoint Creative Limited†

Colourpoint House, Jubilee Business Park,
21 Jubilee Road, Newtownards, Co. Down BT23 4YH
tel 028-9182 6339 (within UK), 048-9182 6339 (Republic of Ireland)
email sales@colourpoint.co.uk
website www.colourpoint.co.uk
Twitter @colourpoint
Publisher Malcolm Johnston, *Head of Educational Publishing* Wesley Johnston, *Marketing* Jacky Hawkes

Irish, Ulster-Scots and general interest including local history; transport (covering the whole of the British Isles), railways, buses, road, aviation; educational textbooks and resources. Short queries by email. Full submission in writing including details of proposal, sample chapter/section, qualification/experience in the topic, full contact details and return postage. Imprints: Colourpoint Educational, Blackstaff Press Ltd (page 156). Founded 1993.

The Columba Press†

23 Merrion Square North, Dublin D02 XE02,
Republic of Ireland
tel +353 (0)16 874096

email info@columba.ie
website www.columba.ie
Facebook www.facebook.com/columbapress/
Twitter @columbapress
Publisher & Managing Director Garry O'Sullivan

Religion (Roman Catholic and Anglican) including pastoral handbooks, spirituality, theology, liturgy and prayer; counselling and self-help. Founded 1985.

Comma Press

Studio 510a, 5th Floor, Hope Mill,
113 Pollard Street, Manchester M4 7JA
email ra.page@commapress.co.uk
website http://commapress.co.uk
Facebook www.facebook.com/Comma-Press/
Twitter @commapress
Founder & Ceo Ra Page

A not-for-profit publishing initiative dedicated to promoting new writing with an emphasis on the short story. In April 2012, Comma became one of the Art's Council's new National Portfolio Organisations (NPOs). For submissions please see 'resources' section of the website: http://commapress.co.uk/resources/submissions/.

Connections Book Publishing Ltd

St Chad's House, 148 King's Cross Road,
London WC1X 9DH
tel 020-7837 1968
email info@eddisonbooks.com
website www.eddisonbooks.com
Director Stéphane Leduc

An imprint of Eddison Books Ltd. Illustrated non-fiction books, kits and gift titles: broad, popular list including mind, body & spirit; health; personal development; and parenting, childcare and brain-training.

Conran Octopus – see Octopus Publishing Group

Constable & Robinson Ltd – see Little, Brown Book Group

The Continuum International Publishing Group Plc – see Bloomsbury Publishing Plc

Cork University Press†

Youngline Industrial Estate, Pouladuff Road, Togher, Cork T12 HT6V, Republic of Ireland
tel +353 (0)21 490 2980
website www.corkuniversitypress.com
Publications Director Mike Collins

Irish literature, history, cultural studies, landscape studies, medieval studies, English literature, musicology, poetry, translations. Founded 1925.

Attic Press and Atrium

email corkuniversitypress@ucc.ie

Books by and about women in the areas of social and political comment, women's studies. Cookery, biography and Irish cultural studies (trade).

Cornerstone

20 Vauxhall Bridge Road, London SW1V 2SA
tel 020-7840 8400
website www.penguin.co.uk
Managing Director Susan Sandon, *Director of Publicity & Media Relations* Charlotte Bush

Part of Penguin Random House UK (page 198). No unsolicited MSS accepted.

Arrow Books Ltd

tel 020-7840 8689
Publisher Selina Walker, *Deputy Publisher* Emily Griffin

Paperback fiction and non-fiction.

Century

tel 020-7840 8414
Publisher Selina Walker, *Deputy Publisher* Ben Brusey

Fiction, biography, autobiography, general non-fiction, true crime, humour.

Hutchinson

tel 020-7840 8733
Publisher Jason Arthur, *Publishing Director* Jocasta Hamilton

Fiction: upmarket and women's fiction, adventure, crime, thrillers. Non-fiction: biography, memoirs, general history, politics, current affairs.

Random House Books

tel 020-7840 8451
Publishing Director Nigel Wilcockson

Non-fiction: social and cultural history, current affairs, popular culture and reference.

Random House Business Books

tel 020-7840 8451
Publishing Director Nigel Wilcockson

Business, finance and economics.

William Heinemann

tel 020-7840 8564
Publisher Jason Arthur, *Editorial Director* Tom Avery

Fiction and general non-fiction: literary fiction, fiction in translation, literary thrillers, narrative non-fiction, history, memoir, biography, popular science, current affairs.

Windmill Books

tel 020-7840 8265
website www.windmillbooks.co.uk
Publisher Jason Arthur

B-format paperback fiction and non-fiction.

Council for British Archaeology

Beatrice de Cardi House, 66 Bootham,
York YO30 7BZ

tel (01904) 671417
email webenquiry@archaeologyuk.org
website www.archaeologyuk.org
Facebook www.facebook.com/Archaeologyuk
Twitter @archaeologyuk
Director Mike Heyworth

British archaeology – academic; practical handbooks; general interest archaeology. *British Archaeology* magazine. Founded 1944.

Country Books

Courtyard Cottage, Little Longstone, Bakewell, Derbyshire DE45 1NN
tel (01629) 640670
email dickrichardson@country-books.co.uk
website www.countrybooks.biz, www.sussexbooks.co.uk

Incorporating Ashridge Press. Local history (new and facsimile reprints), family history, autobiography, general non-fiction, novels, customs and folklore. Books for the National Trust, Chatsworth House, Peak District NPA, Derbyshire County Council. Established 1995.

Countryside Books

2 Highfield Avenue, Newbury, Berks. RG14 5DS
tel (01635) 43816
website www.countrysidebooks.co.uk
Partners Nicholas Battle, Suzanne Battle

Publishes books of local or regional interest, usually on a county basis: walking, outdoor activities, also heritage, aviation, railways and architecture.

CRC Press – see Taylor & Francis Group

Crescent Moon Publishing

PO Box 393, Maidstone, Kent ME14 5XU
tel (01622) 729593
email cresmopub@yahoo.co.uk
website www.crmoon.com
Director Jeremy Robinson *Editors* C. Hughes, B.D. Barnacle

Literature, poetry, arts, cultural studies, media, cinema, feminism. Submit sample chapters or six poems plus sae, not complete MSS. Founded 1988.

Cressrelles Publishing Co. Ltd

10 Station Road Industrial Estate, Colwall, Malvern, Herefordshire WR13 6RN
tel (01684) 540154
email simon@cressrelles.co.uk
website www.cressrelles.co.uk
Directors Leslie Smith, Simon Smith

General publishing. Founded 1973.

J. Garnet Miller

Plays and theatre textbooks.

Kenyon-Deane

Plays and drama textbooks for amateur dramatic societies. Plays for women.

New Playwrights' Network

Plays for amateur dramatic societies.

Croner-i Ltd

240 Blackfriars Road, London SE1 8BF
tel 0844 561 8166
email client.experience@croneri.co.uk
website www.croneri.co.uk

Formerly Croner, CCH Group Ltd. Human Resources, health and safety, tax, audit and accountancy, education, healthcare, manufacturing and construction. Looseleaf, consultancy and online information services.

Crown House Publishing Ltd

Crown Buildings, Bancyfelin, Carmarthen SA33 5ND
tel (01267) 211345
email books@crownhouse.co.uk
website www.crownhouse.co.uk
Facebook www.facebook.com/Crown-House-Publishing/
Twitter @CrownHousePub
Chairman Martin Roberts; *Directors* David Bowman (managing), Glenys Roberts, Karen Bowman

Award-winning education publisher with a large range of classroom resources and materials for professional teacher development. The list includes the Independent Thinking Press imprint, as well as books on health and wellbeing, NLP, hypnosis, counselling, psychotherapy and coaching. Founded 1998.

Independent Thinking Press

email books@independentthinkingpress.com
website www.independentthinkingpress.com

Publishes the thoughts and ideas of some of the UK's leading educational innovators including world-class speakers, award-winning teachers, outstanding school leaders and classroom revolutionaries.

The Crowood Press

The Stable Block, Ramsbury, Marlborough, Wilts. SN8 2HR
tel (01672) 520320
email enquiries@crowood.com
website www.crowood.com
Directors John Dennis (chairman), Ken Hathaway (managing)

Sport, motoring, aviation, military, martial arts, walking, fishing, country sports, farming, natural history, gardening, DIY, crafts, railways, model-making, dogs, equestrian and theatre. Imprints include: Airlife Publishing (aviation, technical and general, military, military history), Robert Hale (general non-fiction), J. A. Allen (equestrian), N. A.

G. Press (horology and gemmology) and Black Horse Westerns (fictions – westerns). Founded 1982.

Crux Publishing

39 Birdhurst Road, London SW18 1AR
tel 020-8871 0594
email hello@cruxpublishing.co.uk
website www.cruxpublishing.co.uk
Publisher Christopher Lascelles

Boutique publisher offering to produce, distribute and market selected high-quality, non-fiction titles. Operates an open submissions policy for new authors and digitally republishes backlist titles for existing authors. Works with individual authors to create and execute a unique marketing plan that drives sales. Founded December 2011.

Benjamin Cummings – see Pearson UK

James Currey – see Boydell & Brewer Ltd

Darf Publishers Ltd

277 West End Lane, London NW6 1QS
tel 020-7431 7009
email enquiry@darfpublishers.co.uk
website www.darfpublishers.co.uk
Facebook www.facebook.com/DarfPublishers
Twitter @DarfPublishers
Contacts Ghassan Fergiani (director), Ghazi Gheblawi (editorial), Sherif Dhaimish (production)

An independent publisher based in London with diversity and inclusion at the heart of the company's work since 1980. The focus is on publishing and reprinting historical, geographic and classical works in English about the Middle East, North Africa and the UK. Also focuses on contemporary works of fiction, non-fiction and children's books from other languages into English, introducing new authors to the British market and the wider English speaking world. Recent published works from Arabic (Libya, Yemen, Sudan, Eritrea), Italian, German with plans to widen to include writers from other European countries, South America, Asia and Africa. Founded 1981.

Darton, Longman and Todd Ltd

1 Spencer Court, 140–142 Wandsworth High Street, London SW18 4JJ
tel 020-8875 0155
email willp@darton-longman-todd.co.uk
website www.darton-longman-todd.co.uk
Editorial Director David Moloney

Spirituality, prayer and meditation; books for the heart, mind and soul; self-help and personal growth; biography; political, environmental and social issues. Founded 1959.

DB Publishing

29 Clarence Road, Nottingham NG9 5HY
tel (07914) 647382
email steve.caron@dbpublishing.co.uk
website www.dbpublishing.co.uk
Directors Steve Caron (managing), Jane Caron (finance)

An imprint of JMD Media Ltd. Primarily: football, sport, local history, heritage. Currently considering all topics including fiction. Unsolicited MSS welcome. Preliminary letter essential. Founded 2009.

Giles de la Mare Publishers Ltd

PO Box 25351, London NW5 1ZT
tel 020-7485 2533
email gilesdelamare@dial.pipex.com
website www.gilesdelamare.co.uk
Chairman Giles de la Mare

Non-fiction: art, architecture, biography, history, music, travel. Telephone before submitting MS. Founded 1995.

Dedalus Ltd

24 St Judith's Lane, Sawtry, Cambs. PE28 5XE
tel (01487) 832382
email info@dedalusbooks.com
website www.dedalusbooks.com
Chairman Margaret Jull Costa, *Publisher* Eric Lane, *Editorial* Timothy Lane

Original fiction in English and in translation; 12–14 titles a year. Imprints include: Original English Language Fiction in Paperback, Dedalus European Classics, Dedalus Euro Shorts, Dedalus Europe Contemporary Fiction, Dedalus Africa, Dedalus Concept books. City Noir, Dark Masters Literary Biography. Founded 1983.

Richard Dennis Publications

The New Chapel, Shepton Beauchamp, Ilminster, Somerset TA19 0JT
tel (01460) 240044
email books@richarddennispublications.com
website www.richarddennispublications.com

Books for collectors specialising in ceramics, glass, illustration, sculpture and facsimile editions of early catalogues.

André Deutsch – see Carlton Publishing Group

diehard

91–93 Main Street, Callander FK17 8BQ
tel (01877) 339449
website http://www.scottishpoetrylibrary.org.uk/poetry/publishers/diehard-publishers
Director Sally Evans (editorial)

Scottish poetry. Founded 1993.

Digital Press – see Elsevier Ltd

Dino Books

3 Bramber Court, 2 Bramber Road, London W14 9PB

tel 020-7381 0666
email help@dinobooks.co.uk
website www.dinobooks.co.uk
Facebook www.facebook.com/dinokidsbooks
Twitter @dinobooks

Popular children's non-fiction.

Discovery Walking Guides Ltd

10 Tennyson Close, Northampton NN15 7HJ
tel (01604) 244869
email ask.discovery@ntlworld.com
website www.dwgwalking.co.uk
Chairman Rosamund C. Brawn

Publishes 'Walk!' walking guidebooks to UK and European destinations; 'Tour & Trail Super-Durable' large-scale maps for outdoor adventures; 'Bus & Touring' maps; and 'Drive' touring maps. Premium content provider to 3G phone/tablet gps apps for Digital Mapping and Hiking Adventures. Publishing in conventional book/map format along with digital platforms. Welcomes project proposals from technologically (gps) proficient walking writers. Founded 1994.

DK

80 Strand, London WC2R 0RL
tel 020-7139 2000
website www.dk.com
Ceo Ian Hudson

Illustrated non-fiction for adults and children: gardening, health and beauty, medical, travel, food and drink, history, science and nature, photography, reference, pregnancy and parenting, popular culture. DK is a company in the Penguin Random House division of Bertelsmann (page 198).

Prima Games

Publisher Mike Degler

Computer games strategy guides and collectors' editions.

Travel

website www.traveldk.com
Publisher Georgina Dee

Travel guides, illustrated travel books, phrasebooks and digital products. Includes *DK Eyewitness Travel*.

Dodo Ink

email sam@dodoink.com
website www.dodoink.com
Facebook www.facebook.com/Dodo-Ink/
Twitter @DodoInk
Directors Sam Mills (managing), Thom Cuell (editorial), Alex Spears (marketing)

An independent press dedicated to publishing daring and difficult literary fiction. Publishes two to three novels a year. Authors include Seraphina Madsen, Monique Roffey and James Miller. No unsolicited MSS by post; see the website for submission guidelines. Founded 2015.

John Donald – see Birlinn Ltd

Dorling Kindersley – see DK

Doubleday Children's Books – see Penguin Random House Children's UK

Doubleday (UK) – see Penguin Random House Children's UK

The Dovecote Press Ltd

Stanbridge, Wimborne Minster, Dorset BH21 4JD
tel (01258) 840549
email online@dovecotepress.com
website www.dovecotepress.com
Editorial Director David Burnett

Books of local interest: natural history, architecture, history. Founded 1974.

Dref Wen

28 Church Road, Whitchurch, Cardiff CF14 2EA
tel 029-2061 7860
website www.drefwen.com
Directors Roger Boore, Anne Boore, Gwilym Boore, Alun Boore, Rhys Boore

Welsh language publisher. Original Welsh language novels for children and adult learners. Original, adaptations and translations of foreign and English language full-colour picture story books for children. Educational material for primary/secondary schoolchildren in Wales and England. Founded 1970.

University College Dublin Press†

H103 Humanities Institute, Belfield, Dublin 4, Republic of Ireland
tel +353 (0)17 164680,
email ucdpress@ucd.ie
website www.ucdpress.ie
Twitter @UCDPress
Executive Editor Noelle Moran

Humanities: Irish studies, history and politics, literary studies, social sciences, sociology. More recently expanded to include music and food science. Founded 1995.

Gerald Duckworth & Co. Ltd

30 Calvin Street, London E1 6NW
tel 020-7490 7300
email info@duckworth-publishers.co.uk
website www.ducknet.co.uk
Twitter @Duckbooks
Publisher Peter Mayer

General trade publishers. Non-fiction: popular science, history, humour, arts, social science, biography, current affairs, humanities, social sciences, language, mind, body & spirit, sport, travel and travel writing. Fiction: crime, thriller, historical, literary, general. Imprints: Duckworth, Duckworth Overlook, Nonesuch Press, Ardis. Founded 1898.

Dunedin Academic Press*

Hudson House, 8 Albany Street, Edinburgh EH1 3QB
tel 0131 473 2397
email mail@dunedinacademicpress.co.uk
website www.dunedinacademicpress.co.uk
Director Anthony Kinahan

Earth and environmental sciences, public health and social sciences (esp. children issues). See website for submission guidelines. Founded 2000.

Dynasty Press

36 Ravensdon Street, London SE11 4AR
tel 020-8675 3435
email david@dynastypresslondon.co.uk
website www.dynastypress.co.uk
Contact David Hornsby

A boutique publishing house specialising in works connected to royalty, dynasties and people of influence. Committed to the freedom of the press to allow authentic voices and important stories to be made available to the public. Usually publishes titles which reveal and analyse the lives of those placed in the upper echelons of society. Founded 2008.

Earthscan

8–12 Camden High Street, London NW1 0JH
tel 020-7387 8558
email earthinfo@earthscan.co.uk
website www.routledge.com/sustainability

Publishes under the Routledge imprint for Taylor & Francis Group (page 209). Academic and professional: sustainable development, climate and energy, natural resource management, cities and built environment, business and economics, design and technology.

Ebury Press – see Ebury Publishing

Ebury Publishing

20 Vauxhall Bridge Road, London SW1V 2SA
tel 020-7840 8400
website www.penguin.co.uk, www.penguinrandomhouse.co.uk
Directors Rebecca Smart (managing), Jake Lingwood (deputy managing), Sarah Bennie (publicity & media relations), Diana Riley (marketing)

Part of Penguin Random House UK (page 198).

Ebury Press Fiction

tel 020-7840 8400
Publishing Director Gillian Green

Commercial fiction, crime, thriller, romance, sci-fi, fantasy. Imprints: Del Rey, Rouge.

Ebury Press

tel 020-7840 8400
Deputy Publisher Andrew Goodfellow

General commercial non-fiction, autobiography, memoir, popular history, sport, travel writing, popular science, humour, film/TV tie-ins, music, popular reference, cookery, lifestyle.

Ebury Enterprises

tel 020-7840 8400
Publishing Director Carey Smith

Gift books, branded and bespoke books.

Rider

tel 020-7840 8400
Publishing Director Judith Kendra

Inspirational titles across the spectrum of psychology, philosophy, international affairs, biography, current affairs, history, travel and spirituality.

Vermilion

tel 020-7840 8400
Publishing Director Susanna Abbott

Personal development, health, diet, relationships, parenting.

Virgin Books (in partnership with Virgin Group)

tel 020-7840 8400
Publishing Director Joel Rickett

Business and smart thinking, health and popular culture: entertainment, showbiz, arts, film and TV, music, humour, biography and autobiography, popular reference, true crime, sport, travel, memoir, environment. Imprints: Black Lace, Nexus, WH Allen.

Eden – see Transworld Publishers

Edinburgh University Press*

The Tun – Holyrood Road, 12 Jackson's Entry, Edinburgh EH8 8PJ
tel 0131 650 4218
email editorial@eup.ac.uk
website www.edinburghuniversitypress.com, www.euppublishing.com
Twitter @EdinburghUP
Chairman Ivon Asquith, *Chief Executive* Timothy Wright, *Head of Editorial* Nicola Ramsey, *Head of Journals* Sarah Edwards, *Head of Sales & Marketing* Anna Glazier

Academic publishers of scholarly books and journals: film, media and cultural studies, Islamic and Middle Eastern studies, history, law, linguistics, literary studies, philosophy, politics, Scottish studies, American studies, religious studies, classical and ancient history. Trade: literature and culture, Scottish history and politics.

The Educational Company of Ireland

Ballymount Road, Walkinstown, Dublin D12 R25C, Republic of Ireland
tel +353 (0)14 500611
email info@edco.ie
website www.edco.ie
Ceo Martina Harford

Educational MSS on all subjects in English or Irish language. A member of the Smurfit Kappa Group plc. Founded 1910.

Educational Explorers (Publishers)

Unit 5, Feidr Castell Business Park, Fishguard SA65 9BB
tel (01348) 874890
website www.cuisenaire.co.uk
Directors J. Hollyfield, D.M. Gattegno

Educational. Recent successes include: mathematics: *Numbers in Colour with Cuisenaire Rods*; languages: *The Silent Way*; literacy, reading: *Words in Colour*; educational films. No longer accepting unsolicited MSS. Founded 1962.

Egmont UK Ltd*

First Floor, The Yellow Building, 1 Nicholas Road, London W11 4AN
email info@egmont.co.uk
website www.egmont.co.uk

The UK's largest specialist children's publisher, publishing books from babies to teens, inspiring children to read. Publishes award-winning books, magazines, ebooks and apps. Egmont has a growing portfolio of digital publishing which includes: the first Flips books for Nintendo DS, apps for iPhone and iPad, ebooks and enhanced ebooks and online virtual worlds. Egmont UK is part of the Egmont Group and owned by the Egmont Foundation, a charitable trust dedicated to supporting children and young people. Founded 1878.

Egmont Press

email childrensreader@euk.egmont.com

Picture book and gift (ages 0+), fiction (ages 5+). Authors include Michael Morpurgo, Enid Blyton, Andy Stanton, Michael Grant, Lemony Snicket, Kristina Stephenson, Giles Andreae, Jan Fearnley and Lydia Monks. Submission details: visit website to see current policy.

Egmont Publishing Group

email charcterpr@euk.egmont.com

The UK's leading licensed character publisher of books and magazines for children from birth to teen. Books portfolio includes *Thomas the Tank Engine*, *Mr Men*, *Fireman Sam*, *Ben 10*, *Bob the Builder*, *Baby Jake* and *Everything's Rosie* and covers a wide range of formats from storybooks, annuals and novelty books to colouring, activity and sticker books. Magazines portfolio includes *Thomas & Friends*, *Disney Princess*, *Toy Story*, *Barbie*, *Ben 10*, *Tinker Bell*, *Fireman Sam*, *We Love Pop* and girls' pre-teen magazine *Go Girl* and boys' lifestyle title *Toxic*.

Eland Publishing Ltd

61 Exmouth Market, London EC1R 4QL
tel 020-7833 0762
email info@travelbooks.co.uk
website www.travelbooks.co.uk
Directors Rose Baring, John Hatt, Barnaby Rogerson

Has a backlist of 125 titles in classic travel literature. No unsolicited MSS. Email in first instance. Founded 1982.

11:9 – see Neil Wilson Publishing Ltd

Edward Elgar Publishing Ltd

The Lypiatts, 15 Lansdown Road, Cheltenham, Glos. GL50 2JA
tel (01242) 226934
email info@e-elgar.co.uk
website www.e-elgar.com
Managing Director Tim Williams

Economics, business, law, public and social policy. Founded 1986.

Elliott & Thompson

27 John Street, London WC1N 2BX
tel 020-7831 5013
email pippa@eandtbooks.com
website www.eandtbooks.com
Twitter @eandtbooks
Chairman Lorne Forsyth, *Director* Olivia Bays, *Publisher* Jennie Condell, *Senior Editor* Pippa Crane

History, biography, music, popular science, gift, sport, business, economics and adult fiction. Founded 2009.

Elsevier Ltd*

The Boulevard, Langford Lane, Kidlington, Oxford OX5 1GB
tel (01865) 843000
website www.elsevier.com
Twitter @ElsevierConnect
Ceo Ron Mobed

Academic and professional reference books; scientific, technical and medical products and services (books, journals, electronic information). No unsolicited MSS, but synopses and project proposals welcome. Imprints: Academic Press, Architectural Press, Bailliere Tindall, Butterworth-Heinemann, Churchill Livingstone, Digital Press, Elsevier, Elsevier Advanced Technology, Focal Press, Gulf Professional Press, JAI, Made Simple Books, Morgan Kauffman, Mosby, Newnes, North-Holland, Pergamon, Saunders, Woodhead Publishing. Division of RELX Corp., Amsterdam.

The Emma Press Ltd

Jewellery Quarter, Birmingham
email queries@theemmapress.com
website https://theemmapress.com
Facebook www.facebook.com/TheEmmaPress
Twitter @TheEmmaPress
Directors Emma Wright (publishing), Rachel Piercey (editorial)

Won the Michael Marks Award for Poetry Pamphlet Publishers in 2016. Publishes themed poetry anthologies, single-author poetry pamphlets and prose pamphlets, including short stories, essays, guides and recipes. Does not consider unsolicited MSS but runs bi-monthly open calls for submissions of poetry for anthologies and biennial calls for poetry and prose pamphlets. Check website for details. Founded 2012.

Encyclopaedia Britannica (UK) Ltd

2nd Floor, Unity Wharf, 13 Mill Street,
London SE1 2BH
tel 020-7500 7800
email enquiries@britannica.co.uk
website www.britannica.co.uk
Managing Director Ian Grant

Global digital educational publisher of instructional products used in schools, universities, homes, libraries and in the workplace.

Endeavour Media

85–7 Borough High Street, London SE1 1NH
email jasmin@endeavourmedia.com
website www.endeavourpress.com
Facebook www.facebook.com/EndeavourPress
Twitter @EndeavourPress
Contacts Matthew, Lynn, Richard Foreman, James Faktor, Alice Rees, Amy Burgwin

Independent publisher of crime fiction, thrillers, historical fiction, history and popular women's fiction.

Enitharmon Editions

10 Bury Place, London WC1A 2JL
tel 020-7430 0844
email info@enitharmon.co.uk
website www.enitharmon.co.uk
Directors Stephen Stuart-Smith, Isabel Brittain

Imprints: Enitharmon Editions: Artists' books, Enitharmon Press: poetry, including fine editions. Some literary criticism, fiction, translations. prints. No unsolicited MSS. No freelance editors or proofreaders required. Founded 1967.

Everyman's Library

50 Albemarle Street, London W1S 4BD
tel 020-7493 4361
email books@everyman.uk.com, guides@everyman.uk.com
website www.everymanslibrary.co.uk
Facebook www.facebook.com/everymanslibrary
Twitter @EverymansLib
Publisher David Campbell

Everyman's Library (clothbound reprints of the classics); *Everyman Pocket Classics*; *Everyman's Library Children's Classics*; *Everyman's Library Pocket Poets*; *Everyman Guides*; P.G. Wodehouse. No unsolicited submissions. Imprint of Alfred A. Knopf.

Everything With Words Ltd

16 Limekiln Place, London SE19 2RE
tel 020-8771 2974
email info@everythingwithwords.com
website www.everythingwithwords.com
Director Mikka Bott

Children's fiction for ages 5 to young adult. Publishes innovative, quality fiction. No picture books. Founded 2016.

University of Exeter Press

Reed Hall, Streatham Drive, Exeter EX4 4QR
tel (01392) 263066
email uep@exeter.ac.uk
website www.exeterpress.co.uk
Facebook www.facebook.com/UniversityofExeterPress
Twitter @UExeterPress
Publisher Simon Baker, *Sales, Marketing & Distribution* Helen Gannon

Academic and scholarly books on European literature, film history, performance studies, local history (Exeter and the South West). Imprints include: University of Exeter Press, Bristol Phoenix Press, The Exeter Press. Distributor in the UK, Europe and the Middle East for US and Canadian academic presses, including American Research Center in Egypt, American Schools of Oriental Research, Archaeological Institute of America, Greece and Cyprus Research Center, Eliot Werner Publications, Freelance Academy Press, Kelsey Museum Publications, Lockwood Press, Michigan Classical Press, Middle East Documentation Center, Truman State University Press, University of Arizona Egyptian Expedition, Yale Egyptological Institute. Distributor for Kapon Editions in UK, Europe and Middle East. Founded 1958.

Helen Exley

16 Chalk Hill, Watford, Herts. WD19 4BG
tel (01923) 474480
website www.helenexleygiftbooks.com
Facebook www.facebook.com/helenexleygifts
Twitter @helen_exley
Ceo Helen Exley

Popular colour gift books for an international market. No unsolicited MSS. Founded 1976.

Eye Books

29 Barrow Street, Much Wenlock,
Shropshire TF13 6EN
tel 020-3239 3027
email dan@eye-books.com
website www.eye-books.com
Twitter @eyebooks
Publisher Dan Hiscocks

Publishes across different imprints both fiction and non-fiction. Founded 1996.

Eyewear Publishing Ltd

Suite 333, 19–21 Crawford Street, London W1H 1PJ
tel 020-7289 0627
email info@eyewearpublishing.com
website www.eyewearpublishing.com
Facebook www.facebook.com/EyewearPublishing
Twitter @EyewearBooks
Director Todd Swift, *Senior Editor* Rosanna Hildyard, *Managing Editor* Alexandra Payne

Celebrates prose and poetry writing in English from the UK and overseas. Through the annual Melita Hume Poetry Prize, Beverly Prize and Sexton Prize, new poets are discovered, supported and developed. Founded 2012.

F&W Media International Ltd

Pynes Hill Court, Pynes Hill, Exeter EX2 5SP
tel (01392) 797680
website www.fwcommunity.com
Managing Director James Woollam

A community-focused, creator of content (for books, ebooks and digital downloads) and marketer of products and services for hobbyists and enthusiasts including crafts, art techniques, writing books, gardening, natural history, equestrian, DIY, military history, photography. Founded 1960.

F100 Group

34–42 Cleveland Street, London W1T 4LB
tel 020-7323 0323
email info@f1000.com
website http://f1000.com
Chairman Vitek Tracz

Life science publishing, electronic publishing and internet communities.

Faber and Faber Ltd*

Bloomsbury House, 74–77 Great Russell Street, London WC1B 3DA
tel 020-7927 3800
website www.faber.co.uk
Facebook www.facebook.com/FaberandFaber
Twitter @FaberBooks
Chief Executive Stephen Page, *Publisher Children's* Leah Thaxton, *Faber Social Creative Director* Lee Brackstone, *Communications Director & Associate Publisher* Rachel Alexander, *Sales & Services Director* Charlotte Robertson, *Operations Director* Nigel Marsh, *Director of Faber Academy* Ian Ellard, *Faber Factory Director* Simon Blacklock

High-quality general fiction and non-fiction, children's fiction and non-fiction, drama, film, music, poetry. Unsolicited submissions accepted for poetry only. For information on poetry submission procedures, ring 020-7927 3800, or consult the website. No unsolicited MSS. Founded 1929.

Fabian Society

61 Petty France, London SW1H 9EU
tel 020-7227 4900
email info@fabians.org.uk
website www.fabians.org.uk
Facebook www.facebook.com/fabiansociety
Twitter @thefabians
General Secretary Andrew Harrop

Current affairs, political thought, economics, education, environment, foreign affairs, social policy. Also controls NCLC Publishing Society Ltd. Founded 1884.

Fairchild Books – see Bloomsbury Publishing Plc

CJ Fallon

Ground Floor, Block B, Liffey Valley Office Campus, Dublin D22 X0Y3, Republic of Ireland
tel +353 (0)16 166400
email editorial@cjfallon.ie
website www.cjfallon.ie
Executive Directors Brian Gilsenan (managing), John Bodley (financial)

Educational textbooks. Founded 1927.

Fat Fox Books

The Den, PO Box 579, Tonbridge TN9 9NG
tel (01580) 857249
email hello@fatfoxbooks.com
website http://fatfoxbooks.com
Facebook www.facebook.com/Fat-Fox/
Twitter @FatFoxBooks
Managing Director Holly Millbank

Independent publisher of children's books for children 3–14 years. Founded 2014.

Featherstone Education – see Bloomsbury Publishing Plc

David Fickling Books

31 Beaumont Street, Oxford OX1 2NP
tel (01865) 339000
website www.davidficklingbooks.com
Publisher David Fickling

Independent publisher of picture books and novels for all ages, as well as graphic novels, with a focus on brilliant storytelling and world-class illustration. Founded 1999.

Fig Tree – see Penguin General

Findhorn Press Ltd

Delft Cottage, Dyke, Forres, Scotland IV36 2TF
tel (01309) 690582
email info@findhornpress.com
website www.findhornpress.com

Mind, body & spirit and healing. Founded 1971.

Fircone Books Ltd

The Holme, Church Road, Eardisley, Herefordshire HR3 6NJ

tel (01544) 327182
email info@firconebooks.com
website www.firconebooks.com
Facebook www.facebook.com/firconebooks
Twitter @firconebooks
Directors Richard Wheeler, Su Wheeler

Nostalgic illustrated children's books, and illustrated books on church art and architecture. Welcomes submission of ideas: send synopsis first. Founded 2009.

Firefly Press Ltd*

25 Gabalfa Road, Llandaff North, Cardiff CF14 2JJ
tel 029-2021 8611
email fireflypress@yahoo.co.uk
website www.fireflypress.co.uk
Facebook www.facebook.com/FireflyPress
Twitter @fireflypress
Publisher Penny Thomas, *Editor* Janet Thomas, *Marketing Officer* Megan Farr

Publishes quality fiction for ages 5 to 19. Founded 2013.

Fisherton Press

email general@fishertonpress.co.uk
website www.fishertonpress.co.uk
Facebook www.facebook.com/FishertonPress
Twitter @fishertonpress
Director Ellie Levenson

A small independent publisher producing picture books for children under 7. Not currently accepting proposals but illustrators are welcome to send links to their portfolio.

Fitzrovia Press Ltd

10 Grafton Mews, London W1T 5JG
tel 020-7380 0749
email info@fitzroviapress.co.uk, pratima@fitzroviapress.co.uk
website www.fitzroviapress.com
Publisher Richard Prime

Fiction and non-fiction: Hinduism and creative writing grounded in Eastern philosophy that explores spirituality in the West. Submit outline plus sample chapter; no complete MSS. Founded 2008.

Flame Tree Publishing

6 Melbray Mews, Fulham, London SW6 3NS
tel 020-7751 9650
email info@flametreepublishing.com
website www.flametreepublishing.com
Ceo/Publisher Nick Wells

Culture, cookery and lifestyle. Currently not accepting unsolicited MSS. Founded 1992.

Fleming Publications

9/2 Fleming House, 134 Renfrew Street, Glasgow G3 6ST
tel 0141 328 1935
email info@flemingpublications.com
website www.flemingpublications.com
Managing Editor Etta Dunn

Fiction, non-fiction, poetry, history, biography, photography and self-help.

Floris Books*

2a Robertson Avenue, Edinburgh EH11 1PZ
tel 0131 337 2372
email floris@florisbooks.co.uk
website www.florisbooks.co.uk
Facebook www.facebook.com/FlorisBooks
Twitter @FlorisBooks
Commissioning Editors Sally Polson, Eleanor Collins

Religion, science, philosophy, holistic health, organics, mind, body & spirit, Celtic studies, crafts, parenting; children's books: board, picture books, activity books. Founded 1976.

Kelpies

website www.discoverkelpies.co.uk

Contemporary Scottish fiction – board books (for 1–3 years), picture books (for 3–6 years), young readers series (for 6–8 years) and novels (for 8–15 years). See website for submission details. Annual Kelpies Prize, see website.

Flyleaf Press

4 Spencer Villas, Glenageary, Co. Dublin A96 P2E9, Republic of Ireland
tel +353 (0)12 854658
email books@flyleaf.ie
website www.flyleaf.ie
Managing Editor James Ryan

Irish family history. Founded 1988.

Folens Publishers

Hibernian Industrial Estate, Greenhills Road, Tallaght, Dublin D24 DH05, Republic of Ireland
tel +353 (0)14 137200
website www.folens.ie
Facebook www.facebook.com/FolensIreland
Twitter @FolensIreland
Chairman David Moffitt

Educational (primary, secondary). Founded 1958.

Fonthill Media Ltd

Stroud House, Russell Street, Stroud, Glos. GL5 3AN
tel (01453) 750505
email office@fonthillmedia.com
website www.fonthillmedia.com
Facebook www.facebook.com/fonthillmedia
Twitter @fonthillmedia
Publisher & Ceo Alan Sutton

General history. Specialisations include biography, military history, aviation history, naval and maritime history, regional and local and history, transport (railway, canal, road) history, social history, sports history, ancient history and archaeology. Also publishes widely in the USA with American regional, local, military and transport history under the imprints of Fonthill, America Through Time and American History House. Founded 2011.

Footprint

Peloton Grey Publishing, 5 Riverside Court,
Lower Bristol Road, Bath BA2 3DZ
tel (01225) 469141
email contactus@footprintbooks.com
website www.footprinttravelguides.com
Facebook www.facebook.com/footprintbooks
Twitter @footprintbooks
Director John Sadler

Travel guides.

W. Foulsham & Co. Ltd

The Old Barrel Store, Brewery Courtyard,
Draymans Lane, Marlow, Bucks. SL7 2FF
tel (01628) 400631
Managing & Editorial Director B.A.R. Belasco

Life issues, general know-how, CMS data, cookery, nutrition, health, therapies, travel guides, parenting, gardening, popular philsophy and practical psychology. Editorial submissions to Annemarie Howe: annemarie.howe@foulsham.com. Founded *c.*1800.

Quantum

Mind, body & spirit, popular philosophy and practical psychology.

Four Courts Press

7 Malpas Street, Dublin D08 YD81,
Republic of Ireland
tel +353 (0)14 534668
email info@fourcourtspress.ie
website www.fourcourtspress.ie
Senior Editor Martin Fanning, *Marketing & Sales Manager* Anthony Tierney

Academic books in the humanities, especially history, Celtic and medieval studies, art, theology. Founded 1970.

4th Estate – see HarperCollins Publishers

Free Association Books

1 Angel Cottages, Milespit Hill, London NW7 1RD
email contact@freeassociationpublishing.com
website www.freeassociationpublishing.com
Twitter @Fab_Publishing
Director Trevor E. Brown, *Publishing Director* Alice Solomons *Marketing Manager* Lisa Findley

Social sciences, psychoanalysis, psychotherapy, counselling, cultural studies, social welfare, addiction studies, child and adolescent studies, mental health. No poetry or fiction. Founded 1984.

Freight Books

49 Virginia Street, Glasgow G1 1TS
tel 0141 5525 303
email info@freightbooks.co.uk
website www.freightbooks.co.uk
Facebook www.facebook.com/FreightBooks
Twitter @freightbooks
Publisher Adrian Searle

Award-winning UK-based independent publisher with a focus on publishing high-quality fiction, though also publishes general illustrated and narrative non-fiction, poetry and humour. Founded 2011.

Samuel French Ltd*

24–32 Stephenson Way, London NW1 2HX
tel 020-7387 9373
email email@samuelfrench.co.uk
website www.samuelfrench.co.uk
Facebook www.facebook.com/samuelfrenchuk
Twitter @samuelfrenchltd
Directors Douglas Schatz (managing), David Webster (operations)

Publisher of plays, performance licensing agent and online theatre bookshop. More information on the the submissions process can be found on the website. Founded 1830.

The Friday Project – see HarperCollins Publishers

Frontline – see Pen & Sword Books Ltd

FT Prentice Hall – see Pearson UK

Gaia Books – see Octopus Publishing Group

The Gallery Press

Loughcrew, Oldcastle,
Co Meath A82 E670 Republic of Ireland
tel +353 (0)49 8541779
email gallery@indigo.ie
website www.gallerypress.com
Editor/Publisher Peter Fallon

Poetry and drama – by Irish authors only at this time. Founded 1970.

Galley Beggar Press

email info@galleybeggar.co.uk
website www.galleybeggar.co.uk
Facebook www.facebook.com/Galley-Beggar-Press/
Twitter @GalleyBeggars
Co-directors Eloise Millar, Sam Jordison

Independent publisher based in Norwich. Looks for authors whose writing shows great ambition and literary merit in their chosen genre. Original publishers of Eimear McBride's *A Girl is a Half-formed Thing* – winner of the Baileys Women's Prize for Fiction 2014. When submitting a MS authors must provide proof that they have read another book that Galley Beggar Press has published. Prefers completed MS; email as PDF or Word document. One submission per author. Considers a wide range of genres including fiction, non-fiction, quality sci-fi, novels and short stories. No poetry or children's. See website for detailed submission guidelines. Founded 2011.

Gallic Books

59 Ebury Street, London SW1W 0NZ
tel 020-7259 9336
email info@gallicbooks.com
website http://belgraviabooks.com/gb/
Facebook www.facebook.com/gallicbooks
Twitter @gallicbooks
Managing Director Jane Aitken

French writing in translation. Only accepts submissions from French publishers or from agents representing French authors. Part of the Belgravia Books Collective. Founded 2007.

Garland Science – see Taylor & Francis Group

J. Garnet Miller – see Cressrelles Publishing Co. Ltd

Garnet Publishing Ltd

8 Southern Court, South Street, Reading RG1 4QS
tel (0118) 9597847
email info@garnetpublishing.co.uk
website www.garnetpublishing.co.uk
Publisher & Commissioning Editor Mitchell Albert

Comprises of three imprints. Founded 1991.

Garnet Publishing

website www.garnetpublishing.co.uk

Trade non-fiction pertaining to the Middle East (art and architecture, cookery, culture, current affairs, history, photography, political and social issues, religion, travel and general). Accepts unsolicited material.

Ithaca Press

website www.ithacapress.co.uk

Leading publisher of academic books with a focus on Middle Eastern studies. Accepts unsolicited material.

Periscope

website www.periscopebooks.co.uk

Literary fiction and trade non-fiction from around the world (biography, crime fiction, current affairs, historical fiction, literary translations, memoir, political and social issues, popular history, popular science, reportage, general literary fiction and general trade non-fiction). Accepts unsolicited material.

Geddes & Grosset

Academy Park, Gower Street (Building 4000), Glasgow G51 1PR
tel 0141 375 1998
email info@geddesandgrosset.co.uk
website www.geddesandgrosset.com
Publishers Ron Grosset, Liz Small

An imprint of The Gresham Publishing Company Ltd. Mass market reference *Word Power* – English language learning and health and wellbeing. Associated imprint: Waverley Books. Founded 1988.

Gibson Square

tel 020-7096 1100
email info@gibsonsquare.com
website www.gibsonsquare.com
Facebook www.facebook.com/gibson.square
Publisher Martin Rynja

Non-fiction: general non-fiction, biography, current affairs, philosophy, politics, cultural criticism, psychology, history, travel, art history. Some fiction. See website for guidelines or email to receive an automated response. Authors include Helena Frith Powell, Alexander Litvinenko, Melanie Phillips, Bernard-Henri Lévy, Diana Mitford, Anthony Grayling, John McCain. Founded 2001.

Gingko Library

4 Molasses Row, London SW11 3UX
tel 020-7823 2312
email gingko@gingkolibrary.com
website www.gingko.org.uk
Publisher Barbara Schwepcke

Gingko works with scholars of diverse backgrounds and research interests to increase understanding of the Middle East, West Asia and North Africa through conferences, public events and cultural programmes as well as publications.

Ginn – see Pearson UK

GL Assessment

9th Floor East, 389 Chiswick High Road, London W4 4AL
tel 020-8996 3333
email information@gl-assessment.co.uk
website www.gl-assessment.co.uk
Chairman Philip Walters

Testing and assessment services for education and health care, including literacy, numeracy, thinking skills, ability, learning support and online testing. Founded 1981.

Godsfield Press – see Octopus Publishing Group

Goldsmiths Press

Room 2, 33 Laurie Grove, New Cross, London SE14 6NW
tel 020-7919 7258
email goldsmithspress@gold.ac.uk
website https://www.gold.ac.uk/goldsmiths-press/
Twitter @goldsmithspress

Director Sarah Kember

Goldsmiths Press is a new university press from Goldsmiths, University of London, which aims to revive and regenerate the traditions and values of university press publishing through the innovative use of print and digital media. Our publishing cuts across disciplinary boundaries and blur the distinction between practice and theory, experimentation and convention and between the academic, literary and artistic. The aim is to create a culture around academic knowledge practices that is more inventive and less constrained than it is now fostering a unique collaboration between academics, librarians and publishing professionals, under the direction of an academic researcher.

Gollancz – see The Orion Publishing Group Ltd

Gomer Press

33–35 Lammas Street, Carmarthen SA31 3AL
tel (01267) 221400
email meirion@gomer.co.uk
website www.gomer.co.uk, www.pontbooks.co.uk
Managing Director Jonathan Lewis, *Editors* Mari Emlyn, Beca Brown (adult Welsh), Dr Ashley Owen (adult English & children's English), Nia Parry (children's, Welsh & learners)

History, travel, photography, biography, art, poetry and fiction of relevance to Welsh culture, in English and in Welsh. Picture books, novels, stories, poetry and teaching resources for children. Preliminary enquiry essential. Welcomes submissions by email. Founded 1892.

Government Publications

Publications Division, Office of Public Works, 52 St Stephen's Green, Dublin D02 DR67, Republic of Ireland
tel +353 (0)16 476834
email publications@opw.ie
website www.opw.ie/en/governmentpublications

Irish government publications.

Gower – see Taylor & Francis Group

Granta Books

12 Addison Avenue, London W11 4QR
tel 020-7605 1360
website www.grantabooks.com
Twitter @GrantaBooks
Publishing Director Alex Bowler, *Editorial Directors* Bella Lacey, Laura Barber, Max Porter, *Commissioning Editor* Anne Meadows, *Junior Editor* Ka Bradley, *Rights Director* Angela Rose, *Publicity Director* Pru Rowlandson, *Production Director* Sarah Wasley

Literary fiction, memoir, nature writing, cultural criticism and travel. No submissions except via a reputable literary agent. An imprint of Granta Publications. Founded 1982.

Green Print – see Merlin Press Ltd

Gresham Books Ltd

The Carriage House, Ningwood Manor, Ningwood, Isle of Wight PO30 4NJ
tel (01983) 761389
email info@gresham-books.co.uk
website www.gresham-books.co.uk
Managing Director Nicholas Oulton

Hymn books, prayer books, service books, school histories and companions.

The Gresham Publishing Company Ltd

Ground floor, 4000 Academy Park, Gower Street, Glasgow G51 1PR
tel 0141 375 1996
email info@waverley-books.co.uk
website www.waverley-books.co.uk, www.geddesandgrosset.com
Facebook www.facebook.com//Waverley-Books/
Twitter @WaverleyBooks
Publishers Ron Grosset, Liz Small

Books for the general trade and Scottish interest books.

The Greystones Press

37 Lawton Avenue, Carterton, Oxon OX18 3JY
tel (01993) 841219
email editorial@greystonespress.com
website www.greystonespress.com
Directors Mary Hoffman, Stephen Barber

A small independent publishing company specializing in good adult and young adult fiction and adult non-fiction in areas of interest, like literature, art, history, music, myths and legends. Full submission guidelines are on the website. No middle grade or younger or illustrated books.

Grub Street Publishing

4 Rainham Close, London SW11 6SS
tel 020-7924 3966, 020-7738 1008
email post@grubstreet.co.uk
website www.grubstreet.co.uk
Principals John B. Davies, Anne Dolamore

Adult non-fiction: military, aviation history, cookery. Founded 1992.

Guild of Master Craftsman Publications Ltd

166 High Street, Lewes, East Sussex BN7 1XU
tel (01273) 477374
email jonathanb@thegmcgroup.com
website www.gmcbooks.com
Twitter @GMCbooks
Joint Managing Directors Jennifer Phillips, Jonathan Phillips, *Publisher* Jonathan Bailey

A diverse publisher of leisure and hobby project books, with a focus on all types of woodworking;

from carving and turning to routing. Craft subjects include needlecraft, paper crafts and jewellery-making. The books are aimed at craftspeople of all skill levels. Founded 1979.

Ammonite Press

email jason.hook@ammonitepress.com
website www.ammonitepress.com
Twitter @AmmonitePress
Publisher Jason Hook

Publishes highly illustrated non-fiction for the international market. Gift books featuring illustration, infographics and photography on pop culture, pop reference, biography and history. Practical photography titles written by professional photographers provide authoritative guides to technique and equipment.

Button Books

website www.buttonbooks.co.uk

A new imprint of GMC Publications publishing children's books and producing stationery for children up to 11 years.

Guinness World Records

3rd Floor, 184–192 Drummond Street,
London NW1 3HP
tel 020-7891 4567
website www.guinnessworldrecords.com

Guinness World Records, *GWR Gamer's Edition*, TV and brand licensing, records processing. No unsolicited MSS. A Jim Pattison Group company. Founded 1954.

Gulf Professional Press – see Elsevier Ltd

Hachette Children's Group*

Carmelite House, 50 Victoria Embankment,
London EC4Y 0DZ
email editorial@hachettechildrens.co.uk
website www.hachettechildrens.co.uk
Ceo Hilary Murray Hill

Children's non-fiction, reference, information, gift, fiction, picture, novelty and audiobooks. Unsolicited material is not considered other than by referral or recommendation. Formed by combining Watts Publishing with Hodder Children's Books in 2005. Part of Hachette UK (see page 176).

Hodder Children's Group

Facebook www.facebook.com/hodderchildrensbooks
Twitter @hodderchildrens
Publishing Director Anne McNeil

Fiction, picture books, novelty, general non-fiction and audiobooks.

Little, Brown Books for Young Readers

Facebook www.facebook.com/lbkidsuk
Twitter @lbkidsuk
Publisher Megan Tingley

Fiction, novelty, general non-fiction and audiobooks.

Orchard Books

Facebook www.facebook.com/orchardchildrensbooks
Twitter @orchardbooks
Publishing Director Megan Larkin

Fiction, picture and novelty books.

Orion Children's Books

Facebook www.facebook.com/TheOrionStar
Twitter @the_orionstar

Fiction, picture books, novelty, general non-fiction and audiobooks.

Pat-a-Cake

New baby, preschool and early years imprint.

Quercus Children's Books

Imprint poducing quality teen and young adult fiction.

Franklin Watts

Twitter @franklinwatts
Publishing Director Rachel Cooke

Non-fiction and information books.

Wayland

Twitter @waylandbooks
Editorial Director Debbie Foy

Non-fiction and information books.

Wren & Rook

Imprint publishing brave, diverse and imaginative books for children and young people.

Hachette UK*

Carmelite House, 50 Victoria Embankment,
London EC4Y 0DZ
tel 020-3122 6000
website www.hachette.co.uk
Chief Executive David Shelley, *Directors* Jamie Hodder Williams (Ceo, Hodder & Stoughton, Headline, John Murray Press, Quercus and Director of Trade Publishing, Hachette UK), Jane Morpeth (Chairman, Headline), Alison Goff (Ceo, Octopus), Hilary Murray Hill (Ceo, Hachette Children's Group), David Shelley (Ceo, Little, Brown Book Group and Orion Publishing Group), Lis Tribe (managing, Hodder Education)

Part of Hachette Livre SA since 2004. Hachette UK group companies: Hachette Children's Group (page 176), Headline Publishing Group (page 179), Hodder Education Group (page 180), Hodder & Stoughton (page 180), John Murray Press (page 190), Little, Brown Book Group (page 186), Octopus Publishing Group (page 192), Orion Publishing Group (page 194), Quercus Publishing Plc (page 201), Hachette Ireland, Hachette Australia (page 218), Hachette New Zealand (page 222), Hachette Book Publishing India Private Ltd, Bookouture (page 159).

Halban Publishers

22 Golden Square, London W1F 9JW
tel 020-7437 9300
email books@halbanpublishers.com
website www.halbanpublishers.com
Twitter @HalbanPublisher
Directors Martine Halban, Peter Halban

General fiction and non-fiction; history and biography; Jewish subjects and Middle East. No unsolicited MSS considered; preliminary letter or email essential. Founded 1986.

Haldane Mason Ltd

North Barrow, Yeovil, Somerset BA22 7LY
tel (01963) 240844
email info@haldanemason.com
website www.haldanemason.com
Directors Sydney Francis, Ron Samuel

Illustrated non-fiction books and box sets, mainly for children. No unsolicited material. Imprints: Haldane Mason (adult), Red Kite Books (children's). Founded 1995.

Robert Hale Ltd

The Crowood Press Ltd, The Stable Block, Crowood Lane, Ramsbury, Wilts. SN8 2HR
tel (01672) 520320
email enquiries@crowood.com
website www.crowood.com

Adult general non-fiction and fiction. Imprint of The Crowood Press (page 165). Founded 1936.

Halsgrove Publishing

Halsgrove House, Ryelands Business Park, Bagley Road, Wellington, Somerset TA21 9PZ
tel (01823) 653777
email sales@halsgrove.com
website www.halsgrove.com
Facebook www.facebook.com/Halsgrove-Publishing-120746011275852/
Twitter @Halsgrove
Managing Director Julian Davidson, *Publisher* Simon Butler

Regional books for local-interest readers in the UK. Also illustrated books on individual artists. Founded 1986.

Hamish Hamilton – see Penguin General

Hamlyn – see Octopus Publishing Group

Patrick Hardy Books – see The Lutterworth Press

Harlequin (UK) Ltd*

HarperCollins Publishers Ltd, Westerhill Road, Bishopbriggs, Glasgow G64 2QT
tel 0844 844 1351
website www.millsandboon.co.uk
Facebook www.facebook.com/millsandboon
Twitter @MillsandBoon
Managing Director Tim Cooper

In 2014 Harlequin (UK) Ltd was acquired by HarperCollins Publishers. Founded 1908.

Mills & Boon Historical

Senior Editor L. Fildew

Historical romance fiction.

Mills & Boon Medical

Senior Editor S. Hodgson

Contemporary romance fiction.

Mills & Boon Cherish

Senior Editor Bryony Green

Commercial literary fiction.

Mira Books

Editorial Director Donna Condon

Women's fiction.

Mills & Boon Modern Romance

Senior Editor Jo Grant

HarperCollins Publishers*

The News Building, 1 London Bridge Street, London SE1 9GF
tel 020-8741 7070
Alternative address Westerhill Road, Bishopbriggs, Glasgow G64 2QT
tel 0141 772 3200
website www.harpercollins.co.uk
Ceo Charlie Redmayne

All fiction and trade non-fiction must be submitted through an agent. Owned by News Corporation. Founded 1817.

Avon

website http://corporate.harpercollins.co.uk/imprints/avon
Executive Publisher Kate Elton, *Publishing Strategy Director* Oliver Malcolm, *Publishing Director* Helen Huthwaite

General fiction, crime and thrillers, women's fiction.

The Borough Press

Publisher Suzie Dooré

Literary fiction.

William Collins

Executive Publisher David Roth-Ey, *Publishing Director* Arabella Pike, *Associate Publisher* Myles Archibald (natural history)

Collins Learning

Managing Director Colin Hughes

Core curriculum and revision resources: books, CD-Roms and online material for UK and international primary schools, secondary schools and colleges.

4th Estate

Executive Publisher David Roth-Ey

Fiction, literary fiction, current affairs, popular science, biography, humour, travel.

HarperCollins
Publishing Director David Brawn

Agatha Christie, J.R.R. Tolkien, C.S. Lewis.

HarperCollins Children's Books
Publisher Ann-Janine Murtagh

Annuals, activity books, novelty books, preschool brands, picture books, pop-up books and book and CD sets. Fiction for 5–8 and 9–12 years, young adult fiction and series fiction; film/TV tie-ins. Publishes approx. 265 titles each year. Picture book authors include Oliver Jeffers, Judith Kerr and Emma Chichester Clark, and fiction by David Walliams, Michael Morpurgo, David Baddiel and Lauren Child. Books published under licence include *Dr Seuss*, *Bing*, *Twirlywoos* and *Paddington Bear*.

HarperElement
Publisher Ed Faulkner

Real-life stories by real people, focusing on inspirational memoir, true crime, animal stories and nostalgia.

HarperFiction
Executive Producer Kate Elton

General, historical fiction, crime and thrillers, women's fiction.

HarperImpulse
Publisher Kimberley Young

Digital first-romance fiction.

Harper NonFiction
Executive Publisher Kate Elton

Autobiographies, entertainment, sport, cookery, lifestyle and culture.

Harper Thorsons
Editor Ed Faulkner

Health and wellbeing, pop-psych, mind, body & spirit, business and personal development.

HQ
Publisher Lisa Milton, *Editorial Director, Fiction* Manpreet Grewal

General, crime and thrillers, women's fiction, historical, book club and young adult.

HQ Digital
Publisher Lisa Milton

Digital-first commercial fiction list, general, crime and thrillers, women's fiction, psychological thrillers, saga.

Mills & Boon
Global Editorial Director Jo Grant

Romance.

Voyager
Publishing Director Natasha Bardon

Fantasy/sci-fi.

Hart Publishing*

Kemp House, Chawley Park, Cumnor Hill, Oxford OX2 9PH
tel (01865) 598648
email mail@hartpub.co.uk
website www.hartpublishing.co.uk
Publisher Sinéad Moloney

Legal academic texts for law students, scholars and practitioners. Will consider unsolicited MSS. Submission guidelines on the website. Books, ebooks and journals on all aspects of law (UK domestic, European and International). An imprint of Bloomsbury Publishing Plc (page 157). Founded in 1996.

Harvill Secker – see Vintage

Haus Publishing Ltd

4 Cinnamon Row, Plantation Wharf, London SW11 3TW
tel 020-7838 9055
email info@hauspublishing.com
website http://hauspublishing.com/
Twitter @HausPublishing
Publisher Harry Hill

Publishes history, literary fiction, translated fiction, biography, memoir and current affairs. Founded 2003.

Hawthorn Press

1 Lansdown Lane, Stroud, Glos. GL5 1BJ
tel (01453) 757040
email info@hawthornpress.com
website www.hawthornpress.com
Director Martin Large, *Accounts/Foreign Rights* Farimah Englefield, *Production & Administration* Claire Percival, *Marketing* Meredith Debonaire

Publishes books and ebooks for a more creative, peaceful and sustainable world. Series include Early Years, Steiner/Waldorf Education, Crafts, Personal Development, Art and Science, Storytelling. Founded 1981.

Hay House Publishers

2nd Floor, Astley House, 33 Notting Hill Gate, London W11 3JQ
tel 020-3675 2450
email info@hayhouse.co.uk
website www.hayhouse.co.uk
Facebook www.facebook.com/HayHouseUK
Twitter @HayHouseUK
Managing Director & Publisher Michelle Pilley, *International Sales & Operations Director* Diane Hill, *Communications Director* Jo Burgess, *Commissioning Editor* Amy Kiberd

Publishers of mind, body & spirit; self-help; personal development; health; spirituality and wellness. Head office in San Diego, California. Founded 1984; in UK 2003.

Haynes Publishing

Sparkford, Yeovil, Somerset BA22 7JJ
tel (01963) 440635
email lmcintyre@haynes.co.uk, srendle@haynes.co.uk, jfalconer@haynes.co.uk
website www.haynes.co.uk
Directors J.H. Haynes (founder director), Eddie Bell (chairman), J. Haynes (chief executive)

Practical manuals for the home: car, motorcycle, motorsport, military, aviation and leisure activities.

Haynes Motor Trade Division

email jaustin@haynes.co.uk

Car and motorcycle service and repair manuals and technical data books.

Head of Zeus

Clerkenwell House, 5–8 Hardwick Street, London EC1R 4RG
tel 020-7253 5557
email hello@headofzeus.com
website www.headofzeus.com
Facebook www.facebook.com//Head-of-Zeus-Books/
Twitter @HoZ_Books
Chairman Anthony Cheetham, *Fiction Publisher* Laura Palmer, *Non-fiction Publishers* Richard Milbank, Neil Belton, *Digital Publisher* Nicolas Cheetham, *Sales Director* Dan Groenewald, *Publicity Director* Suzanne Sangster

General and literary fiction, genre fiction and non-fiction. UK and Commonwealth distributers for MysteriousPress.com, one of the world's largest digital crime fiction lists. Founded 2012.

Zephyr

Publisher Fiona Kennedy

Children's imprint.

Headland Publications

Editorial office Tŷ Coch, Galltegfa, Llanfwrog, Ruthin, Denbighshire LL15 2AR
Alternative address 38 York Avenue, West Kirby, Wirral CH48 3JF
tel 0151 625 9128
email headlandpublications@hotmail.co.uk
website www.headlandpublications.co.uk
Editor Gladys Mary Coles

Poetry, anthologies of poetry and prose. No unsolicited MSS. Founded 1970.

Headline Publishing Group

Carmelite House, 50 Victoria Embankment, London EC4Y 0DZ
tel 020-3122 7222
email enquiries@headline.co.uk
website www.headline.co.uk
Twitter @headlinepg
Chair Mari Evans

Commercial and literary fiction (hardback, paperback and ebook) and popular non-fiction including autobiography, biography, food and wine, gardening, history, popular science, sport, TV tie-ins. Publishes under Headline, Headline Review, Tinder Press, Headline Eternal. Part of Hachette UK (see page 176).

William Heinemann – see Cornerstone

Hermes House – see Anness Publishing

Nick Hern Books Ltd

The Glasshouse, 49A Goldhawk Road, London W12 8QP
tel 020-8749 4953
email info@nickhernbooks.co.uk
website www.nickhernbooks.co.uk
Facebook www.facebook.com/NickHernBooks
Twitter @NickHernBooks
Publisher Nick Hern, *Managing Director* Matt Applewhite

Theatre and performing arts books, professionally produced plays, performing rights. Initial letter required. Founded 1988.

Hesperus Press Ltd

28 Mortimer Street, London W1W 7RD
tel 020-7436 0943
email info@hesperuspress.com
website www.hesperuspress.com
Facebook www.facebook.com/hesperuspress
Twitter @HesperusPress

Under three imprints, publishes over 300 books. Hesperus Classics introduces older works of literature, Hesperus Nova showcases contemporary literature and Hesperus Minor publishes well-loved children's books from the past. Founded 2002.

Hippopotamus Press

22 Whitewell Road, Frome, Somerset BA11 4EL
tel (01373) 466653
email rjhippopress@aol.com, mphippopress@aol.com
Editors Roland John, Mansell Pargitter, *Foreign Editor* (translations) Anna Martin

Poetry, essays, criticism. Submissions from new writers welcome. Founded 1974.

The History Press Ltd

The Mill, Brimscombe Port, Stroud, Glos. GL5 2QG
tel (01453) 883300
website www.thehistorypress.co.uk
Managing Director Gareth Swain, *Publishing Director* Laura Perehinec, *Sales Director* Jamie Kinnear, *Rights* Anette Fuhrmeister

The History Press

General, local, military and transport history: biographies and historical fiction.

Phillimore

British local history and genealogy.

Hodder & Stoughton

338 Euston Road, London NW1 3BH
tel 020-7873 6000
website www.hodder.co.uk
Ceo Jamie Hodder-Williams, *Managing Director* Carolyn Mays, *Deputy Managing Director* Lisa Highton, *Publishing Director* Carole Welch, *Non-fiction Publisher* Drummond Moir, *Non-fiction Publisher* Rupert Lancaster, *Hodder Lifestyle & Yellow Kite Publisher* Liz Gough

Commercial and literary fiction; biography, autobiography, history, humour, mind, body & spirit, travel, lifestyle and cookery and other general interest non-fiction; audio. No unsolicited MSS or synopses. Publishes under Hodder & Stoughton, Sceptre, Mobius. Part of Hachette UK (see page 176).

Hodder Children's Books – see Hachette Children's Group

Hodder Education

338 Euston Road, London NW1 3BH
tel 020-7873 6000
website www.hoddereducation.co.uk, www.galorepark.co.uk, www.risingstars-uk.com
Managing Director Lis Tribe

School and college publishing. Includes Rising Stars, RS Assessment, Hodder Education and Galore Park. Part of Hachette UK (see page 176).

Hodder Faith

338 Euston Road, London NW1 3BH
tel 020-7873 6000
email faitheditorialenquiries@hodder.co.uk
website www.hodder.co.uk/hodder%20faith/index.page
Managing Director Jamie Hodder-Williams

Bibles, Christian books, biography/memoir. Publishes the following versions of the bible: New International Version (NIV), Today's New International Version (TNIV) and New International Reader's Version (NIrV). Part of Hachette UK (see page 176).

Hodder Gibson*

211 St Vincent Street, Glasgow G2 5QY
tel 0141 222 1440
email hoddergibson@hodder.co.uk
website www.hoddergibson.co.uk
Managing Director Paul Cherry

Educational books specifically for Scotland. Part of Hachette UK (see page 176).

Holland House Books

47 Greenham Road, Newbury, Berks. RG14 7HY
email contact@hhousebooks.com
website www.hhousebooks.com
Senior Editor Robert Peett

Literary fiction and non-fiction, crime, historical and speculative fiction welcome. Happy to read traditional and experimental work. Also runs The Novella Project for new authors and interns, and the literary journal The Open Page. Submissions welcome from agents and authors, but please check website first.

Honno Ltd (Welsh Women's Press)

Unit 14, Creative Units, Aberystwyth Arts Centre, Aberystwyth, Ceredigion SY23 3GL
tel (01970) 623150
email post@honno.co.uk
website www.honno.co.uk
Facebook www.facebook.com/honnopress
Twitter @honno
Editor Caroline Oakley

Literature written by women born or living in Wales or women with a significant Welsh connection. All subjects considered – fiction, non-fiction, autobiographies. No poetry or works for children. Honno is a community cooperative. Founded 1986.

Hopscotch

St Jude's Church, Dulwich Road, London SE24 0PB
tel 020-7501 6736
email orders@hopscotchbooks.com
website www.hopscotchbooks.com
Associate Publisher Angela Morano Shaw

A division of MA Education. Teaching resources for primary school teachers. Founded 1997.

Practical Pre-School Books

Early years teacher resources.

Hot Key Books

80–81 Wimpole Street, London W1G 9RE
tel 020-7490 3875
email enquiries@hotkeybooks.com
website www.hotkeybooks.com
Facebook www.facebook.com/HotKeyBooks/
Twitter @HotKeyBooks
Editor-at-Large Emma Matthewson

Part of Bonnier Publishing, publishes books for ages 9–19. Send full MS and synopsis to enquiries@hotkeybooks.com. Only accepts electronic submissions. Founded 2012.

House of Lochar

Isle of Colonsay, Argyll PA61 7YR
tel (01951) 200323
email sales@houseoflochar.com
website www.houseoflochar.com

Scottish history, transport, Scottish literature. Founded 1995.

John Hunt Publishing Ltd

No. 3 East St, Alresford, Hants SO24 9EE
email office1@jhpbooks.net
website www.johnhuntpublishing.com
Director John Hunt

Publishes culture, politics, spirituality, Christianity, history and fiction titles for adults and children. See website for submission procedure, additional author services and trade representation. Imprints include: Zero Books for society, politics and culture; Iff Books for philosophy and popular science; Chronos Books for historical non-fiction; Circle Books for exploring Christian faith; Christian Alternative for liberal Christianity; Changemakers Books for transformation; Moon Books for paganism and shamanism; O Books for broader spirituality; 6th Books for parapsychology; Axis Mundi Books for esoteric thought and practice; Ayni Books for complementary health; Dodona Books for divination; Earth Books for environment; Soul Rocks Books for alternative spirituality; Psyche Books for mind and self; Roundfire Books for exciting, thought-provoking fiction; Cosmic Egg Books for fantasy; Top Hat Books for historical fiction; Our Street Books for children; Lodestone Books for young adults; Liberalis Books for education; and Compass Books for new writers. Founded 1989.

Hutchinson – see Cornerstone

Hutchinson Children's Books – see Penguin Random House Children's UK

Hymns Ancient and Modern Ltd*

Third Floor, Invicta House, 108–114 Golden Lane, London EC1Y 0TG
tel 020-776 7551
website www.hymnsam.co.uk
Publishing Director Christine Smith

Theological books with special emphasis on text and reference books and contemporary theology for both students and clergy. Founded 1929.

Saint Andrew Press

Twitter @standrewpress

Publisher of the Church of Scotland.

Church House Publishing

Twitter @CHPublishingUK

Publisher of the Church of England – church resources, stationery and Common Worship.

Canterbury Press

Norwich Books and Music, 13A Hellesdon Park Road, Norwich NR6 5DR
tel (01603) 785925
website www.canterburypress.co.uk
Twitter @canterburypress

Hymnals, popular religious writing, spirituality and liturgy.

SCM Press

website www.scmpress.co.uk
Twitter @SCM_Press

Academic theology.

Icon Books Ltd

The Omnibus Business Centre, 39–41 North Road, London N7 9DP
tel 020-7697 9695
email info@iconbooks.com
website www.iconbooks.com
Facebook www.introducingbooks.com
Directors Peter Pugh (chairman), Philip Cotterell (managing), Duncan Heath (editorial), Andrew Furlow (sales & marketing), Claire Maxwell (publicity)

Popular, intelligent non-fiction: literature, history, philosophy, politics, psychology, sociology, cultural studies, science, current affairs, computers, women, anthropology, humour, music, cinema, linguistics, economics. Will consider unsolicited MSS (adult non-fiction only). Founded 1991.

ICSA Publishing

Saffron House, 6–10 Kirby Street, London EC1N 8EQ
tel 020-7612 7020
email info@icsa.org.uk
website www.icsa.org.uk/bookshop
Managing Director Susan Richards

Publishing company of the Institute of Chartered Secretaries and Administrators, specialising in information solutions for legal and regulatory compliance. Founded 1981.

Igloo Books Ltd

Cottage Farm, Mears Ashby Road, Sywell, Northants NN6 0BJ
tel (01604) 741116
email editorial@igloobooks.com
website www.igloobooks.com
Twitter @igloo_books

Children's books: licensed books, novelty, board, picture, activity, audio, education, ebooks and apps. Adult books: cookery, lifestyle, gift, trivia and non-fiction. Not currently accepting submissions. Founded 2005.

Impress Books Ltd

Innovation Centre, Rennes Drive, University of Exeter, Devon EX4 4RN
tel (01392) 950910
email enquiries@impress-books.co.uk
website www.impress-books.co.uk
Commissioning Editor Rachel Singleton

Founded as an independent publishing house focusing on previously unpublished writers of non-fiction and fiction, and specialising in crime and historical fiction. Runs the Impress Prize for New Writers. Founded 2004.

Imprint Academic Ltd

PO Box 200, Exeter, Devon EX5 5HY
tel (01392) 851550

email graham@imprint.co.uk
website www.imprint.co.uk
Publisher Keith Sutherland, *Managing Editor* Graham Horswell

Books and journals in politics, society, philosophy and psychology for both academic and general readers. Book series include *St Andrews Studies in Philosophy and Public Affairs*, *British Idealist Studies*, *Societas* (essays in political and cultural criticism) and the *Library of Scottish Philosophy*. Unsolicited MSS, synopses and ideas welcome by email to the Managing Editor or with sae only. Founded 1980.

In Pinn – see Neil Wilson Publishing Ltd

Indigo Dreams Publishing Ltd

24 Forest Houses, Cookworthy Moor, Halwill, Beaworthy, Devon EX21 5UU
email publishing@indigodreams.co.uk
website www.indigodreams.co.uk
Facebook www.facebook.com/indigodreamspublishing
Twitter @IndigoDreamsPub
Editors Ronnie Goodyer, Dawn Bauling

Winners of Ted Slade Award for Services to Poetry 2015. Publishes approx. 35 titles per year. Main subject areas: (poetry) anthologies, collections, pamphlets, competitions, one monthly poetry magazine, two quarterly poetry and prose magazines. New and experienced writers welcome. Also non-fiction for South-West England. Imprint: Tamar Books. Winners of the Most Innovative Publisher Award (Saboteur Awards for Literature) in 2017. Founded 2010.

Infinite Ideas

36 St Giles, Oxford OX1 3LD
tel (01865) 514888
email info@infideas.com
website www.infideas.com
Managing Director Richard Burton

Publishes titles in lifestyle: *52 Brilliant Ideas* series (health, fitness, relationships, leisure and lifestyle, sports, hobbies and games, careers, finance and personal development), *Feel Good Factory* series; *Wine* series (Classic Wine Library). Also business books: *Infinite Success* series (re-interpreted personal development and business classics). Submit business book proposals directly to richard@infideas.com. Founded 2003.

Insight Guides/Berlitz Publishing

1st Floor West, Magdalen House, 136 Tooley Street, London SE1 2TU
tel 020-7403 0284
website www.insightguides.com, www.berlitzpublishing.com
Facebook www.facebook.com/InsightGuides
Twitter @InsightGuides

Travel, language and related multimedia. Founded 1970.

Institute of Public Administration†

57–61 Lansdowne Road, Ballsbridge, Dublin D04 TC62, Republic of Ireland
tel +353 (0)12 403600
email information@ipa.ie
website www.ipa.ie
Publisher Richard Boyle

Government, economics, politics, law, public management, health, education, social policy and administrative history. Founded 1957.

InterVarsity Press

Norton Street, Nottingham NG7 3HR
tel 0115 978 1054
email ivp@ivpbooks.com
website www.ivpress.com
Facebook www.facebook.com/intervarsitypress/
Twitter @thinkivp

A charitable literature ministry, supporting the mission and ministry of the local church. Imprint: Apollos. Founded 1947.

IOP Publishing

Temple Circus, Temple Way, Bristol BS1 6HG
tel 0117 929 7481
email custserv@iop.org
website http://ioppublishing.org/
Editor @IOPPublishing

The company is a subsidiary of the Institute of Physics. It provides a range of journals, ebooks, magazines, conference proceedings and websites for the scientific community. The book publishing arm of the company brings together innovative digital publishing with leading voices in scientific, technical, engineering and medical (STEM) research. Founded 1874.

Irish Academic Press Ltd†

Tuckmill House, 10 George's Street, Newbridge, Co. Kildare W12 PX39, Republic of Ireland
tel +353 (0)45 432497
email info@iap.ie
website www.irishacademicpress.ie
Publisher Conor Graham

General and academic publishing with a focus on modern Irish history, politics, literature, culture and arts. Imprints: Irish Academic Press, founded 1974: Merrion Press, founded 2012.

ISF Publishing

PO Box 71911, London NW2 9QA
email info@idriesshahfoundation.org
website www.idriesshahfoundation.org
Facebook www.facebook.com/idriesshah
Twitter @idriesshah

Dedicated to releasing new editions of the work of Idries Shah, who devoted his life to collecting, selecting and translating key works of Eastern Sufi classical literature, adapting them to the needs of the West and disseminating them in the Occident.

Ithaca Press – see Garnet Publishing Ltd

IWM (Imperial War Museums) Publishing

Lambeth Road, London SE1 6HZ
tel 020-7416 5000
email publishing@iwm.org.uk
website www.iwm.org.uk
Facebook www.facebook.com/iwm.london
Twitter @I_W_M

IWM tells the stories of people who have lived, fought and died in conflicts involving Britain and the Commonwealth since 1914. IWM Publishing produces a range of books drawing on the expertise and archives of the museum. Books are produced both in-house and in partnership with other publishers.

Jacaranda Books Art Music Ltd

Unit 304, Metal Box Factory,
30 Great Guildford Street, London SE1 0HS
tel 020-7609 0891
email office@jacarandabooksartmusic.co.uk
website www.jacarandabooksartmusic.co.uk
Facebook www.facebook.com/jacarandabooks
Twitter @jacarandabooks
Founder & Publisher Valerie Brandes, *Publicity & Digital Manager* Jazzmine Breary, *Editor* Laure Deprez, *Commercial Director* Cynthia Hamilton

Diversity-led independent publisher of literary and genre fiction and non-fiction. The company aims to directly address the ongoing lack of diversity in the industry, and has an interest in Caribbean, African and Diaspora writing. Titles include *Tram 83* by Fiston Mwanza Mujila, *From Pasta to Pigfoot* and *Second Helpings* by Frances Mensah Williams, *Butterfly Fish* and *Speak Gigantular* by Irenosen Okojie, *Beyond the Pale* by Emily Urquhart and *The Elephant and the Bee* by Jess de Boer. Founded 2012.

JAI – see Elsevier Ltd

Jane's Information Group

163 Brighton Road, Coulsdon, Surrey CR5 2YH
tel 020-8700 3700
website www.janes.com

Professional business-to-business publishers in hardcopy and electronic multimedia: military, aviation, naval, defence, reference, police, geo-political. Consumer books in association with HarperCollins Publishers (page 177).

Joffe Books

52 Lion Mills, Hackney Road, London E2 7ST
email office@joffebooks.com
website www.joffebooks.com
Facebook www.facebook.com/joffebooks
Twitter @joffebooks
Publisher Jasper Joffe

Independent publisher of digital and print fiction. Accepts submissions from authors and agents, please see website for guidelines. Bestselling authors include Joy Ellis, Taylor Adams and Helen Durrant. Focuses on high-quality crime thrillers and mysteries. Founded 2012.

Jordan Publishing Ltd

21 St Thomas Street, Bristol BS1 6JS
tel 0117 918 1492
website www.lexisnexis.co.uk/products/jordan-publishing.html

Founded as an independent legal publisher in the UK. Produces practical information, online and in print, for practising lawyers and other professionals. Publishes textbooks, looseleafs, journals, court reference works and news services and also supplies software to law firms in the form of digital service PracticePlus, which combines step-by-step workflows, practice notes, automated court forms and links to core reference works. The company works with partners in key areas, such as the APIL series of guides, and also publishes around 40 new books and editions annually across a wide range of practice areas. Now owned by LexusNexus (page 185)

Michael Joseph

80 Strand, London WC2R 0RL
tel 020-7010 3000
website www.penguinrandomhouse.co.uk/publishers/michael-joseph
Managing Director Louise Moore; *Editors* Louise Moore (general fiction for women, celebrity non-fiction), Maxine Hitchcock (general fiction for women, crime & thriller fiction, general fiction), Jessica Leeke (general fiction), Rowland White (crime, thriller & adventure fiction, commercial non-fiction, popular culture & military), Jillian Taylor (general fiction, historical fiction; general and historical non-fiction) Joel Richardson (crime and thriller fiction), Matilda McDonald (general fiction for women) Daniel Bunyard (commercial non-fiction, popular culture & military), Fenella Bates (commercial non-fiction, popular culture & health), Ione Walder (cookery), Fiona Crosby (general non-fiction)

Part of Penguin Random House UK (page 198).

Kenilworth Press – see Quiller Publishing Ltd

Kenyon-Deane – see Cressrelles Publishing Co. Ltd

Laurence King Publishing Ltd*

361–373 City Road, London EC1V 1LR
tel 020-7841 6900
email enquiries@laurenceking.com
website www.laurenceking.com

Directors Laurence King (managing), Jo Lightfoot (editorial), Maria Treacy-Lord (financial)

Formerly Calmann & King Ltd. Illustrated books on design, architecture, art, fashion and beauty, and photography for the professional, student and general market. Also publishes a children's list and a gift line. Founded 1976.

Kingfisher – see Pan Macmillan

Kings Road Publishing

Suite 2.08 The Plaza, 535 Kings Road,
London SW10 0SZ
tel 020-770 3888
email info@kingsroadpublishing.co.uk
website www.kingsroadpublishing.co.uk
Ceo Perminder Mann, *Managing Director* Ben Dunn, *Acquistions Director & Publisher* Natalie Jerome, *UK Sales & Marketing Director* Andrew Sauerwine, *Head of Children's Publishing* Lisa Edwards

Part of Bonnier Publishing UK. The children imprints of Kings Road Publishing are Studio Press, Weldon Owen, which includes it's new sub imprint 20 Watt, Templar Publishing (page 210), which contains Big Picture Press. They focus on illustrated non-fiction, picture books, novelty titles, activity books, fiction and family reference. Blink (page 157), including 535, Lagom and John Blake Publishing (page 157) are the adult non-fiction imprints. Totally Entwined Group is a leading ebook publisher, which includes Bound Publishing, Pride Publishing and Finch Books. Submissions to be sent to the address above indicating which imprint they are addressed to. Founded 2015.

Jessica Kingsley Publishers*

73 Collier Street, London N1 9BE
tel 020-7833 2307
email hello@jkp.com
website www.jkp.com
Facebook www.facebook.com/JessicaKingsleyPublishers
Twitter @jkpbooks
Managing Director Nick Davies

Books for professionals and general readers on autism and other special needs, social work, arts therapies, mental health, education, practical theology, dementia, parenting, gender, diversity and related issues. The Singing Dragon imprint includes books on Chinese medicine, aromatherapy and qigong. Purchased by Hachette 2017. Founded in 1987.

Charles Knight – see LexisNexis

Kogan Page Ltd*

2nd Floor, 45 Gee Street, London EC1V 3RS
tel 020-7278 0433
website www.koganpage.com
Chairman Phillip Kogan, *Directors* Helen Kogan (managing), Martin Klopstock (digital & operations), Mark Briars (finance), Rex Elston (sales), Alison Middle (marketing), Julia Swales (editorial)

Leading independent global publisher of specialist business books and content with over 900 titles in print. Key subject areas: finance, risk, information management, marketing, branding, human resources, coaching, logistics, supply chain, entrepreneurship and careers. Founded 1967.

Kube Publishing Ltd

Markfield Conference Centre, Ratby Lane,
Markfield, Leics. LE67 9SY
tel (01530) 249230
email info@kubepublishing.com
website www.kubepublishing.com
Managing Director Haris Ahmad

Formerly the Islamic Foundation. Books on Islam and the Muslim world for adults and children.

Kyle Books

Carmelite House, 50 Victoria Embankment,
London EC4Y ODZ
tel 020-3122 6000
email general.enquiries@kylebooks.com
website www.kylebooks.co.uk
Twitter @Kyle_Books
Publisher Joanna Copestick

Food & drink, health, beauty, gardening, reference, style, design, mind, body & spirit. Acquired by Octopus Publishing Group in 2017 (page 192). Founded 1990.

Peter Lang Ltd

52 St Giles, Oxford OX1 3LU
tel (01865) 514160
email oxford@peterlang.com
website www.peterlang.com
Facebook www.facebook.com/Peter-Lang-Oxford/
Twitter @PeterLangOxford
Ceo, Peter Lang Publishing Group Kelly Shergill, *Publishing Director* Lucy Melville, *Senior Commissioning Editors* Christabel Scaife, Laurel Plapp, *Group Commercial Director* Adam Gardner

Part of the international Peter Lang Publishing Group, the company publishes across the humanities and social sciences, producing texts in print and digital formats, as well as Open Access publications. All forms of scholarly research as well as textbooks, readers, student guides. Welcomes submissions from prospective authors. Blog: peterlangoxford.wordpress.com. Founded 2006.

Lawrence & Wishart Ltd

Central Books Building, Freshwater Road,
Chadwell Heath RM8 1RX
tel 020-8597 0090
email lw@lwbooks.co.uk
website www.lwbooks.co.uk

Managing Editors Katharine Harris, Lynda Dyson, Kirsty Capes

Cultural studies, current affairs, history, socialism and Marxism, political philosophy, politics, popular culture. Founded 1936.

Legend Business Ltd

107–111 Fleet Street, London EC4A 2AB
tel 020-7936 9941
email info@legend-paperbooks.co.uk
website www.legendtimesgroup.com
Twitter @LegendBusinessB
Managing Director Tom Chalmers, *Managing Director & Editor* Jonathan Reuvid, *Head of Publicity & Marketing* Lucy Chamberlain, *Sales Manager* Allison Zink

A business book publisher with a wide-ranging and interactive list of business titles. Legend Business is also the publisher of the annual 'Investor's Guide to the United Kingdom'. Submissions can be sent to Tom Chalmers at submissions@legend-paperbooks.co.uk. Founded 2010.

Legend Press Ltd

107–111 Fleet Street, London EC4A 2AB
tel 020-7936 9941
email info@legend-paperbooks.co.uk
website www.legendtimesgroup.com
Twitter @legend_press
Managing Director Tom Chalmers, *Commissioning Editor* Lauren Parsons, *Head of Publicity & Marketing* Lucy Chamberlain, *Sales Manager* Allison Zink

Focused predominantly on publishing mainstream literary and commercial fiction. Submissions can be sent to submissions@legend-paperbooks.co.uk. Founded 2005.

Lewis Mason – see Ian Allan Publishing Ltd

LexisNexis

Lexis House, 30 Farringdon Street, London EC4A 4HH
tel 0330 1611234
email customer.services@lexisnexis.co.uk
website www.lexisnexis.co.uk

Formerly LexisNexis Butterworths. Division of Reed Elsevier (UK) Ltd. Founded 1974.

Butterworths

Legal and tax and accountancy books, journals, looseleaf and electronic services.

Charles Knight

Looseleaf legal works and periodicals on local government law, construction law and technical subjects.

Tolley

Law, taxation, accountancy, business.

The Lilliput Press Ltd†

62–63 Sitric Road, Arbour Hill, Dublin D07 AE27, Republic of Ireland
tel +353 (0)16 711647
email info@lilliputpress.ie
website www.lilliputpress.ie
Facebook www.facebook.com/Lilliput-Press
Twitter @LilliputPress
Managing Director Antony T. Farrell

General and Irish literature: essays, memoir, biography/autobiography, fiction, criticism; Irish history; philosophy; Joycean contemporary culture; nature and environment. Founded 1984.

Frances Lincoln

74–77 White Lion Street, London N1 9PF
tel 020-7284 9300
email reception@frances-lincoln.com
website www.quartoknows.com
Publisher Andrew Dunn

Imprint of The Quarto Group. Illustrated, international co-editions: gardening, architecture, environment, interiors, photography, art, walking and climbing, design and landscape, gift, children's books. Founded 1977.

Lion Hudson Limited (Isle of Man)

Wilkinson House, Jordan Hill Road, Oxford OX2 8DR
tel (01865) 302750
email info@lionhudson.com
website www.lionhudson.com
Managing Director Suzanne Wilson-Higgins

Books for children and adults. Christian spirituality, reference, biography, history, contemporary issues, inspiration and fiction from authors with a Christian world-view. Also specialises in children's bibles and prayer collections, as well as picture storybooks and illustrated non-fiction. Adult submissions: via website, by email or hardcopy with sae if return required. Children's submissions: hardcopy only with sae if return required. Founded 1971 as Lion Publishing; merged with Angus Hudson Ltd in 2003. Purchased by Lion Hudson Limited (Isle of Man), a newly incorporated company controlled by the AFD Group in 2017.

Lion Books

Christian books accessible to all readers: bible related information and reference, history, spirituality and prayer, issues, self-help.

Lion Fiction

Historical fiction, cosy crime, women's fiction and some fantasy from authors with a Christian world-view.

Lion Children's Books

Bible story retellings, prayer books, picture storybooks, illustrated non-fiction and information books on the Christian faith and world religions. Also specialises in gift books, occasion books and seasonal books for Christmas and Easter.

Candle Books
Bible story retellings, prayer books, bible related activity and novelty books, and other resources created in partnership with other publishers and packagers.

Monarch Books
Confessional Christian biography, issues concerning Christian faith and society, bible commentary, church resources and co-publishing with Christian events and organisations.

Little, Brown Book Group*

50 Victoria Embankment, London EC4Y 0DZ
tel 020-3122 7000
email info@littlebrown.co.uk
website www.littlebrown.co.uk
Twitter @LittleBrownUK
Managing Director Charlie King, *Coo* Ben Groves-Raines

Hardback and paperback fiction and general non-fiction. No unsolicited MSS. Part of Hachette UK (see page 176). Founded 1988.

Abacus
Managing Director Richard Beswick
Trade paperbacks.

Atom
website www.atombooks.co.uk
Teen fiction with a fantastical edge.

Blackfriars
website www.blackfriarsbooks.com
Publisher Clare Smith
Digital imprint.

Constable & Robinson
Fiction, non-fiction, psychology, humour, brief histories and how-to books.

Corsair
Twitter @CorsairBooks
Publisher James Gurbutt
Pioneers of literary fiction from groundbreaking debuts to established authors. An imprint of @littlebrownuk.

Dialogue Books
Publisher Sharmaine Lovegrove
Publishes BAME, LGBTQI+, disability and working class communities across fiction, non-fiction, literary and commercial.

Fleet
Publisher Ursula Doyle
A new literary imprint, which publishes six to eight titles a year, both literary fiction and narrative non-fiction.

Hachette Digital
Publisher Sarah Shrubb, *Head of Digital & Online Sales* Ben Goddard
CDs, downloads and ebooks. See page 242.

Little, Brown
Managing Director Richard Beswick, *Publishing Director* Clare Smith
General books: politics, biography, crime fiction, general fiction.

Orbit
website www.orbitbooks.com
Publisher Tim Holman
Sci-fi and fantasy.

Piatkus Constable & Robinson
website www.piatkus.co.uk
Publishing Director Tim Whiting (non-fiction)
Fiction and general non-fiction.

Sphere
Publishing Director Lucy Malagoni
Hardbacks and paperbacks: original fiction and non-fiction.

Virago
website www.virago.co.uk
Publisher Sarah Savitt
Women's literary fiction and non-fiction.

Little Books Ltd

63 Warwick Square, London SW1V 2AL
tel 020-7792 7929
email info@maxpress.co.uk
Contact Helen Nelson

History, biography, fiction and gift books. No unsolicited MSS. Founded 2003.

Little Tiger Group

1 Coda Studios, 189 Munster Road, London SW6 6AW
tel 020-7385 6333
website www.littletiger.co.uk
Ceo Monty Bhatia

Children's picture books, novelty books, board books, pop-up books and activity books for preschool age to 7 years, and fiction for 6–12 years. See imprint websites for submissions guidelines. Imprints: Caterpillar Books (novelty), Little Tiger Press (picture books), Stripes (fiction), 360 Degrees (non-fiction). Founded 1987.

Caterpillar Books
email contact@littletiger.co.uk
website www.littletiger.co.uk/imprint/caterpillar-books
Publisher Thomas Truong, *Editorial Director* Pat Hegarty

Books for preschool children, including pop-ups, board books, cloth books and activity books. Founded 2003.

Little Tiger Press
email contact@littletiger.co.uk
website www.littletiger.co.uk
Publisher Jude Evans, *Editorial Director* Barry Timms

Children's picture books, board books, novelty books and activity books for preschool–7 years. See website for submissions guidelines. Founded 1987.

Stripes
email contact@littletiger.co.uk
website www.littletiger.co.uk/imprint/stripes-publishing
Publisher Thomas Truong, *Editorial Director* Ruth Bennett, *Commissioning Editor* Katie Jennings

Fiction for children aged 6–12 years and young adult. Quality standalone titles and series publishing in all age groups. Will consider new material from authors and illustrators; see website for guidelines. Founded 2005.

360 Degrees
email contact@littletiger.co.uk
website www.littletiger.co.uk/special/360degrees/
Publisher Thomas Truong, *Editorial Director* Pat Hegarty

Non-fiction novelty for children aged 5–12 years. Founded 2015.

Liverpool University Press

4 Cambridge Street, Liverpool L69 7ZU
tel 0151 794 2233
email lup@liv.ac.uk
website www.liverpooluniversitypress.co.uk
Twitter @LivUniPress
Managing Director Andrew Cond

LUP is the UK's third oldest university press, with a distinguished history of publishing exceptional research since 1899, including the work of Nobel prize winners. Rapidly expanded in recent years and now publishes approximately 70 books a year and 25 journals, specialising in literature, modern languages, history and visual culture.

Logaston Press

The Holme, Church Road, Eardisley, Herefordshire HR3 6NJ
tel (01544) 327182
email info@logastonpress.co.uk
website www.logastonpress.co.uk
Twitter @LogastonPress
Proprietors Richard Wheeler, Su Wheeler

History, social history, archaeology and guides to rural West Midlands and Mid and South Wales. Welcomes submission of ideas: send synopsis first. Founded 1985.

LOM ART

16 Lion Yard, Tremadoc Road, London SW4 7NQ
tel 020-7720 8643
email enquiries@mombooks.com
website www.mombooks.com
Facebook www.facebook.com//Lom, www.facebook.com/MichaelOMaraBooks
Twitter @OMaraBooks
Managing Director Lesley O'Mara, *Publisher* Philippa Wingate

Illustrated non-fiction for children and adults. Publishes approx. 10 titles a year. Bestsellers include *Animorphia, How to Draw Animals for the Artistically Anxious, The Modern Art Activity Book* and *Making Winter*, plus a range of artist-led drawing, colouring and picture book titles. Unable to guarantee a reply to every submission received, but the inclusion of a sae is necessary for submission to be returned. Imprint of Michael O'Mara Books Ltd (page 193)

Lonely Planet

240 Blackfriars Road, London SE1 8NW
tel 020-3771 5101
email go@lonelyplanet.co.uk
website www.lonelyplanet.com

A leading travel media company and travel guidebook brand. Over the past four decades, Lonely Planet has published 145 million guidebooks and features content on lonelyplanet.com, mobile, video and in 14 languages, nine international magazines, children's, armchair and lifestyle books and ebooks. Founded 1973.

Longman – see Pearson UK

Lorenz Books – see Anness Publishing

Luath Press Ltd*

543/2 Castlehill, The Royal Mile, Edinburgh EH1 2ND
tel 0131 225 4326
email gavin.macdougall@luath.co.uk
website www.luath.co.uk
Facebook www.facebook.com/LuathPress
Twitter @LuathPress
Director Gavin MacDougall

Publishes modern fiction, history, travel guides, art, poetry, and politics and more. Over 400 titles in print including recent *Sunday Times* Top 10 Bestseller *Poverty Safari: Understanding the Anger of Britain's Underclass* by Darren McGarvey. Award-winning and shortlisted titles include Angus Peter *Campbell's Memory and Straw*, Ann Kelley's *The Bower Bird*, Anne Pia's *Language of My Choosing* and Robert Alan Jamieson's *Da Happie Laand*. UK distributor BookSource. Founded 1981.

Luna Press Publishing*

149/4 Morrison Street, Edinburgh EH3 8AG
email lunapress@outlook.com
website www.lunapresspublishing.com
Directors Francesca T. Barbini (managing), Robert S Malan (editorial)

Fantasy, dark fantasy and science fiction (adult, young adult, teen) in fiction and academia. Publishes novels, illustrated novellas, graphic novels, parodies, academic papers, proceedings. See website for submission guidelines before submitting. Founded 2015.

Lund Humphries

Office 3, Book House, 261A City Road, London EC1V 1JX
email info@lundhumphries.com
website www.lundhumphries.com/
Facebook www.facebook.com/LHArtBooks
Twitter @LHArtBooks
Managing Director Lucy Myers

Independent publishing imprint of quality art and architecture books. Founded 1895.

The Lutterworth Press

PO Box 60, Cambridge CB1 2NT
tel (01223) 350865
email publishing@lutterworth.com
website www.lutterworth.com
website www.lutterworthpress.wordpress.com, www.facebook.com/JamesClarkeandCo
Twitter @LuttPress
Managing Director Adrian Brink

A long-established independent British publishing house trading since the late 18th century. Originally founded as the Religious Tract Society and publisher of *The Boy's Own Paper* and *The Girl's Own Paper*. Now a publisher of educational and adult non-fiction including books and ebooks on: history, biography, literature and criticism, science, philosophy, art and art history, biblical studies, theology, mission, religious studies and collecting. Recent titles include *The Making of Swallows and Amazons* (1974) by Sophie Neville, *The Alfred Wallis Factor: Conflict in Post-War St Ives Art* by David Wilkinson and *The Angel Roofs of East Anglia: Unseen Masterpieces of the Middle Ages* by Michael Rimmer. Imprints: James Clarke & Co, Acorn Editions, Patrick Hardy Books.

Mabecron Books ltd

3 Briston Orchard, St Mellion, Saltash, Cornwall Pl 12 6RQ
tel (01579) 350885
email ronjohns@mabecronbooks.co.uk
website www.mabecronbooks.co.uk
Twitter @mabecronbooks

Award-winning publishers. Producing beautiful children's picture books and books with a Cornish or west country subject. Linked to Bookshops in Falmouth, St Ives, Dartmouth and Padstow.

McGraw-Hill Education*

8th Floor, 338 Euston Road, London NW1 3BH
tel (01628) 502500
email emea_online@mheducation.com
website www.mheducation.co.uk
Managing Director (EMEA) Lloyd Waterhouse (Interim)

Higher education: business, economics, computing, maths, humanities, social sciences, world languages. Professional: business, computing, science, technical, medical, general reference.

Open University Press

email enquiries@openup.co.uk
website www.mheducation.co.uk/openup-homepage
Social sciences.

Macmillan – see Pan Macmillan

Macmillan Education – see Pan Macmillan

Made Simple Books – see Elsevier Ltd

Management Books 2000 Ltd

36 Western Road, Oxford OX1 4LG
tel (01865) 600738
website www.mb2000.com
Directors N. Dale-Harris, R. Hartman

Practical books for working managers and business professionals: management, business and lifeskills, and sponsored titles. Unsolicited MSS, synopses and ideas for books welcome.

Manchester University Press

Floor J, Renold Building, Altrincham Street, Manchester M1 7JA
tel 0161 275 2310
email mup@manchester.ac.uk
website www.manchesteruniversitypress.co.uk
Chief Executive Simon Ross

Works of academic scholarship: social sciences, literary criticism, cultural studies, media studies, art history, design, architecture, history, politics, economics, international law, modern-language texts. Textbooks and monographs. Founded 1904.

Mandrake of Oxford

PO Box 250, Oxford OX1 1AP
tel (01865) 243671
email mandrake@mandrake.uk.net
website www.mandrake.uk.net
Director Mogg Morgan

Art, biography, classic crime studies, fiction, Indology, magic, witchcraft, philosophy, religion. Query letters only. Founded 1986.

Mango Books

18 Soho Square, London W1D 3QL
tel 020-7060 4142
email adam@mangobooks.com
website www.mangobooks.co.uk

Publishers of non-fiction books for lovers of crime, detection and mystery.

Mantra Lingua Ltd

Global House, 303 Ballards Lane, London N12 8NP
tel 020-8445 5123
email info@mantralingua.com
website http://uk.mantralingua.com/, www.discoverypen.co.uk
Facebook www.facebook.com/Mantralingua
Twitter @mantralingua
Managing Directors R. Dutta, M. Chatterji

Publishes picture books and educational resources. The unique talking pen technology enables any book to be sound activated. All resources can be narrated in multiple languages and educational posters for schools and museums have audio visual features. Looking for illustrators, authors, translators and audio narrators. Museums and Heritage: looking for illustrators and trail writers. Looking for specialist audio recordings of birds, frogs and other animals from around the world, tel: 0845 600 1361. Founded 2002.

Kevin Mayhew Ltd

Buxhall, Stowmarket, Suffolk IP14 3BW
tel (01449) 737978
email info@kevinmayhew.com
website www.kevinmayhew.com
Directors Kevin Mayhew, Barbara Mayhew

Christianity: prayer and spirituality, pastoral care, preaching, liturgy worship, children's, youth work, drama, instant art, educational. Music: hymns, organ and choral, contemporary worship, piano and instrumental, tutors. Greetings cards: images, spiritual texts, birthdays, Christian events, musicians, general occasions. Read submissions section on website before sending MSS/synopses. Founded 1976.

Mentor Books

43 Furze Road, Sandyford Industrial Estate, Dublin D18 PN30, Republic of Ireland
tel +353 (0)12 952112
email admin@mentorbooks.ie
website www.mentorbooks.ie
Managing Director Daniel McCarthy

General: non-fiction, humour, biographies, politics, crime, history, guidebooks. Educational (secondary): languages, history, geography, business, maths, sciences. No unsolicited MSS. Founded 1980.

Mercat Press – see Birlinn Ltd

The Mercier Press†

Unit 3B, Oak House, Bessboro Road, Blackrock, Cork T12 D6CH, Republic of Ireland
tel +353 (0)21 4614700
email info@mercierpress.ie
website www.mercierpress.ie
Directors J.F. Spillane (chairman), M.P. Feehan (managing), D. Crowley

Irish literature, folklore, history, politics, humour, academic, current affairs, health, mind and spirit, general non-fiction, children's. Founded 1944.

Merlin Press Ltd

Central Books Building, Freshwater Road, London RM8 1RX
tel 020-8590 9700, 020-8590 9700
email info@merlinpress.co.uk
website www.merlinpress.co.uk
Managing Director Anthony Zurbrugg

Radical history and social studies. Letters/synopses only.

Green Print

Green politics and the environment.

Merrell Publishers Ltd

70 Cowcross Street, London EC1M 6EJ
tel 020-7713 403799
email hm@merrellpublishers.com
website www.merrellpublishers.com
Publisher Hugh Merrell

High-quality illustrated books on all aspects of visual culture, including art, architecture, photography, garden design, interior design, product design and books specially developed for institutions, foundations, corporations and private collectors. Unsolicited carefully prepared proposals welcomed via email. All titles published by Merrell are sold and distributed worldwide through US and UK distributors and international stockholding agents.

Methuen & Co Ltd

Orchard House, Railway Street, Slingsby, York YO62 4AN
(01653) 628152/628195

email editorial@methuen.co.uk, academic@methuen.co.uk
website www.methuen.co.uk
Managing Director Peter Tummons, *Editorial Director* Naomi Tummons, *Sales* Peter Newsom, *Editor-at-Large* Dr Jonathan Tummons, *Accounts* Frank Warn

Literary fiction and non-fiction: biography, autobiography, travel, history, sport, humour, film, children's, performing arts. No unsolicited MSS.

Politico's Publishing

Politics, current affairs, political biography and autobiography.

Metro Books – see John Blake Publishing Ltd

Metro Publications Ltd

PO Box 6336, London N1 6PY
tel 020-8533 7777
email info@metropublications.com
website www.metropublications.com
Twitter @metrolondon

Produces well-researched and beautifully designed guide books on many aspects of London life.

Michelin Maps and Guides

Hannay House, 39 Clarendon Road, Watford, Herts. WD17 1JA
tel (01923) 205240
email travelpubsales@uk.michelin.com
website www.michelin.co.uk/travel

Tourist guides, maps and atlases, hotel and restaurant guides.

Milestone Publications

Forestside House, Broad Walk, Forestside, Rowlands Castle PO9 6EE
tel 023-9263 1888
email andrew@gosschinaclub.co.uk
website www.gosschinaclub.co.uk
Managing Director Andrew O.J. Pine, *Publisher* Nicholas J. Pine

Crested heraldic china, antique porcelain. Milestone Publications – publishing and bookselling division of Goss & Crested China Club. Founded 1967.

Miller's – see Octopus Publishing Group

Mills & Boon Medical – see Harlequin (UK) Ltd

Mills & Boon Modern Romance – see Harlequin (UK) Ltd

Milo Books Ltd

14 Ash Grove, Wrea Green, Preston, Lancs. PR4 2NY
tel (01772) 672900
email info@milobooks.com
website www.milobooks.com
Publisher Peter Walsh

True crime, sport, current affairs. Founded 1997.

Mira Books – see Harlequin (UK) Ltd

Mirror Books

Trinity Mirror, One Canada Square, London E14 5AP
tel 20-7293 3700
email mirrorbooks@trinitymirror.com
website www.mirrorbooks.co.uk
Twitter @themirrorbooks
Executive Editor Jo Sollis, *Publishing Director* Paula Scott, *Head of Syndication & Licensing* Fergus McKenna

Part of Trinity Mirror, one of the UK's leading media companies. The imprint focus is non-fiction real-life (memoir, crime and nostalgia) and popular fiction. Accepts submissions via email: submissions@mirrorbooks.co.uk. Founded 2016.

Mitchell Beazley – see Octopus Publishing Group

Mobius – see Hodder & Stoughton

Morgan Kauffman – see Elsevier Ltd

Morrigan Book Company

Killala, Co. Mayo, Republic of Ireland
tel +353 (0)96 32555
email morriganbooks@gmail.com
website http://conankennedy.com/About.html
Publishers Gerry Kennedy, Hilary Kennedy

Non-fiction: general Irish interest, biography, history, local history, folklore and mythology. Founded 1979.

Mud Pie

43 Leckford Road, Oxford OX2 6HY
tel 07985 935320
email info@mudpiebooks.com
website www.mudpiebooks.com
Facebook www.facebook.com/Mud-Pie-Books-665982096919314
Twitter @mudpiebooks
Founder & Director Tony Morris

Buddhist books and books for Buddhists. An independent specialist online publisher, dedicated to showcasing the best in Buddhist writing. The company's lead title, *The Buddha, Geoff and Me,* has sold over 100,000 copies worldwide. Founded 2016.

Murdoch Books

Ormond House, 26–27 Boswell Street, London WC1N 3JZ
tel 020-8785 5995
email info@murdochbooks.co.uk
website www.murdochbooks.co.uk

Non-fiction: homes and interiors, gardening, cookery, craft, DIY. Owned by Australian publisher Allen & Unwin Pty Ltd.

John Murray Press

338 Euston Road, London NW1 3BH
tel 020-7873 6000
website www.hodder.co.uk/john%20murray/index.page
Facebook www.facebook.com/johnmurraybooks
Twitter @johnmurrays
Publishing Director (fiction) Eleanor Birne, *Publisher (non-fiction)* Georgina Laycock, *Editorial Director (fiction & non-fiction)* Mark Richards

Quality literary fiction and non-fiction: business, travel, history, entertainment, reference, biography and memoir, real-life stories. No unsolicited MSS without preliminary letter. Part of Hachette UK (see page 176). Founded 1768.

Muswell Press

72 Cromwell Avenue, London N6 5HQ
email team@muswell-press.co.uk
website www.muswell-press.co.uk
Facebook www.facebook.com/MuswellPress/
Twitter @MuswellPress
Directors Kate Beal, Sarah Beal

Muswell Press is a proudly independent publisher of great books, both fiction and non-fiction. The current directors bought Muswell Press in 2016, and have subsequently transformed the company with over 60 years publishing experience between them, at Bloomsbury, Faber, Walker Books, HarperCollins amongst others.

Myriad Editions

New Internationalist Publications,
The Old Music Hall, 106–108 Cowley Rd,
Oxford OX4 1JE
tel (01865) 403345
email info@myriadeditions.com
website www.myriadeditions.com
Twitter @MyriadEditions
Directors Candida Lacey (publishing), Corinne Pearlman (creative)

Independent publisher of literary fiction, crime written by women, graphic novels and feminist non-fiction. Merged with New Internationalist in 2017 as part of a joint plan to expand and embrace diversity. Founded 1993.

National Trust – see Pavilion Books

Natural History Museum Publishing

Cromwell Road, London SW7 5BD
tel 020-7942 5336
email publishing@nhm.ac.uk
website www.nhm.ac.uk/publishing
Head of Publishing Colin Ziegler

Natural sciences, entomology, botany, geology, mineralogy, palaeontology, zoology, history of natural history. Founded 1881.

New Holland Publishers (UK) Ltd

The Chandlery Unit 609,
50 Westminster Bridge Road, London SE1 7QY
tel 020-3667 7619
email enquiries@nhpub.co.uk
website www.newhollandpublishers.com
Managing Director Fiona Schultz

Illustrated non-fiction books on natural history, sports and hobbies, animals and pets, travel pictorial, reference, gardening, health and fitness, practical art, DIY, food and drink, outdoor pursuits, craft, humour, gift books. New proposals accepted, send CV and synopsis and sample chapters in first instance; sae essential.

New Island Books†

16 Priory Office Park, Stillorgan,
Co. Dublin A94 RH10, Republic of Ireland
tel +353 (0)12 784225
email info@newisland.ie, editor@newisland.ie
website www.newisland.ie
Facebook www.facebook.com/NewIslandBooks
Twitter @NewIslandBooks
Director Edwin Higel, *Editor* Dan Bolger (commissioning)

Fiction, poetry, drama, humour, biography, current affairs. Submissions by email only to editor@newisland.ie. Send the first three chapters as a Word document, plus a short synopsis, and include details of any previous publications. Founded 1992.

New Playwrights' Network

10 Station Road Industrial Estate, Colwall,
Nr Malvern, Herefordshire WR13 6RN
tel (01684) 540154
email simon@cressrelles.co.uk
website www.cressrelles.co.uk
Publishing Director Leslie Smith

General plays for the amateur, one-act and full length.

New Riders – see Pearson UK

New Theatre Publications/The Playwrights' Co-operative

2 Hereford Close, Woolston, Warrington,
Cheshire WA1 4HR
tel 0845 331 3516, (01925) 485605
email info@plays4theatre.com
website www.plays4theatre.com
Director Alison Hornby

Plays for the professional and amateur stage. Submissions encouraged. Founded 1987.

Newnes – see Elsevier Ltd

Nexus – see Virgin Books (in partnership with Virgin Group), page 168

Nightingale Press

7 Green Park Station, Green Park Road,
Bath BA1 1JB
tel (01225) 478444
email sales@manning-partnership.co.uk
website www.manning-partnership.co.uk
Directors Garry Manning (managing), Roger Hibbert (sales)

Humour, gift. Owned by Manning Partnership Ltd. Founded 1997.

Nobrow Books

27 Westgate Street, London E8 3RL
tel 020-7033 4430
email nobrowsubs@gmail.com
website http://nobrow.net/
Twitter @NobrowPress

Publishes picture books, illustrated fiction and non-fiction and graphic novels. Nobrow Books aims to combine good design and storytelling, quality production value and environmental consciousness. Founded 2008.

Flying Eye Books

email info@nobrow.net
website www.flyingeyebooks.com
Twitter @FlyingEyeBooks

Children's imprint. Focuses on the craft of children's storytelling and non-fiction. Founded 2013.

Nordisk Books Ltd

12 Dove Road, London N1 3GB
tel (07437) 202582
email info@nordiskbooks.com
website www.nordiskbooks.com
Facebook www.facebook.com/nordiskbooks
Twitter @nordiskbooks
Director Duncan J. Lewis

Modern and contemporary fiction from the Nordic countries. Publishing a wide range of exciting literary titles from across the Scandinavian peninsular and beyond. No crime. Founded 2016.

North-Holland – see Elsevier Ltd

Northcote House Publishers Ltd

The Paddocks, Brentor Road, Mary Tavy, Devon PL19 9PY
tel (01822) 810066
email northcotepublishers@gmail.com
website www.writersandtheirwork.co.uk
Directors B.R.W. Hulme, A.V. Hulme (secretary), Sarah Piper (sales & marketing)

Education and education management, educational dance and drama, literary criticism (*Writers and their Work*). Founded 1985.

W.W. Norton & Company

15 Carlisle Street, London W1D 3BS
tel 020-7323 1579
email office@wwnorton.co.uk
website www.wwnorton.co.uk
Facebook www.facebook.com/WW-Norton-UK/
Twitter @wwnortonuk
Managing Director Edward Crutchley

English and American literature, economics, music, psychology, science. Founded 1980.

Nourish Books

Unit 11, Shepperton House, 89 Shepperton Road, London N1 3DF
tel 020-3813 6940
email enquiries@watkinspublishing.com
website https://nourishbooks.com/
Facebook www.facebook.com/nourishbooks
Twitter @nourishbooks

Cookery, wellbeing and health. Part of Watkins Media (page 214).

NWP – see Neil Wilson Publishing Ltd

Oak Tree Press[†]

33 Rochestown Rise, Rochestown, Cork T12 EVT0, Republic of Ireland
tel +353 (0)86 2441633, +353 (0)86 330 7694
email info@oaktreepress.com
website www.SuccessStore.com
Directors Brian O'Kane, Rita O'Kane

Business management, enterprise, accountancy and finance, law. Special emphasis on titles for small business owner/managers. Founded 1991.

Nubooks

Ebooks.

Oberon Books

521 Caledonian Road, London N7 9RH
tel 020-7607 3637
email info@oberonbooks.com
website www.oberonbooks.com
Managing Director Charles Glanville, *Publisher* James Hogan, *Senior Editor* George Spender

New and classic play texts, programme texts and general theatre, dance and performing arts books. Founded 1986.

The O'Brien Press Ltd[†]

12 Terenure Road East, Rathgar, Dublin D06 HD27, Republic of Ireland
tel +353 (0)14 923333
email books@obrien.ie
website www.obrien.ie
Directors Michael O'Brien, Ivan O'Brien, Kunak McGann

Adult non-fiction: biography, politics, history, true crime, sport, humour, reference. Adult fiction, crime (Brandon). No poetry or academic. Children: fiction for all ages; illustrated fiction for ages 3+, 5+, 6+, 8+ years, novels (10+ and young adult): contemporary, historical, fantasy. Unsolicited MSS (sample chapters only), synopses and ideas for books welcome, submissions will not be returned. Founded 1974.

Octopus Publishing Group*

Carmelite House, 50 Victoria Embankment, London EC4Y 0DZ
tel 020-3122 6000
email info@octopusbooks.co.uk, publisher@octopusbooks.co.uk (submissions)

Books

website www.octopusbooks.co.uk
Chief Executive Alison Goff, *Deputy Ceo & Group Sales & Marketing Director* Andrew Welham

Part of Hachette UK (see page 176).

Aster
Publisher Kate Adams

Health and wellbeing.

Bounty
Publisher Lucy Pessell

Promotional/division of Octopus Publishing Group.

Cassell
Popular culture, music, reference.

Conran Octopus
Quality illustrated books, particularly lifestyle, cookery, gardening.

Gaia Books
The environment, natural living and health.

Godsfield Press
email publisher@godsfieldpress.com

Mind, body & spirit with an emphasis on practical application.

Hamlyn
Practical non-fiction, particularly cookery, health and diet, home and garden, sport, puzzles and reference.

Ilex Press
email info@octopusbooks.co.uk

Illustrated books on art, design, photography and popular culture.

Kyle Books
Quality cookery and lifestyle (page 184).

Miller's
Antiques and collectables.

Mitchell Beazley
Quality illustrated books, particularly cookery, wine and gardening.

Philip's
email publisher@philips-maps.co.uk

Atlases, maps and astronomy.

Spruce
Gift and humour.

Summersdale
Gift, humour, travel and health (page 208).

The Oleander Press

16 Orchard Street, Cambridge CB1 1JT
tel (01638) 500784
website www.oleanderpress.com
Managing Director Dr Jane Doyle

Travel, language, Libya, Arabia and Middle East, Cambridgeshire, history, reference, classics. MSS welcome with sae for reply. Founded 1960.

Michael O'Mara Books Ltd*

16 Lion Yard, Tremadoc Road, London SW4 7NQ
tel 020-7720 8643
email enquiries@mombooks.com, publicity@mombooks.com
website www.mombooks.com
Facebook www.facebook.com/MichaelOMaraBooks/
Twitter @OMaraBooks
Chairman Michael O'Mara, *Managing Director* Lesley O'Mara, *Publisher* Clare Tillyer, *Senior Editorial Director* Louise Dixon, *Publishing Director (Buster Books)* Philippa Wingate

General non-fiction: biography, humour, history. See website for submission guidelines. Founded 1985.

Buster Books
website www.busterbooks.com
Facebook www.facebook.com/BusterBooks
Twitter @BusterBooks

Activity, novelty, picture books, fiction and non-fiction for children and young adults.

LOM ART
Activity, arts & crafts, photography, reference, picture books for children (page 187).

Omnibus Press/Music Sales Ltd

14–15 Berners Street, London W1T 3LJ
tel 020-7612 7400
email omniinfo@musicsales.co.uk
website www.omnibuspress.com, www.musicroom.com/omnibus-press
Chief Editor David Barraclough

Rock music biographies, books about music. Founded 1976.

On Stream Publications Ltd

Currabaha, Cloghroe, Blarney, Co. Cork T23 EW08, Republic of Ireland
tel +353 (0)21 4385798
email info@onstream.ie
website www.onstream.ie
Owner Rosalind Crowley

Cookery, wine, travel, human interest non-fiction, local history, academic and practical books. Founded 1986.

Oneworld Publications*

10 Bloomsbury Street, London WC1B 3SR
tel 020-7307 8900
email info@oneworld-publications.com
website www.oneworld-publications.com
Facebook www.facebook.com/oneworldpublications
Twitter @OneworldNews
Director Juliet Mabey (publisher)

Fiction and general non-fiction: current affairs, politics, history, Middle East, business, popular science, philosophy, psychology, green issues, world religions and Islamic studies; literary fiction, plus fiction that sits at the intersection of the literary and commercial, showcasing strong voices and great stories; young adult to children's fiction and upmarket crime/suspense novels, as well as fiction in translation. No unsolicited MSS; email or send proposal via website. Founded 1986.

Open Gate Press*

51 Achilles Road, London NW6 1DZ
tel 020-7431 4391
email books@opengatepress.co.uk
Directors Jeannie Cohen, Elisabeth Petersdorff, Sandra Lovell

Incorporating Centaur Press, founded 1954. Psychoanalysis, philosophy, social sciences, religion, animal welfare, the environment. Founded 1988.

Open University Press – see McGraw-Hill Education

Orbit – see Little, Brown Book Group

Orchard Books – see Hachette Children's Group

Orenda Books

16 Carson Road, West Dulwich, London SE21 8HU
tel 020-8355 4643
email info@orendabooks.co.uk
website www.orendabooks.co.uk
Facebook www.facebook.com/orendabooks
Twitter @OrendaBooks
Publisher Karen Sullivan, *Editor* West Camel

A new independent publisher specialising in literary fiction, with a heavy emphasis on crime thrillers, about half in translation. Founded 2014.

The Orion Publishing Group Ltd*

Carmelite House, 50 Victoria Embankment, London EC4Y 0DZ
tel 020-3122 6444
website www.orionbooks.co.uk
Directors Arnaud Nourry (chairman), David Shelley (chief executive), Katie Espiner (managing director)

No unsolicited MSS; approach in writing in first instance. Part of Hachette UK (see page 176). Founded 1992.

Gollancz

Contact Gillian Redfearn

Sci-fi, fantasy and horror.

Orion Fiction

Contact Harriet Bourton

Trade and mass market fiction.

Orion Spring

Contact Amanda Harris

Wellbeing, health and lifestyle non-fiction.

Seven Dials

Contact Amanda Harris

Trade and mass market: cookery, memoir and autobiography, gift and humour, personal development and parenting, lifestyle, diet and fitness.

Trapeze

Contact Anna Valentine

Trade and mass market fiction: reading group, crime and thriller, women's fiction; trade and mass market non-fiction: memoir and autobiography, lifestyle, gift and humour, popular psychology and entertainment.

Weidenfeld & Nicolson Fiction

Contact Kirsty Dunseath

Literary fiction.

Weidenfeld & Nicolson Non-Fiction

Contact Alan Samson

Biography and autobiography, history, current affairs, popular science and sport.

Osprey Publishing Ltd

Kemp House, Chawley Park, Cumnor Hill, Oxford OX2 9PH
tel (01865) 727022
email info@ospreypublishing.com
website www.ospreypublishing.com

Publishes illustrated military history. Over 1,600 titles in print on a wide range of military history subjects from ancient times to the modern day. Founded 1968; acquired by Bloomsbury Publishing Plc 2014.

Oversteps Books Ltd

6 Halwell House, South Pool, Nr Kingsbridge, Devon TQ7 2RX
tel (01548) 531969
email alwynmarriage@overstepsbooks.com
website www.overstepsbooks.com
Director/Managing Editor Dr Alwyn Marriage

Poetry. Email six poems that have either won major competitions, or been published, giving details of the competitions or magazines in which they appeared, the dates or issue numbers and the email addresses of the editors. Founded 1992.

Peter Owen Publishers

Conway Hall, 25 Red Lion Square, London WC1R 4RL
tel 020-8350 1775
email aowen@peterowen.com
website www.peterowen.com
Facebook www.facebook.com/peter.owen.publishers
Twitter @PeterOwenPubs
Directors Peter L. Owen (managing), Antonia Owen (editorial)

Backlist includes ten Nobel Prize winners. Arts, belles lettres, biography and memoir, literary fiction, general non-fiction, history, theatre and entertainment. Do not send fiction without first emailing the Editorial Department even if an established novelist. No mass-market genre fiction, short stories or poetry; first novels almost never published. Merged with independent publisher Istros Books in August 2016 and formed a new imprint Istros Books. Founded 1951.

Oxford University Press*

Great Clarendon Street, Oxford OX2 6DP
tel (01865) 556767
email enquiry@oup.com
website www.oup.com
Ceo Nigel Portwood, *Group Finance Director* Giles Spackman, *Global Academic Business Managing Director* David Clark, *Managing Director, Oxford Education* Kate Harris, *ELT Division Managing Director* Peter Marshall, *Human Resources Director* Paul Lomas, *Academic Sales Director* Alastair Lewis

Archaeology, architecture, art, belles lettres, bibles, bibliography, children's books (fiction, non-fiction, picture), commerce, current affairs, dictionaries, drama, economics, educational (foundation, primary, secondary, technical, university), encyclopedias, ELT, electronic publishing, essays, foreign language learning, general history, hymn and service books, journals, law, medical, music, oriental, philosophy, political economy, prayer books, reference, science, sociology, theology and religion; educational software; *Grove Dictionaries of Music & Art*. Trade paperbacks published under the imprint of Oxford Paperbacks. Founded 1478.

P8tech

6 Woodside, Churnet View Road, Oakamoor, Staffs. ST10 3AE
tel (01538) 703591
email info@P8tech.com
website www.P8tech.com
Publisher James Lumsden-Cook

IT and computer-related titles, including books on video games and Artificial Intelligence. Specialises in Oracle and Java-related titles. Founded 2012.

Palgrave Macmillan – see Pan Macmillan

Pan Macmillan*

20 New Wharf Road, London N1 9RR
tel 020-7014 6000
email webqueries@macmillan.co.uk
website www.panmacmillan.com
Managing Director Anthony Forbes Watson, *Sales and Brand Director* Anna Bond, *Publishers* Jeremy Trevathan (adult), Robin Harvie (non-fiction), Paul Baggaley (Picador), Carole Tonkinson (Bluebird)

Novels, literary, crime, thrillers, romance, science fiction, fantasy and horror. Autobiography, biography, business, gift books, health and beauty, history, humour, natural history, travel, philosophy, politics, world affairs, theatre, film, gardening, cookery, popular reference. No unsolicited MSS except through Macmillan New Writing. Founded 1843.

Boxtree

Publisher Robin Harvie

Brand and media tie-in titles, including TV, film, music and internet, plus entertainment licences, pop culture, humour in hardback and paperback.

Bluebird

Publisher Carole Tonkinson

Pan Macmillan's wellness and lifestyle imprint, publishing the very latest in diet, popular psychology, self-help as well as career and business, parenting and inspirational memoir.

Campbell Books (preschool)

Editorial Director Stephanie Barton

Early learning, pop-up, novelty, board books for the preschool market.

Kingfisher

tel 020-7014 6000
Publisher Belinda Rasmussen

Non-fiction: imprint of Macmillan Children's Books.

Macmillan

Adult Books Publisher Jeremy Trevathan, *Picador Publisher* Paul Baggaley, *Non-fiction Publisher* Robin Harvie, *Bluebird Publisher* Carole Tonkinson, *Editorial Directors* Georgina Morley (non-fiction), Kate Harvey

Hardback commercial fiction including genre fiction, romantic, crime and thrillers. Hardback serious and general non-fiction including autobiography, biography, economics, history, military history, philosophy, politics and world affairs, popular reference titles.

Macmillan Digital Audio

Digital & Communications Director Sara Lloyd

Audio imprint for the entire Pan Macmillan list. See page 243.

Macmillan Education Ltd

email info@macmillan.com
website www.macmillaneducation.com
Chief Executive Simon Allen, *Managing Director* Helen Melia (Europe & Middle East), *Publishing Directors* Alison Hubert (Africa, Caribbean, Middle East, Asia), Kate Melliss (Spain), Sharon Jervis (Latin America), Sue Bale (dictionaries), Angela Lilley (international ELT)

ELT titles and school and college textbooks and materials in all subjects for the international education market in both book and electronic formats.

Macmillan Science and Education
The Macmillan Campus, 4 Crinan Street, London N1 9XW
tel 020-7833 4000

Mantle
Publisher Maria Rejt

Palgrave Macmillan
website www.palgrave.com

Monographs and journals in academic and professional subjects. Publishes in both hard copy and electronic formats.

Pan
Paperback imprint for Macmillan and Sidgwick & Jackson imprints. Founded 1947.

Picador
Publisher Paul Baggaley

Literary international fiction, non-fiction and poetry published in hardback and paperback. Founded 1972.

Sidgwick & Jackson
Publisher Robin Harvie

Hardback popular non-fiction including celebrity and show business to music and sport. Founded 1908.

Pandora Press – see Rivers Oram Press

Parthian Books
148 Keir Hardie, Swansea University, Singleton Park, Swansea SA2 8PP
(01792) 606605
email info@parthianbooks.com
website www.parthianbooks.com
Facebook www.facebook.com/parthianbooks/
Twitter @parthianbooks
Publishing Editor Susie Wild

Independent publisher of poetry, Welsh literature and translations that reflect a diverse and contemporary Wales. Prizes won by authors include the Dylan Thomas Prize, the Betty Trask, the Wales Book of the Year, the Orange Futures Award, the Rhys Davies Prize, the Journey Prize, the Edge Hill Readers' Award and the Stonewall Award. Currently accepting submissions. See website for guidelines on how to submit MSS. Founded 1993.

Patrician Press
51 Free Rodwell House, School Lane, Mistley CO11 1HW
tel 07968 288651
email patricia@patricianpress.com
website www.patricianpress.com
Facebook www.facebook.com/patricianpress
Twitter @PatricianCom
Publisher Patricia Borlenghi

Paperback and digital publisher of fiction and poetry. Publisher of children's books under the imprint Pudding Press. Founded 2012.

Pavilion Books*
43 Great Ormond Street, London WC1N 3HZ
tel 020-7462 1500
email reception@pavilionbooks.com
website www.pavilionbooks.com
Chief Executive Polly Powell

Formerly Anova Books Group. Founded 2013.

Batsford
Publisher Tina Persaud

Chess, art techniques, film, fashion and costume, textile art, design, embroidery, heritage.

Collins & Brown
Publisher Katie Cowan

Lifestyle and interiors, cookery, gardening, photography, pet care, health and beauty, hobbies and crafts, including *Good Housekeeping* branded books.

National Trust Books
Senior Commissioning Editor Peter Taylor

Heritage, gardens, cookery.

Pavilion
Publisher Katie Cowan

Cookery, gardening, travel, wine, photography, art, popular culture, gift.

Portico
Publisher Tina Persaud

Humour, popular culture, quirky reference, sport.

Robson Books
General non-fiction, biography, music, humour, sport.

Salamander
Packager of made-to-order books on cookery, crafts, military, natural history, music, gardening, hobbies, transport, sports, popular reference.

Pavilion Children's Books*
43 Great Ormond Street, London WC1N 3HZ
tel 020-7462 1500
website www.pavilionbooks.com
Publisher Neil Dunnicliffe

Children's books: from baby books to illustrated non-fiction and classics. Part of Pavilion Books Company Ltd. Submissions via an agent only.

Pavilion Publishing and Media Ltd
Rayford House, School Road, Hove BN3 5HX
tel (01273) 434943
email info@pavpub.com
website www.pavpub.com
Ceo, OLM Group Peter O'Hara, *Head of Publishing Relationships* Graham Hoare

Part of OLM Group. Health and social care training resources, books and assessment tools in a variety of fields including learning disability, mental health, vulnerable adults, housing, drugs and alcohol, staff development, children, young and older people, and forensic services, aimed at front line workers, professionals and academics. Also, English language teaching books and resources aimed at newly-qualified and experienced teachers and teacher trainers in the ELT field. Founded 1987.

Peachpit Press – see Pearson UK

Pearson UK*

Edinburgh Gate, Harlow, Essex CM20 2JE
tel 0845 313 6666
website www.pearsoned.co.uk
President Rod Bristow

Allyn & Bacon

Higher education, humanities, social sciences.

BBC Active

Learning resources for children and adults.

Cisco Press

Cisco-systems authorised publisher. Material for networking students and professionals.

Benjamin Cummings

Higher education, science.

FT Prentice Hall

Business for higher education and professional.

Harcourt

Educational resources for teachers and learners at primary, secondary and vocational level. Provides a range of published resources, teachers' support, and pupil and student material in all core subjects for all ages. Imprints: Ginn, Heinemann, Payne-Gallway, Raintree, Rigby.

Longman

Education for higher education, schools, ELT.

New Riders

Graphics and design.

Peachpit Press

Internet and general computing.

Penguin Longman

ELT.

Prentice Hall

Academic and reference textbooks.

QUE Publishing

Computing.

SAMS Publishing

Professional computing.

Wharton

Business.

York Notes

Literature guides for students.

Pen & Sword Books Ltd

47 Church Street, Barnsley, South Yorkshire S70 2AS
tel (01226) 734555, (01226) 734222
email editorialoffice@pen-and-sword.co.uk
website www.pen-and-sword.co.uk
Managing Director Charles Hewitt, *Publishing Manager* Henry Wilson, *Commissioning Editors* Jonathan Wright, Phil Sidnell, Rupert Harding, Claire Hopkins, Laura Hirst, Michael Leventhal, Julian Mannering, Rob Gardiner

Military history, aviation history, naval and maritime, general history, local history, family history, transport, social history, archaeology, health and lifestyle, natural history, gardening, space, science, sports. Imprints: Leo Cooper, Frontline Books, White Owl, Pen & Sword Aviation, Pen & Sword Naval & Maritime, Remember When, Frontline, Seaforth, Pen & Sword Digital, Pen & Sword Transport, Pen & Sword Discovery, Pen & Sword Social History, Pen & Sword Archaeology.

Penguin General*

80 Strand, London WC2R 0RL
tel 020-7010 3000
Managing Director Joanna Prior

No unsolicited MSS or synopses. Part of Penguin Random House UK (page 198).

Fig Tree

Publishing Director Juliet Annan

Fiction and general non-fiction.

Hamish Hamilton

Publishing Director Simon Prosser

Fiction, biography and memoirs, current affairs, history, literature, politics, travel.

Penguin Life

Publishing Director Emily Robertson

Health, lifestyle, wellbeing, trends.

Portfolio

Editorial Director Martina O'Sullivan

Business, management, technology and finance.

Viking

Publishing Director Venetia Butterfield

Fiction, biography and memoirs, current affairs, popular culture, sport, history, literature, politics, travel.

Penguin Longman – see Pearson UK

Penguin Random House Children's UK*

80 Strand, London WC2R 0RL
tel 020-7139 3000
website www.penguin.co.uk
Managing Director Francesca Dow, *Publishing*

Director (Puffin Fiction, Non-Fiction, Licensing, & Picture Books) Amanda Punter, *Publisher (Puffin Fiction, Non-Fiction & Licensing)* Ruth Knowles, *Publisher (Puffin Fiction)* Ben Horslen, *Publisher (Puffin, Picture books & Partnerships)* Lara Hancock, *Publishing Director (Ladybird Trade, Licensing, & Education)* Shannon Cullen, *Publisher (Ladybird Education)* Kate Heald, *Head of Children's Licensing (Penguin Ventures)* Susan Bolsover, *Art Director* Anna Billson

Part of Penguin Random House UK (see below). Children's paperback and hardback books: wide range of picture books, board books, gift books and novelties; fiction; non-fiction, popular culture, digital and audio. Preschool illustrated developmental books for 0–6 years; licensed brands; children's classic publishing and merchandising properties. No unsolicited MSS or original artwork or text. Imprints: Ladybird, Puffin, Penguin, Bantam Press, Bodley Head Children's Books, Jonathan Cape Children's Books, Corgi Children's Books, Doubleday Children's Books, Hutchinson Children's Books, Red Fox Children's Books.

Penguin Random House UK*

20 Vauxhall Bridge Road, London SW1V 2SA
tel 020-7840 8400
website www.penguinrandomhouse.co.uk
Directors Markus Dohle (Ceo Penguin Random House), Tom Weldon (Ceo Penguin Random House UK), Mark Gardiner (UK Group Finance Director), Robert Waddington (UK Group Sales Director)

Penguin Random House UK publishing divisions: Penguin General (page 197), Cornerstone (page 164), Ebury Press (page 168), Michael Joseph (page 183), Penguin Random House Children's UK (page 197), Transworld (page 211) and Vintage (page 213).

Percy Publishing

9 Warners Close, Woodford, Essex IG8 0TF
tel 020-8504 2570
email enquiries@percy-publishing.com
website www.percy-publishing.com
Twitter @percypublishing
Director Clifford Marker; *Editors* Mike Harrington, Clare Lewis, Harriot Hendington

Publisher of fiction of any genre. Publishes writers who do not normally come from a formerly trained writing background. Wiiner of Peoples Book Prize: Best Publisher 2016. Founded 2012.

Pergamon – see Elsevier (Clinical Solutions)

Persephone Books

59 Lamb's Conduit Street, London WC1N 3NB
tel 020-7242 9292
email info@persephonebooks.co.uk
website www.persephonebooks.co.uk
Managing Director Nicola Beauman

Reprints of forgotten classics by 20th-century women writers with prefaces by contemporary writers. Founded 1999.

Phaidon Press Ltd

Regent's Wharf, All Saints Street, London N1 9PA
tel 020-7843 1000
email enquiries@phaidon.com
website www.phaidon.com
Managing Director James Booth-Clibborn, *Publishers* Emilia Terragni, Deborah Aaronson

Visual arts, lifestyle, culture and food.

Philip's – see Octopus Publishing Group

Phoenix Yard Books

18 Dean House Studios, 27 Greenwood Place, Kentish Town, London NW5 1LB
tel 020-7239 4968
email hello@phoenixyardbooks.com
website www.phoenixyardbooks.com
Facebook www.facebook.com/PhoenixYardBooks
Twitter @phoenixyardbks

Picturebooks, fiction and children's colouring books. No longer accepts unsolicited MSS.

Piatkus – see Little, Brown Book Group

Piccadilly Press

5 Castle Road, London NW1 8PR
tel 020-7267 4492
email books@piccadillypress.co.uk
website www.piccadillypress.co.uk

Early picture books, parental advice, trade paperbacks, trade paperback children's fiction, young adult non-fiction and young adult fiction. Founded 1983.

Pimlico – see Vintage

Pimpernel Press Ltd

22 Marylands Road, London W9 2DY
tel 020-7289 7100
email jo@pimpernelpress.com
website www.pimpernelpress.com
Facebook www.facebook.com/Pimpernel-Press-Ltd-456736654504879
Twitter @PimpernelPress
Publisher Jo Christian, *Commissioning Editor* Anna Sanderson, *Publicity* Emma O'Bryen

Independent publisher of books on art, design, houses and gardens, and also paper books, in association with Sir John Soane's Museum, the British Library, the Victoria & Albert Museum, the Natural History Museum and Glasgow Museums. Founded 2015.

The Playwrights Publishing Company

70 Nottingham Road, Burton Joyce, Notts. NG14 5AL

Books

email playwrightspublishingco@yahoo.com
website www.playwrightspublishing.com
Proprietors Liz Breeze, Tony Breeze

One-act and full-length drama published on the internet. Serious work and comedies, for mixed cast, all women or schools. Reading fee unless professionally produced or unwaged; sae required or email enquiry needed. Founded 1990.

Plexus Publishing Ltd

The Studio, Hillgate Place, 18–20 Balham Hill, London SW12 9ER
tel 020-8673 9230
email plexus@plexusuk.demon.co.uk
website www.plexusbooks.com
Editorial Director Sandra Wake

Film, music, biography, popular culture, fashion, gift. Imprint: Eel Pie. Founded 1973.

Pluto Press

345 Archway Road, London N6 5AA
tel 020-8348 2724
email pluto@plutobooks.com
website www.plutobooks.com
Editorial Director David Castle, *Commissioning Editor* David Shulman

Politics, anthropology, development, media, cultural, economics, history, Irish studies, Black studies, Islamic studies, Middle East, international relations.

Policy Press – see Bristol University Press/ Policy Press

Policy Studies Institute (PSI)

35 Marylebone Road, London NW1 5LS
tel 020-7911 7500
email psi-admin@psi.org.uk
website www.psi.org.uk
Twitter @PSI_London

Economic, cultural, social and environmental policy, political institutions, social sciences.

Politico's Publishing – see Methuen & Co Ltd

Polity Press

65 Bridge Street, Cambridge CB2 1UR
tel (01223) 324315
website www.politybooks.com

Social and political theory, politics, sociology, history, media and cultural studies, philosophy, literary theory, feminism, human geography, anthropology. Founded 1983.

Polygon – see Birlinn Ltd

Pont Books – see Gomer Press

Poolbeg Press Ltd

123 Grange Hill, Baldoyle, Dublin D13 N529, Republic of Ireland
tel +353 (0)18 063825
email info@poolbeg.com
website www.poolbeg.com
Directors Kieran Devlin, Barbara Delvin

Popular fiction, non-fiction, current affairs. Imprint: Poolbeg. Founded 1976.

Portfolio – see Penguin General

Portico – see Pavilion Books

Portland Press Ltd*

Charles Darwin House, 12 Roger Street, London WC1N 2JL
tel 020-7685 2410
email editorial@portlandpress.com
website www.portlandpresspublishing.com
Twitter @PPPublishing
Director of Publishing Niamh O'Connor

Owned by the Biochemical Society, the company is embedded in the global scientific community and dedicated to promoting and sharing research for the advancement of science. Founded 1990.

Portobello Books

12 Addison Avenue, London W11 4QR
tel 020-7605 1380
email mail@portobellobooks.com
website www.portobellobooks.com
Publishing Director Laura Barber, *Editorial Directors* Bella Lacey, Max Porter, *Commissioning Editor* Anne Meadows, *Junior Editor* Ka Bradley

Current affairs, polemic, cultural criticism, history, memoir, travel, fiction in translation. No submissions except via a reputable literary agent. An imprint of Granta Publications. Founded 2005.

Preface Publishing – see Cornerstone

Prestel Publishing Ltd

14–17 Wells Street, London W1T 3PD
tel 020-7323 5004
email editorial@prestel-uk.co.uk
website www.prestel.com
Facebook www.facebook.com/PrestelPublishing
Twitter @Prestel_UK
Managing Director Andrew Hansen

Including pop culture, major exhibition catalogues and artist retrospectives. Publishes in the following genres: art, architecture, photography, fashion, lifestyle, design and children's books. Book submissions: submissions@prestel-uk.co.uk. Press enquiries: publicity@prestel-uk.co.uk. Founded 1924.

Princeton University Press – Europe*

6 Oxford Street, Woodstock, Oxon OX20 1TR
tel (01993) 814500
email claire_williams@press.princeton.edu
website www.press.princeton.edu

Facebook www.facebook.com/PrincetonUniversityPress
Twitter @PrincetonUPress
Publisher for Social Sciences Sarah Caro, *Editor for Humanities* Ben Tate, *Publisher for Sciences* Ingrid Gnerlich

Academic publishing for the social sciences, humanities and sciences. The European office of Princeton University Press. Founded 1999.

Profile Books Ltd

3 Holford Yard, Bevin Way, London WC1X 9HD
tel 020-7841 6300
email info@profilebooks.com
website www.profilebooks.com
Managing Director Andrew Franklin, *Publisher* Mike Jones, *Editorial Deputy* Hannah Westland

General non-fiction: history, biography, current affairs, popular science, politics, business, management, humour. Also publishers of *The Economist* books. No unsolicited MSS. Founded 1996.

Clerkenwell Press

email info@clerkenwellpress.co.uk
Publisher Geoffrey Mulligan

Literary fiction in English and translation. No unsolicited MSS. Founded 2011.

Serpent's Tail

email info@serpentstail.com
website www.serpentstail.com
Publisher Hannah Westland

Fiction and non-fiction; literary and non-mainstream work and work in translation. No unsolicited MSS. Founded 1986.

Tindal Street Press

email info@profilebooks.com

Literary fiction in English. No unsolicited MSS. Founded 1998.

Psychology Press

27 Church Road, Hove, East Sussex BN3 2FA
tel 020-7017 6000
website www.routledge.com/psychology

Psychology textbooks and monographs. Imprint of Taylor and Francis Group (page 209), an informa business.

Psychology Press

website www.routledge.com/psychology

Routledge

website www.routledgementalhealth.com

Puffin – see Penguin Random House Children's UK

Pure Indigo Ltd

Publishing Department, 17 The Herons, Cottenham, Cambridge CB24 8XX
tel 07981 395258
email ashley.martin@pureindigo.co.uk
website www.pureindigo.co.uk/publishing
Commissioning Editor Ashley Martin

Adult books: submissions currently open for romance novels only. Children's books: Pure Indigo Publishing develops innovative junior series fiction. All titles are available in both print and digital formats and are distributed internationally with select partners. The company also develops software products that complement the product range. The junior series fiction titles are developed in-house and on occasion authors and illustrators are commissioned to complete project-based work. For consideration for commissions visit the website. Not currently accepting submissions.

Pushkin Press

Unit 43 Pall Mall Deposit, 124–128 Barlby Road, London W10 6BL
tel 020-3735 9078
email books@pushkinpress.com
website www.pushkinpress.com
Facebook www.facebook.com/PushkinPress
Twitter @pushkinpress
Publisher Adam Freudenheim

Having first rediscovered European classics of the 20th century, Pushkin now publishes novels, essays, memoirs, children's books (Pushkin's Children's) and everything from timeless classics to the urgent and contemporary. Imprints: Pushkin Press, Pushkin Children's Books, Pushkin Vertigo, ONE. Founded 1997.

Quadrille Publishing

5th and 6th Floors, Pentagon House, 52–54 Southwark Street, London SE1 1UN
tel 020-7601 7500
email enquiries@quadrille.co.uk
website www.quadrille.com
Directors Sarah Lavelle (editorial), Vincent Smith (production)

Imprint of Hardie Grant. Non-fiction lifestyle; cookery, food and drink, gift and humour, craft, health and beauty, gardening, interiors, mind, body & spirit. Founded 1994.

Quantum – see W. Foulsham & Co. Ltd

Quartet Books (The Women's Press)

27 Goodge Street, London W1T 2LD
tel 020-7636 3992
email info@quartetbooks.co.uk
website www.quartetbooks.co.uk

Independent publisher with a tradition of pursuing an alternative to mainstream. Books by women in the areas of literary and crime fiction, biography and autobiography, health, culture, politics, handbooks, literary criticism, psychology and self-help, the arts.

Accepting submissions; see website for guidelines. Founded 1978.

The Quarto Group, Inc.

The Old Brewery, 6 Blundell Street, London N7 9BH
tel 020-7700 9000, 020-7700 8066
email dan.rosenberg@quarto.com
website www.quarto.com
Chairman Timothy Chadwick, *Ceo* Marcus Leaver, *Chief Financial Officer* Mick Mousley, *Director, Quarto International Co-editions Group* David Breuer, *President & Ceo, Quarto Publishing Group USA* Ken Fund, *Managing Director, Quarto Publishing Group UK* David Inman

A global illustrated book publisher and distribution group. It is composed of three publishing divisions: Quarto International Co-editions Group; Quarto Publishing Group USA; and Quarto Publishing Group UK (below); plus Books & Gifts Direct (a direct seller of books and gifts in Australia and New Zealand) and Regent Publishing Services, a specialist print services company based in Hong Kong. Quarto International Co-editions Group creates illustrated books that are licensed and printed for third-party publishers for publication under their own imprints in over 30 languages around the world. The division includes: Quarto Publishing, Quarto Children's Books, words & pictures, Qu:id, Quintessence, Quintet Publishing, QED, RotoVision, Marshall Editions, Marshall Editions Children's Books, Harvard Common Press, Small World Creations, Fine Wine Editions, Apple Press, Global Book Publishing, Iqon Editions Ltd, Ivy Press and Quantum Publishing. Book categories: practical art and crafts, graphic arts, lifestyle, reference, food and drink, gardening, popular culture.

Quarto Group Publishing UK

74–77 White Lion Street, London N1 9PF
tel 020-7284 9300
website www.QuartoKnows.com

General adult non-fiction, illustrated and non-illustrated: history, sport, entertainment, biography, autobiography, military, gardening, architecture, environment, interiors, photography, art, walking and climbing, design and landscape, gift, interiors, food and drink, lifestyle and craft.

QUE Publishing – see Pearson UK

Quercus Publishing Plc

Carmelite House, 50 Victoria Embankment, London EC4Y 0DZ
website www.quercusbooks.co.uk
Managing Director Jon Butler

Fiction and non-fiction. Imprints include Quercus, Riverrun, Maclehose Press and Jo Fletcher Books. Founded 2005.

Quiller Publishing Ltd

Wykey House, Wykey, Shrewsbury SY4 1JA
tel (01939) 261616
email info@quillerbooks.com
website www.quillerpublishing.com
Managing Director Andrew Johnston

Quiller

High-quality hardback and paperback biographies, history, food and drink, art and photography, humour and gift books and specialist practical books on country pursuits including dog training, fishing, shooting, stalking, gamekeeping, deer, falconry, natural history and gardening.

Kenilworth Press

Equestrian (riding, training, dressage, eventing, show jumping, driving, polo). Publisher of BHS official publications and exclusive distributor for *The Pony Club*.

Quintet Publishing

Floor 4 Ovest House, 58 West Street, Brighton, East Sussex BN1 2RA
tel (01273) 727268
email mark.searle@quarto.com
website www.quartoknows.com/quintet-publishing

Illustrated books on creative tech, lifestyle, culture, craft and adult activity. Part of The Quarto Group, Inc. (page 201).

Ransom Publishing Ltd

Unit 7, Brocklands Farm, West Meon GU32 1JN
tel (01730) 829091
email ransom@ransom.co.uk
website www.ransom.co.uk
Directors Jenny Ertle (managing), Steve Rickard (creative)

Teen fiction, reading programmes and books for children and adults who are reluctant and struggling readers. Range covers high interest age/low reading age titles, quick reads, reading schemes and titles for young able readers. Series include *Reading Stars, The Outer Reaches, Shades 2.0, Boffin Boy, PIG* and *Dark Man*. Email for submission guidelines. Founded 1995.

Raven Books

Publishes fiction for children and young adults 8–18 years. Actively looking for strong new fiction, either from published authors or new authors.

Reaktion Books

Unit 32 Waterside, 44–48 Wharf Road, London N1 7UX
tel 020-7253 4965
email info@reaktionbooks.co.uk
website www.reaktionbooks.co.uk
Facebook www.facebook.com/ReaktionBooks/
Twitter @reaktionbooks

Publisher Michael R. Leaman

An independent publisher of stimulating and beautifully designed non-fiction books. Reaktion publishes around 100 new titles each year in many fields including art, architecture, design and photography, popular science, food, history, nature, film, music, philosophy, economics and politics. Founded 1985.

Red Rattle Books

23 Thornfield Road, Thornton, Liverpool L23 9XY
tel 07505 700515
email editor@redrattlebooks.co.uk
website www.redrattlebooks.co.uk
Editor Howard Jackson, *Manager* Angela Keith, *Media* Amy Jackson

An independent, family-run publishing company. Produces and promotes four to six books each year. Specialises in crime and horror. Accepts submissions from young writers and unpublished authors. Full MS or samples can be submitted at editor@redrattlebooks.co.uk. Titles accepted for publication are published in paperback and Kindle editions. Fees for MS are negotiated with authors or their agents. If MS not accepted, explanation given as to why not suitable and future advice offered. Founded 2012.

Repeater Books

email enquiries@watkinsmedia.org
website https://repeaterbooks.com/
Facebook www.facebook.com/repeaterbooks/
Twitter @RepeaterBooks
Publisher Tariq Goddard

Publishes books expressing new and radical ideas: counter-culture fiction and non-fiction, politics and current affairs. Part of Watkins Media (page 214). Founded 2014.

Revenge Ink

6D Lowick Close, Hazel Grove, Stockport SK7 5ED
email amita@revengeink.com
website www.revengeink.com
Editor Gopal Mukerjee (with Amita Mukerjee)
Director Amita Mukerjee

Founded by siblings Gopal and Amita Mukerjee, the company publishes adult fiction (all kinds) and prefers unsolicited, first-time novelists or established writers seeking a new outlet for edgier material. Considers poetry if presented in an original, creative manner. Currently publishes approx. seven titles a year. Does not publish children's fiction or non-fiction titles such as cookbooks, gardens and how-to books. The company is aiming to create a non-fiction imprint for new research in philosophy, history, critical theory and political analysis. Submission guidelines can be found on the website. By email, preferably, send short sample and query first. Founded 2007.

Rider – see Ebury Publishing

Rising Stars

PO Box 105, Rochester, Kent ME2 4BE
tel 0800 091 1602
email info@risingstars-uk.com
website www.risingstars-uk.com
Managing Director Andrea Carr

Educational publisher of books and software for primary school age children. Titles are linked to the National Curriculum Key Stages, QCA Schemes of Work, National Numeracy Framework or National Literacy Strategy. Approach by email with ideas for publishing. Acquired by Hodder Education in January 2015.

Rivers Oram Press

144 Hemingford Road, London N1 1DE
tel 020-7607 0823
email ro@riversoram.com
website www.riversoram.com
Directors Elizabeth Rivers Fidlon (managing), Anthony Harris

Non-fiction: social and political science, current affairs, social history, gender studies, sexual politics, cultural studies. Founded 1991.

Pandora Press

Feminist press. General non-fiction: biography, arts, media, health, current affairs, reference and sexual politics.

George Ronald

3 Rosecroft Lane, Oaklands, Welwyn, Herts. AL6 0UB
tel (01438) 716062
email sales@grbooks.com
website www.grbooks.com
Managers E. Leith, M. Hofman

Religion, specialising in the Bahá'í Faith. Founded 1939.

Roundhouse Group

Unit B, 18 Marine Gardens, Brighton BN2 1AH
tel (01273) 603717
email info@roundhousegroup.co.uk
website www.roundhousegroup.co.uk
Publisher Alan T. Goodworth

Non-fiction adult and children's books. No unsolicited MSS. Founded 1991.

Route

PO Box 167, Pontefract, West Yorkshire WF8 4WW
tel (01977) 793442
email info@route-online.com
website www.route-online.com
Twitter @Route_News
Contact Ian Daley, Isabel Galán

Memoir, cultural non-fiction and biography, with a strong interest in music books. Occasional fiction.

Unsolicited MSS discouraged, book proposals in first instance.

Routledge – see Taylor & Francis Group

Rowman & Littlefield International*

Unit A Whitacre Mews, 26–34 Stannary Street, London SE11 4AB
tel 020-3111 1091
email info@rowmaninternational.com
website www.rowmaninternational.com
Facebook www.facebook.com/RowmanLittlefieldInternational
Twitter @rowmaninternat
Chief Executive Oliver Gadsby, *Editorial Director*, Linda Ganster

An independent academic publisher in philosophy, politics and international relations, cultural studies and economics, with a particular focus on the interdisciplinary nature of these subject areas.

Royal Collection Trust

Stable Yard House, St James's Palace, London SW1A 1JR
tel 020-7024 5645
website www.royalcollection.org.uk
Commercial Publisher Jacky Colliss Harvey, *Academic Publisher* Kate Owen, *Content Manager* Elizabeth Silverton, *Content Editor* Rosie Bick, *Academic Publishing Assistant* Polly Atkinson, *Publishing Assistant* Tom Love

The publishing programme at Royal Collection Trust is centred on creating books, exhibition catalogues, guides and children's books to celebrate the royal residences and works of art found within them. Also produces scholarly catalogues raisonnés, which demonstrate the highest standards of academic research. Worldwide distribution is offered by University of Chicago Press in the USA and Canada, and by Thames & Hudson Ltd throughout the rest of the world. Founded 1993.

Royal National Institute of Blind People (RNIB)*

Midgate House, Midgate, Peterborough, Cambs. PE1 1TN
tel 0303 123 9999
email helpline@rnib.org.uk
website www.rnib.org.uk

Magazines, catalogues and books for blind and partially sighted people, to support daily living, leisure, learning and employment reading needs. Includes the charity's flagship Talking Books service, providing more than 25,000 fiction and non-fiction titles to borrow free of charge for adults and children with sight loss, and commercial audio production services. Produced in braille, audio, large/legible print and email. Founded 1868.

Ruby Tuesday Books Ltd

6 Newlands Road, Tunbridge Wells, Kent TN4 9AT
tel (01892) 557767
email shan@rubytuesdaybooks.com
website www.rubytuesdaybooks.com
Twitter @RubyTuesdaybk
Publisher & Author Ruth Owen, *All Sales & Rights* Shan White

Publisher of children's books. Founded 2008.

Ryland Peters & Small

20–21 Jockey's Fields, London WC1R 4BW
tel 020-7025 2200
email info@rps.co.uk
website www.rylandpeters.com
Managing Director David Peters

High-quality illustrated books on food and drink, home and garden, babies and children, gift books. Founded 1995.

Cico Books

tel 020-7025 2280
email mail@cicobooks.co.uk
website www.cicobooks.co.uk

Lifestyle and interiors, crafts and mind, body & spirit. Founded 1999.

Saffron Books

PO Box 13666, London SW14 8WF
tel 020-8392 1122
email saffronbooks@eapgroup.com
website www.saffronbooks.com, www.sajidrizvi.net
Twitter @saffronbooks, @Safnetoffers, @sajidrizvi
Founding Publisher & Editor-in-Chief Sajid Rizvi

Art criticism and art history, history, African and Asian architecture, African and Asian art and archaeology, Central Asian studies, Korean linguistics and new fiction series: Absolute Fiction. Founded 1989.

SAGE Publications Ltd*

1 Oliver's Yard, 55 City Road, London EC1Y 1SP
tel 020-7324 8500
email info@sagepub.co.uk
website www.sagepublishing.com
Twitter @SAGE_News

Independent company that disseminates journals, books, and library products for the educational, scholarly and professional markets. Founded 1965.

St. David's Press

PO Box 733, Cardiff CF14 7ZY
tel 029-2021 8187
email post@st-davids-press.wales
website www.st-davids-press.wales
Facebook www.facebook.com/StDavidsPress
Twitter @StDavidsPress

Sport and popular culture including: rugby, football, cricket, boxing, horse racing, walking, music. Also general Welsh and Celtic interest including the 'Tidy Tales from Welsh History' series. Distributed by Welsh Books Council (Wales), NBNi (UK & Europe), ISBS (North America). Founded 2002.

St Pauls Publishing

St Pauls, Westminster Cathedral, Morpeth Terrace, Victoria, London SW1P 1EP
tel 020-828 5582
email editor@stpauls.org.uk
website www.stpauls.org.uk

Theology, ethics, spirituality, biography, education, general books of Roman Catholic and Christian interest. Founded 1948.

Salariya Book Company Ltd

Book House, 25 Marlborough Place, Brighton BN1 1UB
tel (01273) 603306
email salariya@salariya.com
website www.salariya.com
Facebook www.facebook.com/theSalariya
Twitter @theSalariya
Managing Director David Salariya

Children's art, picture books, fiction and non-fiction. Imprints: Book House, Scribblers, Scribo. No unsolicited MSS. Founded 1989.

Salt Publishing

12 Norwich Road, Cromer, Norfolk NR27 0AX
tel (01263) 511011
email sales@saltpublishing.com
website www.saltpublishing.com
Twitter @saltpublishing
Publishing Director Christopher Hamilton-Emery, Jennifer Hamilton-Emery

Award-winning independent publisher of fiction. Home of the annual Best British Short Story anthology. Founded 1999.

SAMS Publishing – see Pearson UK

Sandstone Press Ltd*

Dochcarty Road, Dingwall, Scotland IV15 9UG
tel (01349) 865484
email info@sandstonepress.com
website www.sandstonepress.com
Facebook www.facebook.com/SandstonePress
Twitter @sandstonepress
Directors Robert Davidson, Moira Forsyth, Iain Gordon

Publishers of quality fiction and non-fiction for adults. Literary fiction, women's fiction, speculative fiction, crime novels and thrillers. Literary biography, memoir, outdoor and Scottish interest. We are also interested in history, music and popular science. Full submission guidelines are available at http://sandstonepress.com/contact/submissions. Founded 2002.

Saqi Books

26 Westbourne Grove, London W2 5RH
tel 020-7221 9347
email lynn@saqibooks.com
website www.saqibooks.com
Facebook www.facebook.com/SaqiBooks
Twitter @SaqiBooks
Publisher Lynn Gaspard, *Editor & Marketing Manager* Elizabeth Briggs, *Editorial & Marketing Assistant* Hassan Ali

An award-winning independent publishing house of quality trade and academic books on North Africa and the Middle East. Links with cutting edge and authoritative voices have led to a rigorous reassessment of Arab cultural heritage. Over the years the company expanded its list to include writers from all over the world and established two imprints: Telegram, releasing the best in international translation and home-grown literary fiction, and The Westbourne Press, releasing engaging and thought-provoking non-fiction from around the globe. Founded 1983.

Saunders – see Elsevier (Clinical Solutions)

Sawday's

Merchants House, Wapping Road, Bristol BS1 4RW
tel 0117 204 7810
email specialplaces@sawdays.co.uk
website www.sawdays.co.uk
Facebook www.facebook.com/sawdays
Twitter @sawdays
Founder Alastair Sawday, *Managing Director* Tom Sawday

Independent travel. Founded 1994.

Scala Arts & Heritage Publishers Ltd

10 Lion Yard, Tremadoc Road, London SW4 7NQ
tel 020-7808 1550
email jmckinley@scalapublishers.com
website www.scalapublishers.com
Twitter @ScalaPublishers
Managing Director Jenny McKinley

Publish high-quality books for the arts and heritage sector: guidebooks, collection highlights, exhibition catalogues, illustrated histories, etc. Offers all aspects of the publishing process: design, editing, production, marketing and distribution throughout the world as part of the Scala list.

Sceptre – see Hodder & Stoughton

Schofield & Sims Ltd*

Dogley Mill, Fenay Bridge, Huddersfield HD8 0NQ
tel (01484) 607080
email post@schofieldandsims.co.uk
website www.schofieldandsims.co.uk

Educational: nursery, infants, primary; posters. Founded 1901.

Scholastic Ltd*

Euston House, 24 Eversholt Street,
London NW1 1DB
tel 020-7756 7756
website www.scholastic.co.uk
Chairman M.R. Robinson, *Co-Group Managing Directors* Catherine Bell, Steve Thompson

Children's fiction, non-fiction and picture books, education resources for primary schools. Owned by Scholastic Inc. Founded 1964.

Chicken House

See page 162.

Scholastic Book Fairs

See page 248.

Scholastic Children's Books

tel 020-7756 7761
email submissions@scholastic.co.uk
website www.scholastic.co.uk
Twitter @scholasticuk
UK Publisher Miriam Farbey, *Editorial Director (non-fiction)* Elizabeth Scoggins, *Publisher (fiction & picture books)* Samantha Smith, *Editorial Director (picture, novelty, gift books)* Pauliina Malinen-Teodoro, Antonia Pelari

Activity books, novelty books, picture books, fiction for 5–12 years, teenage fiction, series fiction and film/TV tie-ins. Imprints: Scholastic, Alison Green Books, Marion Lloyd Books, Klutz. No unsolicited MSS. Unsolicited illustrations are accepted, but do not send any original artwork as it will not be returned.

Scholastic Educational Resources

Book End, Range Road, Witney, Oxon OX29 0YD
tel (01993) 893456
Publishing Director Robin Hunt

Professional books, classroom materials and online resources for primary teachers.

Science Museum Group

Exhibition Road, London SW7 2DD
tel 0870 870 4771
website www.sciencemuseum.org.uk

Science, technology, engineering and mathematics. Museum guides.

SCM Press – see Hymns Ancient and Modern Ltd

Scripture Union

207–209 Queensway, Bletchley, Milton Keynes, Bucks. MK2 2EB
tel (01908) 856000
email info@scriptureunion.org.uk
website www.scriptureunion.org.uk
Director of Ministry Development (Publishing) Terry Clutterham

Christian books and bible reading materials for people of all ages; educational and worship resources for churches; children's fiction and non-fiction; adult non-fiction. Founded 1867.

Search Press Ltd

Wellwood, North Farm Road, Tunbridge Wells, Kent TN2 3DR
tel (01892) 510850
email searchpress@searchpress.com
website www.searchpress.com
Directors Martin de la Bédoyère (managing), Caroline de la Bédoyère (rights), David Grant (sales & marketing), Katie French (editorial)

Arts, crafts, leisure. Founded 1970.

SelfMadeHero

139 Pancras Road, London NW1 1UN
tel 020-7383 5157
email info@selfmadehero.com
website www.selfmadehero.com
Facebook www.facebook.com/SelfMadeHero
Twitter @selfmadehero
Managing Director & Publisher Emma Hayley, *Sales & Marketing Director* Sam Humphrey, *Press Officer* Paul Smith, *Foreign Rights, Editorial & Production Manager* Guillaume Rater

The UK's leading independent publisher of graphic novels and visual narratives. The list of award-winning fiction and non-fiction graphic novels spans literary fiction, biography, classic adaptation, sci-fi, horror, crime and humour. Founded 2007.

September Publishing

161 Algernon Road, London SE13 7AP
tel 020-3637 0116
email info@septemberpublishing.org
website www.septemberpublishing.org
Facebook www.facebook.com/SeptemberPublishing
Twitter @septemberbook
Publisher Hannah MacDonald

Non-fiction publishers of illustrated and narrative adult books, including memoir and biography, travel, humour, art, politics. Founded 2013.

Seren

57 Nolton Street, Bridgend CF31 3AE
tel (01656) 663018
email seren@serenbooks.com
website www.serenbooks.com
Publisher Mick Felton

Poetry, fiction, literary criticism, biography, art – mostly with relevance to Wales. Founded 1981.

Severn House Publishers

Salatin House, 19 Cedar Road, Sutton, Surrey SM2 5DA
tel 020-8770 3930
email sales@severnhouse.com
website www.severnhouse.com
Facebook www.facebook.com/severnhouse

Twitter @severnhouse
Chairman Edwin Buckhalter, *Publisher* Kate Lyall Grant

Hardback, paperback, ebook and large print adult fiction for the library market: mysteries, thrillers, detective, horror, romance. No unsolicited MSS; submissions via literary agents. Imprints: Crème de la Crime. Founded 1974.

Shearsman Books

50 Westons Hill Drive, Emersons Green, Bristol BS16 7DF
tel 0117 957 2957
email editor@shearsman.com
website www.shearsman.com
Facebook www.facebook.com/Shearsman-Books/
Contact Tony Frazer

Contemporary poetry in English and in translation.

Sheldon Press – see Society for Promoting Christian Knowledge

Sheldrake Press

188 Cavendish Road, London SW12 0DA
tel 020-8675 1767
email enquiries@sheldrakepress.co.uk
website www.sheldrakepress.co.uk
Twitter @SheldrakePress
Publisher J.S. Rigge

History and art, travel, architecture, cookery, music; humour; stationery. Founded 1979.

Shepheard-Walwyn (Publishers) Ltd

107 Parkway House, Sheen Lane, London SW14 8LS
tel 020-8241 5927
email books@shepheard-walwyn.co.uk
website www.shepheard-walwyn.co.uk, www.ethicaleconomics.org.uk
Directors A.R.A. Werner, A.L.R. Werner, *Marketing Manager* Catherine Hodgkinson

Independent publishing company. History, biography, political economy, perennial philosophy; illustrated gift books; Scottish interest. Founded 1971.

Shire Publications

Kemp House, Chawley Park, Cumnor Hill, Oxford OX2 9PH
tel (01865) 811332
email shire.editor@ospreypublishing.com
website www.bloomsbury.com/uk/non-fiction/history/heritage
website www.bloomsbury.com/bloomsburybespoke/

Non-fiction publisher of history, heritage and nostalgia. Also provides publishing services to organisations such as museums, schools, universities and charities. Acquired by Bloomsbury Publishing Plc in 2014.

Short Books Ltd

Unit 316, ScreenWorks, 22 Highbury Grove, London N5 2ER
tel 020-7833 9429
email info@shortbooks.co.uk
website www.shortbooks.co.uk
Facebook www.facebook.com/Short-Books/
Twitter @shortbooksuk
Editorial Directors Rebecca Nicolson, Aurea Carpenter

Non-fiction. No unsolicited MSS. Founded 2000.

Sidgwick & Jackson – see Pan Macmillan

Sigma Press

Stobart House, Pontyclerc, Penybanc Road, Ammanford, Carmarthenshire SA18 3HP
tel (01269) 593100
email info@sigmapress.co.uk
website www.sigmapress.co.uk
Directors Nigel Evans, Jane Evans

Leisure: country walking, cycling, regional heritage, ecology, folklore; biographies. Founded 1979.

Silvertail Books

email editor@silvertailbooks.com
website www.silvertailbooks.com
Twitter @silvertailbooks
Publisher Humfrey Hunter

New independent publisher which specialises in commercial fiction and non-fiction. They especially like publishing newsworthy non-fiction and fiction which tells captivating stories well, no matter when or where they're set, or whether it is the author's 1st or 51st novel. Pays high royalties on both ebook and print editions. No children's books. Founded 2012.

Simon & Schuster UK Ltd*

222 Gray's Inn Road, London WC1X 8HB
tel 020-7316 1900
email enquiries@simonandschuster.co.uk
website www.simonandschuster.co.uk
Facebook www.facebook.com/simonschusterUK
Twitter @simonschusteruk
Directors Ian Chapman (Ceo), Suzanne Baboneau (managing, adult), Jo Dickinson (publishing, fiction & audio), Iain MacGregor (publishing, non-fiction), Alexandra Maramenides (managing, children's), Jane Griffiths (children's fiction), Helen Mackenzie Smith (children's picture books), Jane Griffiths (children's fiction)

Adult non-fiction (history, biography, current affairs, science, self-help, political, popular culture, sports books, memoirs and illustrated titles). Adult fiction (mass-market, literary fiction, historical fiction, commercial women's fiction, general fiction). Children's and young adult fiction, picture books, novelty, pop-up and licensed character. Simon & Schuster Audioworks Fiction, non-fiction and business. Founded 1986.

Singing Dragon

73 Collier Street, London N1 9BE
tel 020-7833 2307
email hello@singingdragon.com
website www.singingdragon.com
Facebook www.facebook.com/SingingDragon
Twitter @Singing_Dragon_
Director Nick Davies

An imprint of Jessica Kingsley Publishers (page 184). Authoritative books on complementary and alternative health, Tai Chi, Qigong and ancient wisdom traditions for health, wellbeing and professional and personal development. Includes comics and graphic novels on topics such as pain management and mental health. Founded 2008.

Siri Scientific Press

Arrow Mill, Queensway, Castleton, Rochdale OL11 2YW
tel 07770 796913
email books@siriscientificpress.co.uk
website www.siriscientificpress.co.uk
Facebook www.facebook.com/Siri-Scientific-Press/
Publishing Consultant David Penney

Publisher of specialist natural history books including academic monographs, compiled edited volumes, photographic atlases, field guides and more general works. Specialise in works on entomology, arachnology and palaeontology, but will also consider other topics. Happy to hear directly from potential new authors. Founded 2008.

Smith Gryphon Ltd – see John Blake Publishing Ltd

Colin Smythe Ltd*

38 Mill Lane, Gerrards Cross, Bucks. SL9 8BA
tel (01753) 886000
email info@colinsmythe.co.uk
website www.colinsmythe.co.uk
Directors Colin Smythe (managing & editorial), Leslie Hayward, Ann Saddlemyer

Irish biography, phaleristics, heraldry, Irish literature and literary criticism, Irish history. Other imprints: Dolmen Press, Van Duren Publishers. Founded 1966.

Snowbooks Ltd

112 High Street, Thame, Oxon OX9 3DZ
info@snowbooks.com
website www.snowbooks.com
Directors Emma Barnes (managing), Rob Jones

Genre fiction: steampunk, fantasy, sci-fi and horror. General non-fiction. See website for submission guidelines. No postal submissions or calls please. Founded 2004.

Society for Promoting Christian Knowledge

36 Causton Street, London SW1P 4ST
tel 020-7592 3900
email spck@spck.org.uk
website www.spckpublishing.co.uk
Director of Publishing Sam Richardson

Founded 1698.

IVP

Theology and academic, commentaries, biblical studies, contemporary culture.

Marylebone House

Commercial and literary fiction.

Sheldon Press

Popular medicine, health, self-help, psychology.

SPCK

Theology, bibles, history, contemporary culture, children's picture books and fiction, biography, liturgy, prayer, spirituality, biblical studies, educational resources, social and ethical issues, mission, gospel and culture.

Society of Genealogists Enterprises Ltd

14 Charterhouse Buildings, Goswell Road, London EC1M 7BA
tel 020-7251 8799
email sales@sog.org.uk
website www.sog.org.uk
Chief Executive June Perrin

Local and family history books, software and magazines plus extensive library facilities.

Somerville Press Ltd

Dromore, Bantry, Co. Cork P75 NY22, Republic of Ireland
tel +353 (0)28 32873
email somervillepress@eircom.net
website www.somervillepress.com
Directors Andrew Russell, Jane Russell

Irish interest: fiction and non-fiction. Founded 2008.

Southwater – see Anness Publishing

Souvenir Press Ltd

43 Great Russell Street, London WC1B 3PD
tel 020-7580 9307/8
email souvenirpress@souvenirpress.co.uk
website http://souvenirpress.co.uk/
Managing Director Ernest Hecht OBE

Archaeology, biography and memoirs, educational (secondary, technical), general, humour, practical handbooks, psychiatry, psychology, sociology, sports, games and hobbies, travel, supernatural, parapsychology, illustrated books. No unsolicited fiction or children's books; initial enquiry by letter essential for non-fiction. Founded 1951.

SPCK – see Society for Promoting Christian Knowledge

Speechmark Publishing Ltd
2nd Floor, 5 Thomas More Square,
London E1W 1WY
tel 0845 450 6414
email info@speechmark.net
website www.routledge.com/collections/11164

Education, health, social care. A division of Electric Word. Founded 1990.

Sphere – see Little, Brown Book Group

Spon – see Taylor & Francis Group

SportBooks Ltd
9 St Aubyns Place, York YO24 1EQ
tel (01904) 613475
email info@sportsbooks.ltd.uk
website www.sportsbooks.ltd.uk
Directors Randall Northam, Veronica Northam

Sport. Imprints: SportsBooks, BMM. Not currently accepting submissions. Founded 1995.

Springer-Verlag London Ltd*
236 Gray's Inn Road, Floor 6, London WC1X 8HB
tel 020-3192 2000
website www.springer.com/gb
General Manager Beverley Ford

Medicine, computing, engineering, mathematics, chemistry, biosciences. Founded 1972.

Spruce – see Octopus Publishing Group

Stacey Publishing Ltd
14 Great College Street, London SW1P 3RX
tel 020-7221 7166
email info@stacey-international.co.uk
website www.stacey-international.co.uk
Founder Tom Stacey

Topical issues for *Independent Minds* series, encyclopaedic books on regions and countries, Islamic and Arab subjects, world affairs, children's books, art, travel, belles lettres, biography. Imprints: Capuchin Classics, Gorilla Guides. Founded 1974.

Capuchin Classics
email info@capuchin-classics.co.uk
website www.capuchin-classics.co.uk

Enduring literary fiction, mostly 19th and 20th century. Founded 2008.

Stainer & Bell Ltd
PO Box 110, Victoria House, 23 Gruneisen Road, London N3 1DZ
tel 020-8343 3303
email post@stainer.co.uk
website www.stainer.co.uk
Directors Keith Wakefield (joint managing), Carol Wakefield (joint managing & secretary)

Books on music, religious communication. Founded 1907.

Stenlake Publishing Ltd
54–58 Mill Square, Catrine, Ayrshire KA5 6RD
tel (01290) 552233
email sales@stenlake.co.uk
website www.stenlake.co.uk
Managing Director Richard Stenlake

Local history, Scottish language and literature especially Robert Burns, studio pottery, bee keeping, railways, transport, aviation, canals and mining covering Wales, Scotland, England, Northern Ireland, Isle of Man, Republic of Ireland and Zambia. Founded 1987.

Alloway Publishing
website www.allowaypublishing.co.uk

Oakwood Press
Specialising in railway and transport books. Founded 1931.

Stonewood Press
tel 0845 4564 838
email stonewoodpress@gmail.com
website www.stonewoodpress.co.uk
Facebook www.facebook.com/stonewoodpress
Twitter @stonewoodpress
Publisher & Production Editor Martin Parker

Stonewood Press is a small independent publisher dedicated to promoting new writing with an emphasis on contemporary short stories and poetry. Stonewood aims to publish challenging and high-quality writing in English without the pressures associated with mainstream publishing. Please see our website for up-to-date submission guidelines and submission window. Founded 2011.

Stripes – see Little Tiger Group

Summersdale Publishers Ltd
46 West Street, Chichester, West Sussex PO19 1RP
tel (01243) 771107
email submissions@summersdale.com
website www.summersdale.com
Editorial Director Claire Plimmer

Popular non-fiction, humour and gift books, travel writing and health and wellbeing. See website for guidelines. Acquired by Octopus in 2017 (page 192). Founded 1990.

Sunflower Books
PO Box 36160, London SW7 3WS
tel 020-7589 2377
email info@sunflowerbooks.co.uk
website www.sunflowerbooks.co.uk
Director P.A. Underwood

Travel guidebooks.

Sussex Academic Press
PO Box 139, Eastbourne, East Sussex BN24 9BP
tel (01323) 479220

email edit@sussex-academic.com
website www.sussex-academic.com
Editorial Director Anthony Grahame

Founded 1994.

The Alpha Press

International relations, Middle Eastern studies, cultural studies, theatre, philosophy, literary criticism, biography, history with a special emphasis on Spanish history, first nations studies, Latin American studies, theology and religion, Jewish and Israel studies (history, Holocaust, culture, biography), Asian studies, art history.

Sweet & Maxwell

Thomson Reuters, PO Box 123,
Hebden Bridge HX7 9BF
tel 020-7393 7000
website www.sweetandmaxwell.co.uk

Law. Part of Thomson Reuters Ltd. Founded 1799; incorporated 1889.

Sweet Cherry Publishing

Unit 36, Vulcan Business Complex, Vulcan Road,
Leicester LE5 3EF
tel 0116 253 6796
email info@sweetcherrypublishing.com
website www.sweetcherrypublishing.com
Facebook www.facebook.com/sweetcherrypublishing
Twitter @sweetcherrypub
Director A. Thadha

Children's series fiction specialist. Children's picture books, novelty books, gift books, board books, educational books and fiction series for all ages. Also welcomes young adult novels especially trilogies or longer series. Likes to publish a set of books as a box set or in a slipcase. See website for submission guidelines. Founded 2011.

Tango Books Ltd

PO Box 32595, London W4 5YD
tel 020-8996 9970
email sales@tangobooks.co.uk
website www.tangobooks.co.uk
Directors Sheri Safran, David Fielder

Children's fiction and non-fiction novelty books, including pop-up, touch-and-feel and cloth books. No unsolicited MSS.

Tarquin Publications

Suite 74, 17 Holywell Hill, St Albans AL1 1DT
tel (01727) 833866
email info@tarquinbooks.com
website www.tarquinbooks.com
Director Andrew Griffin

Mathematics and mathematical models, puzzles, codes and logic; paper cutting, paper engineering and pop-up books for intelligent children. No unsolicited MSS; send suggestion or synopsis in first instance. Founded 1970.

Taschen UK Ltd

5th Floor, 1 Heathcock Court, 415 Strand,
London WC2R 0NS
tel 020-7845 8585
email contact-uk@taschen.com
website www.taschen.com

Publishers of art, anthropology and aphrodisia. Founded 1980.

Tate Enterprises Ltd

The Lodge, Millbank, London SW1P 4RG
tel 020-7887 8869
email submissions@tate.org.uk
website www.tate.org.uk/publishing
Publishing & Commercial Director John Stachiewicz, *Merchandise Director* Rosey Blackmore, *Sales & Marketing Manager* Maxx Lundie, *Marketing & Publicity Coordinator* Lucy MacDonald

Publishers for Tate in London, Liverpool and St Ives. Exhibition catalogues, art books, children's books and merchandise. Also product development, picture library and licensing.

I.B. Tauris & Co. Ltd*

6 Salem Road, London W2 4BU
tel 020-7243 1225
website www.ibtauris.com
Facebook www.facebook.com/ibtauris
Twitter @ibtauris
Chairman/Publisher Iradj Bagherzade, *Managing Director* Jonathan McDonnell

History, biography, politics, international relations, current affairs, Middle East, religion, cultural and media studies, film, art, archaeology, travel guides. Acquired by Bloomsbury Publishing (page 157) in 2018. Founded 1983.

Tauris Parke Paperbacks

Non-fiction trade paperbacks: biography, history, travel.

Taylor & Francis Group*

2 and 4 Park Square, Milton Park, Abingdon,
Oxon OX14 4RN
tel 020-7017 6000
email enquiries@taylorandfrancis.com
website http://taylorandfrancis.com/, www.informa.com
Ceo Annie Callanan, *Managing Director (Taylor & Francis Books)* Jeremy North

Academic and reference books.

Ashgate Publishing

Art history, music, history, social work, politics and lterary studies.

CRC Press

website www.crcpress.com

Science: physics, mathematics, chemistry, electronics, natural history, pharmacology and drug metabolism, toxicology, technology, history of science, ergonomics, production engineering, remote sensing, geographic information systems, engineering.

Focal Press

Animation, audio, film, gaming, music technology, photography and theatre.

Garland Science

website www.garlandscience.com
Bioscience textbooks and scholarly works.

Gower

Specialist business and management books and resources.

Psychology Press

See page 200.

Routledge

website www.routledge.com
Addiction, anthropology, archaeology, Asian studies, business, classical studies, counselling, criminology, development and environment, dictionaries, economics, education, geography, health, history, Japanese studies, library science, language, linguistics, literary criticism, media and culture, nursing, performance studies, philosophy, politics, psychiatry, psychology, reference, social administration, social studies/sociology, women's studies, law. Directories, international relations, reference, yearbooks. Imprint of Routledge (page 238).

Spon

website www.sponpress.com
Architecture, civil engineering, construction, leisure and recreation management, sports science.

Templar Publishing

Suite 2.08 The Plaza, 535 Kings Road, London SW10 0SZ
tel 020-3770 8888
email social@bonnierpublishing.co.uk
website www.templarco.co.uk
Facebook www.facebook.com/templarpublishing
Twitter @templarbooks

Templar Publishing is a leading UK children's publisher. Templar is part of the Bonnier Group and was acquired by Bonnier Publishing in 2008. Founded 1978.

Thames & Hudson Ltd*

181A High Holborn, London WC1V 7QX
tel 020-7845 5000
email sales@thameshudson.co.uk
website www.thamesandhudson.com
Facebook www.facebook.com/thamesandhudson
Twitter @thamesandhudson
Chairman T. Evans, *Deputy Chairman* S. Reisz-Neurath, *Ceo* R. Grisebach; *Directors* S. Thompson (publishing), L. Dietrich (international editorial), W. Balliet (US publishing)

Illustrated non-fiction for an international audience (adults and children), specialising in art and art history, photography, design, travel, history, archaeology, architecture, fashion and contemporary media.

Think Books

Think Publishing Ltd, 25 Chapel Street, London NW1 5DH
tel 020-3771 7200
website www.thinkpublishing.co.uk
Chairman Ian McAuliffe, *Chief Executive* Tilly McAuliffe

Specialises in books on the outdoors, gardening and wildlife. Publishes with the Wildlife Trusts, the Royal Horticultural Society and the Campaign to Protect Rural England and others. Founded 2005.

Thistle Publishing

36 Great Smith Street, London SW1P 3BU
tel 020-7222 7574
email david@thistlepublishing.co.uk
website www.thistlepublishing.co.uk
Facebook www.facebook.com/ThistlePublishing
Twitter @ThistleBooks
Publishers David Haviland, Andrew Lownie

Winner of the People's Book Prize 2017. Trade publisher of quality fiction and non-fiction. Accepts unsolicited submissions, please send three chapters and a synopsis by email. Authors include Theo Aronson, Chloe Banks, Charles Beauclerk, Guy Bellamy, Nicholas Best, Joyce Cary, Andrew Crofts, Michael Curtin, Martin Dillon, Patrick Dillon, J. D. Dixon, Piu Eatwell, Duncan Falconer, Richard Falkirk, Anhua Gao, Michael Hartland, Kris Hollington, Lawrence James, Harry Keeble, Norma Major, David McGrath, Richard Mullen, Katharine Quarmby, Siân Rees, Rosalind Russell, Desmond Seward, David Stafford, Peter Thorold, and M.J. Trow.

Thomson Reuters – Round Hall*

13 Exchange Place, Dublin 1, Republic of Ireland
tel +353 (0)16 009355
website www.roundhall.ie
Directors (Ireland) S. Flynn, J. Lanigan, M. McCann

Law. Part of Thomson Reuters.

Three Hares Publishing

2 Dukes Avenue, London N10 2PT
tel 020-8245 8989
email submissions@threeharespublishing.com
website www.threeharespublishing.com
Facebook www.facebook.com/threeharespublishing
Twitter @threeharesbooks
Publisher Yasmin Standen

Submissions are open and will consider fiction/non-fiction, novels, children's books, young adult and short stories. No picture books. Publishes a number of established authors and first-time authors. Interested in discovering new talent. Visit website for submission guidelines – email submissions only. Founded 2014.

Time Out – see Ebury Publishing

Tindal Street Press – see Profile Books Ltd

Tiny Owl Publishing Ltd

1 Repton House, Charlwood Street, London SW1V 2LD
email info@tinyowl.co.uk
website www.tinyowl.co.uk
Facebook www.facebook.com/tinyowlpublishing
Twitter @TinyOwl_Books
Co-founder Delaram Ghanimifard

An independent leading publisher of global children's literature. Publishes high-quality picture books for children 3–11 years. Aims to promote diversity and human rights values.

Titan Books

144 Southwark Street, London SE1 0UP
tel 020-7620 0200
website www.titanbooks.com
Divisional Head Laura Price

Publisher of original fiction under the genres science fiction, fantasy, horror, crime and young adult crossover. Licensed fiction and non-fiction covering TV, film and gaming, including licensed works for *Mass Effect, Star Trek, Alien, Planet of the Apes, Assassin's Creed* and *DC Universe.* Graphic novel collections include The Simpsons and Modesty Blaise. No children's proposals. All fiction submissions must come from an agent. Division of Titan Publishing Group Ltd. Founded 1981.

Tolley – see LexisNexis

Top That! Publishing plc

Marine House, Tide Mill Way, Woodbridge, Suffolk IP12 1AP
tel (01394) 386651
email customerservice@topthatpublishing.com
website www.topthatpublishing.com
Facebook www.facebook.com/topthatpublishing
Twitter @TopThatPub
Chairman Barrie Henderson, *Managing Director* David Henderson

Children's activity books, novelty books, picture books, reference, character, gift books, early learning books, apps and digital animations. Imprint: Top That Publishing. Founded 1999.

Transworld Publishers

61–63 Uxbridge Road, London W5 5SA
tel 020-8579 2652
Publisher Bill Scott-Kerr

Part of Penguin Random House UK (page 198). No unsolicited MSS accepted.

Bantam Press

Publishing Director Doug Young

General non-fiction: business, crime, health and diet, history, humour, military, music, paranormal, self-help, science, travel and adventure, biography, autobiography.

Black Swan

Publisher Bill Scott-Kerr

Paperback quality fiction and non-fiction.

Doubleday (UK)

Publishing Director Marianne Velmans

Literary fiction and non-fiction.

Eden and Expert, Doubleday

Publishing Director Susanna Wadeson

General non-fiction and fiction.

Transworld Crime & Thrillers, Commercial Fiction

Fiction Publisher Sarah Adams

Transworld Commercial Fiction

Publishing Director Frankie Gray

Transworld Ireland

Editorial Director Fiona Murphy

Trentham Books

20 Bedford Way, London WC1H 0AL
tel 020-7911 5383 (production), 020-7911-5538 (editorial)
email trenthambooks@ioe.ac.uk
website www.ucl-ioe-press.com

Imprint of the UCL Institute of Education Press. Education (including specialist fields – social justice and inclusion, race and racism, gender studies and intersectionality, equal opportunities, refugee education), language and literacy, early years, social policy and sociology of education. Does not publish books for parents or children, or fiction, biography, textbooks, reminiscences and poetry.

Troika

Troika Books Ltd, Well House, Green Lane, Ardleigh, Colchester, Essex CO7 7PD
tel (01206) 233333
email martin@troikabooks.com
website www.troikabooks.com
Publisher Martin West, *Rights* Petula Chaplin, *Publicity & Marketing* Andrea Reece, *Sales & Marketing* Roy Johnson

Publishes picture books, poetry and fiction for all ages, with an emphasis on quality and accessibility. Though a determinedly small list, it publishes some big name authors including prize-winners Michelle Magorian, Bernard Ashley, Pippa Goodhart together with new authors Savita Kalhan and Miriam

Halahmy. Our poetry list includes Zaro Weil, Brian Moses, John Foster, Hilda Offen and Neal Zetter. Founded 2012.

Troubador Publishing Ltd

9 Priory Business Park, Wistow Road, Kibworth, Leics. LE8 0RX
tel 0116 279 2299
email books@troubador.co.uk
website www.troubador.co.uk
Facebook www.facebook.com/matadorbooks
Twitter @matadorbooks
Directors Jeremy Thompson (managing), Jane Rowland (operations)

Troubador runs several subsidiaries in the author services sector, and is organiser of the annual Self-Publishing Conference. Subsidiaries include the Matador self-publishing imprint; The Book Guild Ltd partnership/mainstream imprint; and Indie-Go services for independent authors. Founded 1996.

TSO (The Stationery Office)

St Crispins, Duke Street, Norwich NR3 1PD
tel (01603) 696876
email customer.services@tso.co.uk
website www.tso.co.uk

Publishing and information management services: business, directories, pharmaceutical, professional, reference, *Learning to Drive*.

Two Rivers Press Ltd

7 Denmark Road, Reading, Berks. RG1 5PA
tel 0118 987 1452
email tworiverspress@gmail.com
website www.tworiverspress.com
Facebook www.facebook.com/tworiverspress
Twitter @TwoRiversPress
Managing Publisher Sally Mortimore, *Sales* Barbara Morris, *Poetry Editor* Peter Robinson, *Local Interest Editor* Adam Sowan, *Design & Illustration* Nadja Guggi, Sally Castle, Martin Andrews, *Marketing & Website* Karen Mosman

Champions Reading and surrounding area's heritage and culture through contemporary and classic poetry, biography, art and local interest books. Launching an international Botanical Art Portfolios series in 2019. Founded 1994.

Ulric Publishing

35 Sandford Ave, Church Stretton, Shrops. SY6 6BH
tel (01694) 781354
email enquiries@ulricpublishing.com
website www.ulricpublishing.com
Directors Ulric Woodhams, Elizabeth Oakes

Non-fiction military and motoring history. Licensing, bespoke bindings and publishing services. No unsolicited MSS. Visitors by appointment. Founded 1992.

Ulverscroft Group Ltd

The Green, Bradgate Road, Anstey, Leicester LE7 7FU
tel 0116 236 4325
email m.merrill@ulverscroft.co.uk
website www.ulverscroft.co.uk
Facebook www.facebook.com/ulverscroft
Twitter @UlverscroftUK

Offers a wide variety of large print titles in hardback and paperback format as well as abridged and unabridged audiobooks on CD, MP3 CD and digital download, many of which are written by the world's favourite authors and includes award-winning titles. Acquired Oakill Publishing and its range of unabridge audiobooks April 2018. Founded 1964.

Unbound

Unit 18, Waterside, 44–48 Wharf Road, London N1 7UX
tel 020-7253 4230
email hello@unbound.co.uk
website https://unbound.com
Facebook www.facebook.com/unbound
Twitter @unbounders

The world's first crowdfunding publisher and winner of the Bookseller Book of the Year Award 2015, Unbound is home to the *Sunday Times* bestselling *Letters of Note* and the Man Booker prize longlisted *The Wake.* Considers submissions from literary agents and direct from writers. Includes an audio and podcasting arm Unbound Audio. Writers should submit projects using the website submission page: unbound.co.uk/authors. Founded 2011.

Unicorn Publishing Group LLP

101 Wardour Street, London W1F 0UG
tel 07836 633377
email ian@unicornpublishing.org
website www.unicornpublishing.org
Directors Lord Strathcarron, Lucy Duckworth, Simon Perks, Ryan Gearing

Leading independent publisher with three distinct imprints: Unicorn, specialising in the visual arts and cultural history; Uniform, specialising in military history; and Universe, specialising in historical fiction. Unicorn Sales & Distribution is UPG's and its client publishers' marketing arm, with worldwide sales and distribution operations. UPG has corporate and marketing offices in London and Chicago and its design studio in Lewes, Sussex. Founded 1985.

Merlin Unwin Books Ltd

Palmers House, 7 Corve Street, Ludlow, Shrops. SY8 1DB
tel (01584) 877456
email books@merlinunwin.co.uk
website www.merlinunwin.co.uk
Chairman Merlin Unwin, *Managing Director* Karen McCall

Countryside books. Founded 1990.

Usborne Publishing Ltd

Usborne House, 83–85 Saffron Hill, London EC1N 8RT
tel 020-7430 2800
email mail@usborne.co.uk
website www.usborne.com
Directors Peter Usborne, Jenny Tyler (editorial), Robert Jones, Andrea Parsons

Children's books: reference, practical, craft, natural history, science, languages, history, geography, preschool, fiction. Founded 1973.

Vallentine Mitchell

Catalyst House, 720 Centennial Court, Centennial Park, Elstree WD6 3SY
tel 020-8736 4596
email info@vmbooks.com (general), editor@vmbooks.com (submissions)
website www.vmbooks.com
Directors Stewart Cass, A.E. Cass, H.J. Cass

International publisher of books of Jewish interest, both for the scholar and general reader. Subjects published include Jewish history, culture and heritage, modern Jewish thought, Holocuast studies, Middle East studies, biography and reference.

Valley Press

Woodend, The Crescent, Scarborough YO11 2PW
tel (01723) 332077
email office@valleypressuk.com
website www.valleypressuk.com
Facebook www.facebook.com/valleypress
Twitter @valleypress
Publisher Jamie McGarry, *Executive Assistant* Laura McGarry, *Assistant Publisher* Jo Haywood, *Submissions Coordinator* Tess Dennison, *Project Manager (Events/Education)* Vanessa Simmons, *Production Editor* Sasha Hawkes

Publishes poetry (collections, pamphlets and anthologies); fiction (novels and short stories); graphic novels; and non-fiction (memoirs, travel writing, journalism, music, art and more). Founded 2008. Open submissions.

Veritas Publications

Veritas House, 7–8 Lower Abbey Street, Dublin D01 W2C2, Republic of Ireland
tel +353 (0)18 788177
email publications@veritas.ie
website www.veritas.ie

Liturgical and Church resources, religious school books for primary and post-primary levels, biographies, academic studies, and general books on religious, moral and social issues.

Vermilion – see Ebury Publishing

Verso Ltd

6 Meard Street, London W1V 0EG
tel 020-7437 3546
email enquiries@verso.co.uk
website www.verso.com
Directors Jacob Stevens (managing), Rowan Wilson (sales & marketing), Robin Blackburn, Tariq Ali

Current affairs, politics, sociology, economics, history, philosophy, cultural studies. Founded 1970.

Viking – see Penguin General

Vintage

20 Vauxhall Bridge Road, London SW1V 2SA
tel 020-7840 8400
website www.penguin.co.uk/vintage
Managing Director Richard Cable, *Deputy Managing Director* Faye Brewster, *Publishing Directorko* Rachel Cugnoni, *Communications Director* Christian Lewis, *Head of Publicity* Bethan Jones, *Head of Marketing* Chloe Healy

Part of Penguin Random House UK (page 198). Quality fiction and non-fiction. No unsolicited MSS.

The Bodley Head

tel 020-7840 8707
Publishing Director Stuart Williams, *Editorial Director* Will Hammond, *Editor* Anna-Sophia Watts
Non-fiction: history, current affairs, politics, science, biography, economics.

Jonathan Cape

tel 020-7840 8608
Publishing Director Michal Shavit, *Associate Publisher* Dan Franklin, *Associate Publisher* Robin Robertson, *Deputy Publishing Director* Bea Hemming, *Senior Editor* Ana Fletcher
Biography and memoirs, current affairs, drama, fiction, history, poetry, travel, politics, graphic novels, photography.

Chatto & Windus/Hogarth

tel 020-7840 8745
Publishing Director Clara Farmer, *Deputy Publishing Director* Becky Hardie, *Editorial Director* Poppy Hampson, *Editor* Charlotte Humphery, *Assistant Editor* Greg Clowes
Belles lettres, biography and memoirs, current affairs, fiction, history, poetry, politics, philosophy, translations, travel. No unsolicited MSS.

Harvill Secker

tel 020-7840 8893
Publishing Director Liz Foley, *Deputy Publishing Director* Kate Harvey, *Editorial Director (crime)* Jade Chandler, *Editor* Ellie Steel, *Assistant Editor* Mikaela Pedlow
English literature, crime fiction and world literature in translation. Non-fiction (history, current affairs, literary essays, music). No unsolicited MSS.

Pimlico

tel 020-7840 8836
Publishing Director Rachel Cugnoni
History, biography, literature. Exclusively in paperback. No unsolicited MSS.

Square Peg
tel 020-7840 8541
Publishing Director Clara Farmer, *Editorial Director* Rowan Yapp, *Editor* Susannah Otter, *Assistant Editor* Harriet Dobson

Eclectic, idiosyncratic and commercial non-fiction including humour, illustrated and gift books, food, nature, memoir, travel, parenting. Unsolicited MSS with sae.

Yellow Jersey Press
tel 020-7840 8407
Editorial Director Tim Broughton, *Editor* Frances Jessop

Sport and leisure activities. No unsolicited MSS.

Virgin Books – see Ebury Publishing

Virtue Books Ltd

Edward House, Tenter Street, Rotherham S60 1LB
tel (01709) 365005
email info@virtue.co.uk
website www.virtue.co.uk
Directors Peter E. Russum, Margaret H. Russum

Books for the professional chef: catering and drink.

The Vital Spark – see Neil Wilson Publishing Ltd

Voyager – see HarperCollins Publishers

University of Wales Press

10 Columbus Walk, Brigantine Place, Cardiff CF10 4UP
tel 029-2049 6899
email enquiries@press.wales.ac.uk
website www.uwp.co.uk
Director Natalie Williams

Academic, educational and professional publisher (Welsh and English). Specialises in the humanities and social sciences across a broad range of subjects: European studies, political philosophy, literature, history, Celtic and Welsh studies. Founded 1922.

Walker Books Ltd*

87 Vauxhall Walk, London SE11 5HJ
tel 020-7793 0909
website www.walker.co.uk
Facebook www.facebook.com/walkerbooks
Twitter @walkerbooksuk
Directors Karen Lotz, Ian Mablin (non-executive), Roger Alexander (non-executive), Angela Van Den Belt, Jane Winterbotham, Alan Lee, Mike McGrath, John Mendelson, Hilary Berkman

Children's: activity books, novelty books, picture books, fiction for 5–8 and 9–12 years, young adult fiction, series fiction, film/TV tie-ins, plays, poetry, digital and audio. Imprints: Walker Books, Walker Studio and Walker Entertainment. Founded 1980.

Ward Lock Educational Co. Ltd

BIC Ling Kee House, 1 Christopher Road, East Grinstead, West Sussex RH19 3BT
tel (01342) 318980
email wle@lingkee.com
website http://wle.lingkee.com/wle/
Director Wai Kwok Allen Au

Primary and secondary pupil materials, Kent Mathematics Project: *KMP BASIC* and *KMP Main* series covering Reception to GCSE, *Reading Workshops*, *Take Part* series and *Take Part* starters, teachers' books, music books, *Target* series for the National Curriculum: *Target Science* and *Target Geography*, religious education. Founded 1952.

Watkins Media

Unit 11, Shepperton House, 89 Shepperton Road, London N1 3DF
tel 020-813 6940
email enquiries@watkinsmedia.org
website www.watkinsmedia.org
Owner Etan Ilfeld, *Watkins Publisher* Jo Lal, *Angry Robot Publisher* Marc Gascoigne, *Repeater Publisher* Tariq Goddard

Media company that incorporates magazine publishing and retail activities as well as book publishing. Imprints: Watkins Publishing (personal development – page 214), Angry Robot (sci-fi and fantasy – page 154), Nourish Books (health and wellbeing, food and drink – page 192), Repeater (counter-culture fiction and non-fiction, including politics and current affairs – page 202) and Watkins Publishing (self-help, personal development, mind, body & spirit – below). Founded 1893.

Watkins Publishing

Unit 11, Shepperton House, 89 Shepperton Road, London N1 3DF
tel 020-3813-6940
email enquiries@watkinspublishing.com
website https://www.watkinspublishing.com/
Facebook www.facebook.com/WatkinsPublishing
Twitter @WatkinsWisdom
Editor Publisher Jo Lal

Publishes personal development and mind, body & spirit books. Works in partnership with outstanding authors and aims to produce authoritative, innovative titles, both illustrated and non-illustrated. Part of Watkins Media (above).

Franklin Watts – see Hachette Children's Group

Wayland – see Hachette Children's Group

Josef Weinberger Plays Ltd

12–14 Mortimer Street, London W1T 3JJ
tel 020-7580 2827

email general.info@jwmail.co.uk
website www.josef-weinberger.com
Chairman John Schofield

Stage plays only, in both acting and trade editions. Preliminary letter essential.

Welsh Academic Press

PO Box 733, Cardiff CF14 7ZY
tel 029-2021 8187
email post@welsh-academic-press.wales
website www.welsh-academic-press.wales
Facebook www.facebook.com/WelshAcademicPress
Twitter @WelshAcadPress

History, political studies, education, Medieval Welsh and Celtic studies, Scandinavian and Baltic studies. Distributed by: Welsh Books Council (Wales), NBNi (UK & Europe), ISBS (North America). Founded 1994.

Whittet Books Ltd

1 St John's Lane, Stansted, Essex CM24 8JU
tel (01279) 815871
email mail@whittetbooks.com
website www.whittetbooks.com
Director George J. Papa, *Publisher* Shirley Greenall

Natural history, wildlife, countryside, poultry, livestock, horses, donkeys. Publishing proposals considered for the above lists. Please send outline, preferably by email. Founded 1976.

Wide Eyed Editions

74–77 White Lion Street, London N1 9PF
tel 020-7284 9300
website https://www.quartoknows.com/Wide-Eyed-Editions

Imprint of the Quarto Group. Wide Eyed Editions creates original non-fiction for children and families and believes that books should encourage curiosity about the world, inspiring readers to set out on their own journey of discovery. Founded 2014.

John Wiley & Sons Ltd

The Atrium, Southern Gate, Chichester, West Sussex PO19 8SQ
tel (01243) 779777
email customer@wiley.co.uk
Alternative address 9600 Garsington Road, Oxford OX4 2DQ
tel (01865) 776868
website www.wiley.com
Ceo Brian A Napack

Wiley's core businesses publish scientific, technical, medical and scholarly journals, encyclopedias, books and online products and services; professional/trade books, subscription products, training materials, and online applications and websites; and educational materials for undergraduate and graduate students and lifelong learners. Global headquarters in Hoboken, New Jersey, with operations in the USA, Europe, Asia, Canada and Australia.

Neil Wilson Publishing Ltd

226 King Street, Castle Douglas DG7 1DS
tel (01556) 504119
email info@nwp.co.uk
website www.nwp.co.uk
Facebook www.facebook.com/Neil-Wilson-Publishing-170187613028330/
Twitter @NWPbooks
Managing Director Neil Wilson

Independent publisher of print and ebooks covering a broad range of mostly Scottish interests. Submissions by email only. Include covering letter, author CV, synopsis and sample chapter. Genres published include whisky, food, the great outdoors, history and culture, true crime and humour. Imprints: 11:9, Angels' Share, In Pinn, NWP and Vital Spark.

Philip Wilson Publishers Ltd

6 Salem Road, London W2 4BU
tel 020-7243 1225
email cmartelli@philip-wilson.co.uk
website www.philip-wilson.co.uk
Managing Director Jonathan McDonnell, *Senior Commissioning Editor* Anne Jackson

Fine and applied art, architecture, photography, collecting, museums. A subsidiary of I. B. Tauris & Co Ltd. Founded 1975.

Windmill Books – see Cornerstone

Wooden Books

Signature, 20 Castlegate, York YO1 9RP
email info@woodenbooks.com
Alternative address Central Books, 99 Wallis Road, London E9 5LN
website www.woodenbooks.com

Magic, mathematics, ancient sciences, esoteric. Quality b&w illustrators may submit samples. Founded 1996.

words & pictures

The Old Brewery, 6 Blundell Street, London N7 9BH
tel 020-7800 8043
website https://www.quartoknows.com/words-pictures
Publisher Zeta Jones

Imprint of Quarto Publishing for young children. The imprint has three main focuses: imagination, innovation and inspiration. Always on the lookout for authors and artists with creative ideas that enhance and broaden the children's publishing list. See the submission guidelines: https://www.quartoknows.com/Corporate/Submission-Guidelines/.

Y Lolfa Cyf

Talybont, Ceredigion SY24 5HE
tel (01970) 832304

email ylolfa@ylolfa.com
website www.ylolfa.com
Director Garmon Gruffudd, *Editor* Lefi Gruffudd

Welsh language and English books of Welsh/Celtic interest, biographies and sport. Founded 1967.

Yale University Press London

47 Bedford Square, London WC1B 3DP
tel 020-7079 4900
website www.yalebooks.co.uk
Managing Director Heather McCallum, *Editorial Director for Art & Architecture* Mark Eastment, *Editorial Director for Trade & Academic* Julian Loose

Art, architecture, history, economics, political science, religion, history of science, biography, current affairs and music. Founded 1961.

Yellow Jersey Press – see Vintage

Zambezi Publishing Ltd

22 Second Avenue, Camels Head, Plymouth PL2 2EQ
tel (01752) 367300
email info@zampub.com
website www.zampub.com
Contact Sasha Fenton, Jan Budkowski

Mind, body & spirit. Founded 1998.

Zed Books Ltd

2.8 The Foundry, 17 Oval Way London SE11 5RR
tel 020-752 5828 (general)
email info@zedbooks.net
website www.zedbooks.net
Facebook www.facebook.com/ZedBooks
Twitter @ZedBooks
Editorial Directors Ken Barlow, Kim Walker, Kika Sroka-Miller, Dominic Fagan

Social sciences on international issues; gender, sexuality studies and queer identities, politics, economics, development, environmental, sociology, cities and architecture, culture and media, current affairs, history, human rights, philospohy, race and indigenous politics; area studies (Africa, Americas, Asia, and the Middle East). Founded 1976.

ZigZag Education

Unit 3, Greenway Business Centre, Doncaster Road, Bristol BS10 5PY
tel 0117 950 3199
email submissions@publishmenow.co.uk
website www.zigzageducation.co.uk, www.publishmenow.co.uk
Development Director John-Lloyd Hagger, *Strategy Director* Mike Stephens

Secondary school teaching resources: English, maths, ICT, geography, history, science, business, politics, P.E., media studies. Founded 1998.

CROWDFUNDED PUBLISHING

Crowdfunding, the raising of small investments from a wide pool of individuals to fund a project, is becoming a popular and viable option for writers wishing to publish their work.

Indiegogo

website www.indiegogo.com

Acts as a 'launchpad' for creative ideas.

Kickstarter

website www.kickstarter.com

Helps artists, musicians, film-makers, designers find resources and support needed for a project.

Publishizer

website https://publishizer.com/

Books only. Authors submit a proposal and launch a pre-orders campaign. Publishers receive proposals based on targets. If a publisher signals interest, an exchange is initiated between author and publisher. Alternatively approach a crowdfunding publisher to help raise finances with you. The publisher will critically assess your work before presenting it for funding opportunities and will publish and distribute the book. Some publishers seek investment from readers across their operation and not for a specific title.

Eyewear Publishing

website http://stores.eyewearpublishing.com/

Invites readers to be come 'micropatrons'. See Eyewear Publishing Ltd (page 171).

Inkshares

website www.inkshares.com

See Inkshares (page 233).

Unbound

website https://unbound.com

See Unbound (page 212).

Book publishers overseas

Listings are given for book publishers in Australia (below), Canada (page 220), New Zealand (page 222), South Africa (page 224) and the USA (page 226).

AUSTRALIA

**Member of the Australian Publishers Association*

Access Press

PO Box 2300, Geraldton, WA 6530
tel +61 (0)408 943299
Managing Editor Jenny Walsh

Australiana, biography, non-fiction. Commissioned works and privately financed books published and distributed. Founded 1974.

ACER Press*

19 Prospect Hill Road, Private Bag 55, Camberwell, VIC 3124
tel +61 (0)3 9277 5555
email proposals@acer.edu.au
website www.acer.edu.au

Publisher of the Australian Council for Educational Research. Produces a range of books and assessments including professional resources for teachers, psychologists and special needs professionals.

Allen & Unwin Pty Ltd*

83 Alexander Street, Crows Nest, NSW 2065
Postal address PO Box 8500, St Leonards, NSW 1590
tel +61 (0)2 8425 0100
email info@allenandunwin.com
website www.allenandunwin.com
Chairman Patrick Gallagher, *Ceo* Robert Gorman, *Publishing Director* Tom Gilliatt

General trade, including fiction and children's books, academic, especially social science and history. Founded 1990.

Bloomsbury Publishing Pty Ltd*

Level 4, 387 George Street, Sydney, NSW 2000
tel +61 (0)2 8820 4900
email au@bloomsbury.com
website www.bloomsbury.com
Facebook www.facebook.com/bloomsburypublishingaustralia
Twitter @BloomsburySyd
Managing Director Kate Cubitt

Supports the worldwide publishing activities of Bloomsbury Publishing: caters for the Australia and New Zealand territories. See Bloomsbury Publishing Plc (page 157).

Bonnier Publishing Australia*

Level 6, 534 Church Street, Richmond, VIC 3121
tel +61 (0)3 9421 3800
email info@bonnierpublishing.com.au
website www.bonnierpublishing.com.au
Facebook www.facebook.com/bonnierpublishingau
Twitter @bonnierpubau
Ceo Tash Besliev, *Directors* Niki Horin (Five Mile), Kay Scarlett (Echo)

Bonnier Publishing Australia is based in Melbourne. The company represents UK sister-company imprints across the ANZ markets, as well as creating local publishing under Five Mile, a 25-year old children's imprint, and Echo, a fresh voice in Australian adult publishing. Bonnier Publishing Australia is a division of international publishing group, Bonnier Publishing.

Cambridge University Press*

477 Williamstown Road, Private Bag 31, Port Melbourne, VIC 3207
tel +61 (0)3 8671 1400
email educationmarketing@cambridge.edu.au
website www.cambridge.edu.au/education
Executive Director Mark O'Neil

Academic, educational, reference, ESL.

Cengage Learning Australia*

Level 7, 80 Dorcas Street, South Melbourne, VIC 3205
tel +61 (0)3 9685 4111
website www.cengage.com.au

Educational books.

Dominie Pty Ltd

Drama (Plays & Musicals), 8 Cross Street, Brookvale, NSW 2100
tel +61 (0)2 9938 8686
email drama@dominie.com.au
website www.dominie.com.au/drama

Australian representatives of publishers of plays and agents for the collection of royalties for Hanbury Plays, The Society of Authors, Nick Hern Books, Pioneer Drama, IT&M and Dominie Musicals.

ELK Publishing

PO Box 2828, Toowoomba, QLD 4350
tel +61 (0)4 2811 7828
email contactus@elk-publishing.com
website www.elk-publishing.com
Facebook www.facebook.com/elkpublishing
Twitter @elkpublish
Founder & Ceo Selina Kucks, *Correspondance Officer* May Briggs

An Australian grown, independent publishing house of children's and educational literature. Established in Korea, the company is now based in Australia. ELK Publishing creates children's and educational books; provides opportunities for unknown artists and illustrators to collaborate with in-house authors; offers internships to university students who are presently engaged in literary scholarship; supports 'Author In School' visits to educational institutions; produces corporate book gifting; provides book review services; and offers opportunities for authors/writers wanting to break into the literary industry. ELK Publishing is looking to provide future opportunities for new writers to join the in-house team. Founded 2009.

Elsevier Australia*

Tower 1, Level 12, 475 Victoria Avenue, Chatswood, NSW 2067
tel +61 (0)2 9422 8500
email customerserviceau@elsevier.com
website www.elsevierhealth.com.au
Managing Director Rob Kolkman

Science, medical and technical books. Imprints: Academic Press, Butterworth-Heinemann, Churchill Livingstone, Endeavour, Excerpta Medica, Focal Press, The Lancet, MacLennan and Petty, MD Consult, Morgan Kauffman, Mosby, Saunders, Science Direct, Syngress. Founded 1972.

Hachette Australia Pty Ltd*

Level 17, 207 Kent Street, Sydney, NSW 2000
tel +61 (0)2 8248 0800
email auspub@hachette.com.au
website www.hachette.com.au
Publishing Director Fiona Hazard, *Head of Editorial & Production* Anne Macpherson, *Head of Non Fiction* Vanessa Radnidge, *Head of Fiction* Rebecca Saunders

General, children's. Accepts MSS via website: www.hachette.com.au/manuscriptsubmissions.

HarperCollins Publishers (Australia) Pty Ltd Group*

Postal address PO Box A565, Sydney South, NSW 1235
tel +61 (0)2 9952 5000
website www.harpercollins.com.au
Children's Publishing Director Cristina Cappelluto, *Head of HarperCollins Fiction* Catherine Milne, *Head of HarperCollins Non-fiction* Helen Littleton

Literary fiction and non-fiction, popular fiction, children's, reference, biography, autobiography, current affairs, sport, lifestyle, health/self-help, humour, true crime, travel, Australiana, history, business, gift, religion.

Lawbook Co.

Level 5, 16 Harris Street, Pyrmont, NSW 2009
tel +61 (0)2 8587 7980
website www.thomsonreuters.com.au
Ceo Tony Kinnear

Law. Part of Thomson Reuters.

LexisNexis Butterworths Australia*

Tower 2, 475–495 Victoria Avenue, Chatswood, NSW 2067
tel +61 (0)2 9422 2174
Postal address Level 9, Locked Bag 2222, Chatswood Delivery Centre, Chatswood, NSW 2067
website www.lexisnexis.com.au

Accounting, business, legal, tax and commercial.

Lonely Planet*

The Maltstore Level 3, 551 Swanston Street, Carlton, VIC 3053
email go@lonelyplanet.co.uk
Postal address Locked Bag 1, Footscray, Victoria 3011
tel +61 (0)3 8379 8000
website www.lonelyplanet.com

A travel media company, Lonely Planet is the largest travel publisher in the world with 500 titles, content published in 13 languages and products in over 150 countries. The company's ecosystem also includes mobile apps, magazines, an ebook portfolio, a website and a dedicated traveller community. Offices in the US, Australia, the UK and Ireland, India and China. Founded 1973.

McGraw-Hill Australia Pty Ltd*

Level 2, 82 Waterloo Rd North Ryde, NSW 2113
Postal address Private Bag 2233, Business Centre, North Ryde, NSW 1670
tel +61 (0)2 9900 1888
email cservice_sydney@mheducation.com
website www.mheducation.com.au

Educational publisher: higher education, primary education and professional (including medical, general and reference). Division of the McGraw-Hill Companies. Founded 1964.

Melbourne University Publishing*

Level 1, 715 Swanston Street, Carlton, VIC 3053
tel +61 (0)3 9035 3333
email mup-contact@unimelb.edu.au
website www.mup.com.au
Ceo & Publisher Louise Adler

Trade, academic, current affairs and politics; non-fiction. Imprints: Miegunyah Press, Melbourne University Press, MUP Academic, *Meanjin* journal. Founded 1922.

Pan Macmillan Australia Pty Ltd*

Level 25, 1 Market Street, Sydney, NSW 2000
tel +61 (0)2 9285 9100
email pan.reception@macmillan.com.au
website www.panmacmillan.com.au
Directors Cate Paterson (publishing), Katie Crawford (sales), Tracey Cheetham (publicity & marketing)

Commercial and literary fiction; children's fiction, non-fiction and character products; non-fiction; sport.

Penguin Random House Australia Pty Ltd*

Sydney office Level 3, 100 Pacific Highway, North Sydney, NSW 2060
tel +61 (0)2 9954 9966
email information@penguinrandomhouse.com.au
Melbourne office 707 Collins Street, Melbourne, VIC 3008
website www.penguinrandomhouse.com.au
Ceo Julie Burland, *Group Publishing Director* Nikki Christer, *Publishing Director, Penguin Young Readers* Laura Harris, *Publicity & Communications Director* Karen Reid

General fiction and non-fiction; children's, illustrated. MS submissions for non-fiction accepted, unbound in hard copy addressed to Submissions Editor. Fiction submissions are only accepted from previously published authors, or authors represented by an agent or accompanied by a report from an accredited assessment service. Imprints: Arrow, Bantam, Ebury, Hamish Hamilton, Knopf, Lantern, Michael Joseph, Penguin, Viking, Vintage and William Heinemann. Subsidiary of Bertelsmann AG.

University of Queensland Press*

PO Box 6042, St Lucia, QLD 4067
tel +61 (0)7 3365 7244
email uqp@uqp.uq.edu.au
website www.uqp.com.au

Non-fiction and academic in the fields of Australian history, Australian biography, Australian politics and current affairs, Australian social and cultural issues, and Australian indigenous issues. Australian fiction (adult, young adult and children's). Via agents only. Founded 1948.

Scholastic Australia Pty Ltd*

76–80 Railway Crescent, Lisarow, Gostord, NSW 2250
tel +61 (0)2 4328 3555
website www.scholastic.com.au
Chairman Andrew Berkhut

Children's fiction and non-fiction. Founded 1968.

Simon & Schuster (Australia) Pty Ltd*

Office address Suite 19A, Level 1, Building C, 450 Miller Street, Cammeray, NSW 2062
Postal address PO Box 448, Cammeray, NSW 2062
tel +61 (0)2 9983 6600
email cservice@simonandschuster.com.au
website www.simonandschuster.com.au
Facebook www.facebook.com/SimonSchusterAU
Twitter @simonschusterAU
Managing Director Dan Ruffino

Part of the CBS Corporation, the company publishes and distributes in Australia and New Zealand the following: fiction, non-fiction and children's books. Imprints include: Atria, Free Press, Gallery, Howard, Pocket, Scribner, Simon & Schuster and Touchstone. Also acts as the local sales and distribution partner for 4 Ingredients, Watkins Books, Fox Chapel Publishing, Smith Street Books, Cider Mill Press, Regan Arts, Restless Books, Ventura Press, Viz Media, Insight Editions, Manuscript Publishing, Elliott & Thompson and Gallup Press. Founded 1987.

Spinifex Press*

504 Queensberry Street, North Melbourne, VIC 3051
email women@spinifexpress.com.au
Postal address PO Box 5270, North Geelong, VIC 3215
website www.spinifexpress.com.au
Managing Directors Susan Hawthorne, Renate Klein

Feminism and women's studies, art, astronomy, occult, education, gay and lesbian, health and nutrition, technology, travel, ebooks. No unsolicited MSS. Founded 1991.

UNSW Press*

University of New South Wales, UNSW Sydney, NSW 2052
tel +61 (0)2 8936 0100
email enquiries@newsouthpublishing.com
website www.unswpress.com
Ceo Kathy Bail, *Publishing Director* Phillipa McGuinness

Academic and general non-fiction. Politics, history, society and culture, popular science, environmental studies, Aboriginal studies. Includes imprints UNSW Press and New South. Founded 1962.

UWA Publishing*

UWA Publishing, University of Western Australia, M419, 35 Stirling Highway, Crawley, WA 6009
tel +61 (0)8 6488 3670
email admin-uwap@uwa.edu.au
website www.uwap.uwa.edu.au
Director Terri-ann White

Fiction, general non-fiction, natural history, contemporary issues. Founded 1935.

John Wiley & Sons Australia Ltd*

42 McDougall Street, Milton, QLD 4064
tel +61 (0)7 3859 9755
website www.wiley.com.au

Educational, technical, atlases, professional, reference, trade journals. Imprints: John Wiley & Sons, Jacaranda, Wrightbooks, Wiley-Blackwell, Frommer's, Jossey-Bass. Founded 1954.

Wombat Books*

PO Box 1519, Capalaba, QLD 4157
tel +61 (0)7 3245 1938
email info@wombatbooks.com.au
website www.wombatbooks.com.au
Facebook www.facebook.com/wombatbooks

Publisher Rochelle Manners, *Editor & Publicity Coordinator* Emily Lighezzolo

An independent publisher of children's picture books and books for early readers. Always on the lookout for the next story to be shared. Young adult and adult imprint: Rhiza Press. Founded 2009.

CANADA

**Member of the Canadian Publishers' Council*

†Member of the Association of Canadian Publishers

Annick Press Ltd†

15 Patricia Avenue, Toronto, ON M2M 1H9
tel +1 416-221-4802
email annickpress@annickpress.com
website www.annickpress.com
Owner/Director Rick Wilks, *Office Manager* Elaine Burns

Preschool to young adult fiction and non-fiction. Publishes approx. 24 titles each year. Recent successes include: (fiction) *Blue Gold and War Brothers* (novel and graphic novel); (non-fiction) *Before the World Was Ready*, *Bones Never Lie* and *The Bite of the Mango*; (picture books) *The Man With the Violin*. To send MS or illustration submission, please visit website and view submission guidelines. Founded 1975.

The Charlton Press

991 Victoria Street North, Kitchener, ON N2B 3C7
tel +1 416-962-2665
email chpress@charltonpress.com
website www.charltonpress.com

Collectables, Numismatics, Sportscard price catalogues. Founded 1952.

Douglas & McIntyre (2013) Ltd†

4437 Rondeview Road, PO Box 219, Madeira Park, BC V0N 2H0
tel +1 604-883-2730
email info@douglas-mcintyre.com
website www.douglas-mcintyre.com
Publisher Howard White

General list: Canadian biography, art and architecture, natural history, history, native studies, Canadian fiction. Unsolicited MSS accepted. Founded 1971.

Dundurn Press†

500–3 Church Street, Toronto, ON M5E 1M2
tel +1 416-214-5544
email submissions@dundurn.com
Publisher Kirk Howard

Canadian history, fiction, non-fiction and young adult fiction, mystery fiction, popular non-fiction, theatre, drama, translations. Founded 1972.

ECW Press Ltd†

665 Gerrard Street E, Toronto, ON M4M 1Y2
tel +1 416-694-3348
email info@ecwpress.com
website www.ecwpress.com
Facebook www.facebook.com/ecwpress
Twitter @ecwpress
Publishers David Caron, Jack David

Popular culture, TV and film, sports, humour, general trade books, biographies, memoir, popular science, guidebooks. Founded 1979.

Fitzhenry & Whiteside Ltd

195 Allstate Parkway, Markham, ON L3R 4T8
tel +1 800-387-9776
email godwit@fitzhenry.ca
website www.fitzhenry.ca
Publisher Sharon Fitzhenry

Trade, educational, children's books. Founded 1966.

Harlequin Enterprises Ltd*

PO Box 603, Fort Erie, ON L2A 5X3
tel +1 888-432-4879
email customer_ecare@harlequin.ca
website www.harlequin.com/shop/index.html
Publisher Craig Swinwood

Fiction for women, romance, inspirational fiction, African–American fiction, action adventure, mystery. Visit SoYouThinkYouCanWrite.com for the latest writing submissions and contests. Imprints include: Harlequin Blaze, Harlequin Desire, Harlequin Heartwarming, Harlequin Historical, Harlequin Intrigue, Harlequin Kimani Romance, Harlequin Medical Romance, Harlequin Nocturne, Harlequin Presents, Harlequin Romance, Harlequin Romantic Suspense, Harlequin Special Edition, Harlequin Special Releases, Harlequin Superromance, Harlequin Western Romance, Love Inspired, Love Inspired Special Releases, Love Inspired Historical, Love Inspired Suspense. Founded 1949.

HarperCollins Publishers Ltd*

2 Bloor Street East, 20th Floor, Toronto, ON M4W 1A8
tel +1 416-975-9334
email hccanada@harpercollins.com
website www.harpercollins.ca
President & Publisher Michael Morrison

Literary fiction and non-fiction, history, politics, biography, spiritual and children's books. Founded 1989.

Kids Can Press Ltd†

25 Dockside Drive, Toronto, ON M5A 0B5
tel +1 416-479-7000
email customerservice@kidscan.com
website www.kidscanpress.com/canada
Editorial Director Yvette Ghione

Juvenile/young adult books. Founded 1973.

Knopf Canada – see Penguin Random House Canada Ltd

LexisNexis Canada, Inc.*
111 Gordon Baker Road, Suite 900, Toronto, ON M2H 3R1
tel +1 800-668-6481
email info@lexisnexis.ca
website www.lexisnexis.ca

Law and accountancy. Division of Reed Elsevier plc.

Lone Pine Publishing
87 East Pender, Vancouver, BC V6A 1S9
tel +1 780-433-9333
email info@lonepinepublishing.com
website www.lonepinepublishing.com
President Shane Kennedy

Natural history, outdoor recreation and wildlife guidebooks, self-help, gardening, popular history. Founded 1980.

McGill-Queen's University Press†
1010 Sherbrooke Street West, Suite 1720, Montreal, QC H3A 2R7
tel +1 514-398-3750
email info.mqup@mcgill.ca
Alternative address Queen's University, Douglas Library Building, 93 University Avenue, Kingston, Ontario K7L 5C4
tel +1 613-533-2155
email kingstonmqup@queensu.ca
website www.mqup.mcgill.ca

Academic, non-fiction, poetry. Founded 1969.

McGraw-Hill Ryerson Ltd*
300 Water Street, Whitby, ON L1N 9B6
tel +1 905-430-5000
website www.mheducation.ca

Educational and trade books.

Nelson Education*
1120 Birchmount Road, Scarborough, ON M1K 5G4
tel +1 416-752-9448
website www.nelson.com
President Greg Nordal

Educational publishing: school (K–12), college and university, career education, measurement and guidance, professional and reference, ESL titles. Division of Thomson Canada Ltd. Founded 1914.

NeWest Press†
201 8540, 109 Street, Edmonton, AB T6G 1E6
tel +1 780-432-9427
email info@newestpress.com
website www.newestpress.com
President Doug Barbour

Fiction, drama, poetry and non-fiction. Founded 1977.

Oberon Press
205–145 Spruce Street, Ottawa, ON K1R 6P1
tel +1 613-238-3275
email oberon@sympatico.ca
website www.oberonpress.ca

General fiction, short stories, poetry, some biographies, art and children's. Only publishes Canadian writers.

Oxford University Press, Canada*
8 Sampson Mews, Suite 204, Don Mills, ON M3C 0H5
tel +1 416-441-2941
website www.oup.com
General Manager Geoff Forguson

Educational and academic.

Pearson Canada*
26 Prince Andrew Place, Toronto, ON M3C 2T8
tel +1 416-447-5101
website www.pearsoned.ca
President Dan Lee

Academic, technical, educational, children's and adult, trade.

Penguin Random House Canada Ltd*
320 Front Street, Suite 1400, Toronto, ON M5V 3B6
tel +1 416-364-4449
website www.penguinrandomhouse.ca
President & Ceo R. Bradley Martin, *President & Publisher PRHC* Kristin Cochrane

Literary fiction, commercial fiction, memoir, non-fiction (history, business, current events, sports), adult and children's. No unsolicited MSS; submissions via an agent only. Imprints: Anchor Canada, Allen Lane Canada, Appetite by Random House, Bond Street Books, Doubleday Canada, Emblem, Hamish Hamilton Canada, Knopf Canada, McClelland & Stewart, Penguin Canada, Penguin Teen, Portfolio Canada, Puffin Canada, Random House Canada, Seal Books, Signal, Tundra Books, Viking Canada, Vintage Canada. Subsidiary of Penguin Random House. Formed on I July 2013 as part of the worldwide merger of Penguin and Random House.

Pippin Publishing Corporation
PO Box 242, Don Mills, ON M3C 2S2
tel +1 416-510-2918
email arayner@utphighereducation.com
website www.utppublishing.com

ESL/EFL, teacher reference, adult basic education, school texts (all subjects), general trade (non-fiction) – acquired by University of Toronto Press in 2014 (page 222).

Ronsdale Press†
3350 West 21st Avenue, Vancouver, BC V6S 1G7
tel +1 604-738-4688

email ronsdale@shaw.ca
website www.ronsdalepress.com
Facebook www.facebook.com/ronsdalepress
Twitter @ronsdalepress
Director Ronald B. Hatch

Ronsdale is a Canadian publisher based in Vancouver with some 270 books in print. Founded 1988.

Thompson Educational Publishing†

20 Ripley Avenue, Toronto, ON M6S 3N9
tel +1 416-766-2763
email info@thompsonbooks.com
website www.thompsonbooks.com

Social sciences. Founded 1989.

University of Toronto Press

10 St Mary Street, Suite 700, Toronto, ON M4Y 2W8
tel +1 416-978-2239
email publishing@utpress.utoronto.ca
website www.utpress.utoronto.ca
President Meric Gertler

Publishers of academic books, ESL/EFL, teacher reference, adult basic education and school texts. Founded 1901.

Tundra Books

320 Front Street West, Suite 1400, Toronto, ON M5V 3B6
tel +1 416-364-4449
email tundra@mcclelland.com
website www.penguinrandomhouse.ca
Facebook www.facebook.com/tundrabooks
Twitter @TundraBooks
Publisher Tara Walker

Publisher of high-quality children's picture books and novels, renowned for its innovations. Publishes books for children to teens. Imprints: Jordan Fenn, Publisher of Fenn/Tundra (sport-themed children's books). A division of Penguin Random House Canada Ltd. Founded 1967.

NEW ZEALAND

**Member of the Publishers Association of New Zealand (PANZ)*

Auckland University Press*

University of Auckland, Private Bag 92019, Auckland 1142
tel +64 (0)9 373 7528
email press@auckland.ac.nz
website www.press.auckland.ac.nz
Director Sam Elworthy

Archaeology, architecture, art, biography, business, health, New Zealand history, Maori and Pacific studies, poetry, politics and law, science and natural history, social sciences. Founded 1966.

David Bateman Ltd

30 Tarndale Grove, Albany, Auckland 0632
tel +64 (0)9 415 7664
email bateman@bateman.co.nz
website www.batemanpublishing.co.nz
Facebook www.facebook.com/batemanpublishing

General trade non-fiction publisher focusing on craft, natural history, gardening, health, sport, cookery, history, travel, motoring, maritime history, business, art, lifestyle for the international market. Founded 1979.

The Caxton Press

32 Lodestar Ave, Wigram, PO Box 36 411, Christchurch 8042
tel +64 (0)3 366 8516
email peter@caxton.co.nz
website www.caxton.co.nz
Managing Director Bridget Batchelor

Local history, tourist pictorial, Celtic spirituality, parent guides, book designers and printers. Founded 1935.

Cengage Learning New Zealand*

Unit 4B, Rosedale Office Park, 331 Rosedale Road, Albany, North Shore 0632
Postal address PO Box 33376, Takapuna, North Shore 0740
tel +64 (0)9 415 6850
Publishing Editor Jenny Thomas

Educational books.

Dunmore Publishing Ltd

PO Box 28387, Auckland 1541
tel +64 (0)9 521 3121
email books@dunmore.co.nz
website www.dunmore.co.nz

Education secondary/tertiary texts and other, New Zealand society, history, health, economics, politics, general non-fiction. Founded 1970.

Edify Ltd*

Level 1, 39 Woodside Avenue, Northcote, Auckland 0627
tel +64 (0)9 972 9428
email gethelp@edify.co.nz
website www.edify.co.nz
Ceo Adrian Keane

Edify is a publishing, sales and marketing business providing its partners with opportunities for their products and solutions in the New Zealand educational market. Exclusive representatives of Pearson and the New Zealand based educational publisher, Sunshine Books.

Hachette New Zealand Ltd*

PO Box 3255, Shortland Street, Auckland 1140
tel +64 (0)9 379 1480

Books

email contact@hachette.co.nz
website www.hachette.co.nz
Facebook www.facebook.com/HachetteNZ
Managing Director Melanee Winder

International fiction and non-fiction, including cooking and children's.

Halcyon Publishing Ltd

PO Box 1064, Cambridge 3450
tel +64 (0)9 489 5337
email info@halcyonpublishing.co.nz
website www.halcyonpublishing.com
Managing Director/Publisher Graham Gurr

Hunting, shooting, fishing, outdoor interests. Founded 1982.

HarperCollins Publishers (New Zealand) Ltd*

Unit D, 63 Apollo Drive, Rosedale, Auckland 0632
tel +64 (0)9 443 9400
email publicity@harpercollins.co.nz
Postal address PO Box 1, Shortland Street, Auckland 1140
website www.harpercollins.co.nz

General literature, non-fiction, reference, children's. HarperCollins New Zealand does not accept proposals or MSS for consideration, except via the Wednesday Post portal on its website.

Learning Media Ltd

Level 4, Willeston House, 22–28 Willeston Street, Te Aro, Wellington 6021
tel +64 (0)4 472 5522
email info@learningmedia.co.nz
Postal address PO Box 90712, Victoria Street West, Auckland 1142

An award-winning publisher, designer and developer of books, educational resources and interactive programmes for New Zealand and international markets. Texts published in English, Maori and five Pacific languages. Founded 1993.

LexisNexis NZ Ltd

Level 1, 138 The Terrace, Wellington 6011
tel 0800 800 986
email customer.service@lexisnexis.co.nz
Postal address PO Box 472, Wellington 6140
website www.lexisnexis.co.nz
Publisher Christopher Murray

Law, business, academic.

McGraw-Hill Book Company New Zealand Ltd

Level 8, 56–60 Cawley Street, Ellerslie, Auckland 1005
Postal address Private Bag 11904, Ellerslie, Auckland 1005
tel +64 (0)9 526 6200
website www.mcgraw-hill.com.au

Educational publisher: higher education, primary and secondary education (grades K–12) and professional (including medical, general and reference). Division of the McGraw-Hill Companies. Founded 1974.

New Zealand Council for Educational Research

Box 3237, Education House, 178–182 Willis Street, Wellington 6011
tel +64 (0)4 384 7939
email info@nzcer.org.nz
website www.nzcer.org.nz
Publishing Manager David Ellis

Education, including educational policy and practice, early childhood education, educational achievement tests, Maori education, schooling for the future, curriculum and assessment. Founded 1934.

Otago University Press*

University of Otago, PO Box 56, Dunedin, Otago 9054
tel +64 (0)3 479 8807
email university.press@otago.ac.nz
website www.otago.ac.nz/press
Publisher Rachel Scott

New Zealand and Pacific history, social and cultural studies, biography/memoir, poetry as well as a wide range of scholarly to general books. Also publishes New Zealand's longest-running literary journal, Landfall. Founded 1958.

Penguin Random House New Zealand Ltd*

Private Bag 102902, North Shore, Auckland 0745
tel +64 (0)9 442 7400
email publishing@penguinrandomhouse.co.nz
website www.penguinrandomhouse.co.nz
Facebook www.facebook.com/PenguinRandomNZ
Publishing Director Debra Millar, *Managing Director* Margaret Thompson

Adult and children's fiction and non-fiction. Imprints: Penguin, Vintage, Black Swan, Godwit, Viking, Puffin Books. Part of Penguin Random House. Founded 1973.

RSVP Publishing Company

PO Box 93, Oneroa, Waiheke Island, Auckland 1081
tel +64 (0)9 372 5047
email ccpalmer@iconz.co.nz
Managing Director & Publisher Chris Palmer

Fiction, metaphysical, children's. Founded 1990.

Victoria University Press*

Victoria University of Wellington, PO Box 600, Wellington 6140
tel +64 (0)4 463 6580
email victoria-press@vuw.ac.nz
website http://vup.victoria.ac.nz/

Publisher Fergus Barrowman, *Editors* Kyleigh Hodgson, Ashleigh Young, Holly Hunter

Academic, scholarly books on New Zealand history, sociology, law; Maori language; fiction, plays, poetry. Founded 1974.

Viking Sevenseas NZ Ltd

201A Rosetta Road, Raumati 5032
tel +64 (0)4 902 8240
email vikings@paradise.net.nz
website https://vikingsevenseas.co.nz/
Managing Director M.B. Riley

Natural history books on New Zealand only.

SOUTH AFRICA

**Member of the Publishers' Association of South Africa*

Ad Donker – see Jonathan Ball Publishers (Pty) Ltd

Jonathan Ball Publishers (Pty) Ltd*

PO Box 33977, Jeppestown 2043
tel +27 (0)11 601 8000
email services@jonathanball.co.za
Postal address PO Box 33977, Jeppestown 2043
website www.jonathanball.co.za
Publishing Director Jeremy Boraine

Specialises in South African history, politics and current affairs and also publishes some fiction. Also acts as agents for British and American publishers, marketing and distributing books on their behalf in southern Africa. Founded 1977.

Ad Donker

Africana, literature, history, academic.

Jonathan Ball

General publications, current affairs, politics, business history, business, reference.

Delta Books

General South African trade non-fiction.

Sunbird Publishers

Illustrated wildlife, tourism, maps, travel.

Burnet Media

PO Box 53557, Kenilworth, Cape Town 7745
email info@burnetmedia.co.za
website www.burnetmedia.co.za
Facebook www.facebook.com/TwoDogsMercury
Twitter @TwoDogs_Mercury
Publishing Manager Tim Richman

Independent publisher of the Two Dogs and Mercury imprints. Two Dogs: innovative and irreverent non-fiction focusing on contemporary and lifestyle subject matter for the South African market. Numerous local bestsellers. Founded 2006. Imprint: Mercury – publishes interesting, accessible and engaging non-fiction with broader subject matter for both the South African and international markets. Publishes a growing number of internationally-renowned titles. Founded 2010.

Cambridge University Press*

Lower Ground Floor, Nautica Building,
The Water Club, Beach Road, Granger Bay,
Cape Town 8005
tel +27 (0)21) 412 7800
email capetown@cambridge.org
website www.cup.co.za
Publishing Director Johan Traut

Textbooks and literature for sub-Sahara African countries, as well as primary reading materials in 28 African languages.

Delta Books – see Jonathan Ball Publishers (Pty) Ltd

Galago Publishing (Pty) Ltd

PO Box 1645, Alberton 1450
tel +27 (0)11 824 2029
email lemur@mweb.co.za
website www.galago.co.za
Managing Director Fran Stiff

Southern African interest: military, political, hunting. Founded 1980.

Jacklin Enterprises (Pty) Ltd

PO Box 521, Parklands 2121
tel +27 (0)11 265 4200
website www.jacklin.co.za
Managing Director M.A.C. Jacklin

Children's fiction and non-fiction; Afrikaans large print books. Subjects include aviation, natural history, romance, general science, technology and transportation. Imprints: Mike Jacklin, Kennis Onbeperk, Daan Retief.

Juta and Company (Pty) Ltd*

1st Floor, Sunclare Building, 21 Dreyer Street, Claremont 7708
tel +27 (0)21 659 2300
email orders@juta.co.za
website www.juta.co.za
Acting Ceo Megan Marinus

Academic, education, agencies, learning, law and health. Publishers of print and digital print solutions. Founded 1853.

University of KwaZulu-Natal Press*

Private Bag X01, Scottsville, Pietermaritzburg, KwaZulu-Natal 3209
tel +27 (0)33 260 5226
email books@ukzn.ac.za
website www.ukznpress.co.za, http://ukznpress.bookslive.co.za/

Facebook www.facebook.com/UKZNPress
Twitter @UKZNPress
Publisher Debra Primo

Southern African social, political and economic history, sociology, politics and political science, current affairs, literary criticism, gender studies, education, biography. Founded 1948.

Macmillan Education South Africa

4th Floor, Building G, Hertford Office Park, 90 Bekker Road, Vorna Valley, Midrand 1685
tel +27 (0)11 731 3300
Postal address Private Bag X19, Northlands 2116
website www.macmillan.co.za
Managing Director Preggy Naidoo

Educational titles for the RSA market.

NB Publishers (Pty) Ltd*

PO Box 879, Cape Town 8000
tel +27 (0)21 406 3033
email nb@nb.co.za
website www.nb.co.za

General: Afrikaans fiction, politics, children's and youth literature in all the country's languages, non-fiction. Imprints: Tafelberg, Human & Rousseau, Queillerie, Pharos, Kwela, Best Books and Lux Verbi. Founded 1950.

New Africa Books (Pty) Ltd

2nd Floor, 6 Spin Street, Cape Town 8001
tel +27 (0)21 467 5860
email info@newafricabooks.co.za
Postal address PostNet, Suite 144, Private Bag X9190, Cape Town 8000

New Africa Books, incorporating David Philip Publishers, is an independent publishing house. Currently publishes literary, educational and non-fiction books for adults, children and young adults in all South African languages. Formed as a result of the merger of David Philip Publishers (founded 1971), Spearhead Press (founded 2000) and New Africa Educational Publishing.

David Philip

Academic, history, social sciences, politics, biography, reference, education.

Spearhead

Current affairs, also business, self-improvement, health, natural history, travel.

Oxford University Press Southern Africa*

Vasco Boulevard, N1 City, Goodwood, Cape Town 7460
tel +27 (0)21 596 2300
email oxford.za@oup.com
Postal address PO Box 12119, N1 City, Cape Town 7463
website www.oxford.co.za
Managing Director Steve Cilliers

Oxford is one of the leading educational publishers in South Africa, producing a wide range of quality educational material in print and digital format. The range includes books from Grade R to Grade 12, as well as higher education textbooks, school literature, dictionaries and atlases. Committed to transforming lives through education by providing superior quality learning material and support.

Pan Macmillan SA (Pty) Ltd*

2nd Floor, 1 Jameson Avenue, Melrose Estate, 2196
tel +27 (0)11 731 3440
email roshni@panmacmillan.co.za
Postal address Private Bag X19, Northlands, Johannesburg 2116
website www.panmacmillan.co.za
Managing Director Terry Morris, *Marketing & Sales Manager* Gillian Spain, *Children's Books Strategist* Lara Cohen

Imprints: Boxtree, Campbell, Farrar Straus & Giroux, Forge, Franklin Watts, Gateway, Gill & Macmillan, Giraffe Books, Griffin, Guinness, Hachette Children's Books, Henry Holt, Hodder Wayland, Macmillan, Macmillan Children's Books, Mattel, Palgrave, Pan Macmillan, Pan Macmillan Australia, Picador, Picador Africa, Priddy Books, Quadrille, Ravan Press, Rodale, Sidgewick & Jackson, SMP, Tor and Walker Books. Publishes titles in autobiography, biography, business, children's books, cookery and wine, crafts and hobbies, crime, environment, fiction (popular and literary), humour, inspiration, literature, business, reference, sport and stationery.

Pearson South Africa*

4th Floor, Auto Atlantic, Corner Hertzog Boulevard and Herengracht, Cape Town 8001
tel +27 (0)21 532 6000
email pearsonza.enquiries@pearson.com
website www.za.pearson.com
Learning Resources Director (Schools) Jacques Zakarian

Educational and general publishers. Heinemann and Maskew Miller Longman are part of Pearson South Africa.

Penguin Random House (Pty) Ltd*

The Estuaries, No 4, Oxbow Crescent, Century Avenue, Century City 7441
email info@penguinrandomhouse.co.za
Postal address PO Box 1144, Cape Town 8000
tel +27 (0)21 460 5400
website www.penguinrandomhouse.co.za
Managing Director Steve Connolly

Imprints: Penguin Random House, Struik Lifestyle, Struik Nature, Struik Travel & Heritage, Zebra Press, Penguin Non-Fiction, Penguin Fiction, Umuzi.

Genres include general illustrated non-fiction; lifestyle; natural history; South African politics; sport; business; memoirs; contemporary fiction; literary fiction; local fiction; Afrikaans; children's books. Part of Penguin Random House.

Shuter and Shooter Publishers (Pty) Ltd*

110 CB Downes Road, Pietermaritzburg, KwaZulu-Natal 3201
tel +27 (0)33 846 8700
email sales@shuters.com
Postal address PO Box 61, Mkondeni, KwaZulu-Natal 3212
website www.shuters.co.za
Chief Execute Officer P.B. Chetty

Core curriculum-based textbooks for use at foundation, intermediate, senior and FET phases. Supplementary readers in various languages; dictionaries; reading development kits, charts. Literature titles in English, isiXhosa, Sesotho, Sepedi, Setswana, Tshivenda, Xitsonga, Ndebele, isiZulu and Siswati. Founded 1925.

Sunbird Publishers – see Jonathan Ball Publishers (Pty) Ltd

Unisa Press*

University of South Africa, PO Box 392, Unisa, Mackleneuk, Pretoria 0003
tel +27 (0)12 429 3448
email unisa-press@unisa.ac.za
website www.unisa.ac.za/press
Commissioning Editor Hetta Pieterse

All academic disciplines, African history, sustainable development, economics, the arts and the humanities generally. Imprint: UNISA. Email for MS submissions: boshosm@unisa.ac.za. Founded 1957.

Van Schaik Publishers*

PO Box 12681, Hatfield, Pretoria 0028
tel +27 (0)12 342 2765
email vanschaik@vanschaiknet.com
website www.vanschaiknet.com
General Manager Leanne Martini

Texts for the tertiary and private FET markets in South Africa. Founded 1915.

Wits University Press*

Private Bag 3, Wits 2050
tel +27 (0)11 717 8700/1
email veronica.klipp@wits.ac.za
Postal address PO Wits, Johannesburg 2050
website www.witspress.co.za
Publisher Veronica Klipp

Publishes well-researched, innovative books for both academic and general readers in the following areas: art and heritage, popular science, history and politics, biography, literary studies, women's writing and select textbooks.

Zebra Press – see Penguin Random House (Pty) Ltd

USA

**Member of the Association of American Publishers Inc.*

Abbeville Press, Inc.

116 West 23rd Street, New York, NY 10013
tel +1 646-375-2136
website www.abbeville.com
Publisher & President Robert Abrams

Fine art and illustrated books. Founded 1977.

ABC-ClIO

130 Cremona Drive, Ste C, Santa Barbara, CA 93117
tel +1 805-968-1911
website www.abc-clio.com
Facebook www.facebook.com/ABCCLIO
Twitter @ABC_CLIO

Academic resources for secondary and middle schools, colleges and universities, libraries and professionals (librarians, media specialists, teachers). Founded 1955.

Abingdon Press

2222 Rosa L. Parks Boulevard, PO Box 280988, Nashville, TN 37228
tel +1 800-251-3320
website www.abingdonpress.com
Facebook www.facebook.com/abingdonpress
Twitter @AbingdonPress
President & Publisher Neil Alexander

General interest, professional, academic and reference, non-fiction and fiction, youth and children's non-fiction and Vatican Bible School; primarily directed to the religious market. Imprint of United Methodist Publishing House with tradition of crossing denominational boundaries.

Harry N. Abrams, Inc.

195 Broadway, 9th Floor, New York, NY 10007
tel +1 212-206-7715
email abrams@abramsbooks.com
website www.abramsbooks.com

Art and architecture, photography, natural sciences, performing arts, children's books. No fiction. Founded 1949.

Akashic Books Ltd

232 Third Street, Suite A115, Brooklyn, NY 11215
tel +1 718-643-9193
email info@akashicbooks.com
website www.akashicbooks.com
Facebook www.facebook.com/AkashicBooks
Twitter @AkashicBooks
Contacts Ibrahim Ahmad (editorial director), Johanna Ingalls (managing editor)

A Brooklyn-based independent company dedicated to publishing urban literary fiction and political non-fiction by authors who are either ignored by the mainstream, or who have no interest in working within the ever-consolidating ranks of the major corporate publishers.

The University of Alabama Press

Box 870380, Tuscaloosa, AL 35487-0380
tel +1 205-348-5180
website www.uapress.ua.edu
Editor-in-Chief Daniel Waterman

American and Southern history, African–American studies, religion, rhetoric and communication, Judaic studies, literary criticism, anthropology and archaeology. Founded 1945.

Amistad – see HarperCollins Publishers

Applause Theatre and Cinema Book Publishers

19 West 21st Street, Suite 201, New York, NY 10010
tel +1 212-575-9265
email info@halleonardbooks.com
website www.applausepub.com
Facebook www.facebook.com/ApplauseBooks/
Twitter @ApplauseBooks
Publisher Michael Messina

Performing arts. Founded 1980.

Arcade Publishing

11th Floor, 307 West 36th Street, New York, NY 10018
tel +1 212-643-6816
website www.arcadepub.com
Executive Editor Cal Barksdale

General trade, including adult hardback and paperbacks. No unsolicited MSS. Founded 1988. Imprint of Skyhorse Publishing since 2010.

ArcheBooks Publishing, Inc.

6081 Silver King Boulevard, Suite 903, Cape Coral, FL 33914
tel +1 239-542-7595 (toll free)
email info@archebooks.com
website www.archebooks.com
Facebook www.facebook.com/archebooks
Twitter @archebooks
Publisher Robert E. Gelinas

Fiction and non-fiction (history and true crime). Send submissions via a literary agent. Founded 2003.

The University of Arkansas Press

McIlroy House, 105 N. McIlroy Avenue, Fayetteville, AR 72701
tel +1 800-626-0090
email info@uapress.com
website www.uapress.com
Editor-in-Chief David Scott Cunningham

History, humanities, Middle Eastern studies, African–American studies, food studies, poetry. Founded 1980.

Atlantic Monthly Press – see Grove Atlantic, Inc

Avery – see Penguin Publishing Group

Avon – see HarperCollins Publishers

Back Bay Books – see Little, Brown & Company

Baker's Plays

7611 Sunset Boulevard, Hollywood, CA 90046
tel +1 323-876-0579
email info@bakersplays.com
website www.samuelfrench.com
UK Agent Samuel French Ltd

Plays and books on the theatre. Also agents for plays. Division of Samuel French, Inc. Founded 1845.

Barefoot Books

2067 Massachusetts Avenue, Cambridge, MA 02140
tel +1 617-576-0660
email help@barefootbooks.com
website www.barefootbooks.com
Facebook www.facebook.com/barefootbooks
Twitter @BarefootBooks
Ceo Nancy Traversy, *Group Operations Director* Karen Janson, *Senior Director of Product* Stefanie Paige Wieder

Children's picture books, activity decks and board books: diverse, inclusive and global stories that build social-emotional and literacy skills. See website for submission guidelines. Founded 1993.

Barron's Educational Series, Inc.

250 Wireless Boulevard, Hauppauge, NY 11788
tel +1 800-645-3476
email barrons@barronseduc.com
website www.barronseduc.com
Facebook www.facebook.com/Barrons-Educational-Series-Inc-118498041501781/
Twitter @BarronsEduc
Chairman & Ceo Manuel H. Barron, *President & Publisher* Ellen Sibley

Test preparation, juvenile, cookbooks, mind, body & spirit, crafts, business, pets, gardening, family and health, art, study guides, school guides. Founded 1941.

Basic Books

250 West 57th Street, Suite 1500, New York, NY 10107
tel +1 212 340-8101
email basic.books@perseusbooks.com
website www.basicbooks.com
Facebook www.facebook.com/BasicBooks

Twitter @BasicBooks

A member of the Perseus Books Group. Publishes books in history, science, sociology, psychology, politics and current affairs. Also publishes new works in African and African–American studies. Basic Books is an imprint of Perseus Books, a Hachette Book Group company (page 231). Founded 1952.

Beacon Press*

24 Farnsworth, Boston, MA 02110
tel +1 617-742-2110
website www.beacon.org
Director Helene Atwan

General non-fiction in fields of religion, ethics, philosophy, current affairs, gender studies, environmental concerns, African–American studies, anthropology and women's studies, nature. Founded 1854.

Bella Books

PO Box 10543, Tallahassee, FL 32302
tel +1 800-729-4992
email info@bellabooks.com
website www.bellabooks.com

Lesbian fiction: mystery, romance, sci-fi. Founded 1973.

Berkley Books – see Penguin Publishing Group

Bloomsbury Publishing USA*

1385 Broadway, New York, NY 10018
tel +1 212-419-5300
email ChildrensPublicityUSA@bloomsbury.com
website www.bloomsbury.com/us
Vice President & Publishing Director Cindy Loh (consumer publishing)

Supports the worldwide publishing activities of Bloomsbury Publishing Plc: caters for the US market. For submission guidelines see: www.bloomsbury.com/us/authors/submissions/.

Bold Strokes Books, Inc.

648 South Cambridge Road, Building A, Johnsonville, NY 12094
email service@boldstrokesbooks.com
website www.boldstrokesbooks.com
Facebook vwww.facebook.com/BoldStrokesBooks/
Twitter @boldstrokebooks
Publisher Len Barot

Offers a diverse collection of lesbian, gay, bisexual, transgender and queer general and genre fiction. Fiction includes romance, mystery/intrigue, crime, erotica, speculative fiction (sci fi/fantasy/horror), general fiction, and, through the Soliloquy imprint, young adult fiction. Since its inception in 2004, the company's mission has remained unchanged to bring quality queer fiction to readers worldwide and to support an international group of authors in developing their craft and reaching an ever-growing community of readers via print, digital and audio formats. Over 1,000 titles in print. For submission instructions see website.

R.R. Bowker

630 Central Avenue, New Providence, NJ 07974
tel +1 908-286-1090
website www.bowker.com

Bibliographies and reference tools for the book trade and literary and library worlds, available in hardcopy, on microfiche, online and CD-Rom. Reference books for music, art, business, the computer industry, cable industry and information industry. Division of Cambridge Information Group.

Boyds Mills Press

815 Church Street, Honesdale, PA 18431
website www.boydsmillspress.com
Facebook www.facebook.com/BoydsMillsPressBooks
Twitter @boydsmillspress

Fiction, non-fiction, and poetry trade books for children and young adults. Founded 1991.

Burford Books, Inc.

101 E State Street, #301, Ithaca, NY 14850
tel +1 607-319-4373
email pburford@burfordbooks.com
website www.burfordbooks.com
President Peter Burford

Outdoor activities: golf, sports, fitness, nature, travel. Founded 1997.

Cambridge University Press*

1 Liberty Plaza, Floor 20, New York, NY 10006
tel +1 212-337-5000
email customer_service@cambridge.org
website www.cambridge.org/us

Academic and professional; Cambridge Learning (ELT, primary and secondary education).

Candlewick Press

99 Dover Street, Somerville, MA 02144
tel +1 617-661-3330
email bigbear@candlewick.com
website www.candlewick.com
President & Publisher Karen Lotz, *Creative Director & Associate Publisher* Chris Paul, *Executive Editorial Director & Associate Publisher* Liz Bicknell, *Editorial Director & Director of Editorial Operations* Mary Lee Donovan

Books for babies through teens: board books, picture books, novels, non-fiction, novelty books. Submit material through a literary agent. Subsidiary of Walker Books Ltd, UK. Founded 1991.

Candlewick Entertainment

Group Editorial Director Joan Powers
Media-related children's books, including film/TV tie-ins.

Candlewick Studio

Group Editorial Director Karen Lotz, *Group Art Director* Chris Paul

Books for book-lovers of all ages.

Center Street

Hachette Book Group USA, 12 Cadillac Drive, Suite 480, Brentwood, TN 37027
email centerstreetpub@hbgusa.com
website www.centerstreet.com

Books with traditional values for readers in the US heartland. Imprint of Hachette Book Group (page 231). Founded 2005.

University of Chicago Press*

1427 East 60th Street, Chicago, IL 60637
tel +1 773-702-7700
website www.press.uchicago.edu

Scholarly books and monographs (humanities, social sciences and sciences); general trade books; reference books; and 70 scholarly journals.

Chronicle Books*

680 Second Street, San Francisco, CA 94107
tel +1 415-537-4200
email hello@chroniclebooks.com
website www.chroniclebooks.com, www.chroniclebooks.com/titles/kids-teens
Facebook www.facebook.com/ChronicleBooks
Twitter @ChronicleBooks
Chairman & Ceo Nion McEvoy, *Publisher* Christine Carswell

Publishes award-winning, innovative books. Recognized as one of the 50 best small companies to work for in the US. Publishing list includes illustrated books and gift products in design, art, architecture, photography, food, lifestyle, pop culture and children's titles. Founded 1967.

Coffee House Press

79 13th Avenue NE, Suite 110, Minneapolis, MN 55413
tel +1 612-338-0125
website www.coffeehousepress.org
Managing Director Caroline Casey, *Publisher* Chris Fischbach

Literary fiction, essays and poetry; collectors' editions. Founded 1984.

Columbia University Press*

61 West 62nd Street, New York, NY 10023
tel +1 212-459-0600
email jc373@columbia.edu, es3387@columbia.edu
website www.cup.columbia.edu
Twitter @ColumbiaUP
Associate Provost & Director Jennifer Crewe, *Editorial Director* Eric Schwartz

General interest, scholarly, and textbooks in the humanities, social sciences, sciences and professions; reference works in print and electronic formats. Subjects include Asian studies, business, earth science and sustainability, economics, English and comparative literature, film and media studies, global and American history, international relations, journalism, life science, Middle Eastern studies, neuroscience, palaeontology, philosophy, political science and international relations, religion, sociology and social work. Publishes Asian and Russian literature in translation. Founded 1893.

For MSS submission information see http://cup.columbia.edu/manuscript-submissions.

Concordia Publishing House

3558 South Jefferson Avenue, St Louis, MO 63118
tel +1 314-268-1000
website www.cph.org
President & Ceo Bruce G. Kintz

Religious books, Lutheran perspective. Few freelance MSS accepted; query first. Founded 1869.

Contemporary Books

130 East Randolph Street, Suite 400, Chicago, IL 60601
tel +1 800-621-1918
website www.mheducation.com/prek-12/segment/adulted.html

Non-fiction. Imprints: Contemporary Books, Lowell House, Passport Books, VGM Career Books. Division of the McGraw-Hill companies.

The Continuum International Publishing Group, Inc. – see Bloomsbury Publishing Plc

Cooper Square Publishing

4501 Forbes Boulevard, Suite 200, Lanham, MD 20706
tel +1 301-459-3366

Part of the Rowman & Littlefield Publishing Group (page 238). Founded 1949.

Luna Rising

Northland Publishing's bilingual (Spanish–English) imprint.

Northland Publishing

American Southwest themes including home design, cooking and travel. Founded 1958.

NorthWord Books for Young Readers

11571 K–Tel Drive, Minnetonka, MN 55343
tel +1 800-462-6420
email rrinehart@rowman.com

Picture books and non-fiction nature and wildlife books in interactive and fun-to-read formats. Not accepting MSS at present. Founded 1989.

Rising Moon

email editorial@northlandbooks.com

Illustrated, entertaining and thought-provoking picture books for children, including Spanish–English bilingual titles. Founded 1998.

Two-Can Publishing

Non-fiction books and multimedia products for children 2–12 years to entertain and educate. Not accepting MSS at present.

Cornell University Press

Sage House, 512 East State Street, Ithaca, NY 14850
tel +1 607-277-2338
email cupressinfo@cornell.edu
website www.cornellpress.cornell.edu
Director Dean J. Smith

Including LR Press and Comstock Publishing Associates. Scholarly books. Founded 1869.

The Countryman Press

500 Fifth Avenue, New York, NY 10110
tel +1 212-354-5500
email countrymanpress@wwnorton.com
website www.countrymanpress.com
Editorial Director Ann Treistman

Cooking and lifestyle, outdoor recreation guides for anglers, hikers, cyclists, canoeists and kayakers, US travel guides, New England non-fiction, how-to books, country living books, books on nature and the environment, classic reprints and general non-fiction. No unsolicited MSS. Division of W.W. Norton & Co., Inc. Founded 1973.

Crown Publishing Group

1745 Broadway, New York, NY 10019
tel +1 212-572-2537
website http://crownpublishing.com/
President & Publisher Maya Mavjee

One of four adult books divisions at Penguin Random House, the Crown Publishing Group publishes literary and commercial fiction; narrative non-fiction across genres such as history, science, politics, current affairs, biography, memoir, religion and business; as well as in the preeminent culinary and lifestyle illustrated published program in the United States. Imprints: Amphoto Books, Broadway Books, Clarkson Potter, Convergent Books, Crown, Crown Archetype, Crown Forum, Currency, Harmony Books, Hogarth, Hogarth Shakespeare, SJP for Hogarth, Rodale Books, Ten Speed Press, Three Rivers Press, Tim Duggan Books, WaterBrook Multnomah and Watson-Guptill. A division of Penguin Random House (page 236).

DAW Books, Inc.

375 Hudson Street, 3rd Floor, New York, NY 10014
tel +1 212-366-2096
email daw@penguinrandomhouse.com
website www.dawbooks.com
Publishers Elizabeth R. Wollheim, Sheila E. Gilbert

Sci-fi, fantasy, horror and paranormal: originals and reprints. Founded 1971.

Tom Doherty Associates, LLC

175 5th Avenue, New York, NY 10010
tel +1 212-388-0100
email enquiries@tor.com
website www.torforgeblog.com

Fiction: general, historical, western, suspense, mystery, horror, science fiction, fantasy, humour, juvenile, classics (English language); non-fiction: adult and juvenile. Imprints: Tor, Forge, Orb, Starscope, Tor Teen. Founded 1980.

Dover Publications, Inc.

31 East 2nd Street, Mineola, NY 11501
tel +1 516-294-7000
website http://store.doverpublications.com/

Art, architecture, antiques, crafts, juvenile, food, history, folklore, literary classics, mystery, language, music, mathematics and science, nature, design and ready-to-use art. Founded 1941.

Dutton – see Penguin Publishing Group

Elsevier (Clinical Solutions)

1600 John F. Kennedy Boulevard, Philadelphia, PA 19103-2398
tel +1 215-239-3900
website www.elsevierhealth.co.uk, www.elsevier.com/clinical-solutions
President Dr. John Danaher

Medical books, journals and electrical healthcare solutions. No unsolicited MSS but synopses and project proposals welcome. Imprints: Bailliere Tindall, Churchill Livingstone, Elsevier, Mosby, Pergamon, Saunders.

Faber and Faber, Inc. – see Farrar, Straus and Giroux, LLC

Family Tree – see Writer's Digest Books

Farrar, Straus and Giroux, LLC

175 Varick Street, 9th Floor, New York, NY 10014
tel +1 212-741-6900
website www.fsgbooks.com, www.fsgoriginals.com
Facebook www.facebook.com/fsgoriginals
Twitter @FSOriginals
President & Publisher Jonathan Galassi

Sarah Crichton Books

Publishes a wide variety of literary and commercial fiction and non-fiction.

Faber and Faber, Inc.

175 Varick Street, 9th Floor, New York, NY 10014
tel +1 212-741-6900

website http://us.macmillan.com/publishers/farrar-straus-giroux
Publisher Mitzi Angel
Fiction, general non-fiction, drama, poetry, film, music.

FSG Originals
website www.fsgoriginals.com
Original fiction that does not fit into any obvious category.

Hill and Wang
General non-fiction, history, public affairs, graphic novels. Founded 1956.

North Point Press
Literary non-fiction, with an emphasis on natural history, ecology, yoga, food writing and cultural criticism.

Scientific American/Farrar, Straus and Giroux
website http://books.scientificamerican.com/fsg/
Publishes non-fiction science books for the general reader.

Fonthill Media LLC
12 Sires Street, Charleston, SC 29403
tel +1 843-203-3432
email info@fonthillmedia.com
website www.fonthillmedia.com
Publisher & President (Charleston SC Office) Alan Sutton

General history. Specialisations include biography, military history, aviation history, naval and maritime history, regional and local history, transport history, social history, sports history, ancient history and archaeology. US imprints: Fonthill, America Through Time and American History House. Founded 2012.

Samuel French, Inc.
235 Park Avenue South, Fifth Floor, New York, NY 10003
tel +1 212 206 8990
email info@samuelfrench.com
website www.samuelfrench.com

Play publishers and authors' representatives (dramatic).

Fulcrum Publishing
4690 Table Mountain Drive, Suite 100, Golden, CO 80403
tel +1 303-277-1623
website www.fulcrum-books.com

Publishes a wide variety of educational non-fiction texts and children's books, also books and support materials for teachers, librarians, parents and elementary through middle schoolchildren. Subjects include: science and nature, literature and storytelling, history, multicultural studies and Native American and Hispanic cultures.

Getty Publications*
1200 Getty Center Drive, Suite 500, Los Angeles, CA 90049
tel +1 310-440-6536
email booknews@getty.edu
website www.getty.edu

Art, art history, architecture, classical art and archaeology, conservation. Founded 1983.

David R. Godine, Publisher, Inc.
15 Court Square, Suite 320, Boston, MA 02108
tel +1 617-451-9600
website www.godine.com
President David R. Godine

Fiction, photography, poetry, art, biography, children's, essays, history, typography, architecture, nature and gardening, music, cooking, words and writing and mysteries. No unsolicited MSS. Founded 1970.

Grand Central Publishing*
237 Park Avenue, New York, NY 10017
tel +1 212-364-0600
email grandcentralpublishing@hbgusa.com
website www.grandcentralpublishing.com

Previously Warner Books, Inc. Fiction and non-fiction. Imprints: Aspect, Business Plus (business), Forever (romance), Vision (blockbuster fiction), Wellness Central (health and wellbeing), 5 Spot (women's fiction and non-fiction), Twelve, Springboard Press. Division of Hachette Book Group (page 231). Founded 1970.

Grosset & Dunlap – see Penguin Young Readers

Grove Atlantic, Inc*
154 West 14th Street, 12 Floor, New York, NY 10011
tel +1 212-614-7850
website www.groveatlantic.com
Facebook www.facebook.com/groveatlantic
Twitter @groveatlantic
Associate Publisher Judy Hottensen, *Vice-President & Editorial Director* Elisabeth Schmitz

Fiction, biography, autobiography, history, current affairs, social science, belles lettres, natural history. No unsolicited MSS. Imprints: Atlantic Monthly Press, Black Cat, Mysterious Press, Grove Press. Founded 1952.

Hachette Book Group*
1290 Avenue of the Americas, New York, NY 10104
tel +1 212-364-1100
website www.hachettebookgroup.com

Divisions: Center Street (see page 229), Grand Central Publishing (see page 231); Hachette Audio; Hachette Nashville; Hachette Books; Little, Brown and Company (page 233); Little, Brown Books for

Young Readers; Orbit, Perseus Books. Imprints: Grand Central: Business Plus, Forever, Forever Yours, Grand Central Life & Style, Twelve, Vision. Hachette Nashville: Center Street, FaithWords, Hachette Books: Little, Brown and Company: Back Bay Books, Mulholland Books. Little, Brown Books for Young Readers: LB Kids, Poppy Orbit: Orbit, Redhook. Perseus Books: Avalon Travel, Basic Books, Black Dog & Leventhal. Civitas, Da Capo, Nation Books, Running Press, PublicAffairs, Seal Press.

Orbit

website www.orbitbooks.net
Sci-fi and fantasy.

Harcourt Trade Publishers – see Houghton Mifflin Harcourt

HarperCollins Publishers*

195 Broadway, New York, NY 10007
tel +1 212-207-700
website http://corporate.harpercollins.com/us
President & Ceo Brian Murray

Fiction, history, biography, poetry, science, travel, cookbooks, juvenile, educational, business, technical and religious. Founded 1817.

HarperCollins General Books Group

President & Publisher Michael Morrison

Imprints: Amistad, Anthony Bourdain Books, Avon, Avon Impulse, Avon Inspire, Avon Read, Broadside Books, Custom House, Dey Street, Ecco Books, Harper Books, Harper Business, Harper Design, Harper Luxe, Harper Paperbacks, Harper Perennial, Haper Voyager, Harper Wave, HarperAudio, HarperCollins 360, HarperElixir, HarperLegend, HarperOne, William Morrow, William Morrow Paperbacks, Witness.

HarperAudio

A stunning array of bestselling children's books and young adult favorites in audio.

HarperFestival

Books, novelties, and merchandise for the very young: children 0–8 years.

HarperCollins Children's Books

Respected worldwide for publishing quality books for children and home to many classics of children's literature.

Harvard University Press*

79 Garden Street, Cambridge, MA 02138
tel +1 617-495-2600
email contact_hup@harvard.edu
website www.hup.harvard.edu
Director George Andreou, *Editor-in-Chief* Susan Boehmer

History, philosophy, literary criticism, politics, economics, sociology, music, science, classics, social sciences, behavioural sciences, law.

Hill and Wang – see Farrar, Straus and Giroux, LLC

Hippocrene Books, Inc.

171 Madison Avenue, New York, NY 10016
tel +1 718-454-2366
email info@hippocrenebooks.com
website www.hippocrenebooks.com

International cookbooks, foreign language dictionaries, travel, military history, Polonia, general trade. Founded 1971.

Holiday House, Inc.

425 Madison Avenue, New York, NY 10017
tel +1 212-688-0085
email info@holidayhouse.com
website www.holidayhouse.com

General children's books. Send entire MS. Only responds to projects of interest. Founded 1935.

Henry Holt and Company LLC

175 Fifth Avenue, New York, NY 10010
tel +1 646-307-5238
website http://us.macmillan.com/henryholt

History, sports, politics, biography, memoir, novels. Imprints: Henry Holt, Metropolitan Books, Times Books, Holt Paperbacks. Founded 1866.

The Johns Hopkins University Press*

2715 North Charles Street, Baltimore, MD 21218–4319
tel +1 410-516-6900
email tcl@press.jhu.edu
website www.press.jhu.edu

History, literary criticism, classics, politics, environmental studies, biology, medical genetics, consumer health, religion, physics, astronomy, mathematics, education. Founded 1878.

Houghton Mifflin Harcourt*

222 Berkeley Street, Boston, MA 02116
tel +1 617-351-5000
website www.hmhco.com

Educational content and solutions for K-12 teachers and students of all ages; also reference, and fiction and non-fiction for adults and young readers. Founded 1832.

University of Illinois Press*

1325 South Oak Street, Champaign, IL 61820
tel +1 217-333-0950
email uipress@uillinois.edu
website www.press.illinois.edu
Director Laurie Matheson

American studies (history, music, literature, religion), working-class and ethnic studies, communications, regional studies, architecture, philosophy, women's studies, film, sports history, folklore, food studies. Founded 1918.

Indiana University Press

Office of Scholarly Publishing,
Herman B Wells Library 350, 1320 East 10th Street,
Bloomington, IN 47405–3907
tel +1 812-855 8817
email iupress@indiana.edu
website www.iupress.indiana.edu
Director Gary Dunham

Specialises in the humanities and social sciences: African, African–American, Asian, cultural, Jewish and Holocaust, Middle East, Russian and East European, and women's and gender studies; anthropology, film, history, bioethics, music, palaeontology, philanthropy, philosophy and religion. Imprint: Quarry Books (regional publishing). Founded 1950.

Infobase Publishing

132 West 31st Street, New York, NY 10001
tel +1 800-322-8755
website http://www.infobase.com/about/
Editorial Director Laurie E. Likoff

General reference books and services for colleges, libraries, schools and general public. Founded 1940.

Inkshares

114 Linden Street, Oakland, CA 94601
email hello@inkshares.com
website www.inkshares.com
Facebook www.facebook.com/inkshares
Twitter @Inkshares
Co-founder & Ceo Adam Gomolin, *Co-founder & Cpo* Thad Woodman, *Co-founder* Larry Levitsky

A book publisher that has readers, not agents or editors, decide what is published. Publishes books that successfully hit a pre-order threshold on the company's platform, or win a contest run in partnership with an imprint on the platform. The process is as follows: authors pitch, readers pre-order, and the company publishes. Any author can submit a proposal for a book. Once the project goes live, readers support the project by pre-ordering copies of the book. Once the 750 pre-order goal is hit, the work is published: authors are assigned an editor, a designer and the company deals with printing, distribution, marketing and publicity once the MS is finished.

University Press of Kansas

2502 Westbrooke Circle, Lawrence, KS 66045–4444
tel +1 785-864-4154
email upress@ku.edu
website www.kansaspress.ku.edu
Interim Director & Business Manager Conrad Roberts, *Editor-in-Chief* Joyce Harrison, *Acquisitions Editors* Kim Hogeland, David Congdon

American history (political, social, cultural, environmental), military history, American political thought, American presidency studies, law and constitutional history, political science. Founded 1946.

Knopf Doubleday Publishing Group

1745 Broadway, New York, NY 10019
tel +1 212-782-9000
website http://knopfdoubleday.com/
Chairman & Editor-in-Chief Sonny Mehta, *President* Tony Chirico

Alfred A. Knopf was founded in 1915 and has long been known as a publisher of distinguished hardback fiction and non-fiction. Imprints: Alfred A. Knopf, Anchor Books, Doubleday, Everyman's Library, Nan A. Talese, Pantheon Books, Schocken Books and Vintage Books.

Krause Publications

700 East State Street, Iola, WI 54990–0001
tel +1 800-258-0929
website www.krausebooks.com

Antiques and collectables: coins, stamps, automobiles, toys, trains, firearms, comics, records; sewing, ceramics, outdoors, hunting. Imprint of F&W Publications, Inc. Founded 1952.

Little, Brown & Company

1290 Ave of the Americas, New York, NY 10104
tel +1 212-364-1100
email lbpublicity.Generic@hbgusa.com
website www.littlebrown.com

General literature, fiction, non-fiction, biography, history, trade paperbacks, children's. Founded 1837.

Back Bay Books

Fiction and non-fiction. Founded 1993.

Little, Brown Books for Young Readers

website www.lb-kids.com, www.lb-teens.com
Publisher Megan Tingley, *Creative Director* Gail Doobinin

Picture books, board books, chapter books, novelty books and general non-fiction and novels for middle-grade and young adult readers.

Llewellyn Worldwide

2143 Wooddale Drive, Woodbury, MN 55125
tel +1 651-291-1970
email publicity@llewellyn.com
website www.llewellyn.com
Facebook www.facebook.com/LlewellynBooks
Twitter @llewellynbooks
Publisher Bill Krause

For over a century Llewellyn Worldwide Ltd has been a publisher of new age and mind, body & spirit books, including self-help, holistic health, astrology, tarot, paranormal and alternative spirituality titles. Founded 1901.

Lonely Planet

230 Franklin Road, Building 2B, Franklin, TN 37064
email go@lonelyplanet.co.uk
website www.lonelyplanet.com
Facebook www.facebook.com/lonelyplanet
Twitter @lonelyplanet

Lonely Planet is an international travel publisher, printing over 120 million books in 11 different languages. Along with guidebooks and ebooks to almost every destination on the planet. Also produces a range of gift and reference titles, a website, a magazine and a range of digital travel products and apps.

The Lyons Press

246 Goose Lane, Guilford, CT 06437
tel +1 203-458-4500
website www.lyonspress.com, swww.globepequot.com
Editor Contact Stephanie Scott

Fishing, hunting, sports, outdoor skills, horses, history, military history, reference, true crime, entertainment, and non-fiction. An imprint of Globe Pequot Press. Founded 1978.

McGraw-Hill Professional*

2 Penn Plaza, 12th Floor, New York, NY 10121
tel +1 212-904-2000
website www.mhprofessional.com

McGraw-Hill Business

Management, investing, leadership, personal finance.

McGraw-Hill Consumer

Non-fiction: from health, self-help and parenting, to sports, outdoor and boating books. Publishing partnerships include Harvard Medical School and Standard & Poor's.

McGraw-Hill Education

Test-prep, study guides, language instruction, dictionaries.

McGraw-Hill Medical

Harrison's and reference for practitioners and medical students.

McGraw-Hill Technical

Science, engineering, computing, construction references.

Macmillan Publishers, Inc.*

175 Fifth Avenue, New York, NY 10010
tel +1 646-307-5151
email press.inquiries@macmillanusa.com
website http://us.macmillan.com

Imprints: Bedford/St Martins; Farrar, Straus & Giroux; Farrar, Straus & Giroux BYR; Feiwel & Friends; 01 First Second; Henry Holt and Company; Henry Holt BYR; Macmillan Audio; Picador; Square Fish; St Martin's Press; Tor/Forge (see Tom Doherty Associates, LLC on page 230); W.H. Freeman; and Worth.

McPherson & Company

PO Box 1126, Kingston, NY 12402
tel +1 845-331-5807
email bmcphersonco@gmail.com
website www.mcphersonco.com
Facebook www.facebook.com/McPherson-and-Company/
Twitter @bookmaverick
Publisher Bruce R. McPherson

Literary fiction; non-fiction: art criticism, writings by artists, film-making; occasional general titles (e.g. anthropology). No poetry. No unsolicited MSS; query first. Distributed in UK by Central Books, London. Imprints: Documentext, Treacle Press, Saroff Books. Founded 1974.

The University of Massachusetts Press*

671 North Pleasant Street, Amherst, MA 01003
tel +1 413-545-2217
email info@umpress.umass.edu
website www.umass.edu/umpress
Director Mary Dougherty, *Executive Editor* Matt Becker

Scholarly books and works of general interest: American studies and history, Black and ethnic studies, women's studies, cultural criticism, architecture and environmental design, literary criticism, poetry, fiction, philosophy, political science, sociology, books of regional interest. Founded 1964.

The University of Michigan Press*

839 Greene Street, Ann Arbor, MI 48104–3209
tel +1 734-764-4388
email um.press@umich.edu
website www.press.umich.edu/
Director Charles Watkinson

Scholarly and general interest works in literary and cultural theory, classics, history, theatre, women's studies, political science, law, American history, American studies, anthropology, economics, jazz; textbooks in English as a second language; regional trade titles. Founded 1930.

Microsoft Press

One Microsoft Way, Redmond, WA 98052–6399
tel +1 425-882-8080
email 4bkideas@microsoft.com
website https://www.microsoft.com/en-gb/learning/microsoft-press-books.aspx
Publisher Ben Ryan

Computer books. Division of Microsoft Corp. Founded 1983.

Milkweed Editions*

1011 Washington Avenue South, Suite 300, Minneapolis, MN 55415

tel +1 612-332-3192
email editor@milkweed.org
website www.milkweed.org
Editor Abby Travis

Fiction, poetry, essays, the natural world, children's novels (8–14 years). Founded 1979.

University of Missouri Press

113 Heinkel Building, 201 South 7th Street, Columbia, MO 65211
tel +1 573-882-7641
email upress@missouri.edu
website http://upress.missouri.edu
Facebook www.facebook.com/University-of-Missouri-Press/
Twitter @umissouripress
Editor-in-Chief Andrew Davidson

American and European history; African–American studies; U.S. military history; women's studies; sports history; American and British literary criticism; journalism; political science; regional studies. Founded 1958.

The MIT Press

One Rogers Street, Cambridge, MA 02142–1209
tel +1 617-253-5646
website https://mitpress.mit.edu
Director Amy Brand

Architecture, art and design, cognitive sciences, neuroscience, linguistics, computer science and artificial intelligence, economics and finance, philosophy, environment and ecology, new media, information science, game studies, bioethics, communications, education, engineering, physical science, mathematics. Founded 1962.

William Morrow – see HarperCollins Publishers

Thomas Nelson Publisher

PO Box 141000, Nashville, TN 37214
tel +1 800-251-4000
email publicity@thomasnelson.com
website www.thomasnelson.com
Ceo Mark Schoenwald

Acquired by HarperCollins in 2012. Bibles, religious, non-fiction and fiction general trade books for adults and children. Founded 1798.

University of New Mexico Press

1717 Roma NE, MSC05 3185, Albuquerque, NM 87131-0001
tel +1 505-277-3495
email custserv@unm.edu
website www.unmpress.com
Interim Director Richard Schuetz, *Managing Editor* James Ayers

Western history, anthropology and archaeology, Latin American studies, photography, multicultural literature, fiction, poetry. Founded 1929.

The University of North Carolina Press*

116 South Boundary Street, Chapel Hill, NC 27514
tel +1 919-966-3561
website www.uncpress.unc.edu
Editorial Director Mark Simpson-Vos

American history, American studies, Southern studies, European history, women's studies, Latin American studies, political science, anthropology and folklore, classics, regional trade. Founded 1922.

North Light Books – see Writer's Digest Books

North Point Press – see Farrar, Straus and Giroux, LLC

Northland Publishing – see Cooper Square Publishing

NorthWord Books for Young Readers – see Cooper Square Publishing

W.W. Norton & Company, Inc.*

500 Fifth Avenue, New York, NY 10110
tel +1 212-354-5500
website www.wwnorton.com
Vice President & Editor-in-Chief John Glusman

Literary fiction and narrative non-fiction, history, politics, science, biography, music and memoir.

University of Oklahoma Press

2800 Venture Drive, Norman, OK 73069–8216
tel +1 405-325-2000
website www.oupress.com
Director B. Byron Price, *Editor-in-Chief* Adam C. Kane

American West, American Indians, classics, political science. Founded 1928.

OR Books

137 West 14th Street, New York, NY 10011
tel +1 212 514 6485
email info@orbooks.com
website www.orbooks.com
Facebook www.facebook.com/orbooks/
Twitter @orbooks
Co-founders John Oakes, Colin Robinson

OR Books publishes by printing on demand, selling directly to the customer, and focusing on creative promotion through traditional media and the Internet. Publishes non-fiction: literature, history and politics, activism, society, the Internet and the Middle East. Founded 2009.

Orbit – see Hachette Book Group

The Overlook Press

141 Wooster Street #4B, New York, NY 10012
tel +1 212-673-2210
website www.overlookpress.com
Facebook www.facebook.com/overlookpress
Twitter @overlookpress
President & Publisher Peter Mayer

Non-fiction, fiction, children's books (*Freddy the Pig* series). Imprints: Ardis Publishing, Duckworth. Founded 1971.

Oxford University Press*

198 Madison Avenue, New York, NY 10016
tel +1 212-726-6000
website https://global.oup.com/academic
Ceo Nigel Portwood

Academic and trade, bibles; ELT and ESL; dictionaries; higher education and science, technology, medicine and scholarly; law, medicine and music; journals; online; reference. Publishes globally for a range of audiences, across a multitude of cultures, education systems and languages. Currently publishes more than 6,000 titles a year worldwide, in a variety of formats. Many of these titles are created specifically for local markets and are published by regional publishing branches.

Paragon House Publishers

3600 Labore Road, Suite 1, St. Paul, Minnesota, MN 55110–4144
tel +1 651-644-3087
email paragon@ParagonHouse.com
website www.ParagonHouse.com
President Gordon L. Anderson

Textbooks and general interest in philosophy, religion, social sciences and non-fiction.

Pelican Publishing Company

1000 Burmaster Street, Gretna, LA 70053
tel +1 504-368-1175
email editorial@pelicanpub.com
website www.pelicanpub.com
Publisher & President Kathleen Calhoun Nettleton

Art and architecture, cookbooks, biography, history, business, children's, motivational, political science, social commentary, holiday. Founded 1926.

Penguin Publishing Group*

375 Hudson Street, New York, NY 10014
tel +1 212-366-2000
website www.penguin.com
President Allison Dobson

The Penguin Publishing Group is a leading adult trade book division with a wide range of imprints. Imprints: Avery, Berkley, Dutton, Pamela Dorman Books, Penguin Books, Penguin Press, Plume, Portfolio, Putnam, TarcherPerigee, Riverhead, Sentinel and Viking.

Penguin Random House*

1745 Broadway, New York, NY 10019
tel +1 212-782-9000
website www.penguinrandomhouse.com
Ceo Madeline McIntosh

With 250 independent imprints and brands on five continents, more than 15,000 new titles and close to 800 million print, audio and ebooks sold annually, Penguin Random House is the world's leading trade book publisher. The company, which employs about 12,500 people globally, was formed on July 1, 2013 by Bertelsmann and Pearson, who own 75% and 25%, respectively. Like its predecessor companies, Penguin Random House is committed to publishing adult and children's fiction and non-fiction print editions, and is a pioneer in digital publishing. Its book brands include storied imprints such as Doubleday, Viking and Alfred A. Knopf (US); Ebury, Hamish Hamilton and Jonathan Cape (UK); Plaza & Janés and Alfaguara (Spain); and Sudamericana (Argentina); as well as the international imprint DK. See Crown Publishing Group (page 230), Knopf Doubleday Publishing Group (page 233). Penguin Publishing Group (above), Random House Publishing Group (page 237), Penguin Young Readers (below) and Random House Children's Books (page 237).

Penguin Young Readers*

345 Hudson Street, New York, NY 10014
tel +1 212-366-2000
website www.penguin.com/children
President Jen Loja

Penguin Young Readers is one of the leading children's book publishers in the US. The company owns a wide range of imprints and trademarks including Dial Books, Dutton, Grosset & Dunlap, Kathy Dawson Books, Nancy Paulsen Books, Penguin Workshop, Philomel, Puffin, G.P. Putnam's Sons, Viking, Razorbill, Speak and Frederick Warne. Penguin Young Readers is also the proud publisher of perennial brand franchises such as the *Nancy Drew* and *Hardy Boys* series, *Peter Rabbit*, *Spot*, the *Classic Winnie the Pooh*, *The Very Hungry Caterpillar*, *Madeline*, *Mad Libs*, the *Rangers Apprentice*, *Skippyjon Jones*, *Who Was?* and *Flower Fairies* among many others. Penguin Young Readers is a division of Penguin Group LLC, a Penguin Random House company.

University of Pennsylvania Press

3905 Spruce Street, Philadelphia, PA 19104–4112
tel +1 215-898-6261
email custserv@pobox.upenn.edu
website www.pennpress.org
Director Eric Halpern

American and European history, anthropology, architecture, cultural studies, ancient studies, human rights, literature, medieval and early modern studies, Jewish studies, religious studies, current affairs, politics and public policy, urban studies and Pennsylvania regional studies. Founded 1890.

Pennsylvania State University Press*

820 North University Drive, USB1, Suite C, University Park, PA 16802
tel +1 814-865-1329
email info@psupress.org
website www.psupress.org
Director Patrick Alexander

Art history, literary criticism, religious studies, philosophy, political science, sociology, history, Latin American studies and medieval studies. Founded 1956.

The Permanent Press

4170 Noyac Road, Sag Harbor, NY 11963
tel +1 631-725-1101
website www.thepermanentpress.com
Facebook www.facebook.com/ThePermanentPress
Twitter @TPermanentPress
Directors Martin Shepard, Judith Shepard, Chris Knopf

Literary fiction. Imprint: Second Chance Press. Founded 1978.

Philomel – see Penguin Young Readers

Plume – see Penguin Publishing Group

Popular Woodworking – see Writer's Digest Books

Portfolio – see Penguin Publishing Group

Potomac Books, Inc.

c/o Longleaf Services, Inc, 116 S Boundary St, Chapel Hill NC 27514
tel +1 800-848-6224
email customerservice@longleafservices.org
website http://www.nebraskapress.unl.edu/potomac/

National and international affairs, history (military and diplomatic); reference, biography. Purchased by the University of Nebraska Press in 2013. Founded 1984.

Princeton University Press*

Princeton, NJ 08540
tel +1 609-258-4900
Postal address 41 William Street, Princeton, NJ 08540
website www.press.princeton.edu
Director Christie Henry, *Editor-in-Chief* Al Bertrand

Scholarly and scientific books on all subjects. Founded 1905.

Puffin Books – see Penguin Young Readers

Quarto Publishing Group USA

401 Second Avenue North, Suite 301, Minneapolis, MN 55401
website www.quarto.com

Creates and publishes illustrated books in North America and sells co-editions of them internationally. Subject categories include home improvement, gardening, practical arts and crafts, Licensed children's books, transport, graphic arts, food and drink, sports, military history, Americana, health and body, lifestyle, pets and music. The division comprises of 15 imprints; Book Sales, Cool Springs Press, Creative Publishing International, Fair Winds Press, Motorbooks, Quarry Books, QDS, Quiver, Race Point Publishing, Rock Point, Rockport Publishers, Voyageur Press, Walter Foster Publishing, Walter Foster, Jr. and Zenith Press. Details of the imprints can be found on the website. Founded 2004.

Rand McNally

PO Box 7600, Chicago, IL 60680
tel +1 847-329-8100
website www.randmcnally.com

Maps, guides, atlases, educational publications, globes and children's geographical titles and atlases in print and electronic formats.

Random House Children's Books*

1745 Broadway, New York, NY 10019
tel +1 212-782-9000
website www.randomhousekids.com, www.randomhouse.com/teachers
President & Publisher Barbara Marcus

Random House Children's Books (RHCB) is the world's largest English-language children's trade book publisher. Creating books for preschool children through young adult readers, in all formats from board books to activity books to picture books, novels and non-fiction, RHCB brings together award-winning authors and illustrators, world-famous franchise characters and multimillion-copy series. Imprints: Alfred A. Knopf Books for Young Readers, Crown Books for Young Readers, Delacorte Press, Doubleday Books for Young Readers, Random House Books for Young Readers, Rodale Kids, Little Golden Books, Make Me A World, Schwartz & Wade Books, Wendy Lamb Books, Ember, Dragonfly, Yearling Books, Laurel-Leaf, Princeton Review and Sylvan Learning. Part of Penguin Random House (page 236).

Random House Publishing Group*

1745 Broadway, New York, NY 10019
tel +1 212-782-9000
website www.randomhousebooks.com
President & Publisher Gina Centrello

The Random House Publishing Group was formed upon the unification of the Random House Trade Group and the Ballantine Books Group in 2003. In 2008, the group added imprints from the Bantam Dell, Spiegel & Grau and Dial Press divisions, creating a creative powerhouse which publishes many of the best authors in both literary and commercial genres. Imprints: Ballantine Books, Bantam Books, Delacorte Press, Dell, Del Rey, The Dial Press, Modern Library, Random House, and Spiegel & Grau. Part of Penguin Random House (page 236).

Razorbill – see Penguin Young Readers

Rising Moon – see Cooper Square Publishing

Rizzoli International Publications, Inc.

300 Park Avenue South, New York, NY 10010
tel +1 212-387-3400
email publicity@rizzoliusa.com
website www.rizzoliusa.com
Publisher Charles Miers

Art, architecture, photography, fashion, gardening, design, gift books, cookbooks. Founded 1976.

Rodale Book Group

733 Third Avenue, New York, NY 10017
tel +1 212-573-0300
website www.rodale.com
Ceo Maria Rodale

General health, women's health, men's health, senior health, alternative health, fitness, healthy cooking, gardening, pets, spirituality/inspiration, trade health, biography, memoir, current affairs, science, parenting, organics, lifestyle, self-help, how-to, home arts. Founded 1932.

Routledge

711 Third Avenue, New York, NY 10017
tel +1 212-216-7800
website www.routledge.com

Music, history, psychology and psychiatry, politics, business studies, philosophy, education, sociology, urban studies, religion, film, media, literary and cultural studies, reference, English language, linguistics, communication studies, journalism. Editorial office in the UK. Subsidiary of Taylor & Francis, LLC. Imprint: Routledge. Founded 1834.

Rowman & Littlefield

4501 Forbes Boulevard, Suite 200, Lanham, MD 20706
tel +1 301-459-3366
email customercare@rowman.com
website www.rowman.com
Facebook www.facebook.com/rowmanuk
Twitter @rowmanuk
President & Ceo James E. Lyons

Rowman & Littlefield is an independent publisher specialising in academic publishing in the humanities and social sciences, government and official data and educational publishing.

Running Press Book Publishers

2300 Chestnut Street, Suite 200, Philadelphia, PA 19103
tel +1 215-567-5080
email perseus.promos@perseusbooks.com
website www.runningpress.com
Publisher Chris Navratil

General non-fiction, TV, film, humor, history, children's fiction and non-fiction, food and wine, pop culture, lifestyle, illustrated gift books. Imprints: Running Press, Running Press Miniature Editions, Running Press Kids, Running Press Adults. Member of the Perseus Books Group. Founded 1972.

Rutgers University Press

106 Somerset Street, Third Floor, New Brunswick, NJ 08901
tel +1 800-848-6224
website www.rutgersuniversitypress.org
Director Micah Kleit, *Editorial Director* Kimberly Guinta

Women's studies, anthropology, film and media studies, sociology, public health, cultural studies, clinical health, medicine, history of medicine, Asian–American studies, African–American studies, American studies, Jewish studies, regional titles. Founded 1936.

St Martin's Press, Inc.*

175 Fifth Avenue, New York, NY 10010
tel +1 212-677-7456
website http://us.macmillan.com/smp

Trade, reference, college. No unsolicited MSS. Imprints: Griffin, Minotaur, St. Martin's Press, Thomas Dunne Books, Castle Point Books, Wednesday Books and All Point Books. Founded 1952.

Scholastic, Inc.*

557 Broadway, New York, NY 10012
tel +1 212-343-6100
email news@scholastic.com
website www.scholastic.com
Facebook www.facebook.com/scholastic
Twitter @scholastic

Scholastic is the world's largest publisher and distributor of children's books and a leader in education technology and children's media. Divisions: Scholastic Trade Publishing, Scholastic Book Clubs, Scholastic Book Fairs, Scholastic Education, Scholastic International, Media, Licensing and Advertising. Imprints include: Arthur A. Levine Books, Cartwheel Books, Chicken House, David Fickling Books, Graphix, Orchard Books, Point, PUSH, Scholastic en español, Scholastic Focus, Scholastic Licensed Publishing, Scholastic Nonfiction, Scholastic Paperbacks, Scholastic Press, Scholastic Reference and The Blue Sky Press. In addition, Scholastic Trade Books includes Klutz, a highly innovative publisher and creator of "books plus" for children. Founded 1920.

Sentinel – see Penguin Publishing Group

Sheridan House, Inc.
15200 NBN Way, Blue Ridge Summit, PA 17214
tel +1 800-462-6420
email customercare@nbnbooks.com
website www.rowman.com
President James E. Lyons

Sailing, nautical, travel. Founded 1940.

Simon & Schuster Children's Publishing Division*
1230 Avenue of the Americas, New York, NY 10020
tel +1 212-698-7200
website www.simonandschuster.com/kids
President & Publisher Jon Anderson

Preschool to young adult, fiction and non-fiction, trade, library and mass market. Imprints: Aladdin Paperbacks, Atheneum Books for Young Readers, Beach Lane Books, Little Simon, Margaret K. McElderry Books, Simon & Schuster Books for Young Readers, Simon Pulse, Salaam Reads, Simon Spotlight, Paula Wiseman Books. More detail of some of the imprints are given below. Division of Simon & Schuster, Inc. Founded 1924.

Simon & Schuster, Inc*
1230 Avenue of the Americas, New York, NY 10020
tel +1 212-698-7000
website www.simonandschuster.com
President & Ceo Carolyn K. Reidy

General fiction and non-fiction. No unsolicited MSS. Imprints: 37 Ink, Adams Media, Aladdin, Atria Books, Atheneum Books for Young Readers, Beach Lane Books, Beyond Words, Caitlyn Dlouhy Books, Emily Bestler Books, Enliven, Folger Shakespeare Library, Free Press, Gallery Books, Gallery 13, Howard Books, Jeter Publishing, Little Simon, Marble Arch Press, Margaret K. McElderry, Paula Wiseman Books, Pocket Books, Pocket Star, Saga Press, Salaam Reads, Scout Press, Scribner, Simon & Schuster, Simon & Schuster Books for Young Readers, Simon Pulse, Simon Spotlight, Star Trek®, Strebor Books, Threshold Editions, Touchstone, Washington Square Press. Founded 1924.

Soho Press, Inc.
853 Broadway, New York, NY 10003
tel +1 212-260-1900
email soho@sohopress.com
website www.sohopress.com
Facebook www.facebook.com/SohoPress
Twitter @soho_press
Publisher Bronwen Hruska

Literary fiction, commercial fiction, mystery, memoir. Founded 1986.

Sourcebooks Inc.
1935 Brookdale Road, Suite 139, Naperville, IL 60563
tel +1 630-961-3900
website www.sourcebooks.com
Facebook www.facebook.com/sourcebooks
Twitter @Sourcebooks
Publisher & Ceo Dominique Raccah, *Vice President & Editorial Director* Todd Stocke, *Assistant Publisher* Kay Mitchell

A leading independent publisher with a wide variety of genres including fiction, romance, children's, young adult, gift/calendars and college-bound. E-commerce businesses include *Put Me In the Story*, the #1 personalized books platform. Founded 1987.

Stanford University Press*
500 Broadway, Redwood City, CA 94063
tel +1 650-723-9434
email information@www.sup.org
website www.sup.org

Scholarly (humanities and social sciences), professional (business, law, economics and management science), high-level textbooks. Founded 1893.

Ten Speed Press
1745 Broadway, 10th Floor, New York, NY 10019
tel +1 510-559-1600
website http://crownpublishing.com/imprint/ten-speed-press/
President Phil Wood, *Publisher* Lorena Jones

Career/business, cooking, practical non-fiction, health, women's interest, self-help, children's. Imprints: Celestial Arts, Crossing Press, Tricycle Press. Founded 1971.

University of Tennessee Press
110 Conference Center Building, Knoxville, TN 37996
tel +1 865-974-3321
website www.utpress.org
Director Scot Danforth

American studies: African–American studies, Appalachian studies, history, religion, literature, historical archaeology, folklore, vernacular architecture, material culture. New series, *Legacies of War and America's Baptists*. Founded 1940.

University of Texas Press*
3001 Lake Austin Blvd, 2,200 Stop E4800, Austin, TX 78703–4206
tel +1 512-471-7233
email info@utpress.utexas.edu
website www.utexaspress.com
Facebook www.facebook.com/utexaspress
Director David Hamrick

A book and journal publisher – a focal point where the life experiences, insights and specialised knowledge of writers converge to be disseminated in both print and digital format. Founded 1950.

Tuttle Publishing/Periplus Editions

Airport Business Park, 364 Innovation Drive, North Clarendon, VT 05759
tel +1 802-773-8930
email info@tuttlepublishing.com
website http://www.tuttlepublishing.com/
Ceo Eric Oey, *Publishing Director* Ed Walters

Asian art, culture, cooking, gardening, Eastern philosophy, martial arts, health. Founded 1948.

Two-Can Publishing – see Cooper Square Publishing

Viking Press – see Penguin Publishing Group

Walker & Co.

175 Fifth Avenue, New York, NY 10010
tel +1 212-674-5151
website www.walkerbooks.com, www.bloomsburykids.com

General. Walker Books and Walker Books for Young Readers are imprints of Bloomsbury Publishing Plc (page 157).

University of Washington Press

4333 Brooklyn Avenue NE, Seattle, WA 98105
Postal address Box 359570, Seattle, WA 98195-9570
tel +1 206-543-4050
website www.washington.edu/uwpress
Director Nicole Mitchell

American studies; anthropology; art history and visual culture; Asian American studies; Asian studies; critical ethnic studies; environmental history; Jewish studies; Native American and Indigenous studies; nature and environment; Scandinavian studies; sustainable design; women's, gender, and sexuality studies; and Western and Pacific Northwest history. The press also publishes a broad range of books about the Pacific Northwest for general readers, often in partnership with regional museums, cultural organizations, and local tribes. Founded 1920.

WaterBrook Multnomah Publishing Group

10807 New Allegiance Drive Suite 500, Colorado Springs, CO 80921
tel +1 719-590-4999
email info@waterbrookmultnomah.com
website www.waterbrookmultnomah.com
Vice President & Publisher Alexander Field

Fiction and non-fiction with a Christian perspective. No unsolicited MSS. Subsidiary of Penguin Random House (page 236). Founded 1996.

Watson-Guptill Publications

c/o Penguin Random House, 1745 Broadway, New York, NY 10019
tel +1 212-782-9000, +1 212-572-6066
website http://crownpublishing.com/imprint/watson-guptill/

Art, crafts, how-to, comic/cartooning, photography, performing arts, architecture and interior design, graphic design, music, writing, reference. Imprints: Amphoto Books, Watson-Guptill. Founded 1937.

Westminster John Knox Press*

100 Witherspoon Street, Louisville, KY 40202–1396
tel +1 502-569-8400
website www.wjkbooks.com
President & Publisher Marc Lewis

Scholarly reference and general books with a religious/spiritual angle. Division of Presbyterian Publishing Corp.

John Wiley & Sons, Inc.*

111 River Street, Hoboken, NJ 07030
tel +1 201-748-6000
email info@wiley.com
website www.wiley.com
President & Ceo Brian A. Napack

Specialises in scientific, technical, medical and scholarly journals; encyclopedias, books and online products and services; professional/trade books, subscription products, training materials and online applications and websites; and educational materials for undergraduate and graduate students and lifelong learners. Founded 1807.

Workman Publishing Company*

225 Varick Street, New York, NY 10014
tel +1 212-254-5900
email info@workman.com
website www.workman.com
Editor-in-Chief Susan Bolotin

Non-fiction including parenting. Founded 1968.

Writer's Digest Books

10151 Carver Road, Suite 200, Cincinnati, OH 45242
tel +1 513-531-2690
email writersdigest@fwmedia.com
website www.writersdigest.com

Market directories, books and magazine for writers, photographers and songwriters. Imprint of F&W Media Inc. Founded 1920.

Family Tree
Genealogy.

North Light Books

Fine art, decorative art, crafts, graphic arts instruction books.

Popular Woodworking

How-to in home building, remodelling, woodworking, home organisation.

Yale University Press*

PO Box 209040, New Haven, CT 06520-9040
tel +1 203-432-0960
UK office 47 Bedford Square, London WC1B 3DP
website www.yale.edu/yup

Scholarly, trade books and art books.

Yen Press*

Hachette Book Group, 1290 Avenue of the Americas, New York, NY 10104
email yenpress@hbgusa.com
website www.yenpress.com
Facebook www.facebook.com/yenpress
Twitter @yenpress

Graphic novels and manga in all formats for all ages. Currently not seeking original project pitches from writers who are not already working with an illustrator. For submission guidelines see under Contact on website. Division of Hachette Book Group (page 231). Founded 2006.

Audio publishers

Many of the audio publishers listed below are also publishers of print books. As the audio market grows and evolves in line with listeners' preferences, new entrants are offering a range of digital streaming solutions, often on a monthly subscription basis.

Audible

email bizdev_uk@audible.co.uk
website www.audible.co.uk
Twitter @audibleuk

Producer and seller of digital audio entertainment, including fiction and non-fiction audiobooks for adults and children. Publishers keen to enquire about business opportunities with Audible can email on the address above, or find out more about turning print books into audiobooks at www.acx.com. Founded 1995; acquired by Amazon 2008.

Audiobooks.com

website www.audiobooks.com
Twitter @audiobooks_com

Subscription audio book service, offering a wide range fiction and non-fiction genres, as well as some children's titles.

BookBeat

email info@bookbeat.com
website www.bookbeat.com/uk
Twitter @BookBeatUK

Digital streaming service for adult and children's audiobooks across a variety of fiction and non-fiction genres. Monthly subscription model. Owned by Bonnier. Founded 2017.

Canongate Audio Books

14 High Street, Edinburgh EH1 1TE
tel 0131 557 5111
email support@canongate.co.uk
website www.canongate.co.uk
Audio Director Jamie Byng, *Audio and Online Manager* Jo Lord

Classic literature including the works of Jane Austen, Charles Dickens, D.H. Lawrence and P.G. Wodehouse; also current literary authors, such as Yann Martel and Nick Cave. Publishes approx. 25 titles per year and has 150 titles available, including many short stories. Founded 1991 as CSA Word; acquired by Canongate 2010.

Cló Iar-Chonnacht Teo

Indreabhán, Conamara, Co. Galway, Republic of Ireland
tel +353 (0)91 593307
email eolas@cic.ie
website www.cic.ie
Ceo Micheál Ó Conghaile, *General Manager* Deirdre O'Toole

Irish-language novels, short stories, plays, poetry, songs; CDs (writers reading from their works), downloads and bilingual books. Promotes the translation of contemporary Irish poetry and fiction into other languages. Founded 1985.

Creative Content Ltd

Roxburghe House, 273–287 Regent Street, London W1B 2HA
tel 07771 766838
email ali@creativecontentdigital.com
website www.creativecontentdigital.com
Publisher Ali Muirden, *Editorial Director* Lorelei King

Publishes audio digital downloads and ebooks in the business, language improvement, self-improvement, lifestyle, crime fiction, sci-fi, short stories and young adult genres. Founded 2008.

Hachette Audio

Carmelite House, 50 Victoria Embankment, London, EC4Y 0DZ
email louise.newton@littlebrown.co.uk
email sarah.shrubb@littlebrown.co.uk
website www.littlebrown.co.uk
Audio Publisher Sarah Shrubb

Audiobook list that focuses on unabridged titles from Little, Brown's bestselling authors such as Iain Banks, J.K. Rowling, Sarah Waters, Donna Tartt and Mark Billingham, as well as classics including Joseph Heller's *Catch-22*, John Steinbeck's *Of Mice and Men* and Hans Fallada's *Alone in Berlin*. Publishes approx. 200 audiobooks per year. Founded 2003.

HarperCollins Publishers

The News Building, 1 London Bridge Street, London, SE1 9GF
tel 020-8285 4658
website www.harpercollins.co.uk
Twitter @HarperCollinsUK
Audio Director Rachel Mallender, *Senior Audio Editor and Producer* Tanya Hougham, *Senior Audio Editor* Fionnuala Barrett, *Editor* Jack Chalmers, *Audio Assistant* Catriona Morrison

Publishers of award-winning fiction and non-fiction audiobooks for adults and children. An imprint of HarperCollins. Founded 1990.

Hodder & Stoughton Audiobooks

Carmelite House, 50 Victoria Embankment, London EC4Y 0DZ
tel 020-7873 6000

email dominic.gribben@hodder.co.uk
website www.hodder.co.uk
Publisher Dominic Gribben

Fiction and non-fiction audiobooks from within the Hodder group. Authors include Stephen King, John Grisham, Jodi Picoult, Graham Norton, Miranda Hart and Sir Alex Ferguson.

W. F. Howes Ltd

Unit 5, St George's House, Rearsby Business Park, Gaddesby Lane, Rearsby, Leicester LE7 4YH
tel (01664) 423000
email info@wfhowes.co.uk
website www.wfhowes.co.uk

Audiobook and large-print publisher; also digital services provider. Releases c. 60 new and unabridged audiobooks monthly. Works with a range of large UK publishers, including Penguin Random House and HarperCollins. Founded 1999; acquired by RBmedia 2017.

Isis/Soundings

Isis Publishing Ltd, 7 Centremead, Osney Mead, Oxford OX2 0ES
tel (01865) 250333
website www.isis-publishing.co.uk
Twitter @Isisaudio
Chief Executive Michele Petty

Complete and unabridged audiobooks: fiction, non-fiction, autobiography, biography, crime, thrillers, family sagas, mysteries, romances.

Kobo

website www.kobo.com/gb/en
Twitter @kobo

Audiobook streaming service, for a monthly fee. Offers fiction, non-fiction, adult, children's and YA titles.

Library Magna Books Ltd

Magna House, Long Preston, Skipton, North Yorkshire BD23 4ND
tel (01729) 840225
email helen.bibby@magnaprint.co.uk
website www.ulverscroft.co.uk
Managing Director Michele Petty

Publisher of large print and unabridged audio. Supplies libraries worldwide with some of the best-known authors in library lending. Publishes a range of fiction and non-fiction titles and specialises in family sagas. Part of the Ulverscroft Group. Founded 1973.

Macmillan Digital Audio

20 New Wharf Road, London N1 9RR
tel 020-7014 6000
email audiobooks@macmillan.co.uk
website www.panmacmillan.com
Publishing Director for Audio Rebecca Lloyd

Adult fiction, non-fiction and autobiography, and children's. Founded 1995.

Naxos AudioBooks

5 Wyllyotts Place, Potters Bar, Herts. EN6 2JD
tel (01707) 653326
email info@naxosaudiobooks.com
website www.naxosaudiobooks.com
Managing Director Anthony Anderson

Classic literature, modern fiction, non-fiction, drama and poetry on CD. Also junior classics and classical music. Founded 1994.

The Orion Publishing Group Ltd

Carmelite House, 50 Victoria Embankment, London EC4Y 0DZ
tel 020-3122 6876
email salesinformation@orionbooks.co.uk
website https://www.orionbooks.co.uk/
Senior Audio Manager Paul Stark

Adult fiction and non-fiction. Founded 1998.

Penguin Random House UK Audio

20 Vauxhall Bridge Road, London SW1V 2SA
tel 020-7840 8400
website www.penguinrandomhouse.co.uk
Managing Director Hannah Telfer

Includes classic and contemporary fiction and non-fiction, autobiography, poetry and drama. Authors include Jo Nesbø, Lee Child, Kathy Reichs, Nick Hornby, Claire Tomalin, Zadie Smith and Paula Hawkins.

Simon & Schuster Audio

Simon & Schuster UK, 1st Floor, 222 Gray's Inn Road, London WC1X 8HB
tel 020-7316 1900
email enquiries@simonandschuster.co.uk
website www.simonandschuster.co.uk/audio
Publisher Jo Dickinson

Fiction and non-fiction audiobooks. Fiction authors include Philippa Gregory, Milly Johnson and Chris Carter. Non-fiction authors include Rhonda Byrne, Bruce Springsteen, Walter Isaacson and David Grann. Founded 1997.

SmartPass Ltd

15 Park Road, Rottingdean, Brighton, BN2 7HL
tel (01273) 306203
email info@smartpass.co.uk
website www.smartpass.co.uk

Unabridged plays, poetry and dramatisations of novels as guided full-cast dramas for individual study and classroom use. Shakespeare Appreciated: full-cast unabridged plays with an explanatory commentary. SPAudiobooks: full-cast unabridged dramas of classic and cult texts.

Ulverscroft Group Ltd

The Green, Bradgate Road, Anstey, Leicester LE7 7FU
tel 0116 236 4325
email m.merrill@ulverscroft.co.uk
website www.ulverscroft.co.uk
Facebook www.facebook.com/ulverscroft
Twitter @UlverscroftUK

Offers a wide variety of large print titles in hardback and paperback format as well as abridged and unabridged audiobooks on CD, MP3 CD and digital download, many of which are written by the world's favourite authors and includes award-winning titles. Acquired Oakill Publishing and its range of unabridge audiobooks April 2018. Founded 1964.

Book packagers

Many illustrated books are created by book packagers, whose particular skills are in the areas of book design and graphic content. In-house desk editors and art editors match up the expertise of specialist writers, artists and photographers who usually work on a freelance basis.

Aladdin Books Ltd

PO Box 53987, London SW15 2SF
tel 020-3174 3090
email sales@aladdinbooks.co.uk
website www.aladdinbooks.co.uk

Full design and book packaging facility specialising in children's non-fiction and reference. Founded 1980.

Nicola Baxter Ltd

16 Cathedral Street, Norwich NR1 1LX
tel (01603) 766585, 07778 285555
email nb@nicolabaxter.co.uk
website www.nicolabaxter.co.uk
Director Nicola Baxter

Full packaging service for children's books in both traditional and digital formats. Happy to take projects from concept to finished work or supply bespoke authorial, editorial, design, project management or commissioning services. Produces both fiction and non-fiction titles in a wide range of formats, for babies to young adults and experienced in novelty books and licensed publishing. Founded 1990.

Bender Richardson White

PO Box 266, Uxbridge, Middlesex UB9 5NX
tel (01895) 832444
email brw@brw.co.uk
website www.brw.co.uk
Directors Lionel Bender (editorial), Kim Richardson (sales & production), Ben White (design)

Specialises in children's and young people's natural history, science and family information. Opportunities for freelancers. Founded 1990.

Breslich & Foss Ltd

2A Union Court, 20–22 Union Road, London SW4 6JP
tel 020-7819 3990
email sales@breslichfoss.co.uk
website www.breslichfoss.co.uk
Directors Paula G. Breslich, K.B. Dunning

Books produced from MS to bound copy stage from in-house ideas. Specialising in crafts. Founded 1978.

Brown Bear Books Ltd

1st Floor, 9–17 St Albans Place, London N1 0NX
tel 020-7424 5640
website www.windmillbooks.co.uk
Children's Publisher Anne O'Daly

Specialises in high-quality illustrated reference books and multi-volume sets for trade and educational markets. Opportunities for freelancers. Imprint of Windmill Books (page 247).

John Brown Group – Children's Division

8 Baldwin Street, London EC1V 9NU
tel 020-7565 3000
email andrew.hirsch@johnbrownmedia.com
website www.johnbrownmedia.com
Directors Andrew Hirsch (operations), Sara Lynn (creative)

Creative development and packaging of children's products including books, magazines, teachers' resource packs, partworks, CDs and websites.

Cambridge Publishing Management Ltd

Unit 2, Burr Elm Court, Main Street, Caldecote, Cambs. CB23 7NU
tel (01954) 214000
email j.dobbyne@cambridgepm.co.uk
website www.cambridgepm.co.uk
Facebook www.facebook.com/cambridgepm
Twitter @CambridgePM
Managing Director Jackie Dobbyne, *Editorial Manager* Katie Silvester

Provides a streamlined route to publication for publishers, non-profits, charitable foundations and corporate clients. Offers complete project management from author commissioning and management through design, editorial and production to the supply of print-ready or digital files. The company's core activities are conducted in-house. Manages titles in a number of subject areas, from art and business to education and policy reports. Uses an extensive network of trusted freelance specialists who enable the company to provide quality content while the project managers fulfil the pivotal role of ensuring publications are delivered on time, within budget and to clients' exact specification. Founded 1999.

Chase My Snail

19 Darnell House, Royal Hill, London SE10 8SU
tel 0785 267 5689, +27 (0)82 822 8221 (South Africa)
email headsnail@chasemysnail.com
website www.chasemysnail.com
Publishing Director Daniel Ford

Produces top-quality books, especially non-fiction sports, fitness and travel publications, for the co-edition market. Handles writing, editing, proofing and design to take the book through from concept to final files. Has a wide range of book ideas already developed for publishers looking to extend their lists. Operates in London and Johannesburg.

Creative Plus Publishing Ltd

2nd Floor, 151 High Street, Billericay,
Essex CM12 9AB
tel (01277) 633005
email enquiries@creative-plus.co.uk
website www.creative-plus.co.uk
Facebook www.facebook.com/CreativePlusPublishingLtd
Publishing Director Claire Coakley

Provides all editorial and design from concept to final files for books, partworks and magazines. Specialises in female interest, children's, gardening, illustrated non-fiction and instructional video production. Opportunities for freelancers. Founded 1989.

Diagram Visual Information Ltd

34 Elaine Grove, London NW5 4QH
tel 020-7485 5941
email info@diagramgroup.com
website www.diagramgroup.com
Directors Jane Johnson, Patricia Robertson

Research, writing, design and illustration of reference books, supplied as disks. Founded 1967.

Eddison Books Ltd

St Chad's House, 148 King's Cross Road,
London WC1X 9DH
tel 020-7837 1968
email info@eddisonbooks.com
website www.eddisonbooks.com
Director Stéphane Leduc

Illustrated non-fiction books, kits and gift titles for the international co-edition market. Broad, popular list including mind, body & spirit; health; personal development; and parenting, childcare and brain-training.

Edition

PO Box 1, Moffat, Dumfriesshire DG10 9SU
tel (01683) 220808
email jh@cameronbooks.co.uk
Director Jill Hollis

Illustrated non-fiction. Design, editing, typesetting and production from concept to finished book for galleries, museums, institutions and other publishers. Founded 1976.

Elwin Street Productions Ltd

14 Clerkenwell Green, London EC1R 0DP
tel 020-7253 3044
email silvia@elwinstreet.com
website www.elwinstreet.com
Director Silvia Langford, *Rights Director* Elena Battista, *Production Manager* Marion Storz

Trade imprint: Modern Books. Illustrated co-edition publisher of adult non-fiction: reference, visual arts, popular sciences, lifestyle, gastronomy, health and nutrition, parenting, gift and humour.

Global Blended Learning Ltd

Singleton Court, Wonastow Road,
Monmouth NP25 5JA
tel (01993) 706273
email info@hlstudios.eu.com
website www.globalblendedlearning.com

Primary, secondary academic education (geography, science, modern languages) and co-editions (travel guides, gardening, cookery). Multimedia (CD-Rom programming and animations). Opportunities for freelancers. Founded 1985.

Graham-Cameron Publishing & Illustration

59 Hertford Road, Brighton BN1 7GG
tel (01273) 385890
email enquiry@gciforillustration.com
Alternative address The Art House, Uplands Park, Sheringham, Norfolk NR26 8NE
tel (01263) 821333
website www.gciforillustration.com
Partners Helen Graham-Cameron, Duncan Graham-Cameron

Educational and children's books; information publications; sponsored publications. Illustration agency with 37 artists. Do not send unsolicited MSS. Founded 1985.

Hart McLeod Ltd

14A Greenside, Waterbeach, Cambridge CB25 9HP
tel (01223) 861495
email jo@hartmcleod.co.uk
website www.hartmcleod.co.uk
Director Joanne Barker

Primarily educational and general non-fiction with particular expertise in illustrated books, school texts, ELT and electronic and audio content. Opportunities for freelances and work experience. Founded 1985.

Heart of Albion

2 Cross Hill Close, Wymeswold,
Loughborough LE12 6UJ
tel (01509) 881342
email albion@indigogroup.co.uk
website www.hoap.co.uk
Director Bob Trubshaw

Not currently seeking submissions. Founded 1989.

Ivy Press Ltd

Ovest House, 58 West Street, Brighton,
East Sussex BN1 2RA
tel (01273) 487440
email applications@ivy-group.co.uk
website www.ivypress.co.uk
Twitter @QuartoExplores

International Publisher Simon Gwynn

Publishers of illustrated trade books on art, science, popular culture, design, children's non-fiction, natural history and Conscious Living. Opportunities for authors and freelancers. Part of the Quarto Group (page 201). Founded 1996.

Lexus Ltd

47 Brook Street, Glasgow G40 2QW
tel 0141 556 0440
email peterterrell@lexusforlanguages.co.uk
website www.lexusforlanguages.co.uk
Director P.M. Terrell

Publisher of language books, especially language learning material and phrasebooks: *Lexus Travelmate* series (15 titles) and *Chinese Classroom* series (two textbooks and CD-Rom with speech recognition); *Insider China*; *UK4U* (written in Chinese). Also dual language books: *Cross Over into Gaelic* series (*Maggie Midge, Scottish Folk Tales*); *Scottish Folk Tales* in English and French; *ScotlandSpeak*, a wordbook for Scotland. For children: dual language books for young children, *Mess on the Floor*, with audio app (French, German, Spanish and Scottish Gaelic); *Gaelic Gold*, a learner's dictionary/phrasebook; *What's in a Scottish Placename?* Founded 1980.

Little People Books

The Home of BookBod, Knighton,
Radnorshire LD7 1UP
tel (01547) 520925
email littlepeoplebooks@thehobb.tv
website www.littlepeoplebooks.co.uk
Directors Grant Jessé (production & managing), Helen Wallis (rights & finance)

Packager of audio, children's educational and textbooks, digital publications. Parent company: Grant Jessé UK.

Market House Books Ltd

Suite B, Elsinore House, 43 Buckingham Street,
Aylesbury, Bucks. HP20 2NQ
tel (01296) 484911
email books@mhbref.com
website www.markethousebooks.com
Twitter @markethousebook
Directors Jonathan Law (editorial), Anne Kerr (production)

Book packagers with experience in producing reference books from small pocket dictionaries to large multi-volume colour encyclopedias and from specialist academic reference books to popular books for crossword enthusiasts. Deals with publishers worldwide. Services offered include: start-to-finish project management; commissioning of writers and editors; writing and rewriting; editing and copy-editing; proofreading; checking of final pages; keyboarding; typesetting; page design and make-up; text conversion; data manipulation; database management. Founded 1970.

Orpheus Books Ltd

6 Church Green, Witney, Oxon OX28 4AW
tel (01993) 774949
email info@orpheusbooks.com
website www.orpheusbooks.com, www.Q-files.com
Executive Directors Nicholas Harris, Sarah Hartley

Children's illustrated non-fiction/reference books and ebooks. Orpheus Books are the creators of Q-files.com, the free online children's encyclopedia. Founded 1993.

Salamander – see Pavilion Books

Toucan Books Ltd

The Old Fire Station, 140 Tabernacle Street,
London EC2A 4SD
tel 020-7250 3388
website www.toucanbooks.co.uk
Directors Robert Sackville West, Ellen Dupont

International co-editions; editorial, design and production services. Founded 1985.

Windmill Books Ltd

Unit 1/D, Leroy House, 436 Essex Road,
London N1 3QP
tel 020-3176 8603
website www.windmillbooks.co.uk
Children's Publisher Anne O'Daly

Publisher and packager of books and partworks for trade, promotional and international publishers. Opportunities for freelancers. Imprint: Brown Bear Books Ltd (page 245).

Working Partners Ltd

9 Kingsway, 4th Floor, London WC2B 6XF
tel 020-7841 3939
email enquiries@workingpartnersltd.co.uk
website www.workingpartnersltd.co.uk
Managing Director Chris Snowdon, *Operations Director* Charles Nettleton

Children's and young adult fiction series. Genres include: animal fiction, fantasy, horror, historical, detective, magical, adventure. No unsolicited MSS or illustrations. Pays advance and royalty; retains copyright on all works. Selects writers from unpaid writing samples based on specific brief. Looking to add writers to database: to register: www.workingpartnersltd.co.uk/apply/. Founded 1995.

Working Partners Two

Managing Director Charles Nettleton

Adult fiction. Aims to create novels across most adult genres for UK, USA and international houses. See above for submission guidelines. Founded 2006.

Book clubs

Baker Books

Manfield Park, Cranleigh, Surrey GU6 8NU
tel (01483) 267888
email enquiries@bakerbooks.co.uk
website www.bakerbooks.co.uk

International school book club for children aged 3–16. Operates in international and English-medium schools.

Bibliophile

31 Riverside, 55 Trinity Buoy Wharf, London E14 0FP
tel 020-7474 2474
email orders@bibliophilebooks.com
website www.bibliophilebooks.com
Proprietor Annie Quigley

Promotes value-for-money reading. Upmarket literature and classical music on CD available from mail order catalogue (10 p.a.). Over 3,000 titles covering art and fiction as well as travel, history and children's books. Founded 1978.

The Book People Ltd

Park Menai, Bangor LL57 4FB
tel 0845 602 4040
email marketing@thebookpeople.co.uk
website www.thebookpeople.co.uk

Popular general fiction and non-fiction, including children's and travel. Monthly.

The Folio Society

Clove Building, 4 Maguire Street, London SE1 2NQ
tel 020-7400 4222
website www.foliosociety.com
Twitter @foliosociety

Publishers of illustrated fiction, non-fiction and poetry books. Founded 1947.

Letterbox Library

Unit 151, Stratford Workshops, Burford Road, London E15 2SP
tel 020-8534 7502
email info@letterboxlibrary.com
website www.letterboxlibrary.com
Twitter @LetterboxLib

Booksellers, specialising in children's books that celebrate inclusion, equality and diversity.

The Poetry Book Society

c/o Inpress Ltd, Churchill House, 12 Mosley Street, Newcastle upon Tyne, NE1 1DE
tel 0191 230 8100
email pbs@inpressbooks.co.uk
website www.poetrybooks.co.uk
Twitter @PoetryBookSoc

Runs a quarterly poetry book club, with poet selectors choosing the best new collection of the quarter. Also operates online poetry bookshop, and publishes the *Bulletin* quarterly review of new poetry (available to full members). See also page 368.

Red House

PO Box 142, Bangor LL57 4FBZ
tel 0845 606 4280
email enquiries@redhouse.co.uk
website www.redhouse.co.uk

A member of The Book People family. Aims to help parents to select the right books for their children at affordable prices. Founded 1979.

Scholastic Book Fairs

Westfield Road, Southam, Warks. CV47 0RA
tel 0800 212281
email info@scholastic.co.uk
website https://bookfairs.scholastic.co.uk/
Twitter @scholasticuk

Sells directly to children, parents and teachers through 25,000 week-long events held in schools throughout the UK. See Scholastic Ltd.

For the love of language and books

David Lodge notes how, through all the changes and challenges in the today's fast-moving world, aspiring writers must love and treasure the incomparable medium of the English language and all its potential.

I am 83 years old at the time of writing this. I was about 16 when I conceived the ambition to be a writer, and 25 when my first novel was published in 1960. It was a very different world for aspiring writers from the one that they inhabit now. There were no personal computers with word-processing software that makes revision physically effortless; there was no internet, no Amazon for self-publishing and no Google for looking up things without moving from your desk; there were no creative writing courses in universities, very few literary prizes, and not very many literary agents. I did not think of acquiring an agent until after I had published my second novel. As I lived in London, I submitted the typescript of my first novel to publishers by hand to save the cost of postage, and the third one I tried accepted it. I got their addresses from the *Writers' & Artists' Yearbook*.

The *WAYB* is just about the only thing that is common to that world and the world of the writer today. Unlike many once-respected reference books which have succumbed to competition from the internet, the *WAYB* remains an indispensable companion for anyone seriously committed to the profession of author, whether full-time or part-time; and as always it is particularly valued by those who are setting out hopefully on that vocational path. The current edition is twice as thick as the first one I bought in the early 1950s. There are far more publishers, agencies and media in existence than there were then; and more ways in which a writer's words can be communicated to readers, many of which exploit the enormous reach and flexibility of the internet. The modern *WAYB* not only lists the institutions, organizations, companies, etc that operate between writers and the public; it gives practical advice on how to approach them and present work in an appropriate form.

But while there are far more opportunities for writers today than there were when I wrote my first novel, there are also many more people keen to take advantage of them. The struggle to succeed in any particular field, be it prose fiction or non-fiction or poetry or drama or any other form, is intense – much more so, I think, than it was when I started out. The digitalisation of information has made the production and circulation of writing easier and cheaper than ever before, but has also made it more competitive and less remunerative for most authors.

A writer must love the kind of writing that they pursue – and that can only come from immersion in the work of other writers, the great and the good of the past and present – in order to persist in the perennial task of finding something original and interesting to say, often in the face of rejection and indifference. Fortunately there are enough examples of writers who have achieved that to give every aspiring writer hope.

When I am asked for advice on how to write well I say, 'Try to read your own work as if you didn't write it – as if you are a reader coming to it for the first time.' Sometimes it helps to read it aloud. It always helps to put it aside for a while and come back to it with a fresh eye and an alert inner ear. Then you notice the clichés, ambiguities, intrusive sound patterns, unmotivated repetitions of words, and similar flaws that will irritate your reader

– sometimes only subliminally, but they disturb the illusion you are creating, or the continuity of a story you are telling, or of an argument you are presenting.

Basically, you must love your medium, language, and specifically the English language, some variety of which is the first or adopted language of most users of this book. Modern English is incomparable in the range of its vocabulary and the flexibility of its syntax. Historically it evolved from a fusion of Anglo-Saxon, Latin, French and other Romance languages, and incorporated words derived from many other languages. This mix created many synonyms, or near synonyms, which have different tonal effects. The grammar of English also allows for a great variety of rhythm, in prose as well as verse, and a wide range of choice between rhetorical elaboration and colloquial simplicity. With a small adjustment, the same word can often act as a noun, a verb, an adjective or adverb, without the addition of other words. It is impossible to exaggerate what an expressive advantage this protean medium is to a writer. And if you are successful in getting your work published, you have a potential global audience whose first or second language is English.

David Lodge, CBE, FRSL is an award-winning novelist, playwright and screenwriter, and the author of many works of literary criticism. A graduate and Honorary Fellow of University College London, he is Emeritus Professor of English Literature at the University of Birmingham. David's first published novel was *The Picturegoers* (McGibbon & Kee 1960) and subsequent novels include *Out of the Shelter* (Macmillan 1970), his trilogy of campus novels, *Changing Places* (1975), *Small World* (1984) and *Nice Work* (1988), *Therapy* (1995), *Thinks...* (2001) and *Author, Author: A Novel* (2004), all published by Secker & Warburg. *How Far Can You Go?* won the Whitbread Book of the Year 1980 and *Small World* and *Nice Work* were both shortlisted for the Booker Prize for Fiction. David has adapted his own and other writers' novels for television, and his stage plays include *The Writing Game* and *Home Truths*. His latest novels are *Deaf Sentence* (Harvill Secker 2008), based on his own experience of deafness and *A Man of Parts (H.G. Wells)* (2011), and *Quite a Good Time To Be Born: A Memoir 1935–75* was published in 2015. A sequel, *Writer's Luck: A Memoir 1976-1991*, was published in 2018.

Stronger together: writers united

Novelist Maggie Gee encourages writers to get together to cultivate writing friendships and to make full use of the wide range of advice and support writers' organisations have to offer.

Do you remember the YouGov research (February 2015) that found being an author was the most desired 'job' in Britain? Apparently more than 60% of Brits think they would like it. YouGov, slightly oddly, concluded that the 'aura of prestige' around the 'quiet, intellectual life' was what attracted people. I wonder if the real reason that being an author is so popular is because people think authors just stay at home – enjoying a sort of perpetual sickie that protects them from public transport, bosses and colleagues, while their million-pound royalties gracefully accrete of their own accord?

It's not like that any more. Vanishingly rare are the authors who do nothing but write books in solitary studies, self-basting in a silent aura of prestige. Now more than ever authors need meeting-places, networks, publicity, legal and financial support, friends and colleagues, critics and fans, and – far too often – day-jobs. The most recent research commissioned by the Authors' Licensing and Collecting Society (ALCS, see page 707), the highly effective organisation that protects writers' rights and collects, on our behalf, money due from the copying or broadcasting of our work all over the world, tells us that writers' incomes have shrunk by around a third since 2005, and the proportion of full-time professional writers has gone down from 40% to 11%. In that landscape, we need writers' organisations to watch our back. New writers should join ALCS and register for Public Lending Right (PLR, see page 143), the organisation that ensures the government pays authors money every time their books are taken out from libraries.

And don't forget to make good writing friendships. I discovered the importance of this very early on. I had, it's true, been writing poetry and novels in solitary bedsits throughout my twenties. Those hours of lonely application doubtless gave me technique, but they didn't give me a publisher; there were no creative writing MAs back then and I didn't know any writers. But out of the blue I got a letter from a small publisher saying they were starting 'a small, serious fiction list' (this would not happen today) and asking if I had a novel in a bottom drawer which they could look at 'with a view to finding the statue in the stone.'

I sent off my manuscript. Six months later, I got a letter offering publication and a £500 advance. I still vividly remember drinking to the future that had so suddenly arrived, in the open air as the evening sky deepened to indigo over Turnham Green.

If this sounds too good to be true, it was. Not long after the joyous bottle of wine on the grass another letter came from the publisher asking if I would 'support' them in their 'desire to continue publishing serious fiction' by forgoing my advance. I was outraged, not least by that weaselling choice of words. I was working double shifts as a receptionist in a hotel to pay the rent and I could barely support myself – how could I support a publisher? Soon I was trying not to cry with frustration as I constantly ran out of coins in a faulty public phone box, explaining to writer Robert Hewison of the Writers' Guild (WGGB, see page 522) what had happened. To his credit, even though I was not a member, he gave me good advice, and he also told me to join a union. I had got my first taste of a central truth about this business: writing may happen alone but, to get that writing safely out into the world, we need other people.

What else did I learn from that first novel? Put not your faith in princes or publishers, put your faith in publicity and good pals. When a writer-journalist friend of mine, Anthony Holden, loved the novel and arranged for a full-page excerpt to be published in *The Times*, my publisher suddenly contacted me to say they would pay me the money after all.

Though publishers and writers both break them, contracts are vital. The percentage share that authors get of electronic and translation rights for example, or of copies sold at a discount, are vital to our livelihood. It's all in the small print, and a novice eye can't spot problems. New writers, especially if they don't have an agent, should join one of the writers' trades unions when they are offered their first contract. Both the Society of Authors (SoA, see page 519) and the Writers' Guild (the latter typically for film and theatre writers) offer members a free contract-vetting service. Over my 40-year career the Society of Authors has been there for me in a few tight corners: when I couldn't use a computer for six months because of RSI, they gave me a £3,000 Francis Head bequest; when one of my publishers broke a contract, they supported my agent in extracting a payment.

After I had published a few novels I was asked to do a stint with other writers on the Society of Authors' management committee. Every month we heard riveting stories about the disputes between writers and publishers that the Society was trying to sort out. Sometimes the writers had behaved abominably (which was shocking but thrilling), but it seemed to me that, more often, the publishers were trying to get away with murder and the legal weight of the Society was needed to restrain them.

I subesquently served for six years on the Public Lending Right Committee, seven years on the Council of the Royal Society of Literature, four of those as its first woman Chair, and in 2015 I was elected to the Board of ALCS. It's easier for writers to trust organisations run by writers. Novelists Maureen Duffy and Brigid Brophy were the driving force behind the Writers' Action Group (WAG) who set up ALCS and Public Lending Right. ALCS has distributed over £400 million to authors since it began collecting money for rights which authors simply don't have time to collect themselves; it has approximately 90,000 members. My PLR payments, despite ongoing cuts to libraries, have over the decades paid for new computers, research trips and, in the early days, the rent. PLR Registrar Jim Parker has helped other countries set up their own PLR schemes, too, for authors' causes are international. ALCS has founded not only the Parliamentary Writers' Group, where writers lobby ministers, MPs and lords about forthcoming legislation, but also the International Authors' Forum (IAF) which has 52 member organisations from 28 countries and makes sure writers' voices are heard when copyright law is being discussed at the United Nations.

Not everyone is an activist. The Society of Authors has an extensive programme of social events, some in London, some nationwide. Meeting other writers does matter. Despite Samuel Beckett's reputation for proud and lonely artistic innovation, in Paris as a young man he cultivated James Joyce and had a wide range of literary and artistic contacts. Of course publishers want authors to be active and popular on Facebook and Twitter, but virtual friends will never be quite as warm as the ones you meet in the flesh. Plus, using your legs is a good way of avoiding the health hazards of sitting still all day writing and tweeting. Instead, look out for tweets about events and launches and, if the event is public, turn up – in most cities there will be something literary going on, and by getting out there you will be showing interest in other people's work, which may even be returned. Literary salons offer a mix of music, readings and drinks. The longest-lasting and most diverse of these is probably Book Slam (www.bookslam.com), started by the author Patrick Neate.

The Royal Society of Literature holds regular talks, readings and workshops at Somerset House.

One of the best ways of making writer allies near the beginning of a career is to attend a creative writing group or course (see *Writers' retreats and creative writing courses*, page 678). I have taught creative writing in too many places to mention over the years, for ground-breaking organisations like Arvon with its week-long stays for groups of 16 in stunning countryside, from Devon to Moniack Mhor in Scotland, and for London's Spread the Word, with its innovative programme, affordable prices and urban edge. More recently I've taught on the Faber 'Writing a Novel' course, which takes groups of up to 14 through six months of development as novelists in leafy Bloomsbury. Arriving very nervous at the beginning, they are soon meeting up after class every week for shrieks of laughter in the pub.

Currently I am a professor on one of the country's most high-profile Creative Writing MAs, at Bath Spa University, from which novelists like Nathan Filer, Tessa Hadley and Samantha Harvey have graduated, and where, after becoming successful novelists, they now teach part-time. The groups there are small – usually only eight. Regularly reading and commenting on each other's work, these writers start to love each other's projects, and afterwards, when one gets published, the whole group receives a boost. Agents and publishers come and visit. Despite the hard work and occasional blips (for writers are sensitive, sometimes prickly, creatures) all the courses I remember teaching on have been happy places with a huge amount of laughter.

Alas, in the end socialising is not writing – talking is not writing. Complaining to a sympathetic ear about not writing is definitely not writing. The more you get hooked in to the communal aspect of the writers' life, the more fiercely you will have to protect your ability to write the book you want in your own way. Even if there are only eight writers in your group, you can't respond to all their differing comments. What will really help is finding the voice or couple of voices that you trust, probably the ones that correspond to the small internal voice that already knows what is good and bad about your book. Those particular readers are gold dust, yet still you have to make the final decisions yourself.

Writers in groups often find it hard when the regular sessions finish. Frequently their writing stalls for a bit. Writers have to be able to work the central magic by themselves at some point. They have to find a space far enough away from the social, active, competitive world to dream up an alternative one and polish it to an obsessive sheen.

Then, when the story is almost ready to go, other people come in again: a good first reader who you will probably have found and grown to trust already; a good agent; and a good publisher. Then good bookshops to sell your work in; no writer I have ever known has managed to build an actual 'relationship' with Amazon. If you see a book of yours in a bookshop, booksellers are often delighted if you introduce yourself and offer to sign it. Good luck.

Maggie Gee, OBE's most recent novel, *Virginia Woolf in Manhattan* (Telegram 2014) is a comedy that brings Virginia Woolf back to life in the 21st century in New York and Istanbul. She has written a memoir, *My Animal Life* (Telegram 2010); a collection of short stories, *The Blue* (2006); and 12 acclaimed novels, including *The White Family* (Saqi Books 2002), shortlisted for the Orange Prize, and two comedies about the UK and Uganda, *My Cleaner* and *My Driver* (Telegram 2009). She was the first female Chair of the Royal Society of Literature (2004–8) and is currently one of its Vice-Presidents. An international conference about her work was held at St Andrew's University, Scotland, in 2012. She is Professor of Creative Writing at Bath Spa University and a non-executive Director of ALCS. Follow her on Twitter @maggiegeewriter.

Managing a successful writing career

Tony Bradman shares the five guiding principles that have helped him successfully sustain the writing career he has always wanted and worked to achieve, stressing the importance of bolstering talent with market knowledge, all-round professionalism and some much-needed resilience.

I was probably about 15 when I decided I wanted to be a writer. Like most writers, I had become an obsessive bookworm at an early age and, after years of spending all my pocket money on books as well as borrowing them from the local library, I had begun to think it would be marvellous to write some of my own. Imagine having your name on the cover of a book you had written yourself! I couldn't think of anything more amazing, and from that moment on I never seriously considered any other kind of career.

Of course, I had a sneaking feeling it might not be all that easy to get published. But I was convinced I would manage it and that, once I'd written a few books, everything would fall into place. As I explained to my girlfriend at university ('She Who Is Now My Wife'), apparently there were these payments called *royalties*. Each book I published would keep earning money, so that after a while we could just sit back and watch the cash roll in.

I wasn't entirely stupid. I did realise that my writing (which mostly consisted of a few notebooks crammed with unfinished and very mediocre poems) might not be all that attractive to publishers – not yet, anyway. So I applied for jobs in journalism, with the idea that my employer would help me improve my writing and pay me into the bargain – I never doubted that I had talent. The plan seemed to work, too. I was employed by several magazines, and after a while I even began to do a bit of freelancing on the side.

Eventually I found myself working for *Parents*, a magazine about young family life. By then I was a parent myself, and I was surprised the magazine didn't review children's books, even though we were sent lots of review copies. I therefore persuaded the editor to let me write about them, and I started a regular column. Pretty soon I got to know the publicity people at most of the children's book publishers, and I also began to meet editors at book launches and other events. By then I was starting to think that I wanted to write for children myself, so when an editor asked me if I had any ideas for a children's book I seized the opportunity and sent her some rhymes I'd written for my daughters.

Those rhymes became the basis for my first picture book, and the rest, as they say, is history. More commissions followed, and my books sold well in the UK and abroad (this was the mid-1980s, the heyday of 'co-editions' in children's books). The royalties really did flow, and before long I was able to give up my job and become a full-time freelance. That was over 30 years ago, and I've managed to make a pretty good living as a writer ever since. It turned out not to be quite as easy as I had expected – far from it, in fact. But it can be done, and I offer you here the five principles on which I've based my career.

1. Cultivate your talent

I believe there is such a thing as talent. Some people are just better at certain things; you can see that in any artistic pursuit – writing, music, art, acting. And, to be brutal, if you haven't got talent then you're unlikely ever to achieve a career as a professional in any of those fields. Yes, I know from time to time we all read books, or watch plays or TV shows or films, that appear to have been written by someone with no talent whatsoever. But trust me, it would be very hard to sustain a long-term career without any talent at all.

So let's assume you have talent. The question is, what kind of talent do you have? I could have spent years trying to write poetry for grown-ups and not got anywhere at all. In my mid-20s I began to realise I wasn't ever going to be the next Seamus Heaney or Ted Hughes, but by then I'd also started to get interested in children's books. I wrote verse for my daughters, then picture book texts (which often depend on a poet-like ability to use language creatively). After that I steadily moved up the age range with my children, and discovered I had a talent for writing well-plotted stories that kept readers gripped.

I didn't leave it there though. I thought about what I was doing and tried to build on the things that worked, my aim being simply to get better. Back in the 1980s there weren't anywhere near as many creative writing courses, but there were plenty of books about the art and craft of writing, and I read as many as I could. I listened to my editors too, and tried to learn from them, and from anyone else who might give me insight into what makes good writing. I edited anthologies of short stories, which meant I often had to tell writers exactly why I didn't think their stories worked – and that was invaluable experience.

I believe this approach is the foundation of any writing career. Understanding your talent will help to make you a good writer. But you can always make yourself into a better one.

2. Know the market

This is the section of my piece that will be anathema to the purists, those who believe that writing shouldn't ever be about 'satisfying the needs of the market'. Some people believe that great writers simply write what they need to and that it will find its own way to a readership or an audience. Well, good luck with that if you want to make a living as a writer. Of course, your 1,000-page surrealist fantasy written without using the letter 'e' might well become a runaway bestseller and make you a fortune. But what if it doesn't?

I think it's perfectly possible to combine Art and Commerce as a writer; satisfying the needs of the market doesn't mean 'selling out'. If you want a good example, what about the greatest writer of all time – Shakespeare himself? It's clear from his plays that he wrote very consciously for 'the market' in theatre as it was then. But he also managed to produce the most sublime literary art. Awareness of what the market is interested in can often be very stimulating creatively – it may well give you plenty of ideas on what to write.

So how do you study the market? That's easy and fun. Simply read widely, or watch plays, films and TV shows in the areas you find interesting. Find out as much about them as possible – who's hot in your chosen field, and what's doing well. The more you know, the better. Networking is part of this, especially if you see it as something that will help you learn about the business of being a writer. Go on courses, join writing groups; editors and agents sometimes give talks at these, and they're the people you want to meet. Keep it up after you get published – opportunities will usually arise from the contacts you make. You will also be a better prospect for agents and editors if they feel you know the market.

3. Be professional (part one)

… or to put it another way, 'Don't Be Desperate or Grateful'. Begging for a commission won't get you anywhere and, if you are offered an opportunity, there's no need to be thankful. You should always be professional – and that means thinking of what you're doing as a job, the way you earn your living. It's the person who is commissioning you or buying your work who should be grateful. Your editor almost certainly has a target, a number of books to publish in a year, and you're the means of getting that done. *You* are the solution.

Being professional also means making sure you always keep up a high standard as far as your performance is concerned. You should follow the brief, hit the word count, and deliver a clean manuscript, that's as good as you can make it, by the deadline you've been given. If you can't deliver on time for whatever reason (it had better be a good one!), you should let your editor know, and agree a revised delivery date. If you're asked to do edits or revisions (and they're an essential part of being a writer), you should take it as positive criticism that aims to help make your writing better. If you disagree, say so – but be courteous.

The purpose is to present yourself as someone who is good to work with, 'a safe pair of hands' who can be trusted. With that kind of reputation, you will always get work.

4. Be professional (part two)

Being professional also means taking care of business, and that's something you should make a priority. The hard truth is that few writers earn a great deal from their writing, but if you want to make sure you can make a living, then you need to think about money. I've always thought of myself as the owner of a small business, so right from the beginning I took on an accountant, made sure I kept scrupulous records, and paid my taxes.

I've also always tried to think strategically in the way that good businesses have to. I keep track of what I'm earning and think about cashflow, as well as what I'm likely to earn over the next year (for a freelance it's hard to look much further than that). I then make judgements about what kind of work I'm going to do: if it's looking like a good year, I might think about doing something more speculative, maybe that story I've always wanted to write ...; if it's not looking good, then I start trying to drum up new commissions before I run out of money. I do a variety of things too – books, editing, reviews, bits of consultancy and teaching, school visits and festivals – the 'Many-Eggs-In-Many-Baskets' approach.

Having an agent helps, and the commission is tax-deductible. If your books are likely to be in libraries, you should sign up for Public Lending Right (PLR; see page 143), which will pay you for loans of your books. You should also become a member of the Authors' Licensing and Collecting Society (ALCS; see page 707), which collects money for secondary uses of our work such as photocopying, foreign PLR, cable re-transmission and so on. It all adds up, and even a small payment can come at a very useful time. You should also join a union, such as the Writers' Guild of Great Britain (WGGB; page 522), or the Society of Authors (page 519). They're great sources of support, information and networking for writers - you'll find details of all these organisations elsewhere in this excellent book – itself an essential tool for the professional.

5. Be resilient

Last but not least – you should bear in mind that there will be times when everything goes wrong. Books will be rejected or sell poorly, commissions will be hard to come by, favourite editors will move on, your particular area of experience will become unfashionable, royalties that once seemed secure will dry up. I've been through all of those things, and I've had my share of struggles with the usual demons we writers have to deal with – self-doubt, worry, periods of real stress.

But I kept going, through the bad times and the good, and I have my natural resilience (my 'bounce-back-ability') to thank for that. I might get knocked down, but I get up again, and if you don't think you can manage that, well, the life of a professional writer isn't for you. But if you do, and you're prepared to work hard, and have some talent to offer, you'll be fine.

I wish you the best of luck.

Tony Bradman has written for children of all ages, from babies to teenagers. He has edited many anthologies of short stories and poetry, and reviews children's fiction for the *Guardian*. He is also chair of ALCS and the Siobhan Down Trust.

See also...

- *Public Lending Right*, page 143
- *Stronger together: writers united*, page 251
- *Developing talent: support and opportunities for writers*, page 515
- *Society of Authors, page 519*
- *WGGB (Writers Guild of Great Britain)*, page 522
- *Authors' Licensing and Collecting Society*, page 707

First chapters: how to grab your reader's attention

Emma Flint lists the important considerations for a writer embarking on a new book and pinpoints some key elements that make for success when composing that all-important first chapter.

The first chapter of your book is your one chance to hook your reader. If you don't draw your reader in and make them want to continue, it doesn't matter how thrilling the climax in chapter eight is or how thought-provoking the ending is. If your first chapter doesn't work, your reader won't make it past chapter one.

On the plus side, no other part of your book can provide you with the kind of pay-off that a good first chapter can. A good first chapter can get the attention of a reader. Or an agent. Or a publisher.

Viewpoint

There are a number of decisions that you need to make in your first chapter. Firstly, from whose point of view are you telling the story? What kind of voice will work best for the story you're telling?

One of the most common mistakes novelists make is to have too many viewpoints and too many narrators. Keep it as simple as you can and never include more than one narrator if it's not absolutely essential to the plot.

You should never write your opening from a particular viewpoint and then abandon that voice. Don't allow your readers to invest emotionally in a character, and then neglect that character or kill them off early in the story – it will annoy and alienate your audience.

Setting

Your novel will almost certainly have more than one setting. However, in your first chapter you need only set up the rough location and the rough period for the opening of your main character's narrative.

Avoid trying to set up an opening scene in too much depth. Two pages of description about landscape or weather before you've begun the actual story is unlikely to draw a reader in. Conversely, if you can relate the setting of your novel to your characters, you give your reader a reason to care about the history of a building or the colours of a landscape before you start describing it in detail. Sarah Waters does this beautifully: look at how she introduces setting through character.

Character

In your opening chapter, your main character has one job and one job only: *to make your reader care about their story*.

Your readers don't need to like your main character. In the first chapter, they don't need to know everything about her, or understand her childhood. You need to give the reader just enough so that they care about her, about the situation she's in, and about what she wants.

And in order to show these things, you need to work out what you want your reader to learn about that character. If you're writing a murder mystery in which your main character poisons his wife, your reader probably needs to know in the first chapter that the character is having an affair, or that he's desperate for his wife's money.

The easiest way to bore your reader is to *tell* them about your main character, while the most effective way to *show* your readers something about your characters is through dialogue. Dialogue tells you about a person's background – where they're from, sometimes what kind of education they've had, often how old they are. It tells you their beliefs, their prejudices, and how they see the world.

What's the starting point of your story?

Broadly speaking, there are four ways in which you can open a novel:

• **Start with a prologue** – an episode that is not part of chapter one, but that relates somehow to your main story. It might not include the main character, or it might include the main character at a time outside of the central narrative – for example, when she's a child, or when he's looking back on the events of the novel from years later.
• **Put your main character in a scene**, doing something interesting related to the main story. It's almost always more effective to start your story with action rather than description. That action doesn't have to be dramatic – it can be as gentle as someone taking a bath or buying coffee. But what it must *not* be is a description of a character doing nothing – staring out of the window, reflecting on their broken marriage, fantasising. If it wouldn't be interesting to watch a character doing it at the beginning of a film, don't put it in the opening of your novel.
• **Begin in the middle**. Start at a point deep in the story and show a dramatic event; then, at the end of the scene, jump back to an earlier, quieter part of the narrative. To create this effect, you need to bring the reader into the scene late. Bring them in moments before the flight takes off, seconds before the gun is fired.

If you choose to use this method, you need to be aware of two things: firstly, this type of opening is used so often in mysteries and thrillers that it's in danger of becoming a bit of a cliché. Yours must be both original and surprising. Secondly, it can sacrifice suspense for that whole portion of the story until the narrative catches up with the first moment. If you open with your main character fleeing from a guy with a gun, how nervous will the reader be in chapter four when that same character is at risk of drowning? They already know that she survives, at least until she encounters the gunman. The risk is that this kind of opening can deflate any later tension you want to set up.
• **Use a framing device**, where your story is bookended at the front and back (and sometimes in a few instances in the middle) by a story that is outside the main story.

Think of *Alice in Wonderland*, where the main narrative is bookended by dreams. Or Mary Shelley's *Frankenstein*, which uses multiple framed narratives.

If you're writing a story that's very removed from the real life of your reader – perhaps set in a fantasy world – a framing device can be used to show someone like your reader coming in to hear the main story. Show the reader a character like them getting involved, and that way you make it easier for *them* to follow you as well.

In deciding how to open your novel, you need to work out what information is relevant to your story. Your characters have pasts and futures (unless you plan to kill them off).

The setting of your novel also has a past and a future. So, in a sense, every writer jumps into their story midway through.

Create immediacy

One way to plunge your reader into the story is to add detail that makes your writing realistic and credible. If you're writing an historical novel, do your research. If you're writing about a location that you're familiar with, show the reader that you know it well. But be careful to use that detail sparingly, rather than piling it on to show off your knowledge.

Another way is to create tension – and the easiest way to do this – is to set up conflict in the first chapter. Conflict feeds readers. It creates drama.

To generate conflict, you need a mini-plot. A fight scene is an example of conflict. But a fight scene alone isn't enough if the reader doesn't know who the characters are. They're not yet invested in them. A fight scene between two brothers is better. It ups the stakes a little. But a fight scene between two brothers, one of whom suspects the other of killing their mother, is better still. *Now* you have a story.

It's no accident that many great novels have first chapters that could stand as short stories. Every chapter should have its own mini-plot and its own mini-narrative arc, and this element is most important in chapter one.

Move the reader on

As you will know from your own reading, the more of a book you read and enjoy, the more you'll want to read; if you read the first page and liked it, you will read the second. If you read ten pages, you're likely to read twenty.

One of the functions of your first chapter is to get your reader on to the second. As a writer, you're like the witch in Hansel and Gretel … you're giving the reader breadcrumbs to follow. If they pick up one – in the form of a well-crafted line, or a believable character, or a moment of suspense – they'll be looking for the next one.

At the opening of your novel, those breadcrumbs need to be close together – because your reader isn't yet engaged. Following the fairy tale metaphor, they're still looking back at the edge of the forest. You need to *entice* them in.

And your first breadcrumb comes in the form of your first line.

First lines

A great first line is like a welcome marriage proposal: it makes the reader commit.

A first line needs to do one or more of several things:

1. It needs to be well-written, and memorable, and confident. There's no room in a first line for flabby language or clumsy wording.

– Take *Love in the Time of Cholera* by Gabriel Garcia Marquez: 'It was inevitable: the scent of bitter almonds always reminded him of the fate of unrequited love.'

2. The first line needs to give an indication of the story to come. It is a promise, or a question, or an unproven idea, which will be explored in the novel itself.

– Think of Jane Austen's *Pride and Prejudice*: 'It is a truth universally acknowledged, that a single man in possession of a good fortune must be in want of a wife.'

– or Dickens' *A Tale of Two Cities*: 'It was the best of times, it was the worst of times'.

3. A first line needs to say something interesting; it can show the reader a shattered status quo or subvert their expectations.

– Perhaps the best-known example of this is the opening line of George Orwell's *1984*: 'It was a bright cold day in April, and the clocks were striking thirteen.'
– The most effective examples of this type of opening line are often the shortest. Take Iain Banks' opening of *The Crow Road*: 'It was the day my grandmother exploded.'
– or the opening line of *Peter Pan* by J.M. Barrie: 'All children, except one, grow up.'

Ask yourself what questions you are raising in your opening sentence and paragraph, and whether they are interesting or memorable enough to draw readers in.

And two final and key points about opening chapters:

Firstly, your reader needs to understand from the first chapter what your book is about, and why you've written it. They need to feel the interest or the motivation or the passion that made you want to write it.

Secondly, *your first chapter must be interesting*. The absolute worst thing you can do is bore your reader. So be brave. Be bold. Open your book in a way that commands attention and engages curiosity.

Emma Flint graduated from the University of St Andrews with an MA in English Language and Literature and completed a novel-writing course at the Faber Academy. Her debut *Little Deaths*, a crime novel set in 1960s New York and based on a real-life murder, was published to wide acclaim in January 2017 and was longlisted for the Bailey's Women Prize for Fiction, for the Desmond Elliott Prize, and for the Crime Writers' Association Gold Dagger Award. Emma is working on her second novel, also based on a real-life murder, and set in London during the 1920s.

The path to a bestseller

Clare Mackintosh describes the vision, determination and hard work that propelled her along the road to becoming a bestselling author, and the passion and commitment needed to achieve that goal.

In 2011 I made one of the biggest decisions I've ever made. I was a police inspector with 12 years' service, a secure job, good pension, and a promising future ahead of me; and I gave it all up to write. There were other reasons, too – I wanted to see more of my family – but this creative driver was a huge factor. The mantra 'don't give up the day job' is a sound one for those who genuinely lack the skills or the talent to pursue their dreams, and it's a wise one for those who rely on said job to pay the bills. Few are those with the independent means to do exactly what they want. For me, giving up the day job was exactly the impetus I needed to make freelance life work. I had been the biggest wage-earner and, although our childcare costs dropped dramatically, I had no choice but to continue bringing home the bacon. I was determined I would achieve this by writing, but sensible enough to understand that I would need to interpret this loosely. I pitched opinion pieces, securing a commission from *Writers' Forum* and a column in *Cotswold Life*. I wrote for the *Guardian* and for any editor who liked my ideas enough to pay me for them. I wrote blogs for businesses in which I had no interest; social media content for companies about which I knew nothing. I wrote headlines, greetings cards, articles, columns and captions. Hundreds, thousands, millions of words. And every one taught me a little bit more about writing for a living – about deadlines, about working to brief, about budgeting, marketing, selling myself, believing in myself. The modern author is so much more than just a writer, and all these skills are important.

This period in my life lasted two years. Two years in which I was, variously, either 'paying the bills' or 'building a platform', depending on my frame of mind at the time. Building a platform, because my ultimate goal wasn't to be a journalist – although I loved the articles I was writing; and it wasn't to be a copywriter – although I was grateful for the work I had. I wanted to be an author. A novelist. I wanted a traditional publishing deal, with a 'Big Five' publisher and a literary agent who would help me build – and sustain – a career as a writer. I wanted to write a bestseller. It was a big goal; I was open to the idea that I might need to compromise, but at the same time fully committed to working towards it. It happened to other people. Why not me?

I had already dipped a toe into the literary world. Many of the words I had written had been on my own blog, one that had achieved a degree of success in terms of reach. A regular reader had put me touch with a literary agent, who asked to see the novel I was working on at the time – a light-hearted romantic comedy. The agent liked it, spending considerable time over the next year helping me work on a rewrite. Ultimately this proved a false start; I wasn't offered representation, and the novel, whilst funny, wasn't groundbreaking. 'Do you want this book to forever be your debut novel?', the agent asked me. 'Because you only get one shot at that first impression.' Wise advice. Was it my best work? It wasn't. Was I even especially proud of it? I wasn't. It was back to the drawing board.

I started writing *I Let You Go* without any understanding of the genre in which I was writing. Not comedy this time, that was sure, but was it a crime novel? Was it a thriller? I didn't know. I wrote a first draft, then floundered. What now? A chance encounter with a new acquaintance provided the answer. She loved the sound of my book – could she send it to a literary agent friend of hers? She had barely finished speaking before my manuscript was in her inbox.

This new friend and I agreed that she would submit the manuscript anonymously, to an agent whose name I wouldn't know. The goal was to seek objective feedback, with no associated embarrassment if I decided to submit to the same agent in the future. I agreed, but between you and me … I didn't stick to the plan. After all, what former detective in my shoes wouldn't have felt the urge to do a little snooping? I pieced together the facts. Female. A long-time friend. A shared holiday in France. A forthcoming trip to New York. With Morse-like tenacity I narrowed down potential agents to a shortlist I ruthlessly stalked on Twitter. Finally, I pinned it down to just one agent: Sheila Crowley at Curtis Brown. I was heady with excitement. Of all the agencies in the *Writers' & Artists' Yearbook*, Curtis Brown was my number one; of all the agents, Sheila was top of my list. And now she was reading my manuscript.

A week later, in December 2012, she rang and introduced herself. She liked the book. It needed work – a lot of work – but she liked it. I embarked on a rewrite and four months later Sheila decided we'd put it out on submission. 'Quietly,' I remember her saying, 'just to test the waters.' I dreamed of going to auction, of six-figure deals fêted in the *Bookseller*. I prayed for editors fighting over my manuscript. It didn't happen. What happened was a lot of lukewarm feedback. 'It doesn't leap out at me as one I can see how to publish,' one editor said. 'Neither the writing or the hook is quite strong enough to make it stand out,' said another. I tried to be objective, but each rejection was a blow.

In retrospect, I should have shrugged off those comments far more quickly than I did. If I've learned one thing over the last few years, it's the importance of passion in the publishing industry. The passion of an author, in writing a story that demands to be told. The passion of the agent, in pitching the story to an editor. The passion of an editor, not only in committing to the book, but in creating enthusiasm among the rest of a publishing house. This strength of feeling becomes inevitably diluted as it passes along the publishing chain; from editor to sales team, from sales reps to book buyers, from book buyers to store managers, from store managers to members of staff. Imagine how much passion a commissioning editor has to have, to ensure that – dozens of people down the chain – a member of staff in a chain of bookshops will hand-sell your book in such an enthusiastic way the customer cannot bring themselves to leave without buying it. In retrospect, I wouldn't have wanted any of those lukewarm editors to buy my book. I needed passion.

I found it in June 2013, in the form of Lucy Malagoni from Sphere, an imprint of Little, Brown Book Group, whose enthusiasm and vision for *I Let You Go* was evident from our first meeting. We accepted an offer, and then the hard work really started. I don't think I had any real understanding of editing until that point. I imagined some stylistic guidance, some typo correction, perhaps a little character enhancement. Nothing had prepared me for structural editing of such magnitude that each set of notes would plunge me into dark despair for at least 24 hours. I rewrote *I Let You Go* eight times in total, and would have lost all enthusiasm for it had I not been able to see that each draft – each painful, hideous, dragged-from-me draft – was producing a significantly better book. Tighter. Stronger. More suspenseful. Each draft added another layer and stripped out sub-plots that didn't work. Each draft taught me something new.

It was around this time that I looked at the goals I had set myself. I was (although it still feels odd to call myself one) a novelist. I had a publishing deal with a 'Big Five' house, and representation from a superb agent. Had I written a bestseller? I didn't think so. I revised my goals. I decided I wanted my first book to sell sufficient copies to keep my publishers happy. To ensure that bookshops were happy to stock my second book. I decided I would be a 'slow burn' author, hoping that each book would sell more than the last. With this in mind, I set myself a private goal of 50,000 sales. It seemed an extraordinary number, one that would take more than friends and family buying duty copies, so occasionally I told myself I'd be happy with 30,000. Or 15,000. By the time the ebook of *I Let You Go* came out, in November 2014, I had convinced myself I'd be happy if we sold 10,000 copies.

We sold 10,000 copies. In fact, despite very little publicity in the first few months (the marketing push being planned for the paperback) the book sold well. Word-of-mouth should never be underestimated, and the buzz on social media grew daily. Wisely, given I had little control over them, I stopped giving myself sales targets and started focusing on writing another book, wishing I was one of those authors with half a dozen unpublished manuscripts in their bottom drawers. 2015 was extraordinary. There's really no other way to describe it, and several years on it still feels faintly unreal. *I Let You Go* sold a million copies. It was picked as a Richard & Judy Book Club read (and won the readers' vote), and was discussed on ITV's 'Loose Women'. It became 2015's fastest selling debut from a new crime writer, with translation rights now sold to almost 40 territories. It hit the number one spot on Amazon UK for books and Kindle, and spent 12 weeks in the *Sunday Times* top ten. It turned out I had written a bestseller, after all.

Over the last five years I have worked, and continue to work, extremely hard. If you've ever envisaged life as an author to consist of wafting around in a smoking jacket, eating chocolates and occasionally scribbling creative brilliance in a Moleskine notebook, I assure you that the reality is very different (although no less enjoyable, and often featuring no less chocolate).

My advice? Think big. Set goals. Work hard. Talk about what you're doing. It's tempting to keep writing as a private activity, to avoid interminable questions from well-meaning relatives about whether you've finished it, and when can they read it, and are you going to be the next J.K. Rowling? But if you never tell anyone you're writing a book, you'll never benefit from that serendipitous moment when the person you do tell informs you that their neighbour's cousin's teacher's daughter is a literary agent, and would love to see your manuscript.

There's another reason to be out and proud about your writing, and it has to do with self-belief. If no one else knows that you're writing a book, then I would argue that it's hard to take it seriously yourself. Remember that passion I mentioned earlier? It starts with you. Believe in who you are and what you're doing, and others will believe in you too.

Tell people you're a writer. Because you are.

Clare Mackintosh spent 12 years in the police force, including time on CID and as a public order commander. She left the police in 2011 to work as a freelance journalist and social media consultant, and now writes full time. Her psychological thrillers, *I Let You Go* (Sphere 2015) and *I See You* (Sphere 2016) were both *Sunday Times* bestsellers. Her latest novel, *Let Me Lie*, was published in March 2018, also by Sphere. Visit Clare's website www.claremackintosh.com or find her at www.facebook.com/ClareMackWrites and on Twitter @claremackint0sh.

Books

Advice to a new writer

Rachel Joyce advocates that you take yourself seriously as a writer, so that others will too. It's important to 'know your stuff' and allow your writing to find its place in the world.

When I was 14, I finished my first novel. *Sisters* was short, I admit – possibly no more than 500 words. It was written in couplet form and was autobiographical. During the course of this tale, the older sister (*me*) did everything to save her two younger sisters (*mine*) from unhappiness, general uncleanliness and also TB (we had just made a family visit to Haworth). For lots of reasons, it was important for me to tell that story. But here is the thing – as soon as I finished my book, I wanted more. Even then. I wanted it *published*. I tell you this in a light-hearted way but you have to understand that, when I wrote it, it was not light-hearted. That story was a part of me. It marked who I was – and I wanted people to know that.

I find it hard to explain why it isn't enough for me to write a story and keep it to myself; why I must take it into the world; why I need … *what*? What is it I need? The approval of others? The affirmation? The challenge? The sharing? More and more, I feel that writing is about saying, 'This is how the world seems to me' – followed by a question mark. Writing is a deeply solitary process but it is also, I think, the most generous piece of reaching out. I write in order to understand.

But back to *Sisters*. I didn't mention to anyone I had written a book. I didn't dare. I was a quiet child. I wanted people to know who I was, but I didn't seem to be very good at showing it, at least not in a day-to-day way. I decided to give myself a pseudonym as a writer: Mary Thorntons. *Mary* because I thought it sounded intellectual and *Thorntons* because I made a mistake (I misremembered Thornfield from *Jane Eyre*). I had a hunch Mary Thorntons sounded altogether more writerly than Rachel Joyce.

So I had my BOOK. I had my WRITER'S NAME. What next? I went to my local library in West Norwood because that was where we always went for information. I headed for the reference section (I knew it well) and, with a beating heart, I found a heavy manual called the *Writers' & Artists' Yearbook*. We are talking 1976. I sat alone, where no one could see me, and I opened it.

All I can tell you is that it was like discovering a friend – someone who took my writing seriously and who had practical knowledge in spadefuls. It provided a bridge between my story and the professional world of publishing. I couldn't believe that everything I needed to know was in one book. I wrote down the names and addresses of publishers who were interested in rhyming books (there weren't many). I noted the word count they expected (short) and the kind of accompanying letter. I also discovered that it was important to include my name and address (Mary Thorntons, West Norwood).

Now, over 40 years later, I have done at last what I wasn't able or ready to achieve when I was 14. Over the years, I have written in different media: short stories and novels, for radio and television. And here too is a new edition of the *Writers' & Artists' Yearbook* – the 112th to be exact. The book you are holding will give you all the up-to-date information it offered me when I was 14, but it also offers far more. Along with clear detailing of all the contacts you can possibly need, it now provides advice from many well-respected voices in the publishing industry about editing, how to pitch your book, writing for the theatre, copyright law, finance, how to attract the attention of an agent, self-publishing (to name just a few of the topics). If you take your writing at all seriously, and that part of you that wants your writing not only to be finished but to find its place in the world, then … well done, you have come to the right place. There may be a lot of information to be found if you trawl the internet, but here it is all under one roof. Think of yourself as being in the best writers' Christmas market. It is all here.

People ask me sometimes for my advice to a new writer. I say the obvious things: 'Keep going' and 'Don't let go until you really believe you have scraped right down to the bare bones of the truth'. But it might be better to say, 'Take yourself seriously'. If you don't take yourself seriously as a writer then how can you expect anyone else to? Nurture the part of yourself that needs to write. Listen to how it works, what it needs, its ups and downs. Don't think of it as short term. It is a part of you, in the same way that your thoughts are part of you and so is your blood. And when your writing is done, be practical. Know your stuff about the world you are entering. Know where to place what you have done.

Read this book very carefully. Treasure it. Keep it beside you. It is your friend.

Rachel Joyce is the author of the *Sunday Times* and international bestsellers *The Unlikely Pilgrimage of Harold Fry* (Doubleday 2012), *Perfect* (Doubleday 2013) and *The Love Song of Miss Queenie Hennessy* (Doubleday 2014). Her fourth novel, *The Music Shop* was released in 2017 (Doubleday). *The Unlikely Pilgrimage of Harold Fry* was shortlisted for the Commonwealth Book Prize and longlisted for the Man Booker Prize and has been translated into 34 languages. Rachel was awarded the Specsavers National Book Awards 'New Writer of the Year' in December 2012 and shortlisted for the 'Writer of the Year' 2014. She is also the author of the short story, *A Faraway Smell of Lemon*, and the short story collection *A Snow Garden & Other Stories* (Doubleday 2015). Rachel moved to writing after a 20-year career in theatre and television, performing leading roles for the RSC, the Royal National Theatre, the Royal Court, and Cheek by Jowl. She has written over 20 original afternoon plays for BBC Radio 4 and major adaptations for the *Classic Series* and *Woman's Hour*, including *The Professor*, *Villette*, *The Tenant of Wildfell Hall*, *Shirley* and *Jane Eyre* (2016). See more at www.penguin.co.uk/authors/rachel-joyce/1069732.

Writing short stories

Tania Hershman shares her passion for short stories. She introduces the multitude of different forms a short story can take and how to go about writing your own. She also outlines the possibilities for seeing your own short stories published.

The first short stories I read, as a child, were Roald Dahl's *Tales of the Unexpected*, which are horrifyingly wonderful. I couldn't believe so much could happen in only a few pages. Thus my interest in the short story was piqued. Later on, in my late twenties, I read Ali Smith's *Other Stories and Other Stories*, and was similarly astonished. This is *also* a short story? A short story can *also* be so quiet, intimate and just as powerful? And with that, my love for the form was sealed. Having wanted to be a writer from a very early age, I decided to set out to learn how to write short stories.

Short story writers

Some of my favourite short story writers are: Donald Barthelme, Richard Brautigan, Roald Dahl, Anthony Doerr, Janice Galloway, A.L. Kennedy, Ian McEwan, Lorrie Moore, Flannery O'Connor, Grace Paley, George Saunders, Ali Smith, Jeanette Turner Hospital and Tobias Woolf.

What is a short story?

In one respect there is a simple answer: a short story is short, and it's a story. What is short? As short as you like, down to five or six words even, some would say. And at the other end of the scale, the short story butts up against the novella at around 20,000 words, or roughly 100 pages. So, there's a lot of space inside the word 'short'. The question of what constitutes a story is more difficult. Beginning, middle and end? The more we try to define, the less clear it becomes, so let's say we know a complete story when we read one, as opposed to an excerpt from something else.

It's easier to say what a short story is not: it's not a mini-novel; it's not a poem without line breaks. However, it can sometimes seem like either of these. What it comes down to is that the short story is its own thing, a unique creature. Great short stories are great not *despite* their length but because of it. Great short story writers understand the rhythms of brevity, and that what is left out of a short story is just as important as the words it contains.

Tips for writing short stories

1. There is no one way to write, there are no rules, everyone does it differently. Pick and choose from other people's writing tips or make up your own rules, and find the way that works best for you.
2. Pin a note above your writing desk that says, 'No one is ever going to read this' so that you can write freely without any inhibitions!
3. When you write, don't forget that once you've got your first draft down, everything is up for grabs, you can change anything: characters, setting, plot, structure, voice, style, beginning, middle, end. Nothing is sacred.
4. Don't try and write for a particular market or competition; write the kinds of things you love to read. Surprise yourself, delight yourself, tell yourself stories.
5. Don't be afraid to take risks, to stray away from the known into chaos, to get away from labels and boxes. Feel free to make your writing messy, raw and original rather than neat, safe and familiar.

Readers of short stories are required to fill in the gaps themselves, to do a little work, and being involved in the story rather than just watching it unfold makes reading them very rewarding.

There are as many types of short story as there are great short stories. They can be any genre at all – science fiction, historical fiction, mystery, crime, paranormal romance, humour, lit fic, chick lit, magical realism, surrealism – or any combination of these. There are no restrictions on content, style or voice. They can be told in the first person, third person, or even the second person ('You wake up in the morning...') or the first person plural ('When we wake up it is still dark...'). Short stories can be 'experimental' – for example, they might take the form of a list or a recipe, or even a PowerPoint presentation. It is often easier to ask a reader to suspend disbelief and enter into an entirely bizarre world for only a few pages rather than something much longer.

There is a plethora of writing workshops and courses (see page 678) on offer, and undergraduate and postgraduate courses in creative writing (see page 686). The short story world is buzzing with activity.

How to write a short story

There is no right or wrong way to write a short story. Some writers 'splurge' a first draft onto the page and then spend time revising the story. Others write the first paragraph and can't move on until they know what happens next, and generally this is how I write, revising as I go. The American writer Lorrie Moore says she writes the beginning of a short story, then the end, then the middle. A new story comes to me as a first line which demands to be written down. Other writers see an image or hear a voice. Something which took me a long time to internalise is that nothing is sacred in your first draft – not the characters, the plot, the location, the tense (past, present, future), or who is telling the story (main character, narrator...). Anything can be changed, cut entirely or moved around. Where you start writing may not be – and is often not – where the story should actually start. You don't have to start with a blank page: you could grab the nearest book, open it at random, pick a sentence and use that as your first line. Or go to YouTube, pick a video and use it as inspiration. A method that works for me is to compile a set of six prompt phrases taken from six different poems by various authors and write for a fixed amount of time, incorporating these phrases in my story.

Where you finish writing is often not where the story should end. Most of us have a tendency to overwrite endings, trying to tie up all the loose ends, but a good ending is vital. It's not possible to have a fantastic short story with a weak ending, one that stops abruptly so you turn the page and are surprised to find it has finished, or one that peters out, or an ending that goes on and on and doesn't know when to stop. I was told early on that the ending of a short story should be surprising yet inevitable. This is easier said than done. Ending a short story well comes with practice; it's an instinct you develop from reading many short stories as well as writing.

Publishing short stories

It is an excellent time to be a short story writer as the short story is getting a lot of attention – the *Bookseller* reported in January 2018 that 'short story anthologies are enjoying a boom in sales, rising by almost 50% in value, to reach their highest level in seven years'. Canadian short story writer Alice Munro won the 2013 Nobel Prize for Literature; Lydia Davis, American writer of short and very short stories, won the 2013 Man Booker International Prize; and American short story writer George Saunders won the inaugural 2014 Folio Prize for Literature, which is open to all works of fiction.

Literary magazines

Some of my favourite literary magazines are listed here; they all accept short stories.

A3 Review

http://www.writingmaps.com/collections/the-a3-review

A magazine that behaves like a map, with prose and poetry drawn from monthly contests.

Bare Fiction

www.barefictionmagazine.co.uk

Flash fiction, short stories, poetry, plays and more in a large print mag, plus annual contests.

Cease, Cows

www.ceasecows.com

Exploring the contemporary and the strange, flash fiction and prose poetry, online.

Conjunctions

www.conjunctions.com

Innovative writing across fiction, non-fiction and poetry, in print and online.

Gorse

http://gorse.ie

A print journal published in Dublin, featuring original fiction, longform narrative essays, poetry and interviews.

Gutter

See page 59.

Interzone

See page 63.

LabLit

www.lablit.com

'The culture of science in fiction and fact.'

The Letters Page

www.theletterspage.ac.uk

A fabulous, correspondence-themed literary journal.

Litro

See page 67.

Memorious

www.memorious.org

A journal of new verse and fiction.

PANK Magazine

www.pankmagazine.com

Emerging and experimental poetry and prose.

Riptide

www.riptidejournal.co.uk

Short stories with an undercurrent.

SHORT Fiction

www.shortfictionjournal.co.uk

Beautifully illustrated annual journal focusing on short stories.

Southword

www.munsterlit.ie/Southword/issues_index.html

New writing from Ireland.

Stinging Fly

www.stingingfly.org

A beautifully printed magazine showcasing new Irish and international writing with a particular interest in short stories.

Subtropics

http://subtropics.english.ufl.edu

The literary magazine from the University of Florida.

Synaesthesia Magazine

www.synaesthesiamagazine.com

Themed online magazine of art, fiction, poetry and non-fiction articles and interviews. Showcasing weird, unusual, thought-provoking and occasionally bizarre fiction and poetry.

Visual Verse

http://visualverse.org

An online anthology of art and poetry, short fiction and non-fiction, between 50 and 500 words.

Wigleaf

http://wigleaf.com

Features stories under 1,000 words.

There are many places where you can submit your work. When you have a short story ready to send out, a good place to start is with a literary magazine. There are now thousands of literary magazines being published worldwide, both online and in print – and sometimes as audio magazines. The literary magazine is not – as its name might imply – just for 'literary fiction' (another term that is easier to define by what it's *not*) but covers all genres. A literary journal may ask for stories that are only in a particular genre or on a particular theme, or under a certain length, or it may be open to all. Online databases of writers' markets such as Duotrope.com (a small annual fee is charged) allow you to search according to various parameters.

Always read a magazine before submitting anything. Each literary magazine has submission guidelines that should be followed to the letter. One way editors cut down on reading the hundreds of submissions they receive is to discard those that fail to stick to their guidelines – for example, if a story is double the permitted length, or if a science fiction story is sent to a magazine that only wants realist fiction. The majority of literary magazines and competitions stipulate that short stories must not have been previously published, and putting them online where anyone can read them – for example on your blog – counts as 'previously published'. The majority of literary magazines don't charge a fee to submit work but neither do they pay contributors, other than with a copy of the issue in which they are published (if it is a print journal). Although you won't make a living from publishing in literary magazines, it's wonderful to see your name in print (or pixels) and to have your story where it will find readers. It also helps to build your reputation as a writer.

Anthologies are another place where short stories are published. A publisher (mostly small independent presses) will issue a 'Call for Submissions', which is sometimes on a theme or it may be an open call. These can be found on publishers' websites, or via resources such as Duotrope.com and Places for Writers (www.placesforwriters.com). Authors with stories accepted usually receive one or two copies of the anthology and there is sometimes a small payment to the contributors.

BBC Radio 4 has two short story slots, the 15-minute *Afternoon Reading* on Fridays and the Short Reading on Sunday evenings (see *Stories on radio* on page 385), and the BBC

Small presses that publish short story collections

Black Inc Books
www.blackincbooks.com.au

Black Lawrence Press
www.blacklawrence.com

Cinnamon Press
www.cinnamonpress.com

Comma Press
www.commapress.co.uk

Dzanc Books
www.dzancbooks.org

FC2
www.fc2.org

Rose Metal Press
http://rosemetalpress.com

Route
www.route-online.com

Seren Books
www.serenbooks.com

Small Beer Press
http://smallbeerpress.com

Stinging Fly Press
www.stingingfly.org/stinging-press

pays well for short stories. Look out for the Opening Lines competition, which is for writers new to radio (see box below), and for published writers there's also the annual BBC National Short Story Award (see page 566).

There are an increasing number of competitions for short stories. Usually an entry fee is payable, but always check into a competition's reputation before sending off your money and story. Look for competition listings in reputable magazines such as *Mslexia* and other sources (see box below). If something sounds too good to be true, it may well be! While prizes can be up to £1,000 for the winning story – occasionally more – there can, of course, only be one winner. But competitions sometimes offer cash prizes – and publication – to finalists as well, and to be included in a competition anthology such as those published by the Bristol Short Story Prize (www.bristolprize.co.uk), the *The White Review* Short Story Prize for Emerging Writers (www.thewhitereview.org/prize/white-review-short-story-prize-2018), or the Bridport Prize (see page 568) is a very prestigious accomplishment. (See also *Prizes and awards* on page 565 for other short story competitions.) Competitions often make public not just the winners but also the longlisted and shortlisted stories, and to see your story on one of these lists is a great confidence boost – no, you didn't win, but your story rose close to the top out of hundreds, perhaps thousands of entries.

Another place where you can submit your stories is one of the growing number of 'live lit' events, where, if your story is accepted, you will either be invited to the venue to read it or it will be read by an actor (see box on page 272).

Be ready for rejection

It isn't wise to begin submitting anything until you are ready to receive a rejection. There is never a time in the life of a writer when rejection doesn't feature. It just gets easier to deal with as you understand that it is not a rejection of *you* personally and that there are many reasons why an editor may not pick your story. For example, perhaps it doesn't fit with his or her vision for that particular issue of the magazine; or maybe it was a topic that she personally doesn't like to read about; or it could be that you haven't got the ending right yet (sometimes editors can give marvellous feedback in rejection letters and I have found this very useful). Similarly, not getting anywhere in a competition doesn't necessarily

Books

Short story competitions and contests

COMPETITION LISTINGS

BBC

www.bbc.co.uk/programmes/articles/2QXsYTZYWZ40CTc8lbH0FdV/how-to-enter

Mslexia

See page 71.

Poets and Writers' Magazine Tools for Writers

www.pw.org

Places for Writers

www.placesforwriters.com

ShortStops

www.shortstops.info

CRWROPPS list on Yahoo

http://groups.yahoo.com/neo/groups/CRWROPPS-B/info

CHAPBOOK CONTESTS

Black River Chapbook Contest

http://blacklawrence.homestead.com/BRCCContestPage.html

The Diagram Chapbook Contest

http://thediagram.com/contest.html

Gertrude Press Chapbook Competition

www.gertrudepress.org/submit.html

mean the story isn't good. Competitions, too, are judged by human beings, with their own likes and dislikes.

I didn't submit anything for publication during my first seven years of writing short stories. Instead, I went to workshops (the Arvon Foundation, now Arvon, see page 678; and the Iowa Summer Writing Festival in the USA, www.iowasummerwritingfestival.org) and was learning how to write and how to read as a writer. There is no rush: don't risk being put off entirely by receiving a rejection too soon.

Publishing a short story collection

A short story collection may be planned, perhaps with a theme linking the stories (although this is not necessary), or just something that happens when you realise you have enough stories for a book (roughly 30,000 words). If you decide you have a collection, there are

Short story festivals and live events

SHORT STORY FESTIVALS

See also *Literature festivals* on page 597.

Cork International Short Story Festival (Ireland, September)

See page 599.

Flash Fiction Festival

https://www.flashfictionfestival.com

Kikinda Short Story Festival (Serbia, July)

http://kikindashort.org.rs

National Short Story Day

www.nationalshortstoryday.co.uk

National Short Story Week

See page 603.

Small Wonder: The Short Story Festival

See page 604.

LIVE SHORT STORY EVENTS

Bad Language

http://badlanguagemcr.com

Manchester. Promoting new writing in Manchester: a night of spoken word, prose and poetry.

Berko Speakeasy

www.berkospeakeasy.co.uk

Berkhamsted. 'A cabaret of short stories.'

Fictions of Every Kind

http://sjbradleybooks.blogspot.co.uk

Leeds. DIY writers' social night organised by writer S.J. Bradley.

Inky Fingers

http://inkyfingersedinburgh.wordpress.com

Edinburgh. A series of events for people who love words.

Liars League

http://liarsleague.typepad.com

London. A monthly live fiction night, where professional actors read new short stories by writers from around the world.

Rattle Tales

http://rattletales.org

Brighton. A night of interactive storytelling run by local writers.

Short Stories Aloud

http://shortstops.info/short-stories-aloud-live
email sarahefranklin@gmail.com
Contact Sarah Franklin

Oxford. Short stories read aloud by actors.

Story Fridays

www.awordinyourear.org.uk/story-fridays

Bath. Writer-performers read stories inspired by a theme.

Unsung Stories Live

http://www.unsungstories.co.uk

A regular London event featuring readings of science fiction, speculative fiction, fantasy and horror stories.

The Word Factory

www.thewordfactory.tv

London. 'A series of intimate short story salons bringing brilliant writers and readers together.'

several ways to look for a book deal. The traditional route is through a literary agent, although they commonly respond that it is very hard to sell a short story collection without the promise of a novel. Sending your manuscript straight to one of the large publishing houses will probably elicit a similar response. The main publishers of short story collections today are the small, independent presses, often operating on a not-for-profit basis. You can submit to them directly, without an agent. They usually ask for three stories, and then the full manuscript if they are interested. You don't need to submit only to UK-based independent publishers – try further afield too.

Alternatively, you could enter your collection into a contest which has publication as the first prize. A number of American university presses run such contests, and the concept is spreading. There are also 'chapbook' contests (see box on page 271): a chapbook used to refer to slim, often hand-bound, poetry collections, but the term is also now applied to short story collections. The small presses that publish short story chapbooks often invest a great deal in presentation, hand-stitching the covers and experimenting with different formats.

Both my collections are published by very dynamic small presses, which invest a great deal of love and care into each book they produce. Being published by a small press may not carry the prestige of a 'big name' publishing house, and authors will often have to do a great deal of the book promotion themselves and are unlikely to receive an advance on sales. However, these presses pride themselves on their investment and individual attention to every book and author they publish, and small press published books do win major literary prizes. For example, *Grace, Tamar and Laszlo the Great* by Deborah Kay Davies (Parthian Books 2009) won the Wales Book of the Year.

Self-publishing, both in print and as an ebook is becoming increasingly popular, especially with short story writers as their chances of being published by a large publishing house are slim. However, this costs money and the writer is responsible for every element of the publishing process, including marketing and promotion. If you decide to head down this path, hire an editor to edit your stories first. For further information on self-publishing see articles in the *Digital and self-publishing* section starting on page 607.

A passionate affair

I love short stories. This is a passionate affair that I hope will never end. I read upwards of 1,000 short stories a year – some because I am paid to (as a judge of short story contests, as a mentor, and as an editor) but mostly for pleasure – and I frequently find new favourite authors. I am continuously astonished at what writers can do with the short story form, reinventing it time and time again, making it their own. My greatest advice? Read. Read as many short stories as you can to inspire your own writing, to show you possibilities of what a short story can be – and then you can reinvent it for yourself. Good luck!

Tania Hershman is the author of three story collections, *My Mother Was An Upright Piano: Fictions* (Tangent Books 2012), *The White Road and Other Stories* (Salt 2008) and *Some Of Us Glow More Than Others* (Unthank Books 2017), a poetry collection, *Terms and Conditions* (Nine Arches Press 2017) and a poetry chapbook, *Nothing Here Is Wild, Everything Is Open* (Southword 2016). She is co-author of *Writing Short Stories: A Writers' & Artists' Companion* (Bloomsbury 2014) and co-editor of *I Am Because You Are*, an anthology of short stories inspired by Einstein's General Theory of Relativity. Tania is founder and curator of ShortStops (www.shortstops.info), celebrating short story activity across the UK and Ireland. Her website is www.taniahershman.com.

See also...

• *The* Writers' & Artists' Yearbook *Short Story Competition*, page ix

Graphic novels: how to get published

With more graphic novels and comic books being made into films and shortlisted for book prizes, publisher Emma Hayley suggests that there has never been a more exciting time for writers and artists to get their 'GN' published.

When Mary and Bryan Talbot's graphic novel *Dotter of Her Father's Eyes* (Jonathan Cape 2012) was named winner of the biography section in the 2012 Costa Book Awards, it was the first time a graphic novel had won this prestigious literary prize. While others have won major literary awards in the past – Chris Ware won the *Guardian* First Book Award in 2001 for *Jimmy Corrigan: The Smartest Kid on Earth* (Jonathan Cape 2000), and Art Spiegelman won the Pulitzer in 1992 for *Maus* (Penguin 1986/91) – the Costa jury's award marked a renewed enthusiasm for the medium, as well as its acceptance by the broader literary establishment.

Essential books about graphic novels

- Scott McCloud, *Understanding Comics: The Invisible Art* (William Morrow Paperbacks 1994)
- Scott McCloud, *Reinventing Comics* (William Morrow Paperbacks 2000)
- Scott McCloud, *Making Comics* (William Morrow Paperbacks 2006)
- Will Eisner, *Comics and Sequential Art* (WW Norton 2008)
- Will Eisner, *Graphic Storytelling and Visual Narraitve* (WW Norton 2008)
- Michael Dooley and Stephen Heller, *Education of a Comics Artist* (Allworth Press 2005)
- Alan Moore, *Writing for Comics* (Avatar Press 2003)
- Paul Gravett, *1001 Comics You Must Read Before you Die* (Cassell 2011)
- Paul Gravett, *Graphic Novels: Stories to Change Your Life* (Collins Design 2005)

Journalists are dedicating more space to graphic novel reviews, and high-street retailers are devoting more space on their bookshelves to a wider range of graphic novels than ever before. The growth of the graphic novel and comic book market is clear: in the UK it grew from £2m in 2002 to £16m in 2012. That's a staggering *700% increase* over 10 years. This isn't the first time that the market has enjoyed a growth, but it is the first time that such a consistent period of growth has been seen since its peak in the mid-80s with the birth of such classics as *Watchmen*, *Maus* and *The Dark Knight Returns*.

What is a graphic novel?

The term 'graphic novel' was coined in 1964 by American comics reviewer and publisher Richard Kyle, but comics in book form have been around at least since the early 19th century. Not everyone agrees on the definition of a graphic novel: it is generally agreed, however, that it must contain sequential artwork, the narrative of which need not necessarily include words.

The word 'novel' is potentially misleading, since it elsewhere exclusively suggests a work of fiction. It is important to remember, however, that the medium of the *graphic* novel contains many different genres – including reportage, biography and history, as well as the more traditional forms of sci-fi, horror and romance. Essentially, the difference between a graphic novel and a comic is its length: while a comic may contain 24 or 32 pages, a graphic novel will be long enough to warrant a spine. But while a six-issue comic series might be collected into a graphic novel, there are many graphic novels that were only ever conceived as integral, 'long-form' works.

Despite some creators still disliking it (preferring to call their work a 'comic book', plain and simple), the term 'graphic novel' has gone a long way to overcoming preconceptions and prejudice. The usual stereotypical associations of 'comics' with children, geeks, male teenagers or middle-aged nerds (think 'Comic Book Guy' in *The Simpsons*) have to a large degree been replaced by the notion that this unique medium can be a sophisticated form of literature appealing to a broad range of readers.

Getting noticed

The best way to start getting your work noticed is to self-publish short comics. There is no stigma associated with self-publishing in the graphic novel world; in fact there is a long tradition of self-publishing which is actively encouraged. Write or draw your comic, print off some copies, hire yourself a table at a comic 'con' (convention) (see box) and sell it. If you've had an idea, executed it well and sold it, not only will you feel an enormous sense of accomplishment, but you will also have demonstrated your commitment – and this will not go unnoticed by a potential future publisher.

Taking part in a comic con is in any case a great way of meeting people in the industry, from fellow creators and enthusiasts to editors and publishers. Some publishers who exhibit at comic cons will be willing to do 'portfolio reviews', reading and appraising your work – it's a great chance to get your face, name and work in front of a publisher. If you catch

Festivals and comic conventions

UK

There are numerous comic cons in the UK. Here are some of the bigger ones:

LICAF: The Lakes International Comic Art Festival
(Kendal, The Lake District)
www.comicartfestival.com

Thought Bubble
(Leeds)
http://thoughtbubblefestival.com

MCM Expo
(London, Birmingham, Manchester and Glasgow)
Check this website for a complete list:
www.mcmcomiccon.co.uk

EUROPE

You'll find comic cons happening throughout Europe including in Copenhagen, Helsinki, Barcelona, Erlanger, Lucca and Holland. Be sure not to miss:

Angoulême International Comics Festival
www.bdangouleme.com
Book accommodation early to avoid disappointment.

NORTH AMERICA

North America boasts a huge number of comic cons of differing sizes. The big ones include:

Comic-Con International
(San Diego)
www.comic-con.org

New York Comic Con
www.newyorkcomiccon.com

Smaller cons include:

APE: Alternative Press Expo
(San Jose)
www.alternativepressexpo.com

SPX: Small Press Expo
(Bethesda)
www.smallpressexpo.com

MoCCA festival: Museum of Comic and Cartoon Art
(New York)
www.societyillustrators.org/mocca-arts-festival

TCAF: Toronto Comic Arts Festival
www.torontocomics.com

them on their stand at a busy time, then at least drop off your pitch (see **Your pitch** below) and give them your card.

Social media. A good presence on social media can be a prerequisite for some publishers. Make sure you are on the latest social media networks, whether that's Twitter, Facebook or Instagram, etc, and be prepared to build your fan base. One way would be to ask fellow creators to start following you and getting them to endorse or 'like' your work and ideas. Word of mouth is a powerful way to get attention.

Prizes and awards. Another way of enhancing your profile (and broadening your experience of working to a brief) is to enter as many competitions as you can, of which there are an increasing number. The two main awards are the *Observer*/Cape/Comica graphic short story prize and Myriad's First Graphic Novel competition. If your artistic style is more manga-oriented, the Japanese Embassy's annual 'Manga Jiman' contest may be for you. This is a great way of getting your work seen by a wider public, and even if you don't win, your ambition will be noticed by industry professionals.

Know your publisher

Before pitching to a publisher, make sure you've studied their catalogue or website thoroughly. If they don't publish superhero books, don't send them a superhero pitch. Look at the different series they publish, look at the page count ('extent') and size of their books, and try to conform as much as possible with their formats. Check to see if they have any submission guidelines on their website (they usually will) and supply your pitch in accordance with these.

Covering letter. Make sure that you spell the name of your publisher correctly. This may seem basic advice, but you'd be surprised at the number of people who send their covering letters in a rush and make rudimentary errors. Don't let that be you: you may fall at the first hurdle. Spend time on composing your covering letter – it doesn't need to be very long (publishers are busy people), but it does need to introduce you and your work as concisely and effectively as possible. Also ensure that you are addressing your letter to the right person, by finding out the name of the commissioning editor or publishing director.

Your pitch

Getting your pitch to stand out from the rest is one of the most important things you can do. Plan your approach well. One excellent way is to get endorsements for your pitch from those already in the industry, such as other well-known creators. A sentence or two is all that's needed. This shows good marketing skills and gives your project weight. Bribes such as chocolate coins or cookies have been known to send waves of excitement and appreciation through a publisher's office – this may not guarantee your work gets published, but it does get it noticed! The most important way to stand out from the crowd, however, is to make sure that the presentation of your submission is of the highest possible quality.

Usually a publisher will want to see a number of pages of sequential art (I would recommend at least eight pages), together with a 'synopsis' (brief summary of the whole book). A whole script isn't necessary at pitch stage. In fact, to begin with, less is definitely more. Make sure that those pages are of the highest standard possible. If you are a novice letterer, it's worth persuading a more experienced letterer to do it for you; if you're not brilliant at creating speech bubbles, ask someone else to help. Make sure that you don't let your good idea slip under the radar because of a sub-standard presentation.

Agents

Unlike most authors of prose fiction, creators of graphic novels don't need an agent. The graphic novel world is still small enough for you personally to get to know the editors and publishers who make the decisions. However, if you're trying to get your work published in the US, and you don't have the necessary contacts, then an agent could be a useful way in. Many creators are very good at creating, but not so good at selling themselves. If that's you, then perhaps finding an agent is a good option – though of course they don't work for free.

Sequential art courses

Royal Drawing School

http://royaldrawingschool.org/courses/public-courses/drawing-the-graphic-novel-1

Staffordshire University

www.staffs.ac.uk/course/cartoon-comic-arts-ba

University of the Arts London

www.arts.ac.uk/chelsea/courses/short-courses/search-by-subject/illustration/comic-book-art

www.arts.ac.uk/csm/courses/short-courses/animation-interactive-film-and-sound/cartooning-fundamentals

Glyndwr University

www.glyndwr.ac.uk/en/Undergraduatecourses/DesignIllustrationGraphicNovelsandChildrensPublishing

University of Exeter

https://humanities.exeter.ac.uk/english/modules/eas3166/description

Building your library

- Art Spiegelman, *The Complete MAUS* (Penguin 2003)
- Alan Moore and Dave Gibbons, *Watchmen*, International Edition (DC Comics 2014)
- Marjane Satrapi, *The Complete Persepolis* (Random House 2007)
- Frank Miller, *Batman Dark Knight Returns* (DC Comics 2006)
- Frank Miller, *Sin City* series (DC Comics 2010 onwards)
- Neil Gaiman, *Sandman* series (DC Comics 2010 onwards)
- Chris Ware, *Jimmy Corrigan: The Smartest Kid on Earth* (Jonathan Cape 2001)
- Chris Ware, *Building Stories* (Jonathan Cape 2012)
- Craig Thompson, *Blankets* (Top Shelf 2003)
- Charles Burns, *Black Hole* (Jonathan Cape 2005)
- David B., *Epileptic* (Jonathan Cape 2006)
- Bryan Lee O'Malley, *Seconds* (SelfMadeHero 2014)
- Glyn Dillon, *The Nao of Brown* (SelfMadeHero 2012)
- Scott McCloud, *The Sculptor* (SelfMadeHero 2015)
- Posy Simmonds, *Tamara Drewe* (Jonathan Cape 2009)
- Daniel Clowes, *Ghost World* (Jonathan Cape 2000)
- Will Eisner, *A Contract with God* (WW Norton 2007)
- Joe Sacco, *Palestine* (Jonathan Cape 2003)
- Adrian Tomine, *Shortcomings* (Faber & Faber 2012)
- Alison Bechdel, *Fun Home: A Family Tragicomic* (Jonathan Cape 2006)

Collaborations

Some publishers will still accept pitches from a writer without an artist already attached, and vice versa. Increasingly, though, publishers prefer the pitch to be submitted by an established artist-and-writer team, while others prefer to work with a single creator who does both the writing and the artwork. If you're a writer or an artist looking for a collaborator, then there are a number of 'meet-ups' where you can find fellow creators.

Creator meet-ups

WIP Comics

www.meetup.com/WipComics

Laydeez do Comics

https://laydeezdocomics.wordpress.com

Process at Gosh

https://twitter.com/processcomics

Get qualified

A huge number of creators with a background in filmscript or play writing imagine they can easily turn their hand to writing a graphic novel, but it's a different medium and it has different rules. True, if you are used to thinking in visual terms you'll have a head start, but there are unique storytelling techniques you should learn and absorb before taking the plunge. On page 277 there is a list of practical books that might be of help to you (see **Building your library**). On the other hand, if you've never written any kind of script in any medium before, then you should look at the various courses on offer.

Go for it!

If you're passionate about your project, the best thing you can do is believe in yourself and go for it. If it doesn't work out at first, don't be hard on yourself. One of my heroes is the film-maker and comic book writer Alejandro Jodorowsky, whose recent documentary about his doomed attempt to film the sci-fi film *Dune* in the 1970s stands as a triumphant testament to the fact that something that might be deemed a failure can, in so many other ways, prove to be a success. Good luck!

Emma Hayley founded London-based publishing house SelfMadeHero in 2007 after spotting a gap in the UK market for high quality graphic novels for adults. Before launching her own company, she worked as a journalist, a film PR and as an editorial director for several small publishers. She was named UK Young Publishing Entrepreneur of the Year, as part of the British Book Industry Awards 2008. See www.selfmadehero.com/about.php.

The 'how to' of writing how-to books

Author Kate Harrison had published 12 novels when she made the unexpected move of writing a diet book. Here she talks through the six things you need to know to write a how-to book.

Becoming a how-to author was not part of my plan – and as for being a diet guru, my lifelong battle with the scales meant I was surely never going to be a position to tell others how to eat. Yet here I am, the author of four books on the intermittent fasting approach to weight loss: the first, *The 5:2 Diet Book*, was turned down by my own publisher, but I published it myself and it became a bestseller, shifted more copies than my (still successful) novels and, at the last count, has been translated into 16 languages. And I'm two stone lighter than I was before this whole new world opened up …

Maybe dieting isn't your area of expertise, but all of us have some specialist knowledge. Whether you're the go-to person for assembling flat-pack furniture, organising kids' birthday parties or training wilful puppies, there are readers out there who'd love to know how.

But how can you turn your skills into book sales? Here's the 'how to' of how-to books:

1. Know your stuff

What do you know more about than the average Joe or Joanna? Do your friends regularly ask you for help with something? Do you have a job or a hobby that gives you expertise?

Understanding a subject inside out is the key to a great how-to book. But that doesn't mean you need academic qualifications. Decades of experience in a practical skill will give you the understanding – and the short cuts and tips – that readers may prefer.

My experience: I'd spent years of my life losing and regaining weight on different regimes, yet when I tried intermittent fasting after watching the BBC's 'Horizon', I immediately sensed this could be different for me. There wasn't much practical information around, so I tried different approaches, and set up a Facebook group to share tips with friends. I was both an expert in dieting – including emotional factors and the reasons for failure – and a natural sceptic because, as a journalist, I was trained to question everything.

2. Know your readership

Often, the readership of a how-to book will be people like you, but the you *before* you went on the journey that equips you to write the book. Or they might be people you already teach in your day job or as a volunteer.

Whether you're a craftsperson with tricks that have taken you decades to learn, or a therapist who wants to help people in print as well as face to face, you need to understand the readers who might buy your book, so you can get the tone right.

My experience: I knew my ideal reader was me, six months earlier. But I did understand that, while I was fascinated by the science of fasting, not all readers would share my interest. So when I planned the book I aimed for the middle ground, interspersing real-life experiences, with more complex biology. I included a glossary, and lots of hyperlinks – particularly useful in an ebook – so that readers could easily read the research for themselves.

3. Know the question your book will answer

All how-to books answer a question or solve a problem. It's worth spending time thinking through what that question or need is, to help refine what your book will offer. One practical way to do this is to use Google or Amazon search functions. When you type in the beginning of a phrase, search engines predict what the rest of your phrase might be, based on millions of previous searches. It can be hilarious, but useful too.

For example, type 'DIY' into the Amazon books search bar, and you'll see: projects, for women, complete manual ... Or type 'vegan eating' on Google and you'll see other people have searched for 'meal plan' or 'breakfast'. Do this around lots of possible combinations and write down key words.

Once you understand what people want to know, you can structure your book around telling them, dealing with one key point or area per chapter. Use the key words in the title of the book itself: it makes it easier for readers to find your book!

Some questions or needs are very niche, which is not a problem if you're writing an ebook. Because the costs of producing the book are low, you can create shorter books – at lower prices – that address single issues and work well at the shorter length. Or bring different questions on one topic together in a 'complete' guide.

One important point: if you're writing about health, or potentially risky activities, include clear and appropriate warnings to ensure you're not putting readers in danger. If you have any doubt at all, look at the warnings in books on similar topics, or take professional advice. The last thing you want is to be sued!

My experience: 'How can I lose weight and keep it off?' is a need shared by millions of people worldwide. Discovering what worked for me was a life-changer, and I focused on explaining why the approach was different, and on practical ways to fit it into your life.

4. Know your unique story/point of view

Stories aren't just for children. We learn the three-act structure of stories – beginning, middle, end – from movies, books and even jokes. Structuring your non-fiction book around a story makes it more enjoyable. For example, a book about money or changing your job could easily follow the 'rags to riches' Cinderella storyline.

Your book doesn't have to be a fairy tale, but readers will enjoy reading your own story and/or case studies or people you've helped. Explaining your own struggles or problems, and then how you found the solution, establishes you as credible. Your story also makes your book unique. Even if you're a high-powered expert – a brain surgeon or a leading detective – talking as one person to another will make your book accessible, and help you stand out, even if there are many other books already on your topic.

My experience: as a consumer of previous 'diet books' written by scientific experts, I knew they can be patronising. I decided to be 100% honest about my struggles, interspersing research and advice with my own weight-loss diary. After the book was published, I had countless emails from other dieters saying 'it was like reading my own story' and my success, after years of failure, helped inspire them to try the plan.

5. Know how to publish your book

Writing may be a solitary activity, but publishing your book will almost certainly be a team effort!

You have two main options: look for an agent and publishing deal, or self-publish your work as an ebook and a print-on-demand title. The decision is worthy of an article in itself, but how-to books are very well suited to self-publishing. If your subject is quite niche, then it may not be worthwhile for a mainstream publisher, but if you get your title and cover right, readers can find you easily online, and will you will receive the lion's share of the profits. Agents and publishers are more likely to be interested if you're well-known in your field and already have thousands of followers on social media, and they may offer you an advance based on a proposal.

Self-publishing doesn't mean going it alone: you will need an editor/proofreader, and a cover designer who can make your cover as appealing as possible. The investment will help make your book stand out. Formatting an ebook is straightforward, but you may also want to hire someone for that, especially if it contains illustrations or photographs.

My experience: I thought my book had potential, but my publishers didn't agree. So I worked with my agent to self-publish on Amazon Kindle. It went to Number 1 in the diet charts within a few days – and later my publisher did republish an expanded version, plus we worked together on three recipe books and a self-help title, *5:2 Your Life*.

6. Know how to sell your book

Hooray – your book is ready! But the hard work is not over. You need to let potential readers know it exists.

If you already have a blog or a website, post there, and on Twitter or Facebook. Be generous with your knowledge and content; offering free samples of your work is far more convincing than just screaming BUY MY BOOK! Ebooks can be given away for free or at a reduced price, which can help get you early reviews, or increase your visibility by helping the book rise in the charts. But use with caution; don't undersell yourself.

Good reviews on Amazon and other sites are very important, but never post them under fake names or via family members' accounts. You will be found out. A better idea is to put a note to readers at the end of your ebook asking them to review it if they've enjoyed it.

Articles in newspapers or magazines can really boost your sales. Press releases are simple to write but do research the right format online. Offer yourself, or people you've taught, as case studies. Local media often like to feature authors, so approach your local radio station or newspaper.

My experience: I had already shared tips in a private Facebook group I'd set up with a few friends who were also fasting. The group grew massively and when I decided to write the book, I included members' experiences. This meant that, when it went on sale, they were keen to read and discuss it. The group is now 60,000 members strong, and I still use their comments to influence my books.

7. Finally, know what to do next

Whether you find a handful of readers, or many thousands, writing a how-to book can be rewarding and fun. And it can be a platform to so much more: a new book, a podcast or YouTube channel, an e-course, or offering yourself as a public speaker.

The possibilities are endless, but whatever you do, there's nothing like that first email from a reader thanking you for making something easy … or even for changing their lives.

My experience: I've hosted my own podcast now, and also used my research and experiences to create a whole new plan, *The Dirty Diet – Ditch the Guilt, Love your Food*, building on my excitement about helping people feel fantastic.

Kate Harrison worked at the BBC as a TV correspondent and news producer before becoming a full-time writer. Kate wrote nine adult novels, including the *Secret Shopper* series, and a young adult thriller trilogy, *Soul Beach* (Orion 2011), before starting her non-fiction journey. She first self-published *The 5:2 Diet Book* as an ebook in 2012, followed by a print version with Orion, and six more recipe/self-help titles. Her books have been translated into more than 20 languages. Kate also teaches creative techniques and consumer insight to writers and media professionals. Visit Kate's website at www.kate-harrison.com/courses for free resources and courses on publishing and pitching.

Finding my agent

Martina Cole describes how her writing career started.

The *Writers' & Artists' Yearbook* holds a very dear place in my heart. Without it, I would never have been published as quickly, or as well, of that much I am sure.

I had written my first novel, *Dangerous Lady*, when I was 21 and it had been a dream of mine to become an author. I wasn't expecting fortune, or fame; all I had ever wanted was to see my name on the cover of a book. Books are probably the most important things in my life, apart from the family of course! I have loved books since I was a small child, when my father, a merchant seaman, brought home from his travels a cardboard theatre. When I opened the crimson faux velvet curtains, hidden behind them were the smallest books I had ever seen. The stories they contained were all old Aesop fables, and fairy tales, and I was absolutely entranced.

After that, a book was second nature to me. I even played truant from school so I could lie all day long in the park reading books from the local library – books I had taken out in my parents' names as well as my own. Books I would never otherwise have been allowed to read at such a young age. My parents died never knowing they had library memberships!

So, when I wrote *Dangerous Lady* all those years ago, it was the start of my writing career, though I didn't know it at the time.

Over the next nine years I wrote three more novels, film scripts, television scripts, and even a play for the theatre. But I had no confidence in myself as a writer, and I wrote for the sheer pleasure of it. I'm sure many of the people reading this are doing exactly the same thing!

Coming up to 30 was my personal watershed. I was running a nursing agency and had been offered a partnership. I was also moving house, so there were big upheavals all round. I was going to throw out all my writing efforts, and put away the dream of being an author. Then I glanced through *Dangerous Lady* – and I knew instinctively that it was much better than I had ever realised and that I had to at least try and fulfil my ambition, whatever the outcome might be.

I purchased then read the *Writers' & Artists' Yearbook* from cover to cover, and was fascinated by this world I craved but knew absolutely nothing about. It told me the correct way to set out a manuscript, both for a novel and for television, who published what, and more importantly, where I could find them! It was a mine of information, and it gave me the push I needed to pursue my dream.

I found my agent, Darley Anderson, tucked away among the pages, and taking a deep breath I rang him up – I nearly passed out when he answered the phone himself. I explained that I had written a book, what it was about, and he said, 'Send it to me, I'm intrigued'.

I posted it to him on the Thursday night, and he phoned me on the Monday at teatime: Darley's first words were, 'You are going to be a star!' It was the start of a long and happy friendship. It was also the beginning of my career in publishing.

When I am at a writers' conference, or a library event, I always tell the audience they must purchase the *Writers' & Artists' Yearbook*. On signings, if I am approached by someone who is writing a novel and I think they are serious about it, I purchase the book for them, and tell them that if they get published I want the first signed copy!

When I was asked to write this article, I was thrilled because all those years ago when I bought my first copy of the *Yearbook* I never dreamt that one day I would be lucky enough to actually be a small part of it. It's a truly wonderful introduction to the world of literature, and it also contains everything you need to know about writing for television, film *et al.* If it's relevant to what you are writing about, be it a novel or a newspaper article, you can find it in this *Yearbook*.

There's so much of interest, and so much that the budding writer needs explained. By the time I finally had a meeting with Darley in person, the *Writers' & Artists' Yearbook* had helped me understand exactly what I needed to ask about, and more importantly, what to expect from the meeting itself.

I wish you all the very best of luck. Publishing is a great business to be a part of.

I wrote for years in my spare time, for free – I loved it. It was a part of me and who I was. I still love writing, every second of it. I was asked once by a journalist if I ever got lonely – writing is such a solitary occupation, as we all know. But I said no. I spend all day with people that I've created. I put the wallpaper on the walls, and I give them families, lives to live, cars to drive, and in some cases I have even killed them! Not many people can that say about their jobs.

The *Writers' & Artists' Yearbook* is a wonderful tool for any budding writer, so use it and enjoy it. Good luck.

Martina Cole's first novel *Dangerous Lady* caused a sensation when it was published in 1992. 26 years later, Martina is the bestselling author of 24 highly successful novels, and has had more No. 1 original fiction bestsellers than any other author. *The Take*, which won the British Book Award for Crime Thriller of the Year in 2006, was adapted for Sky One, as was *The Runaway*. Three of her novels have been adapted for the stage: *Two Women*, *The Graft* and *Dangerous Lady* were all highly acclaimed when performed at the Theatre Royal Stratford East. Her books have now sold over 16 million copies. Her latest novel, *Damaged*, will be published by Headline in paperback in summer 2018.

See also...

- *How to get an agent*, page 422
- *Getting hooked out of the slush pile*, page 433
- *Literary agents* section, page 419

Changing voices

Alexander McCall Smith suggests that within each writer there is probably more than one author wishing to be expressed and that writers should be ready to push themselves and explore the unfamiliar, to try a new voice. In this article he examines the options and points out when it would be prudent to not write in a different voice.

Every author is used to being asked for a tip for those starting off in the profession. The one that I have tended to give is this: never get stuck on your first novel – move on to the next. That advice comes from meeting so many people who have spent years – sometimes decades – rewriting their first novel. That, in my view, is a bad mistake, particularly if that first novel is unsuitable for publication, as so many first novels are. So why not make one's second novel one's first?

But then comes the question: what other tips? That needs a bit more thought, but my second tip is probably this: be versatile. Being prepared to write more than one sort of thing is, I think, one of the most important abilities that any aspiring writer should seek to develop. Of course there are plenty of writers who find their exact niche and stick to it very successfully: I find it hard to think, for example, of any romantic novels written by John le Carré, or spy thrillers by Barbara Cartland, for that matter. Writers who have the good fortune to master a genre and make it very much their own can indeed get away with doing the same sort of book for their entire careers, but for most people the ability to write on different subjects or in different voices is a very useful weapon in the professional armoury.

Of course there are all sorts of pressures going the other way, not least being those that come from publishers. One of the things that the first-time author may not realise is that publishers prefer to take a long view. When they agree to publish your first book, they are probably already thinking of the second. The commercial reason for this is obvious: a publisher is going to invest time and money in a book that will probably have a reasonably short shelf-life. It is not surprising, then, that they are thinking of your future career and about how your second book can do better than your first. All that is reasonable enough: it takes time to build up a following.

With this long-term strategy in mind, publishers will be keen to pigeon-hole you and present you as a writer of a certain sort of book. If, for example, you write a steamy novel about 50 shades of something or other, your publisher is not going to be pleased if your next book is on moral philosophy or even – and this would cause even greater problems for your publisher – theology. If you write a thriller, then that is how you are going to be marketed – as a writer of thrillers.

This process of categorisation, of course, can be to your advantage. Crime novels, for instance, sell better than many other categories, and to be labelled as a crime writer may help an author get started on a lucrative career. And crime fiction can be extremely well written and psychologically profound; there is no shame in being considered a genre writer, as long as one does not allow the demands of genre to be too constraining. There is a world of difference, though, between the narrow, formulaic romantic novel and the novel about love. The former will be of little literary merit; the latter may be quite the opposite.

Some will be wary of identification with a genre, as being placed in a particular one may be considered limiting. Yet the boundaries of genre may be vague. Think of Patricia

Highsmith with her Ripley novels and her other titles too: those are every bit as good – if not better – than many so-called literary novels, and of course will be read, and enjoyed, by a much wider audience. Ian McEwan is another interesting example: his compelling novel, *Enduring Love*, could be considered crime fiction, or even a thriller, as could his exquisitely frightening novel, *Saturday*. And yet McEwan crosses literary boundaries with ease because he writes so well.

Writing for children brings particular dangers. Children's books are obviously a very distinct genre, marketed and perceived by the public in a very distinctive way. If your first book is a children's book, beware: you will be labelled by publishers – and possibly by everybody else – as a writer of books for children and you may never be able to present yourself as anything but that. I have personal experience of this: at an earlier stage of my writing career I wrote about 30 books for children and remember feeling very frustrated that I could not persuade the people who published those books to consider the manuscripts I wrote for adults. I felt trapped, and I know a number of writers who had a similar experience. It takes a real effort and not infrequently a stroke of luck to venture out from the world of children's books.

Of course there is no real reason why an author should not write for children as well as adults and go backwards and forwards between the genres. Roald Dahl is an example of somebody who did that: his short stories for adults are exceptionally well crafted, but are definitely not children's fare. His children's classics, though, can be read with enjoyment by adults, whether or not one is reading them aloud to one's children or for private pleasure. That is the mark, I think, of the great storyteller: he or she is of universal appeal.

But let us imagine that you are now launched, whether or not with a first book that fits into any narrow genre. What should you do about your second book? Should you try to do much the same thing as you did in the first? An initial question is whether you are interested in writing a sequel. That will depend on the nature of the first book: some books lend themselves to sequels more naturally than others. If you have created strong characters, you may wish to continue those characters and expose them to new challenges. That, of course, is how most real lives are lived: they go on for years – each of us, in a way, finds ourself in a family saga of one sort or another.

A series can be attractive to both author and publisher. From the author's point of view there is a particular pleasure in returning to characters and places with which you are already familiar. Creating a new chapter in a life that you have already got to know in an earlier novel can be rather like sitting down for a chat with an old friend, and may present chances to say much more about character and background than you were able to say in the first encounter. From the publisher's point of view, half the battle of marketing a book is over if there is a readership that already recognises – and likes – the principal character. That is why it is relatively easy for publishers of crime fiction to sell the latest exploits of well-known detectives: everybody knows those detectives and is eager to hear from them. But the same can be said too of other series: readers of Patrick O'Brian were lining up to read about Jack Aubrey and Stephen Maturin as soon as the next instalment was due, just as they did for Harry Potter and his friends.

Again, though, a warning note needs to be sounded. A successful series can become a treadmill for an author and may also frustrate the author's desire to do something different. So it is a good idea to make it clear to publishers that one wants to be able to write something different from time to time. A good publisher will be perfectly happy to allow this if the author has been reasonably successful with an existing series; indeed the publisher should see this as a way of expanding the author's readership as well as allowing existing readers to sample something different from a writer they have come to know.

My own experience of this has involved writing a number of standalone novels as well as a number of existing, regular series. I have found these standalones to be a valuable way of saying things that I might not have been able to say in any of my series, as well as giving me an opportunity to spread my wings stylistically. There is also the sheer stimulation involved in being able to do something new – to accept new challenges.

A few years ago I had one such challenge presented to me by a publisher with whom I had worked in the past. Roger Cazalet, one of the most highly regarded of British publishers, came to me with the suggestion that I should write a new version of Jane Austen's *Emma*. It took me, I think, not much longer than 30 seconds to say yes to this proposal. Not only would this enable me to work again with Roger – and the relationship with your publisher is a very important matter – but it would also allow me to step into the world of Jane Austen, a writer whom I, like virtually everybody else, admire so greatly. I was aware, though, that this was yet another genre of fiction that I was straying into: that of the use of fictional characters developed by another author altogether.

Using another author's characters seems to have become a rather popular pursuit. Not only are people doing it with Jane Austen – there are innumerable versions now of *Pride and Prejudice* – but they are doing it for a whole list of well-known fictional characters. There were the Flashman novels, for instance, that involved the reappearance of the bully in *Tom Brown's Schooldays*. There are also the now fairly numerous reappearances of James Bond, from the pen of various distinguished modern novelists such as William Boyd and Sebastian Faulks. This is itself now a whole new literary genre.

I found writing a new *Emma* one of the most enjoyable literary experiences of my life. Part of that, of course, was the sheer pleasure of Austen's story, but much of the attraction lay in the fact that it was a new thing for me to do. I had not done this sort of thing before, and there was the exciting challenge of an entirely fresh project. And that, I think, is the important thing for any author to remember: you must be ready to push yourself, to explore the unfamiliar, to try a new voice. I am not suggesting that one picks up and then abandons literary styles and genres with careless abandon: what I am suggesting is that within each one of us there is probably more than one author waiting for a chance of self-expression. Let those voices out. Cultivate them. And even if one ends up writing widely differing types of books, there is likely to be the same vision behind each of them that will make them authentically you. And that, of course, is the bit that you must always listen to and never silence – for any reason at all.

Alexander McCall Smith CBE, a former professor of Medical Law, is one of the world's most prolific and most popular authors. His *No 1 Ladies' Detective Agency* series has sold over 20 million copies, and his various series of books have been translated into over 40 languages. These include the 44 *Scotland Street* novels, the *Isabel Dalhousie Novels* series, the *von Igelfeld* series, and the *Corduroy Mansions* novels. Alexander is also the author of collections of short stories, academic works, and over 50 books for children. His numerous awards include the British Book Awards Author of the Year Award (2004) and Bollinger Everyman Wodehouse Prize for Comic Fiction (2015), as well as honorary degrees from 13 universities in Europe and N America. His most recent novels are *The Good Pilot George Woodhouse* (Polygon 2017) and *My Italian Bulldozer* (Little, Brown 2017). In 2017 he was awarded the National Arts Club of America–Medal of Honor for Achievement in Literature.

Notes from a successful crossover author

Neil Gaiman explains how he 'learned to stop worrying and became a crossover author'.

I didn't set out to be a crossover author, it just never occurred to me not to be. To put it another way, what I wanted to be was the kind of writer who told whatever stories he wanted in whatever medium he wanted, and I seem, more or less, to have got to that place. So, I can tell you how I did it. I'm just not sure I could tell you how you could do it too.

My first book was a children's book. I was about 22 when I wrote it, and I sent it to one publisher, and it came back with a nice note from the editor saying that it wasn't quite right for them, and I put it away for ever. I was a journalist for a while (it would be accurate to say that all I knew of being a journalist when I began was what I had gleaned from the 1983 edition of the *Writers' & Artists' Yearbook*). Then I wrote comics – mostly for grown-ups – and once I'd learned to write comics to my own satisfaction and thought it might be good fun to go and explore prose fiction, I was spoiled. The joy of writing comics is that it's a medium that people mistake for a genre: nobody seemed to mind whether I lurched from historical to fantasy to spy stories to autobiography to children's fiction, because it was all comics – a freedom that I treasured.

I started writing my first real children's book in 1991, a scary story for my daughter, Holly, called *Coraline*. I showed the first few chapters to my editor at Gollancz, Richard Evans. Now, Richard was a good editor and a smart man, and had just midwifed a book by Terry Pratchett and me, *Good Omens*, into existence. The next time I was in the Gollancz offices he took me to one side and said, 'Neil. I read the *Coraline* chapters, and I loved it. I think it's the best thing you've ever written. But I have to warn you, it's unpublishable'. I was puzzled: 'Why?' 'Well, it's a horror novel aimed at children and adults,' he told me, 'and I don't think we could publish a horror novel for children, and I really don't know how anyone could publish anything for adults and children at the same time.'

So I put the book away. I planned to keep writing it, in my own time, but there wasn't a lot of my own time about, and I managed about a thousand words on it during the next few years. I knew that unless someone was waiting for it, unless it had a chance of being read, I wasn't going to write it.

By now I had published a couple of books with Avon, and I sent it to my editor, Jennifer Hershey. 'It's great,' she said. 'What happens next?' I told her I wasn't really sure, but if she sent me a contract we would both find out! She did. The contract was for about 5% of what I'd got as an advance for my last novel, but it was a contract, and Jennifer said she would worry about how the book was published when I handed it in.

Two years passed. I didn't have any more time, so I kept a notebook beside my bed and finished the book and handed it in. But I still had an adult novel, *American Gods*, to finish before *Coraline* would be published. Avon was taken over by HarperCollins, a publisher with a healthy children's publishing division, and somewhere in there it was decided that *Coraline* would be published by HarperCollins Children's. In the UK, the book was sold to Bloomsbury.

It was still a horror novel, still aimed at both adults and children, but the publishing landscape had changed in the previous handful of years. The success of the few books that had crossed over from children's fiction to the adult world – the Harry Potter books, Philip Pullman's *His Dark Materials*, the Lemony Snicket books – made it at least a feasible goal.

Coraline was published in the summer of 2002, which was, coincidentally, the first summer without a new Harry Potter book. Journalists had column inches to fill, and they wrote about *Coraline*, imagining a movement of adult novelists now writing children's books. In both the USA and the UK, it's fair to say, adults bought the book at first, not children. That came later, as teachers enjoyed reading it and began introducing it in schools, and news of it spread by word of mouth.

The Wolves in the Walls followed, written by me and illustrated by artist Dave McKean. A children's picture book, again, it was initially bought by adults who liked what I wrote and what Dave painted – essentially the graphic novel audience who had come with us from comics. But it was read to children, and became popular with them, and now most of the copies I sign at signings are for younger readers.

I don't think you can plan for something to be a crossover book. But you can do things to make it easier. In my case, it was useful that I already had a large readership, one that had followed me from comics into prose, and who didn't seem to mind that none of my prose books resembled each other very much, except in having been written by me. It was also wonderful that I had supportive publishers in the USA and the UK, who were willing to take different approaches to the material.

When I wrote *The Graveyard Book*, a book that began with me wondering what would happen if you took Kipling's *The Jungle Book* and relocated it to a graveyard, I wasn't really sure who I was writing it for. I just wanted it to be good. Dave McKean did a book cover for the US edition while I was still writing it, but once the book was done it was obvious that the cover was wrong. It looked like a book for ten year-olds, and only for ten-year-olds. While the book I'd written would work for children, it worked just as well for adults, and we didn't want to exclude them. With tremendous good humour, Dave went back to the drawing board and produced a dozen new sketches. One of them seemed perfect – it showed a gravestone, which became the outline of a boy's face in profile. It could as easily have been a children's book cover or the cover of a Stephen King book; no one picking it up would feel excluded. (Another of Dave's sketches, of a baby walking on a bloody knife-edge in which a graveyard could be seen, would have been perfect for a book aimed at adults, but was thought a bit too edgy for children.)

In the UK, Bloomsbury had come up with their own strategy: two editions of *The Graveyard Book*, one aimed at children, one at adults. The children's edition would be illustrated by Chris Riddell, the adult edition by Dave McKean – and Dave's baby-on-a-knife-edge cover was ideal for what they wanted, something that was unashamedly aimed at adults.

You can do your best to write a book for children that adults will like (or the other way around – in the USA the Young Adult Library Services awards celebrate the books for adults that young readers latch on to); you can try not to mess up the publishing end of things (that first cover for the US version of *The Graveyard Book*, which looked like a book that only 'middle grade readers' might have enjoyed would have been a mis-step); you can try to bring an existing audience with you, if you have one, and a way of letting them know what you've done. But I'm not sure that any of this will guarantee anything. Publishers are less intimidated by crossover books now that there have been many successes, but the mechanics of bookselling, the fact that books have to go somewhere in a bookshop, and that somewhere may be in a place that adults or children don't go, that the adult and children's divisions of publishers are staffed by different people in different groups who don't always talk to each other or have the same objectives (or even the same catalogues) – all of these things serve to make it harder to be a crossover author and encourage you to stay put, to write something people will know where to shelve, to write the same sort of thing you wrote before.

I suppose you become a crossover author by taking risks, but they had better be the kind of risks that you enjoy taking. Don't set out to be a crossover author. Write the books you have to write, and if you write one that crosses boundaries, that finds readers in a variety of ages and types, then do your best to get it published in a way that lets all of them know it's out there. Good luck.

Neil Gaiman is the winner of numerous literary honours and is the *New York Times* bestselling author of novels including *Norse Mythology*, *The Ocean at the End of the Lane*, *American Gods*, *Neverwhere*, *Stardust* and *Anansi Boys*; the *Sandman* series of graphic novels; three short story collections; and he is the first author to win both the Carnegie Medal and the Newbery Medal for one work, *The Graveyard Book*. *American Gods* is a current hit TV series on Starz/Amazon and Neil wrote and is currently showrunning a BBC/Amazon series based on *Good Omens*, the book he wrote with Terry Pratchett. He is also the author of books for readers of all ages including the novels *Fortunately, the Milk* (HarperCollins 2013) and *Coraline* (Bloomsbury 2008) and picture books including *The Sleeper and the Spindle* (Bloomsbury 2014). Recent publications include *The View From The Cheap Seats* (Headline 2016), a collection of his non-fiction, and *Cinnamon* (HarperCollins 2017), a novel for children. Originally from England, Neil now lives in the USA. He is listed in the *Dictionary of Literary Biography* as one of the top ten living post-modern writers and he says he owes it all to reading the *Writers' & Artists' Yearbook* as a young man. Visit him at www.neilgaiman.com.

Notes from a successful children's author

J.K. Rowling shares her experiences of writing success.

I can remember writing *Harry Potter and the Philosopher's Stone* in a cafe in Oporto. I was employed as a teacher at the language institute three doors along the road at the time, and this café was a kind of unofficial staffroom. My friend and colleague joined me at my table. When I realised I was no longer alone I hastily shuffled worksheets over my notebook, but not before Paul had seen exactly what I was doing. 'Writing a novel, eh?' he asked wearily, as though he had seen this sort of behaviour in foolish young teachers only too often before. '*Writers' & Artists' Yearbook*, that's what you need,' he said. 'Lists all the publishers and … stuff,' he advised, before ordering a lager and starting to talk about the previous night's episode of *The Simpsons*.

I had almost no knowledge of the practical aspects of getting published; I knew nobody in the publishing world, I didn't even know anybody who knew anybody. It had never occurred to me that assistance might be available in book form.

Nearly three years later and a long way from Oporto, I had almost finished *Harry Potter and the Philosopher's Stone*. I felt oddly as though I was setting out on a blind date as I took a copy of the *Writers' & Artists' Yearbook* from the shelf in Edinburgh's Central Library. Paul had been right and the *Yearbook* answered my every question, and after I had read and reread the invaluable advice on preparing a manuscript, and noted the time-lapse between sending said manuscript and trying to get information back from the publisher, I made two lists: one of publishers, the other of agents.

The first agent on my list sent my sample three chapters and synopsis back by return of post. The first two publishers took slightly longer to return them, but the 'no' was just as firm. Oddly, these rejections didn't upset me much. I was braced to be turned down by the entire list, and in any case, these were real rejection letters – even real writers had got them. And then the second agent, who was high on the list purely because I like his name, wrote back with the most magical words I have ever read: 'We would be pleased to read the balance of your manuscript on an exclusive basis …'.

This piece was written for the very first edition of the *Children's & Writers' Yearbook*, published in 2004.

J.K. Rowling, CH is the bestselling author of the *Harry Potter* series (Bloomsbury), published between 1997 and 2007, which have sold over 500 million copies worldwide, are distributed in more than 200 territories, translated into over 80 languages and have been turned into eight blockbuster films. In 2012 J.K. Rowling's digital company and digital publisher Pottermore was launched, where fans can enjoy news, features and articles, as well as original content by J.K. Rowling. J.K. Rowling has written a novel for adults: *The Casual Vacancy* (Little, Brown 2012), which was adapted for TV by the BBC in 2015. Her crime novels, written under the pseudonym Robert Galbraith, were published in 2013 (*The Cuckoo's Calling*), 2014 (*The Silkworm*) and 2015 (*Career of Evil*), and have been adapted for TV as a major BBC detective drama, *Strike*, produced by Brontë Film and Television. J.K. Rowling has collaborated on a stage play, *Harry Potter and the Cursed Child Parts One and Two*, which opened in London's West End in the summer of 2016 and on Broadway in 2018. *Harry Potter and the Cursed Child* is based on an original new story by J.K. Rowling, Jack Thorne and John Tiffany, written by Jack Thorne. In 2016 J.K. Rowling made her screenwriting debut and was a producer on the film *Fantastic Beasts and Where to Find Them*, a further extension of the wizarding world and the start of a new five-film series to be written by the author. The second film in the series will be released in November 2018. The script books of both the play *Harry Potter and the Cursed Child Parts One and Two* and the film *Fantastic Beasts and Where to Find Them* were published by Little, Brown in 2016.

About editing and writing

Diana Athill describes the often unnoticed (but by authors generally much appreciated) work of an editor, how she started in the business of editing, and her relationship with one particularly important but needy author, Jean Rhys.

No one taught me to edit. Just before the Second World War's end I joined a Hungarian friend of mine who had decided to be a publisher, although his English was still wobbly, and my job was simply to be English, and well-read.

Almost our first book was a problem: an account of the discovery of Tahiti by a man who knew everything – but everything – about it but who wrote so badly it was painful to read. Most firms would have rejected it, but the subject was interesting and we were trying to build a list, and by chance my partner, at a dinner party, sat next to an old boy recently retired from administering a Pacific Island who said he was looking for some way of using his new leisure. Would he consider editing a book? Yes indeed. So we introduced him to the author who was so pleased that he rashly paid him in advance.

The book came in, and to my dismay I saw that the naughty old boy had become bored after 30 pages and done nothing more. Either the poor author had spent quite a lot of money to no purpose, or I would have to finish the job myself.

I started on it nervously, but soon began to enjoy it. It was like unwrapping a lumpy parcel and finding something beautiful inside it. So I could edit – wow! The book got good reviews, and one reviewer said not only was it informative, but also it was very well-written. The author cut out this review and sent it to me. How kind and appreciative... But oh no! An attached postcard said, 'I always knew all that fuss about the writing was rubbish'. Editor, know your place!

Though in fact that was an unusual case. Never again in almost 50 years did I get anything but gratitude from an author. Provided your comments make sense, a good writer is always glad of them. It is much rarer than one would think for a book to be read with really close attention – something an author longs for – so evidence that an editor has done so is welcome.

Usually my comments were few, and fairly trivial. Perhaps 'it might be better to move your description of x's looks back to his first appearance on the scene', or 'you've used the word "exuberance" four times on the last three pages'. Occasionally I would suggest a little cutting (which can always be done); but usually, once we had got going, I would not take on anything needing a great deal of work on the text. If permissions are needed for quoting from someone else's work, it is of course the editor's job to see that the author has got them, or to get them for him or her, and if something in the text might be libellous or unacceptably obscene it is the editor's job to point it out and get a legal opinion; but on the whole the bulk of the task is nannying. You must keep your author happy by appreciating – genuinely appreciating – his or her work, and you must be helpful and attentive in small ways, making it clear that he or she is truly valued.

In the rare cases when you actually dislike an author, hand him or her over to someone else – unless you are unusually good at brainwashing yourself out of your bad feelings.

It is not often that nannying goes much further than the above, but it can. It did with one of our most valuable writers, Jean Rhys. She was, perhaps, the most extraordinary person I ever knew: extraordinary because of the contrast between her steely control of her art and her incredible inefficiency in her conduct of her life. Jean knew precisely how her writing should be, and why, and was perfectly indifferent to the opinions of anyone else. But in life... Well, I sometimes felt that she had become stuck at the age of eight. She was uncommonly attractive, so as a young woman she was always rescued from disaster by a man – but she was not much good at choosing men. Her first lover had money, but was much older, got bored, and broke her heart. After that, three husbands were each poorer than the last and two of them ended up in prison. Max Hamer, the last one, was there because of foolishness rather than criminality, but he emerged from the experience a broken man, and looking after him for years, with no money, nearly broke Jean. How she managed to finish the novel which finally made her famous, *Wide Sargasso Sea*, heaven knows. It saved her life, but only just.

A woman who knew Jean in her youth said she had never understood the power of the really weak until she met Jean, and I know what she meant. She meant that the feeling one got that unless Jean was rescued she would die in a ditch was *true*. It worked right up to the end of her life, so the nannying one had to provide as her editor was endless. She had to be reassured about money all the time; she had to be rescued from rogue agents; she had to be constantly told how good she was; she had to have home help found for her; she had to have typists found for her... Much of what she had to have was provided by a wonderful friend, Sonia Orwell, who gave her luxurious holidays in London every winter – but even then her editor had to go to her hotel every evening to put her to bed, because Jean filling a hot water bottle meant, inevitably, scalded hands. No one planning to be an editor should *expect* such a situation, but it is not impossible that something similar might happen.

I suppose it is possible that the work helped me to become a writer. I say 'suppose' because the idea did not occur to me at the time, but being concerned every day with the making of sentences may well have taught me what I liked and what I didn't. Although I suspect that reading a lot, and being taught as a child how to parse a sentence played a larger part. (How dreadfully bored I was by grammar lessons, and how grateful I am now for being made to sit through them!)

But I believe what I really gained from being an editor was more important than anything to do with sentence structure. I think it is something simple but important to do with *why* one writes, expressed in words I often say to myself: 'I must get it *like it really was*'. And who said those words – the only words she ever said in my hearing about her art? Jean Rhys.

Diana Athill, OBE is a literary editor and the author of several memoirs, one novel and a collection of short stories. Born in 1917, she was educated at Oxford University and worked throughout the Second World War for the BBC, before helping André Deutsch to establish his publishing company and pursuing a long career as an editor for Deutsch. Diana's first memoir *Stet* was published in 2000 (and was recently re-issued) by Granta Books; this was followed by five further volumes of memoir, most recently *Alive, Alive Oh!: And Other Things That Matter* (Granta 2015). She won the Costa Prize for Biography for her third memoir *Somewhere Towards the End* (Granta 2008). Her novel, *Don't Look at Me Like That,* was published by Chatto & Windus in 1967.

Becoming a comic writer

Marina Lewycka describes how she became a comic writer and makes suggestions on looking at life from a comic writer's point of view. She also offers insights on why the same piece of comic writing can make some people laugh aloud but leave others totally baffled.

When I wrote *A Short History of Tractors in Ukrainian*, I certainly did not think I was embarking on a book in the comic genre; my intention was to write something deep and meaningful about the human condition. My two previous unpublished novels had been rather serious and angst-ridden works. I had wanted to write Literature with a capital L, but alas no one, it seemed, wanted to read my efforts. By the time I was in my late fifties I had more or less given up on the possibility of getting published, but some strange compulsion kept me writing, and I found myself chuckling quite a bit as I wrote. Freed from the obligation to write Literature, my style had lightened up, and so had my view of the human condition.

Getting published was a pleasant surprise, but I was a bit bemused to find myself in 2006 winning the Bollinger Everyman Wodehouse Prize (the UK's only literary award for comic fiction; see page 567). So that's where I've been going wrong, I thought. I must be a comic writer, not a writer of Literature. It was lovely to receive letters from readers who said they had laughed out loud while reading my book. But other readers wrote to me saying they did not know why the book had been described as comic, because they found it profoundly sad. And they had a point. The comic and the tragic are closer than we think. It's the human condition.

With that prize, the die was cast, and keen to experiment with my new craft, I set about writing another comic novel, *Two Caravans*. I was even more bemused to find myself being shortlisted for a prize for political writing.

I soon found that when it comes to comic writing, you can't please everyone. Not long after my third novel *We Are All Made of Glue* was published, I received a letter from a reader in Australia.

'Dear Ms Lewycka, I very much enjoy reading your books, but I am shocked that your spelling is so bad. Don't your publishers employ an editor? In *We Are All Made of Glue* there were two big spelling mistakes on page 14. Because of this, I do not feel able to recommend your books to my friends.'

Needless to say, I immediately turned to page 14 and read:

'My mother had always been a great advocate of past-sell-by-date shopping … She didn't think much of Listernia and Saminella …'

The offending words, for my correspondent, were Listernia and Saminella, which were the character's mangled pronunciation of Listeria and Salmonella. But the reader just didn't get it. In the novel, the narrator's mother uses long words she can't pronounce because she has pretensions to education and culture, and so does my snooty Australian correspondent. How could she be so stupid, I exclaimed under my breath? I wanted to pen a reply pointing out the brilliance of my joke, but alas there was no return address.

That's one of the dangers with comedy – it doesn't travel well. This joke had obviously not made it to this reader in Australia, despite the fact that English and Australian are almost the same language.

Comedy also travels badly in time. The scenes in Shakespeare that had the 16th-century groundlings rolling with laughter, mostly leave modern audiences cold. A good director can still get across the meaning, but the essential quality of comedy is lost when you have to explain it. We may just raise a faint smile, as if to say, 'Oh, I see what you mean.'

And humour even travels badly between generations. The things my parents thought were hilarious seem to me just faintly silly. The jokes that have me and my friends laughing out loud make my daughter and her friends snigger with embarrassment. The things they laugh at, I don't even understand, because they usually refer to music or films or people that I have no knowledge of.

When *Various Pets Alive and Dead* was published, the very same jokes which delighted some reviewers made others groan. For every reviewer who admired a burlesque scene, there was one who derided it as slapstick.

English language and culture are rich in humour: irony, satire, farce, wordplay, wit, silliness, absurdity, teasing. It comes in many forms, and the first rule is that there is no rule to judge whether something is intrinsically funny or not; it all rests on the judgement of the individual. What we find funny is essentially subjective. A good rule of thumb is that if you're chuckling to yourself as you write, the chances are that at least some other people will laugh when they read what you've written. But you can be certain that for every person laughing there will be someone else rolling their eyes and tutting.

Getting the most from rules

Comedy depends on recognition that certain rules commonly accepted by a social group are being broken. Its audience knows those rules, and the humour draws a warm circle of shared understanding around the insiders, 'people like us' who 'get' the joke, and excludes those who are baffled by it. What and who we laugh at defines us just as surely as the clothes we wear or the music we listen to or the books on our shelves.

Language is of course a set of rules, and breaking the rules of language is a rich source of humour. But you have to know the accepted expression to be amused by the mistakes people make. My books, like my life, are peopled by characters of many nationalities. When I was as a child, I learnt 'correct' English at school, while my home was always full of people who got along perfectly well with their own version of it. Later, a spell as a teacher of English to speakers of other languages left me with a lifelong fascination with the way that foreign people talk.

There are as many varieties of 'bad English' as there are languages, and the mistakes a non-native speaker makes often mirror the grammar of their own language. A Slavic native speaker leaves out definite and indefinite articles, whereas a German inserts them even where they don't belong in English, for example in front of abstract nouns. Speakers of Arabic often don't distinguish between 'p' and 'b'. People who speak gendered languages tend to ascribe gender to everything. When I gave Dog a voice in *Two Caravans*, I had to create a new language for him. I studied dogs and I talked to their owners. I learnt that their sense of smell is predominant. They keep tracking and back-tracking over the same ground, in a purposeful, not a random way. But they have no nose at all for punctuation. Even bad English must have its own internal logic. That poses a particular challenge for translators.

In Ukraine my humorous descriptions of Ukrainians have caused controversy because soon after the book was first published it was translated into Russian, not into Ukrainian, and the Russian translators translated all the 'bad English' as Ukrainian. Nor were my Ukrainian characters popular, for despite the great tradition of Ukrainian humour, including Gogol and Bulgakov, modern Ukrainians have only recently achieved independent nationhood, and they want to be taken seriously on the world stage.

Comic writers inevitably offend somebody; it's a risk you have to take, and most writers set their own limits. Just because you can upset someone doesn't mean you have to go out of your way to do so. I draw the line at humour that targets the vulnerable and weak, or diminishes someone's self-esteem. But I prefer humour that also expresses affection, and, like teasing, can offer us the gift of self-knowledge. We can transcend our foibles when we learn to laugh at them. This is one thing I particularly admire and love about the English sense of humour; the English do make fun of others, but they are supremely good at laughing at themselves.

Thinking about writing comedy

Although there is no formula to writing comedy, there has been an enormous amount of academic theory on the subject. From Aristotle through to Lacan and Umberto Eco, thinkers have provided many fascinating insights, but believe me, it's not a bundle of laughs. Umberto Eco is among the most accessible, as witty and stylish in his academic writing as he is in fiction. However, the more one tries to analyse or explain comedy, the more elusive it becomes. In fact when a joke or a comic scene has to be explained, it loses its power to make us laugh. Comedy has to grab you by surprise. It's one of those quirks of the human condition, like the fact that you can't tickle yourself.

If you want to write comedy, the most useful approach is probably to expose yourself to the comic side of life:

- Cultivate eccentric friends and relatives – seek them out, observe their ways, treat them nicely, and let them inhabit your books.
- Be curious – some might say nosy. Ask the slightly impertinent question, peep through the open door, read over the passenger's shoulder, listen in on the hushed conversation. Comedy is often found hidden away among secrets.
- Break rules – talk to strangers, shamelessly explore your host's house, get into arguments. A comic situation often starts out seeming perfectly normal, then incrementally becomes more and more absurd as boundaries are transgressed.
- Keep a notebook – however memorable a joke or an anecdote seems at the time, you will not be able to recall it in an hour's time.
- When things are getting hectic, imagine pushing them one stage further. Ask yourself – what if …?
- Or you can short-cut all these by immersing yourself in the zany world of wonderful comic writers, from Chaucer to Dickens to P.G. Wodehouse to Howard Jacobson. It's hard to imagine a more enjoyable 'homework'.

Comedy, like all drama, originates from a combination of people and circumstances. The same sorts of people often seem to find themselves drawn to tragic or comic situations. You probably have plenty among your acquaintances, and whether their story is comic or tragic depends on how it ends. I am particularly fond of:

- People in the grip of an obsession, like Mrs Bennet in *Pride and Prejudice*.
- People who take themselves too seriously, like Adrian Mole or the characters created by Ricky Gervais.

• People who are perpetual victims or losers, like Eeyore.
• People who live in a world of their own imagining like Don Quixote.
• People driven beyond the bounds of reasonable behaviour by an overriding need or desire, like Valentina in *A Short History of Tractors in Ukrainian.*

Now try placing one of these types of characters in a volatile situation, where some social norms are in danger of being transgressed. Maybe they misunderstand who someone is, or what someone has said, or they have misread the situation. Maybe there are too many people, or a dangerous combination of people together at the same time. Maybe money, honour or love are at stake. You can be sure that something will go terribly wrong. But instead of crying, we will laugh. It's the human condition.

Marina Lewycka was born in a refugee camp in Germany in 1946 and moved to England with her family when she was about a year old. She has been writing for most of her life, and in 2005 published *A Short History of Tractors in Ukrainian* which has sold more than a million copies in the UK alone. This was followed by *Two Caravans* (2007), *We Are All Made of Glue* (2009), *Various Pets Alive and Dead* (2012) and *The Lubetkin Legacy* (2016) – all published by Penguin.

Turning to crime: writing thrillers

Crime writer Kimberley Chambers describes how her life took a new direction when she began writing, and recalls the help and advice that have brought her success. She provides her own top tips for other aspiring authors.

I grew up in Dagenham and left school at 16, with hardly any qualifications. I then spent years working on East End markets such as Roman Road, Petticoat Lane and Whitechapel. When the markets took a turn for the worse, I began DJ-ing and then, in my thirties, I took up minicab driving.

At the age of 38, I was wondering what to do next. I hadn't written anything since school, but always thought that one day I'd have a crack at writing a book. That was the start of my career. Before I started writing my first book, *Billie Jo* (Preface 2008), I made a list of all the main characters. I recall slightly struggling with the first three chapters, but I stuck with it and, from chapter four onwards, it started to get easier. By chapter seven I was flying, and was positive that I'd found my vocation in life.

Because I was still minicabbing, it took me a whole year to write that first book. My friend Pat, who had a bookstall on Romford market at the time, told me about the *Writers' & Artists' Yearbook*. I wasn't particularly great at technical stuff – I'm still not – and if it hadn't been for Pat's advice I wouldn't have had a clue about getting an agent or getting published. She ordered me a copy and I remember reading through it from cover to cover. For someone uneducated like myself, I found it was written in a way that I could understand. I took all the advice on board, including the need to create a strong covering letter and to polish up the first few chapters; they, as the *Yearbook* explains, could be the only chance you have to catch someone's interest.

The day after I sent those chapters off to about 25 agents, an agent rang me up asking to see the rest. Another four agents contacted me the following week. I went to meet a few of them and ended up choosing Tim Bates (then of Pollinger Limited, now at PFD), who is still my agent to this day. And, since then, it really has been a rollercoaster of a journey for both of us.

I recall the initial wait was horrid – waiting to find out if I'd got that first book deal. Every day seemed like a week. I think a few of the publishers were worried because I was so uneducated and because I wrote by hand (which I still do). Penguin Random House had just launched a new imprint called Preface and they decided to take a chance on me. My first book deal was very small but, by the time *Billie Jo* came out in July 2008, I had finished my second novel, *Born Evil* (Preface 2009) and already signed another deal, which enabled me to give up the minicabbing for good. Obviously, there's always a chance, as a new author, that your book will flop or that you won't be able to get your name out there; but my sales still grew, by word of mouth, and I always believed in myself and that one day I would make it to the top.

My fortunes changed when I moved to HarperCollins. They decided to bring out the third book they published for me in hardback, because they knew I had a loyal following. *Payback* (HarperCollins 2013) shot straight to Number One on the *Sunday Times* bestseller list, where it stayed for a couple of weeks. Since that day, I've never looked back.

I'm not the biggest planner when it comes to plotting my books. I tend to mostly go with the flow, and let the storyline come to me as I get into the book. For instance, my novel *The Feud* (Preface 2010) was meant to be a standalone but, when I got five chapters from the end, I decided to change the ending in order to carry on with the story. A similar thing happened with *The Trap* (Harper 2013). That was also meant to be a standalone, but yet again I loved the characters and thought there was so much more to come from them, so I ended up with five books.

I often get asked by others wanting to write a book how to go about it, and I always tell them to get the *Writers' & Artists' Yearbook* and go through it with a fine-tooth comb like I did. I also advise them to write to as many agents as possible. As the old saying goes, one man's trash is another man's treasure. I sometimes wonder what I would be doing now if I hadn't been given the advice that I was.

As far as advising others on their writing, I personally find that I bring more colour to a book when I set it in an era that I'm interested in. I much prefer writing stories set in the '60s, '70s or '80s. I love to recreate the music and fashion of those days and the way life was back then. For example, my parents used to have a caravan on King's Holiday Park in Eastbourne, which back in the day had the biggest nightclub in the Southeast. So I set part of the *Butler* series at King's – my main characters bought a bungalow there – and I went back and recreated those days and how I remembered it. The markets usually pop up in my books too. Queenie Butler, one of my characters, loves shopping with her sister Vivvy up the Roman Road. That was recalling the time I worked there myself and it was like a competition between the women back then, about who was the most glamorous on a Saturday afternoon! As I was writing those scenes, it felt like stepping back in time.

I'm not the biggest reader myself but, as a child, I was addicted to Enid Blyton and I remember reading the *Famous Five* books repeatedly. I didn't pick up a book again until I went on a girls' holiday in my late teens. I found a Jackie Collins novel at the airport, and that's what got me back into reading although, since becoming an author myself, I don't tend to read a great amount. I still enjoy a good holiday book, but I relax by watching a drama or film on TV. I have no set pattern to the hours I work, but I tend to write more in the evening than earlier in the day. In summer I like to sit at the kitchen table because it looks out onto my garden and it's quite tranquil; in winter I prefer sitting in the front room opposite the open fire.

My top tips for anybody who aspires to be a published author are:

1. Think about your **characters** carefully. I tend to visualize what mine would look like, give them strong names that suit them, and focus on their separate personalities.
2. Pick a **genre** you like to read or a world you are familiar with. I chose the genre I write in as it's the one I enjoy reading the most. I had led a reasonably colourful life, so choosing to write crime from the other side of the fence, rather than from the usual police perspective, was much easier for me. I don't like doing hours and hours of research.
3. Think of a strong **beginning, middle and ending**. This might change as your book develops, as it has in a few of mine, but it's always best to know in which direction you are heading.
4. Believe in yourself. If you are having a bad day when you are writing, **don't give up**. Just take a break, then return to the story with a fresh mind and eye.

5. Try to go down the route of getting properly published before considering self-publishing. To do that, you need **an agent**. You will find literary agents listed in this *Yearbook*, along with tips about how to approach them (listings for agents start on page 440). That is exactly how I got published, and I wish all of you doing the same the very best of luck.

Kimberley Chambers worked as a market trader, DJ and minicab driver before becoming a full-time author after the success of her first two books, *Billie Jo* and *Born Evil*. The second book in her *Butler* series, *Payback* (HarperCollins 2013), was No. 1 in the *Sunday Times* bestseller list, as were both *Tainted Love* (Harper Collins 2016) and her most recent book *Life of Crime* (HarperCollins 2018). Kimberley's other books include the Mitchell & O'Haras trilogy: *The Feud*, *The Traitor* and *The Victim*. For more information visit http://kimberleychambers.com and follow her on Twitter @kimbochambers or https://www.facebook.com/kimberleychambersofficial.

See also...

- *The path to a bestseller*, page 262

Writing speculative fiction

Author Claire North considers the nature of 'speculative fiction', and the blurry nature of genres more broadly, and provides advice for writers on the boundless world-building possibilities that writers of fantastical fiction can develop to grab a reader's imagination.

You could spend as much time arguing about what 'speculative fiction' is as writing it. Magic realism? Literature with a twist? Science fiction? Hi-tech social commentary? It's worth asking this question as – although hopefully you are writing out of love for words on the page – your experience of being a published author will vary hugely, depending on where (rather arbitrarily) the world decides your speculative fiction falls.

The question of genre

Revolutions in film, TV and games now mean that science fiction and fantasy have never been more popular and accepted in the mainstream. Yet the world of literary criticism and review frequently still treats genre as if it were less worthy of note than literature, despite its potent selling power. Without making 'literature' a term of exclusions (NOT crime, NOT thriller, NOT romance) it can be hard to say what 'literary' actually means, and the inclusion of writers such as Margaret Atwood, David Mitchell, Kazuo Ishiguro and George Orwell on mainstream shelves only adds to the justified arch of your raised eyebrow.

Partly in response to this, 'speculative fiction' has grown in recent years as a term that tweaks the definition of genre into something mainstream – and therefore perhaps more acceptable. Not quite 'hard' science fiction or pure fantasy, but laced through with an element of something strange, fantastical or other, it is the land of James Smythe, Nick Harkaway, Naomi Alderman, and – in film/TV terms – of *Black Mirror* or *Stranger Things*. Speculative fiction is, in short, an excellent corner to claim for marketing purposes, encompassing the best of so many worlds: if only you can work out what it means.

The simplest truth may be the truth of all genres, namely that the key difference between, say, hard science fiction and speculative fiction is a publisher's marketing choice. In the case of M.R. Carey's *Girl with all the Gifts* (Orbit 2014) this meant removing any reference to 'zombies' from both book and blurb, transforming an excellent apocalypse story into something sold as nuanced character-study in a difficult world. Both aspects are of course true – it is both a character study and a straight-up zombie book – but most books are more than one thing, and it could have been positioned a dozen other ways. Genre is an increasingly blurry line – a comforting tool for helping us find books that we love, as well as an imprisoning categorisation used to define what we don't read as much as what we do. What we read defines us; there is still a social pressure to be seen to read the 'right' thing. Men do not read books about shopping with Comic Sans lettering on pink covers; adults do not read Harry Potter unless they have silver embossed jackets – and so on. The world is changing, perhaps, but social pressures remain.

Does genre even matter?

Of course, appreciating the nuances of how genre is positioned in the changing world of bookshop categories and predictive algorithms may not affect what you write. Indeed, I would argue that at the early stages of writing, it shouldn't. Writing is a business, but it is also a joy, a gift. Forget market positioning, forget reviewer bias; the best book you can possibly write is the one you loved writing the most. And if you have chosen to write speculative fiction – embrace it, enjoy it! In the future you might find yourself making artistic choices based on where a publisher seeks to sell you, but this makes *now* the moment to choose a path that you'll always love walking. That said, there are a few things to bear in mind in those earliest stages, that may help you on your quest:

1. Have confidence

Easier said than done, but this is key, especially in speculative fiction, to bringing a reader into a place where their imagination has never been before. You do not need to explain your choices; you do not need to info-dump your world. If you know every detail of it already, it will manifest in the actions of your text, in the story that you *show* rather than the information that you tell. In doing so, you have already won half the battle.

'Show, don't tell' is one of the classic rules. It is the art of revealing information through story, rather than through exposition.

- 'The witches are coming!'
- *'No – not the witches of the west!'*
- 'Yes, the very ones, who drink the blood of infants!'
- *'Oh my God – and who wear blue robes while chanting to their pagan gods?'*
- 'That's them!'

Nah, mate. Think of the tools you have available to you as a writer to help us **live** a story – third person, first person, extracted texts, second person, biased narrator, past tense, present tense, future tense, flashback. There is the tool out there that is waiting for you to **show** us your world, and to transform information into experience. It is the secret of every great medical drama. Very few people know why the CT scan matters or what the spleen does, but we all hear the truth of **feeling** beneath this language and are caught up by the emotional urgency beneath the technobabble.

Where information must be given, be succinct:

- 'The western witches in robes of blue, who drank the blood of babies and worshipped their pagan gods, came upon the town as it was sleeping.'

Job done. You have imparted data. Now move on; there's a story to tell.

2. Use story for world-building

The same 'show, don't tell' applies to speculative fiction world-building. Show us what we need to know. It is the difference between:

- 'She was one of the sisters, an ancient order of healers, who look after dying men on the battlefield.'

and

- 'The sister's robe was still caked in the blood of the men she had tended on the battlefield ...'.

The immediacy of one brings us into the moment; the other is just information. Resist putting every detail of your world on the page; the story must come first, and the world will unfold as it does. A focus on story allows you to start harder, faster, and let the reader invest more in building the world for themselves.

3. Obey your own rules

It is the classic *Dr Who/Buffy the Vampire Slayer* trope: around 40 minutes into a 45-minute episode (or 250 pages into an average book), when things have got just about as bad as they can possibly get, someone finds a giant button/a mystic spell that fixes everything. In crime, this is the unexpected witness who busts the case wide open; thrillers have the dramatic helicopter rescue. But in speculative fiction, if you try to write yourself out of that plot-hole with an unexpected *deus ex machina*, there is a danger that you will undermine a reader's immersion in what that world is. Don't be afraid of deleting your way to freedom and take time to structure your story. Especially in speculative fiction, death need not be the thing that *matters*. In thrillers in the Chris Ryan vein, soldiers live and soldiers die, but *betrayal* hurts more than actual bullets. Gout doesn't kill Falstaff; the betrayal of Prince Hal does. What matters to the story is not life or death, but what these things mean to our characters. Mount Doom erupting in Middle-Earth has nothing on Frodo succumbing to the dark side. Find what matters to your world and characters; obey your own rules.

4. Humanity is your gift

Speculative fiction is a genre that offers you so many possibilities, from the pure joy of space cowboy adventure through to tales of horror and deceit. But, more than anything, it lets you ask what humanity *is*. What is it to be human, in a world where apps and algorithms run our lives? Are we still ourselves with 30% of our brain grown from something else? 40%? 50%? Are we still ourselves, unique and true, when our clone sits opposite us? Is it human nature to build or to destroy? If we know the thoughts of others, does that elevate us or destroy the very essence of humanity? Is Kafka's twisted human cockroach still a man? Does humankind need gender? Can humans be grown in a lab?

We ask these questions, and in doing so we can tear down the barriers that are used to stratify humanity into exclusionary ideas of 'not I', such as class, race, ethnicity and sex. Fiction tells stories that catch the heart and then bring the head along after. We can do all of this, and we can have fun doing it, poking at the world while having badass, awesome adventures.

This being so, embrace the scope of humanity that is offered to you. Forget normative, oppressive ideas of women, men or culture. Speculative fiction opens up realms of boundless imagination to you; be awesome, and imagine humanity – lots and lots of it.

Claire North is the pen name of Catherine Webb, who also writes under the name Kate Griffin. Her novel, *The First Fifteen Lives of Harry August* (Orbit 2014) was shortlisted for the Arthur C. Clarke Award and was selected for the Richard and Judy Book Club, the Waterstones Book Club and the Radio 2 Book Club. Also published by Orbit, her novel *The Sudden Appearance of Hope* (2017) won the 2017 World Fantasy Award for Best Novel and *The End of the Day* (2017) was shortlisted for the 2017 Sunday Times/PFD Young Writer of the Year Award. In May 2018 Catherine published her fifth book under the Claire North pseudonym, *84K*. For more information see www.kategriffin.net and follow her on Twitter @ClaireNorth42.

Writing (spy) fiction

Mick Herron describes the appeal, range and addictive nature of writing spy novels, and offers his thoughts and advice on developing plot, character, and a rewarding work ethic.

I can't remember when I first realised I was a novelist, but now that the condition has firmly established itself – and seems likely to be terminal – I keep noting new symptoms. Like the habit I've developed of pausing a DVD when a bookshelf hoves into view, to read the titles. Often, set designers remove the dust jackets from novels, to make their spines seem more business-like, which means you can occasionally make out, say, a Jilly Cooper in a Home Secretary's study. And I once spotted a bound set of law reports in the background of a vet's surgery. TV props people buy books by the yard.

Nor am I sure when I became a spy novelist, but it felt like a natural progression. Novelists are spies of a kind, after all; observing the people around them, inventing cover stories for strangers. So it's an attractive genre for the budding writer, offering the opportunity to rely on skills honed by years of nosiness. Which isn't to say that – for me, anyway – it was simply a matter of picking up a pen and wading right in. Starting was difficult. Which is as it ought to be. If you love books, the prospect of adding to their number is an intimidating one, and nobody is going to give you permission to do so; you have to grant this yourself, or find it in the pages of authors you love. For me, that's a long list, but it was the late Reginald Hill whose work provided the necessary encouragement. I'm still not quite sure why this was. There was nothing in his style or plotting to suggest that I, or anyone else, could write anything like as well as he did; but the generosity of his spirit, as exemplified by the humanity of his characters, allowed me to believe there could be no harm in trying.

Assuming, then, that you've already reached that stage, the things you'll need for the road ahead include plot, character, style, a writing routine and some rules. Good luck with all of that. Here's a few loose thoughts to start you off.

Staying off the grid

A good spy novel depends on a tight plot. The classics of the genre dazzle because of the way they deceive – think of *The Spy Who Came In From The Cold*: that moment when the plot cracks like a whip, and the ground shifts beneath the reader. Not all books work like that; still, you need more than the simple desire to produce a novel before embarking on the writing.

But that's not to say you need everything worked out in advance. Beginning a novel is daunting – like setting out on a round-the-world trek – and it's comforting to have an itinerary but, at the same time, it's possible to over-plan and leave no time for the spontaneous experience. If your plot has been designed to the tiniest detail, its every movement choreographed in advance, then writing it becomes less like creating fiction and more like filling in a spreadsheet (symbolic moment: check; character insight: check; action sequence: check). It's a tempting method, largely because it allows you to feel you can sneak up on your book: make your notes, draw up your blueprint, flesh out your jottings, and lo – there's your novel. But the likelihood is that the result will be as lifeless as the process which produced it. A novel needs room to breathe; don't starve it of oxygen. Allow for organic growth. If your plot goes chasing down rabbit-holes, you can always call it to heel on your rewrite. Let yourself enjoy the ride, and this will communicate itself to the reader.

Choose your weapons

As with so many other things, of course, if you're to enjoy the ride, you've got to be in the right vehicle. One you're comfortable with. My editor once had to point out to me, very gently, that car windows don't have handles any more: you open them by pressing a button, which, moreover, won't work when the engine's not on. It's not that I'm a Luddite, or even especially stupid, it's just that the technical stuff – forensic detail – doesn't excite my imagination and I tend not to pay attention to it. Which could be seen as a disadvantage in the world of the spy thriller. After all, any expert in security will tell you that cyber-terrorism is the next big threat. Bullets kill targets, bombs kill crowds, but cyber-villains can knock out infrastructures. So if, like me, you have only the sketchiest notion of how a kettle works, you might feel that the genre isn't for you. How can you write about espionage without being up on the tools of its trade: the latest surveillance techniques, the state-of-the-art weaponry that will have moved one generation forwards before you're halfway through your first draft? How can this be the right car for you?

But just because technology moves like a cheetah doesn't mean the game has changed beyond recognition. As novelist Adam Brookes has pointed out, you can have all the gizmos in the world at your disposal, but sooner or later you're going to need the Sneaker Guy. He's the one who tiptoes across the room in his sneakers, slips a flash-drive into an air-gapped computer, and steals its supposedly secure data. He might be your hero, might be your villain, but the point is: he's a human being. Drones patrol the skies, and malware creeps across the Net, but somewhere down the line, there's a man with a joystick or a woman writing code. And men and women are the novelist's bread and butter.

So if you want a Bond-type scenario, with an evil genius in a volcano-base plotting to conquer the world, go for it. On the other hand, there'll always be overworked civil servants in shabby raincoats, trading classified information at bus stops or on allotments. The spy genre covers both. Which you prefer is a matter of taste.

Start on the inside

And whichever scenario you opt for – whether they're licensed-to-kill Actionwomen or shabby Everymen – your characters should start on the inside. True, there's a readership agog to hear what your character drives, where she shops, what she wears, etc, and you're free to indulge this. The spy genre, after all, has form here; Ian Fleming was among the first to pepper his texts with references to designer names. But this will only take you so far, because readers are only interested in these things for so long. If they don't come to care for your character (note: this is not the same as liking her), they'll pretty soon tire of the cool stuff she has.

How much you reveal of what your characters think and feel – how deeply you delve into the rag-and-bone shops of their hearts – is up to you. You might want them to retain an air of mystery, and not let the reader see too much. That's fine. But regardless of what you put on show, you, the author, have to know what's going on inside them. Without that, you're just pulling strings and watching puppets dance. And the dance will be jerky and uncoordinated, because neither you nor the puppets can hear music.

Nurture your addiction

Of course, having a plot, having characters, choosing your approach: these are all essential, but the tricky part is doing the actual writing. So before you start, remember this: writers are artists, and need creative freedom; they should follow their muse wherever it takes them, and not feel bound by the clock or the petty rules of civilised society. And they should write only when possessed by the urgent need to create, or what they produce will not be authentic.

And now forget all that, because it's nonsense.

The idea that being a writer means only working when you feel like it has a certain attraction, true. Unfortunately, it's one that quickly morphs into not being a writer, in which you can still indulge all the above self-adoring twaddle but without the dreary necessity of squeezing words onto paper. Because, whether you're doing it full time, on your commute, in the half-hour before breakfast or in moments stolen from family life, writing is a job. One you've chosen because you love it, and one you may never be paid for, but still a job, and like any job, if it's to be done effectively you need a routine to follow. You don't need a garret and an absinthe habit; you need a work ethic. And nobody else is going to create one for you.

The handy thing here is, writing fiction can be addictive. It has to be, if you're to accumulate 90,000 words or more, over and again. So feed that feeling. Many habits we try to wean ourselves off, because they're bad for us – drinking, smoking, overeating – or because we're worried we indulge them too much: watching TV, buying shoes, tweeting. With writing, though, you've got to nurture your addiction. Set yourself targets. Reward yourself when you meet them. Feel good about hitting that daily word count, and let it niggle at you when you don't. Before long, it'll become second nature.

Addiction doesn't betoken enjoyment, of course. There are times, many of them, when writing will feel like a chore, but you have to do it anyway. So bear in mind that if it weren't for doing it anyway, most novels wouldn't get written. And that's as true for those gazing down from the top of the bestseller lists as it is for the rest of us.

The Golden Rule

All writers have rules, and I'm no exception. But I'm not about to reveal what they are. In cold stark print they'd look forlorn, like a list of resolutions from New Years gone by; indications of an ambition to do better, not necessarily reflected in subsequent performance. It would just embarrass all of us.

Instead, I'll offer one Golden Rule – not my own; a very familiar commandment, and it's this: *Never use adverbs.* This is a great rule, for at least three reasons. First, it's short; easy to remember. Secondly: it's good. Adverbs weaken sentences; they qualify, they dilute. Is that what you want to do to your prose? And thirdly – and this is the best bit – the word 'never' is an adverb. In other words, what this rule really means is: *When you need to, break the rules.* This will happen, a lot.

Two approaches

There are already a huge number of novelists in the world, but there are a far greater number of people who simply wish they were – a recent survey revealed that 60% of people polled wished they could earn a living by writing. Who'd be left to buy books if they did is a whole other question, but still – if it's that common an ambition, what are the odds on you succeeding? That's the kind of thought that can deter you from ever booting up your laptop.

But ultimately, if you want to write a novel, the best approach to doing so is to write one. You'll encounter problems, but they will mostly be the kind that can be solved by craft and, since craft comes with practice, the more you write, the more able you'll be to deal with them. And after a year or so, you'll have a pile of typescript.

The alternative approach is to not write it, but to angst about it instead. This creates problems too, but of a more existential nature ('Why can't I write? Will I ever achieve my ambition? What am I doing with my life?') that are best addressed through the bottom of a glass. And after a year or so, you'll have a pile of empty bottles.

The choice is yours.

And one last tip ...

Few things are reliable in a novelist's life, but this is: if you publish spy fiction, strangers will ask you, 'Do you write from experience?'.

When this happens, lie.

Mick Herron is a novelist and short story writer whose books include the Sarah Tucker/Zoë Boehm series, the standalone novels *Reconstruction* (Soho Crime 2008) and *Nobody Walks* (Soho Crime 2015), and the award-winning Slough House series. *Dead Lions* (Soho Crime 2013), his second Slough House novel, won the 2013 CWA Goldsboro Gold Dagger; the fourth, *Spook Street* (John Murray 2017) won the 2017 Ian Fleming Steel Dagger. His latest books are *London Rules* and *This Is What Happened* (2018), both published by John Murray. See more at www.mickherron.com.

Then and now: becoming a science fiction and fantasy writer

Aliette de Bodard offers her experience in the special art of science fiction and fantasy writing and the skill of 'world-building'. She provides tips on tools and resources, and stresses the benefits of attending workshops and conventions.

In the beginning: writing books

I was a reader before I became a writer. When I was a child, my parents encouraged me by buying all the books I wanted. I soon became an expert at filing books in double and triple rows on narrow bookshelves. I read a lot, haphazardly – series out of order, children's books, grown-up books, mysteries, science fiction.

I fell into writing much like I fell into reading: at one point, browsing through the library, I found a *How to Write* book, and realised that there was a method to it. There are many such books available. Many apply broadly, the basic building blocks of a story being the same, regardless of genre. But the ones I find myself coming back to are the ones with some sensitivity to writing science fiction and fantasy; some tips and tricks are specific.

The one important thing I learnt from those books is how to manage exposition, which is a problem specific to science fiction and fantasy; when the setting differs a lot from today's world, there is a lot of extra information to get across. The trick, I found, is to remember that the reader only has a few spaces in their mind at a given time for those differences; you don't want to launch into a big, paragraph-long lecture, especially near the beginning, or you will lose them. Rather, you have to do this slowly and in steady trickles. You must build your world gradually, in small touches.

Recommended writing books and resources

- *Beginnings, Middle and Ends*, Nancy Kress (F+W Media 1993)
- *Steering the Craft*, Ursula K Le Guin (Eighth Mountain Press 1998; rev. edn Houghton Mifflin Harcourt 2015)
- *Storyteller*, Kate Wilhelm (Small Beer Press 2005)
- *Wonderbook: the Illustrated Guide to Creating Imaginative Fiction*, Jeff VanderMeer, Jeremy Zerfoss et al. (Abrams Image 2013)
- *Worldbuilding Wednesdays*, Kate Elliott et al. (www.imakeupworlds.com/index.php/category/worldbuilding-wednesday)

The other thing I learnt is how to do world-building. World-building is the basis of science fiction and fantasy: it's the differences between the real world and your imagined ones, and the impact they have on characters, their lives, the plot ... Inspirations for this are numerous; I use history and mythology a lot, because there is so much to be mined there. My novel *The House of Shattered Wings* (Gollancz 2015) had fallen angels in a post-apocalyptic belle époque Paris. Joan D. Vinge's *The Snow Queen* (Doubleday 1980), set in a future of planetary colonisation, draws its inspiration for plot and world from the titular fairy tale.

But you can also change the environment or human condition to arrive at your imagined world. Ken McLeod's *Intrusion* (Orbit 2012) features a benevolent UK dictatorship pushing pregnant women to take a pill that fixes their offsprings' 'anomalies'. Ann Leckie's *Ancillary Justice* (Orbit 2013) features consciousnesses spread over multiple, and sometimes very numerous, host bodies.

One thing I've found that helps is that having only one modification (or 'big idea') will often result in a setting that rings hollow. I've had good results by throwing together two or more totally unrelated ideas and finding with ways to make them mesh.

Honing your craft: software for writing

My first attempt at a novel was swiftly lost when we moved and the computer it was stored on wouldn't start up again ... My second attempt was a 200,000-word fantasy novel that became corrupted when it turned out Word 2000 wouldn't handle large files properly.

Nowadays, of course, there is software for writing and backing up. Dropbox backs up online, and also allows the writer access to a writing folder from different locations like a laptop or a tablet. Microsoft Word has patched up its issues with large files, and is the de facto standard of the science fiction publishing industry: at some point, writers will be handling revisions made with Word's Track Changes (Pages is Apple's slightly cheaper alternative, mostly but not always compatible).

Recommended software

Dropbox

www.dropbox.com

Freedom

https://freedom.to

Microsoft Word

http://office.microsoft.com/en-us/word

Pages (Mac only)

www.apple.com/uk/mac/pages

Scrivener

www.literatureandlatte.com/scrivener.php

I write my first drafts in Word because I find it simpler, and because I often write on the move in public transport. I use an Alphasmart Neo, a keyboard with a small screen and instant on/off that's, alas, no longer manufactured. I've also had good results with a tablet plus Bluetooth keyboard (iPad plus Apple keyboard, in this case). I've found that I need to block out large chunks of time for first drafts; I can do revisions piecemeal, but first drafts require my undiluted attention. My one-hour commute is great for this. You can also try blocking a pre-determined writing time that you spend writing (no internet and no social media). Software like Freedom cuts off your internet connection for a set time-period. For revisions, especially for multiple plot lines and characters, Scrivener, which has been conceived with writers in mind, makes it much easier to change, move and delete scenes, as well as find particular occurrences of sentences or characters, so that's where I do most of my post-first-draft work.

From afar: writing workshops

When I started writing, the internet was just taking off, which was in many ways a godsend. I live in France, which isn't that far from the UK, but might as well be on another planet insofar as writing groups and writing workshops are concerned.

Science fiction and fantasy has a strong culture of peer workshopping: having other people read your manuscript and offer you reader feedback, in exchange for your reader feedback on their manuscript. Even back in 2006, a lot of this community were already online, which enabled me to join them.

You cannot write by committee; there is no pleasing everyone in every detail in a workshop. Equally, you do need to take critiques into account, as it's unlikely your piece will work perfectly as a draft. A good tip is this: if only one person mentions a problem, then you can wonder how important fixing it is to you, and subsequently do the fix or not, as you wish. But if two or more people mention the same issue, then you have to fix it. The fix, though, might be quite different from what the critiquers are suggesting. Someone once wanted me to remove an entire section because it served no purpose. Instead, I rewrote it so that it was far more relevant to the overall plot.

The other thing about critiques is that you can judge how closely a critiquer's tastes mesh with yours by checking what they're saying about other people's stories, and whether you agree with it, because it's easier to judge on things that aren't your own writing. Someone whose critiques on other stories you appreciate should be given more weight.

When it comes to workshops, there are two approaches: a large sample pool of readers (such as Critters), or a smaller pool of people (such as Online Writing Workshop). The large sample is useful because of size and variety of reactions. I know it works great for some people: I've always found the smaller ones more useful because, as a writer, I find it hard to ignore the desire to please everyone, and this can be a disaster when trying to please 40+ people!

Recommended workshops

Clarion
http://clarion.ucsd.edu

Clarion West
www.clarionwest.org

Critters
www.critters.org

Milford
www.milfordsf.co.uk

Odyssey
www.sff.net/odyssey

Online Writing Workshop
http://sff.onlinewritingworkshop.com

Orbit groups, BSFA
www.bsfa.co.uk/orbit

Viable Paradise
http://viableparadise.net

There are also in-person intensive workshops, whether in the UK or US. Many of these are application-based and can be quite competitive. They can be helpful for developing a writer's craft and for connections; being isolated with other like-minded souls for anything from a week to six weeks can be a great boost. It can also be too much, so you should have a good idea of how much intensity you can bear (and such workshops can be expensive and time-consuming, which is the main reason I never went!).

Fantasy and science fiction conventions

RECOMMENDED CONVENTIONS AND EVENTS

BSFA monthly meetings
http://www.bsfa.co.uk

Eastercon
www.eastercon.org
Held over the Easter weekend, various locations depending on the year

Nine Worlds
https://nineworlds.co.uk

Super Relaxed Fantasy Book Club
www.hodderscape.co.uk/introducing-the-super-relaxed-fantasy-club

Worldcon and World Fantasy Con
http://worldcon.org, www.worldfantasy.org

RECOMMENDED READING

- *Conventions and writing, or Schmoozing 101*, Mary Robinette Kowal

http://maryrobinettekowal.com/journal/conventions-and-writing-or-schmoozing-101
- *Thoughts on Conventions*, Zen Cho
http://zencho.org/thoughts-on-conventions

Networking: conventions

I fell into conventions almost by accident. The 2008 Eastercon, one of the UK's big Science Fiction and Fantasy conventions, was taking place in London, and I thought it would be fun to attend. At the time I only had a handful of publishing credits, notably a story in *Interzone*. Fortunately for me, Jetse de Vries, Interzone's assistant editor, introduced me to everyone he knew, which made the whole prospect slightly less intimidating.

In the years since, there have been quite a few new conventions and events set up. They're great fun and also quite useful venues for networking. For all the importance of online social media, nothing quite matches meeting people in the flesh. They're not for everyone; I know writers who do quite well at their careers without ever having set foot at a convention.

The UK has a lot of science fiction and fantasy events and conventions, and there are also a few big ones in the US that are useful. Every convention has a slightly different character, which means you can try a few and see which one suits you best. They can range from huge (thousands of attendees) to quite small (200-300 people), and can be literature or media or gaming focused. My personal comfort level is around 1000 people: large enough to justify a trip, but small enough that I can run into people by accident (as opposed to remembering everyone's email/phones). Events are usually a bit different: they're more circumscribed in time (Super Relaxed Fantasy Club is just one evening; a convention runs continuously over several days).

Conventions are generally very friendly to newcomers, but it's best if you come into them knowing some people already. I was in the position of having published something which made me visible, but if you're not, there are some strong opportunities today to 'e-meet' people before you attend a con. Following people on social media (Twitter, Facebook, Writers' Forum) is a good way to start your network and have people at conventions you already know who can, in turn, introduce you to others.

Only do what you're comfortable with. I'm an introvert (like a lot of writers), and I know I need to recharge my batteries with some quiet time every once in a while, lest I crash. I've found it helpful to have a room in the main convention hotel, or not too far from it. Don't hesitate to hang out in the bar; panels are useful, but a lot of networking happens outside of the official programming. I actually met my agent in a bar at the World Fantasy Convention!

It's been a while since I started writing fantasy and science fiction. Some things have changed, some things haven't. At heart, it's still about time and dedication spent developing and maintaining craft and connections – and sheer bloody perseverance, which always comes in handy!

Aliette de Bodard is a multi-award-winning writer of fantasy and science fiction. In 2016 she became the first writer to win two BSFA awards in the same year for Best Novel and Best Short Fiction. Her novel, *The House of Shattered Wings* (Gollancz 2015), won the BSFA Award for Best Novel. Her Aztec mystery-fantasies, *Servant of the Underworld*, *Harbinger of the Storm*, and *Master of the House of Darts* (Angry Robot) have been reissued by JABberwocky, and her ongoing Xuya universe series includes the short novels *The Tea Master and the Detective* (Subterranean Press 2018) and *The Citadel of Weeping Pearls* (JABberwocky Books 2017). Her latest novel is *The House of Binding Thorns* (Ace/Gollancz 2017). For more information see http://aliettedebodard.com. Follow her on Twitter @aliettedb.

Writing bestselling women's fiction

Penny Vincenzi offers some insight on how she writes her bestselling novels. She highlights the value of writers really knowing the characters they create.

Well, that's a tough one! How to write bestselling women's fiction … Writing: yes, I can tell you about that. Writing women's fiction: yes, I can do that too. But bestselling women's fiction – that's a tough one. You need a bit of magic, a lot of luck, and an ability to believe in yourself – and a refusal to give up. I'll do my best to tell you what I know. Let's start with the writing.

First of all, you know if you're a writer because you'll be doing it already. I believe writers are born not made. You won't suddenly think, 'I don't like nursing, I wonder if I might be a writer instead.' (Although you can certainly do both, and lots of very successful writers have started out as nurses, doctors or vets; the medical profession is rich in plots …) You don't have to think about whether you want to write; you just know.

I started writing stories when I was eight, in the form of fake Enid Blytons, usually about a page long. My stories were hardly works of literature, but they were what I did when other children were sticking stamps in albums or building Meccano models, or playing with dolls. And I really couldn't stop: I was enthralled, happy, utterly satisfied. Two years later I typed my stories on my mother's typewriter with lots of carbon copies, stapled them into a magazine called *Stories* and handed them out in the school playground. (There were few takers.)

Later on, I wrote for the parish magazine and the school magazine (I was the editor), and then moved on to getting paid for writing captions to photographs in *Tatler* magazine where I worked as secretary to the editor. It was humble stuff: 'Lord and Lady Smith enjoying a joke on the stairs' sort of thing. But I knew that when I was writing, I was happy; I felt I was in the right place at the right time. Look out for that feeling; it's all-important.

Writing and inspiration

The next thing you should know is that writing is hard work. A lot of it is sheer hard grind. There is a tendency to romanticise it, but it is not romantic at all. I don't believe in inspiration – unless inspiration is what you call one of those bolt from the blue ideas that gets your spine tingling as it hits you and you recognise it as something that could form a rattling good plot, or really great chapter, or even one wonderful scene. But you are just as likely to get one of those ideas when you're stuck in a traffic jam or leafing through a magazine at the dentist's, or listening to someone chatting on the number 22 bus, as when (as many people seem assume) gazing misty eyed at some beautiful scenery or listening to a glorious piece of music (although don't knock it if it does come then).

You should write because you want to, and more than that even, because you have to. Having got the idea, you then have to start working on it; your book won't get written without you; the words won't drift into your head, page after wonderful page, without effort.

But I'm running away with myself; and also making out writing to be rather joyless when actually it's one of the most joyful, rewarding, exciting things you can possibly do.

When I've had a good day at the plot-face, as I call it, I could fly; I feel literally and perfectly happy.

You need to practise writing; it's a bit like playing the piano, and writing a little every day is better than producing a chunk once a month. Reading is essential too; the more you read, carefully and attentively, paying proper attention to how the author tells the story, weaves the plot, creates the characters, the more you will learn. Read as much and as widely as you can – biographies, thrillers, memoirs and classics, as well as modern fiction.

Squeeze out the time somehow so you can write, however busy you are; getting up an hour earlier never hurt anyone. And don't think you need to have some complex program for your computer – or indeed a computer at all, although it helps. An exercise book and a ballpoint pen will suffice. 'Just do it…' as the song says.

Writing women's fiction

Because I write women's fiction, I feel qualified to tell you about it. I could never write a detective story because I'd be rubbish at the plotting side of it, or a learned literary work because I'm neither learned nor literary; and I couldn't write a self-help book because that sort of thing just doesn't interest me (although I do know they have huge value).

My fiction career began because I wanted to tell stories and I had a cracking idea. I suddenly felt there might be more to life than writing articles about beauty, or even doing interviews with celebrities and then writing about them, which at the time I loved. That writing experience taught me a lot about things like construction and creating a mood and a sense of place, all vital ingredients to successful fiction writing.

So, having cracking ideas is essential. All my books are what one of my editors called 'what-ifs' – each has a strong idea that grabs the reader when she first picks up the book and makes her want to explore it. For instance, a book about a village and the people who live in it sounds charming. But if the village in that book was threatened by a developer moving in and potentially wrecking its most precious beauty spot, describing who opposes him and how, and the relationships formed and/or threatened by him, plus the secrets that get unearthed in the process of the opposition – then you have a plot.

Thus, in *Dilemma* the 'what-if' is: 'What if your husband asked you to perjure yourself to keep him out of jail?', and in *Windfall*, 'What if you inherited an enormous sum of money, how would it affect you, your marriage and your relationships?', and in *The Decision*, 'What if you and your husband were battling over custody of your only child?' People can put themselves into these situations, and wonder: what would I do, how would I behave? And so on.

The greatest and most important rule about writing is an old one: write what you know. If you don't know about something – say, banking or the art world – but feel the subject suits your story, do a lot of research on it. Ignorance of a subject shows horribly in half a page. On the other hand, just because you've done the research it doesn't mean you have to use every syllable of it – that would be boring. Readers get very involved in the world you create; they like to find themselves in a new place – whether it's the world of modelling, law or journalism, they like to be told about something new. A sense of place is important too, from windswept beaches to plush restaurants and from Paris to Peru. If you bring those places alive, your readers will follow you to and through them. It all helps to bring everything in the book to life.

Know your characters

The most important thing about writing fiction for women is the characters you create. They need to leap off the page. For male fiction, in my view, it's less vital as the plot will do a lot more. I think that women need to bond, to become totally involved with their heroines, and to feel she is, for the duration of the book, part of their own lives. Again and again, when I give talks about writing, that's what people say: 'I loved Lady Celia' (in the *Lytton* trilogy), 'I can't get over what happened to Barty' (also in the *Lytton* trilogy and a great favourite of readers), and 'I got so worried about Jocasta [in *Sheer Abandon*] I couldn't sleep'.

And indeed if you start discussing women's favourite fiction, it's the characters people talk about – Jane (in *Jane Eyre*), Cathy (in *Wuthering Heights*), Scarlett (in *Gone with the Wind*) and Lizzie (in *Pride and Prejudice*) as much, if not more, than the book as a whole. A great heroine will, as you write, take over the book and the plot.

I never know what is going to happen in my books. Many writers work in this way, being taken by surprise at what their characters do and actually refusing to do what the writer tells them. The only book I ever planned carefully was my first, *Old Sins*, where I had wanted my heroine to marry her stepson. It was a nice neat plot: her first husband, who was about 25 years older than she was, had died, and I thought and indeed wrote in the synopsis that she would fall in love with his son. But she didn't and moreover, as I continued writing she just wouldn't. Every time I wrote the scene that brings them together, it was awkward and embarrassing. I panicked; what was I going to do with her? Why wasn't my neat plot working out? And then it hit me: she liked older men; of course she did, there was no way she would fall in love with a beautiful boy. So I listened to her for a bit and then abandoned the enforced marriage and allowed to her to choose someone else much more suitable.

It was a huge and truly valuable lesson. I've followed and listened to my characters ever since and I'd advise you to do the same. You need to know them really well – not just what they look like, but their likes and dislikes, what they are afraid of, what makes them happy, what makes them miserable, what they're afraid of. It doesn't all need to be spelt out though. Knowing your characters well makes them leap off the page, and makes your fiction sing and speak to people. It's a wonderful feeling when you create interesting, strong characters and just let them go and you follow them.

Becoming a bestseller

I was lucky; my first book was indeed successful. And I know I had a lot of luck to make it so. I also had some hard-headed practical advice given to me. I knew I needed to have an agent – don't even think about trying to sell your book to a publisher direct. It's difficult to find a good agent who is willing take you on. Agents won't take on an author unless they think they can sell their work. They know all the editors, and which of them will suit your work. Look in this *Yearbook* to find out which agents specialise in what areas. If you're lucky enough to find an agent, listen very attentively to what he or she advises. If they say your typescript is too long, or the language is too flowery, or your grammar isn't too great, or the plot is too convoluted, do what you're told and remember that you're lucky to have an expert working on your book with you.

I was truly lucky to have had a wonderful agent and an amazing editor first off and I never cease to be thankful for both of them. My story would have been very different, and less happy without them.

A good, memorable title is crucial, as is a striking cover. Publishers know a great deal about both and how to make a book stand out from the enormous number of books published every year. So if – and that's a big 'if' – your book is sold to a publisher, you still need a lot of what I call magic.

You need an idea that will catch people's fancy and ensnare their imaginations, a cover that catches the eye on the bookstalls, and a title that promises a heady dash of intrigue in the relationships you've created. It's almost impossible to define but if you can also deliver a considerable element of charm in your characters, that will make people talk about them. If your book provides a positive experience, your readers will want more of it and will also enjoy your other books.

I hope you enjoy your writing and I wish you good luck with it. I think writing is the best fun and if you can promise people fun too, then you could, very possibly, hit the jackpot. Be brave and go for it: believe in yourself and don't be talked out of writing the book you want to write!

Penny Vincenzi was one of Britain's best-loved and most popular novelists. She published her first novel, *Old Sins*, in 1989 and subsequently wrote 17 bestselling novels, most recently *A Question of Trust*, published by Headline in 2017. She died on 25 February 2018 aged 78.

Notes from a successful romantic novelist

Katie Fforde describes how she became published and why she likes writing romantic fiction.

If you want to get a group of writers into a panic, put them on a panel and then ask them, one at a time, what their working practice is. The first one answers confidently enough – after all they probably have several books on the shelves by this time. But the others listen in consternation, convinced that what they do is wrong and they are not proper writers even though the world is reading their books.

This is because there are as many writing methods as there are writers, and it's important to work out what kind of writer you are.

If you are reading this there is a chance that you are a writer; but in case you're not sure, do check. It's hard enough to write if you like doing it, but if you think you might prefer painting water colours or needlepoint, please try those first. At least you might get an acceptable still life or cushion relatively quickly. It takes a long time to write a novel.

I discovered I wanted to write – almost more than anything else in the world – as soon as I started. My mother had given me a writing kit for Christmas. This consisted of paper, pens, a dictionary, a thesaurus and yes, a copy of the *Writers' & Artists' Yearbook*, as well as Tipp-Ex and a nice box to keep it all in.

Having made a New Year's Resolution that I would start writing that year, I started in January. I cleaned the house, made sure my children were out of the way and put the first sheet of paper into my typewriter. When I'd got over my nerves – which I dealt with by starting to rewrite someone else's book – and began a story I'd had in my head for years, I realised what had been missing in my life for so long. I had a lovely family, a lovely house and a lovely dog, and yet I wasn't content. What had been missing was a creative outlet.

One of the joys of starting to write is that no one needs to know you are doing it until you choose to tell them. Most other things people do require a bit of going out in public. While it would be a bit difficult to hide it from the people you live with, the rest of the world doesn't need to know. In fact, I suggest you don't tell anyone unless you're sure they will understand. There is nothing more irritating than being asked 'how the book is going' by people who assume you just need to write one to become a millionaire.

There are annoying examples of people who got their first novel published and became an instant bestseller – some of those authors are even my friends – but I prefer to think it's better to be a tortoise than a hare. If you get there the long slow way at least you know what you've done and can do it again. That said, I have a Pollyanna side to my nature and will always see the advantages to any of life's setbacks if I possibly can. It took me eight years before I found a publisher and ten years – from starting – before I had a book on the shelves.

Now that you're feeling a bit more positive about it, knowing how long it took me to achieve publication, I'll go on with my tips.

My top tip, which I'm assuming you do already, is to read a lot. I believe if you never ever went to any sort of writing course or never read a 'how to' book on writing, you would still be able to write to a publishable standard just by reading enough novels. It would take you longer, probably, because you could set yourself an impossibly high standard and consequently never become Henry James. But once you've decided what sort of book you want to write, which I hope would be the sort of book you want to read, read as many of the genre as you can fit into your busy life.

My second tip – which I sometimes describe as the gift I'd give to baby writers if I was a fairy godmother – is perseverance. This pig-headedness (a less polite but more accurate word) got me through receiving all those rejections. Every time I was rejected I became more determined that one day I would have a book published. But you do have to be very determined. I'd quite like to be a size ten, too, but I'm never going to be one because I don't want it quite enough.

My third tip, which I'll say more about later, is to emulate Nelson's favourite captains and be lucky.

So why did it take me so long? I think it does take quite a long time to learn to write – for most of us anyway – but also I was aiming at a market that wasn't quite suitable for me. I was trying to write for Mills & Boon. Like many people, I read these by the shelf-load and assumed, in my complete ignorance, that because they were easy to read they were easy to write. Not so! But I am eternally grateful to the literary agents that sent me some very encouraging rejection letters, and trying to fit my story into 50,000 words forced me to keep to the point. There is no room in those books for characters who have no function, for any little scene that doesn't further the plot or for a hero who isn't extremely attractive.

How did I finally get a book deal? This is where the luck comes in. I had been a member of the Romantic Novelists' Association for some years (I am now its President) and through its New Writers' scheme (which alas is now hugely oversubscribed) my writing came to the attention of an agent, who was new to the business and so had time to look for new writers and to work with them. This agent told me she couldn't do anything with the books I had been writing but that she liked my style and together we discussed what my next novel should be like. She asked for 100 pages before the end of the year. I felt I couldn't write what amounted to half a Mills & Boon novel and not check I was on the right track so I sent her the first chapter. She liked it and I got into the habit of sending her chunks which she would read and comment on, sometimes asking for changes, at other times saying, crack on with it. This wonderful woman had sold the novel before I'd finished it.

But then came the hard work. There is no tougher writing course than your first professional edit, and although it was hard – no actual blood but certainly sweat and tears – I pity writers who don't have this experience. My lovely story had too little plot and putting one in after it had been written was akin to putting in the foundations to a house after it is built. It is possible with the help of Acrow props and rigid steel joists, but it is not the way round to do it. Books need plots in the same way that bodies need skeletons and it's better to work out what yours is before starting.

My second huge stroke of luck after finding a wonderful agent was to be picked for the WHSmith Fresh Talent promotion. This meant cardboard cutouts of me and the other authors were in the window of every WHSmith shop in the country and our books were reviewed by almost every newspaper. This massive exposure was a terrific start to any writing career.

So what keeps me going nowadays, 20 or so books on? One thing is that I keep having ideas which I want to write and I think this is something that develops along with other neural pathways that you forge. My antennae are constantly twitching when I watch television, go to a party or sit on a train. I am fascinated by relationships and want to explore new ones, and I also like falling in love. If you write romantic fiction you have to fall in love with your hero or you can't expect your readers to. Falling in love with your hero is the affair you're allowed to have and it is a lot less complicated to arrange.

Why do people buy my books? It's hard to say but I'm very glad that they do. I think it's because readers can recognise themselves in my characters and this is the same whatever age you are – I have readers of all ages, from school age girls to elderly women. I and three other authors were asked this question at a literature festival recently and none of us really knew. The general consensus was, life is tough for a lot of people and everyone needs a bit of escape. Some people like a nice gritty crime novel or an edge-of-the-seat thriller, but some like a story where you know the baby – and probably even the dog – is not going to die. You know you're guaranteed a few hours off from your own life in a safe place.

This is why I like writing romantic fiction. I enjoy spending time with people I like, to whom nice things happen. I like being able to choose the wallpaper and have the garden I could never have. I also like deciding it's time we had a good summer, and write about one.

And the very best thing about being a writer is meeting people who have enjoyed your books, read them to cheer themselves up when they were ill (although I do take it amiss when it's implied that you have to be ill to read my books) or going through some sort of hard time. That is the very best reward.

So, if you feel fit for the fight (as Bonnie Tyler might have said) gather your tools and do your research. First of all, decide what you like to read. Don't try and write anything just because it's the current favourite unless you love it. You probably won't succeed if your heart isn't in it; if you do you'll be stuck writing chaste romance novels when you yearn to write raunchy thrillers, and the market will have changed by the time it hits the shelves anyway.

And please do your research before you even think of submitting anything. It may seem blindingly obvious, but the number of people who send their work to any agent in this *Yearbook* without checking that they even handle fiction is enormous.

Be brave and get someone else to read at least part of your book before you submit it. It does have to be someone you can trust to be brutally frank, who will tell you if they don't know who any of the characters are, and if they couldn't care less. It's better to find out things like this before you let the professionals near it.

Make sure you present your script exactly as it's requested. Don't email books to agents who only want hard copy. Make sure the copy is clean and easy to read. Write a covering letter that will encourage the agent to look at the book and if a synopsis is asked for, write one. (Some people find it easier to write after the book is finished.)

If you are lucky enough to receive comments from an agent, take them to heart unless you know them to be wrong. If they say your characters come across as older than they are supposed to be, watch a bit of 'yoof' television and learn some modern slang. If they say no one wants to read about undertakers, consider carefully if this is true. It's possible you've written the one that people would enjoy.

If you're brave enough to join a writers' group, make sure it's not a mutual appreciation society. It's more productive to be told your dialogue is poor than for people to wonder why on earth no one has yet snapped up your masterpiece.

Be in it for the long haul. If (or when) you're rejected, allow yourself a certain amount of time to gnash your teeth and eat chocolate and then get back to it. If you want it enough you will get there and there's no time to waste feeling sorry for yourself. Writing mustn't seem like a hobby, it must be your passion. Eventually it might also become your profession.

Katie Fforde is a *Sunday Times* No. 1 bestselling author. Her first book was *Living Dangerously* (1995) and she has written 21 more novels since. Her most recent books are *The Perfect Match* (2014), *A Vintage Wedding* (2015), *A Summer At Sea* (2016), *A Secret Garden* (2017) and *A Country Escape* (2018), all published by Century. She has published three short story collections, *From Scotland with Love*, *Staying Away at Christmas* and *A Christmas Feast*. Her hobbies, when she has time for them, are singing in a choir and flamenco dancing. Her website is www.katiefforde.com.

Writing popular history books

On turning from fiction to non-fiction, author Tom Holland was able to re-connect fully with his childhood love of history and find a fulfilling place as a writer. He reflects on the importance of historical accuracy in popular history, and on the literary and scholarly giants whose work has combined to influence and inspire him.

When I began writing, I wanted to be Proust. No novel had ever inspired me quite as much as his *À la recherche du temps perdu* (1913-27) – and so, with the lunatic hubris of youth, I decided that I would devote my career to emulating it. Naturally, it did not turn out well. My laborious attempt to write a 'Great Novel' proved abortive. My first published work of fiction, *The Vampyre* (Little, Brown 1995), instead featured Lord Byron as a vampire. Two more in the series followed, set respectively in 1880s London and the Restoration. My final vampire novel featured Howard Carter, a deranged Fatimid caliph, and blood-sucking pharaohs. It was all a long way from madeleines dipped in tea.

Or was it? Proust's great theme was memory – the hold that it has on us, and the tricks that it can play on our minds. My mistake had been to imagine that my formative experiences, my formative passions, were best served by fiction. In truth, the emotions that lived most vividly in my memory, I came to realise, were those bred of my childhood love of history. That all my novels were set in the past was, perhaps, a desperate cry for recognition to my ego from my id. In writing historical fiction, I could now see that what really stirred me was less the fiction than the history. To invent things that had happened in the reign of Akhenaten, the heretic pharaoh who served as the central protagonist in my last vampire novel, was to gild the lily. He was quite extraordinary enough as he was, without me giving him a taste for human blood.

So I decided to turn to non-fiction. Pointedly, though, I chose as my subject the period that had given me my first ever rush of fascination with vanished empires. It was a book on the Roman army (complete with a gory cover showing one of Caesar's officers getting spitted by a Gaul) that had first persuaded me, at the age of eight, to abandon an obsession with palaeontology for one with humanity's past. Rome was the apex predator of the ancient world: like a tyrannosaur, it was lethal, glamorous, and extinct. Yet it was also a civilisation of astonishing brilliance, possessed of poets and historians who, over the course of my studies, and then into my adult life, had allowed my fascination with it to mature as I myself grew older. Rome, as a theme, was unavoidably steeped in my memories. In researching the age of Caesar and the collapse of the Roman Republic, I was exploring an aspect of my own past, as surely as if I been writing an autobiography.

Which is not to say that *Rubicon* (Little, Brown 2003), my first work of non-fiction, did not aspire to stringent accuracy and objectivity. History has always had pretensions to rank as a science. Thucydides, writing back in the 5th century BC, scorned the exaggerations of poets and the meretricious taste for fantasy of chroniclers; presenting his account of the great war between Athens and Sparta, he assured his readers that 'the conclusions I have drawn from the proofs quoted may, I believe, safely be relied upon.'

History today, as an academic discipline, is recognisably the descendant of such a methodology. Scholarship, in university history departments, ranks as a vocation. The books that result tend to be written by experts for experts, and in a style that is distinctively academic. Historians who write for the general reader cannot afford to indulge in jargon; but neither can they afford to jettison the exacting standards that serve to qualify a book published by a university press. With large readerships come large responsibilities. No less than academics, writers of popular history are dependent for their career upon a reputation for not making mistakes.

An evident aspect of history's enduring appeal beyond the groves of academe, though, is precisely the fact that it is *not* a science. Herodotus, Thucydides' great predecessor and rival, declared – in the first sentence of the first work of history ever written – that it was his ambition to ensure that 'human achievement may be spared the ravages of time'. Literally, he spoke of not allowing them to become *exitêla*, a word that could be used in a technical sense to signify the fading of paint from inscriptions or works of art. To Thucydides, the colours applied by Herodotus to his history were too bright, too distracting, to qualify him as a true historian – a criticism that would see him, in due course, named the 'Father of Lies' as well as the 'Father of History'. Herodotus himself, though, might have retorted that Thucydides was too dry, too narrow, too lacking in colour. His own history was rich with the plenitude that is the mark of great literature. If his concern with the means of gathering evidence was something revolutionary, then so too was the sheer scope and range of his interests. No one before him had ever thought to write on such a heroically panoramic scale. Unlike the austere narrative of Thucydides, with its focus on politics and war, that of Herodotus might lead in an often bewildering variety of directions: to a laugh-out-loud story of a drunk man dancing on a table, perhaps, or to the chilling account of a eunuch's revenge on the man who had him castrated as a child. 'Clio,' as Isaiah Berlin once put it, 'is, after all, a muse.'

It is the mark of the direction that my career took, I now recognise, that the great literary influence on my life has turned out to be, not Proust, but Herodotus. He too, like Caesar's legions, was a part of my childhood; and ever since I first read him at the age of 12, he has been a constant companion. I translated him for Penguin Classics, and *Persian Fire* (Little, Brown 2005), the book I wrote after *Rubicon*, was in large part a refraction of his work. Much of what we know about the early 5th century BC – the Persian Empire, the Greek world, and the wars that were fought between them – is dependent upon Herodotus; and it was as a quarry full of data that I gleefully mined him for my own history of the Persian wars. Yet Herodotus – in his love of wonders, in his complex relationship to evidence, and in his style, which today can appear closer to *Tristram Shandy* than to any conventional work of history – was a great literary artist as well as a historian. To write in his shadow is, of necessity, to acknowledge that. Which is why, in academia, the study of Herodotus is as much the prerogative of literary critics as it is of historians; and it is why, to the writer of popular history, he affords quite as many opportunities to meditate upon the nature of memory and narrative as any novelist would.

'*Stat rosa pristina nomine, nomina nuda tenemus.*' So Umberto Eco ended his bestselling novel, *The Name of the Rose* (Secker & Warburg 1983). 'The rose that once was now exists just in name – for bare names are all we have.' It is given to few writers to combine scholarship with fiction to the remarkable degree that Eco did; but to write about the distant past is, perforce, to wrestle with the implications of Eco's Latin tag. Even when the sources are at their most plentiful, uncertainties and discrepancies crop up everywhere. This is the fascination of ancient history, as well as its frustration. Although to write about it is, indeed, to impose upon the past an artificial pattern, that need be no drawback. The ancients, after all, when they wrote their own histories, did the same. Rare, for instance, in the era of Caesar, was the citizen who did not fancy himself the hero of his own history. This was an attitude which did much to bring Rome to disaster, but it also gave the epic of the Republic's fall its peculiarly lurid and heroic hue. Barely a generation after it had occurred, men were already shaking their heads in wonderment, astonished that such a time, and such giants, could ever have been.

A half-century later, the panegyrist of the Emperor Tiberius, Velleius Paterculus, could exclaim that 'It seems an almost superfluous task, to draw attention to an age when men of such extraordinary character lived,' – and then promptly write it up. He knew, as all Romans knew, that it was in action, in great deeds and remarkable accomplishments, that the genius of his people had been most gloriously displayed. Accordingly, it was through narrative that this genius could best be understood.

This intersection between the reliability of ancient sources and their unreliability, between their value as a record of facts and their often incorrigibly literary character, is the furrow which, as a writer, I find I most enjoy ploughing. It has led me to various dimensions in which reality and fantasy can easily seem intermingled: to the court of Nero; to the origins of Islam; to Viking England; to the First Crusade. The pleasure I have taken in writing about all of them is the pleasure of someone who, after years of restless wandering, has finally found somewhere that feels like home. I am not Proust, nor was I meant to be. The relief of this discovery is what enabled me at last, after many false starts, to become fulfilled as a writer.

Tom Holland is the author of the prize-winning history titles *Rubicon: The Triumph and Tragedy of the Roman Republic* (2003) and *Persian Fire* (2005), as well as *Millennium: The End of the World and the Forging of Christendom* (2008), *In the Shadow of the Sword* (2012), and *Dynasty* (2015), all published by Little, Brown. Tom's translation of *Herodotus: The Histories* was published in 2013 by Penguin Classics. His novels include *The Vampyre* (1995), *Deliver Us From Evil* (1997) and *The Bonehunter* (Abacus 2001). His latest book is *Athelstan: The Making of England* (Allen Lane 2016). Tom has adapted Herodotus, Homer, Thucydides and Virgil for BBC Radio 4 and is the presenter of BBC Radio 4's *Making History*. He has written and presented TV documentaries on subjects ranging from religion to dinosaurs. Tom was Chair of the Society of Authors 2009–11. Visit www.tom-holland.org for more information or follow him on Twitter @holland_tom.

Writing historical fiction

Historical fiction gives writers the freedom to use 'informed imagination', rich in authentic detail, to breathe life into history, explains historian and novelist Alison Weir. She explores important aspects of the genre and describes the bridge between biography and fiction in her work, seeing encouraging trends in the market.

Filling in the gaps: enhancing history?

Writing a biography of Eleanor of Aquitaine was my first attempt at recreating the life of a medieval woman, piecing together myriad fragments of evidence in an attempt to construct a cohesive narrative – such is the challenge of medieval biography. It was, to some extent, a frustrating exercise, because there will always be gaps that we cannot hope to fill: no one thought to record what the beautiful Eleanor actually looked like, for example, how much political influence she actually exerted, or why she separated from her husband, Henry II. I found myself itching to fill those gaps, knowing that a historian oversteps the bounds of legitimate speculation at his or her peril, for we can only infer so much from historical sources.

It was while I was researching this biography, it occurred to me that I wanted to write a novel about Eleanor, one in which I could develop ideas and themes that had no place in a history book, but which – based on sound research and educated guesses – could help to illuminate her life and explain her motives and actions. A historian uses such inventiveness at their risk – but a novelist has the power to get inside their subject's head, and that can afford insights that would not be permissible to a historian, and yet can have a legitimate value of their own.

Having decided to have a go at writing a novel, I had to choose a subject. Eleanor of Aquitaine was off limits at the time, because my contract precluded a competing book. A reader had suggested that I write a biography of Lady Jane Grey, and it occurred to me that Jane's tragic tale would be an ideal subject for a novel: it was short, it was dramatic and unbearably poignant, and I knew it well, having researched it for an earlier book. Three months later the novel was finished.

My agent thought it a riveting story, but said I should come down off the fence and forget I was a historian, as the book read like 'faction'. But I had no more time to work on it, so I put it away and forgot about it until 2003, when I rewrote it using the first person and the present tense, a format in which no history book would ever be written. It was this novel that was commissioned by Hutchinson and was published in 2006 as *Innocent Traitor*. Since then I have published seven more historical novels, including one on Eleanor of Aquitaine.

From historical fact to fiction: providing authentic detail

Writing historical fiction affords me a sense of freedom: it is liberating not to have to keep within the strict confines of contemporary sources. I can use my imagination to fill those frustrating gaps, although I strongly feel that what a historical novelist writes must be credible within the context of what is known about the subject. You cannot simply indulge in flights of fancy. That sells short both those who know nothing about the subject, and those who know a great deal. I know – because my readers regularly, and forcefully, tell me so – that people care that what they are reading in a historical novel is close to the truth, if allowing for a little dramatic licence and the novelist's informed imagination.

Consequently I feel that I have a great responsibility towards my readers – and also my subjects, who were, after all, real people. In my novels, I adhere to the facts where they exist, using my informed imagination where they do not. History does not always record people's motives, emotions and reactions, or the intimate details of their relationships or their love lives, so there is plenty of scope for invention there – and I have to confess to having been quite inventive in that respect!

The setting must be authentic. Too many historical novels fall down because the author has not done enough background research. They know the story superficially, but they don't know the period or the social and cultural context. It's an advantage to have studied the history in depth. I find that I am constantly looking up minor details in the interests of authenticity, such as the kind of books that were printed by the Caxton press in Lady Jane Grey's time, the kind of food that Eleanor of Aquitaine would have eaten, or even the Welsh folk song sung by Elizabeth I's nursery maid. One can't afford to be sloppy because this is 'just' fiction.

Readers of history books love such details – I've heard that time and again – and I've found that it's often in the details that we gain a broader picture. For example, Peter Englund's book on the Great War, *The Beauty and the Sorrow* (Knopf Publishing 2011), briefly mentions a soldier watching the body of a fallen comrade decompose over days; he has come to see it as just chemicals and rags. But that speaks volumes about how men coped with the unimaginable carnage of that war. And maybe historians can learn something from historical novelists about bringing history vividly to life.

Finding an authentic voice

A major challenge to any author embarking on a historical novel is the use of language. There are tough choices, and you will never please everyone. You could, if you were stupid enough, adopt pseudo-Tudor speak and alienate your readers with words and phrases such as 'prithee' or 'hey nonny nonny'; or you could go to the other extreme, as Suzannah Dunn does in *The Queen of Subtleties* (Doubleday 2005), where she has Anne Boleyn calling her father 'Dad'. Although I flinched at that, her novel worked well, thanks to the excellent characterisations.

Having spent many years studying Tudor sources, I have become familiar with the idioms of language in use then – although we can never fully know how people actually spoke, only how their words were written down, which may not be the same thing. Wherever possible, I use my characters' own historical quotes, or the quotes of others, lifting them from historical sources but modernising them slightly so that they do not stand out awkwardly in a 21st-century text. In order to appeal to as wide – and as young – an audience as possible, I confess to deliberately using a few modern idioms where I think they sound better than their Tudor equivalent, even if they are anachronistic. But it's impossible to please everyone with the language in a historical novel: while one reviewer of *Innocent Traitor* deplored what he saw as anachronisms, another said I had got the language just right. In my subsequent novels I have used the past tense and the third person, which allows for greater versatility in telling the story.

Inventive freedom: from historical evidence to 'what if ... ?'

How far dare a novelist make things up or manipulate the facts in a novel about a real historical figure who may also be famous? My feeling is that you should have some historical evidence, however flimsy, on which to base your storyline. For a historian, such evidence may not be convincing, but it might be a gift to a novelist. For example, in *The Other Boleyn Girl* (Harper 2007), Philippa Gregory has Anne Boleyn, desperate to have a son, contemplating committing incest with her brother because he is the only man who can safely be relied upon not to betray their intimacy to others. The historical Anne was charged with incest in the indictment drawn up against her, and while other evidence strongly suggests that these were trumped-up charges, a novelist can use them as the basis of a good plot. I have no argument with that.

The issue of Elizabeth I's much-vaunted virginity has been endlessly debated by scholars, so in my view it is quite legitimate for novelists such as Susan Kay in *Legacy* (Bodley Head 1985) and Robin Maxwell in *The Queen's Bastard* (Review 1999) to depict the Queen having a full physical relationship with the Earl of Leicester.

I myself took a similar liberty, going against what I believe as a historian, in my second novel, *The Lady Elizabeth* (Hutchinson 2008). That storyline was based purely on unreliable gossip and a coincidence over dates, but had this contemporary evidence not existed, I would not have ventured so far. Given that it does exist, and even though, as a historian, I would discount it, as a novelist I have the freedom to ask: what if?

My fourth novel, *A Dangerous Inheritance* (Hutchinson 2012), was the sequel to *Innocent Traitor*, with a dramatic sub-plot involving the bastard daughter of Richard III and a few hints of the supernatural, which I have woven into all my novels. But in this one the theme is more prominent – and you might say that Josephine Tey's *The Daughter of Time* (Macmillan 1951) was an inspiration. Yet this book is very different from that much-outdated classic, and it is the first of my novels in which I wrote a fictional tale that had no historical foundation. Even so, it is based on extensive research and set within the context of two documented lives – and an enduring mystery. You could say that I have learned to relax into fiction writing – but my quest for authenticity remains as enthusiastic as ever.

I feel strongly that, where a novelist invents material in a historical novel about real persons or events, they should always include an author's note explaining what is fact and what is fiction. If the book is largely fictional, that should be made clear. Does it matter? Of course it matters, when we are dealing with real history. It is a matter of concern to historians that fiction – in well-publicised novels and films – is often taken as fact.

Publishers, trends and sales

Where do publishers come into this? I want to say from the start that my own publishers have always been supportive of my pursuit of authenticity. But publishers do not have the autonomy they once had, and they need to survive in a difficult world. Supermarket giants, for example, have enormous power: they squeeze publishers' profits (see a 'buy one, get one free' offer and you might depend on it that one has been printed free); they reject jackets and titles as not being commercial enough for their customers, which can result in the dumbing down of a book, making both the publishers and the author very unhappy. I fought for my novel on Eleanor of Aquitaine to be titled *A Marriage of Lions*, which reflects the parallels between evolving heraldry and Eleanor's turbulent marriage to Henry II. But that was rejected out of hand, and I ended up submitting no fewer than 90 titles until a compromise was reached and we went for *The Captive Queen*. It's a title I still hate – it's inane, and echoes so many others on the market. And it has since become clear that many readers preferred *A Marriage of Lions*.

Having made my case somewhat passionately for authenticity in historical novels, which ones would I recommend? Apart from those already mentioned, I must mention C. J. Sansom's compelling Shardlake series; Edward Rutherfurd's epics *Sarum* (Arrow 1991), *London* (Century 1997) and *The Forest* (Century 2000); Sarah Gristwood's *The Girl in the Mirror* (Harper Press 2012); Derek K. Wilson's *The First Horseman* (Sphere 2013); and, of course, Hilary Mantel's *Wolf Hall* (Fourth Estate 2009) and *Bring Up The Bodies* (Fourth Estate 2012), in which she wonderfully evokes a world, even though as a historian I find her portrayal of Thomas Cromwell over-sympathetic. Historical novels have become a respected genre because of novels such as these.

The tide is turning, I think. Having seen the BBC's well-paced and fairly authentic adaptation of *Wolf Hall* (2015), and the huge interest in it, I am more optimistic than I was. Maybe we don't always have to knuckle under to the powerful factors that come into play in the publishing and interpretation of history: market forces; the need to drive sales; the impact of films and blockbuster novels. It seems that people are again seeking – and enjoying – excellence in historical fiction. But historians might not win all the battles. As one lady remarked when she heard me pointing out some inaccuracies to a friend as we toured a well-known castle – 'Please stop spoiling it for me!'

Alison Weir is the top-selling female historian (and the fifth bestselling historian overall) in the UK, and has sold over 2.7 million books worldwide. She has published 18 history books, including *The Six Wives of Henry VIII* (Bodley Head 1991), *The Princes in the Tower* (Bodley Head 1992), *Elizabeth the Queen* (Jonathan Cape 1998), *Eleanor of Aquitaine* (Jonathan Cape 1999), *Henry VIII: King and Court* (Jonathan Cape 2001), *Katherine Swynford* (Jonathan Cape 2007) *The Lady in the Tower* (Jonathan Cape 2009) and *Elizabeth of York* (Jonathan Cape 2013). Alison has also published seven historical novels, including *Innocent Traitor* (Hutchinson 2006) and *Katherine of Aragon: The True Queen* (Headline 2016), the first in her Six Tudor Queens series. The second novel, *Anne Boleyn: A King's Obsession* was published by Headline in 2017 and the third, *Jane Seymour: The Haunted Queen*, in May 2018. Alison's latest non-fiction, *Queens of the Conquest* (Jonathan Cape 2017), the first in her England's Medieval Queens quartet, appeared in September 2017. She is an honorary life patron of Historic Royal Palaces.

See also...

• *Writing popular history books*, page 319

Ghostwriting

Gillian Stern sheds light on the invisible role of the ghostwriter, describing the often intense process involved in the art of writing another person's story in their own voice.

Everyone has a story. I learned this as a Saturday dental nurse at my father's NHS practice in Tottenham. Even the smallest details of people's lives are important, he would tell me. Listen carefully and you will hear.

His tiny surgery vibrated with life. Even before I had a chance to show a patient to the chair, they took up whatever they had been telling him during their last visit, which may have been six months or a year previously. They talked about their children, their families; they pre-emptively repeated their vow to quit eating sugary things; they gave their opinions on what Thatcher was or wasn't doing; told him how they brushed their teeth, what dental problems they were having. And as he filled their mouth with cotton wool rolls and started probing, he would take up the thread of their conversation, to which the patient would nod their head or roll their eyes, trying to make themselves understood.

As I mixed the mercury and amalgam for fillings, or held the hand of a nervous patient, I would listen. Everyone who sat in that chair had a distinctive voice; they were mostly living hard, complex lives. And I learned to hear, I learned to ask questions, and eventually I learned that sometimes what a patient *wasn't* saying was as interesting as what they were saying. My father made each and every one of his patients feel as if they mattered and how I wish now that I had written down the words that filled his surgery, in the rich and varied voices of his patients.

Maybe, then, it is no surprise that I am a ghostwriter – a writer who gives voice to other people's stories. I am paid to listen, to hear, to become someone else, to tell their story in their voice. In this, I am completely invisible, a siphon for their words, their story, their life, their soul. I do not interpret or pass judgement and though I might steer my questions in a direction I think their story should head, ultimately the book I am ghosting is entirely theirs, made up of their words.

While there are a range of ghostwriters – from those who ghost speeches to others ghosting novels – I ghost memoirs. I am a more reactive type of ghost in that I take commissions; many ghosts are more proactive, coming up with the idea of who they are going to ghost, taking responsibility for the outline, and involving themselves in all aspects of the publishing deal to writing the book itself. Ghostwriters are proper writers, often excellent writers, and in a world where we suspend our egos almost entirely, swapping recognition for invisibility, ghostwriters deserve all the accolades the industry and public are so keen not to throw our way. Going into a large, unnamed publishing house, where they were painting beautiful swirls of their author's names up and down the walls, I was completely unsurprised to see my own and other ghostly colleagues' names *not* included.

There is a peculiar snobbery and fuss out there about ghostwritten books and I can't quite work out why. There are plenty of people with book-worthy stories, from the already famous to the completely unknown, who have been busy living their lives – noisily or quietly – but who have never written a book before and are honest enough to know that writing is not one of their talents. While everyone has a story, not everyone has the ability to write that story. So, in order for their *commissioned* book to be the best possible read, they, their agent and publisher decide that it is better to employ the services of a professional writer rather than have them inflict underdeveloped, clumsy prose on their readers. I can see nothing wrong with this. The art is in how that story is told.

I came to ghosting through being a structural editor. A publisher handed me a manuscript by someone pretty famous (signing Non-Disclosure Agreements means I am not allowed to disclose who I am ghosting, before, during and after) and asked me to edit it. It was so tortuously written – so oblique and wooden – that I simply couldn't, and I requested time with the author, persuading them to let me have a go at re-working what they had written. The book went on to do extremely well and so the same publisher commissioned me to ghost another memoir. Publishing is a small world and publishers get used to reading between the lines in acknowledgements. 'A special thank you to Gillian Stern, without whom none of this would have hit the page' is a bit of a giveaway in the industry (and to my family), and so the acknowledgement, on many levels, is everything.

Often I am asked to attend what is, quaintly and oddly, still known as a 'beauty parade', where the person who needs a ghost – the author – with their agent and the publisher interview a number of potential ghosts, offering the job to the person whom the author feels best fits the profile of whatever it is they are looking for. I have walked into some such events and it is obvious immediately, or as the interview proceeds, that there is no way I fit, either because of a massive difference in outlook or voice or a complete lack of connection; I have walked into others and the connection and fit have been instant – not that that means I always then got the job. Mostly, though, because I've been around a bit, I am asked directly by a publisher to meet the author, with a view that I am the right person for the job. I am careful about what I accept; I am likely to be spending a great deal of time with the author, investing a great deal emotionally in them and their story, even 'becoming' them as I get into and develop the writing. I can only write someone's story if I can *imagine* myself in their voice. I will not accept a job if I think I will bring judgment and bias to the page.

Once I accept a commission, I either involve my agent or negotiate the contract myself. I read as much as I can about the author that already exists. Sometimes that can be just the outline on which the publisher has bought the book; in general, though, there is a body of material online, in existing books or articles and often they have diaries or letters or papers. I listen to, or watch, whatever programmes or clips I can and then spend time with the author, chatting, walking, eating (– for one author even frenetically working out with them at their gym while they talked!). I tape as much as I can and in the early stages, as I go about my day, I stick in my headphones and listen to their voice, allowing their way of talking, the patterns in their speech, to become mine too. I try it out as I shop or talk to friends. I try to understand the way they look at the world, the way they see the everyday, what it is they want to convey. I love that aspect of the job, the beginning of becoming part of someone else's life so intimately. It's a strange internal intimacy; *becoming* them – as I write and *am* them – can be overwhelming, although when I'm actually with that person, I can feel oddly detached.

Typically, the author and I have a couple of sessions where we decide how we are going to work and then we get going. I generally spend as much time as I can with them; some like me to tape everything over a number of days or weeks and get writing; others prefer to get together once a week or so, with me writing and them going over what I have written in between times. Most authors I have worked with like to pore over every word, checking that I am expressing them as they believe they express themselves, hearing the flow of the narrative, the timbre of the tone, the sound of their words. I have the world's best transcriber and I download tapes to her as soon as I get home and write from the transcripts. One thing I would strongly advise aspiring ghosts to do is to insist that your publisher or author pay for all transcribing expenses.

Once we settle on style and rhythm, I like my editor or the author's agent to see a few initial draft chapters so that there are no great surprises or disappointments near to the delivery deadline. I didn't do this on the first book I ghosted, and a couple of days before delivery received 18 pages of vicious criticism from the author's agent, none of which I disagreed with.

I get emotionally attached to my authors, of course I do. I have fallen in (appropriate) love; I have wanted to be the person I am ghosting; I have been a part of the lives of people I would never have otherwise had access to and I have seen things that would fill a book I can never write. And I have learned, painfully at first, that once the script is delivered and the book goes into production, I need to get out of there. I don't own the book; I don't own the story and I have no part in the publishing process once the script is delivered. Quite often the author and I stay in touch; quite often they tell me I am the most important person in their lives, the person who 'knows them the best', but that is moonshine and after the launch, after the razzmatazz, after the sales (and even prizes), life moves on. I did ghost two memoirs for one author, two years of our lives spent working together, and she told me shocking things she had genuinely never told anyone before, which was a burden for me but one I was prepared to carry and not include in the book. But I am not in this business to make friends. Ghosting, like editing, is a job and, once a book is written, I need to write the next.

The questions I am most frequently asked are: Why don't you write your own book? and How can you write a book without your name on the front? Here are my answers: I do not have a novel in me; I do not have a story about my life or an aspect of my life that I believe would interest readers; I have no desire to see my name on the front of a book when the story belongs to someone else. I get a great deal of satisfaction bringing interesting stories to life, in capturing someone else's voice so convincingly that they hear themselves come off the page. Ghostwriting is challenging and complex and a great privilege.

These days, well into his eighties, my father is still collecting stories – be it on the streets of his neighbourhood as he goes for his daily 'ball of chalk', in the stands at White Hart Lane, or around the table with his grandchildren. And, if I had time, I would tell you his story. Or maybe, one day, I will ghost it.

Gillian Stern is a former academic publishing commissioning editor, who while on maternity leave discovered a novel that went on to win prizes and become a bestseller. She then crossed over into the world of commercial and literary fiction and has since been a freelance structural editor for literary agents and publishers including Bloomsbury, Hodder and Orion. She combines this with her work as a ghostwriter and to date has ghosted eight books, all memoir, for Penguin and Orion amongst others; her latest ghosted memoir was a prize winner in 2018.

Making facts your mission: the pleasure of writing non-fiction

Jane Robinson describes what led her to become a non-fiction writer, and gives advice on the key elements and requirements of this disciplined and enjoyable work.

I didn't mean to be an author. I've always loved books; my obsession with collecting them began when I was banned from our local library at the age of seven – for using a jam tart as a bookmark in their copy of *Squirrel Nutkin*. After university I bought and sold books for a living, but never dreamed of writing them myself. That happened by accident. One day, while I was working in an antiquarian bookshop, a customer asked me for a guide to all the travel books ever written by women. He wanted to make a complete collection. I asked him to wait a few days; if there wasn't already a published list, I was sure I could work one up. After all, there couldn't be that many female first-hand travel accounts. Didn't history's women traditionally stay at home?

Off I went to the library to begin research. I discovered a handful of volumes by women and then a handful more, and by the time my customer returned I had a catalogue of over 100. He disappeared, disappointed that his task was now probably beyond his purse. And I went back to the library to see how many more forgotten travellers' voices I could find.

I was entranced by these intrepid adventurers. Encouraged by a friend who was a published historian, I decided to attempt a reference bibliography of their work – a book about books – just so that dealers like me could appreciate how many of these surprising authors there were. By now I had unearthed getting on for 1,000, spanning 16 centuries. But when I started reading the books I was only supposed to be listing (how could I resist *On Sledge and Horseback to Outcast Siberian Lepers* or *To Lake Tanganyika in a Bath Chair*?) my life swerved onto a new course. The same friend introduced me to his editor at Oxford University Press. We had a meeting, I wrote a proposal, and a few weeks later was the stunned possessor of a contract for my first book: *Wayward Women: A Guide to Women Travellers* (OUP 1990). One book led to another; I gave up my job at the shop, became self-employed, and now here I am, ten books later, working on the eleventh. I fell into a career as an author specialising in social history through women's eyes – and couldn't enjoy my job more.

I'm making it sound easy, and to some extent it was – back then. I had found a **subject** virtually untouched by other historians by which I was completely enthused; I knew I could **research** it given time; I had an introduction to and subsequently a **commission** from a respectable publisher; and I have never found it hard to **discipline** myself to meet deadlines. When *Wayward Women* came out, the publishing business was not as restricted as it is now by the aggressive need to make money on every book. OUP could afford to take a chance on me. But it is still possible to start from scratch as a non-fiction writer, as I did, and **enjoy success**.

Here's some advice about those five key elements of the job, with reference to my own work as a narrative historian.

1. Subject

Everything begins with this. Fiction writers can make up reality for themselves; we non-fiction authors must stick to the facts. The trick is to root your book in a subject you find irresistibly fascinating (enthusiasm is infectious) and write about it engagingly. Easily said, I know, but you'll develop your style with practice. Read aloud everything you write – that helps you gauge what readers are hearing in their heads as they turn the pages. It's no less important to pay attention to the cadence of a sentence in a biography, for instance, than in a novel. Good writing is good writing.

On a book-by-book level, I seek out well-known historical events or social attitudes and approach them from an unexpected angle, using the testimony of 'ordinary' people rather than history's celebrities. I like challenging stereotypes. The popular assumption is that before the 20th century, for instance, women were mostly seen, not heard, and did what they were told. *Wayward Women* smashes that one. In *Bluestockings* (Penguin 2009), about the first women to fight for higher education, I highlight the drama behind something we take for granted: the right of women to attend university. Did you realise that they were not given degrees at Cambridge until 1948? Or that Victorian medics believed that if women thought too much their wombs would wither? *Hearts and Minds* (Doubleday 2018) focuses on a massed, six-week women's march though the UK which won (some) women the vote in 1918 – and they weren't suffragettes. Who knew?

Choose a common approach like this for each book, and your work will amass a recognisable USP, which helps enormously when pitching for new commissions.

2. Research

Don't choose a subject you can't research thoroughly. While writing *Wayward Women* I had access to the British Library, which is a copyright library. Every book published in the UK must be deposited there by law. Anyone can become a registered reader, provided they have a referee and a valid reason for study. Other copyright libraries are in Aberystwyth, Cambridge, Dublin, Edinburgh and Oxford. It's important, when trying to present a fresh perspective to your readers, to find as many original sources as possible; hence I spend a great deal of research time in local archives and record offices, listening to oral history collections and advertising in judiciously chosen magazines for reader contributions. For *Bluestockings* I asked for family stories through university alumni magazines. Authenticity is crucial – try to get straight to the horse's mouth.

3. Commissions

I was fortunate to have an introduction to my first editor, which helped. If it's your debut you might not have an agent yet, so do try to find a champion – perhaps a friend or mentor in the business. Editors are swamped by unsolicited manuscripts (some refuse them altogether), so they welcome anything that marks you out from the crowd.

I have never written a book, chapter or article without a commission. It's not about the advance – only a quarter of that is due on signing the contract anyway (the rest coming on delivery, hardback and then paperback publication). Very few of us get rich writing. It's more that I need the confidence of a promise to publish and the impetus of having a contractual deadline. I value the framework provided by the proposal I've had to submit to achieve the deal. A good proposal is a thorough document with a detailed chapter-plan, as well as the usual information about why me, why the subject and what's the competition. Mine are blueprints; they are the most important element of the whole process of writing non-fiction. They express the flavour of the book and of my style to a potential editor and guide me through my work until I've finished.

4. Discipline

I happen to be temperamentally incapable of submitting work late. Always was, however hard I tried – even at university. I don't have the bravado to break deadlines, terrified that if something doesn't get done in time, it won't get done at all. I set myself a series of achievable targets. I decide when I'm realistically likely to finish the book, stating this in the proposal. Usually I allow a year for research and a year for writing. That includes a little leeway for other commitments (and life) to get in the way. Within that timeframe I'll mentally apportion periods for: research; collating my notes into a usable resource; completing each chapter; a second draft; and finally organising the notes, bibliography and illustrations.

Like most writers, I suspect, I have a routine. Once the research is done – all of it, so that I have an overview of the whole subject before I metaphorically put pen to paper – I start pretending I have a proper job, by disappearing into my study during office hours, with a break for some exercise at lunch. Because I write at home, I demarcate my working life from my domestic life by (bizarrely) putting on an apron before I sit down at my desk and removing it when I've switched off the computer. Weird, I know, but it works for me. There's probably a psychological fest of hidden agendas swirling around this ritual to do with the subversion of my role as a wife and mother … let's not go there.

5. Enjoy success

Sometimes I dream of being a fiction writer, of sitting somewhere inspirational for a while, inviting some characters into my empty head, then floating off to my study to see where they lead me and eventually lapping up the awards when my tour de force is made into a blockbuster film. Imagine! No research other than my own life and that of my friends and family (more or less disguised); no wearisome checking of the facts, compiling of the bibliography, sifting of the footnotes and fear of having misconstrued the truth.

But then I remember how much I enjoy having the outline of a plot already in place and then colouring it in to my own design. To me, non-fiction is a mission: I aim to restore a voice to people whose part in history has been forgotten. Hence my passion for women's lives. If I write well, I will paint no less involving a picture for my readers than a fiction-writer might; share some astonishing stories with them; inspire them and make them proud of those unknown ancestors who belong to us all. Never think of non-fiction as a poor relation.

Added extras

Don't think that you can't make money from it, either. The days of publishers taking a punt on young authors may have disappeared in the glare of hard-nosed commercialism, but it is possible to supplement your earnings by learning how to deliver a good talk. A significant part of my income comes from author appearances. Publish a blog about your work; interest in that could attract invitations to write opinion pieces elsewhere. Choose your subject carefully enough, and write about it in a lively, revealing way, and – who knows – the film and TV companies might come knocking at your door. It happens. Take advantage of every opportunity offered around publication day in terms of media and speaking engagements; they'll push up sales and, anyway, after all that work you deserve your day in the sun.

Every time a book of mine comes out, I thank that nameless customer who walked into the bookshop all those years ago. He changed the way I look at the world. And by writing non-fiction, I can now do the same for my readers. It's a privilege. Do try it.

Jane Robinson worked in the antiquarian book trade before becoming a full-time writer, social historian and lecturer. Her first book was *Wayward Women: A Guide to Women Travellers* (OUP 1990) and later publications include *A Force To Be Reckoned With: A History of the Women's Institute* (Virago 2011), *In the Family Way* (Viking 2015), and most recently *Hearts and Minds* (Doubleday 2018). For more information see www.jane-robinson.com and read her blog at https://janerobinsonauthor.wordpress.com. Follow her on Twitter @janerobinson00.

See also...

- *How to submit a non-fiction proposal*, page 429
- *Libraries*, page 670

Literary translation

There is more to literary translation than merely translating, as Danny Hahn explains. A self-confessed lobbyist, advocate and proselytiser for the profession, he describes the increasing breadth and diversity of 'being a translator'. He gives advice on how to get started, practical information on the work, and reveals a highly supportive and dynamic working community.

The easy bit

What does a literary translator do? A literary translator takes a literary text in one language, and writes it again in another. It's not particularly difficult, so long as you don't care whether your translation is any good. But ... what about not merely translating, but translating *well*? That's another matter entirely.

We all strive towards an ideal, a perfect translation, even while knowing that such a thing is impossible. Because rewriting a text in a new language doesn't just mean carrying over the sense, it means carrying over everything: the rhythm, the register, the associations, the resonances, the voice. All these things are deeply embedded in the original language, one might say they are inextricable from it – so how could it be possible to keep all of them when you're changing every single word? No, it's *impossible* – simple as that. And yet we translators do it anyway.

Being a literary translator demands all manner of unusual, overlapping skills, but there are just two that are absolutely essential. You need to be: 1) an uncommonly close, sensitive and wise reader; 2) a fantastically accomplished and versatile writer. And in two different languages, of course, because that's what translation is, after all – a process of reading, in language A, followed by a process of writing in which you deploy language B with such spectacular skill that everything you've read is somehow recreated, even if every single word is different. You read a line like 'The cat sat on the mat' and write a line in another language that keeps all of it: the meaning (feline, seated, carpet); the simple, almost childish register; the six absolutely consistent monosyllables; and the fact that the verb and both nouns all rhyme. Want to try it? Like I say – impossible!

How, practically, do translators work?

Literary translators in the UK are freelances, hired usually by a publisher to do a single job (translate a novel, say). There are a number of publishing houses or imprints that have a particular focus on international literature in translation – Harvill Secker, Pushkin Press, And Other Stories, Peirene Press, Maclehose Press and others – but as it becomes more mainstream, translations are nowadays to be found (albeit in small numbers) on all kinds of literary and commercial publishing lists.

Translators do pitch ideas to publishers, but in the overwhelming majority of cases it's the publisher who initiates a project. The publisher finds a book they'd like to publish in English (at one of the big trade fairs, perhaps, such as the Frankfurt or London Book Fair), then they recruit a translator to do the job. (Sometimes they invite several translators each to do a sample and choose the best match for the voice they're after.)

There will be a contract between publisher and translator, specifying the terms of the agreement, which will include a delivery deadline, a rate of payment and a royalty. Payment is calculated on the basis of the word count of the job (I currently charge £90 per 1,000 words of my translation, which is pretty typical, though rates can be negotiated up or down) and this is usually considered an 'advance' on future royalties. The payment is usually made half on signature of the contract and half on delivery of the translation.

The translator will deliver the new text, which will go through a number of editorial stages; it won't usually get a major structural edit as an Anglophone work might, but there will be some editing, copy-editing and proofreading – with the translator involved at every stage. (The translator should have the right to veto unwelcome editorial changes, though most translators – like most writers – are happy to be well edited.)

Eventually the translation will be published, perhaps both in print and ebook form; the translator's name should be clearly credited (ideally on the jacket, but otherwise on the title page), and the translator's copyright in the work asserted. In very rare cases a publisher will ask a translator to agree to a contract in which he or she signs over their copyright, but this should be forcefully resisted! Once the book is out in the world, the translator may well be invited to be a part of promoting it – alongside, or instead of, the original author.

Getting started

Literary translation, like any writing, doesn't have anything as sensible as a career path one might tidily follow. It's not a job that requires a certain series of qualifications, or clear stages of apprenticeship to be served before attaining the hallowed status of Literary Translator (from which time great work just sort of appears magically whenever you need it …).What it does have, however, is an incredible collegial community, a network, which it's really easy to get into.

Organisations like BCLT and Writers' Centre Norwich run residential summer schools and all kinds of other workshops; there's a mentoring scheme which pairs new translators with experienced translators in the same language for six months; and there are now dozens of postgraduate programmes for studying literary translation, some more practice-based, others with a stronger focus on theory. There's a new Emerging Translators Network, too, which is mostly an online community but also hosts occasional events.

And there are plenty of opportunities to meet other translators in the community, whether it's at the Literary Translation Centre at the London Book Fair every April, which hosts its own programme of events every year; or at the International Translation Day event in London, which gathers the whole tribe together – translators but also interested publishers, students, writers, funders. International Translation Day itself is 30 September, St Jerome's Day (he's the patron saint of translators), so the London event is always around that time.

However much you might hate the idea of 'networking', getting yourself known to publishers is an important part of finding your way into this industry, and the existing events, programmes and networks certainly make this easier. You might also want to write to publishers direct and pitch ideas for books you think they should publish (and commission you to translate for them, naturally). Send a cover letter, some information about the book and its author, and an excellent short sample translation. It's very unusual that these cold pitches come to fruition but, if they (and your sample work in particular) are good enough, they are at least a useful calling card; even if they don't buy this book, publishers may remember you and later invite you to audition for something else they acquire. Offer to do reader's reports, too – these are a good way of honing your own critical skills, as well as allowing publishers to get to know you. And don't be shy about pitching short-form translations to magazines; publishing the odd short story or poem is a good

Organisational support

The UK is blessed with a number of extremely effective and collaborative organisations working in the literary translation world. These are just a few of them. Sign up to their newsletters (and/or like on Facebook, follow on Twitter, etc) and you'll quickly get a sense of who else is out there.

The British Centre for Literary Translation (BCLT)

See page 555

Based at the University of East Anglia, the BCLT has recently changed its focus from public, professional and industry work to concentrate principally on its academic side. However, it still hosts an annual summer school (in partnership with Writers' Centre Norwich, see below), and the annual Sebald Lecture. Speakers have included Seamus Heaney, Susan Sontag and Margaret Atwood.
website www.bclt.org.uk

The Emerging Translators Network (ETN)

Just as it sounds, the ETN is a network for emerging translators. It operates mostly as an online forum, offering a welcoming and supportive environment for early-career literary translators and would-be literary translators to exchange information and advice.
website https://emergingtranslatorsnetwork.wordpress.com

English PEN

The founding centre of the PEN International network, English PEN works at the overlap between literature and free speech. Best known perhaps for its work with imprisoned authors around the world, its activities range much wider. Its strapline is 'Freedom to write, freedom to read', and it helps to make as wide a range of books as possible available to English-speaking readers, specifically by supporting literary translation. PEN offers grants to publishers to help cover the translation costs of publishing and promoting foreign books. It is a main player in the consortium of organisations that oversee the Literary Translation Centre at London Book Fair and International Translation Day.
website www.englishpen.org (See also PEN International in *Societies, associations and clubs* page 526.)

Free Word

See page 539

The Free Word Centre in London is home to a number of organisations – both residents (such as English PEN, above) and associates (such as BCLT) – that work in the areas of literature, literacy and free expression.

Free Word has chosen translation as one of the focuses of its work, which has included annual translators in residence who use their time at the Centre to collaborate with resident organisations, work with local schools, programme public events on a translation theme, and so on. Free Word is now the organisation responsible for International Translation Day.
website https://freewordcentre.com

Literature Across Frontiers (LAF)

Founded in 2001, this 'European Platform for Literary Exchange, Translation and Policy Debate' is based in Wales but works right across Europe (and beyond). With a wide network of partners, the organisation uses literature and translation to encourage intercultural dialogue, through workshops and publications, etc, focusing particularly on less-translated languages. It also carries out research into aspects of the translation market.
website www.lit-across-frontiers.org

The Translators Association (TA)

See page 555

Part of the Society of Authors, membership is limited to those who have published a book-length work or equivalent (though there is also associate membership for those who have been offered a first contract, even if it hasn't yet been completed). Among the many benefits is legal advice including clause-by-clause vetting of your contracts.
website www.societyofauthors.org/groups/translators

Writers' Centre Norwich

This literature development agency has recently moved to new premises and is currently evolving into the National Centre for Writing. The transition will involve taking on much of the professional and public work that used to be done by BCLT, including the running of translation mentorships, programming public events that look at literary translation and translated literature, and publishing the journal for literary translators, *In Other Words*.
website www.writerscentrenorwich.org.uk

way to get in the door. There are plenty of good places to start that are particularly receptive to international writing: *Words without Borders*, *Granta*, *Modern Poetry in Translation*, *The White Review*, *Asymptote*, and many others.

I've mentioned the translation 'community', but it's also worth thinking of smaller, more focused communities within it, which may exist for particular languages or regions. Find other translators who work in your language and look for other possible language-specific allies. For example most European countries, and some outside Europe, have organisations that exist to promote their literatures. Drop the appropriate ones a note and introduce yourself; they're usually grateful to meet translators who want to help them get their writers into the wider world, and they'll be useful to you.

'Being a translator'

The world of the professional literary translator in the UK has transformed in the last five or six years, and in almost every respect for the better. So much of this has come about thanks to the dynamism of translators themselves and the way the profession has come to think about itself, and in particular what it means to be a translator. I draw that distinction a lot these days, between 'translating' and 'being a translator'.

Translating is the core of the work, of course – taking an old text and writing a new one. That strange alchemical process (as one of my colleagues beautifully put it) of turning gold into gold. But that's not how I spend most of my time.

I talk to publishers about books – things that interest me, things that interest them; I read foreign-language submissions on their behalf and write reports. I talk to foreign agents and publishers and writers, too, to get a sense of what's going on in the publishing world. I am, in short, part of a big, transnational, translingual, literary conversation. I review translations for newspapers, and write about translation as I'm doing now. I do public events about literary translation and translated literature. I run workshops for newer translators than me (including in universities and schools, primary as well as secondary) and assorted programmes to make translation better, better paid, and more appreciated. In other words, I'm a lobbyist, an advocate, a proselytiser – as most translators are, I think. There's a sense in the profession of a kind of common mission (it seems rather zealous when I say that); we all feel there should be more translation, and more diverse translation, and that translations and translators should be profoundly cherished by the reading public.

That's what 'being a translator' means to me. Yes, doing the translating, but also being part of a community, a conversation – you might almost say a movement; it means seeing one's role as broad and flexible, seeing oneself as a significant and active player in the publishing world, not just an occasional, grateful hired hand. The community itself is an extraordinarily warm and welcoming one, and it's never been easier to join. Our profession and the market for our work are both growing – it's a good time for translating, and for being a translator, too.

Danny Hahn is a writer, editor and translator. He has translated about 20 novels from Portuguese, Spanish and French, including translations of fiction by José Eduardo Agualusa and José Luís Peixoto, and non-fiction by writers ranging from Portuguese Nobel Literature Laureate José Saramago to Brazilian footballer Pelé. He has also written several works of non-fiction and one children's picture book, as well as editing reference books for adults and reading guides for children and teenagers. Formerly National Programme Director of the British Centre for Literary Translation, he is a former chair of the Society of Authors (2014–16) and of the UK Translators Association (2012–15). His most recent publications include the new edition of the *Oxford Companion to Children's Literature* (Oxford University Press 2015).

Being a travel writer

Sara Wheeler paints a vivid picture of life and work as a travel writer, through her own experiences and those of inspirational writers of the past. She reflects on the freedom and flexibility of travel writing as a genre, the personal qualities it demands, and how a sense of place is best captured through the details of daily life.

The happiest moment of my life presented itself one cool February afternoon in the Transantarctic mountains, many years ago. I was hiking up a valley. Fearful of losing my bearings, I stopped to fish an American Geological Survey map out of my pack and spread it on the ice. Tracing my route by topographical landmarks (including an especially pointy mountain glaciologists had baptised 'The Doesn'tmatterhorn'), my finger came to a straight line drawn with a ruler and marked 'Limit of Compilation'. Beyond that, the sheet was blank. I had reached the end of the map …

Getting off the map

Travel writing aims to take the reader off the map, literally and metaphorically. Throughout my own professional life, travel has loaned a vehicle in which to explore the inner terrain of fears and desires we stumble through every day. Writing about travel allows flexibility and freedom within the rigid framework of train journeys, weather and knackered tent. The creative process is an 'escape from personality' (T.S. Eliot said that), and so is the open road. And a journey goes in fits and starts, like life. Not history, not memoir, but a hybrid blend of the two with a generous dose of topographical description, travel writing is *sui generis* – either that, or anything you want it to be, provided the narrative conjures a sense of place. It is a baggy genre. Why not be playful?

In the 5th century BC, Herodotus sniffed around Egypt. Coming upon a handsome obelisk, he asked a gang of workers nearby the meaning of the hieroglyphics carved on the base. 'That', the labourers solemnly announced, 'records the number of onions eaten by the men who constructed the obelisk.' Travel writing can break ground too. In the 14th century, Ibn Battuta set out from the land now known as Morocco and deployed his pen (or was it a quill?) to unveil points east hitherto undreamt of by his contemporaries.

I got started some decades ago with a book on Evia, the second largest Greek island (known to classicists as Euboia). I had studied both ancient and modern Greek at university, had lived in the country for more than a year, and was incubating plenty of ideas about all things Greek. I got a commission, but the resulting book was a labour of love: too much labour, too much love and not enough art (though it's still in print … yeah!). My agent said, 'Next time, go somewhere you don't know anything about.' So I went to Chile, because I had always been fascinated by its shape.

Inspirational writers

Many of the writers who inspired me were on the road and at their desks in the early decades of the 20th century – a kind of golden age for travel writing in Britain. I'm thinking of Evelyn Waugh's *Labels: A Mediterranean Journal* (Duckworth 1930), Norman Douglas' *Old Calabria* (Secker & Warburg 1915), Arthur Grimble's *A Pattern of Islands* (John Murray 1952) and of course Robert Byron, the travel writer's travel writer, whose *Road to Oxiana* (Macmillan 1937) perfectly embraces the frivolous and the deeply serious – a killer combo.

In the '70s, the genre enjoyed a renaissance inspired by Paul Theroux, who set off by train to India, and then to Patagonia. In the aftermath, as the craze worked itself out, a superfluity of travelogues took a bogus motif as their central theme – you know the kind of thing: *Up Everest with One Hand Tied Behind My Back*. The trope reached its logical conclusion with Tony Hawks' bestselling *Round Ireland with a Fridge* (Ebury Press 1998) (he hitchhiked the length of the country with a small item of white goods). This idea has had its day, I feel, and prospective writers would do better to find a more authentic theme.

The 'pattern in the carpet'

The most important thing, in a book or a short piece, is the pattern in the carpet. Travel literature must be *about* something, and not just an account of a great trip. During the glorious six months I spent travelling down Chile, I assumed that journey's end would be Cape Horn. But I learned that the country claimed a slice of Antarctica, which appeared on all the maps – even those on badges on Boy Scouts' arms – like a slice of cake suspended in the Southern Ocean. Damn! So I hitched a lift on a Chilean air-force plane to a snowy base and, as I climbed a hill with a volcanologist and heard him tap-tapping ice into a specimen jar, I looked out at an ice desert bigger than the United States and saw my next book: a travel journey across the Antarctic. I subsequently spent seven months in 'the Big White' and the experience gave me a taste for extreme environments. Some years later I followed up with a book on the Arctic. For both, I had to get people to cooperate, as many of my destinations were not on commercial routes; indeed some, like the far eastern Russian region of Chukotka, were closed to foreigners. Dogged persistence required. Never Give Up!

Books and other ventures . . .

My chief endeavour, in my working life, has been books: travel books and biographies of travellers, of Captain Scott's man Apsley Cherry-Garrard, for example, author of the polar classic *The Worst Journey in the World* (Constable & Co. 1922). But, as for most of my peers, there have been many short pieces along the way. I write essays, reviews and squibs for love – and for money. The freelance travel writer has many avenues to explore. Some of these pieces really are essays – new introductions to classic works of travel literature, for example; some you could call incidental journalism. This latter might be an enemy of promise, but it gets me out of the house, often to places I would not otherwise go. Dropping in to a village in Kerala for six days might not yield any profound experience, but it offers suggestions and opens up possibilities.

There is a difference between the magazine assignment, for which the writer must travel fast and purposefully, and the book, for which the journey evolves its own inner logic. When I turned 50 my publisher suggested I collect some of my incidental articles in a volume which we called *Access All Areas: Selected Writings 1990–2011* (Jonathan Cape 2011). Editing that book revived pleasures of crossing unimportant African borders using a kidney donor card as ID; of sharing a bathroom with a harp seal; of mixing a cocktail of six parts vodka and one part something else (they didn't revive much of that, because I can't remember what happened next …).

The power of detail

I often hear it said that tourism has murdered travel writing. I don't think so. Mass travel has liberated the form. No amount of package tours will stop the ordinary quietly going on everywhere on earth. When I lived in Chile in the early '90s I found my weekly trawl round the supermarket gripping beyond belief: watching women decide between this jar of *dulce de leche* or that one, weighing out their cherimoyas, loading up with boxes of washing powder. In Greece a decade earlier I often joined girlfriends at their weekly weigh-in at the local pharmacy (domestic scales had to wait for more prosperous times). So you don't *actually* have to be off the map. Don't you sometimes find daily life almost unbearably poetic?

Minute curiosity is a requirement of the travel writer – and of the biographer, novelist and poet. The significance of the trivial is what makes a book human. Out there on the road, I have often found that the most aimless and boring interludes yielded, in the long run, the most fertile material. Every journey created energy, joy and, above all, hope. There was always a dash of human dignity to lift a story out of absurdity and farce, however ugly the background. The world everywhere and simultaneously is a beautiful and horrible place.

In short, the notion that all the journeys have been made is just another variation of the theme that the past exists in technicolour while the present has faded to grey – that everything then was good, and everything now is bad. A theme, in other words, as old as literature. I add the point that there are no package tours to the Democratic Republic of Congo, still the heart of darkness, or to the parts of Saudi Arabia where women live in a perpetual ethical midnight.

Tools of the trade

Having established her pattern in the carpet, the writer must work hard to conjure a sense of place: she has to make the reader see, hear, taste, feel and smell (though not all at the same time). Specificity is the key, as it is to all writing. Don't tell the reader so-and-so was eating, or reading – tell them *what* he was eating or reading. Themes and characters can function as scaffolding. Other trusty tools include the use of dialogue, which works on prose like yeast. Quotations from your diary or letters or emails can vary the texture of your narrative. And history is your friend – use judiciously selected quotations from those who have gone before you. I often cruise the topography shelves in the stacks of the London Library, on the lookout.

And do I need to add that to be any kind of writer you have to read all the time? If you are aiming to pursue a career in the field I describe, you can start by devouring one volume by each of the writers I cite here – preferably within a month. Get the habit. Make notes about what you like and don't like. I still keep a log of that kind, and I refer to it all the time.

Travelling heroines

Let me end with a few words from and about the travel writer who inspired me above all others: Mary Kingsley. She belonged to that tribe of tweed-skirted Victorians who battled through malarial swamps, parasols aloft, or scaled the unnamed Pamirs trailed by a retinue of exhausted factotums. History has tended to write them off as benignly mad eccentrics, but the best among their volumes have stood the test of time: Isabella Bird's *A Lady's Life in the Rocky Mountains* (1874), Harriet Tytler's *An Englishwoman in India* (1903–06), Kate Marsden's *On Sledge and Horseback to Outcast Siberian Lepers* (1893) (candidate for title of the millennium?). It is Kingsley, however, who carries the prize with her masterpiece

Travels in West Africa (1897), a book enjoyed by millions since it first appeared more than a century ago. The author's influence on those following in her tracks can scarcely be overestimated. After all, not only did she do what countless men told her could not be done, but she also turned the experience into literature – and had the time of her life to boot.

She was born in London in 1862, high noon of imperial splendour. Amazingly, given the sophistication of her publications, she never went to school. Blue-eyed and slender, with a long face and hair the colour of wet sand, she was 31 when she set off on her first proper trip to Africa in August 1893. *Travels in West Africa* tells the story of Kingsley's second, 11-month voyage. Her ship reached Freetown, Sierra Leone, on 7 January 1895, and she headed southwards through those countries now known as Ghana, Nigeria, Cameroon, Equatorial Guinea and Gabon. The trip involved almost unimaginable hardship. Approaching the Gabonese river Remboué, our heroine wades through swamps for two hours at a stretch, up to her neck in fetid water with leeches round her neck like a frill. She marches 25 miles through forest so dense that the sky is never once visible, and falls 15 feet into a game pit laid with 12-inch ebony spikes ('It is at these times,' she writes, 'you realise the blessing of a good thick skirt.'). Kingsley responds profoundly to the African landscape. 'I believe the great swamp region of the Bight of Biafra is the greatest in the world,' she writes, 'and that in its immensity and gloom it has a grandeur equal to that of the Himalayas.' Like all the very best travel scribes – one thinks of Sybille Bedford, Norman Lewis, Jonathan Raban, and, on form, Freya Stark – Kingsley brilliantly paints a landscape onto the page. The reader can see the silver bubbles of Lake Ncovi as the canoe carves a frosted trail, the rich golden sunlight of late afternoon, or the wreaths of indigo and purple over the forest as day sinks into night. 'To my taste', she writes, 'there is nothing so fascinating as spending a night out in an African forest, or plantation … And if you do fall under its spell, it takes all the colour out of other kinds of living.' Indeed.

Sara Wheeler, FRSL is a travel writer, biographer and journalist. Her books include *Travels in a Thin Country: A Journey Through Chile* (Little, Brown 1994), *Terra Incognita: Travels in Antarctica* (Jonathan Cape 1996), *Cherry: A Biography of Apsley Cherry-Garrard* (Jonathan Cape 2001) and *Too Close to the Sun: A Biography of Denys Finch Hatton* (Jonathan Cape 2006). Her most recent book is *O My America!* (Jonathan Cape 2013). She is a contributing editor of the *Literary Review* and a Trustee of the London Library.

See also...

- *Life's a pitch: how to get your ideas into print*, page 11
- *Writing features for newspapers and magazines*, page 3

Writing a cookbook

Ruby Tandoh describes what is special about a good cookbook, with its vital ingredients of personality, integrity, accessibility and beauty, and how such books continue to be treasured friends, even in our internet age.

We live in a golden age of recipes. Things haven't always been this way. There was a time when families would have just one cookbook – a tome of culinary knowledge that set the standard for every meal they ate. Before that, recipes would be family heirlooms, passed between generations in furtive whispers. Earlier still, the whole concept of the 'recipe' – a set of instructions for preparing a meal – would hardly have made sense; making food was something to be intuited through sight, smell, taste and touch – something impossible to reduce to clunky words and text.

But now, straddling the digital and physical worlds as we do, every day plugging ourselves into the internet, we've grown used to a different kind of cooking: we can search for any recipe, from any time, place or culture, no matter where we are. We have the entire world in our smartphone browsers. We can find videos, tutorials, blog posts, picture guides, scientific breakdowns, nutrition calculators and more. Google 'lasagne recipe' and you'll find over 22 million results. When recipes are so abundant, what's the point of cookbooks?

It might seem pessimistic, but this question is at the heart of good food writing. Because, despite the vastness of the internet and all the resources it offers, people do still buy cookbooks. No matter how many million guacamole recipes litter the virtual landscape, we still do turn to that one stained and food-spattered recipe in the pages of an old book. Clearly there's something special within the pages of a good cookbook that you can't necessarily find online. If you can put your finger on this specialness, *you* can write a good cookbook.

Exactly how this strange, fuzzy-edged 'specialness' manifests itself will be different in every book: for some it'll be in the styling and the aesthetic; in others it'll be a unique voice; some might be brought together by a unifying message; others have a personality at their core. There's no one right way to do this – there are as many ways to write a good cookbook as there are recipes for lasagne on Google – but I find it helps to turn first to the cookbooks that line your shelves. What follows is a little tour through my own cookbook collection – from aspic to avocado toast, celebrity recipe books to scholarly guides – to get a sense of the many, many ways to make a cookbook special.

First up is an unlikely one, because it's important to step outside the old rules and structures if you're going to write a cookbook that holds its own in the here and now. It's *In the Kitchen with Kris: A Kollection of Kardashian-Jenner Family Favorites* (Gallery Books/Karen Hunter Publishing 2014). The food world might not have a lot of time for reality-TV matriarch Kris Jenner and her (most likely ghostwritten) book of recipes, but I think there's a lot to be learnt from it. The recipes are inviting enough, but the core of this book is Kris herself; these are the musings of a home cook, putting herself and her life at the centre of each recipe. Because, as much as cooking is about craft, science and skill, it's also about *who's* cooking, and who they're cooking for. So many cookbooks forget how deeply personal food can be, but Kris Jenner is unapologetic about both who she is (an amateur cook) and why these recipes are important (because they're important to her).

And you don't have to be a reality TV star to put yourself at the centre of the picture like this. From the beginning of her food writing career, Nigella Lawson has followed exactly this approach: weaving personal anecdotes through her recipes, infusing dull how-to sections with in-jokes and wry remarks, and writing herself and her cooking process into the narrative. The recipes in Lawson's books aren't for some exemplar eggs benedict or the platonic pissaladière – they're unique, sometimes odd, and inseparable from the tastes, cravings and idiosyncrasies of the person who devised them. When I cook these meals, I get a taste of what it is to walk in Nigella Lawson's shoes. Now *that's* special.

Even if you're not willing to offer up your life story on a plate, that doesn't mean your voice can't come through loud and clear. So many of the most wonderful cookbooks I own are ones where the author's name is in small print or nestled away with the copyright information; these are the manuals and the collections, books like the *Hamlyn All-Colour Cookbook* (Hamlyn 1979) or your mum's much-used, barely-holding-together, branded slow-cooker recipe book. What keeps these books on the kitchen shelves long after they've gone out of fashion (think dust-jackets with faded photos of aspic, baked alaska and soufflé) is the integrity that they embody. These books are straightforward and unfussy, true to themselves and their readership: if they say home cooking, they mean genuinely easy-to-source ingredients and tried-and-tested recipes. If they claim to give you 100 easy microwave recipes, they do that with unabashed pride. The specialness of these books is about trust: I've got as much faith in the Hamlyn Yorkshire puddings rising as I do in the sun coming up in the morning. This is the stuff that treasured cookbooks are made of.

Creating a book like this isn't easy. The process of recipe testing was completely unlike any kind of home cooking I've ever done. When I was testing and tasting recipes for my two cookbooks, my whole life consisted of going to the shop, trudging home with bags of groceries, cooking until I was exhausted, then getting up the next day to do it all over again. I was forced to think about food in ways that no normal, hungry human being would: I found myself counting grams of pasta, measuring frying times with a stopwatch and agonising over the exact dimensions of 'small cubes' of potato. If I called for half a can of chopped tomatoes in a recipe, I had to think hard about what my readers would do with the other half of the can. If a recipe needed expensive ingredients, I had to question whether or not those costs were worth it, or what cheaper substitutions I could suggest. Jack Monroe's *A Girl Called Jack* (Michael Joseph 2014) takes everyday ingredients and turns them into low-budget meals to feed a family, which meant Jack had to painstakingly calculate exactly how many pennies a teaspoon of cumin would cost. Jamie Oliver's *Jamie's 30-Minute Meals* (Michael Joseph 2010) was no doubt the result of a whole team of home economists working ceaselessly for months to create something that can be recreated in just half an hour.

The glory of these cookbooks is that they take that worry, precision and care – all of those countless questions about whether a recipe is spicy enough, cheap enough, accessible enough or authentic enough – and cook it into something as natural as eating itself. Write a Filipino chicken adobo recipe well, and a week of tireless testing will condense into a single page: a story about your girlfriend's favourite meal, the sweet-sour flavour it's famous for, and the right way to cook the chicken. From all that trial and error comes a recipe as effortless as if you'd just talked your friend through it while sitting idly on their kitchen countertop. A good cookbook is a friend in the kitchen.

With all this talk of recipes and writing, it's easy to forget that cookbooks are seldom comprised of text alone. The modern recipe book is a beautiful object. It's no longer enough just to contain recipes for desirable things; a cookbook has to be a desirable thing in and of itself. I was shocked when I was writing my first cookbook, *Crumb* (Chatto & Windus 2014), at just how much of the book wasn't my work at all: designers chose beautiful fonts and formatted the recipes just so; a photographer took hundreds of photos; the publishing team sourced props that conveyed exactly what kind of cooking the book was all about. The images and design of the book did just as much speaking as the words on the page. Even in wordy, prose-heavy cookbooks such as Nigel Slater's *The Kitchen Diaries* (Fourth Estate 2005), photos play a vital role, giving us a sense of mood, pace and atmosphere. In Samin Nosrat's *Salt, Fat, Acid, Heat* (Canongate 2017), illustrations bring levity to descriptions of the science of cooking, while in Molly Katzen's *The Enchanted Broccoli Forest* (Ten Speed Press 1982), illustrations serve to hint at a natural, back-to-basics style of cooking, at odds with the highly-styled glossiness of the aforementioned *Hamlyn All-Colour Cookbook*.

No matter what type of cuisine you write about, or which audience you write for, these things – voice, narrative, recipe quality, accessibility and aesthetic – should all come together to create a message that runs through every page of your cookbook. For some, this will be a romantic story of love, cooking and family, while in other books it might take shape as a paean to traditional Sicilian food. Your book could be heavy on history and context, or it might immerse you in descriptions of the tactile, sensory joys of the kitchen. Perhaps you're keen to show the world the cooking of your parents and grandparents, preserving a culture that has been passed down to you, or perhaps you want to muddle the rules of good taste, creating something irreverent, inauthentic and fun. In our increasingly self-aware food culture, it might be that you have a more political food message: prioritising affordability, centring marginalised cultures or reframing old culinary histories. Michael W. Twitty's *The Cooking Gene* (Amistad 2017) and Julia Turshen's *Feed the Resistance* (Chronicle Books 2017) are two great examples of the latter.

Whatever your message, it's vital that you have one. It's this message that makes a cookbook more than the sum of its parts, and so, so much more than just a bunch of recipes at the end of a Google search.

Ruby Tandoh is a baker, journalist, and the bestselling author of three books: *Crumb: The Baking Book* (2014) and *Flavour: Eat What You Love* (2016) were published by Chatto & Windus, and her latest book is *Eat Up: Food, Appetite and Eating What You Want* (Profile Books 2018). She is a columnist for the *Guardian*, and co-founder of *Do What You Want*, a zine about mental health. Ruby was a finalist in the 2013 series of 'The Great British Bake Off'. Follow her on Twitter @rubytandoh and her blog at rubyandthekitchen.co.uk.

Writing for the health and wellness market

Health writer Anita Bean offers advice on how to find success in the popular and fast-moving health and wellness market, using some essential ingredients – fresh ideas, careful research, trustworthy content and strong, clever marketing.

When I began writing freelance in 1990, the health and wellness market was quite niche compared to what is today. Back then, it comprised mostly slimming magazines, which were targeted exclusively at women. As a nutritionist, I was – fortunately – in high demand. My first regular commission was a column for *Slimmer* magazine, and after that folded I had a regular column in *Zest* and *She*. In those days, most publications preferred to use freelances rather than staff writers, so there was certainly plenty of work around.

The market has changed hugely over the past 25 years, thanks largely to the internet. So many more people are interested in health and wellness, not just slimmers. You'll find regular health and wellness features in just about every print and digital medium – even the financial and business press! The other major change is the decreased use of freelances by mainstream media, as tighter budgets mean many more health and wellness features are now written in-house.

This is both good and bad for health writers. More media channels and bigger audiences mean there's loads of potential work out there for us. Editors need to fill more column inches and digital space, so they are perpetually on the lookout for new health content. The downside is that every man and his dog now seem to be an 'expert' and there's nothing to stop them writing about health and wellness on the internet. As a result, good (that is, evidence-based) content has become diluted in a tsunami of poor content put out there by bloggers, self-styled 'experts', and social media stars with a large Instagram following and impressive six-packs. The public are often left confused and, nowadays, no longer know who to trust for health advice.

How I got into writing

As a child, I was always curious about the science of food – what's in it, what happens when you add this to that, what happens to food in the body – and I was forever experimenting in the kitchen, cooking and creating recipes. I also loved reading cookery books and built up quite a collection over the years – I would devour every morsel of information I could find about food and nutrition.

At school, I loved home economics (now food technology) but was more fascinated by food chemistry. So I went on to study for a degree in Nutrition and Food Science at the University of Surrey and – unusually for a girl back in the 80s – started lifting weights. I qualified both as a registered nutritionist and, after winning the British bodybuilding championships in 1991, as a fitness instructor.

I honed my writing skills while I worked as a nutritionist for the Dairy Council. I wrote booklets and articles about health and nutrition, and also developed an interest in the organisation's sports sponsorship activities. I realised that there was virtually no nutrition information available for athletes or regular exercisers. There was clearly a gap in the market for such a book! So, I handed in my notice and decided to enter the world of freelance health writing.

Getting your lucky break

As with many things in life, getting that lucky break in writing is often a case of being in the right place at the right time, seizing an opportunity and taking a risk. You also need to have a strong belief in your idea, and be persistent. That's essentially how I got my first book deal in 1992 (*The Complete Guide to Sports Nutrition*) when I sent my proposal to Bloomsbury (then A&C Black), as well as many other publishers. There was nothing on sports and exercise nutrition in the UK trade market but, luckily, this commissioning editor happened to be on the lookout for a sports nutrition book to add to her sports list. My proposal landed at just the right time. But it was a risk for both of us, as it was an untapped and unknown market.

Fortunately, the market turned out to be a lot bigger than anticipated; as well as publicising the book to athletes, I also looked up my contacts list and targeted fitness training providers, schools and universities. The book was soon placed on the recommended list for many higher education courses, which now account for a large proportion of its sales. There's no single secret to a book's success, but it's often a combination of fresh ideas, excellent content and savvy marketing.

Build your brand

The other aspect of writing is longevity. It's tempting to sit back on your laurels after you've published a book and let sales look after themselves. But that won't happen. You need to put sustained effort into building your reputation and marketing yourself and your work. As a new writer, I offered to provide nutrition talks for health clubs and fitness training organisations who then recommended my books to their students. I also gave talks to athletes, spoke at conferences, and provided quotes and commentary to the media. Much of this was either underpaid or unpaid but it was always done in return for a book plug. And any editorial coverage is worth so much more in terms of endorsement. Whether you're a new or an established author, it's important to get your name out there – and keep it there!

In the world of health and wellness, trends change fast, and what's hot one minute can be out of the favour the next. The key to a book's longevity is to update it regularly to reflect new thinking and also the demands of a fast-changing market. I've now written eight editions of my first book. Each time, I re-examine the content to ensure it is current and relevant to my readership. I add extra material and cut sections that I feel are no longer engaging my readers.

Market your work

In the highly competitive world of health and wellness, doing your own marketing is more important than ever before. I strongly recommend having your own website. This is not only a brilliant way of marketing your books and writing services but is also a platform to showcase your published work. Providing free information in the form of articles and recipes is also a great way of establishing your credibility and attracting potential book sales. You don't need to spend a fortune (you can build your own site) but the more time and effort you put into your website, the greater will be the return in terms of future commissions. It's also crucial to update your site regularly, add new content, ditch stuff that has become less relevant and learn a bit about search engine optimisation. I've re-designed my website (www.anitabean.co.uk) three times since 2004. I provide free articles and recipes, and a free downloadable ebook. To sustain a regular readership, I aim to post a new blog a minimum of once a month.

Having a social media presence is also crucial for a health writer. It's not only a great way of letting people know about your work but is also essential for keeping up to date and finding out what people are talking about. I recommend focusing your efforts on just two or three platforms, whichever are most relevant to your target market. For me, Twitter and Instagram work very well. I use Twitter for sharing new information, publicising my work (e.g. new books, blog posts and articles) and finding out what's new in health. I post photos of recipes from my latest book on Instagram to help spread the word.

Seven tips on breaking into the health and wellness market

1. Identify a gap in the market

Read, read, read – find out what's new and emerging. Research what's already out there, your competition, and then work out how you can make your product better. Keep an eye on trends and try to stay ahead of the game – be the first to write about a new topic, not the last.

2. Generate new ideas

Network with colleagues and experts at conferences; this is also useful for building up a contact list of experts for quotes. Mingle with your audience before and after presentations – what do they want to know, what are their concerns? Social media can be a great place to pick up on what's trending and on ideas for blogs, articles and books.

3. Know your readership

Do your research – actually *read* the magazine you want to write for, so you get a feel of who the readers are and what they want to read about. Get on their level and talk their language.

4. Improve your content

Accuracy is paramount; always use evidence (not just 'research says…') and cite or link to the source or study abstract. Always add a practical element ('– now here's how you can use this info...').

5. Adapt your style

Be adaptive and always write to, not at, your reader as if you were speaking to them. Aim to inspire them, and for your reader to say, 'Oh, I didn't know that!' by the end of the piece. Make your article or book unique and different from the competition, not just a companion to what's already out there.

6. Be consistent

Ensure your messages are consistent across everything you write (e.g. you can't be pro-carb one minute and low-carb the next), but be prepared to change your view if new research comes to light.

7. Don't slavishly follow trends

Just because other writers are raving about a new thing – say, coconut oil – doesn't mean you have to. Question a trend; where did it start? Often it stems from clever PR rather than science. And don't believe everything a PR sends you; look beyond the headlines – where did the story come from? Read the original research, and only write about the product if you believe it stands up to scrutiny, not just to fill a column or to generate a grabby headline.

Anita Bean is an award-winning registered nutritionist, freelance health writer and author of 28 books, including *The Complete Guide to Sports Nutrition, The Vegetarian Athlete's Cookbook, Food for Fitness, The Complete Guide to Strength Training, Nutrition for Young Athletes* and *Sod It! Eat Well* (all Bloomsbury). Her latest book, *The Runner's Cookbook*, was published in 2018 (Bloomsbury). She has written features for many national magazines, including *Good Housekeeping, Cycling Weekly, Runner's World, Women's Running* and *Healthy*, and is quoted regularly in the media. Visit Anita's website at www.anitabean.co.uk.

Writing sports books

Frances Jessop describes how, in sports publishing, a quick-thinking and creative author can grasp an opportunity or take advantage of a new angle to find success. Here she gives clear advice on what an editor is looking for in a proposal for a sports book.

A children's book, the autobiography of a player, the biography of a manager, at least seven books telling the story of the season, a book of the manager's quotes, and the story told in the words of Richard III – so many books have been published about the 'fairy tale' of Leicester City winning the Premier League in 2015/16 that this story has almost become a sub-genre in itself. This most unlikely of tales (if it were submitted as a novel, it would surely have had 'a bit unrealistic?' scrawled on the manuscript) has spawned books that perfectly illustrate both the breadth and depth of sports writing and the opportunities open to authors and publishers who can think quickly and imaginatively.

What makes a good (and successful) sports book?

There are as many types of sports books as there are types of non-fiction but, as an editor commissioning sports books for a trade publisher, I mostly see three kinds. Firstly, the autobiography or biography of a sporting figure – what many people imagine when they think of a sports book. Their subjects range from household names to pioneers of a sport and everything in between. What the good ones have in common are insight and access. Many autobiographies are ghostwritten and the more time the writer has had to spend with the subject, the better the book. If they have been able to interview people surrounding their subject, then a much more nuanced and layered portrait will emerge. A gold standard in autobiography (across all genres) is Andre Agassi's *Open* (HarperCollins 2010). As the title suggests, he is breathtakingly honest about his relationship with tennis and the struggles he has faced in his career. This candour and vulnerability, combined, of course, with a highly successful career and an engaging character, make for a terrific book.

Secondly, many of the books we publish at Yellow Jersey Press could be described as narrative non-fiction that happens to be set in the sporting world. One of the best non-fiction books I've read is *Friday Night Lights* by H.G. Bissinger (Yellow Jersey Press 2005), which was subsequently adapted into a film and a long-running television drama. It's 'about' American football in Texas, but it's actually about small town life, growing up, hopes and dreams. The best sporting narratives are often described as books you'd enjoy even if you aren't a fan of the particular sport. Sport is a great leveller; there's a universality to sport that makes it an excellent prism through which to tell bigger stories, something which good books do to great effect.

Sports publishing is opportunistic, as can be seen by the flurry of books that inevitably appear following a successful Olympic Games or the aforementioned Leicester City triumph. A third type of book we see is one that has a clear opportunity of this kind – perhaps due to a tournament, an anniversary or a spectacular result. These books are often a gamble – after all, as every football manager knows, the only result that counts is the most recent one – but when they work can be very successful. It is often said that you need to be the best or the first, and with this type of book being *first* is often what really counts, which makes for some hair-raising schedules! A good sports book of this kind has a clear market, an excellent hook for publicity, and timeliness. Last autumn we published a biography of Liverpool manager Jürgen Klopp. We knew that he was popular with fans, who tend to heavily support books about the club and its players and managers. He was doing well, which meant we hoped he'd be a long-term appointment, plus the book would be out in advance of any trophies he won with the club. And we had the perfect author, someone who had excellent access to Klopp's friends, family and colleagues and could deliver the definitive story of his career.

More than anything, finding a new angle or a story that hasn't been told is key. Some people are brilliant at this, with a knack for spotting sides of their sport that haven't been explored. Most great sports books start with a question, such as: 'Will anyone ever run a marathon in under two hours?' [Ed Caesar's *Two Hours* (Viking 2015)]; 'What's it really like to be a professional athlete? Could I do it?' [George Plimpton's *Paper Lion* (Yellow Jersey Press 2016)].

Pitching a sports book: the proposal

Like any other non-fiction, most sports books are sold on proposal. Whether you're submitting directly to a publisher or to an agent, a good proposal contains an introduction to the project, which includes: an overview of the story; why now is the time to tell it; why you are uniquely qualified (this is just as important as your professional experience – I've commissioned new writers who are perfectly placed to write their book just as often as experienced writers); and research to show the book's place in the market. We also need a detailed summary of the chapters, in order to assess the shape of the story, although, as you write it this might change, so don't be concerned about being beholden to a structure that doesn't work. Finally, a sample of your writing is essential – a chapter or two will do, and make sure it's as polished as possible.

You will need to give an idea of when you'll deliver the manuscript. With most sports books there's likely to be an obvious time to publish it – for example, ahead of the Tour de France for cycling books, before a World Cup or the start of the season for football books. Also important are gifting opportunities – many sports books are given as gifts, so Father's Day and Christmas are sales peaks. Ideally, books are delivered a year in advance of publication to allow time for editorial work, for the cover to be designed, the production process (copy-editing, typesetting, proofreading, etc.), and to have the final book in plenty of time for the sales department to sell it in to retailers and for the publicity and marketing team to plan and execute their campaigns. However, in order to make the most of a window of opportunity, this process is often compressed – so being able to work quickly and deliver in a reasonable timeframe is very attractive to a publisher. But do be realistic: late delivery is intensely frustrating for publishers, resulting in either a book being rushed or it having to be moved on, possibly missing the ideal publication date. Both scenarios can severely affect its commercial potential.

Many publishers only accept submissions from agents, but in sports publishing we do see far more direct approaches from authors. In principle, we're happy to see a well-written and comprehensive proposal, no matter how it comes to us, and if time is a factor then it can make sense to come directly to publishers, particularly if there is an obvious home for a book. However, agents can contribute a great deal to the publishing process, not least by taking care of the contract negotiations, so it's often worth taking advantage of that extra step. See section *Literary agents*, page 419.

Most sports books will require interviews, so it's helpful to have an idea of who you intend to interview and to show if you've already got links to them. By all means include a wish list, but where you do have contacts make this clear, and where you don't, outline how you might get to those interviewees.

Some research into the market and competitor titles is useful. We do this research too, but it helps to be given a view on how you see your book positioned and what the market looks like, particularly in less mainstream sports. And just because a sport isn't mainstream it doesn't mean we won't want to publish it. On the contrary, more diversity in sports writing, such as more books on women's sport and sports that are underrepresented on television, would be very much welcomed. It does mean, though, that author and editor will need to work a bit harder to build a case and to prove there's an audience out there waiting for this book. As well as comparison titles, think about providing viewing figures, attendance numbers, the sport's social media reach, and ways in which the athletes reach their fans.

Finally, it's important to understand that not all books get commissioned and the vast majority are turned down by a least one publisher. Please don't get disheartened. Publishing is an extremely subjective industry: as editors, we must fall in love with a book (or spy an unmissable publishing opportunity), enough to make our colleagues fall for it too; those colleagues, in turn, will make retailers and book reviewers desperate to stock or review it, and they will persuade readers to buy it. We all have different tastes; what leaves one person cold will be perfect for another.

There are many things editors consider when evaluating a proposal, other than simply whether it's good enough to be published. I have numerous questions running through my mind as I look at a proposal: Is it well written? Does the story grab me? Do I know there's a market for it? What publicity and marketing opportunities are there? Is my schedule already full (publishing schedules are usually filled at least a year ahead, barring one or two late must-haves)? What's the balance of the list like – do I have space for another football/cycling/tennis book? We've all turned down books we loved but which just weren't right for us at that particular time, for any of the above reasons and more.

What an editor wants you to know

If you've got a commission, congratulations! Your editor will be excited to publish your book and to share it with colleagues. Here are a few things that we tell almost every writer during the writing and editing process.

Firstly, you're doing a great job – writing a book is hard. Most writers have a wobble at some point and your editor is here to be a sounding board and to offer some advice or just moral support. We'd always rather hear from you than for you to suffer in silence.

Don't panic if you don't already have loads of industry contacts. Most people are willing to help you or to point you in the right direction. Be clear about what you want, polite, and willing to travel or be flexible. Often one interviewee will lead you to another and your network will blossom. Be persistent; PR offices are hectic places, so keep trying in a variety of ways and your patience may well be rewarded. Be creative about who you approach – the star names would be ideal, but you might get more insight (and time) from someone recently retired or the next level down.

When writing, keep notes on your sources. Many sports book need a libel read if the subjects are still living and you will save yourself a lot of time (and money – the cost of libel reads are shared between publishers and authors) if you have this information to hand.

Finally, it's surprising how little sport you actually want in a sports book. Endless descriptions of what happened in a football match are superfluous and drain the pace from a narrative. Save the blow-by-blow detail for when it's necessary and when it adds real drama. On a similar note, the usual adage: *show, don't tell*. Don't tell us why something is important, show it; where possible, let us hear directly from interviewees instead of telling us what they said.

In summary: be curious, be creative, think strategically about where opportunities might be found, and read widely for inspiration and instruction. There are some wonderful stories out there waiting to be turned into brilliant sports books – I look forward to reading your take on them.

Frances Jessop is a commissioning editor within Penguin Random House where she looks after literary sports books at Yellow Jersey Press, as well as fiction and non-fiction paperbacks for Vintage. She started her publishing career at Blackwell Publishing in Oxford and then worked in the literary agency at the William Morris Agency, before joining Random House. Follow her on Twitter @francesjessop.

Poetry

Becoming a published poet

Julia Copus shares insights and advice on getting your poetry published and tells her own personal story from first poem in print to published collections and beyond.

Poetic beginnings

Strictly speaking, I had my first poem published when I was seven. I'd sent it to a girls' comic called *Tammy*, and because I'd forgotten to add my name, the acceptance letter was addressed to 'Tammy Reader' and very nearly got thrown away. Luckily, rather than putting the letter straight back in the post unopened and marked 'return to sender', my mother thought to ask me if I knew anyone of that name. With the £2 postal order they'd enclosed by way of payment, I bought a miniature Pippa doll in a sparkling green evening dress. I say it was lucky because I think encouragements of this kind are tremendously important and though I'd have to wait a long time to see my next poem in print, that early success planted in me the notion that such things were possible.

Throughout school, I loved writing, and filled my exercise books with stories of Alice-like adventures where no one was quite as they seemed and holes in tree roots provided portals into other worlds. I continued writing poems too, and reading a few – mainly classics – but it wasn't until after university that poetry really clicked into place, like the bolt of a great door sliding open. My boyfriend had given me a copy of Sylvia Plath's novel *The Bell Jar* (Heinemann 1963) to read. It was one of those books that left me wanting to know more about the author, so I got hold of a biography and read that too. Finally, I came to the poems. Here was much of the same material (*The Bell Jar* is largely autobiographical) but framed in such a way that the words – visceral and supercharged – left me changed; after looking up from Plath's *Collected Poems* (Harper & Row 1981), the world seemed like a very different place. Mixed with inevitable admiration were feelings of envy and, beyond that, excitement. How had the poet pulled off this conjuring act? I wasn't sure, but somewhere inside me I felt it was something I might be able to emulate.

I spent the next few months trying; you might even say I am trying still, though the traces of Plath – very evident in those early poems – are, I hope, no longer visible. Influences are a good thing and poets, like painters, sculptors and musicians, can learn a great deal from copying the old masters but, for readers, the appeal of poems written 'in the style of...' is limited.

Competitions and other submissions

When I had five or six poems to my name, I entered a local poetry competition, judged by the poet Michael Baldwin who had been friends with Ted Hughes, and I won third prize; I entered another and won first. These were small contests but the affirmation they provided for a novice was vital. I sent off to the Poetry Library in London for a list of magazines and started submitting poems to *Envoi* because it said it welcomed new, as well as established, poets. (The Library still publishes the most comprehensive list, now available online at www.poetrylibrary.org.uk/magazines).

I was careful from the start to follow the standard advice: never send more than six poems; always type the poems; include the briefest of covering letters plus return postage. Though my very first submission was rejected, the editor enclosed an enthusiastic note saying which poems he liked best, where he thought they might be improved, and asking me to send again. Soon, he was accepting my poems and I began sending elsewhere too.

Poetry magazines play a crucial role in the life of any poet, and in the early stages they can act as a barometer of our progress in general, and of the success of individual poems. Until we feel secure enough to allow a second reader into our confidence, we must act as our own readers, editors and critics. For the uncertain, fledgling poet, the impersonal process of submitting to magazines is a godsend: sending a poem out to an unknown editor often feels less daunting than sharing it with someone we know. Editors aren't always right, but the chances are that if a poem is repeatedly rejected you need to work on it, or even start again from scratch. And if you can see beyond the disappointment, a rejection slip can be a useful ally, allowing you to gauge what does and does not work. It's also true that not all rejection slips are the same: if yours is accompanied by an encouraging note – still better a request to 'send more poems' – don't dismiss it. The editor in question has to like your poems a lot to make that kind of effort.

A year or so after I started sending work out to magazines, I read about an award exclusively for poets under 30, run by the Society of Authors. This was the Eric Gregory Award, which you can read about elsewhere in this book (see page 593). By now I had amassed 19 poems that I felt could stand on their own feet. I filled in the form and off they went in their manila envelope to London. Winning one of the five Eric Gregory Awards for that year was a real turning point for me, as it has been for so many poets – Seamus Heaney, Andrew Motion and Carol Ann Duffy among them, but many less well-known names too. I'd go as far as to say that some poetry publishers are on the lookout for the latest 'Gregory winners'; there's no question that the prize opens doors.

Do you need an agent?

People sometimes want to know if an agent will help them in their work as a poet. My answer is no – at least not until you are well established. Even then, while some renowned poets have agents, at least as many of them don't. Remember that an agent will take a commission (generally 15% of everything you earn through your writing). I have now secured an agent , but not for my poetry. I was embarking on two new projects – a children's book and a biography. In the case of the children's book, I wanted someone to help me make sense of the contract I'd been offered and to make sure I was getting a fair deal; in the case of the biography – another field that was new to me – I felt an agent would have a better chance of placing the book in the first place, and would probably be able to secure me a better deal than I could get by myself. Though I'm very glad I found the agent I now have, she has little to do with securing me poetry readings and commissions; to be honest, I had managed perfectly well for 15 years as a published poet without any outside help.

One thing is certain: an agent is not needed to help you place a poetry book with a publisher.

Publishing your first book of poetry

So *how* do you go about publishing a book of poetry? When is the right time? And how big a body of work should you present?

It would certainly be unwise to submit a manuscript to a publisher without first having placed at least a handful of poems (and preferably more) in reputable literary magazines. If you're able to tell a busy publisher that you have a good track record of magazine publication behind you, they are far more likely to take your manuscript seriously. Given that the average poetry collection contains around 56 pages of poetry, once you have, say, 40 poems together, *and you are convinced of their quality*, you might consider submitting your manuscript. Many publishers provide submission guidelines on their websites; in the first instance, they usually want to see a maximum of 15 poems (Faber asks for six; Bloodaxe 'up to a dozen'). If they like those, they will soon ask to see more.

My own route to publication

What of my own story? When the time came, I (along with every poet I know of) went not through an agent but direct to a publisher – and in my case I took a less than conventional route. It is not a route I'd advise others to take, incidentally, but here's how it happened…

After my early reading of Plath, I wanted to find out what poets had been up to in more recent years. The first contemporary poetry collection I read was *Electroplating the Baby* by Jo Shapcott (Bloodaxe Books 1988), which I'd found by chance in Maidstone Reference Library. I was very struck by the poems – surreal, engaging and disarmingly direct in tone. I was also quite taken by the eye-catching cover and started to look out for (and, crucially, *read*) other Bloodaxe titles in bookshops and libraries, as well as books by other publishers.

Soon afterwards I saw an advert in one of the poetry magazines for a competition that was being run by the Kitley Trust. I made up my mind to enter it – not for the prize money, which was £10 for each of the ten winning entries, but because it was being judged by Neil Astley, editor of Bloodaxe Books. I was lucky enough to win one of those prizes, and in due course I travelled up to the prize-giving in Sheffield. At the end of the afternoon, I did something I now shudder to remember: I took a sheaf of 15 poems from my bag and asked Neil if he would read them on the train home. In my defence I can say that, as a shy 24-year-old, I was certainly acting more out of naivety than bravado.

Fortunately for me, the gamble paid off. I remember the moment when Neil Astley's response arrived in the post. It came in a fat Jiffy® bag, postmarked 'Hexham'. I knew by the thickness of the envelope that it wasn't a rejection slip, and ripped it open so fast I cut my thumb on one of the staples. I still have the original letter, complete with its smeared insignia of blood. It says, 'Thank you for leaving me with a sample selection. I was very impressed. Can you send more?' The letter goes on to stress that it would be in my best interests not to publish a book prematurely but to wait until I had 'a consistently strong volume of work'. Sound advice – and over the following year or so I continued publishing in magazines and occasionally sending bundles of poems off to the Bloodaxe offices. The book began to take shape and before I knew it I was at the stage of choosing an image for the cover.

What comes next? Opportunities and possibilities

Perhaps it sounds strange but, for me, holding a book with my name on the cover was not the thrill you might expect. I think that is as it should be. If your overriding ambition is 'to be a published poet', it's unlikely you will ever write really good poems. For one thing, having a book published means that you are no longer anonymous, and for a writer there is great power and freedom in anonymity. Still, I am enormously grateful.

Rather like one of those magical portals I wrote about at primary school, my first book opened up for me a world of new experiences and also professional possibilities: residencies, fellowships, commissions, teaching. In addition, it led to my writing in more forms than I might otherwise have tried. I have gone on to write essays, reviews, radio programmes, children's books – even a pocket writing guide. This is not unusual. Once you have a book published, it is far easier to publish another; it is up to you, then, which direction you want to go in. Poets are, I think, at an advantage here. I know of several who have gone on to be first-class prose writers – novelists, short story writers, essayists – and for a few, they find that the new genre suits them better. It is certainly likely to be more lucrative: most poetry books do not sell in vast quantities. Partly for economic reasons, my own writing has followed several tributaries; even so, the source has always been poetry.

Julia Copus is a poet and children's author. She has published three collections of poetry, *The Shuttered Eye* (Bloodaxe 1995), *In Defence of Adultery* (Bloodaxe 2003) and *The World's Two Smallest Humans* (Faber & Faber 2012); all three are Poetry Book Society Recommendations. Her awards include First Prize in the National Poetry Competition and the Forward Prize for Best Single Poem (2010). She has written four picture books for children, including *The Shrew That Flew* (2016) and *My Bed is an Air Balloon* (2018), both published by Faber & Faber.

See also...

- *Getting your poetry out there*, page 362
- *Poetry organisations*, page 368
- *Notes from a passionate poet*, page 360

How to become a poet

Andrew McMillan knows that poetry is a state of mind and being, a full-time commitment, and has practical advice for would-be poets looking to find their own voice and a path to publication.

The most important thing is to choose exactly the right size of beret to accommodate the shape of your head; everything else will hinge on this first decision.

OK, don't worry, this article will contain much more practical help (hopefully) than that first sentence, though it strikes me that, even in the writing of it, I was doing what one of the key processes of being a poet is: paying attention to the rhythm and feel of language as it is spoken out loud. Originally, my jokey opening line read '...exactly the right shape of beret to accommodate the size of your head'. That didn't quite work, for reasons I can't quite put my finger on. There's a nicer echo between 'right' and 'size'; also, 'shape' and 'head' feel more companionable than 'size' and 'head' which – perhaps because of that 'z' sound and the 'd' – just don't sit well together.

Paying attention to language, then, but also to the world – that's really the only trick to master. Poetry is a state of mind rather than a vocation (disclaimer: it's also impossible to write about it without straying into the realms of vaguely pretentious cliché). Being a poet isn't something you can really sit down at the desk and just 'do', in the same way that you might sit down and turn out 500 more words of your novel. It's not about the fancy notebook that cost £15 that's too nice to ever write in; it's not about berets or fashion choices, or the perfect desk space; it's a mode of being in the world.

I've always thought that if a choreographer witnessed a fight in a bar, they'd probably see it as different dance moves; they'd focus on the movements and the arc of a particular uppercut swing. It's the same with poetry – it's a way of inhabiting every moment, looking at things a certain way, seeing how a certain small thing might speak to something wider. If you're a student studying on a course or at a university, you can't just be a poet for the two or three hours you're in class that day; it has to be a full-time commitment.

Perhaps I'm getting ahead of myself though. The first step towards becoming a poet must be to *read poetry*. Read as much of it as you can. It's a cliché by now, but it certainly has some truth to it, that if everyone who was writing poetry was also actively *buying* it, then all poets would be millionaires. We all come to writing because we were readers first, and that's always important to remember. Every so often I encounter someone who repeats the mantra, 'I don't read other people's work because I don't want to be influenced.' That is basically the same thing as saying, 'I want to be a tennis player, but I don't think I should ever watch a tennis match. It would distract me from my own training to become Wimbledon Champion.'

Obviously, we read poetry because we love poetry and it's the thing that sustains us through our lives, but we also read to see what other people are managing to do with the page, with language, with rhythm, with rhyme, with ideas. So, the first step is to read as much as you can get your hands on. Read widely, from the so-called 'mainstream' across to the avant-garde; read things from the past and read a lot of contemporary poetry. That way you'll get a sense of the lie of the land, too; you'll see which publishers publish which type of work, which publishers are the ones who always seem to be publishing the poets you're really drawn to.

Don't be afraid of reading things you *don't* like as well … spend some time with your discomfort and your displeasure. Why is it you don't like this book? What could it have done differently? What does it make you want to do differently in your own practice? Reading in this way is how we come to find our own 'voice' in poetry. At first you'll wear your influences heavily, but then they will start to become simply your own voice, like the finished soup that is boiling in the pot, made up of all the different ingredients that have been flung in.

Getting published

So … you're reading lots, you're beginning to get a handle on what the world of poetry looks like out there, but it probably still feels impossibly far off. You've got your sheaf of poems, sitting on your desk or on the dining table or in your bottom drawer, and you think you're ready to start sending them off. There is no fixed trajectory for a poet in terms of how it's best to do things, but the perceived wisdom would be that a typical path might be:

Single poems in magazines/competitions ⟶ pamphlet ⟶ first full collection.

I've oversimplified that wildly, so I'll spend some time now unpacking each of those.

Poetry **magazines** are really the coalface of poetry; they're where the really new work is published, and a great way for new poets to begin to get their name out there. They might not have vast readerships, but people do read them and if your name starts turning up on the pages of different ones people will begin to recognize you, and that's how you begin to build a reputation.

There's a huge variety of poetry magazines out there, all of which cater to a different sort of work: new modernism, accessible, experimental (see **Poetry magazines** on page 363). Spend some time with the magazines (libraries, particularly dedicated poetry libraries or university campus libraries, will often stock them). Try and compare your work to the work you're seeing published on their pages, not in terms of quality but in terms of style. There's no point in sending your highly experimental language-breaking poetry to the magazine that likes accessible, anecdotal, 20-line poems, but there will be a magazine out there that suits you much more. When you've found one that does, check the submission guidelines, and send off your work. If the work's accepted, there'll be a few months' wait until it appears, but that thrill of your first poem in print is one that never goes away. If you do get published and the magazine offers you the chance to read at a launch event, or simply invites you there, do go if you can find any way of doing so. That experience of meeting the editors, or possibly even reading, is vital.

Once you've done a few years of that kind of thing, you might have a smallish stack of poems that you think is ready for the world;. this is when you'd begin to think about publishing a **pamphlet**, almost like the EP before the full album. Pamphlets are great as a testing ground for your work; they carry much less weight than a full first collection, and I think of them almost like a business card that you can hand out (or hopefully sell) or send on to the people you're hoping to impress.

Then, far off in the distance, is that first **collection**, but we probably don't need to worry about that … yet. Except to say that it can and will happen, and it will be the most thrilling feeling in the world when you first open the box that contains the books.

I'm saying all this because it's the process I went through myself. When I was still an undergraduate I sent off a couple of my poems to a magazine called *The North* and, by some sort of beginner's fluke, they got accepted … and I thought I'd made it! Of course, what followed were loads and loads of rejections, which if compiled would probably make a volume as thick as this yearbook you're holding. But eventually, I did have enough poems for a pamphlet.

A new pamphlet prize called the Michael Marks Award had just started, and so I looked at a list of the pamphlet publishers who had submitted to it. I found one that seemed as though it would like the sort of stuff I was writing, Red Squirrel Press, and sent an email followed by lots of work to them. They accepted a first pamphlet, which came out in 2009, and then published a second in 2011, and then a third in 2013.

Finally, I felt I was ready for a first collection, and I looked around at the books on my shelves and asked myself whose list would I dream of being on. I wanted to try it; if I failed, I'd work my way down my imaginary list. I chose Jonathan Cape, and was lucky enough to get taken on.

It all started with that love of poetry, staying up too late reading poets, and repeating lines or phrases back to myself as I walked around the house. I knew I wanted, in however small a way, to be a part of that conversation, and that's why I wanted to become a poet. Hopefully that's why you do, as well.

Andrew McMillan's debut collection, *physical* (Jonathan Cape 2015), was the first ever poetry collection to win the *Guardian* First Book Award. It also won the Fenton Aldeburgh First Collection Prize, a Somerset Maugham Award (2016), an Eric Gregory Award (2016) and was shortlisted for the 2015 Costa Poetry Prize and the 2015 Forward Prize for Best First Collection. His second collection, *playtime*, will be published by Jonathan Cape in August 2018. Andrew is senior lecturer at the Manchester Writing School at MMU and lives in Manchester. For more information see www.andrewmcmillanpoet.co.uk.

See also...

- *Becoming a published poet*, page 353
- *Notes from a passionate poet*, page 360
- *Getting your poetry out there*, page 362

Notes from a passionate poet

Benjamin Zephaniah describes his route to being published.

'How did you first get published?' and 'Can you give me any advice on getting published?' must be the two questions I am most regularly asked as I go poeting around this planet. And what really gets me is that for most of my poetic life I have found them so hard to answer without doing a long talk on race and culture, and giving a lesson on the oral traditions of the Caribbean and Africa. I'm trying hard not to do that now but I have to acknowledge that I do come out of the oral tradition and to some extent I am still very much part of the Jamaican branch of that tradition, which has now established itself in Britain. In reality, getting published wasn't that hard for me: I came to the page from the stage. I didn't wake up one day and decide to join the oral tradition, I simply started performing in churches and community centres, on street corners and at political rallies, and I really didn't care about being published in books – I used to say I just want to be published in people's hearts. Now I don't want to sound like a royal seeking sympathy or a surgeon evaluating her or his work, I just feel there's something very special about hearing people recite a poem of yours back to you when you know that it has never been written down: it means that they must have heard me recite the poem and it had such an impact on them that it left an impression on their minds – but I say hearts because it sounds more sensitive.

Someone with a PhD once told me that the most important thing I could do was to get published, so for what seemed like an eternity (in fact it was just a couple of months) I became the most depressed kid on the block as the rejections flooded in, and I took each rejection very personally. I soon stopped punishing myself and went back to performing. Within the black and Asian communities there was a large network of venues to perform in and I was happy there, performing for 'my people'. But it wasn't long before I started to make a bit of a name for myself in what we now call the mainstream, and then the publishers came running back to me, many of them apologising and saying that the person who sent the rejection letter to me had now moved on and they weren't very good anyway. I didn't blame the publishers; I wasn't angry with them. It was a time when the British publishing industry simply didn't understand Reggae and Dub poetry, and the performance scene as we know it today had hardly taken root. It's not practical to advise all budding poets to go down the route that I chose. Some poets simply don't want to perform whilst others want something published before they take to the stage – they literally want something to cling to as they recite – but I have to say there is nothing like looking your audience in the face and delivering your work to them in person.

I used to be able to give a run-down of the poetry publishing and performance scene in Britain in about 30 minutes, but not any longer, with the internet and all that, the universe has changed. Not only are there hundreds of ways to get your poetry published, you can now publish your performance and have a worldwide hit without ever actually having a book or leaving your bedroom. You don't even have to tread the boards to become a performance poet. The choice is now yours: you can be a Dub poet, a pub poet, a cyber poet, a graffiti poet, a rap poet, a naked poet, a space poet, a Myspace poet, or a street poet. You can be a geek poet, a YouTube poet, an underground poet, a Facebook poet, a sound poet, and if you like to keep it short you can be a Twitter poet. You can go any way you want, but you must never forget to be a poet. You must never forget why you started writing (or performing) and you must love your art. The love I had for words as a baby has never left me, and when I was getting all those rejection letters and feeling so unwanted, my love for poetry never waned.

And another thing: read poetry. Many people tell me that they love poetry but after a minute or so of investigation I find that they only love their own poetry, and in many cases they only understand their own poetry. You can get a lot of help from teachers or in workshops, but reading other people's poetry is the best way of understanding poetry, it is the best way of getting into the minds of other poets. This great book that you now have in your hands and learned people who understand the industry are able to give you much better advice on getting published than I can, and if you do get published your publisher or agent should be offering you all the practical help you need. But you have to have the passion, you have to have the inspiration, you have to be a poet. Stay true.

Benjamin Zephaniah has been performing poetry since he was 11 years old. He has also written 13 books of poetry, four novels, and recorded six music CD albums. He spends much of his time encouraging young people to write and perform poetry and has received 16 honorary doctorates in recognition of his work. His latest releases are a martial arts travelogue called *Kung Fu Trip* (Bloomsbury 2011), *To Do Wid Me*, a book and DVD of live performances (Bloodaxe Books 2013) and *Terror Kid* (Hot Key Books 2014). *The Life and Rhymes of Benjamin Zephaniah: The Autobiography* was published in May 2018 by Simon & Schuster UK. He is currently Professor of Poetry and Creative Writing at Brunel University. His website is www.benjaminzephaniah.com.

Getting your poetry out there

Neil Astley knows that you need talent, passion, patience and dedication to become a published poet. He gives valuable advice on the possibilities, pitfalls and rewards that any budding poet might encounter.

Are you a poet – yet?

This article assumes that you have a potential readership or audience for your poetry, and that where you need guidance is in how to reach all those readers. But most poets just starting out believe that. There is, however, *no* readership for poets who *think* they are ready to publish but whose work isn't really *there* yet. If you've *not* immersed yourself in poetry for years – which involves intensive reading and absorbing poetry from all periods – to think of yourself as a poet is self-delusion. No one will want to read you, and your attempts to get your work out there will be met with rejection, frustration and disappointment – and self-righteous indignation if you're one of those would-be writers who think they're geniuses waiting to be discovered. People either have talent or they don't, and no amount of self-promotion and or even education in the way of poetry workshops or MA courses will make you a poet if you don't have an insatiable passion for *reading* poetry (not just your own) and an original way of writing it. But if you've been drawn to poetry, and have *read* as much poetry as you can get hold of, I'd say you're halfway there.

A poet's reading list

One of the poets I publish, Hannah Lowe, was an English teacher who'd always loved poetry but wasn't familiar with the full range of contemporary poetry until her mother gave her a copy of the Bloodaxe anthology *Staying Alive* as a birthday present. That book made her think that *she* could write poetry. With other younger poets writing now, the process has often been the other way round; maybe they've read Simon Armitage, Carol Ann Duffy, Seamus Heaney and Philip Larkin, but they haven't read their Shakespeare, Donne, Keats, Wordsworth, Coleridge, Browning, Dickinson, Frost, Yeats, Auden and Eliot, all essential reading for anyone who wants to write poetry.

Without that groundwork reading, your own work will go nowhere. But all is not lost. If you really do have a gift for poetry, but life circumstances have been such as to make your reading patchy, stop thinking of getting your work out there now, and for the next year, just read and reread judiciously without thinking of writing. Start with the *Norton Anthology of Poetry* (W.W. Norton 1970, 5th edn 2005) and the *Penguin Book of English Verse* (Penguin 1956, new edn 2004), and get hold of books by the major figures they include; then *The Rattle Bag* (Faber & Faber 1982, 2005), *Emergency Kit* (Faber & Faber 2004) and the *Staying Alive* trilogy (Bloodaxe Books 2002, 2004, 2011) and read more by the poets who most appeal to you. When you come back to writing, a year or more later, both you and your poetry will have changed. The poems you had wanted to get out there earlier will go in the bin, and you'll be writing poetry that should interest other readers.

Getting critical feedback

Next you need feedback. If you can find a good writing group or workshop in your area, that can be helpful. Even if you disagree with other people's comments on your work, their feedback should still show what aspects of your poems don't work for other readers. Later, once you've been working on your poetry for at least a year or two, it would be helpful to go on one of the writing courses (which are more week-long workshops than taught courses as such) run by the Arvon Foundation at three centres in England, or by Tŷ Newydd in Wales or Moniack Mhor in Scotland. Or contact the Poetry School in London (www.poetryschool.com) which offers online tuition, downloads, workshops and summer schools. There are also part-time MA courses run by numerous universities and colleges throughout Britain, but I don't think those are right for relative beginners; to gain full benefit from such courses (which cost thousands of pounds in fees) I think you need to have been writing seriously for at least five years. (See page 678 for a list.)

You can also start sending out poems to magazines; their websites will say whether you should submit online or if you need to send half a dozen poems with a stamped addressed envelope for their possible return. It won't be hard to get poems taken by the smallest of the magazines. The real challenge will be in sending work to the long-standing, leading poetry or literary magazines edited by significant poets or critics. These might include *Acumen, Agenda, Ambit, The Dark Horse, Envoi, Iota, The London Magazine, Magma, The North, Orbis, PN Review, Poetry London, The Poetry Review, Poetry Wales* or *The Rialto.* There are also literary and cultural journals that publish poems, but these are much harder for new writers to break into, such as the *London Review of Books* and the *Times Literary Supplement*; somewhat perversely, you may find you have more luck with the political press: the *Morning Star*, *New Statesman* and the *Spectator* all publish newcomers as well as established poets. The fiction quarterly *Granta* was starting to publish poems but had to block further submissions for a year 'due to the unprecedented volume of poetry submissions received' (a salutary lesson there: there are *thousands* of poets trying to get their work out there).

Poetry magazines

Acumen
See page 35

Agenda
See page 36

Ambit
See page 36

The Dark Horse
www.thedarkhorsemagazine.com

Envoi
See page 54

Iota
www.iotamagazine.co.uk

The London Magazine
See page 67

Magma
See page 68

The North
www.poetrybusiness.co.uk/north-menu

PN Review
See page 76

Poetry London
See page 76

The Poetry Review
See page 76

Poetry Wales
See page 76

The Rialto
See page 81

For a fuller list see http://www.bloodaxebooks.com/links

See also *Magazines UK and Ireland* starting on page 35 and *Poetry organisations* on page 368.

Just as important as getting poems accepted is getting them rejected, especially if that includes getting a note back from an editor with a comment on your submission that makes something click. You may think that what you're writing now is great, but there will be flaws. There are always improvements that can be made that make all the difference between a half good poem and a really good one. Poets judging poetry competitions talk about 'the wrong note', a line or phrase in a poem that sticks out as not belonging there or needing to be changed even with just one word added or a phrase taken out, and they can't give the prize to that poem because readers will see it too, but the poet is too close to the work and isn't aware of it.

To submit or not to submit?

So the first lesson in how to get your poetry out there is *not* to send it out, or not yet. Put it in a drawer for six months and come back to it; with that amount of distance from the work, you should be able to fix that 'wrong note' and also make the whole poem read more smoothly. Also – and this is absolutely essential – read the poem aloud. As you're writing it, and when you think you've finished it, and when you come back to it months later. Again, poets who haven't done this all talk about only realising what doesn't work in a poem when they were reading it aloud to an audience; trying not to let their expression show that they've just read a bum line at the live event, but rushing home afterwards to correct it. And if you do all your writing on a computer, print out your poems, and read through and edit them on paper. What may look right on a computer screen will often not *feel* right on paper, and then you'll see what needs to be edited. This is also where magazine rejections are helpful: six months later, going back to the poem you thought was your best but which kept being returned, you see the 'wrong note', fix the problem, send it out, and the poem is taken right away.

Don't submit to magazines unless you're familiar with the kind of work each one publishes. They are all different, and you will not be able to publish much unless you research the field and send to those whose output you like and respect. If you live in or can get to London or Edinburgh, spend a day in the Saison Poetry Library at the Southbank Centre or the Scottish Poetry Library (there's also the Northern Poetry Library in Morpeth, Northumberland) and read the latest issues of the current magazines, and afterwards take out subscriptions to those you like most. Familiarity with the work of other poets is an important part of that process: if you're expecting others to read your work, you should read theirs too and learn from it; and support the magazines which support you. Join the Poetry Society and you'll receive *The Poetry Review* and *Poetry News* every quarter; join the Poetry Book Society and you'll receive their four Choices over the course of the year with the PBS Bulletin (including highly illuminating pieces by the poets about their books). The Saison Poetry Library also has two websites, www.poetrylibrary.org.uk, which includes listings of all the current print and online magazines, and http://poetrymagazines.org.uk, which has an archive covering many of the leading journals where you can read their back issues.

You can familiarise yourself with the editorial taste of online magazines much more easily. Some magazines publish both print and online editions, while others that started out as print have gone over completely to online publication. But so much poetry is published online now – and online imprints come and go – that readers and writers alike find it hard to see the wood for the trees, an appropriate metaphor to use here given that the cost and labour involved in printing and distributing magazines used to discourage poorly edited publications from flourishing. For a list of significant webzines which currently publish poetry (see box). These are the webzines (some quite new, not all exclusively poetry) picked out by poets I've consulted as the places where they'd most like to see their work, and where the younger poets in particular go to read their peers. It's worth adding that they also want their work to be featured or discussed in several webzines which don't take submissions, notably *Prac Crit* (www.praccrit.com), *The Quietus* (http://thequietus.com), *Sabotage Reviews* (http://sabotagereviews.com) and *Wild Court* (http://wildcourt.co.uk). And the ultimate accolade is getting your poems into America's *Poetry* magazine, with all the work it publishes being added to an historic online archive that goes back to 1912. The recently established reciprocal publication by *Poetry* and *The Poetry Review* of selections by US and UK poets has helped make this less of a pipe dream for British poets.

Get noticed through competitions and performance

Building up a coherent body of work can take years. As your work matures, so your confidence grows, and you start getting more and more poems taken by magazines and perhaps win prizes in poetry competitions. And some of the poetry competitions are worth trying, but as with the magazines, don't submit blindly, do your research. Just as you can almost predict which poets will win each year's poetry prizes from who the judges are, or what kind of work the combination of judges on each prize's judging panel is likely to favour, so it is with the poetry competitions. And the timing of their deadlines is such that you can't usually submit the same poems to more than one of the main poetry competitions in any one year. So check out the main competitions and submit to those judged by the poets you admire. As well as the Poetry Society's National Poetry Competition, these might include the Basil Bunting, Bridport, Bristol, Cardiff, Cheltenham, Ledbury, Manchester, Mslexia (women only) and Poetry London competitions. (See *Competitions* on page 374 under *Poetry organisations*.)

Popular webzines

And Other Poems
http://andotherpoems.com

Clinic
http://clinicpresents.com

The Compass
www.thecompassmagazine.co.uk

Ink Sweat and Tears
www.inksweatandtears.co.uk

Likestarlings
www.likestarlings.com

The London Grip
http://londongrip.co.uk

The Manchester Review
www.themanchesterreview.co.uk

Molly Bloom
https://mollybloompoetry.weebly.com

The Open Mouse
https://theopenmouse.wordpress.com

The Poetry Shed
https://abegailmorley.wordpress.com

Stride
http://stridemagazine.blogspot.co.uk

Three Drops from a Cauldron
https://threedropspoetry.co.uk

The White Review
www.thewhitereview.org

The recent growth of festivals and venues with open mic slots has given new writers opportunities to read their work in public; and you don't have to be a performance poet for your work to go down well with audiences, you just have to read strong work and read it well. Don't overrun your time slot and give a straightforward presentation of your work, which means a short introduction only, use your 'natural' voice and don't adopt the highly mannered whining delivery style favoured by poets who should know better.

Once you've published widely in magazines and are starting to do readings, you'll be at the stage of seeking out a small press willing to publish a pamphlet or chapbook (15 to 20 poems). Most pamphlets are sold at readings, and having a pamphlet to give to organisers and to sell at events can lead to more opportunities to read your work. And finally – we're talking about years now – you might have a book-length manuscript (= typescript)

Poetry publishers

THE BIG SIX

Bloodaxe Books
See page 157

Jonathan Cape
See page 213

Carcanet
See page 161

Chatto & Windus
See page 213

Faber and Faber
See page 171

Picador
See page 196

SMALLER PRESSES

Arc Publications
See page 154

Cinnamon Press
www.cinnamonpress.com

Dedalus Press
(Ireland)
www.dedaluspress.com

The Emma Press
https://theemmapress.com

Eyewear Publishing
https://store.eyewearpublishing.com

The Gallery Press
(Ireland) See page 173

Happenstance
www.happenstancepress.com

Knives Forks and Spoons Press
www.knivesforksandspoonspress.co.uk

Nine Arches Press
www.ninearchespress.com

Peepal Tree Press
(Black British & Caribbean)
www.peepaltreepress.com

Penned in the Margins
www.pennedinthemargins.co.uk

Salmon Poetry
(Ireland)
www.salmonpoetry.com

Seren
See page 205

Shearsman Books
See page 206

Shoestring Press
www.shoestringpress.co.uk

Smith/Doorstop Books
www.poetrybusiness.co.uk/smith-doorstop

Smokestack Books
http://smokestack-books.co.uk

Templar Poetry
http://templarpoetry.com

Valley Press
www.valleypressuk.com

The Waywiser Press
https://waywiser-press.com

For a fuller list of poetry publishers visit www.bloodaxebooks.com/links.

of around 50 poems which you think worthy of publication. But the chances of having this taken up by one of the 'big six' leading poetry imprints (Bloodaxe, Cape, Carcanet, Chatto, Faber, Picador) are exceedingly slim. Apart from Picador, which doesn't consider unsolicited submissions, we all receive *thousands* of submissions every year, but the annual output of first collections from *all* six imprints is rarely more than a dozen books *in total*. Much wiser to try the smaller poetry presses you'll find listed in this *Yearbook*, and you won't need an agent to do this. The only poets with agents are writers who are also novelists, journalists or playwrights. Don't think of ebooks as any kind of solution. Ebooks don't give poets the massive readership reached by writers of thrillers or romance, amounting to just 4% of total poetry sales.

Poets, beware!

Finally, a word of warning. There are certain firms which charge poets to publish their work or which require payment for copies of anthologies in which your work appears as a condition of publication. Poets starting out are particularly susceptible to what is known as vanity publishing. Reputable publishers or magazines of any size will pay authors for their work, usually with royalties in the case of books. If you are asked to pay for the production of your book by a publisher who sends you a flattering 'reader's report' on your work, try asking a local printer to give you an estimate for printing a few hundred copies of your book. The likelihood is that the cost will be considerably lower, and if you want your work to be read by friends, colleagues and people in your local community, the circulation you can achieve by this DIY method will be more effective. The normal arrangements for publishing also involve the author receiving complimentary copies of a book or a free contributor's copy of a magazine or anthology. If you're asked to pay to see your own work in print, you are paying to have it published. For more information see the website Vanity Publishing (www.vanitypublishing.info) and also the advice offered by the Society of Authors (www.societyofauthors.org/SOA/MediaLibrary/SOAWebsite/Guides/Vanity-Publishing.pdf).

If you're unable to get your book published but are confident of selling enough copies at readings, there are effective ways of self-publication covered by other articles in the *Writers' & Artists' Yearbook*. As an alternative to local printers, a number of poets use the self-publishing website www.lulu.com which offers a distribution channel as well as well-produced books and ebooks.

Neil Astley is the editor of Bloodaxe Books, which he founded in 1978. His books include novels, poetry collections and anthologies, most notably the Bloodaxe *Staying Alive* trilogy: *Staying Alive* (2002), *Being Alive* (2004) and *Being Human* (2011); and three collaborations with Pamela Robertson-Pearce, *Soul Food: nourishing poems for starved minds* (2008), and the DVD-books *In Person: 30 Poets* (2008) and *In Person: World Poets* (2017). He has published two novels, *The End of My Tether* (Scribner 2002), which was shortlisted for the Whitbread First Novel Award, and *The Sheep Who Changed the World* (Flambard Press 2005).

See also...

- *Becoming a published poet*, page 353
- *Notes from a passionate poet*, page 360
- *What do self-publishing providers offer?*, page 619

Poetry organisations

Below are some organisations which provide budding poets with opportunities to explore, extend and share their work.

WHERE TO GET INVOLVED

A range of organisations – from local groups to larger professional bodies – exists at which emerging and established poets can access support or learn more about others' work. A concise selection appears below.

The British Haiku Society

79 Westbury Road, Barking, Essex IG11 7PL
email membership@britishhaikusociety.org.uk
website www.britishhaikusociety.org.uk

Pioneers the appreciation and writing of haiku in the UK, publishes books concerning haiku and related matters, and is active in promoting the teaching of haiku in schools and colleges. Publishes a quarterly journal, *Blithe Spirit*, an annual members' anthology, and a newsletter. Also runs the prestigious annual British Haiku Society Awards in three categories: haiku, tanka, and haibun. Registered charity. Founded 1990.

Literature Wales

(formerly Academi)
Glyn Jones Centre, Wales Millennium Centre, Bute Place, Cardiff CF10 5AL
tel 029-2047 2266
email post@literaturewales.org
website www.literaturewales.org

Company for the development of literature in Wales. Working collaboratively, bilingually, and in a wide range of communities, Literature Wales ensures that literature is a voice for all. The organisation's many projects and activities include Wales Book of the Year, the National Poet of Wales, Bardd Plant Cymru and Young People's Laureate Wales, Literary Tourism initiatives, Writers on Tour funding scheme, creative writing courses at Tŷ Newydd Writing Centre, Services for Writers (including bursaries and mentoring) and Young People's Writing Squads. Literature Wales is a registered charity (no. 1146560) and works with the support of the Arts Council of Wales and the Welsh Government.

The Poetry Book Society

c/o Inpress Ltd, Churchill House, 12 Mosley Street, Newcastle upon Tyne, NE1 1DE
tel 0191 230 8100
email pbs@inpressbooks.co.uk
website www.poetrybooks.co.uk
Facebook www.facebook.com/poetrybooksoc
Twitter @poetrybooksoc

Book club for readers of poetry founded in 1953 by T.S. Eliot. Every quarter, selectors choose one outstanding publication (the PBS Choice), and recommend four other titles; these are sent to members, who are also offered substantial discounts on other poetry books. The PBS also produces the recently redesigned quarterly membership magazine, the *Bulletin* (available to full members), which contains the Poet Selectors' reviews of the Choice and Recommendations and the selected poets' comments on their own work.

The Poetry Business

Campo House, 54 Campo Lane, Sheffield S1 2EG
tel 0114 438 4074
email office@poetrybusiness.co.uk
website www.poetrybusiness.co.uk

Publishes books, pamphlets and audio under its Smith/Doorstop imprint; runs the literary magazine, *The North*. Also organises a national competition, Writing Days, the Writing School and residential courses.

Poetry Ireland

11 Parnell Square East, Dublin D01 ND60, Republic of Ireland
tel +353 (0)1 6789815
email info@poetryireland.ie
website www.poetryireland.ie

Organisation committed to achieving excellence in the reading, writing and performance of poetry throughout the island of Ireland. Poetry Ireland receives support from The Arts Council / An Chomhairle Ealaíon and The Arts Council of Northern Ireland and enjoys partnerships with arts centres, festivals, schools, colleges and bookshops at home and abroad. Its commitment to creating performance and publication opportunities for poets at all stages of their careers helps ensure that the best work is made available to the widest possible audience. Poetry Ireland publishes the well-regarded poetry journal, *Poetry Ireland Review*.

The Poetry Society

22 Betterton Street, London WC2H 9BX
tel 020-7420 9880
email info@poetrysociety.org.uk
website www.poetrysociety.org.uk

A leading voice for poets and poetry in Britain. Founded in 1909 to promote a more general recognition and appreciation of poetry, the Society has more than 3,000 members. With education initiatives, commissioning and publishing programmes, and a calendar of performances, readings and competitions, the Society champions poetry in its many forms.

The Society offers advice and information to all, with exclusive offers and discounts available to members. Every quarter, members receive copies of *The Poetry Review* and the Society's newsletter, *Poetry News*. The Society also publishes education resources; organises events including an Annual Lecture and National Poetry Day celebrations; runs Poetry Prescription, a critical appraisal service available to members for £40 and non-members for £50; and provides an education advisory and training service, as well as school and youth memberships.

A diverse range of events and readings takes place at the Poetry Café beneath the Society's headquarters in London's Covent Garden. The Society also programmes events and readings throughout the UK.

Competitions run by the Society include the annual National Poetry Competition, with a first prize of £5,000; the biennial Popescu European Poetry Translation Prize; the Ted Hughes Award for New Work in Poetry; SLAMbassadors UK; and the Foyle Young Poets of the Year Award.

The Seamus Heaney Centre for Poetry

c/o School of Arts, English and Languages, Queen's University Belfast, Belfast BT7 1NN
tel 028-9024 5133
email shc@qub.ac.uk
website www.qub.ac.uk/schools/SeamusHeaneyCentreforPoetry
Director Professor Fran Brearton

Designed to promote both the writing and criticism of poetry, fiction and scriptwriting, the Centre houses an extensive library of contemporary poetry volumes. It also hosts regular creative writing workshops, a poetry reading group, and an ongoing series of readings and lectures by visiting poets and critics from all over the world. Its journal, *The Yellow Nib*, is edited by Leontia Flynn and Frank Ormsby. The eminent poet Ciaran Carson, holder of the Seamus Heaney Chair in Poetry, runs its writing group. Other staff include award-winning poet Leontia Flynn, novelists Glenn Patterson, Garrett Carr and Darran McCann and scriptwriters Tim Loane and Jimmy McAleavey, all of whom teach on undergraduate and postgraduate courses in poetry and creative writing. Founded 2003.

Shortlands Poetry Circle

Ripley Arts Centre, 24 Sundridge Avenue, Bromley BR1 2PX
tel 020-8464 9810
email shortlands@poetrypf.co.uk
website www.poetrypf.co.uk/shortlands.html
President Ruth Smith

Founded in 1911, the Circle continues to meet twice a month during term time. Visitors welcome.

Survivors' Poetry

95 Wick Hall, Furze Hill, Hove BN3 1NG
tel (01273) 202876
email info@survivorspoetry.org.uk
email drsimonjenner@gmail.com
website www.survivorspoetry.org
Director Simon Jenner

National charity and survivor-led arts group which coordinates artistic activities using poetry to make connections between creativity and mental health. The quarterly newsletter, *Poetry Express*, is free to download from the website.

Tower Poetry

Christ Church, Oxford OX1 1DP
tel (01865) 276156
email info@towerpoetry.org.uk
website www.towerpoetry.org.uk

Exists to encourage and challenge everyone who reads or writes poetry. Funded by a generous bequest to Christ Church, Oxford, by the late Christopher Tower, the aims of Tower Poetry are to stimulate an enjoyment and critical appreciation of poetry, particularly among young people in education, and to challenge people to write their own poetry.

Ver Poets

tel (01582) 715817
email gregsmith480@gmail.com
website www.verpoets.co.uk
Secretary Gregory Smith
Membership £18 p.a. UK; £24 overseas; £12 students

Encourages the writing and study of poetry. Holds evening meetings and daytime workshops in the St Albans area. Holds members' competitions and the annual Open Competition. Founded 1966.

WHERE TO GET INFORMATION

Your local library is a good first port of call, and should have information about the poetry scene in the area. Many libraries are actively involved in speading the word about poetry as well as having modern poetry available for loan.

Alliance of Literary Societies (ALS)

email ljc1049@gmail.com
website www.allianceofliterarysocieties.org.uk
President Claire Harman

Umbrella organisation for literary societies and groups in the UK. It provides support and advice on a variety of literary subjects, as well as promoting cooperation between member societies. Its publications include a twice-yearly members' newsletter, *Not Only But...*, and an annual journal, *ALSo*. ALS holds an AGM weekend which is hosted by a different member society each year, moving around the UK. Founded 1973.

Arts Council England

Arts Council England, 21 Bloomsbury Street, London WC1B 3HF
tel 0845 300 6200
email enquiries@artscouncil.org.uk
website www.artscouncil.org.uk

Arts Council England is the national development agency for the arts in England, providing funding for a range of arts and cultural activities. It supports creative writing including poetry, fiction, storytelling, spoken word, digital work, writing for children and literary translation. It funds a range of publishers and magazines as well as providing grants to individual writers. Contact the enquiries team for more information on funding support and advice.

Arts Council of Wales

Bute Place, Cardiff CF10 5AL
tel 0845 8734 900
email information@arts.wales
website http://www.arts.wales

Independent charity, established by Royal Charter in 1994. It has three regional offices and its principal sponsor is the Welsh Government. It is the country's funding and development agency for the arts, supporting and developing high-quality arts activities. Its funding schemes offer opportunities for arts organisations and individuals in Wales to apply, through a competitive process, for funding towards a clearly defined arts-related project.

National Association of Writers' Groups (NAWG)

65 Riverside Mead, Peterborough PE2 8JN
email info@nawg.co.uk
website www.nawg.co.uk

Aims to bring cohesion and fellowship to isolated writers' groups and individuals, promoting the study and art of writing in all its aspects. There are many affiliated groups and associate (individual) members across the UK.

The National Poetry Library

Level 5, Royal Festival Hall, Southbank Centre, London SE1 8XX
tel 020-7921 0943
email info@poetrylibrary.org.uk
website www.nationalpoetrylibrary.org.uk
Facebook www.facebook.com/NationalPoetryLibrary
Twitter @WetBlackBough
Membership Free with two forms of ID, one photographic and the other showing a UK address

The largest public collection of modern poetry in the world. It is open to everyone (Tuesday to Sunday, 11 am to 8pm) and free to join (see above stipulations). Members can borrow from the extensive loan collections, including audio items and take advantage of the library's e-loan service through which ebooks can be loaned at distance. The extensive collection of current poetry magazines gives a window into the breadth of poetry in the UK and beyond. The library runs a monthly event series, a programme of exhibitions which run throughout the year, a book club, shared readings and an occasional tutored workshop for budding poets. The library's website features publishers' information, poetry news and a list of UK-wide events.

The National Poetry Library (Children's Collection)

Level 5, Royal Festival Hall, Southbank Centre, London SE1 8XX
tel 020-7921 0943
email info@poetrylibrary.org.uk
website www.nationalpoetrylibrary.org.uk
Facebook www.facebook.com/NationalPoetryLibrary
Twitter @WetBlackBough

Comprises thousands of items for young poets of all ages, including poetry on CD and DVD. The library has an education service for teachers and writing groups, with a separate collection of books and materials for teachers and poets who work with children in schools. Group visits can be organised inviting children to interact with the collection in various ways, from taking a Poetry Word Trail across Southbank Centre, to exploring how the worlds of science and poetry interact, and to engaging with war poetry via the Letters Home booklet to becoming a Poetry Library Poetry Explorer (available to local schools). Nursery schools can also book a Rug Rhymes session for under-5s. Children of all ages can join for free and borrow books and other materials. A special membership scheme is available for teachers to borrow books for the classroom. Contact the library for membership details and opening hours.

The Northern Poetry Library

The Chantry, Bridge Street, Morpeth, Northumberland, NE61 1PD
tel (01670) 620391
email mylibrary@activenorthumberland.org.uk
website www.northernpoetrylibrary.org.uk
Twitter @nplpoetry

Largest collection of contemporary poetry outside London, housing over 15,000 titles and magazines covering poetry published since 1945. Founded 1968.

The Scottish Poetry Library

5 Crichton's Close, Canongate, Edinburgh EH8 8DT
tel 0131 557 2876
email reception@spl.org.uk
website www.scottishpoetrylibrary.org.uk

Houses over 45,000 items: books, magazines, pamphlets, recordings and the Edwin Morgan Archive of his published works. The core of the collection is contemporary poetry written in Scotland, in Scots, Gaelic and English, but historic Scottish poetry as well as contemporary works from almost every part of the world are also available. All resources, advice and information are readily accessible, free of charge. The SPL holds regular poetry events, including reading and writing groups, details of which are available on the library website. Closed Sunday and Monday. Founded 1984.

ONLINE RESOURCES

There is a wealth of information available for poets at the click of a mouse: the suggestions below are a good starting point.

The Poetry Archive

website www.poetryarchive.org

World's premier online collection of recordings of poets reading their work. Free of charge. Features the

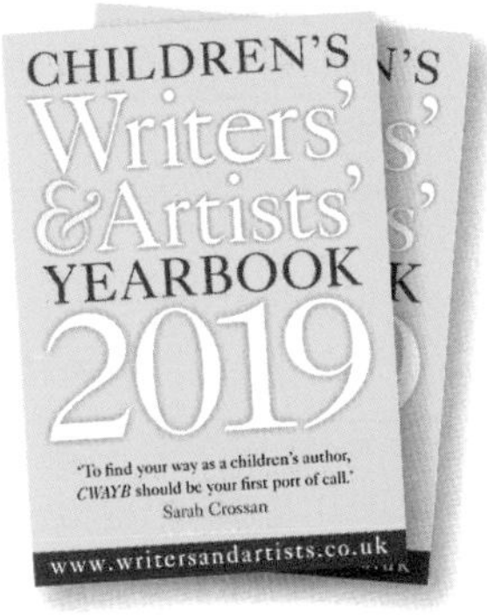

voices of contemporary English-language poets as well as those from the past, including C. Day Lewis, Paul Farley and Dorothea Smartt. The Archive is added to regularly.

The Poetry Kit

email info@poetrykit.org
website www.poetrykit.org

Collates a wide variety of poetry-related information, including events, competitions, courses and more for an international readership.

Poetry Space

website www.poetryspace.co.uk

Specialist publisher of poetry and short stories, as well as news and features, edited by Susan Jane Sims. Operates as a social enterprise with all profits being used to publish online and in print, and to hold events to widen participation in poetry. Poetry submissions accepted all year round for *Poetry Space Showcase Quarterly*, an online and print publication aimed at over-16s. Poems are selected each quarter by a guest editor and if not chosen in that window have another chance with the next guest editor. Poetry submissions also accepted for consideration for pamphlet and full collection publication. Poets are requested to send in a sample of six poems before a full manuscript will be considered; unsolicited manuscripts will not be read. Occasional submission calls for themed anthologies. Subscribers to the Friends of Poetry Space membership scheme receive *Showcase Quarterly* and a surprise pamphlet from the catalogue. Submissions for all of the above should be sent to susan@poetryspace.co.uk. Founded 2010.

Poets and Writers

website www.pw.org
Twitter @poetswritersinc

US-based online magazine and e-newsletter on the craft and business of writing.

Prac Crit

email editors@praccrit.com
website www.praccrit.com
Twitter @praccrit
Editors Sarah Howe, Dai George, Vidyan Ravinthiran

Online journal of poetry and criticism, published three times a year. Features interviews, essays and the reflections of poets themselves; close analysis of poems a hallmark.

Sabotage Reviews

website www.sabotagereviews.com

Small press review site. Welcomes articles and reviews of 500–1000 words on poetry, fiction and the spoken word but check website guidelines carefully prior to submitting any work (http://sabotagereviews.com/about/guidelines) – full poetry collections or novels are rarely covered on the site.

The Wolf

website www.wolfmagazine.co.uk

Archive of original material from the publishers of *The Wolf* magazine, which was active between 2002 and 2017.

Write Out Loud

email info@writeoutloud.net
website www.writeoutloud.net

Poetry news, features and reviews, with comprehensive listings of poetry events, publications, festivals, and competitions. Members may post poems, join discussions, add their profile etc. 50,000+ monthly users.

WHERE TO CELEBRATE POETRY

Festival information should be available from Arts Council England offices (see page 530). See also *Festivals and conferences for writers, artists and readers* on page 597. As well as the list below, major poetry festivals each year include Ledbury, Bridlington, Aldeburgh and Cheltenham. Poetry also features prominently at the Glastonbury and Latitude Festivals.

The British Council

10 Spring Gardens, London SW1A 2BN
tel 020-7389 4385
email general.enquiries@britishcouncil.org
website https://literature.britishcouncil.org/

Visit the website for a list of forthcoming festivals.

Canterbury Festival

Festival House, 8 Orange Street, Canterbury, Kent CT1 2JA
tel (01227) 452853
email info@canterburyfestival.co.uk
website www.canterburyfestival.co.uk
Takes place 20 October–3 November 2018

Kent's international arts festival, one of the most important cultural events in the South East. As an independent charity, the Festival brings a rich mixture of performing arts from around the world to surprise and delight audiences. The Festival inspires artists to create and perform. It commissions new work, champions emerging talent and supports those seeking careers in the cultural industries.

Poems in the Waiting Room (PitWR)

12 Abingdon Court Lane, Cricklade, Wilts. SN6 6BL
email helenium@care4free.net
website www.poemsinthewaitingroom.org
Twitter @poemsintheWR

PitWR is a registered arts in health charity which supplies short collections of poems for patients to read while waiting to see their doctor. First established in 1995, the poems cover both the canon of English verse and contemporary works – poetry from Quill to Qwerty.

StAnza: Scotland's International Poetry Festival

email stanza@stanzapoetry.org
website www.stanzapoetry.org

StAnza is international in outlook and aims to celebrate poetry in all its forms. It is held each March in St Andrews, Scotland's oldest university town. The festival is an opportunity to engage with a wide variety of poetry, to hear world-class poets reading in atmospheric venues, to experience a range of performances where music, film, dance and poetry work in harmony, to view exhibitions linking poetry with visual art and to discover the part poetry has played in the lives of a diverse range of writers, musicians and media personalities. Founded 1988.

WHERE TO PERFORM

Poetry evenings are held all over the UK and the suggestions listed below are worth checking out. Others can be found by visiting your local library or your Arts Council office, or by visiting the What's on section of the Poetry Society website (www.poetrysociety.org.uk/events). The Poetry Library (www.poetrylibrary.org.uk/events) is also an excellent source for upcoming poetry events. Also look out for local groups at which members can share their work.

Allographic

tel 07904 488009
email info@allographic.co.uk
website https://sites.google.com/site/allographica/
Twitter @allographica
Contact Fay Roberts

Cambridge-based live events with new and upcoming names from the spoken word scene and a set of workshops for aspirant poets, storytellers and other writers and performers. Also produces a range of publications, from anthologies to books and pamphlets, that can be purchased online.

Apples and Snakes

The Albany, Douglas Way, London SE8 4AG
tel 020-8465 6140
email programming@applesandsnakes.org
website www.applesandsnakes.org

Performance poetry and spoken word in London and throughout England: see website for full details and contact names.

Bad Language

Gullivers, 109 Oldham Road, Manchester M4 1LW
email openmic@badlanguagemcr.com
website http://badlanguagemcr.com
Contacts Joe Daly, Fat Roland (Manchester); Nicola West, Daniel Carpenter (London)

Saboteur Award-winning literature organisation and spoken word night dedicated to the promotion and development of new writing. See website for up-to-date listing of forthcoming events.

Bang Said the Gun

email info@bangsaidthegun.com
website www.bangsaidthegun.com
Twitter @bangsaidthegun
Contact Daniel Cockrill

High-energy monthly spoken word night with a limited open-mic section. See website for up-to-date gig listings and venues.

Book Slam

Various venues, see website for details
email info@bookslam.com
website www.bookslam.com
Contact Elliott Jack

Founded with the aim of returning literature to the heart of popular culture, Book Slam invites authors, poets, singer-songwriters and comedians to a thinking person's cabaret.

Café Writers Norwich

Louis Marchesi, Tombland, Norwich NR3 1HF
email info@cafewriters.co.uk
website www.cafewriters.co.uk
Twitter @cafewriters
Contacts Martin Figura, Helen Ivory

Readings of poetry and prose in a relaxed and welcoming atmosphere, on the second Monday of every month. Open mic slots available.

CB1 Poetry

CB2 Bistro, 5–7 Norfolk Street, Cambridge CB1 2LD
tel (01223) 508355
email cb1poetry@gmail.com
website www.cb1poetry.org.uk

Regular readings featuring new and well-known artists. Previous participants include Owen Sheers, George Szirtes, Don Paterson and Emily Berry. Check website for dates and times of meetings.

Coffee House Poetry at The Troubadour

PO Box 16210, London W4 1ZP
email coffpoetry@aol.com
website www.coffeehousepoetry.org

Readings & classes take place at The Troubadour, 263–267 Old Brompton Road, London SW5 9JA.

Find the Right Words

The Western, 70 Western Road, Leicester LE3 0GA
email jess_green@hotmail.com
website www.jessgreenpoet.com
Twitter @ftrwpoetry
Editor Jess Green

Monthly poetry and rap event. Two headliners every month, ten open mic spots (five in advance, five on the door) and a free workshop at each event with one of the headliners.

Flint & Pitch Productions

email flintandpitch@gmail.com
website www.flintandpitch.com
Twitter @flintandpitch

Contact Jenny Lindsay

Edinburgh-based spoken word, theatre and music organisation specialising in multi-act revue shows, touring spoken word theatre shows and live literature events across Scotland.

Forked

The B Bar, Barbican Theatre, Plymouth PL1 2NJ
email info@applesandsnakes.org
website www.applesandsnakes.org

Stand-up performance poetry and spectacular spoken word from across the UK. A Plymouth-based seasonal night (three per year) produced by Apples and Snakes.

451 City

Studio 144, Above Bar Street, Southampton, SO14 7DU
email pete@applesandsnakes.org
website www.applesandsnakes.org
Contact Pete Hunter

Southampton-based bi-monthly celebration of the spoken word.

Hammer and Tongue

The Old Fire Station, George Street, Oxford OX1 2AQ
email oxford@hammerandtongue.com
website www.hammerandtongue.com
Twitter @htoxford
Regional Coordinator Steve Larkin

Poetry slam and touring guest artist events in London, Bristol, Brighton, Cambridge, Southampton and Oxford. See website for timings and contact details.

Hit the Ode

email bohdan@applesandsnakes.org
website www.applesandsnakes.org
Twitter @hittheode
Programme Co-ordinator Bohdan Piasecki

Spoken word poetry in Birmingham. Each Hit the Ode features an act from the West Midlands, one from elsewhere in the UK and one international guest.

Inky Fingers

email inkyfingersedinburgh@gmail.com
website https://inkyfingersedinburgh.wordpress.com/
Twitter @InkyFingersEdin
Contacts Ross McCleary, Freddie Alexander, Eleanor Pender

Grass-roots spoken word organisation running a series of wordy events in Edinburgh, from open mic nights to reading and performance workshops.

Jawdance

Rich Mix, 35–47 Bethnal Green Road, London E1 6LA
email nina@applesandsnakes.org
website www.applesandsnakes.org
Host Yomi Sode

Poetry, film and music night, currently every third Wednesday of the month. Check website for details.

Kent & Sussex Poetry Society

The Vittle and Swig, Camden Road, Tunbridge Wells, Kent TN1 2PT
email kentandsussexpoetry@gmail.com
website www.kentandsussexpoetry.com
Secretary Mary Gurr

Local group with national reputation. Organises monthly poetry readings (third Tuesday of each month at 8pm), workshops and an annual poetry competition.

Out-Spoken

100 Club, 100 Oxford Street, London W1D 1LL
website www.outspokenldn.com/live
Facebook www.facebook.com/outspokenLDN
Twitter @OutSpokenLDN
Hosts Joelle Taylor, Anthony Anaxagorou, Karim Kamar, Tom MacAndrew, Sam Bromfield, Craft-D

Monthly poetry and live music event. See website or social media accounts for forthcoming dates and start times; entry £8 online, £10 on the door.

Out-Spoken also runs an annual prize awarded in three categories: Performance; Page; and Film. Submissions open in January, with winners in each category and a cash prize for the overall winner. Submissions can be made via outspokenldn.com and cost £5 per entry. Previous winners include Momtaza Mehri, who was appointed the Young People's Laureate for London in April 2018.

Poetry Unplugged at the Poetry Café

22 Betterton Street, London WC2H 9BX
tel 020-7420 9888
email poetryunplugged@gmail.com
website http://poetrysociety.org.uk/poetry-cafe/
Twitter @poetniall
Host Niall O'Sullivan

Open-mic session, welcoming to new poets. Every Tuesday, sign-up between 6pm and 7pm; spaces are limited.

Poets' Café

21 South Street, Reading RG1 4QU
website www.clairedyer.com/poets-cafe-2
Twitter @Poets_Cafe
Host Reading Stanza c/o Claire Dyer

Reading's longest-running poetry platform, now being organised and hosted by The Poetry Society's Reading Stanza. Held on the second Friday of each month, consisting of an open mic section and a full reading by a leading poet.

Polari

Royal Festival Hall, Southbank Centre, Belvedere Road, London SE1 8XX
email paulburston@btinternet.com
website www.polariliterarysalon.co.uk
Contact Paul Burston

Multi-award-winning LGBT literary salon, held once a month at the Southbank Centre (see website for details). Focuses on established authors but has some pre-arranged spots per event for up-and-coming LGBT writers.

SoapBox

tel 07879 353396
email amy@getonthesoapbox.co.uk
website www.getonthesoapbox.co.uk
Twitter @getonthesoapbox
Contact Amy Wragg

Based in Norfolk and Suffolk, SoapBox promotes and organises live music, poetry and comedy events in a variety of settings, from pubs to arts centres, festivals and street performances.

Stablemates

The Poetry Cafe, 22 Betterton St,
London WC2H 9BX
email jillabram@wordpress.com
website https://jillabram.co.uk/stablemates
Contact Jill Abram

Monthly event presenting three poets from one press. Usually the last Thursday of the month.

Stirred

email stirredwomen@gmail.com
website https://stirredpoetry.wordpress.com
Twitter @StirredPoetry
Team Anna Percy, Rebecca Audra Smith, Jasmine Chatfield, Lenni Sanders

Feminist collective based in Manchester. Runs a monthly themed spoken word and open mic night, as well as facilitating workshops.

That's What She Said

The Book Club, 100–106 Leonard Street,
London EC2A 4RH
website http://forbookssake.net
Twitter @forbookssake

Feminist spoken word and poetry night curated by For Books' Sake at The Book Club. Aims to showcase the best new writing and performance by women, featuring established and emerging authors with a mix of performance, poetry, storytelling, slam and more. Shortlisted for Best Spoken Word Night in the UK (Saboteur Awards, 2017)

Tongue Fu

email tonguefupoetry@gmail.com
website www.tonguefu.co.uk
Twitter @TheTongueFuShow
Founders Chris Redmond, Riaan Vosloo

Lively spoken word night; describes itself as 'a riotous experiment in live literature, music, film and improvisation'. See website for information on forthcoming events. Tours nationally and internationally.

COMPETITIONS

There are now hundreds of competitions to enter and as the prizes increase, so does the prestige associated with winning one, such as the National Poetry Competition.

To decide which competitions are worth entering, make sure you know who the judges are and think twice before paying large sums for an anthology of 'winning' poems which will be read only by entrants wanting to see their own work in print. The Poetry Library publishes a list each month (available free on receipt of a large sae, or online at www.poetrylibrary.org.uk/competitions). See also *Prizes and awards* on page 565.

Literary prizes are given annually to published poets and as such are non-competitive. Information on some high-profile awards can be found on the Booktrust website (www.booktrust.org.uk/prizes).

WHERE TO WRITE POETRY

Apples and Snakes

The Albany, Douglas Way, London SE8 4AG
tel 020-8465 6140
email info@applesandsnakes.org
website www.applesandsnakes.org

Organisation for performance poetry and spoken word, whose goal is to produce engaging and transformative work in performance and participation. Apples and Snakes operates in three main areas: producing, curating and commissioning the spoken word via live events and creative digital content; artist development; participation and outreach. Founded 1982.

Arvon

Lumb Bank – The Ted Hughes Arvon Centre,
Heptonstall, Hebden Bridge,
West Yorkshire HX7 6DF
tel (01422) 843714
email lumbbank@arvon.org
Totleigh Barton, Sheepwash, Beaworthy, Devon EX21 5NS
tel (01409) 231338
email totleighbarton@arvon.org
The Hurst – The John Osborne Arvon Centre,
Clunton, Craven Arms, Shrops. SY7 0JA
tel (01588) 640658
email thehurst@arvon.org
website www.arvon.org

Arvon's three centres run 5-day residential courses throughout the year for anyone over the age of 16, providing the opportunity to live and work with professional writers. Writing genres explored include poetry, narrative, drama, writing for children, song-writing and the performing arts. Bursaries are available to those receiving benefits. Founded 1968.

Cannon Poets

22 Margaret Grove, Harborne, Birmingham B17 9JH
Meets at The Moseley Exchange, The Post Office Building, 149–153 Alcester Road, Moseley, Birmingham B13 8JP usually on the first Sunday of each month (except August) at 2pm
website www.cannonpoets.org.uk
Twitter @Cannonpoets

Cannon Poets have met monthly since 1983. The group encourages poetry writing through:

• workshops run by members or visitors
• break-out groups where poems are subjected to scrutiny by supportive peer groups
• 10-minute slots where members read a selection of their poems to the whole group
• publication of its journal, *The Cannon's Mouth* (quarterly).

Members are encouraged to participate in poetry events and competitions. Cannon Poets' annual poetry competition, *Sonnet or Not*, invites poems of just fourteen lines in length. Entrants may choose any one of the traditional sonnet forms, or experiment with alternative 14-line forms, perhaps using half rhyme, metarhyme or blank verse.

City Lit

1–10 Keeley Street, London WC2B 4BA
tel 020-7492 2600
email infoline@citylit.ac.uk
website www.citylit.ac.uk
Twitter @citylit

Offers classes on poetry appreciation as well as practical workshops.

The Poetry School

1 Dock Offices, Surrey Quays Road, Canada Water, London SE16 2XU
tel 020-7582 1679
website www.poetryschool.com

Teaches the art and craft of writing poetry, with courses in London and around the UK, ranging from evening classes, small seminars and individual tutorials, to one-day workshops, year-long courses and an accredited MA. Activities for beginners to advanced writers, with classes happening face-to-face and online. Three termly programmes a year, plus professional skills development projects and CAMPUS, a social network for poets.

Tŷ Newydd Writing Centre

Llanystumdwy, Cricieth, Gwynedd LL52 0LW
tel (01766) 522811
email tynewydd@literaturewales.org
website www.tynewydd.wales

Runs residential writing courses encompassing a wide variety of genres and caters for all levels, from beginners to published poets. All the courses are tutored by published writers. Writing retreats are also available.

Wey Poets (Surrey Poetry Centre)

Friends Meeting House, 3 Ward Street, Guildford GU1 4LH
tel (01252) 702450 (admin)
email weyfarers@yahoo.co.uk
email bb_singleton@hotmail.com
website www.weyfarers.com
Contact Belinda Singleton

Group meets 2–4.30 each event: third Wednesday of the month for workshops, September to June (first Wednesday in December). Additional speaker events on first Wednesday in November, March, April and May. (Please see website for any changes.) Supportive workshops for original poetry. Small, long-standing group with quality input. New members/visitors and enquiries very welcome.

HELP FOR YOUNG POETS AND TEACHERS

National Association of Writers in Education (NAWE)

Tower House, Mill Lane, off Askham Fields Lane, Askham Bryan, York, YO23 3FS
tel 0330 3335 909
email admin@nawe.co.uk
website www.nawe.co.uk

National membership organisation which aims to further knowledge, understanding and enjoyment of creative writing and to support good practice in its teaching and learning at all levels. NAWE promotes creative writing as both a distinct discipline and an essential element in education generally. Its membership includes those working in Higher Education, the many freelance writers working in schools and community contexts, and the teachers and other professionals who work with them. It runs a national database of writers, produces a weekly opportunities bulletin, publishes two journals – *Writing in Education* and *Writing in Practice* – and holds a national conference.

Poetry Society Education

The Poetry Society, 22 Betterton Street, London WC2H 9BX
tel 020-7420 9880
email educationadmin@poetrysociety.org.uk
website www.poetrysociety.org.uk

An arm of The Poetry Society aiming to facilitate exciting and innovative education work. For over 30 years it has been introducing poets into classrooms, providing comprehensive teachers' resources and producing accessible publications for pupils. It develops projects and schemes to keep poetry flourishing in schools, libraries and workplaces, giving work to hundreds of poets and allowing thousands of children and adults to experience poetry for themselves.

Through projects such as SLAMbassadors UK, the Foyle Young Poets of the Year Award and Young Poets Network, the Poetry Society gives valuable encouragement and exposure to young writers and performers.

Schools membership offers a range of benefits, including quarterly Poetry Society publications, books and posters, and free access to the Poets in Schools placement service. Youth membership is also available (for ages 11–18; £18 p.a.) and offers discounts, publications, poetry books and posters.

Young Poets Network

website http://ypn.poetrysociety.org.uk/
Twitter @youngpoetsnet

Online resource from The Poetry Society comprising features about reading, writing and performing poetry, plus new work by young poets and regular writing challenges. Aimed at young people under the age of 25.

YOUNG POETRY COMPETITIONS

Children's competitions are included in the competition list provided by the Poetry Library: this is free on receipt of a large sae but many details are available online at www.poetrylibrary.org.uk/competitions. Further information on literary prizes can be found on the Book Trust website (www.booktrust.org.uk/prizes).

Foyle Young Poets of the Year Award

The Poetry Society, 22 Betterton Street,
London WC2H 9BX
tel 020-7420 9880
email fyp@poetrysociety.org.uk
website www.foyleyoungpoets.org

Annual competition for writers aged 11–17. Prizes include publication, mentoring and a residential writing course. Deadline 31 July. Free to enter. Founded 2001.

Christopher Tower Poetry Prize

Christ Church, Oxford OX1 1DP
tel (01865) 276156
email info@towerpoetry.org.uk
website www.towerpoetry.org.uk/prize/

Annual poetry competition (open from November to March) from Christ Church, Oxford, aimed at students aged between 16 and 18 in UK schools and colleges. The poems should be no longer than 48 lines, on a different chosen theme each year. Prizes: £3,000 (1st), £1,000 (2nd), £500 (3rd). Every winner also receives a prize for his or her school.

FURTHER READING

Addonizio, Kim, *Ordinary Genius: A Guide for the Poet Within* (W.W. Norton and Co. 2012)

Bell, Jo, and Jane Commane, *How to be a Poet: A 21st Century Guide to Writing Well* (Nine Arches Press 2017)

Bell, Jo, and guests: *52: Write a Poem a Week – Start Now, Keep Going* (Nine Arches Press 2015)

Chisholm, Alison, *A Practical Guide to Poetry Forms* (Compass Books 2014)

Fairfax, John, and John Moat, *The Way to Write* (Penguin Books, 2nd edn revised 1998)

Greene, Roland, *et al.*, *Princeton Encyclopedia of Poetry and Poetics* (Princeton University Press, 4th edn 2012)

Hamilton, Ian, and Jeremy Noel-Tod, *The Oxford Companion to Modern Poetry in English* (Oxford University Press, 2nd edn 2013)

Kowit, Steve, *In the Palm of Your Hand: A Poet's Portable Workshop* (Tilbury House, 2nd edn 2017)

Maxwell, Glyn, *On Poetry* (Oberon Books 2012)

Oliver, Mary, *Rules for the Dance: Handbook for Writing and Reading Metrical Verse* (Houghton Mifflin 1998)

Padel, Ruth, *52 Ways of Looking at a Poem: A Poem for Every Week of the Year* (Vintage 2004)

Padel, Ruth, *The Poem and the Journey: 60 Poems for the Journey of Life* (Vintage 2008)

Roberts, Philip Davies, *How Poetry Works* (Penguin Books, 2nd edn 2000)

Sampson, Fiona, *Poetry Writing: The Expert Guide* (Robert Hale 2009)

Sansom, Peter, *Writing Poems* (Bloodaxe 1993, repr. 1997)

Whitworth, John, *Writing Poetry* (A&C Black, 2nd edn 2006)

See also...

- *Publishers of poetry*, page 763
- *Becoming a published poet*, page 353
- *Notes from a passionate poet*, page 360

Television, film and radio

The calling card script for screen, radio and stage

Breaking in to the competitive world of scriptwriting can be achieved by having an impressive calling card script. Paul Ashton explains what to take into account so that your script is as good as it possibly can be before you send it off to be read.

Many, perhaps most, contemporary professional scriptwriters turn chameleon at some point in their career to work across different mediums, formats and genres – not just to survive, but to thrive. As time marches on, the possibilities open up and some of the seemingly traditional boundaries between different kinds of scriptwriting break down. It has never been more pertinent for scriptwriters to be flexible, and stay flexible. The ever-intensifying competition from other aspiring scriptwriters also means it is equally important to be armed with a great calling card script that speaks your voice.

Where did I go wrong?

The 'how to' of writing scripts will always divide opinion, but the reasons why so many scripts and writers fall short in the eyes of the industry seem to soldier on perennially. From my experience as an industry 'gatekeeper' who has ultimately said 'no' to many thousands of scripts and writers, the recurring problems with the majority include all the usual fundamental mistakes, inconsistencies, lack of care or plain old cliché surrounding:

- Medium and form (what is it?)
- Genre and tone (what kind of story is it?)
- Idea and premise (what is it trying to explore and express?)
- Story (what is engaging the reader's attention from the start right through to the finish?)
- Structure (where is it going and does it get there in surprising ways?)
- Characters (are they distinct? do we connect with them emotionally?)
- Scenes (do they come to dramatic life in the moment?)
- Dialogue (are the characters voiced convincingly, authentically and with individuality?)
- Ending (is the conclusion coherent and satisfying?)

The honest truth is that these are the difficulties faced every day, by every story and every writer. Never send out a script until you have gone back, looked again, rewritten, and given yourself the space to get as many of these things as right as you can. It is certainly possible to over-develop a script by forever tinkering and rewriting all the personality out of it. Your script doesn't need to be perfect or utterly slick. But most scripts from aspiring writers do feel under-developed. And your script does need to be 'ready to be read', because once it has been rejected by someone they will not want to see it again, no matter how much more you develop it. Every script only really has one shot with any given commissioner, producer, director, development executive or literary manager.

Two things (or rather one, stated in two different ways) that you should always remember:

- Writing anything really well is *always* really difficult.
- There are no simple short cuts to writing well – it is *always* really difficult.

Who am I writing for?

Awareness of market and audience is another perennial problem with aspiring writers. Often the writer isn't thinking enough about who might produce their work and who the audience might be. (Or at the other end of the spectrum, they are worrying far too hard about getting a commission and trying/failing desperately to second guess what producers want.) Then there are those who write to satisfy their own creative urge, who write only for themselves. Drama and comedy are audience-driven forms; without an audience, your work means nothing. But there is some hope for the egotist – because one thing you really must never forget is your own voice, your unique, original perspective on the world of your story. This is the thing the gatekeepers are really looking for possibly more than anything else.

So to answer the question: you must always be writing for an audience, but you should always be writing to express yourself.

What is a calling card script?

Written well, it is a script that simply speaks your voice. It is interesting, engaging, intriguing, and in some way unusual. It shows what you can do. It is an opportunity to be truly original. It shows the choices you make when you are not writing to a strict brief or commission. It demonstrates your skill and hints at your potential. It opens doors and starts a dialogue. It is the start of a writer's journey, not the final goal or end point of it. It is a means to any number of ends – yet must not feel like it's been written solely to be expedient, solely to impress, solely to second-guess.

A calling card script is not necessarily the first script you write. You must apply the same rigour to every script until you complete one that you feel speaks your voice. And if you really want to write professionally, then the calling card must not be the only script you ever write. You must *always* be writing anew – again, and again, and again. No matter how successful you ultimately might be, each new original script you write is a kind of calling card of who you are as a writer at any given point in your career. A statement of your intent. An expression of your voice.

What should my script look like?

Film

- Make it no less than 80 and no more than 100 pages long.
- It should be original and a complete, single, self-contained story.
- Think about genre; think about the *big* screen.

Television

- The 60-page pilot episode is ideal – whether for a returning series or a finite serial.
- Do not create your own soap opera and never send out a spec episode of an existing programme to the UK industry.
- Think about where in the small screen schedule it might sit.

Radio

- Aim for the 45-minute single drama.
- The Radio 4 Afternoon Drama is the main window of opportunity, for which you can write all kinds of stories.
- Think about sound and acoustic setting; don't overwrite the dialogue.

Theatre

- You can write with fewer formal restrictions for theatre.
- Make it no less than one hour, or much more than two, in length.
- Think hard about the kind of space/place where you imagine it being staged.

What are you looking for at the moment?

This is the single most repeated question from aspiring (and/or desperate) writers. And it is impossible to answer simply. Commissioners, producers, development executives and literary managers across the new writing industries all like to be surprised. They like to be seen to take risks. They like to be responsible for breaking new talent as well as getting the very best out of established talent. They like being able to identify a new idea as worthy of a commission, development and production investment. They like stamping their personality over their 'slate'. They are looking not only for ideas they have never seen before, but also ideas with which as large an audience as possible can fall in love. This is not crude populism or 'commercialism', by the way. It is the meaning of storytelling: to reach, touch, move, entertain, enthuse, inspire, anger, haunt and surprise as many people as possible.

Further information for writers and film-makers

SUPPORT IN THE UK FILM INDUSTRY

British Film Institute

www.bfi.org.uk

The lead organisation for film in the UK, investing National Lottery funds in British film-making activity. The BFI Film Fund coordinates the NET.WORK, which is comprised of the organisations below offering UK-wide support:

BFI NETWORK

http://network.bfi.org.uk

Creative England

www.creativeengland.co.uk

Northern Ireland Screen

www.northernirelandscreen.co.uk

Ffilm Cymru Wales

www.ffilmcymruwales.com/index.php/en

Scottish Film Talent Network

www.scottishfilmtalent.com

Film London

http://filmlondon.org.uk

BRITISH ORGANISATIONS SUPPORTING FILM

BAFTA

www.bafta.org

BBC Films

www.bbc.co.uk/bbcfilms

BFI Film Academy

www.bfi.org.uk/education-research/5-19-film-education-scheme-2013-2017/bfi-film-academy-scheme

British Council

http://film.britishcouncil.org

Creative Skillset

http://creativeskillset.org/creative_industries/film

Film4

www.film4productions.com

4talent

https://careers.channel4.com/4talent

Hiive

https://app.hiive.co.uk

Lighthouse

www.lighthouse.org.uk/guiding-lights/about-guiding-lights-scheme

Shooting People

https://shootingpeople.org

From tiny studio theatre through to prime-time television and movie blockbusters – everyone should want their particular house to be a *full* house.

Audiences are more discerning, intelligent, hungry, critical, demanding and knowing than you suspect they are, or than we ever give them credit for. You need to know what has and hasn't worked for audiences – and why – in order to know what has already been done and shouldn't be done again in quite the same way. Don't just repeat. Learn from what you see and hear. Dissect it. Analyse it. Criticise it. Digest it. Accept it. Even if you don't like it. And move on to what's distinct about your idea. If you want to write a Radio 4 Afternoon Drama, you need to know what that slot in the schedule is and does. It's always best if you already love a slot/form. It's good if you can learn to love the potential in it. But if you feel nothing for it whatsoever then you are simply being strategic, and this will be seen for what it is very quickly. Write something you care about. Write about what matters to you.

It is important not to write simply for the sake of expediency – because you think it's the kind of thing you ought to write, or everyone else seems to be writing, or, worst of all, because you reckon it will be 'easier'. These scripts are spotted a mile off, and weeded out quickly. What producers are really looking for is a writer with a distinct voice who can deliver an original story that an audience will love. Your calling card script will probably never be made – but if it's good, then it will get you noticed. And that notice is the thing that will get you closer to becoming a real scriptwriter.

So you think your script is ready to be noticed?

If you do think your script is indeed ready to be read, then here's a checklist of key things to do first – and then do next:

- **Don't send it straight out**. Put it in a drawer for a couple of weeks. Give yourself one last chance to spot any problems/errors.
- **Do your research**. Know your market, know your audience. Put in the legwork on where to send it, what opportunities exist, who is and is not accepting scripts, whose taste you might chime with. (If you have a commercially minded romantic comedy, then is the producer of edgy low-budget social realist films really the best place to send your film script?)
- **Follow their guidelines**. Read what they say carefully. If you directly ignore or contradict their guidelines then don't be surprised if and when they reject your script, unread. You may not like their requirements and remits if they don't suit what you want, but they are always there for a reason so ignore them at your peril.
- **Write a simple cover letter/email**. Don't synopsise your script or go into laborious detail. If your writing is strong, then let your script do the talking; if the writing isn't strong enough, then no amount of prefacing or explaining will change that. Long missives immediately put people off reading and enjoying a script.
- **Don't make irrelevant claims, outrageous promises or damaging admissions**. The person reading doesn't need to know if you think it happens to be better than so-and-so's other produced script was (and if you're unlucky they may have been involved with said script, and then you've made an irredeemable *faux pas*). Nor does it really matter if it got a distinction on your MA. Or the script reading service you used told you it ought to get made. Or that your friends loved it. Or that 'it's never been done before' (unless you've seen everything ever made – which nobody has – then this is an impossible assertion).

Never tell them it's 'meant to be ambiguous' or 'it gets better later on' or that you 'know there are areas you could improve it' when what you are really admitting is that you don't know the ending, it isn't very good at the beginning, and it isn't ready to be read. Never claim 'it's the best script you will read all year' as you have no idea what else they will read that year (nor which high-profile award-winning writer they happen to be working with right now).

• **Don't lie about your experience or be economical with the truth**. Really, don't. The creative industries are ultimately quite small, a lot of people know one another, and truth gets out pretty easily and quickly. Whatever experience you do have, you should talk it up; but you should never make it up. Be honest.

• **Be confident in what you think you've achieved**. But don't be arrogant – and do prepare for the worst. For the people looking at your script, it will be just one amongst hundreds or even thousands that year, and you always face stiff competition from other writers.

• **Start your next script**. Don't sit waiting anxiously for a response. Real writers write, all the time, obsessively. Keep writing. And try new things. Never written a radio play? Try it. Want to master final draft screenplay format? Try it.

• **Show initiative**. Don't sit around waiting for floods of interest and commissions to jam up your letterbox/inbox. Find out what useful industry events and networking opportunities of any kind exist within reachable distance to you, and go to them, meet people, network. Use whatever contacts you might have, however tenuous they might seem.

• **Be resilient**. Don't be offended by silence; the sheer volume of spec emails has made life harder for most in the industry. And everyone is rejected at some point. *Everyone*. Learn to deal with rejection, roll with the punches, don't simmer with resentment, argue with someone's decision, or lash out in rejected anger. If someone simply doesn't connect with your work then no amount of telling them that they should will change that. Move on and try to find the person that DOES connect with it. Learn to bounce back better, stronger – happier.

Coda

Embrace the necessary difficulty of writing well. Invest in your own voice. Never be satisfied. Be honest. Be prepared. Be realistic. Be idealistic. Be brave. Be obsessive. Stay sane.

And be lucky.

Paul Ashton is Senior Film Executive at Creative England, where he leads the Sheffield talent team as part of the BFI NETWORK support for new and emerging film-makers towards getting their first feature films made. Paul was previously Development Producer at BBC writersroom (www.bbc.co.uk/writersroom), and before that freelanced across film, television, radio and theatre. He has been involved in finding, developing and producing Academy- and BAFTA-nominated films, and BAFTA, RTS, Sony and Prix Italia award-winning drama and comedy for television and radio. Paul is the author of *The Calling Card Script: A Writer's Toolbox for Stage, Screen and Radio* (Methuen Drama 2011).

See also...

- *Notes from a successful soap scriptwriter*, page 382
- *Stories on radio*, page 385
- *Writing for the theatre*, page 401
- *Bringing new life to classic plays*, page 397

Notes from a successful soap scriptwriter

As the longest serving member of *The Archers'* scriptwriting team, Mary Cutler shares her thoughts about writing for soaps.

A few years ago I was introduced by a friend to someone struggling to establish herself as a playwright. 'I so envy you,' she said, 'writing for *The Archers*. I love soaps.' 'If you love soaps, maybe you should be writing them,' I suggested. I met her again some time later and she said, 'I want to thank you: I took your advice. I gave it a try, and now I'm writing for *Emmerdale*.' So there you are, dear readers. Ten magic words from me might transform your life. I will try to explore why you might love writing for soaps, or equally helpfully, I hope, why you might not.

I have been writing for *The Archers* for 39 years (the programme was first broadcast on Radio 4 in 1951) and such a long career is by no means unique in soaps. During these years I have had a guaranteed audience for my work, and what's more, an affectionate and engaged audience. I've worked collaboratively with some extremely talented people, while retaining control of my own words. I have had the opportunity to cover almost every dramatic situation – tragic, comic, social, political – I could ever have wanted to, in every possible dramatic form. Yes, you may ask – though I hope not as the question fills me with fury – but what about your own work? This is my own work. Who else wrote all those scripts?

The production process

The process of getting a script ready to be recorded starts with the five-weekly Tuesday script conference. This is attended by all the writers (there are 12 of us in the team at the moment) and the production team. We each have in front of us the large script pack which would have been emailed to us on the previous Thursday. We meet to decide on the storyline for the next writing period, for which five of the writers present will each be writing a week's worth of episodes. Those five writers then pitch their week based on the ideas in the pack. But we all work on the storyline together – the writers, whether writing or not – and all the production team, at all levels. That is one of the things I like most. I have never felt plotting was a particular strength of mine, but if someone will give me a starting line I can run from it. The delight of a good script conference is when we start with a strong idea which everyone expands and improves on until it's a thing of beauty, and no one can remember whose idea it was first, and it doesn't matter.

To be part of this engrossing process you have to speak. Most soaps have a script conference element where you will be expected to voice, and if necessary, defend your ideas. That doesn't mean you have to shout, or talk all the time – indeed, these would be positive disadvantages. But you need to stand your ground, especially about what a character might or might not do, and also be ready to yield gracefully if you lose the argument. One of our characters was once torn between two lovers, and the team were, too. On the day of the final decision there was a bad hold-up on the motorway, and three writers rooting for one lover didn't arrive until midday, by which time the other had carried the day. Those writers each had to find their own way to make that decision work for them when they wrote their scripts.

After the script conference, the storyline is emailed two days later to all the writers and members of the production team to arrive on Friday evening. The writers for that writing period have three days to each write their synopsis, which is a scene-by-scene break down of what they intend to write in their six episodes. If it is a well-structured and imaginative synopsis, all that now needs to be written is the dialogue. A script editor speaks with each of the writers for that month the next day, and they then have 12 days to write six scripts – an hour and a quarter of radio. Not everyone can work that fast. One of the best weeks of *The Archers* I ever heard was also that writer's last: he said he could never do it again in the time. It's not a case of locking yourself in your garret and seeing where the muse takes you. The storyline must be covered: while the writer for one week is working on their scripts, the writer for the following week's episodes is writing theirs starting from the point where the storyline is left on the previous week. As all the scripts are written simultaneously each writer needs to let the others know what they're doing. How each writer chooses to dramatise the story is entirely up to them, so there's a lot of scope for individual creative work. There are constraints on the structure of the programme, such as the financial restriction on the number of actors that can be used. Writers may need to tell a story without a character being present because the actor is working elsewhere. Alternatively a writer may swap episodes within their week, or with other writers, to get the actors they need, though we try not to do that.

Until the script editor sees the writing for all five weeks, she can't tell if stories are going too fast or too slow, have become repetitive, or picked up the wrong tone. A few days after the scripts are delivered the editors will ring about any rewrites that need to be done – typically the writer has three days for these too before the scripts are finally accepted. There may well be changes to be made already, following the synopsis discussion. It is only after the synopsis is agreed that the office starts ringing the actors to see if they are still available. Some of them may not be, in which case a writer may have to rethink their beautiful structure and clever stories. But those are just normal run-of-the-mill changes. When we lost the delightful and distinguished actress who played Julia Pargeter (who died suddenly and unexpectedly after a happy day in the recording studio) the team had to deal with not only their individual sorrow and distress, but the fact that this meant rewriting and re-recording scripts that had been completed in the studio, and rewriting those that were about to be recorded, as well as rethinking those that were about to be written. I had two days to turn round my part of this massive undertaking. When the foot-and-mouth crisis hit British farming in 2001 our fictional world was being rewritten practically day by day, so a good soap scriptwriter needs to be fast and flexible. When the Princess of Wales died our redoubtable editor had one day to get something appropriate on air.

My scriptwriting break

So how did scriptwriting for soaps become the job for me? I had always wanted to write, and had been writing since I was quite small. I thought I was going to be a novelist, and wrote several highly autobiographical, very literary quasi novels while at school and university. I should have noticed that the only person prepared to pay me was the editor of *Jackie* magazine to whom I sold three highly autobiographical, although not quite so literary, stories. Then at university I stopped having saleable teenage fantasies, and started having unsaleable literary ones. Real life took over – I decided my ambition to be a writer was a fantasy – I would concentrate on my burgeoning career as a teacher, and stop writing. But I found I couldn't stop. When I realised how I think – rather than seeing images or words, I hear voices (a perpetual radio broadcast!) – I started to write radio plays. To my delight, I found that I could write dialogue till the cows came home(!) though whether it was about anything that would interest even the cows was another matter. I sent my radio plays to the BBC, and sometimes they came back with kind comments (once I was even invited to meet a producer) – and sometimes they just came back. But I persisted.

I am a lifelong fan of *The Archers* (I remember Grace Archer dying when I was six and I used to play Phil and his pigs with my little brothers – naturally I was Phil). When an old school friend started writing for *The Archers* I was fascinated to hear her first week on air: it simultaneously sounded like *The Archers* I had known and loved but also very like my friend – her sense of humour, her preoccupations. I idly wondered what I might find out about my own writing if I tried using these well-loved characters to express myself. So after I heard her Friday episode, I sat down to write the following Monday's, purely as a writing exercise and just for fun, and sent it off.

Some time later I received a letter from the recently appointed editor of *The Archers* saying that although he wasn't looking for new writers my script interested him. He also invited me to meet him. When I went to Pebble Mill the editor offered me a trial week, which I did in the Easter holidays. Following that, he offered me a six-month contract. So my big break was a combination of persistence (I had been sending radio plays to the BBC for at least three years, and writing stories since I could hold a pencil) and sheer luck – the new editor *was* looking for new writers, despite what he'd said in his letter. My script also had the necessary ingredients of craft and, dare I say it, talent. I had, without knowing it, written a script of the right length, with the right number of scenes and the right number of characters – all those years of listening had given me a subliminal feel for the form. According to the editor, my first good line was two-thirds of the way down the first page. I can still remember it: 'She can get up a fair lick of speed when she's pushed'. (Maybe you had to be there but I still think it has a certain ring to it!) But it was also a script I wrote for fun for a programme I loved and admired.

Mary Cutler has been a scriptwriter for *The Archers* since 1979. She has dramatised five of Lindsey Davis's *Falco* novels for Radio 4, the last one being *Poseidon's Gold*, and three dramatic series – *Live Alone and Like It, Three Women and a Boat* and *Three Women and a Baby* for *Women's Hour*. She has also written for the stage and television, including some scripts for *Crossroads* before she was told that her particular talents did not quite fit its special demands. She'd still like to write a novel.

Stories on radio

Getting a story read on BBC Radio 4 is very competitive. Di Speirs outlines how work is selected.

Before they were ever written down, we told stories to each other. And there remains a natural empathy between the written tale and the spoken word. The two make perfect partners in a medium where the imagination has free rein – in other words – radio. And that partnership is particularly effective on the BBC's speech networks, BBC Radio 4 and 4 Extra, which play host to more stories than any other UK stations. Stories, of course, can and do appear in many guises there, from original plays to dramatised adaptations, but above all they work on air as themselves, read by some of the finest actors of our day and listened to by upwards of one million listeners on most slots and now available to download afterwards for 30 days or as podcasts available for a year when we have commissioned them ourselves.

There are two main reading slots for books on Radio 4: the morning non-fiction reading at 9.45am, which is repeated in the late evening and has an audience of around 3.5 million weekly, and every weekday evening a *Book at Bedtime* episode can lull you towards (although hopefully not to) sleep, just after *The World Tonight* at 10.45pm. There are also two short story slots a week, on Friday at 3.30pm and at 7.45pm on a Sunday where both commissioned and extant short stories are broadcast. Sundays in particular are often host to longer story serialisations like *The Reservoir Tapes* by Jon McGregor.

A number of different producers, both in-house and independent, produce readings for these slots – finding the books and stories, getting them commissioned by Radio 4 and then producing the final programmes. The process of successfully translating the written work to the airwaves is as intimate as that of any editor within a publishing house. There is nothing like structuring the abridgement of a novel or a short story – which reduces an author's meticulously crafted work down to 2,000 words an episode – to focus the mind on the essential threads and hidden subtleties of a work, be it originally 3,500 perfectly chosen words or an intricately plotted 300-page novel. The author Derek Longman once described the abridging of his *Diana's Story* (one of the most popular readings ever on *Woman's Hour*) as akin to the book 'having gone on a diet'. You aim to retain the essence, but in a trimmer, slimmer version.

Once cut to the bone, finding the right voice to convey and enhance the story is crucial, as performance, in part, compensates for what has been lost. Casting is vital; so is direction in the studio where different stories demand very different approaches: listen to the output and you'll hear everything from a highly characterised monologue to a narrator-driven piece which demands that the actor also creates a cast of dozens of distinct voices. From the cues that introduce a story, to the music that sets the right mood, a producer works to move a story from the author's original vision into a different but sympathetic medium. As authors mourn what is discarded, it is important to remember what is added by good quality production and top class performance. And of course to remember how effective readings are at taking a book to a whole new audience.

So how do you get your story on air and to all those eager listeners? What is Radio 4 looking for and what works best?

It would be disingenuous to say that it is any easier to get your work read on radio than to get it published. In truth, given the finite number of slots and the volume of submissions it's a tough call. But here are a few hints and guidelines that may help.

Book of the Week

The *Book of the Week* slot is the one that reflects current publishing more than any other. With 42 books a year broadcast on or very close to their original publication date, in five 13-minute episodes, the non-fiction remit is broad and the slot covers everything from biography to humour, politics to travel. Memoir is always an important part of the mix, but so too are good, accessible science books with a narrative thread that can engage the listener, and few subjects are out of bounds if the prose lifts off the page and can catch the attention of what is, by necessity, a largely active and busy audience at that time in the morning.

Submissions come through publishers and agents and in reality are always of published material. (The exceptions to this are about ten fast turnaround commissioned 'letters' and 'essays' series in response to events, like the recent *Letters from South Africa* – these were commissioned by my team to reflect life in the run up to the recent ANC elections.) The *Book of the Week* books need to sustain their story over five episodes but also to work as individual episodes, for this is an audience that won't necessarily hear all of the book (though the BBC's 'Listen Again' facility on iPlayer is increasingly changing this pattern). Overly academic prose doesn't work, nor do too many names and facts. The key is a story and, as discussed below, a voice.

Book at Bedtime

Book at Bedtime is a mix of classic and new fiction. The slot is mostly serialised fiction although occasional harder hitting short story collections – for instance by writers like Julie Orringer and Anne Enright – do find their way in, as do the odd weeks of poetry (*Paradise Lost* and *The Prelude* have been read in the past). The novels divide into, roughly, a quarter classic fiction, a quarter more recent popular fiction, a quarter established names on publication (e.g. new novels, usually transmitted on publication by popular writers, from Arundhati Roy to Tim Winton, Deborah Levy to Jessie Burton); and a quarter newer voices, including a high proportion of debut novels (Jane Harper's *The Dry*, Kate Tempest's *The Bricks that Built the Houses*, Gail Honeyman's *Eleanor Oliphant is Completely Fine*) and some short stories. There are works in translation reflecting Radio 4's broader returning series Reading Europe and novels that tie-in with seasons around authors, e.g. *The Third Man* for the Greene season or whole series of the Adrian Mole novels. What they all share is a quality of writing that works when you pare it to the core. Abridging a work will show up its literary qualities and its flaws – and there is nowhere to hide. Listen to the slot and you will be aware of both the variety (from classics to crime, domestic dramas to lyrical translations) and the quality of the writing.

There are few other hard-and-fast rules – a linear plot, with sub-plots that can be reduced or lost, is preferable – *The Vanishing Act of Esme Lennox* by Maggie O'Farrell was a demanding listen in terms of jumps in time and place but the characters were so vivid and the story so powerful it worked; myriad characters are best avoided, but are manageable with a classic (where familiarity helps). Length is also an important issue. The usual run for a book is ten episodes over two weeks; for almost any novel over 350 pages this becomes a cut too far. Exceptions can be made but they are exceptions; *Atonement* by Ian McEwan, Arundhati Roy's *The Ministry of Utmost Happiness* and *The Interpretation of Murder* by Jed Rubenfeld all ran at 15 episodes, but for new work this is rare. There is an appetite for short novels that can run over five episodes.

New book submissions

New novels are found almost entirely through submissions from agents and publishers to individual producers – the best ones both understand Radio 4 and know the predilections of the main players and play to their tastes. It is extremely rare that an author submits directly; even rarer for them to be successful in what is the most competitive readings slot of all. However, the passion of an individual agent or editor can make a real difference in getting a book read by the producer, which is the first step in the process. Bear in mind that in my office alone we receive upwards of 50 manuscripts and proof sets a week – a lot of work for a team of three producers. Having a reputable champion who can expand on why your novel really is potentially right for the slot is a genuine plus in getting to the top of the scripts pile.

We usually see work at the manuscript or proof stage; this is increasingly submitted online though this is not essential, or even always desirable, as many producers still prefer to read from paper. New titles are ideally broadcast at or near to the hardback publication date, and so producers need to see them in time to get them commissioned and made – ideally six to nine months in advance. And however passionate a producer is about an individual title, the choice is finally in the hands of the commissioning team at Radio 4 who know what else lies in the complex schedule across the network, and must always weigh individual merits against the broader picture.

What makes a good book to read on Radio 4?

Radio 4 is looking for the quality of the writing, coherence of plot (bear in mind though that complex sub-plots can sometimes be stripped out by skilful abridgers), a comprehensible, identifiable and preferably fairly small cast and perhaps above all, a sense of engagement with the listener. Although crime is always popular and increasingly a mainstay of the slot, broadcasting copious amounts of blood and gore at bedtime is unlikely to endear the BBC to the public. Psychological work – like *Engleby* by Sebastian Faulks – works better. Think too, when descriptions are cut, do the clues in the plot stand out like a sore thumb? Consider whether the subject matter is likely to fit with the Radio 4 audience – who are almost certainly much broader-minded and certainly more eclectic than you might imagine – and also highly literate. There is a very real desire to reflect as wide a range of fiction as possible – from a bestseller by Jessie Burton to a Man Booker shortlister like *Exit West* by Mohsin Hamid, from a revisited classic like Muriel Spark to the wide appeal of Matt Haig. It's a broad spectrum but there are of course some issues surrounding language, violence and sexual content; these can be surmountable in many cases – judicious pauses are effective and radio is, after all, a medium that allows the imagination to fill in the blanks as far as you may want to. However, there is no point in submitting a novel filled with expletives or subject matter that will simply shock for the sake of it.

Think too about the voice of a novel – this applies, as much does here, to the short story too. It's an aural medium. Does your book have a 'voice' – can you hear it leaping off the page? Would you want to hear it read to you? And will that be easy to do? There are problems with any story or novel that veers from the third to the first person continually. It can be done – Anna Funder's *All That I Am* was a gift for three narrators, but remember that although every year Radio 4 runs several novels with multiple narrators, they are more expensive to produce and as budgets get ever leaner, slots are even more limited. Be realistic. The competition for this slot is the fiercest of all – and with approximately 26 titles a year, a good number of which are from the ever-popular classic canon, there are really only around a dozen opportunities for the year's new titles.

Short readings

Fifty-two weeks of the year, twice a week, Radio 4 broadcasts a short story or occasionally short non-fiction. The BBC is arguably the largest single commissioner of short stories in the UK, possibly even the world. It is hugely committed to the short story, that most difficult and often underrated of literary forms, and does provide an unparalleled opportunity for writers who want to explore the genre. However, as with *Book at Bedtime*, the competition here is severe.

The vast majority of short stories heard on Radio 4 will be commissioned, though occasional stories, like David Constantine's *Another Country*, are also heard. Producers in a small number of teams will approach writers after agreeing them with the commissioning editor to write individual 2,000-word pieces for Friday afternoons in a slot which is titled 'Short Story of the Week'. Most of these are available for download and increasingly can be found on the Radio 4 Short Story Podcast: www.bbc.co.uk/programmes/p05vff4s. Sunday evenings will have something different. In the last year, Lynne Truss, Gerard Stembridge and Jon McGregor have all been commissioned to write longer runs of inter-connected stories. *The Reservoir Tapes*, which ran over 15 episodes, is also available as a podcast for a year, and after the original broadcast was published as a book. In 2018 more writers, including Lynne Truss and David Szaloy, will follow.

A small group of suppliers, in-house and independent, approach writers whose work they know, often with considerable experience in this genre, to write original material for Radio 4. Publishing a collection, or appearing in many of the excellent literary magazines, winning one of the many short story awards or finding a voice through live literary events, will often bring you to the attention of producers, who also approach novelists and non-fiction writers from time to time. The story slots are as competitive as any others and again a champion in the form of an agent, a magazine editor or a publisher can help.

The short story is a demanding form, and skill and practice are perhaps more vital here than anywhere else. Producers have a certain but sadly limited amount of time to work with an author in an editorial capacity and very little time to read unsolicited material. There is a strong commitment to working with writers and creating original work, and producers are very keen to work with emerging talent that they have identified. Each year a number of slots focus on newer talent, linked for example to the BBC National Short Story Award, and offer a chance to hear the best new writers at work.

With only 2,000 words there's no room for waste and yet you must, as Alice Munro (the Canadian doyenne of the short story) says, 'create a world in a glance'. The subjects may be wide but the bar is high – the best writers in the country and beyond are writing for this slot and you have to match that standard. You may have a better chance of being considered by aiming your story locally (some local BBC radio stations run short fiction from time to time). Be aware of which independent and regional teams work in your geographic area, as the Radio 4 slots reflect the regions and nations of the UK.

The BBC has run the BBC National Short Story Award for 13 years. Initially with partners including Booktrust, this past year has seen exciting new developments with an exciting and expansive partnership with Cambridge University, and with the charity First Story, who are all supporting the BBC Young Writers Award for 14-18 year olds (www.bbc.co.uk/programmes/articles/4PrGlh3csfFgrgdw43K698Q/the-bbc-young-writers-award-2018) and also a new Student Critics Award. The BBC National Short Story Award (www.bbc.co.uk/programmes/b0079gw3; see page 566) was established to celebrate and foster the art of the short story. With an award of £15,000 to the winner, it is one of the largest in the world for a single story. We have received over 12,000 entries from published writers either from, or resident in, the UK since the award began. It is certainly clear that the short story is alive and well across the UK and choosing the winners has been a tremendously hard task each time. If you are a published writer, do consider entering next time around.

In all the readings slots, Radio 4 is looking for terrific writing, a good story and an ear-catching 'voice'. Despite the fierce competition, producers love to 'discover' new writers for the network and every year sees new talent getting their work on air. Keep listening, get to know the slots, and if you have a story – long or short – that demands to be read aloud, try to find a champion for it. Good luck.

Di Speirs worked in theatre and for the Australian Broadcasting Corporation before joining the BBC as a producer for *Woman's Hour*. She edited the *Woman's Hour* serial for three years and produced the first ever *Book of the Week*. She is now Editor, Books for BBC Radio – responsible for the output of the BBC London Readings Unit (about a third of *Book of the Week*, a quarter of *Book at Bedtime*, short stories on Radio 4 and essays on Radio 3 and 4), as well as Radio 4's Bookclub and Open Book, and World Book Club and works closely with the BBC Arts Online team producing BBC Books. She has been instrumental in the BBC National Short Story Award since its inception in 2005 and is a regular judge on the panel. She chaired the Orange Award for New Writers in 2010, and was a nominator for Rolex Mentor and Protégé Arts Initiative 2012 and a judge of the Wellcome Prize in 2017.

See also...

- *Writing short stories*, page 267
- *The calling card script for screen, radio and stage*, page 377

Television and radio

The information in this section has been compiled as a general guide for writers, artists, agents and publishers to the major companies and key contacts within the broadcasting industry. As personnel, corporate structures and commissioning guidelines can change frequently, readers are encouraged to check the websites of companies for the most up-to-date situation.

REGULATION

Ofcom

Riverside House, 2A Southwark Bridge Road, London SE1 9HA
tel 020-7981 3000, 0300 123 3000
website www.ofcom.org.uk
Chief Executive Sharon White

Ofcom is accountable to parliament and exists to further the interests of consumers by balancing choice and competition with the duty to encourage plurality, protect viewers and listeners, promote diversity in the media and ensure full and fair competition between communications providers.

Advertising Standards Authority

Mid City Place, 71 High Holborn, London WC1V 6QT
tel 020-7492 2222
website www.asa.org.uk
Chief Executive Guy Parker

The Advertising Standards Authority is the UK's independent regulator of advertising across all media. Its work includes acting on complaints and taking action against misleading, harmful or offensive advertisements.

TELEVISION

There are five major TV broadcasters operating in the UK: the BBC, ITV, Channel 4 (S4/C in Wales), Channel 5 and Sky. In Ireland, RTÉ is the country's public service broadcaster.

The BBC

website www.bbc.co.uk

The BBC is the world's largest broadcasting organisation, with a remit to provide programmes that inform, educate and entertain. Established by a Royal Charter, the BBC is a public service broadcaster funded by a licence fee. Income from the licence fee is used to provide services including:

- nine national TV channels plus regional programming (BBC3 included)
- 10 national radio stations
- 39 local radio stations
- BBC Online Services
- BBC World Service

Anyone in the UK who watches or records TV programmes (whether via TV, online, mobile phone, games console, digital box, etc) or watches or downloads any BBC programmes from BBC iPlayer needs a TV licence. The Government sets the level of the licence fee; it was announced in 2016 that the licence would rise in line with inflation for five years from 1 April 2017. The annual cost is £150.50. For full details of which services require a TV licence, visit: www.tvlicensing.co.uk.

In addition, the BBC operates separate commercial ventures whose profits help to fund public services.

Governance

BBC Board

Since 3 April 2017, the BBC has been governed by the newly created unitary board, chaired by Sir David Clementi. Tony Hall, Director-General, will sit on the board alongside three other BBC executive members. The Department for Culture, Media and Sport has appointed four non-executive members to represent each of the nations, and the BBC has appointed five non-executive members. More information is available at: www.bbc.co.uk/corporate2/insidethebbc.

Ofcom

Following the closure of the BBC Trust, external regulation of the BBC will be carried out by Ofcom.

What does the BBC do?

It is not possible to list here information about all BBC activities, functions and personnel. The following provides a selective overview of the BBC's main services and key contact information we consider most relevant to our readership.

Television

The BBC operates nine regional national TV channels, providing entertainment, news, current affairs and arts programming for the whole of the UK: BBC One, BBC Two, BBC Three, BBC Four, CBBC, CBeebies, BBC News, BBC Parliament and BBC Alba.

BBC Three has ceased operations as a linear TV channel but remains in operation as an online service.

Director, BBC Content Charlotte Moore
Controller, BBC Two Patrick Holland

Digital Controller, BBC Three Damian Kavanagh
Editor, BBC Four Cassian Harrison
Controller, BBC Daytime Dan McGolpin
Director, Children's Alice Webb
Director of Sport Barbara Slater

BBC Radio and Education

Network radio, arts, music, learning and children's form one division.
Director, Radio and Education James Purnell

BBC Strategy & Digital

BBC Online's services include news, sport, weather, CBBC, CBeebies and BBC iPlayer. BBC Online sites are developed to provide audiences with access to content on a variety of devices including tablets, smartphones, computers and internet-connected TVs. BBC Online also provides access to the BBC's radio and TV programme archives, through BBC iPlayer.
BBC Chief Technology and Product Officer Matthew Postgate

News Group

This is the largest of the BBC's departments in terms of staff, with over 8,000 employed around the UK and throughout the rest of the world. BBC News incorporates network news (the newsroom, news programmes such as Newsnight, political programmes such as Daily Politics, and the weather team), English Regions and Global News.
Director, News & Current Affairs Fran Unsworth

BBC North

BBC North covers Sport, Children's, 5 Live, and parts of Learning and Future Media.

Director, BBC Children's and BBC North Alice Webb

Finance & Business

This operational area manages all aspects of the BBC's Finance and Business division, comprising four areas: finance; operations; commercial development; and legal & business assurance.
Deputy Director-General Anne Bulford

BBC Worldwide

BBC Worldwide is the wholly owned commercial subsidiary of the BBC and sells BBC and other British programming for broadcast abroad, supplementing the BBC's licence fee income. BBC Worldwide helps to keep the licence fee as low as possible. Geographic markets are grouped into three regions: North America; UK, Australia and New Zealand; and Global Markets. The three global business areas are content, brands and digital.
Ceo BBC Worldwide and Director of Global Tim Davie

BBC Studios & Post Production

A wholly owned subsidiary of the BBC, BBC Studios & Post Production works with media companies to create and manage content across all genres for a diverse range of broadcasters and platforms, including ITV, Channel 4 and Sky, as well as the BBC.
Managing Director David Conway

BBC World Service Group

This division incorporates BBC World Service and BBC Global News. This includes the BBC World Service, BBC World News Television Channel, the BBC's international facing online news services in English, BBC Monitoring Service, BBC World Service Group and BBC Media Action (the BBC's international development charity).
Director, BBC World Service Group Jamie Angus

BBC Studios

BBC Studios is a new production division that separates TV production from TV commissioning.
Director, BBC Studios Mark Linsey

Commissioning

For full details of editorial guidelines, commissioning, production and delivery guidelines, and how to submit a proposal, see www.bbc.co.uk/commissioning.

Developing and producing programmes is complex and requires substantial knowledge of production and broadcasting. BBC Pitch is the BBC's commissioning tool designed for UK-based production companies and BBC in-house production teams to submit content proposals for BBC Network Television. See www.bbc.co.uk/commissioning/tv/articles/pitch. Individuals and members of the public cannot use BBC Pitch. If you are a member of the public with an idea, see www.bbc.co.uk/commissioning/tv/ideas-from-the-public.

Who's who in commissioning?

Television (genre commissioning)
Head of Content BBC Children's Cheryl Taylor
Comedy *Controller* Shane Allen, *Commissioning Editors* Gregor Sharp, Alex Moody, Kate Daughton
Daytime & Early Peak *Controller* Dan McGolpin, *Commissioning Editors* Jo Street, Lindsay Bradbury, Alex McLeod, Carla-Maria Lawson, Julie Shaw
Drama *Controller* Piers Wenger, *Commissioning Editors* Lucy Richer, Elizabeth Kilgarriff, Gaynor Holmes, Mona Qureshi, Tommy Bulfin, Ben Irving
Entertainment *Controller* Kate Phillips, *Commissioning Editors* Jo Wallace, Rachel Ashdown, Ruby Kuraishe, Pinki Chambers, Sarah Clay, Kalpna Patel-Knight
Factual (covers arts, current affairs, documentaries, features & formats, history, business, learning, music, religion & ethics, science, natural history, Open

University, acquisitions and BBC iPlayer) *Controller* Alison Kirkham
BBC Nations and Regions *Director* Ken Macquarrie, *Director Northern Ireland* Peter Johnston, *Director BBC Scotland* Donalda MacKinnon, *Director Cymru Wales* Rhodri Talfan Davies, *Director BBC Midlands and BBC Academy* Joe Godwin, *Director South West* Pat Connor

BBC writersroom

website www.bbc.co.uk/writersroom

BBC writersroom is the first port of call at the BBC for unsolicited scripts and new writers. It champions writing talent across a range of genres and is always on the lookout for writers of any age and experience who can show real potential for the BBC. The BBC writersroom blog provides a wealth of behind-the-scenes commentary from writers and producers who have worked on BBC TV and radio programmes: www.bbc.co.uk/blogs/writersroom.

Education and training

The BBC has adopted a recruitment system called the BBC Careers Hub. It allows candidates to apply for jobs, source interview tips, learn about the BBC's recruitment processes and get advice about CVs, applications and assessments: www.bbc.co.uk/careers/home.

Trainee Schemes and Apprenticeships

website www.bbc.co.uk/careers/trainee-schemes-and-apprenticeships

For full details of the BBC's trainee and apprenticeship schemes, see website.

Work Experience

website www.bbc.co.uk/careers/work-experience

For full details of the BBC's work experience placements, see website.

BBC College of Production

website www.bbc.co.uk/academy/production

A free, online learning resource providing practical advice and information on all aspects of working in TV, radio and online.

BBC College of Technology

website www.bbc.co.uk/academy/technology

A free, online learning environment which focuses on providing resources connected with broadcast engineering, software technology and business systems.

BBC College of Journalism

website www.bbc.co.uk/academy/journalism

The College is responsible for the training of BBC news staff and provides in-depth information about core skills, legal and ethical matters and writing techniques. Features a wide range of hints, tips and style guides for writers.

Work in Broadcast

website www.bbc.co.uk/academy/work-in-broadcast

This site provides a wealth of information for anyone wanting to work for the BBC, whether as an employee or freelance.

Writer's Lab

website www.bbc.co.uk/writersroom/writers-lab

The Writer's Lab provides interviews, advice, toolkits, guidelines and other resources to help and support your writing.

ITV plc

The London Television Centre, Upper Ground, London SE1 9LT
tel 020-7157 3000
website www.itv.com, www.itvplc.com

The ITV network is responsible for the commissioning, scheduling and marketing of network programmes on ITV1 and its digital channel portfolio including ITV2, ITV3, ITV4, CiTV and ITVBe. It is the UK's largest commercial TV network. In addition to TV broadcasting services, ITV also delivers programming via a number of platforms, including ITV Player.

ITV Studios is the UK's largest production company and produces over 3,500 hours of original content annually. ITV Studios (UK) produces programming for the ITV network's own channels as well as other UK broadcasters including the BBC, Channel 4, Channel 5 and Sky. ITV also has an international production business which produces for local broadcasters in the USA, Australia, France, Germany and Scandinavia.

Management team
Ceo Carolyn McCall
Group Communications and Corporate Affairs Director Paul Moore
Director of Television Kevin Lygo
Managing Director, Commercial Kelly Williams
Managing Director Julian Bellamy
Director of Strategy and Direct to Consumer Julian Ashworth
Group Legal Director Andrew Garard
Group Finance Director Ian Griffiths
Human Resources Director David Osborn

Commissioning

ITV's commissioning areas include entertainment and comedy, factual, daytime, drama, sport, current affairs, digital and online. Information, FAQs and guidelines for commissioning can be found at www.itv.com/commissioning.

Entertainment & Comedy

email comedy.commissioning@itv.com; entertainment.commissioning@itv.com

Head of Entertainment Siobhan Green, *Controller, Comedy* Saskia Schuster, *Development Coordinator* Emma Barnard

Factual

email factual.commissioning@itv.com
Controller Jo Clinton-Davis, *Head of Factual Entertainment* Sue Murphy, *Commissioning* Priya Singh, Satmohan Panesar, Nicola Lloyd

Daytime

email daytime.commissioning@itv.com
Joint Heads of Daytime Clare Ely, Jane Beacon

Drama

email drama.commissioning@itv.com
Senior Drama Commissioner Victoria Fea, *Commissioning* Jane Hudson, *Head of Drama* Polly Hill

Sport

email niall.sloane@itv.com
Director of Sport Niall Sloane

Current Affairs

email currentaffairs.commissioning@itv.com
Controller of Current Affairs Tom Giles

Digital

Head of Digital Channels and Acquisitions Rosemary Newell, *Controller* Paul Mortimer

Recruitment, training and work experience

Information about training schemes, work experience and recruitment at ITV can be found at www.itvjobs.com, including details of ITV Insight, a volunteering scheme which enables people seeking experience in the TV industry to gain hands-on knowledge.

ITV network regions

The ITV Network is made up of the following regions:
ITV Anglia www.itv.com/news/anglia
ITV Border www.itv.com/news/border
ITV Central www.itv.com/news/central
ITV Granada www.itv.com/news/granada
ITV London www.itv.com/news/london
ITV Meridian www.itv.com/news/meridian
ITV TyneTees www.itv.com/news/tyne-tees
ITV Wales www.itv.com/news/wales
ITV West Country www.itv.com/news/westcountry
STV Group www.stv.tv (Scotland)
UTV www.u.tv (Northern Ireland)
Channel TV www.itv.com/news/channel

Channel 4

124 Horseferry Road, London SW1P 2TX
tel 020-7396 4444
website www.channel4.com

Channel 4 is a publicly owned, commercially funded, not-for-profit public service broadcaster and has a remit to be innovative, experimental and distinctive. Its public ownership and not-for-profit status ensure all profit generated by its commercial activity is directly reinvested back into the delivery of its public service remit. As a publisher-broadcaster, Channel 4 is also required to commission UK content from the independent production sector and currently works with over 400 creative companies across the UK every year. In addition to the main Channel 4 service, its portfolio includes: E4; More4; Film4; 4Music; 4seven; channel4.com; and a digital service, All 4, which presents all of C4's on-demand content, digital innovations and live linear channel streams in one place online for the first time.

Management team

Chief Executive Alex Mahon
Director of Programmes Ian Katz
Chief Marketing and Communications Officer Dan Brooke
Chief HR Officer Caroline Ross

Commissioning

Information about commissioning and related processes and guidelines can be found at www.channel4.com/info/commissioning.

Arts

Commissioning Executive Stephanie Awofisan

Comedy

Head of Comedy Fiona McDermott, *Commissioning* Rachel Springett, Jack Bayles

Daytime

Head of Daytime David Sayer, *Commissioning Programme Coordinator, Daytime, Music and Formats* Cerise Carroll, *Commissioning Editor, Daytime and Features* Tim Hancock

Documentaries

Heads of Documentaries Nick Mirsky, Michelle Chappell, Charlotte Desai, *Commissioning Executive* Madonna Benjamin, *Executive Producer* Rita Daniels

Drama

Head of Drama Beth Willis, *Head of Development* Matthew Wilson, *Commissioning Executives* Lee Mason, Manpreet Dosanjh, Chloe Tucker, Jonny Richards, *Head of International Drama* Simon Maxwell

Entertainment, TV Events and Sport

Head of Entertainment, TV Events and Sport Ed Hàrvard, *Commissioning Editor, Live and TV Events*

Tom Beck, *Commissioning Editor, Entertainment* Syeda Irtizaali, *Commissioning Editor, Factual Entertainment and Entertainment* Sarah Lazenby, *Commissioning Executive, TV Events and Sport* Antonia Howard Taylor, *Commissioning Editor, Sport* Stephen Lyle, *Commissioning Editor, Entertainment and TV Events*, Josh Buckingham

Entertainment Factual

Head of Factual Entertainment Kelly Webb-Lamb, *Commissioning* Ian Dunkley, Lucy Leveugle, Gilly Greenside, Becky Cadman

Features

Head of Features Gill Wilson, *Commissioning* Lizi Wootton, Tim Hancock, Clemency Green, *Commissioning Executive* Vivienne Molokwu

Formats & Music

Head of Formats Dominic Bird, *Commissioning Editors* Simone Haywood, Jonny Rothery, Kate Maddigan, Lee McMurray

Nations and Regions

Nations and Regions Manager Deborah Dunnett

News and Current Affairs

Head of News and Current Affairs Dorothy Byrne, *Commissioning* Siobhan Sinnerton, Tom Porter, Adam Vandermark

All 4

Commissioning editors Pegah Farahmand, Thom Gulseven

Specialist Factual

Head of Specialist Factual Rob Coldstream (Acting), *Commissioning* Alf Lawrie (Science), Shaminder Nahal (History)

4Talent

website http://careers.channel4.com/4talent
Industry Talent Specialist Laura Boswell

Through 4Talent, Channel 4 aims to help people wanting to work in the broadcasting industry gain experience, qualifications and career development.

There are a range of options including apprenticeship, graduate and scholarship programmes, work experience, training, events and workshops. For full details see website.

Channel 5

10 Lower Thames Street, London EC3R 6EN
tel 020-8612 7000
website www.channel5.com
Director of Programmes Ben Frow

Brands include Channel 5, 5* and 5USA, and an on-demand service, Demand 5. Channel 5 works with independent production companies to provide its programmes.

Commissioning

Information about commissioning and related processes and guidelines can be found at: www.channel5.com/commissions.

Factual, News and Current Affairs

Commissioning Emma Westcott, Adrian Padmore, Guy Davies, Lucy Willis

Factual Entertainment, Features and Entertainment

Commissioning Greg Barnett, Sean Doyle

Acquisitions

Head of Acquisitions Katie Keenan, *Channel and Acquisitions Manager* Sebastian Cardwell, *Acquisitions Manager* Cherry Yeandle

Children's Programming: Milkshake!

Head of Children's tba

RTÉ

Donnybrook, Dublin 4, Republic of Ireland
email info@rte.ie
website www.rte.ie
Director General Dee Forbes

RTÉ (Raidio Teilifis Éireann) is Ireland's national public service broadcaster. A leader in Irish media, RTÉ provides comprehensive, free-to-air multimedia services.

Commissioning

RTÉ works in partnership with independent producers to create many of Ireland's favourite TV programmes. RTÉ commissions content in the following areas: lifestyle and formats; entertainment; young people; regional; diversity; wildlife; and education, factual, drama, sport, religion, comedy, talent development and music. Full details of RTÉ's commissioning guidelines, specifications and submissions can be found at www.rte.ie/commissioning.

S4C

Parc Ty Glas, Llanishen, Cardiff CF14 5DU
tel 0870 600 4141
website www.s4c.co.uk

S4C is the only Welsh-language TV channel in the world, broadcasting over 115 hours of programming weekly on sport, drama, music, factual, entertainment and events. See website for full details of commissioning and production guidelines and personnel.

Management team
Ceo Owen Evans
Creative Content Director Amanda Rees
Director of Communications Gwyn Williams
Director of Corporate and Commercial Elin Morris

DIGITAL TV PROVIDERS

Sky
Grant Way, Isleworth TW7 5QD
tel 0333 100 0333
website www.skygroup.ski/corporate/home
Chief Executive Jeremy Darroch

BT
81 Newgate Street, London EC1A 7AJ
Customer postal address BT Correspondence Centre, Providence Row, Durham DH98 1BT
tel 020-7356 5000 (switchboard) or 0800 800 150 (customers)
website http://home.bt.com
Ceo Gavin Patterson

Virgin Media
Media House, Bartley Wood Business Park, Hook, Hants RG27 9UP
website www.virginmedia.com
Ceo Tom Mockridge

Freesat
23–24 Newman Street, London W1T 1PJ
tel 0345 313 0051
website www.freesat.co.uk
Managing Director Alistair Thom

YouView
3rd Floor, 10 Lower Thames Street, London EC3R 6YT
email info@youview.com
website www.youview.com
Ceo Richard Halton

Organisations connected to television broadcasting

BARB
20 Orange Street, London WC2H 7EF
tel 020-7024 8100
email enquiries@barb.co.uk
website www.barb.co.uk
Chief Executive Justin Sampson

The Broadcasters Audience Research Board is the official source of viewing figures in the UK.

Ipsos Connect
(specialist division of Ipsos MORI)
3 Thomas More Square, London E1W 1YW
tel 020-3059 5000
website www.ipsos-mori.com
Managing Director, Ipsos Connect Liz Landy, *Ceo Ipsos MORI* Ben Page

Involved in the work of BARB and RAJAR.

Public Media Alliance
University of East Anglia, Norwich NR4 7TJ
tel (01603) 592335
email info@publicmediaalliance.org
website www.publicmediaalliance.org
Contact Sally-Ann Wilson

World's largest association of public broadcasters. Previously known as the Commonwealth Broadcasting Association.

Royal Television Society
7th Floor, 3 Dorset Rise, London EC4Y 8EN
tel 020-7822 2810
email info@rts.org.uk
website www.rts.org.uk

The leading forum for discussion and debate on all aspects of the TV community. In a fast-changing sector, it reflects the full range of perspectives and views. Hold awards, conferences, seminars, lectures and workshops.

RADIO

UK domestic radio services are broadcast across three wavebands: FM; medium wave; and long wave. A number of radio stations are broadcast in both analogue and digital and there are growing numbers of stations broadcasting in digital alone. Digital radio (DAB – digital audio broadcasting) is available through digital radio sets, car radios, online, and on games consoles and mobile devices such as smartphones and tablets. Radio provision in the UK comprises of public service radio programming provided by the BBC and programming provided by independent, commercial stations.

BBC Radio

The BBC operates 10 national radio stations offering music and speech programming for the whole of the UK: Radio 1, Radio 1 Xtra, Radio 2, Radio 3, Radio 4, Radio 4 Extra, Radio Five Live, Radio Five Live Sports Extra, Radio 6 Music and Asian Network. In addition, there are over 40 regional/local radio stations.
Director, Radio Bob Shennan

Commissioning

For full details of commissioning and delivery guidelines, see www.bbc.co.uk/commissioning/radio/. For details of how to pitch programme ideas to BBC Radio, see www.bbc.co.uk/commissioning/radio/articles/pitching-to-radio.
Radio 1/1Xtra/Asian Network *Controller* Ben Cooper, *Commissioning* Robert Gallacher, *Commissioning Executive (Asian Network)* Khaliq Meer
Radio 2 *Head* Lewis Carnie, *Commissioning Editor* Robert Gallacher, *Manager, Scheduling and Commissioning* Julian Grundy
Radio 3 *Controller* Alan Davey, *Head of Music* Edward Blakeman, *Head of Speech* Matthew Dodd, *Commissioning Manager* David Ireland

Radio 4/4 Extra *Controller* Gwyneth Williams, *Commissioning Editors* James Runcie (Arts), Jeremy Howe (Drama and Fiction), Sioned William (Comedy), Mohit Bakaya (Factual)
Radio 5 Live/5 Live Sports Extra *Controller* Jonathan Wall, *Commissioning Editor* Richard Maddock
Radio 6 Music *Head* Paul Rodgers, *Commissioning Editor* Robert Gallacher
World Service *Controller (English)* Mary Hockaday
Radio & Music Multiplatform *Controller* Mark Friend, *Programme Manager* Helen Cox

Commercial radio

There are around 300 commercial radio stations operating in the UK, most of which serve a local area or region. A small number of commercial radio stations operate nationally, including Classic FM, Absolute Radio, talkSport and LBC. The majority of commercial radio stations are owned by one of three groups:

Global Radio

website www.thisisglobal.com

Bauer Media

website www.bauermedia.co.uk

Wireless Group

website www.wirelessgroup.co.uk

Organisations connected to radio broadcasting

Media.info

website http://media.info/uk

This website provides detailed listings of UK radio stations plus information about TV, newspapers, magazines and media ownership in the UK.

RAJAR

6th Floor, 55 New Oxford Street, London WC1A 1BS
tel 020-7395 0630
website www.rajar.co.uk
Chief Executive Jerry Hill

RAJAR – Radio Joint Audience Research – is the official body in charge of measuring radio audiences in the UK. It is jointly owned by the BBC and the RadioCentre on behalf of the commercial sector.

The Radio Academy

website www.radioacademy.org
Managing Director Roger Cutsforth

The Radio Academy is a registered charity dedicated to the promotion of excellence in UK radio broadcasting and production. For over 30 years the Radio Academy has run the annual Radio Academy Awards, which celebrate content and creativity in the industry.

RadioCentre

6th Floor, 55 New Oxford Street, London WC1A 1BS
tel 020-7010 0600
email info@radiocentre.org
website www.radiocentre.org
Chief Executive Siobhan Kenny

RadioCentre is the voice of UK commercial radio and works with government, policy makers and regulators, and provides a forum for industry-wide debate and discussion.

Theatre

Bringing new life to classic plays

What makes a successful, comfortably off, academic publisher chuck in a safe career and try his hand in the slippery and financially unrewarding world of theatre? Mike Poulton describes how frustration with the style and tone of English productions of classic masterpieces in the past, and persistent neglect of such fine works, drove him to make his successful move into translation and adaptation. He shares his personal golden rules, practical advice and insights.

Becoming an adaptor of classic plays – the motivation

I suppose I became an adaptor of classic plays because, as an avid theatregoer since late childhood, I became increasingly unhappy with what I was seeing and hearing. I had read a lot of Schiller at university and become gripped by it. Why did these powerful epic dramas never, or very rarely, seem to make it into our theatres? Theatre back then was still a going concern, comparatively speaking, and every proud provincial capital supported its producing house. I had also read a lot of Chekhov. On the rare occasions I did see English productions of these Russian masterpieces, they seemed slow, unfunny – sometimes even turgid. Yet in the audiences for them there was an apparent reverence, which seemed unrelated to all the very English over-emoting that was projected woodenly from the acres of silver birch forest on the stage. It was sometimes possible to believe you had wandered out of a *Cherry Orchard* and ended up in *Brief Encounter*. My discontent grew and grew. The material was so much livelier – so much more thrilling in the imagination. I felt cheated. And later, with the arrogance of youth, I deluded myself into a belief that I could do better.

At a rare performance of a Chekhov or an Ibsen play it would seem clear to me that what the actors on the stage were saying, and how they said it, bore very little relationship to how people spoke in *real life* – either now or at the time the plays were written. It was as if the theatre had a style of delivery it reserved unto itself – as did, say, the Church and the BBC. What's more, in a cast of 20 characters, each of them, whatever their status, spoke in the same way. Generals, postmasters and small children all used the same speech patterns and vocabulary – unless they were clowns (who always spoke Mummerset). But for the most part the cast delivered lines with a single voice, and it wasn't difficult to work out that that voice must be the *translator's* voice. I didn't have the same problem with English writers; Shakespeare, though of a different age, seemed real and immediate. It was just that, with the Greeks, the Russians and the European greats performed in translation, there was a middleman, an often dry and academic voice, getting in the way. The immediacy and drive of the original was lost – buried under the literalness of the English text.

An example: in Schiller's great play *Don Carlos* there's a scene where Carlos, the Crown Prince, pleads with his father for a military command and is refused. One very old translation says: 'In this, your refusal, by continually denying my requests you humiliate your son.' Another even older version says: 'Whatever I ask, and I ask for only a very little, is met with your repeated refusals.' It would be difficult for even the most accomplished actor to breathe life into either of those utterances, or even get his tongue round them. So

I went back to the original German. What Schiller makes Carlos say ends in the line: 'Mir alles, alles, alles so verweigern.' This repetition is a gift to an actor when translated as: 'Think how you'll dishonour me, if you refuse me everything – everything – everything! What will the world say of me?' Schiller knew his trade – he knew what an actor needed. The old translations ignored the needs of the actor, and ignored the spirit and passion of the original, in favour of a pedantic slavery to the literal meaning of words. I also began to notice, particularly in performances of Chekhov, that the old translators imposed a tone on their literal translations – refusing to let the characters speak for themselves – and geared their versions towards the tragic, if not the downright dull. I knew, from reading him, that Chekhov had a wonderfully subversive sense of humour. If you watch a Chekhov play in the original with an audience of Russians, they spend half the evening in tears and the other half doubled up with laughter. In English performances that laughter was absent. I realised that the translator was ignoring, once again, the spirit of the original and imposing his or her own opinions and voice on the play. And it was a solemn voice.

But perhaps my strongest motive for wanting to bring great plays to life was a sense of neglect. European theatre eagerly embraces English drama. In any major town in France, Germany or Italy chances are that there will be a Shakespeare and other English (or Irish) work in the theatre programme during the season. (A couple of years ago, Montauban even had posters for *L'éventail de Lady Windermere.*) But in the past it was not a two-way street. English-speaking audiences tended to stick to what they knew. They were not very adventurous. Today though, prompted by some adventurous directors and producing houses, things are improving. There is a vast treasure house of forgotten classics waiting to be brought back to life.

Neglect is still rife. We hardly know how to value our own great works, let alone the masterpieces of the rest of the world. We are unlikely to see a production of *The Great Duke of Florence*, or *The Maid of Honour*, or *The Lie of the Day*, *The World in a Village*, or *Tony Lumpkin in Town*, or even to remember who wrote them. So what chance do Turgenev's *The Old Bachelor*, Goldoni's *The New House*, or Schiller's *Maid of Orleans* stand of a production? Happily, more of a chance today than 20 years ago, but these neglected works still need a producer and a translator to champion them.

Translating classic plays – some practical advice

My rule when starting out was … never accept a commission. I preferred to get a version the way I wanted it and only then to start approaching theatres and artistic directors. I only worked with authors I knew and loved, and had befriended. It's not easy to make a friend of Schiller, say, because he's been dead for such a long time. But I felt I had to get to know him so well I could reach a point where I could confidently answer on his behalf. I did this by reading and rereading everything he ever wrote. If you want to know how Chekhov thinks, for example, read all his short stories and his letters.

At all costs … avoid living authors. The dead ones are a lot less trouble and won't take 50% of your royalties – should there be any. You must believe in the greatness of your author, otherwise why would championing his or her works be a worthwhile expenditure of your time? And, on the question of time, the rule is to work out how long you think you need and double it. When working at full stretch, Ibsen could write a play in a month. To translate that play can't be done successfully, I believe, in under seven.

Another rule of mine was … never translate and adapt a play with the object of making money. I could never have begun a career as a translator/adaptor had I not previously had a successful career as an academic publisher. If you're passionate about the play you want to put before an audience, then some slight financial reward may follow. On occasion you might find you have a smash hit on your hands – but such occasions are, in financial terms, rare. I honestly don't know how playwrights new to the business support themselves. In my first year – over 20 years ago – I had two plays at Chichester. One went into the West End and both went to Broadway. But that was only after working more than a year for nothing, endless readings and workshops, and more good luck and support from the Chichester theatre than I had the right to expect.

Starting out

Every new translator needs to start somewhere. My starting point was a play by Turgenev called *Alien Bread*. I read it in a very old and unplayable translation but I had a strong sense that underneath its lines lay a very powerful play – and great roles for two leading actors. With a lot of help from Russian friends I wrote a version of it I called *Fortune's Fool* and it won a lot of prizes on Broadway. It was a lucky break – and we all need lucky breaks.

So the first thing an adaptor has to do is to look for and find an extraordinary play by an extraordinary but neglected author. Ignore the ones that are out there already, Chekhov, Ibsen, Schiller even. There are plenty of other great works mouldering unregarded on dusty shelves. A fundamental Christian belief is in the communion of saints and the company of angels. The souls of the righteous, saints and martyrs exist in heaven, conversing with the various orders of angels, and with all those down here on Earth waiting to be redeemed and marked out for higher things. I like to imagine that similar communion exists among the great writers of the past. They no longer move on earth but their voices remain – waiting to be translated into English.

Collaboration

Surprisingly, it would be a mistake to think that adapting a play is a solitary business. It's not something you ought to try on your own. If, say, you're working on a Russian play, you have to surround yourself with Russians who will explain to you every layer of meaning in every line. If you are not fluent in the language of the original you have to commission a literal translation – an expensive business – but a good translator is invaluable. I tend to go through the literal translation with the translator in great detail, and then go back to the original and read the two versions together line by line. Only when you are confident that you've absorbed every shade of meaning in the original, and understand it in the context of its time, do you begin your own work – which is to translate the 'spirit' of the original play. This process has very little to do with the words or the order in which they're set down on the page.

I work in drafts. When I have the first rough draft in a speakable form I get a group of actors together and hear it read aloud. However much time you spend pacing up and down and reading your own lines, you'll never accomplish much. You have to sit and listen, notebook in hand, to others reading your work. Then you can begin the serious work of adaptation. For the second draft you'll probably need the cooperation of a theatre. You might need between 10 and 20 actors to spend a week trying out your material. Most actors are very willing to help, but they need feeding! Unless you have a large private income, you're going to need a sponsor, or the involvement of a theatre. And you're only going to get that once you're past Draft One. You might then need another 'workshop' or even two more before you feel you have a script you can confidently take into rehearsal.

I recently adapted *Wolf Hall* and *Bring Up The Bodies* from Hilary Mantel's novels. I could not have done this without the commitment and faith of the Royal Shakespeare Company. And this came because I'd previously worked on six other productions there and the new Artistic Director must have thought I was a good risk. The first draft of *Wolf Hall* was about two-thirds longer than the draft we took into rehearsal a year later. But without the input of 20 RSC actors we'd have never have got the project off the ground, into The Swan, into the West End and onto Broadway. Nobody said it would be easy. I certainly couldn't have called on such resources earlier in my career. Patience is everything.

Maintaining the backlist

Once you have a backlist, a great deal of time is spent in maintenance. I would argue that a 'version' – as we call a play translated and adapted from a classical original these days – has a life in the theatre of five or six years at most. William Archer, the first great translator of Ibsen, now seems florid and unspeakable. Some time ago Michael Mayer breathed new life into Ibsen and became the translator everybody turned to. Now others have overtaken him. A new translation, after a year or so, needs fine-tuning, an overhaul, or in some cases a complete rebuild. For example, my version of Ibsen's *Ghosts* has had six productions in the last 15 years, and for each I have given it a major rethink and a substantial rewrite. Language, we know, is fluid but I wonder if we're aware of how rapidly it dates. I look at my published versions of Schiller, Chekhov, Euripides and Ibsen on my shelves and I think of them in a very different way from the originals standing next to them. The originals are like fine wine maturing and improving. My translations – all translations – are like bottles of milk, open, and rapidly going sour.

The audience

Finally, the most important consideration of all in any adaptation or translation is the audience. If you want to produce a really successful adaptation of any play, go obsessively to the theatre for 20 or 30 years and study your audience. (What makes them laugh? What makes them freeze? What bores them? What gets them on the edge of their seats?) After that you're ready to start.

Mike Poulton is a translator and adaptor of classic plays and novels who began writing for the theatre in 1995 after an earlier successful career as an academic publisher. His first two productions, Chekhov's *Uncle Vanya* and Turgenev's *Fortune's Fool*, were staged the following year at the Chichester Festival Theatre and later went to Broadway. His adaptation of Schiller's *Don Carlos* won an Olivier Award in 2005. Other productions have included Euripides' *Ion*, Schiller's *Wallenstein*, Malory's *Morte d'Arthur* and Dickens' *A Tale of Two Cities*. His Olivier-nominated stage adaptations of Hilary Mantel's *Wolf Hall* and *Bring Up the Bodies* played in Stratford, the West End and on Broadway in 2014/15. In 2016, *Kenny Morgan*, a biographical play about Terence Rattigan opened in London and Mike's adaption of the *York Minster Plays* premiered at York Minister. In 2017 Mike adapted Robert Harris' trilogy of *Cicero* novels for the RSC.

See also...

- *Literary translation*, page 333
- *Writing for the theatre*, page 401

Writing for the theatre

From the perspective of a playwright, David Eldridge describes the process of writing a play, its production, through to a run at a theatre.

Writing the play

Ideas for plays can come from anywhere. Political anger, a riff of dialogue, an image, some experience in your life, a newspaper article, a dream or fantasy, or from a particular actor you admire. As Caryl Churchill says, 'What's the difference between an idea for a play [*sic*]? I think the only difference is that you want to make [it] into a play, the point at which [it] become[s] an idea for a play is when you get some sort of technical or physical way of turning it into a play'. Wherever your ideas for plays come from, the key thing is that you are fired up by your idea.

So you have your idea – a biting political satire or a fantastical farce fuelled by a lost dog – and you've decided whether it's going to be a stichomythic two-hander or a surreally big cast piece. It could be that your story will be told in a form with which an audience is familiar and that inspires you – Chekhovian four-act movement or a fragmented narrative inspired by the plays of Martin Crimp. But what next? Some writers are planners by nature and have everything mapped out on A4 or in notebooks, and spend weeks structuring the drama before any physical action or dialogue is written. Stephen Jeffreys and Simon Stephens are good examples of playwrights who work in this way. But for others, like Robert Holman or David Storey, often even thinking of the possible shape of a play is an anathema, and structuring is a block to them. They like to start with an image or a line, or even a blank page, and find out what 'it' is as they go along. I'm somewhere in the middle; I need to do a little bit of planning to get me going and to avoid false starts, but if there's too much plotting in advance it becomes drained of life. It's true, too, that each play I've written has been made in a different way. So it seems there's not only as many ways to write a play as there are playwrights.

In the absence of a right way to do it, the best thing is just to get on and do your own thing, what feels right for you – anything really, as long as you write. 'Don't get it right, get it written', is how it goes. I always remind myself that I'm under no obligation to show anyone what I've written, so I try not to fear anything. If what I write is rubbish, I can just chuck it away. If what I write is promising but not perfect, I can come back to it later and improve it. The main thing is to write and get to the end. And when you've got to the end, you go back to the beginning again and work on it until you can do no more.

Final draft to producer

When you feel your play is complete and that you've done all you can on it for now, what next? Resist reaching for the stamps or hitting the 'Send' button on your email, and have some time away from it – at least a week or two. Often after the intensive work on a first draft, one comes back to it feeling refreshed both in perspective and in terms of renewed energy. And when you can do no more to improve your script, get one or two (certainly no more than three) people to read it. You need people who will read the script properly and give an honest and generous opinion. They may be a partner, a friend, a colleague or, if you have such a connection, someone who works in the theatre. Choose your readers carefully because you don't want anyone who will focus solely on criticising your script and consequently demoralise you at this stage, and neither do you want unqualified praise as they think this is what you want to hear.

I tend to send out what is in reality a third draft. I usually do a second draft after leaving it for between two and four weeks and then a third draft, which is provoked a bit by the responses or questions of one or two trusted readers. That's my practice now as an established writer, just as it was when I started writing. Today, almost all my work is commissioned but when I first began writing and would send out a play unsolicited, I had some wise advice from playwright Mark Ravenhill. He said I should concentrate on submitting my play to two or three theatres where I believed the play might be of interest and welcome, and where I would like to work. I still think that's good advice. One must be realistic about how few plays that are sent unsolicited actually attract the attention of producing theatres. And plays that are sent unsolicited to too many theatres can often have a feeling of being dog-eared and rejected by everyone, making it harder for those plays to get on anywhere.

Since the mid-1990s, many theatres have grown substantive play development programmes and it is a normal requirement now for new plays to undergo substantial rewrites with the producer's notes in mind. Readings and workshops often take place to see how the scripts work with actors. There's a wide-ranging philosophical debate within the theatre about how much theatres ought to be actively involved in the rewriting of plays and what good it does. My feeling is that writers ought to take on the ideas of theatre professionals when they are good, to be unafraid of saying when you are unsure, and to say 'no' when you don't like the proposed changes to your script. While a network of collaboration brings a play to life, writers must take responsibility for their authorship. Active collaboration is good; passive concession is bad. Around this time, it may be appropriate to get an agent. Most theatres will recommend agents and help you meet those who might be sympathetic to your work.

Rehearsals, production and previews

The play is going ahead. Often the first person you hear from is the theatre's director of marketing as they need to prepare the copy and images for your play for the season's brochure and other publicity. In new writing theatres it is normal for most elements of the pre-production and production of a play to involve the writer. This includes input on the choice of director and creative team, casting the actors, progress of the set design, the development of a marketing and sales strategy, press and media interviews, and even invitations to attend fundraising events for the theatre.

But of course the most significant contribution that the writer makes is to the rehearsal process, particularly in the first week of rehearsal. The acting company and creative team are hungry to mine the writer for every scrap of useful information which may help the play's production. The writer is very much at the centre of the process and what he or she says about their play or how it may be acted and staged has great power. I know from experience how invaluable a playwright's contribution can be to the production of his or her play, both from discussion of the text in rehearsals and from informal discussions during tea breaks, at lunch, or in the pub after rehearsals. Generally, most of what a writer says is useful but care needs to be taken not to squeeze the air from others' contributions.

Sometimes rewrites in rehearsals can be challenging. Changing the odd word or line isn't often contentious but when whole scenes are being cut or rewritten, the excitement of making the play better on the rehearsal room floor should be approached with caution.

Actors tend to think of the script from their character's perspective rather than seeing the writer's whole vision. And, as the point of rehearsal is to practise something until it is right, I'd be wary of actors or directors who want to make changes too quickly.

After the first week or so it is usual and advisable for the writer not to attend rehearsals. Rehearsals can become sticky and actors may grapple with learning their lines. When the writer makes a return towards the end of rehearsals to see bits of the play worked without scripts or a run through, the writer's fresh perspective is very useful to the director.

As public performances approach, the playwright can make everyone feel good about the work by encouraging the company after rehearsals, buying the first drink in the pub, and making the tea during breaks. However, sometimes the writer has to be brave if things aren't right and late changes need to be made to adjust a performance or the staging, etc.

Some writers don't attend all the previews but I do, as most directors continue working and rehearsing the play right up until opening night. You can learn a huge amount by watching the play with an audience, but I have two points of caution. Firstly, you have to be realistic about what is achievable before the opening night. Secondly, while it is important to learn from audience responses, particularly if the storytelling isn't clear or a joke doesn't work properly, I'd stay away from the discussion forums of theatre websites which are routinely populated by people who get off on abusing early performances of plays.

Opening nights are nerve-racking evenings for the writer and seeing the critics and guests forming a crush at the theatre bar can prompt the urge to run away, and for this reason some directors and playwrights don't watch their press night performances. I couldn't be absent as I feel I have to be there for my actors; it is gruelling and all you can do is will the actors and crew on and keep your nerve.

The working writer

Hopefully, the play is a hit and it's a great experience. I tend to see the play once a week because you can learn so much from seeing it again and again and experiencing how it changes and grows over its run.

Often, however successful (or not) a first play is, just the fact that it has been produced will attract the interest of other theatre producers, often radio interviews and sometimes television. If your agent is doing their job, he or she will have brought some of these people to see your play with the hope of opening up future opportunities for you. Offers of commissions for rival theatres, finding yourself pitching radio, television and film ideas, and sometimes being approached to adapt an old play, book or film are all commonplace, particularly if your play is a success.

But the most important thing for the working playwright is to focus on the next play. The longer you leave it after your first play closes the harder it gets to begin something new, and the bigger deal it will seem. So my advice is just to start where you began all those months and years ago, and think about something which in some way intrigues you.

David Eldridge is the author of *Under the Blue Sky*, *The Knot of the Heart*, *In Basildon* and many other plays and adaptations, such as his version of *Miss Julie* by August Strindberg, which ran to critical acclaim at the Royal Exchange Theatre in 2012. His play *Holy Warriors* was premiered at Shakespeare's Globe in 2014 and his screenplay of Hallie Rubenhold's *The Woman in Red* was broadcast on BBC2 in 2015. In August 2015 BBC2 broadcast his screenplay for a 90-minute film *The Scandalous Lady W*. David teaches Creative Writing at Birkbeck, University of London. His latest play is *Beginning*, which premièred at the National Theatre's Dorfman Theatre in 2017 before transferring to London's West End in January 2018. You can find him on Twitter @deldridgewriter.

Writing about theatre: reviews, interviews and more

Mark Fisher compares popular perceptions of the theatre critic with the realities, and outlines what it takes to succeed in the business.

The critic

In the award-winning movie *Birdman*, Michael Keaton plays Riggan Thomson, a mainstream Hollywood actor trying to earn some late-career credibility. He's banking on people seeing him in a different light if he has a Broadway hit with his adaptation of a Raymond Carver story. As opening night approaches, the stakes are high. He loses his lead actor, his last-minute replacement is an unpredictable maverick and his budget is at breaking point.

As the tensions mount, he comes across Tabitha Dickinson in a bar. Played by Lindsay Duncan, she is the lead theatre critic of the *New York Times* and seems to exist less as a character in her own right than as a projection of his actorly neuroses.

In the short time she is in the film, this is what we learn about her:

- She is always alone. We first see her perched at the end of a counter having a drink and writing longhand in a notepad. In the theatre, she sits at the end of a row and leaves before the rest of the audience.
- She is prepared to wield the power of the *New York Times* to shut down a show that she hasn't even seen – at least, she says she is. Having decided Thomson is indulging in a vanity project, she regards him as a threat to Broadway's artistic standards. She tells him she will give him a bad review on principle.
- She gets it all wrong. When, finally, she does file a rave review, she appears not to have realised that the onstage violence was a genuine suicide attempt.

Watching the movie as a theatre critic, I naturally tried to weigh this portrayal against my own experience. If I were the sensitive type, I'd be worried. This is especially the case because the majority of fictional critics share the same characteristics. In films, novels and television programmes, my profession is dominated by misanthropic loners, arrogant opinion-mongers, writers who love the sound of their own voice and destructive zealots who detest the theatre – unless, of course, they happen to be having an affair with someone on stage. Variations on this theme include Addison DeWitt in *All About Eve*, Sheridan Whiteside in *The Man Who Came to Dinner* and Moon and Birdboot in Tom Stoppard's *The Real Inspector Hound.*

Critical characteristics

For anyone considering a career as a theatre critic, it's reasonable to wonder not so much whether the characteristics described above pertain to you, but whether you're prepared for other people to see you in this light. To the theatre profession, you can seem like the only sober guest at the party, the spoilsport who is all head and no heart, the one who's prepared to break the magic spell that keeps the whole enterprise alive. They may not want to be your friend any more.

In reality, the quality common to nearly all the critics I have known is their love of theatre. The job involves long journeys to out-of-the-way venues, spending evenings at work when you could be with friends and family, and sitting through mediocre shows that were not made for someone like you in the first place. Only someone with blind optimism and a passionate belief in the artform would sign up to such working conditions. I've seen cynical critics write entertainingly, but they invariably burn out in a matter of months. In real life, the negativity of a fictional critic is not sustainable.

There is a kind of truth, though, in the solitariness of *Birdman*'s Tabitha. Theatre criticism suits lone wolves. You may be friendly and sociable in the right circumstances, but when it comes to the job, it's just you, your opinion and a blank computer screen. It's not something you can do collectively. You can't get a friend to help. Everything is down to you. This takes a certain resourcefulness. You need to be self-motivated or, at least, motivated by the pressure of a deadline (and not freaked by it) and happy in your own company. You have to be content to work antisocial hours in sociable circumstances. When those around you are on their feet applauding or wiping the tears from their eyes, you have to be thinking of a catchy first sentence.

Becoming a critic

When I told people I was writing a book called *How to Write About Theatre* (Bloomsbury Methuen Drama 2015), some questioned my timing. After all, if you read anything about criticism these days, it tends to be about newspapers cutting back on their arts coverage and laying critics off. Shouldn't I have called it *How Not to Write About Theatre*? Certainly, it seems unlikely that a journalist starting today would have quite the career trajectory I have enjoyed. I was employed in the late 1980s by the *List* magazine, then a fortnightly arts and entertainment guide, and now, since 2015, a predominantly online publication. My first job there was as a production assistant, but with my drama degree and previous interest in writing, it was perhaps inevitable that I would start contributing to the theatre section. Eventually I became the theatre editor and then took up a freelance career in which I founded and edited a quarterly theatre magazine, became theatre critic for the *Herald* in Glasgow and, latterly, Scottish theatre critic for the *Guardian*.

Even if I add that most of the money I have earned has come from feature writing rather than reviewing, there's no question that today's critics have fewer paid opportunities open to them. There are, however, more opportunities than ever for unpaid criticism – and more people than ever writing about theatre. No need for contacts or job interviews, you can just set up a blog right now and start writing. This is having two beneficial effects. One is that a wider range of voices are being heard and the old cultural hegemony – what Nicholas Hytner called the 'dead white men' of the critical establishment – is breaking down. The other is that the idea of what constitutes a 'proper' review is being upturned: the interactive and responsive nature of the internet is well suited to a discursive form of criticism, one that needn't be the final word, just an addition to the debate.

The good news for writers is that it's now possible to make an impression from a standing start. If you have something to say and an arresting way of saying it, you can build up a reputation on the internet without the endorsement of a traditional media publication. The bad news – until somebody comes up with a better idea – is that you're likely to have to treat your writing as a kind of loss leader, an investment in your future career that may (or may not) pay dividends at some later date. The industrious Matt Trueman (http://matttrueman.co.uk) is a case in point. From being a predominantly online critic, he has gone on to pick up paid work from publications including the *Guardian*, the *Stage*, *What's On Stage* and *Variety*.

How typical this route will be in the future remains to be seen, although, as a former editor, I would expect anyone with a serious interest in becoming a professional theatre critic to be doing the job without waiting to be asked. Whether you get published in a student newspaper, a zine, your own website or someone else's, you'll never get a foothold on the critical ladder unless you first do it of your own volition. Without that, you will have no opportunity to develop your writing skills, learn how to translate a live experience into words and extend your knowledge of contemporary theatre. It's also a way to advertise yourself. If you can't show an editor examples of your work, he or she will have nothing to go on and no reason to employ you.

For the first-time critic, the question of authority comes into play. 'Who do you think you are, passing comment on other people's work – what makes you so special?' Your self-confidence is the only adequate answer to this question, especially as there is no expected qualification for the job. Yes, you can study drama, yes, you can take a course in journalism – and there's a strong case to say you should – but nobody will ask to see your certificates. Criticism is a practical occupation and the evidence of whether you can do it or not is in your writing. Taking a course will widen your knowledge, develop your skills and give you confidence, but it will be your passion for communication and passion for theatre, as well as an insatiable desire to get better at both, that will make you a good critic.

Features, interviews and other writing

If you have such a passion, there's no reason you should confine your writing to criticism. On the contrary, there are many more opportunities for writing about theatre – and at greater length – than in reviewing it. For the keen-eyed journalist, the theatre is a rich source of material. The people who work in it, the relationship it has with the wider community, the ideas it deals with and the pragmatics of putting it on all offer potential stories.

Feature writing can range from interviews with the theatremakers to research-based pieces inspired by the themes of a production. If one of the creative team has a fascinating story to tell, you may be able to write a human-interest piece that is only tangentially connected to the show. You may find outlets for think-pieces and blogs about theatrical issues or news stories about artistic fall-outs and funding problems. Think too about publications aimed at special-interest groups such as lighting designers, educationalists and marketing managers. You may also find other ways to exploit your specialist knowledge – I have given seminars to theatre students and led cultural tours for foreign visitors, for example.

Staff or freelance?

My assumption underlying all this is that you will be working freelance. That's not entirely fair because, of course, there are many full-time staff with some responsibility for theatre, whether it be a BBC arts reporter, a theatre editor on a national newspaper or an in-house critic. I worked as an editor back at the *List* magazine from 2000 to 2003, but have been freelance for the majority of my career. Staff jobs have the advantage of relative security, a team of colleagues, pension schemes, wage rises and some kind of career structure. Unsurprisingly, there is tough competition to get one.

It takes a particular temperament to cope with the freelance life. You have to be resilient, thick-skinned and comfortable with unpredictability. If you can't stomach the thought of not knowing where next week's money is going to come from, it probably isn't for you. But in uncertain economic times, when increasing numbers are shifting into portfolio careers, your adaptability can be an asset. It's also a little more likely that you'll be able to spread your knowledge of theatre around a number of publications than to find one publication that can sustain a single theatre-related job.

If that's a life you're happy to lead, then be prepared for a few knocks, keep on generating the ideas and say yes to anything that comes your way (worry about practicalities later). As with any journalistic writing, you need to be accurate, reliable and punctual. If you have a dazzling turn of phrase, your editors will like you even more, but most important is being easy to work with. And as far as the theatre community is concerned, the more you can let your passion and erudition show through, the better they will appreciate you and the more you will enjoy yourself.

Mark Fisher is one of Scotland's foremost commentators on the arts. With over 25 years' experience, he is the Scottish theatre critic for the *Guardian*, a former editor of the *List* and a freelance contributor to *Variety*, the *Scotsman* and *Scotland on Sunday*. He is the author of *The Edinburgh Fringe Survival Guide* (Bloomsbury Methuen Drama 2012) and *How to Write About Theatre* (Bloomsbury Methuen Drama 2015), and editor of *The XTC Bumper Book of Fun for Boys and Girls* (Mark Fisher Ltd 2017).

See also...

- *FAQs for writers*, page 713
- *Income tax*, page 715
- *National Insurance contributions and social security benefits*, page 725

Theatre producers

This list is divided into metropolitan theatres (below), regional theatres (page 411) and touring companies (page 416). See also the articles in this section, which start on page 401 and *Literary agents for television, film, radio and theatre* on page 765.

There are various types of theatre companies and it is helpful to know their respective remits. Many of those that specialise in new writing are based in London (for example, Hampstead Theatre, Royal Court, Bush Theatre, Soho Theatre), but also include the Royal Exchange Manchester, Everyman Theatre Liverpool, West Yorkshire Playhouse etc. Regional repertory theatre companies are based in towns and cities across the country and may produce new plays as part of their repertoire. Commercial production companies and independent producers typically are unsubsidised profit-making theatre producers who may occasionally be interested in new plays to take on tour or to present in the West End. Small- and/or middle-scale companies are companies (mostly touring) which may exist to explore or promote specific themes or are geared towards specific kinds of audiences.

Individuals also have a role. Independent theatre practitioners include, for example, actors who may be looking for interesting plays in which to appear, and independent theatre producers such as young directors or producers who are looking for plays to produce at the onset of their career. There are also drama schools and amateur dramatics companies. See the *Actors and Performers Yearbook* (published annually by Bloomsbury Methuen Drama) for further information.

LONDON

The Bridge Theatre

3 Potters Fields Park, London SE1 2SG
tel 0333 320 0052
email info@bridgetheatre.co.uk
website www.bridgetheatre.co.uk
Twitter @bridgetheatre
Founders Nicholas Hytner, Nick Starr

The home of the London Theatre Company. Commissions and produces new shows, as well as staging occasional classics. Can seat up to 900 in its adaptable auditorium.

Bush Theatre

7 Uxbridge Road, London W12 8LJ
tel (admin) 020-8743 3584
email info@bushtheatre.co.uk
website www.bushtheatre.co.uk
Twitter @bushtheatre
Artistic Director Madani Younis

The Bush has produced hundreds of groundbreaking premieres since its inception in 1972 – many of them Bush commissions – and has hosted guest productions by leading companies and artists from around the world. Check the website for the unsolicited submissions policy and guidelines on when and how to submit.

Michael Codron Plays Ltd

Aldwych Theatre Offices, Aldwych, London WC2B 4DF
tel 020-7240 8291

Finborough Theatre

118 Finborough Road, London SW10 9ED
tel 020-7244 7439
email admin@finboroughtheatre.co.uk
website www.finboroughtheatre.co.uk
Facebook www.facebook.com/FinboroughTheatre
Twitter @finborough
Artistic Director Neil McPherson

Presents new writing, revivals of neglected plays from 1800 onwards, music theatre and UK premieres of foreign work, particularly from Ireland, Scotland, the USA and Canada. Unsolicited scripts are accepted, but see literary policy on website before sending. Founded 1980.

Robert Fox Ltd

6 Beauchamp Place, London SW3 1NG
tel 020-7584 6855
email info@robertfoxltd.com
website www.robertfoxlimited.com
Twitter @RobertFoxLtd

Independent theatre and film production company. Stages productions mainly in the West End and on Broadway. Not currently accepting submissions. Founded 1980.

Hampstead Theatre

Eton Avenue, London NW3 3EU
tel 020-7449 4200
email info@hampsteadtheatre.com
website www.hampsteadtheatre.com
Twitter @Hamps_Theatre
Literary Manager Will Mortimer

The company's theatre, built in 2003, was designed with writers in mind, allowing for flexible staging within an intimate main house auditorium and a second studio space. The theatre accepts unsolicited plays from UK-based writers via email only at certain points in the year. See website for full details of the submission process and new writing initiatives.

Bill Kenwright Ltd

BKL House, 1 Venice Walk, London W2 1RR
tel 020-7446 6200
email info@kenwright.com
website www.kenwright.com
Twitter @BKL_Productions
Managing Director Bill Kenwright

Award-winning commercial theatre and film production company, presenting revivals and new works for the West End, international and regional theatres. Productions include: *Blood Brothers*, *Joseph and the Amazing Technicolor Dreamcoat*, *Evita*, *Cabaret* and *The Sound of Music*. Films include: *Another Mother's Son*, *Broken*, *Cheri* and *Don't Go Breaking My Heart*.

King's Head Theatre

115 Upper Street, London N1 1QN
tel 020-7226 8561
email alan@kingsheadtheatre.com
website www.kingsheadtheatre.com
Twitter @KingsHeadThtr
Artistic Director Adam Spreadbury-Maher

Off-West End theatre producing premieres of plays and musicals.

Lyric Hammersmith

Lyric Square, King Street, London W6 0QL
tel 020-8741 6850
email enquiries@lyric.co.uk
website www.lyric.co.uk
Twitter @LyricHammer
Artistic Director Sean Holmes (stepping down Oct 18), *Executive Director* Sian Alexander

West London's largest producing and receiving theatre. Unsolicited scripts for in-house productions not accepted.

Neal Street Productions Ltd

1st Floor, 26–28 Neal Street, London WC2H 9QQ
tel 020-7240 8890
email post@nealstreetproductions.com
website www.nealstreetproductions.com
Twitter @NealStProds
Founders Sam Mendes, Pippa Harris, Caro Newling

Independent film, TV and theatre producer of new work and revivals. No unsolicited scripts. Founded 2003.

The Old Red Lion Theatre

418 St John Street, London EC1V 4NJ
tel 020-7837 7816
email info@oldredliontheatre.co.uk
website www.oldredliontheatre.co.uk
Twitter @ORLTheatre
Executive Director Damien Devine

Interested in contemporary pieces, especially from unproduced writers. No funding: incoming production company pays to rent the theatre. All submissions via email. Founded 1977.

Orange Tree Theatre

1 Clarence Street, Richmond, Surrey TW9 2SA
tel 020-8940 0141
email literary@orangetreetheatre.co.uk
website www.orangetreetheatre.co.uk
Twitter @OrangeTreeThtr
Artistic Director Paul Miller, *Literary Associate* Guy Jones

Producing theatre presenting a mix of new and rediscovered plays in an intimate in-the-round space. Unsolicited work is not accepted throughout the year. Writers should visit www.orangetreetheatre.co.uk/about/writers for up-to-date information about opportunities. Enquiries can be addressed to the Literary Associate at the email address above.

Polka Theatre

240 The Broadway, London SW19 1SB
tel 020-8543 8320
email stephen@polkatheatre.com
website www.polkatheatre.com
Twitter @polkatheatre
Artistic Director Peter Glanville

Theatre of new work, with targeted commissions. Exclusively for children aged 0–14, the Main Theatre seats 300 and the Adventure Theatre seats 70. Programmed 18 months to two years in advance. Founded 1967.

The Questors Theatre

12 Mattock Lane, London W5 5BQ
tel 020-8567 0011
email enquiries@questors.org.uk
website www.questors.org.uk
Twitter @questorstheatre
Executive Director and Chief Executive Andrea Bath

Largest independent community theatre in Europe. Produces around 20 shows a year, specialising in modern and classical world drama. No unsolicited scripts.

Royal Court Theatre

(English Stage Company Ltd)
Sloane Square, London SW1W 8AS
tel 020-7565 5050
email info@royalcourttheatre.com
website www.royalcourttheatre.com
Twitter @royalcourt
Literary Manager Chris Campbell

Programmes original plays that investigate the problems and possibilities of our time. Looks for outstanding plays which are original in form or theme and unlikely to be produced elsewhere.

Royal National Theatre

South Bank, London SE1 9PX
tel 020-7452 3333
email scripts@nationaltheatre.org.uk
website www.nationaltheatre.org.uk
Twitter @NationalTheatre
Artistic Director Rufus Norris, *New Work Administrator* Sarah Clarke

New Work Department considers submissions from the UK and Ireland. No synopses, treatments or hard copy submissions; full scripts can be sent as pdfs or Word documents to the email addess above.

Soho Theatre

21 Dean Street, London W1D 3NE
tel 020-7478 0117
email deirdre@sohotheatre.com
website www.sohotheatre.com
Twitter @sohotheatre
Artistic Director Steve Marmion

Aims to discover and develop new playwrights, produce a year-round programme of new plays and attract new audiences. Producing venue of new plays, cabaret and comedy. The Writers' Centre offers an extensive unsolicited script-reading service and provides a range of development schemes such as writers' attachment programmes, commissions, seed bursaries and more. Three venues: the main Soho Theatre has 150 seats; Soho Upstairs is self-contained and seats 90; and Soho Downstairs is a 150-seat capacity cabaret space. Also theatre bar, restaurant, offices, rehearsal, writing and meeting rooms. Founded 1972.

Tabard Theatre

2 Bath Road, London W4 1LW
tel 020-8995 6035
email info@tabardtheatre.co.uk
website www.tabardtheatre.co.uk
Twitter @TabardTheatreUK

Hosts a variety of live entertainment, from classical adaptations to revivals and new musical works. Also produces in-house shows.

Theatre Royal, Stratford East

Gerry Raffles Square, London E15 1BN
tel 020-8534 7374
website www.stratfordeast.com
Twitter @stratfordeast
Artistic Director Nadia Fall

Middle-scale producing theatre. Specialises in new writing, including developing contemporary British musicals. Welcomes new plays that are unproduced, full in length, and which relate to its diverse multicultural, Black and Asian audience.

The Tricycle Theatre Company

Tricycle Theatre, 269 Kilburn High Road, London NW6 7JR
tel 020-7372 6611
email info@tricycle.co.uk
website www.tricycle.co.uk
Facebook www.facebook.com/TricycleTheatre
Twitter @tricycletheatre
Artistic Director Indhu Rubasingham

Presents at least six productions per year, aiming to provoke debate and engage the audience. Many of these are commissioned and written specifically for the theatre, or are programmed in collaboration with national or international companies. Unable to accept unsolicited submissions.

Unicorn Theatre

147 Tooley Street, London SE1 2HZ
tel 020-7645 0560
email hello@unicorntheatre.com
website www.unicorntheatre.com
Facebook www.facebook.com/unicorntheatre
Twitter @unicorn_theatre
Artistic Director Purni Morell, *Executive Director* Anneliese Davidsen

Produces a year-round programme of theatre for children and young people under 21. In-house productions of full-length plays with professional casts are staged across two auditoria, alongside visiting companies and education work. Unicorn rarely commissions plays from writers who are new to it, but it is keen to hear from writers who are interested in working with the theatre in the future. Do not send unsolicited MSS, but rather a short statement describing why you would like to write for the Unicorn along with a CV or a summary of your relevant experience.

White Bear Theatre Club

138 Kennington Park Road, London SE11 4DJ
tel 020-7793 9193
email info@whitebeartheatre.co.uk
website http://whitebeartheatre.co.uk/
Twitter @WhiteBearTheatr

Artistic Director Michael Kingsbury

Metropolitan new writing theatre company. Welcomes scripts from new writers: send queries to whitebearliterary@gmail.com. Founded 1988.

Young Vic Theatre Company
66 The Cut, London SE1 8LZ
tel 020-7922 2922
email info@youngvic.org
website www.youngvic.org
Facebook www.facebook.com/youngvictheatre
Twitter @youngvictheatre
Artistic Director Kwame Kwei-Armah

Leading London producing theatre. Founded 1969.

REGIONAL

Abbey Theatre Amharclann na Mainistreach
26 Lower Abbey Street, Dublin D01 K0F1, Republic of Ireland
tel +353 (0)1 8872200
email info@abbeytheatre.ie
website www.abbeytheatre.ie
Twitter @AbbeyTheatre
Directors Graham McLaren, Neil Murray, *New Work* Jesse Weaver, Patricia Malpas

Ireland's national theatre. Produces new Irish writing and contemporary productions of classic plays.

Yvonne Arnaud Theatre Management Ltd
Millbrook, Guildford, Surrey GU1 3UX
tel (01483) 440077
email yat@yvonne-arnaud.co.uk
website www.yvonne-arnaud.co.uk
Twitter @YvonneArnaud

Producing theatre which also receives productions.

The Belgrade Theatre
Belgrade Square, Coventry CV1 1GS
tel 024-7625 6431
email admin@belgrade.co.uk
website www.belgrade.co.uk
Twitter @BelgradeTheatre
Artistic Director Hamish Glen

Repertory theatre producing drama, comedy and musicals. Does not accept unsolicited scripts; email short synopses first to the address above. See also Word document on script submissions, posted online.

Birmingham Repertory Theatre Ltd
Broad Street, Birmingham B1 2EP
tel 0121 245 2000
email stage.door@birmingham-rep.co.uk
website www.birmingham-rep.co.uk
Twitter @BirminghamRep
Artistic Director Roxana Silbert

Producing theatre company and pioneer of new plays whose programme includes new versions of the classics as well as contemporary writing. Recently refurbished alongside the Library of Birmingham, the theatre now includes a 300-seat studio theatre. Founded 1913.

The Bootleg Theatre Company
23 Burgess Green, Bishopdown, Salisbury, Wilts. SP1 3EL
tel (01722) 421476
email colinburden281@gmail.com
website www.bootlegtheatre.com
Contact Colin Burden

New writing theatre company whose recent productions include *Girls Allowed* by Trevor Suthers, *A Rainy Night in Soho* by Stephen Giles, and *The Squeaky Clean* by Roger Goldsmith. Also produces compilation productions of monologues/duologues: these have included *15 Minutes of Fame*, *Tales from The Street* and *Parting Shots* with contributions from Mark Bromley, Annie Cooper, Nick Le Mesurier, Sarah Ryan and Paul Townsend. 2018 productions include *The Other Half of Me* by Sarah Ryan, a compilation based on true crime cases; the company is also co–producing two short filmed documentaries. Founded 1985.

Bristol Old Vic
King Street, Bristol BS1 4ED
tel 0117 949 3993
email admin@bristololdvic.org.uk
website www.bristololdvic.org.uk
Twitter @BristolOldVic
Artistic Director Tom Morris

Oldest theatre auditorium in UK (opened in 1766). See website for more details. Founded 1946.

Chichester Festival Theatre
Oaklands Park, Chichester, West Sussex PO19 6AP
tel (01243) 784437
website www.cft.org.uk
Twitter @chichesterFT
Artistic Director Daniel Evans

Stages annual Summer Festival Season April–Oct in Festival and Minerva Theatres together with a year-round education programme, autumn touring programme and youth theatre Christmas show. Unsolicited scripts are not accepted.

Contact Theatre Company
Oxford Road, Manchester M15 6JA
tel 0161 274 0600
website www.contactmcr.com
Twitter @ContactMcr
Artistic Director Matt Fenton, *Head of Creative Development* Suzie Henderson

Multidisciplinary arts organisation focused on working with and for young people aged from 13 and above.

Creation Theatre Company

tel (01865) 766266
email boxoffice@creationtheatre.co.uk
website www.creationtheatre.co.uk
Facebook www.facebook.co.uk/CreationTheatre
Twitter @creationtheatre
Chief Executive Lucy Askew, *Producer* Ginny Graham, *Education Manager* Crissy O'Donovan

Produces site-specific adaptations of classic texts all over Oxford in unusual spaces, from castles to antique mirror tents, college gardens, bookshops and factories. Also stages summer productions of Shakespeare and eccentric family shows at Christmas, as well as a wide range of education events and workshops. No unsolicited manuscripts.

Curve

Rutland Street, Leicester LE1 1SB
tel 0116 242 3560
email contactus@curvetheatre.co.uk
website www.curveonline.co.uk
Twitter @CurveLeicester
Chief Executive Chris Stafford, *Artistic Director* Nikolai Foster

Regional producing theatre company.

Derby Theatre

Theatre Walk, Westfield, St Peter's Quarter, Derby DE1 2NF
tel (01332) 255800
email tickets@derbyplayhouse.co.uk
website www.derbytheatre.co.uk
Twitter @DerbyTheatre
Artistic Director Sarah Brigham, *Creative Learning Director* Caroline Barth

Regional producing and receiving theatre.

Druid

Flood Street, Galway H91 PWX5, Republic of Ireland
tel +353 (0)91 568660
email info@druid.ie
website www.druid.ie
Twitter @DruidTheatre
Artistic Director Garry Hynes

Producing theatre company presenting a wide range of plays, with an emphasis on new Irish writing. New submission window for scripts: July–November (see website for details). Tours nationally and internationally.

The Dukes

Moor Lane, Lancaster LA1 1QE
tel (01524) 598505
email info@dukes-lancaster.org
website www.dukes-lancaster.org
Twitter @TheDukesTheatre
Artistic Director Sarah Punshon

Producing theatre and cultural centre. Its Young Writers scheme was launched in January 2017. See website for up-to-date information about the theatre's productions and programming approach.

Dundee Rep and Scottish Dance Theatre Limited

Tay Square, Dundee DD1 1PB
tel (01382) 227684
email info@dundeereptheatre.co.uk
website www.dundeereptheatre.co.uk
Twitter @DundeeRep
Artistic Director (Dundee Rep) and Joint Chief Executive Andrew Panton

Regional repertory theatre company with resident ensemble. Mix of classics, musicals and new commissions.

Everyman Theatre Cheltenham

7 Regent Street, Cheltenham, Glos. GL50 1HQ
tel (01242) 512515
email admin@everymantheatre.org.uk
website www.everymantheatre.org.uk
Twitter @Everymanchelt
Creative Director Paul Milton

Regional presenting and producing theatre promoting a wide range of plays. Small-scale experimental, youth and educational work encouraged in The Studio Theatre. Contact the Creative Director before submitting material.

Exeter Northcott Theatre

Stocker Road, Exeter, Devon EX4 4QB
tel (01392) 722414
email info@exeternorthcott.co.uk
website www.exeternorthcott.co.uk
Twitter @ExeterNorthcott
Artistic and Executive Director Paul Jepson

460-seat producing and receiving venue offering a varied programme of shows and touring productions.

The 42nd Theatre Company

Blyth Court, Blyth Road, Bromley, Kent BR1 3RY
email literary@the42ndtheatrecompany.com
website www.the42ndtheatrecompany.com
Facebook www.facebook.com/the42ndtheatrecompany
Twitter @The42ndTheatreC
Artistic Director Adam Bambrough

Small theatre company dedicated to developing new plays by writers who have never had their work produced before. Submissions welcome all year; see website for guidelines. All work commissioned will be compensated. Founded 2013.

Harrogate Theatre

Oxford Street, Harrogate, North Yorkshire HG1 1QF
tel (01423) 502710

email info@harrogatetheatre.co.uk
website www.harrogatetheatre.co.uk
Twitter @HGtheatre
Chief Executive David Bown

Predominately a receiving house, Harrogate Theatre rarely produces productions in-house. Unsolicited scripts not accepted.

HOME: Theatre

2 Tony Wilson Place, First Street, Manchester M15 4FN
tel 0161 200 1500
email info@homemcr.org
website www.homemcr.org
Twitter @HOME_mcr
Artistic Director Walter Meierjohann

World classic drama, international and new writing, adaptations and cross-art projects. Formed following the merger of Cornerhouse and Library Theatre Company. HOME's purpose-built centre for international contemporary art, theatre and film opened in Spring 2015.

Live Theatre

Broad Chare, Quayside, Newcastle upon Tyne NE1 3DQ
tel 0191 232 1232
email wendy@live.org.uk
website www.live.org.uk
Twitter @LiveTheatre
Artistic Director Joe Douglas, *Operations Director* Wendy Barnfather

New writing theatre company and venue. Stages three to four productions per year of new writing, comedy, musical comedy, etc.

Liverpool Everyman and Playhouse

Liverpool and Merseyside Theatres Trust Ltd, 5–11 Hope Street, Liverpool L1 9BH
tel 0151 708 3700
email info@everymanplayhouse.com
website www.everymanplayhouse.com
Facebook www.facebook.com/everymanplayhouse
Twitter @LivEveryPlay
Executive Director Deborah Aydon, *Artistic Director* Gemma Bodinetz

Produces and presents theatre. Looks for original work from writers based within the Liverpool city region: email scripts@everymanplayhouse.com with a pdf or Word document along with a completed submission form (see website for this and further details of submission specifications).

Mercury Theatre Colchester

Balkerne Gate, Colchester, Essex CO1 1PT
tel (01206) 577006
email info@mercurytheatre.co.uk
website www.mercurytheatre.co.uk
Twitter @mercurytheatre
Artistic Director Daniel Buckroyd

Active producing theatre in East Anglia, aiming to put theatre at the heart of the community it serves and to make work in Colchester that reaches audiences regionally and nationally. Runs a comprehensive Creative Learning & Talent programme to support artists and theatre-makers at all stages of their development.

The New Theatre: Dublin

The New Theatre, Temple Bar, 43 East Essex Street, Dublin D02 XH92, Republic of Ireland
tel +353 (0)1 6703361
email info@thenewtheatre.com
website www.thenewtheatre.com
Artistic Director Anthony Fox

Innovative theatre supporting plays by new Irish writers and others whose work deals with issues pertaining to contemporary Irish society. Welcomes scripts from new writers. Seats 66 people. Founded 1997.

New Vic Theatre

Etruria Road, Newcastle under Lyme ST5 0JG
tel (01782) 717954
email admin@newvictheatre.org.uk
website www.newvictheatre.org.uk
Twitter @NewVicTheatre
Artistic Director Theresa Heskins, *Executive Director* Fiona Wallace

Europe's first purpose-built theatre-in-the-round, presenting classics, musical theatre, contemporary plays and new plays.

The New Wolsey Theatre

Civic Drive, Ipswich, Suffolk IP1 2AS
tel (01473) 295900
email info@wolseytheatre.co.uk
website www.wolseytheatre.co.uk
Facebook www.facebook.com/NewWolsey
Twitter @NewWolsey
Chief Executive Sarah Holmes, *Artistic Director* Peter Rowe

Mix of producing and presenting in main house and studio. Hosts annual Pulse Festival. Founded 2000.

Northern Stage (Theatrical Productions) Ltd

Barras Bridge, Newcastle upon Tyne NE1 7RH
tel 0191 242 7210
email info@northernstage.co.uk
website www.northernstage.co.uk
Twitter @northernstage
Executive Director Kate Denby, *Artistic Director* Lorne Campbell

The largest producing theatre company in the north east of England. Presents local, national and international theatre across three stages and runs an extensive participation programme.

Nottingham Playhouse

Nottingham Playhouse Trust Ltd, Wellington Circus, Nottingham NG1 5AF
tel 0115 947 4361
website www.nottinghamplayhouse.co.uk
Twitter @NottmPlayhouse
Artistic Director Adam Penford

Works closely with communities of Nottingham and Nottinghamshire. Seeks to nurture new writers from the East Midlands primarily. Will accept two submissions a year per writer but asks that the second one is not sent until feedback has been received on the first. Scripts should be sent as a pdf or Word document to the email address above, or can be posted; a completed submission form (see www.nottinghamplayhouse.co.uk/about-us/script-submissions/) should also be included.

NST, Nuffield Southampton Theatres

University Road, Southampton SO17 1TR
tel 023-8031 5500
email info@nstheatres.co.uk
website www.nstheatres.co.uk
Twitter @nstheatres

Repertory theatre producing straight plays and occasional musicals. A mix of re-imagined classics and new plays.

Octagon Theatre

Howell Croft South, Bolton BL1 1SB
tel (01204) 529407
email literary@octagonbolton.co.uk
website www.octagonbolton.co.uk
Twitter @octagontheatre
Chief Executive Roddy Gauld, *Artistic Director* Elizabeth Newman

Fully flexible professional theatre. Year-round programme of own productions and visiting companies. The Bill Naughton Studio Theatre for outreach, children's theatre, new work and emerging artists. The theatre is closed from May 2018 to Autumn 2019 for extensive remodelling: see website for information on town-centre venues during this time.

The Oldham Coliseum Theatre

Fairbottom Street, Oldham OL1 3SW
tel 0161 624 1731
email mail@coliseum.org.uk
website www.coliseum.org.uk
Twitter @OldhamColiseum
Chief Executive and Artistic Director Kevin Shaw

Interested in new work, particularly plays set in the North. Alongside the programme in its Main Auditorium, the Studio programme aims to support and showcase the best in new writing and emerging talent to explore issues that affect the local community. The theatre's learning and engagement department runs a variety of outreach programmes and courses for young people, adults and schools.

Queen's Theatre, Hornchurch

(Havering Theatre Trust Ltd)
Billet Lane, Hornchurch, Essex RM11 1QT
tel (01708) 462362
email info@queens-theatre.co.uk
website www.queens-theatre.co.uk
Twitter @QueensTheatreH
Artistic Director Douglas Rintoul, *Executive Director* Mathew Russell

500-seat producing theatre serving outer East London with a permanent company of actors/musicians presenting eight main house and two Theatre in Education (TIE) productions each year. Unsolicited scripts may be returned unread. Also offers writers' groups at various levels.

Royal Exchange Theatre Company Ltd

St Ann's Square, Manchester M2 7DH
tel 0161 833 9833
email suzanne.bell@royalexchange.co.uk
website www.royalexchange.co.uk
Facebook www.facebook.com/rx
Twitter @rxtheatre
Executive Director Mark Dobson, *Artistic Director* Sarah Frankcom, *Dramaturg* Suzanne Bell

Varied programme of major classics, new plays, musicals, contemporary British and European drama. Focus on new writing, writer development, creative collaborations and community participation.

Royal Lyceum Theatre Company

Royal Lyceum Theatre, 30b Grindlay Street, Edinburgh EH3 9AX
tel 0131 248 4800
email info@lyceum.org.uk
website www.lyceum.org.uk
Twitter @lyceumtheatre
Artistic Director David Greig

Scotland's busiest producing theatre, creating a diverse year-round programme of classic, contemporary and new drama in Edinburgh. Interested in work of Scottish writers.

Royal Shakespeare Company

The Royal Shakespeare Theatre, Waterside, Stratford-upon-Avon, Warks. CV37 6BB
tel (01789) 296655
email literary@rsc.org.uk
website www.rsc.org.uk
Twitter @TheRSC
Artistic Director Gregory Doran, *Deputy Artistic Director* Erica Whyman, *Literary Manager* Pippa Hill

On its two main stages in Stratford-upon-Avon, the RST and the Swan Theatre, the Company produces a core repertoire of Shakespeare alongside new plays and the work of Shakespeare's contemporaries. In addition, its studio theatre, The Other Place, produces festivals of cutting-edge new work. For all its stages, the Company commissions new plays, new translations and new adaptations that illuminate the themes and concerns of Shakespeare and his contemporaries for a modern audience. The Literary department does not accept unsolicited work but rather seeks out writers it wishes to work with or commission, and monitors the work of writers in production in the UK and internationally. Writers are welcome to invite the Literary department to readings, showcases or productions by emailing the address above.

Salisbury Playhouse

Malthouse Lane, Salisbury, Wilts. SP2 7RA
tel (01722) 320117; box office (01722) 320333
email info@salisburyplayhouse.com
website www.salisburyplayhouse.com
Twitter @salisburyplay
Artistic Director Gareth Machin, *Executive Director* Sebastian Warrack

Regional producing and presenting theatre with a broad programme of classical and contemporary plays in two auditoria. Does not accept unsolicited scripts. The Playhouse is committed to a programme of original drama with a particular focus on South-West writers. Please check website for current information on script submission.

Stephen Joseph Theatre

Stephen Joseph Theatre, Westborough, Scarborough, North Yorkshire YO11 1JW
tel (01723) 370540
email scripts@sjt.uk.com
website www.sjt.uk.com
Twitter @thesjt
Executive Producer Amanda Saunders, *Artistic Programme & Literary Coordinator* Fleur Hebditch

Regional repertory theatre company presenting approx. eight productions a year, many of which are premieres. Submissions should be emailed to the address above.

Sheffield Theatres

(Crucible, Crucible Studio & Lyceum)
55 Norfolk Street, Sheffield S1 1DA
tel 0114 249 5999
website www.sheffieldtheatres.co.uk
Chief Executive Dan Bates

Large-scale producing house with distinctive thrust stage; studio; Victorian proscenium arch theatre used mainly for touring productions.

Sherman Theatre

Senghennydd Road, Cardiff CF24 4YE
tel 029-2064 6900
website www.shermantheatre.co.uk
Twitter @shermantheatre
Artistic Director Rachel O'Riordan

Produces new work and revivals. Seeks to stage high-quality and innovative drama with a local, national or international perspective. Develops work by Welsh and Welsh-based writers, both in English and Welsh. Supports writers through the New Welsh Playwrights' Programme. Participatory work with youth theatres (age 5 to 25), community engagement, and mentorship of new artists. Currently unable to read and respond to unsolicited scripts. Founded 2007.

Show of Strength Theatre Company Ltd

74 Chessel Street, Bedminster, Bristol BS3 3DN
tel 0117 902 0235
email info@showofstrength.org.uk
website www.showofstrength.org.uk
Twitter @Showofstrength
Creative Producer Sheila Hannon

Small-scale company committed to producing new and unperformed work. Founded 1986.

Swansea Grand Theatre

Singleton Street, Swansea SA1 3QJ
tel (01792) 475715
email swansea.grandmarketing@swansea.gov.uk
email paul.hopkins2@swansea.gov.uk
website www.swanseagrand.co.uk
Facebook www.facebook.com/swanseagrandtheatre
Twitter @swanseagrand
Theatre Manager Paul Hopkins, *Marketing Manager* Helen Dalling

Regional receiving theatre.

Theatr Clwyd

Mold, Flintshire CH7 1YA
tel (01352) 756331
email william.james@theatrclwyd.com
website www.theatrclwyd.com
Twitter @ClwydTweets
Arts centre and producing theatre company producing up to fourteen productions each year, including work for young people, in English, Welsh and bilingually. Plays are a mix of classics, revivals, contemporary drama and new writing. Considers plays by Welsh writers or with Welsh themes and have resident writers on many productions: see website for details.

Theatre Royal Bath

Sawclose, Bath BA1 1ET
tel (01225) 448815
website www.theatreroyal.org.uk
Twitter @TheatreRBath
Director Danny Moar

One of the oldest theatres in Britain. Comprising three auditoria – the Main House, the Ustinov Studio Theatre and the Egg theatre for children and young people – the Theatre Royal offers a varied programme of entertainment all year round.

Theatre Royal Plymouth

Royal Parade, Plymouth PL1 2TR
tel (01752) 668282
website www.theatreroyal.com
Twitter @TRPlymouth
Artistic Director Simon Stokes

Specialises in the production of new plays. Its creative learning work engages young people and communities in Plymouth and beyond. The award-winning waterfront production and learning centre, TR2, offers extensive set, costume, prop-making and rehearsal facilities.

Theatre Royal Windsor

32 Thames Street, Windsor, Berks. SL4 1PS
tel (01753) 863444
email info@theatreroyalwindsor.co.uk
website www.theatreroyalwindsor.co.uk
Facebook www.facebook.com/TheatreWindsor/
Twitter @TheatreWindsor
Executive Producer Bill Kenwright, *Theatre Director* Robert Miles

Regional producing theatre presenting a wide range of productions, from classics to new plays.

Traverse Theatre

10 Cambridge Street, Edinburgh EH1 2ED
tel 0131 228 3223
website www.traverse.co.uk
Twitter @traversetheatre
Artistic Director Orla O'Loughlin

Produces and presents new theatre work from Scotland and internationally. Scripts submissions are accepted at certain points throughout the year; see the website for submission guidelines and further information.

Watford Palace Theatre

20 Clarendon Road, Watford, Herts. WD17 1JZ
tel (01923) 235455
website www.watfordpalacetheatre.co.uk
Twitter @watfordpalace
Artistic Director Brigid Larmour

Regional theatre. Produces and co-produces seasonally, both classic and contemporary drama and new writing. Accepts unsolicited scripts from writers in Hertfordshire.

West Yorkshire Playhouse

Playhouse Square, Quarry Hill, Leeds LS2 7UP
tel 0113 213 7700
website www.wyp.org.uk
Twitter @WYPlayhouse
Artistic Director James Brining, *Executive Director* Robin Hawkes, *Associate Director* Amy Leach, *Literary Associate* Jacqui Honess-Martin, *Youth Theatre Director* Gemma Woffinden

Twin auditoria complex; community theatre. Has a policy of encouraging new writing from Yorkshire and Humberside region. Its Furnace programme for artistic development allows writers at different stages of their professional journey to test out new ideas. See website for full details. The Playhouse Youth Theatre runs weekly sessions for young people aged from 5 to 19, commissions new plays for young audiences, and helps them develop a range of performance skills.

York Theatre Royal

Theatre Royal, St Leonard's Place, York YO1 7HD
tel (01904) 658162
website www.yorktheatreroyal.co.uk
Facebook www.facebook.com/yorktheatreroyal
Twitter @yorktheatre
Executive Director Tom Bird, *Artistic Director* Damian Cruden

Repertory productions, tours.

TOURING COMPANIES

Actors Touring Company

ICA, 12 Carlton Terrace, London SW1Y 5AH
tel 020-7930 6014
email atc@atctheatre.com
website www.atctheatre.com
Facebook www.facebook.com/actorstouringcompany
Twitter @ATCLondon
Artistic Director Ramin Gray

Small- to medium-scale company producing international new writing.

Eastern Angles

Sir John Mills Theatre, Gatacre Road, Ipswich IP1 2LQ
tel (01473) 218202
email admin@easternangles.co.uk
website www.easternangles.co.uk
Twitter @easternangles
Artistic Director Ivan Cutting

Touring company producing new work with a regional theme. Stages three to four productions per year. Welcomes scripts from new writers in the East of England region. Founded 1982.

Graeae Theatre Company

Bradbury Studios,
138 Kingsland Road London E2 8DY
tel 020-7613 6900
email info@graeae.org
website www.graeae.org
Facebook www.facebook.com/graeae
Twitter @graeae
Artistic Director Jenny Sealey MBE, *Operations Director* Kevin Walsh, *Finance Director* Charles Mills, *Marketing and Development Manager* Richard Matthews, *Head of Marketing & Development* Richard Matthews, *Access Manager* Lizzy Leggat, *General*

Manager Kate Baiden, *Literary Manager* Chloe Todd Fordham

Small- to mid-scale touring company boldly placing D/deaf and disabled artists centre stage. Welcomes scripts from D/deaf and disabled writers. Founded 1980.

Headlong Theatre

17 Risborough Street, London SE1 0HG
tel 020-7633 2090
email info@headlong.co.uk
website www.headlong.co.uk
Twitter @HeadlongTheatre
Artistic Director Jeremy Herrin

Mid-/large-scale touring company presenting a provocative mix of new writing, reimagined classics and influential twentieth-century plays.

Hull Truck Theatre Co. Ltd

50 Ferensway, Hull HU2 8LB
tel (01482) 224800
email admin@hulltruck.co.uk
website www.hulltruck.co.uk
Twitter @HullTruck
Artistic Director Mark Babych

Producing and receiving theatre with a national reputation for new writing. Premieres of new plays, including own commissions, have included works by Tanika Gupta, Amanda Whittington, Bryony Lavery, James Graham and Richard Bean.

The London Bubble

(Bubble Theatre Company)
5 Elephant Lane, London SE16 4JD
tel 020-7237 4434
email admin@londonbubble.org.uk
website www.londonbubble.org.uk
Twitter @LBubble
Creative Director Jonathan Petherbridge

Aims to provide the artistic direction, skills, environment and resources to create inspirational, inclusive and involving theatre for the local community and beyond. Also runs a number of groups for children and young people from the age of 6 upwards, as well as an adult drama group, an intergenerational group and the Rotherhithe Shed initiative.

M6 Theatre Company

Studio Theatre, Hamer C.P. School,
Albert Royds Street, Rochdale, Lancs. OL16 2SU
tel (01706) 355898
email admin@m6theatre.co.uk
website www.m6theatre.co.uk
Twitter @M6Theatre
Artistic Director Gilly Baskeyfield

Touring theatre company specialising in creating and delivering innovative theatre for young audiences.

New Perspectives Theatre Company

Park Lane Business Centre, Park Lane, Basford, Nottingham NG6 0DW
tel 0115 927 2334
email info@newperspectives.co.uk
website www.newperspectives.co.uk
Facebook www.facebook.com/newperspectivestheatrecompany
Twitter @NPTheatre
Artistic Director Jack McNamara

Touring theatre company, staging up to four productions a year, many of which are new commissions. The company tours new writing and adaptations of existing works to theatres, arts centres, festivals and rural village halls around the country. Founded 1973.

Northumberland Theatre Company (NTC)

4 Dovecote St, Amble, Morpeth NE65 0DX
tel (01665) 602586
email admin@northumberlandtheatre.co.uk
website www.northumberlandtheatre.co.uk
Twitter @NTCtheatre
Artistic Director Gillian Hambleton

Performs a wide cross-section of work: new plays, extant scripts, classic and modern. Particularly interested in non-naturalism, physical theatre and plays with direct relevance to rural audiences.

Out of Joint

3 Thane Works, Thane Villas, London N7 7NU
tel 020-7609 0207
email ojo@outofjoint.co.uk
website www.outofjoint.co.uk
Twitter @Out_of_Joint

Touring company producing new plays and occasional revivals. Welcomes scripts. Founded 1993.

Paines Plough

4th Floor, 43 Aldwych, London WC2B 4DN
tel 020-7240 4533
email office@painesplough.com
website www.painesplough.com
Facebook www.facebook.com/painesploughHQ
Twitter @painesplough
Joint Artistic Directors George Perrin, James Grieve

Commissions and produces new plays by British and Irish playwrights. Tours at least six plays per year nationally for small- and mid-scale theatres. Also runs The Big Room, a concierge-style development strand for professional playwrights: see website for further details. Welcomes unsolicited scripts and responds to all submissions. Seeks original plays that engage with the contemporary world and are written in a distinctive voice.

Proteus Theatre Company

Proteus Creation Space, Council Road, Basingstoke, Hants RG21 3DH

tel (01256) 354541
email info@proteustheatre.com
website www.proteustheatre.com
Twitter @proteustheatre
Artistic Director and Chief Executive Mary Swan

Small-scale touring company particularly committed to new writing and new work, education and community collaborations. Produces three touring shows a year plus several community projects. Founded 1981.

Real People Theatre Company

37 Curlew Glebe, Dunnington, York YO19 5P
tel (01904) 488870
email sueann@curlew.totalserve.co.uk
website www.realpeopletheatre.co.uk
Artistic Director Sue Lister

Women's theatre company. Welcomes scripts from women writers. Founded 1999.

Red Ladder Theatre Company

3 St Peter's Buildings, York Street, Leeds LS9 8AJ
tel 0113 245 5311
email rod@redladder.co.uk
website www.redladder.co.uk
Twitter @RedLadderTheatr
Artistic Director Rod Dixon

Theatre performances with a radical and dissenting voice. National touring of theatre venues and community spaces. Commissions one or two new plays each year. Runs the Red Grit Project, a free theatre training programme for over-18s.

Sphinx Theatre Company

email info@sphinxtheatre.co.uk
website www.sphinxtheatre.co.uk
Twitter @Sphinxtheatre
Artistic Director Sue Parrish

Specialises in writing, directing and developing roles for women.

Talawa Theatre Company

Rich Mix, 35–47 Bethnal Green Rd, London E1 6LA
tel 020-7251 6644
email hq@talawa.com
website www.talawa.com
Facebook www.facebook.com/TalawaTheatreCompany
Twitter @TalawaTheatreCo
Artistic Director Michael Buffong

Script-reading service available three times a year. Visit the website for further details of submission windows.

Theatre Absolute

Shop Front Theatre, 38 City Arcade, Coventry CV1 3HW
tel 07799 292957
email info@theatreabsolute.co.uk
website www.theatreabsolute.co.uk
Facebook www.facebook.com/TheatreAbsolute
Twitter @theatreabsolute
Contact Julia Negus

Independent theatre producer of contemporary work. Opened the Shop Front Theatre, a 50-seat flexible professional theatre space for new writing, performances, script development, theatre lab and other live art events, in 2009. The company is funded project to project and unfortunately not able to receive unsolicited scripts. Founded 1992 by Chris O'Connell and Julia Negus.

Theatre Centre

Shoreditch Town Hall, 380 Old Street, London EC1V 9LT
tel 020-7729 3066
email admin@theatre-centre.co.uk
website www.theatre-centre.co.uk
Facebook www.facebook.com/TheatreCentreUK
Twitter @TClive
Artistic Director Natalie Wilson

Young people's theatre company producing plays and workshops which tour nationally across the UK. Productions are staged in schools, arts centres and other venues. Recently produced work includes *The Muddy Choir* by Jesse Briton, *Advice for the Young at Heart* by Roy Williams, *The Day the Waters Came* by Lisa Evans and *Layla's Room* by Sabrina Mahfouz. Keen to nurture new and established talent, encouraging all writers to consider writing for young audiences. Also run creative projects and manages writing awards: see website for details. Founded 1953.

Literary agents
How literary agencies work

Catherine Clarke gives an insight into literary agents, both large and small.

When I joined Felicity Bryan as a literary agent in June 2001, I knew I would be making one or two adjustments to my professional mindset. But I didn't fully appreciate how different working for a small agency would be from the publishing job I had left behind – several years as a publishing director for trade books at Oxford University Press, having come up through the editorial route. OUP is a large organisation with a corporate structure and hierarchy, and several divisions which operate effectively as separate companies, not only in the UK but in offices all over the world. I was now joining an agent who had previously been a director at Curtis Brown in London, and had successfully set up her own business in 1988, and who up until this point had operated on her own, with an assistant and a bookkeeper, from a small, pretty office in north Oxford. It was with something of a sigh of relief that I left behind the regular weekly and monthly meetings with colleagues from various publishing departments, which even when they were fun and useful seemed to take up such an inordinate amount of time, and set about learning what the differences were between representing authors and publishing them.

The first eye-opening lesson was that even though the agency itself consisted of just two agents and two staff, it functioned as the hub of a vast, informal network of relationships, not only within the UK but right across the globe. On the day that I started work, an auction was in progress for a new book proposal, a memoir co-written with a ghostwriter. The authors were based in London, but the publishers bidding for it (by phone and email on this occasion) were in Germany. The bids were relayed to Felicity Bryan by our German translation sub-agent at Andrew Nurnberg Associates in London, specialists in translation rights. Felicity called the authors to keep them up to speed with what was happening, and eventually made a recommendation to them for which offer to accept. The deal, once it was done and announced in the trade press, kick-started auctions for the book in many other territories, including the UK and the USA. While all this was happening, Felicity picked up the phone and talked to a London-based agent who deals with film and television rights and agreed that, given the intense interest in the book, it would be a good time to submit it to production companies in London and Los Angeles and get the proposal on track for a film option or sale. The authors were, naturally, over the moon.

Meanwhile I, the novice agent, was learning fast from this on-the-job induction, and was also busy setting up meetings with editors and publishing directors in all the London publishing houses, particularly those who specialised in serious non-fiction – books by historians, literary biographers, and philosophers mostly, as that was my own background as a publisher, and the areas where my earliest clients would be coming from. I wanted to find out what books were selling well for each editor, and what they were looking for. In several cases they were looking for books on particular subjects, and asked if I could help find authors for them.

By the time I attended my first Frankfurt Book Fair in October 2001, I had a small list of my own clients and a few deals already done with UK publishers. In my Filofax (now we all carry Moleskine® notebooks, or type directly into our tablets or smartphones) I had a miniaturised schedule of 50 or so half-hour meetings with European and US publishers in the International Rights Centre, and several invitations to evening parties. I had already had a number of conversations about 'hot' books and who was buying what with publishers at the check-in at Heathrow airport and again waiting at the baggage claim at Frankfurt. Over the mindbogglingly expensive white wine at the Frankfurterhof bar late at night, thronging with publishers from all over the world, I handed over proposals for books that resulted in deals (which took place later, after the adrenalin rush of the Fair was over and everyone could make a sober decision on what they wanted to buy). During the evening I met the New York-based agent who was to become my first port of call for selling my clients' books on my behalf in the US market (later I added two other US agents who had different tastes and close publishing relationships so I could match each project to a really enthusiastic co-agent). I felt well and truly launched by the time I flew back home. The following spring the London Book Fair was to prove just as intense and influential, and when I went on to develop a list of children's writers, the Bologna Children's Book Fair became another annual springtime fixture in my diary for selling rights, meeting new publishers, checking up on how existing deals were progressing, and for trailing exciting new projects that were still in the offing. Very soon I was factoring in a regular trip to New York to see publishers and co-agents, so I could get a sense of the rather different market patterns and pressures in the USA, and also talk up my clients' books.

That experience is probably not very different for any agent, whatever the size of their business, though some will have less emphasis on the international markets. It undoubtedly helps as an agent starting out to have colleagues or contacts already in the business who can effect introductions and help build the necessary networks.

So what might a prospective writer take into account when looking for an agent to represent them?

There are many literary agencies in the UK – the membership of the Association of Authors' Agents is around 100 – and they vary in size from one person working entirely on their own to very large organisations with many agents and support staff. Most agencies are somewhere in between, with several book agents specialising in fiction or non-fiction, children's and adult, or more usually a mixture, and with support staff or freelance services such as royalty management and accounts. The very large agencies, such as Curtis Brown or United Agents also have agents who specialise in film and television rights, scriptwriters, directors, presenters and actors; in other words, they manage a wide range of creative talent. Jonathan Lloyd, Chairman of Curtis Brown, says, 'Compared to almost all publishers, agencies, even the bigger ones, are tiny, but an impressive client list helps us to protect our clients and the "one-stop-shop" ability allows us to exploit clients in the fullest and most effective way.'

At the other end of the spectrum, Rachel Calder at the Sayle Literary Agency, in Cambridge, feels that small is definitely beautiful: 'A small agency can afford to work in the medium- and long-term interest of their writers, not just the short term, because they are under less pressure from having to contribute to large overheads… they can be more flexible in reacting to changing industry circumstances, and still be acting in the writers' best interests.' As Sally Holloway, former publisher and an associate agent with the Felicity Bryan Agency, says, 'Smaller agents, like smaller publishers, are much more aware of their own bottom line, and therefore will pursue that last little foreign rights deal.'

For the writer, several factors might come into the reckoning if they are thinking about who should represent them. The first is that a relationship with an agent is, ideally, for life, or at least for the longer-term career, and should not be entered into lightly on either part. Whether the agent is part of a small or larger agency is not so great a consideration as whether the writer and agent trust one another's judgement and ability to deliver: whether they can both foresee a happy and fruitful collaboration. For some writers, being part of a list of high-profile writers – or more generally of famous 'talent' – may be the highest comfort factor; they might be less concerned about having the full attention of an agent with a very big list of clients than being part of a particular 'brand' created by that list. For others, that is less of a factor than having a hands-on agent who will work hard with the writer to get a proposal or novel into the best possible shape and then doggedly pursue the best deals in all potential markets – and that would not necessarily mean the highest advances. Of course, most agents can happily combine these qualities.

Because literary agenting is a business based not only on contacts and relationships but also personal tastes, every agency will have a slightly different ethos or feel. As Rachel Calder says, 'A good agent is committed to their author's work and career, has excellent industry contacts at home and abroad, wide publishing experience, confidence about their abilities and good literary judgement… what matters is how good the deals are that the agent does for those writers.'

Catherine Clarke is Managing Director at Felicity Bryan Associates.

See also...

- *How to get an agent*, page 422
- *Getting hooked out of the slush pile*, page 433

How to get an agent

Philippa Milnes-Smith demystifies the role of the literary agent.

So, what is a literary agent and why would I want one?

To start, see if you can answer a confident 'yes' to all the questions below:

• Do you have a thorough understanding of the publishing market and its dynamics?

• Do you know who are the best publishers for your book and why? Can you evaluate the pros and cons of each? Do you know the best editors within these publishers?

• Are you up to navigating the fast-changing and fast-growing world of digital publishing?

• Are you financially numerate and confident of being able to negotiate the best commercial deal available in current market conditions?

• Are you confident of being able to understand fully and negotiate a publishing or other media contract?

• Do you know the other opportunities for your work beyond publishing and how these might be exploited? Could you deal with the complexities of a franchise? Or intellectual property development?

• Do you enjoy the process of selling yourself and your work? And do you like this and business affairs so much you would rather be working on the commercial side of things than spending as much time as you can being creative?

An agent's job is to deal with all of the above on your behalf. A good agent will do all of these well – and let you get on with the creative work. They should be able to see the long-term strategy as well as the best deal opportunities.

What else does an agent do?

Some agents will provide more of an editorial role; some may be subject specialists; all should involve themselves in marketing, promotion and social media; all should provide efficient business support and process contracts and money promptly and efficiently; all should work in their clients' best interests; all should understand their clients' work, needs and objectives.

I definitely do want an agent. Where do I begin?

Firstly, using this *Yearbook* and the internet, identify the agents to whom your book will appeal. Then really think about whether you are ready to see your book as a commercial proposition. An agent will only take someone on if they can see how and why they are going to make money for the client and themselves. An agent also knows that if he/she does not sell a client's work, the relationship isn't going to last long. Then do some further research online and see if there are book fairs, festivals, events or local writers group in which an agent is taking part and which you can attend. More and more agents are doing this kind of outreach work to reach new authors.

Do agents just think about deals and money?

A good agent has to think about getting the best deal for their clients. But good agents also care about the quality of work and the clients they represent. They are committed professionals. They also know that good working relationships count. This means that, if and when you get as far as talking to a prospective agent, you should ask yourself the questions:

'Do I have a good rapport with this person? Do I understand and trust what they are saying?' Follow your instinct – more often than not it will be right.

So how do I convince an agent that I'm worth taking on?

Make your approach professional and only approach an appropriate agent who deals with the category of book you are writing/illustrating. Check to whom you should send your work and whether there are any specific ways your submission should be made: some agents enjoy an initial exchange on Twitter and others don't. Some now only accept electronic submissions. Send a short covering letter with your manuscript explaining what it is, why you wrote it, what the intended audience is and providing any other *relevant* context. Always say if and why you are uniquely placed and qualified to write a particular book. Provide your professional credentials, if any. If you are writing an autobiography, justify why it is of public interest and why your experiences set you apart. Supply a relevant short autobiographical piece. But in addition make your approach individual, personal and interesting. You want to make the agent *want* to read your work. And you might only get one go at making your big sales pitch to an agent.

And if I get to meet an agent?

Treat it like a job interview (although hopefully it will be more relaxed than this). Be prepared to talk about your work and yourself. An agent knows that a prepossessing personality in an author is a great asset for a publisher – they will be looking to see how well you communicate. Authors are often required to do publicity interviews, media of all kinds and live events as well as use social networking to promote themselves and their work. Use the opportunity to ask them questions about what they do, including how they work on film, television, theatre, licensing if you are thinking about how your book might work in other formats. It is also worth checking if they are a member of the Association of Authors' Agents.

And if an agent turns my work down? Should I ask them to look again? People say you should not accept rejection.

No means no. Don't pester. It won't make an agent change his/her mind. Instead, move on to the next agency – the agent there might feel more positive. The agents who reject you may be wrong. But the loss is theirs.

Even if an agent turns my work down, isn't it worth asking for help with my creative direction?

No. Agents will often provide editorial advice for clients (some go as far as running their own creative groups) but are under no obligation to do so for non-clients. Submissions are usually sorted into two piles of 'yes, worth seeing more' and 'rejections'. Creative courses and events and writers' and artists' groups are better options to pursue for teaching and advice (see *Creative writing courses* on page 678). However, don't let up on practising and developing your creative skills. If you want to get your work published, you will be competing with professional writers and artists – and those who have spent years working daily at their craft. There is no short cut to success.

Philippa Milnes-Smith is a literary agent and children's and YA specialist at the agency LAW (Lucas Alexander Whitley). She was previously Managing Director of Puffin Books and is a past president of the Association of Authors' Agents.

See also...

• *Getting hooked out of the slush pile*, page 433

Putting together your submission

Hellie Ogden spells out what the time-pressed agent is looking for in a book submission, and provides advice and examples of what *is*, and what *is not*, likely to help a new author secure an agent.

Any agent will tell you they get huge numbers of submissions sent to them daily – perhaps up to 100 or so each week. And it's true, we do, but that fact shouldn't be unduly intimidating. It always amazes me, despite the amount of information available on agents' sites and from resources such as this *Yearbook* and the Writers' & Artists' website (www.writersandartists.co.uk), how many of these submission emails are hastily and sloppily written – full of spelling, punctuation and, in some cases, factual errors. These, not surprisingly, I will reject straightaway. The number of smart, professional cover letters that I receive is much smaller (approximately 25% of all those I see) and these will be instantly bumped up my submission pile.

The cover letter

There are some key points to remember when putting your submission together: personalise your covering letter/email, addressing it to a specific, correctly named agent, and email or post it in line with each agent's guidelines on their site. Include a brief introduction about yourself and your book and what material you are attaching or posting, again as specified by each agency. This would typically include three sample chapters and a synopsis, which should be in two separate documents attached to your cover letter email, and not added to the body of the email itself.

Knowing the market

What will elevate your submission package, in my eyes, comes down to two things. Firstly, knowing where your book sits in the market or what genre it falls within. It may sound obvious, but having market awareness is really smart. It shows that you have done your research and, because of that, that you have an idea of what other published titles it might sit alongside on the booksellers' shelves or in online stores. On top of falling in love with your writing, agents themselves will be strategising and formulating a pitch around how your book will be positioned in the market. Is your book YA, upmarket commercial, narrative non-fiction, literary, psychological suspense? Your agent will have a good idea of what 'type' of book you have written, but it's encouraging to see an author considering these questions too, showing an awareness of the commercial side of publishing and some understanding of the market.

The elevator pitch

The second crucial element of your submission is the 'elevator pitch'. This need only be a paragraph long, around 100-150 words, but contains the most important lines you will write in your cover email. This is your opportunity to be creative in your cover letter and to stand out positively. There are a good and bad example in the cover letters shown below. The elevator pitch is your chance to sell your hook – an agent's eyes will flip to that part of the letter first. Take inspiration from blurbs on the back of published books in your genre; don't rush it and don't overcomplicate; focus on one key plot point and one unique angle.

A good and a not-so-good example

On the next page is an example of a submission letter I received a few years ago. I subsequently took on the author. I was instantly drawn to her letter: in her opening lines, she provides a clear sense of the book's genre and highlights her relevant writing experience. She has an understanding of my client list and her elevator pitch is really strong and compelling. The book's title isn't perfect, but it does feel relevant to the genre. She finishes by including a brief biography and (what I always appreciate) her telephone number, so I can be in touch quickly! It's always useful, too, to mention when you have submitted to other agents and to remain honest and transparent throughout the submission process.

As an extreme example of a bad cover letter(!), overleaf is one that I've cobbled together to highlight the errors a surprising number of authors make:

- It's not directed at an individual agent, it's arrogant in tone, and it's packed full of spelling mistakes.
- The writer has sent in a random selection of chapters – the ones that she thinks are the best. *All* your chapters should be the best examples of your writing and equally strong; send the first three chapters, not a random selection.
- Although I'm a big fan of comparison titles to highlight where your book might sit, the ones included here are contradictory and confusing.

Synopsis

The synopsis can challenge even the most confident of writers, and it shouldn't take precious time away from perfecting the manuscript itself. I would never turn down a manuscript if I loved the book but the synopsis didn't stylistically blow me away. In fact, I won't even open it until I've had a look at the manuscript itself. It's a simple map of the book, ideally a page long, detailing the beginning, middle and end of your story. Concentrate on the key points and don't overload it with detail.

It's an extremely exciting stage getting your manuscript ready to go out to agents, but I can't stress enough the importance of spending a good chunk of time on your approach. Do your research; read widely so you are aware of the market; spend time in bookshops looking at the backs of books and at titles too. Write, rewrite, and write again that pitch! Keep it tight and compelling. Spend time on your synopsis but don't fret over it and, more importantly, try to make those opening three chapters of your work as wonderful as possible.

I often recommend to new writers that they read the *Bookseller* online – the publishing trade magazine (www.thebookseller.com). It's a great resource not only for researching an agent, but also for understanding a little about the market. Remember that agents are reading constantly, so don't nag if you don't hear back from them immediately; do check individual agency guidelines for response times. It's worth noting, too, that around the time of the three major book fairs each year – Bologna, held in March (children's and YA only; www.bookfair.bolognafiere.it), London (April; www.londonbookfair.co.uk) and Frankfurt (October; https://book-fair.com/en) – agents are extremely busy, so I would suggest not submitting during the weeks running up to, during and just after the fairs.

An example of a good submission email

From: Heidi Hopeful 14/02/2018

Subject: Submission of Bones by Heidi Hopeful

To: agent@literaryagency.com

Dear Hellie,

I hope you don't mind me contacting you directly. You have been highly recommended to me by an editor at Faber, who I worked with on the Faber Writing-a-Novel course a few years ago.

I would love you to be one of the first people to look at my upmarket thriller. I have thought long and hard about agents and I would absolutely love to work with you if you felt *Bones* was right for you. You have a wonderful, eclectic list and I hope that I might fit in well alongside your existing clients. I particularly love M.J. Arlidge's *Eeny Meeny*, which is just unputdownable, and the character of Helen Grace is fascinating - a detective who struggles with her demons so differently from other crime novel detectives.

My novel, *Bones*, tells the story of how Beth Chase's life is shattered when her 17-year-old son goes missing. When a body is pulled from the Thames outside her riverside home, Beth is convinced it is her missing son. Although it is soon evident the bones have been in the water far longer, she becomes fixated on them, her search for Louis becoming ever more frantic. As strange things begin to happen in the river house, the life of a former inhabitant emerges and Beth grows obsessed by events that unfolded there centuries ago.
But are these things really happening, or are they all in Beth's mind? Can the house on the river and its secrets lead Beth to her son, or is it spinning her away from him?

In my day job I write for a number of national parenting magazines and websites, on everything from how to travel across a continent with a potty-training toddler, to persuading your monsters that Haribo Sours are not one of the major food groups. Recent titles include *Families Magazine* and *Families Online*. I also write the blog *21stCenturyMum*.

I hope you don't mind but I have taken the liberty of attaching my novel, as well as a brief synopsis.

Thank you so much, and apologies for the excruciating length of this email!
I look forward to hearing from you. My telephone number is *XXX* and I have submitted to a small number of agents.

Best wishes,

Heidi Hopeful

An example of a poor submission email

From: Neil Chance 01/04/2018

Subject: HEY, LOOK AT THIS!!!!

To: agent@literaryagency.com

Dear Sir/Madam/Miss/Mz (that should cover you all),

I am writing to give you an exclusive first look at the future of publishing. A book that will literally change our society.

'The Face of God is an ugly one my son' is a fast-paced but literary thriller that follows the adventures of an innocent postie who gets sucked into the world of forensic archaeology and the dark underbelly of the Christian church, and must race across the world to stop a terrifying prophecy from coming true.

Dan Brown sold buckets of 'The DaVinci Code' and I plan to do the same. But where his book was based on cheap and easy hearsay, the myths and truths exposed in my book are the result of years of my own painstaking research into Christian conspiracies which I undertook during my twenty-five year career as a post office manager. I thin the book will hopefully steal away some of Mr Brown's fans but also appeal to readers of the likes of Graham Greene and John Updike.

If you're interested then read on – I've included the opening, closing and middle chapter to give you a flavour of the novel at its best places! I've already mapped out four possible sequals to this book – each more death defyingly thrilling than the last. I also have a backlist of more historical adventures – very Indiana Jones-esque, when men were men and women were in distress – which I'm sure you'll love as much as 'The Face of God is an ugly one my son.'

I look forward to a long and fruitful career with you,

Best,

N.O. Chance

Good luck! It's the best feeling in the world discovering new talent and nurturing debut writers.

Hellie Ogden is a literary agent at Janklow & Nesbit UK Literary Agency. Hellie featured in the *Bookseller* Rising Stars list 2013 and was shortlisted for the Kim Scott Walwyn Prize 2014. She is looking for series crime, psychological thrillers, commercial and upmarket fiction, YA and children's debuts and accessible, charming literary fiction. She enjoys novels with a strong sense of place, bold twists and enticing protagonists. In non-fiction Hellie is looking for unique personal stories and work that has a large social following with cross-media potential. Her clients include brand names such as M.J. Arlidge, Tilly Bagshawe and Kiran Millwood Hargrave and, as an editorially focused agent, she has a keen interest in helping to develop and nurture debut writers. Follow her on Twitter @HellieOgden.

How to submit a non-fiction proposal

Literary agent and author Andrew Lownie provides a tried-and-tested format for your book proposal, and valuable advice on how to get the attention of an agent or publisher.

Good proposals are essential. The proposal is usually the first – and only – thing publishers will read before making their offer. It will usually determine whether or not you are published, the offer that is made and how your book is published.

The principles of a good non-fiction proposal are the same whether you are submitting to an agent or to a publisher. It needs to give them a good sense of the book, your qualifications to write it, how the book fits into the market and how the book can reach that market. It should also be layered, so that the agent and/or publisher can assess the proposal quickly but obtain more detailed information as they read more of it. Remember – some 30 people in an editorial meeting may be considering your submission, one of dozens they consider each week, so it needs to be concise and it needs to be structured so that even if they only read the first page they will know what it's about.

The format that has served me well over the last 30+ years in publishing is as follows:

1. Introductory page

A first page introducing the ***subject*** in a paragraph, followed by ***bullet-point revelations*** and a note on proposed ***word count*** and ***delivery date***. Word counts vary but are generally around 90,000 words for a commercial book, up to no more than 140,000 words including footnotes for a serious academic book.

Publishers tend to commission for lists about 12-18 months ahead and to take about 12 months to publish from delivery of manuscript. They don't like to put their money down for too long and they worry about competing books sneaking in, so don't they give long delivery periods. Try to hook your publication to an anniversary and be aware that publishers tend to put fiction for heavyweight prizes, as well as their Christmas books, bestselling and gift titles, in the autumn list – which runs from July to end of the year.

The spring list, from January to July, tends to be for books which would be lost in autumn lists with the plethora of titles jostling for Christmas sales. Here are books which need room to breathe while there is less competition in bookshops and in the media. January, as a quiet month of good resolutions, tends to be for diet books and first novelists, along with travel books and commercial fiction for holiday-reading promotions.

The key in this section is to show what makes your book different and commercial. What is its Unique Selling Point or Proposition (USP)? Perhaps it's a new hook, interpretation or information. If you can extrapolate this to one exciting strap line which the editor can use to pitch in a meeting or the salesman can push to a bookshop, then all the better.

A ***strong title*** always helps. I sold a biography of a Tudor poet as *Henry VIII's Last Victim*.

2. Personal profile

A page on you and your qualifications to write the book, together with a photo. Have you an academic background, published widely in the field? Are you respected as an authority on the subject? Have you written lots of successful books before or won awards? Give details of your social media following (Facebook, LinkedIn, Instagram, Twitter) as this shows you are focused on marketing. No need to give your shoe size or GCSE results (as one author proffered) but provide details which might be helpful for publicity, such as links to media appearances, contacts who might endorse the book, and book review extracts.

3. Comparable/competing books

Give the title, author, publisher and date of publication of between five and ten reasonably successful books published in the last 20 years by trade publishers, with a few lines on how they compare to your book. You are trying to plant subliminally in the reader's mind that there is interest in the subject but that you have a slightly different take. This will help the publisher place the book in the market.

Be careful not to make meaningless comparisons, such as 'J.K. Rowling meets John Le Carré' or resort to clichés, such as 'Another *Eat, Pray, Love*'. It may seem fresh to you but will not impress jaded editors and agents. Amazon's search engine is a good place to research not just published titles but also forthcoming ones. Remember that publishers, often run by former sales directors, want 'the same but different'.

4. Sources

The fourth page lists primary sources – whether it's archives or interviews – and demonstrates that there is something new and original in the book rather than simply a synthesis of the existing information.

5. Market

Finally include a note on the market and how it might be reached; who is going to buy the book, why and how can they be reached. Perhaps there are specialist organisations, websites, magazines, television or radio programmes or bloggers with a particular interest in the subject? Give details, if possible, of numbers of members, subscribers, followers, etc.

The purpose is to show you are thinking about the market, but also to give information to the publisher about publicity or marketing outlets of which they might not be aware. If you have particular publicity ideas or contacts, then mention them. Is there potential for extracts in newspapers, for audio or film, or for selling the book in other languages?

When I initially pitch to editors often that's all I send. It's short and should be sufficient for the editor to know if they want to see more.

6. Chapter synopses and samples

The next stage of the layered approach are the chapter ***synopses***. I would suggest about 20-25 of these, each about half a page long and written in continuous prose, numbered, and with chapter titles – as if you were paraphrasing the book. This should give a clear sense of content and structure of the book without being overwhelming.

Now come the ***sample chapters***, perhaps on a separate Word attachment. The more you supply the better – a finished script means the publisher knows exactly what they are buying so they will be less cautious – but certainly include the first chapter. Authors sometimes choose the chapter they feel is best or most exciting, but you have to have confidence that all your chapters are good. Selecting a chapter from the middle of the book can be confusing and suggests that you don't rate your first chapter. Indeed, the first has to be particularly good because that tends to be the chapter the purchaser will dip into first. Chapters should be between 3,000 and 5,000 words – short enough for the reader to feel they are making progress but not so short as to appear superficial.

7. Covering note

The covering note with the proposal doesn't need to be long, but tailor it to the agent or publisher, explaining why you are approaching them by naming specific other books they have handled in the same genre. This is flattering and shows you have done your research and focused your submission.

Don't say you are approaching lots of other agents or publishers, even if you have. No one likes to feel they are in a beauty parade and may be wasting their time assessing the book. I tend to submit in waves of about five, so I can adjust the proposal in the light of the response. Ask if you can have a response within a month and then do a gentle chase. If you don't get a response – I'm afraid a lot of agents and publishers are rude – then move on.

Make sure you address the person properly. I have received supposedly exclusive submissions addressed to other agents and sometimes cc'd to numerous agencies, letters beginning Mr Loonie, Mrs Downie and with the firm described as a litter agency! The covering note may help to explain why you choose that particular agency or publisher. One explanation I received began: 'Warm greetings from Australia. I am very pleased to have found you via a psychic's recommendation to my mother a few weeks ago.'

Make sure the agent you are approaching actually handles what you are offering. Well over half my submissions are for genres which, in all the reference books and on my website, I categorically say I don't represent. It is easy enough, now that agencies have websites, to find out the authors they handle. Look at the acknowledgements pages of books which are comparable to yours and try approaching the agent who handled these.

Important dos and don'ts

• Pitch by email rather than phone as it's the writing which will sell you. If leaving a phone message, explain why you phoned. You are unlikely to receive a return call to Australia if you simply say, 'Steve called.' Agents and editors tend to communicate by email as the easiest method and I suggest you do the same. The days of manuscripts by post are over; just think of the logistical problems and expense of sharing material which isn't in email attachments.
• Don't submit too early. You only have one chance to impress an agent or publisher so make sure the proposal is absolutely right. It shouldn't have grammatical or spelling mistakes, and it should be polished – consistently formatted, fully justified and ideally double-spaced in 12 point – and lucid.
• Don't assume too much knowledge, but equally don't become bogged down in detail.
• Don't underline, use bold or lots of exclamation marks, or write in pencil or green ink.
• Don't boast. Your mother may – indeed should – think the book is wonderful, but her opinion doesn't count in the publishing world.
• Make it easy for an agent to respond. An email address is preferred to an address or phone number. If you are going to submit by post, ensure there is sufficient postage on the envelope, so the receiver isn't surcharged. Including return postage is a courtesy, preferably in UK stamps, and the envelope should be large enough to take the returned material.
• Follow instructions. If agencies have a preferred format, then follow it and customise your proposal. That said, I still think my format is best!
• Don't worry about being rejected. There may be lots of reasons behind it – maybe the book isn't suitable for the list, they already handle authors in the genre and don't want

more, they got out of bed the wrong side that morning, they are incompetent, etc – it doesn't have to mean the book is rubbish. Not every idea makes a book. Perhaps it's better as an article, short-form ebook or would suit being self-published. Don't get upset, even, or write back to point out the error of their ways, but move on to the next person on your list.

Remember that editors and agents are busy people and will be making quick decisions. Anything that jars with them or makes them lose interest means they will move on to the next script. You don't want that to happen – which is why the proposal is so important.

Andrew Lownie has been a Cambridge history fellow, bookseller, publisher, journalist and director of Curtis Brown. He has run his own literary agency (www.andrewlownie.co.uk) since 1988 and according to publishersmarketplace.com is the top-selling non-fiction agent in the world. He is President of the Biographers Club and an award-winning biographer in his own right. *Stalin's Englishman: Guy Burgess, the Cold War, and the Cambridge Spy Ring* was published by St Martin's Press in 2016. Follow him on Twitter @andrewlownie.

Getting hooked out of the slush pile

Literary agents wade through slush piles to find a manuscript that shines out and entices them to read more. Madeleine Milburn offers some helpful tips on how to get your submission noticed, read and hooked by an agent.

I started the Madeleine Milburn Literary, TV & Film Agency six years ago, after ten years of experience at two major UK literary agencies. I've always had a really positive attitude towards my 'slush pile' as it's where I've found the majority of my authors. 'Slush' can conjure some unfairly pejorative images, but it also offers agents the opportunity to wade through these shadowy waters of talent to find that one treasure: a book that melts the icy heart of the literary agent. I receive up to 100 submissions a day and look at them all – but it takes something very special to make me want to read more.

Don't look for an agent too soon

The first, and most important, question when you are thinking of submitting your work to an agent is: am I ready? This might seem like a strange question but it is worth asking. Your book is finished, you've written a smashing covering letter, managed to condense the plot into a one-page synopsis – you've even written the dedication. But you would be surprised how many people submit before they are quite 'there'.

> **Slush pile**
>
> **slush pile** noun *informal* A stack of unsolicited manuscripts that have been sent to a publishing company for consideration.
>
> **slush** noun [mass noun] **1** Partially melted snow or ice. **1.1** Watery mud. **2** *informal* Excessive sentiment.

Asking some pertinent questions will help you to see where you stand. How long ago did you finish the book? Have you come back to it with fresh eyes and read and reread it? Have you asked anyone for a second opinion? Have you self-edited your manuscript – gone through it critically to make sure the pace is right and the characters are authentic? Have you made sure that it captivates the reader from start to finish?

Read your work aloud, and go through it with a fine-tooth comb to weed out any repetition or aspects that don't move the plot along at lightning pace. Once you get past the massive hurdle of getting your full manuscript requested, you'll need to make the agent fall in love with the *entire* book. Unfortunately, so many times, I've loved the opening chapters of a novel only to be sorely let down by an unsuccessful outcome. This is your big chance – don't rush it!

Find an appropriate agent

Having read, reread and polished your manuscript until it's positively shining, you need to find an appropriate agent to submit it to. Start by looking at some agency websites to see what kind of books they represent, or what they are looking to represent. Look out for authors whose work is similar to your own. Has the agent specified that they would welcome a book in the genre you're writing in? Is the agency actively seeking new talent? Are they launching debut authors as well as securing new deals for their existing authors? Do they actively help with their authors' publicity efforts? Are they a member of the Associate of Authors' Agents (AAA)? Do they appear to be aware of all the digital options and alternative ways of launching an author? This is so important in our digital age.

Explore alternative ways of getting to know about agents, such as joining a writing group, reading book trade news, following agents on Twitter, Facebook and Instagram, and going to literary events.

It's often been said that your agent will become your business partner and, whilst I agree with this, I also see the relationship as a close working-friendship. Your agent should be someone you feel comfortable talking with. The very best agents are those who care deeply about their authors and their work, and who will fight for them at every stage of their writing career. If you are fortunate enough to have more than one agent offering you representation, choose the agent who is most passionate about your work.

Sell your book compellingly

Submission packages for agencies are usually of a similar format. Most require you to send a covering letter, synopsis and the first three chapters. When you feel your manuscript is as good as it can be and ready to submit, here are some key tips to consider.

The title

Use a strong and compelling title that grabs an agent's attention. Bestselling titles resonate with a reader before they open a book, for instance *The Essex Serpent*, *Eleanor Oliphant is Completely Fine*, *The Power* and *How to Stop Time*. Don't use a title that only makes sense to a reader once they have read the story. Think of how you, as a reader, approach books in bookshops. What grabs your attention?

The covering letter

A covering letter should include a brief introduction, for example, 'I am currently seeking representation for my debut novel…', followed by an intriguing sentence that will draw the reader into your story; a slightly longer, enticing blurb; a reason why you have chosen the agent you are submitting to; a short profile; and a brief sentence or two about what you will be working on next.

Pitch your book in your letter, *not* in your synopsis. The letter is the place to get an agent excited about your opening chapters and where you need to 'sell' your book. Read the back cover blurb of books in the genre you are writing in, and study why they rouse your attention and interest. Practise pitching your book in a single sentence to get to the core of your story. You need to position your book straight away and make it evident to the agent what genre you are writing in.

Imagine your book on the shelves of a bookshop. Where would it sit? Next to Lee Child or David Nicholls? I want to see that a writer has researched the market and knows that there is a readership for their work. An editor who loves your book will need to persuade the rest of the publishing team that there is a market for it. But when comparing yourself to another author, please don't say you are 'the next' Dan Brown; instead express the hope that your work will appeal to 'readers of' Dan Brown.

Only mention achievements that are relevant to the book you are submitting. I applaud Duke of Edinburgh adventurers, dirt-road bikers, members of Save the Whale foundations and other wonderfully colourful hobbyists, but unless the activity is specifically relevant to your book, for now, please keep the information short and sweet. Use the covering letter to sell the story, not yourself.

Pitch just one book in your letter. If you have written more than one book, choose the one you'd like to launch your writing career with. If an agent loves the book you are submitting, he or she will be interested in all of your work. If you write both adult and children's stories, pick one (for now). A prospective editor will want your next book to appeal to the same readers as your first book – and I like to do two- or even three-book deals with publishers to ensure that they are committed to developing an author's career.

The synopsis

A synopsis is a straightforward chronological account of the *most important* things that happen in a story. A lot of agents read this last, or only read it if they want to see more chapters. Don't include every single detail; try to stick to one A4 page. If there are any twists or plot revelations, don't keep them hidden like you would in a blurb. An agent needs spoilers to see how original your plotting is compared to what is currently on the market, so this aspect can be crucial to deciding whether your manuscript is requested.

Checklist for submitting to an agent

- Make sure your book has a strong title.
- Research the market and check that the length of your novel is appropriate for the genre you are writing in.
- Print out the manuscript and check that all spelling is correct. You will be surprised at how many errors you find.
- Take care to follow the instructions that are specific to each agency. For instance, I like to see 1.5 line spacing for the opening chapters and a one-page synopsis.
- Create a strong and attention-grabbing one-line hook that captures the heart of your story and will entice people to buy and read your book.
- Write a compelling back cover blurb.
- Consider all the selling points for your book. Write a summary of the book's appeal: be clear who the audience is and confident that they will identify with the book. Know the strengths of your manuscript and why it is unique. Think about what previous experience you have that could help promote your book.
- Tailor your profile to be relevant to your writing career. State if you are on a creative writing course, are a member of any writing clubs or societies and if you have won any writing competitions.
- If you have been published before, it is important to be upfront about it. Provide any writing history and say whether you have had an agent in the past.
- Write a synopsis that summarises your book's plot in chronological order with the ending included.

The opening chapters

Your first three chapters are extremely important as, together with your covering letter, they are what an agent judges your work by. They need to be strong, enticing and compelling. There must be a strong sense of atmosphere, empathy or intrigue. Be wary of including irrelevant background information or context at this stage: it never grips readers' attention when they are not yet familiar with the characters. It can also slow the pace.

Strong characters are so important. Everyone remembers characters rather than the intricate details of a plot – just think James Bond, Jack Reacher, Sherlock Holmes and Harry Potter. Let your readers do the work. Create suspense and hook us in with a central character so that we are desperate to know more about them and read on.

Don't make your chapters too long to get around the three-chapter limit. I sometimes get asked whether I'd like to see more than three chapters because theirs are relatively short and, to be similarly brief, the answer is 'no thank you'. I don't count a prologue as a chapter.

I personally read everything that comes into my 'slush pile'. I represent a wide range of adult, young adult and children's fiction, and would be delighted to look at your work.

Madeleine Milburn is founder and director of Madeleine Milburn Ltd, one of the top literary agencies in the UK. Since graduating from the University of St Andrews with a degree in English Literature and Language in 2004, Madeleine has worked for the independent publishing company Trojan Books in Berlin and the oldest literary agency in the UK where she specialised in foreign rights. Prior to having her own agency, Madeleine was the Head of Rights and a Literary Agent at the most commercial agency in the UK, handling the rights to three no.1 bestsellers. In 2011, Milburn (*née* Buston) was chosen as one of the book trade's Rising Stars in the *Bookseller*'s first annual feature on the crop of people who will lead bookselling and publishing for decades to come, and in 2017 she was one of a small handful of agents to be included in the *Bookseller*'s list of the 100 most influential people in the book trade, alongside the likes of J.K. Rowling, Jamie Oliver and the Ceos of the major publishing houses. Follow her on Twitter @agentmilburn.

How to choose your agent

With insights on the important two-way relationship between author and agent, Jo Unwin reflects on how to find the literary agent who's right for you, and how to ensure that the one you've chosen finds you.

I met a woman at a party recently and, when I told her what I did, she declared that my job was surely the best job in the world: 'Oh, to sit about and read all day – and be paid for it!', she swooned.

I *do* actually think my job is the best in the world, but not for that reason. My daily life consists of negotiating contracts, promoting my authors where I can, examining sales figures, dissecting marketing plans, meeting editors, chasing payments, editing manuscripts, submitting new work, reverting old rights, selling rights internationally, envisioning novels as films, brainstorming new directions for authors, tweeting their triumphs ... The list goes on and on, but the one thing there is very rarely time for is sitting about reading. And yet, of course, I can't do my job if I haven't read my clients' work, and they often want a quick response. So I read on my journey to and from work, and in the evenings, and at weekends, and on family holidays. And it's all work. (Reading already-published books uses a very different part of the brain!)

Now it may be hard to believe in some cases but, believe me, it is true: literary agents have lives outside work. We have dogs that need walking, and laundry that needs ironing, and food that needs cooking, and families that need attention. Some of us even have friends! And like the cinema ... and have hobbies ... Finding a dazzlingly exciting new author is what thrills us all, but it's hard work and incredibly time-consuming finding the writer who speaks to us personally, in a voice we can hear, with a story that captivates and fascinates or delights us. Because – and please pardon the cliché – you have to kiss a lot of frogs before you find your prince.

When people submit their work to my agency they are asked to send three chapters and a synopsis, along with a covering letter telling us a bit about the work and the author. On average I get 10-15 submissions a day, let's say 80 a week. If the average submission is 8,000 words long, then ten submissions make up the length of an average novel. I can't read ten novels a week, on top of my existing authors' work. I just can't – not least because you can't speed read when you're panning for gold.

But that's where you – the author – come in. You know when you read something that you adore, and you know exactly *who* to give it to. At Christmas, you're not going to give a book on the history of the reef knot to your 14-year-old electronic-dance-loving nephew, and you know not to give your granny a book by a vlogger about how to colour in their 'Scouse Brow'.

Agents are human too; they have their own likes and dislikes, and it's often nothing to do with the market. I'm not likely to take on either the reef knot book or the vlogger book, and I might well put them on my Reject pile after only a cursory glance. But here's the point: those books do (probably) exist, and there are agents who (possibly) would leap on them. There's no point approaching an agent who specialises in military history with your wonderful YA fantasy, however good it is.

If you're going to be a professional writer you're going to have to harden your hide; it's a career path characterised by multiple rejections. But you really can minimise the number of rejections you receive by making sure you **target the right agent**.

So how are you going to do that? It starts, of course, by writing the best book you possibly can; and then writing it again and again until it's the best it could ever be. Enlist the help of a friend (find one who reads A LOT, and who doesn't owe you money) to read your manuscript and give you notes. Don't be offended if they don't understand what you're trying to do. If you trust them, then find it in yourself to acknowledge that you probably haven't communicated your intentions clearly enough. Be strict with yourself and, when you honestly know that you've done the very best job you're capable of, then – and only then – consider sending it out to agents. **Never use an agent as a sounding board.**

But before you send it out, be sure that you know what it is you've written. I fully understand how hard it is to distil something that's 100,000 words long into a 150-word pitch, but it really helps. And if you can clearly convey the essence of your work in a few sentences, then you can start to get a feel for how it might look in a bookshop. What shelf would it sit on? Which other authors might you be compared to? In a 'three-for-two' offer, which other two books might join yours in the shopping basket?

Then think: who represents the authors of those books? Spend a day in the library, and flick to the acknowledgements pages at the back of all these relevant books. Make a list of names. And then Google them. Do you like the look of them? Do you like the cut of their jib? Do they represent so many grand and famous authors that you might never get a look-in? Do they have an assistant who just has a few clients on her list but is clearly being mentored and encouraged to take on her own clients? And what else does this agent and the agency offer? How will they set about selling your work in translation? Are some of their authors bestsellers? Do they have a book-to-film department? How personally involved do you sense the agent would be? There is an enormous amount of material online, and hours spent sleuthing will repay you by minimising the number of rejections you receive.

Now have a think about what you personally *want*. Creativity is a deeply personal business, so do you want someone you can be very open with? Or do you have friends for that, and instead want an agent who will scrutinise you, your work and your deal in a cool and rigorous fashion? Do you want to be able to phone and talk about your work morning, noon, and night? Do you want a one-to-one personal relationship, or the sense of a large team of people who are all working on your behalf? The best agents will offer all of the above and more, but there is no Literary Agent qualification, and we have all developed our skills in different ways. You need to find the agent who's right for *you*.

Remember that **you are employing us, not the other way round**. So, before you start sending your submission out, think hard about what you want from this very important relationship. It's probably wise to send it out in batches of four to six at a time and, as others will stress in this *Yearbook*, do submit it in the way that the agent specifies. If they like reading in Times New Roman, it'll take you no time to change the font of your submission, and it could make all the difference to the agent's tired old eyes.

When someone offers you representation, don't leap at it. You wouldn't employ the first electrician who said they could rewire your kitchen. You'd check them out, get references, etc. Do the same with literary agents. Tell the other agents you've approached that you have interest, and say you'd like to hear back within a week to ten days. Then, if at all possible, arrange to meet any interested agents, ideally at their offices. Get a sense of who will be answering the phone to you, what the working atmosphere in the office is like. Would you like to sit next to this agent at a drunken awards ceremony? Would they be kind if they had to deliver bad news?

At the point of choosing an agent remember *you* hold the reins. Excitable agents will try to pressure you into signing with them, and you may suddenly feel things are going very fast. Take deep breaths, and keep cool. If it's taken you three years to write this book, you can afford to wait a month or two to be sure that you're employing the very best agent for you.

Remember, it's not just about the one book you've written. You're looking for a long and fruitful career as an author, so take time to find the best possible ally and champion. It might take a while, but once you've found the right person, it may prove to be one of the most important relationships of your life.

Jo Unwin started her career as an actress and writer, before her love of books drew her to work in a bookshop and then to join Conville and Walsh Literary Agency in 2008. She was shortlisted for the *Bookseller* Industry Awards Literary Agent of the Year in 2010, and chosen as one of the *Bookseller*'s Rising Stars in 2011. Jo now runs her own agency, Jo Unwin Literary Agency. For more information see www.jounwin.co.uk. Follow her on Twitter @jounwin.

See also...

- *How literary agents work*, page 419
- *How to get an agent*, page 422
- *Getting hooked out of the slush pile*, page 433

Literary agents UK and Ireland

The *Writers' & Artists' Yearbook*, along with the Association of Authors' Agents and the Society of Authors, takes a dim view of any literary agent who asks potential clients for a fee prior to a manuscript being placed with a publisher. We advise you to treat any such request with caution and to let us know if that agent appears in the listings below. However, agents may charge additional costs later in the process but these should only arise once a book has been accepted by a publisher and the author is earning an income. We urge authors to make the distinction between upfront and additional charges. Authors should also check agents' websites before making an enquiry and should familiarise themselves with submission guidelines.

*Member of the Association of Authors' Agents

A for Authors Ltd

73 Hurlingham Road, Bexleyheath, Kent DA7 5PE
tel (01322) 463479
email enquiries@aforauthors.co.uk
website www.aforauthors.co.uk
Facebook www.facebook.com/aforauthors
Twitter @aforauthors
Directors Annette Crossland, Bill Goodall

Adult fiction, literary and commercial/mass market, including (but not exclusively) crime/thriller and women's/commercial. Home 15%, overseas/translation 20%, film/TV 15% (home)/20% (overseas). No sci-fi/horror, short stories, poetry or children's books. Send synopsis plus first three chapters or 50pp, whichever is shorter, by email as Word attachments. No postal submissions. No reading fee.

Sheila Ableman Literary Agency*

36 Duncan House, 7–9 Fellows Road, London NW3 3LZ
tel 020-7586 2339
email sheila@sheilaableman.co.uk
website www.sheilaableman.com
Contact Sheila Ableman

Non-fiction including history, science, biography, autobiography (home 15%, USA/translation 20%). Not taking any new clients at present. No reading fee. Founded 1999.

The Agency (London) Ltd*

24 Pottery Lane, London W11 4LZ
tel 020-7727 1346
website www.theagency.co.uk
Children's Book Agent Hilary Delamere

Represents picture books, including novelty books, fiction for all ages including teenage fiction and series fiction (home 15%, overseas 20%). Works in conjunction with overseas agents. Submission guidelines on website. No reading fee. The Agency also represents screenwriters, directors, playwrights and composers; for more information please check the website. Founded 1995.

Aitken Alexander Associates Ltd*

291 Gray's Inn Road, London WC1X 8QJ
tel 020-7373 8672
email reception@aitkenalexander.co.uk
website www.aitkenalexander.co.uk
Twitter @AitkenAlexander
Agents Clare Alexander, Lesley Thorne, Lisa Baker (Directors), Chris Wellbelove, Niki Chang; Children's and YA fiction: Gillie Russell; Film/TV/stage rights: Lesley Thorne, Leah Middleton. Associate agent: Matthew Hamilton.

Fiction and non-fiction (home 15%, USA 20%, translation 20%, film/TV 15%). No plays or scripts. Email preliminary letter with half-page synopsis and first 30pp of sample material to submissions@aitkenalexander.co.uk. No reading fee.

Clients include Ayobami Adebayo, Jo Baker, Pat Barker, Tom Bullough, Jung Chang, Clare Clark, John Cornwell, John Crace, Sarah Dunant, Diana Evans, Sebastian Faulks, Helen Fielding, Jeremy Gavron, Germaine Greer, Julia Gregson, Mark Haddon, Mohammed Hanif, Harriet Harman, Philip Hoare, Peter Hook, Armando Iannucci, Virginia Ironside, Oliver James, Liz Jensen, Alan Johnson, Dom Joly, Jonathan Lee, Mark Lowery, Paul Mason, Charles Moore, Lucy Moore, Caroline Moorehead, William Nicholson, Julianne Pachico, Harry Parker, Chris Petit, Max Porter, Jonathan Raban, Piers Paul Reid, P.Z. Reizin, Paul Rees, Jennie Rooney, Lyndal Roper, James Scudamore, Anne Sebba, Nicholas Shakespeare, Gillian Slovo, Brix Smith, Francis Spufford, Nicholas Stargardt, Rory Stewart, Bilal Tanweer, Colin Thubron, Robert Twigger, Amanda Vickery, Penny Vincenzi, Elise Valmorbida, Willy Vlautin, Alexander Watson, Paul Willetts, Sara Wheeler, A.N. Wilson, Andrew Wilson, Robert Wilson, Adam Zamoyski. In association with Anna Stein: Anuk Arudpragasam, Laird Hunt, Maria Semple.

Estates – John Betjeman, Gordon Burn, Bruce Chatwin, Paul Gallico, Ian Hamilton, Ngaio Marsh, Mary Norton, Louise Rennison. UK only: Harper Lee, J.D. Salinger. Founded 1977.

AMP Literary

76 Nowell Road, London SW13 9BS
email anna@ampliterary.co.uk
email submissions@ampliterary.co.uk
Founder Anna Pallai

AMO specialises in commercial non-fiction with a particular interest in bold female voices (15% UK, 20% USA). From journalists and historians to comedians and bloggers, the agency is searching for a fresh generation of unique writers. With strong connections across various media platforms, from digital to TV, AMP develops ideas beyond print to maximise exposure. Submissions to be sent via email, to include synopsis and at least three chapters. No reading fee.

Authors include Natasha Devon, Terri White, Anita Mangan, Linda Papadopolous.

The Ampersand Agency Ltd*

Ryman's Cottages, Little Tew, Oxon OX7 4JJ
tel (01608) 683677/683898
email info@theampersandagency.co.uk
website www.theampersandagency.co.uk
Contacts Peter Buckman, Jamie Cowen, Anne-Marie Doulton

Literary and commercial fiction and non-fiction (home 15%, USA 15–20%, translation 20%). No reading fee. Writers should consult the website for more information and submission guidelines.

Clients include Quentin Bates, Helen Black, Sharon Bolton, Druin Burch, Alan R. Clark, Ben Crane, J.D. Davies, Catherine Deveney, Jamie Doward, James Fahy, Jay Forman, Paul Goodwin, Cora Harrison, Mark Hill, Jin Yong, Beverley Jones, Melissa Josias, Mark Latham, Rachel Lynch, John Matthews, Sarah McGurk, Leo Murray, Bolaji Odofin, Eleanor Porter, Matthew Pritchard, Rebecca Roache, Mark Roberts, Joanne Sefton, Adrian Selby, Paul Robert Smith, Richard Smyth, Ivo Stourton, Vikas Swarup, Michael Walters, Stephen Williams, Phillip Window and the estates of Georgette Heyer, Angela Thirkell, Winifred Foley and John James. Founded 2003.

Darley Anderson Literary, TV and Film Agency*

Estelle House, 11 Eustace Road, London SW6 1JB
tel 020-7386 2674
website www.darleyanderson.com
website www.darleyandersonblog.com
Twitter @DA_Agency
Agents Adult fiction: Darley Anderson (international thrillers, crime, tear-jerking love stories and non-fiction), Camilla Wray (crime, thrillers, suspense, general fiction), Sheila David (TV and film rights), Tanera Simons (women's fiction, accessible literary/reading group fiction). Children's fiction: Clare Wallace (middle grade, YA, picture books and illustrators), Lydia Silver (middle grade), Pippa Archibald (Assistant to Darley Anderson and non-fiction). *Contacts* Celine Kelly (Editorial), Rosanna Bellingham (Financial Controller), Mary Darby (Head of Rights), Emma Winter (Rights Executive), Kristina Egan (Rights Assistant)

All commercial fiction and non-fiction (home 15%,USA/translation 20%, film/TV/radio 20%). No poetry, academic books, scripts or screenplays. Send covering letter, short synopsis and first three chapters. Return postage/sae essential for reply. Overseas associates APA Talent & Literary Agency (LA/Hollywood) and leading foreign agents in selected territories. For the children's agency, visit www.darleyandersonchildrens.com.

Special interests (fiction): all types of thrillers, crime and mystery. All types of American and Irish novels. Comic fiction. All types of popular women's fiction and accessible literary/reading group fiction.

Special interests (non-fiction): autobiographies, biographies, sports books, 'true-life' women in jeopardy, revelatory history and science, popular psychology, self improvement, diet, beauty, health, fashion, animals, humour/cartoon, cookery, gardening, inspirational, religious.

Clients include Samantha Alexander, Tom Bale, Rosie Blake, Constance Briscoe, Rachel Burton, James Carol, Chris Carter, Lee Child, Martina Cole, John Connolly, Gloria Cook, Sophie Cousens, A.J. Cross, Jason Dean, Margaret Dickinson, Clare Dowling, Kerry Fisher, Jack Ford, Tana French, Sandie Jones, Joan Jonker (estate), Emma Kavanagh, T.M. Logan, Imran Mahmood, Cesca Major, Gillian McAllister, Annie Murray, Beth O'Leary, Abi Oliver, B.A. Paris, Phaedra Patrick, Adrian Plass, Jo Platt, Hazel Prior, David Rhodes, Jennifer Ridyard, Jacqui Rose, Rebecca Shaw (estate), Sean Slater, KL Slater, Catherine Steadman, Erik Storey, G.X. Todd, Samantha Tonge, Tim Weaver, Kimberley Willis, David Wishart.

ANDLYN

tel 020-3290 5638
email submissions@andlyn.co.uk
website www.andlyn.co.uk
Facebook www.facebook.com/andlynlit
Twitter @andlynlit
Founder and Agent Davinia Andrew-Lynch

Represents authors and illustrators of picture books, middle grade, YA and crossover fiction. Particularly looking for storytellers whose material has cross-media/platform potential. All genres are welcome; actively looking for new clients. Commission: 15% home and audio, 20% USA, foreign/translation, film/TV, multi-platform and online media rights. No reading fee. See website for submission guidelines. Founded 2015.

Anubis Literary Agency

7 Birdhaven Close, Lighthorne, Warwick CV35 0BE
tel (01926) 642588
Contact Steve Calcutt

Genre fiction: science fiction, fantasy and horror (home 15%, USA/translation 20%). No other material considered. Send 50pp with a one-page synopsis (sae essential). No reading fee. No telephone calls. Works with The Marsh Agency Ltd on translation rights. Founded 1994.

Artellus Ltd*

30 Dorset House, Gloucester Place,
London NW1 5AD
tel 020-7935 6972
email artellussubmissions@gmail.com
website www.artellusltd.co.uk
Twitter @Artellus
Contacts Leslie Gardner (Agent and Director), Gabriele Pantucci (Agent and Chairman), Darryl Samaraweera (Agent and Company Secretary), Jon Curzon (Associate Agent), Angus MacDonald (Associate Agent), Raffaello Pantucci (Consultant)

International literary agency representing writers in all fields and genres (15% UK, 20% direct sales to USA, 15% rest of world). Authors include historians, scientists, economists, investigative journalists and writers on culture, fashion and food. Handles a wide range of fiction, from literary to crime, fantasy and sci-fi. Also interested in fine writers in translation. Submissions in the form of a covering note attaching the first three chapters and synopsis. Submissions also accepted by post. Founded 1986.

Diane Banks Associates Ltd*

email submissions@dianebanks.co.uk
website www.dianebanks.co.uk
Twitter @DianeBanksAssoc

Commercial fiction, non-fiction and children's books (home 15%, overseas and rights in other media 20%). Fiction: women's, crime, thrillers, literary fiction with a strong storyline, young adult, middle grade, children's. Non-fiction: politics, current affairs, memoir, real-life stories, celebrity, autobiography, biography, business, popular history, popular science, self-help, popular psychology, fashion, health & beauty, children's. No poetry, academic books, plays, scripts or short stories. Send brief cv, synopsis and first three chapters as Word or Open Document attachments. Aims to give initial response within two weeks. No reading fee.

Authors include Brian Cox, Jon Butterworth, Peter Bazalgette, Camilla Cavendish, Damian Collins, Carla Valentine, Christopher Harding, Marisa Merico, Shelina Janmohamed, Dani Atkins, Kate Thompson, Rachel Wells and Daisy Styles. Founded 2006.

Tassy Barham Associates

231 Westbourne Park Road, London W11 1EB
tel 020-7229 8667
email tassy@tassybarham.com
Proprietor Tassy Barham

Specialises in representing European and American authors, agents and publishers in Brazil and Portugal, as well as the worldwide representation of Brazilian authors. Founded 1999.

Kate Barker Literary Agency

tel 020-7688 1638
email kate@katebarker.net
website www.katebarker.net

Commercial and literary fiction for adults including crime, thriller, suspense, women's fiction, historical and reading group fiction. Non-fiction including narrative non-fiction, popular psychology and science, smart thinking, business, history, memoir, biography, lifestyle and wellbeing. Commission rates: 15% home, 20% overseas, 15%–20% TV/film by agreement. Does not represent science fiction or fantasy. Submissions via the website. No reading fee.

Bath Literary Agency

5 Gloucester Road, Bath BA1 7BH
tel (01225) 317894
email submissions@bathliteraryagency.com
website www.bathliteraryagency.com
Twitter @BathLitAgency
Contact Gill McLay

Specialist in fiction for children and young adults. Also accepts submissions in picture books, non-fiction and author illustrators. For full submission details, refer to the website. No reading fee. Founded 2011.

The Bell Lomax Moreton Agency*

Suite C, 131 Queensway, Petts Wood, Kent BR5 1DG
tel 020-7930 4447
email agency@bell-lomax.co.uk
website www.belllomaxmoreton.co.uk
Twitter @BLM_Agency
Executives Eddie Bell, Pat Lomax, Paul Moreton, June Bell, Lauren Gardner, Sarah McDonnell, Jo Bell

Will consider most fiction, non-fiction and children's (including picture books, middle grade and young adult) book proposals. Does not represent poetry, short stories or novellas, education textbooks, film scripts or stage plays, or science fiction. Submission guidelines on website. Physical submissions should be accompanied by an sae for return and an email address for correspondence. Founded 2000.

Lorella Belli Literary Agency Ltd (LBLA)*

54 Hartford House, 35 Tavistock Crescent,
London W11 1AY
tel 020-7727 8547
email info@lorellabelliagency.com
website www.lorellabelliagency.com
Facebook www.facebook.com/LorellaBelliLiteraryAgency
Twitter @lblaUK
Proprietor Lorella Belli

Fiction and general non-fiction (home 15%, overseas/dramatic 20%). Particularly interested in first-time writers, books which have international appeal, multicultural writing, books on Italy, successful self-published authors, crime thrillers, psychological suspense, reading group fiction, YA fiction. No children's, science fiction, fantasy, academic, poetry, original scripts. No reading fee. May suggest revision. Send a query email about your work before submitting it. Does not return materials unless the correct sae postage is provided.

Enclose a stamped acknowledgement card with submission if receipt acknowledgment is required. Works with dramatic and overseas associates; represents American and foreign literary agencies in the UK. Sells translation rights on behalf of British publishers, literary agents and independent authors.

Clients include Taylor Adams, Ingrid Alexander, Shahena Ali, Jennifer Armentrout/J. Lynn, Bruno Bara, Gabrielle Bernstein, Michael Bess, Bloodhound Books, Zoë Brân, Lars Brownworth, Theresa Cheung, Misty Copeland, Sally Corner, Crux Publishing, D.B. Nielsen, Renita D'Silva, Karen Dionne, Ruth Dugdall, Ker Dukey, Val Emmich, Erica Ferencik, Marcus Ferrar, Emily Giffin, 'Girl on the Net', Louise Greenberg Books, Kent Greenfield, Jessica Huie, Sophie Jackson, Joffe Books, Ed Kritzler, Dinah Lee Kung, Christopher Lascelles, Diane and Bernie Lierow, William Little, Angela Marsons, Carol Mason, Elisabetta Minervini, Nisha Minhas, Alanna Mitchell, Rick Mofina, Sandro Monetti, Kirsty Moseley, Angela Murrills, Rhiannon Navin, Annalisa Coppolaro-Nowell, Jenni Ogden, Jennifer Ouellette, Panoma Press, Sergio Pistoi, Gerald Posner, Patricia Posner, Robert J. Ray, Burt Reynolds, Sheila Roberts, Ethel Rohan, Jonathan Sacks, Sole Books, Rupert Steiner, Katie Stephens, Justine Trueman, Victoria Van Tiem, P.P. Wong, Carol Wyer. Founded 2002.

The Bent Agency*

21 Melliss Avenue, Richmond TW9 4BQ
email info@thebentagency.com
website www.thebentagency.com
Agents Molly Ker Hawn, Nicola Barr, Gemma Cooper, Sarah Manning (UK); Jenny Bent, Heather Flaherty, Louise Fury, Rachel Horowitz (US)

Represents authors of fiction and non-fiction for adults, children and teenagers. Offices in the UK and US. Unsolicited submissions welcome by email only: query and first ten pages pasted into body of email. See complete guidelines at www.thebentagency.com/submission.php. Founded 2009.

Berlin Associates Ltd

7 Tyers Gate, London SE1 3HX
tel 020-7836 1112
email submissions@berlinassociates.com
website www.berlinassociates.com
Twitter @berlinassocs
Agents Marc Berlin, Stacy Browne, Matt Connell, Alexandra Cory, Rachel Daniels, Julia Mills, Laura Reeve, Fiona Williams, Emily Wraith, Julia Wyatt

A boutique agency representing writers, directors, producers, designers, composers and below-the-line talent across theatre, film, TV, radio and new media. No prose/fiction. The majority of new clients are taken on through recommendation or invitation, however, if you would like your work to be considered for representation, email a cv along with a brief outline of your experience and the work you would like to submit for consideration.

The Blair Partnership*

PO Box 7828, London W1A 4GE
tel 020-7504 2520
email info@theblairpartnership.com
email submissions@theblairpartnership.com
website www.theblairpartnership.com
Founding Partner and Agent Neil Blair, *Agents* Josephine Hayes, Amy Fitzgerald

Considers all genres of fiction and non-fiction for adults, young readers and children. Will consider unsolicited MSS. Email a covering letter, a one-page synopsis and the first three chapters to: submissions@theblairpartnership.com.

Represents a range of people internationally from debut and established writers to broader talent across business, politics, sport and lifestyle. Range of work spans fiction, non-fiction, digital, TV and film production.

Clients include Bana Alabed, Claire Barker, Michael Byrne, Class of 92, Cheryl Tweedy, Emma Farrarons, Bernadette Fisers, Henry Fraser, Deborah Frances-White, Robert Galbraith, Keaton Henson, Sir Chris Hoy, Inbali Iserles, Jennifer Kincheloe, Frank Lampard, Kieran Larwood, Pearl Lowe, Niki Mackay, Jo Malone, Sophie Nicholls, Justine Pattison, Lord Mark Price, Zoom Rockman, Robert Scragg, Svava Sigbertsdottir, J.K. Rowling, Pete Townshend and Brian Wood.

Blake Friedmann Literary, TV & Film Agency Ltd*

First Floor, Selous House, 5–12 Mandela Street, London NW1 0DU
tel 020-7387 0842
email info@blakefriedmann.co.uk
website www.blakefriedmann.co.uk
Agents Books: Isobel Dixon, Juliet Pickering, Tom Witcomb, Hattie Grunewald, Samuel Hodder; Film/TV: Julian Friedmann, Conrad Williams.

Full-length MSS. Fiction: crime, thrillers, women's fiction, literary fiction and YA; a broad range of non-fiction (home 15%, overseas 20%). Media Department handles film and TV rights, and represents scriptwriters, playwrights and directors. Preliminary letter, synopsis and first three chapters preferred via email. No reading fee. See website for full submission guidelines.

Authors include Graeme Macrae Burnet, Edward Carey, Elizabeth Chadwick, Barbara Erskine, Paul

Finch, Janice Galloway, David Gilman, Ann Granger, Kerry Hudson, Peter James, Manu Joseph, Lucy Mangan, Zakes Mda, Deon Meyer, Marlene van Niekerk, Lawrence Norfolk, Joseph O'Connor, Sheila O'Flanagan, Monique Roffey, Julian Stockwin, Ivan Vladislavić.

Scriptwriters, playwrights and directors include Andy Briggs, Steve Hawes, Tim John, Tom Kinninmont, Greg Latter, Stuart Orme, Kaite O'Reilly, Roger Spottiswoode, Martin Thorisson and Stuart Urban. Founded 1977.

The Book Bureau Literary Agency

7 Duncairn Avenue, Bray, Co. Wicklow A98 R293, Republic of Ireland
tel +353 (0)12 764996
email thebookbureau@oceanfree.net
email thebookbureau123@gmail.com
Managing Director Geraldine Nichol

Full-length MSS (home 15%, USA/translation 20%). Fiction preferred – thrillers, crime, Irish novels, literary fiction, women's commercial novels and general fiction. No horror, science fiction, children's or poetry. Strong editorial support. No reading fee. Preliminary letter, synopsis and three sample chapters (single line spacing); return postage required. Email preferred. Works with agents overseas.

BookBlast® Ltd

PO Box 20184, London W10 5AU
tel 020-8968 3089
email gen@bookblast.com
website www.bookblast.com
website www.bookblast.com/blog
Facebook www.facebook.com/bookblastofficial/
Twitter @bookblast

Full-length MSS (home 15%, overseas 20%) Literary and general adult fiction and non-fiction (memoir, travel, popular culture, multicultural writing only). No reading fee. Also offers editorial and translation services. Represents the literary estates of Prof. Elton Mayo, Gael Elton Mayo and Lesley Blanch. Not currently accepting new clients. Promotes cultural diversity and supports the independent publishing sector via The BookBlast® Diary. Founded 1997.

Alan Brodie Representation

Paddock Suite, The Courtyard,
55 Charterhouse Street, London EC1M 6HA
tel 020-7253 6226
email abr@alanbrodie.com
website www.alanbrodie.com
Twitter @abragency
Managing Director Alan Brodie, *Agents* Victoria Williams, Kara Fitzpatrick

Specialises in stage plays, literary estates, radio, TV and film (home 10%, overseas 15%). No prose, fiction or general MSS. Represented in all major countries. No unsolicited scripts; recommendation from known professional required. Founded 1996.

Brotherstone Creative Management

Mortimer House, 37–41 Mortimer Street, London W1T 3JH
tel 020-7502 5037
email info@bcm-agency.com
email submissions@bcm-agency.com
website www.bcm-agency.com
Contact Charlie Brotherstone

Represents an eclectic list of authors, from academics, musicians and cookery writers through to novelists of commercial and literary fiction. Commission rates: UK 15%, US direct 15% (20% if sub-agented); dramatic: 15% direct (20% if sub-agented); translation 20%; TV 15%. The agency guides each client through every part of the publishing process and draws upon a wide contact network to develop their careers across all media. Submissions by email: for fiction, include the first three chapters or 50 pages, a one- to two-page synopsis and a short covering letter; for non-fiction, send a detailed outline with a sample chapter and a covering note. Does not handle scripts for theatre, film or television.

Clients include Brett Anderson, Mel B, A.A. Gill, Kirstin Innes, Nuno Mendes, George The Poet, Anna Stothard. Founded 2017.

Jenny Brown Associates*

31 Marchmont Road, Edinburgh EH9 1HU
tel 0131 229 5334
email info@jennybrownassociates.com
website www.jennybrownassociates.com
Contact Jenny Brown, Lucy Juckes

Literary fiction, crime writing and writing for children; non-fiction: literary memoir, nature, sport, music, popular culture; (home 12.5%, overseas/ translation 20%). No poetry, science fiction, fantasy or academic. No reading fee. A small agency that only reads submissions at certain points in the year; check website before sending work.

Clients include Lin Anderson, Sam Angus, Christopher Edge, Gavin Francis, Alex Gray, Joanna Hickson, Kathleen Jamie, Sara Maitland, Jonathan Meres, Ann O'Loughlin. Founded 2002.

Felicity Bryan Associates*

2A North Parade, Banbury Road, Oxford OX2 6LX
tel (01865) 513816
email agency@felicitybryan.com
website www.felicitybryan.com

Fiction and general non-fiction with emphasis on history, biography, science and current affairs (home 15%, overseas 20%). No scripts for TV, radio or theatre, no crafts, how-to, science fiction, light romance or poetry.

Clients include Carlos Acosta, Karen Armstrong, Mary Berry, Simon Blackburn, Rhidian Brook, Archie Brown, Marcus Chown, Artemis Cooper, Louis de Bernières, Edmund de Waal, John Dickie, Reni Eddo-Lodge, Rebecca Fleet, Peter Frankopan, David

Goldblatt, A.C. Grayling, Tim Harford, Peter Heather, Anna Hope, Gill Hornby, Sadie Jones, Liza Klaussmann, Simon Lelic, Diarmaid MacCulloch, James Naughtie, John Julius Norwich, Iain Pears, Rosamunde Pilcher, Sue Prideaux, Dan Richards, Matt Ridley, Eugene Rogan, Meg Rosoff, Roy Strong, Adrian Tinniswood, Martin Walker, Anna Whitelock, Lucy Worsley.

Juliet Burton Literary Agency*

2 Clifton Avenue, London W12 9DR
tel 020-8762 0148
email juliet@julietburton.com
Contact Juliet Burton

Handles fiction and some non-fiction. Special interests include crime and women's fiction. No science fiction/fantasy, children's, short stories, plays, film scripts, articles, poetry or academic material. Commission: home 15%, USA & translation 20%. Approach in writing in the first instance with synopsis and two sample chapters and sae. No reading fee.

Clients include Rosie Archer, Kay Brellend, Barbara Cleverly, Marjorie Eccles, Edward Enfield, Anthea Fraser, June Hampson, Veronica Heley, Peter Helton, Mick Herron, Maureen Lee, Priscilla Masters, Gwen Moffat, Barbara Nadel, Sheila Norton and Pam Weaver. Founded 1999.

C&W*

(previously Conville & Walsh)
Haymarket House, 28–29 Haymarket, London SW1Y 4SP
tel 020-7393 4200
website www.cwagency.co.uk
Directors Clare Conville, Jake Smith-Bosanquet

Handles all genres of fiction, non-fiction and children's worldwide (home 15%, US and translation 20%). Submissions welcome: first three chapters, cover letter, synopsis by email. No reading fee. Part of the Curtis Brown Group of Companies; simultaneous submission accepted.

Fiction clients include notable prize winners such as D.B.C. Pierre, Nathan Filer, Matt Haig, Ali Shaw, M.L. Stedman, Sara Baume, Kevin Barry, Catherine O'Flynn, Andrew Michael Hurley and Simon Wroe. Other novelists include Colin Barrett, Maxine Beneba Clarke, Joanna Cannon, Tim Clare, Daniel Cole, Fiona Cummins, Esther Freud, Kirsty Gunn, Rowan Hisayo Buchanan, Rachel Joyce, Stephen Kelman, Jess Kidd, John Niven, S.J. Watson, Eley Williams and Isabel Wolff.

Non-fiction clients include Tom Burgis, Dodie Clark, Misha Glenny, Ramita Navai, Ben Rawlence, Tali Sharot, Tim Spector, Liam Vaughan, Christie Watson, Zoe Williams, Ben Wilson and Hannah Witton. Artists represented for books include the estate of Francis Bacon and Harland Miller. Children's and young adult list includes John Burningham, Damian Dibben, Steve Voake, Paula Rawsthorne, Katie Davies, Rebecca James, P.J. Lynch, Piers Torday and the estate of Astrid Lindgren. Founded 2000.

Georgina Capel Associates Ltd*

29 Wardour Street, London W1D 6PS
tel 020-7734 2414
email firstname@georginacapel.com
website www.georginacapel.com
Agents Georgina Capel, Rachel Conway, Philippa Brewster

Literary and commercial fiction, history, biography; film and TV (home/overseas 15%). No reading fee; see website for submission guidelines.

Clients include Simon Barnes, Julia Copus, Flora Fraser, John Gimlette, Adrian Goldsworthy, Andrew Greig, Philip Hoare, Tristram Hunt, Dan Jones, Tobias Jones, Leanda de Lisle, Adam Nicolson, Louise O'Neill, Chibundu Onuzo, Stella Rimington, Andrew Roberts, Ian Sansom, Simon Sebag Montefiore, Diana Souhami, Elizabeth Speller, Lesley Thomson, Fay Weldon. Founded 1999.

Casarotto Ramsay & Associates Ltd

Waverley House, 7–12 Noel Street, London W1F 8GQ
tel 020-7287 4450
email info@casarotto.co.uk
website www.casarotto.co.uk
Directors Jenne Casarotto, Giorgio Casarotto, Mel Kenyon, Jodi Shields, Rachel Holroyd, Ian Devlin

MSS – theatre, films, TV, sound broadcasting only (10%). Works in conjunction with agents in USA and other foreign countries. Preliminary letter essential.

Caskie Mushens*

email juliet@caskiemushens.com
email robert@caskiemushens.com
website www.caskiemushens.com
Twitter @mushenska
Twitter @rcaskie1
Contacts Robert Caskie, Juliet Mushens

Represents all genres except picture books, children's and erotica (home 15%, overseas 20%). Submission guidelines: For Juliet, email with the subject line QUERY, the cover letter in the body of the email, and a synopsis and the first three chapters or approximately first 50pp as attachments. Juliet responds to every submission within 6 to 8 weeks of receipt of email. Does not accept non-fiction. For Robert, email with cover letter, a synopsis and the first three chapters. For non-fiction, please send him a cover letter, introduction, chapter breakdown and sample chapter. Do not submit to both Juliet and Robert.

The Catchpole Agency

53 Cranham Street, Oxford OX2 6DD
tel 07789 588070

email james@thecatchpoleagency.co.uk
website www.thecatchpoleagency.co.uk
Proprietor James Catchpole

Agents for authors and illustrators of children's books from picture books through to young adult novels. Commission from 12.5% to 15%. See website for contact and submissions details. Founded 1996.

Chapman & Vincent*

21 Ellis Street, London SW1X 9AL
email chapmanvincent@hotmail.co.uk
Directors Jennifer Chapman, Gilly Vincent

A specialist agency acting mainly as a packager. Can only consider non-fiction texts suitable for major illustration in heritage, gardening and cookery areas. Not currently seeking clients but will reply to all sensible approaches by email without attachments. No postal submissions. No reading fee. Works with Elaine Markson in the US. Commission: home 15%/ overseas 20%.

Clients include George Carter, Leslie Geddes-Brown, Lucinda Lambton and Eve Pollard.

Teresa Chris Literary Agency Ltd*

43 Musard Road, London W6 8NR
tel 020-7386 0633
email teresachris@litagency.co.uk
website www.teresachrisliteraryagency.co.uk
Director Teresa Chris

All fiction, especially crime, women's commercial, general and literary fiction. No science fiction, horror, fantasy, short stories, poetry, academic books (home 10%, overseas 20%). No reading fee. Send introductory letter describing work, first three chapters and sae. Representation in all overseas territories. Founded 1988.

Anne Clark Literary Agency

email submissions@anneclarkliteraryagency.co.uk
website www.anneclarkliteraryagency.co.uk
Facebook www.facebook.com/anneclarkliterary
Twitter @AnneClarkLit
Contact Anne Clark

Specialist in fiction, picture books and non-fiction for children and young adults (home 15%, overseas 20%). Submissions by email only. See website for submission guidelines. No reading fee. Founded 2012.

Mary Clemmey Literary Agency*

6 Dunollie Road, London NW5 2XP
tel 020-7267 1290
email mcwords@googlemail.com

High-quality fiction and non-fiction with an international market (home 15%, overseas 20%, performance rights 15%). No children's books or science fiction. TV, film, radio and theatre scripts from existing clients only. Works in conjunction with US agent. No reading fee. No unsolicited MSS and no email submissions. Approach first by letter (including sae). Founded 1992.

Jonathan Clowes Ltd*

10 Iron Bridge House, Bridge Approach, London NW1 8BD
tel 020-7722 7674
email rosie@jonathanclowes.co.uk
email cara@jonathanclowes.co.uk
website www.jonathanclowes.co.uk
Directors Ann Evans, Nemonie Craven; *Contacts* Rosie Welsh, Cara Lee Simpson

Literary and commercial fiction and non-fiction, film, TV, theatre (for existing clients) and radio (home 15%, overseas 20%). See website for submission guidelines. No reading fee. Email for general enquiries. Works in association with agents overseas. Founded 1960.

Clients include Dr David Bellamy, Arthur Conan Doyle Characters Ltd, Simon Critchley, Len Deighton, Brian Freemantle, Victoria Glass, Francesca Hornak, Carla Lane, David Nobbs, Gruff Rhys and the literary estates of Doris Lessing, Elizabeth Jane Howard, Michael Baigent and Richard Leigh.

Rosica Colin Ltd

1 Clareville Grove Mews, London SW7 5AH
tel 020-7370 1080
Directors Sylvie Marston, Joanna Marston

All full-length MSS (excluding science fiction and poetry); also theatre, film and sound broadcasting (home 10%, overseas 10–20%). No reading fee, but may take 3–4 months to consider full MSS. Send synopsis only in first instance, with letter outlining writing credits and whether MS has been previously submitted, plus return postage.

Authors include Richard Aldington, Simone de Beauvoir (in UK), Samuel Beckett (publication rights), Steven Berkoff, Alan Brownjohn, Sandy Brownjohn, Donald Campbell, Nick Dear, Neil Donnelly, J.T. Edson, Bernard Farrell, Rainer Werner Fassbinder (in UK), Jean Genet, Franz Xaver Kroetz, Don McCamphill, Heiner Müller (in UK), Graham Reid, Alan Sillitoe, Botho Strauss (in UK), Rina Vergano, Anthony Vivis, Wim Wenders (in UK). Founded 1949.

Jane Conway-Gordon Ltd*

38 Cromwell Grove, London W6 7RG
tel 020-7371 6939
email jane@conway-gordon.co.uk
website www.janeconwaygordon.com

Full length MSS (home 15%, overseas 20%). No poetry, science fiction or children's. Represented in all foreign countries. No reading fee but preliminary letter and return postage essential. Founded 1982.

Coombs Moylett Maclean Literary Agency

120 New Kings Road, London SW6 4LZ
tel 020-8740 0454

website www.cmm.agency
Contacts Lisa Moylett, Jamie Maclean

Specialises in well-written commercial fiction, particularly in the genres of historical fiction, crime/mystery/suspense and thrillers, women's fiction across a spectrum ranging from chick-lit sagas to contemporary and literary fiction. Also looking to build a children's list concentrating on YA fiction. Considers most non-fiction particularly history, biography, current affairs and cookery. Works with foreign agents. Commission: home 15%, overseas 20%, film/TV 20%. No reading fee. Does not handle poetry, plays or scripts for film and TV.

Creative Authors Ltd

11A Woodlawn Street, Whitstable, Kent CT5 1HQ
email write@creativeauthors.co.uk
website www.creativeauthors.co.uk
Twitter @creativeauthors
Director Isabel Atherton

Fiction, women's fiction, literary fiction, non-fiction, humour, history, science, autobiography, biography, business, memoir, health, cookery, arts and crafts, crime, children's fiction, picture books, young adult, graphic novels and illustrators (home 15%, overseas 20%). Only accepts email submissions.

Authors and illustrators include Guojing, Ged Adamson, Zuza Zak, Tristan Donovan, Nick Soulsby, Mark Beaumont, Lucy Scott, Coll Muir, Kenneth Womack, Bompas & Parr, Kelly Lawrence, Colleen Kosinski, Anthony Galving, Dr Keith Souter. Founded 2008.

Rupert Crew Ltd*

6 Windsor Road, London N3 3SS
tel 020-8346 3000
email info@rupertcrew.co.uk
website www.rupertcrew.co.uk
Managing Director Caroline Montgomery

International representation, handling accessible literary and commercial fiction and non-fiction for adult and children's (8+) markets. Home 15%; overseas, TV/film and radio 20%. No picture books, plays, screenplays, poetry, journalism, science fiction, fantasy or short stories. No reading fee. No unsolicited MSS: see website for current submission guidelines. Founded 1927 by F. Rupert Crew.

Curtis Brown Group Ltd*

Haymarket House, 28–29 Haymarket, London SW1Y 4SP
tel 020-7393 4400
email cb@curtisbrown.co.uk
website www.curtisbrown.co.uk
website www.curtisbrowncreative.co.uk
Twitter @CBGBooks
Twitter @CBCreative
Chairman Jonathan Lloyd, *Joint Chief Executives* Jonny Geller and Ben Hall, *Directors* Jacquie Drewe, Nick Marston, Sarah Spear *Books* Jonny Geller (Managing Director), Felicity Blunt, Sheila Crowley, Jonathan Lloyd, Alice Lutyens, Norah Perkins (Estates), Luke Speed (Book to Film), Cathryn Summerhayes, Karolina Sutton, Stephanie Thwaites, Gordon Wise

Represents prominent writers of fiction and non-fiction, from winners of all major awards to international bestsellers, and formats ranging from print and audio to digital and merchandise. In fiction, works across many genres, both literary and those aimed at a popular audience, and looks for strong voices and outstanding storytellers in general fiction, crime, thrillers, psychological suspense, mainstream fantasy, historical fiction, young adult and children's books. Non-fiction list includes leading commentators and thinkers, historians, biographers, YouTubers, lifestyle brands, scientists and writers of quality narrative non-fiction.

Represents a number of well-known personalities, from world-renowned politicians to business leaders and comedians. Curtis Brown also manages the international careers of authors, with strong relationships in translation and US markets. The Book Department works closely with a team of media agents, offering full-service representation in film, TV and theatre. Activities include the creative writing school, Curtis Brown Creative, established with the aim of finding and fostering new talent.

Simultaneous submissions with C&W (previously Conville and Walsh) (see separate entry), also a member of the Curtis Brown Group of companies.

While no longer accepting submissions by post, for more information on submissions and individual agents, as well as the writing courses offered as part of Curtis Brown Creative, consult www.curtisbrowncreative.co.uk. Founded 1899.

Judy Daish Associates Ltd

2 St Charles Place, London W10 6EG
tel 020-8964 8811
email judy@judydaish.com
website www.judydaish.com
Agents Judy Daish, Howard Gooding, Tracey Elliston

Theatre, film, TV, radio (rates by negotiation). No unsolicited MSS. No reading fee. Founded 1978.

Caroline Davidson Literary Agency*

5 Queen Anne's Gardens, London W4 1TU
tel 020-8995 5768
email enquiries@cdla.co.uk
website www.cdla.co.uk

Handles exceptional novels, memoirs and non-fiction of originality and high quality (12.5%). Visit website for further information. All submissions must be in hard copy. Email submissions are not considered. For non-fiction send letter with cv and detailed, well thought-out book proposal, including chapter synopsis. With fiction, send letter, cv, summary and the first 50pp of text. No reply without large sae with correct return postage. CDLA dislikes fantasy, horror, crime and sci-fi.

Authors (frontlist) include Peter Barham, Andrew Beatty, Andrew Dalby, Emma Donoghue, Chris Greenhalgh, Richard Hobday, John Phibbs, Helena Whitbread. Founded 1988.

Felix de Wolfe

20 Old Compton Street, London W1D 4TW
tel 020-7242 5066
email info@felixdewolfe.com
website www.felixdewolfe.com
Agents Caroline de Wolfe, Wendy Scozzaro

Theatre, films, TV, sound broadcasting, fiction (home 10–15%, overseas 20%). No reading fee. Works in conjunction with many foreign agencies. No unsolicited submissions.

DGA Ltd

55 Monmouth Street, London WC2H 9DG
tel 020-7240 9992
email assistant@davidgodwinassociates.co.uk
website www.davidgodwinassociates.com
Twitter @DGALitAgents
Directors David Godwin, Heather Godwin

Broad range of fiction and non-fiction with a strong focus on literary. Send MS with synopsis and cover letter to sebastiangodwin@davidgodwinassociates.co.uk. Founded 1995.

DHH Literary Agency

23–27 Cecil Court, London WC2N 4EZ
tel 020-7836 7376
email enquiries@dhhliteraryagency.com
website www.dhhliteraryagency.com
Facebook www.facebook.com/dhhliteraryagency
Twitter @dhhlitagency
Agents David H. Headley, Broo Doherty, Hannah Sheppard, Harry Illingworth, Natalie Galustian

Fiction, women's commercial fiction, crime, literary fiction, science fiction and fantasy. Non-fiction special interests include memoir, history, cookery and humour. Also children's and YA fiction. No plays or scripts, poetry or short stories. Send informative preliminary email with first three chapters and synopsis. No reading fee. New authors welcome. Founded 2008.

Diamond Kahn & Woods Literary Agency

Top Floor, 66 Onslow Gardens, London N10 3JX
tel 020-3514 6544
email info@dkwlitagency.co.uk
email submissions.ella@dkwlitagency.co.uk
email submissions.bryony@dkwlitagency.co.uk
email submissions.elinor@dkwlitagency.co.uk
website www.dkwlitagency.co.uk
Twitter @DKWLitAgency
Agents Ella Diamond Kahn, Bryony Woods, Elinor Cooper

Literary and commercial fiction (including all major genres) and non-fiction for adults; and children's, young adult and crossover fiction (home 15%, USA/translation 20%). Interested in new writers. No reading fee, email submissions only. Send three chapters and synopsis to one agent only. See website for further details on agents, their areas of interest and submission guidelines.

Clients include Vanessa Curtis, Virginia Macgregor, S.E. Lister, Chris Lloyd, Nicole Burstein, David Owen, Caroline O'Donoghue, Samantha Collett, Sharon Gosling, Sylvia Bishop, Sarah Baker, Katherine Orton, Dan Smith, Meg Fee, Laura Jane Williams, Emma Pass, Tom Percival, Matilda Tristram, Tom Duxbury, Nina de la Mer, Jay Eunji Lee, Jion Sheibani and Laura Kaye.

Elise Dillsworth Agency

9 Grosvenor Road, Muswell Hill, London N10 2DR
email elise@elisedillsworthagency.com
website www.elisedillsworthagency.com
Twitter @EliseDillsworth
Owner/Literary Agent Elise Dillsworth

Represents literary and commercial fiction and non-fiction in the area of memoir, biography, travel and cookery, with a keen aim to reflect writing that is international (home 15%, overseas 20%). Does not represent science fiction, fantasy, poetry, plays, film/TV scripts or children's books. Send preliminary letter, synopsis and first three chapters (or approximately 50 pages). No postal submissions accepted. See website for full submission guidelines.

Authors include Yvonne Battle-Felton, Vanessa Bolosier, Anthony Joseph, Irenosen Okojie, Yewande Omotoso, Ilmar Taska and Stephanie Victoire. Founded 2012.

Robert Dudley Agency

135A Bridge Street, Ashford, Kent TN25 5DP
tel 07879 426574
email info@robertdudleyagency.co.uk
website www.robertdudleyagency.co.uk
Proprietor Robert Dudley

Non-fiction only. Specialises in history, biography, sport, management, politics, military history, current affairs (home 15%, overseas 20%; film/TV/radio 20%). No reading fee. Will suggest revision. Email submissions preferred. All material sent at owner's risk. No MSS returned without sae.

Authors include Nigel Barlow, Ben Barry, Tim Bentinck, Rachel Bridge, Michael Broers, Prit Buttar, David Hanrahan, Halik Kochanski, William Mortimer Moore, Mungo Melvin, Tim Phillips, Brian Holden Reid, Mary Colwell, Elise Schwarz, Chris Sidwells, Martyn Whittock. Founded 2000.

Eddison Pearson Ltd*

West Hill House, 6 Swains Lane, London N6 6QS
tel 020-7700 7763

email enquiries@eddisonpearson.com
website www.eddisonpearson.com
Contact Clare Pearson

Children's and young adult books, fiction and non-fiction, poetry (home 10–15%, overseas 15–20%). Small, personally run agency. Enquiries and submissions by email only; email for up-to-date submission guidelines by return. No reading fee. May suggest revision where appropriate.

Authors include Valerie Bloom, Sue Heap, Caroline Lawrence, Robert Muchamore, Megan Rix.

Edwards Fuglewicz*

49 Great Ormond Street, London WC1N 3HZ
tel 020-7405 6725
Partners Ros Edwards, Helenka Fuglewicz

Literary and commercial fiction (but no children's fiction, science fiction or horror); non-fiction: biography, history and narrative non-fiction (including animal stories), (home 15%, USA/translation 20%). No email submissions. Founded 1996.

Faith Evans Associates*

27 Park Avenue North, London N8 7RU
tel 020-8340 9920
email faith@faith-evans.co.uk

Small agency (home 15%, overseas 20%). Co-agents in most countries. List full. No phone calls or submissions.

Authors include Melissa Benn, Eleanor Bron, Midge Gillies, Ed Glinert, Vesna Goldsworthy, Jim Kelly, Helena Kennedy, Tom Paulin, Sheila Rowbotham, Harriet Walter, Elizabeth Wilson, and the estates of Madeleine Bourdouxhe and Lorna Sage. Founded 1987.

Janet Fillingham Associates

52 Lowther Road, London SW13 9NU
tel 020-8748 5594
website www.janetfillingham.com
Agents Janet Fillingham, Kate Weston

Film, TV and theatre only (home 15%, overseas 15–20%). No books. Strictly no unsolicited MSS; professional recommendation required. Founded 1992.

Film Rights Ltd

11 Pandora Road, London NW6 1TS
tel 020-8001 3040
email information@filmrights.ltd.uk
website www.filmrights.ltd.uk
Directors Brendan Davis, Joan Potts

Theatre, films, TV and sound broadcasting (home 10%, overseas 15%). No reading fee. Represented in USA and abroad. Founded 1932.

Clients include Carlo Ardito, John Chapman, Peter Coke, Ray Cooney OBE, Dave Freeman, John Graham, Robin Hawdon, Jeremy Lloyd (plays), Dawn Lowe-Watson, Glyn Robbins, Edward Taylor, the estate of Dodie Smith, the literary estate of N.C. Hunter, the estate of Frank Baker and the literary estate of Michael Pertwee.

Laurence Fitch Ltd

(incorporating The London Play Company 1922)
11 Pandora Road, London NW6 1TS
tel 020-8001 3040
email information@laurencefitch.com
website www.laurencefitch.com
Directors F.H.L. Fitch, Joan Potts, Brendan Davis

Film and TV (home 10%, overseas 15%).

Authors include Carlo Ardito, John Chapman, Peter Coke, Ray Cooney OBE, Dave Freeman, John Graham, Robin Hawdon, Jeremy Lloyd (plays), Dawn Lowe-Watson, Glyn Robbins, Edward Taylor, the estate of Dodie Smith, the literary estate of N.C. Hunter, the estate of Frank Baker and the literary estate of Michael Pertwee.

Fox & Howard Literary Agency*

39 Eland Road, London SW11 5JX
tel 020-7223 9452
email enquiries@foxandhoward.co.uk
email fandhagency@googlemail.com
website www.foxandhoward.co.uk
Partners Chelsey Fox, Charlotte Howard

General non-fiction: biography, history and popular culture, reference, business, mind, body & spirit, health and personal development, popular psychology (home 15%, overseas 20%). Check website for submission details. The client list is currently closed.

FRA*

(formerly Futerman, Rose & Associates)
91 St Leonards Road, London SW14 7BL
tel 020-8255 7755
email enquiries@futermanrose.co.uk
website www.futermanrose.co.uk
Contacts Guy Rose, Alexandra Groom

Fiction, biography (especially sport, music and politics), show business, current affairs, teen fiction and scripts for TV and film. No children's, science fiction or fantasy. No unsolicited MSS. Send brief résumé, synopsis, first 20pp and sae.

Clients include Jill Anderson, Larry Barker, Christian Piers Betley, Kevin Clarke, Richard Digance, Rt Hon Iain Duncan Smith MP, Sir Martin Ewans, Paul Ferris, John French, Susan George, Keith Gillespie, Paul Hendy, Sarah Heron, Tony Ilott, Sara Khan, Jerry Leider, Keith R. Lindsay, Eric MacInnes, Paul Marx, Tony McMahon, Sir Vartan Melkonian, Joseph Miller, John Moreton, Max Morgan-Witts, His Hon Judge Peter Murphy, His Hon Judge Chris Nicholson, Mary O'Hara, Ciaran O'Keeffe, Antonia Owen, Tom Owen, Zoe Paphitis, Liz Rettig, Kenneth G. Ross, Peter Sallis, Paul Stinchcombe QC, Gordon

Thomas, Bill Tidy, Toyah Willcox, Simon Woodham, Allen Zeleski. Founded 1984.

Fraser Ross Associates

6 Wellington Place, Edinburgh EH6 7EQ
tel 0131 553 2759, 0131 657 4412
email agentlmfraser@gmail.com
email kjross@tiscali.co.uk
website www.fraserross.co.uk
Facebook www.facebook.com/fraserrossassociates
Twitter @FraserRossLA
Partners Lindsey Fraser, Kathryn Ross

Writing and illustration for children's books, fiction and non-fiction for adults. See website for client list and submission guidelines. Founded 2002.

Furniss Lawton*

180 Great Portland Street, London W1W 5QZ
tel 020-8987 6804
email info@furnisslawton.co.uk
website www.furnisslawton.co.uk
Agents Eugenie Furniss, Rowan Lawton, Rory Scarfe, Rachel Mills

Fiction: general commercial, thrillers, historical, crime, suspense, women's fiction, literary and young adult. Non-fiction: biography, memoir, cookery, lifestyle, business, history, popular science, psychology. Submissions by email only to info@furnisslawton.co.uk. Home 15%, overseas 20%.

Authors include S.K. Tremayne, Matt Reilly, Louise Jensen, Caz Frear, Mary Lynn Bracht, Julian Clary, Clare Balding, Tasmina Perry, Lindsey Kelk, Michael Calvin, Jon Sopel.

Jüri Gabriel

35 Camberwell Grove, London SE5 8JA
tel 020-7703 6186
email juri@jurigabriel.com

Quality fiction and non-fiction (i.e. anything that shows wit and intelligence); radio, TV and film, but selling these rights only in existing works by existing clients (home 10%, overseas 20%, performance rights 10%). Submit three sample chapters plus a 1–2 page synopsis and sae (if using snail mail) in the first instance. Will suggest revision where appropriate. No short stories, articles, verse or books for children. No reading fee. Jüri Gabriel was the chairman of Dedalus (publishers) for nearly 30 years.

Authors include Jack Allen, Gbontwi Anyetei, Nick Bradbury, Prof. Christopher Day, Miriam Dunne, Paul Genney, Pat Gray, Mikka Haugaard, Robert Irwin, Pat Johnson, 'David Madsen', Richard Mankiewicz, David Miller, John Outram, Philip Roberts, Roger Storey, Jeremy Weingard.

Graham Maw Christie*

37 Highbury Place, London N5 1QP
email enquiries@grahammawchristie.com
website www.grahammawchristie.com
Twitter @litagencyGMC
Contacts Jane Graham Maw, Jennifer Christie

General non-fiction: autobiography/memoir, business/smart thinking, humour and gift, food and drink, craft, health and wellness, fashion, lifestyle, parenting, self-help/how to, popular science/history/culture/reference, TV tie-in. No fiction, children's or poetry. No reading fee. Email submissions only. Will suggest revisions. Also represents ghostwriters. See website for submission guidelines.

Authors include Bronte Aurell, Elizabeth Bentley, Jane Brocket, Sally Coulthard, Vybarr Cregan-Reid, Simon Dawson, Oli Doyle, Michael Foley, Linda Gask, Clare Gogerty, Amber Hatch, Megan C. Hayes, Dr Jessamy Hibberd, Tim D. James, Cathryn Kemp, Sarah Norris, Lisa Lam, Alex Monroe, Gavin Presman, Andy Ramage, Suzy Reading, Juliet Sear, Fern Taylor, Jo Usmar, Richard Wilson, Brit Williams, Raynor Winn. Founded 2005.

Annette Green Authors' Agency

5 Henwoods Mount, Pembury, Tunbridge Wells TN2 4BH
tel (01892) 263252
website www.annettegreenagency.co.uk
Partners Annette Green, David Smith

Full-length MSS (home 15%, overseas 20/25%). Literary and general fiction and non-fiction, popular culture, history, science, teenage fiction. No picture books, dramatic scripts, poetry, science fiction or fantasy. No reading fee. Preliminary letter, synopsis, sample chapter and sae essential.

Authors include Andrew Baker, Louis Barfe, James Bloodworth, Tim Bradford, Bill Broady, Katherine Clements, Terry Darlington, Elizabeth Haynes, Liz Jones, Frances Kay, Jane Kerr, Claire King, Maria McCann, Adam Macqueen, Ian Marchant, Kirsty Scott, Mel Wells.

Christine Green Authors' Agent*

LSBU Technopark, 90 London Road, London SE1 6LN
tel 020-7401 8844
email info@christinegreen.co.uk
website www.christinegreen.co.uk
Twitter @whitehorsemews
Contact Christine Green

Literary and commercial fiction, narrative (novelistic) non-fiction. General, young adult, women's, crime and historical fiction welcome, but note no genre science fiction or fantasy, travelogues, self-help, picture books, scripts or poetry. Commission: home 15%, overseas 20%. Works in conjunction with agencies in Asia, Europe and Scandinavia. No reading fee. Preliminary queries by email welcome. Email submissions only. Founded 1984.

Louise Greenberg Books Ltd*

The End House, Church Crescent, London N3 1BG
tel 020-8349 1179

email louisegreenberg@msn.com
website www.louisegreenbergbooks.co.uk

Full-length MSS (home 15%, overseas 20%). Literary fiction and non-fiction. No reading fee. Return postage and sae essential. No telephone enquiries. Founded 1997.

Greene & Heaton Ltd*

37 Goldhawk Road, London W12 8QQ
tel 020-8749 0315
email submissions@greeneheaton.co.uk
email info@greeneheaton.co.uk
website www.greeneheaton.co.uk
Twitter @GreeneandHeaton
Contacts Carol Heaton, Judith Murray, Antony Topping, Claudia Young, Eleanor Teasdale, Kate Rizzo (Foreign Rights Director)

Fiction and non-fiction (home 15%, USA/translation 20%). No poetry or original scripts for theatre, film or TV. Email submissions accepted, but no reply guaranteed, or send a covering letter, synopsis and first three chapters with sae and return postage. Handles translation rights directly in all major territories.

Clients include Lucy Atkins, Laura Barnett, Jordan Bourke, Elizabeth Buchan, Helen Callaghan, Emma Chapman, Lucy Clarke, Martha Collison, Suzannah Dunn, Sabine Durrant, Marcus du Sautoy, Samantha Ellis, Hugh Fearnley-Whittingstall, Michael Frayn, Christoph Galfard, Maeve Haran, the estate of P.D. James, Joseph Knox, M.D. Lachlan, William Leith, Dan Lepard, James McGee, Ian McGuire, S.G. MacLean, Thomasina Miers, Lottie Moggach, Kamin Mohammadi, Jo Nadin, Mary-Ann Ochota, Temi Oh, Ian Overton, C.J. Sansom, Andrew Taylor, Sarah Waters, Will Wiles, Benjamin Wood, Jackie Wullschlager, Anne Youngson. *Children's authors* include Helen Craig, Viviane Schwarz. Founded 1963.

The Greenhouse Literary Agency

4th Floor, 9 Kingsway, London WC2B 6XF
tel 020-7841 3959
email submissions@greenhouseliterary.com
website www.greenhouseliterary.com
Twitter @sarahgreenhouse
Twitter @nolanpolly
Director Sarah Davies, *UK Agent* Polly Nolan

Specialist children's book agency with a reputation for impressive transatlantic deals. Represents picture book author-illustrators through to writers for teens/young adults (USA/UK 15%, elsewhere 25%). Represents European and Commonwealth authors writing in English (Polly Nolan) as well as North American authors (Sarah Davies). No non-fiction. No adult fiction. No reading fee. No postal submissions. Queries by email only. Strict submission criteria (see website for details).

Authors include Janine Beacham, Jennifer Bell, Julie Bertagna, Sarwat Chadda/Joshua Khan, Lindsey Eagar, Tae Keller, Dawn Kurtagich, Alice Lickens, Megan Miranda, Sinéad O'Hart, Gavin Puckett, Ali Standish, Louie Stowell, Matilda Woods. Founded 2008.

Gregory & Company Authors' Agents*

(Now part of David Higham Associates)
6th Floor, Waverley House, 7–12 Noel Street, London W1F 8GQ
tel 020-7434 5900
email info@gregoryandcompany.co.uk (general enquiries)
email maryjones@gregoryandcompany.co.uk (submissions)
website www.gregoryandcompany.co.uk
Twitter @GregoryCoAgents
Contacts Jane Gregory (UK, US, film rights), Claire Morris (translation rights), Stephanie Glencross and Mary Jones (editorial), Laura Darpetti (assistant), Sara Langham (assistant)

Fiction (home 15%, USA/translation/radio/film/TV 20%). Special interests (fiction): literary, commercial, women's fiction, crime, suspense and thrillers. Particularly interested in books which will also sell to publishers abroad. No science fiction, fantasy, poetry, academic or children's books, original plays, film or TV scripts (only published books are sold to film and TV). No reading fee. Editorial advice given to own authors. No unsolicited MSS: send preliminary letter with cv, synopsis (3pp maximum), first 10pp of typescript and future writing plans plus return postage. Submissions can also be sent by email, first 50pp of typescript, but due to volume will only respond if interested in reading more. Represented throughout Europe, Asia and USA. Founded 1987.

Authors include Val McDermid, Minette Walters, Belinda Bauer, Tan Twang Eng, Paula Daly.

David Grossman Literary Agency Ltd

9 Lamington Street, London W6 0HU
tel 020-8741 2860
email submissions@dglal.co.uk

Full-length MSS (home 10–15%, overseas 20% including foreign agent's commission, performance rights 15%). Works in conjunction with agents in New York, Los Angeles, Europe, Japan. No reading fee but preliminary letter required. No submissions by fax or email. Founded 1976.

Gunn Media

50 Albemarle Street, London W1S 4BD
tel 020-7529 3745
email douglas@gunnmedia.co.uk
Directors Doug Kean, Sarah McFadden

Commercial fiction and non-fiction including literary, thrillers and celebrity autobiographies (home 15%, overseas 20%).

Authors include Mhairi McFarlane, Dr Liam Fox, Paul Burrell, Mill Millington.

Marianne Gunn O'Connor Literary Agency

Morrison Chambers, Suites 52 & 53,
32 Nassau Street, Dublin D02 RX59,
Republic of Ireland
email mgoclitagency@eircom.net
Contact Marianne Gunn O'Connor

Literary, fiction, upmarket fiction including book club and psychological suspense. We also handle children's books, middle grade, young adult, new adult and crossover fiction, as well as exciting new non-fiction authors with a focus on narrative non-fiction, health, some memoir and biography.

Clients include Liz Nugent, Mike Mccormack, Patrick McCabe, Nana Oforiata Ayim (who brought together the first cultural encyclopaedia for the whole of Africa), Shane Hegarty, Orlagh Collins, Susie Lau aka Stylebubble, Claudia Carroll, Kate Kerrigan, Sinead Moriarty, Emily Gillmor Murphy, Alison Walsh, Kathleen McMahon, Louise Douglas, Kieran Crowley, Christy Lefteri, Julia Kelly, Maureen Gaffney, Chris Binchy, David McWilliams, Vanessa Ronan, Caitriona Perry.

Gwyn Palmer Associates Ltd

225 New King's Road, London SW6 4XE
email robertgwynpalmer@gmail.com
Contact Robert Gwyn Palmer

Non-fiction only including but not limited to self-help, memoir and autobiography, history, cookery, economics, popular science, graphic design, architecture and design (home 15%). Submissions: make initial contact via email with an outline of the proposal.

The Hanbury Agency Ltd, Literary Agents*

53 Lambeth Walk, London SE11 6DX
tel 020-7582 1099
email enquiries@hanburyagency.com
website www.hanburyagency.com
Twitter @HanburyAgency

Represents general fiction and non-fiction. See website for submission guidelines.

Authors include George Alagiah, Tom Bergin, Simon Callow, Oscar de Muriel, Luke Dormehl, Tim Jarvis, Imran Khan, Roman Krznaric, Judith Lennox, Joanna Palani, Katie Price, Kate Raworth, Professor Gina Rippon, the estate of Elizabeth Taylor, Jerry White. The agency has a strong stable of ghostwriters. Founded 1983.

Hardman & Swainson*

S86 Somerset House, London WC2R 1LA
tel 020-3701 7449
website www.hardmanswainson.com
Facebook www.facebook.com/Hardman-Swainson-262825420515276/
Twitter @hardmanswainson
Directors Caroline Hardman, Joanna Swainson

Literary and commercial fiction, crime and thriller, women's, accessible literary, YA and middle grade children's fiction. Non-fiction, including memoir, biography, popular science, history, philosophy. No poetry or screenplays (home 15%, USA/translation/film/TV 20%). No reading fee. Will work editorially with the author where appropriate. Submissions by email only to submissions@hardmanswainson.com.

Clients include Dinah Jefferies, Liz Trenow, Cathy Bramley, Ali McNamara, Giovanna Fletcher, Helen Fields, Isabelle Broom, The Unmumsy Mum. Founded 2012.

Antony Harwood Ltd

103 Walton Street, Oxford OX2 6EB
tel (01865) 559615
email mail@antonyharwood.com
website www.antonyharwood.com
Contacts Antony Harwood, James Macdonald Lockhart, Jo Williamson (children's)

General and genre fiction; general non-fiction (home 15%, overseas 20%). Will suggest revision. No reading fee.

Clients include Louise Doughty, Peter F. Hamilton, Alan Hollinghurst, A.L. Kennedy, Douglas Kennedy, Dorothy Koomson, Amy Liptrot, George Monbiot. Founded 2000.

A.M. Heath & Co. Ltd*

6 Warwick Court, London WC1R 5DJ
tel 020-7242 2811
website www.amheath.com
Twitter @amheathltd
Contacts Bill Hamilton, Victoria Hobbs, Euan Thorneycroft, Alexandra McNicoll (foreign rights), Oliver Munson, Julia Churchill (children's), Rebecca Ritchie, Zoe King

Full-length MSS. Literary and commercial fiction and non-fiction, children's (home 15%, USA/translation 20%), film/TV (15–20% by agreement). No screenplays, poetry or short stories except for established clients. No reading fee. Digital submission via website.

Clients include Christopher Andrew, Lauren Beukes, Sarah Crossan, Lindsey Davies, Katie Fforde, Conn Iggulden, Cynan Jones, Sarah Lean, Sarah Lotz, Sarra Manning, Hilary Mantel, David Mark, Maggie O'Farrell, Kamila Shamsie, Holly Webb and the estates of A.J. Cronin, Winston Graham and George Orwell. Founded 1919.

Rupert Heath Literary Agency*

50 Albemarle Street, London W1S 4BD
tel 020-7060 3395
email emailagency@rupertheath.com
website www.rupertheath.com
Twitter @rupertheathlit

Agents Rupert Heath

Fiction: literary, thrillers, crime, historical, general; non-fiction: history, biography and autobiography, science, nature, politics and current affairs, popular culture and the arts (15% UK, 20% overseas, 20% film/TV/dramatic). Visit website before submitting material. Email submissions preferred. International associates worldwide.

Authors include Michael Arnold, Ros Barber, A.K. Benedict, Andy Bull, Paddy Docherty, Reni Eddo-Lodge, Sarah Govett, Claire Harcup, Martin Lampen, Jo Litchfield, Nina Lyon, Scott Mariani, Lorna Martin, Russell Senior, Merryn Somerset Webb, Robyn Young. Founded 2001.

hhb agency ltd*

62 Grafton Way, London, W1T 5DW
tel 020-7405 5525
email heather@hhbagency.com
email cara@hhbagency.com
website hhbagency.com
Twitter @hhbagencyltd
Contacts Heather Holden-Brown, Cara Armstrong

Non-fiction: journalism, history and politics, contemporary autobiography and biography, ideas, entertainment and TV, business, family memoir, food and cookery a speciality. Fiction: commercial and literary, women's, historical and crime. 15%. No reading fee. Founded 2005.

Sophie Hicks Agency*

email info@sophiehicksagency.com
website www.sophiehicksagency.com
Twitter @SophieHicksAg
Agents Sophie Hicks, Sarah Williams

Adult fiction and non-fiction (UK/USA 15%, translation 20%). Also handles children's books for 9+. No poetry or scripts. Email submissions only, see website for guidelines. No reading fee. Represented in all foreign markets.

Authors include: Herbie Brennan, Anne Cassidy, Lucy Coats, Eoin Colfer, Ruth Fitzmaurice, Tristan Gooley, Jack Higgins, Benedict Jacka, Signe Johansen Andrew Donkin, Sarah Dyer, Kathryn Evans, Emerald Fennell, Padraig Kenny, Amanda Reynolds and Tom Whipple. Founded 2014.

David Higham Associates Ltd*

6th Floor, Waverley House, 7–12 Noel Street, London W1F 8GQ
tel 020-7434 5900
email dha@davidhigham.co.uk
website www.davidhigham.co.uk
Managing Director Anthony Goff, *Books* Veronique Baxter, Jemima Forrester, Georgia Glover, Anthony Goff, Andrew Gordon, Jane Gregory, Lizzy Kremer, Caroline Walsh, Jessica Woollard, *Foreign Rights* Alice Howe, Emma Jamison, Emily Randle, Claire Morris, *Film/TV/Theatre* Nicky Lund, Georgina Ruffhead, Clare Israel

Agents for the negotiation of all rights in literary and commercial fiction, general non-fiction in all genres, children's fiction and picture books, plays, film and TV scripts (home 15%, USA/translation 20%, scripts 10%), offering a full service across all media.

Represented in all foreign markets either directly or through sub-agents. See website for submissions policy. No reading fee.

Clients include literary prize winners: J.M. Coetzee, Tim Winton, Penelope Lively, Alice Sebold, Naomi Alderman; Jane Gardam, bestselling authors: Bernard Cornwell, Jane Green, Paula Hawkins, Alexander McCall Smith, Carole Matthews, Peter May; eminent estates: Anthony Burgess, Graham Greene, Dylan Thomas, John Wyndham; historians: Paul Kennedy, Felipe Fernandez-Armesto; food writers: Claudia Roden, Simon Hopkinson, Rachel Khoo; popular science: John Gribbin; current affairs: John Pilger, Owen Jones, Peter Oborne; biographers: Hilary Spurling, Victoria Glendinning; popular narrative: Lynne Truss; and performers: Stephen Fry, Joanna Lumley, Hugh Laurie. The children's list features Roald Dahl, Jacqueline Wilson, Liz Pichon, Cressida Cowell and Michael Morpurgo. Founded 1935.

Holroyde Cartey*

website www.holroydecartey.com
Contacts Claire Cartey, Penny Holroyde

A literary and artistic agency representing a list of award-winning and bestselling authors and illustrators. Welcomes submissions from debut and established authors. See website for submission guidelines.

Vanessa Holt Ltd*

59 Crescent Road, Leigh-on-Sea, Essex SS9 2PF
tel (01702) 473787
email v.holt791@btinternet.com

General fiction and non-fiction (home 15%, overseas 20%, TV/film/radio 15%). Works in conjunction with foreign agencies and publishers in all markets. No reading fee. No unsolicited MSS and submissions preferred by arrangement. No overseas submissions. Founded 1989.

Kate Hordern Literary Agency Ltd*

email katehordern@blueyonder.co.uk
email annewilliamskhla@googlemail.com
website www.katehordern.co.uk

A small agency with an international reach representing a wide range of fiction, some non-fiction and some children's. See website for further details of what the agency is looking for and for submission guidelines.

Valerie Hoskins Associates Ltd

20 Charlotte Street, London W1T 2NA
tel 020-7637 4490

email vha@vhassociates.co.uk
website www.vhassociates.co.uk
Proprietor Valerie Hoskins, *Agent* Rebecca Watson

Film, TV and radio; specialises in animation (home 12.5%, overseas max. 20%). No unsolicited MSS; preliminary letter essential. No reading fee, but sae essential. Works in conjunction with US agents.

Tanja Howarth Literary Agency

19 New Row, London WC2N 4LA
tel 020-7240 5553
email tanja.howarth@btinternet.com

General fiction and non-fiction, thrillers, contemporary and historical novels (home 15%, USA/translation 20%). No unsolicited MSS, no submissions by email. No reading fee. Specialists in handling German translation rights for Verlag Kiepenheuer & Witsch, Hoffmann & Campe Verlag, AVA International GmbH and others.

Clients include Sebastian Fitzek, Markus Heitz, Frank Schaetzing, Patrick Sueskind, Ferdinand von Schirach, and the estate of Heinrich Boell. English authors represented are Trevor Hoyle, Tom Callaghan and the estate of Zoe Barnes. Founded 1970.

Clare Hulton Literary Agency*

email info@clarehulton.co.uk
website www.clarehulton.com
Director Clare Hulton

Represents numerous bestselling and award-winning authors. Specialises in non-fiction especially cookery and lifestyle, health and fitness, music, humour, television tie-ins, popular philosophy, self-help, commercial non-fiction, history, business and memoir. The agency also has a small fiction and YA list. Submissions consisting of a synopsis and sample chapter should be sent by email. No fantasy, poetry, screenplays or illustrated children's proposals. Founded 2012.

IMG UK Ltd

Building Six, Chiswick Park,
566 Chiswick High Road, London W4 5HR
tel 020-8233 5000
email sarah.wooldridge@img.com
Literary Agent Sarah Wooldridge

Celebrity books, sports-related books, non-fiction and how-to business books (home 15%, USA 20%, elsewhere 25%). No theatre, fiction, children's, academic or poetry. No emails. No reading fee.

Authors include Michael Johnson, Colin Montgomerie, John McEnroe, Katherine Grainger, Ken Brown, Nicole Cooke, Dave Aldred, Judy Murray, Thomas Bjorn, Padraig Harrington. Founded 1960.

Independent Talent Group Ltd

40 Whitfield Street, London W1T 2RH
tel 020-7636 6565
website www.independenttalent.com

Specialises in scripts for film, theatre, TV, radio (home 10%, overseas 10%).

Intercontinental Literary Agency Ltd*

5 New Concordia Wharf, Mill Street,
London SE1 2BB
tel 020-7379 6611
email ila@ila-agency.co.uk
website www.ila-agency.co.uk
Contacts Nicki Kennedy, Sam Edenborough, Clementine Gaisman, Katherine West, Jenny Robson

Represents translation rights only. Founded 1965.

Janklow & Nesbit (UK) Ltd*

13A Hillgate Street, London W8 7SP
tel 020-7243 2975
email submissions@janklow.co.uk
website www.janklowandnesbit.co.uk
Twitter @JanklowUK
Agents Will Francis, Rebecca Carter, Claire Paterson Conrad, Hellie Ogden, *Translation rights:* Rebecca Folland

Represents a bestselling and award-winning range of commercial and literary fiction and non-fiction, children's and YA. Email submissions only. No poetry, plays, film/TV scripts. No reading fee. Send informative covering letter with full outline (non-fiction), synopsis and first three sample chapters (fiction) by email to submissions@janklow.co.uk. See website for full submissions guidelines. Handles translation rights directly or through sub-agents in all territories. US rights handled by Janklow & Nesbit Associates in New York.

Clients include Lily Allen, Maria Alyokhina, Gillian Anderson, M.J. Arlidge, Alex Bellos, Tanya Byron, Isaac Carew, Charles Cumming, Michel Faber, Jasper Fforde, Hannah Fry, Elly Griffiths, Xiaolu Guo, Kiran Millwood Hargrave, Olivia Laing, Derek B. Miller, Adam Rutherford, Sunjeev Sahota, Camilla Way, Juliet West and Gabriel Weston.

JFL Agency Ltd

48 Charlotte Street, London W1T 2NS
tel 020-3137 8182
email agents@jflagency.com
website www.jflagency.com
Agents Alison Finch, Dominic Lord, Gary Wild

TV, radio, film, theatre (10%). No novels, short stories or poetry. Initial contact by preliminary email; do not send scripts in the first instance. See website for further information.

Clients include Humphrey Barclay, Liam Beirne, Adam Bostock-Smith, Tim Brooke-Taylor, Ian Brown, Bill Dare, Ed Dyson, Phil Ford, Ted Gannon, Lisa Gifford, Rob Gittins, Gabby Hutchinson-Crouch, Jane Marlow, Cardy O'Donnell, Gary Russell, David Semple, James Serafinowicz, Pete Sinclair, Paul Smith, Fraser Steele.

Johnson & Alcock Ltd*

Bloomsbury House, 74–77 Great Russell Street, London WC1B 3DA
tel 020-7251 0125
website www.johnsonandalcock.co.uk
Contacts Michael Alcock, Anna Power, Ed Wilson, Becky Thomas

All types of commercial and literary fiction, and general non-fiction (home 15%, USA/translation/film 20%). Young adult and children's fiction (ages 9+). No poetry, screenplays or board/picture books.

For fiction and non-fiction, send first three chapters, full synopsis and brief covering letter with details of writing experience. For email submission guidelines see website. No reading fee but return postage essential. Founded 1956.

Robin Jones Literary Agency (RJLA)

66 High Street, Dorchester on Thames, OX10 7HN
tel (01865) 341486, (07916) 293681
email robijones@gmail.com
Twitter @AgentRobinJones
Director Robin Jones

Adult fiction and non-fiction: literary and commercial. No children's, poetry, fantasy, YA, screenplays or scripts. Russian themed fiction and non-fiction welcomed. High concept non-fiction preferred. In first instance, send synopsis, 50pp sample, and cover letter detailing writing experience. Affordable script consultancy, structural and editorial development, proofreading, self-publishing consultancy and copy editing services also available.

Authors include Sir David Madden, Waqas Ahmed, Chrissie Hynde, Philip Lymbery, Isabel Oakeshott, Paul Jackson. (Home 15%, overseas 20%). Co-founder of independent publisher Unthank Books, Unthology series, Unthank School and UnLit Festival. Founded 2007.

Tibor Jones & Associates

PO Box 74604, London SW2 9NH
email enquiries@tiborjones.com
website www.tiborjones.com
Contact Kevin Conroy Scott

Literary fiction and non-fiction, category fiction, music autobiographies and biographies. Send first 5pp, synopsis and covering letter via email.

Authors include Wilbur Smith, Guillermo Arriaga, Simon Castets, HRH Princess Michael of Kent, Deborah Curtis, Olafur Eliasson, Hala Jaber, Paul Lake, Hans Ulrich Obrist, Bernard Sumner, Christopher Winn. Founded 2007.

Jane Judd Literary Agency*

18 Belitha Villas, London N1 1PD
tel 020-7607 0273
website www.janejudd.com

General non-fiction and fiction (home 10%, overseas 20%). No longer accepting new clients. Works with agents in the US and most foreign countries. Founded 1986.

Michelle Kass Associates Ltd*

85 Charing Cross Road, London WC2H 0AA
tel 020-7439 1624
Proprietor Michelle Kass

Literary and commercial fiction (home 10%, overseas 15–20%) and scripts for film and TV. Works with agents around the world. First three chapters. No reading fee. No unsolicited material, phone in first instance. Founded 1991.

Keane Kataria Literary Agency

website www.keanekataria.co.uk
Partners Sara Keane, Kiran Kataria

Boutique agency representing quality commercial fiction and non-fiction (home 15%, USA/translation 20%). No children's, YA, science fiction/fantasy, academic, short stories, poetry, plays, film/TV scripts. See website for current submission guidelines. No reading fee. Founded 2014.

Frances Kelly Agency*

111 Clifton Road, Kingston-upon-Thames, Surrey KT2 6PL
tel 020-8549 7830

Full-length MSS. Non-fiction: general and academic, reference and professional books, all subjects (home 10%, overseas 20%, TV/radio 10%). No reading fee, but no unsolicited MSS; preliminary letter with synopsis, cv and return postage essential. Founded 1978.

Ki Agency Ltd*

Screenworks Studio 315, 22 Highbury Grove, London N5 2ER
tel 0203-214 8287
email meg@ki-agency.co.uk
website www.ki-agency.co.uk
Twitter @kiagency
Director Meg Davis, *Agent* Ruth Needham (no submissions)

Represents writers of fiction, non-fiction and screenplays. Submission guidelines: letter first with three chapters or full screenplay. No unsolicited MSS. No children's or YA

Clients include Anne Perry, M.R. Carey, Claire North, Jude Morgan, Duncan Falconer (scripts), Angela Slatter, Helena Coggan. Founded 2011.

Kingsford Campbell Literary and Marketing Agents*

38A Minford Gardens, London W14 0AN
email info@kingsfordcampbell.com
website www.kingsfordcampbell.com
Twitter @KCAgents
Directors Charlie Campbell, Julia Kingsford

Fiction and non-fiction (home 15%; USA, film/tv & translation 20%). No plays, poetry or scripts. Submissions via form on website.

Knight Features Ltd

Trident Business Centre, 89 Bickerseth Road, London SW17 9SH
tel 020-3051 5650
email info@knightfeatures.co.uk
website www.knightfeatures.com
Contacts Gaby Martin, Sam Ferris, Andrew Knight

Biography, history, humour, puzzles, general interest. Literary estates management. No poetry, cookery or travel. Send letter accompanied by synopsis, samples and sae. No unsolicited MSS.

Clients include David J. Bodycombe, Frank Dickens, Barbara Minto, Ralph Barker, Frederick Mullaly, and the works by Patrick MacGill. Founded 1985.

Knight Hall Agency Ltd

Lower Ground Floor, 7 Mallow Street, London EC1Y 8RQ
tel 020-3397 2901
email office@knighthallagency.com
website www.knighthallagency.com
Contacts Charlotte Knight, Martin Knight, Katie Langridge

Specialises in writers for stage, screen and radio but also deals in TV and film rights in novels and non-fiction (home 10%, overseas 15%). No reading fee.

Clients include Simon Beaufoy, Jeremy Brock, Liz Lochhead, Tim Lott, Martin McDonagh, Simon Nye, Ol Parker, Lucy Prebble, Philip Ridley, Laura Wade. Founded 1997.

LAW (Lucas Alexander Whitley Ltd)*

14 Vernon Street, London W14 0RJ
tel 020-7471 7900
website www.lawagency.co.uk
Contacts Adult: Mark Lucas, Julian Alexander, Araminta Whitley, Alice Saunders, Ben Clark; Children's: Philippa Milnes-Smith

Full-length commercial and literary fiction, non-fiction, fantasy, young adult and children's books (home 15%, USA/ translation 20%). No plays, poetry or textbooks. Film, TV and stage handled for established clients only. Represented in all markets. Unsolicited MSS considered. See website for further information about the clients and genres represented and essential information on submissions. No reading fee. Founded 1996.

LBA Books*

91 Great Russell Street, London WC1B 3PS
tel 020-7637 1234
email info@lbabooks.com
website www.lbabooks.com
Twitter @LBABooks
Agents Luigi Bonomi, Amanda Preston, Louise Lamont, Danielle Zigner

Fiction and non-fiction (home 15%, overseas 20%). Keen to find new authors and help them develop their careers. Fiction: commercial and literary fiction, thrillers, crime, psychological suspense, young adult, children's, women's fiction, fantasy. Non-fiction: history, science, parenting, lifestyle, cookery, memoir, TV tie-in. No poetry, short stories or screenplays.

Send preliminary letter, synopsis and first three chapters. No reading fee. Works with foreign agencies and has links with film and TV production companies including Endemol, Tiger Aspect, BBC Radio, HatTrick, Plum Pictures, Zodiak and Sega.

Authors include Will Adams, Sarah Alderson, Kirstie Allsopp, Lizzy Barber, Virginia Bergin, Fern Britton, Amanda Brooke, Charlotte Butterfield, Jo Carnegie, Rebecca Cobb, Gennaro Contaldo, Alex Caan, Lucie Cave, Rebecca Chance, Ping Coombes, Emma Cooper, Josephine Cox, Mason Cross, Liz Fenwick, Judy Finnigan, Festival of the Spoken Nerd, Nick Foulkes, Tom Fox, David Gibbins, Rachel Hamilton, Richard Hammond, Helen Hancocks, Fiona Harper, Matt Hilton, Jane Holland, Honey & Co, John Humphrys, Jessica Jarlvi, Annabel Kantaria, Lesley Kara, Simon Kernick, Margaret Kirk, Susan Lewis, Freda Lightfoot, Amy Lloyd, Rachael Lucas, Tom Marcus, Colin McDowell, Richard Madeley, Lucy Mangan, James May, Julie Mayhew, Gavin Menzies, Karen Osman, S.A. Patrick, Gervase Phinn, Madeleine Reiss, Alice Roberts, Simon Scarrow, Lucy Strange, Heidi Swain, Karen Swan, Prof. Bryan Sykes, Alan Titchmarsh, Phil Vickery, Laura Wood, Katherine Woodfine, Emma Yarlett. Founded 2005.

Susanna Lea Associates Ltd*

55 Monmouth Street, London WC2H 9DG
tel 020-7287 7757
email london@susannalea.com
website www.susannalea.com
Facebook www.facebook.com/SLA-London-134576166615645/
Twitter @kerryglencorse
Twitter @slalondon
Directors Susanna Lea, Kerry Glencorse

General fiction and non-fiction. No plays, screenplays or poetry. Send query letter, brief synopsis, the first three chapters and/or proposal via the submissions email address: london@susannalea.com. Established in Paris 2000; New York 2004; London 2008.

Barbara Levy Literary Agency*

64 Greenhill, Hampstead High Street, London NW3 5TZ
tel 020-7435 9046
website barbaralevyagency.com
Director Barbara Levy, *Associate* John Selby (solicitor)

Full-length MSS. Fiction and general non-fiction (home 15%, overseas by arrangement). Film and TV rights for existing clients only. No reading fee, but preliminary letter with synopsis and sae essential, or by email. Translation rights handled by the Buckman Agency; works in conjunction with US agents. Founded 1986.

Limelight Celebrity Management Ltd*

10 Filmer Mews, 75 Filmer Road, London SW6 7JF
tel 020-7384 9950
email mail@limelightmanagement.com
website www.limelightmanagement.com
Contacts Fiona Lindsay, Roz Ellman

Full-length and short MSS. Food, wine, health, crafts, gardening, interior design, literary fiction, biography, travel, history, women's fiction, crime, fashion, business, politics (home 15%, overseas 20%), TV and radio rights (10–20%); will suggest revision where appropriate. No reading fee. Founded 1991.

Lindsay Literary Agency

East Worldham House, Alton, Hants GU34 3AT
tel (01420) 83143
email info@lindsayliteraryagency.co.uk
website www.lindsayliteraryagency.co.uk
Twitter @LindsayLit
Directors Becky Bagnell, Kate Holroyd Smith

Children's books, middle grade, teen/YA, picture books. No reading fee. Will suggest revision. Check website for submissions guidelines as these have changed.

Authors include Pamela Butchart, Sam Gayton, Mike Lancaster, Rachel Valentine, Sue Wallman. Founded 2008.

Christopher Little Literary Agency LLP*

(in association with Curtis Brown Group Ltd)
48 Walham Grove, London SW6 1QR
tel 020-7736 4455
email info@christopherlittle.net
website www.christopherlittle.net
Contact Christopher Little

Commercial and literary full-length fiction and non-fiction (home 15%; USA, Canada, translation, audio, motion picture 20%). No poetry, plays, science fiction, fantasy, textbooks, illustrated children's or short stories. Film scripts for established clients only. No unsolicited submissions.

Authors include Paul Bajoria, Ginny Elliot MBE, Janet Gleeson, Cathy Hopkins, Carol Hughes, General Mike Jackson (Sir), Oskar Cox Jensen, Philip Kazan, Lise Kristensen, Alastair MacNeill, Pippa Mattinson, Robert Mawson, Bruce McCabe, Kate McCann, Haydn Middleton, Shiromi Pinto, A.J. Quinnell, Robert Radcliffe, Darren Shan, Wladyslaw Szpilman, Felix Taylor, Pip Vaughan-Hughes, John Watson, Anne Zouroudi. Founded 1979.

Andrew Lownie Literary Agency*

36 Great Smith Street, London SW1P 3BU
tel 020-7222 7574
email andrew@andrewlownie.co.uk
email david.haviland@andrewlownie.co.uk
website www.andrewlownie.co.uk
Twitter @andrewlownie
Director Andrew Lownie, *Fiction agent* David Haviland

Handles fiction and non-fiction, working in association with a range of sub-agents around the world. Non-fiction submissions should include synopsis, author profile, chapter summaries and sample material. Fiction submissions should comprise synopsis and the first three chapters. The non-fiction list includes biography, history, reference, current affairs and packaging journalists and celebrities for the book market (home and USA 15%, translation and film 20%). Recent sales include the memoirs of *Made in Chelsea*'s Spencer Matthews and *The Only Way is Essex*'s Sam Faiers and Kirk Norcross, and Marina Chapman's *The Girl With No Name*. Represents inspirational memoirs (Cathy Glass, Casey Watson) and ghostwriters. Also handles commercial fiction in all genres, particularly crime, thrillers and historical. No reading fee. Will suggest revision.

Authors include Richard Aldrich, Juliet Barker, the Joyce Cary estate, Roger Crowley, Tom Devine, Patrick Dillon, Duncan Falconer, Timothy Good, David Hasselhoff, John Hatcher, Kris Hollington, Robert Hutchinson, Lawrence James, Ian Knight, Frank Ledwidge, Christopher Lloyd, Sean Longden, the Julian Maclaren-Ross estate, Norma Major, Neil McKenna, Sean McMeekin, Linda Porter, David Quantick, Sian Rees, David Roberts, Desmond Seward, David Stafford, Daniel Tammet, Peter Thompson, Matt Wilven; *The Oxford Classical Dictionary*, *The Cambridge Guide to Literature in English*. Founded 1988.

Lucas Alexander Whitley – see LAW (Lucas Alexander Whitley Ltd)

Luithlen Agency

88 Holmfield Road, Leicester LE2 1SB
tel 0116 273 8863
website www.luithlenagency.com
Agents Jennifer Luithlen, Penny Luithlen

Children's fiction, all ages to YA (home 15%, overseas 20%), performance rights (15%). See website for submission information. Founded 1986.

Lutyens & Rubinstein*

21 Kensington Park Road, London W11 2EU
tel 020-7792 4855
email submissions@lutyensrubinstein.co.uk
website www.lutyensrubinstein.co.uk
Agents Sarah Lutyens, Felicity Rubinstein, Jane Finigan, Daisy Parente, *Contact* Sarah Godman

Fiction and non-fiction, commercial and literary (home 15%, overseas 20%). Send material by email with a covering letter and short synopsis. Submissions not accepted by hand or by post. Founded 1993.

David Luxton Associates Ltd

23 Hillcourt Avenue, London N12 8EY
website www.davidluxtonassociates.co.uk

Agency specialising in non-fiction especially sport, memoir, politics and nature writing. Also handles foerign rights for September Publishing, Judith Murdoch Literary Agency, Eve White Literary Agency and Graham Maw Christie. Unable to accept unsolicited submissions. Please consult website for submission guidelines.

Duncan McAra

3 Viewfield Avenue, Bishopbriggs, Glasgow G64 2AG
tel 0141 772 1067
email duncanmcara@mac.com

Literary fiction; non-fiction: art, architecture, archaeology, biography, military, Scottish, travel (home 15%, USA/translation 20%). Preliminary letter with sae essential. No reading fee. Member of the Association of Scottish Literary Agents. Founded 1988.

Eunice McMullen Ltd

Low Ibbotsholme Cottage, Off Bridge Lane, Troutbeck Bridge, Windermere, Cumbria LA23 1HU
tel (01539) 448551
email eunicemcmullen@totalise.co.uk
website www.eunicemcmullen.co.uk
Director Eunice McMullen

All types of children's fiction, particularly picture books and older fiction (home 15%, overseas 15%). No unsolicited scripts. Telephone or email enquiries only. Founded 1992.

Authors include Caroline Jayne Church, Ross Collins, Emma Dodd, Alison Friend, Charles Fuge, Cally Johnson Isaacs, Sarah Massini, David Melling, Angela McAllister, Angie Sage, Gillian Shields. Founded 1992.

Andrew Mann Ltd*

email info@andrewmann.co.uk
website www.andrewmann.co.uk
Twitter @AML_Literary
Contacts Tina Betts, Louise Burns

Currently closed to new submissions. Founded 1968.

Marjacq Scripts Ltd*

Box 412, 19–21 Crawford Street, London W1H 1PJ
tel 020-7935 9499
email firstname@marjacq.com
website www.marjacq.com
Twitter @MarjacqScripts
Contact Diana Beaumont (commercial fiction and non-fiction), Philip Patterson (commercial and literary fiction, and non-fiction), Imogen Pelham (literary fiction and non-fiction), Catherine Pellegrino (children's and YA), Sandra Sawicka (genre and speculative fiction), Leah Middleton (film & tv)

All full-length MSS (home 15%, overseas/film 20%), including commercial and literary fiction and non-fiction, crime, thrillers, commercial women's fiction, graphic novels, children's, science fiction, history, biography, sport, travel, health. No poetry. No picture book texts. No theatre (especially no musicals). Send first 50pp with synopsis by email to appropriate agent. See website for further submission guidelines. Expanding full-service agency. Handles all rights. In-house legal, foreign rights and book-to-film support.

Clients include: Katarzyna Bonda, Daisy Buchanan, Angela Clarke, Paul Crilley, Helen FitzGerald, Gemma Fowler, Nick Garlick, Jo Jakeman, Stuart MacBride, Claire McGowan, Emily Mayhew, Bryony Pearce, Angela Readman, Kassia St Clair, Luca Veste, Harriet Whitehorn and Tom Wood. Founded 1974 by George Markstein and Jacqui Lyons.

The Marsh Agency Ltd*

50 Albemarle Street, London W1S 4BD
tel 020-7493 4361
email hello@marsh-agency.co.uk
website www.marsh-agency.co.uk

The Marsh Agency offers international representation to a wide range of writers, literary agents and publishing companies. No unsolicited submissions. Founded 1994, incorporating Paterson Marsh Ltd and Campbell, Thomson and McLaughlin Ltd as of April 2011.

Martin Leonardis Literary Management

71–75 Shelton Street, London WC2H 9JQ
tel 020-8316 1878
email info@martinleonardis.com
email submissions@martinleonardis.com
website www.martinleonardis.com
Twitter @missleonardis
Founder & Agent Federica Martin-Leonardis

Fiction: all genres and general fiction. Non-fiction: cookery and food writing, smart thinking, psychology, humour, self-help and inspirational memoirs, business, health and popular science (home 15%; NA/translation 20%). No children/YA, fantasy/space operas, goth/horror, historical non-fiction, poetry/screenplays.

Check the website for full submission guidelines. Do not submit by post. No reading fee. Will consider English and Italian submissions. Interested in new writers and writers from any background. *Authors* include Rachel de Thample, Oliver Rowe, Thom Eagle, Sonya Lalli.

MBA Literary and Script Agents Ltd*

62 Grafton Way, London W1T 5DW
tel 020-7387 2076

website www.mbalit.co.uk
Twitter @mbaagents
Book agents Diana Tyler, Laura Longrigg, David Riding, Susan Smith, Sophie Gorell Barnes, Julia Silk
Film/TV/Radio/Theatre agent Diana Tyler

Fiction and non-fiction, children's books (home 15%, overseas 20%) and TV, film, radio and theatre scripts (TV/theatre/radio 10%, films 15%). See website for submission guidelines. Foreign rights handled by Louisa Pritchard Associates.

Clients include Jonny Bairstow, Jeffrey Caine, estate of B.S. Johnson, Julian Jones, Rosanna Ley, estate of Anne McCaffrey, Clare Morrall, Stef Penney, Iain Sinclair. Founded 1971.

Madeleine Milburn Literary, TV & Film Agency*

10 Shepherd Market, Mayfair, London W1J 7QF
tel 020-7499 7550
email submissions@madeleinemilburn.com
website www.madeleinemilburn.co.uk
Facebook www.facebook.com/MadeleineMilburnLiteraryAgency
Twitter @agentmilburn
Agents Madeleine Milburn, Giles Milburn (Directors); Anna Hogarty, Alice Sutherland-Hawes (children's and YA), *Associate Agent and TV & Film Coordinator* Hayley Steed (overseas associates CAA for film in LA/Hollywood); *Literary Assistant* Sarah-Jayne Carver

Special interest in launching the careers of debut authors. Represents a dynamic and prize-winning range of adult fiction and non-fiction, young adult and children's fiction. Literary and upmarket fiction, women's, reading group, crime, thrillers, historical, romance, mystery, horror, psychological suspense, fantasy and science fiction, true crime, self-help, well being, cookery, narrative non-fiction, history, personal stories, memoir, science, popular psychology, film/TV tie-ins. Film, TV and stage handled for existing clients only.

Children's fiction for all ages including picture books, 6-8 years, 9-12 years, teen, YA, new adult and books that are read by both children and adults. Also represents illustrators. Represents British, American and international authors. Builds the international careers of authors. Handles all rights in the UK, US and foreign markets including film/TV/radio and digital (home 15%, USA/translation/film 20%). No longer accepts submissions by post. See submission guidelines and agency news on website. No reading fee. Works editorially with all clients

Authors include Gail Honeyman, C.J. Tudor, Fiona Barton, C.L. Taylor, Christi Daugherty, Holly Bourne, Teresa Driscoll, Mel Sherratt, Annie Ward, Melanie Golding, Michelle Adams, Katherine May, Kathryn Croft, Nuala Ellwood, Stephen Giles, Pleesecakes, Simon Cherry, Hayley Barker, Fionnuala Kearney, Dave Lowe, Holly Martin, Rupert Wallis, Lara Williamson, Kate Ling. Founded 2012.

Mulcahy Associates (part of MMB Creative)*

The Old Truman Brewery, 91 Brick Lane, London E1 6QL
tel 020-3582 9370
website www.mmbcreative.com
Contacts Ivan Mulcahy, Sallyanne Sweeney

Fiction, non-fiction: biography, crime, finance, historical, lifestyle, sport, thrillers, women's interests, adult, children's, youth, commercial, literary. Send query with synopsis and first three chapters via website only. See website for full guidelines.

Toby Mundy Associates Ltd

38 Berkeley Square, London W1J 5AE
tel 020-3713 0067
email enquiries@tma-agency.com
website www.tma-agency.com
Twitter @tma_agency
Contact Toby Mundy

A management company that represents writers, speakers and brands. Also creates bespoke content for organisations. Works in association with Ed Victor. Fiction and non-fiction (home 15%, USA/translation 20%). Wide range of genres including history, science, biography, autobiography, politics and current affairs, literary fiction, crime, thrillers. No plays, poetry, sci-fi/horror or short stories. Email preliminary letter, brief cv and first 30pp of sample material to submissions@tma-agency.com. No reading fee. Not currently accepting unsolicited submissions. New clients by submission only. Founded 2014.

Judith Murdoch Literary Agency*

19 Chalcot Square, London NW1 8YA
tel 020-7722 4197
website www.judithmurdoch.co.uk
Contact Judith Murdoch

Full-length fiction only, especially commercial women's fiction and crime (home 15%, overseas 20%). No science fiction/fantasy, poetry, short stories or children's. Approach by post, sending the first two chapters and synopsis. Send email address or return postage; no email submissions. Editorial advice given; no reading fee. Translation rights handled by Rebecca Winfield (email: rebecca@rebeccawinfield.com).

Clients include Diane Allen, Trisha Ashley, Frances Brody, Rosie Clarke, Diney Costeloe, Kate Eastham, Leah Fleming, Sarah Flint, Caro Fraser, Elizabeth Gill, Faith Hogan, Emma Hornby, Alex Howard, Arlene Hughes, Lola Jaye, Sheila Jeffries, Pamela Jooste, Jill McGivering, Alison Mercer, Barbara Mutch, Kitty Neale, Sheila Newberry, Mary Wood. Founded 1993.

Kate Nash Literary Agency

1 Swift Way, Brackley, Northants NN13 6PY
tel 0844 415 7844

email submissions.kn@gmail.com
website www.katenashliterary.co.uk
Facebook www.facebook.com/KateNashLiteraryAgency
Twitter @katenashagent
Contact Kate Nash

Represents general and genre fiction, popular non-fiction and children's and YA fiction (no poetry or drama). Open to approaches from both new and established authors. See website for full submission guidelines.

The North Literary Agency

The Chapel, Market Place, Corbridge, Northumberland NE45 5AW
email hello@thenorthlitagency.com
website www.thenorthlitagency.com
Agents Julie Fergusson, Allan Guthrie, Kevin Pocklington, Mark Stanton

Looking for all types of fiction and narrative non-fiction. Does not represent academic writing, poetry, self-help, picture books or screenplays. Does not accept submissions by post. See website for full submission guidelines. Founded 2017.

Andrew Nurnberg Associates International Ltd*

20–23 Greville Street, London EC1N 8SS
tel 020-3327 0400
email info@andrewnurnberg.com
website www.andrewnurnberg.com
Twitter @nurnberg_agency

Represents adult and children's international authors, agent and publisher clients in the fields of literary/commercial fiction and general non-fiction for the sale of rights throughout the world via our offices in the UK and overseas.

Deborah Owen

78 Narrow Street, Limehouse, London E14 8BP
tel 020-7987 5119/5441
Contact Deborah Owen

Small agency specialising in only two authors: Delia Smith and David Owen. No new authors. Founded 1971.

Paper Lion Ltd

13 Grayham Road, New Malden, Surrey KT3 5HR
tel (07748) 786199 / (01276) 61322
email katyloffman@paperlion.co.uk
email lesleypollinger@paperlion.co.uk
website www.paperlion.co.uk
Agents Katy Loffman, Lesley Pollinger

Paper Lion is a cross-media literary agency which brings together the digital publishing expertise of Katy Loffman and Lesley Pollinger's extensive experience as a literary agent. Represents a prestigious list of clients including authors, literary estates, archives, film producers, virtual reality developers and online publishers. Covers all the areas of a traditional literary agency including finding publishers worldwide and selling film and TV rights. In addition, Paper Lion also has a strong focus on the exploration of digital opportunities and solving complex copyright, dramatic rights and literary issues from the present and past.

Clients include Max Allen, Martin Body, Michael Coleman, Kim Erin Cowley, Vince Cross, Fiction Express, Catherine Fisher, Dave Gatward, Bruce Hobson, Bruce Montague, Saviour Pirotta, Summersdale Publishers Ltd and the estates of a number of authors and artists including Grantly Dick-Read, Gene Kemp, Gwynedd Rae and Frieda Lawrence Ravagli.

PBJ & JBJ Management

22 Rathbone Street, London W1T 1LA
tel 020-7287 1112
email general@pbjmanagement.co.uk
website www.pbjmgt.co.uk
Contacts Peter Bennett-Jones, Caroline Chignell

Represents writers, performers, presenters, composers, directors, producers and DJs (theatre 15%, film/TV/radio 12.5%). Specialises in comedy. No reading fee. Founded 1987.

Maggie Pearlstine Associates*

31 Ashley Gardens, Ambrosden Avenue, London SW1P 1QE
tel 020-7828 4212
email maggie@pearlstine.co.uk
Contact Maggie Hattersley

Small agency representing a select few authors. No new authors. Translation rights handled by Aitken Alexander Associates Ltd.

Authors include Matthew Baylis, Lord (Menzies) Campbell, Jamie Crawford, Mark Douglas-Home, Toby Green, Roy Hattersley, Mark Leonard, Prof. Lesley Regan, Winifred Robinson, Christopher Ward. Founded 1989.

Jonathan Pegg Literary Agency*

67 Wingate Square, London SW4 0AF
tel 020-7603 6830
email submissions@jonathanpegg.com
email info@jonathanpegg.com
website www.jonathanpegg.com
Founder & Agent Jonathan Pegg

Specialises in full-length quality fiction and non-fiction (see website for categories). No reading fee. Email submissions accepted; see website for submission guidelines. Founded 2008.

Catherine Pellegrino & Associates

148 Russell Court, Woburn Place, London WC1H 0LR

email catherine@catherinepellegrino.co.uk
website http://catherinepellegrino.co.uk/
Twitter @CatherinePelle8
Director Catherine Pellegrino

Provides a full agenting service for children's writers, from chapter books to new adult. Does not represent picture texts or illustrators. Please see also the entry for Marjacq Scripts Ltd. Founded 2011.

PEW Literary*

46 Lexington Street, London W1F 0LP
tel 020-7734 4464
email submissions@pewliterary.com
website www.pewliterary.com
Agent Patrick Walsh

Boutique agency with a strong list of prize-winning authors. Actively seeking fresh talent. No poetry, children's picture books or screenplays. *Clients* include: literary novelists Nick Harkaway and Tony White, crime writers Luke Jennings and Adam Creed, Keggie Carew (winner of the Costa Biography Prize), Laura Cumming (winner of the James Tait Black Prize), Jim al-Khalili, Tom Holland, Helen Castor, Dame Uta Frith, Andrea Wulf (winner of the Royal Society Prize), Anita Anand, Gaia Vince (winner of the Royal Society Prize), Simon Singh, Professor Richard Wiseman. Artists represented include David Shrigley and Steven Appleby and graphic novels and non-fiction. Founded 2016.

Peters Fraser & Dunlop Ltd*

55 New Oxford Street, London WC1A 1BS
tel 020-7344 1000
email info@pfd.co.uk
website www.petersfraserdunlop.com
Facebook www.facebook.com/pfdagents
Twitter @PFDAgents
Ceo Caroline Michel, *Book agents* Caroline Michel, Annabel Merullo, Michael Sissons, Elizabeth Sheinkman, Tim Bates, Nelle Andrew, Laura Williams, Adam Gauntlett, Silvia Molteni, Marilia Savvides, Fiona Petheram, Tessa David, Laura McNeill, *Theatrical Rights* Adam Gauntlett, *Children's & Audio Rights* Silvia Molteni, *Foreign Rights* Alexandra Cliff, Marilia Savvides, Rebecca Wearmouth, Laura Otal, Silvia Molteni, *Estates* Camilla Shestopal, Ellis Hazelgrove, *Broadcast & Live Events* Jon Fowler, Dan Herron, Vicky Cornforth, *TV & Film Rights* Jonathan Sissons, Zoe Sharples, *Journalism* Kate Evans

Represents authors of fiction and non-fiction, presenters and public speakers throughout the world. Covering letter, synopsis or outline and first three chapters as well as author biographies should be addressed to individual agents. Return postage necessary. No reading fee. See website for submission guidelines. Does not represent scriptwriters. PFD runs its own digital publishing imprint called Ipso Books Ltd (www.ipsobooks.com). Founded 1924.

Shelley Power Literary Agency Ltd*

20 Powell Gardens, South Heighton, Newhaven BN9 0PS
tel (01273) 512347
email sp@shelleypower.co.uk
Contact Shelley Power

General fiction and non-fiction. Full-length MSS (home 12.5%, USA/translation 20%). No children's books, YA, science fiction, fantasy, poetry, screenplays or plays. Works in conjunction with agents abroad. No reading fee, but preliminary letter essential – may be sent by email. Founded 1976.

Redhammer Management Ltd

website www.redhammer.info
Vice President Peter Cox

A boutique literary agency providing in-depth management for a restricted number of clients. Specialises in works with international book, film and television potential. Submissions must follow the guidelines given on the website. Do not send unsolicited MSS by post. No radio or theatre scripts. No reading fee.

The Lisa Richards Agency

108 Upper Leeson Street, Dublin D04 E3E7, Republic of Ireland
tel +353 (0)1 6375000
email info@lisarichards.ie
website www.lisarichards.ie
Contact Faith O'Grady

Handles fiction and general non-fiction (Ireland 10%, UK 15%, USA/translation 20%, film/TV 15%). Approach with proposal and sample chapter for non-fiction and 3–4 chapters and synopsis for fiction (sae essential). No reading fee. *Overseas associate* The Marsh Agency for translation rights.

Clients include Niall Breslin (Bressie), Matt Cooper, Damian Corless, Christy Dignam, Aoife Dooley, Chris Dooley, Austin Duffy, Caroline Foran, Christine Dwyer Hickey, John Giles, Antonia Hart, Maeve Higgins, Paul Howard (aka Ross O'Carroll-Kelly), Amy Huberman, Arlene Hunt, Roisin Ingle, Alison Jameson, Alison Keating, Declan Lynch, Ronan McGreevy, Pauline McLynn, Louise McSharry, Rory O'Neill/Panti, Colm O'Regan (Irish Mammies), David O'Doherty, Mary O'Donoghue, Derval O'Rourke, Damien Owens, Daniel Seery, Rosemary Smith, The Happy Pear Cookbook, Twisted Doodles, Waterford Whispers News, Sheena Wilkinson. Founded 1998.

Richford Becklow Agency

85 Ashburnham Road, London NW10 5SA
tel 020-3737 1068
email enquiries@richfordbecklow.co.uk
website www.richfordbecklow.com
Twitter @richfordbecklow
Contact Lisa Eveleigh

Literary and commercial fiction and non-fiction: first novels, history, biography and popular culture particularly welcome (home 15%, overseas 20%). No fiction for middle grade and younger readers accepted. No reading fee. No postal submissions; will only respond to email submissions. Ensure you visit the website regarding submissions before approaching the agency.

Authors include Amanda Austen, Mary Alexander, Caroline Ashton, Hugo Barnacle, Susan Bassett, Stephen Buck, Anne Corlett, Carol Clewlow, Jane Gordon-Cumming, Lesley Eames, A.D. Lynn, Tim Luscombe, Simon Michael, R.P. Marshall, Ann Victoria Roberts, Grace Wynne-Jones, Sophie Parkin, Lakshmi Raj Sharma, Adrienne Vaughan. Founded 2011.

The Rights Bureau Ltd

The Old Post Office, Kilmacanogue,
County Wicklow, Ireland
tel +353-(0)1-276-5921
email vanessa@therightsbureau.ie
email dominic@therightsbureau.ie
website www.therightsbureau.ie
Contacts Vanessa Fox O'Loughlin, Dominic Perrem

Handles primarily non-fiction: health, wellbeing, lifestyle, MBS, popular psychology, gardening, cooking, sport and leisure, craft, photography, autobiography, biography, travel, history, music, smart thinking (home 15%, overseas 20%, film & TV 20%). Approach with proposal and 3–4 sample chapters. Also represents publishers' rights.

Clients include: Dr Harry Barry, Le Creuset on behalf of Borgerhoff Lamberigts, Andrea Hayes, Karina Melvin, Martin Dillon.

Rocking Chair Books Literary Agency*

2 Rudgwick Terrace, St Stephens Close,
London NW8 6BR
email representme@rockingchairbooks.com
website www.rockingchairbooks.com
Twitter @rockingbooks
Contact Samar Hammam

Dedicated to original and page-turning books and looking for stories that are both inspired and inspiring. Focuses on adult commercial fiction, literary fiction, graphic novels and non-fiction for publication around the world (home 15%, translation/adaptation rights 20%). No children's, YA or science fiction (unless they are crossover). Also works with other agencies to represent their translation or English language rights, including Mulcahy Associates and the Raya Agency. Submission by email only.

Rogers, Coleridge & White Ltd*

20 Powis Mews, London W11 1JN
tel 020-7221 3717
email info@rcwlitagency.com
website www.rcwlitagency.com
Twitter @RCWLitAgency
Chairman Gill Coleridge, *Managing Director* Peter Straus, *Finance Director* Nelka Bell, *Directors* Sam Copeland, Stephen Edwards, Natasha Fairweather, Georgia Garrett, Laurence Laluyaux, Peter Robinson, Zoe Waldie, Claire Wilson, *Agents* Jennifer Hewson, Cara Jones, Emma Paterson.

International representation for all genres of fiction, non-fiction, Children's and YA. RCW clients include Nobel, Man Booker and Pulitzer Prize winners and household names. See website for submissions guidelines. No reading fee. Founded in 1967 by Deborah Rogers.

Elizabeth Roy Literary Agency

White Cottage, Greatford, Nr Stamford,
Lincs. PE9 4PR
tel (01778) 560672
website www.elizabethroy.co.uk

Children's fiction, picture books and non-fiction – writers and illustrators (home 15%, overseas 20%). Send preliminary letter, synopsis and sample chapters with names of publishers and agents previously contacted. Return postage essential. No reading fee. Founded 1990.

The Ruppin Agency

email submissions@ruppinagency.com
website www.ruppinagency.com
Twitter @tintiddle
Director Jonathan Ruppin

Represents both commercial and literary fiction, and serious non-fiction. Commission: 15% home, 20% translation (rights handled by The Marsh Agency). Looking for writing with ambition, scale and relevance. Particularly interested in submissions from writers from under-represented communities: working class, LGBTQ+, people of colour, those with disabilities, those outside London catchment area. No reading fee.

No poetry, plays, graphic novels, children's/YA, professional or academic; full details of areas of interest and submission requirements on website. Founded 2017.

Uli Rushby-Smith Literary Agency

72 Plimsoll Road, London N4 2EE
tel 020-7354 2718
email uli.rushby-smith@btconnect.com
Director Uli Rushby-Smith

Fiction and non-fiction, literary and commercial (home 15%, USA/foreign 20%). No poetry, picture books, plays or film scripts. Send outline, sample chapters (no disks) and return postage. No reading fee. Founded 1993.

The Sayle Literary Agency*

1 Petersfield, Cambridge CB1 1BB
tel (01223) 303035

email info@sayleliteraryagency.com
website www.sayleliteraryagency.com
Proprietor & Agent Rachel Calder

Fiction: general, literary and crime. Non fiction: current affairs, social issues, travel, biographies, history (home 15%, USA/translation 20%). No plays, poetry, textbooks, children's, technical, legal or medical books. No reading fee. See website for submission guidelines. Translation rights handled by The Marsh Agency Ltd. Film and TV rights handled by Sayle Screen Ltd. US rights handled by Dunow, Carlson and Lerner. Represents UK rights for Darhansoff and Verill (USA) and The Naher Agency (Australia). Founded 1896.

Sayle Screen Ltd

11 Jubilee Place, London SW3 3TD
tel 020-7823 3883
email info@saylescreen.com
website www.saylescreen.com
Agents Jane Villiers, Matthew Bates, Kelly Knatchbull

Specialises in scripts for film, TV, theatre and radio. No reading fee. Unable to consider unsolicited material unless recommended by producer, development executive or course tutor. If this is the case, email a cv, covering letter and details of your referee or course tutor to the relevant agent. Please do not email more than one agent at a time. Every submission carefully considered, but responds only to submissions it wishes to take further; not able to return material sent in. Represents film, TV and theatre rights in fiction and non-fiction for The Sayle Literary Agency, Greene & Heaton Ltd and Rogers, Coleridge and White Ltd. Works in conjunction with agents in New York and Los Angeles.

The Science Factory Ltd*

Scheideweg 34c, 20253 Hamburg, Germany
tel +49 (0)40 4327 2959 (Germany), 020-7193 7296 (Skype)
email info@sciencefactory.co.uk
website www.sciencefactory.co.uk
Director/Agent Peter Tallack (Germany), *Agent* Tisse Takagi (New York)

Serious popular non-fiction, particularly science, history and current affairs, by academics and journalists (home 15%, overseas 20%). No fiction. In first instance send proposal with chapter summaries and sample chapter (not the first). Email submissions only (material sent by post not returned). No reading fee. May suggest revision.

Authors include Anjana Ahuja, Anil Ananthaswamy, Jim Baggott, David Bainbridge, Adam Becker, Jesse Bering, Lee Billings, Piers Bizony, Daniel Bor, Dennis Bray, Jeffery Bub, Tanya Bub, Daniel Clery, Matthew Cobb, Enrico Coen, Michael Corballis, Trevor Cox, Seth Darling, Sarah Dry, Nicholas Dunbar, John Duncan, Graham Easton, Richard Elwes, Georgina Ferry, Lone Frank, Marianne Freiberger, Kate Greene, David Hand, Valery Hazanov, Bob Holmes, Simon Ings, Harris Irfan, Stephen Joseph, James Kingsland, Adam Kucharski, Cherry Lewis, Alison Li, Ehsan Masood, Mark Miondownick, Samer Nashef, Ted Nield, Michael Nielsen, Abby Norman, Paul Parsons, Massimo Pigliucci, Aarathi Prasad, John Rhodes, Angela Saini, Ian Sample, Nicholas J. Saunders, Govert Schilling, Andy Scott, Menno Schilthuizen, Doug Sisterson, P.D. Smith, Ian Stewart, Thomas Suddendorf, Frank Swain, Jeremy Taylor, Chris Thomas, Rachel Thomas, Roberto Trotta, Mark Van Vugt, Geerat J. Vermeij, Matt Wilkinson, Caroline Williams. UK-registered limited company established 2008.

Linda Seifert Management Ltd

Screenworks Room 315, 22 Highbury Grove, London N5 2ER
tel 020-3214 8293
email contact@lindaseifert.com
website www.lindaseifert.com
Facebook www.facebook.com/lindaseifert
Twitter @lindaseifert
Agents Edward Hughes, Nick Turner

Represents writers, directors and producers for film, TV and radio only – no book authors (home 10%, overseas 20%). Client list ranges from the highly established to the emerging talent of tomorrow – see website for details. Established 2002.

The Sharland Organisation Ltd

The Manor House, Manor Street, Raunds, Northants NN9 6JW
tel (01933) 626600
email tso@btconnect.com
website www.sharlandorganisation.co.uk
Directors Mike Sharland, Alice Sharland

Specialises in film, TV, stage and radio rights throughout the world (home 15%, overseas 20%). Preliminary letter and return postage is essential. No reading fee. Works in conjunction with overseas agents. Founded 1988.

Sheil Land Associates Ltd

52 Doughty Street, London WC1N 2LS
tel 020-7405 9351
email info@sheilland.co.uk
Twitter @sheilland
Agents UK & US Sonia Land, Vivien Green, Piers Blofeld, Ian Drury, Gaia Banks *Film/theatre/TV* Lucy Fawcett, *Foreign Rights* Gaia Banks, Alba Arnau

Quality literary and commercial fiction and non-fiction, including: politics, history, military history, gardening, thrillers, crime, romance, drama, science fiction, fantasy, young adult, biography, travel, cookery, humour, estates (home 15%, USA/translation 20%). Also film, TV, radio and theatre representation, adult and children's. Welcomes approaches from new clients to start or to develop their careers. See website for submission instructions. No reading fee. Overseas associates Georges Borchardt, Inc. *US film and TV representation* CAA, APA and others.

Clients include Sally Abbott, Peter Ackroyd, Charles Allen, Pam Ayres, Josiah Bancroft, Raffaelle Barker, Karen Bartlett, Christopher Bartley, Dan Berlinka, Hugh Bicheno, Melvyn Bragg, Steven Carroll, Lana Citron, David Cohen, Mackenzie Common, Anna Del Conte, Elspeth Cooper, Elizabeth Corley, Seamus Deane, Angus Donald, Brian Dooley, Nadine Dorries, Amanda Duke, Joe Dunlop, Natalie Dye, Janet Edwards, Rachel Elliott, Robert Fabbri, Ann Featherstone, N.J. Fountain, Michelle Frances, Paola Gavin, Zulfikar Ghose, Alan Gilbey, Dr Claire Guest, Janice Hallett, Graham Hancock, Aidan Harte, Lucinda Hawksley, Felicity Hayes-McCoy, Peter Higgins, Susan Hill, Paterson Joseph, Nina Khrushcheva, Aby King, Mark Lawrence, Julia Lee, Cas Lester, Adam Long, Jane Lythell, Richard Mabey, Sharon Marshall, Ed McDonald, The Brothers McLeod, Peter Morfoot, Rachel Murrell, Chris Ould, Gareth Patterson, Gill Paul, Roger Pearce, Cath Quinn, Catherine Robertson, Graham Rice, David Robinson, Leo Ruikbie, Stephanie Saulter, Eva Schloss, Diane Setterfield, Angela Slatter, Anna Smith-Spark, Laura Summers, Martin Stephen, Jeffrey Tayler, Keith Saha, Sue Teddern, Hazhir Teimourian, Rose Tremain, Prof. Stanley Wells, Michael White, Neil White, J.C. Wilsher, Martin Windrow, James Wyllie and the estates of Catherine Cookson, Helen Forrester, Richard Holmes, Patrick O'Brian, Penelope Mortimer, Jean Rhys, Tom Sharpe, Barry Unsworth, F.A. Worsley and Stephen Gately. Founded 1962.

Caroline Sheldon Literary Agency Ltd*

71 Hillgate Place, London W8 7SS
tel 020-7727 9102
email carolinesheldon@carolinesheldon.co.uk
email felicitytrew@carolinesheldon.co.uk
website www.carolinesheldon.co.uk
Twitter @CarolineAgent
Twitter @FelicityTrew
Contacts Caroline Sheldon, Felicity Trew

Represents fiction, non-fiction, children's books and illustration, women's fiction, contemporary and historical, and all major fiction genres including humour, crime and fantasy. (Home 15%, USA/Translation 20%, Film/TV 20%). All writing for children including picture books, middle grade and young adult. Represents a select list of leading illustrators working mainly in children's books.

Authors – send submissions by email only with Submission/Title of work/Name of author in subject line. Include a three line synopsis, full introductory information about yourself and your writing, and the first three chapters only or equivalent length of work.

Illustrators – send introductory information about yourself by email with Artist's Submission in subject line, and attach samples of your work and/or link to your website. Founded 1985.

Jeffrey Simmons

15 Penn House, Mallory Street, London NW8 8SX
tel 020-7224 8917
email jasimmons@unicombox.co.uk

Specialises in fiction (no science fiction, horror or fantasy), biography, autobiography, show business, personality books, law, crime, politics, world affairs. Full-length MSS (home from 10%, overseas from 15%). Will suggest revision. No reading fee, but preliminary letter essential.

Sinclair-Stevenson

3 South Terrace, London SW7 2TB
tel 020-7581 2550
Directors Christopher Sinclair-Stevenson, Deborah Sinclair-Stevenson

Full-length MSS (home 15%, USA/translation 20%). General – no children's books. No reading fee; will suggest revision. Founded 1995.

Skylark Literary Limited

19 Parkway, Weybridge, Surrey KT13 9HD
tel 020-8144 7440
email info@skylark-literary.com
website www.skylark-literary.com
Facebook www.facebook.com/SkylarkLiteraryLtd
Twitter @skylarklit
Directors Joanna Moult, Amber Caraveo

Specialists in children's and young adult fiction – all genres considered (home 15%, overseas 20%.) Interested in new writers. Will consider unsolicited submissions. Agents have editorial backgrounds. Will work closely with clients on their manuscripts to increase chances of publication. See website for submission guidelines. Submissions by email only to submissions@skylark-literary.com. Will suggest revision where appropriate. No reading fee.

Robert Smith Literary Agency Ltd*

12 Bridge Wharf, 156 Caledonian Road, London N1 9UU
tel 020-7278 2444
email robert@robertsmithliteraryagency.com
website www.robertsmithliteraryagency.com
Directors Robert Smith, Anne Smith

Predominantly non-fiction: autobiography and biography, topical subjects, history, lifestyle, popular culture, entertainment, sport, true crime, health and nutrition, illustrated books (home 15%, overseas 20%). No unsolicited MSS. No reading fee. Will suggest revision.

Authors include Sarbjit Athwal, Richard Baker, Delia Balmer, Juliet Barnes, Peta Bee, Paul Begg, Ralph Bulger, Dr John Casson, Gary Chapman, Shirley Charters, Judy Cook, Clive Driscoll, Robert Driscoll, Russell Edwards, Ryan Edwards, Kate Elysia,

Stewart Evans, Penny Farmer, Helen Foster, Becci Fox, Stephen Fulcher, Charlotte Green, Naomi Jacobs, Albert Jack, Anita Kelsey, Roberta Kray, Carol Ann Lee, Angela Levin, Mary Long, Tony Long, John McDonald, Ann Ming, James Moore, Zana Morris, Alan Moss, Kim Noble, Marnie Palmer, Theo Paphitis, James Reed, Lyn Rigby, Prof. William D. Rubenstein, Tara Shanie, Keith Skinner, Geoffrey Wansell, Monica Weller, Wynne Weston-Davies, Karl Williams. Founded 1997.

The Standen Literary Agency

2 Dukes Avenue, London N10 2PT
tel 020-8245 8989
website www.standenliteraryagency.com
Twitter @YasminStanden
Director Yasmin Standen

Interested in discovering new writers and launching the careers of first-time writers. Literary and commercial fiction, YA and children's fiction – middle grade upwards (home 15%, overseas 20%). Non-fiction: get in touch to see if genre is represented. Send submissions by email only; no submissions by post. Send first three chapters, a synopsis (one side of A4) and a covering letter, all double-line spaced. No reading fee. See website for further information.

Authors include: Sarah Harris, Emily Nagle, Marisa Noelle, Louise Cliffe-Minns, Simon Arrowsmith, Andrew Murray et al. Founded 2004.

Elaine Steel Writers' Agent*

49 Greek Street, London W1D 4EG
tel (01273) 739022
email info@elainesteel.com
website www.elainesteel.com
Contact Elaine Steel

Represents screen, radio, theatre and book writers. Does not read unsolicited material. Any consideration for representation must be by email and accompanied by a cv together with a short outline of the work to be submitted. Founded 1986.

Abner Stein*

Southbank House, Suite 137, Black Prince Road, London SE1 7SJ
tel 020-7373 0456
website www.abnerstein.co.uk
Contacts Caspian Dennis, Sandy Violette

Fiction, general non-fiction and children's (home 15%, overseas 20%). Not taking on any new clients at present.

Micheline Steinberg Associates

Studio 315, ScreenWorks, 22 Highbury Grove, London N5 2ER
tel 020-3214 8292
email info@steinplays.com
website www.steinplays.com
Twitter @SteinbergAssocs
Agent Micheline Steinberg, *Assistant* Grace Carroll

Represents writers/directors for theatre, opera, television, film, radio and animation. Film and TV rights in fiction and non-fiction on behalf of book agents (home 10%, overseas 10–20%). Works in association with agents overseas. No unsolicited submissions. Industry recommendation preferred. Founded 1987.

Rochelle Stevens & Co

2 Terretts Place, Upper Street, London N1 1QZ
tel 020-7359 3900
email info@rochellestevens.com
website www.rochellestevens.com
Directors Rochelle Stevens, Frances Arnold

Adult drama scripts for TV, theatre and radio (10%). Children's drama scripts for TV, film and theatre (10%). Send preliminary letter, cv, short synopsis and opening ten pages of a drama script by post (sae essential for return of material). See website for full submission guidelines. No reading fee. Founded 1984.

Sarah Such Literary Agency

81 Arabella Drive, London SW15 5LL
tel 020-8876 4228
email info@sarah-such.com
website sarahsuchliteraryagency.tumblr.com
Twitter @sarahsuch
Director Sarah Such

High-quality literary and commercial non-fiction and fiction for adults, young adults and children with a particular focus on literary and commercial debut novels, biography, narrative non-fiction, memoir, history, popular culture and humour (home 15%, TV/film 20%, overseas 20%). Always looking for exciting new writers with originality and verve. No reading fee. Will suggest revision. Submit synopsis and a sample chapter (as a Word attachment by email) plus author biography. No postal submissions unless requested. No unsolicited MSS or telephone enquiries. TV/film scripts for established clients only. No radio or theatre scripts, poetry, fantasy, self-help or short stories. Translation representation: The Buckman Agency. Film/TV representation: Lesley Thorne, Aitken Alexander Associates Ltd.

Authors include Matthew De Abaitua, Kirsty Allison, Nick Barlay, Jeffrey Boakye, Salem Brownstone, Kit Caless, Ali Catterall, Rob Chapman, Heather Cooper, Ian Critchley, John Harris Dunning, Rob Harris, John Hartley, Marisa Heath, Wayne Holloway-Smith, Titus Hjelm, Vina Jackson, Maxim Jakubowski, Antony Johnston, Michael Kennedy, Amy Lankester-Owen, Louisa Leaman, Mathew Lyons, Sam Manning, Vesna Maric, Ngaire Mason-Wenn-Wallace, David May, Kit McCall, Benjamin J. Myers QC, Cathy Naden, Ben Osborne, Marian Pashley, Rachel Pashley, John Rowley, Caroline Sanderson, Tony De Saulles, Nikhil Singh, Sara Starbuck, Michael Wendling. Founded 2007.

The Susijn Agency Ltd

820 Harrow Road, London NW10 5JU
tel 020-8968 7435
email info@thesusijnagency.com
website www.thesusijnagency.com
Agents Laura Susijn

Specialises in world rights in English- and non-English-language literature: literary fiction and general non-fiction (home 15%, overseas 20%, theatre/film/TV/radio 15%). Send synopsis and three sample chapters. No reading fee.

Authors include Peter Ackroyd, Uzma Aslam Khan, Robin Baker, Tessa De Loo, Gwynne Dyer, Olivia Fane, Radhika Jha, Sophia Khan, Yan Lianke, Jeffrey Moore, Mark Mulholland, Parinoush Sainee, Karl Shaw, Sunny Singh, Hwang Sok-yong, Paul Sussman, Alex Wheatle, Adam Zameenzad. Founded 1998.

Emily Sweet Associates

35 Barnfield Road, London W5 1QU
tel 020-8997 6696 / 07980 026298
website www.emilysweetassociates.com
Director Emily Sweet

Represents quality fiction and general non-fiction including history, biography, current affairs, topical non-fiction and cookery. No children's or YA. Founded 2014.

The Tennyson Agency

109 Tennyson Avenue, New Malden, Surrey KT3 6NA
tel 020-8942 1039
email submissions@tenagy.co.uk
website www.tenagy.co.uk
Theatre, Radio, Television & Film Scripts Adam Sheldon

Scripts and related material for theatre, film, radio and TV only (home 15%, overseas 20%). No reading fee. Founded 2002.

Tin-Can Telephone Literary Agency

The Melting Pot, 5 Rose Street, Edinburgh EH2 2PR
email mybook@tctliteraryagency.com
website www.tin-can-telephone.com
Facebook www.facebook.com/TCTLiteraryAgency
Twitter @TCTLit
Founder and Agent Cassian Hall

Represents authors in YA, crime/thrillers, historical fiction, science fiction and fantasy. Also interested in non-fiction in the areas of psychology and personal development. Detailed information about what individual agents are looking for can be found on the website. Submissions by email, to include the first three chapters plus a synopsis. Authors should ensure that they have already undertaken editing work on their books before submission. No reading fee. Commission rates: 15% standard commission and up to 20% for overseas representation.

Jane Turnbull*

Postal address Barn Cottage, Veryan Churchtown, Truro TR2 5QA
tel (01872) 501317
email jane@janeturnbull.co.uk
London Office 58 Elgin Crescent, London W11 2JJ
tel 020-7727 9409
website www.janeturnbull.co.uk

High quality non-fiction; biography, history, natural history, lifestyle, humour; TV tie-ins, some literary fiction (home 15%, USA/translation 20%), performance rights (15%). Works in conjunction with Aitken Alexander Associates Ltd for sale of translation rights. No reading fee. Preliminary letter (NOT email) essential; no unsolicited MSS. Founded 1986.

Nick Turner Management Ltd

26 Richborne Terrace, London SW8 1AU
tel 020-7450 3355
email nick@nickturnermanagement.com
website www.nickturnermanagement.com
Twitter @nickturnermgmt
Agents Nick Turner, Phil Adie

Represents writers and directors for film, TV and radio worldwide (home 10%, overseas 15–20%). Specialises in TV drama, comedy, continuing-drama and children's. See website for submission guidelines. Founded 2016.

United Agents LLP*

12–26 Lexington Street, London W1F 0LE
tel 020-3214 0800
email info@unitedagents.co.uk
website www.unitedagents.co.uk
Agents Sarah Ballard, Caroline Dawnay, Jon Elek, Ariella Feiner, James Gill, Jodie Hodges (children's/young adult writers and illustrators), Caradoc King, Robert Kirby, Laura Macdougall, Yasmin McDonald, Amy Mitchell, Zoe Ross, Sophie Scard, Rosemary Scoular, Charles Walker, Anna Webber, Jane Willis.

Fiction and non-fiction (home 15%, USA/translation 20%). No reading fee. See website for submission details. Founded 2008.

Jo Unwin Literary Agency*

West Wing, Somerset House, London WC2R 1LA
email info@jounwin.co.uk
website www.jounwin.co.uk
Twitter @jounwin
Contact Jo Unwin

Represents authors of literary fiction, commercial women's fiction, memoir, YA fiction and fiction for children aged 9+ (picture books only accepted if written by established clients). Also represents comic writing and narrative non-fiction.

Authors include Richard Ayoade, Candice Carty-Williams, Kit de Waal, Sarah Moore Fitzgerald,

Georgia Pritchett, Cathy Rentzenbrink, Nadia Shireen, Maudie Smith, Nina Stibbe.

Wade and Co. Literary Agency Ltd

33 Cormorant Lodge, Thomas More Street, London E1W 1AU
tel 020-7488 4171
email rw@rwla.com
website www.rwla.com
Director Robin Wade

General fiction and non-fiction, excluding children's books (home 15%, overseas 20%). No poetry, plays, screen plays, picture books or short stories. See website for submission guidelines. Email submissions preferred. New authors welcome. No reading fee. Founded 2001.

Watson, Little Ltd*

Suite 315, ScreenWorks, 22 Highbury Grove, London N5 2ER
tel 020-7388 7529
email office@watsonlittle.com
website www.watsonlittle.com
Twitter @watsonlittle
Contacts James Wills (Managing Director), Laetitia Rutherford (Agent), Donald Winchester (Agent), Megan Carroll (Agent)

Adult Fiction: literary, commercial women's, historical, reading group, crime and thriller. Non-fiction: history, science, popular psychology, memoir, humour, cookery, self-help. Childrens: YA and middle-grade fiction, picture books and children's non-fiction in all genres. No poetry, TV, play or filmscripts (home 15%, USA/Translation 20%). Send informative preliminary letter, synopsis and sample chapters by email only to submissions@watsonlittle.com. *Overseas associates* The Marsh Agency Ltd; *Film and TV associates* Ki Agency and The Sharland Agency; *US associates* Howard Morhaim Literary Agency and The Gersh Agency.

Authors include Jenny Blackhurst, Susan Blackmore, Martin Edwards, Christopher Fowler, Tim Hall, Greg Jenner, Alex Marwood, Margaret Mahy, Colin Wilson, James Wong, Evie Wyld

Josef Weinberger Plays Ltd

(formerly Warner/Chappell Plays Ltd)
12–14 Mortimer Street, London W1T 3JJ
tel 020-7580 2827
email plays@jwmail.co.uk
website www.josef-weinberger.com

Specialises in stage plays. Works in conjunction with overseas agents. No unsolicited MSS; preliminary letter essential. Founded 1938.

Whispering Buffalo Literary Agency Ltd

97 Chesson Road, London W14 9QS
tel 020-7565 4737
email info@whisperingbuffalo.com
website www.whisperingbuffalo.com
Director Mariam Keen

Commercial/literary fiction and non-fiction, children's and young adult fiction (home 15%, overseas 20%). Special interest in book-to-screen adaptations; TV and film rights in novels and non-fiction handled in-house. Only accepts submissions by email. No reading fee. Will suggest revision. Founded 2008.

Eve White Literary Agency Limited*

54 Gloucester Street, London SW1V 4EG
tel 020-7630 1155
email eve@evewhite.co.uk
email ludo@evewhite.co.uk
website www.evewhite.co.uk
Twitter @EveWhiteAgency
Contact Eve White, Ludo Cinelli

Boutique agency representing commercial and literary fiction and non-fiction, children's fiction and film/TV tie-ins (home 15%, overseas 20%). No reading fee. Will suggest revision where appropriate. See website for up-to-date submission requirements. No submissions by post.

Eve White's clients include Ruth Ware, Jane Shemilt, Andy Stanton, Yvvette Edwards, Rae Earl, Paul Cooper, Saskia Sarginson, Rebecca Reid, Sarah J. Naughton, Damian Le Bas, Darran Anderson, Sarah Ockwell-Smith, Tracey Corderoy, Elli Woollard, Abie Longstaff. Founded 2003.

Isabel White Literary Agent

email isabel@isabelwhite.co.uk (trade)
email query.isabelwhite@googlemail.com (submissions)
website www.isabelwhite.co.uk
Proprietor Isabel White

Fiction and non-fiction (home 15%, overseas 20%). Books only – no film, TV or stage plays, poetry, short stories or academic monographs. Not currently accepting submissions. No reading fee.

Authors include Suzi Brent, Iain Clark, Graeme Kent. Founded 2008.

Dinah Wiener Ltd*

12 Cornwall Grove, London W4 2LB
tel 020-8994 6011
email dinah@dwla.co.uk
Director Dinah Wiener

Fiction and general non-fiction (home 15%, overseas 20%), film and TV in association (15%). No plays, scripts, poetry, short stories or children's books. Taking on no new clients. Founded 1985.

WME*

(William Morris Endeavour, UK)
100 New Oxford Street, London WC1A 1HB
tel 020-7534 6800

email ldnsubmissions@wmeentertainment.com
website www.wmeauthors.co.uk
Books Simon Trewin, Matilda Forbes Watson, Siobhan O'Neill, Fiona Baird, *TV* Isabella Zoltowski, Antonia Melville

Literary and commercial fiction, crime, thrillers, young adult fiction, middle grade fiction, memoir, self-help, lifestyle, serious non-fiction and popular culture (film/TV 10%, UK books 15%, USA books/translation 20%). No children's picture books. Please submit via email to the address above and see website for submission guidelines. Worldwide talent and literary agency with offices in New York, Beverly Hills, Nashville and Miami.

The Writers' Practice

tel 0845 680 6578, *mobile* 07940 533243
email jemima@thewriterspractice.com
website www.thewriterspractice.com
Twitter @writerspractice
Literary Agent & Editorial Consultant Jemima Hunt, *Editorial Consultant, manuscripts and scripts* Jeremy Page

The Writers' Practice is a boutique literary agency and editorial consultancy that specialises in launching debut authors. Jemima Hunt is interested in commercial and literary fiction and specialises in memoir and narrative non-fiction. She works closely with writers on all aspects of book development. Founded 2011.

The Wylie Agency (UK) Ltd

17 Bedford Square, London WC1B 3JA
tel 020-7908 5900
email mail@wylieagency.co.uk
website www.wylieagency.co.uk
President Andrew Wylie

Literary fiction and non-fiction. No unsolicited MSS. Founded 1996.

Susan Yearwood Agency

2 Knebworth House, Londesborough Road, London N16 8RL
tel 020-7503 0954
email susan@susanyearwood.com
email submissions@susanyearwood.com
website www.susanyearwood.com
Twitter @SYA_Susan
Contact Susan Yearwood

Literary, commercial fiction and non-fiction; children's fiction 9+ and YA (home 15%, overseas 20%). Send submission with covering letter and brief synopsis via email. Submissions not accepted by hand or post. No reading fee. Founded 2007.

Zeno Agency Ltd*

Primrose Hill Business Centre, 110 Gloucester Avenue, London NW1 8HX
tel 020-7096 0927
website www.zenoagency.com
Twitter @zenoagency
Director John Berlyne

Represents most fiction genres (crime, thrillers, YA, historical etc), with particular specialism in science fiction, fantasy and horror. Also some non-fiction (home and direct overseas 15%, overseas via sub-agents 20%). See website for client list and submission guidelines. No reading fee. Founded 2008.

Literary agents overseas

This list includes only a selection of agents across the English-speaking world. Selected lists of agents in non-English speaking territories can be found at www.writersandartists.co.uk/listings. Before submitting material, writers are advised to visit agents' websites for detailed submission guidelines and to ascertain terms.

AUSTRALIA

ALM: Australian Literary Management

tel +61 (0)9 818 8557
email alphaalm8@gmail.com
website www.austlit.com

For full details of genres represented and submission guidelines, see website. Does not consider scripts of any kind or books for children by unpublished authors. Does not accept self-published work or writing by non-Australian authors.

The Authors' Agent

PO Box 577 Terrigal, NSW 2260
email briancook@theauthorsagent.com.au
website www.theauthorsagent.com.au

Specialises in adult fiction, narrative non-fiction and children's books. Does not accept submissions by email. For detailed guidelines, see website.

Curtis Brown (Australia) Pty Ltd

PO Box 19, Paddington, NSW 2021
tel +61 (0)2 9361 6161
email reception@curtisbrown.com.au
website www.curtisbrown.com.au

No reading fee.

Jenny Darling & Associates

email office@jennydarling.com.au
website www.jennydarling.com.au
Facebook www.facebook.com/jennydarlingassociates
Twitter @AgentsJDA
Contact Jenny Darling

Adult fiction and non-fiction, some YA (home 15%, international/translation 20%, film/TV 20%). Currently closed for submissions. Founded 1998.

Drummond Agency

PO Box 572, Woodend, VIC 3442
tel +61 (0)3 5427 3644
email info@drummondagency.com.au
website www.drummondagency.com.au

Considers both fiction and non-fiction for adults and YA fiction but no fantasy or science fiction. Query by telephone, email or letter. Do not send attachments unless requested. See website for full submission guidelines and author listing.

Authors include Randa Abdel-Fattah, Vikki Wakefield, Claire Zorn, Deborah Burrows, Margareta Osborn, Yvette Walker. Founded 1999.

Golvan Arts Management

website www.golvanarts.com.au

Represents a wide range of writers including writers of both adult and children's fiction and non-fiction, poetry, screenwriters and writers of plays. Also represents visual artists and composers. See the General Information section on the website before making contact.

HLA Management

Postal address PO Box 1536 Strawberry Hills, Sydney, NSW 2012
email hla@hlamgt.com.au
website www.hlamgt.com.au

Represents directors, writers, designers, directors of photography, film editors, choreographers, composers, comedians and presenters. Does not represent actors. No unsolicited material. Requests for representation by referral.

HMMG Pty Ltd

email hmm@harrymmiller.com
website www.harrymmiller.com.au
Twitter @HMMG_

Accepts submissions for the following genres: non-fiction (strong female, animals, biography, memoir) and reality-based fiction. Does not accept submissions for poetry, short stories, science fiction, fantasy, screenplays or academic textbooks. For detailed submission guidelines, see website.

Margaret Kennedy Agency

PO Box 1433, Toowong 4066, Brisbane
email info@margaretkennedyagency.com
website www.margaretkennedyagency.com

See website for detailed submission guidelines. Query via email, no attachments.

The Naher Agency

PO Box 249, Paddington, NSW 2021
website www.naher.com.au

Specialises in quality fiction and non-fiction for adults. Does not represent fantasy, science fiction, YA, children's or self-help. Make initial query via form on website.

The Cameron Cresswell Agency/ Cameron's Management

Level 7, 61 Marlborough Street, Surry Hills, NSW 2010
tel +61 (0)2 9319 7199
email info@cameronsmanagement.com.au
website www.cameronsmanagement.com.au

Cameron's Management is an agency representing writers, directors, actors, presenters, designers, cinematographers, editors, composers and book authors across the full range of the film, television, live performance and publishing industries. Only accepts submissions in accordance with guidelines on website. No reading fee.

CANADA

Acacia House Publishing Services Ltd

51 Chestnut Avenue, Brantford, Ontario N3T 4C3
tel +1 519-752-0978
email bhanna.acacia@rogers.com
Managing Director Bill Hanna

Literary fiction/non-fiction, quality commercial fiction, most non-fiction (15% English worldwide, 25% translation, performance 20%). No horror or occult. Works with overseas agents. Query first with sample of 50pp max. Include return postage. No reading fee. Founded 1985.

Rick Broadhead & Associates

47 St. Clair Avenue West, Suite 501, Toronto M4V 3A5
email info@rbaliterary.com
website www.rbaliterary.com

See website for submission guidelines and genres represented. Email queries preferred.

The Bukowski Agency Ltd

14 Prince Arthur Avenue, Suite 202, Toronto M5R 1A9
email info@bukowskiagency.com
website www.bukowskiagency.com
Agent Denise Bukowski

Specialises in international literary fiction and up-market non-fiction for adults. Does not represent genre fiction, children's literature, plays, poetry or screenplays. See website for submission guidelines. Founded 1986.

CookeMcDermid

email submissions@cookemcdermid.com
email admin@cookemcdermid.com
website www.cookemcdermid.com
Agents Dean Cooke, Sally Harding, Martha Webb, Chris Bucci, Suzanne Brandreth, Ron Eckel, Rachel Letofsky

CookeMcDermid was formed when two pre-eminent literary agencies, The Cooke Agency and The McDermid Agency, amalgamated, combining over 47 years of experience. CMD represents authors of literary, commercial and SFF fiction; a broad range of narrative non-fiction; health & wellness resources; and middle grade and young adult books. Sells Canadian and American rights directly. Cooke International represents UK and translation rights, in conjunction with 35 co-agents around the world. CMD also works with associates to sell film and television rights in Canada and abroad. Founded 2017.

Helen Heller Agency

4–216 Heath Street West, Toronto M5P 1N7
email info@helenhelleragency.com
website www.helenhelleragency.com
Twitter @TheHHAgency

Specialises in adult and young adult fiction and non-fiction. Does not open attachments sent with emails. Query letters and any writing samples should be contained within the body of an email. No phone enquiries. See website for full list of genres represented and submission guidelines.

P.S. Literary Agency

2nd Floor, 2010 Winston Park Drive, Oakville, Ontario L6H 5R7
email info@psliterary.com
website www.psliterary.com
Twitter @PSLiterary
President & Principal Curtis Russell, *Vice President & Senior Literary Agent* Carly Watters, *Literary Agents* Maria Vicente, Eric Smith, *Associate Literary Agent* Kurestin Armada

Represents both fiction and non-fiction works to publishers in North America, Europe and throughout the world. Categories include commercial, upmarket, literary, women's fiction, mystery, thriller, romance, science fiction, fantasy, historical, LGBTQ, young adult, middle grade, picture books, memoir, history, politics, current affairs, business, wellness, cookbooks, sports, humour, pop science, pop psychology, pop culture, design and lifestyle. Does not accept submissions via mail or telephone. Send queries to query@psliterary.com. Do not send email attachments unless specifically requested.

Beverley Slopen

131 Bloor Street West, Suite 711, Toronto M5S 1S3
email beverley@slopenagency.ca
email beverley@slopenagency.com
website www.slopenagency.com
Agent Beverley Slopen

Represents a diverse list of authors in fields ranging from literary and commercial fiction to history, non-fiction, anthropology, biography and selected true crime and self-help. Not accepting new children's titles and tends to concentrate on Canadian-based writers. See website for details of authors, titles and submission guidelines.

Carolyn Swayze Literary Agency Ltd

7360-137th Street, Suite 319, Surrey, BC V3W 1A3
email reception@swayzeagency.com
website www.swayzeagency.com
Proprietor Carolyn Swayze

Literary fiction and non-fiction. Some romance and mystery. No science fiction, poetry, self-help, spiritual, screenplays. Eager to discover strong voices writing narrative non-fiction in history, science, nature, popular culture, food and drink. Some memoir. Primarily Canadian authors. No telephone calls: make contact by email. Send query including synopsis and short sample. Provide resume, publication credits, writing awards, education and experience relevant to the book project. Allow six weeks for a reply.

Westwood Creative Artists

386 Huron Street, Toronto M5S 2G6
email wca_office@wcaltd.com
website www.wcaltd.com

Represents literary fiction, quality commercial fiction including mysteries and thrillers and non-fiction in the areas of memoir, history, biography, science, journalism and current affairs. See website for submission guidelines.

NEW ZEALAND

Glenys Bean Writer's Agent

198A Opito Bay Road, Kerikeri 0294
email glenys@glenysbean.com
Directors Fay Weldon, Glenys Bean

Adult and children's fiction, educational, non-fiction, film, TV, radio (10–20%). Send preliminary letter, synopsis and sae. No reading fee. Founded 1989.

Playmarket

PO Box 9767 Wellington 6141
PO Box 5034, Wellesley Street, Auckland 1141
email info@playmarket.org.nz
website www.playmarket.org.nz
Director Murray Lynch

Playwrights' agent, advisor and bookshop. Representation, licensing and script development of New Zealand plays and playwrights. Currently licences over 400 productions of New Zealand plays each year, in New Zealand and around the world. Founded 1973.

Total Fiction Services

PO Box 6292 Dunedin North, Dunedin 9059
email tfs@elseware.co.nz
website www.elseware.co.nz

General fiction, non-fiction, children's books. No poetry, or individual short stories or articles. Enquiries from New Zealand authors only. Email queries but no attachments. Hard copy preferred. No reading fee. Also offers assessment reports, mentoring and courses.

USA

**Member of the Association of Authors' Representatives*

The Axelrod Agency*

55 Main Street, PO Box 357, Chatham, NY 12037
tel +1 518-392-2100
email steve@axelrodagency.com
email lori@axelrodagency.com
President Steven Axelrod, *Foreign Rights Director* Lori Antonson

Full-length MSS. Fiction (home 15%, overseas 20%), film and TV rights (15%); will suggest revision where appropriate. Works with overseas agents. No reading fee. Founded 1983.

The Bent Agency*

19 West 21st Street, #201, New York, NY 10010, USA
email info@thebentagency.com
website www.thebentagency.com
Agents Jenny Bent, Nicola Barr, Victoria Cappello, Gemma Cooper, Heather Flaherty, Louise Fury, Molly Ker Hawn, Sarah Manning, Rachel Horowitz

Represents a diverse range of genres including history, humour, lifestyle, inspiration, memoir, literary fiction, children's and commercial fiction. Only accepts email queries. See website for detailed query and submission guidelines.

Georges Borchardt Inc.*

136 East 57th Street, New York, NY 10022
tel +1 212-753-5785
website www.gbagency.com
Directors Georges Borchardt, Anne Borchardt, Valerie Borchardt

Full-length and short MSS (home/British/performance 15%, translations 20%). Agents in most foreign countries. No unsolicited MSS. No reading fee. Founded 1967.

Bradford Literary Agency

5694 Mission Center Road, Suite 347, San Diego, CA 92108
email queries@bradfordlit.com
website www.bradfordlit.com

Currently looking for fiction (romance, speculative fiction, women's, sci fi/fantasy, mystery, thrillers, historical, magical realism, children's and YA) and non-fiction (relationships, biography, memoir, self-help, lifestyle, business, parenting, narrative humour, pop culture, illustrated/graphic design, food and cooking, mind/body/spirit, history and social issues). Not currently looking for poetry, screenplays, short stories, westerns, horror, New Age, religion, crafts or gift books. Query by email only. For detailed submission guidelines, see website. No reading fee.

Brandt & Hochman Literary Agents Inc.*

1501 Broadway, Suite 2310, New York, NY 10036
tel +1 212-840-5760
website www.brandthochman.com
Contact Gail Hochman

Full-length and short MSS (home 15%, overseas 20%), performance rights (15%). No reading fee.

Barbara Braun Associates Inc.*

7 East 14th Street. 19F, New York, NY 10003, USA
email bbasubmissions@gmail.com
website www.barbarabraunagency.com
President Barbara Braun

Represents literary and commercial fiction and serious non-fiction (home 15%, overseas 20%). Does not represent poetry, science fiction, fantasy, horror or screenplays. Send queries by email. See website for full submission guidelines.

Browne & Miller Literary Associates*

52 Village Place, Hinsdale, IL 60521
tel +1 312-922-3063
email mail@browneandmiller.com
website www.browneandmiller.com
Contact Danielle Egan-Miller

General adult fiction and non-fiction (home 15%, overseas 20%). Works in conjunction with foreign agents. Will suggest revision; no reading fee. Founded 1971.

Maria Carvainis Agency Inc.*

Rockefeller Center, 1270 Avenue of the Americas, Suite 2915, New York, NY 10020
tel +1 212-245-6365
email mca@mariacarvainisagency.com
website www.mariacarvainisagency.com
President & Literary Agent Maria Carvainis

Adult fiction and non-fiction (home 15%, overseas 20%). All categories of fiction (except science fiction and fantasy), especially literary and mainstream; mystery, thrillers and suspense; historical; young adult and middle grade. Non-fiction: biography and memoir, health and women's issues, business, finance, psychology, popular science, popular culture. No reading fee. See website for full submission guidelines.

Frances Collin Literary Agency*

PO Box 33, Wayne, PA 19087-0033
email queries@francescollin.com
website www.publishersmarketplace.com/members/slyyake
website www.francescollin.com
Owner Frances Collin, *Agent* Sarah Yake

Home 15%, overseas 20%, performance rights 20%. Specialisations of interest to UK writers: literary fiction, mysteries, women's fiction, history, biography, science fiction, fantasy. No screenplays. No reading fee. No unsolicited MSS. Query via email only. Query letter in the body of the email with the first five pages of the manuscript pasted in the message, no attachments. Works in conjunction with agents worldwide. Founded 1948; successor to Marie Rodell-Frances Collin Literary Agency.

Don Congdon Associates Inc.*

110 William Street, Suite 2202, New York, NY 10038
tel +1 212-645-1229
email dca@doncongdon.com
website www.doncongdon.com
Agents Michael Congdon, Susan Ramer, Cristina Concepcion, Maura Kye-Casella, Katie Grimm, Katie Kotchman

Full-length and short MSS. General fiction and non-fiction (home 15%, overseas 20%, performance rights 15%). Works with co-agents overseas. No reading fee but no unsolicited MSS – query first with sase (no IRCs) or email for reply. Does not accept phone calls from querying authors. Founded 1983.

The Doe Coover Agency*

PO Box 668, Winchester, MA 01890
tel +1 781-721-6000
email info@doecooveragency.com
website www.doecooveragency.com

Specialises in non-fiction: business, history, popular science, biography, social issues, cooking, food writing, gardening; also literary and commercial fiction (home 15%, overseas 10%). No poetry or screenplays. Email queries only; see website for submission guidelines. Founded 1985.

Richard Curtis Associates Inc.

200 East 72nd Street, Suite 28J, New York, NY 10021
tel +1 212-772-7363
website www.curtisagency.com
President Richard Curtis

All types of commercial non-fiction (home 15%, overseas 25%, film/TV 15%). Foreign rights handled by Baror International. Founded 1970.

Curtis Brown Ltd*

10 Astor Place, New York, NY 10003
tel +1 212-473-5400
email info@cbltd.com
website www.curtisbrown.com
Twitter @CurtisBrownLtd
Ceo Timothy Knowlton, *President* Peter Ginsberg (at CA branch office); *Contacts* Noah Ballard, Tess Callero, Ginger Clark, Katherine Fausset, Jonathan Lyons, Laura Blake Peterson (*Vice President*), Mitchell Waters, *Film & TV rights* Holly Frederick, Kerry D'Agostino, Steven Salpeter, *Translation rights* Jonathan Lyons and Sarah Perillo

Fiction and non-fiction, juvenile (see Agent page on website as not all agents handle juvenile), film and TV rights. No unsolicited MSS. See individual agent's entry on the Agents page of the website for specific query and submission information. No reading fee; no handling fees. Founded 1914.

Liza Dawson Associates

121 West 27th Street, Suite 1201, New York, NY 10001
website www.lizadawsonassociates.com
Twitter @LizaDawsonAssoc
Ceo Liza Dawson

A full-service agency which draws on expertise as former publishers. Fiction and non-fiction. See website for full details of genres represented, submission guidelines and email contacts.

DeFiore and Company*

47 East 19th Street, 3rd Floor, New York, NY 10003
email info@dfliterary.com
website www.defliterary.com

Fiction and non-fiction (home 15%, overseas 20%). See website for submission guidelines. Founded 1999.

Sandra Dijkstra & Associates*

PMB 515, 1155 Camino Del Mar, Del Mar, CA 92014
tel +1 858-755-3115
website www.dijkstraagency.com
Contacts Sandra Dijkstra, Elise Capron, Jill Marr, Roz Foster, Thao Le, Andrea Cavallaro, Jessica Watterson, Suzy Evans, Jennifer Kim

Fiction: literary, contemporary, women's, romance, suspense, thrillers and science fiction. Non-fiction: narrative, history, business, psychology, self-help, science and memoir/biography (home 15%, overseas 20%). Works in conjunction with foreign and film agents. Email submissions only. Please see website for the most up-to-date guidelines. No reading fee. Founded 1981.

Donadio & Olson Inc.*

121 West 27th Street, Suite 704, New York, NY 10001
tel +1 212-691-8077
email mail@donadio.com
website www.donadio.com
Contacts Edward Hibbert, Neil Olson, Darin Webb

Literary fiction and non-fiction.

Dunham Literary, Inc.*

110 William Street, Suite 2202, New York, NY 10038–3901
email dunhamlit@gmail.com
website www.dunhamlit.com
Contact Jennie Dunham, Bridget Smith

Literary fiction and non-fiction, children's books (home 15%, overseas 20%). Send query by post or to query@dunhamlit.com. No reading fee. Founded 2000.

Dunow, Carlson & Lerner*

27 West 20th Street, Suite 1107, New York, NY 10011
email mail@dclagency.com
website www.dclagency.com

Represents literary and commercial fiction, a wide range of non-fiction and children's literature for all ages. Queries should be made by post (include sase) or email (no attachments).

Dystel, Goderich & Bourret LLC*

1 Union Square West, New York, NY 10003
tel +1 212-627-9100
website www.dystel.com
Contacts Jane D. Dystel, Miriam Goderich, Michael Bourret, Jim McCarthy, Lauren Abramo, Stacey Glick, Jessica Papin, John Rudolph, Sharon Pelletier, Eric Myers, Mike Hoogland, Erin Young, Amy Bishop, Kemi Faderin

General fiction and non-fiction (home 15%, overseas 19%, film/TV/radio 15%): literary and commercial fiction, narrative non-fiction, self-help, cookbooks, parenting, science fiction/fantasy, children's and young adults. Send a query letter with a synopsis and up to 50pp of sample MS. Will accept email queries. No reading fee. Will suggest revision. Founded 1994.

The Ethan Ellenberg Literary Agency*

155 Suffolk Street, Suite 2R, New York, NY 10002
tel +1 212-431-4554
email agent@ethanellenberg.com
website www.ethanellenberg.com
President & Agent Ethan Ellenberg, *Senior Agent* Evan Gregory, *Associate Agent* Bibi Lewis

Fiction and non-fiction (home 15%, overseas 20%). Commercial fiction: science fiction, fantasy, romance, thrillers, suspense, mysteries, children's and general fiction; also literary fiction with a strong narrative. Non-fiction: history, adventure, true crime, science, biography. Children's fiction: interested in young adult, middle grade and younger, of all types. Will consider picture books and other illustrated works. No scholarly works, poetry, short stories or screenplays.

Will accept unsolicited MSS and seriously consider all submissions, including first-time writers. For fiction submit synopsis and first three chapters. For non-fiction send a proposal (outline, sample material, author cv, etc). For children's works send complete MS. Illustrators should send a representative selection of colour copies (no original artwork). Unable to return any material from overseas. See website for full submission guidelines. Founded 1983.

Diana Finch Literary Agency*

116 West 23rd Street, Suite 500, New York, NY 10011
tel +1 917-544-4470
email diana.finch@verizon.net
website http://dianafinchliteraryagency.blogspot.com
Facebook www.facebook.com/DianaFinchLitAg

Twitter @DianaFinch
Owner and Agent Diana Finch

Memoirs, narrative non-fiction, science, history, environment, business, literary fiction, science fiction and fantasy, YA fiction (domestic 15%, foreign 20%). No reading fee. Queries through website (preferred) or by email. No queries by telephone.

Clients include Noliwe Rooks, Azadeh Moaveni, Antonia Juhasz, Loretta Napoleoni, Owen Matthews, Greg Palast, Thaisa Frank, Eric Simons, Thomas Goltz, Mark Schapiro, Joanna Russ (estate), Christopher Leonard, Robert Marion MD. Recent sales to W.W. Norton, Farrar, Straus & Giroux, Beacon Press, The New Press, Island Press. Previously agent with Ellen Levine Literary Agency. Founded 2003.

FinePrint Literary Management*

207 West 106th Street, Ste 1D, New York, NY 10025
firstname@fineprintlit.com
website www.fineprintlit.com
Ceo Peter Rubie, *Agents* Laura Wood, Lauren Bieker, June Clark

Represents fiction and non-fiction. Each agent has specific genre interests; these are detailed on the website. Query by email to the appropriate agent, including a query letter, synopsis and first two chapters but do not send any attachments without an invitation to do so.

Folio Literary Management*

The Film Center Building, 630 9th Avenue, Suite 1101, New York, NY 10036
website www.foliolit.com

Represents both first-time and established authors. Seeks upmarket adult fiction, literary fiction, commercial fiction that features fresh voices and/or memorable characters, narrative non-fiction. Folio Jr is devoted exclusively to representing children's book authors and artists. Consult agents' submission guidelines on the website before making contact.

Jeanne Fredericks Literary Agency Inc.*

221 Benedict Hill Road, New Canaan, CT 06840
tel +1 203-972-3011
email jeanne.fredericks@gmail.com
website www.jeannefredericks.com

Quality non-fiction, especially health, science, women's issues, gardening, antiques and decorative arts, biography, cookbooks, popular reference, business, natural history (home 15%, overseas 20%). No reading fee. Query first by email or mail, enclosing sase. Member of Authors Guild and AAR. Founded 1997.

Samuel French, Inc.

235 Park Avenue South, 5th Floor, New York, NY 10003
tel +1 866-598-8449
email info@samuelfrench.com
website www.samuelfrench.com

Play publishers; authors' representatives. No reading fee.

Sarah Jane Freymann Literary Agency

tel +1 212-362-9277
email submissions@sarahjanefreymann.com
website www.sarahjanefreymann.com
Contacts Sarah Jane Freymann, Steven Schwartz, Katherine Sands, Jessica Sinsheimer

Book-length fiction and general non-fiction. Special interest in serious non-fiction, mainstream commercial fiction, contemporary women's fiction, Latino American, Asian American, African American fiction and non-fiction, all children's books. Non-fiction: women's issues, biography, health/fitness, psychology, self-help, spiritual, natural science, cookbooks, pop culture. No reading fee. See website for detailed submission guidelines. Founded 1974.

The Friedrich Agency*

email mfriedrich@friedrichagency.com
email lcarson@friedrichagency.com
email kwolf@friedrichagency.com
website www.friedrichagency.com
Agents Molly Friedrich, Lucy Carson, Kent Wolf

Represents literary and commercial fiction for adults and YA, plus narrative non-fiction and memoir. Accepts queries by email and post. Query only one agent. No unsolicited MSS. No attachments to query emails unless invited. See website for detailed submission guidelines.

Gelfman Schneider ICM Partners*

850 Seventh Avenue, Suite 903, New York, NY 10019
tel +1 212-245-1993
email mail@gelfmanschneider.com
Directors Jane Gelfman, Deborah Schneider

General adult fiction and non-fiction (home 15%, overseas 20%). No reading fee. Send sase for return of material. Query by post only. Works in conjunction with ICM Partners and Curtis Brown, London.

Global Lion Intellectual Property Management, Inc.

PO Box 669238, Pompano Beach, FL 33066
tel +1 754-222-6948
email peter@globallionmgt.com
website www.globallionmanagement.com
Facebook www.facebook.com/GlobalLionManagement/
Twitter @AbundantLion
President/Ceo Peter Miller

Peter Miller has been a literary and film manager for several decades and is President and CEO of Global Lion Intellectual Property Management Inc.

(previously PMA Literary & Film Management Inc. of New York). He has represented more than 1,200 books, including over 20 New York Times bestsellers.

Global Lion specialises in non-fiction and commercial fiction including thrillers and true crime, as well as books with film, TV, or global publishing potential as Global Lion works in conjunction with agents worldwide. Authors and clients include Sir Ken Robinson, Jean Pierre Isbouts, Rabbi Mordecai Schreiber, Anthony DeStefano. Initial submissions should include a synopsis, author biography, manuscript sample and details of personal social media and self-promotion.

Barry Goldblatt Literary LLC*

320 Seventh Avenue, #266, Brooklyn, New York, NY 11215
tel +1 718-832-8787
email query@bgliterary.com
website www.bgliterary.com
Contact Barry Goldblatt

Represents young adult and middle-grade fiction, as well as adult science fiction and fantasy. No non-fiction. Has a preference for quirky, offbeat work. Query only. See website for full submission guidelines.

Frances Goldin Literary Agency*

214 West 29th Street, Suite 410, New York, NY 10001
tel +1 212-777-0047
email agency@goldinlit.com
website www.goldinlit.com
Agents Frances Goldin, Ellen Geiger, Matt McGowan, Sam Stoloff, Ria Julien, Caroline Eisenmann

Fiction (literary and high-quality commercial) and non-fiction. See website for submission guidelines. Founded 1977.

Sanford J. Greenburger Associates Inc.*

55 Fifth Avenue, New York, NY 10003
tel +1 212-206-5600
website www.greenburger.com
Contacts Heide Lange, Faith Hamlin, Daniel Mandel, Matt Bialer, Brenda Bowen, Stephanie Delman, Ed Maxwell

Fiction and non-fiction, film and TV rights. See website for submission guidelines. No reading fee.

The Joy Harris Literary Agency Inc.*

1501 Broadway, Suite 2310, New York, NY 10036
tel +1 212-924-6269
email contact@joyharrisliterary.com
website www.joyharrisliterary.com
President Joy Harris

Represents works of literary fiction and non-fiction. Does not currently accept poetry, screenplays, genre fiction or self-help submissions. Submissions should be emailed, comprising a query letter, an outline or sample letter to submissions@joyharrisliterary.com. See website for detailed submission guidelines.

John Hawkins & Associates Inc.*

80 Maiden Lane, Suite 1503, New York, NY 10038
tel +1 212-807-7040
email jha@jhalit.com
website www.jhalit.com
Agents Moses Cardona (President), Warren Frazier, Anne Hawkins

Fiction, non-fiction, young adult. No reading fee. Founded 1893.

The Jeff Herman Agency LLC

PO Box 1522, Stockblidge, MA 01262
tel +1 413-298-0077
email jeff@jeffherman.com
website www.jeffherman.com

Business, reference, popular psychology, technology, health, spirituality, general non-fiction (home/overseas 15%); will suggest revision where appropriate. Works with overseas agents. No reading fee. Founded 1986.

Hill Nadell Literary Agency

6442 Santa Monica Blvd., Suite 201, Los Angeles, CA 90038
tel +1 310-860-9605
email queries@hillnadell.com
website www.hillnadell.com
Agents Bonnie Nadell, Dara Hyde

Full-length fiction and non-fiction (home 15%, overseas 20%). Send query letter initially with first chapter. If you would like your materials returned, include adequate postage. Due to the high volume of submissions the agency receives, a response to all emailed queries cannot be guaranteed. Works in conjunction with agents in Scandinavia, France, Germany, Holland, Japan, Spain and more. No reading fee. Founded 1979.

ICM Partners*

65 East 55th Street, New York, NY 10022
tel +1 212-556-5600
London office 5th Floor, 28–29 Haymarket, London SW1Y 4SP
tel 020-7393 4400
website www.icmpartners.com

No unsolicited MSS.

InkWell Management

521 Fifth Avenue, 26th Floor, New York, NY 10175
tel +1 212-922-3500
email info@inkwellmanagement.com
email submissions@inkwellmanagement.com
website www.inkwellmanagement.com
Twitter @inkwellmgmt

Fiction and non-fiction (home/overseas 15%). See website for submission guidelines. Founded 2004.

JABberwocky Literary Agency Inc

49 West 5th Street, #12N, New York, NY 10036-4603
website www.awfulagent.com
President Joshua Bilmes

Agency specialising in science fiction and fantasy. There are five acquiring agents; for their individual submission and query guidelines, visit the website. Founded 1994.

Janklow & Nesbit Associates

285 Madison, 21st Floor, New York, NY 10017
tel +1 212-421-1700
email info@janklow.com
website www.janklowandnesbit.com
Chairmen Morton L. Janklow, Lynn Nesbit

Commercial and literary fiction and non-fiction. No unsolicited MSS. Works in conjunction with Janklow & Nesbit (UK) Ltd. Founded 1989.

Keller Media Inc.

578 Washington Boulevard, No. 745, Marina Del Rey, CA 90292
website www.kellermedia.com
Facebook www.facebook.com/KellerMediaInc
Twitter @KellerMediaInc
Ceo/Senior Agent Wendy Keller, *Agent* Megan Close Zavala

Non-fiction for adults: business (all types), self-improvement, pop culture, pop psychology, parenting, relationships, wellness, health and non-traditional health, management, career, entrepreneurship, business, personal finance, science, nature, history, and ecology/green movement. Autobiographies considered only by well-known people. No children's books, young adult, fiction, poetry, memoirs, screenplays or illustrated books. To submit a query, see www.kellermedia.com/query/. Founded 1989.

Virginia Kidd Agency Inc.

538 East Hartford Street, PO Box 278, Milford, PA 18337
tel +1 570-296-6205
website www.vk-agency.com

Fiction, specialising in science fiction and fantasy (home 15%, overseas 20–25%). Send synopsis (1–3pp), cover letter and sase. Founded 1965.

Harvey Klinger Inc.*

queries@harveyklinger.com
website www.harveyklinger.com
Twitter @HKLiterary
Agents Harvey Klinger, David Dunton, Andrea Somberg, Wendy Levinson, Rachel Ridout

Commercial and literary adult and children's fiction and non-fiction – serious narrative through to self-help psychology books by authors who have already established strong credentials in their respective field. (Home 15%, overseas 25%). See website for submission guidelines and submission form. Founded 1977.

The Knight Agency*

website www.knightagency.net

Represents both first-time and established authors across a wide range of genres. For the genre interests of individual agents and detailed submission guidelines, see website. All queries should be made by email. Queries must be addressed to a specific agent, with no attachments.

kt literary*

9249 S. Broadway 200–543, Highlands Ranch, CO 80129
tel +1 720-344-4728
email contact@ktliterary.com
website www.ktliterary.com
Contact Kate Schafer Testerman, Sara Megibow, Hannah Fergesen

Primarily middle-grade and young adult fiction. No picture books. In adult, also seeking romance, science fiction, fantasy and erotica (Sara Megibow and Hannah Fergesen). Email a query letter and the first three pages of manuscript in the body of the email (no attachments) as per website instructions. No snail mail.

Clients include Maureen Johnson, Stephanie Perkins, Matthew Cody, Ellen Booraem, Trish Doller, Amy Spalding, Roni Loren, Tiffany Reisz, Stefan Bachmann, Jason Hough. Founded 2008.

Susanna Lea Associates

331 West 20th Street, New York, NY 10011
tel +1 646-638-1435
email ny@susannalea.com
website www.susannalea.com

General fiction and non-fiction with international appeal. No plays, screenplays or poetry. Send query letter, brief synopsis, the first three chapters and/or proposal via website. Established in Paris 2000, New York 2004, London 2008.

Levine Greenberg Rostan Literary Agency*

307 Seventh Avenue, Suite 2407, New York, NY 10001
email submit@lgrliterary.com
website www.lgrliterary.com

Represents literary and commercial fiction and non-fiction across a diverse range of genres. Refer to the How to Submit section of the website before querying or submitting work.

Julia Lord Literary Management*

38 West Ninth Street, New York, NY 10011
email query@julialordliterarymgt.com
website www.julialordliterarymgt.com
Contacts Julia Lord, Ginger Curwen

Currently looking for submissions in the following genres: narrative non-fiction, reference, biography, history, lifestyle, sports, humour, science, adventure, general fiction, historical fiction, YA fiction, thrillers, mysteries. Email and postal queries accepted. See website for detailed query and submission guidelines.

Donald Maass Literary Agency*

Suite 252, 1000 Dean Street, Brooklyn, NY 11238
tel +1 212-727-8383
email info@maassagency.com
website www.maassagency.com
Agents Donald Maass, Jennifer Jackson, Cameron McClure, Katie Shea Boutillier, Michael Curry, Caitlin McDonald, Paul Stevens, Jennifer Goloboy, Kiana Nguyen

Specialises in fiction, all genres (home 15%, overseas 20%). See website for submission guidelines. Founded 1980.

Margret McBride Literary Agency*

PO Box 9128, La Jolla, CA 92038
tel +1 858-454-1550
email mmla@mcbridelit.com
website www.mcbrideliterary.com
President Margret McBride

Business, mainstream fiction and non-fiction (home 15%, overseas 25%). No poetry or children's books. No reading fee. See website for submission guidelines. Founded 1981.

McIntosh & Otis Inc.*

353 Lexington Avenue, New York, NY 10016
tel +1 212-687-7400
email info@mcintoshandotis.com
website www.mcintoshandotis.com
Agents Eugene H. Winick, Elizabeth Winick Rubinstein, Adam Muhlig, Christa Heschke

Adult and children's literary fiction and non-fiction. No unsolicited MSS; query first via email, see website for instructions. No reading fee. Founded 1928.

MacKenzie Wolf*

email queries@mwlit.com
website www.mwlit.com
Contact Gillian MacKenzie

A full service literary agency and legal consulting company. To submit a project send a query letter along with a 50-page writing sample (for fiction) or a detailed proposal (for non-fiction) to queries@mwlit.com. Samples may be submitted as an attachment or embedded in the body of an email. Does not accept mailed queries. Does not represent screenplays.

Carol Mann Agency*

55 Fifth Avenue, New York, NY 10003
tel +1 212-206-5635
email submissions@carolmannagency.com
website www.carolmannagency.com
Twitter @carolmannagency
Associates Carol Mann, Laura Yorke, Gareth Esersky, Myrsini Stephanides, Joanne Wyckoff, Tom Miller

Psychology, popular history, biography, pop culture, health, advice/relationships, current affairs/politics, parenting, business, memoir, humour, science, general non-fiction, fiction, YA, middle grade (home 15%, overseas 20%). Works in conjunction with foreign and film agents. Submission guidelines: fiction, send a query and the first 25 pages; non-fiction, send a query, synopsis/proposal and the first 25 pages. Founded 1977.

The Evan Marshall Agency*

1 Pacio Court, Roseland, NJ 07068-1121
tel +1 973-287-6216
email evan@evanmarshallagency.com
website www.evanmarshallagency.com
President Evan Marshall

General fiction (home 15%, overseas 20%). Works in conjunction with overseas agents. Will suggest revision; no reading fee. To query: in body of email include query letter, first three chapters and synopsis of entire novel. Founded 1987.

Jean V. Naggar Literary Agency Inc.*

216 East 75th Street, Suite 1E, New York, NY 10021
tel +1 212-794-1082
email jvnla@jvnla.com
website www.jvnla.com
President Jennifer Weltz, *Agents* Alice Tasman, Ariana Philips

Mainstream commercial and literary fiction, non-fiction (narrative, memoir, journalism, psychology, history, pop culture, humour and cookbooks), young readers (picture, middle grade, young adult). Home 15%, overseas 20%. Works in conjunction with foreign agents. Submit queries via form on website. No reading fee. Founded 1978.

Harold Ober Associates Inc.*

425 Madison Avenue, New York, NY 10017
tel +1 212-759-8600
website www.haroldober.com

Full-length MSS (home 15%, UK/overseas 20%), performance rights (15%). No screenplays or playscripts. No email or fax queries; see website for submission instructions. No reading fee. Founded 1929.

Alison Picard, Literary Agent

PO Box 2000, Cotuit, MA 02635
tel +1 508-477-7192
email ajpicard@aol.com

Adult fiction and non-fiction, children's and young adult (15%). No short stories, poetry, plays, screenplays or sci-fi/fantasy. Please send query via email (no attachments). No reading fee. Founded 1985.

Pippin Properties Inc.

110 West 40th Street, Suite 1704, New York, NY 10018, USA
tel +1 212-338-9310
email info@pippinproperties.com
website www.pippinproperties.com
Facebook www.facebook.com/pippinproperties
Twitter @LovethePippins
Contact Holly McGhee, Elena Giovinazzo, Sara Crowe, Larissa Helena, Ashley Valentine

Exclusively children's book authors and artists (home 15%, overseas 25%), from picture books to middle-grade and young adult novels. Query by email. Founded 1998.

Rees Literary Agency*

14 Beacon Street, Suite 710, Boston, MA 02108
email lorin@reesagency.com
website www.reesagency.com
Agents Ann Collette, Lorin Rees, Rebecca Podos

Business books, self-help, biography, autobiography, political, literary fiction, memoirs, history, current affairs (home 15%). No reading fee. Submit query letter with sase. Founded 1982.

The Angela Rinaldi Literary Agency*

email info@rinaldiliterary.com
website www.rinaldiliterary.com
President Angela Rinaldi

Mainstream and literary adult fiction; non-fiction (home 15%, overseas 25%). No reading fee. Founded 1994.

Susan Schulman Literary Agency LLC*

454 West 44th Street, New York, NY 10036
tel +1 212-713-1633
email susan@schulmanagency.com
website www.schulmanagency.com

Agents for negotiation in all markets (with co-agents) of fiction and general non-fiction, children's books, academic and professional works, and associated subsidiary rights including plays, television and film (home 15%, UK 7.5%, overseas 20%). No reading fee. Return postage required. Email enquiries to queries@schulmanagency.com.

Scott Meredith Literary Agency

125 Park Avenue, 25th Floor, New York, NY 10017
email info@scottmeredith.com
website www.scottmeredith.com
President Arthur Klebanoff

General fiction and non-fiction. Founded 1946.

Philip G. Spitzer Literary Agency, Inc.*

50 Talmage Farm Lane, East Hampton, NY 11937
tel +1 631-329-3650
email lukas.ortiz@spitzeragency.com
website www.spitzeragency.com
Agents Philip Spitzer, Anne-Lise Spitzer, Lukas Ortiz, *Office* Kim Lombardini

General fiction and non-fiction; specialises in mystery/suspense, sports, politics, biography, social issues.

The Strothman Agency*

email info@strothmanagency.com
website www.strothmanagency.com
Twitter @strothmanagency

Specialises in history, science, narrative journalism, nature and the environment, current affairs, narrative non-fiction, business and economics, YA fiction and non-fiction, middle grade fiction and non-fiction. Only accepts electronic submissions. Query by email to strothmanagency@gmail.com but first see website for detailed submission guidelines.

Emma Sweeney Agency*

245 East 80th Street, Suite 7E, New York, NY 10075-0506
email queries@emmasweeneyagency.com
website www.emmasweeneyagency.com

Specialises in general fiction, historical fiction and narrative non-fiction including memoir, history, science and religion. Only accepts electronic queries. Query by email with a description of plot/proposal and a brief cover letter containing how you heard about the agency, previous writing credits and a few details about yourself. Do not send attachments unless requested; instead, paste the first ten pages of your novel/proposal into the text of your query email.

Trident Media Group

41 Madison Avenue, New York, NY 10010
tel +1 212-333-1511
email info@tridentmediagroup.com
website www.tridentmediagroup.com

Full-length MSS: see website for genres represented (home 15%, overseas 20%); in conjunction with co-agents, theatre, films, TV (15%). Will suggest revision. See website for submission guidelines.

Watkins/Loomis Agency Inc.

PO Box 20925, Park West Finance Station, New York, NY 10025
website www.watkin-sloomis.squarespace.com
President Gloria Loomis

Fiction and non-fiction. No unsolicited MSS. *Representatives* Abner Stein (UK), The Marsh Agency Ltd (foreign).

Waverly Place Literary Agency

125 Court Street, #3nD, New York, NY 11201
email waverlyplaceliterary@aol.com

Art and illustration

Freelancing for beginners

Fig Taylor describes the opportunities open to freelance illustrators and discusses types of fee and how to negotiate one to your best advantage.

Full-time posts for illustrators are extremely rare. Because commissioners' needs tend to change on a regular basis, most artists have little choice but to freelance – offering their skills to a variety of clients in order to make a living.

Illustration is highly competitive and a professional attitude towards unearthing and targeting potential commissioners, and presenting, promoting and delivering your work will be vital to your success. Likewise, a realistic understanding of how the industry works and of your place within it will be key. Without adequate research into your chosen field(s) of interest, you may find yourself approaching inappropriate clients – a frustrating and disheartening experience for both parties and a waste of your time and money.

Who commissions illustration?

Magazines and newspapers

Whatever your illustrative ambitions, you are most likely to receive your first commissions from editorial clients. The comparatively modest fees involved allow art editors the freedom to take risks, so many are keen to commission newcomers. Briefs are generally fairly loose though deadlines can be short, particularly where daily and weekly publications are concerned. However, fast turnover means you will establish yourself sooner rather than later, thus reassuring clients in other, more lucrative, spheres of your professional status. Given then that it is possible to use magazines as a springboard, it is essential to research them thoroughly when seeking to identify your own individual market. See the directories starting on page 35. Collectively, editorial clients accommodate an infinite variety of illustrative styles and techniques. Don't limit your horizons by approaching only the most obvious titles and/or those you would read yourself. Consider also trade and professional journals, customer magazines (such as in-flight magazines or those produced for supermarkets, insurance companies, etc) and those available on subscription from membership organisations or charities. You will often find obscure titles in the reference section of public or university libraries, where the periodicals they subscribe to will reflect the subjects taught. Seeking out as many potential clients as possible will benefit you in the long term. In addition to the titles listed in this *Yearbook*, the Association of Illustrators (AOI) publishes an *Editorial Directory* which gives specific client contact details, and is updated annually. Don't just confine yourself to the world of print either; online publications commission illustration – and gifs – too. There are also a number of useful online resources to further aid your research such as www.magforum.com, https://magpile.com and https://issuu.com.

Book publishing

With the exception of children's picture books, where illustration is unlikely to fall out of fashion, some publishers are using significantly less illustration than they once did. However, those invested in digital publishing are constantly exploring new formats and platforms enabling books to be experienced in new ways and this could open up fresh avenues for illustrators in time. Some publishers of traditional mass market fiction genres, such as horror, science fiction and fantasy, still favour strong, representational work on their covers, however it no longer predominates entirely and a wider variety of styles has come into use. While photography still predominates in other genres, such as the family saga and historical romance, quirky, humorous and graphic styles continue to be synonymous with the packaging of women's contemporary romance. A very diverse range of styles can be accommodated within literary, upmarket fiction, though a smaller, independent publisher specialising in this area might opt to use stock imagery in order to operate within a limited budget. While specialist and technical illustrators still have a vital part to play in non-fiction publishing, there is also some decorative work being commissioned for the covers and interiors of lifestyle-related subjects, such as cookery, gardening and mind, body & spirit , though again photography continues to predominate – and for those who enjoy detailed line work, the unprecedented rise in popularity of the adult colouring book shows little sign of abating just yet.

Children's publishers use a wide variety of styles, covering the gamut from baby books, activity and early learning, through to full-colour picture books, early readers, covers for YA fiction and black-and-white line illustrations for the 8–11 age group (particularly for boys, who tend to be more reluctant readers than girls). Author/illustrators are particularly welcomed by picture book publishers – though some have a policy of working only with those represented by a literary agent. Whatever your style, being able to develop believable characters and sustain them throughout a narrative is paramount. Some children's book illustrators initially find their feet in educational publishing. However, all ages are catered for within this area, including adults with learning difficulties, those learning languages for business purposes and teachers working right across the educational spectrum. Consequently, a wide variety of illustrators can be accommodated, even those working in comic book or manga styles. With the exception of educational publishing, which tends to have a faster turnover, most publishing deadlines are civilised and mass market covers particularly well paid. There are numerous publishing clients listed elsewhere in this *Yearbook* (see the directories starting on page 152 and page 217)and visiting individual websites is a good way to get a flavour of the kind of illustration they may favour. In addition, the AOI publishes a *Publishing Directory*, which is updated yearly and gives specific client contact details.

Greeting cards

Many illustrators are interested in providing designs for cards and giftwrap. Illustrative styles favoured include decorative, graphic, humorous, fine art, children's, quirky and cute. For specific information on the gift industry which, unlike the areas covered here, works on a speculative basis, see *Card and stationery publishers that accept illustrations and photographs* on page 511. The UK Greeting Card Association also has some excellent resources for those who are new to the industry on their website, www.greetingcardassociation.co.uk/resources.

Design companies

Both designers and their clients (who are largely uncreative and will, ultimately, be footing the bill) will be impressed and reassured by relevant, published work so wait until you're established before approaching them or illustrators' agents who cater to this market. Although fees are significantly higher than those in newspapers, magazines and book publishing, this third-party involvement generally results in a more restrictive brief. Deadlines may vary and styles favoured range from conceptual through to realistic, decorative, humorous and informational – with those involved in multimedia and web design favouring illustrators with character development and flash animation skills.

Magazines such as *Creative Review* and the online-based *Design Week* (both published by Centaur Media Plc) will keep you abreast of developments in the design world and help you identify clients' individual areas of expertise. Meanwhile, online directories such as www.designdirectory.co.uk, www.dbadirectory.org.uk, www.dexigner.com and www.creativematch.com carry listings, though there are any number of well-curated blogs produced by and dedicated to the work of graphic designers you could scour for leads. Individual contact names are also available at a price from database specialists File FX, who can provide creative suppliers with up-to-date information on commissioners in all spheres. A similar service is provided by Bikinilists, an online annual subscription-based resource that specialises in providing categorised contact data. The AOI's annually updated *Advertising Directory* also incorporates a number of design consultancies, reflective of the fact that lines between advertising, marketing and branding are becoming increasingly blurred.

Useful addresses

Association of Illustrators (AOI)
Somerset House, Strand, London WC2R 1LA
tel 020-7759 1010
email info@theaoi.com
website https://theaoi.com

The UK's professional trade organisation. Organisers of the World Illustration Awards and the London Transport Museum Prize for Illustration, and publishers of *Varoom* magazine, *The Illustrator's Guide to Law and Business Practice* and various client directories. See also page 548.

Bikinilists
Unit 18, Govanhill Workspace, 69 Dixon Road, Glasgow G42 8AT
tel 0141 636 3901
website www.bikinilists.com

Maintains an up-to-date database of creative commissioners to creative practitioners. Provides a boutique platform and support to those wishing to create and send promotional email marketing campaigns.

Centaur Media Plc
79 Wells Street, London W1T 3QN
website www.creativereview.co.uk, www.designweek.co.uk

Publishes *Creative Review* magazine and free online resource, *Design Week*.

File FX
201-202 Upper Street, Islington, London N1 1RQ
tel 020-7226 6646
email info@filefx.co.uk
website www.filefx.co.uk

Specialises in providing creative suppliers with up-to-date information on commissioning clients in all spheres.

Haymarket Media Group
Bridge House, 69 London Road, Twickenham TW1 3SP
tel 020-8267 5000
email campaign@haymarket.com
website www.campaignlive.co.uk

Publishes *Campaign* magazine monthly, plus an additional quarterly publication.

Serbin Communications
813 Reddick Street, Santa Barbara, CA 93103
website www.serbin.com, wwwdirectoryofillustration.com

Publishes the *Director of Illustration* and hosts portfolios online.

Workbook LLC
website www.workbook.com

Publishes printed sourcebooks and showcases portfolios online.

Advertising agencies

As with design, you should ideally be established before seeking advertising commissions. Fees can be high, deadlines short and clients extremely demanding. A wide range of styles are used and commissions might be incorporated into direct mail or press advertising, featured on websites or elsewhere in cyberspace, billboards, hoardings or animated for television. Fees will vary, depending on whether a campaign is local, national or even global and how many forms of media are used to attract the target demographic's attention.

Most agencies employ at least one art buyer to look at portfolios, both in person and online. A good one will know what campaigns each creative team is currently working on and may refer you to specific art directors or vice versa. These days some art buyers are open to being approached by freelance illustrators, providing the illustrator has some published work. Monthly periodicals, *Creative Review* and the weekly *Campaign* (see page 44) carry agency news, while the AOI also publishes an *Advertising Directory*, updated annually.

Portfolio presentation

In general, UK commissioners prefer to see someone with a strong, consistent, recognisable style rather than an unfocused jack-of-all-trades type and, in time, the internet will probably make this requirement universal, as the world shrinks and the talent pool widens. Thus, when assembling your professional portfolio – whether print or digital (and many illustrators have both) – try to exclude samples which are, in your own eyes, weak, irrelevant, uncharacteristic or simply unenjoyable to do; focus on your strengths instead. Should you be one of those rare, multi-talented individuals who finds it hard to limit themselves stylistically, try splitting conflicting work into separate portfolios/sections (or even websites) geared towards different kinds of clients to avoid confusion.

A lack of formal training need not be a handicap providing your portfolio accurately reflects the needs of the clients you target. Some illustrators find it useful to assemble 'mock-ups' using existing magazine layouts. By responding to the copy and replacing original images with your own illustrations, it is easier to see how your work will look in context. This is particularly relevant to conceptual illustrators, as commissioners are paying for the way you think in addition to your style/technique. Eventually, as you become more established, you'll be able to replace these with published pieces.

If you are presenting a print portfolio, ideally it should be of the hard or soft, bound, zip-up, ring-bound variety and never exceed A2 in size. A3 or A4 is industry standard these days as clients usually have little desk space; portfolio boxes are also acceptable, though you could run the risk of samples going astray. Alternatively, you may choose to give a laptop or tablet presentation, in which case strive to keep it simple and well organised as if it were a print one. In other words, have a finite number of images and a set running order. If clients wish to see further samples, you have the option of showing some afterwards. Either bring your own device or borrow one with which you are familiar. (Make sure it is fully charged and that you have emergency laptop back-up such as a power brick, USB stick, CDs, etc. If your presentation involves talking a client through your website or blog rather than files or slideshows, check you will have wireless internet access and, if not, take screen captures.) Complexity of style and diversity of subject matter will dictate how many samples to include but if you are opting for a print portfolio presentation, all should be neatly mounted on lightweight paper or card, or printed out with or without a border and placed inside protective plastic sleeves. Originals, high-quality photographs, computer printouts and laser copies are acceptable to clients but tacky out-of-focus snapshots are not. Also avoid including multiple sketchbooks and life drawings, which are anathema to clients. It will be taken for granted that you know how to draw from observation.

Interviews and beyond

Setting up face-to-face meetings can be hard work and clients take a dim view of spontaneous visits from passing illustrators. However, since it's difficult to strike up a working rapport when viewing work remotely, I'd still recommend trying to arrange a physical presentation where geographically practicable. Having established the contact name (either from a written source or by asking the company directly), and making sure your work is suitable to the needs of your target, clients are still best initially approached by letter or telephone call. Emails can be overlooked, ignored or simply end up in the company spam filter. Some publishing houses are happy to see freelances, though others prefer a pdf or weblink or even an old-fashioned print portfolio 'drop-off'. While some commissioners will automatically take photocopies of your printed work and/or bookmark your website for reference, it's always advisable to have some kind of promotional material to leave behind such as a CD, postcard, broadsheet or advertising tearsheet. Always ask an enthusiastic client if they know of others who might be interested in your work. Personal recommendation is more likely to lead to an interview.

Cleanliness, punctuality and enthusiasm are more important to clients than how you dress – as is a professional attitude to taking and fulfilling a brief. A thorough understanding of each commission is paramount from the outset. You will need to know your client's requirements regarding roughs; format and – where relevant – size and flexibility of artwork; preferred medium if you work in more than one; and whether the artwork is needed in colour or black and white. You will also need to know when the deadline is. Never, under any circumstances agree to undertake a commission unless you are certain you can deliver on time and always work within your limitations. Talent is nothing without reliability.

Self-promotion

There are many ways an illustrator can ensure their work stays uppermost in the industry's consciousness, some more expensive than others. See *Selling yourself and your work online* on page 497. On the affordable front, images can be emailed in a variety of formats, burned onto disc, posted in a blog, or showcased on a website/online portfolio. Social networking platforms, such as Twitter, Dribble, Tumblr, Pinterest, Facebook and Instagram, can also be invaluable when raising your professional profile. You might also consider advertising in a professional directory such as the US-based *Workbook* or *Directory of Illustration*, which tend to have a long shelf life and are well respected by industry professionals. While sourcebooks like these are generally available free to commissioners in print and digital format, exposure doesn't come cheap to advertisers. However, those represented by illustration agencies who advertise in them can promote themselves at a cheaper rate. Unlike freelancers, agents purchase multiple pages which can be divided up and shared by their artists.

Competitions are another effective means of self promotion. The annual World Illustration Awards and the London Transport Museum Prize for Illustration, both run by the Association of Illustrators, are open to students and new graduates as well as professional illustrators over the age of 18. There are eight categories and all shortlisted work is published online by the AOI. It is also included, along with that of the category winners, in an annual exhibition and awards catalogue. Keep your eyes open for other competitions too. Even comparatively low-key online challenges such as *Illustration Friday* and *InkTober* can result in commissions.

As commissioners routinely use internet resources, websites have become an essential method of self-promotion. Make sure yours loads quickly, is simple and straightforward to navigate and displays decent-sized images. Use your 'About Me' section to discuss the way you work and the type of commissions you've had or hope to work on. Likewise incorporate links to where else your work can be found on the web. Currently, both AOI members and non-members can promote their work online at https://theaoi.com/folios, though members can do so at a reduced rate.

Be organised

Once you are up and running, it is imperative to keep organised records of all your commissions. Contracts can be verbal as well as written, though details – both financial and otherwise – should always be confirmed in writing (an email fulfils this purpose) and duplicated for your files. Likewise, keep corresponding client faxes, letters, emails and order forms. The AOI publication *The Illustrator's Guide to Law and Business Practice* offers a wealth of practical, legal and ethical information. Subjects covered include contracts, fee negotiation, agents, licences, royalties and copyright issues.

Money matters

The type of client, the purpose for which you are being commissioned and the usage of your work can all affect the fee you can expect to receive, as can your own professional attitude. Given that it is *extremely* inadvisable to undertake a commission without first agreeing on a fee, you will have to learn to be upfront about funds.

Licence *v.* copyright

Put simply, according to current EU legislation (which may of course change post Brexit), copyright is the right to reproduce a piece of work anywhere, *ad infinitum*, for any purpose, for a period ending 70 years after the death of the person who created it. This makes it an extremely valuable commodity.

By law, copyright automatically belongs to you, the creator of your artwork, unless you agree to sell it to another party. In most cases, clients have no need to purchase it, and the recommended alternative is for you to grant them a licence instead, governing the precise usage of the artwork. This is far cheaper from the client's perspective and, should they subsequently decide to use your work for some purpose other than those outlined in your initial agreement, will benefit you too as a separate fee will have to be negotiated. It's also worth noting that even if you were ill-advised enough to sell the copyright, the artwork would still belong to you unless you had also agreed to sell it.

Rejection and cancellation fees

Most commissioners will not expect you to work for nothing unless you are involved in a speculative pitch, in which case it will be up to you to weigh up the pros and cons of your possible involvement. Assuming you have given a job your best shot, i.e. carried out the client's instructions to the letter, it's customary to receive a rejection fee even if the client doesn't care for the outcome: 25% is customary at developmental/rough stage and 50% at finished artwork stage. (Clear this with the client before you start, as there are exceptions to the rule.) Cancellation fees are paid when a job is terminated through no fault of the artist or, on occasion, even the client. Customary rates in this instance are 25% before rough stage, 33% on delivery of roughs and 100% on delivery of artwork.

Fixed *v.* negotiable fees

Editorial and publishing fees are almost always fixed with little, if any, room for haggling and are generally considerably lower than advertising and design fees, which tend to be negotiable. A national full-colour 48-sheet poster advertising Marks & Spencer is likely to pay more than a local black-and-white ad in the local freebie newspaper plugging a poodle parlour. If, having paid your editorial dues, you find yourself hankering after commissions from the big boys, fee negotiation – confusing and complicated as it can sometimes be – will become a fact of life. However you choose to go about the business of cutting a deal, it will help if you disabuse yourself of the notion that the client is doing you a whopping favour by considering you for the job. Believe it or not, the client *needs* your skills to bring his/her ideas to life. In short, you are worth the money and the client knows it.

Pricing a commission

Before you can quote on a job, you'll need to know exactly what it entails. For what purpose is the work to be used? Will it be used several times and/or for more than one purpose? Will its use be local or national? For how long is the client intending to use it? Who is the client and how soon do they want the work? Are you up against anyone else (who could possibly undercut you)?

Next, ask the client what the budget is. There's a fair chance they might tell you. Whether they are forthcoming or not, don't feel you have to pluck a figure out of thin air or agree to their offer immediately. Play for time. Tell them you need to review your current workload and that you'll get back to them within a brief, specified period of time. If nothing else, haggling over the phone is less daunting than doing it face to face. If you've had no comparable commissions to date and are an AOI member, check out the going rate by contacting them online for pricing advice (or check out their survey on illustration fees and standards of pricing in the members-only section of the AOI website). Failing that, try speaking to a friendly client or a fellow illustrator who's worked on similar jobs.

When you begin negotiating, have in mind a bottom-line price you're prepared to do the job for and always ask for slightly more than your ideal fee as the client will invariably try to beat you down. You may find it useful to break down your asking price in order to explain exactly what it is the client is paying for. How you do this is up to you. Some people find it helpful to work out a daily rate incorporating overheads such as rent, heating, materials, travel and telephone charges, while others prefer to negotiate on a flat fee basis. There are also illustrators who charge extra for something needed yesterday, time spent researching, model hire if applicable and so on. It pays to be flexible, so if your initial quote exceeds the client's budget and you really want the job, tell them you are open to negotiation. If, on the other hand, the job looks suspiciously thankless, stick to your guns. If the client agrees to your exorbitant demands, the job might start to look more appetising.

Getting paid

Once you've traded terms and conditions, done the job and invoiced the client, you'll then have the unenviable task of getting your hands on your fee. It is customary to send your invoice to the accounts department stating payment within 30 days. It is also customary for them to ignore this entreaty, regardless of the wolf at your door, and pay you when it suits them. Magazines pay promptly, usually within 4–6 weeks; everyone else takes 60–90 days.

Be methodical when chasing up your invoice. Send out a statement the moment your 30 days has elapsed and call the accounts department as soon as you like. Take names, note dates and the gist of their feeble excuses, and keep on chasing. Don't worry about your incessant nagging scuppering your plans of further commissions as these decisions are solely down to the art department, and they think you're a gem. Should payment still not be forthcoming three months down the line, it might be advisable to ask your commissioner to follow things up on your behalf. Chances are they'll be horrified you haven't been paid yet and things will be speedily resolved. In the meantime, you'll have had a good deal of practice talking money, which can only make things easier next time around.

And finally . . .

Basic book-keeping – making a simple, legible record of all your financial transactions, both incoming and outgoing – will be crucial to your sanity once the tax inspector starts to loom. It will also make your accountant's job easier, thereby saving you money. If your annual turnover is less than £85,000, it is unnecessary to provide HM Revenue & Customs with detailed accounts of your earnings. Information regarding your turnover, allowable expenses and net profit may simply be entered on your tax return. Although an accountant is not necessary to this process, many find it advantageous to employ one. The tax system is complicated and dealing with HM Revenue & Customs can be stressful, intimidating and time consuming. Accountants offer invaluable advice on tax allowances, National Insurance and tax assessments, as well as dealing expertly with HM Revenue & Customs on your behalf – thereby enabling you to attend to the business of illustrating.

Further reading

- Fig Taylor, *How To Create A Portfolio and Get Hired* (Laurence King Publishing, 2nd edn 2013)
- Derek Brazell and Jo Davies, *Understanding Illustration* (Bloomsbury 2014)
- Derek Brazell and Jo Davies, *Becoming a Successful Illustrator* (Bloomsbury, *Creative Careers* series, 2nd edn 2017)
- Darrel Rees, *How To Be An Illustrator* (Laurence King Publishing, 2nd edn 2014)

Fig Taylor initially began her career as an illustrators' agent in 1983. She has been the resident 'portfolio surgeon' at the Association of Illustrators since 1986 and also operates as a private consultant to non-AOI member artists. She lectures extensively in Professional Practice to illustration students throughout the UK and is the author of *How to Create a Portfolio and Get Hired* (Laurence King Publishing, 2nd edn 2013).

See also...

- *Art agents and commercial studios*, page 507
- *Selling yourself and your work online*, page 497
- *Copyright questions*, page 693
- *Income tax*, page 715
- *National Insurance contributions and social security benefits*, page 725

How to get ahead in cartooning

Earning a living from creating cartoons is highly competitive. But if you feel that you were born to be a cartoonist, Martin Rowson offers some advice on how to get your work published.

I can't say precisely when I first realised I wanted to be a cartoonist. I personally believe that cartoonists are born and not made so perhaps I should be talking about when I realised I *was* a cartoonist. I do know that, aged ten, I nicked my sister's 1950s British history textbook, which was illustrated throughout by cartoons (from Gillray via Tenniel to Low) and somewhere inside me stirred an unquantifiable yearning to draw – to express myself in the unique style that is the equally unique talent of the 'cartoonist'. So, shortly afterwards I started copying the way Wally Fawkes (better known by his *nom de plume* 'Trog') drew the then Prime Minister Edward Heath.

I've spent most of my life drawing. I drew cartoons for school magazines, designed posters for school societies which invariably turned into political cartoons displayed, in the good old-fashioned way, on walls. I also developed a useful party trick of caricaturing teachers on blackboards. I did Art 'O' and 'A' levels (only a grade B in the latter) but that didn't have much to do with cartoons, and I certainly never contemplated for a moment going to art school. Instead I went to Pembroke College, Cambridge, to read English Literature, and as things turned out I hated it and I spent most of my time doing cartoons for two-bit student magazines, which partly explains how I ended up with a truly terrible degree. More on this later.

At the same time I was half-heartedly putting together a portfolio of work, in the hope that what I'd always done for fun (despite the fact that it was also a compulsion) might just end up being what I did for a living. I'd occasionally send off the portfolio to magazines, never to hear anything back. Then, shortly after graduating I had an idea for a series which I hoped would appeal to a particular demographic at the time (1982). It was called 'Scenes from the Lives of the Great Socialists' and consisted of a number of stylised depictions of leading socialist thinkers and politicians from history, with the added value of an appallingly bad pun thrown into the mixture. One example is 'Proudhon and Bakunin have tea in Tunbridge Wells', which showed the 19th century French and Russian anarchists sitting round a tea table, with Bakunin spitting out his cup of tea and exclaiming 'Proudhon! This tea is disgusting! This isn't proper tea at all!', to which Proudhon replied 'Ah, my dear Bakunin, but Property is Theft!'

I sent about half a dozen of these drawings to the *New Statesman* (then going through one of its periodic lefty phases) and, as usual, heard nothing for months. Then, just before Christmas 1982, in bed suffering from chickenpox, I received a phone call from the art director who said they were going to publish four of the cartoons in their Christmas issue, and would like me to do a series. (I was paid £40 a cartoon, which throughout 1983 meant I was earning £40 a month, which also meant I still had to sign on in order to stay alive.) Thus began my career as a cartoonist.

My three-year deadline

Now living in London, I found myself an agent and *She* magazine was the first offer to come in. They proposed to pay their standard fee of £6 for anything they published. I instructed my agent to inform them that this barely covered my expenses for materials and postage and they could forget it (although I used two other words, one of them also beginning with 'f') – I don't know if he passed on the message. Then someone wanted to do a book of the *New Statesman* cartoons, with the offer of an advance of £750. This took my earned income for that year to somewhere perilously close to a thousand pounds.

At around this time I went to a College reunion and remember skulking around in my Oxfam suit listening with growing irritation to my contemporaries outlining how they'd got into computing/merchant banking/systems analysis or whatever at just the right time, and were earning 50 times more than I was. But I knew I was in for the long haul. As a slight nod to my father's ceaseless injunctions that it was time I got a proper job, I'd set myself a limit of three years, sort of promising that, if I wasn't making a fist of it by then I'd give up (although I doubt I actually meant it).

Luckily, a year into my putative career other contemporaries from university were starting out in journalism, and found they could earn important brownie points from their editors by bringing in a cartoonist to liven up the dull magazines they worked for. That's how I found myself working for *Satellite and Cable TV News* and *One Two Testing....* The fact that I neither knew nor cared about what I was illustrating and lampooning didn't matter. It was work, and also an essential lesson in how to master a brief, however obscure.

However, the true catalyst for my career came when another university acquaintance started working on *Financial Weekly* and, for the usual self-aggrandising reasons, suggested to the editor that they might use me. Again, this was something I knew and cared nothing about but it offered plenty of scope to lampoon truly awful people and of course frequently crossed over into political satire, where my real interest lay. More significantly, the editor himself was so nice, kind and amenable that he consequently drove his staff mad with frustration to the point that they would leave for better things. And when they went, they often took me with them.

Part of the *Financial Weekly* diaspora fled to Eddie Shah's infant *Today* newspaper, and so, just inside my self-imposed three-year time limit, I was producing a daily pocket cartoon for the business pages as well as drawing editorial cartoons for both *Today* and its short-lived sister paper *Sunday Today*. From there, another university friend brought me onto the books pages of the *Sunday Correspondent* and, in doing so, to broadsheet respectability. After that I never really had to solicit for work again. I'd reached cartooning critical mass; the people commissioning knew who I was and, more importantly, knew my work so the hard part was over. And, rather nicely, when I went to another College reunion, I discovered that all the smart boys in computing and banking had been sacked in the recession of the early 1990s.

How can other people get ahead in cartooning?

At one level you could say, between gritted teeth, that all that I've written above proves is that it's just about the old boy network – not what you know but who you know. To an extent that's true, but I'd like to think that none of the publications I'd worked for would have given me a second glance if I couldn't cut the mustard and deliver the goods. So, what do you need to get ahead in cartooning?

First of all, and most importantly, you need to recognise whether or not you truly are a cartoonist, and to do that you need to know what cartoons are. It won't do just to be able to draw; nor is it enough to have a sense of humour. You need to combine the two, and understand that in so doing you are creating something that can't be expressed in any other way. This requires a mindset which, I believe, is innate. Moreover, I don't believe you can teach people how to be cartoonists – they have to teach themselves, and from an early age at that. If you copy other cartoonists to find out how it's done, then slowly but surely you'll develop a style of your own which you feel comfortable with.

Once you recognise what you are, and that you're determined to embark on a career that, like poetry or acting, offers a dream of glamour out of all proportion to its guaranteed financial reward, you then need to create a frame of mind which combines, in equal measure, arrogance and sloth. In other words, you *know* that you're good, and actually better than anyone else who's ever lived, but you're also, crucially, too lazy to do anything else, like accountancy.

Then comes the hard part, which is not for the faint-hearted. You have to work very hard, to make sure what you're producing is really good, and is the best you can do (of which you will always, ultimately, be the best judge). If you're a caricaturist, practice your caricature (and by all means steal other, more established cartoonists' tricks in order to develop your own; after all, they do). If you're a gag cartoonist, hone the gag and work on the drawing so it's clear what's going on (cartooning is the last bastion of realism in the visual arts – abstract cartoons don't work). If you're a political cartoonist, immerse yourself in current affairs and, most importantly, either develop or clearly express your point of view, which can be either right or left wing (a fair, unopinionated cartoonist is as useless and boring as a newspaper columnist with no opinions and nothing to say). A good editorial cartoon is a newspaper column by other means, and is best described as visual journalism, using tricks – like irony, humour, violence and vile imagery – that the big boys in newspaper punditry are too dumb to understand. But remember – while you go through this stage you'll be papering your bedroom wall with rejection slips.

Practical advice

Always try to make your artwork look professional. This means using good paper drawn on in indelible ink, centrally placed. This might sound obvious, but I've seen many cartoons by aspiring cartoonists drawn in crayon on lined file paper going right up to the edge of the sheet. This won't even get halfway out of the envelope before any editor bins it.

Second, always remember that, although you are a genius you have to start somewhere, and some work is always better than no work. If you want to get into newspapers or magazines (which is all there really is if you want to earn some money and not just feel complacent about your beautiful website), identify parts of the press that would benefit from your input.

Journalists producing gardening or travel or, most of all, personal finance sections are crying out for something to liven their pages, something other than a photo which will mark them out as different. In other words, be arrogant enough to be sufficiently humble to illustrate copy you'd never in a million years personally read. Many famous and established cartoonists still knock out stuff for trade papers of crashing obscurity and dullness, this being as good a way as any other of paying the mortgage.

Once you've identified a potential gap in the market, *always* submit your idea or portfolio to the editor of that section, and *never* send it to the art director (despite my experience with the *New Statesman*). There are several reasons for this. First, art directors are inundated with unsolicited work, and so the odds are immediately pitched against you. Second, there's the danger that, in the endless little territorial feuds that pertain in journalism, you will become the exclusive property of the art director who, because he or she hates the gardening editor, will never pass your work on. Third, the section editor will be flattered and delighted to receive something different from the usual dross of press releases and letters of pedantic complaint. If your work tickles their fancy, then you're in, and a section editor always pulls rank over an art director, whatever anyone may imagine.

From these first steps, you will have the beginnings of a portfolio of published work which will stand you in excellent stead on your way to reaching that critical mass of recognition I mentioned earlier.

Finally, never forget that cartoons are something different from anything else. While they combine text journalism and illustration, they end up as something greater than their component parts. In a way, a cartoon is a kind of voodoo, doing harm to someone (whether a politician or a castaway on a desert island) at a distance with a sharp object, which in this case is a pen. It's hard to get established, the number of successful cartoonists earning a decent wedge is tiny and there will always be a generational logjam as the clapped-out old has-beens whose work enrages and disgusts you cling tenaciously to the precious few slots. But if you're determined and tough enough, stick with it and you, too, could become one of those clapped-out has-beens. Until then, just bear in mind that it's a small and crowded profession, and despite everything I've said, the last thing I need is anyone good coming along and muscling in on my territory. In my heart of hearts, I should really advise all aspiring young cartoonists to give up now. Such churlishness apart, however, I'll stick with wishing you good luck.

Martin Rowson is a cartoonist and writer whose work appears regularly in the *Guardian*, the *Daily Mirror* and many other publications. His awards include Political Cartoonist of the Year in 2001, 2003 and 2010, Caricaturist of the Year in 2011, and he produced the Political Cartoon of the Year in 2002 and 2007. His books include comic book versions of *The Waste Land*, *Tristram Shandy* and *Gulliver's Travels*, and *Stuff*, a memoir of clearing out his late parents' house which was longlisted for the Samuel Johnson Prize for Non-fiction. *The Coalition Book* (SelfMadeHero 2014), a collection of his cartoons covering the ConLibDem government 2010-15, won the Political Book Awards Satire Book of the Year in 2015. Martin most recently illustrated *Gimson's Prime Ministers: Brief Lives from Walpole to May* (Square Peg 2018). He is Chairman of the British Cartoonists' Association, a trustee and a vice-president of the Zoological Society of London, an Honorary Fellow of Goldsmiths College and a Visiting Fellow of Teesside University.

See also...

- *Freelancing for beginners*, page 481
- *DACS (Design and Artists Copyright Society)*, page 709
- *Making waves online*, page 633

How to make a living: money matters

Alison Branagan explores the ways in which the self-employed artist, illustrator or writer can make their creative work pay in the current financial environment.

> 'It is easier to write about money than to acquire it...'
> Voltaire, *Philosophical Dictionary* (1764)

As professional writers, illustrators or artists we are all vulnerable to periods of economic uncertainty, often temporary in nature, but which might be anything from a sudden shortage of ready cash to suffering longer-term hardship and poverty. This is largely due to the increasing erosion of rights and fees triggered by a range of factors, including the collapse of traditional print media – caused partly by the loss of advertising revenue – inexpensive stock illustration portals, and harsh client commissioning terms, such as requests for unpaid advertorial content or copyright assignment. The result is that budgets have been squeezed and less is spent on commissioning original work.

Undertaking free work is now expected, but I would suggest only writing a one-off pro-bono blog piece or offering artwork or illustrations if the association with the business, brand, publication or organisation is of longer-term use to you. This might be in terms of gaining experience if you are just starting out, or of raising your profile, introducing you to new contacts, or promoting your literary or illustrative services. Otherwise, creative work needs to be paid for, or politely turned down if a suitable fee can't be negotiated. Taking the opportunity to recommend a competitor who regularly charges the most eye-watering sums (with a wry smile to yourself, of course) might be an even more fitting resolution!

In this article, I consider various aspects of money management, including taxation, royalty payments, fees, negotiation strategies and raising funds from trusts, as well as other options, such as crowdfunding and sponsorship.

Free royalties

Unclaimed royalties from the ALCS (Authors' Licensing and Collecting Society; see page 707), PLR (Public Lending Right; see page 143) and DACS (Design and Artists' Copyright Society; see page 709) do add up. If you are a member or associate of the SoA (Society of Authors), which is highly recommended, you gain free membership of the ALCS which usually costs £36. The annual 'payback' royalty claimed by an illustrator from images printed in books, newspapers, magazines or even captured on television via DACS can amount to anywhere between £40 to £4,000.

If you are currently a member of ALCS you can now also submit claims for illustrations, photographs and diagrams you have submitted to publications. However, you can't claim twice, meaning if you are already claiming through DACS Payback, you can't also apply through ALCS Visual Claims.

Though some of these annual royalty payments are often quite small for most of us, over time they can mount up; they are well worth the tiny amount of effort involved in signing up and submitting your claim online at: www.alcs.co.uk; www.plr.uk.com; and www.dacs.org.uk.

Trusts, grants and charities

Grants are difficult to come by, but I recommend contacting charitable organisations who have funds for artists or writers experiencing financial difficulty. Turn2Us is a website (www.turn2us.org.uk) that can be used to find trusts and foundations for which you might be eligible, simply by entering your postcode into their 'Search for a Grant' section.

The SoA (Society of Authors) has a number of trusts that members can apply to, such as those set up to allay general financial difficulty or to assist with a specific publishing project by way of a research or writing grant.

If illustration is not your main focus and you are a visual artist, then subscribing to 'a-n' The Artists Information Company (www.a-n.co.uk), is recommended. The Arts Council website (www.artscouncil.org.uk) and the 'Grants' tab on Artquest (www.artquest.org.uk) are also good places to look for funding. The Elephant Trust (http://elephanttrust.org.uk) is one such charity for fine artists.

Trusts, grants and charities: useful websites

a-n The Artists Information Company
www.a-n.co.uk

Artquest
www.artquest.org.uk

The Arts Council
www.artscouncil.org.uk

The Elephant Trust
http://elephanttrust.org.uk

SoA (Society of Authors)
www.societyofauthors.org

Turn2Us
www.turn2us.org.uk

In-work and out-of-work benefits

Working Tax Credit and Child Tax Credit, Housing Benefit, Council Tax Reduction and claiming state support if you are out of work or unwell are available. (See *National Insurance contributions and social security benefits*, on page 725). I would strongly urge you to apply for any of these for which you are eligible if you have been without any paid commissions for some time, especially if you have dependents, rent or a mortgage to pay. It is worth bearing in mind that if you have substantial savings this can limit your eligibility for assistance.

Although the new Universal Credit system is slowly being rolled out, at present it isn't very supportive of being self-employed with a low turnover. I must stress, this benefit is in development and how it is administered may change. UC is an 'in-work' and also 'out-of-work' payment, which may support you in the first year of self-employment. However, if claiming UC you may still have to look for a job if trading income continues to be at subsistence levels and you still require financial support. Visit the UK Government portal (www.gov.uk/browse/benefits) and look at revised eligibility guidelines, try out the online calculators or contact Citizens Advice (www.citizensadvice.org.uk) if you are bewildered by the complexity of it all.

Understanding how taxation works

Many creative people fail to fully understand what they can count as expenses as part of their self-employment, and thereby reduce their net profits, and in turn their income tax or Class 4 National Insurance liability. Visit www.gov.uk/income-tax-rates/current-rates-and-allowances or see *National Insurance contributions and social security benefits*, on page 725 for more information. You can offset any trading losses against tax paid on a salary, or possibly become eligible for Tax Credits if you record a reduced level of income on your tax return. If you are a member of the AOI (Association of Illustrators), SoA (Society of Authors), or other professional body, you may have access to advice from an accountant as part of your membership.

Tax Aid (http://taxaid.org.uk) is a very useful organisation if your annual income is under £20,000. They offer free advice and are used to working with artists, illustrators and writers.

Saving small sums

Credit Unions (www.findyourcreditunion.co.uk) are like local community banks, whereby you can join and save regular small amounts of money. In return there are a number of benefits, including access to personal and business loans. Equally, if you only save a small amount each week there will always be a small sum of money held in reserve to pay for the odd unexpected bill or tax demand.

What is crowdfunding?

Crowdfunding is a new way of raising money to help creative projects get off the ground – it is a godsend, and well worth exploring. It works by attracting pledges from a number of sources to help fund or pay for a new (creative) project; the best way to see how this can work successfully is by visiting some of the websites listed in the box (see **Crowdfunding platforms**). It can be helpful to have some form of social media presence to make the opportunity work best for you, but it is also now the case that these platforms are garnering their own brand of enthusiastic supporters.

Crowdfunding platforms

GoFundMe
https://uk.gofundme.com

Indiegogo
www.indiegogo.com

Kickstarter
www.kickstarter.com

Spacehive
www.spacehive.com

Unbound
https://unbound.com

Kickstarter and Indiegogo are two of the leading platforms, but there are more specialist publishing platforms aimed at authors and illustrators such as Unbound. If Unbound supports your proposed campaign, once the advance, print and distribution costs are raised they will print your book and make it available to buy through their online bookshop.

GoFundMe is a crowdfunding platform closer in nature to traditional sponsorship or philanthropic support. Spacehive supports projects that benefit the wider community both socially and culturally.

Sponsorship

Major art festivals and book competitions are often sponsored by large businesses, but sponsorship can also work at a more localised and personal level. Attracting sponsorship often isn't just about money; it can take other forms such as the loan of a vehicle, assistance with travel costs, access to accommodation, resources, materials, hospitality, technology or a space to work. Often businesses like to become involved with interesting projects that not only work in a commercial sense, e.g. by attracting new consumers, but also provide a positive association with an emerging or established writer, illustrator, artist or collective.

Negotiation

Developing the skills of negotiation and persuasion are vital if you want to gain a better financial deal for your work. Negotiation is not just about money.

It is helpful, as a starting point, to obtain some guidance about what to charge, and the SoA (Society of Authors) provides helpful factsheets on rates to its members. The AOI (Association of Illustrators) also provides access to an extensive pricing survey and can offer bespoke advice to members.

These days, many people are using email and texts to negotiate fees. I usually wouldn't advise this as you don't know what frame of mind the other party is going to be in when they see your communication. It is possible to negotiate on the phone, but face-to-face is always best. Suitable non-verbal cues, facial expressions and tone of voice are important factors in any discussion.

Building relationships which withstand the test of time is essential and nurturing trust and goodwill with your clients will improve the likelihood of gaining a successful outcome when it comes to agreeing commissions, rates, licensing, and securing further opportunities.

Persuasion is something that needs to be cultivated as a personal attribute; you should never let a little thing like a potential client being utterly disinterested in your ideas or work put you off from pitching another idea! If you experience difficulties with a client, try to remain professional, upbeat and confident. A shiny disposition and outlook will always be attractive to those who commission, buy and hire creative freelancers.

Alison Branagan is an author and visual arts consultant. She is currently the Creative Enterprise Coordinator for the University for the Creative Arts (UCA) for the Surrey campuses and is an associate lecturer at Central Saint Martins. She has written several business start-up and enterprise books, including *The Essential Guide to Business for Artists and Designers* (Bloomsbury, 2nd edn 2017). For more information see www.alisonbranagan.com. Her Twitter handle is @AlisonBranagan.

See also...

- *National Insurance contributions and social security benefits*, page 725
- *Authors' Licensing and Collecting Society, page 707*
- *DACS (Design and Artists Copyright Society)*, page 709
- *Public Lending Right*, page 143

Selling yourself and your work online

To succeed as an illustrator, it is essential to build and maintain a strong online presence. Fig Taylor outlines the tools and practices that are indispensable for promoting your work.

Over the past couple of decades, technological advancement has gradually reduced the size of the average art department, impacting the commissioning landscape considerably. Today's commissioner is often too busy to conduct face-to-face interviews with emerging talent on a regular basis, much less dispense helpful career advice. Consequently many are turning to the internet – itself a commissioning game-changer – to familiarise themselves with what's on offer both locally and globally. As a result, having a strong online presence has become a must for any illustrator hoping to stay on top of their game. Fortunately this need not be too costly an exercise and there are many different modes of promotion available.

First on the list: a website

A professional website is industry standard for any creative practitioner and should function as a virtual portfolio and creative CV combined. In addition to showcasing your best and/or most recent work and providing contact details, you can namecheck significant commissioners you have worked for and link to other places your work may be found online, for example: video-sharing platforms for moving image; other web-based portfolios; online stores or galleries; personal or industry-themed blogs; and social media outlets. If you are an established practitioner you may also want to include testimonials from satisfied clients. Lastly, the 'About Me' section can be used to provide information about preferred media, technique and subject matter, plus information about the type of commissions you are seeking and/or enjoy working on. Too many fledgling illustrators produce flimsy or uninformative bios. Commissioners aren't mind-readers, especially those you've never worked with before, so be sure to put some thought into the content you provide.

While getting a bespoke website is always an option, it can be an expensive one – so be sure to shop around if your heart is set on doing so. For those in search of a more affordable means of self-promotion, however, help is at hand in the form of numerous DIY options such as Wix, Squarespace, Mr Site, Moonfruit and Weebly. No knowledge of HTML is required to customise the various templates on offer and, for the cash-challenged, some even offer a variation of the service for free. However, the number of images you're permitted to show in this instance is usually quite limited and you'll probably be expected to carry advertisements for the web-builder on your site. Since these are likely to divert attention away from your work, I wouldn't personally recommend it post-graduation. For an ad-free site with back-up support and more in the way of whistles and bells, expect to pay something in the region of £5-8 a month to begin with, though some offer a discount for making a yearly payment. Most also offer you a free domain for the first year. Meanwhile, for those overwhelmed by the plethora of web-builders available, comparison websites such as www.websitebuilderexpert.com and www.top10bestwebsitebuilders.co.uk can be invaluable in helping you determine the best host for your particular needs.

Last but not least, having weighed up all your options, take care to make functionality and user-friendliness a priority. Your website should load quickly, perform consistently across a variety of platforms and be simple and straightforward to negotiate. Images that take ages to load, minuscule or misleading thumbnails that give little clue to image content, annoying musical soundtracks (and, trust me, they're all annoying when they start playing from the top every time you click on an image or return to the home page), or anything that makes it difficult for a commissioner to share your images with a client or colleague, will be a deal-breaker.

Next up: start a blog. Yes, really.

Given their omnipresence, you might feel that adding yet one more voice to an over-crowded blogosphere would be be a waste of time and energy. You might even be scathing about blogs in general since the emergence of the 'superstar' blogger. But this isn't about giving Zoella a run for her money or taking snapshots of your artfully arranged elevenses. It's about finding a viable way to give potential commissioners a more detailed understanding of your working practice than a bunch of samples and a brief bio, however pithy, can convey alone. Because it's that much harder to blag a speculative face-to-face meeting these

Useful websites

WEB BUILDERS

Jimdo
www.jimdo.com

Mr Site
www.mrsite.com

Moonfruit
www.moonfruit.com

Site Builder
www.sitebuilder.com

SquareSpace
www.squarespace.com

Weebly
www.weebly.com

Wix
www.wix.com

Word Press
www.wordpress.org

PORTFOLIO HOSTING

Association Of Illustrators
www.theaoi.com/portfolios

Carbonmade
www.carbonmade.com

Children's Illustrators
www.childrensillustrators.com

Directory of Illustration
www.directoryofillustration.com

Dunked
www.dunked.com

Fabrik
www.fabrik.io

Foliolink
www.foliolink.com

Format
www.format.com

Hire an Illustrator
www.hireanillustrator.com

The i-Spot
www.theispot.com

Workbook
www.workbook.com

BLOGGING PLATFORMS

Blogger
www.blogger.com

Tumblr
www.tumblr.com

Word Press
www.wordpress.com

Typepad
www.typepad.com

days, a blog can provide you with a means to share your passions and influences, and – most importantly of all – a window into your creative process, thus giving clients an inkling of what you might be like to work with. Style can only take an illustrator so far. Never underestimate the importance of shared interests and chemistry in the client/illustrator relationship. It is, after all, a collaboration, a meeting of creative minds.

Before you start checking out blogging platforms, however, a word to the wise: an image or three, accompanied by a single sentence, does not an effective blog post make. In fact, it might do more harm to your career than good (the case of a cartoonist who accompanied an image of a man contemplating suicide off the end of a seaside pier with the ominous caption, 'Well, that's the summer gone then', haunts me to this day).

You don't have to use high fallutin' language, nor do you have to blog on a daily basis, but I would advise talking about your work in some depth when you do. Think *re-cap*. Who was the client? What was the brief? Was there research involved? Did you have some creative freedom or was the art direction style-crampingly restrictive? How did you approach the job to make it more enjoyable? Did you include some ideas of your own when you gave the client the rough? Did they respond positively? Would you have liked to have done something differently? You get my drift.

A blog is also a place to document more personal or experimental work that might currently look out of place on your website, and even to get feedback from your peers. The key is to believe that some commissioner somewhere will be reading, because, given the prevalence of tweets, re-blogs, virtual pinboards, and the creative industry's insatiable appetite for novelty, they almost certainly will be.

As with website builders there are a myriad blogging platforms out there, many of them free, and a quick Google of 'best blogging sites for artists and designers' or a gander at the likes of www.dearblogger.org will bring up plenty of options and helpful advice. Since you aren't planning to make blogging your career, it's not strictly necessary to opt for a paid service. If you do opt for a free blog though, the web host technically owns it. This means that, if you choose a platform that goes belly up or gets bought out by an industry giant, you could potentially lose your archive. With this in mind you'll probably want to opt for one that has stood the test of time, such as Blogger, Tumblr, or WordPress (which also offers a paid option). Conversely, some website builders, such as Weebly and Squarespace, come with a blog option as part of the package. If yours doesn't, be sure to include a prominent link to your blog along with whatever social networking platforms you use. Oh – and if you do opt for Tumblr to host your blog, don't run the risk of confusing future commissioners by re-blogging other illustrators' work; not only is it potentially embarrassing, it's also a great way to lose a job to the artist whose work you re-blogged. If you want to keep tabs on your favourite movers and shakers, start a separate Tumblr or a Pinterest board.

Maintaining an additional online portfolio

Although they don't offer the comprehensiveness of a website, there are alternative and/or complimentary ways of archiving your work online. As with website builders, most are simple to use and some, such as Cargo Collective, Behance and Carbonmade, offer a basic free option with the option of paid upgrades. While these all host illustrators' portfolios, they aren't however solely dedicated to showcasing illustration. You may, depending on personal preference, prefer one that does – for instance, Hire An Illustrator, Children's

Illustrators, or the i-Spot. Alternatively, the Association of Illustrators hosts a portfolio site on which members and non-members can upload and maintain a portfolio comprised of 20 images, plus a brief bio and link to their main website. Non-members pay £100 per year for the service which includes bi-monthly promotion to key commissioners, while members benefit from a hefty 60% discount.

If money is tight and you are already maintaining a paid website, consider going the free route for a back-up web-based portfolio of around 20 images. Try, if possible, to vary the samples across platforms too, so that there is always fresh work to be discovered by anyone clicking on your links; commissioners are apt to pigeonhole artists, so it's always good to keep them on their toes. If, on the other hand, you are searching for an alternative to a website, I would recommend going the paid portfolio route as you will be able to showcase more work and there will be additional benefits as part of the package.

And finally ... social networking

Whether you tweet, pin, Instagram, Google+, Dribble, Snapchat, WhatsApp or Facebook, if used adroitly social media has the power to put you on the map and keep you there. Creative people tend to know other creative people and that includes online, so keep peers and commissioners abreast of your activities. Embarking on InkTober? Got an exhibition coming up? Published your first zine? Bagged the commission of a lifetime? Or maybe you just doodled something in your sketchbook and fancy some instant feedback. Whatever it is, if it's related to your work in any way, just get it out there. You have nothing to lose and a turbo-charged career to gain.

Fig Taylor initially began her career as an illustrators' agent in 1983. She has been the resident 'portfolio surgeon' at the Association of Illustrators since 1986 and also operates as a private consultant to non-AOI member artists. She lectures extensively in Professional Practice to illustration students throughout the UK and is the author of *How to Create a Portfolio and Get Hired* (Laurence King Publishing, 2nd edn 2013).

See also...

- *Freelancing for beginners*, page 481
- *Making waves online*, page 633

The freelance photographer

Becoming a successful freelance photographer is as much about marketing as photographic talent. Professional photographer Ian Thraves highlights possibilities for freelancers.

Having an outstanding portfolio is one thing, but to receive regular commissions takes a good business head and sound market knowledge. Although working as a professional photographer can be tough, it is undoubtedly one of the most interesting and rewarding ways of earning a living.

Entering professional photography

A good starting point is to embark on one of the many college courses available, which range from GCSE to degree level, and higher. These form a good foundation, though most teach only the technical and artistic aspects of photography and very few cover the basics of running a business. But a good college course will provide students with the opportunity to become familiar with photographic equipment and develop skills without the restrictions and pressures found in the workplace.

In certain fields, such as commercial photography, it is possible to learn the trade as an assistant to an established photographer. A photographer's assistant will undertake many varied tasks, including preparing camera equipment and lighting, building sets, obtaining props and organising locations, as well as general mundane chores. It usually takes only a year or two for an assistant to become a fully competent photographer, having during that time learnt many technical aspects of a particular field of photography and the fundamentals of running a successful business. There is, however, the danger of a long-standing assistant becoming a clone of the photographer worked for, and it is for this reason that some assistants prefer to gain experience with various photographers rather than working for just one for a long period of time. The Association of Photographers (AOP) can help place an assistant.

However, in other fields of photography, such as photojournalism or wildlife photography, an assistant is not generally required, and photographers in these fields are usually self-taught.

Identifying your market

From the outset, identify which markets are most suitable for the kind of subjects you photograph. Study each market carefully and only offer images which suit the client's requirements.

Usually photographers who specialise in a particular field do better than those who generalise. By concentrating on one or two subject areas they become expert at what they do. Those who make a name for themselves are invariably specialists, and it is far easier for the images of, for example, an exceptional fashion photographer or an award-winning wildlife photographer to be remembered than the work of someone who covers a broad range of subjects.

In addition, photographers who produce work with individual style (e.g. by experimenting with camera angles or manipulating images to create unusual and distinctive effects) are far more likely to make an impact. Alternative images that attract attention and can help sell a product or service are always sought after. This is especially true of advertising photography, but applies also to other markets such as book and magazine publishers, who are continually seeking eye-catching images, especially for front cover use.

Promoting yourself

Effective self-promotion tells the market who you are and what service you offer. A first step should be to create an outstanding portfolio of images, tailored to appeal to the targeted market. Photographers targeting a few different markets should create an individual portfolio for each rather than presenting a single general one, including only a few relevant images. A portfolio should only contain a photographer's most outstanding work. Including substandard images will show inconsistent quality, leaving a potential client in doubt about the photographer's ability.

Images should be presented in a format that the client is used to handling. Usually, a high-quality printed portfolio, backed up by a well-designed website is adequate. Many photographers also produce an additional portfolio in the form of a DVD slideshow or movie. These can be very cheap to create and duplicate and can be handed or posted out to potential and existing clients. Any published material (often referred to as 'tearsheets') should also be added to a portfolio. Tearsheets are often presented mounted and laminated in plastic and also can be included in the portfolio section of a photographer's website.

Business cards and letterheads should be designed to reflect style and professionalism. Consider using a good graphic designer to create a logo for use on cards, letterheads and any other promotional literature. Many photographers produce postcard-size business cards and include an image as well as their name and logo.

Other than word of mouth, advertising is probably the best way of making your services known to potential clients. Whether targeting local or global markets, web-based promotion has become the photographer's preferred method of gaining business. Compared to print advertising media, web-based is generally much cheaper and more accessible to

Professional organisations

The Association of Photographers (AOP)
Studio 9, Holborn Studios,
49/50 Eagle Wharf Road, London N1 7ED
tel 020-7739 6669
email info@aophoto.co.uk
website www.the-aop.org
See page 549.

BAPLA (British Association of Picture Libraries and Agencies)
59 Tranquil Vale, Blackheath, London SE3 0BS
tel 020-8297 1198
email enquiries@bapla.org.uk
website www.bapla.org.uk
See page 549.

British Institute of Professional Photography (BIPP)
Ardenham Court, Oxford Road, Aylesbury, Bucks. HP19 8HT
tel (01296) 642020
email info@bipp.com
website www.bipp.com
See page 549.

Master Photographers Association
Jubilee House, 1 Chancery Lane, Darlington, Co. Durham DL1 5QP
tel (01325) 356555
email membership@thempa.com
website www.masterphotographersassociation.co.uk
See page 551.

The Royal Photographic Society
Fenton House, 122 Wells Road, Bath BA2 3AH
tel (01225) 325733
email reception@rps.org
website www.rps.org
See page 533.

potential global markets, plus it allows the photographer more opportunity to showcase a greater number of portfolio images, supported by an unlimited amount of textor copy.

Cold calling by telephone is probably the most cost-effective and productive way of making contacts, and these should be followed up by an appointment to meet potential clients in person, if possible.

Photographers should regard the internet as a primary promotion medium. A cleverly designed website is essential and is a stylish and cost-effective way to expose a photographer's portfolio to a global market, as well as being a convenient way for a potential client to view a photographer's work. Your website address should be included in all business stationery and other forms of advertising.

As with any business, it is essential that professional photographers have online presence in the form of a well-designed website, but customised web design can be difficult and time-consuming and is a job that's probably best left to a professional website designer. However, many photographers have now taken to using simple website platforms, such as Squarespace and Format, which both feature website templates with photographers' needs in mind. These are simple to create, look impressive, and most importantly work well on multiple devices, whether viewed on a desktop computer, tablet or phone.

In addition to a traditional website, many photographers use blogs as another form of web-based marketing. The beauty of a blog is the ease at which the owner can update the content. Updatable items may include your latest images, news articles and equipment reviews, plus any other interesting posts that relate to the industry. Blogs and other types of social media, such as Twitter, Facebook, Instagram and LinkedIn, can all work together to increase a photographer's 'fan-base' or 'following', all serving to strengthen a photographer's market presence on a global basis. In recent years, many photographers have also adopted video as an additional format of self-promotion, uploading content to online platforms such as YouTube and Vimeo.

A well-organised exhibition of images is a very effective way of bringing a body of work to the attention of current and potential new clients. Some photographers promote themselves by throwing a preview party with refreshments for friends, colleagues and specially invited guests from the industry. A show that is well reviewed by respected newspaper and magazine journalists can generate additional interest.

As a photographer's career develops, the budget for self-promotion should increase. Many established photographers will go as far as producing full-colour mailers, posters, and even calendars, which all contain examples of their work.

Digital photography

Most photographers now use digital cameras, and image-enhancement and manipulation using computer technology are widely used in the photographic industry. There are various levels of quality produced by digital cameras and photographers should consider the requirements of their market prior to investing in expensive hardware which is prone to rapid change and improvement. At the cheaper level, digital SLR cameras (DSLRs) manufactured by companies such as Nikon and Canon can produce outstanding quality images suitable for many end uses. Cameras like these are used predominantly for press, PR and general commercial work.

At a higher level, many commercial studio photographers have invested in medium- or large-format digital cameras, which incorporate high-quality sensors that can be adapted to fit many of the conventional studio cameras. This system is far more expensive, but is capable of producing images where maximum quality is required by the client. Thus the images are suitable for any end use, such as top-quality advertisements. Photographers thinking of supplying stock libraries with digital images should consider the quality of the camera they use. Stock libraries often supply a diverse range of clients, including advertising, and will therefore only accept the highest standard in order to meet the demands of the market.

Image-enhancement and manipulation using software such as Adobe Photoshop provides photographers with an onscreen darkroom where the possibilities for creating imaginative images are endless. As well as being useful for retouching purposes and creating photo compositions, it provides the photographer with an opportunity to create images that are more distinctive.

Using a stock library

As well as undertaking commissions, photographers have the option of selling their images through a photographic stock library or agency. There are now many globally based stock libraries, some specialising in specific subject areas, such as wildlife photography, and others covering general subjects.

Stock libraries are fiercely competitive, all fighting for a share of the market, and it is therefore best to aim to place images with an established name, although competition amongst photographers will be strong. Each stock library has different specific requirements and established markets, so contact them first before making a submission. Some agencies will ask to see a large number of images from a photographer in order to judge for consistency of quality and saleability, while others will consider an initial submission of just a few images.

Useful information

British Journal of Photography
1854 Media, Subscriptions Department, Anchorage House, 9th Floor, 2 Clove Street, London E14 2BE
0207 9932243
email subscriptions@1854.media
website www.bjp-online.com

UK photography trade magazine (web and print).

Bureau of Freelance Photographers
Vision House, PO Box 474, Hatfield AL10 1FY
tel (01707) 651450
email info@thebfp.com
website www.thebfp.com
Membership £54 p.a.

Helps the freelance photographer by providing information on markets and a free advisory service. Publishes *Market Newsletter* (monthly).

Centaur Media Plc
Centaur Media Plc, Wells Point, 79 Wells Street, London W1T 3QN
tel 020-7970 4000
website www.creativereview.co.uk

Publishes *Creative Review*.

Images placed with a library usually remain the property of the photographer and libraries do not normally sell images outright to clients, but lease them for a specific use for a fee, from which commission is deducted. This means that a single image can accumulate many sales over a period of time. The commission rate is usually around 50% of every sale generated by the library. This may sound high, but it should be borne in mind that the library takes on all overheads, marketing costs and other responsibilities involved in the smooth running of a business, allowing the photographer the freedom to spend more time taking pictures.

As a result of the current boom in online advertising, many libraries now offer video clips, in addition to still photographs. The majority of professional DSLR cameras are now capable of capturing high-resolution video footage and this has opened new doors to photographers willing to diversify and exploit the new demand for high-quality video.

Photographers should realise, however, that stock photography is a long-term investment and it can take some time for sales to build up to a significant income. Clearly, photographers who supply the right images for the market, and are prolific, are those who do well, and there are a good number of photographers who make their entire living as full-time stock photographers, never having to undertake commissioned work.

Running your own library

Photographers choosing to market their own images or start up their own library have the advantage of retaining a full fee for every picture sale they make. But it is unlikely that an individual photographer could ever match the rates of an established library, or make the same volume of sales per image. However, the internet continually progresses, offering new marketing avenues for photographers and providing many opportunities to sell images worldwide. Previously, only an established stock library would have been able to do this. Before embarking on establishing a 'home' library, photographers should be aware that the business of marketing images is essentially a desk job which involves a considerable amount of admin work and time, which could be spent taking pictures.

When setting up a picture library, your first consideration should be whether to build up a library of your own images, or to take on other contributing photographers. Many photographers running their own libraries submit additional images to bigger libraries to increase the odds of making a good income. Often, a photographer's personal library is made up of work rejected by the larger libraries, which are usually only interested in images that will regularly sell and generate a high turnover. However, occasional sales can generate a significant amount of income for the individual. Furthermore, a photographer with a library of specialised subjects stands a good chance of gaining recognition with niche markets, which can be very lucrative if the competition for those particular subjects is low.

If you take on contributing photographers, the responsibility for another's work becomes yours, so it is important to draw up a contract with terms of business for both your contributing photographers and your clients. Since images are now predominantly distributed as digital files, there is no real problem with loss or damage, which used to be a big problem in the days of film-based originals. However, another issue has emerged since the advent of digital technology in the form of copyright abuse, which is now rife in the industry. Therefore, if representing another's work, it will be the library or agent's responsibility to protect image copyright on behalf of the photographer and also take any necessary legal steps in cases where copyright has been abused.

Reproduction fees should also be established on a strict basis, bearing in mind that you owe it to your contributing photographers to command fees that are as high as possible when selling the rights to their images. It is also essential that you control how pictures will be used and the amount of exposure they will receive. The fees should be established according to the type of client using the image and how the image itself will be reproduced. Important factors to consider are where the image will appear, to what size it will be reproduced, the size of the print run, and the territorial rights required by the client. However, many online agencies have now simplified their pricing structure and base fees on the specific image file size that's required by the client. A smaller file size (or lower resolution) limits the extent to which an image can be reproduced and therefore dictates final reproduction quality.

Working in any field of professional photography is fiercely competitive and successful practitioners commonly spend a great deal of time researching their client's needs and then marketing accordingly – the ultimate goal to ensure their name is always ahead of the ever-increasing competition.

Ian Thraves is a self-employed photographer and former picture editor at Bruce Coleman The Natural World Photo Agency (www.thravesphoto.co.uk).

See also...

- *Freelancing for beginners*, page 481
- *Making waves online*, page 633
- *DACS (Design and Artists Copyright Society)*, page 709
- *Copyright questions*, page 693

Art agents and commercial art studios

*Member of the Society of Artists Agents
†Member of the Association of Illustrators

Before submitting work, artists are advised to make preliminary enquiries and to ascertain terms of work. Commission varies but averages 25–30%. The Association of Illustrators (see page 548) provides a valuable service for illustrators, agents and clients.

Advocate Art Ltd

Suite 7, The Sanctuary, 23 Oakhill Grove, Surbiton, Surrey KT6 6DU
tel 020-8390 6293
email mail@advocate-art.com
website www.advocate-art.com
Director Edward Burns

Has seven agents representing 300 artists and illustrators. Bespoke Illustration for children's books, greeting cards and fine art publishers, gift and ceramic manufacturers. For illustrators' submission guidelines see website. New animation, design and original content represented through LaB – Writers and Artists colLaBorate. Also original art gallery, stock library and website in German, Spanish and French. Founded 1996.

Allied Artists/Artistic License

tel 07971 111256
email info@allied-artists.net
website www.alliedartists-illustration.com
Contact Gary Mills

Represents over 90 illustrators ranging in styles from realistic, through stylised to cute for all types of publishing but particularly children's illustration. Commission: 33%. Founded 1983.

Arena Illustration Ltd*†

Arena Illustration Ltd, 31 Eleanor Road, London E15 4AB
tel 020-8555 9827
website www.arenaillustration.com
Contact Tamlyn Francis

Represents 27 artists illustrating mostly for book covers, children's books and design groups. Average commission: 25%. Founded 1970.

The Art Agency

21 Morris Street, Sheringham, Norfolk NR26 8JY
tel (01263) 823424
email artagency@me.com
website www.the-art-agency.co.uk

Provides non-fiction, reference and children's book illustration. Specialises in non-fiction illustrations across a wide variety of subjects and age groups. Submit by email up to six samples along with a link to your website. Founded 1990.

The Art Market

51 Oxford Drive, London SE1 2FB
tel 020-7407 8111
email info@artmarketillustration.com
website www.artmarketillustration.com
Director Philip Reed

Represents 40 artists creating illustrations for publishing, design and advertising. Founded 1989.

Artist Partners Ltd*

22 Albion Hill, Ramsgate, Kent CT11 8HG
tel 020-7401 7904
email chris@artistpartners.demon.co.uk
website www.artistpartners.com
Managing Director Christine Isteed

Represents artists, including specialists, producing artwork in every genre for advertising campaigns, storyboards, children's and adult book covers, newspaper and magazine features and album covers. New artists are considered if their work is of high standard. Submission should be by post and include a sae. Commission: 30%. Founded 1951.

The Artworks†

12–18 Hoxton Street, London N1 6NG
tel 020-7729 1973
email mail@theartworksinc.com
website www.theartworksinc.com
Contacts Lucy Scherer, Stephanie Alexander-Jinks, Alex Gardner

Represents 25 illustrators for design and advertising work as well as for non-fiction children's books, book jackets, illustrated gift books and children's picture books. Commission: 25% advances, 15% royalties, 25% book jackets.

Beehive Illustration

42A Cricklade Street, Cirencester, Glos. GL7 1JH
tel (01285) 885149
email enquiries@beehiveillustration.co.uk
website www.beehiveillustration.co.uk
Contact Paul Beebee

Represents 200 artists specialising in ELT, education and general children's publishing illustration. Commission: 25%. Founded 1989.

The Big Red Illustration Agency

tel 0808 120 0996
email enquiries@bigredillustrationagency.com
website www.bigredillustrationagency.com
Director Adam Rushton

Presents portfolios of over 50 artists creating work for children's book publishers, design agencies, greeting cards and toy companies. Founded 2012.

Central Illustration Agency

17b Perseverance Works, 38 Kingsland Road, London E2 8DD
tel 020-3222 0007
email info@centralillustration.com
website www.centralillustration.com
Contact Benjamin Cox

Represents 70 artists producing illustrations for design, publishing, animation and advertising. Commission: 30%. Founded 1983.

Column Arts Agency*

33 Kelmscott Road, Harborne, Birmingham B17 8QW
tel 07803 244202
email hi@columnartsagency.co.uk
website www.columnartsagency.co.uk
Facebook www.facebook.com/ColumnArtsAgency
Twitter @columnartagency
Artists' Agent & Project Manager William Ashbury

An illustration, design and animation agency that represents a range of author-cum-illustrators, artists and commercial creatives. Represents portfolios of individuals in both the UK and US. Founded 2012.

Creative Coverage

49 Church Close, Locks Heath, Southampton, Hants SO31 6LR
tel (01489) 564536
email info@creativecoverage.co.uk
website www.creativecoverage.co.uk
Facebook www.facebook.com/CreativeCoverage
Twitter @CreativeCov
Co-founders Tim Saunders, Caroline Saunders

Fine art book publisher and artists agent. Marketing for professional artists. Founded 2013.

David Lewis Agency

3 Somali Road, London NW2 3RN
tel 020-7435 7762, 07931 824674
email davidlewis34@hotmail.com
Director David Lewis

Considers all types of illustration for a variety of applications but mostly suitable for book and magazine publishers, design groups, recording companies and corporate institutions. Also offers a comprehensive selection of images suitable for subsidiary rights purposes. Send return postage with samples. Commission: 30%. Founded 1974.

Début Art & The Coningsby Gallery*†

30 Tottenham Street, London W1T 4RJ
tel 020-7636 1064
email info@debutart.com
website www.debutart.com, www.coningsbygallery.com
Directors Andrew Coningsby, Jonathan Hedley, Laura Lee

Represents 153 leading illustrators and illustration studios, motion artists and illustrative designers. Commission re: illustration: 25–30%. Worldwide commissioning client and artist base. Email submissions from illustrators and fine artists welcome. Founded 1985.

Eastwing*†

99 Chase Side, Enfield EN2 6NL
tel 020-8367 6760
email representation@eastwing.co.uk
website www.eastwing.co.uk
Contacts Andrea Plummer, Abby Glassfield

Represents artists who work across advertising, design, publishing and editorial. Commission: 25–30%. Founded 1985.

Eye Candy Illustration

Field Cottage, Saintbury WR12 7PX
tel 020-8291 0729
email info@eyecandyillustration.com
website www.eyecandyillustration.com
Managing Director Mark Wilson

Represents 50+ artists producing work for advertising campaigns, packaging, publishing, editorials, greeting cards, merchandising and a variety of design projects. Submit printed samples with sae or email low-res jpg files via website. Founded 2002.

Ian Fleming Associates – see Phosphor Art Ltd

Folio Illustration Agency

10 Gate Street, Lincoln's Inn Fields, London WC2A 3HP
tel 020-7242 9562
email info@folioart.co.uk
website www.folioart.co.uk

All areas of illustration. Founded 1976.

Good Illustration Ltd

71–75 Shelton Street, Covent Garden, London WC2H 9JQ
tel 020-8123 0243, (US) +1 347-627-0243
email draw@goodillustration.com
website www.goodillustration.com
Directors Doreen Thorogood, Kate Webber, Tom Thorogood

Represents 50+ artists for advertising, design, publishing, animation. Send return postage and samples. Commission: 25% publishing, 30% advertising. Founded 1977.

Graham-Cameron Illustration

59 Hertford Road, Brighton BN1 7GG
tel (01273) 385890
email enquiry@gciforillustration.com
Alternative address The Art House, Uplands Park, Sheringham, Norfolk NR26 8NE
tel (01263) 821333
website www.gciforillustration.com
Partners Helen Graham-Cameron, Duncan Graham-Cameron

Represents 37+ artists and undertakes illustration for publishing and communications. Specialises in educational, children's and information books. Phone before sending A4 samples with sae or email samples or link to a website. No MSS. Founded 1985.

The Guild of Aviation Artists

Studio 100, Rye House, 113 High Street, Ruislip HA4 8JN
tel (03331) 302233
email admin@gava.org.uk
website www.gava.org.uk
President Michael Turner FGAvA, *Secretary* Tony Nicholls GAvA

Specialising in aviation art in all hand-applied mediums and comprising approx. 450 members, the Guild sells, commissions and exhibits members' work. Founded 1971.

Illustration Ltd*†

2 Salamanca Place, Albert Embankment, London SE1 7HB
tel 020-7720 5202
email hello@illustrationweb.com
website www.illustrationweb.com
Contacts Juliette Lott, Victoria Pearce, Alice Ball, Mike Cowley

Represents 150 artists producing illustrations and animation for international advertisers, designers, publishers and editorial clients. Artists should send submissions via the website. Founded 1929.

Image by Design Licensing

Suite 3, 107 Bancroft, Hitchin, Herts. SG5 1NB
tel (01462) 451190
email hugh@ibd-licensing.co.uk
website www.ibd-licensing.co.uk
Contact Hugh Brenham

Well-known art licensing agency representing artists from around the world. Representing a large portfolio of on trend artwork licensed on a wide range of products including greeting cards, wall art, stationery, calendars, ceramics, table top, jigsaws, giftware, napkins, craft and needlecraft. New artists always considered. Commissions welcome. Founded 1987.

B.L. Kearley Ltd

16 Chiltern Street, London W1U 7PZ
tel 020-7935 9550
email christine.kearley@kearley.co.uk
website www.kearley.co.uk
Agent C.R. Kearley

Represents over 30 artists and has been supplying top-quality illustrations for over 60 years. Mainly specialises in children's book and educational illustration for the domestic market and overseas. Known for realistic figurative work. Specialises in the sale of original book illustration artwork. Commission: 25%. Founded 1948.

Kids Corner

The Old Candlemakers, West Street, Lewes BN7 2NZ
tel 020-7593 0506
email claire@meiklejohn.co.uk
website www.kidscornerillustration.co.uk
Managing Director Claire Meiklejohn

Represents illustrators, from award-winning to emerging artists for children's publishing. Styles include fun, cute, stylised, picture book, young fiction, reference, graphic, traditional, painterly and digital. See also Meiklejohn Illustration (page 510) and New Division (page 510). Founded 2015.

Lemonade Illustration Agency

Hill House, Suite 231, 210 Upper Richmond Road, London SW15 6NP
tel (07891) 390750
email lucy@lemonadeillustration.com
US office 347 Fifth Ave, Suite 1402, New York, NY 10016
website www.lemonadeillustration.com
Contact Lucy Quinn

Represents 130+ illustrators and animators for all kinds of media from TV to children's books. Also has a specialist division, Fizzy, which represents 100+ artists working for the children's picture book and educational market. Any submissions from illustrators by email must contain a website link (no attachments) or hard copies of samples can be sent by post with a sae. Offices in London, New York and Sydney.

Frances McKay Illustration

17 Church Road, West Mersea, Essex CO5 8QH
tel (01206) 383286
email frances@francesmckay.com
website www.francesmckay.com
Proprietor Frances McKay

Represents 15–20 artists for illustration mainly for children's books. For information on submissions please look at the website. Submit email with low-res scans or colour copies of recent work; sae essential for return of all unsolicited samples sent by post. Commission: 25%. Founded 1999.

Meiklejohn Illustration*

The Old Candlemakers, West Street, Lewes BN7 2NZ
tel 020-7593 0506
email claire@meiklejohn.co.uk
website www.meiklejohn.co.uk
Managing Director Claire Meiklejohn

Represents illustrators, covering a wide range of styles, from traditional, children's publishing, photorealistic, cartoon to contemporary. See also Kids Corner (page 509) and New Division (page 510).

NB Illustration

40 Bowling Green Lane, London EC1R 0NE
tel 07720 827328
email info@nbillustration.co.uk
website www.nbillustration.co.uk
Directors Joe Najman, Charlotte Dowson, Paul Najman

Represents over 50 artists and will consider all material for the commercial illustration market. For submission details see website. Commission: 30%. Founded 2000.

New Division*

The Old Candlemakers, West Street, Lewes BN7 2NZ
tel 020-7593 0505
email claire@newdivision.co.uk
website www.newdivision.co.uk
Managing Director Claire Meiklejohn

Represents illustrators, artists and new graduates. Represents a select group of lifestyle, fashion and stylised artists. See also Kids Corner (page 509) and Meiklejohn Illustration (page 510). Founded 1983.

The Organisation

6 Manor Wood, Chepstow, Gwent NP16 6DS
tel 07973 172902
email info@organisart.co.uk
website www.organisart.co.uk
Contact Lorraine Owen

Represents over 60 international illustrators. Contemporary and traditional styles for all areas of publishing. Stock illustration also available. See website for submission guidelines. Founded 1987.

Oxford Designers & Illustrators Ltd

Suite M, Kidlington Centre, High Street, Kidlington, Oxford OX5 2DL
tel (01865) 512331
email info@odi-design.co.uk
website www.o-d-i.com
Twitter @ODIoxford

An independent company with a long history of working with prestigious educational organisations. Offers a varied range of design and illustration skills, and particular expertise with educational materials, such as ELT, science and maths textbooks. Also offers a wide range of creative services, including production of 3D images, animations, ebooks, maps, scientific and technical illustrations, as well as project management. Not an agency. Founded 1968.

Phosphor Art Ltd*

19 Acacia Way, The Hollies, Sidcup, Kent DA15 8WW
tel 020-7064 4666
email info@phosphorart.com
website www.phosphorart.com
Directors Jon Rogers, Catriona Wydmanski

Represents 46 artists and specialises in innovative graphic digital illustration with artists working in watercolour, oil and gouche as well as pen and ink, scraper, charcoal and engraving styles. Also animation. Incorporates Ian Fleming Associates and The Black and White Line. Commission: 33.3%.

Plum Pudding Illustration

Chapel House, St. Lawrences Way, Reigate, Surrey RH2 7AF
tel (01737) 244095
email letterbox@plumpuddingillustration.com
website www.plumpuddingillustration.com
Director Mark Mills *Associate Director* Hannah Whitty

Represents 100+ artists, producing illustrations for children's publishing, advertising, editorial, greeting cards and packaging. See website for submission procedure. Commission: 30%. Founded 2006.

Sylvie Poggio Artists Agency

36 Haslemere Road, London N8 9RB
tel 020-8341 2722
email sylviepoggio@blueyonder.co.uk
website www.sylviepoggio.com
Directors Sylvie Poggio, Bruno Caurat

Represents 40 artists producing illustrations for publishing and advertising.

Vicki Thomas Associates

195 Tollgate Road, London E6 5JY
tel 020-7511 5767
email vickithomasassociates@yahoo.co.uk
website www.vickithomasassociates.com
Facebook www.facebook.com/vickithomasassociates
Twitter @VickiThomasA
Consultant Vicki Thomas

Considers the work of illustrators and designers working in greetings/gift industries, and promotes work to gift, toy, publishing and related industries. Email sample images, covering letter and CV. Commission: 30%. Founded 1985.

Card and stationery publishers that accept illustrations and photographs

*Member of the Greeting Card Association

Before submitting work, artists and photographers are advised to ascertain requirements of the company they are approaching, including terms and conditions. Only high-quality material should be submitted.

The Almanac Gallery*

Waterwells Drive, Gloucester, Glos. GL2 2PH
tel (01452) 888999
email submissions@greatbritishcards.co.uk
website www.greatbritishcards.co.uk

Specialises in contemporary art and beautiful Charity Christmas cards.

Card Connection Ltd*

Park House, South Street, Farnham, Surrey GU9 7QQ
tel (01252) 892300
email enquiries@cardconnection.co.uk
website www.card-connection.co.uk
Managing Director Michael Johnson

Everyday and seasonal designs. Styles include cute, fun, traditional, contemporary, humour and photographic. Humorous copy and jokes plus sentimental verse. Founded 1992.

CardsWorld Ltd t/a 4C For Charity

114 High Street, Stevenage, Herts. SG1 3DW
tel 0845 230 0046
email design@charitycards.org
website www.charitycards.org

Contemporary and traditional Christmas cards for the corporate and charity market (London, international and festive themes). Submit low-res artwork by email no larger than 5MB. No verses or cute styles. Works with over 70 charities. Founded 1966.

Caspari Ltd

Linden House, John Dane Player Court, East Street, Saffron Walden, Essex CB10 1LR
tel (01799) 513010
email info@caspari.co.uk
website www.casparionline.com

Traditional fine art/classic images; 5 x 4in transparencies. No verses. Founded 1990.

Colneis Marketing Ltd*

3 Manning Road, Felixstowe IP11 2AS
tel (01394) 271668
email colneiscards@btconnect.com
website www.colneisgreetingcards.com
Proprietor John Botting

Photographs (preferably medium format) and colour artwork of nature and cute images. Founded 1994.

Colour House Graphics Ltd*

3 Manning Road, Felixstowe, Suffolk IP11 2AS
tel (01394) 271668
email colourhousegraphics@btinternet.com
website www.colourhousegraphics.co.uk
Contact John Batting

Contemporary styles of painting of subjects relating to people's everyday lives. Particularly interested in sophisticated, loose, graphic styles. No verses. Founded 1990.

Simon Elvin Ltd*

Wooburn Industrial Park, Wooburn Green, Bucks. HP10 0PE
tel (01628) 526711
email studioadmin@simonelvin.com
website www.simonelvin.com
Art Director Fiona Buszard *Studio Manager* Rachel Green

Female/male traditional and contemporary designs, female/male cute, wedding/anniversary, birth congratulations, fine art, photographic animals, flowers and male imagery, traditional sympathy, juvenile ages, special occasions and giftwrap.

Looking for submissions that show flair, imagination and an understanding of greeting card design. Artists should familiarise themselves with the ranges, style and content. Submit a small collection of either colour copies or prints (no original artwork) and include a sae for return of work. Alternatively email jpg files.

Gallery Five Ltd

The Old Bakery, 1 Bellingham Road, London SE6 2PN
tel 07984 138061
website www.galleryfive.co.uk
Managing Director Frank Larkin

Send samples of work FAO 'Gallery Five Art Studio'. Colour photocopies, Mac-formatted zip/CD acceptable, plus sae. No verses.

Gemma International Ltd*

Linmar House, 6 East Portway, Andover, Hants SP10 3LU
tel (01264) 388400
email esales@gemma-international.co.uk
website www.gemma-international.co.uk

Directors William Harris, A. Parkin, T. Rudd-Clarke, David Wesson

Cute, contemporary, leading-edge designs for children, teens and young adults. Founded 1984.

Graphic Humour Ltd

PO Box 717, North Shields, Tyne & Wear NE30 4WR
tel 0191 280 5019
email enquiries@graphichumour.com
website www.graphichumour.com

Risqué and everyday artwork ideas for greeting cards; short, humorous copy. Founded 1984.

The Great British Card Company

(incorporating Paper House, Medici Cards and The Almanac Gallery)
Waterwells Drive, Gloucester, Glos. GL2 2PH
tel (01452) 888999
email art@paperhouse.co.uk
website www.greatbritishcards.co.uk

Publishers of everyday, Christmas and spring greeting cards, notecards, gift wrap and gift bags. Particularly welcomes new humorous submissions. For a full listing of brands published visit website.

Green Pebble*

Roos Hall Studio, Bungay Road, Beccles, Suffolk NR34 8HE
tel (01502) 710427
email ruby@greenpebble.co.uk
website www.greenpebble.co.uk
Publisher Michael Charles

Publisher of fine art greeting cards and associated products by artists. See website for style before submitting. Send a minimum of six design thumbnails via email. Founded 2010.

Hallmark Cards Plc*

Dawson Lane, Dudley Hill, Bradford BD4 6HN
tel (01274) 252000
email creativesubmissions@hallmark-uk.com
website www.hallmark.co.uk

See website for freelance opportunities and submission details.

Leeds Postcards

4 Granby Road, Leeds LS6 3AS
email xtine@leedspostcards.com
website www.leedspostcards.com
Contact Christine Hankinson

Publisher and distributor of postcards; feminism, animal rights and socialism. Send only suitable and relevant jpg files to email above. If published, paid by advance royalty on print run.

Ling Design Ltd*

Westmoreland House, Westmoreland Street, Bath BA2 3HE
tel (01225) 489760
email info@lingdesign.co.uk
website www.lingdesign.co.uk
Creative Director Rebecca Mcculloch

Artwork for greeting cards, stationery and giftwrap.

Medici Cards

Waterwells Drive, Gloucester, Glos. GL2 2PH
tel (01452) 888999
email submissions@greatbritishcards.co.uk
website www.greatbritishcards.co.uk

Specialises in market-leading art and photographic cards. Brands include National Geographic, English Heritage, Royal Horticultural Society and Medici Cards Blue Label.

Miko Greetings*

85 Landcroft Road, East Dulwich, London SE22 9JS
tel 020-8693-1011 / 07957 395739
email info@miko-greetings.com
website www.miko-greetings.com
Head Creative & Illustrator, Mik Brown aka Miko, *Creative Photographer* Toby Brown, *Consultant* Annie Horwood

Produces high-end, quality, humorous illustrated and photographic greetings cards. Cards are mainly blank for any occasion. Currently introducing some occasions cards. Also produces high-quality 'Wall Art' of all the company's designs. Founded 2014.

Paper House

Waterwells Drive, Gloucester, Glos. GL2 2PH
tel (01452) 888999
email art@paperhouse.co.uk
website www.greatbritishcards.co.uk

Producers of everyday birthday, special occasions and family relations greeting cards; plus spring seasons and Christmas. Specialising in the following: funny/humorous cards and always looking for new copy/ideas; photographic ranges; and contemporary and trend-driven imagery.

Paperlink Ltd*

356 Kennington Road, London SE11 4LD
tel 020-7582 8244
email info@paperlink.co.uk
website www.paperlink.co.uk

Publishes a range of humorous and contemporary art greeting cards. Produce products under licence for charities. Founded 1986.

Pineapple Park*

Unit 9, Henlow Trading Estate, Henlow Camp, Beds. SG16 6DS
tel (01462) 814817
email sally@pineapplepark.co.uk
website www.pineapplepark.co.uk
Main contact Sally Kelly *Directors* Peter M. Cockerline, Sarah M. Parker

Illustrations and photographs for publication as greeting cards. Contemporary, cute, humour: submit artwork or laser copies with sae. Photographic florals always needed. Humour copy/jokes accepted without artwork. Founded 1993.

Nigel Quiney Publications Ltd*

Cloudesley House, Shire Hill, Saffron Walden, Essex CB11 3FB
tel 01799 520200

email carl.pledger@nigelquiney.com
website www.nigelquiney.com
Contact Carl Pledger (Head of Product)

Everyday and seasonal greeting cards including fine art, photographic, humour, contemporary and cute. Submit by email or colour copies, photographs, transparencies or disk by post: no original artwork.

Really Good*

The Old Mast House, The Square, Abingdon, Oxon OX14 5AR
tel (01235) 537888
email ello@reallygood.uk.com
website www.reallygood.uk.com
Director David Hicks

Always looking for fun, trendy and quirky artwork to publish on cards, stationery or gifts. Check the website first, and if there is a fit, email website/blog link or small jpg or pdf files to view. Please do not post submissions. Really Good is the sister company of Soul (page 513). Founded 1987.

Felix Rosenstiels Widow & Son Ltd

Fine Art Publishers, 33–35 Markham Street, London SW3 3NR
tel 020-7352 3551
email artists@rosentiels.com
website www.rosentiels.com

Invites offers of artwork of a professional standard for reproduction as picture prints for the picture framing trade. Any type of subject considered. See website for submission details.

Royle Publications Ltd – see Medici Cards

Santoro London

Rotunda Point, 11 Hartfield Crescent, London SW19 3RL
tel 020-8781 1100
email submissions@santorographics.com
website www.santoro-london.com
Directors Lucio Santoro, Meera Santoro

Publishers of innovative and International award-winning designs for three-dimensional pop-up cards, greeting cards, giftwrap and gift stationery. Bold, contemporary images with an international appeal. Subjects covered: contemporary, pop-up, cute, kawaii, quirky, fashion, retro. Submit samples as colour copies or digital files (jpg or pdf files). Founded 1985.

Second Nature Ltd*

10 Malton Road, London W10 5UP
tel (01983) 209590
email design@secondnature.co.uk
website www.secondnature.co.uk
Facebook www.facebook.com/SecondNatureLtd

Contemporary artwork for greeting cards and handmade cards; jokes for humorous range; short modern sentiment; verses. Founded 1981.

Soul*

Old Mast House, The Square, Abingdon, Oxon OX14 5AR
tel (01235) 537816
email smile@souluk.com
website www.souluk.com
Director David Hicks

Publishers of contemporary trend gifts, cards and stationery. Also wrapping paper and notebooks. Consult website for suitability, then email link to your website or blog link, small jpg or pdf files. Please do not post artwork. Soul is the sister company of Really Good (page 513).

Noel Tatt Group/Impress Publishing*

Appledown House, Barton Business Park, Appledown Way, New Dover Road, Canterbury, Kent CT1 3TE
tel (01227) 811600
email mail@noeltatt.co.uk
website www.noeltatt.co.uk

General everyday cards – broad mix; Christmas. Will consider verses. Founded 1964.

UK Greetings Ltd

Mill Street East, Dewsbury, West Yorkshire WF12 9AW
tel (01924) 465200
website www.ukgreetings.co.uk
Sales & Marketing Director James Conn *Director of Marketing* Ceri Stirland

For creative submissions, please visit the website.

Wishing Well Studios (Carte Blanche Group Ltd)*

R11 Block N4,
Chorley Business & Technology Centre, East Terrace, Euxton Lane, Chorley, Lancs. PR7 6TE
tel (01243) 792642
email nicky.harrison@cbg.co.uk
website www.carteblanchegreetings.com
Creative Director Nicky Harrison

Part of Carte Blanche Group. Rhyming and prose verse 4–24 lines long; also jokes. All artwork styles considered. Don't send originals (sae needed for return of work). Email attachments less than 3MB.

Woodmansterne Publications Ltd*

1 The Boulevard, Blackmoor Lane, Watford, Herts. WD18 8UW
tel (01923) 200600
website www.woodmansterne.co.uk

Publisher of greeting cards and social stationery featuring fine and contemporary art and photography (colour and b&w). Submit colour copies, photographs or jpg files by email.

Societies, prizes and festivals

Developing talent: support and opportunities for writers

Helen Chaloner shares her knowledge of the many agencies, networks, awards and opportunities available to writers, to provide funding, inspiration and encouragement as they develop their talents.

Prizes, bursaries, awards and other opportunities for developing your writing are widespread and can really support your efforts. The process of putting yourself forward for one of these provides focus in the form of a deadline. It can lift your horizons and help you view your writing ambitions in a wider context. However, there is a balance to be sought, as always; the hard graft of seeking and applying for opportunities will eat into precious writing time.

Writer development agencies

A good place to start is your regional literature development agency. These agencies are Arts Council England-funded, not-for-profit organisations that exist to support writers and generate opportunities. I am writing this article in my role as Chief Executive Officer of Literature Works (http://literatureworks.org.uk), the literature development agency for South West England. The other agencies are: New Writing South (www.newwritingsouth.com), New Writing North (http://newwritingnorth.com), Spread the Word, London (www.spreadtheword.org.uk), Writers' Centre Norwich, covering the East of England (www.writerscentrenorwich.org.uk), Writing East Midlands (www.writingeastmidlands.co.uk) and Writing West Midlands (www.writingwestmidlands.org). There are non-regional agencies, too, such as Speaking Volumes (www.speakingvolumes.org.uk), which produces *Breaking Ground: Celebrating British Writers of Colour*, a resource aimed at improving representation and diversity in live literature events.

Signing up for your regional agency's online newsletter will instantly connect you to networks and opportunities. Amongst other things, we run writing courses, offer mentoring and bursaries, administer prizes, oversee festivals and tour live literature. Some of us have membership schemes, through which you can access advance information and connect with other writers. Creative Scotland supports an equivalent in Scottish Book Trust (www.scottishbooktrust.com), and the Arts Council of Wales supports Literature Wales (www.literaturewales.org). We all survey writers on a regular basis about their priorities and needs, so that you can have your say and feed into what we offer as well.

See also *Arts councils, Royal Societies and funding* on page 530.

Prizes

In a constantly changing landscape, there are hundreds of writing prizes. They sometimes charge a small fee per entry and often offer publication in an anthology as part of the prize package. A significant number recognise new talent or previously unpublished work.

• The Bridport Prize (see page 568) is one of the biggest and aims specifically to encourage emerging writers, with categories for short stories, poems, flash fiction and first novels.
• The Royal Society of Literature's annual V.S. Pritchett Memorial Prize (see page 583) is for the best unpublished short story of the year, which is then published in *Prospect Magazine* and the *RSL Review*.
• The Betty Trask Prize (see page 589) distributes substantial prize money every year to the best published or unpublished first novels by writers under the age of 35.
• The Creative Future Literary Awards (see page 571) showcase the work of talented writers from under-represented groups, with prizes and mentoring offered for writers of poems and flash fiction.

There are many others and the smaller prizes should not to be overlooked. They offer better odds of winning, with closely defined areas of interest that may just dovetail nicely with your interests. See full listings in the *Prizes and awards* section, page 565. To give just one example, Literature Works runs an annual poetry prize to accompany a project about the positive impact of poetry on people living with memory loss. In order to focus attention on the meaning of our project, we have a prize category for poems by a primary carer who is looking after a loved one with dementia.

Awards

Awards and bursaries are another prospect. They can provide crucial cash support that reduces financial pressure and frees up time for writing and research.
• The Deborah Rogers Foundation Writers' Award supports an unpublished prose writer to complete their first book.
• The Royal Society of Literature's Giles St Aubyn Awards help writers complete their first commissioned work of non-fiction.
• The Royal Society of Literature (RSL) and the Society of Authors (SoA) both offer a range of support and awards.
• For more experienced writers, the Royal Literary Fund (www.rlf.org.uk) runs year-long writers' fellowships at universities and colleges to help students with their academic writing.

Be aware, though, that demand outstrips supply for all high-profile awards; your regional literature development agency may well be running similar schemes on a smaller, more attainable scale.

Do also sign up for information about Arts Council England's funding streams (see www.artscouncil.org.uk/funding). These are generally grants for activities over a set period that engage people in arts activities and help artists and arts organisations to carry out their work. Individual writers can apply to the 'Developing Your Creative Practice Fund' for a grant of between £2,000 and £10,000 to support periods of research, developing new ideas, international work and training, networking or mentoring.

Feedback, writing courses and residencies

If you are looking for objective external feedback on your writing, there are a number of services on offer.The Literary Consultancy's 'Free Reads' scheme (https://literaryconsultancy.co.uk/editorial/ace-free-reads-scheme) produces detailed assessments from professional readers for promising writers on low incomes or from under-represented groups. The regional literature development agencies select and submit work to the scheme each year and the same service is also available from The Literary Consultancy (on a paid basis).

Perhaps you crave time and space to write, away from day-to-day responsibilities and in the company of other writers? Arvon (see page 678) has been making this possible for 50 years at residential writers' centres in secluded locations in Devon, Shropshire and West Yorkshire. Course members make the house their home for five days and immerse themselves in writing. They are tutored and guided by two established authors, who encourage them to take themselves seriously as writers. Courses run all year round, in many genres and for different writing stages. The list of tutors, past and present, is an impressive roll call of contemporary writing talent. Arvon offers substantial bursaries to people who cannot afford the full course fee and works in partnership with other organisations to provide bespoke courses for particular interest groups. Moniack Mhor runs a similarly impressive programme in the Scottish Highlands and Tŷ Newydd, on the Llŷn Peninsula in North Wales is the National Writing Centre of Wales. (See *Writers' retreats and creative writing courses* on page 678.)

If you enjoy time away from the desk, bringing writing to other people, opportunities for paid writer-in-residence work come in many other forms and settings. A writers' residency can be a one-off event, or it may actually involve a writer living at a property. Usually it entails some combination of activities for the writer, between running workshops and developing their own work.

Writers can be paid to work in prisons, in commercial firms and, in the south west, at National Trust properties with a literary heritage. Literature Works also places poets in community dementia care settings, remembering and creating poetry with people living with memory loss and their loved ones.

Schools will often engage a local writer to work with children and there is good guidance on this from the National Association of Writers in Education (NAWE; see page 375). It is well worth looking out for opportunities to train as a facilitator or writing workshop leader. This can not only provide you with essential guidance on things like safeguarding and insurance, but will sometimes feed directly into projects as well.

Festivals and promotions

Literary festivals are springing up everywhere and there will be at least one near you. Get to know the organisers; volunteer if you can spare the time. The big ones are well established and attract high-profile media sponsorship. Smaller ones are thriving, too, and they are often keen to promote local writers. (See *Festivals and conferences for writers, artists and readers* on page 597.)

There are now a range of themed literary days or weeks throughout the year:

- **World Book Day**, in early spring, is a celebration of books and reading marked by many schools and a great opportunity for author events.
- The most prominent of the longstanding generic promotions must be **National Poetry Day**, celebrated in the autumn and firmly on the agenda of publishers, booksellers, schools and poets.
- A relatively new and welcome addition is **National Writing Day**, which takes place in the summer and provides a focus for all sorts of writing courses and opportunities. Check the dates for these and others, and put them in your calendar. Opportunities may well arise for events, volunteering and connecting.

Libraries

In the south west of England, we have a long track record of working closely with libraries, based on the absolute knowledge that writers need readers and vice versa. Libraries often host or run writing groups and these, for many people, are a great place to start and sustain your writing. Libraries run regular author events and themed or local promotions. Though operating in a harsh climate and often under-resourced, they can be fantastic early champions of local writers and it's worth letting them know that you're around.

For an up-to-date overview of library sector innovations and latest news, the Libraries Taskforce blog (https://librariestaskforce.blog.gov.uk) is well worth a read.

In summary, there is vibrant culture of development opportunities for writers, whether just starting out or more established. It is worth doing your research and it's very easy these days to keep informed by signing up for newsletters. If you can meet face to face, pop into your local library, or get involved with writers' group that will pay dividends, too. None of this replaces precious hours spent writing, but writing is a craft that can be improved over time and there are many people and organisations out there, ready to share their expertise with you.

Helen Chaloner is Ceo of Literature Works, the literature development agency for SW England. After studying French and Comparative Literature at UEA, Helen worked in publishing PR at Penguin Books and at Faber and Faber, before taking up leadership positions with the Arvon Foundation and with the educational charity, Farms for City Children. Before joining Literature Works, Helen ran her own consultancy offering charities support with developing, funding and growing their organisations. Follow her on Twitter @ChalonerHelen.

See also...

- *Festivals and conferences for writers, artists and readers*, page 597
- *Prizes and awards*, page 565
- *Writers' organisations*, page 557
- *Arts councils, Royal Societies and funding*, page 530

Society of Authors

The SoA is the UK trade union for all types of writers, illustrators and literary translators at every stage of their careers.

Founded in 1884, the Society of Authors now has over 10,000 members. Members receive unlimited free advice on all aspects of the profession, including confidential clause-by-clause contract vetting, and a wide range of exclusive offers. It campaigns and lobbies on the issues that affect authors, and holds a wide range of events across the UK, offering opportunities for authors to network and learn from each other. It manages more than 50 literary estates, the income from which helps to fund their work. It also administers a range of literary grants and prizes, awarding more than £400,000 to authors annually.

Members

SoA members include household names, such as J.K. Rowling, Philip Pullman and Joanne Harris, but they also include authors right at the start of their careers. Amongst the SoA membership are academic writers, biographers, broadcasters, children's writers, crime writers, dramatists, educational writers, ELT writers, health writers, ghostwriters, graphic novelists, historians, illustrators, journalists, medical writers, non-fiction writers, novelists, poets, playwrights, radio writers, scriptwriters, short story writers, translators, spoken word artists, YA writers, and more.

The benefits available to all SoA members include:

• assistance with contracts, from negotiation and assessment of terms to clause-by-clause, confidential vetting;

• unlimited advice on queries, covering any aspect of the business of authorship;

Membership

The Society of Authors
84 Drayton Gardens, London SW10 9SB
(from March 2019) 24 Bedford Row, London WC1R 4TQ
tel 020-7373 6642
email info@societyofauthors.org
website www.societyofauthors.org
Chief Executive Nicola Solomon
President Philip Pullman

We have two membership bands: Full and Associate membership.

Full membership is available to professional writers, poets, translators and illustrators working in any genre or medium. This includes those who have: had a full-length work traditionally published, broadcast or performed commercially; self-published or been published on a print-on-demand or ebook-only basis and who meet sales criteria; published or had broadcast or performed an equivalent body of professional work; or administrators of a deceased author's estate.

Authors at the start of their careers are invited to join as Associates.

Associate membership is available to anyone actively working to launch a career as an author. This includes: authors who are starting out in self-publishing but who are not yet making a profit; authors who have been offered a contract for publication or agent representation but who are not yet published; students engaged on a course of at least one academic year's duration that will help them develop a career as an author, as well as other activities that mark the early stages of an author's career. Associate members enjoy all the same services and benefits as Full members. Full eligibility details can be found at www.societyofauthors.org/join.

Membership is subject to election and payment of subscription fees.

The subscription fee (tax deductible) starts at £25.50 per quarter, or £18 for those aged 35 or under. From the second year of subscription there are concessionary rates for over 65s who are no longer earning a significant amount of income from writing. Annual payment schedules are also available.

• taking up complaints on behalf of members on any issue concerned with the business of authorship;
• pursuing legal actions for breach of contract, copyright infringement, and the non-payment of royalties and fees, when the risk and cost preclude individual action by a member and issues of general concern to the profession are at stake;
• conferences, seminars, meetings and other opportunities to network and learn from other authors;
• regular communications and a comprehensive range of publications, including the SoA's quarterly journal, the *Author*;
• discounts on books, exclusive rates on specialist insurance, special offers on products and services, and free membership of the Authors' Licensing and Collecting Society (ALCS; see page 707);
• Academic and Medical Writers Groups – investigating and highlighting the issues faced by these authors, including confusion and concern around Open Access requirements and Creative Commons licensing.
• Broadcasting Group – representing members working in radio, TV and film;
• Children's Writers and Illustrators Group – a professional community of writers and illustrators who create content for the children's publishing market;
• Educational Writers Group – protecting the interests of educational authors in professional matters, especially contracts, rates of pay, digitalisation and copyright;
• Poetry and Spoken Word Group – a new, increasingly active group to which all new member poets are subscribed on joining SoA;
• Society of Authors in Scotland – organises a varied and busy calendar of activities in Scotland through a committee of volunteers;
• Translators Association – a source of expert advice for individual literary translators and a collective voice representing the profession. See page 555;
• Writers as Carers Group – a new group designed to help keep writers writing when they take on caring responsibilities for someone with an illness or disability.

The SoA also facilitates many local groups across the UK.

Campaigning and lobbying

The SoA is a voice for authors and works at a national and international level to improve terms and treatment of authors, negotiating with all parties including publishers, broadcasters, agents and governments. Current areas of campaigning include contract terms, copyright, freedom of expression, tax and benefits arrangements and Public Lending Right (PLR, see page 143) – which the SoA played a key role in establishing. It also campaigns on wider matters which affect authors, such as libraries, literacy and a fair playing field for publishing.

In the UK the SoA lobbies parliament, ministers and departments and makes submissions on relevant issues, working closely with the Department for Culture, Media and Sport and the All Party Parliamentary Writers Group. The SoA is a member of the British Copyright Council and was instrumental in setting up ALCS. It is recognised by the BBC in the negotiation of rates for authors' contributions to radio drama, as well as for the broadcasting of published material.

The SoA is highly active and influential at a European level and is a member of the European Writers' Council and applies pressure globally, working with sister organisations as part of the international Authors' Foundation.

The SoA also works closely with other professional bodies, including the Association of Authors' Agents, the Booksellers Association, the Publishers Association, the Independent Publishers Guild, the British Council, the National Union of Journalists and the Writers' Guild of Great Britain. (See the societies listings that start on page 526)

Awards and grants

The SoA supports authors through a wide range of awards and grants. Over £100,000 is given in prizes each year and more than £230,000 is distributed in grants.
As of 2018, the SoA administers:
• the Authors' Foundation and K Blundell Trust, which give grants to assist authors working on their next book;
• the Francis Head Bequest and the Authors' Contingency Fund, which assist authors who, through physical mishap, are temporarily unable to maintain themselves or their families;
• the Women's Prize for Fiction;
• the *Sunday Times*/Peters, Fraser & Dunlop Young Writer of the Year Award;
• the *Sunday Times* EFG Short Story Award;
• Travelling Scholarships, which give honorary awards;
• two prizes for first novels: the Betty Trask Awards and the McKitterick Prize;
• the Somerset Maugham Awards for a full-length published work;
• two poetry awards: the Eric Gregory Awards and the Cholmondeley Awards;
• the Tom-Gallon Award for short story writers;
• two audio drama prizes: the Imison Award for a writer new to radio drama and the Tinniswood Award;
• awards for translations from Arabic, Dutch/Flemish, French, German, Greek, Italian, Spanish and Swedish into English;
• the ALCS Educational Writers' Awards.

WGGB (Writers' Guild of Great Britain)

The WGGB is the TUC-affiliated trade union for writers.

WGGB represents writers working in film, television, radio, theatre, books, poetry, animation, comedy and videogames. Formed in 1959 as the Screenwriters' Guild, the union gradually extended into all areas of freelance writing activity and copyright protection. In 1974, when book authors and stage dramatists became eligible for membership, substantial numbers joined. In June 1997 the Theatre Writers' Union membership unified with that of the WGGB to create a larger, more powerful writers' union.

Apart from necessary dealings with Government and policies on legislative matters affecting writers, the WGGB is, by constitution, non-political, has no involvement with any political party, and members pay no political levy.

WGGB employs a permanent general secretary and other permanent staff and is administered by an Executive Council of around 20 members. WGGB comprises professional writers in all media, united in common concern for one another and regulating the conditions under which they work.

Membership

The Writers' Guild of Great Britain (WGGB)
First Floor, 134 Tooley Street, London SE1 2TU
tel 020-7833 0777
email admin@writersguild.org.uk
website www.writersguild.org.uk
Facebook www.facebook.com/thewritersguild
Twitter @The WritersGuild
General Secretary Ellie Peers
Full membership: Members pay approximately 1.2% of earnings from professional writing using a banding system (min. £198, max. £2,000 p.a.)
Candidate membership: £108 p.a. restricted to writers who have not had work published or produced at WGGB-approved rates
Affiliate membership: £300 p.a. for people who work professionally with writers, e.g. agents, technical advisers

Members receive a weekly email newsletter. The WGGB website contains full details of collective agreements and WGGB activities, plus a 'Find a Writer' service and a dedicated Members' area; information is also made available on Twitter and Facebook. Other benefits include: legal advice and contract vetting; free training; member events, discounts and special offers, including free entry to the British Library reading rooms.

WGGB agreements

WGGB's core function is to negotiate minimum terms in those areas in which its members work. Those agreements form the basis of the individual contracts signed by members. Further details are given below. WGGB also gives individual advice to its members on contracts and other matters which the writer encounters in his or her professional life. It also maintains a benevolent fund to help writers in financial trouble.

Television

WGGB negotiates minimum terms agreements with the BBC, ITV, Pact (Producers' Alliance for Cinema and Television, see page 554) and has also talked to Channel 4 about internet services. There is also a minimum terms agreement in place with TAC (representing Welsh-language television producers).

WGGB TV agreements regulate minimum fees, residuals and royalties, copyright, credits, and general conditions for television plays, series and serials, dramatisations and adaptations, soaps, sitcoms and sketch shows. One of the WGGB's most important achievements has been the establishment of pension rights for members. The BBC, ITV and independent producers pay a pension contribution on top of the standard writer's fee on the understanding that the WGGB member also pays a contribution.

The switch to digital television, video-on-demand and download-to-own services, mobile phone technology and the expansion of the BBC's commercial arm have seen WGGB in constant negotiation over the past decade. WGGB now has agreements for all of the BBC's digital channels and for its joint venture channels. In May 2012 WGGB signed ground-breaking new agreements with the BBC extending minimum terms over online services such as iPlayer. From April 2015 the first payments under the Writers Digital Payments scheme were paid out to writers whose work had been broadcast on BBC iPlayer and ITV Player (Writers Digital Payments is a not-for-profit company set up by WGGB and the Personal Managers' Association). In 2016 WGGB negotiated a 75% fee increase for writers working under its 2003 Pact agreement, and also started work on rewriting the agreement. In 2017 it negotiated a new script agreement for television and online with the BBC.

Film

In 1985 an agreement was signed with the two producer organisations: the British Film and Television Producers' Association and the Independent Programme Producers' Association (now known as Pact). Since then there has been an industrial agreement covering UK film productions. Pension fund contributions have been negotiated for WGGB members in the same way as for the BBC and ITV. The Agreement was renegotiated in February 1992 and consultations on an updated arrangement, led by the WGGB Film Committee, are in progress.

Radio

WGGB has a standard agreement for Radio Drama with the BBC, establishing a fee structure that is reviewed annually. This was comprehensively renegotiated in 2005, with input from the WGGB Radio Committee, resulting in an agreement covering various new developments such as digital radio. In 1985 the BBC agreed to extend the pension scheme already established for television writers to include radio writers. WGGB has special agreements for Radio 4's *The Archers* and for BBC iPlayer. A separate agreement covers the reuse of old comedy and drama material on digital BBC Radio 4 Extra.

Books

WGGB fought long, hard and successfully for the loans-based Public Lending Right (PLR, see page 143) to reimburse authors for books lent in libraries. The scheme is now administered by the British Library and WGGB is represented on its advisory committee.

WGGB has a Books Committee, which works on behalf of book writers and poets. Issues affecting members include self-publishing, print-on-demand services and ebooks.

Theatre

In 1979 WGGB, together with the Theatre Writers' Union, negotiated the first industrial agreement for theatre writers. The Theatres National Committee Agreement (TNC) covers the Royal Shakespeare Company, the Royal National Theatre Company and the English Stage Company at the Royal Court. When their agreement was renegotiated in 2007,

WGGB achieved a long-standing ambition of a minimum fee of £10,000 for a new play; this has since risen to £12,554.

In June 1986, a new agreement was signed with the Theatrical Management Association (now UK Theatre), which covers 95 provincial theatres. In 1993, this agreement was comprehensively revised and included a provision for a year-on-year increase in fees in line with the Retail Price Index. The agreement was renegotiated in 2015.

After many years of negotiation, an agreement was concluded in 1991 between WGGB and the Independent Theatre Council (ITC), which represents 200 of the smaller and fringe theatres as well as educational and touring companies. This agreement was revised in 2002 and the minimum fees are reviewed annually. WGGB is currently talking to the ITC about updating the agreement again and making it more user-friendly.

The WGGB Theatre Committee holds an annual forum for Literary Managers, runs the Olwen Wymark Theatre Encouragement Award scheme and meets with Arts Council England to inform its theatre policy.

Other activities

WGGB is in touch with Government and national institutions wherever and whenever the interests of writers are in question or are being discussed. It holds cross-party Parliamentary lobbies with Equity and the Musicians' Union to ensure that the various artforms they represent are properly cared for. Working with the Federation of Entertainment Unions, WGGB makes its views known to Government bodies on a broader basis. It keeps in touch with Arts Council England, the BBC Trust, Ofcom and other national bodies.

WGGB is an active affiliate of the British Copyright Council, Creators' Rights Alliance and other organisations whose activities are relevant to professional writers. An Anti-Censorship Committee has intervened strongly to protect freedom of speech.

Internationally, WGGB plays a leading role in the International Affiliation of Writers Guilds, which includes the American Guilds East and West, the Canadian Guilds (French and English), and the Irish, Mexican, French, Israeli, South African and New Zealand Guilds. When it is possible to make common cause, the Guilds act accordingly. WGGB takes a leading role in the European Writers' Council and the Fédération des Scénaristes d'Europe. On a European level, WGGB continues to represent writers on issues like copyright, and since the referendum of 2016 has been lobbying government ministers on protecting writers' rights during the Brexit negotiations.

On a day-to-day basis, WGGB gives advice on contracts, and takes up issues that affect the lives of its members as professional writers. Other benefits include access to free and discounted training, exclusive events and discounts, and a dedicated online members' area. Full members are entitled to submit a profile for inclusion in the WGGB online *Find A Writer* directory; pay no joining fee for membership to Writers Guild of America East or West; and are eligible for Cannes accreditation. Regular committee meetings are held by various specialist WGGB Craft Committees. WGGB has active branches across the UK. They organise a range of events such as panel discussions, talks and social occasions.

Each year WGGB presents the much-prized Writers' Guild Awards, covering all the areas in which its members work. These are the only cross-media awards in which writers are honoured by their peers, and as such are highly valued by the recipients.

The writer is an isolated creator in a world in which individual voices are not always heard. WGGB brings writers together to make common cause on many important matters, making full use of its collective strength.

Alliance of Independent Authors

The ALLi is a professional association of self-publishing writers and advisors.

The Alliance of Independent Authors (ALLi) is a global collaborative collective of self-publishing writers. It was founded in 2012 at the London Book Fair by former trade published author and literary agent, Orna Ross, in response to her personal experience of self-publishing and she has been named 'One of the 100 most influential people in publishing' for this work.

ALLi has an Advisory Board of world-class authors and educators, bloggers and service providers, all of whom hold self-publishing in high esteem and all with exceptional knowledge and skills. Their contribution is supplemented by ALLi's global ambassadors, who aid writers to create vibrant self-publishing literary communities in their local areas or online.

A rapidly growing organisation, with members all over the world, ALLi invites 'indie' authors to come together in a spirit of mutual cooperation, empowerment and service to the reading and writing community. As well as encouraging ethics and excellence in the writing, printing, formatting and promotion of self-published books, ALLi advances, supports and advocates for the interests of independent, self-publishing authors everywhere. Its 'Open Up To Indie Authors' Campaign promotes the interests of indie authors within the literary and publishing industries – engaging with booksellers, festivals, prize-giving committees, libraries, book clubs and the media.

ALLi's core mission is the democratisation of writing and publishing.

Membership

The Alliance of Independent Authors
Freeword Centre, 60 Farringdon Road,
London EC1G 2RA
email press@allianceindependentauthors.org
website http://allianceindependentauthors.org, www.SelfPublishingAdvice.org

At ALLi, 'independent' is an inclusive description, including trade-published, self-published and hybrid authors. There are four grades of membership:

Author membership (£75 p.a.) is open to writers or translators of books for adults who have self-published a full-length title (55,000+ words); writers of children's/young adult books who have self-published; and previously trade-published writers or translators who are now preparing to self-publish.

Partner membership (100+ employees £399 p.a.; 10–99 employees £299 p.a.; 1–9 employees £129 p.a.) is open to organisations or sole traders offering necessary services to self-publishing authors and bloggers (e.g. editing, design, publicity, printing, distribution, etc) or an individual who works within an organisation that offers such services. All partner members are vetted by the ALLi watchdog desk.

Professional membership (£99 p.a.) is open to full-time self-publishing authors who earn their living through book sales, though this may be in some cases combined with service to the writing and reading community. All applications for professional membership are carefully assessed.

Associate membership (£55 p.a.) is open to writing/publishing students with an interest in self-publishing and non-published writers (or translators) preparing a book for self-publication.

Benefits include self-publishing advice and guidance; collaboration and contacts; discounts and deals; author promotion and advancement; and campaigns on behalf of indie authors. See website for full information.

Societies, associations and clubs

This list is divided into the following sections: Representation and publishing; Arts councils, Royal Societies and funding; Copyright and licensing; Editorial, journalism and broadcasting; Literacy; Libraries and information; Literary; Art, illustration and photography; Film, theatre and television; Translation; Bibliographical and academic; Members' Clubs; Writers' organisations; and Music. Some also offer prizes and awards (see page 565).

REPRESENTATION AND PUBLISHING

Association of American Publishers

website www.publishers.org
Twitter @AmericanPublish
President & Ceo Maria A. Pallante

AAP is the largest trade association for US books and journal publishers, providing advocacy and communications on behalf of the industry and its priorities nationally and worldwide. Founded 1970.

The Association of Authors' Agents

c/o Watson, Little Ltd, Suite 315 ScreenWorks, 22 Highbury Grove, London N5 2ER
tel 020-7388 7529
website www.agentsassoc.co.uk
President Gordon Wise, *Secretary* Donald Winchester

The AAA exists to provide a forum which allows member agencies to discuss issues arising in the profession; a collective voice for UK literary agencies in public affairs and the media; and a code of conduct to which all members commit themselves. Founded 1974.

Association of Authors' Representatives Inc.

302A West 12th Street, #122, New York, NY 10014
email administrator@aaronline.org
website www.aaronline.org

A professional organisation of over 400 agents who work with book authors and playwrights. Founded 1991.

Association of Canadian Publishers

174 Spadina Avenue, Suite 306, Toronto, Ontario M5T 2C2
tel +1 416-487-6116
email admin@canbook.org
website www.publishers.ca
Executive Director Kate Edwards

Represents approximately 120 Canadian-owned and controlled book publishers from across the country. Founded 1976.

Australian Publishers Association

60–89 Jones Street, Ultimo, NSW 2007
website www.publishers.asn.au
Twitter @AusPublish

The APA is the peak industry body for Australian book, journal and electronic publishers. Founded 1948.

The Australian Society of Authors

Suite C1.06, 22–36 Mountain Street, Ultimo, NSW 2007
tel +61 (0)2 9211 1004
email asa@asauthors.org
website www.asauthors.org

The ASA is the professional association for Australia's authors and illustrators. Provides advocacy, support and advice for authors and illustrators in matters relating to their professional practice. Founded 1963.

Australian Writers' Guild

Level 4, 70 Pitt Street, Sydney, NSW 2000
tel +61 (0)2 9319 0339
email admin@awg.com.au
website www.awg.com.au

The professional association for all performance writers, including writers for film, TV, radio, theatre, video and new media. The AWG is recognised throughout the industry in Australia as being the voice of performance writers. Founded 1962.

The Booksellers Association of the United Kingdom & Ireland Ltd

6 Bell Yard, London WC2A 2JR
tel 020-7421 4640
email mail@booksellers.org.uk
website www.booksellers.org.uk
Managing Director Meryl Hall

A membership organisation for all booksellers in the UK and Ireland, representing over 95% of bookshops. Key services include National Book Tokens and World Book Day. Founded 1895.

Canadian Authors Association

6 West Street North, Suite 203, Orillia, Ontario L3V 5B8
tel +1 705-325-3926
website www.canadianauthors.org
National Chair Margaret A. Hume, *Executive Director* Anita Purcell

Provides writers with a wide variety of programmes, services and resources to help them develop their skills in both the craft and the business of writing. A membership-based organisation for writers in all areas of the profession. Branches across Canada. Founded 1921.

Canadian Publishers' Council

3080 Yonge Street, Toronto, Ontario M4N 3N1
email dswail@pubcouncil.ca
website www.pubcouncil.ca
Executive Director David Swail

Represents the interests of Canadian publishing companies that publish books and other media for schools, colleges and universities, professional and reference markets, the retail and library sectors. Founded 1910.

CANSCAIP (Canadian Society of Children's Authors, Illustrators & Performers)

720 Bathurst Street, Suite 503, Toronto, Ontario M5S 2R4
tel +1 416-515-1559
email office@canscaip.org
website www.canscaip.org
Administrative Director Helena Aalto
Membership $85 p.a.

A non-profit support network for Canadian children's artists. Promotes children's literature and performances throughout Canada and internationally. Founded 1977.

Creative Access

9th Floor, London Television Centre, Upper Ground, London SE1 9LT
email info@creativeaccess.org.uk
website https://creativeaccess.org.uk
Facebook www.facebook.com/CreativeAccessUK
Twitter @_CreativeAccess

Creative Access aims to help young people from black, Asian and other non-white minority ethnic (BAME) backgrounds to secure paid training opportunities in the creative industries and support them into full-time employment. Working with the UK's most successful creative companies in publishing, film, museums and galleries, music, broadcasting, PR, advertising and threatre, Creative Access provides a range of services to help bring diverse talent to organisations, including internships and employer training. Founded 2012.

Creative Industries Federation

22 Endell Street, London WC2H 9AD
tel 020-3771 0350
website www.creativeindustriesfederation.com
Twitter @Creative_Fed

The national organisation for the UK's creative industries, cultural education and arts, spanning advertising and architecture to video games, performance and publishing. The Federation is entirely independent and works with members in towns, cities and the rural economy nationwide, as well as with politicians, mayors and local authorities on a wide range of policy issues. Founded 2014.

Cwlwm Cyhoeddwyr Cymru

Elwyn Williams, Bryntirion Villa, Ffordd Penglais, Aberystwyth SY23 2EU
tel 07866 834109
email elwyn_williams@btinternet.com
website www.bedwen.com
Facebook www.facebook.com/bedwenlyfrau

Represents and promotes Welsh-language publishers and organises Bedwen Lyfrau, the only national Welsh-language book festival, held annually in April. Founded 2002.

Equality in Publishing

The Publishers Association, 50 Southwark Street, London SE1 1UN
website www.publishers.org.uk/activities/inclusivity/equip

Equality in Publishing (EQUIP) is a joint initiative of the Publishers Association and the Independent Publishers Guild to promote inclusivity across UK publishing, bookselling and agenting.

Federation of European Publishers

Rue Montoyer 31 Bte 8, B–1000 Brussels, Belgium
tel +32 2-7701110
email info@fep-fee.eu
website www.fep-fee.eu
President Henrique Mota, *Director* Anne Bergman-Tahon

Represents the interests of European publishers on EU affairs; informs members on the development of EU policies which could affect the publishing industry. Founded 1967.

Independent Publishers Guild

PO Box 12, Llain, Login SA34 0WU
tel (01437) 563335
email info@ipg.uk.com
website www.ipg.uk.com
Chief Executive Bridget Shine
Membership Open to new and established publishers and book packagers

Provides an information and contact network for independent publishers. Also voices concerns of member companies within the book trade. Founded 1962.

International Authors Forum

1st Floor, Barnard's Inn, 86 Fetter Lane, London EC4A 1EN
tel 020-7264 5707
email luke.alcott@internationalauthors.org
website www.internationalauthors.org
Executive Administrator Luke Alcott

A forum for discussion, where authors' organisations can share information and take action on issues affecting them worldwide. Organises events, publications and discussions, and collaborates with other organisations representing authors to promote the importance of creative work financially, socially and culturally. Keeps members up to date with international developments in copyright law.

International Publishers Association

23 Avenue de France, 1202 Geneva, Switzerland
tel +41 22-704 1820
email info@internationalpublishers.org
website www.internationalpublishers.org
President Dr Michiel Kolman, *Secretary-General* José Borghino

The IPA is a federation of national, regional and international publishers associations. It promotes and protects publishing worldwide, with a focus on copyright and freedom to publish. Its membership comprises 76 organisations from 65 countries worldwide. Founded 1896.

Irish Writers Centre

19 Parnell Square, Dublin D01 E102, Republic of Ireland
tel +353 (0)1 872 1302
email info@writerscentre.ie
website www.irishwriterscentre.ie
Director Valerie Bistany, *Manager* Bernadette Greenan

The national resource centre for Irish writers, the Irish Writers Centre supports and promotes writers at all stages of their development. It runs workshops, seminars and events related to the art of writing which are run by established writers across a range of genres. It hosts professional development seminars for writers, and provides space for writers, writing groups and other literary organisations.

Irish Writers' Union/Comhar na Scríbhneoirí

Irish Writers' Centre, 19 Parnell Square, Dublin D01 E102, Republic of Ireland
email info@irishwritersunion.org
website www.irishwritersunion.org
Chairperson Helen Dwyer, *Secretary* Lissa Oliver, *Treasurer* Roy Hunt

The Union aims to advance the cause of writing as a profession, to achieve better remuneration and more favourable conditions for writers and to provide a means for the expression of the collective opinion of writers on matters affecting their profession. Offers free contract advice and negotiation for members. Founded 1986.

New Zealand Association of Literary Agents

PO Box 6292, Dunedin North 9059
email tfs@elseware.co.nz
website www.elseware.co.nz/nzala

Set up to establish standards and guidelines for literary agents operating in New Zealand. All members subscribe to a code of ethics which includes working on commission and not charging upfront fees for promotion or manuscript reading.

New Zealand Writers Guild

PO Box 47 886, Ponsonby, Auckland 1144
tel +64 (0)9 360 1408
email guildhq@nzwg.org.nz
website www.nzwg.org.nz

Represents the interests of New Zealand writers (TV, film, radio and theatre); to establish and improve minimum conditions of work and rates of compensation for writers; to provide professional services for members. Founded 1975.

The Personal Managers' Association Ltd

30 Bristol Gardens, Brighton, BN2 5JR
tel 0845 602 7191
email info@thepma.com
website www.thepma.com

Membership organisation for agents representing talent in film, television and theatre.

Professional Publishers Association

2nd Floor, 35–38 New Bridge Street, London EC4V 6BW
tel 020-7404 4166
email info@ppa.co.uk
website www.ppa.co.uk
Chief Executive Barry McIlheney

Represents around 250 companies, ranging from consumer and online magazine publishers to business-to-business data and information providers, customer magazine publishers and smaller independent companies.

The Publishers Association

First Floor, 50 Southwark Street, London SE1 1UN
tel 020-7378 0504
email mail@publishers.org.uk
website www.publishers.org.uk
Twitter @PublishersAssoc
Ceo Stephen Lotinga, *President* Charlie Redmayne, *Deputy Ceo* Emma House, *Director of Operations* Mark Wharton

The leading representative voice for book, journal, audio and electronic publishers in the UK. The Association has over 100 members and its role is to support publishers in their political, media and industry stakeholder communications. Founded 1896.

Publishers Association of New Zealand

PO Box 33319, Takapuna, Auckland 0740
tel +64 (0)9 280 3212
email catriona@publishers.org.nz
website www.publishers.org.nz
Association Director Catriona Ferguson

PANZ represents book, educational and digital publishers in New Zealand. Members include both the largest international publishers and companies in the independent publishing community.

Publishers' Association of South Africa

House Vincent, Wynberg Mews, 1st Floor, Unit 104, Brodie Road, Wynberg
tel +27 (0)21 762 9083
email pasa@publishsa.co.za
website www.publishsa.co.za

PASA is the largest publishing industry body in South Africa and is committed to creativity, literacy, the free flow of ideas and encouraging a culture of reading. It aims to promote and protect the rights and responsibilities of the publishing sector in South Africa.

Publishers Publicity Circle

email publisherspublicitycircle@gmail.com
Secretary/Treasurer Madeline Toy

Enables all book publicists to meet and share information regularly. Monthly meetings provide a forum for press journalists, TV and radio researchers and producers to meet publicists collectively. Awards are presented for the best PR campaigns. Monthly newsletter includes recruitment advertising. Founded 1955.

Publishing Ireland/Foilsiú Éireann

63 Patrick Street, Dun Laoghaire,
Co Dublin A96 WF25, Republic of Ireland
tel +353 (0)1 6394868
email info@publishingireland.com
website www.publishingireland.com

Publishing Ireland enables publishers to share expertise and resources in order to benefit from opportunities and solve problems that are of common concern to all. It comprises most of the major publishing houses in Ireland with a mixture of trade, general and academic publishers as members.

Publishing Scotland

Scott House, 10 South St Andrew Street,
Edinburgh EH2 2AZ
tel 0131 228 6866
email enquiries@publishingscotland.org
website www.publishingscotland.org
Chief Executive Marion Sinclair

A network for trade, training and development in the Scottish publishing industry. Founded 1973.

Society of Artists Agents

website www.saahub.com

Formed to promote professionalism in the illustration industry and to forge closer links between clients and artists through an agreed set of guidelines. The Society believes in an ethical approach through proper terms and conditions, thereby protecting the interests of the artists and clients. Founded 1992.

The Society of Authors – see page 519

Society of Young Publishers

c/o The Publishers Association, First Floor,
50 Southwark Street, London SE1 1UN
email sypchair@thesyp.org.uk
website www.thesyp.org.uk
Twitter @SYP_UK
Membership Open to anyone employed in publishing or hoping to be soon, catering specifically to those in the first 10 years of their career; £30 p.a. standard; £24 student/unwaged; £18 digital only

Organises monthly events which offer the chance to network, develop skills and hear senior figures talk on topics of key importance to the publishing industry. Organises industry mentor schemes, book clubs and two annual conferences. Publishes a quarterly print magazine *InPrint*. Provides a job database advertising the latest vacancies and internships; online forum The Network; and a blog, PressForward. Has branches in London, Oxford, Scotland, Ireland and North (Manchester/Leeds), overseen by a UK steering committee. Founded 1949.

Theatre Writers' Union – see page 522

Women in Publishing

website www.womeninpublishing.org.uk

Promotes the status of women within publishing; encourages networking and mutual support among women; provides a forum for the discussion of ideas, trends and subjects to women in the trade; offers advice on publishing careers; supports and publicises women's achievements and successes. Each year WiP presents two awards: the Pandora Award is given in recognition of significant and sustained contribution to the publishing industry, and the New Venture Award is given for pioneering work on behalf of under-represented groups in society. Founded 1979.

Writers Guild of America, East Inc.

250 Hudson Street, 7th Floor, New York, NY 10013
tel +1 212-767-7800
website www.wgaeast.org/

WGAE represents writers in screen, TV and new media for collective bargaining. It provides member services including pension and health, as well as educational and professional activities. Founded 1954.

Writers Guild of America, West Inc.

7000 West 3rd Street, Los Angeles, CA 90048
tel +1 323-951-4000
website www.wga.org

WGAW represents and services 12,000 writers in film, broadcast, cable and multimedia industries for purposes of collective bargaining, contract administration and other services, and functions to protect and advance the economic, professional and creative interests of writers. Bi-monthly publication, *Written By*, published in January, February/March, April/May, Summer, September/October, November/December. Available by subscription. Founded 1933.

Writers Guild of Canada

366 Adelaide Street West, Suite 401, Toronto, Ontario M5V 1R9
tel +1 416-979-7907; toll free +1-800-567-9974
email info@wgc.ca
website www.writersguildofcanada.com

Represents professional screenwriters. Negotiates and administers collective agreements with independent producers and broadcasters. The Guild also publishes *Canadian Screenwriter* magazine.

WGGB - The Writers' Union – see page 522

Writers Guild of Ireland

Art House, Curved Street, Temple Bar, Dublin 2, Republic of Ireland
tel +353 (0)1 6709970
email info@script.ie
website http://script.ie/
Chairperson Thomas McLaughlin, *Ceo* David Kavanagh

Represents writers' interests in theatre, radio and screen. Founded 1969.

The Writers' Union of Canada

600–460 Richmond Street West, Suite 600, Toronto, Ontario M5V 1Y1
tel +1 416-703-8982
email info@writersunion.ca
website www.writersunion.ca

National arts service organisation for professionally published book authors. Founded 1973.

ARTS COUNCILS, ROYAL SOCIETIES AND FUNDING

Arts Council England

tel 0845 300 6200
email enquiries@artscouncil.org.uk
website www.artscouncil.org.uk

The national development agency for the arts in England, distributing public money from Government and the National Lottery. Arts Council England's main funding programme is Grants for the Arts, which is open to individuals, arts organisations, national touring companies and other people who use the arts in their work. Founded 1946.

East

24 Brooklands Avenue, Cambridge CB2 8BU
tel 0845 300 6200

East Midlands

Room 005-005A, Arkwright Building, Nottingham Trent University, Burton Street, Nottingham NG1 4BU
tel 0845 300 6200

London

21 Bloomsbury Street, London WC1B 3HF
tel 0845 300 6200

North East

Central Square, Forth Street, Newcastle upon Tyne NE1 3PJ
tel 0845 300 6200

North West

The Hive, 49 Lever Street, Manchester M1 1FN
tel 0845 300 6200

South East

New England House, New England Street, Brighton BN1 4GH
tel 0845 300 6200

South West

Third Floor, St Thomas Court, Thomas Lane, Bristol BS1 6JG
tel 0845 300 6200

West Midlands

82 Granville Street, Birmingham B1 2LH
tel 0845 300 6200

Yorkshire

1st Floor South, Marshall's Mill, Marshall Street, Leeds LS11 9YJ
tel 0845 300 6200

Arts Council/An Chomhairle Ealaíon

70 Merrion Square, Dublin D02 NY52, Republic of Ireland
tel +353 (0)1 6180200
website www.artscouncil.ie

The national development agency for the arts in Ireland. Founded 1951.

Arts Council of Northern Ireland

1 The Sidings, Antrim Road, Lisburn BT28 3AJ
tel 028-9262 3555
email info@artscouncil-ni.org
website www.artscouncil-ni.org
Chief Executive Roisín McDonough

Promotes and encourages the arts throughout Northern Ireland. Artists in drama, dance, music and jazz, literature, the visual arts, traditional arts and community arts can apply for support for specific schemes and projects. The value of the grant will be set according to the aims of the programme. Artists of all disciplines and in all types of working practice, who have made a contribution to artistic activities in Northern Ireland for a minimum period of one year within the last five years, are eligible.

Arts Council of Wales

Bute Place, Cardiff CF10 5AL
tel 0845 873 4900
email info@arts.wales
website www.arts.wales

National organisation with specific responsibility for the funding and development of the arts in Wales; operates in both English and Welsh languages. Arts Council of Wales receives funding from the Welsh Government and also distributes National Lottery funds for the arts in Wales. Makes grants to support arts activities and facilities, including annual revenue grants to full-time arts organisations such as Literature Wales and to individual artists or projects. Wales Arts International is the international arm of the Arts Council of Wales and works in partnership with the British Council, which works to promote knowledge about contemporary arts and culture from Wales and encourages international exchange and collaboration.

North Wales Regional Office
Princes Park II, Princes Drive, Colwyn Bay LL29 8PL
tel (01492) 533440

Mid and West Wales Regional Office
The Mount, 18 Queen Street, Carmarthen SA31 1JT
tel 0845 873 4900

Central Office
Bute Place, Cardiff CF10 5AL
tel 0845 873 4900

Australia Council

PO Box 788, Strawberry Hills, NSW 2012
tel +61 (0)2 9215 9000
website www.australiacouncil.gov.au
Ceo Tony Grybowski

Provides a broad range of support for the arts in Australia, embracing music, theatre, literature, visual arts, crafts, Aboriginal arts, community and new media arts.

British Academy

10–11 Carlton House Terrace, London SW1Y 5AH
tel 020-7969 5200
email enquiries@britac.ac.uk
website www.britishacademy.ac.uk
Twitter @britac_news
Chief Executive Alun Evans

The British Academy is the voice of humanities and social sciences. The Academy is an independent fellowship of world-leading scholars and researchers; a funding body for research, nationally and internationally; and a forum for debate and engagement. It produces a wide range of publications, for academic and more general readerships.

The British Council

10 Spring Gardens, London SW1A 2BN
tel 020-7389 3194
email general.enquiries@britishcouncil.org
website www.britishcouncil.org
Twitter @BritishCouncil
Chief Executive Ciarán Devane, *Director of Arts* Graham Sheffield

The British Council connects people worldwide with learning opportunities and creative ideas from the UK. It has 6,000 staff in offices, teaching centres, libraries and information and resource centres in the UK and over 100 countries and territories worldwide. Working in close collaboration with book trade associations, British Council offices participate in major international book fairs.

The British Council Literature Department works with hundreds of writers and literature partners in the UK and collaborates with offices overseas to broker relationships and create activities which link artists and cultural institutions around the world. The Department works with writers, publishers, producers, translators and other sector professionals across literature, publishing and education.

The Visual Arts Department promotes the UK's visual arts sector internationally. It stages and supports contemporary art projects in areas of the developing world via exhibitions, training and development, professional study visits and the management of the British Pavilion at the Venice Biennale and an expansive collection of British art.

Creative Scotland

Waverley Gate, 2–4 Waterloo Place, Edinburgh EH1 3EG
tel 0330 333 2000 (switchboard); 0345 603 6000 (enquiries line)
email enquiries@creativescotland.com
website www.creativescotland.com

Creative Scotland is the public body that supports the arts, screen and creative industries across all parts of Scotland on behalf of everyone who lives, works or visits there. Through distributing funding from the Scottish Government and the National Lottery, Creative Scotland enables people and organisations to work in and experience the arts, screen and creative industries in Scotland by helping others to develop great ideas and bring them to life.

The Gaelic Books Council/Comhairle nan Leabhraichean

32 Mansfield Street, Glasgow G11 5QP
tel 0141 337 6211
email rosemary@gaelicbooks.org
website www.gaelicbooks.org
Director Rosemary Ward

Stimulates Scottish Gaelic publishing by awarding publication grants for new books, commissions new works from established and emerging authors and provides editorial advice and guidance to Gaelic writers and publishers. Has a bookshop in Glasgow that stocks all Gaelic and Gaelic-related books in print. All stock is listed on the website. Founded 1968.

Guernsey Arts Commission

North Esplanade, St Peter Port, Guernsey GY1 2LQ
tel (01481) 709747
email info@arts.gg

The Commission's aim is to help promote, develop and support the arts in Guernsey through exhibitions, a community arts programme and public events.

Literature Wales

Glyn Jones Centre, Wales Millennium Centre, Bute Place, Cardiff CF10 5AL
tel 029-2047 2266
email post@literaturewales.org
website www.literaturewales.org
Facebook www.facebook.com/LlenCymruLitWales/
Twitter @LitWales
Chief Executive Lleucu Siencyn

The National Company for the development of literature in Wales. It works collaboratively, bilingually, and in a wide range of communities.

The organisation's many projects and activities include Wales Book of the Year, the National Poet of Wales, Bardd Plant Cymru and Young People's Laureate Wales, Literary Tourism initiatives, Writers on Tour funding scheme, creative writing courses at Tŷ Newydd Writing Centre, Services for Writers (including bursaries and mentoring) and Young People's Writing Squads. Works with the support of the Arts Council of Wales and the Welsh Government.

Literature Works

Peninsula Arts, Plymouth University, Roland Levinsky Building, Drake Circus, Plymouth PL4 8AA
tel (01752) 585073
email info@literatureworks.org.uk
website www.literatureworks.org.uk

Literature Works is the strategic literature charity for South West England and is a national portfolio organisation of Arts Council England. It helps develop both writers and readers, providing a central resource for literature in the South West. It supports the wider literature sector through large-scale projects and evaluation. A small grants scheme known as the Annual Fund supports community-based literature initiatives around the region.

Royal Academy of Arts

Burlington House, Piccadilly, London W1J 0BD
tel 020-7300 8000
website www.royalacademy.org.uk
President Christopher Le Brun, *Keeper* Eileen Cooper

Royal Academicians are elected from the most distinguished artists in the UK. Holds major loan exhibitions throughout the year including the Annual Summer Exhibition (June–Aug). Also runs Royal Academy Schools for 60 postgraduate students in painting and sculpture.

Royal Birmingham Society of Artists

RBSA Gallery, 4 Brook Street, St Paul's, Birmingham B3 1SA
tel 0121 236 4353
email rbsagallery@rbsa.org.uk
website www.rbsa.org.uk
Facebook www.facebook.com/pages/Royal-Birmingham-Society-of-Artists/143050305709122
Twitter @rbsgallery
Membership Friends £34 p.a.

The Royal Birmingham Society of Artists (RBSA) is an artist-led charity, which supports artists and promotes engagement with the visual arts through a range of exhibitions, workshops and events. The Society is one of the oldest in the UK. It owns and runs its own exhibition venue, the RBSA Gallery, which has a changing programme of exhibitions including various yearly, two-yearly and three-yearly open exhibitions, providing opportunities for all artists working in all media. The Gallery is open seven days a week and admission is free.

Royal Institute of Oil Painters

17 Carlton House Terrace, London SW1Y 5BD
tel 020-7930 6844
email enquiries@theroi.org.uk
website www.theroi.org.uk
President Tim Benson

Promotes and encourages the art of painting in oils. Open Annual Exhibition at the Mall Galleries, The Mall, London SW1.

Royal Institute of Painters in Water Colours

17 Carlton House Terrace, London SW1Y 5BD
tel 020-7930 6844
email info@mallgalleries.com
website www.royalinstituteofpaintersinwatercolours.org
Facebook www.facebook.com/RIwatercolours
Twitter @RIwatercolours
President Rosa Sepple
Membership Elected from approved candidates' list

Promotes the appreciation of watercolour painting in its traditional and contemporary forms, primarily by means of an annual exhibition at the Mall Galleries, The Mall, London SW1 of members' and non-members' work and also by members' exhibitions at selected venues in Britain and abroad. The Royal Institute of Painters in Water Colours is one of the oldest watercolour societies in the world. Founded 1831.

The Royal Musical Association

Dr Jeffrey Dean, 4 Chandos Road,
Chorlton-cum-Hardy, Manchester M21 0ST
tel 0161 861 7542
email exec@rma.ac.uk
website www.rma.ac.uk
Twitter @RoyalMusical
President Prof. Simon McVeigh
Membership See website for details

Promotes the investigation and discussion of subjects connected with the art and science of music. Sponsors conferences, study days, and research training events. Publishes the *Journal of the Royal Musical Association*, *Royal Musical Association Research Chronicle*, and the RMA Monographs series. Founded 1874.

The Royal Photographic Society

Fenton House, 122 Wells Road, Bath BA2 3AH
tel (01225) 325733
email reception@rps.org
website www.rps.org
Facebook www.facebook.com/royalphotographicsociety
Twitter @The_RPS
Membership UK £120; overseas £106; discounts for over 65s, under 25s, students, the disabled

The Society promotes photography in all its forms and supports and encourages individuals to develop their skills, which it does through exhibitions, workshops and a distinctions and qualifications programme. It also acts as an advocate for photography and photographers and speaks to the media on relevant matters. Membership is open to anyone with an interest in photography. Founded 1853.

The Royal Scottish Academy of Art and Architecture

The Mound, Edinburgh EH2 2EL
tel 0131 225 6671
website www.royalscottishacademy.org
Director Colin R. Greenslade

Led by eminent artists and architects, the Royal Scottish Academy (RSA) is an independent voice for cultural advocacy and one of the largest supporters of artists in Scotland. It administers a number of scholarships, awards and residencies and has an historic collection of Scottish artworks and an archive, recognised by the Scottish Government as being of national significance. The Academy cherishes its independence from local or national government funding, relying instead on bequests, legacies, sponsorship and earned income. For information on open submission exhibitions, artist scholarships and residencies, or to discuss making a bequest to the Academy visit the website. Founded 1826.

The Royal Society

6–9 Carlton House Terrace, London SW1Y 5AG
tel 020-7451 2500
email library@royalsociety.org
website royalsociety.org
Facebook www.facebook.com/theroyalsociety
Twitter @royalsociety
President Sir Venki Ramakrishnan PRS, *Treasurer* Prof. Andrew Hopper FRS, *Biological Secretary* Sir John Skehel FRS, *Physical Secretary* Prof. Alex Halliday FRS, *Foreign Secretary* Prof. Richard Catlow FRS, *Executive Director* Dr Julie Maxton

The independent scientific academy of the UK and the Commonwealth, dedicated to promoting excellence in science.

Royal Society for the Encouragement of Arts, Manufactures and Commerce (RSA)

8 John Adam Street, London WC2N 6EZ
tel 020-7930 5115
email general@rsa.org.uk
website www.thersa.org

The RSA works to remove the barriers to social progress, driving ideas, innovation and social change through an ambitious programme of projects, events and lectures. Supported by over 27,000 Fellows, an international network of influencers and innovators from every field and background across the UK and overseas. Welcomes women and men of any nationality and background who will support the organisation's aims. Its activities are detailed in the *RSA Journal*. Founded 1754.

Royal Society of British Artists

email info@royalsocietyofbritishartists.org.uk
website www.royalsocietyofbritishartists.org.uk
Hon. Secretary Judith Gardner

Incorporated by Royal Charter for the purpose of encouraging the study and practice of the arts of painting, sculpture and architectural design. Annual Open Exhibition at the Mall Galleries, The Mall, London SW1, open to artists working in any two- or three-dimensional medium.

Royal Society of Literature

Somerset House, Strand, London WC2R 1LA
tel 020-7845 4679
email info@rsliterature.org
website www.rsliterature.org
Membership £50 p.a.; £30 for those aged 18–30

The RSL is Britain's national charity for the advancement of literature. It encourages and honours writers, engages people in appreciating literature and acts as a voice for the value of literature through its events programme, awards and prizes and schools outreach programme. Founded 1820.

Royal Society of Marine Artists

17 Carlton House Terrace, London SW1Y 5BD
tel 020-7930 6844
email rmsa.contact@gmail.com
website www.rsma-web.co.uk

The aim of the society is to promote and encourage the highest standards of marine art and welcomes submissions for their Annual Open Exhibition at The Mall Galleries in London, which is usually held in October (more information at www.mallgalleries.org.uk). Membership is achieved by a consistent record of success in having work selected and hung at this event and ultimately by election by the members.

The Royal Society of Miniature Painters, Sculptors and Gravers

email info@royal-miniature-society.org.uk
website www.royal-miniature-society.org.uk
Twitter @royalminiature
President Rosalind Pierson, *Executive Secretary* Claire Hucker
Membership By selection and standard of work over a period of years (ARMS associate, RMS full member)

Annual Open Exhibition in November at the Mall Galleries, The Mall, London SW1. Submission date 18 November; entry forms available from the website. Applications and enquiries to the Executive Secretary. Founded 1895.

Royal Society of Painter-Printmakers

Bankside Gallery, 48 Hopton Street, London SE1 9JH
tel 020-7928 7521
email info@banksidegallery.com
website www.banksidegallery.com
website www.re-printmakers.com

Open to British and overseas artists. An election of Associates is held annually; for details check the website. New members are elected by the Council of the Society based on the quality of their work alone, in a tradition reaching back over one hundred years. Holds three members' exhibitions per year. Founded 1880.

Royal Society of Portrait Painters

17 Carlton House Terrace, London SW1Y 5BD
tel 020-7930 6844
email enquiries@therp.co.uk
website www.therp.co.uk
website www.mallgalleries.org.uk
President Richard Foster

Annual Exhibition at the Mall Galleries, The Mall, London SW1, of members' work and work drawn from an open section. Six artists' awards are made: the Ondaatje Prize for Portraiture (£10,000), the De Laszlo Prize (£3,000), the Prince of Wales's Award for Portrait Drawing (£2,000), the Changing Faces Prize (£2,000), the Burke's Peerage Foundation Award (£2,000), Smallwood Architects' Contextual Portraiture Prize (£1,000). A commissions consultancy service to help those wishing to commission portraits runs throughout the year. Founded 1891.

Royal Watercolour Society

Bankside Gallery, 48 Hopton Street, London SE1 9JH
tel 020-7928 7521
email info@banksidegallery.com
website www.royalwatercoloursociety.co.uk
President Jill Leman PRWS, HON HE
Membership Open to British and overseas artists; election of Associates held annually. Friends membership is open to all those interested in watercolour painting.

Arranges lectures and courses on watercolour painting; holds an annual open exhibition in February. Exhibitions in the spring and autumn. Founded 1804.

Royal West of England Academy

Queens Road, Clifton, Bristol BS8 1PX
tel 0117 973 5129
email info@rwa.org.uk
website www.rwa.org.uk
Director Alison Bevan

An art academy/gallery/museum and drawing school whose objectives are to advance the education of the public in the fine arts and in particular to promote the appreciation and practice of the fine arts and to encourage and develop talent in the fine arts. Founded 1844.

Welsh Books Council/Cyngor Llyfrau Cymru

Castell Brychan, Aberystwyth, Ceredigion SY23 2JB
tel (01970) 624151
email castellbrychan@books.wales
website www.books.wales
website www.gwales.com
Ceo Helgard Krause

A national body funded directly by the Welsh Government which provides a focus for the publishing industry in Wales. Awards grants for publishing in Welsh and English. Provides services to the trade in the fields of editing, design, marketing and distribution. The Council is a key enabling institution in the world of books and provides services and information in this field to all who are associated with it. Founded 1961.

COPYRIGHT AND LICENSING

Australian Copyright Council

PO Box 1986, Strawberry Hills, NSW 2012
tel +61 (0)2 9101 2377
email info@copyright.org.au
website www.copyright.org.au

Facebook www.facebook.com/AustralianCopyrightCouncil
Twitter @AusCopyright
Chief Executive Officer Grant McAvaney

Provides easily accessible and affordable practical information, legal advice, education and forums on Australian copyright law for content creators and consumers. It represents the peak bodies for professional artists and content creators working in Australia's creative industries and Australia's major copyright collecting societies, including the Australian Society of Authors, the Australian Writers' Guild and the Australian Publishers Association.

The Council advocates for the contribution of creators to Australia's culture and economy; the importance of copyright for the common good. It works to promote understanding of copyright law and its application, lobby for appropriate law reform and foster collaboration between content creators and consumers. Founded 1968.

Authors' Licensing and Collecting Society Ltd – see page 707

British Copyright Council

2 Pancras Square, London N1C 4AG
tel 020-3290 1444
email info@britishcopyright.org
website www.britishcopyright.org
Vice-President Geoffrey Adams, *President of Honour* Maureen Duffy, *Chairman* Trevor Cook

Aims to defend and foster the true principles of copyright and its acceptance throughout the world, to bring together bodies representing all who are interested in the protection of such copyright, and to keep watch on any legal or other changes which may require an amendment of the law.

Copyright Clearance Center Inc.

222 Rosewood Drive, Danvers, MA 01923, USA
tel +1 978-646-2600
email info@copyright.com
website www.copyright.com

Aims to remove the complexity from copyright issues and make it easy for businesses and academic institutions to use copyright-protected materials while compensating publishers and content creators for their work.

The Copyright Licensing Agency Ltd – see page 705

DACS (Design and Artists Copyright Society) – see page 709

Federation Against Copyright Theft Ltd

Regal House, 70 London Road, Twickenham, Middlesex TW1 3QS
tel 020-8891 1217
email contact@fact-uk.org.uk
website www.fact-uk.org.uk
Twitter @factuk

FACT protects the interests of its members and others against infringement in the UK of copyright in cinematograph films, TV programmes and all forms of audiovisual recording. Founded 1982.

The Irish Copyright Licensing Agency

63 Patrick Street, Dun Laoghaire, Co Dublin A96 WF25, Republic of Ireland
tel +353 (0)1 6624211
email info@icla.ie
website www.icla.ie
Executive Director Samantha Holman

Licences schools and other users of copyright material to photocopy or scan extracts of such material, and distributes the monies collected to the authors and publishers whose works have been copied. Founded 1992.

Picture Industry Collecting Society for Effective Licensing (PICSEL)

112 Western Road, Brighton, East Sussex BN1 2AB
email info@picsel.org.uk
website www.picsel.org.uk

PICSEL is a not-for-profit organisation that ensures that all visual artists, creators and representative rights holders of images receive fair payment for various uses of their works. It works to ensure that all licence fees collected are distributed equitably, efficiently and in a transparent manner. Founded 2016.

EDITORIAL, JOURNALISM AND BROADCASTING

American Society for Indexing

1628 E. Southern Ave. 9-223, Tempe, AZ 85282, USA
tel +1 480-245-6750
email info@asindexing.org
website www.asindexing.org
Executive Director Gwen Henson

Increases awareness of the value of high-quality indexes and indexing; offers members access to educational resources that enable them to strengthen their indexing performance; keeps members up to date on indexing technology; advocates for the professional interests of indexers.

Association of American Correspondents in London

PO Box 645, Pinner HA5 9JJ
email secretary@theaacl.co.uk
website www.theaacl.co.uk

An independent, not-for-profit organisation whose members represent North American media organisations with staff based in London.

Association of Freelance Editors, Proofreaders and Indexers of Ireland

Contact 1 Averill Buchanan (Chair)
tel 07875 857278
email averill@averillbuchanan.com
Contact 2 Kate Murphy (Treasurer/Secretary)
tel +353 (0)87 2363922
email kate@katemurphy-indexing.ie
Contact 3 Bernadette Kearns (Vice-Chair)
+353 (0)85 8887253
email booknannyeditor@gmail.com
website www.afepi.ie
Twitter @AFEPI_Ireland

AFEPI protects the interests of members, and serves as a point of contact between publishers/independent authors and members. Membership is available to experienced professional editors, proofreaders and indexers. For services for publishers and authors, see our directory of freelance professional editors, proofreaders and indexers based in Ireland and Northern Ireland. Founded 1985

British Association of Journalists

website www.bajunion.org.uk

Non-political trade union for professional journalists. Aims to protect and promote the industrial and professional interests of journalists. Founded 1992.

British Guild of Agricultural Journalists

444 Westwood Heath Road, Coventry CV4 8AA
tel 07584 022909
email gajsec@gmail.com
website www.gaj.org.uk
Twitter @gajinfo
President Lord Curry of Kirkharle, *Chairman* Ben Briggs, *General Secretary* Nikki Robertson
Membership £68 p.a.

The Guild promotes high standards among journalists, photographers and communicators who specialise in agriculture, horticulture, food production and other rural affairs, and contributes towards a better understanding of agriculture. Founded 1944.

British Society of Magazine Editors

137 Hale Lane, Edgware, Middlesex HA8 9QP
tel 020-8906 4664
email admin@bsme.com
website www.bsme.com
Twitter @bsmeinfo

The only society in the UK exclusively for magazine and digital editors. Represents the needs and views of editors and acts as a voice for the industry.

Campaign for Press and Broadcasting Freedom

2nd Floor, Vi & Garner Smith House,
23 Orford Road, London E17 9NL
tel 07729 846146
email freepress@cpbf.org.uk
website www.cpbf.org.uk

Organisation dedicated to the promotion of diverse, democratic and accountable media. Founded 1979.

The Chartered Institute of Journalists

2 Dock Offices, Surrey Quays Road,
London SE16 2XU
tel 020-7252 1187
email memberservices@cioj.co.uk
website www.cioj.co.uk

The senior organisation of the profession, the Chartered Institute has accumulated funds for the assistance of members. A Freelance Division links editors and publishers with freelances and a Directory is published of freelance writers, with their specialisations. There are special sections for broadcasters, motoring correspondents, public relations practitioners and overseas members. Occasional contributors to the media may qualify for election as Affiliates. Founded in 1884; incorporated by Royal Charter in 1890.

Editors' and Proofreaders' Alliance of Northern Ireland

tel 07875 857278
email info@epani.org.uk
website www.epani.org.uk
Twitter @epa_ni
Coordinator Averill Buchanan

The Alliance aims to establish and maintain high professional standards in editorial skills in Northern Ireland. Membership is free, but a small fee is charged for inclusion in EPANI's online directory. For services for authors, see our directory of freelance professional editors, proofreaders and indexers based in Northern Ireland. Founded 2011.

European Broadcasting Union

L'Ancienne Route 17A, CH–1218 Grand-Saconnex, Geneva, Switzerland
tel +41 (0)22-717 2111
email ebu@ebu.ch
website www.ebu.ch
Twitter @EBU_HQ
Director General Noel Curran

The European Broadcasting Union (EBU) is the world's foremost alliance of public service media (PSM). Its mission is to make PSM indispensable. It has 73 members in 56 countries in Europe, and an additional 33 Associates in Asia, Africa and the Americas. Members operate over 2,000 television and radio channels, broadcasting in more than 120 different languages and reach audiences of more than one billion people around the world. EBU's television and radio services operate under the trademarks of Eurovision and Euroradio.

Foreign Press Association in London

website www.fpalondon.net

The first and oldest association of foreign journalists in the world. All major news outlets are represented. Provides access and accreditation to a wide variety of events in the UK. See website for membership details. Founded 1888.

Association of Freelance Writers

8–10 Dutton Street, Manchester M3 ILE
tel 0161 819 9922
email studentservices@writersbureau.com
website www.writersbureau.com/writing/association-of-freelance-writers.htm
Membership £24.99 p.a.

Members to the association receive resources to help with their writing career including: a membership card identifying them as a freelance writer, free online course, bi-annual newsletter, plus discounts on writing resources, competitions, courses, self-publishing and more.

Independent Press Standards Organisation

Gate House, 1 Farringdon Street, London EC4M 7LG
tel 0300 1232220
email inquiries@ipso.co.uk
website www.ipso.co.uk

IPSO is the independent regulator of the newspaper and magazine industry. It exists to promote and uphold the highest professional standards of journalism in the UK and to support members of the public in seeking redress where they believe that the Editors' Code of Practice has been breached.

Journalists' Charity

Dickens House, 35 Wathen Road, Dorking, Surrey RH4 1JY
tel (01306) 887511
email enquiries@journalistscharity.org.uk
website www.journalistscharity.org.uk
Director David Ilott

For the relief of hardship amongst journalists, their widows and dependants. Financial assistance and retirement housing are provided.

Magazines Canada (Canadian Magazine Publishers Association)

425 Adelaide Street West, Suite 700, Toronto, Ontario M5V 3C1
tel +1 416-504-0274
email info@magazinescanada.ca
website www.magazinescanada.ca
Chief Executive Officer Matthew Holmes

The national trade association representing Canadian-owned, Canadian-content consumer, cultural, speciality, professional and business media magazines.

The Media Society

Broadgate Tower, 3rd Floor, 20 Primrose Street, London EC2A 2RS
email admin@themediasociety.com
website www.themediasociety.com
Hon. President Peter York
Membership £60 p.a., retired members £45 p.a., students £5 p.a.

Exists to promote and encourage collective and independent research into the standards, performance, organisation and economics of the media and hold regular discussions and debates on subjects of topical or special interest and concern to print and broadcast journalists and others working in or with the media. Up to 15 evening debates and events organised throughout the year. Founded 1973.

Mediawatch-UK

3 Willow House, Kennington Road, Ashford, Kent TN24 0NR
tel (01233) 633936
email info@mediawatchuk.org
website www.mediawatchuk.org
website mediawatch-UK.blogspot.com
Facebook www.facebook.com/MediawatchUK
Twitter @mediawatch_uk
Director Helen Lewington
Membership £15 p.a.

Aims to encourage viewers and listeners to react effectively to broadcast content; to initiate and stimulate public discussion and parliamentary debate concerning the effects of broadcasting, and other mass media, on the individual, family and society; to work for effective legislation to control obscenity and pornography in the media. Founded 1965.

National Association of Press Agencies

c/o Cavendish Press (Manchester) Ltd, 5th Floor, The Landing, BLUE, MediaCityUK, Salford Quays, Manchester M50 2ST
email enquiries@napa.org.uk
website www.napa.org.uk
Membership £250 p.a.

NAPA is network of independent, established and experienced press agencies serving newspapers, magazines, TV and radio networks. Founded 1983.

National Council for the Training of Journalists

The New Granary, Station Road, Newport, Essex CB11 3PL
tel (01799) 544014
email info@nctj.com
website www.nctj.com
Facebook www.facebook.com/nctjpage

Twitter @NCTJ_news

The NCTJ is a registered charity and awarding body which provides multimedia journalism training. Full-time accredited courses run at various colleges/ independent providers/universities in the UK. Distance learning programmes and short courses are also available.

National Union of Journalists

Headland House, 72 Acton Street,
London WC1X 9NB
tel 020-7843 3700
email info@nuj.org.uk
website www.nuj.org.uk

Trade union for journalists and photographers, including freelances, with over 30,000 members and branches in the UK, Republic of Ireland, Paris, Brussels and the Netherlands. It covers the newspaper press, news agencies, magazines, broadcasting, periodical and book publishing, public relations departments and consultancies, information services and new media. The NUJ mediates disputes, organises campaigns, provides training and general and legal advice. Official publications: *The Journalist* (bi-monthly), e-newsletters called *NUJ Active* and *NUJ Informed*, the online *Freelance Directory* and *Freelance Fees Guide*, *The NUJ Ethical Code of Conduct* and policy pamphlets and submissions.

News Media Association

292 Vauxhall Bridge Road, London SW1V 1AE
tel 020-7963 7480
email nma@newsmediauk.org
website www.newsmediauk.org

Serves and promotes the shared interests of national, regional and local news media publishers in the UK by working across a broad range of issues which affect the industry.

Scottish Newspaper Society

17 Polwarth Grove, Edinburgh EH11 1LY
email info@scotns.org.uk
website www.scotns.org.uk
Represents the interests of the Scottish newspaper industry.

Society for Editors and Proofreaders (SfEP)

Apsley House, 176 Upper Richmond Road,
London SW15 2SH
tel 020-8785 6155
email administrator@sfep.org.uk
website www.sfep.org.uk
Facebook www.facebook.com/EditProof
Twitter @TheSfEP

The SfEP works to promote high editorial standards and achieve recognition of its members' professional status, through local and national meetings, an annual conference, discussion forums and a regular e-magazine. The Society publishes an online directory of experienced members. It also runs online courses and workshops and offers in-house training, which help newcomers to acquire basic editorial skills, and enable experienced editors and proofreaders to update their skills or broaden their competence. Training also covers aspects of professional practice and business for the self-employed. The Society supports moves towards recognised standards of training and accreditation for editors and proofreaders and is working towards chartership. It has close links with the Publishing Training Centre and the Society of Indexers, is represented on the BSI Technical Committee dealing with copy preparation and proof correction (BS 5261), and works to foster good relations with all relevant bodies and organisations in the UK and worldwide. Founded 1988.

Society of Editors

University Centre, Granta Place, Mill Lane,
Cambridge CB2 1RU
tel (01223) 304080
email office@societyofeditors.org
website www.societyofeditors.org
Director Ian Murray
Membership up to £230 p.a. depending on category

Formed from the merger of the Guild of Editors and the Association of British Editors, the Society of Editors has members in national, regional and local newspapers, magazines, broadcasting and digital media, journalism education and media law. It campaigns for media freedom, self regulation, the public's right to know and the maintenance of standards in journalism.

Society of Indexers – see page 668

Society of Women Writers & Journalists (SWWJ)

email enquiries@swwj.co.uk
website www.swwj.co.uk

The SWWJ aims to encourage literary achievement, to uphold professional standards, to promote social contact with fellow writers and to defend the dignity and prestige of the writing profession in all its aspects. Founded 1894.

Sports Journalists' Association

tel 020-8916 2234
email info@sportjournalists.co.uk
website www.sportsjournalists.co.uk

The SJA represents sports journalists across the country and is Britain's voice in international sporting affairs. Offers advice to members covering major events, acts as a consultant to organisers of major sporting events on media requirements. Member of the BOA Press Advisory Committee. Founded 1948.

Voice of the Listener & Viewer Ltd

The Old Rectory Business Centre, Springhead Road, Northfleet DA11 8HN
tel (01474) 338716
email info@vlv.org.uk
website www.vlv.org.uk
Twitter @vlvuk
Administrator Sue Washbrook

VLV's mission is to campaign for accountability, diversity and excellence in UK broadcasting, seeking to sustain and strengthen public service broadcasting to the benefit of civil society and democracy in the UK. It holds regular conferences and seminars and publishes a Bulletin and an e-newsletter. Founded 1983.

Yachting Journalists' Association

website www.yja.co.uk
President The Lord Greenway, *Honorary Secretary* Chris English
Membership £50 p.a.

Aims to further the interests of yachting, sail and power, and yachting journalism. Members vote annually for the Yachtsman of the Year and the Young Sailor of the Year Award and host several important functions annually on both the British and international maritime calendar. Founded 1969.

LITERACY

BookTrust

G8 Battersea Studios, 80 Silverthorne Road, London SW8 3HE
tel 020-7801 8800
email query@booktrust.org.uk
website www.booktrust.org.uk
Director Diana Gerald, *Chair of Board* Karen Brown

BookTrust is the UK largest children's reading charity dedicated to getting children reading. Children who read are happier, healthier, more empathetic and more creative. They also do better at school.

BookTrust works with a variety of partners to get children excited about books, rhymes and stories because if reading is fun, children will want to do it. BookTrust administers the Blue Peter Book Awards, Children's Book Weeks and the Waterstones Children's Laureate.

The Children's Book Circle

website www.childrensbookcircle.org.uk
Membership £25 p.a.

Provides a discussion forum for anybody involved with children's books. Monthly meetings are addressed by a panel of invited speakers and topics focus on current and controversial issues. Holds the annual Patrick Hardy lecture and administers the Eleanor Farjeon Award. Founded 1962.

Children's Books Ireland

17 North Great George's Street, Dublin D01 R2F1, Republic of Ireland
tel +353 (0)1 8727475
email info@childrensbooksireland.com
website www.childrensbooksireland.ie
Director Elaina Ryan, *Publications & Projects Manager* Jenny Murray, *Programme & Events Manager* Aoife Murray, Administrator Ciara Houlihan

Children's Books Ireland (CBI) is the national children's books resource organisation of Ireland. Its mission is to make books part of every child's life. It champions and celebrates the importance of authors and illustrators and works in partnership with the people and organisations who enhance children's lives through books. Core projects include: the CBI Annual Conference; the CBI Book of the Year Awards and its shadowing scheme for school groups and book clubs; the annual nationwide reading campaign which promotes books and reading and which coincides with the publication of the *Inis Reading Guide*, a guide to the best books of the year; nationwide Book Clinics, the Robert Dunbar Memorial Libraries and *Inis* magazine in print and online, a forum for discussion, debate and critique of Irish and international books. CBI administers the Laureate na nÓg project on behalf of the Arts Council and runs live literature events throughout the year. Founded 1996.

Free Word

Free Word Centre, 60 Farringdon Road, London EC1R 3GA
tel 020-7324 2570
email info@freewordcentre.com
website www.freewordcentre.com

Free Word is an international centre for literacy, literature and free expression. Provides a home for organisations working across literature, literacy and free expression. Current residents are: Apples & Snakes, ARTICLE 19, Arvon, English PEN, The Literary Consultancy and The Reading Agency. Free Word promotes, protects and democratises the power of words. With residents, associates and other partners, Free Word develops a year-round programme of cultural projects and events to explore important contemporary issues. Works worldwide with writers and thinkers.

National Literacy Trust

68 South Lambeth Road, London SW8 1RL
tel 020-7587 1842
email contact@literacytrust.org.uk
website www.literacytrust.org.uk

An independent charity that aims to help change lives through literacy. It campaigns to improve public understanding of the importance of literacy, as well as delivering projects and working in partnership to reach those most in need of support.

Read for Good

26 Nailsworth Mills, Avening Road, Nailsworth, Glos. GL6 0BS
tel (01453) 839005
email reading@readforgood.org
website www.readforgood.org

Read for Good aims for all children in the UK to be given the opportunity, space and motivation to develop their own love of reading, benefiting them throughout their lives. Many studies show that reading changes lives: from educational outcomes and social mobility to emotional wellbeing. Runs a readathon programme in schools and a hospital programme, which focuses on the supply of books and storyteller visits to brighten up the days of children in the UK's main children's hospitals.

The Reading Agency

Free Word Centre, 60 Farringdon Road, London EC1R 3GA
email info@readingagency.org.uk
website www.readingagency.org.uk
Twitter @readingagency

A charity whose mission is to inspire more people to read more, encourage them to share their enjoyment of reading and celebrate the difference that reading makes to everyone's lives. It has a close partnership with public libraries in creating equal access to reading, and works closely with publishers to bring author events and reading promotions to every kind of community. Funded by the Arts Council.

The Reading Agency supports a wide range of reading initiatives for children, young people and adults including: the Summer Reading Challenge, run in partnership with libraries, which helps get three-quarters of a million children reading each year; Reading Ahead, designed to build people's reading confidence and motivation; and World Book Night, an annual celebration of books and reading which takes place on 23 April.

Scottish Book Trust (SBT)

Sandeman House, Trunk's Close, 55 High Street, Edinburgh EH1 1SR
tel 0131 524 0160
email info@scottishbooktrust.com
website www.scottishbooktrust.com
Facebook www.facebook.com/scottishbktrust
Twitter @ScottishBkTrust

Scottish Book Trust (SBT) is Scotland's national agency for the promotion of reading, writing and literature. Programmes include: Bookbug, a free universal book-gifting programme which encourages families to read with their children from birth; an ambitious school's programme including national tours, the virtual events programme Authors Live and the Scottish Children's Book Awards; the Live Literature funding programme, a national initiative enabling Scottish citizens to engage with authors, playwrights, poets, storytellers and illustrators; a writer development programme, offering mentoring and professional development for emerging and established writers; and a readership development programme featuring a national writing campaign as well as Book Week Scotland during last week in November.

Seven Stories – The National Centre for Children's Books

30 Lime Street, Ouseburn Valley, Newcastle upon Tyne NE1 2PQ
tel 0300 330 1095
email info@sevenstories.org.uk
website www.sevenstories.org.uk
Facebook www.facebook.com/7stories
Twitter @7stories

Seven Stories champions the art of children's books to ensure its place as an integral part of childhood and national cultural life. The world of children's books is celebrated through unique exhibitions, events for all ages and a national archive. The work of over 200 British authors and illustrators, including Judith Kerr, Enid Blyton, Michael Morpurgo and David Almond is cared for in the archive collection – and it is still growing. Seven Stories is a charity – all the money earned and raised is used to save, celebrate and share children's books so that future generations can enjoy Britain's rich literary heritage. Arts Council England and Newcastle Culture Fund regularly fund Seven Stories' work, giving children's literature status and establishing new ways of engaging young audiences.

LIBRARIES AND INFORMATION

Campaign for Freedom of Information

Free Word Centre, 60 Farringdon Road, London EC1R 3GA
tel 020-7324 2519
email admin@cfoi.demon.co.uk
website www.cfoi.org.uk
Twitter @CampaignFOI

A non-profit organisation working to improve public access to official information and to ensure that the Freedom of Information Act is implemented effectively. The Campaign is a non-profit organisation which seeks to improve and defend the Freedom of Information. Advises members of the public about their rights to information under FOI and related laws, helps people challenge unreasonable refusals to disclose information, encourages good practice by public authorities and provides FOI training.

CILIP (The Library and Information Association)

7 Ridgmount Street, London WC1E 7AE
tel 020-7255 0500

website www.cilip.org.uk
Twitter @CILIPinfo
Membership Varies according to income

The leading professional body for librarians, information specialists and knowledge managers, with members in the UK and internationally. CILIP's objective is to put library and information skills at the heart of a democratic, equal and prosperous information society. Offices in London, Wales, Scotland and Northern Ireland.

English Association

University of Leicester, University Road, Leicester LE1 7RH
tel 0116 229 7622
email engassoc@leicester.ac.uk
website www.le.ac.uk/engassoc
Chair Martin Halliwell, *Chief Executive* Helen Lucas

Aims to further knowledge, understanding and enjoyment of English literature and the English language, by working towards a fuller recognition of English as an essential element in education and in the community at large; by encouraging the study of English literature and language by means of conferences, lectures and publications; and by fostering the discussion of methods of teaching English of all kinds

English Speaking Board (International) Ltd

9 Hattersley Court, Burscough Road, Ormskirk L39 2AY
tel (01695) 573439
email customer@esbuk.org
website www.esbuk.org
Ceo Tina Renshaw

English Speaking Board (International) Ltd is a national awarding body and charity, with a mission to promote clear, effective communication at all levels by providing high quality educational products and training services, domestically and internationally. Produces products for schools and vocational and business contexts. Qualifications include Graded Examinations in speech and drama, presentation skills, debating qualifications, interview and employability skills, English for speakers of other languages (ESOL).

ESB assessments are designed for enterprises who teach English as a second language, who want to use spoken language to raise pupil achievement or those who wish to develop their enrichment programmes to include spoken language skills.

The English-Speaking Union

Dartmouth House, 37 Charles Street, London W1J 5ED
tel 020-7529 1550
email esu@esu.org
website www.esu.org

Aims to promote international understanding and human achievement through the widening use of the English language throughout the world. The ESU is an educational charity which sponsors scholarships and exchanges, educational programmes promoting the effective use of English, and a wide range of international and cultural events. Members contribute to its work across the world. Founded 1918.

Institute of Internal Communication

Suite G10, Gemini House, Sunrise Parkway, Linford Wood, Milton Keynes MK14 6PW
tel (01908) 232168
email enquiries@ioic.org.uk
website www.ioic.org.uk

The only independent professional body solely dedicated to promoting a deeper understanding of internal communication and helping its members to be the best they can be. Founded 1949.

Private Libraries Association

29 Eden Drive, Hull HU8 8JQ
email maslen@maslen.karoo.co.uk
website www.plabooks.org
President Giles Mandelbrote, *Hon. Secretary* Jim Maslen, *Hon. Journal Editors* David Chambers, David Butcher, James Freemantle
Membership £30 p.a.

International society of book collectors and lovers of books. Publications include *The Private Library* (quarterly), annual *Private Press Books*, and other books on book collecting. Founded 1956.

LITERARY

Alliance of Literary Societies

website www.allianceofliterarysocieties.wordpress.com
President Claire Harman

Aims to act as a valuable liaison body between member societies as a means of sharing knowledge, skills and expertise, and may also act as a pressure group when necessary. The Alliance can assist in the preservation of buildings, places and objects which have literary associations. Its publications include a twice-yearly newsletter, *Not Only But...*, as well as it annual journal, *ALSo*. Holds an annual literary weekend, hosted by a different member society each year.

Association for Scottish Literary Studies

c/o Dept of Scottish Literature, 7 University Gardens, University of Glasgow G12 8QH
tel 0141 330 5309
email office@asls.org.uk
website www.asls.org.uk
President Alison Lumsden, *Secretary* Craig Lamont, *Director* Duncan Jones

Membership £50 p.a. individuals; £12 UK students; £75 corporate

ASLS promotes the study, teaching and writing of Scottish literature and furthers the study of the languages of Scotland. Publishes annually *New Writing Scotland*, an anthology of new Scottish writing; an edited text of Scottish literature; a series of academic journals; the online e-zine *The Bottle Imp*; and a newsletter (two p.a.). Also publishes *Scotnotes* (comprehensive study guides to major Scottish writers), literary texts and commentaries designed to assist the classroom teacher, and a series of occasional papers. Organises three conferences a year. Founded 1970.

The Jane Austen Society

Sospiri, 9 George Street, Dunfermline, Fife KY11 4TQ
tel (01383) 727491
email memsec@jasoc.org.uk
website www.janeaustensociety.org.uk
Membership Secretary Sharron Bassett
Membership £28 from 1 January to 31 December each year; £33 joint membership for 2 people living at the same address; £12 student membership (UK), on production of tutor reference or ID; £38 overseas. Joint overseas rate £43.

Promotes interest in, and enjoyment of, the life and works of Jane Austen (1775–1817). Regular publications, meetings and conferences. Eleven branches and groups in UK. Founded 1940.

The Beckford Society

The Timber Cottage, Crockerton, Warminster BA12 8AX
tel (01985) 213195
email sidney.blackmore@btinternet.com
website www.beckfordsociety.org
Membership from £20 p.a.

Promotes an interest in the life and works of William Beckford of Fonthill (1760–1844) and his circle. Encourages Beckford studies and scholarship through exhibitions, lectures and publications, including *The Beckford Journal* (annual) and occasional newsletters. Founded 1995.

Arnold Bennett Society

4 Field End Close, Trentham, Stoke-on-Trent ST4 8DA
email arnoldbennettscty@btinternet.com
website www.arnoldbennettsociety.org.uk
Facebook Arnold Bennett Society
Twitter @BennettSoc
Secretary Carol Gorton
Membership £15 p.a. individuals; £17.50 p.a. family. Add £2 if living outside Europe

Promotes the study and appreciation of the life, works and times not only of Arnold Bennett (1867–1931), but also of other provincial writers with a particular relationship to north Staffordshire.

The E.F. Benson Society

The Old Coach House, High Street, Rye, East Sussex TN31 7JF
tel (01797) 223114
email info@efbensonsociety.org
website www.efbensonsociety.org
Secretary Allan Downend
Membership £12 p.a. single; £15 p.a. for two people at same address; £20 overseas

Promotes interest in the author E.F. Benson (1867–1940) and the Benson family. Arranges annual literary evening, annual outing to Rye (July) and other places of Benson interest, talks on the Bensons and exhibitions. Archive includes the Austin Seckersen Collection, transcriptions of the Benson diaries and letters. Publishes postcards, anthologies of Benson's works, a Mary Benson biography, books on Benson and an annual journal, *The Dodo*. Also sells out-of-print Bensons to members. Founded 1984.

The George Borrow Society

60 Upper Marsh Road, Warminster, Wilts. BA12 9PN
email mkskillman@blueyonder.co.uk
website http://georgeborrow.org/home.html
Membership Secretary Michael Skillman
Membership £25 p.a.; £37.50 joint members at same address; £10 students

Promotes knowledge of the life and works of George Borrow (1803–81), traveller and author. Publishes *Bulletin* (bi-annual). Founded 1991.

The Brontë Society

Brontë Parsonage Museum, Haworth, Keighley, West Yorkshire BD22 8DR
tel (01535) 642323
email bronte@bronte.org.uk
website www.bronte.org.uk

The Society cares for and promotes the accredited collections and literary legacy of the Brontë family. It is an Arts Council National Portfolio Organisation and presents an exciting contemporary arts programme, alongside changing exhibitions and learning and engagement programmes. *Brontë Studies* and the *Brontë Gazette* are published three times a year. The museum is open all year round, except in January.

The Browning Society

64 Blyth Vale, London SE6 4NW
email browningsociety@hotmail.co.uk
website www.browningsociety.org
Honorary Secretary Jim Smith
Membership £15 p.a.

Aims to widen the appreciation and understanding of the lives and poetry of Robert Browning (1812–89) and Elizabeth Barrett Browning (1806–61), as well as other Victorian writers and poets. Founded 1881; refounded 1969.

The John Buchan Society

72 Ravensdowne, Berwick-upon-Tweed, Northumberland TD15 1DQ
tel (01573) 229068
email akgallico@gmail.com
website www.johnbuchansociety.co.uk
Membership Secretary Alison Gallico
Membership £20 p.a. full; overseas and other rates on application

Promotes a wider understanding of the life and works of John Buchan (1875–1940). Encourages publication of Buchan's works and supports the John Buchan Story Museum in Peebles, EH45 8AG (www.johnbuchanstory.co.uk). Also holds regular meetings and social gatherings; produces a newsletter and a journal. Founded 1979.

Byron Society (Newstead Abbey)

Acushla, Halam Road, Southwell, Notts. NG25 0AD
website www.newsteadabbeybyronsociety.org
Chairman P.K. Purslow
Membership £25 p.a.

Promotes research into the life and works of Lord Byron (1788–1824) through seminars, discussions, lectures and readings. Publishes *The Newstead Review* (annual, £12.50 plus postage). Founded 1988.

Randolph Caldecott Society

website www.randolphcaldecott.org.uk
Membership £12.50 p.a. individual; £17.50 p.a. families/corporate

Aims to encourage an interest in the life and works of Randolph Caldecott (1846–86), the Victorian artist, illustrator and sculptor. Meetings held in Chester. Liaises with the American Caldecott Society. Founded 1983.

The Lewis Carroll Society

6 Chilton Street, London E2 6DZ
email membership@lewiscarrollsociety.org.uk
website www.lewiscarrollsociety.org.uk
Facebook www.facebook.com/groups/68678994062/
Twitter @LewisCarrollSoc
Membership £20 p.a. UK; £23 Europe; £26 elsewhere. Special rates for institutions

Promotes interest in the life and works of Lewis Carroll (Revd Charles Lutwidge Dodgson) (1832–98) and to encourage research. Activities include regular meetings, exhibitions, and a publishing programme that includes the first annotated, unexpurgated edition of his diaries in nine volumes, the Society's journal *The Carrollian* (two p.a.), a newsletter, *Bandersnatch* (quarterly) and the *Lewis Carroll Review* (occasional). Founded 1969.

Lewis Carroll Society (Daresbury)

email secretary@lewiscarrollsociety.org.uk
website www.lewiscarrollsociety.org.uk
Membership £7 p.a.; £10 families/corporate

Encourages an interest in the life and works of Lewis Carroll (1832–98), author of *Alice's Adventures*. Meetings take place at Carroll's birth village (Daresbury, Cheshire). Founded 1970.

The John Clare Society

tel (01353) 668438
email sueholgate@hotmail.co.uk
website http://johnclaresociety.blogspot.com/
Membership £15 p.a. UK individual; other rates on application

Promotes a wider appreciation of the life and works of the poet John Clare (1793–1864). Founded 1981.

The William Cobbett Society

6 Lynch Road, Farnham, Surrey GU9 8BD
email information@williamcobbett.org.uk
website www.williamcobbett.org.uk
Twitter @RuralRides

Aims to make the life and work of William Cobbett (1763–1835) better known. Founded 1976.

The Wilkie Collins Society

4 Ernest Gardens, London W4 3QU
email paul@paullewis.co.uk
website www.wilkiecollins.org
Secretary Paul Lewis
Membership £16 p.a. EU; £28 international

Aims to promote interest in the life and works of Wilkie Collins (1824–89). Publishes a newsletter, an annual scholarly journal and reprints of Collins's lesser known works. Founded 1981.

The Joseph Conrad Society (UK)

c/o The Polish Social and Cultural Association, 238–246 King Street, London W6 0RF
email theconradian@aol.com
website www.josephconradsociety.org
Chairman Robert Hampson, *Honorary Secretary* Hugh Epstein, *Editor of The Conradian* Alex Fachard

Activities include an annual international conference; publication of *The Conradian* and a series of pamphlets; and maintenance of a substantial reference library as part of the Polish Library at the Polish Social and Cultural Association. Administers the Juliet McLauchlan Prize, a £200 annual award for the winner of an essay competition, and travel grants for scholars wishing to attend Conrad conferences. Founded 1973.

Walter de la Mare Society

3 Hazelwood Close, New River Crescent, Palmers Green, London N13 5RE
website www.walterdelamare.co.uk
Hon. Secretary & Treasurer Frances Guthrie
Membership £15 p.a.

Established to promote the study and deepen the appreciation of the works of Walter de la Mare (1873–1956) through a magazine, talks, discussions and other activities. Founded 1997.

Dickens Fellowship

The Charles Dickens Museum, 48 Doughty Street, London WC1N 2LX
tel 020-7405 2127
email postbox@dickensfellowship.org
website www.dickensfellowship.org
Hon. Secretary Paul Graham
Membership £17 p.a.

Based in the house occupied by Charles Dickens (1812–70) during the period 1837–9. Publishes *The Dickensian* (3 p.a.). Founded 1902.

The Arthur Conan Doyle Society

PO Box 1360, Ashcroft, BC V0K 1A0, Canada
tel +1 250-453-2045
email sirhenry@telus.net
website www.ash-tree.bc.ca/acdsocy.html

Promotes the study of the life and works of Sir Arthur Conan Doyle (1859–1930). Publishes *ACD* journal (bi-annual) and occasional reprints of Conan Doyle material. Occasional conventions. Founded 1989.

The George Eliot Fellowship

39 Lower Road, Barnacle, Coventry CV7 9LD
tel 024-7661 9126
email johnkburton43@gmail.com
website www.georgeeliot.org
Facebook www.facebook.com/TheGeorgeEliotFellowship/
Twitter @GeorgeEliotLove
President Jonathan G. Ouvry, *Chairman* John Burton
Membership £18 p.a. (£15 concessions) individuals; £23 p.a. (£20 concessions) for couples; £15 p.a. students (under 25)

Promotes an interest in the life and work of George Eliot (1819–80) and helps to extend her influence; arranges meetings, study days and conferences; produces an annual journal (*The George Eliot Review*), newsletters and other publications. Back numbers of all editions of the *George Eliot Review* are now online, via the website. Works closely with educational establishments in the Nuneaton area. Awards the annual George Eliot Fellowship Prize (£500) for an essay on Eliot's life or work, which must be previously unpublished and not exceed 4,000 words. The Fellowship is planning a wide variety of events and activities during 2019 to celebrate the bicentenary of George Eliot's birth in 1819. Founded 1930.

The Folklore Society

c/o The Warburg Institute, Woburn Square, London WC1H 0AB
tel 020-7862 8564
email thefolkloresociety@gmail.com
website www.folklore-society.com

Collection, recording and study of folklore. Founded 1878.

The Gaskell Society

37 Buckingham Drive, Knutsford, Cheshire WA16 8LH
tel (01565) 651761
email pamgriff54@gmail.com
website www.gaskellsociety.co.uk
Twitter @EGaskell
Secretary Mrs Pam Griffiths
Membership £23 p.a.; £28 joint annual member/European member/institutions; £15 student in full time education; £30 non-European member

Promotes and encourages the study and appreciation of the work and life of Elizabeth Cleghorn Gaskell (1810–65). Holds regular meetings in Knutsford, London, Manchester and Bath, visits and residential conferences; produces an annual journal and bi-annual newsletters. Founded 1985.

Graham Greene Birthplace Trust

website www.grahamgreenebt.org
Facebook www.facebook.com/Graham-Greene-International-Festival-55327438605/
Twitter @GreeneFestival
Membership £12, £16 and £20 p.a. for the UK, Europe and ROW respectively; £32, £38 and £50 respectively for three years, all including the quarterly newsletter.

Exists to study the works of Graham Greene (1904–91). The Trust promotes the Annual Graham Greene Festival (20–23 September 2018) and Graham Greene trails in Berkhamsted. It publishes a quarterly newsletter, occasional papers, videos and CDs, and maintains a small library. It administers the Graham Greene Memorial Awards. Founded 1997.

The Thomas Hardy Society

c/o Dorset County Museum, High West Street, Dorchester, Dorset DT1 1XA
tel (01305) 251501
email info@hardysociety.org
website www.hardysociety.org
Membership £24 p.a.; £35 overseas

Promotes and celebrates the work of Thomas Hardy (1840–1928). Publishes *The Thomas Hardy Journal* (annual) and *The Hardy Society Journal* (2 p.a.). Biennial conference held in Dorchester. Founded 1967.

The James Hilton Society

22 Well House, Woodmansterne Lane, Banstead, Surrey SM7 3AA
website www.jameshiltonsociety.co.uk
Chairman R. Hughes
Membership £13 p.a.; £10 concessions; £18 overseas

Promotes interest in the life and work of novelist and scriptwriter James Hilton (1900–54). Publishes a newsletter three times a year and a bi-annual scholarly journal, and organises conferences. Founded 2000.

The Sherlock Holmes Society of London

email shjournal@btinternet.com
website www.sherlock-holmes.org.uk
Press & Publicity Officer Roger Johnson

The Society is open to anyone with an interest in Sherlock Holmes, Dr John H. Watson and their world. A literary and social society, publishing a bi-annual scholarly journal and occasional papers, and holding meetings, dinners and excursions. Founded 1951.

Housman Society

Abberley Cottage, 7 Dowles Road, Bewdley DY12 2EJ
email info@housman-society.co.uk
website www.housman-society.co.uk
Membership £15 p.a. UK; £20 p.a. overseas

Aims to foster interest in and promote knowledge of A.E. Housman (1859–1936) and his family. Sponsors a lecture at the Hay Festival. Publishes an annual journal and bi-annual newsletter. Founded 1973.

The Johnson Society

Johnson Birthplace Museum, Breadmarket Street, Lichfield, Staffs. WS13 6LG
tel (01543) 264972
email info@thejohnsonsociety.org.uk
website www.johnsonnew.wordpress.com
General Secretary Marilyn Davies

Aims to encourage the study of the life and works of Dr Samuel Johnson (1709–84); to preserve the memorials, associations, books, manuscripts and letters of Dr Johnson and his contemporaries; and to work with the local council in the preservation of his birthplace.

Johnson Society of London

email memsec@johnsonsocietyoflondon.org
website www.johnsonsocietyoflondon.org
President Lord Harmsworth
Membership £25 p.a. individual; £30 joint, £20 student

Promotes the study the life and works of Dr Johnson (1709–84) and perpetuates his memory in the city of his adoption. Founded 1928.

Keats-Shelley Memorial Association

website www.keats-shelley.co.uk

Owns and supports house in Rome where John Keats died, as a museum open to the public; celebrates the poets Keats (1795–1821), Shelley (1792–1822) and Leigh Hunt (1784–1859). Regular meetings; poetry competitions; annual *Review;* two literary awards; and progress reports. The Keats-Shelley Memorial Association runs the annual Keats-Shelley Poetry and Essay Prize, and the Young Romantics Poetry and Essay Prize, open to young writers aged 16–18. Founded 1903.

The Kipling Society

31 Brookside, Billericay, Essex CM11 1DT
email john.lambert1@btinternet.com
website www.kipling.org.uk
Hon. Secretary John Lambert
Membership £29 p.a.; £14 under age 23

Encourages discussion and study of the work and life of Rudyard Kipling (1865–1936), to assist in the study of his writings, to hold discussion meetings, to publish a quarterly journal and website, with a Readers' Guide to Kipling's work, and to maintain a Kipling Library in London.

The Charles Lamb Society

BM-ELIA, London WC1N 3XX
website www.charleslambsociety.com
Chairman Nicholas Powell, *Membership Secretary* Cecilia Powell
Membership Personal: £24/$45 p.a. individual; £32 couple; £32/$60 corporate

Publishes the academic journal *The Charles Lamb Bulletin* (twice a year). The Society's extensive library of books and MSS by and about Charles Lamb (1775–1834) is housed at the Guildhall Library, Aldermanbury, London EC2P 2EJ. Founded 1935.

The D.H. Lawrence Society

email dhlawrencesociety@gmail.com
website www.dhlawrencesociety.com
Chairman M.J. Gray, *Treasurer* Sheila Bamford
Membership £20 p.a. ordinary; £22 overseas; £18 UK retired persons and students

Aims to bring together people interested in D.H. Lawrence (1885–1930), to encourage study of his work, and to provide information and guides for people visiting Eastwood. Founded 1974.

The T.E. Lawrence Society

PO Box 728, Oxford OX2 9ZJ
email chairman@telsociety.org.uk
website www.telsociety.org.uk
Membership £24 p.a. UK; £32 overseas (discounts available for membership benefits received via email)

Promotes the memory of T.E. Lawrence (1888–1935) and furthers education and knowledge by research into his life; publishes *Journal* (bi-annual) and *Newsletter* (three p.a.). Founded 1985.

The Marlowe Society

email kenneth.pickering@marlowe-society.org
website www.marlowe-society.org
Chairman Ken Pickering, *Secretary* Peter Cherry

Aims to extend appreciation and widen recognition of Christopher Marlowe (1564–93) as the foremost poet and dramatist preceding Shakespeare, whose development he influenced. Holds meetings and cultural visits, and issues a bi-annual magazine and an occasional research journal. See website for subscription rates. Founded 1955.

The John Masefield Society

40 Mill Way, Bushey, Herts. WD23 2AG
tel (01923) 246047
email robert.vaughan110@gmail.com
website www.ies.sas.ac.uk/node/496
Chairman Bob Vaughan
Membership £5 p.a.; £10 overseas; £8 family/institution

Promotes the life and works of the poet John Masefield (1878–1967). Holds an annual lecture and other, less formal, readings and gatherings; publishes an annual journal and frequent newsletters. Founded 1992.

William Morris Society

Kelmscott House, 26 Upper Mall, London W6 9TA
tel 020-8741 3735
email info@williammorrissociety.org.uk
website www.williammorrissociety.org
Honorary Secretary Natalia Martynenko-Hunt

Spreads knowledge of the life, work and ideas of William Morris (1834–96); publishes newsletter (quarterly) and journal (two p.a.). Library and collections open to the public Thurs and Sat, 2–5pm. Founded 1955.

The Edith Nesbit Society

21 Churchfields, West Malling, Kent ME19 6RJ
email edithnesbit@gmail.com
website www.edithnesbit.co.uk
Membership £10 p.a. individual; £12 p.a. joint; £15 organisations

Promotes an interest in the life and works of Edith Nesbit (1858–1924) by means of talks, a regular newsletter and other publications, and visits to relevant places. Founded 1996.

Wilfred Owen Association

email woa@1914-18.co.uk
website www.wilfredowen.org.uk

Commemorates the life and work of Wilfred Owen (1893–1918); encourages and enhances appreciation of his work through visits, public events and a bi-annual journal. Founded 1989.

The Beatrix Potter Society

email info@beatrixpottersociety.org.uk
website www.beatrixpottersociety.org.uk
Membership £30 p.a. UK; £36 overseas; £35/£41 commercial/institutional

Promotes the study and appreciation of the life and works of Beatrix Potter (1866–1943) as author, artist, diarist, farmer and conservationist. Regular lecture meetings, conferences and events in the UK and USA. Quarterly newsletter. Small publishing programme. Founded 1980.

The Powys Society

Flat D, 87 Ledbury Road, London W11 2AG
tel 020-7243 0168
email chris.d.thomas@hotmail.co.uk
website www.powys-society.org
Hon. Secretary Chris Thomas
Membership £22 p.a. UK; £26 overseas

Promotes the greater public recognition and enjoyment of the writings, thought and contribution to the arts of the Powys family, particularly John Cowper (1872–1963), Theodore (1875–1953) and Llewelyn (1884–1939) Powys, and the many other family members and their close friends. Publishes an annual scholarly journal (*The Powys Journal*) and three newsletters per year as well as books by and about the Powys family, and holds an annual weekend conference in August, as well as organising other activities throughout the year. Founded 1967.

The J.B. Priestley Society

Eldwick Crag Farm, High Eldwick, Bingley, W. Yorkshire BD16 3BB
email reavill@globalnet.co.uk
website www.jbpriestleysociety.com
General Secretary Rod Slater (rodslater7@gmail.com), *Information Officer* Roger Statham (stathamwass@btinternet.com), *Membership Secretary* Tony Reavill
Membership £15 p.a. single; £20 family; £10 concessions

Promotes the knowledge, understanding and appreciation of the published works of J.B. Priestley (1894–1984) and the study of his life and career. Holds lectures and discussions and shows films. Publishes a newsletter and journal. Organises walks to areas with Priestley connections, Annual Priestley Luncheon and other social events. Founded 1997.

The Ruskin Society

email info@theruskinsociety.com
website www.theruskinsociety.com
Membership £15 p.a.

Celebrates the life, work and legacy of John Ruskin (1819–1900). Organises lectures and events exploring Ruskin's ideas and placing them in a modern context. Awards an annual book prize for new books about Ruskin. Founded 1997.

The Malcolm Saville Society

11 Minster Court, Windsor Close, Taunton TA1 4LW
email mystery@witchend.com
website www.witchend.com
Facebook www.facebook.com/MalcolmSaville
Twitter @MSavilleSociety
Membership £15 p.a. UK; £17.50 Europe; £21 elsewhere

Promotes interest in the work of Malcolm Saville (1901–82), children's author. Regular social activities, library, contact directory and magazine (four p.a.). Founded 1994.

The Dorothy L. Sayers Society

Gimsons, Kings Chase, Witham, Essex CM8 1AX
tel (01376) 515626
email info@sayers.org.uk
website www.sayers.org.uk
Chair Seona Ford, *Secretaries* Lenelle Davis, Jasmine Simeone
Membership £20 p.a. UK and worldwide for electronic version of *Bulletin*. Paper version (mailed): £24 UK, £27 Europe, £30 rest of world; under 25s £10 for electronic version of *Bulletin* only.

Aims to promote and encourage the study of the works of Dorothy L. Sayers (1893–1957); to collect archive materials and reminiscences about her and make them available to students and biographers; to hold an annual conference and other meetings; to publish *Proceedings*, pamphlets and a bi-monthly *Bulletin*; to make grants and awards. Founded 1976.

The Shaw Society

tel 020-7435 6497
email contact@shawsociety.org.uk
website www.shawsociety.org.uk
Chairman Dr Anne Wright CBE
Membership £25/$40 p.a.

Works towards the improvement and diffusion of knowledge of the life and works of Bernard Shaw (1856–1950) and his circle. Publishes *The Shavian*. Meets monthly (not July, August or December) at The Actors Centre, 1A Tower Street, off Earlham Street, London WC2H 9NP for script-in-hand performances and discussion. Play-reading Group meets on the first Thursday (for details see website or telephone).

The Robert Louis Stevenson Club

website www.robert-louis-stevenson.org

Aims to foster interest in Robert Louis Stevenson's life (1850–94) and works through various events and its newsletter. Founded 1920.

The Tennyson Society

Lincolnshire Archives, St Rumbold Street, Lincoln LN2 5AB
tel (01522) 687837
email kathleen.jefferson@lincolnshire.gov.uk
website www.tennysonsociety.org.uk
Membership £14 p.a.; £16 family; £25 institutions

Promotes the study and understanding of the life and work of the poet Alfred, Lord Tennyson (1809–92) and supports the Tennyson Research Centre in Lincoln. Holds lectures, visits and seminars; publishes the *Tennyson Research Bulletin* (annual), Monographs and Occasional Papers; tapes/recordings available. Founded 1960.

Angela Thirkell Society

website www.angelathirkellsociety.co.uk
Facebook www.facebook.com/angelathirkellappreciationgroup
Membership £10 p.a.

The Society aims 'to honour the memory of Angela Thirkell (1890–1960) as a writer, and to make her works available to new generations'. Publishes an annual journal, encourages Thirkell studies and works in cooperation with its North American branch (www.angelathirkell.org). Founded 1980.

The Edward Thomas Fellowship

Fairlands, Finchmead Lane, Stroud, Petersfield, Hampshire GU32 3PF
email mitchjd.etf@outlook.com
website www.edward-thomas-fellowship.org.uk
Chairman Jeremy Mitchell
Membership £15 p.a.

Celebrates the life and work of Edward Thomas (1878–1917), poet and writer, and assists in the preservation of places associated with him and arranges events which extend fellowship amongst his admirers. In partnership with Petersfield Museum, the Fellowship has established the Edward Thomas Study Centre at the museum based around the Tim Wilton-Steer collection of books by and about Edward Thomas. There are over 2,000 books and artefacts in the collection, which are available to researchers and readers. Contact Jeremy Mitchell for access arrangements. Founded 1980.

Dylan Thomas Society

email info@dylandthomassociety.com
website dylanthomassociety.com
Chairman Geoff Haden
Membership £10 p.a. single; £15 p.a. double; Patrons £25

Promotes an interest in the works of Dylan Thomas (1914–53) and other writers. Founded 1977.

The Tolkien Society

email membership@tolkiensociety.org
website www.tolkiensociety.org
Membership £30 p.a.; £10 student; £2 p.a. Entings (under 16s)

The Trollope Society

PO Box 505, Tunbridge Wells, TN2 9RW
tel (01747) 839799
email info@trollopesociety.org
website www.trollopesociety.org
Chairman Michael Williamson JP DL
Membership £26 p.a. UK; £36 international

Has produced the first ever complete edition of the novels of Anthony Trollope (1815–82). Founded 1987.

The Turner Society

BCM Box Turner, London WC1N 3XX
website www.turnersociety.com
Membership £30 p.a. individuals; £30 p.a. overseas surface mail; £45 p.a. overseas airmail; Life Member £600

Fosters a wider appreciation of all aspects of the work of J.M.W. Turner RA (1775–1851); to encourage exhibitions of his paintings, drawings and engravings. Publishes *Turner Society News* (two p.a.). Founded 1975.

The Walmsley Society

April Cottage, 1 Brand Road, Hampden Park, Eastbourne, East Sussex BN22 9PX
website www.walmsleysoc.org
Secretary Fred Lane

Promotes and encourages an appreciation of the literary and artistic heritage left to us by Leo Walmsley (1892–1966) and J. Ulric Walmsley (1860–1954). Founded 1985.

Mary Webb Society

Old Barn Cottage, 10 Barrow Hall Farm, Village Road, Great Barrow, Chester, Cheshire CH3 7JH
tel (01829) 740592
email suehigginbotham@yahoo.co.uk
website www.marywebbsociety.co.uk
Secretary Sue Higginbotham

For devotees of the literature and works of Mary Webb (1881–1927) and of the Shropshire countryside of her novels. Publishes two newsletters p.a., organises four events p.a. including a two-day Summer School in various locations related to Webb's life and works. Lectures and tours arranged for individuals and groups. The Society archive is continually being added to. Founded 1972.

The H.G. Wells Society

153 Kenilworth Crescent, Enfield, Middlesex, EN1 3RG
email secretaryhgwellssociety@hotmail.com
website www.hgwellssociety.com
Chairman Dr Emelyne Godfrey (emelynegodfrey@yahoo.com), *Secretary* Brian Jukes
Membership £20 p.a. UK (£13 retired/student/unwaged); £24 EU (£17); £27 rest of world (£20); Institutions: £25 p.a. UK, £30 EU, £35 rest of world

Promotes an active interest in and an appreciation of the life, work and thought of H.G. Wells (1866–1946). Publishes *The Wellsian* (annual) and *The Newsletter* (bi-annual). Founded 1960.

The Oscar Wilde Society

email secretary@oscarwildesociety.co.uk
website www.oscarwildesociety.co.uk
Membership Secretary Veronika Binoeder, *Hon. Secretary* Vanessa Heron

Promotes knowledge, appreciation and study of the life, personality and works of the writer and wit Oscar Wilde (1854–1900). Activities include meetings, lectures, readings and exhibitions, and visits to associated locations. Members receive a journal, *The Wildean* (two p.a.), a newsletter/journal, *Intentions* (four p.a.) and regular e-newsletters. Founded 1990.

The Henry Williamson Society

General Secretary Will Harris, 46 Brambledown Road, Wallington SM6 0TF
020-8395 9978
email wjh@blueyonder.co.uk
Membership Secretary Margaret Murphy, 16 Doran Drive, Redhill, Surrey RH1 6AX
(01737) 763228
email margaretmurphy567@gmail.com
website www.henrywilliamson.co.uk

Encourages a wider readership and greater understanding of the literary heritage left by Henry Williamson (1895–1977). Founded 1980.

The P.G. Wodehouse Society (UK)

email info@pgwodehousesociety.org.uk
website www.pgwodehousesociety.org.uk
Membership £22 p.a.

Promotes the enjoyment of P.G. Wodehouse (1881–1975). Publishes *Wooster Sauce* (quarterly) and *By The Way* papers (four p.a.) which cover diverse subjects of Wodehousean interest. Holds events, entertainments and meetings throughout Britain. Founded 1997.

Virginia Woolf Society of Great Britain

Fairhaven, Charnleys Lane, Banks, Southport PR9 8HJ
tel (01704) 225232
email stuart.n.clarke@btinternet.com
website www.virginiawoolfsociety.co.uk
Facebook www.facebook.com/VWSGB
Membership Secretary Stuart N. Clarke
Membership £18 p.a.; £23 Europe; £26 outside Europe

Acts as a forum for British admirers of Virginia Woolf (1882–1941) to meet, correspond and share their enjoyment of her work. Publishes the *Virginia Woolf Bulletin*. Founded 1998.

Francis Brett Young Society

92 Gower Road, Halesowen, West Midlands B62 9BT
tel 0121 422 8969
email michael.hall10@gmail.com
website www.fbysociety.co.uk
Chairman Dr Michael Hall, *Secretary* Mrs J. Hadley
Membership £7 p.a., £70 life for individual; £10 p.a., £100 life joint; £5 p.a. full-time students; £7 p.a. societies and institutions

Provides opportunities for members to meet, correspond, and to share the enjoyment of the works of Francis Brett Young (1884–1954). Publishes a journal (two p.a.). Founded 1979.

ART, ILLUSTRATION AND PHOTOGRAPHY

The Association of Illustrators

Somerset House, Strand, London WC2R 1LA
tel 020-7759 1010
email info@theaoi.com
website www.theaoi.com

Facebook www.facebook.com/theaoi
Twitter @theaoi

Trade association which supports illustrators, promotes illustration and encourages professional standards in the industry. Publishes *Varoom* magazine (two p.a.); presents an annual programme of events; annual competition, exhibition and tour of the World Illustration Awards in partnership with the *Directory of Illustration* (www.theaoi.com/awards). Founded 1973.

The Association of Photographers

Studio 9, Holborn Studios, 49/50 Eagle Wharf Road, London N1 7ED
tel 020-7739 6669
email info@aophoto.co.uk
website www.the-aop.org
Facebook www.facebook.com/AssociationOfPhotographers
Twitter @AssocPhoto
Membership See website for options

Exists to protect and promote the interests of fashion advertising and editorial photographers. Founded 1968.

Axisweb

email hello@axisweb.org
website www.axisweb.org
Facebook www.facebook.com/axisweb.org
Twitter @axisweb

Axisweb is an indepedent charity providing a platform to support artists and profile what they do. Axisweb's programme reflects the artists' voice, presenting new aspects and forms of expression to local, national and international audiences. Through membership, Asixweb supports artists and art professionals with insurance, networking, space, opportunities, awards, profiling, advice and mentoring.

BAPLA (British Association of Picture Libraries and Agencies)

59 Tranquil Vale, Blackheath, London SE3 0BS
tel 020-8297 1198
email enquiries@bapla.org.uk
website www.bapla.org.uk
Membership Manager Susanne Kittlinger

The British Association of Picture Libraries and Agencies (BAPLA) is the trade association for picture libraries in the UK, and has been a trade body since 1975. Members include the major news, stock and production agencies as well as sole traders and cultural heritage institutions.

The Blackpool Art Society

The Studio, Wilkinson Avenue, Off Woodland Grove, Blackpool FY3 9HB
tel (01253) 768297
email sec@blackpoolartsociety.co.uk
website www.blackpoolartsociety.co.uk

Various exhibitions (members' work only). Studio meetings, demonstrations, workshops, lectures, out-of-door sketching. New members always welcome. See website for more details. Founded 1884.

British Institute of Professional Photography

Ardenham Court, Oxford Road, Aylesbury, Bucks HP19 8HT
tel (01296) 642020
email info@bipp.com
website www.bipp.com
Chief Executive Chris Harper

Represents all who practise photography as a profession in any field; to improve the quality of photography; establish recognised qualifications and a high standard of conduct; to safeguard the interests of the public and the profession. Admission can be obtained by submission of work and other information to the appropriate examining board.

Fellows, Associates and Licentiates are entitled to the designation FBIPP, ABIPP or LBIPP in accordance with the qualification awarded. Organises numerous meetings and conferences in various parts of the country throughout the year; publishes *The Photographer* magazine (bi-monthly), plus various pamphlets and leaflets on professional photography. Founded 1901; incorporated 1921.

British Interactive Media Association

49 Greek Street, London W1D 4EG
tel 020-3538 6607
website www.bima.co.uk
Membership Open to any organisation or individual with an interest in multimedia

BIMA is Britain's digital community which connects, develops and champions the industry. Membership of BIMA can lead to the extension of professional networks, attracting and developing talent, business growth and raising professional profiles. It also gives members a voice on issues affecting the industry. Founded 1985.

Bureau of Freelance Photographers

Vision House, PO Box 474, Hatfield AL10 1FY
tel (01707) 651450
email mail@thebfp.com
website www.thebfp.com
Chief Executive John Tracy
Membership £54 p.a. UK; £70 p.a. overseas

Exists to help the freelance photographer by providing information on markets, and free advisory service. Publishes *Market Newsletter* (monthly). Founded 1965.

Cartoonists Club of Great Britain

email secretary@thecartoonistsclub.com
email membership@thecartoonistsclub.com
website www.ccgb.org.uk
Facebook www.facebook.com/TheCartoonistsClub/

The UK's largest cartoonists' organisation, started by Fleet Street cartoonists in the 1960s and providing a social base for cartoonists wherever they may live/work. It has grown to include many different types of cartoonist. In addition to events around the country, members also visit events abroad, including a regular annual convention in Malta. It has a thriving online presence with its own website with several forums, including one for non-members that helps interested budding cartoonists to raise their game. Members have their own private forum and a members portfolio so that they can promote their work. The club's Facebook page is another lively cartoon-related news source as is the monthly magazine *The Jester*.

The Chartered Society of Designers

1 Cedar Court, Royal Oak Yard, Bermondsey Street, London SE1 3GA
tel 020-7357 8088
email info@csd.org.uk
website www.csd.org.uk

Works to promote and regulate standards of competence, professional conduct and integrity, including representation on government and official bodies, design education and awards. The services to members include general information, publications, guidance on copyright and other professional issues, access to professional indemnity insurance, as well as the membership magazine *The Designer*. Activities in the regions are included in an extensive annual programme of events and training courses.

Event & Visual Communication Association (EVCOM)

23 Golden Square, London W1F 9JP
tel 020-7287 1002
email info@evcom.org.uk
website www.evcom.org.uk
Twitter @EVCOMUK

Created from two highly successful organisations, eventia and IVCA, EVCOM is comprised of a wide variety of leading professionals, agencies, freelances, destinations, production companies and suppliers; all working throughout the events and visual communications sector.

Federation of British Artists

17 Carlton House Terrace, London SW1Y 5BD
tel 020-7930 6844
email info@mallgalleries.com
website www.mallgalleries.org.uk
Facebook www.facebook.com/mallgalleries
Twitter @mallgalleries

Administers nine major National Art Societies as well as the Threadneedle Prize at the Mall Galleries, The Mall, London SW1.

Fine Art Trade Guild

2 Wye House, 6 Enterprise Way, London SW18 1FZ
tel 020-7381 6616
email info@fineart.co.uk
website www.fineart.co.uk
Managing Director Louise Hay

Promotes the sale of fine art prints and picture framing in the UK and overseas markets; establishes and raises standards amongst members and communicates these to the buying public. The Guild publishes *Art + Framing Today*, the trade's longest established magazine, and various specialist books. Founded 1910.

FOCAL International Ltd (Federation of Commercial AudioVisual Libraries International Ltd)

79 College Road, Harrow, Middlesex, HA1 1BD
tel 020-7663 8090
email info@focalint.org
website www.focalint.org

A not-for-profit trade association for the commercial audio visual library industry, with over 300 members. Founded 1985.

Free Painters & Sculptors

Registered office 14 John Street, London WC1N 2EB
email info@freepaintersandsculptors.co.uk
website www.freepaintersandsculptors.co.uk

Promotes group shows twice a year in prestigious galleries in London. Sponsors all that is exciting in contemporary art.

The Greeting Card Association

United House, North Road, London N7 9DP
tel 020-7619 0396
email gca@max-publishing.co.uk
website www.greetingcardassociation.org.uk
Facebook www.facebook.com/GreetingCardAssociation
Twitter @GCAUK
Chief Executive Sharon Little

The trade association for greeting card publishers. See website for information and contacts for freelance designing and writing for greeting cards. Official magazine: *Progressive Greetings Worldwide*. Founded 1919.

The Guild of Aviation Artists

(incorporating the Society of Aviation Artists)
Studio 100, Rye House, 113 High Street, Ruislip HA4 8JN
tel (03331) 302223
email admin@gava.org.uk
website www.gava.org.uk
President Michael Turner
Membership £65 p.a. Full (by invitation); £50 Associates (by selection); £30 Friends; £15 Young Friends (aged under 25 years and in continuing education)

Formed to promote aviation art through the organisation of exhibitions and meetings. Holds annual open exhibition in July in London; £1,000 prize for 'Aviation Painting of the Year'. Quarterly members' newsletter. Founded 1971.

Guild of Railway Artists

website www.railart.co.uk

Aims to forge a link between artists depicting railway subjects and to give members a corporate identity; also stages railway art exhibitions and members' meetings and produces books of members' works. Founded 1979.

Hesketh Hubbard Art Society

17 Carlton House Terrace, London SW1Y 5BD
tel 020-7930 6844
email info@mallgalleries.com
website www.mallgalleries.org.uk
President Simon Whittle
Membership £225 p.a.

Offers both amateur and professional artists the opportunity to work from life models in untutored sessions. Membership includes 48 drawing sessions and no cover charge. Prospective members are invited to attend one session free before deciding if they wish to apply for membership.

The Hilliard Society of Miniaturists

c/o 26 St Cuthbert Avenue, Wells, BA5 2JW
email hilliardsociety@aol.com
website www.hilliardsociety.org
President Joyce Rowsell, *Executive Secretary* Heather Webb
Membership £60 p.a.; Friend Member £25 p.a.

Aims to increase knowledge and promote the art of miniature painting. Annual exhibition held in June at Wells; produces a newsletter. Founded 1982.

Institute of Designers in Ireland

Fumbally Exchange, 5 Dame Lane,
Dublin D02 HC67, Republic of Ireland
email info@idi-design.ie
website www.idi-design.ie

Irish design profession's representative body, covering every field of design. Founded 1972.

International Society of Typographic Designers

ISTD Ltd, PO Box 7002, London W1A 2TY
website www.istd.org.uk

Working closely with graphic design educationalists and the professional community, the International Society of Typographic Designers establishes, maintains and promotes typographic standards through the forum of debate and design practice.

Membership is awarded to practising designers, educators and students who demonstrate, through the quality of their work, their commitment to achieving the highest possible quality of visual communication. It publishes a journal, *Typographic*. Students of typography and graphic design are encouraged to gain membership of the Society by entering the annual student assessment scheme. Founded 1928.

Master Photographers Association

Jubilee House, 1 Chancery Lane, Darlington,
Co. Durham DL1 5QP
tel (01325) 356555
email membership@thempa.com
website www.thempa.com

Promotes and protects professional photographers. With over 60 years in the professional photography industry, the MPA prides itself in developing some of the industry's leading photographers.

National Acrylic Painters' Association

website www.napauk.com
Director Anthony Gribbin

Promotes interest in, and encourages excellence and innovation in, the work of painters in acrylic. Holds an annual exhibition and regional shows: awards are made. Worldwide membership. Publishes a newsletter known as the *International NAPA Newspages*. Founded 1985 by Ken Hodgson; American Division established 1995, now known as International Society of Acrylic Painters (ISAP).

National Society for Education in Art and Design

3 Mason's Wharf, Potley Lane, Corsham,
Wilts. SN13 9FY
tel (01225) 810134
email info@nsead.org
website www.nsead.org
Facebook www.facebook.com/groups/NSEADOnline
Twitter @LBNSEAD
General Secretary Lesley Butterworth, *Assistant General Secretary* Sophie Leach

The leading national authority concerned with art, craft and design across all phases of education in the UK. Offers the benefits of membership of a professional association, a learned society and a trade union. Has representatives on national and regional committees concerned with art and design education. Publishes *International Journal of Art and Design Education* online (three p.a.; Wiley Blackwell) and *AD* magazine for teachers. Founded 1888.

National Society of Painters, Sculptors and Printmakers

website www.nationalsociety.org

Formed to communicate innovative painting, sculpture and printmaking with a wide audience. Founded 1931.

The Pastel Society

email info@mallgalleries.com
website www.thepastelsociety.org.uk
Facebook www.facebook.com/thepastelsociety
Twitter @pastelsociety

Pastel and drawings in all dry media. Annual Exhibition open to all artists working in dry media held at the Mall Galleries, The Mall, London SW1. Members elected from approved candidates' list. Founded 1898.

The Picture Research Association

tel 07825 788343
email chair@picture-research.org.uk
website www.picture-research.org.uk
Facebook www.facebook.com/PictureResearchAssociation
Twitter @PRA_Association

The PRA is a professional organisation of picture researchers and picture editors specifically involved in the research, management and supply of visual material to the media industry. Its aims are:

- To promote the recognition of picture research, management, editing, picture buying and supplying as a profession requiring particular skills and knowledge.
- To bring together all those involved in the picture profession and provide a forum for information exchange and interaction.
- To encourage publishers, TV and video production organisations, internet companies, and any other users of images to use the PRA freelance register and engage a member of PRA to obtain them, thus ensuring that professional standards and copyright clearances are adhered to and maintained.
- To advise those specifically wishing to embark on a profession in the research and supply of pictures for all types of visual media information, providing guidelines and standards in so doing.

Registered members are listed on the website and can be located through the Find Researchers page, along with lots of useful information about the picture industry. Founded 1977.

Printmakers Council

Ground Floor Unit, 23 Blue Anchor Lane, London SE16 3UL
tel 07531 883250
email printpmc@gmail.com
website www.printmakerscouncil.com
Facebook www.facebook.com/PrintmakersCouncil/
Twitter @PMCouncil
Membership £75 p.a.; £30 students, join online

Artist-led group which aims to promote the use of both traditional and innovative printmaking techniques by: holding exhibitions of prints; providing information on prints and printmaking to both its membership and the public and; encouraging cooperation and exchanges between members, other associations and interested individuals.

Archives held by the V&A and Scarborough Museums Trust. Founded 1965.

Professional Cartoonists' Organisation

email info@procartoonists.org
website www.procartoonists.org
Membership £80 p.a.

An organisation dedicated to the promotion of UK cartoon art in new media and old. Cartoons provide much-needed humour and satire to society and are a universally appreciated, effective method of communication for business. The organisation showcases UK cartoonists via its magazine, *Foghorn,* cartoon news blog (*Bloghorn*), and public events such as the annual Big Draw and cartoon festivals. Founded 2006.

SAA (Society for All Artists)

PO Box 50, Newark, Notts. NG23 5GY
tel 0800 980 1123
email info@saa.co.uk
website www.saa.co.uk
Facebook www.facebook.com/WeAreTheSAA
Twitter @The_SAA
Membership from £32 p.a.

Aims to encourage and inspire all artists. Members range from complete beginners to professionals. SAA is the largest art society with over 43,000 members, and welcomes new members. Membership includes paintings insurance for exhibitions and third-party public liability, exclusive discounts and offers on art materials from the society's *Home Shop* catalogue and the inspirational *Paint* magazine (bi-monthly). Founded 1992.

The Society of Botanical Artists

Registered office: 1 Knapp Cottages, Wyke, Gillingham, Dorset SP8 4NQ
tel (01747) 825718
email pam@soc-botanical-artists.org
website www.soc-botanical-artists.org
President Sandra Wall Armitage, *Executive Secretary* Mrs Pam Henderson
Membership Through selection. £175 p.a.; £25 friend members

Aims to encourage the art of botanical painting. No open exhibition in 2018 in the UK, but entry details for 2019 will be available on the website. Founded 1985.

Society of Graphic Fine Art

email enquiries@sgfa.org.uk
website www.sgfa.org.uk
President Jackie Devereux PSGFA

The Society of Graphic Fine Art (The Drawing Society) exists to promote and exhibit works of high quality in colour or black and white, with the emphasis on good drawing and draughtsmanship, in pencil, pen, brush, charcoal or any of the forms of original printmaking. The Society holds an annual Open Exhibition with prizes and awards in many categories. The Society's journal can be found at http://sgfajournal.wordpress.com. Founded 1919.

Society of Heraldic Arts

53 Hitchen Street, Baldock, Hertfordshire, SG7 6AQ
email sha.honsec@gmail.com
website www.heraldic-arts.com
Hon. Secretary John J. Tunesi of Liongam

Serves the interests of heraldic artists, craftsmen, designers and writers, to provide a 'shop window' for their work, to obtain commissions on their behalf and to act as a forum for the exchange of information and ideas. Also offers an information service to the public. Candidates for admission as craft members should be artists or craftsmen whose work comprises a substantial element of heraldry and is of a sufficiently high standard to satisfy the requirements of the Society's advisory council. Founded 1987.

The Society of Limners

Contact Diana Altman, 41 Canal Wharf, Chichester, West Sussex PO19 8EY
tel (01243) 527422
email societyoflimners@outlook.com
website www.societyoflimners.co.uk
Membership £45 p.a., £25 Friends (open to non-exhibitors); £55/£35 overseas

The Society's aims are to promote an interest in miniature painting (in any medium), calligraphy and heraldry and encourage their development to a high standard. New members are elected after the submission of four works of acceptable standard and guidelines are provided for new artists. Members receive up to three newsletters a year and an annual exhibition is arranged. At least one painting weekend is held each year and occasional seminars. Founded 1986.

Society of Scribes and Illuminators

Hon. Secretary 6 Queen Square, London WC1N 3AT
email honsec@calligraphyonline.org
website www.calligraphyonline.org
Membership £46 Fellows; £37 Lay members; £30 Friends

Aims to promote and preserve the art of calligraphy, bringing the beauty of handwritten letters to the modern world, moving with the times to embrace contemporary lettering whilst upholding the traditions of the craft. Education programme includes a correspondence course, an advanced training scheme, mentorship towards fellowship, a programme of study days, a series of masterclasses and recommendations for local learning opportunities. A specialist sales shop and an archive/library are available to members. Founded 1921.

Society of Wildlife Artists

17 Carlton House Terrace, London SW1Y 5BD
tel 020-7930 6844
website www.swla.co.uk
President Harriet Mead

Aims to promote and encourage the art of wildlife painting and sculpture. Open Annual Exhibition at Mall Galleries, The Mall, London SW1, for any artist whose work depicts wildlife subjects (botanical and domestic animals are not admissable).

The Society of Women Artists

Foxcote Cottage, Foxcote, Andoversford, Cheltenham, Glos. GL54 4LP
tel 07528 477002
email rebeccacottonswa@gmail.com
website www.society-women-artists.org.uk
President Soraya French, *Executive Secretary* Rebecca Cotton
Membership Election by invitation, based on work submitted to the exhibition

Receiving day in July for annual open exhibition held in September at Mall Galleries, The Mall, London SW1. Founded in 1855, the Society continues to promote art by women.

FILM, THEATRE AND TELEVISION

AITA/IATA asbl International Amateur Theatre Association

email secretariat@aitaiata.org
website www.aitaiata.net
Facebook www.facebook.com/aitaiata/
President Rob Van Genechten, *Vice-President & Councillor* Tim Jebsen, *Treasurer & Councillor* Villy Dall

Encourages, fosters and promotes exchanges of community and non-professional theatre and of student, educational and adult theatre activities at international level. Organises international seminars, workshops, courses and conferences, and collates information of all types for national and international dissemination. Holds a biennial General Assembly and International Amateur Theatre Festival and a biennial World Festival of Children's Theatre. Every other General Assembly is held in Monaco and every other Festival of Children's Theatre is held in Lingen, Germany.

BAFTA (British Academy of Film and Television Arts)

195 Piccadilly, London W1J 9LN
tel 020-7734 0022
email info@bafta.org
website www.bafta.org
Chief Executive Amanda Berry OBE

The UK's pre-eminent, independent charity supporting, developing and promoting the art forms of the moving image (film, TV and games) by identifying and rewarding excellence, inspiring practitioners and benefiting the public. BAFTA's awards are awarded annually by its members to their peers in recognition of their skills and expertise. BAFTA's year-round learning programme offers unique access to some of the world's most inspiring talent through workshops, masterclasses, lectures and mentoring schemes, connecting with audiences of all ages and backgrounds across the UK, Los Angeles and New York. Founded 1947.

BFI (British Film Institute)

21 Stephen Street, London W1T 1LN
tel 020-7255 1444
website www.bfi.org.uk

The BFI is the lead organisation for film in the UK with the ambition to create a flourishing film environment in which innovation, opportunity and creativity can thrive by:

• connecting audiences to the widest choice of British and World cinema;
• preserving and restoring the most significant film collection in the world for today and future generations;
• championing emerging and world class film-makers in the UK;
• investing in creative, distinctive and entertaining work;
• promoting British film talent to the world;
• growing the next generation of film makers and audiences.

The BFI is a Government arm's-length body and distributor of Lottery funds for film. The BFI serves a public role which covers the cultural, creative and economic aspects of film in the UK. It delivers this role:

• as the UK-wide organisation for film, a charity core funded by Government;
• by providing Lottery and Government funds for film across the UK;
• by working with partners to advance the position of film across the UK.

Founded 1933.

BECTU (Broadcasting Entertainment Communications and Theatre Union)

373–377 Clapham Road, London SW9 9BT
tel 020-7346 0900
email info@bectu.org.uk
website www.bectu.org.uk
Head of BECTU G. Morrissey

BECTU (a sector of the Prospect union) aims to defend the interests of writers in film, TV and radio. By virtue of its industrial strength, the Union is able to help its writer members to secure favourable terms and conditions. In cases of disputes with employers, the Union can intervene in order to ensure an equitable settlement. Its production agreement with Pact lays down minimum terms for writers working in the documentary area. Founded 1991.

Independent Theatre Council

The Albany, Douglas Way, London SE8 4AG
tel 020-7403 1727
email admin@itc-arts.org
website https://www.itc-arts.org/
Twitter @itc_arts

The Independent Theatre Council exists to enable the creation of high quality professional performing arts by supporting, representing and developing the people who manage and produce it. It has around 500 members from a wide range of companies, venues and individuals in the fields of drama, dance, opera, musical theatre, puppetry, mixed media, mime, physical theatre and circus. Founded 1974.

Little Theatre Guild of Great Britain

tel (01388) 730042
website www.littletheatreguild.org

Promotes closer cooperation amongst the little theatres constituting its membership; to act as a coordinating and representative body on behalf of the little theatres; to maintain and advance the highest standards in the art of theatre; and to assist in encouraging the establishment of other little theatres.

Pact (Producers' Alliance for Cinema and Television)

3rd Floor, Fitzrovia House,
153–157 Cleveland Street, London W1T 6QW
tel 020-7380 8230
email info@pact.co.uk
website www.pact.co.uk
Twitter @PactUK
Chief Executive John McVay

The UK trade association that represents and promotes the commercial interests of independent feature film, television, animation and interactive media companies. Headquartered in London, it has regional representation throughout the UK, in order to support its members. An effective lobbying organisation, it has regular and constructive dialogues with government, regulators, public agencies and opinion formers on all issues affecting its members, and contributes to key public policy debates on the media industry, both in the UK and in Europe. It negotiates terms of trade with all public service broadcasters in the UK and supports members in their business dealings with cable and satellite channels. It also lobbies for a properly structured and funded UK film industry and maintains close contact with other relevant film organisations and government departments.

Player–Playwrights

email lynneplay@gmail.com
website www.playerplaywrights.co.uk

Facebook www.facebook.com/groups/playerplaywrights/
Secretary Lynne O'Sullivan
Membership £12 in first year and £8 thereafter (plus £2.50 per attendance). Guests and audience welcome (non-members £4 entrance).

Meets on Monday evenings upstairs in the North London Tavern, 375 Kilburn High Road, London NW6 7QB; 7.30p.m., just turn up. The society reads, performs and discusses plays and scripts submitted by members, with a view to assisting the writers in improving and marketing their work and enabling actors to showcase their talents. New writers and new acting members are always welcome. Founded 1948.

The Society for Theatre Research

c/o Theatres Trust, 22 Charing Cross Road, London WC2H 0QL
email contact1@str.org.uk
website www.str.org.uk
Joint Hon. Secretaries Diana Fraser and Chris Abbot

Supporting and promoting theatre research since 1948. Publishes the journal *Theatre Notebook* along with at least one major book per year, holds public lectures, and makes annual research grants. Also awards an annual prize for best book published in English on British Theatre.

TRANSLATION

American Literary Translators Association

email elisabeth@literarytranslators.org
website www.literarytranslators.org
Executive Director Elisabeth Jaquette

ALTA is a broad-based professional association dedicated to the promotion of literary translation through services to literary translators, forums on the theory and practice of translation, collaboration with the international literary community, and advocacy on behalf of literary translators. Founded 1978.

British Centre for Literary Translation

School of Literature, Drama & Creative Writing, University of East Anglia, Norwich Research Park, Norwich NR4 7TJ
tel (01603) 592785
email bclt@uea.ac.uk
website www.bclt.org.uk
Facebook www.facebook.com/bcltuea
Twitter @bcltuea

The BCLT raises the profile of literary translation in the UK through events, publications, activities and research aimed at professional translators, the publishing industry, students and the general reader. Activities include the annual Sebald Lecture in London, Summer School and public talks and events. It is joint sponsor of the John Dryden Translation Prize. Member of the international RECIT literary translation network. Founded 1989.

Chartered Institute of Linguists

Dunstan House, 14A St Cross Street, London EC1N 8XA
tel 020-7940 3100
email info@ciol.org.uk
website www.ciol.org.uk
Twitter @ciolinguists

The Chartered Institute of Linguists (CIOL) is the foremost international membership organisation for all language professionals and is the only one offering a pathway to Chartership. Its diverse membership includes translators and interpreters, language teachers, university lecturers and linguists who use their foreign language skills in business, the professions and government.

CIOL's associated charity, IoL Educational Trust, is an Ofqual accredited awarding body offering professional qualifications in translation and public service interpreting. CIOL publishes a bi-monthly magazine, *The Linguist*, free to members and available to non-members by subscription. *The Linguist* offers its readers a wide range of articles that are of interest to anyone working with languages. Founded 1910.

The Institute of Translation & Interpreting

Milton Keynes Business Centre, Foxhunter Drive, Linford Wood, Milton Keynes MK14 6GD
info@iti.org.uk
website www.iti.org.uk

The ITI is the independent professional association of practising translators and interpreters. With the aim of promoting the highest standards in the profession, ITI serves as a focal point for all those who understand the importance of translation and interpreting to the economy and community. It offers guidance to those entering the profession and advice to both people offering their language services and their potential customers. Founded 1986.

Translators Association

84 Drayton Gardens, London SW10 9SB
tel 020-7373 6642
email info@societyofauthors.org
website www.societyofauthors.org/translators-association

Specialist unit within the membership of the Society of Authors (see page 519), exclusively concerned with the interests of literary translators into English whose work is published or performed commercially in Great Britain. Members are entitled to advice on all aspects of their work, including remuneration and contractual arrangements with publishers, editors and broadcasting organisations. Members receive a free copy of the journal *In Other Words*. Founded 1958.

BIBLIOGRAPHICAL AND ACADEMIC

The Association of Learned and Professional Society Publishers

Egale 1, 80 St Albans Road, Watford, Herts. WD17 1DL
email admin@alpsp.org
website www.alpsp.org

The ALPSP is the international membership trade body which works to support and represent not-for-profit organisations and institutions that publish scholarly and professional content around the world. Its membership also encompasses those that partner with and provide services to not-for-profit publishers. ALPSP has over 300 members in 30 countries. Its mission is to connect, inform, develop and represent the international scholarly and professional publishing community.

Bibliographical Society

c/o Institute of English Studies, University of London, Senate House, Malet Street, London WC1E 7HU
tel 020-7782 3279
email admin@bibsoc.org.uk
website www.bibsoc.org.uk

Acquisition and dissemination of information on subjects connected with historical bibliography. Publishes the journal *The Library*. Founded 1892.

Cambridge Bibliographical Society

University Library, West Road, Cambridge CB3 9DR
email cbs@lib.cam.ac.uk
website www.lib.cam.ac.uk/cambibsoc

Aims to encourage the study of bibliography, including book and MS production, book collecting and the history of libraries. It publishes *Transactions* (annual) and a series of monographs, and arranges a programme of lectures and visits. Founded 1949.

Classical Association

email canews@classicalassociation.org
website www.classicalassociation.org
Hon. Secretary Dr E.J. Stafford

Exists to promote and sustain interest in classical studies, to maintain their rightful position in universities and schools, and to give scholars and teachers opportunities for meeting and discussing their problems.

Early English Text Society

Faculty of English, St Cross Building, Manor Road, Oxford OX1 3UL
website www.eets.org.uk
Twitter @EEngTextSoc
Hon. Director Prof. V. Gillespie, *Executive Secretary* Prof. D. Wakelin
Membership £30 p.a.

Aims to bring unprinted early English literature within the reach of students in sound texts. Founded 1864.

Edinburgh Bibliographical Society

102A Findhorn Place, Edinburgh EH9 2NZ
email derek.annetaylor@gmail.com
website www.edinburghbibliographicalsociety.org.uk
Secretary D. Taylor, *Treasurer* R. Betteridge
Membership £18 p.a.; £25 corporate; £12 full-time students

Encourages bibliographical activity through organising talks for members, particularly on bibliographical topics relating to Scotland, and visits to libraries. See website for submission guidelines and prizes. Publishes *Journal* (annual, free to members) and other occasional publications. Founded 1890.

Oxford Bibliographical Society

Bodleian Library, Broad Street, Oxford OX1 3BG
email secretary@oxbibsoc.org.uk
website www.oxbibsoc.org.uk
Membership £30 p.a.

Exists to encourage bibliographical research. Publishes monographs. Founded 1922.

MEMBERS' CLUBS

Arts Club

40 Dover Street, London W1S 4NP
tel 020-7499 8581
email membership@theartsclub.co.uk
website www.theartsclub.co.uk
Twitter @The_Arts_Club

A private members' club for all those connected with or interested in the arts, literature and science. Founded 1863.

Authors' Club

Whitehall Place, London SW1A 2HE
email info@authorsclub.co.uk
website www.authorsclub.co.uk
Facebook www.facebook.com/authorsclub1891
Twitter @AuthorsClub
President John Walsh, *Chairperson* Sunny Singh

A club for all those professionally engaged with literature, the Authors' Club welcomes as members writers, publishers, critics, journalists and academics. Administers the Authors' Club Best First Novel Award, the Art Book Prize and the Stanford Dolman Travel Book of the Year Award. Founded 1891.

New English Art Club

email info@neac.co.uk
website www.newenglishartclub.co.uk

The New English represents the very best of contemporary British figurative painting. Members of the public can send in work to the Annual Open Exhibition at The Mall Galleries, The Mall, London SW1, open to all working in painting, drawing, pastels and prints.

Scottish Arts Club

24 Rutland Square, Edinburgh EH1 2BW
tel 0131 229 8157
website www.scottishartsclub.com

The Scottish Arts Club has been a social hub for the arts and professional members include painters and sculptors, movie-makers and musicians, planners, playwrights and poets, novelists and journalists, architects and designers, dancers and diplomats. There are a number of lay members, all with an interest in the arts. Founded 1873.

WRITERS' ORGANISATIONS

All Party Parliamentary Writers Group

tel 020-7264 5700
email barbara.hayes@alcs.co.uk
website www.allpartywritersgroup.co.uk
Chair John Whittingdale MP, *Administrator* Barbara Hayes

The Group has some 60 Members from both Houses and seeks to represent the interests of all writers; to safeguard their intellectual property rights and ensure they receive a fair level of recognition and reward for their contribution to the economy and society as a whole. Founded 2007.

Alliance of Independent Authors – see page 525

Association of British Science Writers

email info@absw.org.uk
website www.absw.org.uk
Facebook www.facebook.com/Association-of-British-Science-Writers-ABSW-124733480870885/
Twitter @absw
Chair Mico Tatlovic, *Hon. President* Pallab Ghosh

Association of science writers, editors, and radio, film and TV producers concerned with the presentation and communication of science and technology. Aims to improve the standard of science journalism and to assist its members in their work. Runs the annual ABSW Science Writers' Awards, the Biennial UK Conference of Science Journalists and Science Journalism Summer School. Membership details/ application through website only.

Association of Christian Writers

email admin@christianwriters.org.uk
website www.christianwriters.org.uk
Facebook www.facebook.com/groups/24831838019
Twitter @ACW1971
Membership From 2019: £29 per annum with PayPal (because of fees levied); £26 PayPal auto. Renewal: £28 cash or cheque; £25 direct debit; £33 overseas. Membership year runs from 1 April to 31 March and includes quarterly issues of Christian Writer magazine sent by post.

ACW aims to inspire excellence in writing from a Christian world view. Equips Christian writers through writing days around the UK, workshops and writing competitions. Members encourage each other online and in affiliated local groups. Please note that ACW is not a publisher.

Authors Aloud UK

72 Castle Road, St Albans, Herts. AL1 5DG
tel (01727) 893992
email info@authorsalouduk.co.uk
website www.authorsalouduk.co.uk
Facebook www.facebook.com/Authors-Aloud-UK-497942623573822/
Twitter @AuthorsAloudUK
Directors Anne Marley, Naomi Cooper, Annie Everall

Authors Aloud UK is an author booking agency which brings together authors, illustrators, poets, storytellers and trainers with schools, libraries and festivals to promote enthusiasm for reading, both for enjoyment and information. Happy to take on new speakers, published by mainstream children's publishers, who meet the relevant criteria and guidelines. Keen to work with new and debut authors who wish to visit schools and libraries.

Book Aid International

39–41 Coldharbour Lane, London SE5 9NR
tel 020-7733 3577
email info@bookaid.org
website www.bookaid.org

Book Aid Interantional is the UK's leading international book donation and library support charity. The group provides books, resources and training to support an environment in which reading for pleasure, study and lifelong learning can flourish.

Book Marketing Society

website www.bookmarketingsociety.co.uk

The Book Marketing Society was launched with the objective of becoming the representative body of marketing within the book industry. As such, it champions marketing professionalism with the ultimate goal of expanding the UK book market. Anyone who works for a book publisher, book retailer or book wholesaler is eligible for membership, including those working in associated areas of the publishing and book retailing industry. Founded 2004.

The British Fantasy Society

email secretary@britishfantasysociety.org
website www.britishfantasysociety.org

Membership £35 p.a. single; £40 joint; £45 Europe; £60 rest of world for the print editions. £10 p.a. for digital membership.

For readers, writers and publishers of fantasy, horror and related fields, in literature, art and the cinema. There is an annual convention, FantasyCon, and The British Fantasy Awards are sponsored by the Society. Founded 1971.

British Guild of Beer Writers

44 Hurst Road, Horsham, West Sussex, RH12 2EP
tel (07841) 694137
email secretary@beerguild.co.uk
website www.beerwriters.co.uk
Twitter @Britbeerwriters
Secretary Ros Shiel
Membership £40 p.a.

Aims to improve standards in beer writing and at the same time extend public knowledge of beer and pubs. Awards are given annually to writers, broadcasters and other communicators judged to have made the most valuable contribution to this end. Publishes a directory of members with details of their publications and their particular areas of interest, which is circulated to the media. Founded 1988.

The British Guild of Travel Writers

335 Lordship Road, London N16 5HG
tel 020-8144 8713
email secretariat@bgtw.org
website www.bgtw.org
Facebook www.facebook.com/TravelBGTW
Twitter @TravWriters

Arranges meetings, discussions and visits for its members (who are all professional travel journalists) to promote and encourage the public's interest in travel. Publishes a monthly newsletter (for members only), website and annual Yearbook, which contains details of members and lists travel industry PRs and contacts. Annual awards for journalism (members only) and the travel trade. Founded 1960.

The British Haiku Society

79 Westbury Road, Barking, Essex IG11 7PL
email membership@britishhaikusociety.org.uk
website www.britishhaikusociety.org.uk

Pioneers the appreciation and writing of haiku in the UK, publishes books concerning haiku and related matters, and is active in promoting the teaching of haiku in schools and colleges. Publishes a quarterly journal, *Blithe Spirit*, an annual members' anthology, and a newsletter. Also runs the prestigious annual British Haiku Society Awards in three categories: haiku, tanka, and haibun. Registered charity. Founded 1990.

British Science Fiction Association Ltd

email info@bsfa.co.uk
website www.bsfa.co.uk
Chair Donna Bond

For authors, publishers, booksellers and readers of science fiction, fantasy and allied genres. Publishes *Focus*, an amateur writers' magazine; *Vector*, a critical magazine and the Orbiter Service, a network of email/postal writers' workshops. Trophies are awarded annually to the winner in each category of the BSFA Awards: best UK-published novel (previous winners include Christopher Priest, Adam Roberts, China Mieville), best short story, best artwork, best non-fiction. Founded 1958.

British Society of Comedy Writers

61 Parry Road, Ashmore Park, Wolverhampton, West Midlands WV11 2PS
tel (01902) 722729
email info@bscw.co.uk
website www.bscw.co.uk
President Kenneth Rock
Membership £75 p.a. full, £40 p.a. subscriber

Aims to bring together writers and industry representatives in order to develop new projects and ideas. Holds an annual international comedy conference, networking days and workshops to train new writers to professional standards. Founded 1999.

Circle of Wine Writers

tel (01753) 882320
email administrator@circleofwinewriters.org
website www.circleofwinewriters.org
Membership By election.

An association for those engaged in communicating about wines and spirits. Produces *The Circlular* (monthly online newsletter), organises tasting sessions as well as a programme of meetings, talks and trips. Founded 1960.

Crime Writers' Association

email secretary@thecwa.co.uk
website www.thecwa.co.uk
Secretary Dea Parkin

Membership is open to traditionally published crime writers, plus anyone whose business is concerned with publishing, bookselling or representing crime writers. Provisional membership is available for writers with a valid contract whose first book will be published within the next two years. Associate and corporate membership is open to editors, reviewers, bloggers, publishers, journalists, booksellers specialising in crime literature and literary agents.

The CWA runs the world-renowed Dagger awards. Membership benefits include monthly magazine *Red Herrings*, local chapters for social events, Find an Author profile, blogging opportunities on the Crime Readers' Association website and book promotional platforms such as Case Files and the CRA Newsletter, read by around 11,000 subscribers, plus diverse social media outlets. The CWA initiates National Crime Reading Month in May where members participate in library and bookshop events, and runs the Debut

Dagger and Margery Allingham Short Story competitions. Founded 1953.

The Critics' Circle

c/o Rick Jones, 17 Rosenthal Road, Catford, London SE6 2BX
tel 020-8698 2460
email criticscircleallsections@gmail.com
website www.criticscircle.org.uk
President Anna Smith, *Hon. General Secretary* Rick Jones, *Hon. Treasurer* Peter Cargin
Membership By invitation of the Council

Promotes the art of criticism, to uphold its integrity, to foster and safeguard the professional interests of its members, to provide opportunities for socialising and networking, and to support the advancement of the arts. Membership is by invitation only and granted only to persons engaged regularly and substantially in the writing or broadcasting of criticism of dance, drama, film, literature, music and the visual arts. Founded 1913.

TheFED – A Network of Writing and Community Publishers

Flat 2 Clydesdale, 5 College Road, Buxton, Derbyshire SK17 9DZ
tel 07549 862495
email fedonline1@gmail.com
website www.thefed.btck.co.uk
Facebook www.facebook.com/groups/TheFEDfriends
Membership Secretary/Treasurer Louise Glasscoe
Membership £25 p.a. funded groups; £15 unfunded; £10 waged/higher income individuals; £5 unwaged/ low income

TheFED is a not-for-profit organisation, run by volunteers, and continues the work started by the Federation of Worker Writers and Community Publishers. Details of the 2019 annual Festival of Writing and AGM at Syracuse University's London campus, as well as other activities associated with TheFED, will be advertised on the website.

TheFED runs a monthly writing challenge and hosts TheFED archive in collaboration with TUC Library Collections, London Metropolitan University and Syracuse University, New York; it has associations with other local and national events and encourages networking between member groups.

The Garden Media Guild

Katepwa House, Ashfield Park Avenue, Ross-on-Wye, Herefordshire HR9 5AX
tel (01989) 567393
email admin@gardenmediaguild.co.uk
website www.gardenmediaguild.co.uk
Facebook www.facebook.com/gardenmediaguild
Twitter @gdnmediaguild
Chairman Clare Foggett
Membership £70 p.a.; associate membership £105 p.a.; probationary membership £52.50 p.a. Full membership is open to those who earn a significant part of their income from communicating information on the subject of gardening and horticulture.

Aims to raise the quality of garden writing, photography and broadcasting, to help members operate efficiently and profitably, to improve communication between members and to promote liaison between members and the broader horticultural industry. The Guild administers annual awards to encourage excellence in garden writing, photography, trade and consumer press journalism, TV and radio broadcasting. Founded 1991.

Gay Authors Workshop

BM Box 5700, London WC1N 3XX
email eandk2@btinternet.com
website http://gayauthorsworkshop.uk/
Contact Kathryn Bell
Membership £8 p.a.; £5 unwaged

Exists to encourage writers who are lesbian, gay or bisexual. Quarterly newsletter, bi-annual magazine and monthly meetings. Founded 1978.

Guild of Food Writers

255 Kent House Road, Beckenham, Kent BR3 1JQ
tel 020-8659 0422
email guild@gfw.co.uk
website www.gfw.co.uk
Administrator Jonathan Woods
Membership £85 p.a.

Aims to bring together professional food writers including journalists, broadcasters and authors, to print and issue an annual list of members, to extend the range of members' knowledge and experience by arranging discussions, tastings and visits, and to encourage the development of new writers by every means, including competitions and awards. There are 14 awards and entry is not restricted to members of the Guild. Founded 1984.

Guild of Health Writers

Dale Lodge, 88 Wensleydale Road, Hampton, Middlesex TW12 2LX
tel 020-8941 2977
email admin@healthwriters.com
website www.healthwriters.com
Twitter @HealthWritersUK
Membership £50 p.a.; students £12 p.a.

The Guild of Health Writers is a national, independent membership organisation representing Britain's leading health journalists and writers. It was founded to encourage the provision of readable and accurate health information to the public. Members write on every aspect of health and wellbeing, from innovative medical science to complementary therapies and lifestyle issues. They value the training and networking opportunities that the Guild provides. Founded 1994.

The Guild of Motoring Writers

Secretariat, 40 Baring Road, Bournemouth BH6 4DT
tel (01202) 422424
email generalsec@gomw.co.uk
website www.gomw.co.uk/
Facebook www.facebook.com/gomwuk
Twitter @gomw_uk

The Guild of Motoring Writers is the largest organisation of its kind in the world representing automotive journalists, photographers, broadcasters and artists. Based in the UK, it represents more than 500 members. It aims to raise the standard of motoring journalism, to encourage motoring, motorsport and road safety, promote professional training of journalists, works closely with the motor industry and provides a link between fellow members around the world and to safeguard the interests of members in relation to the aims of the Guild. Founded 1944.

Hakluyt Society

c/o The Map Library, The British Library,
96 Euston Road, London NW1 2DB
tel (07568) 468066
email office@hakluyt.com
website www.hakluyt.com

Publication of original narratives of voyages, travels, naval expeditions, and other geographical records. Founded 1846.

Harleian Society

College of Arms, 130 Queen Victoria Street,
London EC4V 4BT
tel 020-7236 7728
email norroy&ulster@college-of-arms.gov.uk
website http://harleian.org.uk
Chairman T. Woodcock CVO, DL, FSA, Garter King of Arms, *Hon. Secretary* T.H.S. Duke, Norroy and Ulster King of Arms

Instituted for transcribing, printing and publishing the heraldic visitations of Counties, Parish Registers and any manuscripts relating to genealogy, family history and heraldry. Founded 1869.

Historical Novel Society

Marine Cottage, The Strand, Starcross,
Devon EX6 8NY
tel (01626) 891962
email richard@historicalnovelsociety.org
website http://historicalnovelsociety.org/
Facebook www.facebook.com/historicalnovelsociety
Twitter @histnovsoc
Contact Richard Lee
Membership £40 p.a.

Promotes the enjoyment of historical fiction. Based in the US and UK but welcomes members (who can be readers or writers) from all over the world. Publishes print magazines, organises conferences and local chapters. Founded 1997.

Historical Writers' Association

email admin@historicalwriters.org
website www.historicalwriters.org

Association created by authors, publishers and agents of historical writing, both fiction and non-fiction, which provides professional and social support to members and creates opportunities online and in person for members to meet with fellow writers and enthusiasts of all things historical. Ogranises a range of regional events.

Horror Writers Association

email hwa@horror.org
website www.horror.org
Facebook www.facebook.com/groups/Horrorwritersassoc/
Twitter @horrorwriters
President Lisa Morton

The HWA is a worldwide organisation of 1,300 writers and publishing professionals dedicated to promoting the interests of writers of horror and dark fantasy. There are five levels of membership: for new writers, established writers, professionals, academics and non-writing horror professionals. The HWA gives the iconic Bram Stoker Awards® on an annual basis, as well as hosting horror conventions, and provides a range of services to its horror writer, editor and publisher membership base. Founded 1987.

International Association of Conscious & Creative Writers

PO Box 3703, Trowbridge BA14 6ZW
tel (01380) 871331
email iaccw@juliamccutchen.com
website www.iaccw.com
Founder & Creative Director Julia McCutchen
Membership Free

Membership-based organisation for writers offering monthly teleseminar training and interviews with bestselling authors and experts from around the world. Topics include all aspects of creativity, writing and contemporary publishing options, plus marketing and building an author platform. Highlights the importance of discovering your authentic voice both on the page and in the world. Founded 2010.

The Mythopoeic Society

secretary@mythsoc.org
website www.mythsoc.org

A non-profit international literary and educational organisation for the study, discussion and enjoyment of fantastic and mythic literature, especially the works of Tolkien, C.S. Lewis and Charles Williams. The word 'mythopoeic' (myth-oh-PAY-ik or myth-oh-PEE-ic), meaning 'mythmaking' or 'productive of myth', aptly describes much of the fictional work of the three authors who were also prominent members of an informal Oxford literary circle (1930s–1950s) known as the Inklings. Membership is open to all scholars, writers and readers of these literatures. The Society sponsors three periodicals: *Mythprint* (a bulletin of book reviews, articles and events), *Mythlore* (scholarly articles on mythic and fantastic literature), and *Mythic Circle* (a literary annual of original poetry and short stories). Each summer the Society holds an annual conference, Mythcon. Founded 1967.

National Association of Writers' Groups (NAWG)

email info@nawg.co.uk
website www.nawg.co.uk
Facebook www.facebook.com/NAWGNews/
Twitter @NAWGnews
Secretary Chris Huck
Membership £50 p.a. per group; £25 Individuals

NAWG aims to advance the education of the general public throughout the UK, including the Channel Islands, by promoting the study and art of writing in all its aspects. Publishes *LNK*, a bi-monthly magazine. Festival of Writing held annually in August/September. New members always welcome. Founded 1995.

New Writers UK

Facebook www.facebook.com/New-Writers-UK-257055444333315/

New Writers UK supports and advises independently published authors and those who do not have financial backing or marketing to promote their books. This is an organisation of authors working on a voluntary basis to assist other authors and encourage imaginative literacy in young people and adults. New members welcome. NWUK holds a number of events throughout the year, produces an online quarterly newsletter. NWUK has an associate membership of copy editors, proofreaders, graphic designers, reviewers and illustrators. Founded 2006.

New Writing North

email office@newwritingnorth.com
website www.newwritingnorth.com

The literature development agency for the North of England. Specialises in developing writers and acts as a broker between writers, producers, publishers and broadcasters. Flagship projects include Northern Writers' Awards, Gordon Burn Prize and Durham Book Festival.

New Writing South

9 Jew Street, Brighton, East Sussex BN1 1UT
tel (01273) 735353
email admin@newwritingsouth.com
website www.newwritingsouth.com
Facebook www.facebook.com/newwritingsouth
Twitter @newwritingsouth
Chief Executive Lesley Wood
Membership Friends £20 p.a. (concessions available at £10 p.a.)

New Writing South champions all kinds of new creative writing in the South East and beyond. It develops writers' careers and helps fresh talent to flourish by providing development opportunities and commissioning new work. Join the new membership scheme, NWS Friends, and you will not only become part of a vibrant community of writers – you will be supporting New Writing South to nurture diverse talent across the region, including writers who would not ordinarily have access to professional development opportunities.

Outdoor Writers and Photographers Guild

The Oast House Huntsbarn, Piccadilly Lane, Mayfield, East Sussex TN20 6RH
tel (07813) 855820
email secretary@owpg.org.uk
website www.owpg.org.uk
Membership £80 p.a.

Association of the leading practitioners in outdoor media; represents members' interests to representative bodies in the outdoor industry; circulates members with news of media opportunities; provides a forum for members to meet colleagues and others in the outdoor industry. Presents annual literary and photographic awards. Members include writers, journalists, broadcasters, illustrators, photographers, bloggers, editors and publishers. Founded 1980.

PEN International

Unit A Koops Mill Mews, 162 Abbey Street, London SE1 2AN
tel 020-7405 0338
email info@pen-international.org.uk
website www.pen-international.org.uk

A world association of writers. PEN was founded by C.A. Dawson Scott under the presidency of John Galsworthy, to promote friendship and understanding between writers and to defend freedom of expression within and between all nations. The initials PEN stand for Poets, Playwrights, Editors, Essayists, Novelists – but membership is open to all writers of standing (including translators), whether men or women, without distinction of creed or race, who subscribe to these fundamental principles. PEN takes no part in state or party politics. Founded 1921.

English PEN Centre

email enquiries@englishpen.org
website www.englishpen.org

Scottish PEN Centre

email info@scottishpen.org
website www.scottishpen.org

Irish PEN Centre
email info@irishpen.com.com
website www.irishpen.com

The Poetry Book Society – see page 368

The Poetry Society – see page 368

The Romantic Novelists' Association

email rnahonsec@romanticnovelistsassociation.org
website www.romanticnovelistsassociation.org
Chairman Nicola Cornick, *Hon. Secretary* Julie Vince

Promotes romantic fiction and encourages good writing within the genre. Represents around 1,000 writers, agents, editors and other publishing professionals. See also The Romantic Novel of the Year Awards page 584.

Scattered Authors' Society

email scatteredauthorssociety@gmail.com
website www.scatteredauthors.org

Provides a forum for informal discussion, contact and support for professional writers in children's fiction. Founded 1998.

Scottish Association of Writers

16 Norval Place, Rosyth, Fife KY11 2RJ
email secretary@sawriters.org.uk
website www.sawriters.org.uk
Facebook www.facebook.com/groups/Sawriters
Twitter @ScotAWriters
President Marc Sherland (president@sawriters.org.uk), *Vice-President & Secretary* Jen Butler, *Treasurer* Jacklin Murray (treasurer@sawriters.org.uk)

Promotes writing in Scotland. Organises an annual conference attended by writers who are members of affiliated clubs and runs alternating annual satellite events: Write Up North and Write Down South. Competitions organised throughout the year in a range of categories (contact the Competition Secretary: competition@sawriters.org.uk). Website features group and writer resources. For further information about joining the Association or to volunteer to help form new writing groups and and individual club matching service, contact the Club Development Secretary: development@sawriters.org.uk. The Council organises outreach visits to writing clubs to promote good practice, offer workshops and advise on the current writing market. This can often be coupled with competitions and specific talks. Founded 1969.

Scottish Fellowship of Christian Writers

website www.sfcw.info
Facebook www.facebook.com/Scottish-Fellowship-of-Christian-Writers-393556520670479/
Membership £10 p.a.

To encourage Christians living in Scotland to make use of their creative writing talents. Over 100 members. Founded 1980.

SCBWI (Society of Children's Book Writers and Illustrators)

email ra@britishscbwi.org
website www.britishisles.scbwi.org
Facebook www.facebook.com/groups/122794234418913/
Co-Regional Advisers, SCBWI–British Isles Natascha Biebow and Kathy Evans
Membership approx. £50 p.a.

An international network for the exchange of knowledge between professional writers, illustrators, editors, publishers, agents, librarians, educators, booksellers and others involved with literature for young people. Sponsors conferences on writing and illustrating children's books and multimedia as well as dozens of regional conferences and events throughout the world. Publishes a quarterly newsletter, *The Bulletin*, and information publications. Awards grants for: works in progress, portfolios, humour, marketing your book, excellence in non-traditional publishing and diversity in books. The SCBWI also presents the annual Golden Kite and Crystal Kite Awards for the best fiction and non-fiction books, and the Spark Award for the best book published through a non-traditional publishing route.

The SCBWI British Isles region meets regularly for speaker, networking or professional development events, including the annual two-day conference, industry insiders series, PULSE events for published members, agents' party, masterclasses for writers and illustrators and annual fiction and picture book retreats. Also sponsors local and online critique groups and publishes Words and Pictures blog magazine (www.wordsandpics.org). Founded 1971.

The Society of Civil and Public Service Writers

email membership@scpsw.co.uk
website www.scpsw.org
Membership £15 p.a.; Poetry Workshop add £7

Welcomes serving and retired members of the civil service, armed forces, police, local government, NHS and other public servants. Members can be aspiring or published writers. Holds annual competitions for short stories, articles and poetry, plus occasional competitions for longer works. Offers postal folios for short stories and articles; holds an AGM and occasional meetings; publishes *The Civil Service Author* (quarterly) magazine. Poetry Workshop offers magazine (*Wavelengths*), postal and e-folios, anthology and one-day events. Send email or sae for details. Founded 1935.

The Society of Medical Writers
Dr R. Cutler, 30 Dollis Hill Lane, London NW2 6JE
website www.somw.org.uk

Recruits members from all branches of the medical profession, together with all professions allied to medicine, to foster interest in literature and in writing – not solely about medicine but also about art, history, music, theatre, etc. Members are encouraged to write fiction, poetry, plays, book reviews, non-fiction articles. Poetry, short story and biography (Roger Bacon Award) prizes, for best non-fiction and best written clinical paper. Publishes *The Writer* (two p.a.) and a register of members and their writing interests. Holds a bi-annual conference in which various aspects of literature and writing are explored in a relaxed and informal atmosphere. Founded 1989.

South African Writers' Circle
email southafricanwriterscircle@gmail.com
website www.sawriters.org.za
Membership R205 p.a. (single), R270 (couple); R160 (pensioner single), R210 (pensioner couple), R160 (student single)

Encourages all writers, new and experienced, in the art of writing. Publishes a monthly newsletter, and runs competitions with prizes for the winners. Founded 1960.

Southwest Scriptwriters
email info@southwestscriptwriters.co.uk
website www.southwestscriptwriters.co.uk
Facebook www.facebook.com/southwestscriptwriters
Twitter @swscriptwriters

Workshops members' drama scripts for stage, screen, radio and TV with the aim of improving their chances of professional production, meeting at Watershed in Bristol. Also hosts talks by professional dramatists. Projects to present members' work to a wider audience have included theatre and short film productions, as well as public rehearsed readings. Bi-monthly e-newsletter. Founded 1994.

Spread the Word
The Albany, Douglas Way, London SE8 4AG
tel 020-8692 0231 extension 249
email hello@spreadtheword.org.uk
website www.spreadtheword.org.uk
Facebook www.facebook.com/spreadthewordwriters
Twitter @STWevents

London's writer development agency, helping London's writers make their mark on the page, the screen and in the world. Kick starts the careers of London's best new writers, and energetically campaigns to ensure mainstream publishing truly reflects the diversity of the city. Supports the creative and professional development of talent, by engaging those already interested in literature and those who will be, and by advocating on behalf of both.

Worshipful Company of Stationers and Newspaper Makers
Stationers' Hall, Ava Maria Lane,
London EC4M 7DD
tel 020-7248 2934
email admin@stationers.org
website www.stationers.org
Master Nick Steidl, *Clerk* William Alden MBE DL

One of the Livery Companies of the City of London. Connected with the printing, publishing, bookselling, newspaper and allied trades. Founded 1403.

Writers Advice Centre for Children's Books
Shakespeare House, 168 Lavender Hill,
London SW11 5TG
tel 020-7801 6300
email info@writersadvice.co.uk
website www.writersadvice.co.uk
Facebook www.facebook.com/writersadvice
Twitter @writersadvice
Managing Editor Louise Jordan

Dedicated to helping new and published children's writers by offering both editorial advice and tips on how to get published. The Centre also runs workshops, an online children's writing correspondence course and publishes a small list of its own under the name of Wacky Bee Books (www.wackybeebooks.com). Founded 1994.

MUSIC

American Society of Composers, Authors and Publishers
website www.ascap.com

An organisation owned and run by its members, it is the leading performance rights organisation representing over 555,000 songwriters, composers and music publishers.

British Academy of Songwriters, Composers and Authors
2 St Pancras Square, London, N1C 4AG
tel 020-7636 2929
website www.basca.org.uk

BASCA represents the interests of composers and songwriters across all genres, providing advice on professional and artistic matters. It administers a number of major events, including the annual Ivor Novello Awards and British Composer Awards.

The Guild of International Songwriters & Composers
Northland House, 32 Hillgarth, Castleside, Consett, Co. Durham DH8 9QD

tel (01207) 500825
email gisc@btinternet.com
website www.songwriters-guild.co.uk
Secretary Anne Eade
Membership £60

Gives advice to members on contractual and copyright matters; assists with protection of members rights; free members online copyright service; international collaboration register free to members; outlines requirements of record companies, publishers, artists. Publishes *Songwriting & Composing* (quarterly).

Incorporated Society of Musicians

4–5 Inverness Mews, London W2 3JQ
tel 020-7221 3499
email membership@ism.org
website www.ism.org
Facebook www.facebook.com/ISMusicians
Twitter @ISM_music
Chief Executive Deborah Annetts
Membership £176 p.a.

Professional body for musicians. Aims to promote the art of music; protect the interests and raise the standards of the musical profession; provide unrivalled services and expert advice for its members. Publishes *Music Journal* and a handbook annually. Founded 1882.

Music Publishers Association Ltd

8th Floor, 2 Pancras Square, London N1C 4AG
tel 020-3741 3800
email info@mpagroup.com
website www.mpaonline.org.uk
Facebook www.facebook.com/MusicPublishersAssociation
Twitter @the_MPA
Membership Details available on request

Trade organisation representing over 270 UK music publisher members: promotes and safeguards its members' interests in copyright, trade and related matters. Sub-committees and groups deal with particular interests. Founded 1881.

PRS for Music

2 Pancras Square, London N1C 4AG
tel 020-7580 5544
website www.prsformusic.com

PRS for Music represents the rights of over 125,000 songwriters, composers and music publishers in the UK. As a membership organisation it ensures creators are paid whenever their music is played, performed or reproduced, championing the importance of copyright to protect and support the UK music industry. PRS for Music provides business and community groups with easy access to over 10 million songs through its music licences. Founded 1914.

Prizes and awards

This section has two parts: an alphabetical listing of prizes, competitions and awards; and an alphabetical list of grants, bursaries and fellowships for writers and artists, and the organisations that award them. See page 767 for details of prizes and awards by genre.

PRIZES, COMPETITIONS AND AWARDS

Academy of British Cover Design: annual cover design competition

website https://abcoverd.co.uk
Twitter @abcoverd

The Academy of British Cover Design's annual competition awards covers produced for any book published between 1 January and 31 December each year, by any designer in the UK, for a UK or overseas publisher. Ebooks are eligible. Designers may enter their own work or the work of other designers. There are ten categories: children's, young adult, sci-fi/fantasy, mass market, literary fiction, crime/thriller, non-fiction, series design, classic/reissue and women's fiction. A cover can only be submitted in one category unless it is entered as an individual cover and again as part of a series design. Entry is free.

The Aeon Award

Albedo One, 8 Bachelor's Walk, Dublin 1, Republic of Ireland
email fraslaw@yahoo.co.uk
website www.albedo1.com

An annual contest for short fiction (up to 10,000 words) in genres of fantasy, science fiction, horror or anything in between. A grand prize of €1,000 will be awarded to the winner (2nd prize €200, 3rd €100) plus publication in *Albedo One*. The contest runs for four rounds throughout the year; deadlines are 31 March (1st round), 30 June (2nd round), 30 September (3rd round) and 30 November (final round). At the end of each round the best story submissions will be shortlisted for the award. Email submissions only. Entry fee: €8.50.

ALCS Educational Writers' Award

The Society of Authors, 84 Drayton Gardens, London SW10 9SB
tel 020-7373 6642
email prizes@societyofauthors.org
website www.societyofauthors.org/ALCS-award

This is an annual award alternating each year between books in the 5–11 and 11–18 age groups. It is given to an outstanding example of traditionally published non-fiction (with or without illustrations) that stimulates and enhances learning. The work must have been first published in the UK, in the English language, within the previous two calendar years. Deadline 30 June.

Dinesh Allirajah Prize for Short Fiction

email commaprizes@gmail.com
website https://commapress.co.uk/resources/prizes

Hosted by Comma Press and the University of Central Lancashire, the Dinesh Allirajah Prize for Short Fiction is open to anyone 18 years or over who is a UK resident, and the story submitted must not have been published anywhere previously in print or online. One entry per author. Entries for the 2018/19 competition will be on the theme of 'Scent', which was the title of Dinesh Allirajah's posthumous collected works. For full details regarding entry and submission guidelines, see the website.

The Hans Christian Andersen Awards

International Board on Books for Young People, Nonnenweg 12, Postfach CH–4009 Basel, Switzerland
tel +41 61-272 2917
email ibby@ibby.org
website www.ibby.org

The Medals are awarded every other year to a living author and an illustrator who by the outstanding value of their work are judged to have made a lasting contribution to literature for children and young people. The 2018 winners were Eiko Kadono of Japan (writing) and Igo Olyenikov of Russia (illustration).

Audio & Radio Industry Awards (ARIAS)

website www.radioacademy.org
Twitter @UKARIAS

The ARIAS recognise the best in the UK audio and radio industry and celebrate outstanding achievement. The awards offer stations, podcasters, publishers, presenters and production companies an annual opportunity to enter work in a range of categories reflecting today's UK audio and radio landscape. See website for further information. Founded 1982.

The Australian/Vogel's Literary Award

email vogel@allenandunwin.com
website www.allenandunwin.com

An annual award of $20,000 for a chosen unpublished work of fiction, Australian history or biography. Entrants must be under 35 years of age on the closing date and must normally be residents of

Australia. The MS must be between 30,000 and 100,000 words and must be an original work entirely by the entrant written in English. It cannot be under consideration by any publisher or award. See website for details. Closing date: 31 May. Founded 1980.

Authors' Club Awards

email info@authorsclub.co.uk
website www.authorsclub.co.uk

Best First Novel Award

The Authors' Club Best First Novel Award was inaugurated in 1954 and past winners have included Brian Moore, Alan Sillitoe, Paul Bailey, Diran Adebayo, Jackie Kay, Susan Fletcher, Nicola Monaghan, Anthony Quinn, Jonathan Kemp and Jack Wolf. The £2,500 prize is open to any debut novel written in English and published in the UK during the previous calendar year: novels first published in another country will not be considered. All imprints may submit two titles. Please send two copies of each title to Suzi Feay, The Authors' Club, c/o The National Liberal Club, 1 Whitehall Place, SW1A 3HE. Please mark packages 'BFNA' and send a confirmation email to suzifeay@aol.com with details of the titles submitted.

The Art Book Prize

The Art Book Prize (formerly the Banister Fletcher Prize) is presented each year for the best book on architecture or the arts (architecture, fine art, painting, sculpture, photography, graphic art, design etc). The book needs to be published in the previous calendar year, with a preferred emphasis on works illuminating art for the intelligent lay reader. It must be in English, but may be published anywhere in the world. Please send two copies of each title to Sunny Singh, The Authors' Club, c/o The National Liberal Club, 1 Whitehall Place, SW1A 3HE. Please mark packages 'Art Book Prize' and send a confirmation email to ssingh@authorsclub.co.uk with details of the titles submitted.

The Stanford-Dolman Best Travel Book Award

The award is presented annually for the best literary travel book (no guidebooks accepted) published in the previous calendar year. It is open to writers from across the globe, although submissions must be available in English. Instituted by the Reverend Dr William Dolman in 2005, the £5,000 prize is now jointly sponsored by Stanfords, the world's largest travel bookshop. Please send two copies of each title to John Walsh, The Authors' Club, c/o The National Liberal Club, 1 Whitehall Place, SW1A 3HE. Please mark packages 'Stanford-Dolman Award' and send a confirmation email to j.walshindependent@gmail.com with details of the titles submitted.

The Baillie Gifford Prize for Non-Fiction

website www.thebailliegiffordprize.co.uk
Twitter @BGPrize

The Baillie Gifford Prize aims to reward the best of non-fiction and is open to authors of any nationality. It covers all non-fiction in the areas of current affairs, history, politics, science, sport, travel, biography, autobiography and the arts. Formerly known as The Samuel Johnson Prize (1999–2015) it is the most prestigious non-fiction prize in the UK, worth £30,000 to the winner.

Bardd Plant Cymru (Welsh-Language Children's Poet Laureate)

Welsh Books Council, Castell Brychan, Aberystwyth, Ceredigion SY23 2JB
tel (01970) 624151
email castellbrychan@books.wales
website www.books.wales

The main aim is to raise the profile of poetry amongst children and to encourage them to compose and enjoy poetry. During his/her term of office the bard will visit schools as well as helping children to create poetry through electronic workshops. The scheme's partner organisations are: S4C, the Welsh Government, the Welsh Books Council, Urdd Gobaith Cymru and Literature Wales.

Verity Bargate Award

Soho Theatre, 21 Dean Street, London W1D 3NE
email vba@sohotheatre.com
website www.sohotheatre.com/writers/verity-bargate-award

The Verity Bargate Award was established to honour Soho Theatre's co-founder and is presented biennially to an artist resident in the UK or Ireland with fewer than three professional productions. The winner receives £7,000 in respect of an exclusive option to produce the winning play at Soho Theatre. See website for information on workshops and events associated with the award. Founded 1982.

The Bath Novel Award

PO Box 5223, Bath BA1 0UR
email info@bathnovelaward.co.uk
website www.bathnovelaward.co.uk
Twitter @bathnovelaward

This annual international prize is for unpublished or independently published writers of novels for adults or young adults. Submissions: first 5,000 words plus one-page synopsis. Prize: £2,500 plus introductions to literary agents. Entries open December until May. Entry fee: £25 per novel. See website for full entry and submission guidelines.

BBC National Short Story Award

website www.bbc.co.uk/writersroom/opportunities/nssa-ywa

The BBC National Short Story Award is one of the most prestigious awards for a single short story, aims to expand opportunities for British writers, readers and publishers of the short story, and to honour the UK's finest exponents of the form. Founded 2005.

BBC Young Writers' Award

email bbcywa@bbc.co.uk
website www.bbc.co.uk/ywa

The BBC Young Writers' Award seeks out writers between 14 and 18 who submit a story of no more than 1,000 words on any topic they choose. Run in conjunction with the BBC National Short Story Award, the winner receives a mentorship with an author and their story is broadcast on BBC Radio 1. Closing date: April. Shortlist announced: September. Winner announced: October.

The David Berry Prize

Administrative Secretary of the Royal Historical Society, University College London, Gower Street, London WC1E 6BT
tel 020-7387 7532
email m.ransom@royalhistsoc.org
website www.royalhistsoc.org/prizes/david-berry/

Candidates may submit an essay/article of between 6,000 and 10,000 words in length on any subject dealing with Scottish history. Essays/articles already published or selected for future publication are eligible. Value of prize: £250. Closing date: 31 December each year.

Besterman/McColvin Medals – see The K&IM Information Resources Awards

The Biographers' Club Slightly Foxed Best First Biography Prize

tel 07985 920341
email ariane.bankes@gmail.com
website www.biographersclub.co.uk
Prize Administrator Ariane Bankes

The prize is awarded to the best book written by a first-time biographer. The Prize, worth £2,500, is sponsored by *Slightly Foxed, The Real Reader's Quarterly*. Only entries submitted by publishers will be accepted for consideration. Literary memoirs are also eligible but celebrity autobiographies and ghostwritten books are not.

To qualify, books must have a publication date between 1 January and 31 December (proofs are acceptable). Four copies of each book should be submitted no later than 1 November (enclose a press release to confirm publication date) along with an entry form (downloadable from the website) and entry fee of £25 per title. Delivery address: The Slightly Foxed Best First Biography Prize, c/o Jane Mays, 21 Marsden Street, London NW5 3HE.

The Biographers' Club Tony Lothian Prize

E6 Albany, Piccadilly, London W1J 0AR
tel 07985 920341
email ariane.bankes@gmail.com
website www.biographersclub.co.uk
Prize Administrator Ariane Bankes

The £2,000 Tony Lothian Prize (sponsored by her daughter, Elizabeth, Duchess of Buccleuch) supports uncommissioned first-time writers working on a biography. Applicants should submit a proposal of no more than 20 pages including a synopsis and ten-page sample chapter (double-spaced, numbered pages), cv and a note on the market for the book and competing literature (all unbound), to the prize administrator. Entry fee: £15. For further details and mandatory entry form, see website.

Blue Pencil Agency First Novel Award

website https://bluepencilagency.com/first-novel-award-2018/

The Award is open to unrepresented and unpublished authors for a novel in any adult fiction genre. Winner receives £1,000 plus an introduction to a literary agent. Runner up receives £250 plus a manuscript review from a Blue Pencil Agency editor. The inaugural prize was awarded in 2017. See website for submission guidelines, entry deadlines, eligibility, and announcement of future awards.

Blue Peter Book Awards

BookTrust, G8 Battersea Studios, 80 Silverthorne Road, London SW8 3HE
tel 020-7801 8843
email bluepeter@booktrust.org.uk
website www.booktrust.org.uk/books/awards-and-prizes

Awarded annually, winners are shortlisted by a panel of expert adult judges, then a group of young *Blue Peter* viewers judge the two categories, which are: the Best Story and the Best Book with Facts. Winning books are announced on *Blue Peter* in March. Founded 2000.

The Boardman Tasker Prize

website www.boardmantasker.com

This annual prize is given for a work of fiction, non-fiction or poetry, the central theme of which is concerned with the mountain environment. Authors of any nationality are eligible but the work must be published or distributed in the UK. Entries from publishers only. Founded 1983.

The Bollinger Everyman Wodehouse Prize for Comic Fiction

Four Colman Getty, 20 St Thomas Street, London SE1 9BF
tel 020-3697 4251
email hanna.davies@fourcolmangetty.com
email arthur.dimsdale@fourcolmangetty.com

The UK's only prize for comic fiction. Awarded to the most original comic novel of the previous 12 months. The winner receives a case of Bollinger Special Cuvée, a jeroboam of Bollinger, a complete set of the Everyman Wodehouse collection and a rare breed pig named after the winning novel. Eligible novels are published in the UK between 1 June and 31 May. The winner is announced at the Hay Festival in late May/early June. Closing date: February; shortlist announced in late March/early April. Launched in 2000 on the 25th anniversary of the death of P.G. Wodehouse.

The Branford Boase Award

8 Bolderwood Close, Bishopstoke, Eastleigh, Hants SO50 8PG
tel 023-8060 0439
email anne.marley@tiscali.co.uk
website www.branfordboaseaward.org.uk

An annual award of £1,000 is made to a first-time writer of a full-length children's novel (age 7+) published in the preceding year; the editor is also recognised. Its aim is to encourage new writers for children and to recognise the role of perceptive editors in developing new talent. The Award was set up in memory of the outstanding children's writer Henrietta Branford and the gifted editor and publisher Wendy Boase who both died in 1999. Closing date for nominations: end of December. Founded 2000.

The Bridport Prize

PO Box 6910, Dorset DT6 9BQ
email kate@bridportprize.org.uk
website www.bridportprize.org.uk

Annual prizes are awarded for poetry and short stories (1st £5,000, 2nd £1,000, 3rd £500) in both categories, and £1,000 for flash fiction stories (under 250 words). The Peggy-Chapman Andrews First Novel Award launched in 2014. Enter first chapter(s) of novel, up to 8,000 words, plus 300-word synopsis. 1st prize £1,000 plus mentoring from The Literary Consultancy through their Chapter & Verse mentoring scheme and possible publication. Novel award open to writers based in Britain and Republic of Ireland only, all other categories open internationally. Entry fees: £8 flash fiction, £9 poems, £10 short stories, £20 novel.

Closing date 31 May each year. Enter by post or online. See website for rules and eligibility. Entries should be in English, original work, typed or clearly written, and never published or read on radio/TV/stage. Winning stories are read by a leading London literary agent, without obligation, and an anthology of winning entries is published each autumn. Top three poems are submitted to the Forward Poetry Prizes and top 13 eligible stories are submitted to the National Short Story Award and *The Sunday Times* Short Story Prize. Send sae for entry form or enter online.

The British Book Awards

The Bookseller, 10th Floor, Westminster Tower, 3 Albert Embankment, London, SE1 7SP
email emma.lowe@thebookseller.com
website www.thebookseller.com/british-book-industry-awards

Awards to celebrate the best in bookselling, publishing, and other aspects of the UK book industry.

British Academy Medals and Prizes

The British Academy, 10–11 Carlton House Terrace, London SW1Y 5AH
tel 020-7969 5200
email prizes@britac.ac.uk
website www.britishacademy.ac.uk

A number of prizes and medals are awarded by the British Academy for outstanding work in various fields of the humanities and social sciences on the recommendation of specialist committees: Brian Barry Prize in Political Science; British Academy Medal; Burkitt Medal (Biblical studies); Derek Allen Prize (made annually in turn for Musicology, Numismatics and Celtic studies); Edward Ullendorff Medal (Semitic languages and Ethiopian studies); Grahame Clark Medal (Prehistoric Archaeology); Sir Israel Gollancz Prize (English studies); Kenyon Medal (Classical Studies and Archaeology); Nayef Al-Rodhan Prize for Transcultural Understanding; Peter Townsend Prize (Social Policy); Rose Mary Crawshay Prize (English Literature); Serena Medal (Italian studies); Leverhulme Medal and Prize (Humanities and Social Sciences); The Landscape Archaeology Medal; Wiley Prize in Economics; Wiley Prize in Psychology.

British Czech and Slovak Association Writing Competition

24 Ferndale, Tunbridge Wells, Kent TN2 3NS
tel (01892) 543206
email prize@bcsa.co.uk
website www.bcsa.co.uk
Contact BCSA Prize Administrator

Annual BCSA competition (1st prize: £400; 2nd prize: £150) for fiction or non-fiction on the theme of the links between Britain and the Czech and Slovak Republics, at any time in their history, or society in transition in those republics since the Velvet Revolution in 1989. See website for suggested (optional) theme for 2019. Winning entries published in *British Czech & Slovak Review*. Length: 2,000 words max. Entry is free. Closing date: 30 June each year. Founded 2002.

British Fantasy Awards

tel 07557 389878
email bfsawards@britishfantasysociety.org
website www.britishfantasysociety.org
Facebook www.facebook.com/britishfantasysociety
Twitter @BritFantasySoc
Awards Administrator Katherine Fowler

The British Fantasy Awards are awarded in up to 14 categories including best novel, novella, short story and collection, and are presented each autumn at FantasyCon to works published the previous year.

Past winners include Neil Gaiman, Angela Slatter, Lavie Tidhar and Tanith Lee. Publishers, writers, editors and readers are able to contribute to a list of eligible works. The shortlist is currently decided by a vote of British Fantasy Society members and FantasyCon attendees, and the winners decided by a jury. Founded 1972.

The Caine Prize for African Writing

51 Southwark Street, London SE1 1RU
tel 020-7378 6234
email info@caineprize.com
website www.caineprize.com
Twitter @caineprize
Director Lizzy Attree

An annual award of £10,000 for a short story published in English (may be a published translation into English) by an African writer in the five years before the closing date, and not previously submitted. Indicative length 3,000–10,000 words. Shortlisted writers will each be awarded £500. Submissions only by publishers. Closing date: 31 January each year. Founded 1999.

Carnegie Medal – see The CILIP Carnegie and Kate Greenaway Children's Book Awards

The CBI Book of the Year Awards

Children's Books Ireland, 17 North Great George's Street, Dublin 1 D01 R2F1, Republic of Ireland
tel +353 (0)1 8727475
email info@childrensbooksireland.ie
website www.childrensbooksireland.ie

These awards are made annually to authors and illustrators born or resident in Ireland and are open to books written in Irish or English. The awards are: CBI Book of the Year, the Eilís Dillon Award (for a first children's book), the Honour Award for Fiction, the Honour Award for Illustration, the Judges' Special Award and the Children's Choice Award. Schools and reading groups nationwide take part in a shadowing scheme: each group reads the shortlisted books and engages with them using the suggested questions and activities in the CBI shadowing packs. Each group then votes for their favourite book, the results of which form the basis for the Children's Choice Award. Closing date: December for work published between 1 January and 31 December of an awards year. Shortlist announced in March; winners announced in May. Founded 1990.

Peggy Chapman-Andrews First Novel Award

The Bridport Prize, PO Box 6910, Dorset DT6 9BQ
email kate@bridportprize.org.uk
website www.bridportprize.org.uk/content/peggy-chapman-andrews-award-first-novel

Enter first chapter(s) of novel, up to 8,000 words, plus 300-word synopsis. 1st prize £1,000 plus mentoring from the Literary Consultancy, through their Chapter & Verse mentoring scheme, and possible publication. Closing date 31 May each year. Enter by post or online. Entry fees £20 per novel. Open to writers based in Britain and Republic of Ireland only. See website for rules and eligibility. Founded 2014.

Cheltenham Illustration Awards

email eevans@glos.ac.uk
website www.cheltenham-illustration-awards.com

Exhibition and Annual submissions are invited and can be freely interpreted in a narrative context. Submissions of work are free and open to all students, emerging and established illustrators and graphic novelists. A selection panel will assess entries. The selected work will be showcased in an exhibition and published in the *Cheltenham Illustration Awards Annual*, which will be distributed to education institutions and publishers. Deadline for submissions: June. See website for further information.

The Children's Book Award

10 St. Laurence Road, Bradford on Avon, BA15 1JG
email info@fcbg.org.uk
website www.fcbg.org.uk

This award, founded by Pat Thomson and run by the Federation of Children's Book Groups, is given annually to authors and illustrators of children's fiction published in the UK. Children participate in the judging of the award. Awards are made in the following categories: Books for Younger Children, Books for Young Readers and Books for Older Readers. Founded 1980.

The Children's Laureate

BookTrust, Studio G8, Battersea Studios, 80 Silverthorne Road, London SW8 3HE
tel 020-7801 8800
email childrenslaureate@booktrust.org.uk
website www.childrenslaureate.org.uk
Contact Charlotte Copping

The idea for the Children's Laureate originated from a conversation between (the then) Poet Laureate Ted Hughes and children's writer Michael Morpurgo. The post was established to celebrate exceptional children's authors and illustrators and to acknowledge their importance in creating the readers of tomorrow. Quentin Blake was the first Children's Laureate (1999–2001), followed by Anne Fine (2001–2003), Michael Morpurgo (2003–2005), Jacqueline Wilson (2005–2007), Michael Rosen (2007–2009), Anthony Browne (2009–2011), Julia Donaldson (2011–2013), Malorie Blackman (2013–2015), Chris Riddell (2015–17) and Lauren Child (2017–19). Founded 1999.

Cholmondeley Awards

The Society of Authors, 84 Drayton Gardens, London SW10 9SB

tel 020-7373 6642
email prizes@societyofauthors.org
website www.societyofauthors.org
Twitter @Soc_of_Authors

These honorary awards recognise the achievement and distinction of individual poets. Submissions cannot be accepted. Total value of awards is about £8,000.

The CILIP Carnegie and Kate Greenaway Children's Book Awards

CILIP, 7 Ridgmount Street, London WC1E 7AE
tel 020-7255 0650
email ckg@cilip.org.uk
website www.ckg.org.uk

Nominations for the following two awards are invited from members of CILIP (the library and information association), who are asked to submit up to two titles for each award, accompanied by a 50-word appraisal justifying the recommendation of each book. The awards are selected by judges from the Youth Libraries Group of CILIP. One title from each shortlist will be named the recipient of the Amnesty CILIP Honour, a joint commendation for a book that most distinctinvely illuminates, upholds or celebrates freedoms.

Carnegie Medal

Awarded annually for an outstanding book for children (fiction or non-fiction) written in English and first published in the UK during the preceding year or co-published elsewhere within a three-month time lapse. The Carnegie Medal winner is awarded £5,000 prize money from the Colin Mears Award annually.

Kate Greenaway Medal

Awarded annually for an outstanding illustrated book for children first published in the UK during the preceding year or co-published elsewhere within a three-month time lapse. Books intended for older as well as younger children are included, and reproduction will be taken into account. The Colin Mears Award (£5,000) is awarded annually to the winner of the Kate Greenaway Medal.

Arthur C. Clarke Award

website www.clarkeaward.com

An annual prize consisting of a number of pounds sterling equal to the current year (e.g. £2,019 in 2019) plus an engraved bookend is given for the best science fiction novel with first UK publication during the previous calendar year. Titles are submitted by publishers. Founded 1985.

The David Cohen Prize for Literature

PO Box 1277, Newcastle upon Tyne NE99 5BP
tel 0191-204 8850
email office@newwritingnorth.com
website www.newwritingnorth.com
website www.davidcohenprize.com

The David Cohen Prize for Literature is one of the UK's most distinguished literary prizes. It recognises writers who use the English language and are citizens of the United Kingdom or the Republic of Ireland, encompassing dramatists as well as novelists, poets and essayists. Former winners include Harold Pinter, William Trevor, Doris Lessing, Seamus Heaney, Hilary Mantel and Tony Harrison.

The biennial prize, of £40,000, is for a lifetime's achievement and is donated by the John S. Cohen Foundation. Established in 1965 by David Cohen and his family, the trust supports education, the arts, conservation and the environment. Arts Council England funds an additional prize of £10,000 (The Clarissa Luard Award) which is given by the winner to a fellow author or literary organisation. The David Cohen Prize for Literature is not open to applications but is awarded by an independent judging panel. Founded 1993.

Commonwealth Short Story Prize

Commonwealth Foundation, Marlborough House, Pall Mall, London SW1Y 5HY
email writers@commonwealth.int
website www.commonwealthwriters.org
Facebook www.facebook.com/commonwealthwriters
Twitter @cwwriters

The Short Story Prize is part of Commonwealth Writers, the cultural initiative of the Commonwealth Foundation. Commonwealth Writers develops and connects writers across the world. It believes that well-told stories can help people make sense of events, engage with others and take action to bring about change. The Commonwealth Short Story Prize is awarded for the best piece of unpublished short fiction (2,000–5,000 words) in English. The overall winner receives £5,000. Regional winners receive £2,500. Short stories translated into English from other languages are also eligible.

The Pol Roger Duff Cooper Prize

email info@theduffcooperprize.org
website www.theduffcooperprize.org

An annual prize for a literary work in the field of biography, history, politics or poetry published in English and submitted by a recognised publisher during the previous 12 months. The prize of £5,000 comes from a Trust Fund established by the friends and admirers of Duff Cooper, 1st Viscount Norwich (1890–1954) after his death.

Cordon d'Or – Gold Ribbon Culinary Academy Awards

7312 6th Avenue North, St Petersburg, FL 33710, USA
tel +1 727-347-2437
email ambassadornoreen@tampabay.rr.com
email nmekinney@tampabay.rr.com
website www.florida-americasculinaryparadise.com

website www.cordondorcuisine.com
website www.culinaryambassadorofireland.com
President Noreen Kinney

Awards for authors, writers, journalists, photographers, newsletters, websites, cookbooks and culinary literature. Overall winner receives $1,000. See website for details. Founded 2003.

Costa Book Awards

The Booksellers Association, 6 Bell Yard, London WC2A 2JR
tel 020-7421 4693
email naomi.gane@booksellers.org.uk
website www.costa.co.uk/costa-book-awards
Contact Naomi Gane

The awards celebrate and promote the most enjoyable contemporary British writing. There are five categories: Novel, First Novel, Biography, Poetry and Children's. Each category is judged by a panel of three judges and the winner in each category receives £5,000. Nine final judges then choose the Costa Book of the Year from the five category winners. The overall winner receives £30,000. Authors of submitted books must have been resident in the UK or Ireland for over six months of each of the previous three years (although UK or Irish nationality is not essential). Books must have been first published in the UK or Ireland between 1 November of the previous year and 31 October of the current year. Books previously published elsewhere are not eligible. Submissions must be received from publishers. Closing date: end of June.

The Rose Mary Crawshay Prize

The British Academy, 10–11 Carlton House Terrace, London SW1Y 5AH
tel 020-7969 5200
website www.britishacademy.ac.uk

The Rose Mary Crawshay Prize, worth £500, is awarded each year to a woman of any nationality for a historical or critical work on any subject connected with English literature. Nominations are invited from Fellows of the British Academy and, under the original terms of the prize, preference is given to a work regarding Byron, Shelley or Keats. Founded 1888.

Creative Future Literary Awards

tel (01273) 234780
email literary@creativefuture.org.uk
website https://literary.creativefuture.org.uk

The Creative Future Literary Awards are the UK's only national writing competition and high-profile awards ceremony for under-represented writers. The Awards showcase talented writers who lack opportunities due to mental health issues, disability, identity or other social circumstance. Prizes are awarded for poetry and short fiction, including £1,000 of cash prizes and writing development support. See website for information about eligibility, rules and how to apply.

Cundill History Prize

3463 Peel Street, Montreal, Quebec H3A 1W7 Canada
email cundill.prize@mcgill.ca
website www.cundillprize.com

The Cundill History Prize is offered each year to an individual who has published a book in English determined to have had, or likely to have, a profound literary, social and intellectual impact. Administered by Montreal's McGill University, the Cundill Prize recognises outstanding works of non-fiction that are grounded in scholarly research while retaining wide appeal and interest to the general public. Submissions are judged on their literary merits, their scholarship, and their contribution to historical understanding. The Prize is the largest non-fiction history prize in the world and welcomes submissions on any historical period or subject, regardless of the nationality or place of residence of the author. See website for submission guidelines.

The Curtis Brown Prize for Prose Fiction (University of East Anglia)

email ldc.schooloffice@uea.ac.uk
website www.uea.ac.uk/literature/scholarships-and-funding/prizes

The prize of £1,500 is awarded annually to the best writer of prose fiction on the University of East Anglia MA in Creative Writing (Prose Fiction) course. The prize is open to all students enrolled on the MA in Prose Fiction in a given year and based on the material submitted by students for their MA assessment. The winner will be chosen by a panel of Curtis Brown agents from a shortlist comprising all students in the year who achieve MA with Distinction. For further details, contact the School of Literature, Drama and Creative Writing.

CWA Dagger Awards

c/o CJAM, Peershaws, Berewyk Hall Court, White Colne, Colchester CO2 2QB
email secretary@thecwa.co.uk
email dagger.liaison@thecwa.co.uk
website www.thecwa.co.uk
website www.cwadaggers.co.uk
Contacts Dea Parkin, Mike Stotter

CWA Awards for crime writing: the Diamond Dagger, with the winner nominated by CWA members. The Gold Dagger, the Ian Fleming Steel Dagger, the John Creasey Dagger, the International Dagger, the Gold Dagger for Non-Fiction, the Dagger in the Library, the Short Story Dagger and the Historical Dagger are nominated by publishers via cwadaggers.co.uk. The Debut Dagger is a competition for the opening of a crime novel for unpublished writers, and the CWA Margery Allingham Short

Story Competition welcomes unpublished stories of up to 3,500 words, from both published and unpublished authors. Deadlines: 28 February. See CWA website for competition details.

Deutsche Börse Photography Foundation Prize

email foundation@deutsche-boerse.com
email info@tpg.org.uk
website www.deutscheboersephotography foundation.org

Rewards a living photographer, of any nationality, who has made the most significant contribution to the medium of photography during the past year (1st prize £30,000). Founded by the Photographers' Gallery and awarded together with the Deutsche Börse Photography Foundation, a non-profit organisation dedicated to the collection, exhibition and promotion of contemporary photography. Visit the website. Founded 1996.

DSC Prize for South Asian Literature

email admin@dcsprize.com
website www.dscprize.com

This Prize celebrates the rich and varied world of literature of the South Asian region. Authors can belong to the region through birth or be of any ethnicity but the writing should pertain to the South Asian region in terms of content and theme. The prize aims to bring South Asian writing to a new global audience through a celebration of the achievements of South Asian writers. Prize value: $25,000. See website for submission guidelines and eligibility. Founded 2010.

East Anglian Book Awards

email info@writerscentrenorwich.org.uk
website www.writerscentrenorwich.org.uk

Awarded annually, the Awards comprise six categories: fiction; general non-fiction, poetry, children's history and tradition and biography/memoir, with the £1,000 prize money going to the East Anglian Book of the Year. Additional categories: Book by the Cover, sponsored by East Anglian Writers, offering £100 to the best cover, and Outstanding Contribution Award given to a key figure in the world of literature, publishing, writing and editing etc. Books must be largely set in or around East Anglia, or the author of the book should be based in the area of Norfolk, Suffolk and the Fenland District. Awards are staged in partnership with *Eastern Daily Press*, Jarrold, Writers' Centre Norwich, sponsored by the University of East Anglia Faculty of Humanities and the PACCAR Foundation.

Closing date for entries: July. Books must have been published within the calendar year of the previous award's closing date and the one for the current year. Once entries are open (May), two copies of the book and a covering note explaining which category it is to be submitted to should be sent to Trevor Heaton at the *Eastern Daily Press*.

Edge Hill Short Story Prize

Edge Hill University, St Helens Road, Ormskirk, Lancs. L39 4QP
tel (01695) 584133
email cowanb@edgehill.ac.uk
website www.edgehill.ac.uk/shortstory
Contact Billy Cowan

This prize is awarded annually by Edge Hill University for excellence in a published single author short story collection. The winner will receive £10,000 and a Readers' Choice prize of £1,000 is awarded to a writer from the shortlist. Publishers are entitled to submit collections published during the preceding year. Authors must be born or normally resident in the British Isles (including Ireland). Deadline: 23 March.

The T.S. Eliot Prize

50 Penn Road, London N7 9RE
website http://tseliot.com/prize/
Director Chris Holifield

An annual prize of £25,000, with £1,500 for each of the ten shortlisted poets, is awarded by the T.S. Eliot Foundation to the best collection of new poetry published in the UK or the Republic of Ireland during the year. Submissions are invited from publishers in June with a closing date of early August. The shortlist is announced in October and the winner in January, the day after the T.S. Eliot Prize Readings in the Royal Festival Hall.

The Desmond Elliott Prize

The Desmond Elliott Charitable Trust, 84 Godolphin Road, London W12 8JW
tel 020-8222 6580
email emma.manderson@desmondelliottprize.org
website www.desmondelliottprize.org
Literary Director Emma Manderson

An annual prize for a first novel written in English by an author resident in the UK or Ireland and published in the UK. Worth £10,000 to the winner, the prize is named after the literary agent and publisher, Desmond Elliott, who died in 2003. Qualities the judges will be looking for are: a debut novel of depth and breadth with a compelling narrative, original and arresting characters, vividly written and confidently realised. Founded 2007.

The European Publishers Award

website www.europhotobookaward.eu

Annual competition for the best set of photographs suitable for publication as a book. All photographic material must be completed and unpublished in book form and be original. Projects conceived as anthologies are not acceptable. Copyright must belong to the photographer. See website for details. Founded 1994.

European Union Prize for Literature

email info@euprizeliterature.eu
website www.euprizeliterature.eu

Celebrating its 10th anniversary in 2018, the aim of the European Prize for Literature is to celebrate creativity and diversity of contemporary literature in the field of fiction, to promote the circulation of literature within Europe and to encourage greater interest in non-national literary works. The prize is financed by the Culture Programme of the European Union and is open to all countries currently involved in the EU Culture Programme. See website for full details and eligibility criteria. Founded 2008.

FAB Prize for Undiscovered BAME Talent

email fab@faber.co.uk
website www.faber.co.uk/blog/fab-prize-2018/

The FAB Prize is the Faber and Andlyn BAME Prize for undiscovered BAME writers and illustrators of children's books. Entrants must be of black, Asian or minority ethnic background, and previously unpublished. Entries must be text or artwork for children aged 1 to 18 years. First prize of £500 for text and £500 for illustration. For full entry guidelines and submission criteria, see the website. Founded 2017.

The Geoffrey Faber Memorial Prize

An annual prize of £1,500 is awarded in alternate years for a volume of verse and for a volume of prose fiction, first published originally in the UK during the two years preceding the year in which the award is given which is, in the opinion of the judges, of the greatest literary merit. Eligible writers must be not more than 40 years old at the date of publication of the book and a citizen of the UK and Colonies, of any other Commonwealth state or of the Republic of Ireland. The three judges are reviewers of poetry or fiction who are nominated each year by the literary editors of newspapers and magazines which regularly publish such reviews. Faber and Faber invite nominations from reviewers and literary editors. No submissions for the prize are to be made. Founded 1963 by Faber and Faber Ltd, as a memorial to the founder and first Chairman of the firm.

The Alfred Fagon Award

email info@alfredfagonaward.co.uk
website www.alfredfagonaward.co.uk
Facebook www.facebook.com/alfredfagonaward/
Twitter @AlfredFagonAwrd

An annual award of £6,000 for the Best New Play of the Year (which need not have been produced) for the theatre in English. TV and radio plays and film scripts will not be considered. Only writers of Caribbean and African descent resident in the UK are eligible. Applicants should submit two copies of their play plus sae for return of their script and a CV which includes details of the writer's Caribbean and African connection. Closing date: end August. Founded 1997.

The Eleanor Farjeon Award

website www.childrensbookcircle.org.uk

An annual award which may be given to an individual or an organisation. Librarians, authors, publishers, teachers, reviewers and others who have given exceptional service to the children's book industry are eligible for nomination. It was instituted in 1965 by the Children's Book Circle (page 539) for distinguished services to children's books and named after the much-loved children's writer Eleanor Farjeon.

Financial Times and McKinsey Business Book of the Year Award

email bookaward@ft.com
website www.ft.com/work-careers/business-book-award

This award aims to identify the book that provides the most compelling and enjoyable insight into modern business issues including management, finance and economics. Submissions should be made via the publisher. The winner will receive £30,000 and each runner up £10,000.

First Novel Prize

c/o Daniel Goldsmith Associates Ltd,
Gridiron Building, One Pancras Square,
London N1C 4AG
email hello@danielgoldsmith.co.uk
website www.firstnovel.co.uk

A literary contest organised by the literary consultancy Daniel Goldsmith Associates, open to previously unpublished and independently published debut novelists. Open to novels of more than 50,000 words and of an adult genre. Judges include a leading literary agent and an adult fiction editor. First prize £1,000, second prize £250 and third prize £100. For full entry guidelines and entry fees, see the website.

Fish Publishing Writing Prizes

Fish Publishing, Durrus, Bantry, Co. Cork,
Republic of Ireland
email info@fishpublishing.com
website www.fishpublishing.com
Honorary Patrons Colum McCann, Roddy Doyle

International writing prizes set up to publish and encourage new writers. There are a number of prizes available including the Fish Short Story Prize, the Fish Short Memoir Prize, the Fish Flash Fiction Prize and the Fish Poetry Prize. Ten winners from each prize are published in the Annual Fish Anthology and each competition has cash and other prizes including residencies and other courses. For full details see website. Founded 1994

FOCAL International Awards

email info@focalint.org
website www.focalint.org/focal-international-awards

The FOCAL International Awards celebrate achievement in the use of footage in all variety of genres, across all media platforms plus its restoration. Producers, film-makers and other creative professionals who have used library footage in a documentary, feature film or any other form of production are encouraged to submit their work for consideration. See website for full submission guidelines and further information.

The Rathbones Folio Prize

email minna.fry@rathbonesfolioprize.com
website www.rathbonesfolioprize.com
Twitter @RathbonesFolio
Executive Director Minna Fry

Open to any book (written primarily for adults) in the given year and, uniquely, is nominated exclusively by The Folio Prize Academy, an international group of writers and critics. The prize is worth £20,000. The Rathbones Folio Prize is open to all books written in English and published in the UK. All genres and forms are eligible. The format of first publication may be print or digital. See the website for submission details and dates.

Fool for Poetry Chapbook Competition

Frank O'Connor House, 84 Douglas Street, Cork T12 X802, Republic of Ireland
email foolforpoetry@munsterlit.ie
website www.munsterlit.ie

An annual poetry chapbook competition run by the Munster Literature Centre. The competition is open to new, emerging and established poets from any country but at least one of the winners will be previously unpublished. First prize €1,000 and second prize €500. Both winners will receive a chapbook publication and 50 complimentary copies. The published chapbooks will be reviewed in *Southword Journal* and elsewhere. See website for entry fees and submission guidelines.

Forward Prizes for Poetry

Forward Arts Foundation, Somerset House, Strand, London WC2R 1LA
tel 020-7845 4655
email info@forwardartsfoundation.org
website www.forwardartsfoundation.org

Three prizes are awarded annually:

• The Forward Prize for Best Collection published in the UK and Republic of Ireland between 19 September 2018 and 18 September 2019 (£10,000);
• The Felix Dennis Prize for Best First Collection published between 19 September 2018 and 18 September 2019 (£5,000); and
• The Forward Prize for Best Single Poem in memory of Michael Donaghy, published but not as part of a collection, pamphlet or anthology between 25 March 2018 and 24 March 2019 (£1,000).

All poems entered are also considered for inclusion in the *Forward Book of Poetry*, an annual anthology. Entries for the Best Collection and Best First Collection must be submitted by book publishers and, for Best Single Poem, by editors of newspapers, periodicals, magazines or online journals, or by competition organisers, in the UK and Ireland.

Entries accepted online. See website for details. Entries from individual poets of their unpublished or self-published work will not be accepted. Established 1992.

The Franco-British Society's Literary Prize

Franco–British Society, 3 Dovedale Studios, 465 Battersea Park Road, London SW11 4LR
email francobritsoc@gmail.com
website www.franco-british-society.org/
Executive Secretary Isabelle Gault

This annual prize is given for a full-length work of literature which contributes most to Franco–British understanding. It must be first published in the UK between 1 January and 31 December, and written in English by a citizen of the UK, British Commonwealth or the Republic of Ireland. Closing date: 31 December.

Gladstone History Book Prize

Royal Historical Society, University College London, Gower Street, London WC1E 6BT
tel 020-7387 7532
email m.ransom@royalhistsoc.org
website www.royalhistsoc.org/prizes/gladstone-history-book-prize
Administrative Secretary Melanie Ransom

An annual award (value £1,000) for a history book. The book must:

• be on any historical subject which is not primarily related to British history;
• be its author's first solely written history book;
• have been published in English during the previous calendar year;
• be an original and scholarly work of historical research.

One non-returnable copy of an eligible book should be submitted by the publisher before 31 December. Should the book be shortlisted, two further copies will be required.

The Goethe-Institut Award for New Translation

The Society of Authors, 84 Drayton Gardens, London SW10 9SB
tel 020-7373 6642
email prizes@societyofauthors.org
website www.societyofauthors.org/prizes/translation-prizes/Goethe-Institut

This biennial award is open to emerging British translators of literature who translate from German into the English language. The winner will be awarded prize money of €1,000 and a place at the International Translator's seminar, including a visit to the Leipzig Book Fair. The next award will be open for entries in summer 2019 and will be presented in 2020.

The Goldsmiths Prize

c/o Department of English & Comparative Literature, Goldsmiths University of London, New Cross, London SE14 6NW
email goldsmithsprize@gold.ac.uk
website www.gold.ac.uk/goldsmiths-prize/
Twitter @GoldsmithsPrize
Literary Director Tim Parnell

Celebrates the qualities of creative daring associated with the University and to reward fiction that breaks the mould or extends the possibility of the novel form. The annual prize of £10,000 is awarded to a book that is deemed genuinely novel and which embodies the spirit of invention that characterises the genre at its best.

Prize open for submissions late January; closing date for submission of entry forms late March; closing date for submission of books early July; shortlist announced late September/early October; winner announced November. Founded 2013.

The Gourmand World Cookbook Awards

Pintor Rosales 50, 28008, Madrid, Spain
tel +34-91-541-67-68
email pilar@gourmandbooks.com
email edouard@gourmandbooks.com
website www.cookbookfair.com
President Edouard Cointreau

The annual Gourmand World Cookbook Awards were created by Edouard Cointreau. Entries are free and any book published within the year can be entered by sending three copies of the book to the Gourmand Library at: Luis Velez de Guevara, 8, bajo A, 28012, Madrid, Spain. The Gourmand Library was created in 2013 to house the reference collection of cookbook and wine book titles of the awards. For further details about past winners, see the website. Founded 1995.

Kate Greenaway Medal – see The CILIP Carnegie and Kate Greenaway Children's Book Awards

The Griffin Poetry Prize

The Griffin Trust for Excellence in Poetry,
363 Parkridge Crescent, Oakville, Ontario L6M 1A8, Canada
tel +1 905-618 0420
email info@griffinpoetryprize.com
website www.griffinpoetryprize.com

Two annual prizes of Can$65,000 (and an additional Can$10,000 to each shortlisted poet) are awarded for collections of poetry published in English during the preceding year. One prize goes to a living Canadian poet, the other to a living poet from any country. Collections of poetry translated into English from other languages are also eligible and are assessed for their literary quality in English. Submissions are accepted from publishers only. Founded 2000.

Harvill Secker Young Translators' Prize

email youngtranslatorsprize@randomhouse.co.uk
website www.penguinrandomhouse.co.uk/publishers/vintage/harvill-secker

The Harvill Secker Young Translators' Prize recognises the achievements of young translators at the start of their careers. The prize is open to anyone between the ages of 18 and 34, with no restriction on the country of residence. The first prize includes £1,000 and a selection of Vintage titles. Founded 2010.

The Hawthornden Prize

The Prize Administrator,
International Retreat for Writers,
Hawthornden Castle, Lasswade,
Midlothian EH18 1EG
email office@hawthornden.org

This £15,000 prize is awarded annually to the author of what, in the opinion of the judges, is the best work of imaginative literature published during the preceding calendar year by a British author. Books are chosen rather than received by submission.

The Hessell-Tiltman History Prize

English PEN, 60 Farringdon Road,
London EC1R 3GA
tel 020-7324 2535
email enquiries@englishpen.org
website www.englishpen.org/events/prizes/hessell-tiltman-prize

An annual prize of £2,000 awarded to a non-fiction work of high literary merit covering any historical period. Biography and autobiography are excluded. Submissions must come through publishers. Full details can be found on the English PEN website. Founded 2002.

William Hill Sports Book of the Year Award

website www.williamhillplc.com

The world's longest established and most valuable literary sports-writing prize. Winner receives £30,000, a free £2,000 bet and a trophy. Shortlisted authors receive a leather-bound copy of their book and £3,000. See website for rules and submission guidelines. Founded 1989.

The Calvin and Rose G. Hoffman Memorial Prize for Distinguished Scholarly Essay on Christopher Marlowe

The King's School, 25 The Precincts, Canterbury, Kent CT1 2ES
email bursar@kings-bursary.co.uk
Contact The Hoffman Administrator

This annual prize is awarded to the writer of the best distinguished scholarly essay on Christopher Marlowe. Closing date: 1 September. An application form and further details must be obtained from the Hoffman Administrator.

The Ted Hughes Award for New Work in Poetry

The Poetry Society, 22 Betterton Street, London WC2H 9BX
tel 020-7420 9886
email tedhughesaward@poetrysociety.org.uk
website www.poetrysociety.org.uk

An annual award of £5,000 for a living UK poet, working in any form, who has made the most exciting contribution to poetry over the year. Organised by the Poetry Society and funded by Carol Ann Duffy with the honorarium which the Poet Laureate traditionally receives from H.M. the Queen.

HWA Dorothy Dunnett Short Story Competition

email admin@historicalwriters.org
website www.historicalwriters.org/dorothydunnett/

Short story competition run by the Historical Writers' Association for unpublished short stories of up to 3,500 words. Stories must be set at least 35 years in the past. Entry fee £5. First prize £500. For full entry guidelines and submission dates, see website.

The Imison Award

The Broadcasting Committee, The Society of Authors, 84 Drayton Gardens, London SW10 9SB
tel 020-7373 6642
email info@societyofauthors.org
website www.societyofauthors.org/prizes/audio-drama/imison

This annual prize of £3,000, sponsored by the Peggy Ramsay Foundation, is awarded to any new writer of original audio drama first produced and broadcast (nationally or online) in the UK. Founded 1994.

The Impress Prize for New Writers

Innovation Centre, Rennes Drive, University of Exeter, Devon EX4 4RN
tel (01392) 950910
email enquiries@impress-books.co.uk
website www.impress-books.co.uk
Contact Natalie Clark

The prize was created to discover and publish new writing talent in fiction and non-fiction. The winner is offered a publishing contract with Impress Books in both print and ebook and a £500 advance. Writers submit a 6,000 word sample of the manuscript, a synopsis, publishing rationale and author biography. Entries to the prize are assessed by the Impress team and a shortlist is produced from which a panel of representatives from the publishing industry, chooses the winner.

In the past the winners and shortlisted candidates have gone on to be represented by agents and received subsequent publishing contracts. Previous winners of the prize include Annabel Abbs with *The Joyce Girl* and Magdalena McGuire with *Home Is Nearby*. See the website for details. Entry fee: £25. Founded 2006.

Independent Bookshop Week Book Awards

6 Bell Yard, London WC2A 2JR
tel 020-7421 4694
email sharon.benton@booksellers.org.uk
website www.indiebookshopweek.co.uk

Awards are given in three categories: adult, children's and picture book, as well as a Best of the Best award. For entry guidelines and shortlist details, see the website.

International Dublin Literary Award

Dublin City Library & Archive, 138–144 Pearse Street, Dublin D02 HE37, Republic of Ireland
tel +353 (0)1 6744802
email literaryaward@dublincity.ie
website www.dublinliteraryaward.ie

This award is the largest and most international prize of its kind. Administered by Dublin City Public Libraries, nominations are made by libraries in capital and major cities throughout the world. Novels are nominated solely on the basis of 'high literary merit'. Books may be written in any language, but must be translated into English. The prize is €100,000 which is awarded to the author if the book is written in English. If the winning book is in English translation, the author receives €75,000 and the translator €25,000. Founded 1996.

International Prize for Arabic Fiction

133 Hill House, 210 Upper Richmond Road, London SW15 6NP
email fleurmontanaro@yahoo.co.uk
website www.arabicfiction.org/en
Prize Administrator Fleur Montanaro

The International Prize for Arabic Fiction (IPAF) is the most prestigious literary prize in the Arab world.

Its aim is to reward excellence in contemporary Arabic creative writing and to encourage the readership of high quality Arabic literature internationally through the translation and publication of winning and shortlisted novels in other major languages. Shortlisted authors receive $10,000 and the winning author goes on to receive a further $50,000. For full entry and submission guidelines, see the website.

Irish Book Awards

137 Hillside, Dalkley, County Dublin A96 DP86, Republic of Ireland
tel +353 (0)85 1449574
email bert@agile-ideas.com
website www.irishbookawards.irish/
Administrator Bert Wright

The Irish Book Awards are a set of industry-recognition awards set up by a coalition of Irish booksellers. The awards are owned by Irish Book Awards Ltd, a not-for-profit company, and were established to celebrate the extraordinary quality of Irish writing, to help bring the best books to a wider readership annually, and to promote an industry under severe competitive pressures. The awards include fifteen categories spanning the literary genres. Thousands of ordinary readers vote to select the winners every year.

At the time of writing, the Awards are in negotiations for a replacement headline sponsor after an eight-year partnership with Bord Gáis Energy. Submissions open: 1 June; shortlist announced: late October; Awards Ceremony: late November. Founded 2007.

Jewish Quarterly – Wingate Literary Prizes

email customerservices@thejc.com
website www.thejc.com

Celebrating its 41st anniversary in 2018, an annual prize of £4,000 is awarded for a work of fiction or non-fiction which best stimulates an interest in and awareness of themes of Jewish concern among a wider reading public. Founded 1977.

The K&IM Information Resources Awards

CILIP, 7 Ridgmount Street, London WC1E 7AE
tel 020-7255 0500
email isgrefawards@cilip.org.uk
email jdburntoak@virginmedia.com
website www.cilip.org.uk/isg

Information Resources Award

Awarded annually for outstanding information resources that are available and relevant to the library and information sector in the UK within the preceding year. There are two categories, one for electronic formats and one for printed works. Recommendations are invited from Members of CILIP (the Chartered Institute of Library and Information Professionals), publishers and others, who are asked to submit a preliminary list via email. Winners receive a certificate.

The Walford Award

Awarded annually to an individual for an outstanding contribution to the world of reference and information services in the UK. Recommendations may be made for the work of a living person or persons, or for an organisation. The winner receives a certificate and a cheque for £100.

Kent and Sussex Poetry Society Open Poetry Competition

26 Courtlands, Teston, Maidstone, Kent, ME18 5AS
email kentandsussexpoetry@gmail.com
website www.kentandsussexpoetry.com

This competition is open to all unpublished poems, no longer than 40 lines. Prizes: 1st: £1,000, 2nd: £300, 3rd: £100, 4th: four at £50. Closing date: 31 January. Entry fee £5 per poem (£4 per poem if submitting 3+ poems). Founded 1985.

Kerry Group Irish Novel of the Year Award

Listowel Writers' Week, 24 The Square, Listowel, Co. Kerry V31 RD93, Republic of Ireland
tel +353 (0)68 21074
email info@writersweek.ie
website www.writersweek.ie
Facebook www.facebook.com/writersweek
Contacts Maire Logue, Eilish Wren

An annual award of €15,000 for a published novel by an Irish author. Listowel Writers' Week is an acclaimed literary festival devoted to bringing together writers and audiences at unique and innovative events in the historic and intimate surroundings of Listowel, County Kerry. Events include workshops, readings, seminars, lectures, book launches, art exhibitions and a comprehensive children's and teenagers' programme. See website for submission guidelines and dates. Founded 1971.

Kindle Storyteller Prize

website www.amazon.co.uk

The Kindle Storyteller Prize is open to submissions of new English language books in any genre. Titles must be previously unpublished and be available as an ebook and in print via Kindle Direct Publishing or CreateSpace (print edition only). The winning author will receive £20,000 and will be recognised at a central London award ceremony. Competition entry period runs from 1 May to 31 August.

The Kitschies

email submissions@thekitschies.com
website www.thekitschies.com
Twitter @thekitschies

Director Glen Mehn

The Kitschies reward the year's most progressive, intelligent and entertaining works that contain elements of the speculative or fantastic. Open for submissions in late spring/early summer and closed in late autumn/early winter, with awards presented in late winter each year. Prizes total £2,000. There is no fee to enter. Founded 2009.

Kraszna-Krausz Awards

email info@kraszna-krausz.org.uk
website www.kraszna-krausz.org.uk

Awards totalling over £10,000 are made each year for the best photography book and best moving image book published in English. Entries to be submitted by publishers only. The Foundation also presents the Outstanding Contribution to Publishing Award and supports the First Book Award. Founded 1985.

Listowel Writers' Week Poetry Competitions

Listowel Writers' Week, 24 The Square, Listowel, Co. Kerry V31 RD93, Republic of Ireland
tel +353 (0)68 21074
email info@writersweek.ie
website www.writersweek.ie
Facebook www.facebook.com/writersweek
Contacts Maire Logue, Eilish Wren

Holds four poetry competitions (poetry book: €5,000; poetry single: €700; poetry collection: €1,500; short poem: €250). Contact for full details and submission guidelines. No entry form required. No entry fee. Founded 1971.

Little, Brown Award for Crime Fiction (University of East Anglia)

email ldc.schooloffice@uea.ac.uk
website www.uea.ac.uk/literature/scholarships-and-funding/prizes

This prize of £3,000 is awarded annually for the best writer of crime fiction on the University of East Anglia MA in Creative Writing (Crime Fiction). The prize is open to all students enrolled on the MA in Crime Fiction in a given year and will be based on the material submitted by students for their final assignment of a full-length crime fiction manuscript. The winner will be chosen by a panel of Little, Brown editors. For further information, contact the School of Literature, Drama and Creative Writing.

The London Magazine Short Story, Poetry and Essay Competitions

email info@thelondonmagazine.org
website www.thelondonmagazine.org
Facebook www.facebook.com/thelondonmagazine1732
Twitter @TheLondonMag

A chance to be published in the UK's oldest literary magazine, established in 1732. Annual competitions held for Poetry, Essays and Short Stories. Dates announced online throughout the year. First Prize: £500, Second Prize: £300, Third Prize: £200, plus publication in the magazine. £10 per entry and £5 for subsequent entries.

The London Hellenic Prize

The Hellenic Centre, 16–18 Paddington Street, London W1U 5AS
email jason.leech@londonhellenicprize.org
website www.londonhellenicprize.org

Established by the London Hellenic Society, the Prize is worth £10,000 and runs annually with a submission deadline of 31 January for books published in the preceding calendar year. It is awarded to authors of original works written in (or translated into) English and inspired by Greece or Greek exploits, culture or history at any time from the ancient past to the present day. Although the Prize will always strive to recognise works of excellence, any winner must be accessible to a broad readership. Individual applicants or their publishers may submit any number of titles (two copies of each). Further details are available on the website or by contacting the email address above. Founded 1996.

London Press Club Awards

c/o London & Partners, 6th Floor, 2 More Riverside, London SE1 2RR
tel 020-7520 9082
email info@londonpressclub.co.uk
website www.londonpressclub.co.uk
Twitter @londonpressclub

The London Press Club is a membership organisation for journalists and other media professionals. It organises debates, Q&As and social events at exclusive venues across the capital, as well as the annual Press Ball. The London Press Club Awards take place each year, honouring the following categories: Daily Newspaper of the Year, Sunday Newspaper of the Year, Business Journalist of the Year, Scoop of the Year, Blog of the Year, Reviewer of the Year, Broadcast Journalist of the Year, the Edgar Wallace Award and Londoner of the Year.

The Elizabeth Longford Prize for Historical Biography

The Society of Authors, 84 Drayton Gardens, London SW10 9SB
tel 020-7373 6642
email prizes@societyofauthors.org
website www.societyofauthors.org/prizes/non-fiction/Elizabeth-Longford
website www.elhb.uk
Twitter @Soc_of_Authors

A prize of £5,000 is awarded annually for an historical biography published in the year preceding the prize in memory of acclaimed biographer Elizabeth Longford, and sponsored by Flora Fraser and Peter Soros. Founded 2003.

Longman-History Today Awards

email admin@historytoday.com
website www.historytoday.com/longman-history-today-awards

The Longman-*History Today* awards are made jointly by the publishers Longman and *History Today* magazine to foster a wider understanding of, and enthusiasm for, history. The winning book receives an award of £2,000 and must display innovative research and interpretation in its field. It will also have contributed significantly to making its subject accessible to the general reader. Founded 1997.

The Sir William Lyons Award

The Guild of Motoring Writers' Secretariat, 40 Baring Road, Bournemouth BH6 4DT
tel (01202) 422424
email generalsec@gomw.co.uk
website www.gomw.co.uk
Facebook www.facebook.com/gomwuk
Twitter @gomw_uk

Sponsored by Jaguar Cars in memory of Sir William Lyons, founder and president of Jaguar Cars, this annual award was set up to encourage young people to foster interest in motoring and the motor industry through automotive journalism. Open to any person of British nationality resident in the UK aged 17–23 years at the closing date of 1 October. Full details are available on the website.

The McKitterick Prize

The Society of Authors, 84 Drayton Gardens, London SW10 9SB
tel 020-7373 6642
email prizes@societyofauthors.org
website www.societyofauthors.org/prizes/fiction/mckitterick
Twitter @Soc_of_Authors

This annual award of £4,000 is open to first published novels (excluding works for children) and unpublished submissions by authors over the age of 40. The runner-up receives £1,000. Closing date: 31 October.

Bryan MacMahon Short Story Award

Listowel Writers' Week, 24 The Square, Listowel, Co. Kerry V31 RD93, Republic of Ireland
tel +353 (0)68 21074
email info@writersweek.ie
website www.writersweek.ie
Facebook www.facebook.com/writersweek
Twitter @ListowelWW18
Contacts Maire Logue, Eilish Wren

An annual award for the best short story (up to 3,000 words) on any subject. Prize: €2,000. Entry fee: €10. No entry form required, enter online. There is a subsidiary award, Writers' Week Originals Short Story, for stories of up to 1,500 words as part of Listowel Writers' Week, an acclaimed literary festival devoted to bringing together writers and audiences at unique and innovative events in the intimate and historic surroundings of Listowel, County Kerry. Founded 1971.

The Macmillan Prize for Children's Picture Book Illustration

Macmillan Children's Books, 20 New Wharf Road, London N1 9RR
email macmillanprize@macmillan.co.uk
website www.panmacmillan.com/macmillanprize

Three prizes are awarded annually for unpublished children's book illustrations by art students in higher education establishments in the UK. Prizes: 1st: £1,000, 2nd: £500 and 3rd: £250.

Magic Oxygen Literary Prize

The Flat, 53 Broad Street, Lyme Regis, Dorset DT7 3QF
tel (01297) 442824
website www.magicoxygen.co.uk/molp/

The Magic Oxygen Literary Prize is the only short story and poetry writing competition in the world to plant a tree for every entry, in conjunction with the Word Forest Organisation. Short stories should be up to 4,000 words, excluding title. Poetry of up to 50 lines can be entered, excluding title and lines between stanzas. Online entries preferred. Open to writers worldwide and entrants must be 15 or over at the time of submission. Prizes: 1st: £1,000, 2nd: £300, 3rd: £100, 2 x Highly Commended prizes of £50. For full details, entry guidelines and deadlines, see the website.

The Man Booker International Prize

Four Colman Getty, 20 St Thomas Street, London SE1 9BF
tel 020-3697 4256
email marion.evans@fourcolmangetty.com
website www.themanbookerprize.com

The Man Booker International Prize is awarded annually for a single work of fiction, translated into English and published in the UK. Both novels and collections of short stories are eligible. As a further acknowledgement of the importance of translation, the £50,000 prize will be divided equally between the author and the translator. Each shortlisted author and translator will receive £1,000. Entries only from UK publishers. Sponsored by Man Group plc.

The Man Booker Prize

Four Colman Getty, 20 St Thomas Street, London SE1 9BF
tel 020-3697 4256
email marion.evans@fourcolmangetty.com
website www.themanbookerprize.com

This annual prize for fiction of £50,000, plus £2,500 to each of six shortlisted authors, is awarded by the Booker Prize Foundation to the author of the best (in the opinion of the judges) eligible novel. Any novel in print or electronic format, written originally in English and published in the UK and Ireland by an imprint formally established in the UK or Ireland is eligible. Entries only from UK and Irish publishers who may each submit novels based on their previous longlisting with scheduled publication dates between 1 October of the previous year and 30 September of the current year, but the judges may also ask for other eligible novels to be submitted to them. In addition, publishers may submit eligible titles by authors who have either won or been shortlisted in the past. Sponsored by Man Group plc.

The Manchester Fiction Prize

The Manchester Writing School,
Manchester Metropolitan University,
70 Oxford Street, Manchester M1 5NH
tel 0161 247 1787
email writingschool@mmu.ac.uk
website www.manchesterwritingcompetition.co.uk
Twitter @McrWritingSchl
Manager James Draper

The Manchester Writing School, the home of creative writing within the Department of English at Manchester Metropolitan University, hosts this competition which was created by UK Poet Laureate Carol Ann Duffy and which is designed to attract and celebrate the best new writing from around the world. Entrants are asked to submit a short story of up to 2,500 words. An award of £10,000 will be made each year to the overall winner, or winners. The deadline for entries for the 2018 competition is 30 September and the award ceremony will be held in December. See website for further information.

The Manchester Poetry Prize

The Manchester Writing School,
Manchester Metropolitan University,
70 Oxford Street, Manchester M1 5NH
tel 0161 247 1787
email writingschool@mmu.ac.uk
website www.manchesterwritingcompetition.co.uk
Twitter @McrWritingSchl
Manager James Draper

Entrants are asked to submit a portfolio of three to five poems totalling up to 120 lines. An award of £10,000 will be made to the overall winner, or winners. The deadline for entries for the 2018 competition is 30 September and the award ceremony will be held in December. See website for further information.

The Michael Marks Awards for Poetry Pamphlets

Wordsworth Trust, Dove Cottage, Grasmere,
Cumbria LA22 9SH
tel (01539) 435544
website www.wordsworth.org.uk

Inaugurated by the British Library and supported by the Michael Marks Charitable Trust, to raise the profile of poetry pamphlets and also recognise and reward the enormous contribution that poets and their pamphlet publishers make to the poetry world in the UK. There are three awards:

- The Michael Marks Poetry Award to recognise a single outstanding work of poetry published in pamphlet form in the UK during the eligible period. This award is open to self-published work. Winner receives £5,000.
- The Michael Marks Publishers' Award to recognise an outstanding UK publisher of poetry in pamphlet form, based on their publishing programme during the eligible period. Winner receives £5,000.
- The Michael Marks Illustration Award to recognise outstanding illustration of a poetry pamphlet. Winner receives £1,000. Founded 2009.

See website for full details and submission guidelines.

The Somerset Maugham Awards

The Society of Authors, 84 Drayton Gardens,
London SW10 9SB
tel 020-7373 6642
email prizes@societyofauthors.org
website www.societyofauthors.org/somerset-maugham
Twitter @Soc_of_Authors

These annual awards are for writers under the age of 35. Candidates must be ordinarily resident in the UK or Northern Ireland. Poetry, fiction, non-fiction, belles lettres or philosophy, but not dramatic works, are eligible. Entries should be submitted by the publisher. Total prize money of £10,000 which should be used for foreign travel. Closing date: 30 November.

McIlvanney Prize for the Scottish Crime Book of the Year

Bloody Scotland, c/o The Mitchell Library,
North Street, Glasgow G3 7DN
website www.bloodyscotland.com/the-mcilvanney-prize/
Twitter @BloodyScotland

Novels, collections of short stories and non-fiction crime titles are eligible for submission. A Scottish crime book is eligible if it is written by a writer born in Scotland or a writer domiciled in Scotland, or the book submitted for the award is largely set in Scotland. See website for full submission guidelines.

The Mogford Prize for Food and Drink Short Story Writing

36 St Giles, Oxford OX1 3LD
email steve@mogford.co.uk
website www.mogfordprize.co.uk
Facebook www.facebook.com/mogfordcoll
Twitter @mogfordcoll

Contact Steve Holmes

The Mogford Prize is a £10,000 annual award for a short story based, to a greater or lesser extent, on the theme of food and/or drink. The story can be any form of fiction – a romance, a mystery, an observation on life, a comedy, or any other theme. The Prize is open to all published or unpublished writers. Each year judging is conducted by Prize founders Jeremy and Hilary Mogford as well as a different acclaimed literary author and an established food/cookery writer. In addition to the winning story, there are three runners-up. The winning story is published in small booklet form and distributed throughout the Mogford Group's venues. For 2019, submissions open in November 2018 and close in January 2019. See the website for full details. Founded 2013.

The Moth Art Prize

email mothartprize@themothmagazine.com
website www.themothmagazine.come

The Moth Art Prize is awarded annually to an artist for a body of figurative or representational work (images of which can be sent electronically). Anyone over 16 can enter, and the winner receives €1,000 plus a two-week stay at The Moth Retreat in rural Ireland. There is a fee of €20 per portfolio. Closes 30 May. For full entry details and guidelines, see the website.

The Moth Poetry Prize

email enquiries@themothmagazine.com
website www.themothmagazine.com

The Moth Poetry Prize is awarded annually to four unpublished poems, chosen by a different judge each year. Prizes: 1st €10,000, with three runner-up prizes of €1,000. Anyone over 16 can enter. There is a fee of €12 per poem. All four poems appear in *The Moth* magazine. Closes 31 December. For full entry details and guidelines, see the website.

The Moth Short Story Prize

email enquiries@themothmagazine.com
website www.themothmagazine.com

The Moth Short Story Prize is awarded annually to three unpublished stories, chosen by a different judge each year. Prizes: 1st: €3,000, 2nd: a week-long retreat at Circle of Misse in France plus €250, 3rd: €1,000. Anyone over 16 can enter. There is a fee of €12 per story. All three stories appear in *The Moth* magazine. Closes 30 June. For full entry details and guidelines, see the website.

The Mythopoeic Fantasy Award for Adult Literature

email awards@mythsoc.org
website www.mythsoc.org

Given to the fantasy novel, multi-volume novel or single-author story collection for adults published during the previous year that best exemplifies the spirit of the Inklings.

The Mythopoeic Scholarship Award in Myth and Fantasy Studies

email awards@mythsoc.org
website www.mythsoc.org

Given to scholarly books on specific authors in the Inklings tradition, or to more general works on the genres of myth and fantasy.

The Mythopoeic Scholarship Award in Inklings Studies

email awards@mythsoc.org
website www.mythsoc.org

Given to books on J.R.R. Tolkien, C.S. Lewis and/or Charles Williams that make significant contributions to Inklings scholarship.

National Poetry Competition

The Poetry Society, 22 Betterton Street, London WC2H 9BX
tel 020-7420 9880
email info@poetrysociety.org.uk
website www.poetrysociety.org.uk

One of the UK's major annual open poetry competitions. Accepts poems up to 40 lines long on any theme (previously unpublished and written in English). Prizes: 1st £5,000, 2nd £2,000, 3rd £1,000, plus seven commendations of £200. Judged by a panel of three leading poets. For rules and an entry form send a sae or visit the website. Closing date: 31 October each year. Founded 1978.

New Angle Prize for East Anglian Literature

Ipswich Institute, Reading Room & Library, 15 Tavern Street, Ipswich IP1 3AA
tel (01473) 253992
email library@ipswichinstitute.org.uk
website www.ipswichinstitute.org.uk/NAP.html
Twitter @PrizeNewAngle
Prize Coordinator Hugh Pierce

The New Angle Prize is a biennial award for a recently published book of literary merit, associated with or influenced by the UK region of East Anglia (defined here as Norfolk, Suffolk, north Essex, Cambridgeshire and the Fens).

The 2019 award will be open to works of fiction or poetry, first published between 1 January 2017 and 31 December 2018. Past winners include Jim Kelly (*Death Watch*), Jules Pretty (*This Luminous Coast*), Kate Worsley (*She Rises*) and Julia Blackburn (*Threads, the Delicate Life of John Craske*). Current sponsors of the £2,000 single category first prize (£500 for runner-up) are Suffolk-based Gotelee Solicitors.

The New Poets Prize

The Poetry Business, Bank Street Arts,
32–40 Bank Street, Sheffield S1 2DS
tel 0114-346 3037
email office@poetrybusiness.co.uk
website www.poetrybusiness.co.uk
Directors Peter Sansom, Ann Sansom

A pamphlet competition for writers between the ages of 16 and 22. Entrants are invited to submit short poetry collections of 12 pages. Four outstanding collections are selected to receive a year of support and mentoring led by Peter and Ann Sansom of the Poetry Business. The four winners will receive guidance on submitting to magazines, other competitions and publishers.

One first prize winner's collection will be published by smith|doorstop books following a year of mentoring and editorial support. Poets between the ages of 16 and 22 writing in English from anywhere in the world are eligible. Entry £8. Entries can be submitted by post (with a cheque and completed entry form) or online via the website.

New Venture Award

website www.womeninpublishing.org.uk
Twitter @WIPublishingUK

The New Venture Award is given for pioneering work on behalf of under-represented groups in society. Run by Women in Publishing.

The Nobel Prize in Literature

website www.nobelprize.org

One of the annual awards stipulated in the will of the Swedish scientist Alfred Nobel. No direct application for a prize will be taken into consideration. For a full list of literature Laureates, visit www.nobelprize.org/nobel_prizes/literature/laureates/ml.

The Observer/Jonathan Cape/Comica Graphic Short Story Prize

website www.theguardian.com/books/series/observer-graphic-short-story-prize

An annual graphic short story competition offering a £1,000 cash prize and the chance to see your story printed in the *Observer New Review*. £250 runner-up prize. Founded 2007.

Ockham New Zealand Book Awards

c/o Auckland Writers Festival, Suite 9A,
44–52 Wellesley Street West, Auckland 1010
tel +64 (0)9 376 8074
email awards@nzbookawards.org.nz
website www.nzbookawards.nz

Annual awards to celebrate excellence in, and provide recognition for, the best books published annually in New Zealand. Awards are presented in four categories: fiction, poetry, illustrated non-fiction and general non-fiction. The winner of the fiction category, the Acorn Foundation Fiction Award, wins $50,000. The winners of the other three categories each win $10,000. Special awards include a Maori Language Award and a Best First Book Award for each of the four categories. Eligible books must have been published in New Zealand in the year preceding the awards ceremony date.

OCM Bocas Prize for Caribbean Literature

email awards@bocaslitfest.com
website www.bocaslitfest.com

An annual prize for literary books by Caribbean writers (writers must have been born in the Caribbean or hold Caribbean citizenship). Books published in the calendar year 2018 will be eligible for the 2019 prize. There are two deadline dates for entries: books published before November 2018 (which should be received by the prize administrators by mid-November) and books published between 1 November and 31 December 2018 (which should be received by the prize administrators by the first week of January 2019). Books are judged in three categories: poetry; fiction (including novels and short stories); and literary non-fiction (including books of essays, biography, autobiography, history, current affairs, travel and other genres which demonstrate literary qualities and use literary techniques, regardless of subject matter). Textbooks, technical books, coffee-table books, specialist publications and reference works are not eligible. There is an entry fee of US$35. The overall winner will receive an award of US$10,000. Prize guidelines and entry forms available via the website.

The Orwell Prize

The Institute of Advanced Studies,
University College London, Gower Street,
London WC1E 6BT
tel 020-3108 1618
email robyn.donaldson@theorwellprize.co.uk
website www.orwellfoundation.com
Contact Robyn Donaldson

The Orwell Prize is awarded annually for books and journalism that come closest to George Orwell's ambition to 'make political writing into art'. Three prizes are awarded annually: the Orwell Prize for Books, the Orwell Prize for Journalism and the Orwell Prize for Exposing Britain's Social Evils (sponsored by the Joseph Rowntree Foundation). Each prize is worth £3,000 to the winner; shortlists and longlists published on the website and widely publicised. Deadline for entry is December for Books, early January for Journalism and Social Evils. Work with a British or Irish connection first published in the calendar year before the date of the prize is eligible; books must be first published in the UK or Ireland. Please see website for further details. Founded 1994.

Pandora Award

website www.womeninpublishing.org.uk
Twitter @WIPublishingUK

The Pandora Award is made for significant and sustained contributions to the publishing industry. Run by Women in Publishing.

PEN Ackerley Prize for Autobiography and Memoir

English PEN, 60 Farringdon Road,
London EC1R 3GA
tel 020-7324 2535
email enquiries@englishpen.org
website www.englishpen.org

An annual prize of £2,000 is given for an outstanding work of literary autobiography/memoir written in English and published during the previous year by an author of British nationality. No submissions: books are nominated by the judges only. Founded 1982.

The People's Book Prize

email thepeoplesbkpr@aol.com
website www.peoplesbookprize.com
Facebook www.facebook.com/pages/The-Peoples-Book-Prize/108823565880728
Twitter @PeoplesBkPrize
Founder & Prize Administrator Tatiana Wilson, *Patron* Frederick Forsyth CBE, *Founding Patron* Dame Beryl Bainbridge DBE

The People's Book Prize awards prizes in six categories: fiction, non-fiction, children's, first time author (the Beryl Bainbridge First Time Author Award), TPBP Best Achievement Award and TPBP Best Publisher Award. Titles must be submitted by publishers, with a limit of one title per category. Winners are announced at an awards ceremony at the end of May at Stationers' Hall Livery Company. For entry rules and submission guidelines, see the website.

The Samuel Pepys Award

Paul Gray, Haremoor House, Faringdon,
Oxon SN7 8PN
tel 07802 301297
email plgray@btinternet.com
website www.pepys-club.org.uk

A biennial prize is given to a book published in English making the greatest contribution to the understanding of Samuel Pepys, his times, or his contemporaries. The winner receives £2,000 and the Robert Latham Medal. Closing date: 30 June 2019 (for publication between 1 July 2017 and 30 June 2019). Founded by the Samuel Pepys Award Trust in 2003 on the tercentenary of the death of Pepys.

The Plough Prize

The Plough Arts Centre, 9–11 Fore Street,
Great Torrington, Devon EX38 8HQ
tel (01805) 624624
website www.theploughprize.co.uk

Poetry competition; poems should contain no more than 40 lines. There are three top prizes: 1st: £1,000, 2nd: £750, 3rd: £250. Visit website for full entry criteria and submission guidelines.

The Poetry Business Book & Pamphlet Competition

The Poetry Business, Bank Street Arts,
32–40 Bank Street, Sheffield S1 2DS
tel 0114 346 3037
email office@poetrybusiness.co.uk
website www.poetrybusiness.co.uk
Directors Peter Sansom, Ann Sansom

An annual award is made for a poetry collection. The judges select up to five short collections for publication as pamphlets; on further submission of more poems, one of these will be selected for a full-length collection. To be published under the Poetry Business's smith|doorstop imprint. All winners share a cash prize of £2,000. Poets over the age of 18 writing in English from anywhere in the world are eligible. Founded 1986.

The Portico Prize

Portico Library, 57 Mosley Street,
Manchester M2 3HY
tel 0161 236 6785
email librarian@theportico.org.uk
website www.theportico.org.uk

This biennial prize is awarded for a published work of fiction or non-fiction, of general interest and literary merit set wholly or mainly in the North of England with prizes for fiction and non-fiction totalling up to £20,000. The prize is currently under review and the next projected prize year is 2019. Founded 1985.

The Press Awards

Society of Editors, University Centre, Granta Place,
Cambridge CB2 1RU
tel (01223) 304080
email office@societyofeditors.org
website www.pressawards.org.uk

Annual awards for British journalism judged by a number of influential judges as well as representatives from all the national newspaper groups.

The V.S. Pritchett Memorial Prize

The Royal Society of Literature, Somerset House,
Strand, London WC2R 1LA
tel 020-7845 4679
email info@rsliterature.org
website www.rsliterature.org

An annual prize of £1,000 is awarded for a previously unpublished short story of between 2,000 and 4,000 words. Entry fee: £5 per story. Closing date for entries: June. See website for full details and submission guidelines. Founded 1999.

Trevor Reese Memorial Prize

Institute of Commonwealth Studies,
School of Advanced Study, University of London,
Senate House, Malet Street, London WC1E 7HU
tel 020-7862 8853
email ics@sas.ac.uk
website http://commonwealth.sas.ac.uk/publications/trevor-reese-memorial-prize

Established in the name of Dr Trevor Reese, a distinguished scholar of Australian and Commonwealth history, who was Reader in Imperial Studies at the Institute of Commonwealth Studies until his death in 1976. He was the author of several leading works in his field, and was both founder and first editor of the *Journal of Imperial and Commonwealth History*.

The prize of £1,000 is awarded every three years to the author of a work which has made a wide-ranging, innovative and scholarly contribution in the broadly-defined field of Imperial and Commonwealth History. The next award of the prize will be in 2019, for books in the relevant field published in 2016, 2017 or 2018. Queries should be sent by email. Founded 1979.

Deborah Rogers Foundation Writers Award and David Miller Bursary

email info@deborahrogersfoundation.org
website www.deborahrogersfoundation.org/writers-award
website www.deborahrogersfoundation.org/bursary

Set up in memory of Deborah Rogers, a literary agent, who died in 2014. The Foundation aims to seek out and support emerging talent by means of two biennial awards: the Writers Award, which gives £10,000 to an unpublished author to enable them to complete a first book; and the DRF David Miller Bursary, which offers work placements in publishing houses worldwide together with £10,000 to help a young agent or publisher gain international work experience. For full submission guidelines, see the website.

The Romantic Novel of the Year Awards

website www.romanticnovelistsassociation.org
Awards Organiser Celia Anderson

The Romantic Novelists' Association gives annual awards for the very best romantic fiction. These awards, presented in early March, include a Best Debut Book Award and Romantic Novel of the Year Award. The awards are open to both members and non-members of the RNA. Novels must be first published between 1 January and 31 December of the year of entry. Four copies of each novel are required and there is a small entry fee. The entry form can be found on the website or obtained from the organiser.

The Joan Hessayon Award is only open to members of the Romantic Novelists' Association's New Writers' Scheme who submit a MS from January until the end of August. All will receive a critique. Any MSS subsequently accepted for publication become eligible for the Award.

The RSL Giles St Aubyn Awards for Non-Fiction

The Royal Society of Literature, Somerset House, Strand, London WC2R 1LA
tel 020-7845 4679
email info@rsliterature.org
website www.rsliterature.org

Awards offering financial assistance to authors engaged in writing their first major commissioned works of non-fiction. The awards are open to UK and Irish writers and writers who have been resident in the UK for at least three years. These awards are made possible thanks to a generous bequest from author and RSL Fellow Giles St Aubyn. See website for further details.

The RSL Ondaatje Prize

The Royal Society of Literature, Somerset House, Strand, London WC2R 1LA
tel 020-7845 4679
email info@rsliterature.org
website www.rsliterature.org

This annual £10,000 award, administered by the Royal Society of Literature and endowed by Sir Christopher Ondaatje, is awarded to a book of literary merit: fiction, poetry or non-fiction, best evoking the spirit of a place. The writer must be a citizen of the UK, Commonwealth, Republic of Ireland or have been a resident of the UK for three years. Books may be entered only by publishers based in the UK. See website for further details.

The Royal Society Insight Investment Science Book Prize

The Royal Society, 6–9 Carlton House Terrace, London SW1Y 5AG
tel 020-7451 2500
email sciencebooks@royalsociety.org
website https://royalsociety.org/awards/science-books
Facebook www.facebook.com/theroyalsociety
Twitter @royalsociety

This prestigious prize is open to authors of science books written for a non-specialist audience. The winner will receive £25,000 and each shortlisted author will receive £2,500. Eligible books should be written in English and their first publication in the UK must have been between 1 October and 30 September the following year.

Publishers may submit any number of books for the Prize. Entries may cover any aspect of science and technology but educational textbooks published for professional or specialist audiences are not eligible. Founded 1988.

The Royal Society Young People's Book Prize

The Royal Society, 6–9 Carlton House Terrace, London SW1Y 5AG
tel 020-7451 2500
email sciencebooks@royalsociety.org
website www.royalsociety.org/young-peoples-book-prize
Facebook www.facebook.com/theroyalsociety
Twitter @royalsociety

This prize is open to books for under-14s that have science as a substantial part of their content, narrative or theme. An expert adult panel choose the shortlist, but the winner is chosen by groups of young people in judging panels across the UK. The winning entry receives £10,000 and shortlisted entries receive £2,500. Entries open in December each year. Pure reference works including encyclopedias, educational textbooks and descriptive books are not eligible. The Prize is offered thanks to the generosity of an anonymous donor. Founded 1988.

RSL Encore Award

Royal Society of Literature, Somerset House, London WC2R 1LA
tel 020-7845 4679
email info@rsliterature.org
website www.rsliterature.org/award/rsl-encore-award

The £10,000 Encore Award for the best second novel of the year was first awarded in 1990 and is sponsored by Lucy Astor. The award fills a niche in the catalogue of literary prizes by celebrating the achievement of outstanding second novels. See the website for full submission guidelines. The RSL has administrated the award since 2016.

RSPCA Young Photographer Awards

Brand Marketing and Content Department Department, RSPCA, Wilberforce Way, Southwater, Horsham, West Sussex RH13 9RS
email ypa@rspca.org.uk
website www.rspca.org.uk/ypa

Annual awards open to anyone aged 18 or under. The aim of the competition is to encourage young people's interest in photography and to show their appreciation and understanding of the animals around them. See website for a full list of categories and submission guidelines. Founded 1990.

RTÉ Radio 1 Francis MacManus Short Story Competition

RTÉ Radio Centre, Donnybrook, Dublin 4, Republic of Ireland
website www.rte.ie/radio1/francis-macmanus-short-story

An annual competition for short stories, open to writers born or living in Ireland. Entries, in Irish or English, should not have been previously published or broadcast. See website for details. Winning entries are broadcast on RTÉ Radio 1.

RTÉ Radio Drama P.J. O'Connor Awards for Radio Drama

RTÉ Radio, Drama on One, Radio Centre, Donnybrook, Dublin 4, Republic of Ireland
email dramaonone@rte.ie
website www.rte.ie/dramaonone

Rubery Book Award

PO Box 15821, Birmingham, B31 9EA
email enquiries@ruberybookaward.com
website www.ruberybookaward.com

An annual award for published books on any subject, including children's books, with prizes totalling £2,000 (Book of the Year receives £1,500 and category winners £150 each). Books published by independent presses and self-published books are eligible. See website for entry fees and submission guidelines. Deadline (book award) end March.

Runciman Award

Rectory House, Brandon Road, Hilborough, Thetford, Norfolk IP26 5BW
tel (01760) 756086
email rcarden2@btinternet.com
website www.runcimanaward.org

An annual award of £9,000, given by the Anglo-Hellenic League, to promote Anglo-Greek understanding and friendship. Named after Sir Steven Runciman, former chairman of the League and sponsored by Elias Paraskevas Attorneys 1933. Works must be wholly or mainly about some aspect of Greece or the world of Hellenism, and must have been published in English, though in any country of the world, in a first edition during (with the imprint of) the preceding year. No category of writing will be excluded from consideration: history, literary studies, biography, travel/topography, the arts, architecture, archaeology, the environment, social and political sciences or current affairs, fiction, poetry or drama. Works in translation, with the exception of translations from Greek literature, will not be considered.

The judges normally announce a short list in April, and the prize is awarded to the winner at a ceremony in June, held at the Hellenic Centre, London. More information at www.anglohellenicleague.org. Founded 1986.

The Saltire Society Awards

The Saltire Society, 9 Fountain Close, 22 High Street, Edinburgh EH1 1TF
tel 0131 556 1836
email saltire@saltiresociety.org.uk
website www.saltiresociety.org.uk
Twitter @saltire_society

Books published between 1 September and 31 August are eligible. The Scottish Book of the Year is an annual award selected from the Saltire Society Book Award categories. The categories are:

Scottish First Book of the Year

Annual award open to any author who has not previously published a book. Authors of Scottish descent or living in Scotland, or any book which deals with the work or life of a Scot or with a Scottish problem, event or situation are eligible.

Scottish Fiction Book of the Year

Annual award for all fiction by an author of Scottish descent or living in Scotland, or for any book which deals with the work or life of a Scot or with a Scottish problem, event or situation.

Scottish Non-Fiction Book of the Year

Annual award for non-fiction books such as biography, travel and political writing. Authors of Scottish descent or living in Scotland, or any book which deals with the work or life of a Scot or with a Scottish problem, event or situation are eligible.

Scottish History Book of the Year

Annual award for a work of Scottish historical research from authors of Scottish descent or living in Scotland, or for any book which deals with the work or life of a Scot or with a Scottish problem, event or situation. Editions of texts are not eligible. Nominations are invited from professors of Scottish history and editors of historical reviews.

Scottish Poetry Book of the Year

Annual award for a collection of new poetry from authors of Scottish descent or living in Scotland, or for any book which deals with the work or life of a Scot or with a Scottish problem, event or situation. Collections which include previously published are not eligible (excludes magazine/pamphlet publication).

Scottish Research Book of the Year

Annual award for a books representing a significant body of research by authors of Scottish descent or living in Scotland, or for any book which deals with the work or life of a Scot or with a Scottish problem, event or situation. Research books must offer insight or dimension to the subject and add to the knowledge and understanding of Scotland and the Scots.

Walter Scott Prize for Historical Fiction

c/o StonehillSalt PR, 10 Brewery Park Business Centre, Haddington, East Lothian EH41 3HA
tel (01620) 829800
email rebecca@stonehillsalt.co.uk
website www.walterscottprize.co.uk
Facebook www.facebook.com/walterscottprize
Twitter @waltscottprize
Administration, Publicity & Marketing Rebecca Salt

The Walter Scott Prize for Historical Fiction was founded by the Duke and Duchess of Buccleuch and Alistair Moffat, the Chair of Judges. Awarded annually, it rewards fiction of exceptional quality which is set in the past (according to Walter Scott's subtitle for *Waverley*, at least 'sixty years since'). The Prize is among the richest UK book prizes, with a total value of £30,000. The winner receives £25,000, and shortlisted authors receive £1,000 each. The Prize is awarded at the Borders Book Festival in Melrose each June, with a longlist announced in February and a shortlist announced in March or April.

The rules governing submission are on the website. Books must be written in English and have been published in the UK, Eire or the Commonwealth during the previous calendar year. Books written in English by authors of British nationality first published outside the UK, Eire or the Commonwealth are also eligible provided they are also published in the UK in that calendar year, and books published in the Commonwealth the year before the UK publication are also eligible. Books must be submitted by publishers, and self-published authors are not eligible. Founded 2010.

The Kim Scott Walwyn Prize

website https://kimscottwalwyn.org

The Kim Scott Walwyn Prize honours the life and career of Kim Scott Walwyn (who was Publishing Director at Oxford University Press and who died in 2002), and celebrates exceptional women in publishing. The 2017 Prize was awarded to Alice Curry, founder of Lantana Publishing. The Prize is open to any woman who has worked in publishing in the UK for up to seven years and recognises the professional achievements and promise of women in the industry. Founded 2003.

Scottish Book of the Year – see The Saltire Society Awards

Scottish Children's Book Awards

Scottish Book Trust, Sandeman House, Trunk's Close, 55 High Street, Edinburgh EH1 1SR
tel 0131 524 0160
email info@scottishbooktrust.com
website www.scottishbooktrust.com

Scotland's largest book awards for children and young people. Awards are given to new and established authors of published books in recognition of high standards of writing for children. Visit the Scottish Book Trust website for more details.

Scottish First Book of the Year – see The Saltire Society Awards

Scottish Research Book Award – see The Saltire Society Awards

Segora International Writing Competitions

email simms.gordon@orange.fr
website www.poetryandplays.com
Organisers Gordon and Jocelyn Simms

Segora International Writing Competitions are held annually for poetry, short story, vignette (short prose) and one-act play. Deadline for all competitions 15th June each year. Full details available on the website.

The André Simon Memorial Fund Book Awards

1 Westbourne Gardens, Glasgow G12 9XE
tel 07801 310973
email katie@andresimon.co.uk
website www.andresimon.co.uk

Celebrating excellent new writing in the fields of food and drink. Two awards of £2,000 are given annually, one each for the best new books on food and on drink. There is also a Special Commendation of £1,500 in either category. All works first published in the calendar year of the award are eligible (publisher entry only). See website for entry guidelines and form. Founded 1978.

The Jill Smythies Award

The Linnean Society of London, Burlington House, Piccadilly, London W1J 0BF
tel 020-7434 4479
email info@linnean.org
website www.linnean.org

A prize of £1,000 for a botanical artist for outstanding illustrations. Established in honour of Jill Smythies whose career as a botanical artist was cut short by an accident to her right hand. The rubric states that 'the Award, to be made by Council usually annually consisting of a silver medal and a purse … is for published illustrations, such as drawings and paintings, in aid of plant identification, with the emphasis on botanical accuracy and the accurate portrayal of diagnostic characteristics. Illustrations of cultivars of garden origin are not eligible.' Closing date for nominations: 30 November. Founded 1988.

Specsavers Bestseller Awards

website www.specsaversbestsellerawards.com

The Nielsen Book Gold and Platinum Awards were originally launched in September 2001, and were presented to publishers and authors of books that achieved outstanding sales through the UK retail book trade. Any one title, in all its print editions, that had sold more than 500,000 copies (Gold) or 1,000,000 copies (Platinum) over a period of five consecutive years qualified.

In 2017, the Awards were re-launched with new criteria and a three-year sponsorship from Specsavers. For the first time, both print and ebook sales will be counted and all sales from publication (or from when Nielsen BookScan UK TCM records began: 1998 for print books and January 2014 for ebooks), will be included. In addition, a new Award has been added: Silver, for sales of over 250,000 copies in all editions over the same time period. The former Nielsen Book Gold and Platinum Awards are now called the Specsavers Bestseller Awards, powered by Nielsen Book.

Sports Book Awards

c/o Agile Marketing, Magnolia House, 172 Winsley Road, Bradford-on-Avon, Wiltshire BA15 1NY
tel (01225) 302266
email alastair@agile-ideas.com
website www.sportsbookawards.com
Twitter @SportBookAwards
Contact Danielle Bowers

The Sports Book Awards is the major annual promotion for sports writing and publishing. The awards exist to highlight the most outstanding sports books of the previous calendar year, to showcase their merits and to enhance their reputation and profile. Winners are announced at an annual awards ceremony in May/June. See website for full details.

The Sunday Times/Peters Fraser Dunlop Young Writer of the Year Award

email prizes@societyofauthors.org
website www.societyofauthors.org/sunday-times-pfd
website www.youngwriteraward.com

A prize of £5,000 is awarded for a full-length published or self-published (in book or ebook format) work of fiction, non-fiction or poetry, by a British or Irish author aged 35 years or under. Runners-up receive £500 each. The winning book will be a work of outstanding literary merit. For submission information, see the website. The prize is administered by the Society of Authors.

The Sunday Times EFG Short Story Award

The Society of Authors, 84 Drayton Gardens, London, SW10 9SB
tel 020-7373 6642
email STEFGqueries@societyofauthors.org
website www.societyofauthors.org.uk/prizes/SundayTimesEFG
website www.shortstoryaward.co.uk

Founded by Lord Matthew Evans, former chairman of EFG Private Bank and Cathy Galvin from *The Sunday Times*, The Sunday Times EFG Short Story Award is the richest prize for a single short story in the English language open to any novelist or short story writer from around the world who is published in the UK. Worth £30,000 to the winner, and £1,000 to each of the shortlisted authors, the annual award aims to promote and celebrate the excellence of the modern short story, and has attracted entries from some of the world's finest writers. Winners of the competition, which is open to stories of up to 6,000 words written in English, have come from all over the world, and have included the Pulitzer Prize-winning American writer Junot Diaz, C.K. Stead from New Zealand and Kevin Barry from Ireland. Founded 2009.

The James Tait Black Memorial Prizes

English Literature, School of Literatures, Languages and Cultures, The University of Edinburgh, 50 George Square, Edinburgh EH8 9LH
tel 0131 650 3619
email nicola.mccartney@ed.ac.uk
website www.ed.ac.uk/events/james-tait-black
Contact Nicola McCartney

The James Tait Black Fiction and Biography Prizes

Two prizes of £10,000 are awarded annually: one for the best biography or work of that nature, the other for the best work of fiction, published during the calendar year 1 January to 31 December. The adjudicators are Professors of English Literature at the University of Edinburgh, with the assistance of teams of postgraduate readers. Eligible novels and biographies are those written in English and first published or co-published in Britain in the year of the award. Both prizes may go to the same author, but neither to the same author a second time.

Publishers should submit a copy of any appropriate biography, or work of fiction, as early as possible with a note of the date of publication, marked 'James Tait Black Prize'. Closing date for submissions: 1 December. Founded 1918.

The James Tait Black Prize for Drama: University of Edinburgh in association with Playwrights Studio Scotland

A prize of £10,000 for a professionally produced play which displays an original voice in theatre and one that has made a significant and unique contribution to the art form. The prize is open to any new work originally written in English, Scots or Gaelic, by playwrights from any country at any stage in their career. The judges will be students and staff of the University's School of Literatures, Languages and Cultures and representatives from the wider European theatre industry.

Plays must be formally commissioned and have had a full professional production. Eligible plays will have been produced between 1 January and 31 December in the year preceding the year of the award, and run for a minimum of six performances. A typed copy of the script and a digital copy must be sent with details of the first production, which should include venue, company and date, and proof of production if possible. The submissions must come from the producing company or the agent of the playwright, and should be submitted with the submission form to the Department of English Literature by the date specified on the website.

Applications which do not have the submission form complete will be considered ineligible. For full criteria visit the website.

Reginald Taylor and Lord Fletcher Essay Competition

British Archaeological Association, 18 Stanley Road, Oxford OX4 1QZ
email jsmcneill@btinternet.com
Hon. Secretary John McNeill

A prize of a medal and £500 is awarded biennially for the best unpublished essay of high scholarly standard, which shows original research on a subject of archaeological, art-historical or antiquarian interest within the period from the Roman era to AD1830. The successful competitor will be invited to read the essay before the Association and the essay may be published in the Association's *Journal*. Competitors should notify the Hon. Editor in advance of the intended subject of their work. Next award: Spring 2020. The essay should be submitted not later than 1 November 2019 to the Honorary Editor, Dr Zoe Opacic, Department of History of Art, Birkbeck College, 43–46 Gordon Square, London WC1H 0PD. Founded in memory of E. Reginald Taylor FSA and Lord Fletcher FSA.

International Dylan Thomas Prize

tel (01792) 606245
website www.swansea.ac.uk/dylan-thomas-prize/

The £30,000 Swansea University International Dylan Thomas Prize is awarded to the best published literary work in the English language, written by an author aged 39 or under. Previous winners include: Lucy Caldwell, Claire Vaye-Watkins, Joshua Ferris, Max Porter and Fiona McFarlane. Launched in 2006.

The Times/Chicken House Children's Fiction Competition

Chicken House, 2 Palmer Street, Frome, Somerset BA11 1DS
tel (01373) 454488
email hello@chickenhousebooks.com
website www.chickenhousebooks.com
Twitter @chickenhsebooks
Contact Kesia Lupo

This annual competition is open to unpublished writers of a full-length children's novel (age 7–18). Entrants must be over 18 and novels must not exceed 80,000 words in length. The winner will be announced in *The Times* and will receive a worldwide publishing contract with Chicken House with a royalty advance of £10,000. The winner is selected by a panel of judges which includes children's authors, journalists, publishers, librarians and other key figures from the world of children's literature.

Submissions are invited between July and December, with a shortlist announced the following April and the winner chosen in June. See website for further details.

The Tinniswood Award

Society of Authors, 84 Drayton Gardens, London SW10 9SB
website www.societyofauthors.org/prizes/audio-drama/the-tinniswood-award

The Tinniswood Award is presented annually for the best original audio drama script of the year. The Society of Authors perpetuate the memory of radio and TV comedy scriptwriter, Peter Tinniswood through the Award, which aims to celebrate and encourage high standards in radio drama. Prize: £3,000. Submissions will be accepted from any party (producer, broadcasting organisation, writer, agent etc). For entry guidelines and details of the application procedure, see the website.

Tir na n-Og Awards

Welsh Books Council, Castell Brychan, Aberystwyth, Ceredigion SY23 2JB
email wbc.children@wbc.org.uk
website www.wbc.org.uk
Facebook www.facebook.com/LlyfrDaFabBooks

The Tir na n-Og Awards were established with the intention of promoting and raising the standard of children's and young people's books in Wales. Three awards are presented annually by the Welsh Books Council and are sponsored by the Chartered Institute of Library and Information Professionals Cymru/ Wales and Cymdeithas Lyfrau Ceredigion:

- The best English-language book of the year with an authentic Welsh background. Fiction and factual books originally in English are eligible; translations from Welsh or any other language are not eligible. Prize: £1,000.
- The best original Welsh-language book aimed at the primary school sector. Prize: £1,000.
- The best original Welsh-language book aimed at the secondary school sector. Prize: £1,000. Founded 1976.

The Tom-Gallon Trust Award

The Society of Authors, 84 Drayton Gardens, London SW10 9SB
tel 020-7373 6642
email prizes@societyofauthors.org
website www.societyofauthors.org/tom-gallon
Twitter @Soc_of_Authors

An annual award of £1,000 with £500 for a runner-up is made on the basis of a submitted short story to fiction writers who have had at least one short story accepted for publication and are ordinarily resident in the UK or Northern Ireland. The submission should be traditional, not experimental, in character. Closing date: 31 October.

The Translation Prizes

The Society of Authors, 84 Drayton Gardens, London SW10 9SB
tel 020-7373 6642
email prizes@societyofauthors.org
website www.societyofauthors.org/prizes/translation-prizes
Twitter @Soc_of_Authors

The Society of Authors offers a number of prizes for published translations into English from Arabic, Dutch, French, German, Hebrew, Italian, Spanish and Swedish. The Society also administers the TA First Translation Prize, which is an annual prize of £2,000 for debut literary translation published in the UK. See website for entry guidelines and deadlines.

The Betty Trask Prize and Awards

The Society of Authors, 84 Drayton Gardens, London SW10 9SB
tel 020-7373 6642
email prizes@societyofauthors.org
website www.societyofauthors.org/betty-trask
Twitter @Soc_of_Authors

An annual prize for first novels (published or unpublished), of a traditional or romantic nature, by authors under the age of 35. Total prize money from £20,000. Closing date: 30 November.

The V&A Illustration Awards

Victoria & Albert Museum, London SW7 2RL
email villa@vam.ac.uk
website www.vam.ac.uk/illustrationawards

These annual awards are open to illustrators living or publishing in the UK market and students who have attended a course in the UK over the last two years. Awards are made in the following categories: best illustrated book, book cover, editorial illustration and student illustrator.

Ver Poets Open Competition

181 Sandridge Road, St Albans, Herts. AL1 4AH
tel (01727) 762601
email gillknibbs@yahoo.co.uk
website www.verpoets.co.uk
Competition Secretary Gill Knibbs

A competition open to all for poems of up to 30 lines of any genre or subject matter, which must be unpublished work in English. Prizes: 1st: £600, 2nd: £300, 3rd: £100. Send two copies of each poem with no name or address; either put address on separate sheet or send sae or email for entry form. Closing date: 30 April. Anthology of winning and selected poems with Adjudicator's Report usually available from mid-June, free to those included. See website for details.

The Wainwright Prize

email alastair@agile-ideas.com
website www.wainwrightprize.com
Twitter @wainwrightprize

The Wainwright Prize seeks to reward the best writing on the outdoors, nature and UK-based travel writing and is sponsored by Wainwright Golden Beer. The prize will be awarded to the work which best reflects Wainwright's core values of Great British writing and culture and a celebration of the outdoors. See website for submission guidelines and key dates.

Wales Book of the Year Award

Literature Wales, 4th Floor, Cambrian Buildings, Mount Stuart Square, Cardiff CF10 5FL
tel 029-2047 2266
email post@literaturewales.org
website www.literaturewales.org/our-projects/wales-book-year
website www.literaturewales.org
Facebook www.facebook.com/LlenCymruLitWales
Twitter @litwales
Literature Wales Chief Executive Lleucu Siencyn

Wales Book of the Year, administered by Literature Wales, is an annual award which is presented to the best Welsh and English-language works first published in the year preceding the ceremony in the fields of creative writing and literary criticism in three categories: Poetry, Fiction and Creative Non-fiction. Past winners include Owen Sheers, Rhian Edwards, Patrick McGuinness, Thomas Morris and Alys Conran.

Wasafiri New Writing Prize

email wasafiri@qmul.ac.uk
website www.wasafiri.org/new-writing-prize

The Wasafiri New Writing Prize is awarded in three categories. Poetry, Fiction and Life Writing, and is open to anyone worldwide who has not published a complete book in the category they wish to enter. The prize was launched to support new writers, with no limits on age, gender, nationality or background. The three category winners will be published by Wasafiri and receive a cash prize. They will also be offered a mentoring scheme (depending on eligibility). See website for submission guidelines and entry fees. Founded 2009.

The Wellcome Book Prize

email bookprize@wellcome.ac.uk
website www.wellcomebookprize.org

Celebrates the best of medicine in literature by awarding £30,000 each year for the finest fiction or non-fiction book centred around medicine. This prize aims to stimulate interest, excitement and debate about medicine and literature, reaching audiences not normally engaged with medical science. Founded 2009.

The White Review Short Story Prize

website www.thewhitereview.org/prizes/white-review-short-story-prize-2018/

An annual short story competition for emerging writers, established with support from a Jerwood Charitable Foundation Small Grant in 2013. The prize awards £2,500 to the best piece of short fiction by a writer resident in the UK or Ireland who has yet to secure a publishing deal. For the first time in 2017, the Prize was run concurrently on both sides of the Atlantic, with the usual competition running in Britain and Ireland, and a separate contest taking place simultaneously in the US and Canada. For submission guidelines and entry terms and conditions, see the website.

The Whitfield Prize

Administrative Secretary, Royal Historical Society, University College London, Gower Street, London WC1E 6BT
tel 020-7387 7532
email m.ransom@royalhistsoc.org
website http://royalhistsoc.org/prizes/

The Prize of £1,000 is awarded for the best work on a subject within a field of British or Irish history. It must be its author's first solely written history book, an original and scholarly work of historical research and published in English. For full information on how to enter and for eligibility guidelines, see the website.

Wildlife Photographer of the Year

The Natural History Museum, Cromwell Road, London SW7 5BD
website www.nhm.ac.uk/visit/wpy/competition.html

This annual award is given to the photographer whose individual image is judged to be the most striking and memorable. There is an adult competition for photographers aged 18 or over and a young competition for photographers aged 17 or under. See website for submission guidelines.

Winchester Writers' Festival Competitions and Scholarships

University of Winchester, Winchester, Hants SO22 4NR
tel (01962) 827238
email judith.heneghan@winchester.ac.uk
website www.writersfestival.co.uk
Festival Director Judith Heneghan

Ten writing competitions are attached to this major international festival for emerging writers, which takes place in June. Entrants do not have to attend the Festival and can opt to receive a written adjudication (with the exception of the writing for children competitions).

Categories are: First Three Pages of a Novel, Poetry, Short Stories, Flash Fiction, Children's Picture Book, Children's Funny Fiction, Memoir, Writing Can Be Murder, Young Writers' Competition and Skylark Soaring Stories. Deadline for entries: second week in April. Winners announced: third week in May. Fee £6 without written adjudication; £16 with written adjudication.

Prizes include editorial consultations, subscriptions, cash prizes and books. First place winning entries and their adjudications are published in the Festival anthology. The Festival also offers ten full weekend scholarships for young writers aged 18–25 to attend the Festival for free and a number of £50 bursaries for writers of all ages. Apply to the Festival Director.

The Wolfson History Prize

The Prize Administrator, The Wolfson Foundation, 8 Queen Anne Street, London W1G 9LD
tel 020-7323 5730
website www.wolfson.org.uk/history-prize
Facebook www.facebook.com/WolfsonHistoryPrize
Twitter @wolfsonfdn

Awarded annually to promote and recognise outstanding history written for a general audience. Books are judged on the extent to which they are both scholarly and accessible to the lay reader. Books must be published in the UK in the calendar year preceding the year of the award. The subject matter of the book may cover any aspect of history, including historical biography. The author must be normally resident in the UK during the year of publication and not be a previous winner of the Prize. Previously shortlisted authors are eligible. The winning author will receive a prize of £40,000. The five remaining shortlisted authors will be awarded a prize of £4,000 each. All submissions must come via the publisher. Full details on the process are available online. Founded 1972.

Women's Prize for Fiction

The Society of Authors, 84 Drayton Gardens, London, SW10 9SB
tel 020-7373 6642
email womensprize@societyofauthors.org
website www.societyofauthors.org/prizes/womens-prize

The Women's Prize for Fiction celebrates excellence, originality and accessibility in writing by women in English from throughout the world. It is the UK's most prestigious annual book award for fiction written by a woman and also provides a range of educational, literacy or research initiatives to support reading and writing.

The Women's Prize for Fiction is awarded annually for the best full novel of the year written by a woman and published in the UK. Any woman writing in English – whatever her nationality, country of residence, age or subject matter – is eligible. The winner receives £30,000 and a limited edition bronze figurine known as a 'Bessie', created and donated by the artist Grizel Niven.

World Illustration Awards

Association of Illustrators, Somerset House, Strand, London WC2R 1LA
tel 020-7759 1012
email awards@theaoi.com
website www.theaoi.com/awards/
Facebook www.facebook.com/theaoi
Twitter @theaoi
Twitter @WIA2018
Awards Manager Sabine Reimer

The World Illustration Awards, in partnership with the Directory of Illustration, is an awards programme that sets out to celebrate contemporary illustration across the globe. A panel of international judges create a shortlist, which is displayed at an exhibition in Somerset House and subsequently tours the UK and internationally.

An accompanying publication is distributed to commissioners worldwide. Entries can be submitted by practising illustrators or students from around the world, created in any medium into any of eight categories. Two awards are given for Best in each category and to one overall winner of Professional and New Talent respectively. Call for entries: November to February; shortlist announced May; exhibition and publication June; UK tour for one year thereafter.

Writers' & Artists' Yearbook 2019 Short Story Competition

website www.writersandartists.co.uk/competitions

See information panel on page ix of this edition or visit our website for details.

YouWriteOn.com Book Awards

tel 07948 392634
email edward@youwriteon.com
website www.youwriteon.com

Arts Council-funded site publishing awards for new fiction writers. Random House and Orion, the publishers of authors such as Dan Brown and Terry Pratchett, provide free professional critiques for the highest rated new writers' opening chapters and short stories on YouWriteOn.com each month. The highest rated writers of the year are then published, three in each of the adult and children's categories, through YouWriteOn's free paperback publishing service for writers. The novel publishing awards total £1,000. Writers can enter at any time throughout the year: closing date is 31 December each year. Join YouWriteOn.com to participate. Previous YouWriteOn.com winners have been published by mainstream publishers such as Random House, Orion, Penguin and Hodder including Channel 4 TV Book Club winner and bestseller *The Legacy* by Katherine Webb. Founded 2005.

Zooker Award

Arkbound, Backfields House, Upper York Street, Bristol BS2 8QJ
email editorial@arkbound.com
website http://arkbound.com/zooker-award/

The Zooker Award aims to encourage first-time authors from disadvantaged backgrounds and to reward works of social value; principally those that touch upon the themes of environmental sustainability and social inclusion, encouraging positive changes in behaviour or attitude for readers. Submitted work must have been published (not self-published) in the last two years. Entry fee £4.50. The prize is £500 and in the event that there is insufficient sponsorship or entry fees, the Award will be carried over to the next year. For full details, visit the website.

GRANTS, BURSARIES AND FELLOWSHIPS

Arts Council England

Arts Council England, 21 Bloomsbury Street, London WC1B 3HF
tel 0845 300 6200
email enquiries@artscouncil.org.uk
website www.artscouncil.org.uk

Arts Council England is the national development agency for the arts in England, providing funding for a range of arts and cultural activities. It supports creative writing including poetry, fiction, storytelling, spoken word, digital work, writing for children and literary translation. It funds a range of publishers and magazines as well as providing grants to individual writers. Contact the enquiries team for more information on funding support and advice.

The Arts Council/An Chomhairle Ealaíon

70 Merrion Square, Dublin D02 NY52, Republic of Ireland
tel +353 (0)1 6180200
website www.artscouncil.ie

Outlines all of its funding opportunities for individuals, groups and organisations on website. Also publishes regular information on grants and awards, news and events, and arts policy.

The Authors' Contingency Fund

Grants, The Society of Authors, 84 Drayton Gardens, London SW10 9SB
tel 020-7373 6642
email grants@societyofauthors.org
website www.societyofauthors.org

This fund makes modest grants to established, published authors who find themselves in sudden financial difficulty. Apply for guidelines and application form.

The Authors' Foundation

The Society of Authors, 84 Drayton Gardens, London SW10 9SB
tel 020-7373 6642
email prizes@societyofauthors.org
website www.societyofauthors.org/grants/grants-for-works-in-progress
Twitter @Soc_of_Authors

The Authors' Foundation provides grants to writers to assist them while writing books. There are two rounds of grants each year (deadlines April and September). The Authors' Foundation provides funding (in addition to a proper advance) for research, travel or other necessary expenditure.

Applicants are welcome who have been commissioned by a commercial British publisher to write a full-length work of fiction, poetry or non-fiction, or those without a contractual commitment by a publisher who have had at least one book published commercially, and where there is a strong likelihood that a further book will be published in the UK. Download application guidelines from the website or send an sae for an information sheet. Founded 1984.

Carole Blake Open Doors Project

email hattie@blakefriedmann.co.uk
website www.blakefriedmann.co.uk/carole-blake-open-doors-project/

The Carole Blake Open Doors Project is a programme specifally aimed at encouraging candidates from a diverse range of backgrounds to enter the publishing industry. The programme offers ten days of work shadowing to a selected applicant over a two-week period, including funding for travel and up to twelve nights' accommodation in London. The programme runs twice a year, includes close mentorship with Blake Friedmann agents, the opportunity to attend meetings with editors and clients and the chance to be involved in the day-to-day life of a literary agent. For full details of candidate specifications, how to apply and terms and conditions, see the website.

The K. Blundell Trust

The Society of Authors, 84 Drayton Gardens, London SW10 9SB
tel 020-7373 6642
email prizes@societyofauthors.org
website www.societyofauthors.org/grants/grants-for-works-in-progress
Twitter @Soc_of_Authors

Grants are given to published writers under the age of 40 to assist them with their next book. This work must 'contribute to the greater understanding of existing social and economic organisation' and may be fiction or non-fiction. Closing dates: April and September. Download application guidelines from the website or send sae for an information sheet.

Alfred Bradley Bursary Award

website www.bbc.co.uk/writersroom

This biennial development opportunity is awarded to a writer or writers resident in the North of England.

This scheme allows the winning writer to devote a period of time to writing and to develop an idea for a radio drama commission. Founded 1992.

Creative Scotland

tel 0330 333 2000 (main switchboard), 0345 603 6000 (enquiries line)
email enquiries@creativescotland.com
website www.creativescotland.com/funding

Creative Scotland is the national funding and development agency for the arts, screen and creative industries in Scotland. Funding support is available to writers, playwrights, illustrators and publishers based in Scotland through Open Project Funding. Additionally, other fellowships, residencies and developmental programmes are available through organisations we fund directly or in partnership with.

The Julia Darling Travel Fellowship

email office@newwritingnorth.com
website www.newwritingnorth/projects/the-julia-darling-travel-fellowship
website www.juliadarling.co.uk

New Writing North, in conjunction with the family and friends of the late writer, Julia Darling, have established a travel fellowship for creative writers in her name. Julia's work covered a variety of forms, from plays and novels to poetry and performance. The fellowship is worth £2,000, to be used to fund travel and accommodation both in the UK and internationally. It will also support group applications from writers who would like to undertake joint residential retreats.

Open to novelists, poets and playwrights over the age of 18 who live and work in the North of England and who have at least one professionally produced or published work to their name. Entry is by online submission only. See the website for full details.

E.M. Forster Award

American Academy of Arts and Letters,
633 West 155th Street, New York, NY 10032, USA
tel +1 212-368-5900
email academy@artsandletters.org
website www.artsandletters.org

The distinguished English author, E.M. Forster, bequeathed the American publication rights and royalties of his posthumous novel *Maurice* to Christopher Isherwood, who transferred them to the American Academy of Arts and Letters, for the establishment of an E.M. Forster Award, currently $20,000, to be given annually to a British or Irish writer for a stay in the USA. Applications for this award are not accepted.

The Eric Gregory Awards

The Society of Authors, 84 Drayton Gardens,
London SW10 9SB
tel 020-7373 6642
email prizes@societyofauthors.org
website www.societyofauthors.org/eric-gregory
Twitter @Soc_of_Authors

These awards are for poets under the age of 30, made annually for the encouragement of young poets who can show that they are likely to benefit from an opportunity to give more time to writing. Candidates must be ordinarily resident in the UK or Northern Ireland. Candidates must be under the age of 30 on 31 March in the year of the Award (i.e. the year following submission). The work submitted may be a published or unpublished volume of poetry, drama-poems or belles lettres, and no more than 30 poems should be submitted. Closing date: 31 October.

Hawthornden Fellowships

The Administrator, International Retreat for Writers,
Hawthornden Castle, Lasswade,
Midlothian EH18 1EG
tel 0131 440 2180
email office@hawthornden.org

Applications are invited from novelists, poets, dramatists and other creative writers whose work has already been published. The Retreat provides four-week fellowships in a peaceful setting. Application forms are available from January for Fellowships awarded in the following year. Deadline for applications 30 June.

Francis Head Bequest

Grants Department, The Society of Authors,
84 Drayton Gardens, London SW10 9SB
tel 020-7373 6642
email grants@societyofauthors.org
website www.societyofauthors.org

This fund provides grants to published British authors over the age of 35 who need financial help during a period of illness, disablement or temporary financial crisis. Apply for guidelines and application form.

The P.D. James Memorial Fund

Society of Authors, 84 Drayton Gardens,
London SW10 9SB
email info@societyofauthors.org
website www.societyofauthors.org/grants/P-D-James-memorial-fund

This fund offers regular payments to a small number of Society of Authors members who find themselves in financial hardship. Awards are given by committee to long-term members who are either aged 60 or over or who are completely incapacitated for work. The fund currently distributes £2,000 per annum to each recipient. For more information, see the website.

Jerwood Compton Poetry Fellowships

email info@jerwood.charitablefoundation.org
website www.jerwoodcharitablefoundation.org

Funded by the Jerwood Charitable Foundation and Arts Council England, the Jerwood Compton Poetry

Fellowships offer a significant new development opportunity for poets. Running between 2017 and 2022 and supporting a total of nine artists, successful artists will receive £15,000 to support their Fellowship, during which time they will be matched with a mentor and given access to a range of advisers to support their work. For further details, see the website.

Leverhulme Research Fellowships

The Leverhulme Trust, 1 Pemberton Row,
London EC4A 3BG
tel 020-7042 9861
email agrundy@leverhulme.ac.uk
website www.leverhulme.ac.uk
Twitter @LeverhulmeTrust

The Leverhulme Trust Board offer annually approximately 100 fellowships to experienced researchers in aid of original research. These awards are not available as replacement for past support from other sources. Applications in all subject areas are considered, with the exception of clinical medical or pharmaceutical research. Applications must be completed online by early November 2018 for 2019 awards. Refer to the website for further details. Founded 1933.

The John Masefield Memorial Trust

Grants, The Society of Authors, 84 Drayton Gardens,
London SW10 9SB
tel 020-7373 6642
email grants@societyofauthors.org
website www.societyofauthors.org

This trust makes occasional grants to professional poets who find themselves with sudden financial problems. Apply for guidelines and application form.

Northern Writers' Awards

email awards@newwritingnorth.com
website www.northernwritersawards.com

Established by New Writing North, the Northern Writers' Awards support work-in-progress by new, emerging and established writers across the North of England. The Awards support writers creatively as they develop their work through publication, as well as helping them to progress professionally and to navigate their way through the publishing industry. Founded 2000.

The Frank O'Connor International Short Story Fellowship

The Munster Literature Centre,
Frank O' Connor House, 84 Douglas Street, Cork,
Republic of Ireland
tel +353 (0)21 431 2955
email info@munsterlit.ie
website www.munsterlit.ie
website www.corkshortstory.net

For a non-Irish writer, not resident in Ireland to take up residency in Cork City for three months. The fellow will have plenty of time to concentrate on his/her own work but will be expected to contribute a four-morning masterclass and reading to the Cork International Short Story Festival, and to offer six contact hours per week over eight weeks, mentoring local fiction authors. A stipend of €9,000, accommodation and flights to Ireland are on offer. Annual deadline for applications 30 August (for residency one year later).

Charles Pick South Asia Fellowship

School of Literature, Drama and Creative Writing,
University of East Anglia, Norwich NR4 7TJ
tel (01603) 597599
email charlespickfellowship@uea.ac.uk
website www.uea.ac.uk/literature/fellowships

The Charles Pick Fellowship is dedicated to the memory of the distinguished publisher and literary agent, Charles Pick, whose career began in 1933 and continued until shortly before his death in January 2000. He encouraged young writers at the start of their careers with introductions to other writers and offered practical and financial help. The Charles Pick Fellowship seeks to continue this spirit of encouragement by giving support to the work of a new and, as yet, unpublished writer of fictional or non-fictional prose based in South Asia. The writer must be from Bangladesh, Burma/Myanmar or Pakistan but does not need to be domiciled there. Preference will be given to mature students, and candidates who have completed their education and who have embarked on a career path. The 2017/18 Charles Pick Fellow is Rahad Abir.

The Peggy Ramsay Foundation

Hanover House, 14 Hanover Square,
London W1S 1HP
email prf@harbottle.com
website www.peggyramsayfoundation.org

Grants are made to writers of stage plays in accordance with the criteria on the Foundation's website. Awards are made at intervals during each year. A total of approx. £200,000 is expended annually. Founded 1992.

The Royal Literary Fund

3 Johnson's Court, off Fleet Street,
London EC4A 3EA
tel 020-7353 7150
website www.rlf.org.uk

The RLF is a benevolent fund for writers in financial difficulties. It does not offer grants to writers who can earn their living in other ways, nor does it provide financial support for writing projects, but it helps authors who have fallen on hard times due to personal or professional setbacks. Applicants must have published several works of approved literary merit. Applicants are requested to send copies of their books with their completed application forms. Founded 1790.

Robert Louis Stevenson Fellowship

Scottish Book Trust, Sandeman House,
Trunk's Close, 55 High Street, Edinburgh EH1 1SR
tel 0131-524 0160
email info@scottishbooktrust.com
website www.scottishbooktrust.com

The Robert Louis Stevenson Fellowship is an annual award that allows professional writers living in Scotland to enjoy a month-long residency at the Hotel Chevillon International Arts Centre at Grez-sur-Loing in France, with a stipend of £1,200. Each year, four writers are invited to spend time with other artists and develop their work in a peaceful and inspiring environment. For full eligibility criteria and application details, visit the website.

TLC/Arts Council England Free Reads Scheme

The Literary Consultancy Ltd, Free Word Centre,
60 Farringdon Road, London EC1R 3GA
tel 020-7324 2563
email info@literaryconsultancy.co.uk
website www.literaryconsultancy.co.uk/editorial/ace-free-reads-scheme/
Director Aki Schilz

In 2001, TLC received funding from Arts Council England to enable the provision of bursaried manuscript assessments for writers from low-income households. The scheme is known as the Free Reads Scheme and offers access to TLC's core services to writers who might not be able to afford them. Free Reads are selected by a range of literature development bodies from across the UK, and there are currently thirteen organisations benefitting from the scheme. For detailed submission guidelines and eligibility information, see the website.

The Travelling Scholarships

The Society of Authors, 84 Drayton Gardens,
London SW10 9SB
tel 020-7373 6642
email prizes@societyofauthors.org
website www.societyofauthors.org/prizes/fiction/travelling-scholarships
Twitter @Soc_of_Authors

These honorary awards were established in 1944 by an anonymous benefactor. See website for more information.

David T.K. Wong Fellowship

School of Literature, Drama and Creative Writing,
University of East Anglia, Norwich NR4 7TJ
tel (01603) 597599
email davidtkwongfellowship@uea.ac.uk
website www.uea.ac.uk/literature/fellowships

The David T.K. Wong Fellowship is an annual award of £26,000 to enable a fiction writer who wants to write in English about the Far East to spend a year in the UK, at the University of East Anglia in Norwich. The Fellowship is named after its sponsor David T.K. Wong, a retired Hong Kong businessman, who has also been a teacher, journalist and senior civil servant, and is a writer of short stories. The Fellowship will be awarded to a writer planning to produce a work of prose fiction in English which deals seriously with some aspect of life in the Far East (Brunei, Cambodia, Hong Kong, Indonesia, Japan, Korea, Laos, Macau, Malaysia, Mongolia, Myanmar, People's Republic of China, Philippines, Singapore, Taiwan, Thailand and Vietnam). The 2017/18 Fellow is Nathaniel Go.

PRIZE WINNERS

This is a selection of high-profile literary prize winners from 2017–18 presented chronologically. Entries for many of these prizes are included in the *Yearbook*, starting on page 565.

May 2017

Man Booker International Prize
A Horse Walks into a Bar by David Grossman (translated from Hebrew by Jessica Cohen)

The CILIP Carnegie Medal
Salt to the Sea by Ruta Sepetys

The CILIP Kate Greenaway Medal
There is a Tribe of Kids illustrated by Lane Smith

Commonwealth Writers' Short Story Award
The Sweet Sop by Ingrid Persaud

June

Baileys Women's Prize for Fiction
The Power by Naomi Alderman

October

BBC National Short Story Award
The Edge of the Shoal by Cynan Jones

BBC Young Writers' Award
The Roses by Elizabeth Ryder

The Nobel Prize in Literature
Kazuo Ishiguro

The Man Booker Prize
Lincoln in the Bardo by George Saunders
The Bridport Prize
Siren Call by Mary-Jane Holmes (Poetry); *Esther* by Nicholas Ruddock (Short Story); *Buttercups* by Terry Warren (Flash Fiction)

November

National Book Awards (USA)
Sing, Unburied, Sing by Jesmyn Ward (Fiction); *The Future is History: How Totalitarianism Reclaimed Russia* by Masha Gessen (Non-fiction); *Far from the Tree* by Robin Benway (Young People's Literature); *Half-light: Collected Poems 1965-2016* by Frank Bidart (Poetry)

Waterstones Book of the Year
La Belle Sauvage: Book of Dust, Vol. 1 by Philip Pullman

January 2018

T.S. Eliot Prize for Poetry
Night Sky With Exit Wounds by Ocean Vuong

Costa Book of the Year
Inside the Wave by Helen Dunmore

Bookbug Picture Book Award
Gorilla Loves Vanilla by Chae Strathie

February

Scottish Teenage Book Prize
Children of Icarus by Caighlan Smith

March

Blue Peter Book Awards
The Wizard of Once by Cressida Cowell (Best Story); *Real-Life Mysteries* by Susan Martineau, illustrated by Vicky Barker (Best Book with Facts)

Waterstones Children's Book Prize
The Hate U Give by Angie Thomas (Best Older Fiction and Overall Winner); *The Secret of Black Rock* by Joe Todd-Stanton (Best Illustrated Book); *Nevermoor* by Jessica Townsend (Best Younger Fiction)

April

The Pulitzer Prize (USA)
Less by Andrew Sean Greer (Fiction); *Half-light: Collected Poems 1965-2016* by Frank Bidart (Poetry); *The Gulf: The Making of an American Sea* by Jack E. Davis (History); *Locking Up Our Own: Crime and Punishment in Black America* by James Forman Jr. (General Non-fiction); *Prairie Fires: The American Dreams of Laura Ingalls Wilder* by Caroline Fraser (Biography or Autobiography); *Cost of Living* by Martyna Majok (Drama); *DAMN.* by Kendrick Lamar (Music)

The Sunday Times EFG Private Bank Short Story Award
Peanuts Aren't Nuts by Courtney Zoffness

Festivals and conferences for writers, artists and readers

There are hundreds of arts festivals and conferences held in the UK each year – too many to mention in this *Yearbook*. We list a selection of literature, writing and general arts festivals which include literature events. Space constraints and the nature of an annual publication together determine that only brief details are given; contact festival organisers for a full programme of events.

Ageas Salisbury International Arts Festival

87 Crane Street, Salisbury, Wilts. SP1 2PU
tel (01722) 332241
email info@salisburyfestival.co.uk
website www.salisburyfestival.co.uk
Facebook www.facebook.com/SalisburyArtsFestival
Twitter @AgeasSalisFest
Takes place May–June

A thriving, annual multi-arts festival that delivers over 150 arts events each year, including concerts, comedy, poetry, dance, exhibitions, outdoor spectacles and commissioned works.

Aldeburgh Poetry Festival

website www.poetryinaldeburgh.org
Takes place November

Annual festival of contemporary poetry with venues in Aldeburgh and at Snape Maltings. Readings, workshops, talks, discussions, public masterclass and children's event. Founded 1989.

Appledore Book Festival

Festival Office, Docton Court Gallery,
2 Myrtle Street, Appledore, Bideford,
Devon EX39 1PH
email info@appledorebookfestival.co.uk
website www.appledorebookfestival.co.uk
Takes place 21–29 September 2018

Founded by children's author Nick Arnold this annual festival includes a schools programme covering North Devon and public events for all ages; also book fairs and a bookshop. Founded 2007.

Asia House Bagri Foundation Literature Festival

Asia House, 63 New Cavendish Street,
London W1G 7LP
tel 020-7307 5454
email arts@asiahouse.co.uk
website www.asiahouse.org
Takes place May

The Festival remains the only festival in the UK dedicated exclusively to pan-Asian literature. It has earned a reputation as the Festival for people with an interest in Asia and its rich literary heritage. It hosts remarkable, witty, sensitive and inspiring guest speakers, from Nobel laureates and Man Booker prize winners to local language writers and debut novelists.

Aspects Irish Literature Festival

website www.aspectsfestival.com
Facebook www.facebook.com/aspectsfestival/

An annual celebration of contemporary Irish writing with novelists, poets and playwrights. Includes readings, discussion, workshops, comedy, music and an Aspects showcase day for young writers.

Autumn International Literary Festival

University of East Anglia, Norwich NR4 7TJ
tel (01603) 592286
email literaryevents@uea.ac.uk
website www.uea.ac.uk/litfest
Facebook UEA Literary Festival
Twitter @UEALitFest
Takes place late September–early December

An annual festival of events bringing established writers of fiction, biography and poetry to a public audience in the Eastern region.

The Bath Festival

Bath Festivals, 9/10 Bath Street, Bath BA1 1SN
tel (01225) 614180 Box Office (01225) 463362
email info@bathfestivals.org.uk
website https://bathfestivals.org.uk/the-bath-festival/
website https://bathfestivals.org.uk/childrens-literature
Takes place May

An annual festival with leading guest writers. Includes readings, debates, discussions and workshops and events for children and young people.

Birmingham Literature Festival

Unit 204, Custard Factory, Gibb Street,
Birmingham B9 4AA
tel 0121 246 2770
email abigail@writingwestmidlands.org
website www.birminghamliteraturefestival.org
Twitter @BhamLitFest
Programmes Director Abigail Campbell
Takes place April and October

The annual Birmingham Literature Festival is firmly

established in the cultural calendar as the region's brightest literary event. It gathers household names and rising stars to celebrate the power of words. The Festival is always a varied, ambitious programme that has won a loyal and growing audience over the years. A project of Writing West Midlands.

Borders Book Festival

Harmony House, St Mary's Road, Melrose TD6 9LJ
tel (01896) 822644
email info@bordersbookfestival.org
website www.bordersbookfestival.org
Takes place June

An annual festival with a programme of events featuring high-profile and bestselling writers. Winner of the Walter Scott Prize for Historical Fiction is announced during the festival. Founded 2004.

Bread and Roses

c/o Five Leaves Bookshop, 14a Long Row, Nottingham NG1 2DH
email bookshop@fiveleaves.co.uk
website www.fiveleavesbookshop.co.uk

An annual weekend of radical politics, music and literature held at various venues in Nottingham. The only book festival supported by trade unions.

Brighton Festival

tel (01273) 700747
email info@brightonfestival.org
website www.brightonfestival.org
Takes place May

An annual arts festival with an extensive national and international programme featuring theatre, dance, music, opera, literature, outdoor and family events.

Buxton International Festival

3 The Square, Buxton, Derbyshire SK17 6AZ
tel (01298) 70395
email info@buxtonfestival.co.uk
website www.buxtonfestival.co.uk
Takes place July

The renowned opera and music programme is complemented by a Literary Series, featuring distinguished authors, which takes place every morning and afternoon.

Cambridge Literary Festival

7 Downing Place, Cambridge CB2 3EL
email info@cambridgeliteraryfestival.com
website www.cambridgeliteraryfestival.com
Takes place April and November

The Cambridge Literary Festival welcomes writers and readers from around the world and provides a space for debate and diversity, and showcases creativity. It encourages children and young people to be enthused by reading and writing, and provides a forum for authors and readers to mingle, converse and develop their craft.

Canterbury Festival

Festival House, 8 Orange Street, Canterbury, Kent CT1 2JA
tel (01227) 452853
email info@canterburyfestival.co.uk
website www.canterburyfestival.co.uk
Takes place 20 October–3 November 2018

Kent's international arts festival, one of the most important cultural events in the South East. As an independent charity, the Festival brings a rich mixture of performing arts from around the world to inspire artists to create and perform. It commissions new work, champions emerging talent and supports those seeking careers in the cultural industries.

Charleston Festival

The Charleston Trust, Charleston, Firle, Lewes, East Sussex BN8 6LL
email festivals@charleston.org.uk
website www.charleston.org.uk/charleston-festival
Twitter @charlestontrust
Takes place late May

Charleston, country home of Bloomsbury artists Duncan Grant and Vanessa Bell, hosts an annual literary festival involving writers, performers, politicians and thinkers – both high profile and up and coming, national and international. It also holds a dedicated short story festival – Small Wonder – for a long weekend in late September. The artistic director normally issues invitations for both festivals and is rarely able to accept unsolicited requests to take part.

The Times and The Sunday Times Cheltenham Literature Festival

109–111 Bath Road, Cheltenham, Glos. GL53 7LS
tel (01242) 511211
website www.cheltenhamfestivals.com
Facebook www.facebook.com/cheltenhamfestivals
Twitter @cheltlitfest
Takes place 5–14 October 2018

The annual festival is one of oldest literary events in the world and is one of the largest of its kind in Europe. Events include debates, talks and lectures, poetry readings, novelists in conversation, exhibitions, discussions, workshops and more. The festival has both an adult and family programme with events for toddlers to teenagers. Founded 1949.

Cliveden Literary Festival

tel 020-3488 3401
email info@clivedenliteraryfestival.org
website www.clivedenliteraryfestival.org

Set in Cliveden, the magnificent English country house with a unique and extraordinary history of politics and intrigue, the Cliveden Literary Festival aims to evoke the spirit of the great writers and potentates who have stayed there and to continue the tradition of the house as a sanctuary for literature lovers. Since 1666, the house has been known for its literary salon, helping to inspire writers from Alexander Pope and George Bernard Shaw, Jonathan Swift and Lord Tennyson to Sir Winston Churchill. Various events, key speakers and panel discussions.

Cork International Short Story Festival

Frank O'Connor House, 84 Douglas Street, Cork T12 X802, Republic of Ireland
tel +353 (0)21 4312955
email info@munsterlit.ie
website www.munsterlit.ie
website www.corkshortstory.net
Takes place September

Run by the Munster Literature Centre, this festival includes readings, seminars and public interviews, and is host to several short story awards, including the Frank O'Connor Short Story Award. The Centre also hosts the annual Cork International Poetry Festival.

CrimeFest

email info@crimefest.com
website www.crimefest.com
Facebook www.facebook.com/crimefest.bristol
Twitter @CrimeFest
Takes place May

CrimeFest is an annual, Bristol-based convention for people who like to read an occasional crime novel as well as for die-hard fanatics. Drawing top crime novelists, readers, editors, publishers and reviewers from around the world, it gives all delegates the opportunity to celebrate the genre in a friendly, informal and inclusive atmosphere. The CrimeFest programme consists of interviews with its featured and highlighted guest authors; over 60 events with more than 150 participating authors; a gala awards dinner; and one or two surprises!

Cúirt International Festival of Literature

Galway Arts Centre, 47 Dominick Street, Galway H91 X0AP, Republic of Ireland
tel +353 (0)91 565886
email info@galwayartscentre.ie
website www.cuirt.ie
Twitter @CuirtFestival
Takes place Last week in April

An annual week-long festival to celebrate great writing, bringing together national and international authors to promote literary discussion and ideas. Events include readings, performances, workshops, seminars, lectures, poetry slams, music, exhibitions, theatre and talks. The festival is renowned for its convivial atmosphere. ('Cúirt' means a 'bardic court or gathering'.) Founded 1985.

Dalkey Creates

tel +353 (0)87 2235124
email dalkeycreates@gmail.com
website www.dalkeycreates.com
Festival Director Anna Fox
Takes place mid-October

Held annually in the picturesque seaside town of Dalkey in Dublin, Ireland, Dalkey Creates aims to encourage and inspire writers with an excellent range of workshops and writer-focused events. It also features an annual Short Story Competition with a winning prize of €1,000. Details on the website.

The Daunt Books Festival

83-84 Marylebone High Street, London W1U 4QW
tel 020-7224 2295
email orders@dauntbooks.co.uk
website www.dauntbooks.co.uk
Twitter @dauntbooks
Festival Organiser Samantha Meeson
Takes place Spring

The Daunt Books Festival takes place in a beautiful Edwardian bookshop in Marylebone. This annual celebration of literature goes to show that a bookshop is not just a place to buy books but a space to bring readers together, to foster a literary community and to have a great deal of fun in the process. Key speakers over the years have included Michael Palin, Antonia Fraser, Colin Thubron, Claire Tomalin, Owen Jones, George Saunders, Sebastian Barry, Sarah Perry, Peter Frankopan and Michael Morpurgo.

Dublin Book Festival

email info@dublinbookfestival.com
website www.dublinbookfestival.com
Takes place 8-11 November 2018

Dublin Book Festival brings together the best of Irish publishing, offering a chance for the voices of both established and up-and-coming authors to be heard. Mostly held in Smock Alley Theatre, the festival's events include book launches, interviews, workshops, a children's and schools programme and lots more.

Durham Book Festival

New Writing North, PO Box 1277, Newcastle upon Tyne NE99 5PB
email office@newwritingnorth.com
website www.durhambookfestival.com
Takes place 6–14 October 2018

A book festival for new and established writers, taking place in the historic city of Durham.

East Riding Festival of Words

Libraries and Information Services, c/o East Riding Supplies, Gibson Lane, Melton HU14 3HN
email lama.admin@eastriding.gov.uk
Twitter @erwordfest

Takes place October

This is one of the UK's leading literature festivals. The festival includes authors' events, readings, panel events, workshops, children's activities and performances. Founded 2000.

Edinburgh International Book Festival

5 Charlotte Square, Edinburgh EH2 4DR
tel 0131 718 5666
email admin@edbookfest.co.uk
website www.edbookfest.co.uk
Twitter @edbookfest
Takes place August

The largest celebration of books and reading in the world. In addition to a unique independent bookselling operation, around 1,000 UK and international writers appear in over 800 events for adults and children. Programme details available in June.

Ennis Book Club Festival

tel +353 (0)87 9723647
email info@ennisbookclubfestival.com
website www.ennisbookclubfestival.com
Takes place First weekend in March

An annual literary weekend which brings together book club members, book lovers, writers and other artists. Includes lectures, readings, discussions, theatre, music and more.

Essex Poetry Festival

Flat 3, 1 Clifton Terrace, Southend-on-Sea, Essex SS1 1DT
email adrian@essex-poetry-festival.co.uk
website www.essex-poetry-festival.co.uk
Contact Adrian Green
Takes place October

A poetry festival across Essex. Also includes the Young Essex Poet of the Year Competition.

Festival at the Edge

39 Fawdry Street, Whitmore Reans, Wolverhampton WV1 4PA
tel 07544 044126
website www.festivalattheedge.org
Takes place July

A storytelling festival with a mix of stories, music and performance, held at Dearnford Lake, Whitchurch, Shropshire.

The Festival of Writing

Jericho Writers, Belsyre Court, 57 Woodstock Road, Oxford OX2 6HJ
tel 0345 459 9560
email info@jerichowriters.com
website https://jerichowriters.com
Takes place in York 7–9 September 2018

A festival for aspiring writers providing the opportunity to meet literary agents, publishers and professional authors. Now in its 12th year, it is the country's biggest writing festival specifically for writers looking to get published.

Folkestone Book Festival

tel (01303) 760740
email info@folkestonebookfest.com
website www.folkestonebookfest.com
Facebook www.facebook.com/FolkestoneBookFestival
Twitter @FstoneBookFest
Takes place 16–25 November 2018

An annual festival with many events, including a Children's Day.

Free the Word!

PEN International, Unit A, Koops Mill Mews, 162–164 Abbey Street, London SE1 2AN
tel 020-7405 0338
email info@pen-international.org
website http://www.pen-international.org/events-festivals/free-the-word/

Free the Word! is PEN International's roaming event series of contemporary literature from around the world. The Free the Word! team works with PEN Centres, festivals and book fairs to develop an international network of literary events. 'Free the Word! is PEN International in spirit and actions – events for authors and readers to make sparks across the divide between national literatures' – Sir Tom Stoppard.

Guildford Book Festival

c/o Tourist Information Office, 155 High Street, Guildford GU1 3AJ
tel (01483) 444334
email director@guildfordbookfestival.co.uk
website www.guildfordbookfestival.co.uk
Twitter @gfordbookfest
Co-directors Jane Beaton, Alex Andrews
Takes place 7–14 October 2018

An annual festival. A diverse programme of outstanding conversation and lively debate to inspire and entertain. Held throughout the historic town and drawing audiences from throughout London and the South East. Author events, workshops and schools programme. Its aim is to further an interest and love of literature by involvement and entertainment. Founded 1989.

The Hay Festival

The Drill Hall, 25 Lion Street, Hay-on-Wye HR3 5AD
tel (01497) 822620
email admin@hayfestival.org
website www.hayfestival.org
Takes place May/June

This annual festival of literature and the arts in Hay-on-Wye, Wales, brings together writers, musicians, film-makers, historians, politicians, environmentalists and scientists from around the world to communicate challenging ideas. More than 700 events over ten days. Within the annual festival is a festival for families and children, HAYDAYS, which introduces children, from toddlers to teenagers, to their favourite authors and holds workshops to entertain and educate. Programme published April.

Huddersfield Literature Festival

email office@huddlitfest.org.uk
website www.huddlitfest.org.uk
Festival Director Michelle Hodgson
Takes place March

An award-winning 10-day festival held annually. Showcasing major names, new, emerging and established writers/artists, the programme includes author talks, writing and performance workshops, multi-arts performances, innovative spoken word events and family-friendly events. Includes many free and low-cost events, and several with subtitling by Stagetext. Founded 2006.

Ilkley Literature Festival

9 The Grove, Ilkley LS29 9LW
tel (01943) 601210
email info@ilkleyliteraturefestival.org.uk
website www.ilkleyliteraturefestival.org.uk
Facebook www.facebook.com/ilkleyliteraturefestival/
Twitter @ilkleylitfest
Festival Director Rachel Feldberg, *Programme Coordinator* Pakeezah Zahoor
Takes place 28 September–14 October 2018

The North of England's oldest, largest and most prestigious literature festival with over 250 events, from author discussions to workshops, readings, literary walks, children's events and a festival fringe. Founded 1973.

Independent Bookshop Week

email sharon.benton@booksellers.org.uk
website www.indiebookshopweek.co.uk
Twitter @IndieBound_UK
Takes place June

Independent Bookshop Week is an annual celebration of independent bookshops and is part of the IndieBound campaign to promote independent bookshops, strong reading communities and the idea of shopping locally and sustainably. Independent Bookshop Week brings together bookshops, publishers and consumers through events such as National Reading Group Day, author visits and storytime sessions, and offers from publishers.

International Literature Festival Dublin

GEC, Taylor's Lane, Dubline 8
email info@ilfdublin.com
website www.ilfdublin.com
Twitter @ILFDublin
Takes place May

The International Literature Festival Dublin (formerly the Dublin Writers Festival) is Ireland's premier literary event and gathers the finest writers to debate, provoke and delight. The Festival continues to champion Dublin's position as a UNESCO City of Literature, celebrating the local alongside the global and the power of words to change the world. With readings, discussions, debates, workshops, performances and screenings, the Festival creates a hotbed of ideas for all ages. Founded 1998.

Jewish Book Week

Jewish Book Council, ORT House, 126 Albert Street, London NW1 7NE
tel 020-7446 8771
email info@jewishbookweek.com
website www.jewishbookweek.com
Production Manager Sarah Fairbairn
Takes place February/March

A 10-day festival of writing, arts and culture, with contributors from around the world and sessions in London and nationwide. Includes events for children and teenagers.

King's Lynn Festival

Fermoy Gallery, King Street, King's Lynn, Norfolk PE30 1HA
tel (01553) 767557
email info@kingslynnfestival.org.uk
website www.kingslynnfestival.org.uk
Administrator Ema Holman
Takes place July

An annual arts festival with a music focus, including literature events featuring leading guest writers. Founded 1951.

King's Lynn Literature Festivals

email enquiries@lynnlitfests.com
website www.lynnlitfests.com
Chairman Tony Ellis
Takes place September/March

Poetry Festival (28–30 September 2018): An annual festival which brings 12 published poets to King's Lynn for the weekend for readings and discussions.

Fiction Festival (March 2018): An annual festival which brings ten published novelists to King's Lynn for the weekend for readings and discussions.

Knutsford Literature Festival

website www.knutsfordlitfest.org
Takes place October

An annual festival to celebrate writing and performance, with distinguished national, international and local authors. Events include readings and discussions, a literary lunch and theatrical performances.

Laureate na nÓg/Ireland's Children's Laureate

Children's Books Ireland,
17 North Great George's Street, Dublin 1, D01 R2F1
tel +353 (0)18 727475
email info@childrenslaureate.ie
email info@childrensbooksireland.ie
website www.childrenslaureate.ie

This is a project recognising the role and importance of literature for children in Ireland. This unique honour was established to engage young people with high quality literature and to underline the importance of children's literature in our cultural and imaginative life and was awarded for the first time in 2010. The position is held for a period of two years. The laureate participates in selected events and activities around Ireland and internationally during their term.

The laureate is chosen in recognition of their widely recognised high-quality children's writing or illustration and the considerably positive impact they have had on readers as well as other writers and illustrators. Laureate na nÓg 2010–2012, Siobhán Parkinson; 2012–2014, Niamh Sharkey; 2014–2016, Eoin Colfer; 2016–2018, PJ Lynch. The fifth Laureate na nÓg commenced their term in May 2018.

Ledbury Poetry Festival

Master's House, St Katherines, Bye Street,
Ledbury HR8 1EA
tel (01531) 634156
email manager@poetry-festival.co.uk
website www.poetry-festival.co.uk
Twitter @ledburyfest
Festival Manager Phillippa Slinger
Takes place July

An annual festival featuring nationally and internationally renowned poets, together with a poet-in-residence programme, slams, competitions (see rules and download form from website), workshops, community events and exhibitions.

Listowel Writers' Week

24 The Square, Listowel, Co. Kerry V31 RD92,
Republic of Ireland
tel +353 (0)68 21074
email info@writersweek.ie
website www.writersweek.ie
Facebook www.facebook.com/writersweek
Twitter @ListowelWW18
Festival Managers Eilish Wren, Maire Logue

Listowel Writers' Week is an annual literary festival devoted to bringing together writers and audiences at unique and innovative events in the historic and intimate surroundings of Listowel, County Kerry. At its heart is a commitment to developing and promoting writing talent, underpinned by the values of partnership, inclusivity and civic responsibility. Events include workshops, readings, seminars, lectures, book launches, art exhibitions and a comprehensive children's and teenagers' programme. Founded 1971.

Litfest

The Storey, Meeting House Lane, Lancaster LA1 1TH
tel (01524) 62166
email marketing@litfest.org
website www.litfest.org
Takes place March

Annual literature festival featuring local, national and international writers, poets and performers. Litfest is the literature development agency for Lancashire with a year-round programme of readings, performances and workshops.

London Literature Festival

email customer@southbankcentre.co.uk
website www.southbankcentre.co.uk
Takes place October

The Southbank Centre runs a year-round programme of readings, talks and debates. Highlights include the annual London Literature Festival and bi-annual Poetry International; the biggest poetry festival in the British Isles, bringing together a wide range of poets from around the world.

Manchester Children's Book Festival

Manchester Metropolitan University,
Rosamond Street West, Off Oxford Road,
Manchester M15 6LL
tel 0161 247 2424
email mcbf@mmu.ac.uk
website www.mcbf.org.uk

A festival of year-round activities celebrating the very best writing for children, inspiring young people to engage with literature and creativity across the curriculum, and offering extended projects and training to ensure the event has an impact and legacy in classrooms.

Manchester Literature Festival

The Department Store, 5 Oak Street,
Manchester M4 5JD
email office@manchesterliteraturefestival.co.uk
website www.manchesterliteraturefestival.co.uk
Twitter @McrLitFest
Co-Directors Cathy Bolton and Sarah-Jane Roberts
Takes place October

An annual two-week festival showcasing new commissions and celebrating the best literature and imaginative writing from around the world. Note that MLF only accepts a small number of submissions each year with the majority of the Festival being curated by the team.

May Festival

Festivals & Events Team, University of Aberdeen,
King's College, Aberdeen AB24 3FX

tel (01224) 273233
email festival@abdn.ac.uk
website www.abdn.ac.uk/mayfestival
Takes place May

The May Festival programme aims to engage people of all ages and backgrounds, providing a culturally-enriching experience of the North East, Scotland and beyond. It aims to build on the success of research projects and past and present activities such as Word, Director's Cut, the British Science Festival and the music concert series. Events include debates, lectures, readings, workshops and concerts spanning areas such as literature, science, music, film, Gaelic, food and nutrition.

National Eisteddfod of Wales

40 Parc Ty Glas, Llanisien, Cardiff CF14 5DU
tel 0845 409 0300
email gwyb@eisteddfod.org.uk
website www.eisteddfod.org.uk
Twitter @eisteddfod
Chief Executive Betsan Moses
Takes place August

Wales's largest cultural festival. Activities include competitions in all aspects of the arts, fringe performances and majestic ceremonies. In addition to activities held in the main pavilion, it houses over 250 trade stands along with a literary pavilion, arts exhibition, an outdoor performance stage and a purpose-built theatre. The event is set in a different location each year; Cardiff in 2018 and Conwy in 2019.

National Short Story Week

website www.nationalshortstoryweek.org.uk

An annual awareness week aimed at encouraging more people to write, read and listen to short stories. Events held around the UK with involvement from publishers, writers, libraries, universities, writing organisations and readers. See website for details of the Annual Young Writers' competition. Founded 2010.

*Noir*wich Crime Writing Festival

tel (01603) 597582
email literaryevents@uea.ac.uk
website www.noirwich.co.uk
Twitter @NOIRwichFEST
Takes place 13–16 September 2018

*Noir*wich Crime Writing Festival celebrates the sharpest noir and crime writing over four days of author events, film screenings and writing masterclasses in Norwich, UNESCO City of Literature. A collaboration between the National Centre for Writing and the University of East Anglia.

Norfolk & Norwich Festival

Festival Office, Augustine Steward House, 14 Tombland, Norwich NR3 1HF
tel (01603) 877750
email info@nnfestival.org.uk
website www.nnfestival.org.uk
Takes place May

For 17 days each year the Festival transforms public spaces, city streets, performance venues, parks, forests and beaches, bringing people together to experience a variety of events spanning music, theatre, literature, visual arts, circus, dance and free outdoor events.

Off the Shelf Festival of Words Sheffield

Cathedral Court, 46 Church Street, Sheffield S1 2GN
tel 0114 222 3895
email offtheshelf@sheffield.ac.uk
website www.offtheshelf.org.uk
Takes place 6–27 October 2018

Meet great writers, historians, artists, scientists, journalists and musicians at this diverse and innovative festival. Events city-wide for all ages. Listen, question, be part of the story.

Oundle Festival of Literature

email oundlelitfestival@hotmail.co.uk
website www.oundlelitfest.org.uk
Facebook www.facebook.com/OundleFestivalOfLiterature/
Twitter @OundleLitFes
Festival Manager Helen Shair

The Festival runs a programme of all-year-round events aimed at exciting, informing, entertaining and educating a wide variety of people through talks, discussions and workshops by award-winning and local authors and poets. Uses a variety of venues in the beautiful market town of Oundle.

FT Weekend Oxford Literary Festival

Registered office, Greyfriars Court, Paradise Square, Oxford OX1 1BE
email info@oxfordliteraryfestival.org
website www.oxfordliteraryfestival.org
Festival Director Sally Dunsmore
Takes place March/April

An annual festival for both adults and children. Presents topical debates, fiction and non-fiction discussion panels, and adult and children's authors who have recently published books. Topics range from contemporary fiction to discussions on politics, history, science, gardening, food, poetry, philosophy, art and crime fiction.

Port Eliot Festival

email info@porteliotfestival.com
website www.porteliotfestival.com

The idyllic Port Eliot estate in Cornwall plays host to one of the UK's most imaginative arts festival; over 100 performances on ten different stages, presenting a wealth of creative talent from the worlds of books, music, fashion, food and film. Port Eliot aims to raise the spirits of and inspire its audience, and the festival prides itself on offering something a little bit different.

Raworths Harrogate Literature Festival

The Crown Hotel, Crown Place, Harrogate HG1 2RZ
tel (01423) 562303
email literature@harrogate-festival.org.uk
website www.harrogateinternationalfestivals.com
Twitter @RaworthsHGLit
Takes place 18–21 October 2018

Four days of literary events designed to inspire and stimulate.

Richmond upon Thames Literature Festival

tel 020-8831 6494
email artsinfo@richmond.gov.uk
website www.richmondliterature.com
Twitter @richmondlitfest
Takes place November

An annual literature festival featuring a diverse programme of authors, commentators and leading figures from sport, television, politics and journalism in a range of interesting and unique venues across the borough. The festival includes something for everyone, with an exciting programme for all ages and interests.

Rye Arts Festival

email secretary@ryeartsfestival.org.uk
website www.ryeartsfestival.org.uk
Chairman Michael Eve
Takes place Last 2 weeks of September

Annual festival of literary events across 15 days featuring biographers, novelists, political and environmental writers with book signings and discussions. Runs concurrently with festival of music and visual arts.

The Self-Publishing Conference

tel 0116 279 2299
email books@troubador.co.uk
website www.selfpublishingconference.org.uk
Twitter @Selfpubconf

The UK's ony dedicated self-publishing conference. Now in its sixth year, this annual event covers all aspects of self-publishing from production through to marketing and distribution. The conference offers plenty of networking opportunities and access to over 16 presentations. Founded 2013.

Small Wonder: The Short Story Festival

The Charleston Trust, Charleston, Firle, Lewes, East Sussex BN8 6LL
email info@charleston.org.uk
website www.charleston.org.uk/smallwonder

Charleston, home of Bloomsbury artists Duncan Grant and Vanessa Bell, hosts this respected annual short story jamboree. Small Wonder celebrates the most innovative short fiction in a variety of forms from top practitioners of the art, and also incorporates a fringe programme of participatory events for all ages.

Spring Literary Festival

University of East Anglia, Norwich NR4 7TJ
tel (01603) 592286
email literaryevents@uea.ac.uk
website www.uea.ac.uk/litfest
Facebook UEA Literary Festival
Twitter @UEALitfest
Takes place February to May

An annual festival of events bringing established writers of fiction, biography and poetry to a public audience in the Eastern region.

StAnza: Scotland's International Poetry Festival

tel (01334) 475000 (box office), (01334) 474610 (programmes)
email stanza@stanzapoetry.org
website www.stanzapoetry.org
Facebook www.facebook.com/stanzapoetry
Twitter @StAnzaPoetry
Festival Director Eleanor Livingstone
Takes place March

The festival engages with all forms of poetry: read and spoken verse, poetry in exhibition, performance poetry, cross-media collaboration, schools work, book launches and poetry workshops, with numerous UK and international guests and weekend children's events. Founded 1997.

States of Independence

email info@fiveleaves.co.uk
website www.statesofindependence.co.uk
Takes place March

An annual one-day festival celebrating independent publishing. Held in mid-March at De Montfort University in Leicester. Involves independent publishers from the region and elsewhere in the country. A free event with a varied programme of sessions and a book fair.

Stratford-upon-Avon Poetry Festival

website www.shakespeares-england.co.uk/event/stratford-upon-avon-poetry-festival/
Takes place June/July

An annual festival to celebrate poetry past and present with special reference to the works of Shakespeare. Events include: evenings of children's verse, a Poetry Mass and a local poets' evening.

Stratford-upon-Avon Literary Festival

email info@stratfordliteraryfestival.co.uk
website www.stratfordliteraryfestival.co.uk

Takes place April with events in Autumn

Stratford-upon-Avon Literary Festival is an annual feast of workshops, panel discussions and celebrity author events. In addition, there is a programme of education events in Stratford and local schools aimed at entertaining and inspiring children, as well as events in the community and workshops in prisons.

Swindon Festival of Literature

Lower Shaw Farm, Shaw, Swindon, Wilts. SN5 5PJ
tel (01793) 771080
email swindonlitfest@lowershawfarm.co.uk
website www.swindonfestivalofliterature.co.uk
Festival Director Matt Holland
Takes place May

An annual celebration of live literature through prose, poetry, drama and storytelling, with readings, discussions, performances and talks in theatres, arts centres, parks and pubs. A festival of ideas with leading authors, speakers and performers.

Theakston Old Peculier Crime Writing Festival

Old Swan Hotel, Swan Road, Harrogate HG1 2SR
tel (01423) 562303
email crime@harrogate-festival.org.uk
website www.harrogateinternationalfestivals.com
Twitter @TheakstonsCrime
Takes place July

Europe's largest celebration of crime fiction, featuring over 90 authors.

The Dylan Thomas Exhibition

The Dylan Thomas Centre, Somerset Place, Swansea SA1 1RR
tel (01792) 463980
email dylanthomas.lit@swansea.gov.uk
website www.dylanthomas.com
Facebook www.facebook.com/dylanthomascentre
Twitter @DTCSwansea
Events Manager Jo Furber

A year round resource celebrating the life and work of Swansea's most famous son: performances, family friendly events, poetry, and workshops. Dylan Thomas talks and tours by arrangement.

Warwick Words History Festival

The Court House, Jury Street, Warwick CV34 4EW
tel (07944) 768607
email info@warwickwords.co.uk
website www.warwickwords.co.uk
Takes place beginning of October

Founded 1999.

Ways With Words Festivals of Words and Ideas

Droridge Farm, Dartington, Totnes, Devon TQ9 6JG
tel (01803) 867373
website www.wayswithwords.co.uk
Facebook www.facebook.com/wayswithwords/
Twitter @Ways_With_Words

Leading writers give talks, interviews and discussions. Numerous events take place throughout the year including Words by the Water, Ways With Words Festival of Words and Ideas, a literature festival in Southwold and writing, art and language holidays in Italy.

Wells Festival of Literature

email admin@wellsfestivalofliterature.org.uk
website www.wellsfestivalofliterature.org.uk
Facebook www.facebook.com/Wellslitfest/
Twitter @wellslitfest
Takes place 19–27 October 2018

Celebrates its 26th year in 2018. An eight-day festival, featuring leading writers of fiction and non-fiction, poets and performers. Programme includes talks, discussions, workshops, bookclub and competitions. Events in local schools and the community throughout the year. Helps fund a variety of educational projects locally to encourage young people to love literature.

Wigtown Book Festival

Wigtown Festival Company, 11 North Main Street, Wigtown, DG8 9HN
tel (01988) 402036
email mail@wigtownbookfestival.com
website www.wigtownbookfestival.com
Facebook www.facebook.com/WigtownBookFestival
Twitter @wigtownbookfest
Operational Director Anne Barclay
Takes place 21–30 September 2018

An annual celebration of literature and the arts in Scotland's National Book Town. More than 200 events including author events, theatre, music, film and children's and young people's programmes.

Winchester Poetry Festival

41 Nuns Road, Hyde, Winchester, SO23 7EF
email hello@winchesterpoetryfestival.org
website www.winchesterpoetryfestival.org
Twitter @WinPoetryFest
Contact Madelaine Smith
Takes place 5–7 October 2018

Winchester Poetry Festival is a biennial festival dedicated to poetry. It is intended to celebrate poetry within a civic environment in order to ensure the widest possible degree of public awareness and enjoyment.

The Winchester Writers' Festival

University of Winchester, Winchester, Hants SO22 4NR
tel (01962) 827238
email judith.heneghan@winchester.ac.uk
email sara.gangai@winchester.ac.uk

website www.writersfestival.co.uk
Twitter @WinWritersFest
Director Judith Heneghan, *Events Manager* Sara Gangai
Takes place Third weekend in June

This major festival of writing, celebrating its 38th year in 2018, attracts new and emerging writers from the UK and around the world who come for day-long courses, talks, workshops and up to four one-to-one appointments each with literary agents, commissioning editors and established novelists, poets and screenwriters to help them harness their creativity, develop their writing and editing skills and pitch their work to industry professionals. Recent keynote speakers include Sebastian Faulks, Meg Rosoff, Michael Morpurgo, Joanne Harris, Patrick Gale and Lemn Sissay. Open mics and festival readings. Ten free weekend Scholarship places available to writers aged 18–25. For information and registration, visit the website. Also available: ten writing competitions open to all. No need to attend the Festival to enter.

World Book Day

6 Bell Yard, London WC2A 2JR
email wbd@education.co.uk
website www.worldbookday.com
Takes place First Thursday in March

An annual celebration of books and reading aimed at promoting their value and creating the readers of the future. Every schoolchild in full-time education receives a £1 (€1.50) book token and events take place all over the UK and Ireland in schools, bookshops and libraries. World Book Day was designated by UNESCO as a worldwide celebration of books and reading and is marked in over 100 countries.

YALC (Young Adult Literature Convention)

website www.londonfilmandcomiccon.com/index.php/zones/yalc
Twitter @yalc_uk
Takes place July

YALC is a celebration of the best young adult books and authors. It is an interactive event where YA fans can meet their favourite authors, listen to panel discussions and take part in workshops. YALC is run by Showmasters, which runs the London Film and Comic Con.

Self-publishing

Self-publishing online: the emerging template for sales success

With the self-publishing revolution rapidly transforming the industry, Harry Bingham explains how indie authors can now unlock huge sales through some simple techniques for connecting with readers online.

In a past era – not long ago in terms of years, but whole aeons in terms of the industry – self-publishing involved the creation and sale of print books. Lacking access to major national distribution chains, that activity was inevitably small-scale. If you sold 500 books and broke even in the exercise, you had done well. If you sold 1,000, you were a self-pub superstar.

That version of self-publishing still exists, and is perfectly reputable. But the rise of Amazon and the advent of the ebook have, together, utterly transformed the boundaries of the possible. You want to reach readers worldwide? Sure, no problem. You want to earn good money from every book sold? Consider it done. You want to sell tens of thousands of copies, make a prosperous living, have a close bond with thousands of readers? Of course. These things aren't easy to achieve exactly, but they're no longer remarkable. These truths, however, are weirdly invisible, in part because of the continuing cultural authority of print and the High Street. A typical traditional trade publisher today sells about 75% of its work in print. The remaining quarter will be made up mostly of ebooks, together with a small but rapidly growing slice of audio.

But these – very familiar – figures are deeply misleading. For one thing, they ignore Amazon's own publishing activity; the firm is, after all, a publisher as well as a retailer. They also ignore all the sales generated by indie authors (or self-publishers; I use the terms interchangeably).

These two non-traditional sources, Amazon plus the indies, now account for a stonking 42% share of all adult fiction sales. And never mind format! If you look at *where* books are sold – print, digital and audio – it turns out that around 75% of all adult books – fiction and non-fiction – are sold online. The same is true of almost half of all books for children. (These stats come via AuthorEarnings.com and relate to the US market only, as no comparable estimates exist for the UK. That said, although the British trajectory is broadly similar, online penetration in the US has probably proceeded further.)

These data lead us to the two rocket-fuelled propellants of the self-pub revolution:

1. Traditional publishers have a lock on high-street bookselling. Indie authors simply can't gain access to national chains without a corporate publisher on side. But *anyone* has access to Amazon. All you need is an email address. Uploading an ebook is particularly simple, but creating print books isn't much harder, and most big-selling indies will be profiting from audio too.
2. Amazon's royalties are extraordinary. If you sell £100 worth of ebooks (post-VAT) on Amazon, the firm will pay you just a shade under £70. If you sell the same value of ebooks

via a traditional publisher and literary agent, you're likely to see less than £15. In most industries, would-be insurgents have to do something better than the incumbents in order to thrive. In this industry, the royalty gap is such that you can sell fewer books, *and* price them more cheaply, *and* still make a ton more money.

Those royalties are the golden flame that attracts self-pubbers – a commercial advantage of vast potential. But how to unlock it? Because the beauty of Amazon – its accessibility – is also its terror. Amazon currently lists 5,000,000 ebooks for sale. Every three months, that number increases by 250,000. How do you compete against those millions? How will your book find its readers?

Hit and hope is not the answer. That has never worked, and never will. Equally, you can't just use social media to bellow in people's faces: 'Buy my book, it's great.' The problem there isn't just that it's repellent to act that way. It's also – and mostly – that no one buys books because people are shouting at them. And OK, if you're deft enough and committed enough, if you blog and tweet and post and engage with enough people, on enough sites, and do so while making sure that no more than one in ten of your messages are sales-related – then, sure, you'll sell some books. But not many. It's not a way to succeed. So what is?

The answer is simple: you connect with readers. You get people to read your work and, if they like it, to give you their email address, so you can be in touch whenever you have a new work out. Some readers will give you an address, but forgetfully and without commitment. Many, however, will stay committed to you and your books, so that they will buy and *buy when you prompt them to*. That fact means you can, as your list builds up, create little sale tsunamis. Fifty sales in a day. Then a hundred and fifty. Then a thousand. That, in itself, doesn't sound so impressive. Sure, if you have a mailing list of 3,000 names, and a third of those buy your book within 24 hours of your email, you'll sell 1,000 books. But what comes next? You need to be selling in the tens of thousands to make a living.

The answer is Amazon. Its marketing algorithms are constantly on the lookout for books that sell. And if those data-bots encounter a surge of sales in a new title, they recognise that the product is hot. It's something that Amazon wants to market. And it does that, automatically, via marketing emails, by popping you onto bestseller lists, by elevating you on relevant searches, and much else. A small list can generate revenues out of all proportion to its size.

In 2015, I marketed my crime novel *This Thing of Darkness* in the US using what was then a very small email list of just 330 names. I was dealing with new-born twins at the time and did nothing to sell that book beyond one email to those readers. Over the next 12 (sleepless) months, I earned about $30,000 from that book and its sisters. A small list; a stunning result.

This technique lies at the heart of almost every recent indie success story. Better still: it's totally ethical. *It's how things should work*. It's word of mouth re-engineered for the digital age. So all those questions about how to market your books now narrow down to just three:

- How do you most effectively collect email addresses?
- How do you maximise the effectiveness of your email-driven sales surge?
- How do you make sure that *all* your titles get that Amazon-love, not just the one you're currently launching?

The first question is easily answered. No one likes giving away their personal data, so you don't *ask* the reader for anything. Rather, you *offer* them something: 'Get an exclusive free story to download.' You make that offer, or something along those lines, in the front- or end-material of your ebook. That call to action links to a page on your website, where your reader can give you the email address to which you'll send the story. (All that stuff can be automated, of course. You can do it yourself or pay a tech-guy, as I do.) Naturally, you disclose that readers will receive further emails from you, but that's not some kind of small-print marketing subterfuge. On the contrary: readers *like* to be in direct contact with favoured authors. This is 'permission marketing' at its truest.

In terms of maximising sales effectiveness, you need to make sure that your book's metadata is as solid as it can be. That means writing a strong book description. It means making sure that your choice of Amazon category is logical. It means making sure that your keywords are well-chosen to get you on the right sub-bestseller lists and the right thematic searches. Those things sound scary and technical, but they're not hard. It's a morning's work, no more.

As for making sure that sales success in one title bleeds over to the rest, the answer there is also simple. The moment to market another of your books to a reader is in the glow of that moment when they've just finished one. So make sure you list *all* of your titles in the back of *all* of your books. When it comes to your ebooks, don't just provide a boring, unclickable list; you need to insert links direct to the e-stores where your books are available. Those links mean that your reader doesn't have to be more than two or three clicks from making another purchase. Two or three clicks from placing more money in your pocket.

And that, in essence, is that. To be sure, a number of tricks remain. Instafreebie (www.instafreebie.com) is an extraordinary way to kick your mailing list off from scratch. Facebook lead-generation ads still work well for some authors, in some contexts. If properly used, Bookbub (www.bookbub.com) is a delightful machine whose primary purpose is to make you richer. Launch teams can ensure a flurry of great reviews when your book launches on Amazon. The sequencing of things like pre-orders, Kindle Countdown deals, email blasts, pricing changes and so on can make serious differences to how well you do overall.

And do remember that, while ebooks are likely to dominate your self-pub revenue stream (as they do mine), you can succeed in any format. 2015 was the Year of the Colouring Book, as far as the publishing industry was concerned, and indeed Amazon.com duly reported that 11 of its top 35 print sellers were adult colouring books. That much is well known, but get this: *five of those 11 top-sellers were indie-published*. The issue isn't format, it's sales channel. And, if you create great content and work hard to connect with your readers (or crayon-wielding adults), there's no reason why you can't succeed.

Likewise, while Amazon is likely to provide a clear majority of your revenues, the other e-stores can start to perform well for you too. Some indies report that Amazon represents less than 50% of their overall income, though, if you're just starting out, you should probably work with Amazon exclusively.

But all these things are refinements. They're not the strategy. The strategy is simply this: you write a great book; you find your first readers, probably via giveaways on Facebook or Instafreebie; those readers like your stuff and choose to give you their email address in return for some exclusive material; you use those email addresses to kick start your sales for the next book. Then – rinse and repeat, rinse and repeat, rinse and repeat.

The very best part about all this? The more you use this motor, the more powerful it becomes. Your mailing list increases and your sales grow. Each year, a higher income than the year before. The self-pub revolution is still young, but it's mighty. It has given authors wholly new options, a wholly new authority. I don't know what the industry will look like in ten years' time, but it's changing fast, and changing radically. And, just for once, authors are on the winning side.

Harry Bingham is the author of the *Fiona Griffiths* series of crime novels (and much else). The sixth book in the series, *The Deepest Grave*, was released by Orion in 2017. He is traditionally published in the UK and self-published in the US, and greatly relishes both routes. He also runs Jericho Writers, an online club for writers. Readers wanting more detail on the techniques mentioned in this article can get them via https://jerichowriters.com/academy.

See also...

- *The dos and don'ts of self-publishing*, page 615
- *Making waves online*, page 633
- *Electronic publishing*, page 124

Getting your book stocked in a high-street bookshop

So you've written your book. It's finally finished, you have it printed, and you're ready to share it with readers. But how do you get you self-published novel onto the shelves of a high-street bookshop? Independent bookseller, Sheila O'Reilly, guides you on your way.

How to contact booksellers

• Ideally booksellers like to be emailed. It gives us time to think about your proposal; it gives us time to chat to our colleagues, and it gives us the opportunity to deal with the request within our normal day.
• If you do decide to show us the book in person, please don't visit unannounced. It's beneficial instead to email ahead so we can arrange a quick appointment for you with the appropriate buyer, at a time that works with the shop diary.

What booksellers need to know

To help us make our decision, you should include the following information on your proposal:
• A quick synopsis of the book - two or three sentences is perfect.
• A couple of lines about who you are.
• The sales details:
  - How much your book retails for.
  - Include a professional invoice outlining your terms of business.
  - How much you are selling it to bookshops for. (Trade terms vary between publishers.) The market research agency, Nielsen, reports that the average discount received by bookshops from publishers is just over 40% off the recommended retail price. In the UK, the publisher almost always pays for the carriage charge in getting the books to the bookshop.
  - The format (paperback/hardback). We would always recommend that the book has a spine; that the title is printed on the spine; and that there is a 13-digit EAN bar code (based on the ISBN) printed on the book.
  - Returns information. The most usual trade practice for independently published titles would be for the books to be supplied on 'consignment terms' (which means that the bookshop will pay for the stock once it has sold and can return unsold stock when it chooses). An alternative is 'sale or return', where the bookshop pays for the stock according to the payment terms of your invoice, but has the right to return unsold stock for a full refund.
  - Think about payment terms and the length of time the bookshop should have the stock for sale. If after this agreed length of time the books have not sold it is your responsibility to collect unsold stock. If the books are not collected after three months, the bookseller can dispose of the stock as they deem fit.
  - A few sample pages for us to read.
  - Why you think the book will sell in our bookshop.
  - Who the competitors – or comparable authors – are in your eyes.
  - In which section we should display the book.

- A jpg image of the jacket.
- If the book has any local ties; is it set in our area? Did you go to school around the corner?
- Do you have any local publicity lined up or in the pipeline (e.g. features, interviews or extracts in local news media)? This can have real value in improving local sales.

Do not call the bookshop on a regular basis checking on sales (tempting as that might be).

Tips

• Be competitive regarding the pricing of your book. A standard paperback is around £8.99.

• Look at the production quality; a well-presented finished product speaks volumes. Look at books in similar genres to your own on bookshop shelves and note the current design styles/finishes/fonts being used.

• Give important consideration to the jacket design. Review the competition, check out the award-winning designs from the latest British Book Design Awards (www.britishbookawards.org). If you want your book to take up space on a shelf face out (the most popular display method) the jacket must be of stunning design and quality. Book cover design is a specialist discipline, so commissioning an experienced designer is often the best way to give your book an edge alongside other publications.

• Pick your time of year carefully. The majority of new writers are launched in the beginning of the year. If you release too close to Christmas, your book will get lost on the shelves. If you come in February or March, we often have the space to display your book where it has a better chance of selling.

• Booksellers would not welcome being sent an Amazon link in your proposal. Whilst, of course, Amazon is likely to be another outlet for your book, most high-street bookshops choose to have no commercial dealings with Amazon because of the perceived negative impact they have had on Britain's high streets and physical bookshops.

• Think about how you might promote your book and direct people to the bookshop for sales. We send our sales information to Nielsen/Book Scan, so if we sell a lot of copies your book will get noticed around the book industry.

• Outline what will be your marketing and publicity plan for the book if we take stock to generate interest.

• Supply: make sure your book can be distributed via the national trade wholesalers Gardners (www.gardners.com) or Bertrams (www.bertrams.com), at a standard trade discount, with returns. If in the Republic of Ireland, use either Easons (www.easons.com) or Argosy (www.argosybooks.ie).

• Ask your printer how they can help to distribute your book via the wholesalers mentioned above. Many will take care of this on your behalf. For instance, a traditional book printer like Clays will warehouse copies of your books then distribute them when wholesale orders come in, while Ingram Sparks/Lightning Source will print each copy to order and distribute them to retailers via the main wholesale routes.

• Fix a realistic wholesale discount when you set up your book for distribution, whether you do this directly via the wholesalers, or via your printer. It might be tempting to keep the discount as low as possible to increase your royalties, but the lower you make it the less realistic it will be for a bookshop to stock it. Do your research – find out how much of a cut the wholesaler will take (as a very general guide, it could be in the area of 15%), and remember that the average discount bookshops receive is in the region of 40% of the cover price.

• Thinking through and planning for these elements of distribution will simplify our ordering/ reordering of your book and increases your chance of being stocked by us tenfold. Whilst bookshops might from time to time agree to being supplied directly by an author, each time a separate supplier is set up for an individual book it adds greatly to the bookshop's paperwork and accounting burden and, more importantly, means that it takes longer to reorder the book once it sells. Most bookshops order every day from Gardners, Bertrams, Easons or Agrosy at the click of a button, and so ensuring those wholesalers have stock of your book is the best way to make it easily accessible to every bookshop in the country.

• Months before the book is due to be published, begin the social media campaign and include your local bookshops.

• Gather the email contact details of friends and contacts, and once the book is published tell them that they can order it through such-and-such a bookshop. This will show the local bookshop that there is interest and they, in turn, are more likely to say 'yes' to stocking your book.

• If you sell copies direct to all your friends and family, it is unlikely that the local bookshop will have a market to sell to. If you persist in taking this step, don't be surprised if after a month or so you get an email from them announcing they have sold none and want to return the books.

• If you have a website, please direct potential customers to any bookshops that have agreed to stock your book.

• If a bookshop does order copies of your book and agrees to be supplied by you directly, then don't forget to deliver the books along with an invoice. It is very important the latter has your contact details (for future orders) and bank details (for payment).

How a typical high-street bookshop decides on the books to stock

Every bookshop has a finite amount of space and budget to spend each month. The book buyers will go through a series of decisions before saying 'yes' or 'no' to any particular book.

For many bookshops the decision is helped by the representatives from publishers, who will brief them on the new books, why they believe it will sell in the bookshop, and what promotion the publisher is putting behind the book.

Here is an outline of some of the decisions taken by a bookseller before deciding to stock a book:

Our market: we understand what our customers like to read and what genres sell well. We tailor our stock around that (we also try and find the books they didn't know they liked).

Our tastes: if we read and love a book, you can be sure we're going to be telling our customers about it.

The subject: if a book is on a topic that we feel will be of interest to our customers, then that is a huge swaying factor for us.

The author: if we know their work and their track record, we can make a judgement on how well we think the book will sell for us. Also, if the author is local and is likely to have a local following and/or supportive friends and family, then this will influence us.

Marketing: we look at what sort of promotion the book will be getting locally, further afield and on social media (is there already a buzz around it?).
Format and price: this is a major selling point for us; it's not unusual to wait for a paperback to come out before taking a chance on a title.
Design: as with the format, we look at the jacket. Sometimes a stunning cover can be the swaying point between us taking a book or not.

After all this, the bookseller may decline to stock your book. Don't take that personally or expect an explanation. Time does not allow for an explanation for every book we decline to stock.

One thing to remember is, please don't be disheartened if we say 'no' to your book. What works for some bookshops doesn't work for others. What sells huge numbers in, say, the Edinburgh Bookshop might not sell in Bath and what sells in Bath may not sell in Oswestry. That's the beauty of high-street bookshops – they are all different. You can find lists of Britain's bookshops at www.booksellers.org.uk/bookshopsearch.aspx.

What can you expect from a bookshop?

Despite the many one-way tips above, getting a book into a reader's hands is very much a team effort between an author, a publisher and a bookseller. Here's what you can expect from a bookshop when you approach them with your book:

- In all circumstances, to be treated with the respect and consideration you'd expect any business to give to a potential business partner.
- Once the bookseller has had a chance to consider the book properly, a clear and prompt answer as to whether or not the bookshop is willing to accept the book into its stock.
- If the bookshop is not willing to take the book, then a considered reason should be given for not doing so.
- If the bookshop does take the book and the book sells, to pay you promptly in accordance with the payment terms you have specified and to give quick consideration to reordering more stock.
- If the bookshop is included in any social media campaign around a book it has agreed to stock, to participate actively in that campaign.

Extracted from the Booksellers Association *Want to get your Book stocked in a High Street Bookshop?* written by **Sheila O'Reilly**, an experienced independent bookseller, from Village Books in Dulwich, London. For the complete Guide see www.societyofauthors.org/SOA/MediaLibrary/SOAWebsite/Guides/tipsforauthors0117oreilly.pdf.

The dos and don'ts of self-publishing

Alison Baverstock gives valuable advice to any writer considering, or already active in, the empowering and increasingly accepted process of self-publishing.

My interest in self-publishing began about ten years ago, when I was researching and writing a book on how authors could market their own work. What struck me was how all authors, both traditionally and self-published, were increasingly being relied upon to get actively involved in marketing their work, and how this was disrupting publishing's traditional business model. Now that the public had an ever-expanding range of options for spending their free time it became increasingly difficult for publishers to predict and hence find the market for each book they planned to publish. So who better than the author to think about how to find their readership, and to help reach them?

Author involvement in marketing had other consequences. Most notably, it taught them about the processes of publishing. These were previously little understood by authors, who generally had contact only with their editor; the rest of their relationship with their publishing house was managed either by their agent or, possibly, not at all. (See *What do publishers do?* on page 107.) Authors came to understand that being published involves far more than providing a passable manuscript. It also means giving interviews to newspapers and online media, taking part in literary festivals, experimenting with social media, and being willing to write blogs for no money; all are now part of the process of being published, whoever's logo is on the book spine.

In addition, the practice of self-publishing as a writing apprenticeship has emerged. In the process, writers have the opportunity to hear directly from readers about how their work is perceived (feedback can be brutally frank), to discover what kind of publishing decisions shape the buyer's actions (does adding 50p to the price affect willingness to purchase?), and to offer additional materials to extend the relationship (background information on some of the characters; ideas on new writing projects). This is a complete change from the existing reader-writer interaction, when the most authors could hope for was an occasional respectful letter of appreciation sent via their publishing house, often passed on months later. This direct contact has empowered many authors, leaving them less reliant on traditional publishers, and frankly less grateful. Having experimented with the presentation of their work, and heard directly back from their readers about what they do and don't like, many decide to carry on self-publishing – even if subsequently offered a conventional deal.

Whether you are just considering self-publishing, or are already an experienced practitioner, I hope this list of dos and don'ts will be useful to you.

Do take your time in finalising the material you want to publish

It's common for writers to set themselves a deadline, such as getting published by a particular birthday (30, 40, 50) or specific stage in life (by the time the children start school/leave home/you retire). Effective writing is best developed through application and effort than correlation with a particular point in life, so take your time and get it right before you share. Making work available yourself also means the response tends to be unmediated (there's no supportive publisher or agent hovering around in the background, to tell you to ignore an unpleasant review and carry on writing). Hearing directly from your market what they think about your work, or seeing it negatively discussed on social media can be devastating to a new writer's confidence. So, if you are asking readers to invest their time in your writing, make it something worth reading.

If you want to offer a manuscript that is worth the time and effort of others, do allocate specific time to its creation. The world is full of people who intend to write a book one day but just never quite get around to it. How you plan eventually to publish your work is irrelevant; writing is a long process of drafting, shaping, editing and redrafting. Very, very few writers get it right on their first attempt, and everyone needs editing. How you equip yourself with enough time for writing is therefore very important. You could consider making an appointment with yourself at a particular time of day (first thing in the morning; last thing at night), or putting a line through days in your diary when writing hours can be allocated and therefore 'found'. This really matters. While there are a wealth of ways for storing and making work available, these are largely irrelevant if you don't value the process enough to allocate sufficient time.

Don't assume you have to do everything yourself

Deciding to self-publish *does* mean you have to assume responsibility for every stage of the book's creation. But that *does not* mean you have to do everything yourself. One of the most interesting developments promoted by the rise of self-publishing has been the appearance of a new range of services to support writers, such a literary festivals that include a strand on 'how to get published', traditional publishers who see a market in selling their wider range of expertise to authors, and completely new firms offering relevant services. (See the list of *Self-publishing providers* on page 644.)

A comparison with cooking works well; you can either buy a complete ready-cooked meal, or buy the ingredients and cook everything from scratch, and all stages in between. So the job of the self-published author can be that of a coordinator, or project manager – or painstaking and hands-on involvement in each stage. There is no right answer, and the approach you take will depend on the outcomes you seek. For example, if you are researching your family history, or writing as part of a process of bereavement, you might prefer to handle every stage yourself – and thus find the process therapeutic. If you are focused on a history project that has to be completed in time for an important anniversary, you might want to subcontract particular stages to others.

Do think carefully about which suppliers to instruct

You will find a wealth of options exist and, in general, the more time the supplier takes in getting to know you and your needs, the better the likely outcome. So organisations that confidently inform you how thrilled they are by the prospect of publishing your wonderful book, when they have not yet seen your manuscript, or those whose website talks about all the attractive options on offer but shows you no accompanying images, may be best avoided.

Do realise that it's a very labour-intensive process

The finished product will be in direct relation to the resources you allocate, and that means time as much as money. So investigate those you will be instructing. An editor to help you develop your work should be someone with relevant experience in the type of book you are producing – and this should be clear through the information they provide about themselves. Reputable agencies offering publishing services make clear the experience of those whose services they represent. For example, if you are writing a romantic novel you want someone with relevant experience of the structure and development of romantic novels, and a method of giving feedback you can relate to – probably not an editor with experience of managing scientific papers, however brilliant they may sound. You can find editors with relevant experience by consulting the Society for Editors and Proofreaders www.sfep.org.uk.(For more information, see *Editing your work*, page 661.)

Don't assume it all has to be done in one go

Self-publishing can be a staged process, where you edge towards a final conclusion. It can be something that takes months or years. I know someone who worked on the story of his relationship with a step-parent for a very long time. He produced the first draft, had it edited, and then printed it out and bound it in an informal format, photocopied and spiral bound. The process was cathartic – out of his head and onto the page. One day he may take this and develop it into something that can be more widely shared. For now, he is just happy that it exists. Along similar lines, self-publishing a single copy of a book you intend for wider circulation can be a very helpful stage in the development of your work, allowing you to see how the book feels in the reader's hands, and promoting greater objectivity about your writing.

Don't underestimate the amount of effort it takes to get your work noticed

The other by-product of lots of people getting involved in self-publishing is that there is significantly more content competing for readers' attention. It is possible to get marketing support for self-published books, but you will need to do so professionally and effectively. This may be best achieved by giving yourself a specific time to devote to marketing; a time of the day or day of the week when you stop writing and concentrate on promoting your book. Some authors also give themselves a different name or persona before making calls to journalists – it can be easier to talk your work up in the third person. Being a self-published author may even make you more appealing to the media, you have not only the story of what your book is about, but the second strand of plucky self-published author who had the grit to keep going.

Do highlight any idiosyncracies that make you sound appealing

What individual aspects might spark a response from the seemingly vast numbers of the public who think that they, too, would like to write a book? How you managed to achieve your goal, despite the difficulties you faced, can be really inspiring to them – and hence of great interest to the press and in social media. So what time of day did you write, and what were your writing implements of choice? Did any music or specific foods help you keep going? One self-published author I spoke to broke the back of her novel by borrowing a garden shed in the garden of a friend, which gave her the necessary time away from familiar surroundings – and associated distractions.

Don't feel you need a long print run to justify self-publishing

Small-scale projects can be of immense social and personal relevance, within your immediate family or society as a whole. For example, historians today are delighted to find the personal memoirs of soldiers who fought in the world wars; they offer a more complete understanding of what went on – the official histories having already been written. Writing the story of your life so that your wider family have access, whenever they are mature enough to decide they want to know, can be a process that brings satisfaction, reconciliation and the profoundly satisfying knowledge that your story will live on.

Similarly, when deciding on a print run, ***do* print the exact number you realistically think you can sell/distribute** – bearing in mind that however much you think people ought to be interested/feel obliged to buy your work, they will probably be less motivated to purchase than you anticipate. Buying an additional thousand, so the unit cost falls to a more acceptable rate, is a slippery slope towards a spare bedroom full of boxes or a declining relationship with friends, as they too are persuaded to take stock pending a sudden surge in demand!

Do benefit from the wisdom and support of the self-publishing community

In my experience, and somewhat to my surprise, self-publishing writers seem to be remarkably generous towards each other; they share information on reliable suppliers and seem genuinely pleased by each other's successes. So find out if there is a community of local writers that you could join or contribute to online and get involved. You would almost certainly benefit from joining The Alliance of Independent Authors (http://allianceindependentauthors.org; see page 525) who offer much related guidance and the chance to contribute. What goes around comes around.

Don't, above all, be apologetic about the fact that you are self-publishing

Whereas at one time it was seen as a second-rate option, for those lacking external investment, today it's a badge of proactivity. It is evidence of your belief in your own material and your desire to be taken seriously. Indeed, traditional publishers and agents are now looking to see what has been self-published and has found a market; this may be strong evidence of new interests within the reading public – and of authors able to satisfy them.

Associate Professor **Alison Baverstock** is a publisher and publishing consultant who jointly established the Publishing MA at Kingston University in 2006 (which includes self-publishing). Her research into self-publishing has been published in a range of journals, magazines for writers and the national press. She is the author of *The Naked Author* (Bloomsbury 2011) and *Marketing your book: an author's guide* (Bloomsbury 2009). She was awarded the Pandora Prize for Services to Publishing in 2007. Her Twitter handle is @alisonbav.

See also...

- *Making waves online*, page 633
- *How self-publishing started my publishing journey*, page 622

What do self-publishing providers offer?

Jeremy Thompson presents the options for engaging an author services company.

Now that self-publishing is widely accepted and it is easier to do it than ever before, authors are presented with a broader range of opportunities to deliver their book or ebook to readers. This brings with it a greater responsibility to you, the author and publisher, to make the right choices for your publishing project. The various options for self-publishing may seem bewildering at first, and each has their pros and cons. But some relatively simple research will prove invaluable in ensuring you make the right choices for your book.

Motivation influences method

There are many reasons why authors choose to self-publish, and contrary to popular belief, the decision to do so is not always motivated by the aspiration to be a bestselling novelist! That is only one reason; others include the wish to impart knowledge to a wider audience; the desire to publish a specialist book with a relatively small target audience; the fulfilment of a hobby; publishing as part of a business or charity; and yes, vanity (a wish to see one's name on a book cover is fine, as long as you have realistic expectations of your work).

Understanding why you are self-publishing is important, as the reasons for doing so can help point to the best way in which to go about it. For example, if you are publishing simply for pleasure, and have few expectations that your book will 'set the world alight', then you'd be wise not to invest in a large number of copies; using 'print on demand' (POD) or producing an ebook could be a good way forward. If you have a book that you're publishing to give away or sell as part of your business to a relatively captive audience, then a short print run of a few hundred copies might be wise. If you want your novel to reach as many readers as possible and to sell it widely, you'll need to have physical copies to get into the retail supply chain and in front of potential readers, so opt for a longer print run of perhaps 500 or more. The more copies you print, the greater the economies of scale.

Decisions on how to self-publish are often influenced by the money you are prepared to invest in (and risk on) your project. Making a decision on what self-publishing route to take based on financial grounds alone is fine, as long as you understand the implications of that decision. For example, as the name implies, print-on-demand (POD) books are only printed when someone actually places an order for a copy; there are no physical copies available to sell. As POD books are largely sold on a 'firm sale' basis, bookshops will rarely stock them, so most POD sales will be made through online retailers. In addition, as the POD unit cost is higher than if a quantity of books are printed in one go, the retail price of a book is likely to be fairly high in order to cover the print cost and retailer's discount, and make you, the publisher, some profit. Authors often assume that POD is some miracle form of low-cost book publishing, but if that were so, why aren't all the major commercial publishers distributing all of their books in this way? The disadvantages of POD include limited retail distribution and high print cost; these can work for many types of book, like specialist non-fiction titles or academic books that command high cover prices, but it can be difficult to make it cost-effective for mass market books.

At the other end of the scale, printing 3,000 copies of a novel will only pay off if you can get that book onto the retailers' shelves and in front of potential readers, or if you have some other form of 'captive' readership that you can reach with your marketing. Distribution to retailers works largely on the 'sale or return' model, using distribution companies and sales teams to sell new books to bookshops (and whatever you may have heard to the contrary, bookshops are still the largest sellers of books in the UK). If you can't get your book into that distribution chain, you are limiting the prospect of selling your 3,000 copies, and money tied up in unsaleable stock is money wasted.

Publishing an ebook is also an increasingly popular method of self-publishing, but it too has its pros and cons. On the up side, it can be done very cheaply and quickly; the flip side is that, as hundreds of new ebooks are published each day, how do you get yours noticed? Making your ebook available through one retailer (e.g. Kobo) effectively limits your potential readership … what about readers with a Kindle, an iPad or a Nook? How and where should you market your ebook?

As a self-publisher, you need to make sure you understand the limitations of each form of publishing method before you decide on the best route for your book(s). It can make the difference between success or failure for your book before it's even produced.

Choosing an author services company

In its truest sense, self-publishing means that you as author undertake all the processes undertaken by a commercial publisher to bring a book to market: editing, design, production, marketing, promotion and distribution. If you're multi-talented and have a lot of spare time, then you may want to do all of these things yourself, but for most authors it's a question of contracting an author services company to carry out some or all of the tasks required. From the start it should be understood that most author services companies make their money by selling their services to you as the author; very few have a lot of market knowledge and even fewer offer any real form of active marketing or have a retail distribution set-up. Choosing the right company to work with is crucial in ensuring that your self-publishing expectations stand a chance of being met. Author services companies come in various guises, but they can broadly be broken into three categories:

- **DIY POD services.** You upload your manuscript and cover design, and your book (or ebook) is simply published 'as is'. It's relatively cheap, and great if you are not too concerned about the design quality and POD or electronic distribution is what you want.
- **Assisted services companies.** These companies offer typesetting and cover design, and perhaps some limited distribution and marketing options. If you're looking for a better product and some basic help in selling your book then this could be right for you.
- **Full service companies.** These suppliers tend to work at the higher quality end of the self-publishing market, offering authoritative advice, bespoke design, active trade and media marketing and, in a couple of cases, real bookshop distribution options.

In addition, there is a plethora of companies and individuals offering component parts of the book production and marketing process, such as copy-editing, proofreading, cover design, public relations, etc.

The key for any self-publisher in choosing a company to work with is research. Having decided why you are self-publishing and set your expectations from doing so, the next step is to see who offers what, and at what cost, and to match the right company with what you are seeking. A search on the internet for 'self-publishing' will present you with many choices, so explore the company websites, compare what is being offered, and generally get a feel for what each says they do. Are they just selling services to authors, or are they selling their authors' books? Do they offer active marketing or just 'marketing advice'? Don't take their word for it, though: seek independent advice from other authors or independent industry commentators – there are three sources of reliable, independent information on self-publishing service providers: this *Yearbook* and associated website (www.writersandartists.co.uk); ALLi (see page 525); and the Independent Publishing Magazine (www.theindependentpublishingmagazine.com), which gives authoritative reviews of self-publishing companies and a monthly ranking of the best (and worst) based upon author feedback.

Having identified some companies that look as if they will help you meet your publishing expectations, you need to establish how much it will cost. Get detailed quotations from companies and compare like-for-like. Ask questions of those companies if anything is in doubt: ask to see a contract; ask for a sample of their product (many companies still produce terrible quality books!). Time spent at this stage will ensure that you get a good feel for the company you're considering working with, and that can be the difference between a happy self-publishing experience and a disastrous one.

Marketing and distribution

Authors often concentrate on producing a book or ebook and ignore the part of the equation that actually sells the book. Examine carefully what author services companies offer. Distribution includes all the processes involved in getting a book or ebook in front of potential readers, but many companies offer only a limited, online-only service. Marketing is the process of alerting both the media (whether in print, on air or online) and potential readers that a book is available. Similarly, very few companies spend much effort to actively market their authors' work. The right choice of marketing and distribution service can make or break a book even before production has started.

As the author and self-publisher, you must decide how to get it into the hands of readers. You will need to make decisions on whether POD or wider retail distribution is required; whether the marketing services offered by an author services company are enough for your book; or if a public relations company might be the way forward. And, of course, all of this has a cost implication.

A brave new world

Self-publishing offers authors a host of opportunities to make their work available to readers. Making the right decisions to meet your expectations for your book or ebook in the early stages of the publishing process will pay dividends. Understand your motivations; research the production options well; understand distribution choices; give marketing the importance it requires; and above all, enjoy your self-publishing experience.

Jeremy Thompson founded Troubador Publishing (www.troubador.co.uk) in 1996 and started the Matador (www.troubador.co.uk/matador) self-publishing imprint in 1999, which has since helped over 9,000 authors to self-publish. Troubador also runs the annual Self-Publishing Conference (in its sixth year in 2018) and holds a 'Self-Publishing Experience' Day three times a year at its offices near Leicester. Troubador also runs Indie-Go (www.indie-go.co.uk), offering component author services, and in 2015 it acquired The Book Guild Ltd, an independent partnership publisher.

How self-publishing started my publishing journey

Mel Sherratt describes her route from aspiring writer to successful self-published author and beyond, and offers advice on how to stay ahead in a challenging business.

I've wanted to write for as long as I can remember. My first ever short story was about a gobstopper called Gerry who was kidnapped by the Black Jacks and Fruit Salads in a sweet shop.

When I was in my teens, I used to go to the library every week to see which 'how-to-write' books on writing were new or available. I borrowed books about writing children's novels, crime, romance, horror, screenplays, short stories, magazine articles – you name it, I wanted to try it. It was most disappointing when there were no new books to read, and equally exciting when a new one popped up on the shelves. I just wanted to write.

My route to success

I tried for 12 years to get a traditional deal before self-publishing my debut novel, *Taunting the Dead* (2011). In the early 2000s, I would religiously wait for the new edition of the *Writers' & Artists' Yearbook* to come out. I'd sit down with a notepad and write a list of agents I could approach, what genres they represented and their submission details. Any new agents that hadn't been included the year before were a bonus! Back then, most submissions – the first three chapters, a synopsis and covering letter, had to be sent by snail mail. Then came the wait. Most of the rejections slips would be delivered on a Saturday – so that would be another weekend ruined.

I found my first agent in 2004, when I was writing contemporary women's fiction (which I have since self-published on Kindle Direct Publishing Services under a pen name). By that time, I had written the first of the three novels in my first series, *The Estate Series*, which are about fear and emotion, friendships and gritty lifestyles. As well as enjoying books by Martina Cole and Lynda la Plante, I began to read more authors I admired in the crime genre, such as Peter James, Ian Rankin and Mark Billingham. From all of them I learned about hooks, scene-setting, character-building, cliffhangers, how to show not tell, how less is often more, and how to evoke a sense of place. As I began to find my love for crime, I wanted to portray much more than fear and emotion in my own books. I wanted to delve deeper into darker storylines, often with a crime that was solved by the police. So my writing went from shopping and gossip, to gossip and emotion, to emotion and fear, to justice and murder.

When *Taunting The Dead* was originally rejected by several publishers, I was devastated. It was the fifth book I had written, and it wasn't the first of my books to be turned down. *Somewhere to Hide* and *Behind a Closed Door*, the first two books in *The Estate Series*, had been rejected because they were too much of a mixture between women's fiction and crime. So when I wrote something more 'to type', it then became too similar to Martina Cole or Lynda la Plante. Was I still trying to find my own voice? *Taunting the Dead* did go to acquisition meetings, but in the end it wasn't accepted – again because it didn't fit into an established niche.

So I changed tack. I decided to self-publish *Taunting the Dead* to see if a traditional publisher might then take an interest. But getting the book noticed wasn't easy. You can't just put a book online and expect it to sell. It needs to be marketed – discoverability being the main objective. I had been a blogger for several years prior to publication and had built up a lot of support online which helped to spread the word about my self-published novel. I discovered that through my blog and Twitter I was able to create a 'network' of contacts who would recommend my books of their own accord.

I studied what was popular in the Kindle charts: the bestsellers and series that were selling well, books by unknown authors as well as books by bestselling writers, debut novelists and established ones too. I checked out covers and blurbs, and which genres were selling consistently.

Why self-publishing worked for me

When I first self-published in 2011–12, I was worried that if I couldn't get a publisher to sign up my gritty novel, making it available direct to the public might scupper my writing 'career' before it had really started. But in fact, using the strategy I had adopted for *Taunting the Dead*, over the space of six months I self-published three more books in a series.

I write under a number of different genres – police procedurals, psychological thrillers, women's fiction with a punch, and contemporary women's fiction novels under the pen name Marcie Steele. But the main thing I like to write about is emotion, whether that is fear and emotion or love and emotion. These subjects cover a vast area of the commercial fiction market. Readers who enjoy digital copies devour books so quickly that they always want more. I very often find that if a reader likes one of my books, they tend to seek out the others.

For novels that I publish with traditional publishers, I work well in advance of publication date; it is months after the manuscript is finished that the book is scheduled for release. I have a fantastic editing and cover design team, promotion, and the backing of a great editor who schedules everything in for me. Until a writer has had a structural edit of a book, they are unlikely to know how valuable such interventions are. Only now do I realise the huge difference between development editing and copy edits. My editor has added the glitter to my words.

In between the times I have work to do for my publisher, I concentrate on my other books. With the self-published novels, I can try new things all the time. I can try out free promotions, lower prices for a limited period or change prices on a regular basis to tempt new and existing readers. This year, I changed the covers on *The Estate Series* to give it a boost. I'm constantly refreshing things, such as tweaking the product description (or blurb). You have to be organised – a good project manager; most of the time I am, but it often means working evenings and weekends to fit everything in.

What have I learned along the way?

Just like any fledgling business, I learned as I went along and I strive to keep learning a little more every day. Having lots of books to market is a challenge. I am writing number 14 now – imagine trying to keep tabs on all those! There are many people who help keep my business afloat. I have a bookkeeper who looks after all my accounts for me (I'm terrible with figures) and I have an accountant who deals with the more complicated side of things. I have a cover designer, who also does all my banners and advertising images. I hire a structural editor and a copy-editor. I'm in the process of finding a PR aide. And my husband is a great sounding board for plots and twists. He helps keep my ideas realistic: 'That's a bit *Die Hard 7*, Mel,' he'll say. 'You need to bring it back to *Die Hard 4*.'

Why I chose to work with an agent

After I parted company with my second agent early in 2012, due to my success with self-publishing, I was approached by seven agents in a matter of weeks. I'm now able to work with a fantastic lady, Madeleine Milburn, who really understands my work. Through her, I've been offered five two-book deals and I feel my writing is going from strength to strength. My agent encourages me to be who I am – a gritty, raw writer, producing work steeped in emotion.

Some advice

These are my top pieces of advice for any writer:

- Write, write, write.
- Read, read, read in the genre you want to conquer.
- Edit until you are sick of the work.
- Hire an editor to work with you.
- Get the best cover you can if you're going to publish it yourself.
- Stay positive on social media – it leads to so many opportunities and great friendships.
- Read about marketing yourself.
- Experiment and have fun.

Madeleine came looking for me. I still remember the Saturday afternoon I received an email from her. She had been reading my books, checking out my website and my online presence, and asked if we could meet. We had learned a lot about each other over a stream of emails and when we met in person, we clicked. Madeleine told me what she could do for me and has since put her plans into action. For example, I'm finally getting foreign rights and TV deals. There's a lot of self in self-publishing and sometimes I just want to sit down and write. Madeleine takes some of the burden from me, leaving me with more time to do what I love. She even tells me to stop worrying, to get a grip if I'm panicking, and gives me a stern telling-off when the self-doubt eats at me too much.

I've been represented by Madeleine for nearly six years and, not only has she become a great friend, she is also my business partner. She treats me as an equal. We can chat about strategies and sales and long-term plans, and we bounce ideas off one another too. I have knowledge of self-publishing and try to keep up to date with what is going on in the digital world and she in turn keeps me up to date with the publishing world she inhabits.

Prizes and other successes

In 2014, I was one of the first four authors to appear on a panel for 'indies' at Crimefest. From there, I was delighted to take part in a panel at Theakston Old Peculier Crime Writing Festival, called 'The Good Old Days', tracking several writers' stories to success. I've been going to Harrogate for this festival for the past seven years, and it was at the top of my writer's bucket list to get up on that stage. This was topped when I found out that I was longlisted, and then shortlisted, for the Crime Writer's Association Dagger in the Library Award 2014, which was voted for by readers. That was a fantastic feeling and, as it was in December, it ended an incredible year.

For the past three years, I have been named as one of the top 100 most influential people in my city of Stoke-on-Trent, which is an honour. Even more astonishing is that I have now surpassed sales of one million books.

What next?

I'm not self-publishing at the moment because I'm working on a new series for HarperCollins Avon. I've recently signed a six-figure deal to write another police procedural series, the first of which is out in October 2018. It's very exciting. It's very scary too. But that's what keeps me on my toes. So, for now, I'm going to do what I do best – and that is to keep learning and keep writing. I have a saying – 'Keep on keeping on.' I feel very lucky to do what I do, but there were numerous times over those 12 years of rejection that I would convince myself that I couldn't do it, that I didn't have what it takes . . .

If there is a writer inside you, you'll do it because you have to. It compels you, even if you're getting nowhere to start with. Words have always been a huge part of my life. I love making things up! By writing more, your skills will improve, your words will get better and others will take notice. I still can't quite believe it when I get reviews and emails from readers saying how much they have enjoyed my books. Self-publishing *Taunting the Dead* helped me to start my career as well as my own business. Now I see writers not only taking the self-publishing path but choosing to pursue that route rather than a traditional publishing deal. Either way is fine – and doing both is good too. Writers have more choices now; that's real progress.

Mel Sherratt is a writer of psychological thrillers, suspense, police procedurals and women's fiction 'with a punch'. She self-published *Taunting the Dead* in 2011 and a further two books in the DS Allie Shenton series, *Follow the Leader* and *Only the Brave* in 2015 with Thomas & Mercer. She has also published *Watching Over You* (Thomas & Mercer 2014) and four titles in her psychological suspense *The Estate Series*. Her books as Marcie Steele have now been republished by Bookouture and she also has two crime dramas published with them, *The Girls Next Door* and *Don't Look Behind You*, as Mel Sherratt. *She Did It* was her last self-published book in 2017. *Hush Hush* is the next book to be published by Avon, due out in October 2018. See more at http://melsherratt.co.uk/ or on Twitter @writermels.

See also...

- *Finding my agent*, page 282
- *Getting hooked out of the slush pile*, page 433
- *Notes from a hybrid author*, page 630

Should I make an audiobook?

James Peak looks at the rapid growth, popularity and profitability of the audiobook market that has been made possible by new technology, and lays out a clear route and valuable tips for anyone considering producing their own audiobook.

It was 1999. I was lost and disoriented at the London Book Fair. I staggered into a lopsided little tent right at the back, where a wizened old lady whose palm I crossed with silver peered into her misty orb. 'What does the future of book publishing hold?', I asked her. Then, more stridently (thinking of the small Caribbean island I so richly deserve), 'And how can it make me some money?' Focusing deep inside the glass, she muttered something about young wizards, colouring-in for adults, and rebooted ladybirds. Staring deeper, she whispered a mysterious incantation: 'Buy amazon' and rushed outside to phone her stockbroker. I seized her crystal ball. The mist inside cleared to reveal a strange vision: some books would become peculiar electronic files, beamed straight to the pockets and handbags of readers via their tiny, shiny, computery-phoney things; some books would be read on scrolling screens; some would even be listened to with stylish white headphones. I ran from the tent. I'd seen the future. I was going to be rich.

Twenty years later that future is here – and 70,000 of my colouring books about wizarding ladybirds have been pulped. Authors today must expect to be heard as well as read. It's a change that begs several questions: should I write differently if my words are destined for the ear as well as the eye? Whose voice will my readers be hearing? What will this all cost me? Should I bother to make an audiobook at all?

The market is growing

Over the last few years, the UK's big four publishers have been racing to hire teams of audio editors, build in-house studios and forge links with independent audio producers, in order that they may deep-fill their back catalogues with spoken versions, not only of their bestsellers but their midsellers too. Penguin Random House audio now has a catalogue of over 11,000 titles, and Harper's audio business grew 47% year on year to June 2017. Why is this land-grab for audio making good business sense? One reason might be that audiobook distribution has vastly simplified. Publishers no longer need to cough up to burn CDs, expensively design and package boxed sets, and lobby for shelf space in high-street bookshops. Instead, the ubiquity of the smartphone has enabled a streamlined distribution network from printed page to listener's ear.

The economics look great. In common with ebooks, the endless replicability of the mp3 file negates all physical costs of production. An eight-hour book can retail at well over £20. Once produced, it's re-deliverable, pretty much free, forever (or at least until the tech changes again). As a result, the entire audiobook market has digitised and found millions of new listeners ready to put their hands into their pockets. According to a 2017 American Publishing Association report, 26% of the entire US population listened to an audiobook in the last year, and US sales were up from \$2.1 billion in 2016 to \$2.5 billion in 2017. Voice-enabled home smart speakers, like Amazon Echo and Google Home, support digital audiobooks, with 19% of listeners already using this new tech to listen.

Excitingly, the same report found that, with audiobooks, people multitask. 68% do housework and listen; 65% bake and listen and 56% exercise and listen. This is big. It means people are finding entirely new hours in their days to consume book content. Print books demand a reader's full attention. If you exercise or bake with a printed book on the go, you'll sustain terrible injuries and your muffins will be dreadful.

Who is behind all this?

So who is behind this sensational reboot? Amazon – through its subsidiary Audible, the early-to-market US audiobook producer that was snapped up back in 2008 for a mere bagatelle ($300 million) and which now presides over an estimated 90% of the global audiobook market. There are other players on the audiobook market (Scribed, Kobo, Storytel) but competition-wise, the dominance has raised hackles. In 2015 anti-trust regulators began investigating, as simply too much, an exclusivity agreement that made Audible the only provider of audiobooks to Apple's massive, global iStore. The Amazon-Apple arrangement came to an end in 2017, which the European Commission said was 'likely to improve competition' in the future. For now, though, the Amazon-Audible platform is overwhelmingly the biggest game in town, and it is most probably the main place where your audiobook will live.

Audiobooks are not just for big publishers. Amazon has extended its jaw-droppingly efficient infrastructure to the self-publishing sector, through Audible's Audiobook Creation Exchange (ACX). It is aimed at book rights-holders and self-publishing authors in the US, UK and, since 2017, Canada too. Although the quality of the most cheaply produced audiobooks can vary, it has lowered the barriers to entry. An audiobook can now cost just a few hundred pounds to produce if you are prepared to narrate and edit it yourself, and a couple of thousand if working with a professional voice actor and studio. Amazon then advertises the audiobook on the same page as the printed book on amazon.com. Royalties of up to 40% of cover price can quickly add up to significant sums, if it sells. After an initial production outlay, writers are finding it's possible to turn a profit. How much of a profit is difficult to establish, as Amazon are cagey about releasing their sales data.

How to do it

If you are going to make an audiobook, there are pitfalls into which you should not stumble. Here is an overview of a linear route to market:

Writing > voice casting > recording > editing > releasing > marketing

Writing

Your book is a strong candidate to become an audiobook if it's literary, historical, thrilling, romantic, fantastical or erotic, or if it's a memoir, diary or self-help book. Sci-fi can also be enormously popular, and a few specialist UK audio companies (including Big Finish Ltd) found success with audio products before the current land grab, working within classic sci-fi like *Dr Who* and *Blake's 7*. Graphic novels, art books and cookbooks may struggle with audio, as they depend so heavily on a visual element. However, some big publishers are experimenting with recording children's picture books, using familiar voices, high-end sound design and music to create adaptations. Imelda Staunton's version of *The Gruffalo* (Macmillan 1999) is a lovely example of this. If you have a children's picture book that you can adapt to work without pictures, its brevity can be its saving grace, as the finished audiobook might be only five or ten minutes long, and costs or recording and editing correspondingly low.

Voice casting

Deciding whose voice to use may be easy if cost is an issue: your own will be cheapest, and nobody knows the nuances of your book like you do. However, if time is a factor, or you are not sure if your own voice is strong enough, you could book a test session at a local recording studio (£50-£100) or find a quiet space and read into your smartphone for a full 30 minutes, taking feedback from sample listeners. At the end of a test session you'll know if narrating is something you have an appetite for and if your voice will do your book justice.

Alternatively, hiring a professional narrator can be a really effective way to draw out the drama, romance, thrills and mystery in your book, particularly if there is lots of multi-character dialogue or if it needs careful pacing or tone. The best narrators are absolutely spellbinding, bringing emotion and passion to your words.

A typical 100,000-word novel might be 8-10 hours long and will take a professional 'voice' 20-25 hours to record properly. Their services do not have to be horrifically expensive if you have your negotiating hat on. Often, voices combine audiobook work with lucrative commercial work and acting careers. Many are represented by agents keen to monetise time, and recording audiobooks can soak up spare hours. Reasonable charges for audiobook voices are around £200-£400 per day, and for this you can expect adequate preparation and reading time thrown in.

If only a particular (high-profile, celebrity) narrator will do, or you really need transparency on costs at the outset, try passing your book on via that person's agent, with a letter explaining why they simply must do it! If you can enthuse them, you might be able to 'buy them out' to record the whole thing for a fixed price.

Recording

If you decide to voice your own book in your own home, you'll need a very quiet and small space, and ideally it should be soundproofed and acoustically deadened. Bare, flat walls reverberate sound, but hanging heavy fabrics at angles can minimize this.

You'll need a decent condenser microphone, a 'pop shield' to stop plosive sounds like 'P' and 'B' distorting your recording, and a computer with a solid-state drive or the fan turned off so that it is near silent.

You'll need decent audio recording software, like ProTools or the open-source programme Audacity, with Garageband being a simple entry-level programme that is already pre-installed on many Apple computers.

Make sure you read your book from a tablet, as rustling noises from paper scripts will be picked up by your microphone. Regular hydration will stop horrid clicky mouth noises being picked up by the microphone. You will quickly get into the habit of re-doing sentences that you've fluffed, and these mistakes can be edited out afterwards.

Recording in a studio with an engineer can be expensive (£75-£150 per hour) but many will consider buy-outs for a project, particularly if they can schedule sessions around other work. As the author, you should be welcome at all recording sessions, to review production and comment on pace and narration style. Beware of studios that don't welcome you to sit in, as it might indicate quality isn't key. Many studios provide a producer to sit alongside the engineer, to listen to performances, ask for retakes and rewrite sentences that were better on the page than they sound. Having several pairs of ears in these recording sessions can eliminate the need to re-record later.

Editing

If you are producing your own audiobook at home, you'll have to review and edit every page into chapter-sized chunks for ACX. This can be fiddly, but it is immensely satisfying if you are a tech-savvy multitasker. Editing consists of: removing extraneous noises from the recording; joining different takes together without losing the sense of drama and pace; adding music and effects; and delivering sound files to exact technical specifications.

To pass ACX's quality control for release for sale on Audible and Amazon, you'll need to deliver audio files 'at 44.1khz . . . measuring between -23dB and -18dB RMS . . . with a maximum -60dB noise floor.' This sounds more difficult that it is.

If you recorded in a professional studio, then you'd be well advised to keep the editing with the same team, because they know your book very well by this stage.

Releasing

Once edited, your audiobook's individual chapters are uploaded onto ACX, where it enters a quality control queue. Audible learned quickly that consumers won't pay £20-odd for distorted or echoing audio recordings. Their quality control is stringent but, equally, their feedback about problems with files is helpful and precise.

If all is well, a couple of weeks after submission your book will appear for sale. Because of the quality-control filter, and a greater volume of audiobooks being submitted than even a year ago, you'd be well advised to pause advance marketing activity until your new audiobook is confirmed as available.

Marketing

Increasingly, reviewers are listening to audiobooks and plumbing them into their blogs and channels. There are many audiobook specialists, e.g. at www.rtbookreviews.com, https://audiobookreviewer.com, www.hotlistens.com and http://briansbookblog.com.

Just as for books, marketing audiobooks is effort-based. If you're prepared to run a campaign of social media ads, serenade bloggers, lobby to appear on podcasts, organise online book tours and engage in all those dark arts, then your sales will benefit. Upon request, ACX provides free download codes to send out to reviewers, so you may push your audiobook as much or as little as you please.

Making an audiobook is a fascinating, exacting, collaborative process that can give your book another dimension, and, hopefully, your bank balance a boost. There are many brilliant audio engineers and narrators out there who can help your words reach ears as well as eyes. If you decide to start production, good luck, and don't forget your pop shield.

... As I was roaming around the London Book Fair in 2018, the old lady in her lopsided little tent beckoned me in. Inside her crystal ball was another glimpse of book publishing's future: a dazzling mishmash of text, audio, video, animation, graphics, music, sound effects and artwork, all inside a virtual ecosystem of content verticals delivered on space-age devices. And then another image appeared, of a dog-eared paperback. It reminded me that, as long as your writing is wonderful, readers will buy it – however it's delivered.

James Peak co-owns Essential Music Ltd (http://essentialmusic.co.uk), which has been producing BBC dramas and documentaries since 1996, and audiobook and podcasts since they were invented. He co-writes BBC Radio 4's *John Cleese Knows Nothing* with John Cleese, and is co-author, with Duncan Crowe, of *Scoundrels*, a series of comic novels published by Black Door Press (www.blackdoorpress.com). He welcomes questions about your audiobook projects at james@essentialmusic.co.uk.

Notes from a hybrid author

Nick Spalding's success with writing comedy fiction and self-publishing ebooks led him to be noticed by publishers and literary agents. Deals followed that have seen him published in print both in the UK and abroad. Epitomising a new breed of 'hybrid author', he describes his publishing choices so far and stresses the value of always keeping your options open.

I'm not sure if the term 'hybrid author' is one that sits all that well with me, to be honest. It makes me sound like some kind of hideous experiment, conducted in one of those sterile laboratories you see in badly made sci-fi horror movies. In my mind's eye, I can see myself stumbling out of a glass pod, surrounded by cold gas, covered in green goo and moaning loudly about royalty payments. There's probably a Kobo grafted onto one hand, an iPad grafted onto the other, and a Kindle shoved up my arse. Not a pretty sight.

Nevertheless, hybrid author is the accepted term for what I am, so I'm just going to have to lump it. What authors don't have to lump these days is a single path to publication. You now have more options than ever when it comes to getting your book into the grubby hands of readers all over the world.

You can submit the book to agents and publishers in order to get your book into print 'the old-fashioned way', with one of the large publishing companies that have dominated the industry for decades, or you can go smaller scale and try to get your work published via one of the new digital-only publishers that have sprung up in recent years. Lastly, you can choose to self-publish both ebook and paperback versions of your book via the various companies available online that provide such a service – the most powerful and successful of which, of course, is Amazon. The most important word here is *choice*. Writers have a clear choice these days – and consequently far greater control over their careers.

It was Amazon's KDP (Kindle Direct Publishing) platform that gave me my springboard to a career as a writer. Without it, I wouldn't be covered in all that green goo and walking round with a Kindle up my backside – metaphorically speaking.

So what exactly is a hybrid author then? I would describe a hybrid author as one who uses as many different paths to publication as possible. A hybrid author is a writer who likes to keep his or her options open. Someone who keeps a foot in as many camps as they possibly can – without rupturing something important.

The publishing industry is about as predictable as an episode of *Game Of Thrones*, so I think it's vitally important to avoid putting all your eggs in one basket – if you are lucky enough to have more than one basket available to you. I do, so that's why I continue to self-publish books, alongside securing traditional publishing contracts when appropriate (and I always find it *very* appropriate when people offer me a lot of cash, funnily enough).

My road to being a successful hybrid author was largely through trial and error, with a fair bit of luck thrown in for good measure. Five years ago, I wrote a semi-fictional memoir, *Life . . . With No Breaks*, in a 30-hour period as an experiment, and had no idea what to do with it. So when the Amazon KDP service came to my attention it seemed like the perfect place for it to find a home.

I then wrote a second memoir called *Life . . . On A High* and a fantasy adventure called *The Cornerstone*, and released both in the summer of 2011. My sales then started to pick up – proving that the more books you have out, the more books you sell, as your platform grows and people start to recognise your brand name.

Then one evening I was discussing with my girlfriend what to do next. I wanted to write a book that would appeal to as many ebook readers as possible, and from the year or so I'd spent self-publishing it had become very apparent that a majority were female. A popular genre for female readers is romance, so I decided to combine Spalding-style humour with a romantic storyline. *Love . . . From Both Sides* was born – and the rest (as people who like to indulge in obvious cliché would say) is history.

Love . . . From Both Sides was released in September 2011. In the first six months of its life, it shifted 1,500 copies. Not a bad haul if you're just starting out – but I'd been around a while, had built a pretty good reputation, and all of my other books were selling far better. I was quite the disappointed lad, I can tell you. It took a cover change and a price drop for *Love . . . From Both Sides* to take off. I cut the price from £1.49 to 99p, and added two cartoon images of Jamie and Laura to the cover. That was at the start of March 2012. By the end of April I'd sold over 36,000 copies, and developed a nosebleed.

Given the rampant sales, I figured I'd better write a sequel, so in the middle of May I released *Love . . . And Sleepless Nights* and sat back to await developments. And developments turned out to be combined sales of 300,000 for the two books by the end of October, along with another 100,000 sales of my other three titles.

You don't sell that many books without somebody sitting up and paying attention. I started to get emails from both agents and publishers during the summer, and by the autumn I'd sewn up a deal with Hodder & Stoughton to republish *Love . . . From Both Sides* and *Love . . . And Sleepless Nights*, along with a third title, *Love . . . Under Different Skies*.

So why change from a purely self-published author, to one also published by a traditional publishing company? My decision was due to a combination of things. The first – and I'm not going to lie to you here – was the rather large advance Hodder offered. The second was the fact they could get me into the paperback market – something which I was unable to do as a self-publisher. Thirdly – and separate to the Hodder deal – having an agent enabled me to secure several foreign rights deals, which I would not have been able to negotiate on my own.

I believed (and still do) that forming a relationship with an agent and a publisher is still ultimately the best way to secure a long-term livelihood as a writer. Self-publishing is a brilliant way to establish a career, but for longevity you need help.

That help doesn't just have to come from agents or publishers though. Your fellow authors can be incredibly helpful too. Around the time I was writing *Love . . . Under Different Skies*, I was fortunate enough to be asked to join a collective of successful authors, working together under the banner of Notting Hill Press. Made up of several of the UK's best romance and humour writers, it is an absolutely fantastic thing to be a part of, and I was more than happy to place *Life . . . With No Breaks* and its sequel with them. I'm still fairly new to this industry, so having a group of experienced and talent authors to turn to for advice has been a godsend. I now have five titles published with NHP (and I retain control over all of my rights) and plan on publishing more with them over the coming years.

After all that excitement, the next step in my career was to write and sell a new book called *Fat Chance* (Lake Union Publishing 2014). This was an entirely new project, so I was bloody nervous about getting a deal for it. It's one thing to write sequels to a story that you know is already popular; it's quite another to write about an entirely new set of characters in a brand new setting. Luckily, my agent stepped up to the plate again magnificently, and scored me a contract with the newly created publishing arm over at Amazon.

This was an absolutely brilliant deal for me, as Amazon are the industry leaders right now when it comes to selling books, so who better to be published by? I'm sure that *Fat Chance* has done better with their Lake Union imprint than it would have with any other publisher, given the clout that Amazon can exert when it comes to promotion and publicity. Proof? When I wrote this article, *Fat Chance* was in the Amazon UK Kindle Top Ten. I hope to have further titles with Amazon Publishing over the next few years.

So right now I find myself in the position of being published by Hodder & Stoughton with the *Love* . . . series, published by Amazon with *Fat Chance*, a member of Notting Hill Press with five other titles, and still self-published under my own steam with a further three. You don't get much more hybrid than that! Unless I buy my own printing press and start churning books out to throw at passers-by in the street, I think I've covered as many bases as I possibly can for the moment.

None of this means I am guaranteed any kind of success in the future of course, but by diversifying as much as possible, I feel that I've given myself the best chance of having some longevity in this business.

So what does all this tell you – other than the fact I am a jammy bastard, obviously? Probably that the way an author goes about his or her work in the 21st century is vastly different from the way things were 15 years ago. The march of technological progress has multiplied the avenues through which a writer can sell a book to the reading public, and changed his or her relationship with publishers and agents.

Making sure you investigate each and every avenue open to you is a must. Even if you choose not to walk down them (and I'm fully aware of how laboured this metaphor is becoming – don't worry, I won't mention it again after this sentence) you should at least consider each one thoroughly, because not doing so may cut off a potential revenue stream for your work. And if there's one thing no writer should ever do, it's miss out on an opportunity to make money!

Are there downsides to being a hybrid author? Yes, absolutely. Juggling all these different ways of working can be extremely stressful. I am not only a writer, I am also a marketer, a publicist, an editor, a proofreader, a webmaster, an admin secretary, an amateur accountant and an online researcher. I would stick a broom up my backside and sweep the floor at the same time, but the Kindle keeps getting in the way.

It's not a career choice for everyone, certainly. But it's the only way to be a writer that I've ever known, so I don't know any better! Being a hybrid has worked for me in the past, and I very much hope it will continue to do so in the future. While it is a lot of hard work, it is also a lot of fun, and I wouldn't change it for the world.

What I would change is the first paragraph of this feature, because I am painfully aware that while I've tried my best to give you an idea of what it's like to be a hybrid author, there's every chance that the only thing you're actually going to take away from this article is the image of a snot-covered Nick Spalding with a Kindle stuck up his arse.

Nick Spalding previously worked in the communications industry, mainly in media and marketing. Because Nick concluded that talking rubbish for a living can get tiresome (for anyone other than a politician), he thought he'd have a crack at writing comedy fiction – and has now sold nearly 1.3 million books. His novels include the bestselling comedies *Love . . . From Both Sides* (2012), *Fat Chance* (2014), *Bricking It* (2015) and *Checking Out* (2018). You can contact him via Twitter: @nickspalding and Facebook: www.facebook.com/spaldingauthor. See also his website and blog: www.nickspalding.com.

Making waves online

Simon Appleby outlines how writers can use the internet to get noticed.

Make some noise!

Whether you're a published writer with an ongoing deal, or an aspiring writer with lots of ideas or even a finished manuscript, the challenge remains the same. How do you get your name known, your words read, your manuscripts taken on, your book bought? Whether you're looking for a traditional publishing deal, you're considering self-publishing, or have some other approach in mind, this article is intended to help you promote your work online.

The prevalence of smartphones, tablets and mobile internet means that book and author websites are, more than ever, in direct competition with every form of media, not just other websites. This includes TV-on-demand services such as Netflix, social media platforms, instant messaging and online gaming.

> **The smartphone phenomenon**
>
> Internet statistics company Statista estimated that the number of smartphone users in the UK will have reached approximately 46.4 million by 2018.

But it's crucial to find a way to get people's attention and build a devoted following of your own. Readers are bombarded with options and are unlikely to stumble upon your site by accident. You need to lure readers and critics to your writing, and, in turn, attract publishers.

Risk-averse publishers (and agents) look to the internet for inspiration and to gauge marketability. Much of your activity should demonstrate to a publisher that people like your work and would pay to read more of it. The E.L. James's global phenomenon *Fifty Shades of Grey* began life on an internet fan-fiction forum, the ultimate reminder that there are many ways to be discovered as a writer. Equally, Hugh Howey achieved extraordinary success – which included worldwide fame and lucrative publishing and film-rights deals – from self-publishing his books, as did paranormal romance writer Amanda Hocking.

But it didn't come easily and even those who've achieved international recognition still need to work hard. Published authors are expected to show a continued commitment to their own success – marketing, publicity, social media. Gone are the days when landing a publishing deal meant you could sit back and let the publisher do all the work. It's important to develop the skills first, because you'll have far less trouble adjusting to the work once the publishing deal is in place.

The technologies, platforms and communities involved in online promotion evolve constantly. But the concepts behind developing a manageable approach to promoting your writing on the internet – to get you closer to your readers and them closer to you – stay virtually the same. This article doesn't deliver detailed DIY instructions, but it does, hopefully, offer ideas for developing your internet presence in a structured and accessible fashion.

There's a lot of noise out there, and to be heard you will have to make some of your own. The technical side of things is not rocket science – there are numerous (and free) solutions which do most of the hard work for you. But it does take persistence and a good idea of what you want to accomplish and who you want to appeal to. This means setting aside some time to plan your approach. It's just like writing – you put the building blocks in place and then, once you start, you won't be able to stop!

Set up your own website and blog

Chances are you're already doing this, but if not you should be. To get started, check out authors who are selling themselves well (and badly). Websites that are easy to navigate, visually appealing, functional and up to date tend to generate the best response. Your website should reflect your style, allowing your visitors to get a sense of who you are. You can look at professional authors' websites for inspiration, but it's also possible to find great examples among lesser-known authors. A good website needn't be expensive or difficult to maintain. Many household names use basic, off-the-shelf website themes.

It's important to include as much information about your published books as your visitors can find on major retailer websites. Ideally, give them extra content they won't find anywhere else. If you can, let visitors in on little secrets or give them insight into the writing process. For example, you might include some interesting copy you wrote for your book but didn't include in the final version.

Include a blog on your website. It's a great way to impart useful or interesting information and drive users to your site. For example, you could publish some of your work to find out what people think about it, or discuss other authors' work, the writing market, or the processes you go through in your writing. Perhaps you could write about the books you liked as a child, topics you researched to write a book, or places you went while researching. Google looks for information it hasn't seen before, and a blog is a great way to update your site.

Place your blog at the centre of your online universe so that all your social media presences point to it. Also, decide what level of engagement you want to offer visitors. Do you want to allow people to comment on your blog posts, for example?

Finally, remember what you write will be available on the internet for a long time, so think carefully about how you talk about yourself, your life and about other writers. And don't put anything in writing that you wouldn't want a potential reader or publisher to see.

Get discovered

Good content will only help promote your writing if people are aware of it, so make sure you have a solid understanding of search engine optimisation (SEO). Research the key terms people use to search (there are many keyword research tools available) and include them in your content, but take care to ensure they only appear in context. Search engines prioritise unique, high-quality information, which your readers find useful and interesting, so keep it relevant, fresh and clearly written.

Explore social networking and communities

To help people find your website or blog, you must be a willing participant of the social internet. There are innumerable online communities relevant to authors. But you can find them just as you would find a good book – by searching according to your tastes and listening to the recommendations of your friends. By joining these communities, you can potentially transform your online reputation. It won't happen overnight, but if you continue to engage and participate in discussions, you'll increase your friends and visitor numbers, encourage people to read your words, and boost your reputation. Here are the main categories of community that could be relevant to you:

- Writing communities – where you can get your work evaluated and rate the work of others. These are both a source of useful feedback and encouragement, and a place to get noticed by publishers (sometimes even leading to book deals).
- General book communities – where book owners, librarians, collectors and authors come together – an instant source of like-minded people. Popular communities include Goodreads, LibraryThing and Shelfari.
- Forums – these can be wide-ranging or focused on one subject, but if you find one you like, hang around and join in. However, don't expect to drop in, plug your work and reap the gratitude of other users if you're not prepared to stick around.
- Social networking – this is the broadest category, encompassing thousands of sites large and small. Find the ones that are right for you and that you're comfortable with. Don't set up a Twitter page if you don't want to spend time engaging with other users, for example.

Make 'friends'

There was a time when 'social media' meant Facebook and Twitter to most people. The social media landscape is now much more fragmented – you also have to consider Instagram, Tumblr, Flickr, SoundCloud and many more, as well as book-oriented networks such as Goodreads and LibraryThing. You can't work with all of them and do a great job. The key is to focus on platforms that allow you to reach your audience, and, more importantly, suit the content you want to create.

Some quality author websites

Roald Dahl

www.roalddahl.com

A great wealth of content available, but avoids any unnecessary visual whizbanggery.

Laline Paull

www.lalinepaull.com

Simple and elegant, this site feels very much on brand to promote Laline's debut novel, *The Bees*.

Shannon Selin

www.shannonselin.com

Shannon's focused content marketing has resulted in over 100 weekly blog posts on all things Napoleonic.

Haruki Muarakami

www.harukimurakami.com

US site that embraces the aesthetic of Muarakami's book cover designs.

Gillian Flynn

www.gillian-flynn.com

Helps broaden Flynn's appeal by showcasing all her writing and not just her most famous book.

Anthony Horowitz

www.anthonyhorowitz.com

A welcoming, fresh and engaging site, recently revamped.

Chris Cleave

http://chriscleave.com

A site that demonstrates how, with WordPress and an off-the-shelf theme, you can make a site that has good content and a high level of engagement with its audience.

Nick Harkaway

www.nickharkaway.com

Just like one of Nick's books, this is a website that draws the visitor in via his the slightly anarchic, off-kilter 'pathways'.

Joe Wicks

www.thebodycoach.co.uk

Great selling inducements wrapped up in a very clean, modern and inspirational package.

Don't forget LinkedIn. While this was once the province of traditional professionals, today authors, agents and publishing people use LinkedIn. And there are numerous groups for discussing topics of interest to authors. You may be able to use it to find collaborators (perhaps an illustrator or photographer), and a smartly completed LinkedIn profile is your online CV – essential if you want to be taken seriously.

Use the right tool for the job

It may not be so simple in life, but online there's a tool for almost every situation. I can't tell you every item a good toolkit should contain, but I can suggest some general principles and a few key tools, all of which are free and easy to use.

• **Stay on 'brand'**: keep a standard biography and a decent photo of yourself handy when setting up your user profiles. It helps to represent yourself consistently across every platform. Always try to use the same username as well. Keep a note of the profiles you set up and update them periodically.

• **Social conversation**: use social networking sites, micro-blogging services (i.e. Twitter) and your own site to engage with your current and potential readers and your fellow authors.

• **Share and enjoy**: there's a platform on which to share any type of content you create, from video (YouTube, Vimeo) and photos (Flickr, Photobucket), to audio/podcasts (SoundCloud). Research the most visited platforms in each category – there's no point targeting unpopular ones. When you share content, think about whether you need to maintain your copyright, or whether you want to grant people permission to share or use your work by choosing a Creative Commons license (http://creativecommons.org).

• **Listening and measuring tools**: it's good to know when to drop in and contribute to a conversation that's taking place about you or your work. It's also great to know when someone has just linked to your website. You can set up Google Alerts to notify you when these things happen. Or, to follow the blogs that interest you and keep track of new writers and industry trends, use Really Simple Syndication (RSS), which could also provide you with topics to blog about. I suggest NewsBlur or feedly, but there are numerous feed readers available.

To understand what tools work for you, you need to measure their impact. Monitoring websites can help, as can blog statistics within packages such as Google Analytics. You can also find tools that will help you identify how often you, or your chosen genre of writing, are being discussed.

• **Cheat**: to keep the content on your social media channels flowing, use tools that suggest news articles and blog posts for you to share, based on your preferences and interests. These can be real time-savers if you want to post something every day. Similar to functionality within social media dashboards such as Hootsuite, these tools also enable you to schedule content so you can spread out your activities over a longer period.

• **Stay current**: make sure any information about you is current and detailed. Keep your Wikipedia entry up to date if you have one, taking care to stay factual. Update information about yourself on sites such as LibraryThing, and make sure your publishing company knows about your online activities so it can promote them.

Engage with your audience

As a writer spending time online, you are inevitably going to come across comments about your work at some point – sometimes positive, sometimes critical, and occasionally abusive. Keep your cool and remember, when deciding how to react to something, one of these four responses will usually be appropriate:

• **Endorse**: a positive comment, such as a good review, or someone saying they've been inspired by your work, is worth shouting about. Link to it in your own social media, tell your publisher and respond to the creator, helping to cement his or her enthusiasm. It's good to endorse others' work too. Link to the work of another author who has inspired you, or who has recently created interesting content. It's possible that author or others may return the favour at some point.

• **Engage**: talk to fans and critics on their forums of choice. Respond to constructive criticism professionally and never take it personally.

• **Ignore**: if you can't say anything nice …

• **Enforce**: if anyone becomes abusive, infringing your rights or just going too far, take measured steps to do something about it (such as contacting their forum moderator or ISP), but never descend to their level. Anything you say in anger may come back to haunt you later.

One more thing. *Never* pretend to be someone you're not, anywhere, for any reason. Always represent yourself honestly as 'the author in question'. Successful authors, who shall remain nameless here, have seriously damaged their credibility and careers through the practice of 'sock puppetry': leaving glowing reviews of their own work under false names and trashing their rivals' books. There really is such a thing as bad publicity.

Delve into some online PR

Put simply, this involves talking to people about your work to get them to write about it. If you're willing to take the time to contact bloggers and offer review copies, interviews, competition prizes or other content they can use, some of them are likely to respond positively. Understand their pressures – they want to find things to write about, but they may also be bombarded with offers every day.

Use some of the same organisational skills that you use when researching and talking to agents and publishers, and when looking through the *Writers' & Artists' Yearbook*. Do your homework on blogs too. Before you approach a blogger, read the blog thoroughly to make sure your work is right for that blog. And read any submission guidelines the site may have. Keep a record of who you contact, and when, to make sure you don't send repeated messages to the same person. And follow up any communications you've made with sites that offer to look at your work. Finally, always present yourself professionally. It's all common sense, but in my experience that doesn't mean everyone does it properly.

Promote your book on a budget

You can get creative and be noticed even with little or no money to spend. By creating content to promote your book yourself, you can save expensive marketing costs.

Ways to do this include writing blogs or articles 'in character'. Or, you could set up a Twitter feed in your character's name, or write microfiction. Enlist the services of friends and family, and their cameras, video cameras, computers and, most importantly, skills to create images or videos that you can promote yourself with. I know you're creative, or you wouldn't be reading this, so there's no doubt you can think of a way to get yourself noticed (and don't get hung up on being wholly original, or you might never get started).

Look to the future

Self-publishing and digital reading have changed the publishing environment permanently. The economics have changed, as has the ease with which new publishing companies can be created and authors can self-publish their books. That's both good and bad news for an aspiring author. While your chances of seeing your work on sale are higher than ever, the competition for attention from both readers and publishers is fierce.

Today, no author can afford to neglect his or her digital profile. It's vital you take digital self-promotion seriously and treat it as an ongoing campaign that needs regular thought, attention and time throughout your writing career.

Simon Appleby is the Founder and Managing Director of Bookswarm, the only digital agency in the UK dedicated to delivering projects for publishers, authors and others in the world of books. Bookswarm has extensive experience in website design and development. It has delivered author websites for a wide range of writers including Martina Cole, Stephen King, Patrick Ness, Penny Vincenzi, Karen Maitland, Clare Furniss, Hanif Kureishi, Katy Birchall, Peter Fisk and Marcus Chown.

Book sites, blogs and podcasts

This is a small selection of the best book sites, blogs and podcasts recommended by the editors of the *Yearbook*.

BOOK SITES AND BLOGS

The Artist's Road

website http://artistsroad.wordpress.com
Founder Patrick Ross

Blog created to record the cross-USA road trip that the author Patrick Ross took in the summer of 2010 while interviewing over 40 artists with the aim of discussing the motivations, challenges and rewards of their lifestyles, and passing on their creative wisdom. It now details his insights into living an 'art-committed life' through writing and creativity.

Better Novel Project

website www.betternovelproject.com/blog
Founder Christine Frazier

Deconstructs bestselling novels to discover what common elements they all share and shows how writers can use these to create reliable story structures.

Book Patrol

website http://bookpatrol.net
Founder Michael Lieberman

Founded in 2006 in the US as a blog to promote books and literacy, it is now a hub for all things book-related. Posting about book news, book reviews, technology and related content, the site has its own online shop selling a large collection of curated material.

Books & Such

website www.booksandsuch.com/blog
Founder Janel Kobobel Grant

Blog from a literary agent's perspective, advising on writing query letters and improving MSS before submitting them to agents. Also addresses how to find an agent and get published. Highlights the importance of the editing process in adding to writing quality. Discusses the various aspects of traditional publishing and self-promotion for authors.

Nathan Bransford

website http://blog.nathanbransford.com
Founder Nathan Bransford
From the perspective of an author and former literary agent advising about the writing, editing and publishing process, based on his own experience. Added tips on improving plots, dialogue and characters, writing a query letter and synopsis and finding a literary agent. Analyses and debates a range of topics including ebooks and their pricing, social media options, marketing, cover design and plot themes. Includes a publishing glossary and FAQs.

Cornflower Books

website www.cornflowerbooks.co.uk
Founder Karen Howlett

Reviews a wide range of books and has a monthly online book club, debates cover designs and includes a 'writing and publishing' section. Also includes interviews with well-known authors about their books, writing process and routine. Selects 'books of the year' in different genres, and discusses literary festivals and prizes.

Courage 2 Create

website http://thecourage2create.com
Founder Ollin Morales

Ollin Morales shares the experience of writing his first novel: pitfalls to avoid, dealing with stress, overcoming challenges, how his lifestyle benefits from writing, and inspirational quotes. Blog chapters describe his creative journey and what he has learned about life through the writing process.

The Creative Penn

website www.thecreativepenn.com
Founder Joanna Penn

Focuses on the writing process and how to market and sell your book. Advises writers on dealing with criticism, finding an agent and writing query letters. Debates traditional publishing, 'hybrid' and self-publishing options, and also advises on POD, ebook publishing as well as online and social media marketing. Includes audio/video interviews with mainly self-published authors.

Daily Writing Tips

website www.dailywritingtips.com
Founder Maeve Maddox and others

Publishing new content every day with articles covering the whole writing spectrum: from grammar and punctuation to usage and vocabulary.

Dear Author

website www.dearauthor.com
Founder Jane Litte

Focuses on romantic novels. All reviews are written in the form of a letter to the author. Includes interviews with authors about their writing style.

Fiction Notes

website www.darcypattison.com
Founder Darcy Pattison

Darcy Pattison is a published non-fiction writer and children's author, as well as an experienced speaker. Her blog collates her own articles and thoughts on children's writing, reviews of her work and information on her speaking engagements where she specialises in novel revision and metamorphosis.

Jane Friedman

website http://janefriedman.com
Founder Jane Friedman

Focuses on digital publishing and discusses the future of publishing. Provides tips for writers on how to beat writers' block, DIY ebook publishing, marketing your writing and publicising it online through blogs, social media and websites to create your 'author platform' and publish your book. Includes guidance on copyright and securing permissions.

Goins, Writer

website http://goinswriter.com
Founder Jeff Goins

Focuses on advising authors about their writing journey and how to enhance their writing style. Highlights how authors can build a core fanbase 'tribe' through a focused approach and adding value to social media and blogs.

Goodreads

website www.goodreads.com

Founded in 2006 to help people find and share the books they love. Users can see what their friends and favourite authors are reading, rate books they've read on a scale of one to five stars and write reviews, and customise bookshelves full of books 'Read' and books 'To Read'. Users can receive news on books, poetry, author interviews and more via their regular newsletter. Now owned by Amazon.

Helping Writers Become Authors

website www.helpingwritersbecomeauthors.com
Founder K.M. Weiland

Tips on story structure, creating memorable characters and plot development. Advice about finding writing inspiration and the writing process, as well as addressing the story revision and MS editing stages. Includes an extensive list of books for aspiring authors.

Live Write Thrive

website www.livewritethrive.com
Founder C.S. Lakin

Set up by a writer specialising in fiction, fantasy and YA, this blog focuses on helping writers discover what kind of copy-editing and critiquing services their work will need once it is finished. As a copy-editor and writing coach, Lakin offers her own editorial services and advice on how to choose the right editor. There are also articles by guest bloggers and tips on grammar.

Lovereading

website www.lovereading.co.uk

Independent book recommendation site designed to inspire and inform readers, all with the aim of helping them choose their next read. Features include: categories broken down by interest; downloadable opening extracts of featured books; like-for-like recommendations for discovering new authors; expert reviews and reader review panels. Direct purchase available.

A Newbie's Guide to Publishing

website http://jakonrath.blogspot.co.uk
Founder Joe Konrath

Blog by a self-published author which discusses the writing process and focuses on self-publishing, encourages writers to self-publish ebooks, and looks at developments and trends in this area. Includes interviews with self-published authors about their books and guest posts.

Omnivoracious

website http://www.omnivoracious.com

This blog from Amazon covers an eclectic range of genres. Casting a wide but focused lens over publishing the posts include: reviews and articles; the best books of the month; current news and discussions; tips for writers; awards in writing and interviews with authors.

Positive Writer

website http://positivewriter.com
Founder Bryan Hutchinson

A motivational and inspirational blog for creatives, particularly writers, focusing on how to overcome doubt and negativity and to unlock your inner creativity. It includes handy tips on marketing and interviews with other authors.

Reading Matters

website http://readingmattersblog.com
Founder Kim Forrester

Created in 2004, Reading Matters offers reviews of modern and contemporary fiction on a clean and navigable website. The site's main focus is Irish and Australian literature and reviews are personable and informative. Every Tuesday the site acts as a platform for guest bloggers to share their favourite books and promote their own blogs.

Romance University

website http://romanceuniversity.org
Co-founders Tracey Devlyn, Kelsey Browning, Adrienne Giordano

An online 'university' for all who are hoping to learn the craft of writing romance. Three new blog post lectures are added by contributors and industry professionals weekly. Each Monday, posts focus on the theme of 'crafting your career', which include the business of writing, agents, publishing and self-publishing options, and marketing your work on social media and blogs. Wednesdays focus on 'the anatomy of the mind' in relation to different facets of romance writing and Fridays on the elements of the manuscript writing process, e.g. creating characters and plot.

Lauren Sapala

website http://laurensapala.com
Founder Lauren Sapala

This blog gives pep talks to writers in moments of self-doubt. With posts about how to get inspired and stay focused, its aim is to nurture and empower your creative flame.

Savidge Reads

website https://savidgereads.wordpress.com
Founder Simon Savidge

Follows the reading of Simon Savidge whose writing has featured in several literary and lifestyle magazines. Comprised mainly of books in the literary fiction genre from modern classic to contemporary fiction. His chatty reviews are entertaining and open, and give insight into the mind of a self-proclaimed 'book-a-holic'.

Terribleminds

website http://terribleminds.com/ramble/blog
Founder Chuck Wendig

Comical, easy-to-read blog about author Chuck Wendig's trials and tribulations whilst writing.

There Are No Rules

website www.writersdigest.com/editor-blogs/there-are-no-rules

Blog by the editors of Writer's Digest. Focuses on the writing process, plot and character development, writing query letters and creating your author platform through social media and public speaking. Tips on how to overcome writing challenges, improve your writing and revise your MS so that it is more likely to be accepted by an agent. Includes a range of regular webinars with industry professionals including agents offering advice. Also discusses and advises on the self-publishing process.

This Itch of Writing

website http://emmadarwin.typepad.com/thisitchofwriting
Founder Emma Darwin

An author's advice on the craft of authoring successful books both fiction and creative non-fiction.

Well-Storied

website www.well-storied.com
Founder Kristen Kieffer

Articles, resources and podcasts, offering all the necessary tips and tools to turn your writing dreams into reality.

The Write Life

website http://thewritelife.com
Founder Alexis Grant

This blog, by writers for writers, is designed to encourage individuals to connect and share experiences. There is no single expert, but a running dialogue connecting fellow writers during the stages in their writing. Posts tend to focus on how to become a writer rather than the writing process itself, with advice on blogging, freelancing, finding an agent, promoting and self-publishing amongst other topics.

The Write Practice

website http://thewritepractice.com
Founder Joe Bunting

Focuses on how to get published; includes advice for writers on different stages of the writing process and submitting MSS to agents (e.g. '8 Tips for Naming Characters', 'Your Dream vs. Rejection' and 'Bring Your Setting to Life').

Writer Unboxed

website http://writerunboxed.com
Co-founders Therese Walsh (Editor-in-Chief), Kathleen Bolton

Comical tips on the art and craft of writing fiction, the writing process, and marketing your work. Includes interviews with established authors also offering advice.

Writers & Artists

website www.writersandartists.co.uk

You can join over 40,000 subscribers to receive informed and up-to-date news, views and advice on all aspects of writing and publishing on the site brought to you by the creators of this *Yearbook*. As well as guest blogs, videos and articles from established and debut writers across all genres, there are sections on self-publishing, a community area for sharing work, a calendar of book-related events, including those hosted by Writers & Artists, and much else besides.

Writers Helping Writers

website http://writershelpingwriters.net
Co-founders Angela Ackerman, Becca Puglisi

Writing tools for authors, to help them visualise and create dynamic characters and improve their plot and writing, including a 'Character Pyramid Tool', 'Character Profile Questionnaire' and 'Reverse

Backstory Tool'. Also provides multiple thesauruses such as the 'Character Trait Thesaurus', 'Emotion Thesaurus' and 'Setting Thesaurus' to help authors improve their descriptive writing. Downloadable advice sheets on blogs and social media marketing for authors also available.

PODCASTS

This is a small selection of podcast series that are readily available and published on a regular basis. They seek to inform the listener about the publishing industry and provide guidance to aspiring and established writers on how to improve their writing.

Begin Self-Publishing Podcast

website https://beginselfpublishing.com
Host Tim Lewis

Aims to promote self-publishing by demystifying the whole process and gives advice on how to safely navigate all services available to self-published writers.

Books and Authors

website www.bbc.co.uk/programmes/p02nrsfl/episodes/downloads
Hosts Mariella Frostrup, Harriett Gilbert
Provider BBC Radio 4

A weekly podcast with highlights from BBC Radio 4 programmes *Open Book*: Mariella Frostrup interviews publishers and bestselling authors about their work; and *A Good Read*, in which Harriett Gilbert hosts a lively discussion with her guests about their favourite books.

The Creative Penn Podcast

website www.thecreativepenn.com/podcasts
Host Joanna Penn

Published on Mondays, this weekly podcast informs aspiring authors about available publishing options and book marketing through useful information and interviews.

Creative Writing Career

website http://creativewritingcareer.com
Hosts Stephan Bugaj, Justin Sloan, Kevin Tumlinson

Hosted by leading industry professionals whose credits include writing for Pixar, FOX and HBO, this US podcast provides practical advice to writers on all forms of multimedia writing. Topics covered include books and comics, video games and e-publishing, and writing screenplays for television and film.

Dead Robots' Society

website http://deadrobotssociety.com
Hosts Justin Macumber, Terry Mixon, Paul E. Cooley

Created *for* aspiring writers *by* aspiring writers, this fun podcast offers advice and support by sharing anecdotes and discussing current topics of interest.

The Drunken Odyssey

website https://thedrunkenodyssey.com
Host John King

Started to create a community hub for writers, this podcast is a forum to discuss all aspects of creative writing and literature.

Grammar Girl Quick and Dirty Tips for Better Writing

website www.quickanddirtytips.com/grammar-girl
Host Mignon Fogarty
Provider QuickandDirtyTips

This award winning weekly podcast provides a bitesize guide to the English language. Each week tackles a specific feature from style and usage, to grammar and punctuation, all in the hope of providing friendly tips on how to become a better writer.

The *Guardian* Books Podcast

website www.theguardian.com/books/series/books
Hosts Claire Armitstead, Richard Lea, Sian Cain
Provider theguardian.com

The *Guardian*'s book editor, Claire Armitstead, provides a weekly podcast that looks at the world of books, poetry and great writing, including interviews with prominent authors; recordings of *Guardian* live events; panel discussions examining current themes in contemporary writing; and readings of selected literary works.

Helping Writers Become Authors

website www.helpingwritersbecomeauthors.com/podcasts
Host K.M. Weiland

As a published author, K.M. Weiland produces these podcasts on a weekly basis to help guide aspiring authors on how to craft and edit a manuscript ready to be sent to a literary agent.

I Should Be Writing

website http://murverse.com/subscribe-to-podcasts/
Host Mur Lafferty

This award-winning podcast is about the process science fiction writer Mur Lafferty went through to go from a wannabe writer to a professional and published author. It documents the highs and lows of a writing career and provides comprehensive how-to tips and interviews.

The *New Yorker* : Fiction

website www.newyorker.com/podcast/fiction
Host Deborah Treisman
Provider WNYC Studios and The *New Yorker*

Published monthly. *New Yorker* fiction editor, Deborah Treisman, invites an author whose work is being published by the magazine that month to join her in the podcast. Each author selects a piece of short fiction from the magazine's archive to read and analyse.

The Penguin Podcast

website www.penguin.co.uk/articles/in-conversation/podcasts/penguin-podcast
Provider Penguin Books UK

This series, published fortnightly, gives intimate access to bestselling authors through interviews where they discuss their work and give examples of five things that have inspired and shaped their writing.

Reading and Writing Podcast

website http://readingandwritingpodcast.com
Host Jeff Rutherford

This interview-style podcast encourages readers to call in and leave voicemail messages and questions ready for the host to ask the guest writer, who discusses their work and writing practices.

The Self-Publishing Podcast

website https://sterlingandstone.net/series/self-publishing-podcast
Hosts Johnny B. Truant, Sean Platt, David Wright
Provider Sterling & Stone

As the hosts of this podcast proclaim, self-publishing is a new publishing frontier. The trio explore how a writer can become truely 'authorpreneurial', getting their books published and making money without resorting to agents and traditional publishing models.

Story Grid

website https://storygrid.simplecast.fm
Hosts Shawn Coyne, Tim Grahl

Hosted by a book editor with more than 25 years' experience in publishing and a struggling writer, the duo discuss what features bestselling novels have in common and how authors can utilise these to write a great story that works.

Write Now With Sarah Werner

website www.sarahwerner.com/episodes
Host Sarah Werner

A weekly podcast produced specifically with aspiring writers in mind. Sarah Werner provides advice, inspiration, and encouragement to writers to find a suitable work-life balance that will enable them to take their hobby to the next level.

The Writer Files

website https://rainmaker.fm/series/writer
Host Kelton Reid

This long-running podcast explores productivity and creativity, seeing how accomplished writers tackle writer's block and keep the ink flowing and cursor moving.

WRITER 2.0: Writing, Publishing, and the Space Between

website http://acfuller.com/writer-2-0-podcast/episodes
Host A.C. Fuller

This podcast tackles both traditional and self-publishing. It includes interviews with bestselling authors from every genre, as well as leading industry professionals such as agents, book marketers and journalists to give a broad update on the publishing industry.

The Writership Podcast

website https://writership.com/episodes
Hosts Leslie Watts, Clark Chamberlain (a member of the Author Marketing Institute's podcasting network)

This podcast provides help, support and advice to fiction writers on how they can develop the appropriate skills to self-edit their completed manuscript.

Writing Excuses

website www.writingexcuses.com
Hosts Maurice Broaddus, Valynne E. Maetani, Amel El-Mohtar, Mary Robinette Kowal, Brandon Sanderson, Howard Tayler, Dan Wells

This weekly educational podcast is in its 12th season. Written by writers for writers, it offers sensible and strategic advice to all who write, whether for pleasure or for profit, on how they can revise and edit their work to create a better story. Each week there is a homework assignment and suggested reading that complements the theme of each podcast.

Editorial services and self-publishing providers

This is a selection of the rapidly expanding list of companies that offer editorial, production, marketing and distribution support predominantly for authors who want to self-publish. As with all the organisations mentioned in the *Yearbook*, we recommend that you check carefully what companies offer and precisely what they would charge.

@YouCaxton

23 High Street, Bishops Castle, Shropshire SY9 5BE
tel (Shropshire) (01588) 638728
tel (Oxford) (01865) 693429
email newbooks@youcaxton.co.uk
website www.youcaxton.co.uk
Facebook www.facebook.com/pages/YouCaxton-Publishing/133150206770479
Twitter @YouCaxton
Partners Robert Fowke, Robert Branton and Steven Edwards

Specialises in high-quality memoir and general non-fiction, selected fiction and high-end, full-colour productions and art books. Offers support for self-publishers: structural editing; copy-editing; proofreading, cover design and interior layout; print and ebook production and distribution. Authors are able to follow progress of their project via an online reporting system. Additional services include: a range of marketing tools for self-publishing author websites and web pages; a book packaging and design service for publishers; a publication project management service for academic and corporate clients; and a high-quality fine-art printing service for photographers and artists. Founded 1986 as Lazy Summer Books Ltd of Oxford.

Albury Books

Albury Court, Albury, Thame, Oxon OX9 2LP
tel (01844) 337000
email hannah@alburybooks.com
website www.alburybooks.com
Twitter @AlburyBooks

Collaborates with writers and illustrators to republish and/or self-publish their work through the Albury BookShelf platform. Provides print-on-demand and/or short print runs and co-edition deals to small publishers and individuals. Rights management also available. Clients may publish under their own imprint, or an Albury-managed imprint. Each book published is listed for sale in the Albury online store and made available to major booksellers. Founded 2013.

Amolibros

Loundshay Manor Cottage, Preston Bowyer, Milverton, Somerset TA4 1QF
tel (01823) 401527
email amolibros@aol.com
website www.amolibros.com
Director Jane Tatam

Offers print and ebook design, production, copy-editing and distribution through online retailers. Sales and marketing services include design and production of adverts, leaflets, author websites, distribution of press releases and direct mail campaigns.

arima publishing

ASK House, Northgate Avenue, Bury St Edmunds, Suffolk IP32 6BB
tel (01284) 700321
email info@arimapublishing.com
website www.arimapublishing.co.uk

Offers print-on-demand options in hardback and paperback formats. Distributes print books through wholesalers, and to online retailers. Proofreading and image scanning also available; prices on application. Also provides a typing service for handwritten manuscripts. Authors receive a royalty rate of 30% of full cover price for direct sales from the arima online bookshop, and 20% for general sales.

Arkbound

Backfields House, Upper York Street, Bristol BS2 8QJ
tel 0871 268 2929
email editorial@arkbound.com
website http://arkbound.com

Social enterprise supported by the Prince's Trust: can offer fully sponsored publishing to talented writers from disadvantaged backgrounds, but also provides a range of services and packages to authors who can afford to self-publish. Editorial services include copy-editing and proofreading; enhanced book promotion and mentoring also available. Arkbound is founder of the Zooker literary award and runs an annual writing competition. Founded 2015.

Author Design Studio

email contact@authordesignstudio.com
website www.authordesignstudio.com
Twitter @authordesigner
Contact Aimee Coveney

Creative design and digital marketing consultancy specialising in author services including award-winning book and ebook design, website design, book trailers, social media training and more.

Author House UK

1663 Liberty Drive, Bloomington, IN 47403, USA
tel 0800 197 4150
website www.authorhouse.co.uk
Facebook www.facebook.com/AuthorHouseUK
Twitter @AuthorHouse

Offers editorial services, interior and cover design, illustration, marketing and publicity advice and distribution for hardcover and paperback print-on-demand books, as well as ebook conversion and distribution services. Colour and b&w publishing packages start at £799, speciality packages at £1,499 and ebook-only packages at £499.

Authoright

53–59 Chandos Place, London WC2N 4HS
tel 020-7993 8225
email info@authoright.com
website www.authoright.com
Twitter @Authoright
Ceo & Co-founder Gareth Howard, *Coo & Co-founder* Hayley Radford

Marketing and publicity firm for new and unpublished writers, based in London and New York. Offers a range of services to traditionally published and self-published authors, including structural editing, copy-editing and proofreading, cover design, website design, press releases, blog tours and marketing and publicity campaigns in the UK and US. Case studies and testimonials available on request.

Azimuth Print Ltd

Unit 2A, Princess Street, Bedminster, Bristol BS3 4AG
tel (0117) 332 0055
email sales@azimuthprint.co.uk
website www.azimuthprint.co.uk
Contact Mike Edmonds

Produces wirebound, perfect-bound and hardback books in a variety of sizes, in colour or b&w. Authors can send their own artwork, use the artwork templates supplied by Azimuth Print or commission their own designers. Also prints promotional materials including leaflets and posters. Founded 1989.

Blue Ocean Publishing

tel (01763) 208887
email blueoceanpublishing@btconnect.com
website www.blueoceanpublishing.biz

Professional, personal self-publishing of books, ebooks, brochures, CDs, DVDs and games for individuals and organisations. Complete design and editorial services are available, as are advice on MSS and assistance with marketing, writing and distribution. Founded 2007.

Blurb

website www.blurb.co.uk
Twitter @BlurbBooks
Founder and Executive Chairman Eileen Gittins, *Ceo* Rix Kramlich

Self-publishing platform and creative community that enables individuals to design, publish, share, sell, and distribute photo books, trade books and magazines in both print and digital formats. Publications can be sold online through the Blurb bookshop and the iBooks Store. Photobooks and trade books, novels or poetry can be printed in hardcover or softcover and in a variety of sizes. Prices are based on extent; for details see www.blurb.co.uk/pricing-calculator.

Book Create Service Ltd

22 Coleman Ave, Teignmouth, Devon TQ14 9DU
tel (01626) 870999
email enquiries@bookcreateservice.com
website www.bookcreateservice.com
Facebook www.facebook.com/bookcreateservice
Twitter @BookCreateS

Book layout and cover design services for new and experienced authors, as well ebook conversion. Price information available on the website or via a telephone call.

Bookollective

email hello@bookollective.com
website www.bookollective.com
Facebook www.facebook.com/bookollective
Twitter @bookollective
Contacts Esther Harris (editorial), Aimee Coveney (design), Helen McCusker (publicity)

One-stop agency for authors, publishers and industry professionals. A collaboration of experienced service providers, Bookollective offers a range of bespoke packages, including editing, design, digital marketing, blog tours and publicity. Fiction and non-fiction covered. Named as one of the *The Bookseller*'s Rising Stars list, 2017.

BookPrinting UK

Remus House, Coltsfoot Drive, Woodston, Peterborough PE2 9BF
tel (01733) 898102
email info@bookprintinguk.com
website www.bookprintinguk.com
Twitter @BookPrintingUK
Contact Naz Stewart

Offers colour and b&w printing and print-on-demand books in a range of bindings. Can provide custom illustration and interior layout options, as well as typesetting. Supplies templates for formatting manuscript files before sending. Can also distribute print books direct to customers. Prints bookmarks, posters and flyers.

Daniel Burton Editing

tel 07519 707490
email daniel@dburtonediting.com
website www.dburtonediting.com
Facebook www.facebook.com/D. Burton Editing
Twitter @dburton_editing
Contact Daniel Burton

Offers copy-editing and proofreading services, as well as providing engaging content for blogs, newsletters, websites and social media. A range of PR services also available. Works with authors across a variety of genres, including children's fiction and crime thriller. Founded 2014.

Cameron Publicity and Marketing Ltd

180 Piccadilly, London W1J 9HF
tel 020-7917 9812
email info@cameronpm.co.uk
website www.cameronpm.co.uk
Facebook www.facebook.com/CameronPublicity
Twitter @CameronPMtweets
Director Ben Cameron

Publicity and marketing campaigns for publishers and independent authors including media awareness, websites and social media. Founded 2006.

The Choir Press

132 Bristol Road, Gloucester GL1 5SR
tel (01452) 500016
email enquiries@thechoirpress.co.uk
website www.selfpublishingbooks.co.uk
Contact Miles Bailey

Self publishing company offering short- and long-run printing and print-on-demand options in a variety of sizes and bindings, as well as ebook conversion and distribution. Preferred formats for printed editions are illustrated non-fiction. Offers custom cover design or can incorporate author-supplied images. Copy-editing, structural editing and proofreading services also available. Founded 1982.

Clink Street Publishing

53–59 Chandos Place, London WC2N 4HS
tel 020-7993 8225
email info@clinkstreetpublishing.com
website www.bookpublishing.co.uk

Boutique self-publishing imprint from Authoright, with an experienced team of editors, project managers, designers and publicists publishing and promoting writers across all genres. Also has links with literary scouts with a view to securing foreign translation rights. Case studies and testimonials available on request.

CompletelyNovel

website http://completelynovel.com
Twitter @completelynovel

Provides online publishing tools for authors to upload their manuscripts to create and distribute print-on-demand books and ebooks. A number of sales and distribution options are available. Website also offers a cover-creator option, as well as self-publishing advice on topics including editing, cover design and social media marketing.

Dissect Designs

email timbarberart@gmail.com
website www.dissectdesigns.com
Twitter @dissectdesigns

Bespoke book cover designs for ebooks and print editions at affordable prices. Non-fiction and fiction. 50% deposit payable via PayPal required.

eBook Versions

27 Old Gloucester Street, London WC1N 3AX
website www.ebookversions.com

Offers ebook and paperback self-publishing and distribution through online retailers and trade wholesalers including Amazon Kindle Direct Publishing, Apple iBookstores, Kobo Books, Gardners Books and more than 300 independent high street booksellers. Fees begin at £95 for ebook conversion of a manuscript of up to 100,000 words. Print-on-demand paperback pre-press production is available from £295. OCR scanning of hardbacks, paperbacks and typescripts is also offered.

eBookPartnership.com

PO Box 2173, Seaford, BN25 9EL
tel 0845 123 2699
email helpdesk@ebookpartnership.com
website www.ebookpartnership.com
Twitter @ebookpartners

Ebook conversion and distribution services. Conversion to standard and fixed layout ebook files. Complex conversion specialists. Worldwide distribution and management of ebook files for authors, publishers, businesses and non-profit organisations. Extensive network of retailers, libraries and subscription services. Set-up fee; clients retain 100% of royalties. Client admin system, no fees for changes to listings. Founded 2010.

Frank Fahy Publishing Services

5 Barna Village Centre, Barna, Galway, Republic of Ireland
tel +353 (0)86 2269330
email frank.fahy0@gmail.com
website www.frank-fahy.com

Specialises in preparing manuscripts for book production, either as printed books or digital ebooks. This can include, as required, copy-editing and/or proofreading, or preparing presentations for submission to publishers. Estimates are free of charge and authors' individual requirements discussed. Publishing projects of all kinds considered, from individuals, institutions or businesses. Founded 2007.

FictionAtelier

email fictionatelier@gmail.com
website fictionatelier.wordpress.com
Contacts Lucy Ellmann, Todd McEwen

Two published novelists give independent, experienced, one-to-one, anti-workshop editorial help to serious writers of fiction. Editing and line editing £75 per hour. Flat rates available for reading and a detailed response.

Firsty Group

4 The Courtyard, London Road, Newbury, Berks. RG14 1AX
tel (01635) 581185
email info@firstygroup.com
website http://firstygroup.com
Twitter @firstygroup

Provides web development and e-commerce solutions for the publishing industry, from bespoke projects to bolt-on software as a service. Enables publishers to sell print, ebooks and audiobooks (with or without DRM) directly to customers through open-source content management systems, API links to distribution partners and a thorough understanding of metadata. Also provides direct-to-customer publisher support and assistance within customer service, financial accounting and marketing.

Grammar Factory

c/o Morgan James Publishing, Level 32, 367 Collins St, Melbourne 3000, Australia
tel +61 423 441 701
email info@grammarfactory.com
website https://grammarfactory.com
Founder Jacqui Pretty

Self-publishing company offering ghostwriting, editing and publishing services for speakers, business leaders and entrepreneurs. Over the past four years the team has worked with over 150 authors across the fields of leadership and motivation, business, finance, personal development and health and wellness.

Grosvenor House Publishing

Link House, 140 The Broadway, Tolworth, Surrey KT6 7HT
tel 020-8339 6060
website www.grosvenorhousepublishing.co.uk
Co-founders Kim Cross, Jason Kosbab

Publishes across a range of genres including children's and non-fiction in colour, b&w, print-on-demand, paperback, hardback and ebook formats. Offers a £795 publishing package which includes typesetting and five free print copies as well as an ISBN, and print and ebook distribution via online retailers. Authors can design covers online. Marketing services include producing posters and postcards, and website set-up from template with two years' hosting. Ebook publishing costs £195 if the print edition of the book has been produced by the company and £495 otherwise. Print costs and royalties depend on book specification. A proofreading service is offered at a rate of £5 per 1,000 words. See website for full list of costs.

I AM Self-Publishing

82 Southwark Bridge Road, London SE1 0AS
tel 020-3488 0565
email hello@iamselfpublishing.com
website www.iamselfpublishing.com
Facebook www.facebook.com/iamselfpub
Twitter @iamselfpub

Professional publishing services include: design; typesetting; editing; proofreading; print-on-demand and short-run printing; ebook conversion; author branding, marketing; and backlist republication. Assistance available for authors at all stages of the process. No royalty taken: authors retain 100% of earnings. Packages start from £450.

iBooks Author

website www.apple.com/uk/ibooks-author

App that allows authors to create interactive e-textbooks and other types of ebooks, such as photo books, travel, or craft/cookery books for iPad. Features include video and audio, interactive diagrams, photos and 3D images. They can then be sold through the iBooks Store. Authors may choose fonts and template page layouts or design their own. Charts, tables, text, images and interactive features can also be added.

Jelly Bean Self-Publishing

Candy Jar Ltd, Mackintosh House, 136 Newport Road, Cardiff, CF24 1DJ
tel 029-211 57202
email submissions@jellybeanselfpublishing.co.uk
website www.jellybeanselfpublishing.com
Twitter @Jelly_BeanUK
Director Shaun Russell

Self-publishing imprint of Candy Jar Books. Offers a bespoke service for new and experienced authors at all stages of the process, including but not limited to editing and typesetting, illustration, cover design, website design and other marketing services. Submissions are welcomed, and face-to-face meetings are available on request. Founded 2012.

Kindle Direct Publishing

website https://kdp.amazon.com
Facebook www.facebook.com/KindleDirectPublishing
Twitter @AmazonKDP

Ebook self-publishing and distribution platform for Kindle and Kindle Apps. Its business model offers up to a 70% royalty (on certain retail prices between $2.99–$9.99) in many countries and availability in Amazon stores worldwide. Print-on-demand options are also available. Note that KDP Select makes books exclusive to Amazon (which means they cannot be sold through an author's personal website, for example), but authors can share in the Global Fund amount every time the book is borrowed from the Kindle Owners' Lending Library.

Kobo Writing Life

website www.kobo.com/writinglife
Facebook www.facebook.com/KoboWritingLife
Twitter @KoboWritingLife

Ebook self-publishing platform where authors can upload manuscripts and cover images. These files are then converted into ebooks before being distributed through the Kobo ebookstore. Authors are able to set pricing and DRM territories, as well as track sales. Royalty rates vary depending on price or territory; enquire directly. Free to join.

Lavender and White Publishing

Snipe Lodge, Moycullen, County Galway, Republic of Ireland
email info@lavenderandwhite.co.uk
website www.lavenderandwhite.co.uk
Facebook www.facebook.com/Lavender-and-White-Publishing-201996279902790/
Twitter @LavenderandW
Editorial Director Jacqueline Broderick, *Editor* Sarah Lewis

Offers a range of services for self-publishing authors, including: editing; proofreading; cover design; typesetting; ebook conversion; print-on-demand; marketing and sell-through services; mentoring; and ghostwriting. Costs vary depending on services required; email for a quote. Easy payment options available.

Lulu

website www.lulu.com/gb
Facebook www.facebook.com/Luludotcom
Twitter @Luludotcom

Self-publishing platform and distributor for ebooks and print-on-demand books through online retailers including Amazon and iBooks. Authors can upload a file and design their own cover for free. Optional paid-for services include cover design, editorial, publicity services and associated materials. See website for full breakdown of costs and royalty information.

Manuscripts & Mentoring

25 Corinne Road, London N19 5EZ
tel 020-7700 4472
email manuscriptmentoring@gmail.com
website www.genevievefox.com
Twitter @genevievefox21
Contact Genevieve Fox

Helps both fledgling and experienced writers of fiction, non-fiction and YA fiction get from first draft to finished manuscript. Primary services: editing; manuscript overviews; advice on structure, plot, themes and characterisation; and submission to agents. Also available: mentoring; writing plans; and coaching for interviews and promotional talks. Published author, journalist and creative writing tutor.

Margie's Mark

email margie@margiesmark.com
website http://margiesmark.com
Twitter @MargieMark
Contact Margie Markevicius

Supplies graphic design services, including logo design, and can apply designs to social media accounts. Also offers: book cover design and formatting for print and print-on-demand; design of ebook ePub files; website design and maintenance; content updates. US-based.

Matador

Troubador Publishing Ltd, 9 Priory Business Park, Wistow Road, Kibworth Beauchamp, Leicester LE8 0RX
tel 0116 279 2299
email matador@troubador.co.uk
website www.troubador.co.uk/matador
Facebook www.facebook.com/matadorbooks
Twitter @matadorbooks
Managing Director Jeremy Thompson, *Operations Director* Jane Rowland

The self-publishing imprint of Troubador Publishing. Offers print-on-demand, short-run digital- and litho-printed books and ebook production, with distribution through high-street bookshops and online retailers, plus worldwide ebook distribution. Author services include all book and ebook production, trade and retail marketing, plus bookshop distribution via Orca Book Services and Sales Representation by Star Book Sales. Founded 1999.

Mereo Books

1A The Wool Market, Dyer Street, Cirencester, Gloucestershire GL7 2PR
tel (01285) 640485
email info@mereobooks.co.uk
website www.mereobooks.com
Twitter @MereoBooks
Director Toni Tingle, *Editor-in-Chief* Chris Newton

Specialises in editing, typesetting, and cover design of both fiction and non-fiction books. Publishes in hardback, paperback and ebook formats. Also offers ghostwriting services. Allocates ISBNs and distributes to online retailers including Amazon and Barnes & Noble, as ebooks or print-on-demand and from stock through Orca Book Services trade distribution. Books sold through the Mereo website as well as via trade sales representation with Harbour Publishing Services and trade distribution by Orca Book Services, and listed with wholesalers. Costs dependent on specification. Mereo is actively looking for authors for its new romantic fiction imprint, Romaunce (www.romaunce.com). Part of Memoirs Publishing.

MJV Literary Author Services

71–75 Shelton Street, London WC2H 9JQ
email authors@mjvliterary.com
website www.mjvliterary.com
Contact Matt McAvoy

Offers copy-editing and promotion services for book authors of all genres, including fiction, non-fiction and children's books. Services include translation into English, proofreading, complete copy-editing, formatting for e-book creation and print-ready typesetting for paperback. Senior Editor Matt McAvoy also carries out book review and beta-reading services, and is a member of the Society for Editors and Proofreaders. Editing services start from £3.50 per 1,000 words; promotion services include Twitter campaigns, reviewer submissions and interview requests. Clients include self-published and traditionally published authors, as well as publishers.

Molten Publishing Ltd

14 Clachar Close, Chelmsford, Essex, CM2 6RX
tel 07861 211740
email molly@moltenpublishing.co.uk
website www.moltenpublishing.co.uk
Facebook www.facebook.com/moltenpublishing
Twitter @MoltenPublish
Directors Molly Terry, Nick Looby

Hybrid publisher of young adult fiction and non-fiction business books by new or established authors. Editing services also available. Founded 2015.

M-Y Books Ltd

187 Ware Road Hertford Herts. SG13 7EQ
tel (01992) 586279
email jonathan@m-ybooks.co.uk
website www.m-ybooks.co.uk
Facebook www.facebook.com/MYBookspublishingandmarketing
Twitter @jonathanbooks
Editorial Director Jonathan Miller

Self-publishing service provider for authors at all stages of their careers. Offers a concierge-style service aimed at authors who are either new to self-publishing or who require a bespoke package. Author visits welcome. Online marketing also available. Audio book production specialists. Clients include international bestselling authors. Founded 2002.

New Generation Publishing

107–111 Fleet Street, London EC4A 2AB
tel 020-7936 9941 (production queries)
tel (01234) 711956 (publishing enquiries)
email info@newgeneration-publishing.com
website www.newgeneration-publishing.com
Facebook www.facebook.com/NewGenerationPublishing
Twitter @NGPublishing

Provides publication in paperback, hardback and ebook with global distribution. Publishing packages range from Standard Paperback to the Bestseller options; bespoke packages are also available. Services include layout, cover design, ISBN allocation, editing, proofreading, bookselling, bookstore placement, website design and manuscript critique. Distribution provided via online retailers, high-street shops, libraries and wholesalers. Promotional materials available including distributed press releases and social media. Free marketing and promotional support service also offered. Offices in London and Buckinghamshire; author visits welcome. Free guide to publishing available on request.

Noveleditingservices

PO Box 95, Liverpool L17 8WY
tel 07801 055556
email susan@storieswanted.com
website www.storieswanted.com
Contact Susan Wallace

High-level, thorough edits from experienced journalist for emerging and established authors. Prices: £25 per 4–5, double-spaced pages; fixed fee/deadline to be agreed for full manuscript following a test read. Confidentiality assured.

Oodlebooks Ltd

Shortwall Court, Pontefract WF8 4SZ
email info@oodlebooks.com
website www.oodlebooks.com
Managing Director Gail Powell

Online book marketing platform for self-published authors. Aims to help authors to connect with their readers and grow their fan-base. Offers advice and support to authors on the best marketing techniques specific to their needs, including the use of social media. If an author's book is accepted, a one-off joining fee as well as a small monthly subscription fee are payable. See website for details.

Paragon Publishing

4 North Street, Rothersthorpe, Northants NN7 3JB
tel (01604) 832149
email intoprint@live.com
website www.intoprint.net
Proprietor Mark Webb

Packagers of non-fiction and fiction books for independent authors and small publishers, working regularly with schools, colleges, associations and writers' groups. Provides a range of editorial, design and typesetting services to create PDFs in black and white or colour, as well as print-on-demand options. Also publishes Kindle and ePub editions, as are multilingual editions. Experienced at working with new writers to help them to publish, providing ISBN, marketing consultancy and distribution to booksellers worldwide. Ghostwriting and illustration services also available. Founded 1992.

Pomegranate PA

Clavering House, Clavering Place,
Newcastle upon Tyne NE1 3NG
tel 07443 490752
email karen@pomegranatepa.co.uk
website www.pomegranatepa.co.uk
Twitter @pomegranatepa
Freelance Proofreader Karen Stubbs

Proofreading and editorial service. All subjects considered. Founded 2013.

Prepare to Publish Ltd

Blackbirds Studio, Bayliss Yard, Charlbury OX7 3RS
(01865) 922923
email mail@preparetopublish.com
website www.preparetopublish.com
Editor Andrew Chapman

Editorial and typesetting agency for book and magazine production. A team of more than a dozen experienced freelancers provides development-editing, copy-editing and proofreading services (fiction and non-fiction, but not poetry or children's books), plus typesetting. Clients typically include: publishers looking to outsource the editorial process; businesses planning publications; and authors who have completed a first draft.

Publishing Services

9 Curwen Road, London W12 9AF
tel 07984 585861
email susanne@susannelumsden.co.uk
website www.susannelumsden.co.uk
Twitter @SusanneLumsden
Contact Susanne Lumsden

Former non-fiction director of Faber & Faber offers mentoring and full book publishing services for quality non-fiction titles, including trade sales and distribution (via Central Books). Suited to those who wish to publish traditional printed books (with POD/ebooks as add-ons) that meet mainstream publishing standards.

Offers initial publishing appraisal covering goals, resources and publishing requirements: format/s, pricing, level of editorial work, production spec, sales & marketing, and timing.

Rigorous editing is a speciality. The first stages (structural and line editing) are conducted personally, before experienced freelancers are commissioned for copy-editing, proofreading and proof-correction collation. Also provides access to a curated network of tested external service providers in design, typesetting, printing, ebook conversion and publicity.

PublishNation

Suite 544, Kemp House, 152 City Road,
London EC1V 2NX
email david@publishnation.co.uk
website www.publishnation.co.uk
Publisher David Morrison

Offers print-on-demand paperback and Kindle format ebooks, available through Amazon. Publication in both print and digital formats costs £250 or £150 for Kindle format. Images may be included from £2.95 each. A range of book sizes is available, as are free template book covers. Enhanced cover design costs £40. Marketing services include creation of a press release, social media accounts and author website. Standard proofreading is £7 per 1,000 words, while an 'express' option from £125 focuses on the beginning of the manuscript. Editorial critique reports range in price from £99 for manuscripts of up to 15,000 words to £219 for manuscripts of up to 120,000 words.

Reedsy

email service@reedsy.com
website https://reedsy.com
Twitter @ReedsyHQ
Founders Emmanuel Nataf, Matt Cobb, Ricardo Fayet, Vincent Durand

Online marketplace that helps authors and publishers connect with editors, designers and marketers. Reedsy also offers free publishing courses via its Learning platform, available from: https://reedsy.com/learning. Founded 2014.

The Right Book Company

c/o SRA Books, Unit 53, Spike Island,
133 Cumberland Road, Bristol BS8 4TY
tel 01789 761345
email waayb@therightbookcompany.com
website http://therightbookcompany.com
Twitter @therightbookco
Managing Director Sue Richardson

Publishing and book marketing consultancy and services for businesses, small publishers and non-fiction authors. Also offers book trade distribution services to qualifying self-published authors and other small independent imprints.

Rowanvale Books Ltd

The Gate, Keppoch Street, Roath, Cardiff CF24 3JW
email info@rowanvalebooks.com
website www.rowanvalebooks.com
Twitter @RowanvaleBooks
Managing Director Cat Charlton

Provider of publishing services such as proofreading and copy-editing, cover design and illustration, ebook conversion, paperback printing and marketing. Distribution to over 40,000 online and print retailers and libraries worldwide. Founded 2012.

Scotforth Books

Carnegie House, Chatsworth Road,
Lancaster LA1 4SL
tel (01524) 840111
email info@scotforthbooks.com
website www.scotforthbooks.com
Twitter @ScotforthBooks

Specialises in the complete design and production of books of all kinds, from manuscript to finished printed copies. This can include, as required, editing/proofreading, processing and placement of pictures, page layout, covers and jacket design, printing and binding of any number of copies, sales and marketing advice and leaflet/poster design etc. Estimates are free of charge and author visits and phone calls to discuss requirements are welcomed. Founded 1984.

Selfpublishbooks.ie

Springhill House, Carrigtwohill,
Co. Cork T45 NX81, Republic of Ireland
tel + 353 (0)2 14883370
email info@selfpublishbooks.ie
website www.selfpublishbooks.ie
Facebook www.facebook.com/selfpublishbooks
Twitter @printbooks

Services include digital printing and binding options, including perfect binding and saddle stitching. Offers custom cover design or can include author-supplied images and artwork. Also offers editing, proofreading and formatting services. Can design promotional materials including posters and bookmarks and allocate ISBNs. Printing prices start from 100 copies but fewer can be printed on request.

The Self-Publishing Partnership

7 Green Park Station, Green Park Road,
Bath BA1 1JB
tel (01225) 478444
email enquiries@selfpublishingpartnership.co.uk
website www.selfpublishingpartnership.co.uk
Twitter @SelfPublishBath
Contacts Douglas Walker, Garry Manning

Providers of full self-publishing services with personal guidance and support. Services include: proofreading/copy-editing; page design and typesetting; cover design (bespoke or standard): ebooks; ISBNs, trade & legal cataloguing; and trade-order fulfilment (invoicing & distribution).

SilverWood Books

14 Small Street, Bristol BS1 1DE
tel 0117 910 5829
email info@silverwoodbooks.co.uk
website www.silverwoodbooks.co.uk
Twitter @SilverWoodBooks
Publishing Director Helen Hart

Offers bespoke author services tailored to individual projects, as well as three comprehensive publishing packages, with prices dependent on specification. Services include professional cover and page design, typesetting, ebook hand-formatting and conversion, b&w and colour print-on-demand, short-run and lithographic printing, one-to-one support and coaching. Distributes to bookshops via wholesalers and to online retailers including Amazon. Also provides the Amazon Look Inside feature, and lists books in its own SilverWood online bookstore. UK wholesale distribution via Central Books. Nielsen Enhanced Data Listing. Marketing services include author websites, social media set-up, online book trailer campaign and blog tours. Editorial services include an initial assessment and manuscript appraisal. VAT at the standard rate added to services but not print. See www.silverwoodbooks.co.uk/packages for guidance on prices and packages.

Smart Quill Editorial

email info@smartquilleditorial.co.uk
website http://smartquilleditorial.co.uk
Facebook www.facebook.com/pages/Smart-Quill-Editorial/185221901518383
Twitter @SmartQuill
Literary Consultant and Book-to-Film Scout Philippa Donovan

Offers structural edits and line edits, with prices from £600. An agent submission report, priced at £600, analyses covering letter, synopsis and first three chapters. Agent-recommendation service, film/tv producer introduction and book-to-film adaptation expertise. Fiction (all genres), narrative non-fiction, YA, middle grade and picture books. Named as a Publishing Rising Star 2014 by *The Bookseller* magazine and Unsung Publishing Hero 2016.

Spiderwize

Remus House, Coltsfoot Drive, Woodston,
Peterborough, PE2 9BF
tel (01733) 898103
email info@spiderwize.com
website www.spiderwize.com
Facebook www.facebook.com/pages/Spiderwize-Publishing/124594357569927
Twitter @S_piderwize

Offers print-on-demand self-publishing packages for several genres including fiction, autobiography and poetry. See website for full information.

Stairwell Books

161 Lowther Street, York YO31 7LZ
tel 01904 733767
email rose@stairwellbooks.com
website www.stairwellbooks.co.uk
Facebook www.facebook.com/pages/Stairwell-Books/108430809178357
Owner and Operations Alan Gillott, *Owner, Editor and Marketing* Rose Drew

Publisher of novels, memoirs, anthologies and collections focussed mainly, but not exclusively, on York and Yorkshire writers. Publishers of *Dream Catcher* international literary journal. Services include preparation and design of books, managing new book launches, event management, proofreading, content advice, fact-checking with particular reference to physical anthropology, archaeology and history, as well as a range of author services and writing projects. Founded 2002.

Tantamount

Coventry University Technology Park, Puma Way, Coventry CV1 2TT
tel 024 7722 0299
email hello@tantamount.com
website www.tantamount.com, www.authorbranding.co.uk
Twitter @TantamountBooks

Specialists in enhanced digital publications and author branding. Offer a wide range of editorial, design and publishing services to individual authors and publishing houses. Integrated online presence and self-publishing service allows writers to deal with a single supplier for all digital, design and publishing requirements, and to achieve a unified and coherent personal brand image for their work. Founded 2002.

Michael Terence Publishing

Two Brewers House, 2A Wellington Street, Thame OX9 3BN
tel (0203) 582 2002
email admin@mtp.agency
website www.mtp.agency
Founders Karolina Robinson, Keith Abbott

Publishes across a range of genres – fiction (including biography, true stories, crime, science fiction, historical) and non-fiction. Special consideration given to new and little-published authors. Open for submissions from authors worldwide at www.mtp.agency/submissions. See website for full details. Founded 2016.

JM Thurley Management

Archery House, 33 Archery Square, Walmer, Deal, Kent CT14 7JA
tel (01304) 371721
email thurleyjon@gmail.com
website www.thecuttingedge.biz
Contact Jon Thurley

Provides rewriting and advice services to writers of full-length adult fiction and non-fiction; see website for full details and pricing. Also continues to act as a literary agent dealing with fiction, non-fiction, film, television, theatre. Founded 1976.

TJ INK

Trecerus Industrial Estate, Padstow, Cornwall PL28 8RW
tel (01841) 534 264
email hello@tjink.co.uk
website www.tjink.co.uk
Twitter @TJINKtweets

Independent publishing services company that works with writers and industry professionals to create quality publishing projects. Offers services for each stage of the publishing process including editorial, design and production, and marketing and distribution. Part of TJ International Ltd, book manufacturers for the publishing industry for over 40 years. Founded 2014.

2QT Ltd (Publishing)

Unit 5, Commercial Courtyard, Duke Street, Settle, North Yorkshire BD24 9RH
tel (01729) 268010
website www.2qt.co.uk
Facebook www.facebook.com/2QTPublishing
Director Catherine Cousins

Offering flexible, tailored packages. Services include editing and proofreading, manuscript critique, cover design and typesetting. Also offers ebook conversion and distribution, print-on-demand and other printing options. Allocates ISBNs and barcodes.

whitefox

2nd Floor, Stapleton House, 110 Clifton Street, London EC2A 4HT
tel 020-8638 0536
email info@wearewhitefox.com
website http://wearewhitefox.com/
Facebook www.facebook.com/wearewhitefox
Twitter @wearewhitefox
Partners Annabel Wright, John Bond

Aims to provide the largest curated network of professional services available to publishers, agents, writers and brands. Specialises in a range of books, from fiction to non-fiction, including genre fiction, illustrated and business guides, and is able to handle all aspects of the publishing process. Offers support and solutions for independent writers and publishers including: editorial reports; structural editing; copy-editing; proofreading; design; typesetting; copywriting; marketing and publicity; interior layout; print and ebook production; and distribution. Founded 2012.

Wise Words Editorial

email info@wisewordseditorial.com
website www.wisewordseditorial.com
Twitter @WiseWordsEd

Provides proofreading services for fiction and non-fiction manuscripts and ebooks. Rate is £5/$7 per 1,000 words for proofreading documents over 50,000 words. Authors are sent a file showing edits as well as the final proofread file.

Wrate's Editing Services

14C Woodland Road, London SE19 1NT
tel 020-8670 0660
email danielle@wrateseditingservices.co.uk
website http://wrateseditingservices.co.uk
Twitter @WratesEditing
Contact Danielle Wrate

Helps authors with all aspects of the self-publishing process, from draft manuscript to publication. Primary services include proofreading, copy-editing, structural editing, cover design, internal layout, ebook conversion, printing, ISBN registration and marketing. Works with both novelists and non-fiction authors; free, no-obligation sample edit and publishing guide available. Founded 2013.

WRITERSWORLD

2 Bear Close Flats, Bear Close, Woodstock, Oxon OX20 1JX
tel (01993) 812500
email enquiries@writersworld.co.uk
website www.writersworld.co.uk
Founder & Owner Graham Cook

Specialises in self-publishing, print-on-demand books and book reprints. Also issues ISBNs on behalf of authors, pays them 100% of the royalties and supplies them with copies of their books at print cost. Established 2000.

The Writing Hall

33 Mount Pleasant, Ackworth, Pontefract, West Yorkshire, WF7 7HU
tel (01977) 614799
email info@thewritinghall.co.uk
website www.thewritinghall.co.uk
Facebook www.facebook.com/thewritinghall
Twitter @thewritinghall
Contact Diane Hall

Services include: developmental and copy-editing; proofreading; typesetting; cover design; small run printing; ebook formatting; author landing page and/or website creation; writing workshops, book launches and literary events; marketing and social media coaching. Additional services include: writing coaching/mentoring; manuscript critique; developmental editing; ghostwriting; and literary consultancy and advice.

Submissions for TWH's traditional royalty-based publishing, under the HallGoodBooks imprint are welcome, in the following genres: contemporary fiction (all sub-genres); business titles; romance; comedy. Founded 2007.

Xlibris

Victory Way, Admirals Park, Crossways, Dartford, Kent DA2 6QD
tel 0800 056 3182
email info@xlibrispublishing.co.uk
website www.xlibrispublishing.co.uk
Twitter @XlibrisUK

Established print-on-demand publisher, offering b&w, colour and speciality publishing packages (such as poetry and children's). Services range from design and editorial to ebook creation and distribution with online booksellers, website creation and marketing materials including a press release and book video. Royalties: 10% to author if sold via retail partner, and 25% if sold via Xlibris directly; 50% for ebook net sales. A subsidiary of Author Solutions LLC.

York Publishing Services

64 Hallfield Road, Layerthorpe, York YO1 7ZQ
tel (01904) 431213
email enqs@yps-publishing.co.uk
website www.yps-publishing.co.uk
Twitter @ypspublishing

Offers print and ebook publishing options, as well as distribution to bookshops and online retailers including Amazon. Services include copy-editing, proofreading, page and cover design, and printing. Provides page proofs and sample bound copy before main print run. Marketing services include compiling a press pack with press release sent to media; social media set-up (£250 plus VAT); posters; and direct mail campaigns. Book is also listed on the YPS online bookstore. Printing and editing price dependent on specification.

Resources for writers
Glossary of publishing terms

The selected terms in this glossary relate to the content of this *Yearbook* and includes terms used widely across the media industries.

advance

Money paid by a publisher to an author before a book is published which will be covered by future royalties. A publishing contract often allows an author an advance payment against future royalties; the author will not receive any further royalties until the amount paid in advance has been earned by sales of the book.

AI (advance information sheet)

A document that is put together by a publishing company to provide sales and marketing information about a book before publication and can be sent several months before publication to sales representatives. It can incorporate details of the format and contents of the book, key selling points and information about intended readership, as well as information about promotions and reviews.

auction

An auction, usually arranged by a literary agent, takes place when multiple publishing houses are interested in acquiring a manuscript and bid against one another to secure the domestic or territorial rights.

backlist

The range of books already published by a publisher that are still in print.

blad (book layout and design)

A pre-publication sales and marketing tool. It is often a printed booklet that contains sample pages, images and front and back covers, which acts as a preview for promotional use or for sales teams to show to potential retailers, customers or reviewers.

blurb

A short piece of writing or a paragraph that praises and promotes a book, which usually appears on the back or inside cover of the book and may be used in sales and marketing material.

book club edition

An edition of a book specially printed and bound for a book club for sale to its members.

book proof

A bound set of uncorrected reading proofs used by the sales team of a publishing house and as early review copies.

C format

A term most often used to describe a paperback edition published simultaneously with, and in the same format as, the hardback original.

co-edition

The publication of a book by two publishing companies in different countries, where the first company has originated the work and then sells sheets to the second publisher (or licenses the second publisher to reprint the book locally).

copyright

The legal right, which the creator of an original work has, to only allow copying of the work with permission and sometimes on payment of royalties or a copyright fee. An amendment to the Copyright, Designs and Patents Act (1988) states that in the UK most works are protected for 70 years from the creator's death. The 'copyright page' at the start of a book asserts copyright ownership and author identification.

edition

A quantity of books printed without changes to the content. A 'new edition' is a reprint of an existing title that incorporates substantial textual alterations. Originally one edition meant a single print run, though today an edition may consist of several separate printings, or impressions.

endmatter

Material at the end of the main body of a book which may be useful to the reader, including references, appendices, indexes and bibliography. Also called back matter.

EPUB files

Digital book format compatible with all electronic devices and e-readers (excluding Kindles).

extent

The number of pages in a book.

first edition

The first print run of a book. It can occasionally gain secondhand value if either the book or its author become collectable.

folio

A large sheet of paper folded twice across the middle and trimmed to make four pages of a book. Also a page number.

frontlist

New books just published (generally in their first year of publication) or about to be published by a publisher. Promotion of the frontlist is heavy, and the frontlist carries most of a publisher's investment. On the other hand, a backlist which continues to sell is usually the most profitable part of a publisher's list.

impression

A single print run of a book; all books in an impression are manufactured at the same time and are identical. A 'second impression' would be the second batch of copies to be printed and bound. The impression number is usually marked on the copyright/imprint page. There can be several impressions in an edition, all sharing the same ISBN.

imprint

The publisher's or printer's name which appears on the title page of a book or in the bibliographical details; a brand name under which a book is published within a larger publishing company, usually representing a specialised subject area.

inspection copy

A copy of a publication sent or given with time allowed for a decision to purchase or return it. In academic publishing, lecturers can request inspection copies to decide whether to make a book/textbook recommended reading or adopt it as a core textbook for their course.

ISBN

International Standard Book Number.

ISSN

International Standard Serial Number. An international system used on periodicals, magazines, learned journals, etc. The ISSN is formed of eight digits, which refer to the country in which the magazine is published and the title of the publication.

kill fee

A fee paid to a freelance writer for material written on assignment but not used, typically a percentage of the total payment.

manuscript

The pre-published version of an author's work, now usually submitted in electronic form.

metadata

Data that describes the content of a book to aid online discoverability – typically title, author, ISBN, key terms, description and other bibliographic information.

mobi files

Digital book format for Kindle devices (owned by Amazon).

moral right

The right of people such as editors or illustrators to have some say in the publication of a work to which they have contributed, even if they do not own the copyright.

MS (*pl* MSS)

The abbreviation commonly used for 'manuscript'.

nom de plume

A pseudonym or 'pen-name' under which a writer may choose to publish their work instead of their real name.

out of print or o.p.

Relating to a book of which the publisher has no copies left and which is not going to be reprinted. Print-on-demand technology, however, means that a book can be kept 'in print' indefinitely.

page proofs

A set of proofs of the pages in a book used to check the accuracy of typesetting and page layout, and also as an advance promotional tool. These are commonly provided in electronic form, rather than in physical form.

paper engineering

The mechanics of creating novelty books and pop-ups.

PDF/pdf

Portable Document Format. A data file generated from PostScript that is platform-independent, application-independent and font-independent. Acrobat is Adobe's suite of software used to generate, edit and view pdf files.

point of sale

Merchandising display material provided by publishers to bookshops in order to promote particular titles.

prelims

The initial pages of a book, including the title page and table of contents, which precede the main text. Also called front matter.

pre-press

Before going to press, to be printed.

print on demand or POD

The facility to print and bind a small number of books at short notice, without the need for a large print run, using digital technology. When an order comes through, a digital file of the book can be printed individually and automatically.

print run

The quantity a book printed at one time in an impression.

public lending right

An author's right to receive from the public purse a payment for the loan of works from public libraries in the UK.

publisher's agreement

A contract between a publisher and the copyright holder, author, agent or another publisher, which lays down the terms under which the publisher will publish the book for the copyright holder.

publishing contract

An agreement between a publisher and an author by which the author grants the publisher the right to publish the work against payment of a fee, usually in the form of a royalty.

query letter

A letter from an author to an agent pitching their book.

reading fee

Money paid to somebody for reading a manuscript and commenting on it.

recto

Relating to the right-hand page of a book, usually given an odd number.

reprint

Copies of a book made from the original, but with a note in the publication details of the date of reprinting and possibly a new title page and cover design.

review copy

An advance copy of a book sent to magazines, newspapers and/or other media for the purposes of review. A 'book proof' may be sent out before the book is printed.

rights

The legal right to publish something such as a book, picture or extract from a text.

royalty

Money paid to a writer for the right to use his or her property, usually a percentage of sales or an agreed amount per sale.

royalty split

The way in which a royalty is divided between several authors or between author and illustrator.

royalty statement

A printed statement from a publisher showing how much royalty is due to an author.

sans serif

A style of printing letters with all lines of equal thickness and no serifs. Sans faces are less easy to read than seriffed faces and they are rarely used for continuous text, although some magazines use them for text matter.

serialisation

Publication of a book in parts in a magazine or newspaper.

serif

A small decorative line added to letters in some fonts; a font that uses serifs, such as Times. The addition of serifs (1) keeps the letters apart while at the same time making it possible to link one letter to the next, and (2) makes the letters distinct, in particular the top parts which the reader recognises when reading.

slush pile

Unsolicited manuscripts which are sent to publishers or agents, and which may never be read.

STM

The accepted abbreviation for the scientific, technical and medical publishing sectors.

style sheet

A guide listing all the rules of house style for a publishing company which has to be followed by authors and editors.

submission guidelines

Instructions given by agents or publishers on how they wish to receive submissions from authors.

subscription sale or 'sub'

Sales of a title to booksellers in advance of publication, and orders taken from wholesalers and retailers to be supplied by the publisher shortly before the publication date.

subsidiary rights

Rights other than the right to publish a book in its first form, e.g. paperback rights; rights to adapt the book; rights to serialise it in a magazine; film and TV rights; audio, ebook, foreign and translation rights.

synopsis

A concise plot summary of a manuscript (usually one side of A4) that covers the major plot points, narrative arcs and characters.

territory

Areas of the world where the publisher has the rights to publish or can make foreign rights deals.

trade discount

A reduction in price given to a customer in the same trade, as by a publisher to another publisher or to a bookseller.

trade paperback (B format)

A paperback edition of a book that is superior in production quality to and larger than a mass-market paperback edition, size 198 x 129mm.

trim size or trimmed size

The measurements of a page of a book after it has been cut, or of a sheet of paper after it has been cut to size.

type specification or 'spec'

A brief created by the design department of a publishing house for how a book should be typeset.

typeface

A set of characters that share a distinctive and consistent design. Typefaces come in families of different weights, e.g. Helvetica Roman, Helvetica Italic, Bold, Bold Italic, etc. Hundreds of typefaces exist and new ones are still being designed. Today, 'font' is often used synonymously with 'typeface' though originally font meant the characters were all the same size, e.g. Helvetica italic 11 point.

typescript or manuscript

The final draft of a book. This unedited text is usually an electronic Word file but may be typewritten. The term 'typescript' (abbreviated TS or ts) is now used more commonly than 'manuscript' (abbreviated MS or ms; pl. MSS or mss), though they are synonymous.

typographic error or typo

A mistake made when keying text or typesetting.

unsolicited manuscript

An unpublished manuscript sent to a publisher without having been commissioned or requested.

verso

The left-hand page of a book, usually given an even number.

voice casting

The process of finding a suitable voice artist to narrate audiobooks.

volume rights

The right to publish the work in hardback, paperback or ebook.

XML tagging

Inserting tags into the text that can allow it to be converted for ebooks or for use in electronic formats.

See also...

- *Who's who in publishing,* page 136

Software for writers

This is a selection of software programmes and applications designed to enhance your writing experience and aid productivity. Each product has its own selection of features; we recommend you check the cost carefully, as many involve a fixed-term subscription or licence fee but do also offer free trials.

WRITING SOFTWARE

Aeon Timeline

www.aeontimeline.com
£42.00

Includes tools and features to help you understand characters, avoid plot holes and inconsistencies, and visualise your story in new ways.

Atomic Scribbler

www.atomicscribbler.com
$47.00

Organically build your book one scene or one chapter at a time, then drag and drop to arrange these on your document tree. Store your research images, URLs and notes alongside work for easy access, plus export your manuscript into a single Word document when ready.

Bibisco

www.bibisco.com
Free

Designed to allow a writer to focus on their characters and develop rounded and complex narratives, with particular emphasis on the manuscript's geographical, temporal and social context.

Dabble

www.dabblewriter.com
$9.99 a month

Gives writers the freedom to plot, write and edit on a desktop, in a browser or offline, and automatically syncs all versions across your devices. Features include plot grids, progress tracking and goal setting.

FocusWriter

https://gottcode.org/focuswriter
Free

Provides a simple and distraction-free writing environment with a hide-away interface, so you can focus solely on your writing.

Novelize

https://getnovelize.com
$45 p.a. or $5 a month

Developed for fiction writers, this web-based writing app means you can work on your book anywhere on any device. Keep your research in one place in the notebook displayed on the writing screen and track your progress.

Novel Factory

www.novel-software.com
£24.99

Plan your book with confidence by using the Roadmap feature which provides tools and structures to suit your needs. Includes detailed character overviews including biographies and images, as well as scene tabs and writing statistics about your work.

Novel Suite

www.novelsuite.com
$99 p.a. or $12 a month

An all-in-one novel writing application that can be used across all devices. Manage multiple books using character profiles, scene outlines and writing template tools.

Scrivener

www.literatureandlatte.com
$45

Tailored for long writing projects with everything you need housed in one place; it is a typewriter, ring binder and scrapbook, allowing you to optimise your digital workspace.

Ulysses

https://ulyssesapp.com
£35.99 p.a. or £4.49 a month

Document management for all writing projects, with flexible export options including pdf, Word, ebook and HTML which are appropriately formatted and styled.

WriteItNow

www.ravensheadservices.com
from $59.99

Includes sophisticated world-building features to create detailed and complex settings and characters. Recommends suitable names for your characters based on the historical period and geographical setting of your story.

EDITING SOFTWARE

After the Deadline

www.afterthedeadline.com
Free

A context-driven grammar and spelling checker, it underlines potential issues and gives a suggestion with an explanation of how you can rectify the error.

AutoCrit

www.autocrit.com
$29.97 a month

Analyses your entire manuscript and suggests insightful improvements in the form of an individual summary report, showing where your strengths and weaknesses lie.

Grammarly

www.grammarly.com
Premium from $11.66 a month (standard version free via certain browsers)

Provides accurate and context-specific suggestions when the application detects grammar, spelling, puncuation, word choice and style mistakes in your writing.

Hemingway Editor

www.hemingwayapp.com
$19.99 (desktop), free online

Helps you write with clarity and confidence. This application is like a spellchecker, but for style. It will highlight any areas that need tightening up by identifying: adverbs, passive voice, and uninspiring or over-complicated words.

ProWritingAid

https://prowritingaid.com
from $50

For use via the web, or as an add-on to word processing software, it interrogates your work for a multitude of potential issues such as passive voice, clichés, missing dialogue tags and pace, and suggests how you can rectify any errors or make style improvements.

SmartEdit

www.smart-edit.com
$77

Sits inside Microsoft Word and runs 20 individual checks whilst you work, flagging areas that need attention, including: highlighting repeated words, listing adverbs and foreign phrases used and identifying possible misused words.

WordRake

www.wordrake.com
from $129

When you click the 'rake' button in Microsoft Word, the text editor will read your document and suggest edits to tighten and add clarity to your work.

Editing your work

If you are publishing, via a traditional publisher or independently, editing your work is an essential part of the process. This article outlines for authors what is involved.

What is editing?

Broadly speaking, editing involves refining your writing ('copy') to make it as readable as possible and thus ready to be published. There are four main editorial stages:

• **Manuscript assessment/critique** is an initial assessment of the strengths and weaknesses of your work, with general suggestions for improvement.

• **Developmental/structural editing** gives more in-depth feedback on aspects of your work such as pace, writing style and appropriate language for your readership, and technical features such as characterisation (fiction) or reference styles (non-fiction).

• **Copy-editing** focuses on the detail, accuracy, completeness and consistency of your text, including grammar, spelling and punctuation.

• **Proofreading** is the final check of the layout and also picks up anything overlooked earlier.

Should I edit my work before submitting it to an agent or publisher?

Most fiction is not submitted direct to a publisher but will find its way to a commissioning or acquisitions editor via a literary agent (see the articles in this *Yearbook* in the *Literary agents* section, which starts on page 419). Some specialist non-fiction can be submitted directly to an appropriate publisher. The listings under *Book publishers*, starting on page 152, will indicate if a company accepts unsolicited scripts. In all cases it is important to follow the agent or publisher submission guidelines.

You should always check any submission for basic spelling and grammatical mistakes ('typos') and to ensure that there are no blatant inconsistencies or factual inaccuracies. It is up to you whether you pay a professional editor to do this for you, but you are unlikely to need a full copy-edit of your whole work at this stage. It may help, though, to have an outsider or beta-reader give you feedback.

If your manuscript is accepted for publication, it is usually the publisher who will arrange and pay for the editing of your complete work (see *What do publishers do?* on page 107). However, in academic publishing some authors are now asked to arrange and/or pay for their own copy-editing (and index). Beware of companies who ask you to pay for publishing your novel or non-fiction book – this is not traditional publishing. There are legitimate companies who do offer paid-for self-publishing packages (see below and *What do self-publishing providers offer?* on page 619), but tread carefully. A publisher who asks you to contribute to the publishing costs is a 'vanity' publisher and should be avoided.

What if I am self-publishing?

Independent authors do not have to obtain or pay for editorial advice, but if you want to sell a book that looks as good and reads as well as a professionally produced one, you are unlikely to achieve this on your own. There are a host of individuals and companies available to review and edit your work at all stages in the writing process, and to guide you through design and layout to publication and marketing.

When engaging a professional editor, be cautious and read the small print about what services are being offered and what qualifications the provider has to do the job. Decide what type of help you require and employ people with a track record and recommendations. Importantly, agree a fair price for the work. If you seek out the cheapest offering you are unlikely to get the best result. Writers & Artists offer editorial services for authors. Look also at the advice, rates and directory of editorial professionals provided by the Society for Editors and Proofreaders (www.sfep.org.uk).

What happens during editing?

While processes differ from publisher to publisher, the sequence of events from draft manuscript to published copy is roughly similar. If you are self-publishing and working direct with an editor the sequence of events will be determined by which services you buy.

- If your work needs structural or developmental editing the publisher or freelance editor will make suggestions and you will need to revise your work accordingly.
- You will then submit the finished work for copy-editing. You should make sure you follow your publisher's style and formatting guidelines or ask your freelance editor to devise a style guide for you. This will save time in the detailed copy-edit, and therefore save you money.
- The editor or publisher may ask you to answer queries that arise during copy-editing.
- When the text is finalised it will be sent for typesetting or layout. If you are publishing independently, unless you are very experienced, you should find a reputable professional to do your interior page layout for print and ebook and commission a professional cover designer.
- You may be sent one or more sets of proofs of the layout, or your publisher may handle this stage. Again, if you are self-publishing then checking the proofs carefully is up to you. See the handy checklist in the 'Mistakes to look out for' box.
- Your work is now ready for publication – and the all-important marketing.

What are the differences between copy-editing and proofreading?

Copy-editing and proofreading are crucial stages of the publishing process and, while the two can often be confused or referred to interchangeably, there are important differences. The copy-editing function normally takes place when your work is complete but before typesetting or design, allowing substantial revisions to be made at minimal cost. Proofreading, on the other hand, typically takes place after your work has been copy-edited and typeset/designed and serves to 'fine-polish' the text to ensure that it is free from editorial and layout inaccuracies.

Copy-editing

This is the essential stage for all writers and should be done after you are happy with the general structure and content of your work. As this is the detailed, line-by-line edit, if you rewrite or add material after this stage your work will need to be edited again. The aim of copy-editing is to ensure that whatever appears in public is accurate, easy to follow, fit for purpose and free of error, omission, inconsistency and repetition. This process picks up embarrassing mistakes, ambiguities and anomalies, alerts you to possible legal problems and marks up your work for the typesetter/designer.

Typically, copy-editing involves:
• checking for mistakes in spelling, grammar and punctuation;
• creating a style sheet; applying consistency in spelling, punctuation, capitalisation, etc;
• making sure the text flows well, is logically ordered and is appropriate for your target audience;
• marking up or formatting the structure for the designer – e.g. headings, tables, lists, boxed items, quotes;
• checking any illustrations and figures correspond with what's written in the text;
• checking that any bibliographical references and notes are correctly ordered and styled and that none are missing;
• making sure you have any necessary introductory pages (prelims);
• querying obvious errors of fact, misleading information or parts that are unclear.

How much editing your copy will require (and therefore how long it will take) depends on a number of factors, including:
• the complexity of the subject matter;
• how consistent you have been;
• whether you have correctly followed a publisher's house style (or your own);
• the quality of your writing.

In the past, manuscripts were copy-edited on paper, which was labour-intensive and time consuming. These days, nearly all copy-editing is carried out electronically, usually using

Common mistakes to look out for when editing and proofreading

- Punctuation mistakes, especially with direct speech and quotations.
- Inadvertently repeated words, e.g. 'and and . . .'.
- Phrases used inappropriately, e.g. 'should of' instead of 'should have' or 'compare to' instead of 'compare with'.
- Apostrophe misuse, e.g. its/it's and plurals (*not* banana's).
- Words with similar spelling or pronunciation but with different meanings used incorrectly, e.g. their/they're/there and effect/affect.
- Mixed use of past and present tenses.
- Use of plural verbs with single subjects (or vice versa), e.g. 'one in five children *are*... ' instead of 'one in five children *is*...' or '[the company] *has* 100 employees and [the company] *provide* free childcare' instead of 'provides' (or 'have' and 'provide').
- Obvious factual errors, e.g. 'the Battle of Hastings in 1766'.
- Inconsistent use of abbreviations and acronyms.
- Abbreviations/acronyms that have not been defined at least once in full.
- Missing bullet points or numbers in a sequenced list.
- Typing errors, e.g. '3' instead of '£'.
- Inconsistent layout of names, addresses, telephone numbers and email/web addresses.
- Incorrect or no use of trademarks, e.g. 'blackberry' instead of 'BlackBerry™'.
- References in the text that do not correspond to footnotes.
- Inaccurate or inadequate cross-referencing.
- Index listings not found on the page given in the index.
- Text inadvertently reordered or cut during the typesetting process.
- Headings wrongly formatted as body text.
- Running heads (at the top of pages) that do not correspond to chapter headings.
- Fonts and font sizes used incorrectly.
- Formatting inconsistencies such as poorly aligned margins or uneven columns.
- Captions/headings omitted from illustrations, photographs or diagrams.
- Illustrations/photographs/diagrams without appropriate copyright references.
- Widows and orphans, i.e. text which runs over page breaks and leaves a word or a line stranded.

Microsoft Word (or sometimes a bespoke publishing system). Suggested changes are usually made using the Track Changes function; queries for the author or publisher are often inserted using Comments. Copy-editors and publishers work in different ways. You may be asked to work through the changes and comments accepting, rejecting or answering each one; you may be sent a 'clean' edited version to approve; or you may just be sent queries to answer.

Proofreading

As this is the final check for errors and layout problems, you should not make major changes at this stage. These days you will normally receive proofs as pdf documents, which should be marked up using in-built commenting tools or the correct proof correction marks (see below) – check with your publisher or editor which method you are expected to use. Some publishers still work with hard copy paper proofs, or you may prefer to work this way yourself, in which case you should learn to use the main proof correction marks.

What are proofreading symbols and why do I need to know them?

Proofreading symbols (proof correction marks) are the 'shorthand' that copy-editors and proofreaders use for correcting written material and they are set by the British Standards Institution (BSi). Typesetters, designers and printers also require this knowledge as part of correcting page layout, style and format.

If you are sent a set of page proofs it is important that you have at least a basic understanding of the main marks so that you can interpret corrections that have been made or add your own corrections quickly, uniformly and without any ambiguity. The main proof correction marks you need to know are shown in the tables which follow.

Using the marks

- When proofreading, make a mark in the text to show exactly where the correction needs to be made. The marginal mark is used to specify what needs to be done.
- If there is more than one mark in a line, mark from left to right and use both margins if you need to.
- Every marginal mark should be followed by an oblique stroke, unless it is already followed by the insert mark or the amendment is a delete symbol.
- Circle any comments or notes you write in the margins to distinguish them from the corrections.
- For copy-editing (on hard copy), marks are made in the text only.

Handy proofreading tips

Effective proofreading takes time and practice but by following these tips you'll be able to spot mistakes more quickly and accurately:

- Set aside adequate time for proofreading. It requires concentration and should not be rushed.
- Before starting on a proofreading task, make sure you have easy access to a dictionary and thesaurus, and ensure that you have any relevant style guides for spellings, use of capitals and format/design.
- If possible, proofread the document several times and concentrate on different aspects each time, e.g. sense/tone, format, grammar/punctuation/use of language.

Marks/symbols for general instructions

INSTRUCTIONS	MARGIN	TEXT
Leave the text in its original state and ignore any marks that have been made, commonly referred to as 'stet'	✓ (circled)	- - - - under the characters to be left as they were
Query for the author/typesetter/ printer/publisher.	? (circled)	A circle should be placed around text to be queried
Remove non-textual marks	×	A circle should be placed around marks to be removed
End of change	/	None

Marks/symbols for inserting, deleting and changing text

INSTRUCTIONS	MARGIN	TEXT
Text to be inserted	New text, followed by ⅄	⅄
Additional text supplied separately	⅄ followed by a letter in a diamond which identifies additional text ◇A	⅄
Delete a character	ꝺ	/ through the character
Delete text	ꝺ	⊢⊣ through text
Delete character and close space	ꝺ (with close-up marks)	/ through the character (with close-up marks)
Delete text and close space	ꝺ (with close-up marks)	⊢⊣ through text (with close-up marks)
Character to replace marked character	New character, followed by /	/ through the character
Text to replace marked text	New text, followed by /	⊢⊣ through text

Marks/symbols for grammar and punctuation

INSTRUCTIONS	MARGIN	TEXT
Full stop	⊙	⅄ at insertion point or / through character
Comma	,	As above
Semi-colon	;	As above
Colon	: (circled)	As above
Hyphen	⊢-⊣	As above
Single quote marks	‘ or ’ (in ⅄)	As above
Double quote marks	“ or ” (in ⅄)	As above
Apostrophe	’ (in ⅄)	As above
Ellipses or leader dots	... (circled)	As above
Insert/replace dash	⊢1en⊣ Size of dash to be stated between uprights	As above

Marks/symbols for altering the look/style/layout of text

INSTRUCTIONS	MARGIN	TEXT
Put text in italics	⊔⊔	——— under text to be changed
Remove italics, replace with roman text	⊔⊔ with vertical stroke	Circle text to be changed
Put text in bold	~~~~	~~~~ under text to be changed
Remove bold	~~~~ with vertical stroke	Circle text to be changed
Put text in capitals	≡	≡ under text to be changed
Put text in small capitals	=	= under text to be changed
Put text in lower case	≢ or ≠	Circle text to be changed
Change character to superscript	Y under character	/ through character to be changed
Insert a superscript character	Y under character	⅄ at point of insertion
Change character to subscript	⅄ above character	/ through character to be changed
Insert a subscript character	⅄ above character	⅄ at point of insertion
Remove bold and italics	~~~~ with ⊔⊔ and vertical stroke	Circle text to be changed
Paragraph break	__⌐	__⌐
Remove paragraph break, run on text	⁀	⁀
Indent text	⊏	⊏
Remove indent	⊐	⊐
Insert or replace space between characters or words	Y	⅄ at relevant point of insertion or / through character
Reduce space between characters or words	⊤	|
Insert space between lines or paragraphs	Mark extends into margin	—(or)—
Reduce space between lines or paragraphs	Mark extends into margin	—→) or (←—
Transpose lines	⊆⊇	⊆⊇
Transpose characters or words	⊔⊓	⊔⊓
Close space between characters	⁀‿	character ⁀‿ character
Underline words	(underline)	◯ circle words
Take over character(s) or word(s) to next line/column/page	Mark extends into margin	⊏
Take back character(s) or word(s) to previous line/column/page	Mark extends into margin	⊐

• Always double-check scientific, mathematical or medical symbols as they can often be corrupted during the typesetting process. Accented characters and currency symbols can also cause problems.
• If possible, have a version of the copy-edited text to refer to while you proofread – it might help solve minor inaccuracies or inconsistencies more quickly.

Further resources

Butcher, Judith; Drake, Caroline and Leach, Maureen, *Butcher's Copy-editing: The Cambridge Handbook for Editors, Copy-editors and Proofreaders* (Cambridge University Press, 4th edn 2006)

Burchfield, R.W., *Fowler's Modern English Usage* (Oxford University Press, 4th edn 2015)

Ritter, R.M. *New Oxford Dictionary for Writers and Editors: The Essential A-Z Guide to the Written Word* (Oxford University Press, 2nd revised edn 2014)

The Chicago Manual of Style: The Essential Guide for Writers, Editors, and Publishers (University of Chicago Press, 17th edn 2017; www.chicagomanualofstyle.org/home.html)

Waddingham, A. (ed.), *New Hart's Rules: The Oxford Style Guide* (Oxford University Press, 2nd edn 2014)

The Society for Editors and Proofreaders (SfEP), offers training, mentoring, support and advice for editors and proofreaders and a freely searchable directory of editorial professionals, www.sfep.org.uk (see page 538)

The Publishing Training Centre (PTC) offers courses on editing, proofreading and all aspects of publishing, www.train4publishing.co.uk.

This article has been written by three professional editors. **Lauren Simpson** (lauren.simpson73@gmail.com) is a freelance editor, writer, publishing consultant and proofreader with over 20 years' experience. Lauren offers an extensive range of editorial, writing and project management services to businesses and individuals. **Margaret Hunter** (daisyeditorial.co.uk) offers copy-editing, proofreading and layout services to businesses, organisations and independent authors. She joined the SfEP council in 2015. **Gerard M-F Hill** (much-better-text.com) served on the SfEP council from 2007 to 2016 and is currently its chartership adviser. He has worked as a copy-editor, indexer, proofreader, consultant and ghostwriter.

Indexing

A good index is essential to the user of a non-fiction book; a bad index will let down an otherwise excellent book. The functions of indexes, and the skills needed to compile them, are explained here by the Society of Indexers.

An index is a detailed key to the contents of a document, unlike a contents list, which shows only the sections into which the document is divided (e.g. chapters). An index guides readers to information by providing a systematic arrangement of entries (single words, phrases, acronyms, names and so on) in a suitably organised list (usually alphabetical) that refers them to specific locations using page, column, section, frame, figure, table, paragraph, line or other appropriate numbers or hyperlinks.

Professional indexing

A well-crafted analytical index produced by a skilled professional with appropriate subject expertise is an essential feature of almost every non-fiction book. A professional indexer not only has subject knowledge, but also analyses the document from the readers' perspectives, anticipating how they will approach the subject and what language they will use. The indexer analyses the content of the text and provides a carefully structured index to guide readers efficiently into the main text of the book.

A detailed, comprehensive and regularly updated directory of freelance professional indexers, *Indexers Available*, is on the Society of Indexers' website. Professional competence is recognised in three stages by the Society. Professional Members (MSocInd) have successfully completed initial training (see below) or have many years' continuous experience. Advanced Professional Members (MSocInd(Adv)) have demonstrated skills and experience gained since their initial training, while Fellows of the Society of Indexers (FSI) have been through a rigorous assessment procedure to demonstrate the quality of their work.

Indexing fees depend on many factors, particularly the complexity of the text, but for an index to a straightforward text the Society recommends £25.00 an hour, £2.75 a page or £7.50 per 1,000 words (in 2018).

Indexing should normally be organised by the publisher, but may be left to the author to do or to arrange. It is rarely a popular task with authors, and they are often not well suited to the task, which takes objectivity, perspective, speed, patience, attention to detail and, above all, training, experience and specialist software. Moreover, authors are generally too close to the text by this stage. Authors who do need to construct their own indexes for whatever reason should consult the further reading list at the end of this article.

Ebooks and other electronic material

An index is necessary for ebooks and other electronic material. It is a complete myth that users of ebooks can rely solely on keyword-based retrieval systems; these pick out far too much information to be usable and far too little to be reliable. Only careful analysis by the human brain creates suitable index terms for non-fiction ebooks. There are no shortcuts for judging relevance, for extracting meaning and significance from the text, for identifying complex concepts, or for recognising different ways of expressing similar ideas. Index entries must also be properly linked to the text when a printed book is converted into an ebook.

The Society of Indexers

The Society of Indexers was founded in 1957 and is the only autonomous professional body for indexers in the UK. The main objectives of the Society are to promote high standards in all types of indexing and highlight the role of indexers in the organisation of knowledge; to provide, promote and recognise facilities for both the initial and the further training of indexers; to establish criteria for assessing conformity to indexing standards; and to conduct research and publish guidance, ideas and information about indexing. It seeks to establish good relationships between indexers, librarians, publishers and authors, both to advance good indexing and to ensure that the contribution of indexers to the organisation and retrieval of knowledge is properly recognised.

The Society holds an annual conference and publishes a learned journal, the *Indexer* (quarterly), a newsletter and *Occasional Papers on Indexing*. Additional resources are published on its website.

Further information

Society of Indexers
Woodbourn Business Centre, 10 Jessell Street, Sheffield S9 3HY
tel 0114 244 9561
email admin@indexers.org.uk
website www.indexers.org.uk
Membership (2017) £140 p.a. UK/Europe, £175 overseas; for corporate rates see website

Publishers and authors seeking to commission an indexer should consult *Indexers Available* on the website.

Indexing as a career

Indexing is often taken up as a second career, frequently drawing on expertise developed in some other field. Both intellectually demanding and creative, it requires considerable and sustained mental effort. Indexers need to be well-organised, flexible, disciplined and self-motivated, and resilient enough to cope with the uncertainties of freelance work. The Society of Indexers long-established training course, which has received the CILIP Seal of Recognition (see CILIP page 540, gives a thorough grounding in indexing principles and plenty of practice on real documents. Based on the principle of open learning, it enables students to learn in their own way and at their own pace. A web-based platform offers access to study materials, practice exercises and quizzes, and links to a wide range of useful resources. Online tutorials are undertaken at various stages during the course. After completing the four assessed modules, which cover the core indexing skills, students undertake a book-length practical indexing assignment. Successful completion of the course leads to Accreditation, designation as a Professional Indexer (MSocInd), and entry in the Society's online directory, *Indexers Available*.

Further reading

Booth, P.F., *Indexing: The Manual of Good Practice* (K.G. Saur 2001)

British Standards Institution, *British Standard Recommendations for Examining Documents, Determining their Subjects and Selecting Indexing Terms* (BS6529:1984)

'Indexes' (chapter from *The Chicago Manual of Style*, 16th edn; University of Chicago Press 2010)

International Standards Organisation, *Information and Documentation – Guidelines for the Content, Organization and Presentation of Indexes* (ISO 999:1996)

Mulvany, N.C., *Indexing Books* (University of Chicago Press, 2nd edn 2005)

Stauber, D.M., *Facing the Text: Content and Structure in Book Indexing* (Cedar Row Press 2004)

Libraries

Libraries are no longer just repositories for books and a source of reference. They provide an increasing range of different services, using a multitude of media to reach a more diverse audience.

TYPES OF LIBRARIES

• **Public libraries** are accessible to the general population and are usually funded by a local or district council. They typically offer a mix of lending and reference facilities. Public libraries are distinct from research libraries, subscription libraries and other specialist libraries in terms of their funding and access, but may offer some of the same facilities to visitors. Public library services are facing financial challenges and cuts to funding so many library authorities are looking towards new approaches to working with communities in order to build sustainable library services for the future.
• A list of **community libraries** in the UK can be found at www.publiclibrariesnews.com.
• An **academic library** is usually affiliated to an educational institution and primarily serves the students and faculty of that institution. Some are accessible to the public.
• A **subscription library** is one that is funded via membership or endowments. Access is often restricted to members but membership is sometimes extended to groups who are non-members, such as students.
• Many libraries belong to the Association of Independent Libraries and a list of members can be found on the Association's website (see below).
• This website is a tool to find your nearest and local UK public libraries http://www.findmylibrary.co.uk/. It is also designed to share reviews and provide information on collections and facilities offered (and within various other institutions around the country such as museums and galleries).

SOME OF THE BEST

Britain has such a wealth of comprehensive and historic libraries that a full list of them is not possible in this publication. Here is just a small selection of the best.

Barbican Library

Barbican Centre, Silk Street, London EC2Y 8DS
tel 020-7638 0569
email barbicanlib@cityoflondon.gov.uk
website www.barbican.org.uk
Facebook www.facebook.com/Barbicanlibrary
Twitter @barbicanlib

The largest of the City of London's lending libraries with a strong arts and music section, a London collection, literature events programme and reading groups.

Belfast Central Library

Royal Avenue, Belfast BT1 1EA
tel 028-9050 9150
email belfast.central@librariesni.org.uk
website www.librariesni.org.uk/Libraries/Pages/Belfast-Central-Library.aspx
Facebook www.facebook.com/BelfastCentralLibrary
Twitter @BelfastCentLib

The library's reference library is the largest in stock terms in Northern Ireland. The library houses a number of special collections including a digital film archive and the Northern Ireland Music Archive.

Library of Birmingham

Centenary Square, Broad Street, Birmingham B1 2ND
tel 0121 242 4242
email enquiries@libraryofbirmingham.com
website www.libraryofbirmingham.com
Facebook www.facebook.com/libraryofbirmingham
Twitter @LibraryofBham

The Library of Birmingham replaced Birmingham Central Library in September 2013 and is the largest public library in the UK and the largest regional library in Europe.

Cardiff Central Library

The Hayes, Cardiff CF10 1FL
tel 029-2038 2116
email centrallibrary@cardiff.gov.uk
website www.cardiff.gov.uk/ENG/resident/Libraries-and-archives/Find-a-library/Pages/Central-Library.aspx

The largest public library in Wales, opened in 2009, houses 90,000 books, 10,000 of which are in Welsh.

Liverpool Central Library

William Brown Street, Liverpool L3 8EW
tel 0151 233 3069
email refbt.central.library@liverpool.gov.uk
website https://liverpool.gov.uk/libraries/find-a-library/central-library/

Liverpool Central Library has undergone major refurbishment and reopened in May 2013. The collection includes 15,000 rare books.

London Library

14 St James's Square, London SW1Y 4LG
tel 020-7766 4700

email reception@londonlibrary.co.uk
website www.londonlibrary.co.uk
Facebook www.facebook.com/thelondonlibrary
Twitter @thelondonlib

A subscription lending library containing more than one million books and periodicals in over 50 languages, the collection includes works from the 16th century to the latest publications in print and electronic form. Membership is open to all.

Manchester Central Library

St Peter's Square, Manchester M2 5PD
tel 0161 234 1983
email libraries@manchester.gov.uk
website http://www.manchester.gov.uk/centrallibrary

Manchester's main library, the second biggest public lending library in the UK, reopened in March 2014 after major refurbishment.

Mitchell Library

North Street, Glasgow G3 7DN
tel 0141 287 2999
email libraries@glasgowlife.org.uk
website www.glasgowlife.org.uk/libraries/the-mitchell-library/pages/home.aspx
Facebook www.facebook.com/GlasgowLibraries
Twitter @GlasgowLib

The largest public reference library in Europe housing almost two million volumes. Holds an unrivalled collection of material relating to the city of Glasgow.

Newcastle City Library

Charles Avison Building, 33 Newbridge Street West, Newcastle upon Tyne NE1 8AX
tel 0191 277 4100
email information@newcastle.gov.uk
website www.newcastle.gov.uk/leisure-libraries-and-tourism/libraries/branch-libraries-and-opening-hours/city-library
Facebook www.facebook.com/NewcastleLibraries
Twitter @ToonLibraries

Newcastle's main public library includes a café, exhibition spaces, a rare books and watercolours collection, a viewing deck and six floors of books.

Westminster Reference Library

35 St Martin's Street, London WC2H 7HP
tel 020-7641 6200 (press 2)
email referencelibrarywc2@westminster.gov.uk
website www.westminster.gov.uk/westminster-reference-library

Specialist public reference library with collections in performing arts and art & design. Hosts regular and varied events, includes an exhibition space and a Business Information Point. Also has a range of business resources including market research, company and legal databases.

LIBRARIES OF LEGAL DEPOSIT IN THE UK AND IRELAND

A library of legal deposit is a library that has the power to request (at no charge) a copy of anything published in the UK. There are six legal deposit libraries in the UK and Ireland. To obtain a copy of a book, five out of the six legal deposit libraries must make a request in writing to a publisher within one year of publication of a book, newspaper or journal. Different rules apply to the British Library in that all UK libraries and Republic of Ireland publishers have a legal responsibility to send a copy of each of their publications to the library, without a written request being made. The British Library is the only legal deposit library with its own Legal Deposit Office. Since April 2013, legal deposit also covers material published digitally and online, so that the legal deposit libraries can provide a national archive of the UK's non-print published material, such as websites, blogs, e-journals and CD-ROMs.

Agency for the Legal Deposit Libraries (ALDL)

161 Causewayside, Edinburgh EH9 1PH
tel 0131 623 4680
email publisher.enquiries@legaldeposit.org.uk
website www.legaldeposit.org.uk

The Agency for the Legal Deposit Libraries (ALDL) requests and receives copies of publications for distribution to five major libraries (not the British Library). It is maintained by five legal deposit libraries and ensures that they receive legal deposit copies of British and Irish publications. The legal deposit libraries belong to the agency, which sends out written requests on behalf of member libraries and acts as a depot for books received. The agency must request copies on behalf of the libraries within 12 months of the date of publication. On receiving such a request from the agency, a publisher must supply a copy for each of the requesting libraries under the terms of the Legal Deposit Libraries Act 2003 (UK) and the Copyright and Related Rights Act 2000 (Ireland).

Bodleian Libraries of the University of Oxford

Broad Street, Oxford OX1 3BG
tel (01865) 277162
email reader.services@bodleian.ox.ac.uk
website www.bodleian.ox.ac.uk
Facebook www.facebook.com/bodleianlibraries
Twitter @bodleianlibs

With over 12 million printed volumes and over 80,000 e-journals and vast quantities of materials in many other formats, the Bodleian Libraries together form the second-largest library in the UK after the British Library, and is the main reference library of

Oxford University. It is one of the oldest libraries in Europe.

The British Library

St Pancras Building, 96 Euston Road,
London NW1 2DB
tel 0330 333 1144 (switchboard), 020-7412 7676 (reader information, St Pancras), (01937) 546070 (reader information, enquiries, Boston Spa), 020-7412 7831 (humanities, librarianship, information science service), 020-7412 7513 (maps and manuscripts)
Legal Deposit Office: The British Library, Boston Spa, Wetherby, West Yorkshire LS23 7BQ
tel (01937) 546268
email legal-deposit-books@bl.uk
website www.bl.uk
Facebook www.facebook.com/britishlibrary
Twitter @britishlibrary

The British Library holds books, journals, newspapers, sound recordings, patents, original manuscripts, maps, online images and texts, plays, digital books, and poet and author recordings. With a holding of over 14 million UK books, over 150 million published items from around the globe, around a million journals and newspapers, and three million sound recordings, it is the largest library in the world in terms of number of items held. Three million new items are added each year.

Cambridge University Library

West Road, Cambridge CB3 9DR
tel (01223) 333000
email library@lib.cam.ac.uk
website www.lib.cam.ac.uk

Cambridge University Library houses its own collection and also comprises four other libraries within the university. The library dates back to the 15th century and now has a collection of over eight million books. It is the only legal deposit library that keeps a large percentage of its books on open access.

National Library of Scotland

George IV Bridge, Edinburgh EH1 1EW
tel 0131 623 3700
email enquiries@nls.uk
website www.nls.uk
Facebook www.facebook.com/NationalLibraryOfScotland
Twitter @natlibscot

The National Library of Scotland holds over 15 million printed items including seven million books and more than two million maps. It is the world's central source for research relating to Scotland and the Scots. The library also holds a copy of the Gutenberg Bible, a First Folio of Shakespeare, and the last letter written by Mary Queen of Scots. In 2005 the library bought the John Murray Archive for £31 million; it contains important items relating to Jane Austen, Lord Byron and Sir Arthur Conan Doyle.

National Library of Wales

Aberystwyth, Ceredigion SY23 3BU
tel (01970) 632800
email gofyn@llgc.org.uk
website www.llgc.org.uk
Facebook www.facebook.com/llgcymrunlwales
Twitter @llgcymru

The National Library of Wales was established in 1907 and holds over five million books, including many important works such as the first book printed in Welsh and the first Welsh translation of the Bible.

Trinity College Library Dublin

College Green, Dublin 2, Republic of Ireland
tel +353 (0)1 896 1127
email library@tcd.ie
website www.tcd.ie/library
Facebook www.facebook.com/tcdlibrary
Twitter @tcdlibrary

Trinity College Library is the largest library in Ireland and is home to the *Book of Kells* – two of the four volumes are on permanent public display. The library houses sound recordings, maps, databases, and a digital collection. Currently it has over six million printed volumes with extensive collections of journals, manuscripts, maps and music reflecting over 400 years of academic development.

DESIGNATED OUTSTANDING COLLECTIONS

The Designated Outstanding Collections scheme was established in 1997 by the Museums and Galleries Commission to identify collections of national and international importance in non-national museums and galleries. In 2005 the scheme was extended to include libraries and archives. The scheme is now administered by Arts Council England and there are 140 Designated Outstanding Collections in England. To find out if there is a Designated Outstanding Collection library near you, visit the Designation section of the Arts Council website (www.artscouncil.org.uk).

SPECIALIST LIBRARIES IN THE UK

Writers often need access to specialised information sources in order to research their work. The following are a sample of specialist libraries in the UK.

BBC Written Archives Centre

Peppard Road, Caversham Park, Reading RG4 8TZ
tel 0118 948 6281
email heritage@bbc.co.uk

Home of the BBC's written records. Holds thousands of files, scripts and working papers, dating from the BBC's formation in 1922 to the 1980s together with information about past programmes and the history of broadcasting. Does not have recordings or information about current programmes.

BFI National Archive and Reuben Library

21 Stephen Street, London W1T 1LN
tel 020-7255 1444
website www.bfi.org.uk
Facebook www.facebook.com/BritishFilmInstitute
Twitter @BFI

Established in 1933, the BFI National Archive is one of the largest film and television collections anywhere. Dating from the earliest days of film to the 21st century, it contains nearly a million titles. The Archive contains over 50,000 fiction films, over 100,000 non-fiction titles and approx. 625,000 television programmes. The majority of the collection is British material but it also features internationally significant holdings from around the world. The Archive also collects films which feature key British actors and the work of British directors. Using the latest preservation methods, the BFI cares for a variety of often obsolete formats. The BFI Reuben Library at BFI Southbank is home to a huge collection of books, journals, documents and audio recordings about the world of film and television.

British Library for Development Studies (BLDS)

Institute of Development Studies at the University of Sussex, Brighton BN1 9RE
tel (01273) 678163
email library@sussex.ac.uk
website www.ids.ac.uk/about-us/who-we-are/blds

Europe's largest research collection on economic and social change in developing countries.

British Newspaper Archive

tel (01382) 210100
website www.britishnewspaperarchive.co.uk
Facebook www.facebook.com/TheBritishNewspaperArchive
Twitter @BNArchive

The British Newspaper Archive gives access to over three million historical local, national and regional newspaper pages from across the UK and Ireland. The Archive is a partnership between the British Library and findmypast to digitise up to 40 million newspaper pages from the British Library's vast collection over the next ten years.

Catholic National Library

Centre for Catholic Studies, University of Durham, Stockton Road, Durham DH1 3LE
tel 0191 334 1656
email ccs.admin@durham.ac.uk
website www.dur.ac.uk/theology.religion/ccs

The Catholic National Library is housed by the Centre for Catholic Studies at Durham University. It holds over 70,000 books, pamphlets and periodicals on theology, spirituality and related subjects, biography and history.

Chawton House Library

Chawton, Alton, Hants GU34 1SJ
tel (01420) 541010
email info@chawton.net
website www.chawtonhouse.org
Twitter @chawtonhouse

A collection of over 8,000 volumes focusing on women's writing in English from 1600 to 1830 including some manuscripts. The library also houses the Knight Collection, which is the private library belonging to the Knight family, the owners of Chawton House for over 400 years.

City Business Library

Aldermanbury, London EC2V 7HH
tel 020-7332 1812
email cbl@cityoflondon.gov.uk
website www.cityoflondon.gov.uk/business/economic-research-and-information/city-business-library/Pages/default.aspx
Facebook www.facebook.com/CityBusinessLibrary
Twitter @CBL_London

One of the leading business information sources in the UK.

Library of the Commonwealth Secretariat

Commonwealth Secretariat, Marlborough House, Pall Mall, London SW1Y 5HX
tel 020-7747 6164 (librarian), 020-7747 6167 (archivist)
email library@commonwealth.int
website http://thecommonwealth.org/library-and-archives
Facebook www.facebook.com/commonwealthsec
Twitter @commonwealthsec

Collection covers politics and international relations, economics, education, health, gender, environment and management. Holds a comprehensive collection of Commonwealth Secretariat publications and its archives.

Crafts Council Research Library

Crafts Council, 44A Pentonville Road, London N1 9BY
tel 020-7806 2500
email reception@craftscouncil.org.uk
website www.craftscouncil.org.uk
Facebook www.facebook.com/CraftsCouncilUK/
Twitter @CraftsCouncilUK

This is a reference library open to the public two days a week by appointment. Houses a large collection of contemporary craft books and catalogues as well as journals. Covers ceramics, textiles, jewellery, fashion accessories and paper.

Goethe-Institut London Library

50 Princes Gate, Exhibition Road, London SW7 2PH
tel 020-7596 4000
email library@london.goethe.org
email info-london@goethe.org
website www.goethe.de/london
Facebook www.facebook.com/goethe.institut.london
Twitter @GI_London1

Specialises in German literature, especially contemporary fiction and drama, film DVDs and books/audiovisual material on German culture and recent history. E-library gives access to Goethe Institut libraries in the UK, Ireland and the Netherlands and allows electronic downloading of ebooks, e-audiobooks and electronic newspapers for a predetermined period of time.

Guildhall Library

Aldermanbury, London EC2V 7HH
tel 020-7332 1868/1870
email guildhall.library@cityoflondon.gov.uk
website www.cityoflondon.gov.uk/guildhalllibrary
Twitter @GuildhallLib

The Library's printed books collection comprises over 200,000 titles dating from the 15th century to the 21st century and includes books, pamphlets, periodicals, trade directories and poll books. The collection covers all aspects of life in London, past and present.

Lambeth Palace Library

Enquiries, Lambeth Palace Library, London SE1 7JU
tel 020-7898 1400
email archives@churchofengland.org
website www.lambethpalacelibrary.org
Facebook www.facebook.com/LambethPalaceLibrary
Twitter @lampallib

The historic library of the Archbishops of Canterbury and the principal library and record office for the Church of England.

Library Services, The Open University

Open University, Walton Hall,
Milton Keynes MK7 6AA
tel (01908) 659001
email lib-help@open.ac.uk
website www.open.ac.uk/library
Facebook www.facebook.com/OULibrary
Twitter @OULibrary

The Open University's electronic library service.

Linen Hall Library

17 Donegall Square North, Belfast BT1 5GB
tel 028-9032 1707
email info@linenhall.com
website www.linenhall.com
Facebook www.facebook.com/LinenHallLibraryBelfast
Twitter @thelinenhall

Renowned for its Irish and Local Studies Collection ranging from early Belfast and Ulster printed books to the approx. 250,000 items in the internationally acclaimed Northern Ireland Political Collection (NIPC). Also expansive General Lending Collection.

National Art Library

Victoria & Albert Museum, Cromwell Road,
South Kensington, London SW7 2RL
tel 020-7942 2000
email contact@vam.ac.uk
website https://www.vam.ac.uk/info/national-art-library
Facebook www.facebook.com/victoriaandalbertmuseum/
Twitter @V_and_A

A major reference library and the Victoria & Albert Museum's curatorial department for the art, craft and design of the book.

National Maritime Museum

Greenwich, London SE10 9NF
tel 020-8312 6516
email library@rmg.co.uk
website www.rmg.co.uk/national-maritime-museum

Specialist maritime research library.

Natural History Museum Library and Information Services

Cromwell Road, London SW7 5BD
tel 020-7942 5000 (switchboard), 020-7942 5460 (archives), 020-7942 5460 (general library), 020-7942 6156 (ornithology library, Tring)
email library@nhm.ac.uk
website http://www.nhm.ac.uk/research-curation/science-facilities/library/
Facebook www.facebook.com/naturalhistorymuseum
Twitter @NHM_Library

Online catalogue contains all library material acquired since 1989 and about 80% of earlier items. The library collection contains more than one million items, including almost 400,000 books, 22,000 ongoing journal titles, 350,000 artworks and over 100,000 catalogued archival items. Contact via the website.

RNIB National Library Service

105 Judd Street, London WC1H 9NE
tel 0303 123 9999
email library@rnib.org.uk
website www.rnib.org.uk/library
Facebook www.facebook.com/rnibuk
Twitter @RNIB

The largest specialist library for readers with sight loss in the UK. The Talking Books service is free, providing access to over 25,000 titles. Offers a comprehensive range of books and accessible information for children and adults in a range of formats including braille, large print and unabridged audio. Also provides free access to online reference material, braille sheet music, themed book lists and a quarterly reader magazine.

Science Museum Library

The Dana Research Centre and Library,
165 Queens Gate, London SW7 5HD
tel 020-7942 4242
email smlinfo@sciencemuseum.ac.uk
website https://www.sciencemuseum.org.uk/researchers/dana-research-centre-and-library
Facebook www.facebook.com/sciencemuseumlondon
Twitter @sciencemuseum

Allows access to around 6,000 books and journals covering museum studies, the history and biography of science technology and medicine and the philosophical and social aspects of these subjects.

Tate Library & Archive

Tate Library and Archive, Tate Britain, Millbank, London SW1P 4RG
tel 020-7887 8838
email reading.rooms@tate.org.uk
website www.tate.org.uk/research/library

Broadly covers those areas in which the Tate collects. The library includes British art from the Renaissance to the present day and international modern art from 1900. The archive covers British art from 1900 and contains a wealth of unpublished material on artists, art world figures and organisations.

Wellcome Library

Wellcome Library, Part of Wellcome Collection, 183 Euston Road, London NW1 2BE
tel 020-7611 8722
email library@wellcome.ac.uk
website http://wellcomelibrary.org/
Facebook www.facebook.com/Wellcomelibrary/
Twitter @WellcomeLibrary

One of the world's major resources for the study of medical history. Also houses an expanding collection of material relating to contemporary medicine and biomedical science in society.

Moving Image and Sound Collections

tel 020-7611 8899
email collections@wellcome.ac.uk
website https://wellcomelibrary.org/collections/about-the-collections/moving-image-and-sound-collection/

Physical materials in the collection are held in closed stores, and can be requested through the catalogue to view or listen to in the Library.

Wellcome Images

tel 020-7611 8348
email images@wellcome.ac.uk
website https://wellcomecollection.org/works
Facebook www.facebook.com/WellcomeImages
Twitter @wellcomeimages

Westminster Music Library

Victoria Library, 160 Buckingham Palace Road, London SW1W 9UD
tel 020-7641 6200
email musiclibrary@westminster.gov.uk
website www.westminster.gov.uk/libraries

Holds a wide range of scores, orchestral sets, books on music, music journals and a collection of Mozart sound recordings, formerly the GLASS collection.

Women's Library @ LSE

Lionel Robbins Building,
The London School of Economics and Political Science, 10 Portugal Street, Westminster, London WC2A 2HD
tel 020-7955 7229
email library.enquiries@lse.ac.uk
website www.lse.ac.uk/library/collections/featuredCollections/womensLibraryLSE.aspx
Twitter @LSELibrary

Houses the most extensive collection of women's history in the UK. Part of the London School of Economics.

Working Class Movement Library

Jubilee House, 51 The Crescent, Salford M5 4WX
tel 0161 736 3601
email enquiries@wcml.org.uk
website www.wcml.org.uk
Facebook www.facebook.com/wcmlibrary
Twitter @wcmlibrary

Records over 200 years of organising and campaigning by ordinary men and women. The collection provides an insight into working people's daily lives. Collection contains: books, pamphlets, archives, photographs, plays, poetry, songs, banners, posters, badges, cartoons, journals, biographies, reports.

Zoological Society of London Library

Outer Circle, Regent's Park, London NW1 4RY
tel 020-7449 6293
email library@zsl.org
website www.zsl.org/about-us/library
Facebook www.facebook.com/officialzsl
Twitter @officialzsl

Contains a unique collection of journals and books on zoology and animal conservation.

ORGANISATIONS AFFILIATED TO LIBRARIES

Aslib (The Association of Information Management)

Howard House, Wagon Lane, Bingley BD16 1WA
tel (01274) 777700
website www.aslib.co.uk

Actively promotes best practice in the management of information resources. Aslib represents its members and lobbies on all aspects of the management of and legislation concerning information at local, national and international levels. Aslib provides consultancy and information services, professional development training, conferences, specialist recruitment, internet products, and publishes primary and secondary journals, conference proceedings, directories and monographs. Founded 1924.

Association of Independent Libraries

The Portico Library, 57 Mosley Street, Manchester M2 3HY
tel (0161) 236 6785
email keasson@litandphil.org.uk
website http://independentlibraries.co.uk

Aims to develop the conservation, restoration and public awareness of independent libraries in the UK. Together, its members possess over two million books and have many listed buildings in their care. Founded 1989.

Association of Senior and Children's Education Librarians (ASCEL)

website www.ascel.org.uk

A national membership network of Senior Children's and Education Librarians. It aims to stimulate developments and share initiatives relating to children and young people using public libraries and educational services.

CILIP (Chartered Institute of Library and Information Professionals)

7 Ridgmount Street, London WC1E 7AE
tel 020-7255 0500
email info@cilip.org.uk
website www.cilip.org.uk

The leading professional body for librarians, information specialists and knowledge managers. Aims for a fair and economically prosperous society underpinned by literacy, access to information and the transfer of knowledge. CILIP is a registered charity. Offices in London, Wales, Scotland and Northern Ireland.

Internet Library for Librarians

email info@itcompany.com
website www.itcompany2.com/inforetriever/index.htm

Internet Library for Librarians has been one of the most popular information resource sites for librarians since 1994. It is an information portal specifically designed for librarians to locate internet resources related to their profession.

Private Libraries Association

email info@plabooks.org
website www.plabooks.org

An international society of book collectors and lovers of books. Membership: £30 p.a. Publications include *The Private Library* (quarterly), annual *Private Press Books*, and other books on book collecting. Founded 1956.

School Library Association (SLA)

1 Pine Court, Kembrey Park, Swindon SN2 8AD
tel (01793) 530166
email info@sla.org.uk
website www.sla.org.uk

The main goal of the SLA is to support people involved with school libraries, promoting high-quality reading and learning opportunities for all. Founded 1937.

Society of Chief Librarians (SCL)

email societyofchieflibrarians@gmail.com
website www.goscl.com

SCL leads and manages public libraries in England, Wales and Northern Ireland. It is made up of the head of service of every library authority, and advocates for continuous improvement of the public library service on behalf of local people.

ORGANISATIONS THAT SUPPORT AND ENCOURAGE LIBRARY USE

There are many non-profit organisations which champion the use of libraries in the UK. These include:

Arts Council England

website www.artscouncil.org.uk

Arts Council England is the developmental agency for libraries in England and has responsibility for supporting and developing libraries. See also page 530.

BookTrust

website www.booktrust.org.uk

Aims to give everyone access to books and the chance to benefit from reading. See also page 539.

The Community Knowledge Hub for Libraries

website http://libraries.communityknowledgehub.org.uk

Unites expert guidance and resources with an interactive community of organisations and local authorities involved with community-managed and supported libraries.

Libraries All Party Parliamentary Group (APPG)

The goal of the Libraries APPG is to povide information and opportunities for debate about the important role libraries play in society and their future; to highlight the contribution that a wide variety of library and information services make, including those in public, school, government, health sector, colleges, private companies and university libraries; and to promote and discuss themes in the wider information and knowledge sector including the impact of technology, skills and training, professional standards and broader issues.

Libraries Taskforce

website https://librariestaskforce.blog.gov.uk

Set up to implement the Independent Library Report for England and reinvigorate public library services. Aims to build upon existing good practice and support partnerships of public libraries.

The Library Campaign

website www.librarycampaign.com

Aims to advance the lifelong education of the public by the promotion, support, assistance and improvement of libraries through the activities of friends and user groups.

National Libraries Day

website www.nationallibrariesday.org.uk

The first National Libraries Day took place in February 2012 and is now an annual event in the UK dedicated to the celebration of libraries and librarians. Author talks and competitions are arranged by local authorities, universities, library services and local community groups.

National Literacy Trust

website www.literacytrust.org.uk

Aims to improve the reading, writing, speaking and listening skills in isadvantaged communities, in part through access to libraries. See also page 539.

Public Libraries News

website www.publiclibrariesnews.com

Promotes knowledge about libraries in the UK.

The Reading Agency

website https://readingagency.org.uk

Aims to give everyone an equal chance in life by helping people become confident and enthusiastic readers, and that includes supporting library use.

Speak Up For Libraries

website http://speakupforlibraries.org/

A coalition of organisations and campaigners working to protect libraries and library staff.

Voices for the Library

website www.voicesforthelibrary.org.uk

Provides information about the public library service in the UK and the role of professional librarians. Library users can share their stories about the difference public libraries have made to their lives on the website.

Writers' retreats and creative writing courses

The following list of creative writing courses and writers' retreats is not exhaustive but is intended to give our readers a flavour of the many options available. Anyone wishing to participate in a writing course or writers' retreat should first satisfy themselves as to its content and quality. Details of postgraduate courses follow on page 686.

Anam Cara

tel +353 277-4441
email anamcararetreat@gmail.com
website www.anamcararetreat.com
Facebook www.facebook.com/anamcararetreat

An all-inclusive residential retreat, Anam Cara offers private and common working rooms and five acres of walking paths, quiet nooks and crannies, a river island and a labyrinth meadow. Set on a hillside between Coulagh Bay and Mishkish mountain on the Kealincha River, Anam Cara is a tranquil spot to provide sanctuary for people who seriously want to enhance their craft. Whether writers and artists want to work by themselves or as part of a workshop, or special interest group, Anam Cara provides support, creature comforts and peace to help everyone produce their best work. For further information or to make a booking, contact Sue Booth-Forbes.

Arvon

Free Word, 60 Farringdon Road, London EC1R 3GA
tel 020-7324 2554
email national@arvon.org
website www.arvon.org
Facebook www.facebook.com/arvonfoundation
Twitter @arvonfoundation
Chief Executive Ruth Borthwick

See individual entries for Arvon's four writing houses: The Hurst – The John Osborne Arvon Centre, Lumb Bank – The Ted Hughes Arvon Centre, Totleigh Barton and Writers Retreat at The Clockhouse. Arvon hosts 5-day residential creative writing courses and retreats in four beautiful writing houses, set in inspiring countryside locations. Courses include morning workshops, one-to-one tutorials with leading authors and plenty of time and space to write. Courses cover a range of genres including fiction, poetry, theatre, creative non-fiction, writing for children and many more. Arvon runs a grants system for those who would not be able to afford the full course fee.

Arvon Writers Retreat at the Clockhouse

Arvon Writers Retreat at the Clockhouse, Clunton, Craven Arms, Shropshire SY7 0JA
tel (01588) 640658
email thehurst@arvon.org
website www.arvon.org
Centre Director Natasha Carlish, *Centre Administrator* Dan Pavitt

A dedicated Writers Retreat at The Clockhouse, in the grounds of Arvon's Shropshire centre. The Clockhouse has four apartments, each with bedroom, study and en-suite bathroom, and all food provided, for six-day and four-day writing retreats.

Anne Aylor Creative Writing Courses

46 Beversbrook Road, London N19 4QH
020-7263 0669
email admin2019@anneaylor.co.uk
website www.anneaylor.co.uk
Contact Anne Aylor

Offers a range of short, weekend and overseas courses, as well as customised courses for all levels of ability.

The Book Doctor and Creativity Coach

132 Canalot Studios, 222 Kensal Road, London W10 5BN
tel 020-8964 1444; 07710 672318
email philippa_pride@yahoo.co.uk
website www.thebookdoctor.co.uk
Contact Philippa Pride

How to Free Your Creativity, Write a Book and Get it Published writing courses in the UK and abroad as well as one-to-one coaching and consultancy.

University of Cambridge Institute of Continuing Education

Institute of Continuing Education, Madingley Hall, Madingley, Cambridge CB23 8AQ
tel (01223) 746262
email enquiries@ice.cam.ac.uk
website www.ice.cam.ac.uk
Facebook www.facebook.com/CambridgeICE
Twitter @Cambridge_ICE
Contact Admissions Team

A wide range of short and part-time courses at introductory and advanced levels on literature, film, creative writing, art and art history. See website for details.

Casa Ana Creative Writing Programme

Calle Artesa 7, Ferreirola, 18414 La Taha, Granada, Spain
tel +34 678 298 497
email info@casa-ana.com
website www.casa-ana.com
Contact Anne Hunt

Casa Ana is a 400-year old house in the Alpujarra, the southern slopes of the Sierra Nevada mountains in Andalusia. Offers three or four residential writers' retreats each year in spring, summer and autumn. There are eight places available in each retreat and they last for two weeks. As well as providing a quiet and inspiring setting in which to write, Casa Ana offers a one-to-one mentoring service and optional reading/critiquing sessions. Also hosts week-long, residential creative writing courses at various times during the year.

Central St Martins College of Arts & Design, Short Course Office

Granary Square, 1 Granary Building, King's Cross, London N1C 4AA
website www.arts.ac.uk/csm/courses/short-courses/
Twitter @CSMShortCourses

Central Saint Martins offers an annual programme of courses in a variety of subjects taught by expert practitioners.

Centre for Open Learning

University of Edinburgh, Paterson's Land, Holyrood Road, Edinburgh EH8 8AQ
tel 0131-650 4400
email COL@ed.ac.uk
website www.ed.ac.uk/lifelong-learning

Offers a wide range of short courses including subjects such as art, film and creative writing.

Chalk the Sun Creative Writing

tel 07852 483001
email creativewriting@chalkthesun.co.uk
website www.chalkthesun.co.uk
Facebook www.facebook.com/CreativeWritingChalktheSun
Twitter @ChalktheSun
Programme Director Ardella Jones

Offers creative writing courses from beginners to specialist workshops for novelists, children's writers and scriptwriters with a team which includes CBBC producer Jonathan Wolfman, playwright Danusia Iwaszko, novelist Sheena Joughin, crime writer Claire McGowan, thriller novelist and screenwriter Simon Lewis and children's publisher and editor Simon Sideri. Also runs reading events, an Italian writing retreat, writing courses in Andalusia, one-to-one development tutorials, personalised distance learning and manuscript editing services. Classes are taught in small groups in the relaxed atmosphere of the Trafalgar Arms, Tooting Broadway, London SW17 0RT.

Château de Lavigny International Writers' Residence

Le Château, Route d'Etoy 10, 1175 Lavigny, Switzerland
tel +41 21-808 6143
email chlavigny@hotmail.com
website www.chateaudelavigny.ch

An international residence for writers in the canton of Vaud in Switzerland. The residence was created in 1996 by the Ledig-Rowohlt Foundation and has since welcomed each summer 20 or more writers from around the world. Writers come for four weeks, in groups of five or six, from early June through to mid-September. They are housed in the former home of German publisher Heinrich Maria Ledig-Rowohlt and his wife Jane, an 18th-century manor house among vineyards and hills overlooking Lake Geneva. There is no charge for the writers invited; food and lodging for the duration is free. Sessions are in English or French and writers must be published.

City Lit

Keeley Street, London WC2B 4BA
tel 020-7492 2717
email writing@citylit.ac.uk
website www.citylit.ac.uk

Situated in the heart of London, the writing department at City Lit offers affordable courses on approaching agents, impressing publishers, writing fiction, poetry, stage and screenwriting, memoir and non-fiction. From introductory courses to advanced masterclasses, City Lit has something for everyone.

Community Creative Writing and Publishing

Sea Winds, 2 St Helens Terrace, Spittal, Berwick-upon-Tweed, Northumberland TD15 1RJ
tel (01289) 305213
email mavismaureen@btinternet.com
Author/Tutor Moderator Maureen Raper MBE, (member of the Society of Authors and the Royal Society of Literature)

Classes in creative writing for beginners and intermediates in Writing for Radio and Television, Writing for Children, Writing Romantic Fiction. Writing groups monthly; reading groups monthly at Berwick Library. Distance learning available for all.

The Complete Creative Writing Course

email jamie@writingcourses.org.uk
website www.writingcourses.org.uk/
Contact Jamie Winter

Inspiring creative writing courses held at the Groucho Club in Soho and nearby locations, starting in January, April and September on Mondays and

Saturdays, daytime and evenings. Offers beginner, intermediate and advanced courses, and runs weekend workshops and a summer school. Tutors are all published writers and experienced teachers. Courses of six to eight three-hour sessions include stimulating exercises, feedback, discussion and homework. Cost ranges from £295 to £425.

Cove Park

Peaton Hill, Cove, Argyll and Bute, Scotland G84 0PE
tel (01436) 850123
email information@covepark.org
website www.covepark.org
Director Julian Forrester

Cove Park is Scotland's international artist residency centre and offers a year-round programme of residencies for writers and artists from all disciplines. For details of the funded residency programme, see the website.

The Creative Writer's Workshop

Kinvara, Co. Galway, Republic of Ireland
tel +353 (0)86 2523428
email office@thecreativewritersworkshop.com
website www.thecreativewritersworkshop.com
Facebook www.facebook.com/IreneGrahamWritingCourses
Founder Irene Graham

The Creative Writer's Workshop provides:

• fiction and memoir writing retreats in the west of Ireland;
• private writing classes in person and online;
• creative writing study abroad credit programme
• professional development workshops
• book writing coach services.

Irene Graham is the founder of the Creative Writer's Workshop (1991) and the Memoir Writing Club. She is also author of *The Memoir Writing Workbook*. Her fiction and memoir writing workshops are accredited by George Mason University in the US as part of its undergraduate and graduate degree programmes.

CreativeWordsMatter

Chinook, Southdown Road, Shawford, Hants SO21 2BY
tel (01962) 712307
email b.a.large@gmail.com
website www.creativewordsmatter.co.uk
Contact Barbara Large MBE, FRSA, HFUW

Offers individual and group editorial advice; nurturing, mentoring and line-editing of manuscripts for publication; and helps writers to build partnerships with literary agents and commissioning editors. In addition, this team of professional writers offers talks, workshops and one-to-one appointments on all genres of adult and children's fiction and non-fiction to art centres, festivals, universities, colleges, schools and businesses to stimulate new ideas and to develop writing projects for pleasure and publication.

Day courses on How To Successfully Self-Publish Your Book are offered in conjunction with CPI Group UK, part of Europe's largest printing group, to help writers plan a strategy that will produce the best product; well-written, with an attractive cover, a joy to market, to read and to share.

CreativeWordsMatter Saturday Workshops

Discovery Centre, Winchester, Hants SO21 2BY (and other venues)
tel (01962) 712307
email b.a.large@gmail.com
website www.creativewordsmatter.co.uk

For new and established writers. Offers the opportunity, throughout the year, for aspiring writers to work in small groups, under the guidance of professional writers, to improve their writing projects towards the goal of publication. At most longer workshops a literary agent or commissioning editor will offer one-to-one appointments. Phone or email for a free brochure.

Emerson College

Emerson College, Forest Row, East Sussex RH18 5JX
tel (01342) 822238
email bookings@emerson.org.uk
website www.emerson.org.uk
Facebook www.facebook.com/emersoncollegeuk
Twitter @Emerson_College

A holistic centre for education based on the works of Rudolf Steiner. Emerson is a rich environment for personal, artistic and spiritual growth. Visual, verbal, performing arts and many other courses held September to June every year; one-term and shorter blocks available. Founded 1962.

Faber Academy

74–77 Great Russell Street, London WC1B 3DA
tel 020-7927 3868
email academy@faber.co.uk
website www.faberacademy.co.uk
Facebook www.facebook.com/faberacademy
Twitter @faberacademy

Faber Academy offers high-quality creative writing courses, run by hand-picked authors, editors and agents. Provides the time, space and support needed to write and write well.

Fictionfire Literary Consultancy

110 Oxford Road, Old Marston, Oxford OX3 0RD
tel 07827 455723
email info@fictionfire.co.uk
website www.fictionfire.co.uk
Facebook www.facebook.com/FictionfireLiteraryConsultancy
Twitter @LornaFergusson
Contact Lorna Fergusson

Fictionfire offers in person and online creative writing courses, retreats and workshops. Guest talks and workshops can be arranged for writers' groups, libraries, conferences and festivals. Manuscript appraisal, editing, mentoring and consultation also available. Founded 2009.

Fire in the Head

email roselle@fire-in-the-head.co.uk
website www.fire-in-the-head.co.uk
website www.thewildways.co.uk
Twitter @Qualiabird
Contact Roselle Angwin

Courses and mentoring in poetry, novel, life writing, creative, reflective, psychospiritual and therapeutic writing, outdoor eco-writing, journaling and personal development; retreats; short courses; online/distance learning courses; tuition and appraisals.

The French House Party, Carcassonne

The Jaylands, Abberley, Worcs. WR6 6BN
mobile 07900 322791
email frenchhouseparty@gmail.com
website www.frenchhouseparty.eu
Director Moira Martingale

Luxury learning holidays in SW France include a creative writing tutored course plus a writing retreat and songwriting course with Dean Friedman.

Garsdale Retreat

tel (01539) 234184
email garsdaleretreat@gmail.com
website www.thegarsdaleretreat.co.uk
Contact Rebecca Nouchette

The Garsdale Retreat is a creative writing centre in the remote and beautiful setting of the Yorkshire Dales National Park, opened in May 2017. It provides inspirational residential courses tutored by professional writers, enabling participants to develop their individual creativity in a place of peace and tranquility. All levels of ability are welcomed and a high level of individual tuition is offered in classes with a maximum of eight. All courses and retreats are fully catered with delicious, locally sourced food, allowing participants to focus entirely on their writing.

The Grange

9 Eastcliff Road, Shanklin, Isle of Wight PO37 6AA
tel (01983) 867644
email info@thegrangebythesea.com
website www.thegrangebythesea.com

The Grange is an offshoot of Skyros with its renowned Writers' Lab that has attracted some very well-respected authors. The Grange hosts weekend residential creative writing workshops in a 4-star B&B, in the old village of Shanklin on the south coast of the Isle of Wight. Nestled in greenery, it is very secluded, yet only moments from thatched pubs, cosy tearooms, the local train station, shops, restaurants and the long sandy beach. A beautiful and peaceful place to write.

Green Ink Writers' Gym

tel 07870 630788
email info@greeninkwritersgym.com
website www.greeninkwritersgym.com
Contact Rachel Knightley

Welcomes writers of all genres and levels of experience. Creative and inspiring courses provide the skills, motivation and sense of fun to guide you from work-in-progress to the end of your project. Runs six- and eight-week courses at Waterstones Piccadilly, the Barbican Library and the Olympic Cinema and Members' Club, and venues across London.

Hawthornden Castle

International Retreat for Writers, Lasswade, Midlothian EH18 1EG
tel 0131 440 2180
email office@hawthornden.org
Contact The Director

Exists to provide a peaceful setting where published writers can work without disturbance. The Retreat houses up to six writers at a time, who are known as Hawthornden Fellows. Writers from any part of the world may apply for the fellowships. No monetary assistance is given, nor any contribution to travelling expenses, but fellows board as guests of the Retreat. Application forms are available from January for the following calendar year. Deadline for applications 30 June.

The Hurst – The John Osborne Arvon Centre

Arvon, The Hurst, Clunton, Craven Arms, Shropshire SY7 0JA
tel (01588) 640658
email thehurst@arvon.org
website www.arvon.org
Centre Director Natasha Carlish, *Centre Administrator* Dan Pavitt

Offers residential writing courses April to December. Grants available. The Hurst is situated in the beautiful Clun Valley in Shropshire, 12 miles from Ludlow, and is set in 30 acres of woodland, with gardens and a lake.

Indian King Arts

Garmoe Cottage, 2 Trefrew Road, Camelford, Cornwall PL32 9TP
tel (01840) 212161
email indianking@btconnect.com

Weekly morning poetry group and monthly afternoon poetry workshop, facilitated by Helen Jagger; occasional all day poetry workshops and readings by guest poets; and bi-monthly novel workshop led by Karen Hayes. Also the home of the Poetry Society's North Cornwall Stanza.

The Inkwell Group

The Old Post Office, Kilmacanogue,
Co. Wicklow A98 V215, Republic of Ireland
tel +353 (0)1 2765921, +353 087 2835382
website www.inkwellwriters.ie
website www.writing.ie
Facebook www.facebook.com/TheInkwellGroup
Twitter @inkwellHQ
Contact Vanessa Fox O'Loughlin

The Inkwell Group works with writers at all stages of their career to improve their work and to achieve their goals. Inkwell is a literary scout for some of Ireland and the UK's top agents and has assisted bestselling and award-winning authors to publication. Inkwell developed www.writing.ie, Ireland's national writing resources magazine and the National Emerging Writer Programme with Dublin UNESCO City of Literature (free writing advice from experts on DVD and online). Founded 2006.

Irish Writers Centre – Áras Scríobhneoirí na hÉireann

19 Parnell Square, Dublin D01 E102,
Republic of Ireland
tel +353 (0)1 8721302
email info@writerscentre.ie
website www.writerscentre.ie

The national resource centre for Irish writers. It runs workshops, seminars and events related to the art of writing, hosts professional developments seminars for writers, provides space for writers, writing groups and other literary organisations. It also provides information to writers and the general public.

Isle of Wight Writing Courses and Workshops

F&F Productions, 39 Ranelagh Road, Sandown,
Isle of Wight PO36 8NT
tel (01983) 407772
email felicity@writeplot.co.uk
website www.felicityfair.co.uk
website www.learnwriting.co.uk
website www.wightdiamondpress.com
Contact Felicity Fair Thompson

Residential and non-residential occasional weekends through the year for beginners and experienced writers. Individual advice and workshops. Time to write and to enjoy the beautiful Isle of Wight in comfortable and roomy B&B accommodation, two minutes from beach path and coastal walks to Sandown and Shanklin. Also offers postal MS critiques and one-to-one advice on film scripts and fiction.

Jericho Writers

Belsyre Court, 57 Woodstock Road, Oxford OX2 6HJ
tel 0345 459 9560
email info@jerichowriters.com
website https://jerichowriters.com
Twitter @JerichoWriters
Founder Harry Bingham, *Operations* Samantha Novak

A writers' club which helps members to grow their careers through access to the best teaching materials, tools and practical advice. Membership benefits include access to video courses, masterclasses with advice from industry experts, information about UK literary agents and discounts and priority booking on editorial services, tutored courses and events.

Knuston Hall

Irchester, Wellingborough, Northants NN29 7EU
tel (01604) 362200
email enquiries@knustonhall.org.uk
website www.knustonhall.org.uk
Twitter @knustonhall

Knuston Hall offers an extensive programme of courses and events which can be attended on a residential or non-residential basis.

Le Verger

Savignac-Lédrier, Dordogne 24270, France
tel (01223) 316539 (UK)
email info@retreatfrance.co.uk
Contact David Lambert

Le Verger offers residential writers' retreats or tutored courses (poetry, drama, fiction and life writing) from May to September with experienced tutors. Guests stay in a comfortable stone house outside a picturesque village in the rolling Dordogne countryside of south-west France. Shared or individual accommodation in the main house, the Piggery or writer's cabins, full board (with wine) for up to ten writers. Besides creative and academic writers, Le Verger welcomes artists, photographers and anyone working on a creative project. Offers Yoga, Mindfulness & Creativity retreats. Transfers to/from Limoges and Brive. Listed with the National Association of Writers in Education (NAWE).

Limnisa Centre for Writers

Agios Georgios, 18030, Methana, Greece
tel +31 681 027701
email mariel@limnisa.com
website www.limnisa.com

International retreats and workshops for writers. Two hours by ferry from Piraeus, Limnisa stands in its own shaded garden with access to a tranquil beach, in a stunning position on the Methana Peninsula with views to Epidavros and the island of Aegina. Offers single rooms, studios or tents and all vegetarian meals. Check website for details and dates.

Lumb Bank – The Ted Hughes Arvon Centre

Arvon, Lumb Bank, Heptonstall, Hebden Bridge,
West Yorkshire HX7 6DF

tel (01422) 843714
email lumbbank@arvon.org
website www.arvon.org
Centre Director Rosie Scott, *Assistant Centre Director* Jill Penny, *Administrator* Becky Liddell

Offers residential writing courses April to December. Grants available. Lumb Bank is an 18th-century former mill-owner's house set in 20 acres of steep pasture land.

Annie McKie

Writer's Retreat, Keystone, Blakeney Hill, Glos. GL15 4BT
email annie@anniemckie.co.uk
website www.anniemckie.co.uk
Contact Annie McKie

A peaceful retreat in the Forest of Dean, Gloucestershire. Beautiful room with private access and en suite bathroom. Balcony with wide reaching views across woodland and the Severn Valley. A few steps from the garden gate take you into the Forest with its mile upon mile of public footpaths. Retreats are a minimum of two nights. The price includes all homemade vegetarian meals and an hour of one-to-one tuition. Additional feedback is available at an extra cost. All retreats are geared to the individual. Accepts only one guest at a time.

Marlborough College Summer School

Marlborough, Wilts. SN8 1PA
tel (01672) 892388
email admin@summerschool.org.uk
website www.summerschool.co.uk
Facebook www.facebook.com/MarlboroughCollegeSummerSchool
Twitter @MCol_Summer

Marlborough College Summer School runs during July and August each year. See website for dates. This multi-generational event will play host to a wide range of courses, many of which specialise in the creative arts. Whether you're into poetry, scriptwriting or wish to write your memoirs, there's sure to be a course to inspire you. Founded 1974.

The Memoir Writing Club

tel +353 (0)86 2523428
email office@thememoirwritingclub.com
website www.thememoirwritingclub.com
Facebook www.facebook.com/IreneGrahamWritingCourses
Founder Irene Graham

The Memoir Writing Club provides:

• 12-week online memoir writing course, interactive with audios and the *Memoir Writing Workbook*;
• private writing classes in person and online;
• memoir writing retreat in the west of Ireland;
• book writing coach services.

Irene Graham is the founder of The Creative Writer's Workshop and The Memoir Writing Club. She is also the author of *The Memoir Writing Workbook*. Her fiction and memoir writing workshops are accredited by George Mason University in the USA, as part of its undergraduate and graduate degree programmes.

Missenden Abbey School of Creative Arts

c/o Jessamine House, King Street, Tring, Herts. HP23 6BE
tel 07955 484605
email info@missendenschoolofcreativearts.co.uk
website www.missendenschoolofcreativearts.co.uk

Weekend and summer school creative writing courses for all abilities.

Moniack Mhor

Moniack Mhor, Teavarran, Kiltarlity, Beauly, Inverness-shire IV4 7HT
tel (01463) 741675
email info@moniackmhor.org.uk
website www.moniackmhor.org.uk
Centre Director Rachel Humphries

Moniack Mhor is Scotland's Creative Writing Centre, running residential creative writing courses, retreats and residencies throughout the year. In addition, the centre offers a programme of awards, residencies and retreats for writing groups and organisations. Tuition is by established writers, and the range of courses is designed to suit writers at all stages. Grants are available on all courses. High on a hill close to Loch Ness, the centre is an inspirational, inclusive and nurturing setting for writers to spend an intensive period focusing on their work. Established in 1993.

Monkton Wyld Court

Elsdon's Lane, Nr Charmouth, Bridport, Dorset DT6 6DQ
tel (01297) 560342
email info@monktonwyldcourt.org
website http://monktonwyldcourt.co.uk/writers-retreats/

A Victorian country house in a secluded valley on the Dorset/Devon border. Monkton Wyld Court is an educational charity offering affordable, full board, short- and long-term accommodation to writers of all sorts. Email or call to discuss availability.

Morley College

61 Westminster Bridge Road, London SE1 7HT
tel 020-7450 1889
website www.morleycollege.ac.uk
Facebook www.facebook.com/morleycollegewaterloo
Twitter @morleycollege

Offers a number of creative writing courses throughout the year.

Open College of the Arts

The Michael Young Arts Centre, Redbrook Business Park, Wilthorpe Road, Barnsley S75 1JN

tel 0800 731 2116
email enquiries@oca.ac.uk
website www.oca.ac.uk

Distance learning creative arts courses. Study part-time foundation, undergraduate and postgraduate course anywhere, any time as part of a UK and international student community.

Oxford University Summer School for Adults

Department for Continuing Education,
Rewley House, 1 Wellington Square,
Oxford OX1 2JA
tel (01865) 270360
email summerschools@conted.ox.ac.uk
website www.conted.ox.ac.uk/about/oussa

A four-week programme consisting of over 40 week-long courses, including creative writing and specialist literature courses.

Pitch to Publication

tel 07952 724299
email pitchtopublication@gmail.com
Twitter @glyniskoz
Twitter @liathughesjoshi
Contacts Glynis Kozma, Liat Hughes Joshi

Pitch to publication is an eight-week online course with telephone tuition and coaching. It is designed to take prospective non-fiction authors to the point where they are ready to submit a well-honed pitch to agents and publishers. Taught by two experienced, published non-fiction writers. Open to all. Courses run every 8-10 weeks.

Responsible Travel

First Floor, Edge House, 42 Bond Street,
Brighton BN1 1RD
tel (01273) 823700
email rosy@responsibletravel.com
website www.responsibletravel.com
Facebook www.facebook.com/responsibletravel
Twitter @r_travel

Offers a range of holidays, secluded retreats and specialist writing, painting and photography holidays. For writers and artists with confirmed commissions, can also help source press trips, dependent on the type of commission and publication involved.

SCBWI-BI Writer's Retreat

email scbwi@scbwi.org
website www.britishisles.scbwi.org/events

Providing an ideal opportunity for space to write, away from day-to-day demands, the programme is streamlined to allow maximum writing time. See website for further details and information about other writing and literary events organised by SCBWI-BI.

Scottish Universities', International Summer School

21 Buccleuch Place, Edinburgh EH8 9LN
tel 0131 650 4369
email suiss@ed.ac.uk
website www.suiss.ed.ac.uk
Facebook www.facebook.com/ScottishUniversitiesInternationalSummerSchool/

See the website for full details of the creative writing programme and the theatre and performance programme.

Skyros Writers' Lab

9 Eastcliff Road, Shanklin, Isle of Wight PO37 6AA
tel (01983) 865566
email holidays@skyros.com
website www.skyros.com
Facebook www.facebook.com/skyroshols
Twitter @SkyrosHolidays

The Skyros Writers' Lab, situated on the island of Skyros in Greece, offers writers of all levels the opportunity to learn from distinguished writers, share the joys and struggles of the creative process, discover their strengths and polish their skills. Courses are open to novices with a passion for writing as well as writers with a book under their belt. Arrive with work in progress or just an empty page; all are welcome.

The Skyros Writers' Lab has built up an excellent reputation over the years for its visiting authors who have included Steven Berkoff, Mez Packer, Leigh Russell, Sophie Hannah, Rachel Billington, Margaret Drabble, Hanif Kureishi, D.M. Thomas, Sue Townsend, Marina Warner, Hugo Williams, Hilary Mantel, James Kelman, Barry Unsworth, Bernice Rubens and Alison Lurie.

Maria Stephenson Creative Writing Courses

tel 07464 310998
email mariastephenson1973@outlook.com
website www.mariastephenson.com
website www.writeanovelinsixmonths.com
Facebook www.facebook.com/distancelearningcreativewritingcourses/
Twitter @writermaria2017
Contact Maria Stephenson

Author, poet and creative writing teacher, Maria Stephenson, offers the following courses: Write a Novel in Six Months and Write a Collection of Poetry in Six Months. The courses support all stages of completing a novel or poetry collection from planning to publication and follow a progressive 26-week online programme (currently priced at £195) which is classroom taught but adapted for distance learning. Visit the website or contact to receive a free introductory session by email.

Stiwdio Maelor

Maelor, Corris, Machynlleth SY20 9SP
tel 07480 231003

email stiwdiomaelor@gmail.com
website www.stiwdiomaelor.wordpress.com
Contact Veronica Calarco

Provides one to 12 week residencies with individual studios and accommodation for writers and artists. Writers and artists are able to take time out of their busy lives, visit a stunning area in North Wales, refocus on their work and find new inspiration. Maelor has a bursary programme and a competition every year to enable creatives to complete residencies fee free. Founded 2014 by artist Veronica Carlarco.

Swanwick, The Writers' Summer School

Hayes Conference Centre, Swanwick,
Derbyshire DE55 1AU
tel 07452 283652
email secretary@swanwickwritersschool.org.uk
website www.swanwickwritersschool.org.uk
Facebook www.facebook.com/SwanwickWriters
Twitter @swanwickwriters
Takes place August

Celebrating its 70th year in 2018, Swanwick offers the opportunity to learn new skills and hone existing ones. There is an extensive choice of courses, talks and workshops. Offers several highly subsidised places for writers aged between 18 and 30, and assistance for writers unable to afford the full course fee. Full details of the programme and information on how to apply for the TopWrite Programme and Assisted Places Scheme are available on the website.

TLC Literary Adventures

The Literary Consultancy, Free Word Centre,
60 Farringdon Road, London EC1R 3GA
tel 020-7324 2563
email info@literaryconsultancy.co.uk
website www.literaryconsultancy.co.uk
website http://literaryconsultancy.co.uk/literary-adventures
Facebook www.facebook.com/pages/The-Literary-Consultancy/331088000235106
Twitter @TLCUK
Director Aki Schilz

TLC's annual writing retreat is held at the idyllic Casa Ana in Andalusia, Spain. Workshops are led by experienced tutor, bestselling ghostwriter, novelist, and former commissioning editor in publishing Tom Bromley. TLC Literary Adventures offers an environment where inspiration and improvisation meet. Guests have access to world-class teaching and get a chance to work, read, listen and relax in a stunning setting which opens the mind and the senses. The retreat is open to writers of fiction, memoir and general non-fiction. Groups are limited to a maximum of 12.

Totleigh Barton

Arvon, Totleigh Barton, Sheepwash, Beaworthy,
Devon EX21 5NS
tel (01409) 231338
email totleighbarton@arvon.org
website www.arvon.org
Twitter @TotleighBarton
Centre Director Mary Morris, *Assistant Centre Director* Eliza Squire, *Administrator* Sue Walker

Offers residential writing courses April to December. Grants available. Totleigh Barton is a thatched, 16th-century manor house, surrounded by farmland in Devon, two miles from the village of Sheepwash.

Travellers' Tales

58 Summerlee Avenue, London N2 9QH
email info@travellerstales.org
website www.travellerstales.org
Director Jonathan Lorie

UK's leading training agency for travel writers and travel photographers. Offers vocational courses with the UK's top travel photographers and travel writers in London, Marrakech, Istanbul and Andalusia including beginners' weekends, masterclasses and creative retreats. Hosts the Travellers' Tales Festival of the world's leading travel writers and photographers. Online tuition also available. Founded 2004.

Tŷ Newydd Writing Centre

Tŷ Newydd, Llanystumdwy, Cricieth,
Gwynedd LL52 0LW
tel (01766) 522811
email tynewydd@literaturewales.org
website www.tynewydd.wales
Twitter @ty_newydd

Tŷ Newydd, the former home of Prime Minister David Lloyd George, has hosted residential creative writing courses for writers of all abilities for over 25 years. Whether you're interested in a poetry masterclass, writing for the theatre, developing a novel for young adults or conquering the popular fiction market, there'll be a course in the programme suitable for you. Courses are open to everyone over the age of 16 and no qualifications are necessary. Tŷ Newydd can advise on the suitability of courses, and further details about each individual course can be obtained by visiting the website, or contacting the team by phone or email. Tŷ Newydd also offers courses for schools, corporate courses and away days for companies. Tŷ Newydd Writing Centre is run by Literature Wales, the national company for the development of literature in Wales.

Upton Cressett Foundation

Upton Cressett Hall, Upton Cressett, Nr Bridgnorth,
Shrops. WV16 6UH
tel (01746) 714616
email laura@uptoncressett.co.uk
website www.uptoncressetthall.co.uk

Guest fellows are invited to stay and write in the Foundation's historic Grade I Elizabethan gatehouse for up to four weeks (off season) to make progress with a literary project. The idea is to give established writers an opportunity to make headway with a work-in-progress in a remote and beautiful creative environment away from domestic or second career distractions. This could be 100 pages of a novel, a major rewrite after an editor's marks, a new play/screenplay or a monograph. Previous fellows include Dr Lara Feigel, the historian Juliet Gardiner and the playwright Ella Hickson.

Urban Writers' Retreat

email hello@urbanwritersretreat.co.uk
website www.urbanwritersretreat.co.uk
Facebook www.facebook.com/UrbanWritersRetreat
Twitter @urbanwriters
Contact Charlie Haynes

Urban Writers' Retreat creates time and space so you can focus and just write. Escape the real world and all its distractions at one-day retreats in London and blissful residential retreats in the countryside, or get online courses and support to help you kick procrastination into touch.

The Writers Bureau

8–10 Dutton Street, Manchester M3 1LE
tel 0161 819 9922
email studentservices@writersbureau.com
website www.writersbureau.com
Facebook www.facebook.com/pages/The-Writers-Bureau/65033531276
Twitter @writersbureau

The Writers Bureau offers a wide range of writing-related distance-learning courses including: Creative Writing, Freelance Journalism, Proofreading and Copy-Editing, Writing for Children, Copywriting, Poetry, How to Market Your Book, Non-Fiction Writing, Article Writing, Fiction Writing, Novel and Short Story Writing, Biographies, Memoirs and Family Histories, How to Write for Competitions, Writing for the Internet, Report Writing, Business Writing and Effective Time Management.

The courses are suitable for both beginners and writers wanting to brush up on their skills. The only requirement for enrolment is a good command of English and plenty of enthusiasm! Also holds annual writing competitions with cash and free courses as prizes. See www.wbcompetition.com.

Writers' Holiday at Fishguard

website www.writersholiday.net

Workshops and courses for writers of all standards from absolute beginner to bestselling author.

Writingclasses.co.uk

tel 0131-554 1857
email marianne@writingclasses.co.uk
website www.writingclasses.co.uk

Established to help beginner and emerging writers hone their writing skills and develop story ideas in a nurturing online environment. The school offers a range of short online courses throughout the year.

Experienced tutors, who are professional writers, give full feedback on all written work and are available to support students with all aspects of the course. Students come from throughout the UK and around the world. As long as you have a passion for telling stories and a desire to improve your writing skills, you can sign up for a writingclasses.co.uk course. Founded 2002.

www.writing.ie

The Old Post Office, Kilmacanogue,
Co. Wicklow A98 V215, Republic of Ireland
tel +353 (0)1 2765921, +353 (0)87 2835382
email vanessa@writing.ie
Contact Vanessa Fox O'Loughlin

A national online writing resources magazine packed full of author tips and assistance for new, emerging and established writers. Features author interviews plus information on competitions, submission opportunities, festivals and events as well as writing courses and workshops. Contains agent and publisher listings, guest blogs, plus services for writers listings, book reviews, writers' groups, book club information and giveaways. View the National Emerging Writer Programme (video), a joint project with Dublin UNESCO City of Literature, free online at www.writing.ie; vital tips and advice from three of Ireland's top writers, Carlo Gebler, Sinead Moriarty and Declan Hughes..

POSTGRADUATE COURSES

Aberystwyth University

Department of English and Creative Writing,
Hugh Owen Building, Penglais Campus,
Aberystwyth, Ceredigion SY23 3DY
tel (01970) 621946
email jxr@aber.ac.uk
website www.aber.ac.uk/en/english
Facebook www.facebook.com/aberystwyth.university
Contact Julie Roberts

MA in Creative Writing. PhD in Creative Writing. A new low residency PhD in Creative Writing for international students.

Bath Spa University

Bath Spa University, Newton Park, Newton St Loe,
Bath BA2 9BN
tel (01225) 875875
email admissions@bathspa.ac.uk
website www.bathspa.ac.uk

MA Creative Writing, MA Writing for Young People, MA Travel and Nature Writing, MRes Transnational Writing, PhD in Creative Writing.

Birkbeck College, University of London

Malet Street, London WC1E 7HX
tel 020-7631 6000

website www.bbk.ac.uk
Facebook www.facebook.com/BirkbeckUniversityofLondon
Twitter @BirkbeckNews

MA in Creative Writing: full- and part-time evening teaching. Applications from students writing fiction for young adults welcome. Tutors include: Julia Bell, Toby Litt and Russell Celyn Jones. PhD students also welcome but prospective students should consult with individual tutors before making an application. BA Creative Writing: four-years part-time, evening study. Course covers all genres from fiction to playwriting to poetry and practical courses on publishing and journalism. Screenwriting: MA/postgraduate certificate.

University of Bolton

Deane Road Campus, Bolton BL3 5AB
tel (01204) 903903
website www.bolton.ac.uk
Facebook www.facebook.com/UniversityofBolton
Twitter @BoltonUni
Contact Admission Tutor, Creative Writing: Dr Simon Holloway

MPhil/PhD in Creative Writing Specialisms.

Brunel University London

College of Business, Arts and Social Sciences, Brunel University London, Uxbridge, Middlesex UB8 3PH
tel (01895) 265599
email course-enquiries@brunel.ac.uk
website www.brunel.ac.uk/creativewriting

MA Creative Writing: The Novel, and MA Creative Writing.

Cardiff University

Cardiff School of English and Philosophy, John Percival Building, Colum Drive, Cardiff CF10 3EU
tel 029-2087 4722
email encap-pg@cardiff.ac.uk
website www.cf.ac.uk

MA and PhD in Creative Writing.

University of Chichester

Bishop Otter Campus, College Lane, Chichester, West Sussex PO19 6PE
tel (01243) 816000
email h.frey@chi.ac.uk
email h.dunkerley@chi.ac.uk
website www.chi.ac.uk
Contacts Prof. Hugo Frey, Head of Department; Dr Hugh Dunkerley, MA in Creative Writing Programme Coordinator

BA in Creative Writing; MA in Creative Writing, PhD in Creative Writing. One of the most established creative writing programmes in the country. Students can work with practising writers to develop themselves as a novelist, short story writer, dramatist, screenwriter or poet. Hosts regular visits by high profile writers, editors and agents. Many students go on to publish and win prizes.

City University

City University, Northampton Square, London EC1V 0HB
email enquiries@city.ac.uk
website www.city.ac.uk
Facebook www.facebook.com/cityuniversitylondon
Twitter @CityUniLondon

MA Creative Writing (Non-Fiction), MA Creative Writing (Literary Novels, Crime/Thriller Novels), MA Creative Writing (Screenplay and Screenwriting), MA Creative Writing & Publishing.

University of Cumbria

Bowerham Road, Lancaster LA1 3JD
tel 0845 606 1144
email enquirycentre@cumbria.ac.uk
website www.cumbria.ac.uk
Facebook www.facebook.com/universityofcumbria
Twitter @CumbriaUni

MA in Scriptwriting. MA in Creative Writing.

De Montfort University

Admissions Team, De Montfort University, The Gateway, Leicester LE1 9BH
tel 0116 255 1551
website www.dmu.ac.uk/home.aspx

MA in Television Scriptwriting. This long-established course concentrates on the craft of television scriptwriting and prepares students for the competitive world of professional writing. It offers direct links and networking opportunities within the industry by introducing students to professional writers, script editors, agents and producers through a regular programme of guest lectures, workshops, location visits and one-to-one mentoring.

University of East Anglia

Admissions Office, School of Literature, Drama and Creative Writing, Faculty of Arts and Humanities, University of East Anglia, Norwich Research Park, Norwich NR4 7TJ
tel (01603) 591515
email admissions@uea.ac.uk
website www.uea.ac.uk/ldc
Contact Admissions Office

MA Creative Writing: Poetry. MA Creative Writing: Prose Fiction. MA Creative Writing: Scriptwriting. MA Biography and Creative Non-Fiction. MFA Creative Writing. MA Creative Writing: Crime Fiction. MA Literary Translation. MA Medieval and Early Modern Textual Cultures 1381–1688. MA Modern and Contemporary Writing. MA Theatre Directing: Text and Production. Master's by research,

MPhil and PhD. For academic enquiries, contact Thomas Rutledge at t.rutledge@uea.ac.uk.

Edge Hill University

Department of English and History, St Helens Road, Ormskirk L39 4QP
tel (01695) 584274
website www.edgehill.ac.uk

For MA in Creative Writing (full- and part-time, established 1989) and PhD programmes in creative writing, contact Prof. Robert Sheppard (shepparr@edgehill.ac.uk). For BA in Creative Writing, contact Rodge Glass (rodge.glass@edgehill.ac.uk).

University of Edinburgh

website www.ed.ac.uk
Twitter @UniofEdinburgh

Various postgraduate courses in Creative Writing.

University of Essex

Wivenhoe Park, Colchester CO4 3SQ
tel (01206) 872624
email thorj@essex.ac.uk
website www.essex.ac.uk
Contact Dept of Literature, Film, and Theatre Studies

MA in Creative Writing.

University of Exeter

College of Humanities, Department of Drama, Thornlea, New North Road, Exeter EX4 4LA
tel (01392) 722427
email drama@exeter.ac.uk
website www.exeter.ac.uk/drama

MA in International Contemporary Performance Practice with specialist pathways.

Falmouth University

Falmouth Campus, Woodlane, Falmouth, Cornwall TR11 4RH
tel (01326) 213730
website www.falmouth.ac.uk
Contact Admissions Team

Writing & Journalism at Falmouth has a reputation for excellence in teaching, renowned MA courses and internationally recognised research. Blending a solid foundation in the study of English literature and a practical engagement with the craft and vocation of creative writing and a choice of four undergraduate degrees in journalism, Falmouth focuses on the development of imaginative thinking and professional skills that are more important than ever to writers, editors and multimedia communicators. Falmouth offers postgraduate MA courses in Professional Writing and Writing for Script & Screen.

University of Glasgow

Creative Writing, School of Critical Studies, 5 Lilybank Gardens, Glasgow G12 8QQ
tel 0141 330 8372
website www.gla.ac.uk/schools/critical/creativewriting/

MLitt, MFA and DFA in Creative Writing, MLitt by distance learning, Low Residency MFA/DFA.

University of Hull

English and Creative Writing Subject Group, School of Arts, Culture & Education, University of Hull, Cottingham Road, Hull HU6 7RX
tel (01482) 466604
email pgenglish@hull.ac.uk
email englishoffice@hull.ac.uk
website www.hull.ac.uk

MA/PhD courses.

Kingston University

River House, 53–57 High Street, Kingston upon Thames, Surrey KT1 1LQ
tel 020-8417 9000
website www.kingston.ac.uk
Facebook www.facebook.com/KingstonUni
Twitter @KingstonUni

Courses in Creative Writing, Journalism, Publishing.

Lancaster University

Dept of English Literature & Creative Writing, County College, Lancaster University, Lancaster LA1 4YD
tel (01524) 593089
email l.j.atkinson@lancaster.ac.uk
website www.lancaster.ac.uk/english-literature-and-creative-writing/
Contact The Postgraduate Coordinator

MA in Creative Writing by Independent Project. MA in Creative Writing by Distance Learning. MA in Creative Writing (Modular). MA in Creative Writing with English Literary Studies. MA in English Literary Studies with Creative Writing. MA in English Literary Studies. MA in English Literary Research. PhD in Creative Writing. PhD in English Literature and Creative Writing. PhD in English Literature

University of Leeds

website www.leeds.ac.uk

Various postgraduate courses in design; media and communication; fine art; history of art; cultural studies; music and performance.

Leeds Beckett University

email admissionenquiries@leedsbeckett.ac.uk
website www.leedsbeckett.ac.uk
Facebook www.facebook.com/beckett
Twitter @leedsbeckett

MA in Film-making.

Liverpool John Moores University

Faculty of Arts, Professional & Social Studies, Redmonds Building, Brownlow Hill, Liverpool L3 5UG

tel 0151 231 5175
email APSadmissions@ljmu.ac.uk
website www.ljmu.ac.uk

MA in Screenwriting and MA in Writing.

University of London, Goldsmiths

Dept of English and Comparative Literature,
Goldsmiths, University of London,
London SE14 6NW
tel 020-7919 7752
email english@gold.ac.uk
website www.gold.ac.uk
Facebook www.facebook.com/GoldsmithsUoL
Twitter @GoldsmithsEng
Contact Department Business Manager

MPhil/PhD in Creative Writing, MA in Creative and Life Writing, BA in English with Creative Writing, among others. The Department of English and Comparative Literature is also the home of the Goldsmiths Writers' Centre and the Goldsmiths Prize for fiction at its most novel, as well as the Centre for Caribbean and Diaspora Studies and the Centre for Philosophy and Critical Thought.

University of London, Goldsmiths

Goldsmiths College, University of London,
London SE14 6NW
email course-info@gold.ac.uk
website www.gold.ac.uk

MA in Dramaturgy and Writing for Performance.

University of London, Royal Holloway

Dept of English, Royal Holloway,
University of London, Egham, Surrey TW20 0EX
tel (01784) 434455/437520
website www.rhul.ac.uk/English
Facebook www.facebook.com/pages/Royal-Holloway-University-of-London/6449932074
Twitter @RoyalHolloway

Contact Jo Shapcott

MA in Creative Writing, taught in central London.

London College of Communication

website www.arts.ac.uk
Facebook www.facebook.com/UniversityoftheArtsLondon
Twitter @UniArtsLondon

Various full-time, part-time and short courses.

The London Film School

London Film School, 24 Shelton Street,
London WC2H 9UB
tel 020-7836 9642
email info@lfs.org.uk
website www.lfs.org.uk

MA in Screenwriting. MA in Film-making

University of Manchester

University of Manchester, Oxford Road,
Manchester M13 9PL
tel 0161 306 1259
email info-cnw@manchester.ac.uk
website www.manchester.ac.uk/centrefornewwriting

Whether you want to study creative writing at an undergraduate, MA or PhD level, Manchester has a programme in poetry, prose or literature to meet your needs. MA and PhD in Creative Writing MA and PhD in Contemporary Literature and Culture and the MA in Screenwriting.

The Manchester Writing School at Manchester Metropolitan University

70 Oxford Street, Manchester M1 5NH
tel 0161 247 1787
email writingschool@mmu.ac.uk
website www.manchesterwritingschool.co.uk
Twitter @McrWritingSchl
Contact (admission and general enquiries) James Draper, Manager

Master of Fine Arts (MFA) and Master of Arts (MA) in Creative Writing with specialist routes in Novel, Poetry, Writing for Children & Young Adults and Place Writing. Campus-based and international online distance learning, available to study full-time (MA: one year, MFA two years) or part-time (MA: two years; MFA three years). September and January enrolment. Scholarships available (including Joyce Nield Fund for non-UK Commonwealth students). Evening taught, with strong industry links. MFA students complete a full-length book. PhD in Creative Writing – including PhD by practice and PhD by published work. Tutors include Susan Barker, Andrew Biswell, Carol Ann Duffy, Nikolai Duffy, Catherine Fox, Rachel Genn, Andrew Michael Hurley, Anjum Malik, Andrew McMillan, Livi Michael, Helen Mort, Gregory Norminton, Adam O'Riordan, Michael Symmons Roberts, Monique Roffey, Jean Sprackland, Simon Stephens, Joe Stretch and Alex Wheatle.

Tutors include Andrew Biswell, Carol Ann Duffy, Nikolai Duffy, Catherine Fox, Rachel Genn, Andrew Hurley, Anjum Malkik, Livi Michael, Helen Mort, Gregory Norminton, Adam O'Riordan, Michael Symmons Roberts, Monique Roffey, Jacqueline Roy, Nicholas Royle, Jean Sprackland, Joe Stretch, Julie Wilkinson. Home of the Manchester Children's Book Festival, 'Manchester Writing' event series, Manchester Poetry and Fiction Prizes, anthology publishing, and Carol Ann Duffy's national Laureate Education Projects.

Middlesex University

tel 020-8411 5555
email info@mdx.ac.uk
website www.mdx.ac.uk

MA Novel Writing. MA Writing for Creative and Professional Practice. Research degrees and journalism courses.

National Film and Television School

National Film and Television School,
Beaconsfield Studios, Station Road, Beaconsfield, Bucks. HP9 1LG
tel (01494) 671234
email info@nfts.co.uk
website www.nfts.co.uk

MA, diploma, certificate and short courses covering a wide range of disciplines relating to television and film.

Newcastle University

School of English Literature,
Language and Linguistics, Percy Building,
Newcastle upon Tyne NE1 7RU
tel 0191 222 7199
email pgadmissions@ncl.ac.uk
website www.ncl.ac.uk/elll
Twitter @NewUniPress
Contact Postgraduate Admission Secretary

MA in Creative Writing. Postgraduate Certificate in Creative Writing. PhD in Creative Writing.

Northumbria University

Faculty of Arts, Design and Social Sciences,
Lipman Building, Newcastle upon Tyne NE1 8ST
tel 0191 227 4444
email ar.admissions@northumbria.ac.uk
email laura.fish@northumbria.ac.uk
email michael.m.green@northumbria.ac.uk
website www.northumbria.ac.uk
Contacts Laura Fish, Programme Leader (MA Creative Writing), Tony Williams, Prof. Michael Green, Programme Leader (PhD Creative Writing)

MA in Creative Writing, PhD in Creative Writing.

Nottingham Trent University

School of Arts and Humanities,
Nottingham Trent University, Clifton Lane,
Nottingham NG11 8NS
tel 0115 848 4200
email rory.waterman@ntu.ac.uk
email hum.enquiries@ntu.ac.uk
website www.ntu.ac.uk/creativewriting
Facebook www.facebook.com/ntucreative/
Twitter @TrentUni
Contact Dr Rory Waterman, Programme Leader

MA in Creative Writing. A practice-based course in Nottingham UNESCO City of Literature, and one of the longest-established and successful programmes of its kind in the UK, with close links to the writing industry, an annual anthology, a programme of guest talks and workshops, and many highly successful graduate writers. Diverse module options include: Fiction; Poetry; Writing for Stage, Radio and Screen; Children's and Young Adult Fiction.

Oxford University

Department for Continuing Education,
Rewley House, 1 Wellington Square,
Oxford OX1 2JA
tel (01865) 280145
website www.conted.ox.ac.uk

Short online courses in creative writing: Getting Started in Creative Writing, Writing Drama, Writing Fiction, Writing Fiction for Young Adults, Writing Lives, Writing Poetry. Three intakes a year, in October, January and April. *Email*: onlinecourses@conted.ox.ac.uk.

Creative Writing Summer School: held at Exeter College in July/August. *Email*: ipwriters@conted.ox.ac.uk.

Master of Studies in Creative Writing (two years part-time): covering prose fiction, narrative non-fiction, radio and TV drama, poetry, stage drama and screenwriting. *Email*: mstcreativewriting@conted.ox.ac.uk.

The Undergraduate Diploma in Creative Writing is a two-year course structured around Saturday day schools (four per term). Students develop their skills in three major areas: poetry, prose and drama. *Email*: ppaward@conted.ox.ac.uk

Plymouth University

Faculty of Arts, University of Plymouth,
Drake Circus, Plymouth PL4 8AA
tel (01752) 600600
email admissions@plymouth.ac.uk
website www.plymouth.ac.uk
Facebook www.facebook.com/plymouthuni
Twitter @PlymUni

MA/Postgraduate Diploma in Creative Writing.

Queen's University, Belfast

Queen's University, Belfast, Belfast BT7 1NN
tel 028-9097 3319
website www.qub.ac.uk
Facebook www.facebook.com/QueensUniversityBelfast
Twitter @QueensUBelfast

MA/Postgraduate Diploma in Creative Writing. PhD in Creative Writing.

The Royal Central School of Speech and Drama

Embassy Theatre, Eton Avenue, London NW3 3HY
tel 020-7722 8183
email sarah.grochala@cssd.ac.uk
website www.cssd.ac.uk
Twitter @CSSDLondon

MA and MFA in Writing for Stage and Broadcast Media.

University of St Andrews

School of English, University of St Andrews,
St Andrews, Fife KY16 9AR

tel (01334) 462668
email pgeng@st-andrews.ac.uk
website www.st-andrews.ac.uk/english/postgraduate
Contact Alexandra Wallace, PG Administrator

MFA or MLitt in Creative Writing: Poetry or Prose MFA or MLitt in Playwriting and Screenwriting.

University of Salford

The Crescent, Salford M5 4WT
tel 0161 295 4545
website www.salford.ac.uk
Facebook www.facebook.com/salforduni/
Twitter @SalfordUni

Courses in journalism, scriptwriting and creative writing.

Sheffield Hallam University

City Campus, Sheffield S1 1WB
tel 0114 225 5555
email enquiries@shu.ac.uk
website www.shu.ac.uk
Facebook www.facebook.com/sheffieldhallamuniversity
Twitter @sheffhallumuni

MA Creative Writing.

University of South Wales

School of Humanities and Social Science, University of South Wales, Treforest, Pontypridd CF37 1DL
tel (01443) 654195
email philip.gross@southwales.ac.uk
website http://courses.southwales.ac.uk/courses/297-mphil-in-writing
Contact Prof. Philip Gross, Course Director

MPhil/PhD in Writing programme. One of the original creative writing master's programmes in the UK, this is a research degree with one-to-one supervision enhanced by three weekend workshopping residencies per year. Also an international students' version with a single five-day residency.

University of Wales Trinity Saint David

tel (01570) 422351
email admissions@uwtsd.ac.uk
website www.uwtsd.ac.uk
Facebook www.facebook.com/trinitysaintdavid
Twitter @UWTSD

MA in Creative Writing, MA in Creative and Script Writing.

University of Warwick

Dept of English and Comparative Literary Studies, Humanities Building, University of Warwick, Coventry CV4 7AL
tel 024-7652 3665
email pgenglish@warwick.ac.uk
website www.warwick.ac.uk
website www2.warwick.ac.uk/fac/arts/english/applying/postgraduatestudies/masters/writing

MA in Writing.

University of Winchester

Sparkford Road, Winchester SO22 4NR
tel (01962) 841515
email course.enquiries@winchester.ac.uk
website www.winchester.ac.uk
Facebook www.facebook.com/universityofwinchester
Twitter @_UoW

MA Writing for Children and MA Creative and Critical Writing.

Law and copyright

Copyright questions

Gillian Haggart Davies answers questions to draw out some of the legal issues and explain the basics of how copyright works, or should work, for the benefit of the writer.

What is copyright?

Copyright is a negative right in the sense that it is not a right of possession but is a right of *exclusion*. However, if you know your rights it can be a strong legal tool because copyright law affords remedies in both the civil and criminal courts. Material will automatically be protected by copyright without registration (in the UK) if it is original, i.e. not copied. The onus is on you, the writer, and your publisher to do the work of protecting, policing and enforcing your valuable intellectual property. Copyright is different in every country – registration is not possible in the UK, Japan or the Netherlands; it is optional in the USA (for some works), China and India; and mandatory for some works in other jurisdictions (e.g. for some works in the Kyrgyz Republic, Mauritius and Nepal). Unfortunately, generally speaking, people do not respect copyright and there are ongoing issues to do with copyright, especially online, with large expanses of 'grey areas'.

I am a freelance writer and submitted an article to a magazine editor and heard nothing back. Six months later I read a feature in a Sunday newspaper which looks very similar. Can I sue someone?

Pitching ideas can be fraught with difficulty. In legal terms you do not have any protection under copyright law for 'ideas', but only for 'the expression of those ideas' – for the way in which the ideas have been 'clothed in words' to paraphrase a Learned Judge. It could be argued that in many ways this distinction between ideas and their expression does not work for writing and 'literary works'. But that won't help you in court or get you legal recompense if you are ripped off.

In the situation described, you would need to prove that your work came first in time; that your work was seen by the second writer or publisher; and that the second person copied unlawfully a 'substantial part' of your work (this is qualitative not quantitative), which these days involves a very woolly and subjective judicial comparison of one work weighed against the other. You would also need to be able to counter any claims that the subject matter is not capable of being monopolised by you and show that there is actual language copying. Further, you might then have to fend off counter-arguments from the other party that you did not have copyright in the first place. The other writer can rely on a 'defence' that she has 'incidentally included' the text; or that her use is 'fair dealing' (because she is using it for a permitted purpose, for example of reporting news or current affairs; or that it is for research for non-commercial purposes; is included in educational materials (Indian case); or for private use; or for 'criticism or review'; or that it is parody, pastiche or satire). These defences are actually referred to in the legislation as 'exceptions' and are very strict, i.e. they have always been difficult to make out. On parody and pastiche see a recent situation on using Enid Blyton headings in an Edinburgh Fringe performance 'Five Go Off on One!', reminding us that trade mark law also protects headings, which are generally too short to be protected by copyright law (www.thetimes.co.uk/article/five-go-to-their-solicitor-so-now-there-are-four-for-fringe-show-kwwdjwstr).

In addition, the person doing the 'copying' or publishing could say that she had an 'implied licence' from you to do so; or that she had a common law right under trusts law: this would arise, say, if she and you had been accustomed to dealing with each other in such a way that you commonly gave her original work and she used/copied it.

Avoid these difficulties by taking practical pre-emptive steps: mark your speculative pieces 'in confidence' and add '© Your Name 201X'. Using the © symbol puts people on notice that you are aware of your rights. It would also have an effect later on if it came to litigation evidentially, i.e. if a person sees the copyright sign but nevertheless goes ahead and uses work without permission, the defence of 'innocent dissemination' cannot be relied upon.

You did not have copyright in the first place: if the subject matter is 'out there', i.e. common knowledge, copyright law may not protect the first work. The law is very contradictory in this area, as can be seen in these three cases which went to court: the persistent lifting of facts from another newspaper, even with rewriting, was deemed a copyright infringement; but copyright did protect a detailed sequence of ideas where precise wording was not copied; the fact that an author went to primary sources did not necessarily ensure that he was not copyright-infringing. However, copyright law does weigh heavily in favour of protecting the originator.

If a newspaper pays for an article and I then want to sell the story to a magazine, am I free under copyright law to do so?

Yes, provided that you have not assigned copyright or licensed exclusive use to the newspaper. When selling your work to newspapers or magazines, make it clear in writing that you are selling only First or Second Serial Rights, not your copyright.

Does being paid a kill fee affect my copyright in a given piece?

No, provided that you have not assigned or licensed your copyright to the magazine or newspaper. Broadly, never agree to an assignation; it is irreversible. Always license: those parts of copyright you want to license, for example print-only; UK only; not television rights, etc. Copyright rights are infinitely divisible and negotiable. If you have inadvertently or purposely granted copyright permission to the publisher and the publisher prints the piece, and you have taken a kill fee, don't forget that you can at least also claim 'secondary licence' income from the collective pool of monies collected on behalf of UK authors by both the ALCS (see page 707) and PLR (see page 143) if you are named on the piece. This may amount to only a tiny amount of money but it may take the sting out of the tail.

I am writing an (unauthorised) biography of a novelist. Can I quote her novels – since they are published and 'public domain'?

Using extracts and quotes is a very difficult area and there is no easy answer to this. If the author has definitely been deceased for 70 years or more, you may be fine; the work may have passed into the 'public domain'. However, unpublished works require caution. In general, unpublished works are protected by copyright as soon as they are 'expressed' and copyright belongs to the author until/unless published and rights are transferred to a publisher. Protection for unpublished works lasts for 50 years (usually); Crown copyright lasts for 125 years for unpublished works, etc.

Generally, copyright law requires you to ask permission and (usually) pay a fee for reuse. There is no exact recipe for the amount of money payable or the number of words you can 'take' before you need to pay. A law passed on 1 October 2014 says, somewhat vaguely, that you can take 'no more than is required for the specific purpose for which it is needed'. To quote from the legislation: 'Copyright in a work is not infringed by the use of a quotation from the work (whether for criticism or review or otherwise) provided that (a) the work has been made available to the public, (b) the use of the quotation is fair dealing with the work, (c) *the extent of the quotation is no more than is required by the specific purpose for which it is used* [emphasis added], and (d) the quotation is accompanied by a sufficient acknowledgement (*unless this would be impossible for reasons of practicality or otherwise* [emphasis added])' [Copyright and Rights in Performances (Quotation and Parody) Regulations 2014, No. 2356 (in force since 1 October 2014)]. But does this help? Is it not a bit woolly? In the biography example here, how much would 'no more than is necessary' be? A line from every work? A paragraph from every work? A page? The entirety of one work but excerpts only of others … or none at all? What if the biography is authorised, not unauthorised? These are all unanswered questions and untried by case law.

I want to use a quote from another book but don't know who owns the copyright. Can I just put it in quotes and use it?

If you cannot identify the source of the quote, we enter the murky waters of 'orphan works'. A scheme is now in place whereby you can buy a non-exclusive licence for the UK commercial or non-commercial use of an 'orphan work' from the IPO (Intellectual Property Office), for an application fee of £20 (for a single 'work', e.g. book), up to £80 for 30 'works', plus a licence fee, which will depend on the work and what you say about its use on the application form. The licence will last for seven years, which is the window of time allowed for a copyright owner to 'claim' the work (which goes on the IPO orphan works register when it becomes a licensed subject under the scheme).

The IPO will not grant an orphan-use licence if it thinks your use will be 'derogatory' of the copyright work, or if you are unable to show that you have made diligent attempts to trace the copyright owner, so the old rules about making such efforts now apply in statutory form. 'Diligent' efforts to trace the copyright owner could include contacting publishers, searching the WATCH (Writers Artists and their Copyright Holders) database (http://norman.hrc.utexas.edu/watch), and placing an advertisement in the *TLS*, the *Bookseller*, etc). Keep a record of all your efforts in case the copyright question comes back to bite you later, and use a disclaimer on your material. In an ideal world, all content would be tagged with details of what is permissible and how to contact the owner. [See www.alcs.co.uk/wiseup; IPO orphan works guidance at https://www.gov.uk/government/collections/orphan-works-guidance; and the section above relating to quoting from a novel.]

The US Supreme Court ruled in 2015 that Google's use of scanned text extracts and images, used in its search engine to let users choose whether to go ahead and read/see the full work, was not in breach of copyright. The US Copyright Office said the defence is decided on a case-by-case basis. 'The distinction between what is fair use and what is infringement in a particular case will not always be clear or easily defined. There is no specific number of words, lines, or notes that may safely be taken without permission. Acknowledging the source of the copyrighted material does not substitute for obtaining permission,' the US Copyright Office said. There are, however, at least four factors that judges must consider when deciding fair use: the purpose of use, the nature of the copyrighted work, the amount and substantiality of the portion taken, and the effect of the use upon the potential market. Google had urged the justices to side against the writers because, in the end, their works would be more readily discovered: 'Google Books gives readers a dramatically new way to find books of interest.' Google has stated that 'By formulating their own text queries and reviewing search results, users can identify, determine the relevance of, and locate books they might otherwise never have found.'

My publisher has forgotten to assert my copyright on the imprint page. What does that mean for me?

Technically, what is usually asserted on the imprint page is the moral right to be identified as author of the work. This 'paternity right' is lost if it is not 'asserted', so if it is not on the imprint page or anywhere else you lose the right. Moral rights are copyrights, separate to and additional to what we normally refer to as '('economic') copyright': they protect the personal side of creation, in that they are about the integrity of the work and the person/reputation of the creator; whereas the 'main'/economic copyright protection is there to ensure you get revenues from your work, for example licence fees and royalties. Both economic copyrights and moral rights were conferred by the 1988 UK statute and Berne Convention. They exist separately, so you can keep moral rights and 'licence away' copyright (economic copyrights). And so in reverse, even if your moral right to be identified as author is lost, your other rights – economic copyright and the moral right to not have your work subjected to 'derogatory treatment' – remain with you. Moral rights cannot be licensed or assigned because they are personal to the author, but they can be 'waived'; for example, a ghostwriter may well waive the right to be identified as author. Moral rights are very flexible and useful, but are not widely used.

I've found an illustration I want to use for the cover of a book that I'm self-publishing. I chose the picture (dated 1928) on purpose because the artist is out of copyright and the picture is in the 'public domain'. Why is the picture library, which holds the image, charging a reproduction fee?

You have to pay a reproduction fee under copyright law because of the separate copyright issue for photography. Because the original artwork was photographed, copyright vests separately in the photograph (of the artwork) as opposed to the artwork itself. It is a controversial area and one where the UK/US legal systems are split. Make sure that standing behind this is a contract with your publishing services provider identifying you as the copyright holder. Do not cede any rights. You should be granting the publisher a non-exclusive licence to publish your book only.

You should also be aware of changes which took effect in the UK in July 2016, which apply to all publishers of any illustrative or photographic pictures of 2D objects (e.g. chairs and furniture), 3D artworks, and possibly architecture (widely held by the design community as absurd). Publishers must now clear UK copyright permissions and pay any relevant fees for use of such images, unless that change to the law is undermined by judicial review, a sort of appeal procedure which could be instigated by, for example, the Publishers Association and/or the designers themselves, artists, photographers, publishers or authors.

I included someone's work on my blog, but as I blog for free and it's not a money-making thing, can I be sued for copyright infringement?

Yes you can. If the person alleging copyright infringement can show she has copyright in the work, that you had access to her work, can show you copied the whole of that work or a 'substantial part' of it, and that you did not have permission, you could well be infringing criminal and civil copyright laws. The point of copyright law – the economic as opposed to the moral rights aspect – is to protect the economic interests of the original copyright owner. If she can demonstrate that her position has been undermined by your blog in terms of her market share having diminished and/or that sales have been adversely affected, etc or if she can show that you have not paid her any reuse fee or asked permission or acknowledged her authorship, you are on very thin ice.

I retweeted, edited, two lines from Twitter. I tweet for free and it's not a money-making exercise; can I be sued for copyright infringement?

A similar answer to the above. 'Yes' or at least 'probably yes'. A ruling of the Court of Justice of the European Union (CJEU) interpreting EU copyright law strongly suggests copyright vests in anything that is the original author's creation, and in the EU case in point (*Infopaq*, 2009) that applied to an 11-word extract. This is in spite of the fact that there is a broader general principle in copyright that an 'insubstantial part' of a work does not enjoy copyright protection in the first place, and therefore there could be no breach. A good lawyer could argue either way as this is a grey area. The situation in the USA may be different but seems certainly arguable. An alternative way of viewing the situation is that this is a 'quote', and therefore 'exceptional', i.e. non-infringing under legislation introduced in 2014 (see above). But the issues have not been tested in court and, again, are wide open to argument. Keep an eye on the Great Repeal [Brexit] Bill.

In the UK the courts have moved in a different direction on this matter. The old 'test' looked at the author's 'labour', skill and effort. In continental EU countries a literary, dramatic or artistic work must generally possess a creative element or express its author's personality.

My book has been made available by a free book download site but I never agreed to this. What can I do?

Contact your publisher or ask the site direct (if it's a self-published work) to remove it from their website. If they do not act or do not respond, get legal advice: a lawyer will be able to issue a warning followed by a 'take down notice', followed if necessary by a court injunction. However, this is very difficult for cases worth under £10,000. And it is no understatement to say that the present system of access to justice and costs of lawyers and litigation will prove to be a significant hurdle for most writers. Take practical steps to protect copyright in your own works yourself by setting up a Google Alert for every title you own.

First steps legal advice may be available from the Society of Authors (see page 519), the Writers' Guild of Great Britain (see page 522), the National Union of Journalists (NUJ), the Society for Editors and Proofreaders (SfEP, page 538) or your local BusinessLink or an intellectual property specialist adviser like Own-It or Artquest (which deals with the visual arts but carries advice applicable to writers too).

May I reproduce and share a selfie taken in an art gallery or museum?

If you take a selfie in front of a sculpture and use the photo for a T-shirt and post and share it on Facebook, that picture violates the sculptor's copyright protection against high-commercialisation. **Artists, designers, photographers and crafters are protected too.** Since 28 July 2016, those creating for sale reproduction furniture have been restricted by a tighter UK copyright law, and those designers now enjoy the same protection as is afforded to makers of 'plastic graphic works', musicians, writers, broadcasters and film-makers, i.e. 75 years (not 25) post creator's death, following the repeal of section 52 of the 1988 UK Act which applies to reproductions of e.g. anglepoise lamps, the 'Barcelona' chair, and Eames' furniture, all going up in price x12. In line with 'the rest of the EU', the loop exempting pre-1957 designs closed. The repeal of section 52 of the 1988 Act became effective on 28 July 2016 (see www.gov.uk/government/uploads/system/uploads/attachment_data/file/606207/160408_guidance_s52_final_web_accessible.pdf).

Gillian Haggart Davies MA (Hons), LLB is the author of *Copyright Law for Artists, Designers and Photographers* (A&C Black 2010) and *Copyright Law for Writers, Editors and Publishers* (A&C Black 2011).

See also...

- *UK copyright law and publishing rights*, page 699
- *Writing features for newspapers and magazines*, page 3
- *Copyright Licensing Agency Ltd*, page 705
- *DACS (Design and Artists Copyright Society)*, page 709
- *Publishers' Licensing Services*, page 711

UK copyright law and publishing rights

Publisher Lynette Owen outlines the basic principles of copyright and how UK copyright law provides a framework for the protection of creative works, with particular reference to publishing.

Creators including writers and artists are dependent on copyright to protect their works and to underpin the arrangements they make with the publishers who bring their works to market. The United Kingdom has the oldest tradition of copyright legislation, starting with the Statute of Anne which came into force in 1710. The last full revision of UK copyright law resulted in the Copyright, Designs and Patents Act 1988 (CDPA); this replaced the 1956 Copyright Act, which in turn replaced the 1911 Copyright Act. Since the 1988 Act, there have been a number of revisions, usually undertaken via Statutory Instrument.

What is copyright?

Copyright is one aspect of intellectual property rights (IPR), which are often defined as relating to 'works of the mind'. Other aspects include design and patent rights. Copyright has both positive and negative aspects – it enables rightsholders to authorise the use of their work in a variety of ways and also to take action against unauthorised use. It is worth flagging here that there are different philosophies of copyright; the UK, in common with other Anglophone countries, operates under common law, based on factual case law, and views copyright works as property which can be traded and transferred. By contrast, countries which operate under civil law, based on civil codes, (e.g. the countries of mainland Europe) view copyright (referred to as *droit d'auteur*) more as a human right belonging to the creator, with far more restrictive regulations on how it can be exploited.

How does it work?

Each country has its own national copyright legislation which normally covers works created by citizens of that country, creators normally resident in that country, and works first published in that country. There is also normally an obligation to respect the creative works originating in other countries which belong to the same international copyright conventions; this is normally undertaken in the form of 'national treatment', i.e. each member country provides to the creative works from other member states the same standard of protection it would grant to the works of its own citizens. This means that there may be varying standards of protection from country to country, for example in terms of the duration of copyright protection; there may also be differing exceptions to copyright from country to country. Most countries in the world now belong to one or more of the international copyright conventions: the Berne Convention (1886), the Universal Copyright Convention (1952) and the World Intellectual Property Organization (WIPO) Copyright Treaty (1996, but in force from 2002 – this convention reinforces the concept of copyright in the digital age). Membership of a convention requires member states to observe certain minimum standards of copyright protection.

What types of work are protected by copyright?

The CDPA (Copyright, Designs and Patents Act 1988; see above) provides copyright protection to three main categories of creative works:

1. Original literary, dramatic, musical and artistic works

'Literary works' includes any work which is written, including tables, graphs, compilations and computer programs. It also includes databases which involve creativity in terms of selection by the compiler. Dramatic and musical works include performable works such as plays and dances, with the lyrics of musical works protected separately. Artistic works include graphic works (paintings, drawings, maps, engravings or similar works), sculptures, collages, works of architecture and works of artistic craftsmanship (although these can also be protected under design rights). All works must be original and in written or other fixed form.

2. Sound recordings, films and broadcasts

These are also protected and may involve the many different copyrights of performers, producers and broadcasters. Broadcasts traditionally covered transmission by radio and television, but now include satellite broadcasts and transmissions via the internet.

3. Copyright in typographical arrangements

This is a specific right under UK copyright law which does not appear in the legislation of many other countries. This right covers the design and layout of text and, as such, is a right quite separate from that of the creative content of the text; it belongs to the publisher in recognition of their skill and investment in the layout of a work and lasts for 25 years from the date of first publication of that version of the text.

Who owns the copyright?

The first owner of copyright is normally the creator, e.g. the writer, artist, composer, etc. The major exception to this, in UK copyright law, is if a work is created as part of the creator's regular employment, in which case copyright belongs to the employer. A good example of this would be when a publisher employs a team of lexicographers in-house to compile dictionary entries. US copyright law has a provision for 'works for hire' where content (text, illustrations, etc) may be commissioned by a publisher, usually on the basis of an outright fee, with copyright then belonging to the commissioning entity.

In the case of copyright controlled by the creator, he or she will then have a choice on how to deal with the question of copyright when dealing with a publisher. For an author or illustrator seeking to contract with a publisher, there are two possibilities:

i) They may retain ownership of the copyright and grant an exclusive licence or licences to one or more publishers for publication of the work in an agreed language, in agreed format/s, within agreed sales territories and for an agreed period of time. For example, an author could grant an exclusive licence to a UK publisher for the UK and Commonwealth markets, and a separate licence to a US publisher for the American market. This is a common scenario in trade (general) publishing.

ii) In educational, academic and professional publishing, the scenario may be different. The author may be asked to assign copyright to the publishing house – this is often a requirement for academic journal articles but may also be requested for books, even when the author is receiving an advance and ongoing royalties; it is particularly logical for multiauthor works where individual contributors may each be paid an outright fee. There is often much misunderstanding of copyright assignment and publishers should always be prepared to explain to authors and illustrators their reasons for requesting it. One particularly powerful reason is that it is often much simpler to take action against piracy if copyright is in the name of the publishing house.

With the rise of the internet, there is a need for protection of internet transmissions and for user-generated works; these are covered under provisions for 'communication to the public' and 'making available to the public'. However, the question of copyright ownership in user-generated works is complex, given the scale of material which is uploaded to social media sites such as YouTube, Facebook, Twitter, Instagram and others. If the material uploaded is original to the person undertaking the uploading, then copyright will belong to them, but a lot of such material may belong to other parties and may have been uploaded without their knowledge or consent.

What are moral rights?

Moral rights are personal to the creator and were introduced into UK copyright legislation for the first time in the CDPA 1988; they had long been a feature of civil law. They are quite separate from the economic rights of the creator and in the UK they last for the same period as copyright protection; in some other legislations they are inalienable and perpetual. They include the right of paternity (the right to be recognised as the creator), the right of integrity (the right to object to derogatory or damaging treatment of the work), and the right to object to false attribution of a work. UK legislation is unusual in that it requires the creator to assert his or her right of paternity (this is often done via a notice on the title verso page of a book); it also allows for the creator to waive his or her moral rights, something which may be necessary for certain forms of publication or when a book is used as the basis for film or television exploitation.

How long does copyright last?

In the case of the UK, the period of protection is now 70 years from the end of the year in which the creator dies – in the case of works of collaborative authorship, from the end of the year in which the last author dies. The term of protection was extended from 50 to 70 years for all works still in copyright as at 1 July 1995, as a result of an EU directive to harmonise the term of copyright within the European Union. Works published in the USA since 1 January 1978 also now have a similar period of protection. However, many countries in the world still have a shorter period of protection (e.g. Japan and China have a period of 50 years *post mortem auctoris*).

What does copyright enable the owner to do?

It enables the owner to undertake or authorise reproduction and distribution of the work to the public, as well as a range of other methods of exploiting the work, including performance, broadcasting and adaptations (which would include translations). It is normally an infringement of copyright for anyone to undertake any of these activities without authorisation from the copyright holder.

What action can be taken against copyright infringement?

UK copyright legislation permits action to be taken under civil or criminal law, depending on the nature of the infringement; penalties are decided by the courts. By contrast, the legislation of some countries defines the penalties in terms of maximum financial fines or terms of imprisonment. There are many possible categories of infringement – these could include unauthorised reproduction, unauthorised adaptation, plagiarism and passing off. In the internet age, unauthorised use of copyright content has increased; some is undertaken for commercial purposes via torrent sites, whilst other cases may be file sharing (e.g. of textbooks amongst students). The Publishers Association has a website which enables its members to issue 'notice and takedown' to infringing sites (see www.copyrightinfringementportal.org.uk).

Are there exceptions to copyright?

Most national copyright laws list a number of uses of copyright material which can be undertaken without permission from or payment to the copyright owner, subject to certain conditions. The CDPA 1988 provides for a number of these:

- Fair dealing with a literary, dramatic, musical or artistic work for the purposes of research or study;
- Fair dealing for the purposes of criticism or review;
- Fair dealing with a work (other than a photograph) for the purpose or reporting current events.

These uses are permitted subject to due acknowledgement to the creator and the source, provided they do not adversely affect the normal interests of the copyright holder. There is no statutory definition of *fair dealing*, but most publishers would consider that fair dealing does not apply to use in the context of a commercial publication, so an author wishing to include copyright text or illustrations from outside sources in his or her own book should not assume that this is covered by fair dealing, however short the material may be.

The CDPA also provides for the copying of material for educational purposes, provided this is not undertaken by a reprographic process; thus, for example, displaying a passage of text on an interactive whiteboard is permitted. Large-scale copying of limited amounts of copyright material via photocopying or scanning (e.g. for course-packs for schools or universities, or on a company intranet) is covered under collective licences issued by the Copyright Licensing Agency (CLA) which negotiates licences to schools, colleges, universities, government departments and private businesses for such use; a share of licence revenue is paid to authors via the Authors Licensing and Collecting Society (ALCS), to visual artists via the Design and Artists Collecting Society (DACS) or the Picture Industry Collecting Society for Effective Licensing (PICSEL), and to publishers via Publishers' Licensing Services (PLS).

Useful websites

Authors Licensing and Collecting Society (ALCS): www.alcs.co.uk

Copyright Licensing Agency (CLA): www.cla.co.uk

Design and Artists Copyright Society (DACS): www.dacs.org.uk

Intellectual Property Office (IPO): www.ipo.gov.uk

Picture Industry Collecting Society for Effective Licensing (PICSEL): www.picsel.org.uk

Publishers' Licensing Services (PLS): www.pls.org.uk

Publishers Association: www.publishers.org.uk

Society of Authors: www.societyofauthors.org

World Intellectual Property Organisation (WIPO): www.wipo.int/portal/en/index.html

Organisations similar to CLA exist in many overseas countries and revenue from the copying of extracts from UK copyright works abroad is channelled to CLA via bilateral agreements with those organisations.

There are also provisions for the inclusion of short passages of published literary and dramatic works in educational anthologies, provided this does not affect the interests of the copyright holders and that such material does not represent the majority of the anthology.

The CDPA 1988 permits the making of a single copy of a copyright work by a library on behalf of a person undertaking research or private study, and it also permits libraries to make copies for the purposes of preservation or replacement of a damaged item.

There has been a copyright exception for visually impaired people since the Copyright (Visually Impaired Persons) Act 2002, giving them the right to accessible versions of copyright content (e.g. in Braille, audio or text-to-speech versions).

2014 saw the introduction of a number of amendments to existing copyright exceptions and some new exceptions, introduced via statutory instruments. Among them was an exception for copying for private use; fair dealing for non-commercial research or private study; a fair dealing exception for criticism or review or otherwise (the latter term undefined); a new exception for caricature, parody or pastiche; a new exception for text and data analysis for non-commercial research; and an extension of the exception for visually impaired persons to cover persons whose ability to read is affected by their disability (either physical or e.g. dyslexia). It remains the case that any fair dealing use must acknowledge the source and must not affect the normal interests of the rightsholder.

Copyright acts

- Copyright, Designs and Patents Act 1988 (but it is vital to use an up-to-date amended version). See www.gov.uk/government/organisations/intellectual-property-office.
- Duration of Copyright and Rights in Performances Regulations 1995 (SI 1995 No. 3297)
- Copyright and Rights in Database Regulations 1997 (SI 1997/3032) amended by the Copyright and Rights in Databases (Amendment) Regulations 2003 (SI 2003/2501)
- Copyright and Related Rights Regulations 2003 (SI 2003 No. 2498)
- Intellectual Property (Enforcement, etc) Regulations 2006 (SI 2006 No. 1028)
- Performances (Moral Rights, etc) Regulations 2006 (SI 2006 No. 18)
- Copyright and Rights in Performances (Quotation and Parody) Regulations 2014
- Copyright and Rights in Performances (Personal Copies for Private Use) Regulations 2014

How has UK copyright law changed?

In particular, UK copyright law has been influenced by a number of EU directives over the years, which have normally been implemented via statutory instruments. The most significant have been: the 1993 Directive on the Duration of Copyright and Authors' Rights (93/98/EEC), implemented via the Duration of Copyright and Rights in Performance Regulations 1995 (SI 1995 No 3297); the EC Database Directive 96/9 EC which was implemented via the Copyright and Rights in Databases Regulations 1997; and the EU Directive 2001/29/EC on the Harmonisation of Certain Aspects of Copyright and Related Rights in the Information Society, which included a transmission right and the right for copyright holders to use encryption and identifier systems to protect their works (implemented by SI 2003 No. 2498, the Copyright and Related Rights Regulations).

The EC is currently considering a major copyright review, but with the UK due to leave EU membership by 29 March 2019 and a transition period until 31 December 2020, it is unclear what effect that might have on UK copyright legislation.

Copyright under the microscope?

The last 20 years have seen a plethora of reviews of copyright – at international, multinational and national level – raising the question of the balance of interest between rightsholders and users, and questioning whether copyright remains fit for purpose. The rise of the internet has raised expectations amongst many users that content should be instantly available and preferably free of charge. The dangers of this have been seen all too clearly, in particular with the adverse impact on the music, film and computer software industries and their creators. On the other hand, some creators have been happy to make their work available under a range of Creative Commons licences, some more restrictive than others. There is an ongoing move towards Open Access in the academic sector, with its impact being felt particularly in the area of academic journals.

Copyright has had a long history of adapting to developments in technology and to changing market needs; hence it remains fit for purpose and is a necessary framework that enables creators to receive a just reward for the use of their work and to recognise the skills and investment of those who, like publishers, bring their works to market.

Further reading

Cornish, William et al., *Intellectual Property, Patents, Copyrights, Trademarks and Allied Rights* (Sweet & Maxwell, 9th edn due 30 September 2018)

Bently, Lionel and Sherman, Brad, *Intellectual Property Law* (OUP, 4th edn 2014)

Caddick, Nicholas et al., *Copinger and Skone James on Copyright* (Sweet & Maxwell, 17th edn 2016)

Jones, Hugh and Benson, Christopher, *Publishing Law* (Routledge, 5th edn 2016)

Haggart Davies, Gillian, *Copyright for Artists, Photographers and Designers* (A&C Black 2010)

Haggart Davies, Gillian, *Copyright for Writers, Editors and Publishers* (A&C Black 2011)

Owen, Lynette (Gen. Ed.), *Clark's Publishing Agreements: A Book of Precedents* (Bloomsbury Professional, 10th edn 2017)

Lynette Owen, OBE has worked at Cambridge University Press, Pitman Publishing, Marshall Cavendish and Pearson Education, and is now a freelance copyright and rights consultant at Lynette Owen consultancy. Her book, *Selling Rights*, published by Routledge, is now in its 7th edition (2014).

See also...

- *Copyright questions*, page 693
- *Copyright Licensing Agency Ltd*, page 705
- *Authors' Licensing and Collecting Society*, page 707
- *DACS (Design and Artists Copyright Society)*, page 709
- *Publishers' Licensing Services*, page 711

Copyright Licensing Agency Ltd

Since 1983, the CLA has been the recognised UK collective rights licensing body for text and images from book, journal and magazine content.

CLA provides rights, content and licensing services to customers in the academic, professional and public sectors. It performs collective licensing on behalf of ALCS (the Authors' Licensing and Collecting Society) and the PLS (Publishers' Licensing Service) and other copyright owners. With streamlined workflow systems and over 35 years' experience it is uniquely positioned to help content users access, copy and share the content they need while making sure copyright owners are paid the royalties they are due.

CLA's licences permit limited copying from print and digital publications. This copying includes photocopying, scanning and emailing of articles and extracts from books, journals and magazines, as well as digital copying from electronic publications, online titles and websites. CLA issues its licences to schools, further and higher education, businesses and government bodies. The money collected is distributed to the copyright owners to ensure that they are fairly rewarded for the use of their intellectual property.

Why was CLA established?

CLA was set up in 1983 by its founding members, the ALCS (see page 707) and PLS (see page 711). CLA represents creators and publishers by licensing the copying of their work and promoting the role and value of copyright. By championing copyright it is helping to sustain creativity and maintain the incentive to produce new work. It also collects money for visual artists and has two other collective management organisation members who represent visual artists; DACS (Design and Artists Copyright Society (page 709) and PICSEL (Picture Industry Collecting Society for Effective Licensing) distribute money from CLA licence fees to visual artists such as illustrators and photographers.

Further information

The Copyright Licensing Agency Ltd
Barnard's Inn, 86 Fetter Lane, London EC4A 1EN
tel 020-7400 3100
email cla@cla.co.uk
website www.cla.co.uk

How CLA helps creators and users of copyright work

CLA provides content users with access to millions of titles worldwide. In return, CLA ensures that creators, artists, photographers and writers, along with publishers, are paid royalties for the copying, sharing and re-use of limited extracts of their published work.

Through this collective licensing system CLA is able to provide users with the simplest and most cost-effective means of obtaining authorisation for the use of their work.

CLA has licences which enable digitisation of existing print material, enabling users to scan and electronically send extracts from print copyright works as well as copy digital electronic and online publications, including websites.

Who is licensed?

CLA offers licences to three principal sectors:

- education (schools, further and higher education);
- government (central departments, local authorities, public bodies); and
- business (businesses, industry and the professions).

The licences meet the specific needs of each sector and user groups within each sector. Depending upon the requirement, there are both blanket and transactional licences available. Every licence allows copying from most print and digital books, journals, magazines and periodicals published in the UK.

The international dimension

Many countries have established equivalents to CLA and the number of such agencies is set to grow. Nearly all these agencies, including CLA, are members of the International Federation of Reproduction Rights Organisations (IFRRO).

Through reciprocal arrangements covering 36 overseas territories, including the USA, Canada and most EU countries, CLA's licences allow copying from an expanding list of international publications. CLA receives monies from these territories for the copying of UK material abroad, passing it on to UK rights holders.

Distribution of licence fees

The fees collected from licensees are forwarded to ALCS, PLS, DACS and PISCEL for distribution to publishers, writers and visual artists. The allocation of fees is based on subscriptions, library holdings and detailed surveys of copying activity (see www.cla.co.uk/who-receives-royalties and read the 'Distribution Model Report'). CLA has collected and distributed over £1.4 billion as royalties to copyright owners since 1983. For the year 2016/17, £65.5 million was paid to creators and publishers in the UK and abroad.

Copyright. Made simple

CLA exist to simplify copyright for content users and copyright owners. They help their customers to legally access, copy and share published content while making sure copyright owners are paid royalties for the use of their work.

Their rights, licences and innovative digital services make it easy for content users across the academic, professional and public sectors to use and manage content from books, journals, magazines and online publications, including websites. By doing so they simplify access to the work of 87,000 authors, 25,000 visual artists and 3,500 publishers and play an important part in supporting the creative industries.

See also...

- *Copyright questions*, page 693
- *Authors' Licensing and Collecting Society*, page 707
- *DACS (Design and Artists Copyright Society)*, page 709
- *UK copyright law and publishing rights*, page 699

Authors' Licensing and Collecting Society

ALCS is the rights management society for UK writers.

ALCS (The Authors' Licensing and Collecting Society) is the UK collective rights management society for writers. Established in 1977, it represents the interests of all UK writers and aims to ensure that they are fairly compensated for any works that are copied, broadcast or recorded.

A non-profit company, ALCS was set up in the wake of the campaign to establish a Public Lending Right (see page 143) to help writers protect and exploit their collective rights. Today, it is the largest writers' organisation in the UK with a membership of approximately 90,000. In the financial year of 2016/17, over £32.6 million (net) in royalties were paid out to more than 78,000 writers.

ALCS is committed to ensuring that the rights of writers, both intellectual property and moral, are fully respected and fairly rewarded. It represents all types of writers and includes educational, research and academic authors drawn from the professions: scriptwriters, adaptors, playwrights, poets, editors and freelance journalists, across the print and broadcast media.

Internationally recognised as a leading authority on copyright matters and authors' interests, ALCS is committed to fostering an awareness of intellectual property issues among the writing community. It maintains a close watching brief on all matters affecting copyright, both in the UK and internationally, and makes regular representations to the UK government and the European Union.

ALCS collects fees that are difficult, time-consuming or legally impossible for writers and their representatives to claim on an individual basis, money that is nonetheless due to them. To date, it has distributed over £450 million in secondary royalties to writers. Over the years, ALCS has developed highly specialised knowledge and sophisticated systems that can track writers and their works against any secondary use for which they are due payment. A network of international contacts and reciprocal agreements with foreign collecting societies also ensures that UK writers are compensated for any similar use overseas.

Membership

Authors' Licensing and Collecting Society Ltd
1st Floor, Barnard's Inn, 86 Fetter Lane,
London EC4A 1EN
tel 020-7264 5700
email alcs@alcs.co.uk
website www.alcs.co.uk
Chief Executive Owen Atkinson

Membership is open to all writers and successors to their estates at a one-off fee of £36 for Ordinary membership. Members of the Society of Authors, the Writers' Guild of Great Britain, National Union of Journalists, Chartered Institute of Journalists and British Association of Journalists have free Ordinary membership of ALCS. Operations are primarily funded through a commission levied on distributions and membership fees. The commission on funds generated for Ordinary members is currently 9.5%. Most writers will find that this, together with a number of other membership benefits, provides good value.

The primary sources of fees due to writers are secondary royalties from the following:

Photocopying and scanning

The single largest source of income, this is administered by the Copyright Licensing Agency (CLA, see page 705). Created in 1982 by ALCS and the Publishers Licensing Society (PLS), CLA grants licences to users for copying books and serials. This includes schools, colleges, universities, central and local government departments, as well as the British Library, businesses and other institutions. Licence fees are based on the number of people who benefit and the number of copies made. The revenue from this is then split between the rights holders: authors, publishers and artists. Money due to authors is transferred to ALCS for distribution. ALCS also receives photocopying payments from foreign sources.

Foreign Public Lending Right

The Public Lending Right (PLR) system pays authors whose books are borrowed from public libraries. Through reciprocal agreements, ALCS members receive payment whenever their books are borrowed from German, Belgian, Dutch, French, Austrian, Estonian and Irish libraries. Please note that ALCS does not administer the UK Public Lending Right; this is managed directly by the UK PLR Office (see page 143).

ALCS also receives other payments from Germany. These cover the loan of academic, scientific and technical titles from academic libraries; extracts of authors' works in textbooks and the press, together with other one-off fees.

Simultaneous cable retransmission

This involves the simultaneous showing of one country's television signals in another country, via a cable network. Cable companies pay a central collecting organisation a percentage of their subscription fees, which must be collectively administered. This sum is then divided by the rights holders. ALCS receives the writers' share for British programmes containing literary and dramatic material and distributes it to them.

Educational recording

ALCS, together with the main broadcasters and rights holders, set up the Educational Recording Agency (ERA) in 1989 to offer licences to educational establishments. ERA collects fees from the licensees and pays ALCS the amount due to writers for their literary works.

Other sources of income include a blank tape levy and small, miscellaneous literary rights.

Tracing authors

ALCS is dedicated to protecting and promoting authors' rights and enabling writers to maximise their income. It is committed to ensuring that royalties due to writers are efficiently collected and speedily distributed to them. One of its greatest challenges is finding some of the writers for whom it holds funds and ensuring that they claim their money.

Any published author or broadcast writer could have some funds held by ALCS for them. It may be a nominal sum or it could run into several thousand pounds. Either call or visit the ALCS website – see **Membership** box for contact details.

DACS (Design and Artists Copyright Society)

Established by artists for artists, DACS is the UK's leading visual artists' rights management organisation.

As a not-for-profit organisation, DACS translates rights into revenues and recognition for a wide spectrum of visual artists. It collects and distributes royalties to visual artists and their estates through its different services, including Payback, Artist's Resale Right, Copyright Licensing and Artimage – in addition to lobbying, advocacy and legal advice for visual artists.

Contact details

DACS
33 Old Bethnal Green Road, London E2 6AA
tel 020-7336 8811
email info@dacs.org.uk
website www.dacs.org.uk

DACS is part of an international network of rights management organisations. Today DACS acts as a trusted broker for 100,000 artists and in 2016 it distributed £14 million in royalties to artists and estates. See website for more information about DACS and its services.

Payback

Each year DACS pays a share of royalties to visual artists whose work has been reproduced in UK magazines and books or broadcast on UK television channels. DACS operates this service for situations where it would be impractical or near impossible for an artist to license their rights on an individual basis, for example when a university student wants to photocopy pages from a book that features their work.

Artist's Resale Right

The Artist's Resale Right entitles artists to a royalty each time their work is resold for more than €1,000 by an auction house, gallery or dealer. DACS ensures artists receive their royalties from qualifying sales not just in the UK but also from other countries in the European Economic Area (EEA). Since 1 January 2012 in the UK, artists' heirs and beneficiaries can now benefit from these royalties. (See website for details of eligibility criteria.)

Copyright Licensing

This service benefits artists and their estates when their work is reproduced for commercial purposes, for example on t-shirts or greetings cards, in a book or on a website. DACS can take care of everything on behalf of the artist, ensuring terms, fees and contractual arrangements are all in order and in their best interests. Artists who use this service are also represented globally through the DACS international network of rights management organisations.

Copyright facts

- Copyright is a right granted to visual artists under law.
- Copyright in all artistic works is established from the moment of creation – the only qualification is that the work must be original.

• There is no registration system in the UK; copyright comes into operation automatically and lasts the lifetime of the visual artist plus a period of 70 years after their death.
• After death, copyright is usually transferred to the visual artist's heirs or beneficiaries. When the 70-year period has expired, the work then enters the public domain and no longer benefits from copyright protection.
• The copyright owner has the exclusive right to authorise the reproduction (or copy) of a work in any medium by any other party.
• Any reproduction can only take place with the copyright owner's consent.
• Permission is usually granted in return for a fee, which enables the visual artist to derive some income from other people using his or her work.
• If a visual artist is commissioned to produce a work, he or she will usually retain the copyright unless an agreement is signed which specifically assigns the copyright. When visual creators are employees and create work during the course of their employment, the employer retains the copyright in those works.

See also...

- *Freelancing for beginners*, page 481
- *How to get ahead in cartooning*, page 489
- *Copyright questions*, page 693
- *Copyright Licensing Agency Ltd*, page 705
- *UK copyright law and publishing rights, page 699*

Publishers' Licensing Services

The core business of Publishers' Licensing Services (formerly Publishers' Licensing Society) is to manage collective licensing. PLS has been serving the collective interests of publishers since 1981 and it is owned and governed by four publisher trade associations.

Key activities

• Collective licensing

Collective licensing offers a simple and cost-effective solution for those who wish to copy from published materials without breaking the law, and for rights-holders where direct licensing is inefficient and not cost-effective.

Contact details

PLS
Barnard's Inn, 86 Fetter Lane, London EC4A 1EN
tel 020-7079 5930
email pls@pls.org.uk
website www.pls.org.uk

PLS appoints licensing organisations, including Copyright Licensing Agency (CLA) which licenses the rights granted to it by publishers. CLA licenses organisations in the education, public and business sectors, allowing them to copy extracts from a broad range of titles in return for a licence fee. CLA also has reciprocal agreements with equivalent organisations around the world. CLA is able, therefore, to collect licensing revenue for the use of UK publications abroad. PLS licenses some magazine publishers' rights to businesses and government through NLA media access. PLS distributes the resulting licensing revenue to publishers according to the usage data collected from users; it distributed over £34m to publishers between April 2017 and March 2018.

• Permissions

PLS Permissions is a suite of services designed to help publishers optimise efficiencies in their permissions management processes and reduce the administrative burden. A new feature launched in 2017 is fee payable licensing. The service is particularly useful for editorial staff and authors seeking to clear permissions.

The suite comprises:

PermissionsDirect, which enables publishers to manage their own permissions requests in one simple online account;

PermissionsAssist, a service by which publishers outsource the entire management of their permissions to PLS;

PermissionsRequest, a free service that enables anyone seeking to reuse published content to get permission to do so quickly and easily.

PLS won the 'Innovator of the Year' award at the Stationers' Innovation Excellence Awards in 2017 for its new PLS Permissions services.

Find out more at www.PLS-Permissions.com.

• Access to research

The Access to Research service provides free access to over 15 million academic articles in public libraries across the UK. More than 80% of UK local authorities have signed up.

Access to Research was launched in response to a key recommendation of the Finch Group, namely that the major journal publishers should grant public libraries a licence to provide free access to their academic articles. Access to Research is the result of a unique collaboration between publishers, who have made their journal content available for free to UK libraries and librarians. The content is searchable through the Summon discovery service, generously provided by ProQuest.

Find out more at www.accesstoresearch.org.uk.

See also...

- *Authors' Licensing and Collecting Society*, page 707
- *Copyright Licensing Agency Ltd*, page 705
- *UK copyright law and publishing rights*, page 699

Finance for writers and artists

FAQs for writers

Peter Vaines, a tax barrister, addresses some frequently asked questions.

What can a working writer claim against tax?

A working writer is carrying on a business and can therefore claim all the expenses which are incurred wholly and exclusively for the purposes of that business. A list showing most of the usual expenses can be found in the article on *Income tax* (see page 715) but there will be other expenses that can be allowed in special circumstances. Strictly, only expenses which are incurred for the sole purpose of the business can be claimed; there must be no 'duality of purpose' so an item of expenditure cannot be divided into private and business parts. However, HM Revenue & Customs are now able to allow all reasonable expenses (including apportioned sums) where the amounts can be commercially justified.

Allowances can also be claimed for the cost of business assets such as a car, personal computers, printers and scanners and all other equipment (including books) which may be used by the writer. An allowance of 100% of the cost can now be claimed for most assets except cars, for which a lower allowance can be claimed. See the article on *Income tax* for further details of the deductions available in respect of capital expenditure.

Can I request interest on fees owed to me beyond 30 days of my invoice?

Yes. A writer is like any other person carrying on a business and is entitled to charge interest at a rate of 8% over bank base rate on any debt outstanding for more than 30 days – although the period of credit can be varied by agreement between the parties. It is not compulsory to claim the interest; it is your decision whether to enforce the right.

What can I do about bad debts?

A writer is in exactly the same position as anybody else carrying on a business over the payment of his or her invoices. It is generally not commercially sensible to insist on payment in advance but where the work involved is substantial (e.g. a book), it is usual to receive one third of the fee on signature, one third on delivery of the manuscript and the remaining one third on publication. On other assignments, perhaps not as substantial as a book, it could be worthwhile seeking 50% of the fee on signature and the other 50% on delivery. This would provide a degree of protection in case of cancellation of the assignment because of changes of policy or personnel at the publisher.

What financial disputes can I take to the Small Claims Court?

If somebody owes you money you can take them to the Small Claims section of your local County Court, which deals with financial disputes up to £10,000. It is much less formal than normal court proceedings and involves little expense. It is not necessary to have a solicitor. You fill in some forms, turn up and explain why you are owed the money (see www.gov.uk/make-court-claim-for-money/overview).

If I receive an advance, can I divide it between two tax years?

Yes. There is a system known as 'averaging'. This enables writers (and others engaged in the creation of literary or dramatic works or designs) to average the profits of two or more consecutive years if the profits for one year are less than 75% of the profits for the highest year. This relief can apply even if the work takes less than 12 months to create and it allows the writer to avoid the higher rates of tax which might arise if the income in respect of a number of years' work were all to be concentrated in a single year.

How do I make sure I am taxed as a self-employed person so that tax and National Insurance contributions are not deducted at source?

To be taxed as a self-employed person you have to make sure that the contract for the writing cannot be regarded as a contract of employment. This is unlikely to be the case with a professional author. The subject is highly complex but one of the most important features is that the publisher must not be in a position to direct or control the author's work. Where any doubt exists, the author might find the publisher deducting tax and National Insurance contributions as a precaution and that would clearly be highly disadvantageous. The author would be well advised to discuss the position with the publisher before the contract is signed to agree that he or she should be treated as self-employed and that no tax or National Insurance contributions will be deducted from any payments. If such agreement cannot be reached, professional advice should immediately be sought so that the detailed technical position can be explained to the publisher.

Is it a good idea to operate through a limited company?

It can be a good idea for a self-employed writer to operate through a company but generally only where the income is quite large. The costs of operating a company can outweigh any benefit if the writer is paying tax only at the basic rate. Where the writer is paying tax at the higher rate of 40% (or 45%), being able to retain some of the income in a company at a tax rate of only 19% is obviously attractive. However, this will be entirely ineffective if the writer's contract with the publisher would otherwise be an employment. The whole subject of operating through a company is complex and professional advice is essential.

When does it become necessary to register for VAT?

Where the writer's self-employed income (from all sources, not only writing) exceeds £85,000 in the previous 12 months or is expected to do so in the next 30 days, he or she must register for VAT and add VAT to all his/her fees. The publisher will pay the VAT to the writer, who must pay the VAT over to HM Revenue & Customs each quarter. Any VAT the writer has paid on business expenses and on the purchase of business assets can be deducted. It is possible for some authors to take advantage of the simplified system for VAT payments which applies to small businesses. This involves a flat rate payment of VAT without any need to keep records of VAT on expenses.

If I make a loss from my writing can I get any tax back?

Where a writer makes a loss, HM Revenue & Customs may suggest that the writing is only a hobby and not a professional activity, thereby denying any relief or tax deduction for the loss. However, providing the writing is carried out on a sensible commercial basis with an expectation of profits, any resulting loss can be offset against any other income the writer may have for the same or the previous year.

Income tax

Despite attempts by successive governments to simplify our taxation system, the subject has become increasingly complicated. Peter Vaines, a chartered accountant and barrister, gives a broad outline of taxation from the point of view of writers and other creative professionals. The proposals in the November 2017 Budget are broadly reflected in this article.

How income is taxed

Generally

Authors are usually treated for tax purposes as carrying on a profession and are taxed in a similar fashion to other self-employed professionals. This article is directed to self-employed persons only, because if a writer is employed he or she will be subject to the much less advantageous rules which apply to employment income.

Employed persons may try to shake off the status of 'employee' to attain 'freelance' status so as to qualify for the tax advantages, but such attempts meet with varying degrees of success. The problems involved in making this transition are considerable and space does not permit a detailed explanation to be made here – individual advice is necessary if difficulties are to be avoided.

Particular attention has been paid by HM Revenue & Customs (HMRC) to journalists and a number of sectors such as those engaged in the entertainment industry with a view to reclassifying them as employees so that PAYE is deducted from their earnings. This blanket treatment has been extended to other areas and, although it is obviously open to challenge by individual taxpayers, it is always difficult to persuade HMRC to change its views.

There is no reason why employed people cannot carry on a freelance business in their spare time. Indeed, aspiring authors, artists, musicians, etc often derive so little income from their craft that the financial security of an employment, perhaps in a different sphere of activity, is necessary. The existence of the employment is irrelevant to the taxation of the freelance earnings, although it is most important not to confuse the income or expenditure of the employment with that of the self-employed activity. HMRC is aware of the advantages which can be derived by an individual having 'freelance' income from an organisation of which he or she is also an employee, and where such circumstances are contrived, it can be extremely difficult to convince an Inspector of Taxes that a genuine freelance activity is being carried on. Where the individual operates through a company or partnership providing services personally to a particular client, and would be regarded as an employee if the services were supplied directly by the individual, additional problems arise from the notorious IR35 legislation and professional advice is essential.

For those starting in business or commencing work on a freelance basis there is a useful section called 'Working for yourself' on the GOV.UK website (www.gov.uk/working-for-yourself/overview).

Income

For income to be taxable it need not be substantial, nor even the author's only source of income; earnings from casual writing are also taxable but this can be an advantage because occasional writers do not often make a profit from their writing. The expenses incurred in connection with writing may well exceed any income receivable and the resultant loss may then be used to reclaim tax paid on other income. Certain allowable expenses and capital allowances may be deducted from the income, and these are set out in more detail below. The possibility of a loss being used as a basis for a tax repayment is fully appreciated by HMRC, which sometimes attempts to treat casual writing as a hobby so that any losses incurred cannot be used to reclaim tax; of course by the same token any income receivable would not be chargeable to tax. This treatment may sound attractive but it should be resisted vigorously because HMRC does not hesitate to change its mind when profits begin to arise. However, in exceptional or non-recurring writing, such as the autobiography of a sports personality or the memoirs of a politician, it could be better to be treated as pursuing a hobby and not as a professional author. Sales of copyright cannot be charged to income tax unless the recipient is a professional author – but the proceeds of sale of copyright may be charged to capital gains tax in the hands of an individual who is not a professional author.

Royalties

Where the recipient is a professional author, the proceeds of sale of copyright are taxable as income and not as capital receipts. Similarly, lump sums on account of, or in advance of royalties are also taxable as income in the year of receipt, subject to a claim for averaging relief (see below).

Copyright royalties are generally paid without deduction of income tax. However, if royalties are paid to a person who normally lives abroad, tax must be deducted by the payer or his agent at the time the payment is made unless arrangements are made with HMRC for payments to be made gross under the terms of a Double Taxation Agreement with the other country.

Grants, prizes and awards

Persons in receipt of grants from the Arts Council or similar bodies will be concerned whether or not such grants are liable to income tax. Many years ago HMRC issued a Statement of Practice after detailed discussions with the Arts Council regarding the tax treatment of the awards. Grants and other receipts of a similar nature were divided into two categories (see box) – those which were to be treated by HMRC as chargeable to tax and those which were not. Category A awards were considered to be taxable; awards made under category B were not chargeable to tax.

The Statement of Practice has not been withdrawn but it is no longer publicly available – although there is nothing to suggest that the treatment of awards in these categories will not continue to be treated in this way. In any event, the statement had no legal force and was merely and expression of the view of HMRC. It remains open to anybody in receipt of a grant or award to challenge the HMRC view on the merits of their own case.

The tax position of persons in receipt of literary prizes will generally follow a decision by the Special Commissioners in connection with the Whitbread Book Awards (now called the Costa Book Awards). In that case it was decided that the prize was not part of the author's professional income and accordingly not chargeable to tax. The precise details are not available because decisions of the Special Commissioners were not, at that time, reported unless an appeal was made to the High Court; HMRC chose not to appeal against this decision. Details of the many literary awards that are given each year start on page 565, and this decision is of considerable significance to the winners of these prizes. It would be unwise to assume that all such awards will be free of tax as the precise facts which were present in the case of the Whitbread awards may not be repeated in another case; however, it is clear that an author winning a prize has some very powerful arguments in his or her favour, should HMRC seek to charge tax on the award.

Allowable expenses

To qualify as an allowable business expense, expenditure has to be laid out wholly and exclusively for business purposes. Strictly there must be no 'duality of purpose', which means that expenditure cannot be apportioned to reflect private and business usage, for example food, clothing, telephone, travelling expenses, etc. However, HMRC will usually allow all reasonable expenses (including apportioned sums) where the amounts can be commercially justified.

It should be noted carefully that the expenditure does not have to be 'necessary', it merely has to be incurred 'wholly and exclusively' for business purposes. Naturally, however, expenditure of an outrageous and wholly unnecessary character might well give rise to a presumption that it was not really for business purposes. As with all things, some expenses are unquestionably allowable and some expenses are equally unquestionably not allowable – it is the grey area in between which gives rise to all the difficulties and the outcome invariably depends on negotiation with HMRC.

Arts Council awards

Arts Council category A awards

- Direct or indirect musical, design or choreographic commissions and direct or indirect commission of sculpture and paintings for public sites.
- The Royalty Supplement Guarantee Scheme.
- The Contract Writers' Scheme.
- Jazz bursaries.
- Translators' grants.
- Photographic awards and bursaries.
- Film and video awards and bursaries.
- Performance Art Awards.
- Art Publishing Grants.
- Grants to assist with a specific project or projects (such as the writing of a book) or to meet specific professional expenses such as a contribution towards copying expenses made to a composer or to an artist's studio expenses.

Arts Council category B awards

- Bursaries to trainee directors.
- Bursaries for associate directors.
- Bursaries to people attending full-time courses in arts administration (the practical training course).
- In-service bursaries to theatre designers and bursaries to trainees on the theatre designers' scheme.
- In-service bursaries for administrators.
- Bursaries for actors and actresses.
- Bursaries for technicians and stage managers.
- Bursaries made to students attending the City University Arts Administration courses.
- Awards, known as the Buying Time Awards, made not to assist with a specific project or professional expenses but to maintain the recipient to enable him or her to take time off to develop his or her personal talents. These include the awards and bursaries known as the Theatre Writing Bursaries, awards and bursaries to composers, awards and bursaries to painters, sculptors and print makers, literature awards and bursaries.

Great care should be taken when claiming a deduction for items where there may be a duality of purpose and negotiations should be conducted with more than usual care and courtesy – if provoked, the Inspector of Taxes may well choose to allow nothing. An appeal is always possible although unlikely to succeed as a string of cases in the Courts has clearly demonstrated. An example is the case of *Caillebotte* v. *Quinn* where the taxpayer (who normally had lunch at home) sought to claim the excess cost of meals incurred because he was working a long way from his home. The taxpayer's arguments failed because he did not eat only in order to work, one of the reasons for his eating was in order to sustain his life; a duality of purpose therefore existed and no tax relief was due.

Other cases have shown that expenditure on clothing can also be disallowed if it is the kind of clothing which is in everyday use, because clothing is worn not only to assist the pursuit of one's profession but also to accord with public decency. This duality of purpose may be sufficient to deny relief – even where the particular type of clothing is of a kind not otherwise worn by the taxpayer. In the case of *Mallalieu* v. *Drummond* a barrister failed to obtain a tax deduction for items of sombre clothing that she purchased specifically for wearing in Court. The House of Lords decided that a duality of purpose existed because clothing represented part of her needs as a human being.

Allowances

Despite the above, Inspectors of Taxes are not usually inflexible and the following list of expenses are among those generally allowed.

(a) Cost of all materials used up in the course of the work's preparation.

(b) Cost of typewriting and secretarial assistance, etc; if this or other help is obtained from one's spouse then it is entirely proper for a deduction to be claimed for the amounts paid for the work. The amounts claimed must actually be paid to the spouse and should be at the market rate, although some uplift can be made for unsocial hours, etc. Payments to a spouse are of course taxable in their hands and should therefore be most carefully considered. The spouse's earnings may also be liable for National Insurance contributions and it is important to take care because otherwise you may find that these contributions outweigh the tax savings. The impact of the National Minimum Wage should also be considered.

(c) All expenditure on normal business items such as postage, stationery, telephone, email, printers and scanners, agent's fees, accountancy charges, photography, subscriptions, periodicals, magazines, etc may be claimed. The cost of daily papers should not be overlooked if these form part of research material. Visits to theatres, cinemas, etc for research purposes may also be permissible (but not the costs relating to guests). Unfortunately, expenditure on all types of business entertaining is specifically denied tax relief.

(d) If work is conducted at home, a deduction for 'use of home' is usually allowed providing the amount claimed is reasonable. If the claim is based on an appropriate proportion of the total costs of rent, light and heat, cleaning and maintenance, insurance, etc (but not the Council Tax), care should be taken to ensure that no single room is used 'exclusively' for business purposes, because this may result in the Capital Gains Tax exemption on the house as the only or main residence being partially forfeited. However, it would be a strange household where one room was in fact used exclusively for business purposes and for no other purpose whatsoever (e.g. storing personal bank statements and other private papers); the usual practice is to claim a deduction on the basis that most or all of the rooms in the

house are used at one time or another for business purposes, thereby avoiding any suggestion that any part was used exclusively for business purposes.
(e) The appropriate business proportion of motor running expenses may also be claimed although what is the appropriate proportion will naturally depend on the particular circumstances of each case. It should be appreciated that the well-known scale of benefits, whereby employees are taxed according to the size of the car's CO_2 emissions, do not apply to self-employed persons.
(f) It has been long established that the cost of travelling from home to work (whether employed or self-employed) is not an allowable expense. However, if home is one's place of work then no difficulties are likely to arise.
(g) Travelling and hotel expenses incurred for business purposes will normally be allowed but if any part could be construed as disguised holiday or pleasure expenditure, considerable thought would need to be given to the commercial reasons for the journey in order to justify the claim. The principle of 'duality of purpose' will always be a difficult hurdle in this connection – although not insurmountable.
(h) If a separate business bank account is maintained, any overdraft interest on the account will be an allowable expense. This is the only circumstance in which overdraft interest is allowed for tax purposes.
(i) Where capital allowances (see below) are claimed for a personal computer, laptop, iPad, printer, mobile phone, television, CD or DVD player, etc used for business purposes, the costs of maintenance and repair of the equipment may also be claimed.

Clearly many other allowable items may be claimed in addition to those listed. Wherever there is any reasonable business motive for some expenditure it should be claimed as a deduction although it is necessary to preserve all records relating to the expense. It is sensible to avoid an excess of imagination as this would naturally cause the Inspector of Taxes to doubt the genuineness of other expenses claimed.

The question is often raised whether the whole amount of an expense may be deducted or whether the VAT content must be excluded. Where VAT is reclaimed from HMRC by someone who is registered for VAT, the VAT element of the expense cannot be treated as an allowable deduction. Where the VAT is not reclaimed, the whole expense (inclusive of VAT) is allowable for income tax purposes.

Capital allowances

Where expenditure of a capital nature is incurred, it cannot be deducted from income as an expense – a separate and sometimes more valuable capital allowance being available instead. Capital allowances are given for many different types of expenditure, but authors and similar professional people are likely to claim only for 'plant and machinery'; this is a very wide expression which may include cars, personal computers, laptops, iPads, printers, televisions, CD and DVD players used for business purposes. Plant and machinery will normally qualify for an allowance of 100%.

The reason capital allowances can be more valuable than allowable expenses is that they may be wholly or partly disclaimed in any year that full benefit cannot be obtained – ordinary business expenses cannot be similarly disclaimed. Where, for example, the income of an author is not large enough to bring him above the tax threshold, he would not be liable to tax and a claim for capital allowances would be wasted. If the capital allowances were to be disclaimed their benefit would be carried forward for use in subsequent years.

This would also be advantageous where the income is likely to be taxable at the higher rate of 40% (or the 45% rate) in a subsequent year. Careful planning with claims for capital allowances is therefore essential if maximum benefit is to be obtained.

Leasing is a popular method of acquiring fixed assets, and where cash is not available to enable an outright purchase to be made, assets may be leased over a period of time. Whilst leasing may have financial benefits in certain circumstances, in normal cases there is likely to be no tax advantage in leasing an asset where the alternative of outright purchase is available.

Books

The question of whether the cost of books is eligible for tax relief has long been a source of difficulty. The annual cost of replacing books used for the purposes of one's professional activities (e.g. the cost of a new *Writers' & Artists' Yearbook* each year) has always been an allowable expense; the difficulty arose because the initial cost of reference books, etc (e.g. when commencing one's profession) was treated as capital expenditure but no allowances were due as the books were not considered to be 'plant'. However, the matter was clarified by the case of *Munby* v. *Furlong* in which the Court of Appeal decided that the initial cost of law books purchased by a barrister was expenditure on 'plant' and eligible for capital allowances. This is clearly a most important decision, particularly relevant to any person who uses expensive books in the course of exercising his or her profession.

Pension contributions

Where a self-employed person makes contributions to a pension scheme, those contributions are usually deductible.

These arrangements are generally advantageous in providing for a pension as contributions are usually paid when the income is high (and the tax relief is also high) and the pension (taxed as earned income when received) usually arises when the income is low and a lower rate of tax may be payable. There is also the opportunity to take part of the pension entitlement as a tax-free lump sum. It is necessary to take into account the possibility that the tax advantages could go into reverse. When the pension is paid it could, if rates rise again, be taxed at a higher rate than the rate of tax relief presently available for the contributions.

Each individual is allowed a lifetime pension pot (which has been gradually reduced and is now down to £1 million). When benefits crystallise, which will generally be when a pension begins to be paid, this is measured against the individual's lifetime pension pot with any excess being taxed at the individual's marginal rate of tax.

Each individual also has an annual allowance for contributions to the pension fund, which is £40,000 but this is severely reduced for those paying the higher rates of tax. If the annual increase in an individual's rights under all registered schemes of which he is a member exceeds the annual allowance, the excess is chargeable to tax.

For many writers and artists this means that they can contribute a significant part of their earnings to a pension scheme (if they can afford to do so) without any of the previous complications. It is still necessary to be careful where there is other income giving rise to a pension because the whole of the pension entitlement has to be taken into account.

Flexible retirement is possible allowing members of occupational pension schemes to continue working while also drawing retirement benefits.

Class 4 National Insurance contributions

Allied to pensions is the payment of Class 4 National Insurance contributions, which are payable in addition to the normal Class 2 (self-employed) contributions. The rates are changed each year and for 2018/19 self-employed persons will be obliged to contribute 9% of their profits between the range £8,424–£46,350 per annum plus 2% on earnings above £46,350. This amount is collected in conjunction with the annual income tax liability.

Averaging relief

Relief for copyright payments

Professional authors and artists engaged in the creation of literary or dramatic works or designs may claim to average the profits of two or more consecutive years if the profits for one year are less than 75% of the profits for the highest year. This relief can apply even if the work took less than 12 months to create and is available to people who create works in partnership with others. It enables the creative artist to utilise their allowances fully and to avoid the higher rates of tax which might apply if all the income were to arise in a single year.

Collection of tax: self-assessment

Under 'self-assessment' you submit your tax return and work out your tax liability for yourself. If you get it wrong, or if you are late with your tax return or the payment of tax, interest and penalties will be charged. Completing a tax return is a daunting task but the term 'self-assessment' is not intended to imply that individuals have to do it themselves; they can (and often will) engage professional help. The term is only intended to convey that it is the taxpayer, and not HMRC, who is responsible for getting the tax liability right and for it to be paid on time.

The deadline for filing your tax return is 31 January following the end of the tax year. You must now file online; a paper tax return cannot be filed in most cases.

Income tax on self-employed earnings remains payable in two instalments on 31 January and 31 July each year. Because the accurate figures may not necessarily be known, these payments in January and July will therefore be only payments on account based on the previous year's liability. The final balancing figure will be paid the following 31 January together with the first instalment of the liability for the following year.

When HMRC receives the self-assessment tax return, it is checked to see if there is anything obviously wrong; if there is, a letter will be sent to you immediately. Otherwise, HMRC has 12 months from the filing date in which to make further enquiries; if it doesn't, it will have no further opportunity to do so and your tax liabilities are final – unless there is an error or an omission. In that event, HMRC can raise an assessment later to collect any extra tax together with appropriate penalties. It is essential that all records relevant to your tax return are retained for at least 12 months after the filing date in case they are needed by HMRC. For the self-employed, the record-keeping requirement is much more onerous because the records need to be kept for nearly six years. If you claim a tax deduction for an expense, it will be necessary to have a receipt or other document proving that the expenditure has been made. Because the existence of the underlying records is so important to the operation of self-assessment, HMRC will treat them very seriously and there are penalties for a failure to keep adequate records.

Interest

Interest is chargeable on overdue tax at a variable rate, which is presently 3% per annum. It does not rank for any tax relief, which can make HMRC an expensive source of credit.

However, HMRC can also be obliged to pay interest (known as repayment supplement) tax-free where repayments are delayed. The rules relating to repayment supplement are less beneficial and even more complicated than the rules for interest payable but they do exist and can be very welcome if a large repayment has been delayed for a long time. Unfortunately, the rate of repayment supplement is only 0.5% and is always less than the rate charged by HMRC on overdue tax.

Value added tax

The activities of writers, painters, composers, etc are all 'taxable supplies' within the scope of VAT and chargeable at the standard rate. (Zero rating which applies to publishers, booksellers, etc on the supply of books does not extend to the work performed by writers.) Accordingly, authors are obliged to register for VAT if their income for the past 12 months exceeds £85,000 or if their income for the coming month will exceed that figure.

Delay in registering can be a most serious matter because if registration is not effected at the proper time, HMRC can (and invariably do) claim VAT from all the income received since the date on which registration should have been made. As no VAT would have been included in the amounts received during this period the amount claimed by HMRC must inevitably come straight from the pocket of the author.

The author may be entitled to seek reimbursement of the VAT from those whom he or she ought to have charged VAT but this is obviously a matter of some difficulty and may indeed damage his or her commercial relationships. Apart from these disadvantages there is also a penalty for late registration. The rules are extremely harsh and are imposed automatically even in cases of innocent error. It is therefore extremely important to monitor the income very carefully because if in any period of 12 months the income exceeds the £85,000 limit, HMRC must be notified within 30 days of the end of the period. Failure to do so will give rise to an automatic penalty. It should be emphasised that this is a penalty for failing to submit a form and has nothing to do with any real or potential loss of tax. Furthermore, whether the failure was innocent or deliberate will not matter. Only the existence of a 'reasonable excuse' will be a defence to the penalty. However, a reasonable excuse does not include ignorance, error, a lack of funds or reliance on any third party.

However, it is possible to regard VAT registration as a privilege and not a penalty, because only VAT registered persons can reclaim VAT paid on their expenses such as stationery, telephone, professional fees, etc and even computers and other plant and machinery (excluding cars). However, many find that the administrative inconvenience – the cost of maintaining the necessary records and completing the necessary forms – more than outweighs the benefits to be gained from registration and prefer to stay outside the scope of VAT for as long as possible.

Overseas matters

The general observation may be made that self-employed persons resident and domiciled in the UK are not well treated with regard to their overseas work, being taxable on their worldwide income. It is important to emphasise that if fees are earned abroad, no tax saving can be achieved merely by keeping the money outside the country. Although exchange control regulations no longer exist to require repatriation of foreign earnings, such income remains taxable in the UK and must be disclosed to HMRC; the same applies to interest or other income arising on any investment of these earnings overseas. Accordingly, whenever foreign earnings are likely to become substantial, prompt and effective action is required to limit the impact of UK and foreign taxation. In the case of non-resident authors it is important that arrangements concerning writing for publication in the UK, for example in newspapers, are undertaken with great care. A case concerning the wife of one of the great train robbers who provided detailed information for a series of articles published in a Sunday newspaper is most instructive. Although she was acknowledged to be resident in Canada for all the relevant years, the income from the articles was treated as arising in this country and fully chargeable to UK tax.

The UK has double taxation agreements with many other countries and these agreements are designed to ensure that income arising in a foreign country is taxed either in that country or in the UK. Where a withholding tax is deducted from payments received from another country (or where tax is paid in full in the absence of a double taxation agreement), the amount of foreign tax paid can usually be set off against the related UK tax liability.

Many successful authors can be found living in Eire because of the complete exemption from tax which attaches to works of cultural or artistic merit by persons who are resident there. However, such a step should only be contemplated having careful regard to all the other domestic and commercial considerations and specialist advice is essential if the exemption is to be obtained and kept; a careless breach of the conditions could cause the exemption to be withdrawn with catastrophic consequences. Consult the Revenue Commissioners in Dublin (www.revenue.ie) for further information concerning the precise conditions to be satisfied for exemption from tax in the Republic of Ireland.

Companies

When authors become successful the prospect of paying tax at high rates may drive them to take hasty action, such as the formation of a company, which may not always be to their advantage. Indeed some authors seeing the exodus into tax exile of their more successful colleagues even form companies in low tax areas in the hope of saving large amounts of tax. HMRC is fully aware of these possibilities and has extensive powers to charge tax and combat avoidance. Accordingly, such action is just as likely to increase tax liabilities and generate other costs and should never be contemplated without expert advice; some very expensive mistakes are often made in this area which are not always able to be remedied.

To conduct one's business through the medium of a company can be a very effective method of mitigating tax liabilities, and providing it is done at the right time and under the right circumstances very substantial advantages can be derived. However, if done without due care and attention the intended advantages will simply evaporate. At the very least it is essential to ensure that the company's business is genuine and conducted properly with regard to the realities of the situation. If the author continues his/her activities unchanged, simply paying all the receipts from his/her work into a company's bank account, he/she cannot expect to persuade HMRC that it is the company and not himself/herself who is entitled to, and should be assessed to tax on, that income.

It must be strongly emphasised that many pitfalls exist which can easily eliminate all the tax benefits expected to arise by the formation of the company. For example, company directors are employees of the company and will be liable to pay much higher National Insurance contributions; the company must also pay the employer's proportion of the contribution and a total liability of nearly 26% of gross salary may arise. This compares most unfavourably with the position of a self-employed person. Moreover, on the commencement of the company's business the individual's profession will cease and the possibility of revisions being made by HMRC to earlier tax liabilities means that the timing of a change has to be considered very carefully.

The tax return

No mention has been made above of personal reliefs and allowances; this is because these allowances and the rates of tax are subject to constant change and are always set out in detail in the explanatory notes which accompany the tax return. The annual tax return is an important document and should be completed promptly with extreme care. If filling in the tax return is a source of difficulty or anxiety, *Money Which? – Tax Saving Guide* (Consumer Association, annual, March) is very helpful.

Peter Vaines is a barrister at Field Court Tax Chambers in Gray's Inn. He writes and speaks widely on tax matters.

See also...

- *FAQs for writers*, page 713
- *National Insurance contributions and social security benefits*, page 725

National Insurance contributions and social security benefits

Most people who work in Great Britain either as an employee or as a self-employed person are liable to pay Class 1 National Insurance contributions. The law governing this subject is complex and Peter Arrowsmith FCA and Sarah Bradford summarise it here for the benefit of writers and artists. This article also contains an outline of the benefits system and should be regarded as a general guide only.

All contributions are payable in respect of years ending on 5 April. See box (below) for the classes of contributions.

Employed or self-employed?

Employed earners pay Class 1 contributions and self-employed earners currently pay Class 2 and Class 4 contributions. It is therefore essential to know the status of a worker to ensure that the correct class of contribution is paid. The question as to whether a person is employed under a contract *of* service and is thereby an employed earner liable to Class 1 contributions, or performs services (either solely or in partnership) under a contract *for* service and is thereby self-employed and liable to Class 2 and Class 4 contributions, often has to be decided in practice. One of the more longstanding guides can be found in the case of *Market Investigations Ltd* v. *Minister of Social Security* (1969 2 WLR 1) when Cooke J. remarked:

Classes of contributions

Class 1 Payable by employees (primary contributions) and their employers (secondary contributions), based on earnings.

Class 1A Payable only by employers in respect of all taxable benefits in kind.

Class 1B Payable only by employers in respect of PAYE Settlement Agreements entered into by them.

Class 2 Weekly flat rate contributions payable by the self-employed.

Class 3 Weekly flat rate contributions, payable on a voluntary basis in order to provide, or make up entitlement to, certain social security benefits.

Class 3A Voluntary contributions payable from 12 October 2015 until 5 April 2017 by those reaching state pension age before 6 April 2016. Amount depends on age.

Class 4 Payable by the self-employed in respect of their trading or professional income, based on earnings.

'...the fundamental test to be applied is this: "Is the person who has engaged himself to perform these services performing them as a person in business on his own account?" If the answer to that question is "yes", then the contract is a contract for services. If the answer is "no", then the contract is a contract of service. No exhaustive list has been compiled and perhaps no exhaustive list can be compiled of the considerations which are relevant in determining that question, nor can strict rules be laid down as to the relative weight which the various considerations should carry in particular cases. The most that can be said is that control will no doubt always have to be considered, although it can no longer be regarded as the sole determining factor; and that factors which may be of importance are such matters as:

- whether the man performing the services provides his own equipment,
- whether he hires his own helpers,
- what degree of financial risk he takes,

• what degree of responsibility for investment and management he has, and
• whether and how far he has an opportunity of profiting from sound management in the performance of his task.'

The above case has often been considered subsequently in Tribunal cases, but there are many factors to take into account. Increasingly, workers do not fit neatly into either category, and following the Taylor Review into Modern Working Practices, the government published a consultation in February 2018 on proposals to make the employment status rules clearer. The consultation document is available on the GOV.UK website at www.gov.uk/government/consultations/employment-status. Further guidance on employment status can be found on the GOV.UK website at www.gov.uk/government/collections/employed-or-self-employed. HMRC also produce an employment status tool which can be used to determine if a worker is an employed or self-employed earner (see www.gov.uk/guidance/check-employment-status-for-tax).

Exceptions

There are exceptions to the above rules, those most relevant to artists and writers being:
• the employment of a spouse or civil partner is disregarded for National Insurance purposes unless it is for the purposes of a trade or profession (e.g. the employment of one's spouse by an author would not be disregarded and would result in a liability for contributions if their spouse's reached the minimum levels);
• the employment of certain relatives in a private dwelling house in which both employee and employer reside is disregarded for social security purposes provided the employment is not for the purposes of a trade or business carried out at those premises by the employer. This would cover the employment of a relative (as defined) as a housekeeper in a private residence.

Personal service companies

Since 6 April 2000, those who have control of their own 'one-man service companies' are subject to special rules (commonly referred to as IR35). If the work carried out by the owner of the company for the company's customers would be – but for the one-man company – considered as an employment of that individual (i.e. rather than self-employment), a deemed salary may arise. If it does, then some or all of the company's income will be treated as salary liable to PAYE and National Insurance contributions (NICs). This will be the case whether or not such salary is actually paid by the company. The same situation may arise where the worker owns as little as 5% of a company's share capital.

The calculations required by HMRC are complicated and have to be done very quickly at the end of each tax year (even if the company's year-end does not coincide). It is essential that affected businesses seek detailed professional advice about these rules which may also, in certain circumstances, apply to partnerships.

The rules, as they apply where the end client is a public service body, were reformed from 6 April 2017. Under these rules, the responsibility for deciding whether IR35 applies (i.e. would the worker be an employee if employed under a direct contract) is shifted to the public sector body and responsibility for deducting PAYE and NIC due on the deemed payment (which is calculated without the 5% cost allowance) is transferred to the fee-payer, which may be an agency.

At the time of the 2018 Spring Statement, the government confirmed that they would be consulting on reforms where the end client is in the private sector, and looking at extending the scope of the public sector reforms where services are provided via an intermediary to a private-sector end client.

In order to escape the application of the IR35 rules, a number of workers arranged their engagements through 'managed service companies', etc where the promoter is heavily involved in all the company management to the exclusion of the workers themselves. Such companies are subject to similar, but different, rules, which apply from 6 April 2007 for tax and 6 August 2007 for NICs.

For further information, see www.gov.uk/business-tax/ir35.

State pension age

Workers, both employed and self-employed, stop paying NICs once they reach state pension age. However, employers must continue to pay secondary Class 1 contributions in respect of earnings paid to employees who have reached state pension age.

The current state pension age for men is 65. The state pension age for women is gradually being increased so as to equalise it with that for men; it is being increased gradually from 6 April 2010 and will reach age 65 on 6 November 2018. From that date, the state pension age for both men and women will rise to 66 to achieve a state pension age of 66 on 6 September 2020. The state pension age will be further increased from 66 to 67 between 2026 and 2028. Provisions included in the Pensions Act 2014 provide for the state pension age to be reviewed every 5 years. In July 2017, following such a review, the government announced plans to bring forward the increase in the state pension age to 65 to between 2037 and 2039, rather than between 2044 and 2046 as under existing legislation.

Until November 2018, women will reach state pension age on the dates shown below, depending on their date of birth. The state pension age for women will be equalised with men from November 2018. Men will reach state pension age at age 65 until November 2018. The state pension age for both men and women will then increase from 65 to 66.

Date of birth *(women)*	**Date state pension age reached**	**Pension age**
6 Oct. 1953 to 5 Nov. 1953	6 July 2018	64 yrs 8 mths–64 yrs 9 mths
6 Nov. 1953 to 5 Dec. 1953	6 Nov. 2018	64 yrs 11 mths–65 yrs

The state pension age for **men** born before 6 December 1953 is 65.

Men and women born between 6 December 1953 and 5 January 1954 will reach state pension age on 6 March 2018 (65 yrs 2 mths–65 yrs 3 mths).

Class 1 contributions

Primary Class 1 contributions are payable by employed earners and secondary Class 1 contributions are payable by self-employed workers by reference to their earnings.

Primary Class 1 National Insurance contributions are payable by employees on earnings that exceed the primary threshold (£162 per week for 2018/19) and by employers on earnings that exceed the secondary threshold (£162 per week for 2018/19). However, where the employee is under the age of 21 or an apprentice under the age of 25, employer contributions are only payable on earnings that exceed, respectively, the upper secondary threshold for under 21s or the apprentice upper secondary threshold. Both thresholds are aligned with the upper earnings limit for primary Class 1 contributions (£892 per week for 2018/19). Contributions are normally collected via the PAYE tax deduction machinery, and there are penalties for late submission of returns and for errors therein and also for PAYE and NICs paid late on more than one occasion in the tax year. Interest is charged automatically on PAYE and social security contributions paid late.

Employees' liability to pay

Contributions are payable by any employee who is aged 16 years and over (even though they may still be at school) and who is paid an amount equal to, or exceeding, the primary earnings threshold (£162 per week for 2018/19). Where the employee has earnings between the lower earnings limit and the primary threshold, contributions are payable at a notional zero rate. This preserves the employee's contributions record and entitlement to the state pension and contributory benefits. Nationality is irrelevant for contribution purposes and, subject to special rules covering employees not normally resident in Great Britain, Northern Ireland or the Isle of Man, or resident in EEA countries or those with which there are reciprocal agreements, contributions must be paid whether the employee concerned is a British subject or not provided he/she is gainfully employed in Great Britain.

Persons over state pension age are exempt from liability to pay primary contributions, even if they have not retired. However, the fact that an employee may be exempt from liability does not relieve an employer from liability to pay secondary contributions in respect of that employee.

Employees' (primary) contributions

From 6 April 2018, the rate of employees' contributions on earnings from the employee earnings threshold (£162 per week) to the upper earnings limit (£892 per week) is 12%. Contributions are payable at a rate of 2% on earnings above the upper earnings limit. Certain married women who made appropriate elections before 12 May 1977 may be entitled to pay a reduced rate of 5.85% on earnings between the primary threshold and upper earnings limit. However, they have no entitlement to benefits in respect of these contributions. Where a reduced rate election is in force, contributions are payable at the additional rate of 2% on earnings above the upper earnings limit.

Employers' (secondary) contributions

All employers are liable to pay contributions on the gross earnings of employees above the age of 16 where their earnings exceed the secondary earnings threshold (£162 per week for 2018/19). However, where the employee is under 21 or an apprentice under the age of 25, employer contributions are only payable on earnings in excess of, respectively, the upper secondary threshold for under 21s or the apprentice upper secondary threshold (AUST). Both thresholds are set at £892 per week for 2018/19. As mentioned above, an employer's liability is not reduced as a result of employees being exempted from contributions, or being liable to pay only the reduced rate (5.85%) of contributions.

For earnings paid on or after 6 April 2017, employers are liable at a rate of 13.8% on earnings paid above the secondary earnings threshold (or, where the employee is under 21). Most employers are entitled to an annual employment allowance, which is set at £3,000 for 2018/19 and which is offset against their secondary Class 1 liability. However, the allowance is not available to employers where the sole employee is a director. The allowance is claimed through the employer's real time information (RTI) software.

The employer is responsible for the payment of both employees' and employer's contributions, but is entitled to deduct the employees' contributions from the earnings on which they are calculated. Effectively, therefore, the employee suffers a deduction in respect of his or her social security contributions in arriving at his weekly or monthly wage or salary. Special rules apply to company directors and persons employed through agencies.

Items included in, or excluded from, earnings

Contributions are calculated on the basis of a person's gross earnings from their employment.

Earnings include salary, wages, overtime pay, commissions, bonuses, holiday pay, payments made while the employee is sick or absent from work, payments to cover travel between home and office, and payments under the statutory sick pay, statutory maternity pay, statutory paternity pay and statutory adoption pay schemes.

However, certain payments, some of which may be regarded as taxable income for income tax purposes, are ignored for Class 1 purposes. These include:

- certain gratuities paid other than by the employer;
- redundancy payments and some payments in lieu of notice;
- certain payments in kind;
- reimbursement of specific expenses incurred in the carrying out of the employment;
- benefits given on an individual basis for personal reasons (e.g. birthday presents);
- compensation for loss of office.

Booklet CWG 2 (2016 edition) gives a list of items to include in or exclude from earnings for Class 1 contribution purposes (available from www.gov.uk). Some such items may, however, be liable to Class 1A (employer-only) contributions.

Class 1A and Class 1B contributions

Class 1A contributions are employer-only contributions payable in respect of most taxable benefits. All taxable benefits provided to employees regardless of the employee's earnings rate are liable to Class 1A National Insurance contributions unless the benefit in question is within the charge to Class 1 or 1B or specifically exempt. Class 1A contributions are payable at a rate of 13.8%.

Class 1B contributions are payable by employers using PAYE Settlement Agreements in respect of small and/or irregular expense payments and benefits, etc. This rate is also 13.8%.

Rates of Class 1 contributions and earnings limits from 6 April 2018

Earnings per week	*Rates payable on earnings in each band*	
	Employee	*Employer*
£	*%*	*%*
Below 116.00	–	–
116.00–161.99	0**	–
162.00–891.99	12	13.8***
Over 892.00	2	13.8

** Contributions payable at a notional zero rate.

*** No employer contributions where employee is under 21 or an apprentice under 25.

Class 2 contributions

Class 2 contributions are payable at the weekly rate of £2.95 as from 6 April 2018. They are currently the mechanism by which the self-employed earn entitlement to the state pension and certain contributory benefits. They are payable annually with income tax and Class 4 contributions via the self-assessment system and are due by 3 January after the end of the tax year to which they relate. The liability is based on the number of weeks of self-employment in the tax year. Certain persons are exempt from Class 2 liability as follows:

- a person over state pension age;
- a person who has not attained the age of 16;
- a married woman or, in certain cases, a widow, either of whom elected prior to 12 May 1977 not to pay Class 2 contributions;
- persons with earnings below the small profits threshold (see below);
- persons not ordinarily self-employed (see below).

As part of the reform of National Insurance contributions for the self-employed, Class 2 contributions are to be abolished from April 2019 – one year later than originally planned. Class 4 contributions are to be reformed from the same date to provide for pension and benefit entitlement.

Small profits threshold

No liability to Class 2 contributions arises unless earnings from self-employment exceed the small profits threshold, which is set at £6,205 for 2018/19.

Persons not ordinarily self-employed

Part-time self-employed activities (including as a writer or artist) are disregarded for contribution purposes if the person concerned is not ordinarily employed in such activities and has a full-time job as an employee. There is no definition of 'ordinarily employed' for this purpose.

Payment of contributions

Class 2 contributions are payable via the self-assessment system with income tax and Class 4 contributions. Class 2 contributions for 2018/19 are due by 31 January 2020.

Class 3 and Class 3A contributions

Class 3 contributions are payable voluntarily. For 2018/19 they are payable at the weekly rate of £14.65 per week by persons aged 16 or over with a view to enabling them to qualify for a limited range of benefits if their contribution record is not otherwise sufficient. In general, Class 3 contributions can be paid by employees, the self-employed and the non-employed.

Broadly speaking, no more than 52 Class 3 contributions are payable for any one tax year, and contributions cannot be paid in respect of tax years after the one in which the individual concerned reaches state pension age. Class 3 contributions may be paid by monthly direct debit, quarterly bill or by annual cheque in arrears.

Class 3A contributions were introduced from October 2015, payable for a limited window, and provided those who reach state pension age before 6 April 2016 with an opportunity to top up their state pension. The Class 3A contribution 'bought' up to £25 per week of additional state pension. The amount of the Class 3A contribution depends on the contributor's age and was payable by 5 April 2017.

Class 4 contributions

In addition to Class 2 contributions, self-employed persons are liable to pay Class 4 contributions. These are calculated at the rate of 9% on the amount of profits or gains chargeable to income tax which exceed the lower profits limit (£8,424 per annum for 2018/19) but which do not exceed the upper profits limit (£46,350 per annum for 2018/19). Profits above the upper profits limit attract a Class 4 charge at the rate of 2%. The income tax profit on which Class 4 contributions are calculated is after deducting capital allowances and losses, but before deducting personal tax allowances or retirement annuity or personal pension or stakeholder pension plan premiums.

Class 4 contributions currently produce no additional benefits. However, as part of the reforms to National Insurance contributions for the self-employed, Class 2 contributions are to be abolished from April 2019 (delayed from 6 April 2018) and Class 4 contributions are to be reformed from the same time to provide benefit entitlement. From 6 April 2019 onwards, the structure of Class 4 contributions will more closely resemble that of Class 1 contributions. A new limit – the small profits limit – will be introduced, which will be aligned with the lower earnings limit for Class 1 purposes. Class 4 contributions at a notional zero rate will be deemed to be paid on profits between the small profits limit and the lower profits limit.

Payment of contributions

In general, Class 4 contributions are self-assessed and paid to HMRC together with the income tax as a result of the self-assessment income tax return, and accordingly the contributions are due and payable at the same time as the income tax liability on the relevant profits. Under self-assessment, payments on account of Class 4 contributions are payable at the same time as interim payments of tax.

Class 4 exemptions

The following persons are exempt from Class 4 contributions:

- persons over state pension age at the start of the tax year (i.e. on 6 April);
- an individual not resident in the UK for income tax purposes in the year of assessment;
- persons whose earnings are not 'immediately derived' from carrying on a trade, profession or vocation;
- a person under 16 years old on 6 April of the year of assessment;
- persons not ordinarily self-employed.

Married persons, civil partners and partnerships

Under independent taxation, each spouse or civil partner is responsible for his or her own Class 4 liability.

In partnerships, each partner's liability is calculated separately. If a partner also carries on another trade or profession, the profits of all such businesses are aggregated for the purposes of calculating their Class 4 liability.

When an assessment has become final and conclusive for the purposes of income tax, it is also final and conclusive for the purposes of calculating Class 4 liability.

Maximum contributions

There is a limit to the total liability for social security contributions payable by a person who is employed in more than one employment, or is also self-employed or a partner.

Where a person would otherwise pay more than the permitted maximum it may be possible to defer some contributions. The calculations are complex and guidance on the permitted maximum and deferment can be found on the GOV.UK website (see www.gov.uk/defer-self-employed-national-insurance).

Social security benefits

Benefits may be contributory (i.e. dependent upon set levels of social security contributions and/or NIC-able earnings arising in all or part of one or more tax years) or means-tested (i.e. subject to a full assessment of the income and capital of the claimant and their partner). Child benefit is one of a handful falling outside either category being neither contributory nor means-tested, although the high income child benefit tax charge claws back child benefit where anyone in the household has taxable income over £50,000 per annum. The benefit is clawed back at a rate of 1% for each £100 of income over £50,000 such that the tax is equal to the child benefit received where income is £60,000 or above.

Most benefits are administered by the Department for Work and Pensions and its agencies (such as Jobcentre Plus and The Pension Service). Some are administered wholly or partly by HMRC and the latter are marked with an asterisk in the following lists.

Universal Credit is replacing a number of benefits and is in the process of being phased in.

Universal benefits

- Child Benefit*
- Carer's Allowance (for those looking after a severely disabled person)
- Disability Living Allowance (DLA) – progressively being replaced by Personal Independence Payment (PIP)
- Personal Independence Payment (PIP) (help with some of the extra costs caused by long-term ill-health or disability for those aged 16–64)

Contributory benefits

- State Pension – basic and earnings-related
- Bereavement benefits
- Contribution-based Jobseeker's Allowance (JSA) (time limited, i.e. unemployment)
- Contribution-based Employment and Support Allowance (ESA) (time limited for some, i.e. sickness and incapacity)
- Statutory Sick Pay* (SSP) (for employees only, paid by the employer)
- Statutory Maternity Pay* (SMP) (for employees only, paid by the employer)
- Maternity Allowance (for self-employed and others meeting the conditions)
- Statutory Paternity Pay* (SPP) (for employees only, paid by the employer)

Further information

GOV.UK
www.gov.uk/national-insurance
For guidance on National Insurance.

DWP benefits
www.gov.uk/browse/benefits

Tax Credits
www.gov.uk/browse/benefits/tax-credits

Child benefit
www.gov.uk/child-benefit

Statutory payments
For SSP, SMP, SPP, SAP and ShPP contact your employer in the first instance.

National Insurance Contributions & Employer Office, International Caseworker
Newcastle upon Tyne NE98 1ZZ
tel 0300 200 3506
For enquiries for individuals resident abroad.

• Shared Parental Pay* (ShPP) (for employees only, paid by the employer)
• Statutory Adoption Pay* (SAP) (for employees only, paid by the employer)
• Guardian's Allowance*

Means-tested benefits

• Income-based Jobseeker's Allowance (JSA) (i.e. unemployment)
• Income-based Employment and Support Allowance (ESA) (i.e. sickness and incapacity)
• Income Support (low-income top up for those of working age, not working but neither unemployed nor sick/incapacitated)
• Working Tax Credits* (WTC) (low-income top up for those of working age)
• Child Tax Credit* (low-income top up for those of working age with children, in addition to Working Tax Credit if applicable)
• Disabled Person's Tax Credits* (DPTC) (low-income top up for disabled people)
• Pension Credit (low-income top up for those of pension age)
• Social Fund grants (one-off assistance for low-income household with unexpected, emergency expenditure)

In addition, help with rent and rates is available on a means-tested basis from local authorities.

Many of the working age benefits are in the process of being replaced with 'Universal Credit', starting with new claimants. Universal Credit will eventually replace Income-based Jobseeker's Allowance, Income-related Employment and Support Allowance, Income Support, Working Tax Credit, Child Tax Credit and Housing Benefit.

Peter Arrowsmith FCA is a former sole practitioner specialising in National Insurance matters, and member and former chairman of the Employment Taxes and National Insurance Committee of the Institute of Chartered Accountants in England and Wales. **Sarah Bradford** BA (Hons), ACA CTA (Fellow) is the director of Writetax Ltd and the author of *National Insurance Contributions 2018/19* (and earlier editions) published by Bloomsbury Professional. She writes widely on tax and National Insurance contributions and provides tax consultancy services.

Subject indexes
Magazines by subject area

These lists provide a broad classification and pointer to possible markets.
Contacts for *Magazines UK and Ireland* start on page 35.

Advertising, design, printing and publishing

Agriculture, farming and horticulture

Architecture and building

Art and collecting

Aviation

Business, industry and management

Cinema and films

Computing

Economics, accountancy and finance

Education

Engineering and mechanics

Fiction

Food and drink

Gardening

Health and home

History and archaeology

Hotel, catering and leisure

Humour and satire

Legal and police

Leisure interests, pets

Literary (see also Poetry)

Local government and civil service

Marketing and retailing

Medicine and nursing

Military

Motor transport and cycling

Music and recording

Natural history

Nautical and marine

Photography

Poetry

Some magazines only take the occasional poem. Check with the Editor before submitting.

Politics

Radio and TV

Religion, philosophy and New Age

Rural life and country

Sciences

Sports and games

Theatre, drama and dancing (see also Cinema and films, Music and recording)

Travel and geography

. . .

Magazines aimed at women

Magazines aimed at men

Publishers of fiction (UK)

Contacts for *Book publishers UK and Ireland* start on page 152.

Adventure/westerns

BME

Comedy/humour

Crime/detective/mystery

Erotica

General

Graphic/cartoons

Historical

Horror

LGBT+

Literary

New/experimental

Romantic/chick-lit/women's

Sci-fi/fantasy/speculative

Short stories

Teen/YA

Translation/international

War

Westerns

Publishers of non-fiction (UK)

Contacts for *Book publishers UK and Ireland* start on page 152.

Academic and professional

Agriculture, farming and horticulture

Animals and birds

Archaeology

Architecture and building

Art and craft

Astronomy

Aviation

Bibliography

Biography, autobiography and memoir

Business, industry and management

Cartography/maps

Comedy, humour

Computers and computing

Cookery, food and drink

Crime

Cultural studies

Current affairs

Design

Economics, accountancy and finance

Education

Engineering and mechanics

Environment and development

Fashion

Film and cinema

Fine art and antiques

Gardening

Gender studies and LGBT+

General non-fiction

Health

Heritage

History

Illustrated books

International issues

Irish interest

Languages and ELT

Law

Leisure interests and hobbies

Lifestyle, home and DIY

Literary criticism and essays

Local government and civil service

Local interest

Medicine and nursing

Military

Mind, body & spirit (MBS)

Music

Natural history

Nautical and marine

Novelty, gift books

Parenting, relationships and self-help

Performing arts

Photography

Politics

Popular culture

Popular reference

Reference

Religion, philosophy and New Age

Rural life and country

Science

Scottish interest

Social sciences

Sports and games

The media

Transport, including cycling

Travel and geography

TV, TV tie-ins and radio

Welsh interest

Writers' guides

Children's book publishers and packagers (UK)

Listings for *Book publishers UK and Ireland* start on page 152
and listings for *Book packagers* start on page 245.

Activity and novelty

Book publishers

Book packagers

Audiobooks

Book publishers

Children's fiction

Book publishers

Book packagers

Children's non-fiction

Book publishers

Book packagers

Multimedia

Book publishers

Book packagers

Picture books

Book publishers

Book packagers

Poetry

Book publishers

Book packagers

Religion

Book publishers

Book packagers

Publishers of plays (UK)

Playwrights are reminded that it is unusual for a publisher of trade editions of plays to publish plays which have not had at least reasonably successful, usually professional, productions on stage first. See listings starting on page 152 for contacts.

Publishers of poetry (UK)

See listings starting on page 152 for contacts.

Literary agents for children's books

The following literary agents will consider work suitable for children's books, from authors and/or illustrators of children's books. Listings start on page 440.

See also *Art agents and commercial art studios* on page 507.

Literary agents for television, film, radio and theatre

Listings for these and other literary agents start on page 440.

Newspapers and magazines that accept cartoons

Listed below are newspapers and magazines which take cartoons – either occasionally, or on a regular basis. Approach in writing in the first instance to ascertain the Editor's requirements (for addresses see listings starting on page 15 for newspapers and page 35 for magazines).

Newspapers and colour supplements

Consumer and special interest magazines

Business and professional magazines

Prizes and awards by subject area

This index gives the major subject area of each entry in the main listings which start on page 565.

Biography

Children

Theatre, TV and radio

Essays

Fiction

Grants, bursaries and fellowships

Illustration

Journalism

Non-fiction

Photography

Poetry

Short stories

Translation

General index

Key topics and terms that appear in the articles within this *Yearbook* are listed here.

Listings index

All companies, public and commercial organisations, societies, festivals and prize-giving bodies, that have a listing in the *Yearbook* are included in this index.